CONTEMPORARY'S

GED

Coordinating Editor
Patricia Mulcrone, Ed.D.
Professor/Chair
Adult Educational Development
William Rainey Harper College
Palatine, Illinois

Reviewers
Kathryn Coleman
GED Instructor
Kishwaukee College
Malta, Illinois

Mary Ann Corley, Ph.D.
GED Administrator
Baltimore, Maryland

Mary Kay Gray
GED Coordinator
Mott Adult High School
Flint, Michigan

Carrie Robinson
Assistant Professor
Staten Island Community College
Staten Island, New York

CB

CONTEMPORARY BOOKS

a division of NTC/CONTEMPORARY PUBLISHING GROUP
Lincolnwood, Illinois USA

Library of Congress Cataloging-in-Publication Data

GED : how to prepare for the high school equivalency examination. —
   Newly rev.
      p.   cm.
      Rev. ed. of: Contemporary's new GED. © 1985.
      ISBN 0-8092-3777-6
      1. General educational development tests—Study guides.
  I. Contemporary Books, inc.   II. Contemporary's new GED.
  LB3060.33.G45G14   1994
  373.12'62—dc20

                                             94-1956
                                             CIP

Contributing Writers

Reading Skills
Noreen Giles
Patricia Mulcrone

Test 1: Writing Skills
Karen A. Fox
Judith Gallagher

Test 2: Social Studies
Dan M. Fox
Karen Gibbons
Virginia Lowe

Test 3: Science
Bruce R. Brown
Robert P. Mitchell

Test 4: Literature and the Arts
Karen A. Fox
Noreen Giles
Anne V. McGravie

Test 5: Mathematics
Jerry Howett
Janice Phillips

ISBN: 0-8092-3777-6

Published by Contemporary Books,
a division of NTC/Contemporary Publishing Group, Inc.,
4255 West Touhy Avenue,
Lincolnwood (Chicago), Illinois 60646-1975 U.S.A.
© 1994 by NTC/Contemporary Publishing Group, Inc.
Manufactured in the United States of America.

8 9 0 CU 14 13 12 11

CONTENTS

ACKNOWLEDGMENTS

Article on page 13 from the *Chicago Tribune*. Copyright 1986 by Reuters. Reprinted by permission.

Cartoon on page 14 by Jim Morin. Copyright 1992 by the *Miami Herald*. Reprinted by permission.

Excerpt on page 16 from *Indian Oratory: Famous Speeches by Noted Indian Chieftains* by W. C. Vanderwerth. Copyright 1971 by the University of Oklahoma Press. Reprinted by permission.

Cartoon on page 19 by Larry Wright, © 1986. Reprinted by permission of the *Detroit News*, a Gannett newspaper.

Map on page 21 from *World Geography* by Preston E. James and Nelda Davis, © 1985. Reprinted by permission of the Glencoe division of the Macmillan/McGraw-Hill School Publishing Company.

Excerpt on page 39 from *Song of Solomon* by Toni Morrison. Permission granted by International Creative Management, Inc. Copyright 1977 by Toni Morrison.

Poem on page 39, "Tom Merritt," in *Spoon River Anthology* by Edgar Lee Masters. Originally published by the Macmillan Company. Permission by Ellen C. Masters.

Excerpt on pages 40–41 from *Pygmalion* in *Four Modern Plays* by George Bernard Shaw. Reprinted by permission of The Society of Authors Ltd.

Excerpt on page 209 from "The Night the Ghost Got In," © 1961 by James Thurber. From *My Life and Hard Times*, published by Harper & Row.

Excerpt on pages 209–210 from *Seize the Day* by Saul Bellow. Copyright 1956, 1974, renewed by Saul Bellow. Used by permission of Viking Penguin, a division of Penguin Books USA Inc.

Review on page 212, "Game Shows," by Dorothy Scheuer in *Senior Scholastic Magazines*. Reprinted by permission of Scholastic Inc. © 1982.

Cartoon on page 236 by Dana Summers, © 1983, Washington Post Writers Group, reprinted by permission.

Cartoon on page 237 by Don Wright, © 1992 the *Palm Beach Post*, reprinted by permission.

Excerpt on page 249 from "The Sacred Rac" in *Learning About Peoples and Cultures* by Patricia Hughes Ponzi, © 1972.

Article on page 252, "He's Reborn After 51 Years in an Attic," by Jack Mabley. Copyright December 18, 1986, Chicago Tribune Company, all rights reserved. Used by permission.

Excerpt on page 265 from *The Shaping of Colonial Virginia* by Thomas J. Wertenbaker, © 1958.

Cartoon on page 317 by Hugh S. Haynie. Reprinted by permission. Copyright by the *Courier-Journal*, Louisville Times Company, and Hugh S. Haynie.

Cartoon on page 325 by Arthur Bok, © 1993. Reprinted by permission of the *Akron Beacon Journal*.

Excerpt on page 456 from "A Certain Beginning" by Kim Chi-won in *Words of Farewell: Stories by Korean Women Writers*. Copyright 1989 by Kim Chi-won. Reprinted by permission of Seal Press.

Excerpt on page 458 from *Of Mice and Men* by John Steinbeck. Copyright 1937, renewed © 1965 by John Steinbeck. Used by permission of Viking Penguin, a division of Penguin Books USA Inc.

Excerpt on page 460 from *The Woman Warrior* by Maxine Hong Kingston. Copyright 1975, 1976 by Maxine Hong Kingston. Reprinted by permission of Alfred A. Knopf, Inc.

Excerpt on page 463 reprinted by permission of Faber and Faber Ltd. and The Putnam Publishing Group from *Lord of the Flies* by William Golding. Copyright 1954 by William Golding; renewed 1982.

Excerpt on page 466 from "The Short Happy Life of Francis Macomber." Reprinted by permission of Charles Scribner's Sons, an imprint of Macmillan Publishing Company, from *The Short Stories of Ernest Hemingway*. Copyright 1936 by Ernest Hemingway; renewal © 1964 by Mary Hemingway.

Excerpt on page 467 from "The Possibility of Evil" by Shirley Jackson. Copyright 1965 by Stanley Edgar Hyman. Reprinted by permission of Brandt & Brandt Literary Agents, Inc.

Excerpt on page 470 from "Everything That Rises Must Converge" in *The Complete Stories* by Flannery O'Connor. Copyright 1961, 1965 by the Estate of Mary Flannery O'Connor. Reprinted by permission of Farrar, Straus & Giroux, Inc.

Excerpt on page 472 from *The Bell Jar* by Sylvia Plath. Copyright 1971 by Harper & Row Publishers, Inc. Reprinted by permission of HarperCollins Publishers, Inc.

Story on pages 476–478, "The Sniper," in *Spring Sowing* by Liam O'Flaherty, reprinted by permission of Harcourt Brace & Company.

Review on page 482 by Anne Whitehouse. Copyright 1993 by the New York Times Company. Reprinted by permission.

Poem on page 483, "Oh, When I Was in Love with You," from *The Collected Poems of A. E. Housman* by A. E. Housman. Copyright 1939, 1940, © 1965 by Henry Holt and Company, Inc. Copyright 1967, 1968 by Robert E. Symons. Reprinted by permission of Henry Holt and Company, Inc.

Excerpt on page 484 from "Southbound on the Freeway" by May Swenson. Copyright 1963 and renewed 1991. Used by permission of The Literary Estate of May Swenson.

Poem on page 486, "On Being a Woman," in *The Portable Dorothy Parker* by Dorothy Parker. Introduction by Brendan Gill. Copyright 1928, renewed © 1956 by Dorothy Parker. Used by permission of Viking Penguin, a division of Penguin Books USA Inc.

Poem on page 487, "History." Copyright 1977 by Gary Soto. Used by permission of Gary Soto.

Poem on page 489, "maggie and milly and molly and may," is reprinted from *Complete Poems, 1904–1962* by E. E. Cummings. Edited by George J. Firmage, by permission of Liveright Publishing Corporation. Copyright 1923, 1925, 1926, 1931, 1935, 1938–1940, 1944–1962 by E. E. Cummings. Copyright 1961, 1963, 1966–1968 by Marion Morehouse Cummings. Copyright 1972–1991 by the Trustees for the E. E. Cummings Trust.

Poem on page 490, "Jazz Fantasia," in *Smoke and Steel* by Carl Sandburg, © 1920 by Harcourt Brace & Company and renewed 1948 by Carl Sandburg, reprinted by permission of the publisher.

Poem on page 491, "My Papa's Waltz," © 1942 by Hearst Magazines, Inc., from *The Collected Poems of Theodore Roethke* by Theodore Roethke. Used by permission of Doubleday, a division of Bantam Doubleday Dell Publishing Group, Inc.

Poem on page 493, "Memory," by Trevor Nunn in *Cats: The Book of the Musical*, incorporating lines from "Rhapsody on a Windy Night" in *Collected Poems 1909–1962* by T. S. Eliot, © 1936 by Harcourt Brace & Company, © 1964, 1963 by T. S. Eliot, reprinted by permission of the publisher.

Poem on page 493, "Memory," from *Cats: The Book of the Musical*. Words by Trevor Nunn after T. S. Eliot. Reprinted by permission of Faber and Faber Ltd. © 1981 by Trevor Nunn/Set Copyrights Ltd.

Poem on page 494, "The Negro Speaks of Rivers," in *Selected Poems* by Langston Hughes. Copyright 1926 by Alfred A. Knopf, Inc., and renewed 1954 by Langston Hughes. Reprinted by permission of the publisher.

Excerpt on page 495 from "Chicago" in *Chicago Poems* by Carl Sandburg, reprinted by permission of Harcourt Brace & Company.

Poem on pages 496–497 from *The Poetry of Robert Frost* edited by Edward Connery Latham. Copyright 1923, © 1969 by Henry Holt and Company, Inc. Copyright 1942, 1951 by Robert Frost. Copyright 1970 by Lesley Frost Ballantine. Reprinted by permission of Henry Holt and Company, Inc.

Excerpt on page 497 from "An Indian Summer Day on the Prairie" in *Collected Poems of Vachel Lindsay* (New York: Macmillan, 1925).

Poem on page 497, "Dreams," in *The Dream Keeper and Other Poems* by Langston Hughes. Copyright 1932 by Alfred A. Knopf, Inc., and renewed 1960 by Langston Hughes. Reprinted by permission of the publisher.

Poem on page 498, "Barter." Reprinted by permission of Macmillan Publishing Company from *Collected Poems of Sara Teasdale* (New York: Macmillan, 1937).

Poem on page 499, "Wind and Silver," from "What's O'Clock" in *The Complete Poetical Works of Amy Lowell*. Copyright 1955 by Houghton Mifflin Company, © renewed 1983 by Houghton Mifflin Company, Brinton P. Roberts, and G. D'Andelot Belin, Esquire. Reprinted by permission of Houghton Mifflin Company. All rights reserved.

Poem on page 499, "Because I Could Not Stop for Death," by Emily Dickinson. Reprinted by permission of the publishers and the Trustees of Amherst College from *The Poems of Emily Dickinson*, Thomas H. Johnson, ed., Cambridge, Mass.: The Belknap Press of Harvard University Press, © 1951, 1955, 1979, 1983 by the President and Fellows of Harvard College.

Poem on page 501, "The Man from Washington," by James Welch in *Tales from American Authors* edited by Natachee Scott Momaday. Used by permission of editor.

Review on page 502 by Stephen C. Levi, October 1992. Reprinted by permission of *Small Press Review*.

Excerpt on pages 512–513 from *'night, Mother* by Marsha Norman. Copyright 1983 by Marsha Norman. Reprinted by permission of Hill and Wang, a division of Farrar, Straus & Giroux, Inc.

Excerpt on pages 514–515, *I Never Sang for My Father*, by Robert Anderson. Reprinted by permission of International Creative Management.

Excerpt on page 519 from *Parent Effectiveness Training* by Dr. Thomas Gordon. Copyright 1970 by Dr. Thomas Gordon. Reprinted by permission of David McKay Co., a division of Random House, Inc.

Excerpt on page 523 from *Hard Times* by Studs Terkel. Copyright 1970 by Studs Terkel. Reprinted by permission of Pantheon Books, a division of Random House, Inc.

Excerpt on pages 525 from *Nigger: An Autobiography* by Dick Gregory. Copyright 1964 by Dick Gregory Enterprises, Inc. Used by permission of the publisher, Dutton, an imprint of New American Library, a division of Penguin Books USA Inc.

Essay on pages 531–532, "The Computer Is Down." Reprinted by permission of The Putnam Publishing Group from *You Can Fool All of the People All of the Time* by Art Buchwald. Copyright 1985 by Art Buchwald.

Excerpt on page 533 from "The Dark Side of the Boom" by Mary S. Glucksman. Reprinted by permission of *Omni*, © 1991, Omni Publications International, Ltd.

Excerpt on page 535 from "Red Jacket Speech" in *A Treasury of Great American Speeches* by Charles Hurd, editor. Copyright 1959 by Hawthorn Books; 1987 by Charles Hurd. Used by permission of the publisher, Dutton, an imprint of New American Library, a division of Penguin Books USA Inc.

Review on page 539 reprinted by permission of *People Weekly* © 1993 Time Inc.

Review on page 541 of the book *The Pentagon Catalog*. Reviewed by Clarence Petersen. Copyright June 15, 1986, Chicago Tribune Company, all rights reserved, used by permission.

Review on page 545 reprinted by permission from *TV Guide® Magazine*. Copyright 1993 by News America Publications, Inc.

Excerpt on page 759 from *Scholastic Update*, December 1, 1986, vol. 119, no. 7. Reprinted by permission of Scholastic, Inc.

Excerpt on page 761 from the *News-Sun*, © 1985. Reprinted by permission of the *News-Sun*, Waukegan, Illinois.

Excerpt on page 763 from "Giving Children a Good Start" by Carol A. Emig, © 1986. Reprinted by permission of the author.

Illustration on page 767 from *Scholastic Update*, March 21, 1986, vol. 118, no. 14. Reprinted by permission of Scholastic, Inc.

Excerpt on page 768 from "Still at the Bottom of the Ladder" by Mary Elson. Copyright 1987, Chicago Tribune Company, all rights reserved, used by permission.

Map of Mexico on page 770 from *World Geography Workbook* by Preston E. James and Nelda Davis, © 1985. Reprinted by permission of the Glencoe division of the Macmillan/McGraw-Hill School Publishing Company.

Cartoon on page 772 by Rob Rogers, *Pittsburgh Press*, © 1992. Reprinted by permission of UFS, Inc.

Table on page 773 from *World Geography Workbook* by Preston E. James and Nelda Davis, © 1985. Reprinted by permission of the Glencoe division of the Macmillan/McGraw-Hill School Publishing Company.

Cartoon on page 774 by Mike Thompson, the *State Journal-Register*, © 1993. Reprinted by permission of Copley News Service.

Excerpt on page 801 from "American History" by Judith Ortíz-Cofer. Reprinted by permission of the author.

Excerpt on page 802 from *Medal of Honor Rag*, © 1977, 1983 by Tom Cole. Reprinted by permission of Lois Berman, The Little Theatre Building.

Excerpt on page 803 from "Suburban Prophecy" in *The Collected Poems of Howard Nemerov*. University of Chicago Press, 1977. Reprinted by permission of the author.

Excerpt on page 805 from "Narrow 'Realism' Misses the Point of Real Vision" in *Pieces of Eight* by Sydney J. Harris. Copyright 1982 by Houghton Mifflin Co. Reprinted by permission of Houghton Mifflin Co. All rights reserved.

Excerpt on page 807 from *Main Street* by Sinclair Lewis, © 1920 by Harcourt Brace & Company and renewed 1948 by Sinclair Lewis, reprinted by permission of the publisher.

Excerpt on pages 809–810 from "Beauty Marks." Copyright 1986 Time Inc. Reprinted by permission.

Cartoon on page 852 by Dan Wasserman, © 1986, *Boston Globe*. Distributed by Los Angeles Times Syndicate. Reprinted by permission.

Graphic on page 856, "Amount Spent on TV Ads," © 1992, Time Inc. Reprinted by permission.

Cartoon on page 862 by Tom Toles, © 1991, the *Buffalo News*. Reprinted by permission of Universal Press Syndicate. All rights reserved.

Cartoon on page 867 by Jorgensen, copyright 1992, Extra Newspaper Features. Reprinted by permission.

Excerpt on page 868 from *Newsweek*, May 14, © 1993, Newsweek, Inc. All rights reserved. Reprinted by permission.

Map and key on page 869 from *U.S. News & World Report*, © January 28, 1991. Reprinted by permission of *U.S. News & World Report*.

Excerpt on page 899 from *Gather Together in My Name* by Maya Angelou. Copyright 1974 by Maya Angelou. Reprinted by permission of Random House, Inc.

Excerpt on page 900 from "Girls of Summer" by Marie Brenner. Copyright 1993 by The New York Times Company. Reprinted by permission.

Excerpt on pages 901–902 from *There Will Come Soft Rains* by Ray Bradbury. Reprinted by permission of Don Congdon Associates, Inc. Copyright 1950, renewed 1977 by Ray Bradbury.

Excerpt on page 903 from "Reunion" in *The Brigadier and the Golf Widow*, © 1964 by John Cheever, reprinted by permission of Wylie, Aitken & Stone, Inc.

Excerpt on page 904 from "He" in *Flowering Judas and Other Stories*, © 1930 and renewed 1958 by Katherine Anne Porter, reprinted by permission of Harcourt Brace & Company.

Poem on page 905, "25th High School Reunion," by Linda Pastan in *The Five Stages of Grief*. Reprinted by permission of W. W. Norton & Company, Inc.

Excerpt on pages 906–907 from *The House of Ramon Iglesia*. Copyright 1983 by Jose Rivera.

Review on pages 907–908, " 'White Rose' Celebrates Anti-Nazi Heroes," by Lawrence Bommer, theater critic for the *Chicago Tribune*. Reprinted by permission of the author.

Review on page 909 of the book *In My Place*. Reprinted by permission of Phoebe-Lou Adams, *The Atlantic Monthly*.

The editor has made every effort to trace the ownership of all copyrighted material, and necessary permissions have been secured in most cases. Should there prove to be any question regarding the use of any material, regret is here expressed for such error. Upon notification of any such oversight, proper acknowledgment will be made in future editions.

TO THE STUDENT

If you're studying to pass the GED Tests, you're in good company, In 1994, the most recent year for which figures are available, over 750,000 people took the tests. Of this number, nearly 450,000 actually received their certificates. Why do so many people choose to take the GED Tests? Some do so to get a job or to get a better one than they already have. Others take the tests so that they can go on to college or vocational school. Still others pursue their GED diplomas to feel better about themselves or to set good examples for their children.

Americans and Canadians alike, from all walks of life, have passed their GED Tests and obtained diplomas. Some well-known graduates include country music singers Waylon Jennings and John Michael Montgomery, comedian Bill Cosby, Olympic gold medalist Mary Lou Retton, former New Jersey Governor James J. Florio, Wendy's Old-Fashioned Hamburgers founder Dave Thomas, Delaware State Senator Ruth Ann Minner, U.S. Senator Ben Nighthorse Campbell of Colorado, motion picture actor Kelly McGillis, Famous Amos Chocolate Chip Cookies creator Wally Amos, *Parade* magazine editor Walter Anderson, NBA referee Tommy Nuñez, and Triple Crown winner jockey Ron Turcotte.

This book has been designed to help you, too, succeed on the test. It will provide you with instruction in the skills you need to pass, background information on key concepts in the subject areas of writing skills, social studies, science, literature and the arts, and mathematics, and plenty of practice with the kinds of test items you will find on the real test.

WHAT DOES GED STAND FOR?

GED stands for the Tests of General Educational Development. The GED Test is a national examination developed by the GED Testing Service of the American Council on Education. The credential received for passing the test is widely recognized by colleges, training schools, and employers as equivalent to a high school diploma.

While the GED Test measures skills and knowledge normally acquired in four years of high school, much that you have learned informally or through other types of training can help you pass the test.

The GED Test is available in English, French, and Spanish and on audio-cassette, in Braille, and in large print.

WHAT SHOULD I KNOW TO PASS THE TEST?

The GED Test consists of five examinations in the areas of writing skills, social studies, science, literature and the arts, and mathematics. The chart on the next page outlines the main content areas, the breakdown of questions, and the time allowed per test.

THE GED TESTS			
Test	*Minutes*	*Questions*	*Percentage*
1: Writing Skills Part 1: Conventions of English Part 2: The Essay	 75 45	 55 1 topic	Sentence Structure 35% Usage 35% Mechanics 30%
2: Social Studies	85	64	History 25% Economics 20% Political Science 20% Geography 15%* Behavioral Sciences 20%*
3: Science	95	66	Life Sciences 50% Physical Sciences 50%
4: Literature and the Arts	65	45	Popular Literature 50% Classical Literature 25% Commentary 25%
5: Mathematics	90	56	Arithmetic 50% Algebra 30% Geometry 20%

*In Canada, 20% of the test is based on Geography and 15% on Behavioral Sciences.

On all five tests, you are expected to demonstrate the ability to think about many issues. You also are tested on knowledge and skills you have acquired from life experiences, television, radio, books and newspapers, consumer products, and advertising. In addition to the above information, keep these facts in mind:

1. Three of the five tests—Literature and the Arts, Science, and Social Studies—require that you answer questions based on reading passages or interpreting cartoons, diagrams, maps, charts, and graphs in these content areas. Developing strong reading and thinking skills is the key to succeeding on these tests.

2. The Writing Skills Test requires you to be able to detect and correct errors in sentence structure, grammar, punctuation, and spelling. You also will have to write a composition of approximately 200 words on a topic familiar to most adults.

3. The Mathematics Test consists mainly of word problems to be solved. Therefore, you must be able to combine your ability to perform computations with problem-solving skills.

WHO MAY TAKE THE TESTS?

In the United States, Canada, and many territories, people who have not graduated from high school and who meet specific eligibility requirements (age, residency, etc.) may take the tests. Since eligibility requirements vary, it would be useful to contact your local GED testing center or the director of adult education in your state, province, or territory for specific information.

WHAT IS A PASSING SCORE ON THE GED?

Again, this varies from area to area. To find out what you need to pass the test, contact your local GED testing center. However, you must keep two scores in mind. One score represents the minimum score you must get on each test. For example, if your state requires minimum scores of 40, you must get at least 40 points on every test. Additionally, you must meet the requirements of a minimum average score on all five tests. For example, if your state requires a minimum average score of 45, you must get a total of 225 points to pass. The two scores together, the minimum score and the minimum average score, determine whether you pass or fail the GED Test.

To understand this better, look at the scores of three people who took the test in a state that requires a minimum score of 40 and a minimum average score of 45 (225 total). Ann and Willie did not pass, but Ramon did. See if you can tell why.

	Ann	*Willie*	*Ramon*
Test 1	44	42	43
Test 2	43	43	48
Test 3	38	42	47
Test 4	50	40	52
Test 5	50	40	49
	225	207	239

Ann made the total of 225 points but fell below the minimum score on Test 3. Willie passed each test but failed to get the 225 points needed; just passing the individual tests was not enough. Ramon passed all the tests and exceeded the minimum score. Generally, to receive a GED credential, you must correctly answer half or a little more than half of the questions on each test.

MAY I RETAKE THE TEST?

You are allowed to retake some or all of the tests. Again, the regulations governing the number of times that you may retake the tests and the time you must wait before retaking them are set by your state, province, or territory. Some states require you to take a review class or to study on your own for a certain amount of time before taking the test again.

HOW CAN I BEST PREPARE FOR THE TEST?

Many libraries, community colleges, adult education centers, churches, and other institutions offer GED preparation classes. Some television stations broadcast classes to prepare people for the test. If you cannot find a GED preparation class locally, contact the director of adult education in your state, province, or territory or call the GED Hotline (800-62-MY-GED). This hotline will give you telephone numbers and addresses of adult education and testing centers in your area. The hotline is staffed 24 hours a day, seven days a week.

IF I STUDY ON MY OWN,
HOW MUCH TIME SHOULD I ALLOW TO PREPARE?

It depends on your readiness in each of the five subject areas; however, you should probably allow three to six months to do the following:

1. Read the introductory section of the book.

2. Take and score the five Pre-Tests. Decide which areas you need to focus on the most. Use the Countdown Checklist on pages xxi–xxii to help you plan your study program.

3. Complete the Reading Skills section of the book.

4. Read and complete the exercises in those areas that you decided to focus on.

5. Take the Post-Tests to determine how much improvement you've made.

6. Take the Practice Tests to determine whether you're ready for the real test.

7. Review the test-taking tips below.

8. Contact the GED Administrator or the director of adult education in your state, province, or territory and arrange to take the GED.

TEST-TAKING TIPS FOR SUCCESS

1. **Prepare physically.** Get plenty of rest and eat a well-balanced meal before the test so that you will have energy and will be able to think clearly. Last-minute cramming will probably not help as much as a relaxed and rested mind.

2. **Arrive early.** Be at the testing center at least 15 to 20 minutes before the starting time. Make sure you have time to find the room and to get situated. Keep in mind that many testing centers refuse to admit latecomers.

3. **Think positively.** Tell yourself you will do well. If you have studied and prepared for the test, you should succeed.

4. **Relax during the test.** Take half a minute several times during the test to stretch and breathe deeply, especially if you are feeling anxious or confused.

5. **Read the test directions carefully.** Be sure you understand how to answer the questions. If you have any questions about the test or about filling in the answer form, ask before the test begins.

6. **Know the time limit for each test.** Some testing centers allow extra time, while others do not. You may be able to find out the policy of your testing center before you take the test, but always work according to the official time limit. If you have extra time, go back and check your answers.

7. **Have a strategy for answering questions.** You should read through the reading passages, or look over the materials, once and then answer the questions that follow. Read each question two or three times to make sure you understand it. It is best to refer back to the passage or illustration in order to confirm your answer choice. Don't try to depend on your memory of what you have just read or seen. Some people like to guide their reading by skimming the questions before reading a passage. Use the method that works best for you.

8. **Don't spend a lot of time on difficult questions.** If you're not sure of an answer, go on to the next question. Answer easier questions first and then go back to the harder questions. However, when you skip a question, be sure that you have skipped the same number on your answer sheet. Although skipping difficult questions is a good strategy for making the most of your time, it is very easy to get confused and throw off your whole answer key.

   Lightly mark the margin of your answer sheet next to the numbers of the questions you did not answer so that you know what to go back to. To prevent confusion when your test is graded, be sure to erase these marks completely after you answer the questions.

9. **Answer every question on the test.** If you're not sure of an answer, take an educated guess. When you leave a question unanswered, you will always lose points, but you can possibly gain points if you make a correct guess.

   If you must guess, try to eliminate one or more answers that you are sure are not correct. Then choose from the remaining answers. Remember, you greatly increase your chances if you can eliminate one or two answers before guessing. Of course, guessing should be used only when all else has failed.

10. **Clearly fill in the circle for each answer choice.** If you erase something, erase it completely. Be sure that you give only one answer per question; otherwise, no answer will count.

11. **Practice test-taking.** Use the exercises, reviews, and especially the Post-Tests and Practice Tests in this book to better understand your test-taking habits and weaknesses. Use them to practice different strategies such as skimming questions first or skipping hard questions until the end. Knowing your own personal test-taking style is important to your success on the GED Test.

HOW TO USE THIS BOOK

1. You do not have to work through all of the five sections in this book. In some areas you are likely to have stronger skills than in others. However, before you begin this book you should take the Pre-Tests. These will give you a preview of what the five tests include, but more important, they will help you to identify which areas you need to concentrate on most. Use the **Evaluation Charts** at the end of the Pre-Tests to pinpoint the types of questions you answered incorrectly and to determine what skills you need extra work in.

2. Complete the sections of the book that the Pre-Tests indicate you need to review. However, to prepare yourself best for the test, work through the entire book.

3. After you have worked through the subject areas that needed strengthening as indicated by the Pre-Test scores, you should take the Post-Tests and Practice Tests at the end of this book. These tests will help you determine whether you are ready for the actual GED Test and, if not, what areas of the book you need to review. The Evaluation Charts are especially helpful in making this decision.

4. If you determine that you need still more practice at the GED level in answering the kinds of questions to be found on the GED Test, we recommend that you work through Contemporary's satellite series, available for each of the five GED subject areas:

   Test 1: Writing Skills
   Test 2: Social Studies
   Test 3: Science
   Test 4: Literature and the Arts
   Test 5: Mathematics

   Additional titles that Contemporary offers for effective test preparation in math and writing include *The GED Math Problem Solver* and *The GED Essay*.

   This book has a number of features designed to help make the task of preparing for the actual GED Test easier as well as effective and enjoyable:

   - A special essay section helps to prepare you for the Writing Skills portion of the GED Test.

   - A preliminary reading skills section of two chapters isolates the four thinking skills—comprehension, application, analysis, and evaluation—and provides plenty of practice in using these skills; it also provides practice in interpreting graphics and illustrations (these make up at least one-third of the Science and Social Studies Tests and a good portion of the Mathematics Test).

   - Skill builders, hints, and tips help you increase your proficiency in the Writing Skills, Reading, and Literature and the Arts sections.

   - A variety of exercise types maintain interest—matching, fill-in-the-blank, true-false, multiple-choice, and short essay questions.

   - Writing across the curriculum—writing activities in science, social studies, and literature help you practice the skills introduced earlier in the Writing Skills section.

- U.S. history and science "trivia"—fascinating little-known facts add spice to the reading activities and exercises.

- Full-length Post-Tests and Practice Tests that are simulated GED Tests present questions in the format, level of difficulty, and percentages you will find on the actual tests.

- An answer key (coded by skill level) for each section explains the correct answers for the exercises.

- Evaluation charts for the Pre-Tests, Post-Tests, and Practice Tests help pinpoint weaknesses and refer you to specific pages for review.

- Hundreds of questions for strengthening your reading, writing, and thinking skills are provided.

Contemporary Books publishes a wide range of materials to help you prepare for the tests. These books are designed for home study or classroom use. Our GED preparation books are available through schools and bookstores and directy from the publisher. Our toll-free number is (800) 621-1918. For the visually impaired, a large-print version is available. For further information, call Library Reproduction Service (LRS) at (800) 255-5002.

COUNTDOWN CHECKLIST

This checklist will assist those who are studying on their own in planning their course of preparation for the GED examination. It will also be helpful as a guide in GED review classes. It is designed to help students spread out their study, pace themselves wisely, and be prepared for the GED Test.

Step 1

- Begin your review by taking and checking the Pre-Tests on pages 1–53. Take one Pre-Test at a time. Read as much as you can in your spare time.

Step 2

- Read and study the Reading Skills section—Chapters 1 and 2, pages 189–237. In addition, do as much extra reading as you can.

- If you think you need extra reading help, consider taking a reading test and a reading course at a local school or adult education center.

Step 3

- Go over the Evaluation Charts on the Pre-Tests, circling those areas in which you had the most trouble.

- Divide the instructional material into about ten weeks of work, focusing on those areas in which you need the most time to prepare.

- Below, fill in the pages you plan to complete each week. As you complete each assignment, check it off.

Week 1: pages _____   Week 6: pages _____
Week 2: pages _____   Week 7: pages _____
Week 3: pages _____   Week 8: pages _____
Week 4: pages _____   Week 9: pages _____
Week 5: pages _____   Week 10: pages _____

Step 4

- Take and check the Post-Tests and Practice Tests on pages 737–926.

- Based on where you had trouble, target pages you still need to review. Plan a three-week course to get yourself completely ready to take the GED Test.

  Week 1: pages _____
  Week 2: pages _____
  Week 3: pages _____

The night before the test—

- Review the test-taking tips on pages xviii–xix.

- Relax. Don't study.

- Get a good night's sleep.

The day of the test—

- Eat a good breakfast, but don't eat heavily.

- Think positively and relax.

- Leave yourself plenty of time to get there; arrive 15–20 minutes early.

Finally, we'd like to hear from you. If our materials have helped you to pass the test or if you feel that we can do a better job preparing you, write to us at the address on the back of the book to let us know. We hope you enjoy studying for the GED Test with our materials and wish you the greatest success.

The Editors

Pre-Tests

The Pre-Tests will help you determine what you need to study in this book. They are half-length tests in the format and level of difficulty of the real GED Test. The results of these tests, along with the Countdown Checklist on pages xxi–xxii, will help you map out a plan of study. We recommend the following approach to the Pre-Tests.

1. Take only one Pre-Test at a time. Don't attempt to do all of the tests at one sitting. Read the directions before you start a test. Use the answer sheets at the beginning of each test to mark your choices.

2. After you finish each Pre-Test, check the answers in the answer key and fill in the Evaluation Chart for that test. An answer key and an Evaluation Chart follow each test. For all of the questions that you miss, read explanations of the correct answers.

3. Based on the information in the Evaluation Charts, you may choose to do one of two things:

   • If you miss half or more of the questions in a Pre-Test, you should work through the entire subject area.
   • If you miss fewer than half of the questions, focus on particular areas of the test that gave you difficulty.

4. Even if you do well on a subject area Pre-Test, for best results you will want to review the chapters on Critical Thinking Skills, beginning on page 189, and Interpreting Graphs and Illustrations, beginning on page 223.

The order of the Pre-Tests and the time allotted for each is listed below.

Time Allowed for Each Test		
Writing Skills	Part 1	75 minutes
	Part 2	45 minutes
Social Studies		85 minutes
Science		95 minutes
Literature and the Arts		65 minutes
Mathematics		90 minutes

Although these are Pre-Tests, you should give them your best effort. If an item seems difficult, mark it and come back later. Always answer every question—even if you have to make an "educated guess." Sometimes you may know more than you give yourself credit for. Also, on the real GED Tests a blank counts as a wrong answer. It's always wise to answer every question as best you can.

PRE-TEST 1: WRITING SKILLS
Part 1: Conventions of English

Part 1 of the Writing Skills Pre-Test consists of 30 multiple-choice questions. The questions are based on paragraphs that contain numbered sentences. Most sentences contain errors, but a few may be correct as written. Read the paragraphs and then answer the questions based on them. For each item, choose the answer that would result in the best rewriting of the sentence or sentences. The best answer must be consistent with the meaning and tone of the rest of the paragraph.

Answer each question as carefully as possible, choosing the best of five answer choices and blackening in the grid. If you find a question too difficult, do not waste time on it. Work ahead and come back to it later when you can think it through carefully.

When you have completed the test, check your work with the answers and explanations at the end of the section.

Use the Evaluation Charts on page 11 to determine which areas you need to review most.

PRE-TEST 1: WRITING SKILLS ANSWER GRID

1 ① ② ③ ④ ⑤	9 ① ② ③ ④ ⑤	17 ① ② ③ ④ ⑤	24 ① ② ③ ④ ⑤
2 ① ② ③ ④ ⑤	10 ① ② ③ ④ ⑤	18 ① ② ③ ④ ⑤	25 ① ② ③ ④ ⑤
3 ① ② ③ ④ ⑤	11 ① ② ③ ④ ⑤	19 ① ② ③ ④ ⑤	26 ① ② ③ ④ ⑤
4 ① ② ③ ④ ⑤	12 ① ② ③ ④ ⑤	20 ① ② ③ ④ ⑤	27 ① ② ③ ④ ⑤
5 ① ② ③ ④ ⑤	13 ① ② ③ ④ ⑤	21 ① ② ③ ④ ⑤	28 ① ② ③ ④ ⑤
6 ① ② ③ ④ ⑤	14 ① ② ③ ④ ⑤	22 ① ② ③ ④ ⑤	29 ① ② ③ ④ ⑤
7 ① ② ③ ④ ⑤	15 ① ② ③ ④ ⑤	23 ① ② ③ ④ ⑤	30 ① ② ③ ④ ⑤
8 ① ② ③ ④ ⑤	16 ① ② ③ ④ ⑤		

Choose the best answer to each question that follows.

Questions 1–9 refer to the following passage.

(1) Most fire-related death's result from household fires, yet many people do not have fire extinguishers in their homes. (2) There is smoke detectors in many homes to warn residents of a fire, but fire extinguishers can actually help people fight fires. (3) In most cases, everyone should evacuate a home when a fire has started or the smoke alarm sounds. (4) Someone outside the home should call the fire department. (5) However, if a fire extinguisher is handy, a quick-thinking person often can use them to put out a small fire. (6) There are several types of fire extinguishers on the market, and each are suitable for particular types of fire. (7) Most extinguishers come with instructions, they are very easy to operate. (8) Fire departments may be contacted for training in operating extinguishers. (9) A person should keep in mind some basic safety rules when you are deciding whether or not to use a fire extinguisher. (10) Buying a fire extinguisher knowing how to use it, and placing it in a location familiar to all family members can help protect families against fire.

1. Sentence 1: **Most fire-related death's result from household fires, yet many people do not have fire extinguishers in their homes.**

   What correction should be made to this sentence?

   (1) replace *death's* with *deaths*
   (2) change *result* to *results*
   (3) remove the comma after *fires*
   (4) change *have* to *has*
   (5) replace *their* with *there*

2. Sentence 2: **There is smoke detectors in many homes to warn residents of a fire, but fire extinguishers can actually help people fight fires.**

   Which of the following is the best way to write the underlined portion of this sentence? If you think the original is the best way, choose option (1).

   (1) There is
   (2) Their is
   (3) They're is
   (4) There are
   (5) Their are

3. Sentences 3 and 4: **In most cases, everyone should evacuate a home when a fire has started or the smoke alarm sounds. Someone outside the home should call the fire department.**

   The most effective combination of sentences 3 and 4 would contain which of the following groups of words?

   (1) sounds, and someone
   (2) sounds and call
   (3) sounds, or someone
   (4) sounds unless someone
   (5) sounds and should call

4. Sentence 5: **However, if a fire extinguisher is handy, a quick-thinking person often can use them to put out a small fire.**

   Which of the following is the best way to write the underlined portion of this sentence? If you think the original is the best way, choose option (1).

   (1) them
   (2) him
   (3) it
   (4) they
   (5) theirs

5. Sentence 6: **There are several types of fire extinguishers on the market, and each are suitable for particular types of fire.**

What correction should be made to this sentence?

(1) replace *There are* with *There is*
(2) remove the comma after *market*
(3) replace *and* with *or*
(4) replace *each are* with *each is*
(5) change the spelling of *particular* to *particuler*

6. Sentence 7: **Most extinguishers come with <u>instructions, they are</u> very easy to operate.**

Which of the following is the best way to write the underlined portion of this sentence? If you think the original is the best way, choose option (1).

(1) instructions, they are
(2) instructions and are
(3) instructions, are
(4) instructions and they are
(5) instructions; and are

7. Sentence 8: **Fire departments may be contacted for training in operating extinguishers.**

What correction should be made to this sentence?

(1) replace *departments* with *Departments*
(2) replace *may be* with *were*
(3) change the spelling of *operating* to *opperating*
(4) replace departments with department's
(5) no correction is necessary

8. Sentence 9: **A person should keep in mind some basic safety <u>rules when you are deciding</u> whether or not to use a fire extinguisher.**

Which of the following is the best way to write the underlined portion of this sentence? If you think the original is the best way, choose option (1).

(1) rules when you are deciding
(2) rules when deciding
(3) rules you decide
(4) rules when you decided
(5) rules. You are deciding

9. Sentence 10: **Buying a fire extinguisher knowing how to use it, and placing it in a location familiar to all family members can help protect families against fire.**

What correction should be made to this sentence?

(1) insert a comma after *extinguisher*
(2) change *placing* to *place*
(3) replace *members* with *member's*
(4) insert a comma after *help*
(5) change the spelling of *families* to *familys*

Questions 10–19 refer to the following passage.

(1) A european concept in overnight lodging known as "bed and breakfast" is becoming popular in the United States. (2) Private citizens act as hosts and rent out spare bedrooms in there homes. (3) The hosts provide a home-cooked breakfast and a bedroom appropriatly designed to offer their guests privacy in a cozy setting. (4) While most American travelers expect to find lodging in a hotel or motel, the recent popularity of bed and breakfasts offer a new alternative to travelers. (5) Staying in a private home offers travelers a more personal atmosphere; as a result, they feel pampered and enjoy visiting with the hosts. (6) Saying that they feel safer and like being treated as guests, the bed and breakfast hosts make them feel at home. (7) Travelers can learn much about the history and people of the local area; for example, visitors currently stayed on Wisconsin dairy farms and in restored log cabins in Kentucky. (8) If travelers cannot afford a long trip, they can still enjoy a peaceful getaway weekend as houseguests. (9) The hosts also benefit from running such a business because they can stay at home, make money, and meeting a variety of people. (10) Most State tourism departments and some travel agencies have bed and breakfast listings.

10. Sentence 1: **A european concept in overnight lodging known as "bed and breakfast" is becoming popular in the United States.**

What correction should be made to this sentence?

(1) change *european* to *European*
(2) replace *known* with *is known*
(3) replace *is* with *are*
(4) replace *States* with *states*
(5) no correction is necessary

11. Sentence 2: **Private citizens act as hosts and rent out spare bedrooms in there homes.**

What correction should be made to this sentence?

(1) replace *citizens* with *citizen's*
(2) change *act* to *acted*
(3) change *rent* to *renting*
(4) add a comma after *hosts*
(5) replace *there* with *their*

12. Sentence 3: **The hosts provide a home-cooked breakfast and a bedroom appropriatly designed to offer their guests privacy in a cozy setting.**

What correction should be made to this sentence?

(1) change *provide* to *provides*
(2) insert a comma after *breakfast*
(3) change the spelling of *appropriatly* to *appropriately*
(4) replace *designed* with *design*
(5) no correction is necessary

13. Sentence 4: **While most American travelers expect to find lodging in a hotel or motel, the recent popularity of bed and breakfasts offer a new alternative to travelers.**

What correction should be made to this sentence?

(1) change *expect* to *expects*
(2) remove the comma after *motel*
(3) change *offer* to *offers*
(4) replace *new* with *knew*
(5) replace *to* with *too*

14. Sentence 5: **Staying in a private home offers travelers a more personal atmosphere; as a result, they feel pampered and enjoy visiting with the hosts.**

    If you rewrote sentence 5 beginning with

    Because staying in a private home offers travelers a more personal atmosphere,

    the next word should be

    (1) as
    (2) feeling
    (3) hosts
    (4) they
    (5) the

15. Sentence 6: **Saying that they feel safer and like being treated as guests, the bed and breakfast hosts make them feel at home.**

    Which of the following is the best way to write the underlined portion of this sentence? If you think the original is the best way, choose option (1).

    (1) the bed and breakfast hosts make them feel at home.
    (2) feeling at home with the bed and breakfast hosts.
    (3) the bed and breakfast hosts feel at home with travelers.
    (4) are the bed and breakfast hosts feeling at home.
    (5) the travelers feel at home with the bed and breakfast hosts.

16. Sentence 7: **Travelers can learn much about the history and people of the local area; for example, visitors currently stayed on Wisconsin dairy farms and in restored log cabins in Kentucky.**

    What correction should be made to this sentence?

    (1) replace *can* with *did*
    (2) remove the comma after *example*
    (3) replace *stayed* with *can stay*
    (4) add a comma after *farms*
    (5) no correction is necessary

17. Sentence 8: **If travelers cannot afford a long trip, they can still enjoy a peaceful getaway weekend as houseguests.**

    If you rewrote sentence 8 beginning with

    Travelers who cannot afford a long trip

    the next word should be

    (1) they
    (2) can
    (3) if
    (4) a
    (5) enjoying

18. Sentence 9: **The hosts also benefit from running such a business because they can stay at home, make money, and meeting a variety of people.**

    Which of the following is the best way to write the underlined portion of this sentence? If you think the original is the best way, choose option (1).

    (1) and meeting
    (2) and meet
    (3) to meet
    (4) and be meeting
    (5) get to meet

19. Sentence 10: **Most State tourism departments and some travel agencies have bed and breakfast listings.**

    What correction should be made to this sentence?

    (1) change *State* to *state*
    (2) change *tourism* to *Tourism*
    (3) insert a comma after *departments*
    (4) insert a comma after *agencies*
    (5) change *have* to *has*

Questions 20–30 refer to the following passage.

(1) Recently, educators exammined the effectiveness of computer instruction in American schools. (2) The educators were dismayed to find the issue of sexism and immediately analyzed the results. (3) The studies revealing that, for various reasons, girls spent less time working with computers than boys. (4) By the 1980s many American schools had began to offer computer classes or clubs. (5) Only half as many girls as boys were enrolled in computer-programming classes. (6) Schools with computer clubs and camps reported that membership consisted of many more boys than girls. (7) Some educators were frustrated because they have not become as interested in using computers.

(8) One factor to explain this discrepancy was that many of the early computer games were similar to the Space Invader video games that girls viewed as boys games. (9) Researchers also speculate that some teachers might have given boys more computer time because parents and teachers expected boys to need computers for future careers. (10) Some schools, especially at the elementary level, had only a few computers, so teachers had to choose the students which got to use them. (11) Not surprisingly, boys will be more likely to be chosen to use computers than girls. (12) Because of these findings, educators have recommended that teachers and parents encourage girls to use computers by providing opportunities and exposure to the machines.

20. Sentence 1: **Recently, educators exammined the effectiveness of computer instruction in American schools.**

What correction should be made to this sentence?

(1) replace *educators* with *educator's*
(2) change the spelling of *exammined* to *examined*
(3) replace *computer* with *computer's*
(4) change *schools* to *Schools*
(5) no correction is necessary

21. Sentence 2: **The educators were dismayed to find the issue of sexism and immediately analyzed the results.**

If you rewrote sentence 2 beginning with
Dismayed to find the issue of sexism,
the next words should be

(1) the American schools
(2) their analysis
(3) the educators
(4) computers
(5) the results

22. Sentence 3: **The <u>studies revealing</u> that, for various reasons, girls spent less time working with computers than boys.**

Which of the following is the best way to write the underlined portion of this sentence? If you think the original is the best way, choose option (1).

(1) studies revealing
(2) studies' revelations
(3) studies revealed
(4) studies will reveal
(5) revealing studies

23. Sentence 4: **By the 1980s many American schools had began to offer computer classes or clubs.**

    What correction should be made to this sentence?

    (1) replace *American* with *american*
    (2) change *had began* to *had begun*
    (3) replace *classes* with *class's*
    (4) change *clubs* to *Clubs*
    (5) no correction is necessary

24. Sentences 5 and 6: **Only half as many girls as boys were enrolled in computer-programming classes. Schools with computer clubs and camps reported that membership consisted of many more boys than girls.**

    The most effective combination of sentences 5 and 6 would include which of the following groups of words?

    (1) classes, schools
    (2) classes in schools
    (3) classes; furthermore, schools
    (4) classes, or schools
    (5) classes; however, schools

25. Sentence 7: **Some educators were frustrated because <u>they</u> have not become as interested in using computers.**

    Which of the following is the best way to write the underlined portion of this sentence? If you think the original is the best way, choose option (1).

    (1) they
    (2) educators
    (3) computers
    (4) girls
    (5) boys

26. Sentence 8: **One factor to explain this discrepancy was that many of the early computer games were similar to the Space Invader video games that girls viewed as boys games.**

    What correction should be made to this sentence?

    (1) add a comma after *was*
    (2) change *were* to *was*
    (3) replace *girls* with *girls'*
    (4) change the spelling of *viewed* to *veiwed*
    (5) replace *boys* with *boys'*

27. Sentence 9: **Researchers also speculate that some teachers might have given boys more computer time because parents and teachers <u>expected</u> boys to need computers for future careers.**

    Which of the following is the best way to write the underlined portion of this sentence? If you think the original is the best way, choose option (1).

    (1) expected
    (2) will have expected
    (3) expecting
    (4) will expect
    (5) will be expecting

28. Sentence 10: **Some schools, especially at the elementary level, had only a few computers, so teachers had to choose the students which got to use them.**

    What correction should be made to this sentence?

    (1) change the spelling of *especially* to *especialy*
    (2) remove the comma after *level*
    (3) remove the comma after *computers*
    (4) replace *which* with *who*
    (5) no correction is necessary

29. Sentence 11: **Not surprisingly, boys will be more likely to be chosen to use computers than girls.**

Which of the following is the best way to write the underlined portion of this sentence? If you think the original is the best way, choose option (1).

(1) boys will be
(2) boys' will be
(3) boys are
(4) boys' were
(5) boys were

30. Sentence 12: **Because of these findings, educators have recommended that teachers and parents encourage girls to use computers by providing opportunities and exposure to the machines.**

Which of the following is the best way to write the underlined portion of this sentence? If you think the original is the best way, choose option (1).

(1) findings, educators
(2) findings educators
(3) findings; educators
(4) findings. Educators
(5) findings, and educators

Answers begin on page 10.

Part 2: The Essay

Directions: This part of the test is designed to find out how well you write. The test has one question that asks you to present an opinion on an issue or to explain something. In preparing your answer to this question, you should take the following steps:

1. Read all of the information accompanying the question.

2. Plan your answer carefully before you write.

3. Use scratch paper to mark any notes.

4. Write your answer on a separate sheet of paper.

5. Read carefully what you have written and make any changes that will improve your writing.

6. Check your paragraphing, sentence structure, spelling, punctuation, capitalization, and usage and make any necessary corrections.

Take 45 minutes to plan and write on the following topic. Write legibly and use a ballpoint pen.

Topic

People decide to obtain a GED certificate for a wide variety of reasons. Some are interested in changing jobs, while others simply want to finish something they started a long time ago.

Why have you decided to study for the GED? Explain your decision and what you hope to gain by it. Be sure to give examples and to be specific.

Information on evaluating your essay is on page 11.

PRE-TEST 1: WRITING SKILLS ANSWER KEY
Part 1: Conventions of English

1. **(1)** The plural of *death* is *deaths*. No possession (*death's*) is shown.
2. **(4)** The subject is *detectors*, so the verb must agree with the plural subject.
3. **(1)** The new sentence would read, "In most cases, everyone should evacuate a home when a fire has started or the smoke alarm sounds, and someone outside the home should call the fire department."
4. **(3)** The pronoun *them* incorrectly refers to the singular noun *extinguisher*. The pronoun *it* is singular.
5. **(4)** The indefinite pronoun *each* is always singular, so the verb must agree with a singular subject.
6. **(2)** The original sentence is a comma splice. It incorrectly joins two complete thoughts with only a comma. Only choice (2) is punctuated correctly.
7. **(5)** No correction is necessary.
8. **(2)** This choice eliminates the incorrect pronoun *you*, which does not fit in the passage.
9. **(1)** This sentence contains a series of three items that should be separated by commas.
10. **(1)** The word *European* is derived from the name of a continent, *Europe*, so it should always be capitalized.
11. **(5)** The possessive pronoun *their* should be used here to show that the homes belong to the hosts.
12. **(3)** Keep a silent *e* when adding *ly* to *appropriate*.
13. **(3)** The subject, *popularity*, is singular, so the verb must agree with a singular subject: *popularity offers*.
14. **(4)** The new sentence would read, "Because staying in a private home offers travelers a more personal atmosphere, they feel pampered and enjoy visiting with the hosts."
15. **(5)** The phrase *Saying that they feel safer and like being treated as guests* describes the travelers, not the hosts. Choice (5) puts the phrase next to *travelers*.
16. **(3)** This sentence, as well as the passage as a whole, is written in present tense: travelers *can stay*.
17. **(2)** The new sentence would read, "Travelers who cannot afford a long trip can still enjoy a peaceful getaway weekend as houseguests."
18. **(2)** Each of the parts of the series, *can stay at home, make money,* and *meet a variety of people*, must be parallel in wording.
19. **(1)** The term *state tourism departments* is not the name of a specific agency. *State* should not be capitalized.
20. **(2)** This commonly misspelled word has one *m*, not two.
21. **(3)** The new sentence would read, "Dismayed to find the issue of sexism, the educators immediately analyzed the results."
22. **(3)** The original sentence is a fragment because the verb, *revealing*, requires a helping verb. The verb form *revealed* is complete.
23. **(2)** The past participle of the irregular verb *begin* is *begun*: *had begun*.
24. **(3)** The new sentence would read, "Only half as many girls as boys were enrolled in computer-programming classes; furthermore, schools with computer clubs and camps reported that membership consisted of many more boys than girls."
25. **(4)** The pronoun *they* is vague. It should be replaced by *girls* to make the meaning of the sentence more clear.
26. **(5)** The plural possessive, *boys'*, should be used to show that the sentence means "games for boys."
27. **(1)** There is no error.
28. **(4)** The pronoun *who* should be used to refer to people.
29. **(5)** The passage as a whole is written in the past tense, so *were* is correct.
30. **(1)** There is no error.

Use the answer key on page 10 to check your answers to the Pre-Test. Then find the item number of each question you missed and circle it on the chart below to determine the writing content areas in which you need more practice. Pay particular attention to areas where you missed half or more of the questions. The page numbers for the content areas are listed below on the chart. For those questions that you missed, review the skill pages indicated.

PRE-TEST 1: WRITING SKILLS EVALUATION CHART

Content Area	Item Number	Review Pages
Nouns, Pronouns	1, 26	60–64, 80–92
Verbs	23, 29	65–76
Subject-Verb Agreement	2, 5, 13	76–79
Pronoun Reference	4, 8, 25, 28	82–92
Sentence Fragments	22	93–98
Sentence Combining	3, 6, 14, 17, 21, 24	95–107
Sequence of Tenses	16	109–110
Misplaced/Dangling Modifiers	15	111–112
Parallel Structure	18	112–116
Capitalization	10, 19	117–119
Punctuation	9	119–125
Spelling	11, 12, 20	126–141
No Error	7, 27, 30	—

Part 2: The Essay

If possible, give your essay to an instructor to evaluate. That person's opinion of your writing will be useful in deciding what further work you need to write a good essay.

If, however, you are unable to show your work to someone else, you can try to evaluate your own essay. If you can answer *yes* to the five questions in the Essay Evaluation Checklist, your essay would *probably* earn an upper half score (4, 5, or 6) on Part 2 of the Writing Skills Test. If you receive any *no* answers on your evaluation checklist, you should read your essay carefully to see how it could be improved and review Chapter 4 of the Writing Skills section.

Essay Evaluation Checklist

YES   NO

____   ____   **1.** Does the essay answer the question asked?

____   ____   **2.** Does the main point of the essay stand out clearly?

____   ____   **3.** Does each paragraph contain specific examples and details that help prove the main point?

____   ____   **4.** Can you follow how the writer has arranged and linked ideas in sentences and paragraphs?

____   ____   **5.** Is the writer's control of grammar and usage effective enough so that you were able to read the essay easily and smoothly?

PRE-TEST 2: SOCIAL STUDIES

The Social Studies Pre-Test consists of 30 multiple-choice questions. Some of the questions are based on maps, charts, graphs, cartoons, and reading passages.

Answer each question as carefully as possible, choosing the best of five answer choices and blackening in the grid. If you find a question too difficult, do not waste time on it. Work ahead and come back to it later when you can think it through carefully.

When you have completed the test, check your work with the answers and explanations at the end of the section.

Use the Evaluation Chart on page 24 to determine which areas you need to review most.

PRE-TEST 2: SOCIAL STUDIES ANSWER GRID

1 ① ② ③ ④ ⑤   9 ① ② ③ ④ ⑤   17 ① ② ③ ④ ⑤   24 ① ② ③ ④ ⑤

2 ① ② ③ ④ ⑤   10 ① ② ③ ④ ⑤   18 ① ② ③ ④ ⑤   25 ① ② ③ ④ ⑤

3 ① ② ③ ④ ⑤   11 ① ② ③ ④ ⑤   19 ① ② ③ ④ ⑤   26 ① ② ③ ④ ⑤

4 ① ② ③ ④ ⑤   12 ① ② ③ ④ ⑤   20 ① ② ③ ④ ⑤   27 ① ② ③ ④ ⑤

5 ① ② ③ ④ ⑤   13 ① ② ③ ④ ⑤   21 ① ② ③ ④ ⑤   28 ① ② ③ ④ ⑤

6 ① ② ③ ④ ⑤   14 ① ② ③ ④ ⑤   22 ① ② ③ ④ ⑤   29 ① ② ③ ④ ⑤

7 ① ② ③ ④ ⑤   15 ① ② ③ ④ ⑤   23 ① ② ③ ④ ⑤   30 ① ② ③ ④ ⑤

8 ① ② ③ ④ ⑤   16 ① ② ③ ④ ⑤

Choose the best answer to each question that follows.

Questions 1–3 are based on the following news report.

KAMPALA, Uganda [Reuters]—A young boy with all the behavioral traits of a monkey has been found living wild in the jungle of the notorious Luwero Triangle, site of massacres and killings during Uganda's civil war.

The boy, believed to be 5 to 7 years old, shuns human company and moves by jumping from place to place like a monkey with his fists clenched. If he is approached, he scratches. When he is still, he squats on his rump. He eats grass or anything else he can find.

Last September, Ugandan government troops retreating from a rebel army found him living with monkeys. He is now at the Naguru orphanage in Kampala, where nurses have given him the name Robert.

Staffers at the orphanage believe Robert lost his parents when he was about a year old during the fighting in the Luwero area and was mothered by a [primate] chimpanzee or a gorilla.

He is about 2½ feet tall and weighs 22 pounds. He grunts and squeals but does not speak.

Theresa Nansikombi, who runs the orphanage, said that when Robert was brought to Naguru he fled from humans, cried all the time and tried to hide his face.

"He ate anything and still does—grass, clothes, blankets and sheets—even stones," she said.

"He looks miserable all the time."

1. The findings in this case support the belief that

   (1) humans can survive in only one environment or culture
   (2) people know what skills and tools are necessary to survive
   (3) humans are descended directly from the monkeys
   (4) human behavior is not instinctive; it is learned
   (5) primates are the only species to teach their young

2. Robert was raised by the monkeys because he

   (1) ran away from home
   (2) lost his parents during a war
   (3) was intentionally abandoned
   (4) was kidnapped and later abandoned
   (5) chose to be raised by them

3. This passage illustrates how Robert has learned certain behaviors from the primates. Which one of the following is an example of a learned, not an instinctive, behavior.

   (1) Babies tend to respond to bright colors.
   (2) Babies babble and squeal before they can talk.
   (3) Infants can be taught to swim because they have not yet learned to fear water.
   (4) Children like security blankets because the blankets give them comfort.
   (5) Infants tend to put objects they can grasp into their mouths.

4. American consumers are not spending their money as freely as they have in the past. As a result, sales of personal computers have been affected. According to the dynamics of supply and demand, what will happen to the price of computers? The price will

   (1) increase to make up for the loss in profits
   (2) remain the same because the cost to manufacture computers stays the same
   (3) decrease to encourage consumers to buy them
   (4) increase in order for manufacturers to improve the quality of computers
   (5) remain the same because fewer computers will be available for sale

Questions 5 and 6 are based on the following cartoon.

Morin
Miami Herald

5. The cartoonist is suggesting that

(1) terrorists have bigger and better weapons than ever before

(2) terrorists deliberately use the media to publicize and promote their causes

(3) terrorists cover their faces because they are afraid to be identified by the media

(4) to terrorists, the media is the real enemy

(5) terrorists want to dominate the world

6. In recent years, the media has been criticized for "glamorizing" certain news events such as terrorist activities. Some people feel that this excessive coverage contributes to an increase in the number of incidents. The media's handling of which of the following could be criticized largely for the same reasons?

(1) the AIDS epidemic affecting Americans

(2) the bloody casualties suffered in Central America

(3) anti-apartheid violence in South Africa

(4) teen suicides in recent years

(5) widespread drug busts in major cities

Questions 7–9 are based on the bar graph below.

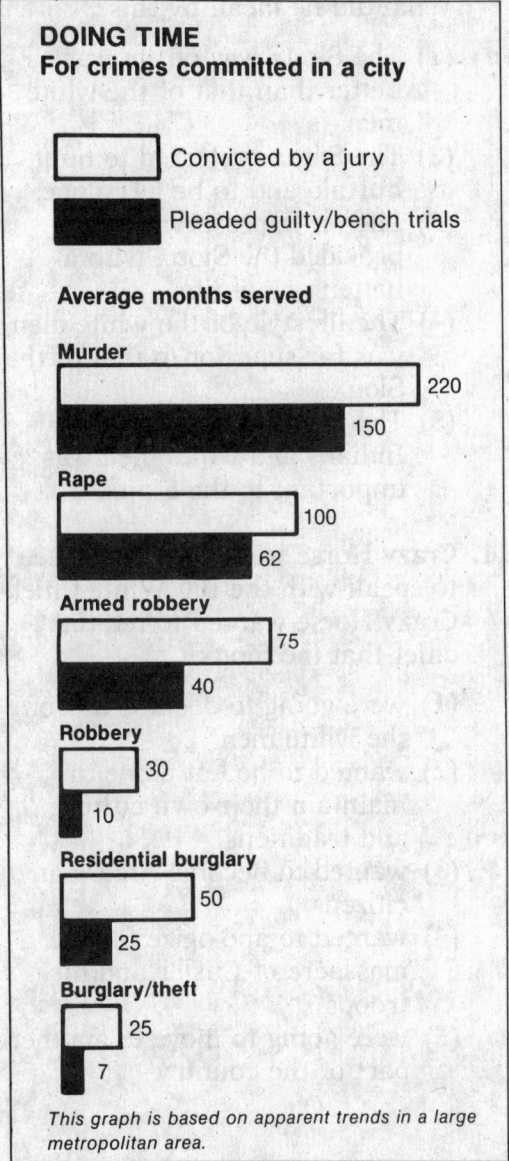

DOING TIME
For crimes committed in a city

☐ Convicted by a jury

■ Pleaded guilty/bench trials

Average months served

Murder
220
150

Rape
100
62

Armed robbery
75
40

Robbery
30
10

Residential burglary
50
25

Burglary/theft
25
7

This graph is based on apparent trends in a large metropolitan area.

7. Which of the following statements is best supported by the information in the graph?

    (1) Accused criminals are better off insisting on their right to a jury trial.
    (2) In this city, accused criminals are better off pleading guilty and accepting a bench trial presided over by a judge.
    (3) Juries do not understand the impact of their decisions.
    (4) Criminal courts in this city are harsher on criminals than in most other cities.
    (5) Criminal courts in this city are more lenient with convictions than in most cities.

8. What values are being given priority by juries in criminal cases in this city?

    (1) the punishment of the criminal over the safety of the community
    (2) the needs of the criminal over the advice of the judge
    (3) the life of the criminal over the needs of the community
    (4) the safety of the community over sympathy for the criminal
    (5) the rights of the criminal over a strict interpretation of the law

9. If defendants have knowledge of the information in the graph, it is reasonable to predict that

    (1) the number of jury trials will increase
    (2) the number of jury trials will remain the same
    (3) the number of bench trials will increase
    (4) juries will give lighter sentences
    (5) judges presiding over bench trials will give harsher sentences

Questions 10 and 11 are based on the following passage.

"We Preferred Our Own Way of Living"

My friend, I do not blame you for this. Had I listened to you this trouble would not have happened to me. I was not hostile to the white men. Sometimes my young men would attack the Indians who were their enemies and took their ponies. They did it in return.

We had buffalo for food, and their hides for clothing and for our teepees. We preferred hunting to a life of idleness on the reservation, where we were driven against our will. At times we did not get enough to eat, and we were not allowed to leave the reservation to hunt.

We preferred our own way of living. We were no expense to the government. All we wanted was peace and to be left alone. Soldiers were sent out in the winter, who destroyed our villages.

Then "Long Hair" (Custer) came in the same way. They say we massacred him, but he would have done the same thing to us had we not defended ourselves and fought to the last. Our first impulse was to escape with our squaws and papooses, but we were so hemmed in that we had to fight.

After that I went up on the Tongue River with a few of my people and lived in peace. But the government would not let me alone. Finally, I came back to the Red Cloud Agency. Yet I was not allowed to remain quiet.

I was tired of fighting. I went to the Spotted Tail Agency and asked that chief and his agent to let me live there in peace. I came here with the agent (Lee) to talk with the Big White Chief, but was not given a chance. They tried to confine me. I tried to escape, and a soldier ran his bayonet into me.

I have spoken.

10. Crazy Horse, chief of the Sioux Indians in the 1870s, said, "We preferred our own way of living." What did he mean by this?

(1) The Sioux way of life was better than that of the white men.
(2) The Sioux preferred to hunt buffalo and to be left alone.
(3) Life on the reservation provided the Sioux with a better way of life.
(4) The lifestyle of the white men was far superior to that of the Sioux.
(5) The hostility between the Indians and white men was important to the Sioux.

11. Crazy Horse went with agent Lee to speak with the Big White Chief. Crazy Horse wanted to tell the chief that the Sioux

(1) were going to declare war on the white men
(2) wanted to be left alone to maintain their own culture and traditions
(3) wanted to become American citizens
(4) wanted to apologize for the massacre of Custer and his troops
(5) were going to move to another part of the country

Questions 12–14 are based on the following passage.

The great rule of conduct for us in regard to foreign nations is, in extending our commercial relations, to have with them as little *political* connection as possible. So far as we have already formed engagements, let them be fulfilled with perfect good faith. Here let us stop.

Europe has a set of primary interests which to us have none or a very remote relation. Hence she must be engaged in frequent controversies, the causes of which are essentially foreign to our concerns. Hence, therefore, it must be unwise in us to implicate ourselves by artificial ties in the ordinary vicissitudes [changes] of her politics or the ordinary combinations and collisions of her friendships or enmities. . . .

It is our true policy to steer clear of permanent alliances with any portion of the foreign world. . . .

from George Washington's
Farewell Address

12. Which one of the following statements reflects George Washington's attitude as expressed in this address?

The United States should

(1) offer its assistance wherever needed in the world
(2) avoid becoming involved in world political affairs
(3) stay out of European affairs while assisting other areas of the world
(4) become as politically connected with Europe as possible
(5) support policies that would increase the territory under its control

13. Based on this quote, Washington may be described *best* as a(n)

(1) patriot
(2) imperialist
(3) isolationist
(4) colonialist
(5) expansionist

14. Based on his address, what would George Washington think of America's position today as a world power? He would think that the United States

(1) has been successful in leaving other nations alone
(2) has achieved its primary goal of being a world power
(3) should continue to control the other nations of the world
(4) has become involved in affairs that are none of America's business
(5) has not changed much from the time when he was president

Question 15 is based on the following chart.

THE RELATIONSHIP BETWEEN INCOME AND EDUCATION, 1990	
Level of Education	Median Income
Elementary 8 years or less	$14,336
High School 1 to 3 years 4 years	$17,155 $21,642
College 1 to 3 years 4 years	$26,094 $32,056

Source: U.S. Bureau of the Census

15. Which of the following conclusions is supported by the chart?

(1) No relationship exists between education level and income.
(2) All people with an elementary school education will earn at least $14,336 per year.
(3) A college education is required to earn over $26,000 per year.
(4) Education alone determines a person's income.
(5) People who have more education are more likely to earn a higher income.

Question 16 is based on the paragraph below.

The Monroe Doctrine demanded that Europe stay out of the affairs of the Americas. President Theodore Roosevelt used the doctrine to support a position on imperialism that he called the "Roosevelt Corollary." It stated that the United States had a right to move into areas of the Americas needing our civilizing power.

16. In which incident would Roosevelt have used the corollary to defend his actions?

(1) his approval of England's colonization of India and Egypt

(2) the United Nations' participation in a conference to end French-German rivalry in Morocco

(3) his support for the Open Door policy for trade with China

(4) his negotiating an informal understanding between the United States and Japan to end unwanted immigration

(5) the aiding of Panamanian rebels against the Colombian government

---

17. Before the Civil War, Virginia was united; however, in 1863, West Virginia chose to become independent. Which is the most reasonable cause of West Virginia's secession from the rest of the state?

(1) The state was too large for only one legislature.

(2) West Virginia was defeated by the North early in the war.

(3) Richmond, Virginia, became the capital of the Confederacy.

(4) There were no slave owners in West Virginia.

(5) Political differences existed between western Virginia and the eastern part of the state.

Questions 18 and 19 are based on the following graph and passage.

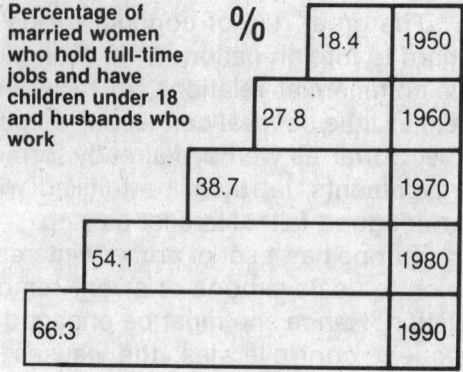

Percentage of married women who hold full-time jobs and have children under 18 and husbands who work	%		
		18.4	1950
		27.8	1960
	38.7		1970
54.1			1980
66.3			1990

Source: Scholastic Update Magazine

The way a male or female acts or is expected to act in society is called a *role*. The traditional role in the American family for the husband has been breadwinner while the wife's role has been homemaker. According to the bar graph above, however, family roles are changing.

18. Which of the following is *least likely* to be considered a cause of the changing role of married women in the family?

(1) increased expenses requiring a second income in many families

(2) more women wanting careers in addition to raising a family

(3) the lack of respect accorded the traditional role of homemaker

(4) increased availability of day care centers and professional baby-sitters

(5) more job opportunities for women than ever before

19. According to the bar graph, during which time period was there the greatest increase in the percentage of married women in the work force?

(1) Before 1950

(2) 1950–1960

(3) 1960–1970

(4) 1970–1980

(5) 1980–1990

Questions 20 and 21 are based on the following cartoon.

LARRY WRIGHT
Courtesy Detroit News

20. Which of the following would most likely agree with the cartoonist's viewpoint?

(1) an opponent of high-rise office development

(2) a conservative politician who is concerned about too many government regulations

(3) the surgeon general who lobbied in favor of printed warnings on cigarette packages

(4) a liberal politician who believes the government should protect the interests of its citizens

(5) a congressman who favors mandatory seat belt laws in all fifty states

21. The main idea the cartoonist is expressing is that the FDA

(1) should be abolished because it violates civil liberties

(2) is experiencing a hiring freeze and is firing longtime employees

(3) has gone to ridiculous extremes in safeguarding the public against potentially harmful products

(4) has control over too many products sold to consumers

(5) focuses too much on products the public considers harmless

22. Between 1935 and 1957, the birth rate rose from 16.9 to 25 per 1,000 people. The most likely cause of this "baby boom" was

(1) the return of young American soldiers from war

(2) the growth of the urban/suburban areas after World War II

(3) the increased mobility of the American family of the 1950s

(4) the continuing expansion of the middle class and its new wealth

(5) the relaxing of moral sanctions against artificial birth control methods

23. Increased personal income lets people purchase more goods and services. For example, spending for houses and cars increases as people feel comfortable in making long-term investments. In such a climate, business would likely

(1) increase production to provide greater quantities of goods

(2) lower the sales tax on the products

(3) spend less money on new equipment and machinery

(4) sell the products to foreign nations

(5) distribute the products equally throughout the country

Questions 24 and 25 are based on the following graph.

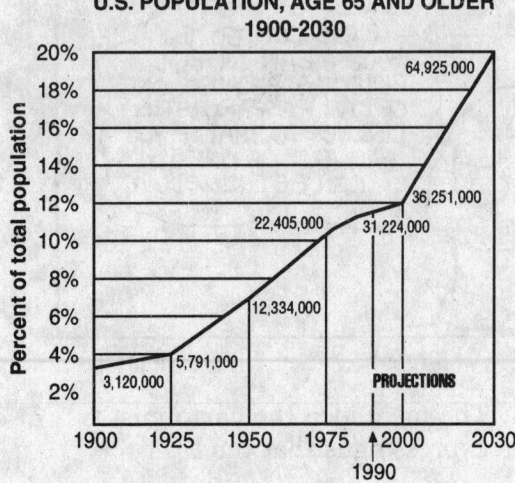

U.S. POPULATION, AGE 65 AND OLDER
1900–2030

Percent of total population

64,925,000
36,251,000
22,405,000
31,224,000
12,334,000
5,791,000
3,120,000
PROJECTIONS

1900 1925 1950 1975 2000 2030
1990

24. The number of people in the United States over the age of 65 is increasing dramatically. Which one of the following governmental programs would be most directly affected by this growth?

(1) veterans' benefits
(2) national defense
(3) job training and employment programs
(4) food stamps
(5) social security

25. The largest increase in the number of people in the U.S. age 65 years and older occurred during which of the following time periods?

(1) 1900–1925
(2) 1925–1950
(3) 1950–1975
(4) 1975–1990
(5) 1990–2000

Questions 26 and 27 are based on the following passage.

In 1992, Australia's Prime Minister, Paul Keating, urged that the country cut its remaining political ties with Britain and become a republic instead of a commonwealth. Britain is no longer a major factor in Australia's economic security. Today, almost half of Australia's exports go to Asia, and Asian immigration to Australia is on the rise. With a declining economy, Australians must decide where their best interests lie.

26. Based on the information in the passage, you can conclude that

(1) Paul Keating is in favor of continued commonwealth status.
(2) Australia's economy will most likely improve if it develops further relations with Asia.
(3) Australia is isolated to maintain its economy.
(4) Politics has nothing to do with geographical location.
(5) Many Australians agree with the prime minister.

27. The decision facing the Commonwealth of Australia is most similar to

(1) the decision to transfer Hong Kong from British rule to Chinese rule
(2) the decision of the Commonwealth of Kentucky to join the United States
(3) the decision to adopt Guam as a territory of the United States
(4) the decision of Puerto Rico about whether to request statehood or remain a commonwealth
(5) the decision of the thirteen original American colonies to form a new nation

Questions 28 and 29 are based on the following map.

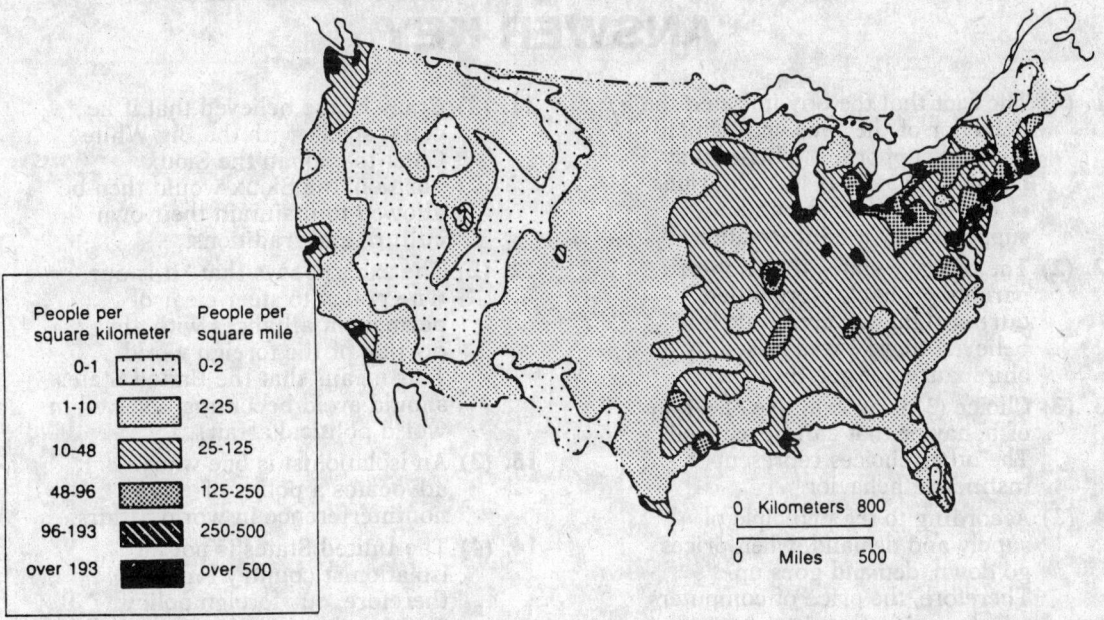

People per square kilometer		People per square mile
0-1		0-2
1-10		2-25
10-48		25-125
48-96		125-250
96-193		250-500
over 193		over 500

0   Kilometers   800

0   Miles   500

28. Based on the map, which one of the following pairs of cities has over 500 people per square mile?

  (1) Miami/Los Angeles
  (2) Houston/New York
  (3) Atlanta/Boston
  (4) Chicago/San Francisco
  (5) Detroit/Dallas

29. The region of the country with the greatest population density is the

  (1) Midwest
  (2) Southwest
  (3) Northwest
  (4) Southeast
  (5) Northeast

Question 30 is based on the following passage.

Vice President Andrew Johnson succeeded Lincoln as president after Lincoln's assassination. Johnson was from Tennessee and was the only southern senator not to join the Confederacy when war broke out. Lincoln had trusted him totally, but many in Congress did not. In spite of Johnson's refusal to join the Confederacy, his every action appeared to be suspiciously pro-South to them.

30. Which of the following actions of Johnson's does *not* support these congressmen's opinion of him?

  (1) his issuing a proclamation forgiving most Confederates
  (2) his demand that Confederate states ratify the Thirteenth Amendment abolishing slavery
  (3) his veto of the civil rights bill that guaranteed rights to freed slaves
  (4) his veto of the Freedman's Bureau bill that had been approved without the input of the southern states
  (5) his opposition to the Fourteenth Amendment that toughened Congress's stand against former Confederate loyalists

Answers begin on page 22.

PRE-TEST 2: SOCIAL STUDIES
ANSWER KEY

1. (4) The fact that the boy imitated the behavior of the apes with which he lived supports the belief that human behavior is learned. None of the other choices can be supported by the information.

2. (2) The passage states that Robert's parents probably were killed during Uganda's civil war. It is believed that he was raised by a chimpanzee or gorilla.

3. (3) Choice (3) is an example of a type of behavior that can be learned. The other choices represent instinctive behavior.

4. (3) According to the principle of supply and demand, when prices go down, demand goes up. Therefore, the price of computers will be reduced to encourage more people to buy them.

5. (2) Terrorist acts get wide publicity. For this reason, terrorists are perceived as using the media to promote their causes.

6. (4) Psychologists have noted that incidents of teenage suicides increase after the reporting of such acts. This is the only case shown in which the glamour attached to an act leads to increased incidence.

7. (2) The graph shows that the average number of months served by criminals convicted by a jury is greater than the sentence imposed by a judge at a bench trial. Therefore, you can conclude that accused criminals are better off pleading guilty and accepting a bench trial instead of a jury trial.

8. (4) The longer sentences imposed by juries suggest that they value the community's safety over mercy for the criminal.

9. (3) If bench trials continue to provide shorter sentences than jury trials for convicted criminals, then you could predict that more defendants will demand bench trials and that the number of bench trials will increase.

10. (2) The Sioux were content with their lifestyle and did not want the white men to interfere with them, as suggested by choice (2).

11. (2) Crazy Horse believed that if he could speak with the Big White Chief to explain the Sioux position, the Sioux would then be allowed to maintain their own culture and traditions.

12. (2) The excerpt says that "It is our true policy to steer clear of permanent alliances with any portion of the foreign world. . . ." This means that the United States should avoid becoming involved in world political affairs.

13. (3) An isolationist is one who advocates a policy of noninterference in world affairs.

14. (4) The United States is not an isolationist country today; therefore, our foreign policy position does not conform to the spirit of isolationism expressed in Washington's address.

15. (5) The chart indicates a higher income as the level of education increases.

16. (5) Like the Monroe Doctrine, the Roosevelt Corollary applied only to countries in the Americas; Panama and Colombia are located in Central and South America respectively.

17. (5) West Virginia was different from eastern Virginia in culture, religion, nationality, and economy. Therefore, it is most reasonable to conclude that West Virginia seceded from the rest of the state because of political differences.

18. (3) Choices (1), (2), (4), and (5) are all plausible reasons for married women joining the work force. Choice (3) is least likely to be a reasonable explanation for married women entering the work force.

19. (4) Between 1970 and 1980, the percentage of married women who work increased by 15.4 percent—from 38.7 to 54.1 percent.

20. (2) The FDA is a government agency that protects consumers. In the cartoon, the cartoonist is criticizing the tendency for regulators to "go overboard." Of all the choices, a conservative politician who is concerned about too much government regulation would most likely agree with the cartoonist's viewpoint.

21. (3) It is obvious that a person who falls out of a tall building can die. The FDA's proposal to ban the construction of tall buildings for this reason can be viewed as ridiculous. None of the other choices is suggested by the cartoon.

22. (1) Quick marriages after soldiers returned from war is the most reasonable explanation for the surge in births. Choices (2), (3), and (4) did not contribute directly to the baby boom. Choice (5) is not a reasonable explanation.

23. (1) When consumers spend more money, businesses capitalize on the increased spending by producing more goods to sell.

24. (5) The social security program would be the most affected because it provides payments to the retired and the elderly.

25. (3) From 1950 to 1975, the population of Americans 65 years of age and older increased from 12,334,000 to 22,405,000—an increase of over 10,000,000 people.

26. (2) The passage states that almost half of Australia's exports already go to Asia. Further relations with Asia would most probably improve the economy.

27. (5) Both Australia and the thirteen original American colonies were dominated by another nation. Like the colonies, Australia wants to be politically and economically independent. By becoming a republic, Australia would also become an independent nation. The other choices involve incorporation of one country into another.

28. (4) Chicago, located at the southern tip of Lake Michigan, and San Francisco, located along the central Pacific coast, make up the only pair of cities that has over 500 people per square mile.

29. (5) The areas of the country with the greatest number of people per square mile are represented in black. The northeastern part of the country has more black areas than any other.

30. (2) Johnson's demand that the states ratify an amendment abolishing slavery was not a pro-southern action, while all of the other choices could be interpreted as being pro-southern.

Use the answer key on pages 22–23 to check your answers to the Pre-Test. Then find the item number of each question you missed and circle it on the chart below to determine the reading skill and content areas in which you need more practice. Pay particular attention to areas where you missed half or more of the questions. The reading skills are covered on pages 187–243. The page numbers for the content areas are listed below on the chart. Knowledge of reading skill and content area–based questions is absolutely essential for success on the GED Social Studies Test. The numbers in boldface are questions based on graphics. For those questions that you missed, review the skill pages indicated.

PRE-TEST 2: SOCIAL STUDIES EVALUATION CHART

Skill Area/ Content Area	Comprehension (pages 189–195)	Application (pages 195–199)	Analysis (pages 200–210)	Evaluation (pages 211–222)
Behavioral Sciences (pages 247–262)	25	3, **24**	2, 22	1, **18**
U.S. History (pages 263–300)	10, 11	13, 16	14, 17	12, 30
Political Science (pages 301–318)	**7, 21**	6	**5, 9**	**8, 20**
Economics (pages 319–332)	19	23	4	**15**
Geography (pages 333–342)	**29**	27	**28**	26

PRE-TEST 3: SCIENCE

The Science Pre-Test consists of 30 multiple-choice questions. Some of the questions are based on charts, graphs, diagrams, and reading passages.

Answer each question as carefully as possible, choosing the best of five answer choices and blackening in the grid. If you find a question too difficult, do not waste time on it. Work ahead and come back to it later when you can think it through carefully.

When you have completed the test, check your work with the answers and explanations at the end of the section.

Use the Evaluation Chart on page 34 to determine which areas you need to review most.

PRE-TEST 3: SCIENCE ANSWER GRID

1 ① ② ③ ④ ⑤   9 ① ② ③ ④ ⑤   17 ① ② ③ ④ ⑤   24 ① ② ③ ④ ⑤

2 ① ② ③ ④ ⑤   10 ① ② ③ ④ ⑤   18 ① ② ③ ④ ⑤   25 ① ② ③ ④ ⑤

3 ① ② ③ ④ ⑤   11 ① ② ③ ④ ⑤   19 ① ② ③ ④ ⑤   26 ① ② ③ ④ ⑤

4 ① ② ③ ④ ⑤   12 ① ② ③ ④ ⑤   20 ① ② ③ ④ ⑤   27 ① ② ③ ④ ⑤

5 ① ② ③ ④ ⑤   13 ① ② ③ ④ ⑤   21 ① ② ③ ④ ⑤   28 ① ② ③ ④ ⑤

6 ① ② ③ ④ ⑤   14 ① ② ③ ④ ⑤   22 ① ② ③ ④ ⑤   29 ① ② ③ ④ ⑤

7 ① ② ③ ④ ⑤   15 ① ② ③ ④ ⑤   23 ① ② ③ ④ ⑤   30 ① ② ③ ④ ⑤

8 ① ② ③ ④ ⑤   16 ① ② ③ ④ ⑤

Choose the best answer to each question that follows.

Question 1 is based on the following passage.

Our blood consists of a liquid, the straw-colored *plasma*, in which are suspended red blood cells, white blood cells, and *platelets*. Red blood cells are used to transport oxygen throughout the body. The different types of white blood cells are used to fight infections. Platelets are important in blood clotting.

1. Based on the passage above, which of the following blood components would be used to repair an open wound?

   (1) plasma and white blood cells
   (2) red blood cells
   (3) white blood cells
   (4) platelets
   (5) white blood cells and platelets

Questions 2 and 3 are based on the following information.

The leaf is a flat organ composed of two layers of photosynthetic cells sandwiched between the epidermal, or outer, layers. The epidermal layers are coated with a waxy covering called the *cuticle*, which prevents the loss of gas and water. Tiny holes, called *stomata*, provide openings for the entry of carbon dioxide and the exit of oxygen.

2. Based on the information above, the leaf "breathes" through its

   (1) photosynthetic cells
   (2) veins
   (3) cuticle
   (4) epidermal layers
   (5) stomata

3. Stomata in plants are most similar to which of the following?

   A. lungs in mammals
   B. pores in animal skin
   C. gills in fish

   (1) A
   (2) B
   (3) C
   (4) A and B
   (5) B and C

Questions 4 and 5 are based on the table below.

Energy Expenditure	
Activity	Calories per Hour
sitting at rest	15
walking	130–200
running	500–900
bicycling	240
swimming	200–700
writing	20

4. According to the table above, which of the people listed below would need to consume 720 calories to maintain body weight after three hours of his or her chosen activity?

   (1) a runner
   (2) a bicyclist
   (3) an office worker
   (4) a writer
   (5) a swimmer

5. For a person concerned with weight loss, which would be the most efficient weight-loss exercise for the time spent?

   (1) bicycling
   (2) swimming
   (3) walking
   (4) writing
   (5) running

Question 6 is based on the following illustration.

| S | N | N | S |

6. As the two bar magnets above are brought closer together, what do you predict will happen?

   (1) They will attract each other.
   (2) They will repel each other.
   (3) They will cancel out each other's magnetic field.
   (4) They will create an alternating current.
   (5) Nothing will happen.

Questions 7–10 are based on the following passage.

Charles Darwin proposed the theory of natural selection in 1859. The theory holds that those species that are best adapted to the conditions under which they live will survive, and those that are not adapted will perish.

An example of this theory is illustrated by the experience of the peppered moth that was once common near Manchester, England, an industrial city.

Before the industrial revolution, the light-colored form of this moth was common and the dark-colored form was rare. As Manchester's environment became increasingly polluted, however, the tree trunks on which the peppered moth lived became blackened by soot. The light-colored form of the moth stood out against the dark tree trunks and was eaten by birds, which destroyed 99 percent of the light-colored moths.

In the absence of the light-colored moths, the rare dark moths became more common and filled the vacancy left by the light-colored moths. In the 1950s, however, Manchester's industries were cleaned up, the tree trunks became lighter, and the light-colored moth became the more common type again.

7. Based on the passage above, the cause of the light-colored moth's disappearance was

   (1) an inability to tolerate a polluted environment
   (2) the birds' preference for its taste
   (3) an insecticide that killed it
   (4) the reduced number of eggs laid by female moths
   (5) its inability to blend in with its environment

8. Which of the following was not a factor in the disappearance of the light-colored moth?

   (1) the industrial pollution found near Manchester
   (2) the presence of moth-eating birds
   (3) the change in the color of the tree trunks
   (4) the interbreeding of light-colored moths with dark-colored moths
   (5) the moth's inability to adapt to a changing environment

9. Based on the information in the passage, you can infer that

   (1) forms of life in a community are influenced by nature's laws
   (2) human activity can have significant ecological impact on an environment
   (3) Darwin's theory works only under ideal circumstances
   (4) all forms of life must fend for themselves
   (5) moths can thrive under the worst conditions

10. Which of the following trees would have bark most favorably suited to the light-colored moth, enabling it to blend in with its surroundings?

    (1) elm
    (2) pine
    (3) paper birch
    (4) red maple
    (5) oak

11. Acetylsalicylic acid (aspirin) is known to retard the blood-clotting process. This can have both positive and negative effects. One positive application of this knowledge is the use of aspirin to

    (1) relieve pain
    (2) reduce inflammation
    (3) reduce the possibility of stroke
    (4) act as a stimulant
    (5) stop bleeding

Questions 12–14 are based on the following passage.

There is, perhaps, no part of the world where the early geological periods can be studied with so much ease and precision as in the United States. Along the northern border between Canada and the United States, there runs a low line of hills known as the Laurentian Hills. Insignificant in height, nowhere rising more than two thousand feet above the level of the sea, these are nevertheless the first mountains that broke the uniform level of Earth's surface and lifted themselves above the waters. Their low stature, as compared with that of other, loftier mountain ranges, is in accordance with an invariable rule by which the relative age of mountains may be estimated. The oldest mountains are the lowest, while the younger and more recent ones tower above their elders and are usually more jagged and dislocated.

12. In the United States, early geological periods

    (1) can be studied only along the country's northern border
    (2) can be studied only in the Rocky Mountains
    (3) can be studied easily and precisely
    (4) are not as visible as in the rest of the world
    (5) can be studied only in the Appalachian Mountains

13. The relationship between low mountain ranges and high mountain ranges can be described *best* in terms of

    (1) old age and youth
    (2) the Laurentian Hills
    (3) the Swiss Alps and the Himalayas
    (4) dislocation and thickness
    (5) their location in either Canada or the United States

14. The Appalachian Mountains are lower than the Rocky Mountains. Therefore, based on the passage, the Appalachian Mountains would be

    (1) younger than the Rocky Mountains
    (2) older than the Rocky Mountains
    (3) the same age as the Rocky Mountains
    (4) more scenic than the Rocky Mountains
    (5) more torn and dislocated than the Rocky Mountains

Question 15 is based on the information and table below.

Heat is able to pass from one molecule to another. This is called *heat conduction*. In the table that follows, the numbers (called coefficients) indicate the relative rates of heat transfer in the materials listed.

HEAT CONDUCTION COEFFICIENTS	
Material	**Coefficient**
silver	100
copper	92
aluminum	50
iron	11
glass	0.20
water	0.12
wood	0.03
air	0.006
perfect vacuum	0

15. The table identifies the best conductors as

    (1) gases
    (2) natural materials
    (3) metals
    (4) liquids
    (5) compounds

Question 16 is based on the following passage.

Tsunamis are seismic sea waves that may be produced by earthquakes, volcanic eruptions, or submarine landslides. They travel at speeds from 500 to 800 kilometers per hour and in the open ocean may be only 30 to 60 centimeters in height. However, as they approach land they are compressed and may reach 30 meters in height.

16. Tsunamis would be very dangerous to humans because of the potential for causing

    (1) earthquakes
    (2) severe flooding
    (3) submarine landslides
    (4) fault lines
    (5) volcanic eruptions

Questions 17 and 18 are based on the following passage.

Loess is a deposit of windblown dust that slowly blankets large areas and often covers existing landforms. A distinctive sedimentary deposit, loess was laid down long ago. It may cover as much as one-tenth of Earth's surface and is particularly widespread in semi-arid regions along the margins of great deserts. The equatorial tropics and the areas once covered by continental glaciers are free of loess.

17. A nation in which loess would likely be found today is

    (1) Republic of the Congo
    (2) Iceland
    (3) Japan
    (4) United States
    (5) Ecuador

18. The equatorial tropics are free of loess most probably because of the absence of which of the following?

    (1) sun
    (2) aridity
    (3) rain
    (4) glaciers
    (5) running water

Question 19 is based on the diagram below.

19. In order to balance the lever in the diagram above, how much must object A weigh?

    (1)   50 pounds
    (2)   100 pounds
    (3)   200 pounds
    (4)   500 pounds
    (5) 1,000 pounds

Question 20 is based on the following information.

The Fathometer is a device used for determining ocean depths. It operates by sending sound waves under water. A sudden pulse of sound is transmitted by a ship and then picked up again after it has been reflected, or echoed, from the sea bottom, and the elapsed time is recorded. Knowing the time and the speed of sound waves through water, the depth of the sea at any point may be computed, often to the nearest foot.

20. From the information in the passage, you can conclude that

(1) the depth of the ocean is already known
(2) the speed at which underwater sound waves travel from the ocean's surface to the bottom remains constant
(3) Fathometers show only approximate depths and are, therefore, unreliable
(4) Fathometers work best in shallow waters
(5) Fathometers operate on scientific and not mathematical principles

Questions 21–23 are based on the following information.

The most common organic acids are formic acid and acetic acid. Formic acid occurs naturally in red ants and in pine needles. In concentrated form it can burn the skin; however, diluted formic acid is used for its germicidal properties. Acetic acid is responsible for the sour taste of pickles and sharp odors that can burn the nostrils. Cider vinegar contains 3 to 6 percent acetic acid and is made by the natural oxidation of apple cider.

21. The main idea of the passage above is that

(1) organic acid can be both harmful and beneficial
(2) formic acid is a part of vinegar
(3) pine needles contain acetic acid
(4) undiluted formic acid is used as a germicide
(5) apple cider turns into formic acid

22. Which of the following organic acids occurring in low concentrations is essential to humans but is highly dangerous when humans are exposed to high concentrations of it?

(1) citric acid found in citrus fruits
(2) lactic acid found in milk products
(3) hydrochloric acid found in the stomach's gastric juices
(4) oxalic acid found in rhubarb leaves
(5) folic acid, a form of Vitamin B used to treat anemia

23. The passage supports the statement that

(1) all acids are harmful to humans
(2) only organic acids are useful to humans
(3) organic acids in diluted form are useful to humans
(4) inorganic acids in diluted form are useful to humans
(5) only diluted inorganic acids are beneficial to humans

Question 24 is based on the following passage.

In a normal person, glutamic acid, a protein-based acid, is found in hemoglobin; however, in persons who have sickle-cell anemia, valine is found in the hemoglobin instead of glutamic acid. This mutation becomes part of the genetic code and is passed on from generation to generation. Sickle-cell anemia occurs in about 10 percent of African-Americans in the United States and in approximately 25 percent of native African blacks.

24. The facts in this passage support which of the following?

   (1) Sickle-cell anemia is not a serious health problem in the United States.
   (2) Sickle-cell anemia is gradually declining worldwide.
   (3) Sickle-cell anemia is related to the physical environment.
   (4) Sickle-cell anemia cannot be cured by means of drugs or medication.
   (5) Sickle-cell anemia has been discovered only recently.

---

25. Which of the following represents the three states of matter?

   (1) water, vinegar, and vegetable oil
   (2) rocks, water, and sand
   (3) salt, pepper, and sugar
   (4) air, helium, and carbon dioxide
   (5) ice, water, and water vapor

Questions 26–28 are based on the chart below.

TRANSFUSION RELATIONSHIP		
Blood Type	Can Receive Blood from	Acts as Donor to
O	O	O, A, B, AB
A	A, O	A, AB
B	B, O	B, AB
AB	O, A, B, AB	AB

26. What type(s) of blood can be given to a person with blood type A?

   (1) only type O
   (2) only types O and A
   (3) only types O and B
   (4) only types A and AB
   (5) any blood type

27. If a person with blood type AB wishes to donate blood, those with which blood type(s) may receive the blood?

   (1) only type O
   (2) only types O and B
   (3) only types B and AB
   (4) only type AB
   (5) all types of blood

28. Which of the following blood types can be regarded as a universal donor?

   (1) O
   (2) A
   (3) B
   (4) AB
   (5) all blood types

Question 29 is based on the following information.

An unusual flowering plant is the *hydrangea*, a shrub that produces showy flowers in the shape of a pom-pom. The hydrangea is unusual in that the color of its flower indicates the type of soil in which it grows. An acidic soil produces a pink bloom, and an alkaline soil produces a blue flower.

29. The characteristic of a change in color is most similar to which of the following tests?
    A. the pH test for alkalinity and acidity
    B. the iodine test for the presence of starch
    C. the litmus-paper test

    (1) A
    (2) B
    (3) C
    (4) A and B
    (5) A and C

Question 30 is based on the following information.

Have you ever wondered how a photograph is made? What actually happens when you push that button to record an image?

When you push the button on a camera, the shutter opens, allowing light to strike the film in the camera. The film is usually coated with silver bromide. The light rays strike the film and reduce the silver bromide, making it less stable.

In black-and-white film, the silver bromide particles that are struck by light turn black when the film is developed. Particles that have not been struck by light will not change. Since the chemical reduction depends on the intensity of light, the film becomes a detailed chemical picture of the object photographed. The developing process converts the chemical pictures into film negatives.

30. What could you conclude if a negative turned out completely black?

    (1) The silver and bromide had been resynthesized into silver bromide.
    (2) The light rays were not strong enough to reduce the silver bromide.
    (3) The film was too old to use.
    (4) The film had not been developed.
    (5) The film had been overexposed to light.

Answers begin on page 33.

PRE-TEST 3: SCIENCE ANSWER KEY

1. **(5)** The passage says that white blood cells fight infections and that platelets are important in clotting of blood. Fighting infections and blood clotting are two processes needed to repair a wound.

2. **(5)** According to the passage, the only opening in the leaf is the stomata. This must be the "mouth" through which a plant breathes.

3. **(2)** Pores, tiny openings in the skin's epidermis, allow the skin to breathe, thus serving a function similar to the stomata in plant leaves.

4. **(2)** A bicyclist would consume approximately 720 calories in three hours ($240 \times 3 = 720$).

5. **(5)** Running consumes the most calories per hour, so it is the most efficient weight-loss activity among those listed.

6. **(2)** Like charges repel; unlike charges attract. The north poles of each magnet are alike, so they will repel each other.

7. **(5)** According to the passage, the light-colored moth was preyed upon by birds when it was no longer able to blend in with the soot-darkened tree trunks on which it lived.

8. **(4)** The interbreeding of light-colored moths with dark-colored moths was not mentioned in the passage.

9. **(2)** The industrial pollution in Manchester that darkened the tree trunks was caused by humans.

10. **(3)** Of the trees listed, the paper birch has the lightest bark, which would enable the light-colored peppered moth to blend in with the environment.

11. **(3)** Since aspirin retards clotting, it is used to reduce the possibility of a stroke, which is caused by the arteries in the brain being blocked by clotted blood.

12. **(3)** The passage says that the early geological periods can be studied with ease and precision.

13. **(1)** The passage describes the relationship between old age and youth; the low mountains are the oldest, and the high mountains are the youngest.

14. **(2)** The Appalachian Mountains are lower than the Rocky Mountains; therefore, the Appalachian Mountains are older.

15. **(3)** The metals silver, copper, aluminum, and iron have the highest heat conduction coefficients; therefore, they are the best conductors among the materials listed.

16. **(2)** Tsunamis are giant waves of water. They would create severe flooding and damage in populated coastal areas.

17. **(4)** Of the countries listed, only the United States has semiarid regions bordering the desert.

18. **(2)** The passage says that loess is widespread in semiarid regions along the margins of great deserts. The tropics are not semiarid but are extremely humid.

19. **(3)** If object A is half as far away from the middle of the lever as the 100-pound weight, then to balance, it must weigh twice as much, or 200 pounds.

20. **(2)** Sound waves must travel at a constant speed through the sea in order for the principle under which a Fathometer works to be valid.

21. **(1)** The passage shows how organic acids can be both beneficial and harmful. Diluted formic acid has germicidal properties, but concentrated formic acid is corrosive and burns. Acetic acid is beneficial because it is used to make pickles but is harmful because its sharp odors can irritate the nostrils.

22. **(3)** Diluted hydrochloric acid is found in the stomach's gastric juices, but undiluted hydrochloric acid is harmful when humans are exposed to it.

23. **(3)** The passage demonstrates how organic acids are beneficial to humans. Examples of beneficial organic acids are formic acid, which can be used as a germicide, and acetic acid, which is used in the processing of cucumbers to make pickles.

24. **(4)** Since sickle-cell anemia is genetic, it has no medical cure. Only a change in genetic material would eliminate the disease.

25. **(5)** The three states of matter are solid, liquid, and gas. Ice is a solid, water is a liquid, and water vapor is a gas.

26. **(2)** Look across the row that starts with blood type A. You can see that a person with blood type A can receive blood from blood types O and A.

27. **(4)** Look across the row on the table that starts with blood type AB. You can see that a person with blood type AB can act as a donor only to a person with blood type AB.

28. **(1)** Since people with blood type O can donate blood to people of all blood types, a person with blood type O is known as a universal donor.

29. **(3)** The characteristic of the hydrangea is most similar to the litmus-paper test. According to the litmus-paper test, acids turn the coloring matter in the litmus paper red, and bases or alkalies turn it blue.

30. **(5)** The last paragraph states that reduced particles of silver bromide turn black when film is developed. If a negative is completely black, then all of the silver bromide must have been reduced by light, indicating overexposure.

Use the answer key on pages 33–34 to check your answers to the Pre-Test. Then find the item number of each question you missed and circle it on the chart below to determine the reading skill and content areas in which you need more practice. Pay particular attention to areas where you missed half or more of the questions. The reading skills are covered on pages 187–243. The page numbers for the content areas are listed below on the chart. Knowledge of reading skill and content area–based questions is absolutely essential for success on the GED Science Test. The numbers in boldface are questions based on graphics. For those questions that you missed, review the skill pages indicated.

PRE-TEST 3: SCIENCE EVALUATION CHART

Skill Area/ Content Area	Comprehension (pages 189–195)	Application (pages 195–199)	Analysis (pages 200–210)	Evaluation (pages 211–222)
Biology (pages 355–374)	1	**4**, 7, 9, **30**	3, 10, **26**, **27**, **28**	5, 8
Earth Science (pages 375–398)	12, 16	13, 14, 18	17	
Chemistry (pages 399–418)	21	2	11, 22, 29	23, 24
Physics (pages 419–440)	15, 25	6, 19		20

PRE-TEST 4: LITERATURE AND THE ARTS

The Literature and the Arts Pre-Test consists of 24 multiple-choice questions. These questions are based on passages of fiction and nonfiction prose, poetry, drama, and commentaries on literature and the arts.

Answer each question as carefully as possible, choosing the best of five answer choices and blackening in the grid. If you find a question too difficult, do not waste time on it. Work ahead and come back to it later when you can think it through carefully.

When you have completed the test, check your work with the answers and explanations at the end of the section.

Use the Evaluation Chart on page 44 to determine which areas you need to review most.

PRE-TEST 4: LITERATURE AND THE ARTS ANSWER GRID

1 ① ② ③ ④ ⑤   7 ① ② ③ ④ ⑤   13 ① ② ③ ④ ⑤   19 ① ② ③ ④ ⑤

2 ① ② ③ ④ ⑤   8 ① ② ③ ④ ⑤   14 ① ② ③ ④ ⑤   20 ① ② ③ ④ ⑤

3 ① ② ③ ④ ⑤   9 ① ② ③ ④ ⑤   15 ① ② ③ ④ ⑤   21 ① ② ③ ④ ⑤

4 ① ② ③ ④ ⑤   10 ① ② ③ ④ ⑤   16 ① ② ③ ④ ⑤   22 ① ② ③ ④ ⑤

5 ① ② ③ ④ ⑤   11 ① ② ③ ④ ⑤   17 ① ② ③ ④ ⑤   23 ① ② ③ ④ ⑤

6 ① ② ③ ④ ⑤   12 ① ② ③ ④ ⑤   18 ① ② ③ ④ ⑤   24 ① ② ③ ④ ⑤

Read each excerpt and choose the best answer to each question.

Questions 1–4 refer to the following biographical sketch.

HOW DID ELVIS PRESLEY ACHIEVE RECOGNITION?

Success often comes to those with humble beginnings. Elvis Aron Presley was born on January 8, 1935, in Tupelo, Mississippi. He first
5 sang in a church choir and taught himself to play the guitar, but he never learned to read music. By 1953, he had moved to Memphis, Tennessee, graduated from high
10 school, and enrolled in night school to become an electrician. That year, at Sun Records, Presley recorded a personal record for his mother, a song that was heard by the com-
15 pany's president. As a result of the president's recognition, Presley's first record, "That's All Right, Mama," was cut in 1954.

He toured the South, and in
20 1955 five of his records were released simultaneously. His first national television appearance was that year on Jackie Gleason's "The Stage Show," but Presley became
25 known for his appearance on "The Ed Sullivan Show," where the young singer gyrated as he sang "rock 'n' roll" music. During the live television performance, Presley was photo-
30 graphed only from the waist up because his motions were considered obscene.

"Elvis the Pelvis" began his film career in 1956 with *Love Me Tender*
35 and signed a long-term film contract. The movie critics were not always kind, but teenagers flocked to Presley's films. Within a few short years, Presley had established a ca-
40 reer that would span twenty-five years of ups and downs and make him one of the most popular entertainers in history. Long after his untimely death at age 42, Presley
45 would be remembered as "The King of Rock 'n' Roll."

1. The author uses the phrase *ups and downs* to refer to Presley's

   (1) use of drugs, "uppers and downers"
   (2) gyrations as he performed
   (3) the best of rock 'n' roll music
   (4) successes and disappointments in his career
   (5) increasing and decreasing finances

2. The last sentence reveals that the author's attitude toward Presley is one of

   (1) indifference
   (2) admiration
   (3) disgust
   (4) disbelief
   (5) sarcasm

3. The main idea of the sketch is that

   (1) there has always been obscenity on television
   (2) singers are more successful if they appear in films
   (3) celebrities are usually more famous after their death
   (4) success always comes to those who work hard
   (5) opportunity and luck are often as important as hard work

4. The statement that "success often comes to those with humble beginnings" would apply best to which of the following historical figures?

   (1) multimillionaire Pierre DuPont
   (2) John F. Kennedy
   (3) Franklin D. Roosevelt
   (4) Abraham Lincoln
   (5) oil billionaire J. Paul Getty

Questions 5–10 refer to the following excerpt from a short story.

WHAT DOES
GOLDIE KRAMER WANT?

"Are you ready to be a citizen of the United States of America?" His voice was suddenly stern.

5 She became rigid. "Sure, sure, Judge!" Her hand jerked. "Of course, I want to be a citizner." Tears welled in her eyes.

"Do you understand what is meant by the Constitution?"

10 Fear blanched her face. *Constitution*! She wanted to talk but couldn't.

He looked at her keenly. "Constitution. Do you know what that 15 means?"

Her eyes wandered from his face to the flag, to the clerk, to the bailiff. Where was Krakauer? Where was Slemo Marcus? She looked at 20 the pictures of Washington and Lincoln on the wall behind the bench. "Ye-ye-yeah!" she stuttered.

She saw the clerk smiling, and she remembered. "Oh, Constitu-25 tion!" she cried. "Constitution! Judge, I'm surprised! Constitution is the laws of the land. 'We, the People of the United States because we want to make a perfect govern-30 ment—' We have Congress, is Senators, two to a State, and Representatives, lots of them, and a President, a Supreme Court—" She tittered. "Oh Judge, I been studying the 35 Constitution. Ask me anything, Judge!"

He brushed at his mouth and chin. "So you know the Constitution, Goldie Kramer? Good. Now 40 tell me what is the capital of the United States?"

Again she was horror-stricken. She heard Jacob Krakauer harumphing at her side. "Vashington," 45 she replied nervously. Her fingers knit together and her lips quivered to pronounce the name: "Washington."

"Who makes the laws? Do you 50 know that?"

Her tongue was thick and her knees were trembling. "Congress makes the laws."

"What does the Supreme Court 55 do?"

"You want," she began timidly, "I should say the truth?"

He nodded. His eyes crinkled.

"Then, Judge, if it's the truth—60 the Supreme Court they say if the law that Congress makes is any good."

The gavel rapped as an audible chuckling rattled about the bench. 65 "Goldie Kramer, what do you know about the President?"

She beamed. "Oh, the President is thirty-five years old. At least. He has a job four years. Maybe 70 more if the people want him. He works hard, Judge. Then he becomes an ex-President."

Gravely the Judge studied his papers. He spoke briefly to the wit-75 nesses. "That's all, Goldie Kramer."

She frowned. "That is all you are going to ask me, Judge?"

"That's all."

"But I learned so much, Judge!" 80 She gestured excitedly. Krakauer and Marcus nudged her, but she ran on. "For three months now I studied and you don't ask me—"

The Judge pulled at his ear. 85 "Very good, Goldie Kramer. One more question. Do you love this country?"

She smiled. "Oh, Judge, what a question! Do I love it? Who wouldn't 90 love such a country? Forty years I been here. My oldest boy he died in France. My grandson will fly an airplane soon for the Army." Her dark eyes flashed. "Judge, even if you 95 gave me some other countries, gave them to me free—just like that—I wouldn't take them. But America, Judge—America is for me—and me, I'm for America!"

100 The courtroom applauded. The Judge smiled.

—Louis Zara, excerpted from
"The Citizner," 1946

5. If you were to make a film of the excerpt, which of the following locales would make the best setting?

   (1) a criminal courtroom
   (2) a naturalization court
   (3) an Ellis Island immigration processing office
   (4) a police station
   (5) U.S. Senate chambers

6. Goldie Kramer is a

   (1) recent immigrant to the United States
   (2) Native American
   (3) citizen seeking employment outside the United States
   (4) U.S. resident seeking citizenship
   (5) grandmother seeking custody of her grandson

7. Goldie can best be described as

   (1) anxious and emotional
   (2) self-assured and calm
   (3) overly confident
   (4) defeated and troubled
   (5) lighthearted and eager

8. " 'But I learned so much, Judge!' She gestured excitedly. Krakauer and Marcus nudged her, but she ran on." The author includes this to show that

   (1) the judge was angered by Goldie's behavior
   (2) her friends encouraged her to continue speaking
   (3) the tension was increasing in the room
   (4) Goldie was too frightened to speak
   (5) her friends were trying to silence her

9. A writer may use different methods to create characters and make them come to life. Which of the five methods below is *not* used in the excerpt above?

   (1) showing the character's actual speech patterns
   (2) showing what others say about the character
   (3) revealing the character's private thoughts
   (4) describing the character
   (5) showing the character in action

10. The title of the excerpt is "The Citizner." Although no such word exists, it is, nevertheless, an appropriate title. The author most likely chose such a title mainly to

   (1) arouse the reader's curiosity
   (2) test the reader's knowledge of standard English
   (3) impart a lighthearted tone to a serious subject
   (4) show that Goldie Kramer needs to learn to speak English
   (5) ridicule the entire naturalization process

Questions 11–13 refer to the following excerpt from a novel.

HOW DOES THE PERSON FEEL?

Once again he did his Christmas shopping in a Rexall drugstore. It was late, the day before Christmas Eve, and he hadn't had the spirit or
5 energy or presence of mind to do it earlier or thoughtfully. Boredom, which had begun as a mild infection, now took him over completely. No activity seemed worth the doing,
10 no conversation worth having. The fluttery preparations at home seemed fake and dingy. His mother was going on as she did every year about the incredible price of trees
15 and butter. As though their tree would be anything other than it had always been: the huge shadowy thing in a corner burdened with decorations she had had since she was
20 a girl. As if her fruitcakes were edible, or her turkey done all the way to the bone. His father gave them all envelopes of varying amounts of money, never thinking that just once
25 they might like something he actually went into a department store and selected.

—Toni Morrison, excerpted from
Song of Solomon, 1977

11. The son waits until the last minute to do his Christmas shopping because he

  (1) is following the example set by his father
  (2) couldn't go shopping until he received his paycheck
  (3) hasn't any idea what to buy for his parents
  (4) doesn't really care what gifts he buys
  (5) spent all his money on a Christmas tree

12. The character's attitude is one of

  (1) sadness and resentment
  (2) suspense and fear
  (3) cheerfulness
  (4) peace and tranquility
  (5) nostalgia

13. Which of the following methods does the author rely on most heavily in creating character in this excerpt?

  (1) showing the character's actual speech patterns
  (2) showing what other characters say about the character
  (3) revealing the character's private thoughts
  (4) describing the character's physical features
  (5) showing the character in action

Questions 14–17 refer to the following poem.

WHAT HAPPENED TO TOM MERRITT?

Tom Merritt

At first I suspected something—
She acted so calm and absent-minded.
And one day I heard the back door shut,
As I entered the front, and I saw him slink
5 Back of the smokehouse into the lot,
And across the field.
And I meant to kill him on sight.
But that day, walking near Fourth Bridge,
Without a stick or a stone at hand,
10 All of a sudden I saw him standing,
Scared to death, holding his rabbits,
And all I could say was, "Don't, Don't, Don't,"
As he aimed and fired at my heart.

—Edgar Lee Masters, 1915

14. Who is the speaker of this poem?

  (1) Merritt's wife
  (2) a murderer
  (3) Tom Merritt
  (4) God
  (5) the sheriff

15. "At first I suspected something—
    She acted so calm and absent-
    minded. And one day I heard the
    back door shut . . ." (lines 1–3)
    The poet introduces the poem
    with these lines to show us that
    Tom Merritt

    (1) was a very suspicious person
    (2) was sure that his wife was ill
    (3) had suspected that his wife
        was losing her mind
    (4) had suspected that his wife
        was seeing another man
    (5) was sure that his wife still
        loved him

16. The poem mainly uses which of
    the following techniques?

    (1) rhyme—the repetition of two
        or more vowel sounds
    (2) verse—a division of a poem
        into distinct parts
    (3) rhythm—an emphasis
        on certain words or
        syllables (beat)
    (4) free verse—the absence
        of rhyme and a regular
        rhythmic pattern
    (5) personification—the
        attributing to an animal or
        thing some human activity
        or quality

17. "Don't, Don't, Don't . . ." (line 12)
    The way in which the poet
    presents these words implies
    that Tom

    (1) did not want to hurt the other
        man
    (2) tried to annoy the other man
    (3) begged the man to stop seeing
        Tom's wife
    (4) turned to run away from the
        other man
    (5) was shot before he finished
        the statement

Questions 18–20 refer to the following excerpt from a play.

WHAT DOES HIGGINS THINK OF WOMEN?

PICKERING: Excuse the straight question, Higgins. Are you a man of good character where women are concerned?

HIGGINS: [*Moodily.*] Have you ever met a man of good character where women are concerned?

PICKERING: Yes: very frequently.

HIGGINS: [*Dogmatically, lifting himself on his hands to the level of the piano, and sitting on it with a bounce.*] Well, I haven't. I find that the moment I let a woman make friends with me, she becomes jealous, exacting, suspicious, and a damned nuisance. I find that the moment I let myself make friends with a woman, I become selfish and tyrannical. Women upset everything. When you let them into your life, you find that the woman is driving at one thing and you're driving at another.

PICKERING: At what, for example?

HIGGINS: [*Coming off the piano restlessly.*] Oh, Lord knows! I suppose the woman wants to live her own life; and the man wants to live his; and each tries to drag the other on to the wrong track. One wants to go north and the other south; and the result is that both have to go east, though they both hate the east wind. [*He sits down on the bench at the keyboard.*] So here I am, a confirmed old bachelor, and likely to remain so.

PICKERING: [*Rising and standing over him gravely*.] Come, Higgins! You know what I mean. If I'm to be in this business I shall feel responsible for that girl. I hope it's understood that no advantage is to be taken of her position.

HIGGINS: What! That thing! Sacred, I assure you. [*Rising to explain.*] You see, she'll be a pupil; and teaching would be impossible unless pupils were sacred. I've taught scores of American millionairesses how to speak English: the best looking women in the world. I'm seasoned. They might as well be blocks of wood. I might as well be a block of wood.

—George Bernard Shaw, excerpted from *Pygmalion*, 1913

18. Higgins's negative attitude toward women is based on his

   (1) recent divorce
   (2) lack of contact with women
   (3) desire to meet beautiful women
   (4) previous experience with women
   (5) upcoming marriage

19. "One wants to go north and the other south; and the result is that both have to go east, though they both hate the east wind."

The playwright includes this reference to show that

   (1) relationships are stronger if both parties sacrifice
   (2) couples often come from different regions of the country
   (3) compromise can have negative effects upon a relationship
   (4) trust is the most important element of a relationship
   (5) women have equal rights in all relationships

20. The playwright uses the image of blocks of wood to show Higgins's

   (1) strictness as a teacher
   (2) dislike of inflexibility
   (3) pride in his teaching skills
   (4) will to "break" his clients
   (5) lack of emotions toward his clients

Questions 21–24 refer to the following excerpt from a commentary.

DOES TV STEREOTYPE?

Hispanics may be the fastest-growing minority group in the USA, but they are sorely underrepresented on prime-time television.

5 While 9% of the U.S. population is Hispanic, only 2% of prime-time characters were during a week surveyed by *USA TODAY*. Asians and Native Americans also were underrepresented, with Asians 1% of
10 TV's players vs. 3% of the U.S. population and Native Americans .4% of TV's characters vs. 1% in real life.

The problem lies in perceptions, says Ray Blanco of the Na-
15 tional Hispanic Academy of Media Arts & Sciences.

"People tend to think that all Hispanics don't speak English, only
20 watch Spanish-language TV and don't have a disposable income, which is not the case," Blanco says.

Hispanic roles that do exist, Blanco adds, often reinforce derog-
25 atory stereotypes.

Actor Marco Sanchez agrees.

"I can't tell you how frustrating it was to go on auditions and know I'd be considered for one of four
30 roles: the drug dealer, the gang member, the lover or the streetwise youth with a heart of gold."

Sanchez, the son of Cuban immigrants, says his mother sug-
35 gested he change his name, "but I refused to compromise a part of myself to get a job."

—Donna Gable, excerpted from "TV's Limited Visions of Hispanics," August 30, 1993, *USA Today*

21. According to the excerpt, the fastest-growing minority group in the United States is

(1) Hispanics
(2) Asians
(3) Native Americans
(4) Cubans
(5) African Americans

22. Which of the following statements best sums up the main idea of the excerpt?

(1) It's a myth that Hispanics don't watch programs broadcast in English.
(2) Prime-time TV programs tend to ignore or stereotype minorities.
(3) Native Americans and Asians are underrepresented on television.
(4) There are not enough good roles on television for Cuban actors.
(5) The perception that TV does not represent all Americans is mistaken.

23. The mother of actor Marco Sanchez suggested that he change his name because

(1) casting agents found it hard to remember
(2) people kept misspelling and mispronouncing the name
(3) it was not an appropriate name for a stage and screen star
(4) people kept mistaking him for someone with a similar name
(5) it limited the kinds of characters he was allowed to play

24. If Marco Sanchez were offered the following roles, which would he most likely pick?

(1) a drug dealer in a made-for-TV movie
(2) the lead in a Shakespearean comedy
(3) a gang leader on a weekly drama series
(4) a streetwise youth in a feature film
(5) the love interest of a married woman in a soap opera

Answers begin on page 43.

PRE-TEST 4: LITERATURE AND THE ARTS ANSWER KEY

1. **(4)** The term *ups and downs* refers to high and low points in the entertainer's long career.

2. **(2)** The word *King* implies admiration. The entire passage discusses Presley's early career and the attitude throughout is one of admiration.

3. **(5)** Although hard work is important, being in the right place at the right time also contributes to success. Presley's move to Memphis and his recognition by the record company president were circumstances that were crucial to his success.

4. **(4)** "Humble beginnings" suggests a lack of wealth and influence. Abraham Lincoln, who was born in a log cabin and became president, is the only choice listed who rose from humble beginnings. All the other men were born into wealthy families.

5. **(2)** The judge is asking Goldie questions required of one seeking U.S. citizenship, as would be done in a naturalization court.

6. **(4)** Goldie has been living in the United States for forty years and is asking to become a U.S. citizen.

7. **(1)** Goldie expresses fear, panic, relief, and excitement. Her lips quiver and her knees tremble, but she beams with pride.

8. **(5)** Goldie studied hard for the interrogation and is upset that the judge is not asking her more questions. Her friends do not want her to offend the judge, so they attempt to stop her.

9. **(2)** The writer employs all of the methods listed except showing what other characters say about Goldie.

10. **(3)** Many people take the naturalization process very seriously. The author appears to treat a serious proceeding lightheartedly. While the title does arouse the reader's curiosity, it goes beyond arousing curiosity to establish a lighthearted mood.

11. **(4)** Lines 4–6 say that he "hadn't had the spirit or energy or presence of mind to do it [shop] earlier or thoughtfully." In other words, the son doesn't care what he buys.

12. **(1)** The character is depressed and resents his parents' activities.

13. **(3)** The excerpt is based almost entirely on the private thoughts of the character; none of the other methods is used.

14. **(3)** The title and the reference to the other characters implies that Tom, a dead man, is speaking as "I."

15. **(4)** Her strange behavior and someone's leaving his house aroused his suspicion.

16. **(4)** The poem is written in free verse; there is no rhyme or regular rhythmic pattern.

17. **(5)** The sentence *"Don't"* is unfinished. We assume Tom was killed.

18. **(4)** Higgins refers to "the moment I let a woman make friends with me" and "the moment I let myself make friends with a woman," so we know he has had some experience.

19. **(3)** The reference to directions implies that couples settle for a new direction neither one wants.

20. **(5)** Blocks of wood do not feel or express emotions.

21. (1) The first sentence states that Hispanics are "the fastest-growing minority group in the USA."

22. (2) The first two paragraphs present statistics that show minorities are underrepresented on prime-time TV. The last six paragraphs are about the problem of "derogatory stereotypes."

23. (5) In lines 26–32, Sanchez complains that, as a Cuban-American, he was offered only stereotypical roles. He then goes on to explain that his mother suggested that he change his name. The implication is that Sanchez's Hispanic name was keeping him from being offered a wide variety of roles.

24. (2) In lines 26–32, Sanchez says, "I can't tell you how frustrating it was to go on auditions and know I'd be considered for one of four roles: the drug dealer, the gang member, the lover or the streetwise youth with a heart of gold." Sanchez would probably welcome the opportunity to play against these stereotypes in a Shakespeare comedy.

Use the answer key on pages 43–44 to check your answers to the Pre-Test. Then find the item number of each question you missed and circle it on the chart below to determine the reading skill and content areas in which you need more practice. Pay particular attention to areas where you missed half or more of the questions. The reading skills are covered on pages 187–243. The page numbers for the content areas are listed below on the chart. Knowledge of reading skill and content area–based questions is absolutely essential for success on the GED Literature and the Arts Test. For those questions that you missed, review the skill pages indicated.

PRE-TEST 4: LITERATURE AND THE ARTS EVALUATION CHART

Skill Area/ Content Area	Comprehension (pages 189-195)	Application (pages 195-199)	Analysis (pages 200-210)
Prose Fiction (pages 453-482)	6, 7, 11	5	8, 9, 10, 12, 13
Poetry (pages 483-502)	14, 17		15, 16
Drama (pages 503-518)	18		19, 20
Nonfiction Prose (pages 519-536)	1, 3	4	2
Commentaries (pages 537-546)	21, 22	24	23

PRE-TEST 5: MATHEMATICS

The Mathematics Pre-Test consists of 40 items. It offers you the opportunity to test both your computational and problem-solving skills. These are not multiple-choice items so you will have to work as accurately and carefully as possible. Be sure to use any diagrams or charts that are provided with the problems.

Use the Evaluation Chart on page 53 to determine which areas you need to review most.

PRE-TEST 5: MATHEMATICS ANSWER GRID

1 _____	11 _____	21 _____	31 _____
2 _____	12 _____	22 _____	32 _____
3 _____	13 _____	23 _____	33 _____
4 _____	14 _____	24 _____	34 _____
5 _____	15 _____	25 _____	35 _____
6 _____	16 _____	26 _____	36 _____
7 _____	17 _____	27 _____	37 _____
8 _____	18 _____	28 _____	38 _____
9 _____	19 _____	29 _____	39 _____
10 _____	20 _____	30 _____	40 _____

You may find these formulas useful in solving some of the following problems.

FORMULAS

Description	Formula
AREA (A) of a:	
square	$A = s^2$ where s = side
rectangle	$A = lw$ where l = length, w = width
triangle	$A = \frac{1}{2}bh$ where b = base, h = height
circle	$A = \pi r^2$ where $\pi \cong 3.14$, r = radius
PERIMETER (P) of a:	
square	$P = 4s$ where s = side
rectangle	$P = 2l + 2w$ where l = length, w = width
circle—circumference (C)	$C = \pi d$ where $\pi \cong 3.14$, d = diameter
VOLUME (V) of a:	
cube	$V = s^3$ where s = side
rectangular container	$V = lwh$ where l = length, w = width, h = height
Pythagorean theorem	$c^2 = a^2 + b^2$ where c = hypotenuse, a and b are legs of a right triangle
distance (d) between two points in a plane	$d = \sqrt{(x_2 - x_1)^2 + (y_2 - y_1)^2}$ where (x_1, y_1) and (x_2, y_2) are two points in a plane
slope of a line (m)	$m = \dfrac{y_2 - y_1}{x_2 - x_1}$ where (x_1, y_1) and (x_2, y_2) are two points in a plane

Solve each problem.

1. Subtract 386 from 72,000.

2. Divide 5310 by 9.

3. In a recent village election, six precincts recorded the following voter turnout.

Precinct	Number of Voters
#26	168
#15	240
#10	195
#7	180
#21	312
#25	87

What was the average number of voters per precinct?

4. Find 1.43 plus .5.

5. What is .38 divided by .4?

6. Corey needs $120 to buy a new coat. She has saved the money she received from four dividend checks of $16.75 each. How much more money must she add to those savings to pay for the coat?

7. $1\frac{1}{4}$
   $-\frac{3}{4}$

8. $4\frac{1}{5} \times \frac{1}{2} =$

Questions 9 and 10 are based on the chart below, which compares the growth of four local companies.

	Sales	
	1989	1993
Magic Marketing	$323,000	$904,400
Futures International	$630,000	$925,000
Townley Agency	$264,000	$1,497,000
Billings Printing	$2,000,000	$6,000,000

9. Billings Printing's 1993 sales were what percent of its 1989 sales?

10. If Magic Marketing continues to have approximately the same rate of growth for the 4 years to 1997, what will be the projected sales in 1997 (to the nearest 500,000 dollars)?

11. Martha had $12\frac{2}{3}$ yards of drapery material. She used $\frac{3}{4}$ of it to make the drapes for her family room. How much does she have left to make matching throw pillows?

12. On the first day of their vacation, the Morales family drove 312 miles in 6 hours. At that rate, how far will they travel the next day if they drive for 8 hours?

13. During the last winter carnival, the local college students built a 30-foot snowman out of 100 tons of snow. How much snow will be needed to build a 36-foot snowman this year?

14. Find 72% of $350.

15. Find the length of the diagonal brace used to reinforce the barn door.

12 ft

5 ft

16. Nick's time card shows his hours for one week. If he works 8 hours per day before earning overtime, find Nick's total pay before deductions.

PHILLIPS CORPORATION time card

Name: Nick Acino   **SS #:** 002-00-0021

Date	From	To
7/8	8:30 A.M.	4:30 P.M.
7/9	8:30 A.M.	5:15 P.M.
7/10	8:00 A.M.	4:30 P.M.
7/11	8:30 A.M.	6:00 P.M.
7/12	8:30 A.M.	4:45 P.M.

Total Regular Hours _____ at $8.40

Overtime Hours _____ at $12.60 (over 40 hours)

17. In the formula for the circumference of a circle, the *d* stands for the diameter, which is twice the radius, *r*. If $\pi \cong 3.14$ and $r = 3$ m, choose the expression below that could be used to find the circumference of the circle.

(1) (3.14)(3)
(2) (3.14)(6)
(3) (3.14)(1.5)
(4) $(3.14)(3^2)$
(5) not enough information is given

18. Write 273,000 in scientific notation.

19. There were many increases in gasohol sales over a nine-year period. What is the difference between the smallest annual increase and the largest annual increase?

GASOHOL SALES
(in millions of gallons)

20. Find the number of square *yards* of sod needed to cover the circular putting green shown below. (*Hint*: 9 sq ft = 1 sq yd)

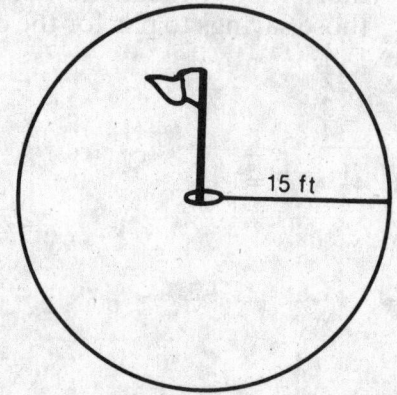

15 ft

21. Margaret wants to put a wallpaper border around her bedroom walls. The room is a rectangle 15 feet by 20 feet. How many complete *yards* of the wallpaper must she buy?

22. How much sand is needed to fill a sandbox 8 feet by 6 feet to a depth of 18 inches?

23. Find the measure of angle *x* in the illustration below.

x   78°

24. Main Street and Union Avenue are parallel roads as shown below.

The railroad tracks cut across both streets. What is the angle measure of the land on which the station rests, based on the information given in the diagram above?

25. Solve for x: $14 = \frac{x}{5}$

26. Solve for x: $4x - 9 = 7$

27. Solve for x: $3(x - 2) - 3 = x + 5$

28. Evaluate: $-4 + (-3) - (-2)$

29. Find the average temperature of most of Illinois for the frigid day reported on this weather map.

30. If $x = -2$ and $y = 5$, find the value of the expression $5y - 3x^2$.

31. Miguel has fourteen coins in his pocket. He has one more dime than quarters and three more nickels than dimes. How many of each coin does he have?

32. Using the diagram below, find the measure of angle A.

33. If 6 inches of decorative ribbon costs $3.25, how much does a yard cost?

34. If one kilogram = 2.2 pounds, does a 3-kilogram roast beef weigh more or less than a 6-pound roast?

35. To find the height of the evergreen in his backyard, Doug sketched the information shown here.

He placed a yardstick parallel to the tree and compared its shadow on the ground with the length of the shadow of the tree. How tall is the tree?

Questions 36 and 37 are based on this drawing.

36. Find the length of the line segment from point A to point B.

37. Find the slope of the line AB.

38. Look at the triangle below. What is the measure of $\angle b$?

39. In a standard deck of 52 playing cards, what is the probability of drawing an ace on one draw?

40. Evaluate:

$$\sqrt{25} + (4 \times 3)^2 - (5 \times 2)$$

Answers begin on page 51.

PRE-TEST 5: MATHEMATICS ANSWER KEY

1. **71,614**

$$\begin{array}{r} 72,000 \\ -386 \\ \hline 71,614 \end{array}$$

2. **590**

$$\begin{array}{r} 590 \\ 9\overline{)5310} \\ -45 \\ \hline 81 \\ 81 \\ \hline 00 \end{array}$$

3. **197 voters**

   Find the total:
   $168 + 240 + 195 + 180 + 312 + 87 = 1182$
   Find the average:
   $1182 \div 6 = 197$

4. **1.93**

$$\begin{array}{r} 1.43 \\ +.5 \\ \hline 1.93 \end{array}$$

5. **.95**

$$\begin{array}{r} .95 \\ .4.\overline{)3.80} \\ \underline{3\ 6} \\ 20 \\ \underline{20} \\ 0 \end{array}$$

6. **$53**

   First, find the total in checks:
   $\$16.75 \times 4 = \$67$
   Then, find the difference:
   $\$120 - \$67 = \$53$

7. **$\frac{1}{2}$**

$$1\frac{1}{4} = \frac{5}{4}$$
$$-\frac{3}{4} = \frac{3}{4}$$
$$\frac{2}{4} = \frac{1}{2}$$

8. **$2\frac{1}{10}$**

   $4\frac{1}{5} \times \frac{1}{2} =$
   $\frac{21}{5} \times \frac{1}{2} = \frac{21}{10} = 2\frac{1}{10}$

9. **300%**

   Write a ratio:
   $\frac{\$6 \text{ million}}{\$2 \text{ million}} = \frac{3}{1}$
   Change the ratio to a percent:
   $\frac{3}{1} = 300\%$

10. **$2.5 million**

    First compare 1993 to 1989:
    $\frac{\$904,400}{\$323,000} = 2.80 = 280\%$

    *Then multiply 1993 sales by 280%
    to find the 1997 projection:*
    $\$904,400 \times 2.8 = \$2,532,320$

    Then round to the nearest $500,000:
    $\$2,500,000$

11. **$3\frac{1}{6}$ yards**

    First, find $\frac{3}{4}$ of the material:
    $12\frac{2}{3} \times \frac{3}{4} = \frac{38}{3} \times \frac{3}{4} = \frac{38}{4} = 9\frac{1}{2}$

    Then, find the difference:

    $$\begin{array}{r} 12\frac{2}{3} = 12\frac{4}{6} \\ -9\frac{1}{2} = 9\frac{3}{6} \\ \hline 3\frac{1}{6} \text{ yd} \end{array}$$

12. **416 miles**

    $\frac{312 \text{ miles}}{6 \text{ hours}} = \frac{x}{8 \text{ hours}}$

    $= \frac{312 \times 8}{6} = 416$

13. **120 tons**

    $\frac{30 \text{ feet}}{100 \text{ tons}} = \frac{36 \text{ feet}}{x}$

    $= \frac{36 \times 100}{30} = \frac{3600}{30} = 120$

14. **$252**

    $\frac{x}{\$350} = \frac{72}{100}$

    $= \frac{\$350 \times 72}{100} = \frac{\$25,200}{100} = \$252$

    or
    $350 \times .72 = 252$

15. **13 feet** $c^2 = a^2 + b^2$
    $c^2 = 12^2 + 5^2$
    $c^2 = 144 + 25$
    $c^2 = 169$
    $c = \sqrt{169} = 13$

16. **$373.80**

    Find Nick's hours, including overtime:

    $8 + 8\frac{3}{4} + 8\frac{1}{2} + 9\frac{1}{2} + 8\frac{1}{4} = 43$

    40 hours regular; 3 hours overtime
    Find Nick's total pay:

    $$\begin{array}{r} 40 \times \$\ 8.40 = \$336.00 \\ +3 \times \$12.60 = \$\ 37.80 \\ \hline \$373.80 \end{array}$$

17. **(2) (3.14)(6)**

    The formula for circumference is
    $C = \pi d$; d = twice the radius or
    $2 \cdot 3 = 6$
    $C = \pi d$
    $= (3.14)(6)$

18. 2.73×10^5

19. **218 million gallons**

    Smallest increase:
    85 million − 80 million = 5 million
    Largest increase:
    790 − 567 = 223 million
    Find the difference:
    223 − 5 = 218 million

20. 78.5 sq yd
$$A = \pi r^2$$
$$A = \pi(15)^2$$
$$A = 3.14 \cdot 225$$
$$A = 706.5 \text{ sq ft}$$
$$A = 706.5 \div 9 = 78.5 \text{ sq yd}$$

21. 24 yd
$$P = 2l + 2w$$
$$P = 2(20) + 2(15)$$
$$P = 40 + 30 = 70 \text{ ft}$$
$$(1 \text{ yd} = 3 \text{ ft})$$
$$P = 70 \div 3 = 23\tfrac{1}{3} \text{ yards needed,}$$
so she must buy 24 yards

22. 72 cu ft
$$V = lwh$$
$$V = 8 \cdot 6 \cdot 1\tfrac{1}{2} \quad (18 \text{ in} = 1\tfrac{1}{2} \text{ ft})$$
$$V = 72 \text{ cu ft}$$

23. 102° $180° - 78° = 102°$

24. 105° The angle above the station is 75°, the same as the angle above Main Street. To find its supplement:
$$180° - 75° = 105°$$

25. $x = 70$
$$14 = \frac{x}{5}$$
$$14 \cdot 5 = x$$
$$70 = x$$

26. $x = 4$
$$4x - 9 = 7$$
$$4x = 7 + 9$$
$$4x = 16$$
$$x = \frac{16}{4} = 4$$

27. $x = 7$
$$3(x - 2) - 3 = x + 5$$
$$3x - 6 - 3 = x + 5$$
$$3x - 9 = x + 5$$
$$3x - x - 9 + 9 = x - x + 5 + 9$$
$$2x = 14$$
$$x = 7$$

28. -5
$$-4 + (-3) - (-2)$$
$$-4 - 3 + 2$$
$$-7 + 2 = -5$$

29. $-13°$
Find the total:
$$-19°$$
$$-12°$$
$$-18°$$
$$-10°$$
$$-13°$$
$$-12°$$
$$\underline{-\ 7°}$$
$$-91°$$
Find the average:
$$-91° \div 7 = -13°$$

30. 13
$$5y - 3x^2$$
$$5(5) - 3(-2)^2$$
$$25 - 3(4)$$
$$25 - 12 = 13$$

31. 3 quarters, 4 dimes, 7 nickels
$$\text{Let } x = \text{quarters}$$
$$x + 1 = \text{dimes}$$
$$x + 1 + 3 = \text{nickels}$$
$$x + x + 1 + x + 1 + 3 = 14$$
$$3x + 5 = 14$$
$$3x = 14 - 5$$
$$3x = 9$$
$$x = \frac{9}{3} = 3$$
$$x = 3 \text{ quarters}$$
$$x + 1 = 4 \text{ dimes}$$
$$x + 4 = 7 \text{ nickels}$$

32. 30°
$$\angle C = 180° - 110° = 70°$$
$$\angle B = 180° - 100° = 80°$$
$$\angle A = 180° - (80° + 70°) = 30°$$

33. $19.50
Find 1 ft of ribbon:
$$(6 \text{ in} = \tfrac{1}{2} \text{ ft})$$
$$2 \times \$3.25 = \$6.50$$
Find 1 yd of ribbon:
$$(3 \text{ ft} = 1 \text{ yd})$$
$$3 \times \$6.50 = \$19.50$$

34. more
$$\frac{1 \text{ kg}}{2.2 \text{ lb}} = \frac{3 \text{ kg}}{x \text{ lb}}$$
$$= \frac{3 \times 2.2}{1} = 6.6 \text{ lb}$$

Therefore, the 3-kg roast weighs more than the 6-lb roast.

35. $16\tfrac{1}{2}$ feet $\dfrac{3}{4} = \dfrac{x}{22}$
$$= \frac{22 \times 3}{4} = \frac{66}{4} = 16\tfrac{1}{2}$$

36. $2\sqrt{5}$
$$d = \sqrt{(x_2 - x_1)^2 + (y_2 - y_1)^2}$$
$$= \sqrt{(5 - 1)^2 + (4 - 2)^2}$$
$$= \sqrt{4^2 + 2^2}$$
$$= \sqrt{16 + 4}$$
$$= \sqrt{20} = \sqrt{4 \cdot 5} = 2\sqrt{5}$$

37. $\dfrac{1}{2}$
$$\frac{y_2 - y_1}{x_2 - x_1}$$
$$\frac{4 - 2}{5 - 1} = \frac{2}{4} = \frac{1}{2}$$

38. 70°
First, find $\angle c$:
The measure of angle c is 55° since both side ab and side bc are 6 inches.
Then, find $\angle b$:
$$180° - 2(55°) =$$
$$180° - 110° = 70°$$

39. $\dfrac{1}{13}$ $\dfrac{4 \text{ aces}}{52 \text{ cards}} = \dfrac{1}{13}$

40. 139
$$\sqrt{25} + (4 \times 3)^2 - (5 \times 2)$$
$$5 + 12^2 - 10$$
$$5 + 144 - 10 = 149 - 10 = 139$$

Use the answer key on pages 51–52 to check your answers to the Pre-Test. Then find the item number of each question you missed and circle it on the chart below to determine the mathematics content areas in which you need more practice. Pay particular attention to areas where you missed half or more of the questions. The page numbers for the content areas are listed below on the chart. The numbers in boldface are questions based on graphics. For those questions that you missed, review the skill pages indicated.

PRE-TEST 5: MATHEMATICS EVALUATION CHART

Skill Area/ Content Area	Item Number	Review Pages
Whole Numbers & Problem Solving	1, 2	559–572
Decimals	4, 5, 6	573–586
Fractions	7, 8, 11	587–604
Ratio & Proportion	**10**, 12, 13	605–610
Percent	**9**, 14	611–620
Measurement	**16**, 33, 34	621–636
Graphs, Statistics & Probability	**3**, **19**, **29**, 39	637–648
Numeration	18, 40	649–656
Geometry	**15**, 17, **20**, 21, 22, **23**, **24**, **32**, **35**, **38**	657–674
Algebra	25, 26, 27, 28, 30, 31, **36**, **37**	675–710

Test 1: Writing Skills

The GED Writing Skills Test consists of two parts. Each part is discussed separately below.

Part 1: Conventions of English

What's on the test?

Part 1 is a multiple-choice test of 55 questions. You will have 75 minutes to answer these questions. In this part, several passages will be followed by questions about the sentences within the passage. Some questions will ask you to locate errors in the passage, while other questions may ask you to restate an idea in different words. The questions will test your knowledge of sentence structure, grammar and usage, punctuation, spelling, and capitalization.

Part 1 of the test can be broken down into the following content areas:

Sentence Structure	35%
Usage	35%
Mechanics	30%

What kinds of questions are on the test?

Three types of questions will appear on the GED Writing Skills Test. In the *sentence correction* type, you'll see a sentence followed by the question, "What correction should be made to this sentence?" The five answer choices will focus on different parts of the sentence and deal with different grammar and usage issues.

Example Sentence 1: **Time flies, when you're having fun.**

What correction should be made to this sentence?

(1) replace *flies* with *flys*
(2) remove the comma after *flies*
(3) replace *you're* with *your*
(4) insert a comma after *having*
(5) no correction is necessary

Note that this question tests your understanding of spelling, comma rules, possessives, and contractions. The correct answer is (2) remove the comma after *flies.*

In another question type, *sentence revision*, a sentence from the passage will be given with a part underlined. You will need to choose the best way to rewrite that underlined portion. The first answer choice in this question type is always the original version of the sentence, and this version is sometimes the correct answer.

Example Sentence 2: **Frustration is an emotion we all have to deal <u>with, the</u> question is how to handle it well.**

Which of the following is the best way to rewrite the underlined portion of this sentence? If you think the original is the best way to write the sentence, choose option (1).

(1) with, the
(2) with the
(3) with and the
(4) with. The
(5) with however the

This question tests your understanding of sentence structure and combining. Choice (4) is the best way to write these two sentences. The other choices create incorrect sentence structures.

The last question type, *construction shift*, asks you to choose the best way to rewrite a sentence or combine two sentences. In this type of question, *the original sentences contain no error*. Your job is to understand how the ideas are related in a sentence and which of the answer choices has the same meaning as the original sentence.

Example Sentence 3: **Although the female candidate ran a good race, she didn't receive enough votes.**

If you rewrote sentence 3 beginning with

The female candidate ran a good race,

the next word should be

(1) and
(2) which
(3) but
(4) so
(5) to

As you can see, the original sentence has no error. To answer this question, you must see the contrasting relationship between the two ideas of the sentence, then choose (3) but, the word that correctly shows this contrast.

Part 2: The Essay

You will be given 45 minutes to complete Part 2 of the Writing Skills Test. In this part, you will be given a topic and told to write a composition of about 200 words. You will not be given a choice of topics, but you will not need any special information or knowledge in order to write the essay. The topic will draw on your general knowledge and ask you to explain something about a common issue or problem. In this part of the Writing Skills Test, you should be able to plan and organize your thinking on an issue, and you should be able to communicate these thoughts clearly on paper.

1
BASIC ENGLISH USAGE

What Is Standard English?

We first learn language by listening to people speak. As children, our only language is a spoken one. We learn the meaning of words such as *me* and *cookie*, and we learn to put these ideas together to communicate a need. "Me cookie" might be easily understood by family and friends to mean "I would like a cookie."

As we grow older, we learn that there is a right and a wrong way to say things. By hearing others speak, we understand that "Me want go outside" is unacceptable English. While someone may understand what we mean by this phrase, it is still an incorrect use of the English language. Gradually, through speaking and listening, we learn what is acceptable and unacceptable in our language.

The Writing Skills Test examines your knowledge of standard written English, language that is acceptable at all times and places. It is the language of all kinds of communication, such as in books, newspapers, and magazines, as well as in school and business. In general, when you read something in print, you are reading standard English. When someone gives a prepared presentation or speech, the speaker usually uses standard English.

Nonstandard English does not follow the rules of grammar and usage. In casual conversation, we may use nonstandard English. In fact, incorrect expressions we use in our daily speech may sound "right" to our ears because we are used to hearing them. In this chapter, you'll learn how to correct many common usage errors we make in both speech and writing—problems with pronouns and verb tenses, for example. Of course, whether or not you follow all the rules of standard English in conversation, you will need to know these rules for the Writing Skills Test.

Writing in Complete Sentences

One major difference between spoken and written English is that we do not always speak in complete sentences. For example, in a telephone conversation you might mix complete sentences with *fragments*, groups of words that are not complete sentences. In the following conversation, the fragments are in bold type.

RIPOFF'S APPLIANCE COMPANY: Good morning. This is Ripoff's. You buy 'em, then try 'em.

CUSTOMER: Do you sell air conditioners?

RIPOFF'S: **Yeah, sometimes.**

CUSTOMER: Do you have any in stock now?

RIPOFF'S: **Might have some.**

CUSTOMER: Where is your store located?

RIPOFF'S: **On Airport Road. Next to the Wal-Mart.**

As you will learn in Chapters 1 and 2, a complete sentence has the following three characteristics.

CHARACTERISTICS OF A COMPLETE SENTENCE
1. A complete sentence contains a *complete thought*. It does not leave unanswered questions.
2. A complete sentence must have a *subject* that tells whom or what the sentence is about.
3. A complete sentence must have a *predicate* that tells what the subject is or does.

Look at the following sentences. The subjects and predicates are labeled for you. Compare these sentences with the characteristics listed in the box.

Subject		Predicate
Ripoff's Appliance Co.	/	is located on Airport Road next to the Wal-Mart.
We	/	sell air conditioners sometimes.
The warehouse	/	might have some.

For practice in working with subjects and predicates, try matching a subject from the left column with a predicate from the right. Notice that you are connecting *whom* or *what* the sentence is about with what this subject *is* or *does*.

Subject	Predicate
The carpenter	malfunctioned and exploded.
The Hawaiian Islands	has six nieces and a nephew.
Some of the equipment	are full of tourists.
The unexpected tornado	built four bookshelves.
My Aunt Louise	destroyed fifty homes.

While we often *speak* without including both a subject and a predicate in our sentences, we must always *write* in complete sentences—sentences containing both a subject and a predicate. Complete sentences are a feature of standard written English that will be important on the Writing Skills Test, both Part 1 and Part 2.

EXERCISE 1: SUBJECTS AND PREDICATES

Directions: The following trivia quiz is based on Academy Award winners. Match the following actors, actresses, and movies (Column 1) with what they were or did (Column 2). As you work through the exercise, notice that you are connecting subjects and predicates to make *complete sentences*. The first one is done for you.

Column 1

_g_ **1.** The first Academy Awards

_____ **2.** Julie Andrews

_____ **3.** Katharine Hepburn and Spencer Tracy

_____ **4.** Dustin Hoffman and Tom Cruise

_____ **5.** _Gone With the Wind, Stagecoach_, and _The Wizard of Oz_

_____ **6.** Awards for "Best Film," "Best Actor," "Best Actress," and "Best Director"

_____ **7.** _Terminator 2_

_____ **8.** Clint Eastwood

Column 2

(a) costarred in _Rain Man_, "Best Film" of 1988.

(b) were nominated for "Best Film" in 1939.

(c) acted together for the last time in 1967's _Guess Who's Coming to Dinner?_

(d) were given to _Silence of the Lambs_ in 1991.

(e) finally won an Academy Award for directing _Unforgiven_ in 1992.

(f) won the award for Special Effects in 1991.

(g) went to films made in 1927 and 1928.

(h) won an award for her performance in _Mary Poppins_ in 1964.

Answers are on page 179.

Parts of Speech

Subjects and predicates are built from the **_parts of speech_**. You will not have to define or explain these terms on the Writing Skills Test, but a knowledge of these major parts of speech and their functions will help you understand how standard English is put together. You'll be studying the following parts of speech closely in this book.

BASIC PARTS OF SPEECH		
Part of Speech	**Function**	**Examples**
noun	names person, place, thing, or idea	**John** drove to **Milwaukee** to give a **speech** about **democracy**.
pronoun	replaces a noun	**Somebody** showed **him** and **me** a picture of **it**.
verb	shows action or state of being (is, are, was, were, being, be, been)	Jim **is** tall. He **plays** basketball. Lew **looked** for a job.
conjunction	joins words and groups of words	Meg was here, **but** she left. Misha **and** I got home at noon.

Other parts of speech used all the time include adverbs and adjectives. However, in this book we will focus on the points covered on Part 1 of the Writing Skills Test.

What Is a Noun?

A *noun* names a person, place, thing, or idea. Whether or not you realize it, you are very familiar with nouns. Complete the lists of nouns under each of the following headings.

entertainers (people)

a. Bill Cosby

b. _____

c. _____

grocery list (things)

a. tomatoes

b. _____

c. _____

types of buildings (places)

a. school

b. _____

c. _____

qualities of a good leader (ideas)

a. patience

b. _____

c. _____

People, places, and things are usually easy to recognize as nouns. Sometimes ideas are a little harder. Read the following words carefully to get a better sense of this category of nouns: *democracy, capitalism, courage, love, time, anger.*

Noun as a Subject

A noun can be the *subject* of a sentence. Think of the subject as the main noun or the *actor* in the sentence. Ask yourself this question to find the subject of a sentence: "Who or what is doing something or being described in this sentence?"

The following sentence contains several nouns, but only one is the subject. Which one?

The **movers** packed the **truck** with **furniture** such as **beds**, **chairs**, and **tables**.

All of the nouns are in bold type. If you ask yourself, "What is this sentence about?" you might answer, "A truck of furniture." But if you ask, "Who or what is doing something?" your answer will be "movers." The noun *movers* is the subject of this sentence.

EXERCISE 2: NOUNS AND SUBJECTS

Directions: Underline all of the nouns in each of these sentences; then label the subject of each sentence with an *S.*

Example: Since August, my brother has lived in the green house at the end of

the block.

1. Bud missed the bus and had to take a cab to the concert.

2. Because of her poor health, Sheila will move to Arizona.

3. Did Mary apply for the new position at the bank?

4. The men stopped off for a drink on their way home.

5. Our children do their own laundry and clean the house.

6. Here is your pickle.

Answers are on page 179.

Singular and Plural Nouns

Singular means "one" (single). *Plural* means "more than one." You are probably familiar with the most common way to form plural nouns: adding an *s* to the end of the noun. Sounds simple, right? Not always. There are several ways to form plural nouns, as you'll see now.

Rules for forming plurals often depend on combinations of *vowels* and *consonants* at the ends of words. You may know that all the letters of the alphabet are divided into these two groups. The vowels are *a, e, i, o,* and *u* (and sometimes *y*). All the other letters are consonants.

Study the following rules for forming plurals correctly and practice each one as you go.

Rules for Forming Plural Nouns

★ 1. **Add *s* to most nouns.**

      cup ⟶ cups

      boy ⟶ _____

      desk ⟶ _____

      pencil ⟶ _____

★ 2. **Add *es* to words ending with *s*, *sh*, *ch*, *x*, and *z*.**

      boss ⟶ bosses

      bush ⟶ _____

      church ⟶ _____

      fox ⟶ _____

★ 3. **Add *s* to nouns ending in *y* if a vowel comes before the *y*.**

      driveway ⟶ driveways

      bay ⟶ _____

      toy ⟶ _____

      valley ⟶ _____

★ **4. Change the *y* to *i* and add *es* to a word ending in *y* if a consonant comes before the *y*.**

candy ⟶ candies

lady ⟶ _____

party ⟶ _____

company ⟶ _____

★ **5. Change the *f* to *v* and add *es* to <u>some</u> words ending in *f* or *fe*.**

loaf ⟶ loaves

leaf ⟶ _____

half ⟶ _____

wife ⟶ _____

For most words ending in *f* or *ff* simply add an *s*.

chief ⟶ chiefs

staff ⟶ _____

roof ⟶ _____

bluff ⟶ _____

★ **6. A few nouns do not change form when they are made plural.**

deer ⟶ deer

sheep ⟶ _____

moose ⟶ _____

★ **7. A few nouns are made plural by changing their spelling.** You probably know the plurals of the words below, but if you don't, you can find them in any dictionary.

goose ⟶ geese

man ⟶ _____

child ⟶ _____

mouse ⟶ _____

foot ⟶ _____

These rules cover most plural forms, but not all. Whenever you're not sure how to form a plural, look up the singular word in the dictionary. The plural will sometimes be listed there.

EXERCISE 3: PLURAL NOUNS

Directions: Write the correct plural forms of each of the following words.

Singular	Plural	Number of Rule That Applies
1. country	_____	_____
2. home	_____	_____
3. business	_____	_____
4. alloy	_____	_____
5. car	_____	_____
6. factory	_____	_____
7. race	_____	_____
8. life	_____	_____
9. woman	_____	_____
10. dish	_____	_____

Answers are on page 179.

Possessive Nouns

Many people confuse possessive nouns and plural nouns. Look at *neighbors* and *neighbor's* in the following sentences. Which shows ownership, or possession?

My neighbors have loud parties on the weekends.
My neighbor's car had to be dragged out of the ditch.

In the second sentence, *neighbor's* shows possession—the neighbor owns a car. Notice the possessive ending: *'s*.

Study the following rules for forming possessive nouns, filling in the blanks for practice as you go.

Rules for Forming Possessive Nouns

★ 1. Add 's to form most singular possessive nouns.

desk of the secretary ⟶ the secretary's desk

policy of the state ⟶ _____

gift of my niece ⟶ _____

friend of Laurie ⟶ _____

★ 2. Add $\boxed{'}$ to plural nouns to form most plural possessive nouns.

decision of the managers → the managers' decision

union of teachers ⟶ _____

house of the Joneses ⟶ _____

shirts of the babies ⟶ _____

★ 3. Add $\boxed{'s}$ to plural nouns that do not end in *s*.

department for children → children's department

magazine for women ⟶ _____

eggs of geese ⟶ _____

hoofprints of deer ⟶ _____

BE CAREFUL NOT TO USE 's TO FORM PLURALS.

INCORRECT: I saw three bus's at the station.

CORRECT: I saw three buses at the station.

EXERCISE 4: POSSESSIVE NOUNS

Directions: Insert apostrophes wherever they belong in the following sentences. Remember, not all nouns ending in *s* are possessive.

Example: The girls meeting ended when their votes had been counted.

1. My cats favorite food never stays long in her dish.

2. Over the past two years, the Wagners house has become worn around the doors and windows.

3. Childrens pants and toddlers playsuits are marked down at Emilys favorite shop.

4. The presidents plan to restrict imports was abandoned due to several allies protests.

5. For days after the volcanos eruption, ashes and dust in the atmosphere partially blocked the suns rays.

Answers are on page 179.

What Is a Verb?

The daily news consists of events—actions—that have taken place locally, nationally, or internationally. Read the following headlines and choose the appropriate word to complete each one.

President _____ Legislation   Marries

Hurricane _____ Florida Coastline   Rise

Starlet _____ Prince!   Signs

Jaycees _____ Raymond   Elect

Insurance Rates _____   Demolishes

In any sentence, the **verb** is the key word that names what the subject is or does. The two types of verbs are **action verbs** and **linking verbs**. The words in the blanks above are action verbs, words that show action. Some verbs show mental action (*think, believe, wish*), and others show physical action (*run, leave, swim*).

While an action verb tells what the subject is doing, linking verbs do not express action. Instead, they link the subject to words that describe the subject. No action is shown in the following sentences, but the subjects, *Joel* and *We*, are connected to words that describe them, *tall* and *angry*.

Joel **is** tall.

We **are** angry.

Is and *are* are forms of the most common linking verb, the verb *to be*. Forms of *to be* as well as some other common linking verbs are shown in the box below.

COMMON LINKING VERBS

is, am, are, was, were, be, being, been, appear, seem, become

---

For practice in using linking verbs, fill in the blanks in the sentences below with forms of the linking verbs in the box.

She _____ calm during the GED test.

David _____ very nervous about his job interview.

I _____ tired of exercising.

Victor _____ bored during dance class.

Tenses of Regular Verbs

When you read, you are generally aware that what you are reading about either has already happened, is happening now, or will happen in the future. One of the ways writers let you know when events take place is through *verb tense*.

PAST: Yesterday Brandon **wanted** to play outside.

PRESENT: Today Brandon **wants** to play outside.

FUTURE: Tomorrow Brandon **will want** to play outside.

Some verb tenses are formed using a single word, such as *wants*. Other tenses require a verb phrase, such as *will want*. In the verb phrase *will want*, *want* is the **base verb** and *will* is a **helping verb**. To form all verb tenses, you need the base verb. For some, you also need to use helping verbs, as you will see as you review the verb tenses.

Knowing how to form different verb tenses correctly is very important for the Writing Skills Test. *Regular verbs* are verbs that form the simple past tense and the *past participle* (used to form the perfect tenses) by adding *ed* to the base verb. Naturally, the tenses of regular verbs are the easiest to master. However, knowing how to form the different tenses won't help you very much unless you know when to use the different tenses. As you study verb forms, take careful note of when they are used.

The Simple Tenses

The *simple present* tense is used for something that is happening now, something that happens regularly, or something that is always true. The simple present is the base form of the verb unless the subject is *he, she, it,* or a singular noun. For these subjects, add *s* (or *es* if the verb ends in a hissing sound such as *s, sh, ch, x,* and *z*).

I **look** terrible today.

Gary **washes** his car every morning.

The sun **rises** in the east.

The *simple past* tense shows action that occurred in the past. To form the simple past of any regular verb, add *ed* to the base verb.

Wilson **dunked** his cat in the bathtub last night.

The *simple future* tense shows action that will happen in the future. Form the simple future for any subject by using *will* with the base verb.

Tomorrow Becky Brown **will learn** to juggle.

EXERCISE 5: THE SIMPLE TENSES

Directions: Fill in the correct simple tense form of the verb indicated in parentheses. Time clues such as *yesterday, today,* and *tomorrow* in the sentences will help you decide whether to use past, present, or future.

Example: (mix) Last night Mr. Fricks _____*mixed*_____ the batter for his son's birthday cake.

1. (walk) Next week Fred _____ to work while his car is being fixed.

2. (appear) Right now the store manager _____ very distressed.

3. (plant) In March of 1994 Rayleen _____ those daffodils.

4. (play) Tomorrow night Brian and his buddies _____ Go Fish and drink orange juice until bedtime.

5. (love) Cats _____ tuna fish.

Answers are on page 179.

The Continuing Tenses

The *continuing tenses* show action continuing in the past, present, or future, as in the following examples.

PAST: The crew **was working** on the roof all last week.

PRESENT: Right now the children **are watching** a dreadful TV show.

FUTURE: I **will be knitting** this sweater for months.

As you can see, the continuing tenses are formed by combining helping verbs with the base form of the verb plus *ing*. The following chart shows how to form all the continuing tenses.

CONTINUING TENSES			
Present continuing	I he, she, it* we, you, they**	am is are	I am looking. He is looking. You are looking.
Past continuing	I, he, she, it* we, you, they**	was were	I was looking. We were looking.
Future continuing	all subjects	will be	They will be looking.
*or any singular noun **or any plural noun			

EXERCISE 6: THE CONTINUING TENSES

Directions: Fill in the correct continuing tense form of the verb indicated in parentheses. Time clues such as *yesterday, today,* and *tomorrow* in the sentences will help you decide whether to use past, present, or future.

Example: (print) Wannamaker's Copy Shop ___*is printing*___ the programs today.

1. (lick) At the moment, my brother _____ his ice cream cone frantically.

2. (bark) Now that blasted dog _____ again!

3. (cook) By next month I _____ in the kitchen of my own restaurant.

4. (pick) The workers _____ that big crop of beans for the next two weeks.

5. (sleep) On yesterday's show, Tad _____ during the fight between Hillary and Roy.

Answers are on page 179.

The Perfect Tenses

The *perfect tenses* show action completed before or continuing to a specific time. These tenses are used to show more specific time relationships than the simple or continuing tenses.

The *present perfect* tense shows that an action started in the past and either continues into the present or has just been completed.

Al **has fished** in this river since 1920.

The Barhams **have repaired** their back porch.

The *past perfect* tense shows that an action was completed before a specific time in the past.

By midnight last Tuesday, the boys **had washed** forty-six cars.

The *future perfect* tense shows that an action will be completed by a specific time in the future.

By 4:00 tomorrow, I **will have mowed** every blade of this grass.

PERFECT TENSES			
Present perfect	he, she it* I, you, we, they**	has have	She has looked. You have looked.
Past perfect	all subjects	had	We had looked.
Future perfect	all subjects	will have	They will have looked.

*or any singular noun   **or any plural noun

EXERCISE 7: THE PERFECT TENSES

Directions: Fill in the correct perfect tense form of the verb indicated in parentheses. Pay careful attention to the meaning of each sentence before you decide whether to use the past, present, or future perfect.

Example: (paint) Merle Watson recently ___*has painted*___ his house lavender with purple trim.

1. (walk) I _____ my dog by bedtime tonight.

2. (curl) My daughter _____ her hair every day since her seventh birthday.

3. (order) By 9:00 last night, Palmer already _____ several rounds of cocoa for everyone.

4. (attend) Lucy is enrolled in a Lamaze class. She _____ every session so far.

5. (work) Before going into the army, Warren _____ in a fish canning factory.

6. (mail) By next October, Ms. Eggebraaten _____ Christmas gifts to her relatives in Europe.

7. (miss) In the last twenty-five years, Ginger _____ the company picnic only once.

8. (travel) Before coming to Chicago last summer, I _____ throughout the Midwest.

Answers are on page 179.

Spelling Regular Verb Forms

So far you have been writing different forms of verbs by adding *ed* or *ing* to the base verb. However, not all verbs change form so simply. Following are five rules for adding *ed* and *ing* that cover all regular verbs. Study each rule.

★ 1. **When *ed* and *ing* are added to most regular verbs, the spelling of the base verb does not change.**

watch → watched, watching

walk → walked, walking

reach → _____, _____

jump → _____, _____

kick → _____, _____

★ 2. **If the base verb ends in *y* preceded by a consonant, change the *y* to *i* when adding *ed*, but keep the *y* when adding *ing*.**

rely → relied, relying

cry → cried, crying

marry → _____, _____

study → _____, _____

carry → _____, _____

★ 3. **If the base verb ends with a silent *e*, drop the *e* before adding *ed* or *ing*.**

like → liked, liking

memorize → memorized, memorizing

live → _____, _____

hope → _____, _____

★ 4. **If the base verb ends in *ie*, drop the silent *e* when adding *ed*, but change the *ie* to *y* when adding *ing*.**

tie → tied, tying

die → _____, _____

lie → _____, _____

★ 5. **If the base verb ends in a single vowel and a single consonant other than *h*, *w*, or *x*, and if the accent falls on the last (or only) syllable of the verb, double the final consonant of the base verb when adding *ed* or *ing*. Otherwise, keep the normal spelling.**

refer → referred, referring

relax → relaxed, relaxing

commit → _____, _____

prefer → _____, _____

rot → _____, _____

EXERCISE 8: REGULAR VERB REVIEW

Directions: This exercise tests your understanding of simple, continuing, and perfect tenses. Fill in the blank in each sentence with the correct form of the base verb indicated. Be sure to spell all the verb forms correctly. Read each sentence carefully for clues to the correct tense.

1. (wait) At the time of my arrival last week, Wendell _____ at the wrong bus station.

2. (enter) Someday Reba _____ the glamorous world of TV game shows.

3. (sketch) On her way home from work every day, Fairbanks _____ the other passengers on the train.

4. (plunge) By 8:00 this morning, I already _____ into my projects for the day.

5. (wait) I _____ for this moment for many a year.

6. (lie) By the end of his term two years from now, the executive _____ to his staff about many major issues.

7. (ship) Yesterday afternoon Debra secretly _____ the documents from her office mailroom.

8. (study) For the next few months, I _____ math.

9. (feel) Currently Henry _____ miserable because of his girlfriend's betrayal.

10. (seem) Today Ray _____ to have given up any hope of his friend's survival.

11. (live) Since the day she was born, Therese Ruffing _____ in Texas.

12. (decide) Last night Mary Beth _____ to name her daughter Esmerelda Ophelia after her husband's mother.

Answers are on page 180.

Irregular Verbs

English would be a much easier language to write if all verbs shifted to different tenses according to the regular patterns you have just been studying. However, many English verbs are irregular—they do not change according to these regular patterns. When you study irregular verbs, you need to learn the simple present, the simple past, and the past participle, which is used to form the perfect tenses.

Have, Do, and *Be*

Make sure you know the three most common irregular verbs: *have, do,* and *be.* If you are not sure of the forms of these verbs in the following box, you should memorize them.

	Present	Past	Past Participle
I, you, we, they** he, she, it*	have has	had	had
I, you, we, they** he, she, it*	do does	did	done
I he, she, it* you, we, they**	am is are	was were	been
*or any singular noun **or any plural noun			

The most common mistake people make with irregular verbs is confusing the past participle with the simple past tense. Remember, the past participle is used to form the perfect tenses, so a helping verb (*has, have,* or *had*) must always be used with a past participle.

INCORRECT: I done my chores.

CORRECT: I did my chores.

CORRECT: I have done my chores.

Other Common Irregular Verbs

On the following two pages is a list of the simple present, simple past, and past participle forms of common irregular verbs. Verbs that follow similar patterns are grouped together. You may already use most of these verbs correctly. Study this list by following these steps:

1. Cover the second and third columns of the list.

2. Read the simple present form in a short sentence using *I* as the subject. *I fall.*

3. Test to see if you know the simple past form by putting the sentence in the past tense. *I fell.*

4. Test to see if you know the past participle by putting the sentence in the present perfect. *I have fallen.*

5. Check your answers against the forms listed in the second and third columns.

6. Study the forms you missed by repeating the sentences over and over in each tense until you have memorized them.

Present	Past	Past Participle
cost	cost	cost
put	put	put
read	read	read
set	set	set
bring	brought	brought
buy	bought	bought
think	thought	thought
catch	caught	caught
teach	taught	taught
lay (put or place)	laid	laid
pay	paid	paid
say	said	said
send	sent	sent
feel	felt	felt
keep	kept	kept
leave	left	left
mean	meant	meant
meet	met	met
sleep	slept	slept
build	built	built
get	got	got, gotten
lose	lost	lost
find	found	found
feed	fed	fed
hold	held	held
lead	led	led
hear	heard	heard
sell	sold	sold
tell	told	told
understand	understood	understood
make	made	made
fall	fell	fallen
choose	chose	chosen
speak	spoke	spoken
take	took	taken
drive	drove	driven
eat	ate	eaten
give	gave	given
ride	rode	ridden
write	wrote	written

Present	Past	Past Participle
begin	began	begun
drink	drank	drunk
ring	rang	rung
sing	sang	sung
draw	drew	drawn
grow	grew	grown
know	knew	known
throw	threw	thrown
become	became	become
come	came	come
run	ran	run
see	saw	seen
go	went	gone
lie	lay	lain

There are many more irregular verbs than the ones on this list. Whenever you are unsure of the simple past or past participle of an irregular verb, look up the base verb in the dictionary. The forms of the verb will be listed there.

Correct Verb Tense in a Passage

On the Writing Skills Test, you will have to be able to correct verb tense in the context of a whole passage. Not every sentence in a passage will contain clues such as *at the present* or *next week* to tell you what tense to use. Read the following paragraph and cross out the two incorrect verbs. Write the correct form in the margin.

Melissa had a hard time sleeping last night. It was her first night alone in her new apartment. The tap in the bathroom drips constantly. The refrigerator rattled and hummed. The neighbors' dog barked all night long. The streetlight was shining in her eyes. Finally she goes to sleep around 3:00 A.M.

Did you change *drips* to *dripped* and *goes* to *went*? The passage as a whole is written in the past tense. Notice the words *last night* in the first sentence. In the following GED practice exercise, make sure that you choose consistent verb tenses to correct the passage. First, identify the tense of the paragraph. Then, identify verbs. Next, determine which are similar and which are different. Finally, change those that need to be changed.

EXERCISE 9: VERBS

Directions: Read the following passage and answer the questions. Be sure that all verb tenses are correct and that verb forms are spelled correctly.

(1) Videocassette recorders (VCRs) give TV watchers more choice in television programs. (2) Many viewers taped shows to watch later. (3) For example, people who work during the day had recorded daytime news programs, talk shows, movies, and soap operas. (4) Parents make collections of children's shows to give their children "rainy day" entertainment. (5) Sometimes a family has went out for the evening. (6) However, their VCR kept them from missing their favorite prime time shows. (7) Because of VCRs, TV viewers will be seeing more good television.

1. Sentence 2: **Many viewers <u>taped</u> shows to watch later.**

Which of the following is the best way to write the underlined portion of this sentence? If you think the original is the best way to write the sentence, choose option (1).

(1) taped
(2) tapped
(3) tape
(4) had tapped
(5) had taped

2. Sentence 3: **For example, people who work during the day <u>had recorded</u> daytime news programs, talk shows, movies, and soap operas.**

Which of the following is the best way to write the underlined portion of this sentence? If you think the original is the best way to write the sentence, choose option (1).

(1) had recorded
(2) record
(3) will be recording
(4) will have recorded
(5) recorded

3. Sentence 4: **Parents <u>make</u> collections of children's shows to give their children "rainy day" entertainment.**

Which of the following is the best way to write the underlined portion of this sentence? If you think the original is the best way to write the sentence, choose option (1).

(1) make
(2) were making
(3) were makeing
(4) made
(5) will be making

4. Sentence 5: **Sometimes a family <u>has went</u> out for the evening.**

Which of the following is the best way to write the underlined portion of this sentence? If you think the original is the best way to write the sentence, choose option (1).

(1) has went
(2) has gone
(3) will have gone
(4) went
(5) goes

5. Sentence 6: **However, their VCR <u>kept</u> them from missing their favorite prime time shows.**

Which of the following is the best way to write the underlined portion of this sentence? If you think the original is the best way to write the sentence, choose option (1).

(1) kept
(2) keeps
(3) keeped
(4) had kept
(5) keepes

6. Sentence 7: **Because of VCRs, TV viewers <u>will be seeing</u> more good television.**

Which of the following is the best way to write the underlined portion of this sentence? If you think the original is the best way to write the sentence, choose option (1).

(1) will be seeing
(2) will have seen
(3) are seeing
(4) will be seen
(5) had seen

Answers are on page 180.

Subject-Verb Agreement

As adults, we get a great deal of pleasure when someone agrees with us. When we express our opinions, we get support from others saying, "I agree. That's right." Agreement between people makes everything easier.

Agreement also makes the English language easier to understand. When you are writing, it is important to make subjects agree with verbs. ***Subject-verb agreement*** means that you have chosen the correct verb form to match the number and person of the subject. In this section you will learn how to make sure you have this agreement.

The Basic Pattern

If the subject of a present-tense verb is *he, she, it,* or any singular noun (except *I* or *you*), the verb must end in *s* or *es*. Verbs ending in a hissing sound (*s, sh, ch, x,* and *z*) take an *es* ending.

Note that the forms of irregular verbs for *he, she,* and *it* always end in *s*. Test this for yourself by looking back at the forms of *have, do,* and *be* on page 72.

In the following examples, are the subjects singular or plural? Fill in the correct form of the verb *walk* in each sentence.

The elderly women _____ in the mall every day.

The elderly woman _____ in the mall every day.

You should have written *walk* in the first sentence because the subject, *women,* is plural. The subject of the second sentence, *woman,* is singular, so the correct verb is *walks.*

Subject-Verb Agreement Problems

You have to worry about subject-verb agreement only in the present tense, with one exception. The irregular verb *be* changes form for different subjects in the past tense as well. You can review this pattern in the chart on page 72.

Keep subject-verb agreement in mind when you see contractions. If you have trouble figuring out the correct form, take the contraction apart. For example, *doesn't* means *does not*, and *don't* means *do not*.

INCORRECT: She don't (do not) care.

CORRECT: She doesn't (does not) care.

1. Compound Subjects

The following rules apply to compound subjects and verbs.

★ **If the parts of a compound subject are connected by *and*, the subject is always plural and the verb does not end in *s*.**

Mr. Tidwell and his daughter **row** the boat together.

★ **If the parts of a compound subject are connected by *or* or *nor*, the verb agrees with the part of the subject closer to it.**

Mr. Tidwell or his daughters (row, rows) the boat.
His daughters or Mr. Tidwell (row, rows) the boat.

In the first sentence, the verb must agree with *daughters*. You should have chosen *row*. In the second, the verb must agree with *Mr. Tidwell*. You should have chosen *rows*.

2. Inverted Order

In three common types of sentences, the verb comes before the subject. Underline the subject of each of the following sentences; then underline the correct verb.

(Is, Are) the twins hiding in the garage?

Here (goes, go) the Bensons on their way to the races.

In the storeroom (sits, sit) an almond-colored refrigerator.

If you have trouble finding the subject of these sentences, mentally rearrange the word order:

The twins (is, are) hiding in the garage.

The Bensons (goes, go) here on their way to the races.

An almond-colored refrigerator (sits, sit) in the storeroom.

You should have chosen *twins are* for the first example, *Bensons go* for the second, and *refrigerator sits* for the third.

EXERCISE 10: SUBJECT-VERB AGREEMENT
Directions: Underline the subject; then underline the correct verb in parentheses.

1. Down the street (runs, run) the racers in the Boston Marathon.

2. Neither her sons nor Letitia (visits, visit) the dentist often.

3. Time and money (was, were) all he lacked.

4. (Wasn't, Weren't) the secretary really paid $25 per hour?

5. (Has, Have) your mother given away her old clothes?

6. A sandwich and a glass of juice (is, are) plenty of lunch for me.

7. Here (lies, lie) the remains of my dog Roberta.

Answers are on page 180.

3. Interrupting Phrases
The subject and verb of a sentence are often separated by two types of phrases: prepositional phrases, and phrases that add information to the subject. Neither type of phrase affects agreement between subject and verb.

Some of the most common prepositions are *of, in, for, to, from, with, on,* and *by.* The prepositional phrases in the following example sentences are in bold type. They are not part of the subject. Underline the subject and then underline the correct verb.

The papers **on the desk** (is, are) very important.

The bushel **of peaches** (has, have) been sold.

You should have chosen *papers are* and *bushel has.*

Other interrupting phrases may seem to make the subject plural, but they do not. They often start with words such as *as well as, in addition to,* and *like.* These phrases are set off by commas. Underline the subject and then underline the verb in the following examples.

Clay, along with his parents, (is, are) headed for the game.

Marcia, like her coworkers, (is, are) going on strike.

You should have chosen *Clay is* and *Marcia is.*

4. Indefinite Pronouns

There are three groups of indefinite pronouns. Some are always singular, some are always plural, and some can be either singular or plural depending on their antecedents (see page 82). Singular indefinite pronouns almost always end in *one* or *body.*

INDEFINITE PRONOUNS			
Singular		**Plural**	**Singular or Plural** *(depending upon their use)*
everyone	everybody	both	some
someone	somebody	few	any
no one	nobody	many	none
anyone	anybody	several	most
one	each (one)		all
either (one)	neither (one)		

Underline the indefinite pronoun in the following sentences and then underline the correct verb.

Each of the children (is, are) here.

Some of the cake (tastes, taste) stale.

Most of the cookies (looks, look) burned.

You should have chosen *Each is, Some tastes,* and *Most look.* Did the interrupting phrase *of the children* throw you off in the first sentence? *Each* is always singular, no matter what comes between it and the verb. In the second sentence, *Some* refers to the singular noun *cake,* making the indefinite pronoun singular. In the third sentence, *most* refers to the plural noun *cookies,* making the indefinite pronoun plural. See the section on antecedents beginning on page 82.

EXERCISE 11: MORE SUBJECT-VERB AGREEMENT

Directions: Underline the subject; then underline the correct verb in parentheses for each sentence.

*1. Mrs. Bundt, along with her children, (attends, attend) the Lutheran church.

2. Each of the captains (receives, receive) the award.

3. Some of the students (was, were) absent.

4. A breakfast of cereal and toast (keeps, keep) me going all day.

5. If anyone (wants, want) to go, call me!

6. Most of the figures (is, are) accurate.

7. The new property tax, like our other taxes, (is, are) unreasonably high.

8. None of the water (is, are) fit to drink.

Answers are on page 180.

What Is a Pronoun?

A *pronoun* is a word that replaces and refers to a noun. Usually, you use pronouns to avoid repeating the same nouns over and over. Instead of saying, "Jane told Bob Bob was a liar, and Bob told Jane Jane was a liar, too," you would say, "Jane told Bob he was a liar, and he told her she was a liar, too." *He, she,* and *her* are pronouns.

Types of Personal Pronouns

In the following chart are three important groups of pronouns. Each group has different functions in a sentence.

Subject Pronouns	Object Pronouns	Possessive Pronouns	
act as the subject of a verb	*never act as the subject of a verb*	*show ownership* (appear with another noun)	(stand alone)
I	me	my	mine
you	him	your	yours
he	her	his	his
she	us	her	hers
it	them	its	—
we	whom	our	ours
they		their	theirs
who		whose	whose

Subject and Object Pronouns

The following hints will help you decide when to use subject and object pronouns.

HINT 1: Ask yourself whether the pronoun is the subject of a verb.

In the following sentence, what is the verb? Will the pronoun be the subject of that verb?

Rebecca brought the flowers to (they, them).

In this sentence, the verb is *brought.* The subject of *brought* is *Rebecca,* so the pronoun will not be the subject. The object pronoun *them* is correct.

> **HINT 2:** Cross out any nouns connected to the pronoun with *and*. Then look at the pronoun alone to see if it is the subject of a verb.

Which pronoun is correct in the following example?

Bill and (they, them) went to a movie.

Cross out *Bill and*. Will the pronoun be the subject of the verb *went*? Which is correct, *they went to a movie* or *them went to a movie*? The correct pronoun is *they*.

EXERCISE 12: PRONOUN FORM

Directions: Replace the parts of each sentence in bold type with the correct pronoun. Read the sentence carefully to determine whether to use a subject, object, or possessive pronoun. Remember that there are two types of possessive pronouns.

Example: The ~~children's~~ *Their* hair is the same color as ~~Tom's~~ *his*.

1. **Jeanette** is going to the circus with **Sandy and Lucy**.

2. Give the pearls to **Mother and me**.

3. John and **John's** friends left the meeting.

4. **Phil and I** read **Kate's** paper with great delight.

5. Nancy was planning to bring her husband, so I brought **my husband**.

Answers are on page 180.

Possessives and Contractions

A possessive noun such as *Gerald's* shows ownership. So does the possessive pronoun *his*, which you could use to substitute for *Gerald's*. However, unlike the possessive noun, the possessive pronoun does not contain an apostrophe ('). If you remember that no possessive pronouns contain apostrophes, you should be able to avoid confusing the possessive pronouns and their sound-alike contractions.

Possessive Pronoun	Sound-Alike Contraction
its	it's (it is)
theirs	there's (there is)
their	they're (they are)
your	you're (you are)
whose	who's (who is)

If you can't decide whether to use a contraction in a sentence, try substituting the two words that the contraction stands for.

I can't believe (your, you're) going to do that!

Test the sentence with *you are*, the two words that *you're* stands for: *I can't believe you are going to do that!* The sentence makes sense, so the contraction *you're* is the correct choice.

(Whose, Who's) house do you think this is, young lady?

Test the sentence with *Who is*: *Who is house do you think this is, young lady?* The sentence makes no sense, so the possessive pronoun *whose* is the correct choice.

EXERCISE 13: POSSESSIVE PRONOUNS AND CONTRACTIONS

Directions: Underline the correct word to complete each sentence.

1. (Your, You're) not ready to move out of the house at age twelve.

2. (Theirs, There's) no one here by that name, Officer.

3. I have given up hope that (your, you're) father will ever stop telling bad jokes.

4. (Whose, Who's) coat is lying in the back corner of the bar?

5. (Its, It's) not likely that Reginald will ever darken (its, it's) door again.

6. (Their, They're) going on a vacation to Alaska.

Answers are on page 180.

Identifying Antecedents

The noun that a pronoun replaces and refers to is called its **antecedent**. The relationship between a pronoun and its antecedent must be clear and correct. There are several specific pronoun problems that you are likely to find on the Writing Skills Test. But before you turn to those problems, first practice identifying the antecedents of pronouns in correctly written sentences.

Draw an arrow from the pronoun in this sentence to its antecedent.

Jenny told Bob how much she loves roses.

Did you draw the arrow from *she* to *Jenny*? The pronoun *she* replaces and refers to the noun *Jenny*.

Pronouns often refer to antecedents in other sentences. Draw arrows from *him* in the second sentence and *they* in the third sentence to their antecedents.

Jim has the children for the weekend. I'll be getting them back from

him Sunday night. Then they'll be with me all week.

Did you choose *Jim* as the antecedent for *him* and *children* for *they*?

EXERCISE 14: IDENTIFYING ANTECEDENTS

Directions: In the following paragraph, the pronouns are numbered. Fill in the correct antecedent for each pronoun. The first two are done for you.

Murray and Dee went to church yesterday with their new baby Marissa
                                                      1

for the first time. Upon getting her out of the car, they were surrounded by
                                       2   3

eager friends who wanted to see Marissa. Finally the three of them escaped
                   4   5

to the nursery. Marissa seemed to like her temporary crib and the bubble
                                         6

mobile that dangled above it. The nursery worker was nervous about having
                             7

such a young baby to care for, though. He asked Murray and Dee where they
                                            8   9

would be sitting during the service in case he needed to find them.
                                             10   11

Pronoun	Antecedent	Pronoun	Antecedent
1. their	*Murray and Dee*	7. it	
2. her	*Marissa*	8. He	
3. they		9. they	
4. who		10. he	
5. them		11. them	
6. her			

Answers are on page 180.

Pronoun-Antecedent Agreement

Relative Pronouns

Relative pronouns (*who*, *which*, and *that*) are often used to link two ideas in a sentence.

> The eggs that I bought yesterday were brown.
>
> The man who came to dinner was her future son-in-law.
>
> This suitcase, which I have had since 1970, is falling apart.

These relative pronouns must agree with their antecedents according to the following rules.

★ 1. *Who* (*whom*, *whose*) can refer only to humans.

★ 2. The relative pronoun *which* can refer only to nonhumans.

★ 3. *That* can refer to either humans or nonhumans.

Look again at the three example sentences above. Draw an arrow from each relative pronoun to its antecedent.

You should have marked *eggs* as the antecedent of *that*, *man* as the antecedent of *who*, and *suitcase* as the antecedent of *which*.

EXERCISE 15: RELATIVE PRONOUNS

Directions: Underline the antecedent for the relative pronoun in each sentence. Then underline the correct relative pronoun in parentheses.

Example: This <u>exercise</u>, (who, <u>which</u>) is not hard, is quite short.

1. The woman (who, which) is sitting on the floor is the photographer.

2. The door (who, that) is slightly ajar leads to the chamber of horrors.

3. Time, (who, which) waits for no man, waits for no woman either.

4. Dorothy, (who, which) is friends with Glenda, would like to move back to Kansas.

5. The people (that, which) answer the phone there sound as though they have been dead for years.

Answers are on page 180.

Agreement in Number

In the following sentence, the pronoun *they* is used because its antecedent, *cities*, is plural.

> Cities often use tax incentives to stimulate the economic growth they need.

Is *they* used correctly in the next example sentence also? Decide if *they* agrees in number with its antecedent.

> Birmingham used tax incentives to stimulate the economic growth they needed.

Here the plural pronoun *they* incorrectly refers to *Birmingham*, a singular noun. The singular pronoun *it* should be used instead:

> Birmingham used tax incentives to stimulate the economic growth it needed.

As you check for pronoun agreement errors on the GED Writing Skills Test, keep in mind that the antecedent of a pronoun is not always in the same sentence as the pronoun. Find the pronoun in the following passage that does not agree in number with the rest of the passage and correct it.

> Word processors are miracles of technology. Because of them, correction fluid no longer stains the clothing and fingers of typists. They have eliminated typing and retyping drafts of the same material. Its quiet clicking has replaced the noisy thudding of typewriters. Many of them even check grammar and spelling.

Did you find the singular possessive pronoun *its*? The rest of the pronouns in the passage are plural—*they* and *them* are used to refer to *word processors*. Therefore, *its* should be replaced with *their*.

Compound Antecedents

The antecedent of a pronoun is not always a single noun. Sometimes the antecedent is made up of two nouns connected by *and, or,* or *nor*. In this example, the two nouns in the antecedent are connected by *and.* The pronoun is plural.

> **Mark and Tim** showed up for **their** swim team practice.

And makes a ***compound antecedent*** (an antecedent of more than one noun) plural. Use a plural pronoun to refer to a compound antecedent joined by *and.*

When a compound antecedent is joined by *or* or *nor,* the rule is different. *Or* and *nor* separate the nouns in a compound antecedent. The pronoun must agree with the closest noun in the antecedent.

> Either **Mark or his brothers** will show up for **their** swim practice.

> Either **his brothers or Mark** will show up for **his** swim practice.

In the first example above, *his brothers* is closest to the pronoun, so the pronoun is plural, *their.* In the second example, *Mark* is closest to the pronoun, so the pronoun is singular, *his.*

EXERCISE 16: AGREEMENT IN NUMBER
PART A

Directions: Underline the antecedent of the pronoun; then underline the singular or plural pronoun in parentheses that agrees with it.

Example: Every <u>boy</u> must be checked by (<u>his</u>, their) physician before entering the program.

1. Japan has greatly increased (its, their) industrial capacity.

2. Either Allison or Muriel will give up (her, their) turn at bat.

3. Neither Bobby nor the twins have told us (his, their) new address.

4. Neither the hamsters nor the dog has been fed (its, their) breakfast.

5. This company has sold (its, their) holdings in South Africa.

PART B

Directions: Cross out incorrect pronouns in this passage and write in correct ones, making sure the pronouns agree in number.

Over the last twenty years, Knoxville's population center, once clustered around their small downtown area, has shifted westward. However, their downtown area may become more important again in future years. Many of the city's older buildings are being restored, and its newer downtown buildings are lovely too.

Answers are on page 180.

More than One Antecedent

The meaning of a pronoun is unclear if the pronoun can refer to more than one antecedent. In the following example, whose dress is it?

Jane told Mary about her dress.

Because two females are mentioned in the same sentence, the pronoun *her* is confusing. Here is one way the sentence could be corrected:

Jane told Mary about Mary's dress.

Or, depending on the intended meaning of the original sentence, it might be rewritten this way:

Jane told Mary about Jane's dress.

Now look at another example. Whom does *they* seem to be referring to?

I invited my best friends and my family to the party, but they couldn't come.

The writer does not clearly tell you whether both her best friends and her family couldn't come, just her family, or just her best friends. In this case, she may have to do a little more rewriting to make the sentence clear, depending on her actual meaning. On a piece of scratch paper, jot down a possible revision of the sentence.

Here is one way to correct the problem:

> I invited my best friends and my family to the party, but none of the people I invited could come.

No Antecedent

Some pronouns are used without any antecedent at all. The pronouns *it*, *this*, and *they* commonly appear without an antecedent. Here's an example:

VAGUE: When I went to the public library, they told me I needed two pieces of identification to get a library card.

CLEAR: When I went to the public library, **a librarian** told me I needed two pieces of identification to get a library card.

The following sentences contain a very common example of a pronoun with no antecedent. Circle the vague pronoun. On a piece of scratch paper, rewrite the sentence it appears in to make the meaning clear.

> Joe drove sixteen hours in one day to get home for Christmas. As soon as he walked in the door, his mother started nagging him to pay some bills and buy the Christmas tree. This gave him a bad headache.

Did you circle *This*? You might have revised the last sentence several ways. One possibility would be *Her nagging gave him a bad headache.*

EXERCISE 17: CLARIFYING ANTECEDENTS

Directions: Read the following sentences carefully, looking for confusing pronoun reference. If a sentence or group of sentences is written clearly and does not need to be revised, write *C* in the blank. If revision is needed, write *X* in the blank and revise on a separate sheet of paper.

Example: _____X_____ When I went to the hospital, they gave me eighteen stitches.

When I went to the hospital, the doctor gave me eighteen stitches.

_____ **1.** I wrote to Ken and his sisters, but they did not respond.

_____ **2.** They say that drinking peppermint tea is good for an upset stomach.

_____ **3.** Herd the sheep away from the cattle and feed them.

_____ **4.** Dion asked Tony if he thought he would win the contest.

_____ **5.** When the quarterback made the touchdown in the final seconds of the game, it went wild in the stands.

_____ **6.** Sam thought he left his checkbook at home but later couldn't find it.

_____ **7.** Darleen never wants to go out anymore, and she is not eating or sleeping well. This worries her husband.

_____ **8.** Mr. Olivetti followed Dominick into his storeroom.

_____ **9.** Many people drink too much on New Year's Eve and then try to drive home. This drinking and driving makes the roads dangerous for everyone on that holiday night.

Possible answers are on page 181.

Keeping Track of Person

Read this paragraph and try to keep track of the pronouns.

> A person should register to vote as soon as you turn eighteen. He should realize that it is your right to vote in a democracy. To register, he must be a U.S. citizen and a resident of the area in which you vote. Two convenient places he can register to vote are his local library and your post office.

The pronouns in this paragraph are all mixed up between *he* and *you*. The pronouns are all singular, so they agree in number, but they shift in **person** (from *you* to *he* and back again). Within a passage, the pronouns should not shift from one person to another.

> *First person:* I, me, my, mine, we, us, our, ours
>
> *Second person:* you, your, yours
>
> *Third person:* he, she, it, him, her, his, hers, its, they, them, they, theirs

Here is one way to correct the paragraph:

> You should register to vote as soon as you turn eighteen. You should realize that it is your right to vote in a democracy. To register, you must be a U.S. citizen and a resident of the area in which you vote. Two convenient places you can register to vote are your local library and your post office.

EXERCISE 18: AGREEMENT IN PERSON

Directions: Find which of the pronouns in bold type need to be corrected in the following passage.

Most of us think that having running water and electricity is normal. As a result, **you** might be surprised at the simple mud huts many Africans live in. Even when **you** are out of work here, **we** can get help from government agencies, including welfare or unemployment income. **We** may not all have lives of luxury, but **you** easily forget that people in many other countries feel lucky to earn only pennies per day.

Answers are on page 181.

EXERCISE 19: SENTENCE STRUCTURE

Directions: The following items are based on paragraphs that contain numbered sentences. Some of the sentences may contain errors in usage. A few sentences, however, may be correct as written. Read the paragraph and then answer the items based on it. For each item, choose the answer that would result in the most effective writing of the sentence or sentences. The best answer must be consistent with the meaning and tone of the rest of the paragraph.

(1) One of our most popular American artists are Norman Rockwell, who was a painter. (2) His paintings show such detail that some people have mistaken it for photography. (3) His paintings were on the cover of *The Saturday Evening Post* magazine for several years, and you collected those covers. (4) Although he is no longer alive, those masterpieces of his lives on in art galleries, in bookstores, and even on calendars and greeting cards.

1. Sentence 1: **One of our most popular American artists are Norman Rockwell, who was a painter.**

   What correction should be made to this sentence?

   (1) change *our* to *ours*
   (2) change *are* to *is*
   (3) replace *who* with *which*
   (4) change *was* to *were*
   (5) no correction is necessary

2. Sentence 2: **His paintings show such detail that some people have mistaken it for photography.**

   Which of the following is the best way to write the underlined portion of this sentence? If you think the original is the best way to write the sentence, choose option (1).

   (1) it
   (2) its
   (3) they
   (4) them
   (5) him

3. Sentence 3: **His paintings were on the cover of *The Saturday Evening Post* magazine for several years, and you collected those covers.**

What correction should be made to this sentence?

(1) change *paintings* to *painting's*
(2) change *were* to *was*
(3) change *you* to *people*
(4) change *collected* to *collecting*
(5) no correction is necessary

4. Sentence 4: **Although he is no longer alive, those masterpieces of his lives on in art galleries, in bookstores, and even on calendars and greeting cards.**

What correction should be made to this sentence?

(1) replace *he* with *they*
(2) change *is* to *are*
(3) change the spelling of *alive* to *alife*
(4) change *lives* to *live*
(5) change the spelling of *galleries* to *gallerys*

(1) Born in Boston in 1857, Fannie Farmer was a famous woman who's accomplishments benefit us today. (2) In high school, a stroke will cause her to end her formal education. (3) While recovering, she helped with household duties and begun to cook. (4) Fannie's cooking was noticed by her parents, which enrolled her in the Boston Cooking School. (5) Upon Fannie's graduation, they asked her to stay on as an assistant director. (6) Within two years, she had become the school's director. (7) In 1902 she left and openned Miss Farmer's School of Cookery, a school that trained housewives. (8) She also taught a course in invalid cooking at Harvard for a year. (9) In addition, she and her sister writed a regular column for ten years in *Woman's Home Companion*. (10) Still popular among best-selling cookbooks today are her *Boston Cooking School Cookbook*, which is now known as *The Fannie Farmer Cookbook*. (11) Moreover, the cup or teaspoon that we measure with got its standard size from Fannie Farmer.

5. Sentence 1: **Born in Boston in 1857, Fannie Farmer was a famous woman who's accomplishments benefit us today.**

What correction should be made to this sentence?

(1) change *was* to *were*
(2) change *woman* to *women*
(3) replace *who's* with *whose*
(4) change *benefit* to *benefited*
(5) change *us* to *we*

6. Sentence 2: **In high school, a stroke <u>will cause</u> her to end her formal education.**

Which of the following is the best way to write the underlined portion of this sentence? If you think the original is the best way, choose option (1).

(1) will cause   (2) may cause   (3) causing   (4) were causing   (5) caused

7. Sentence 3: **While recovering, she helped with household duties and begun to cook.**

    What correction should be made to this sentence?

    (1) change the spelling of *recovering* to *recoverring*
    (2) change *she* to *her*
    (3) change the spelling of *duties* to *dutys*
    (4) change *begun* to *began*
    (5) no correction is necessary

8. Sentence 4: **Fannie's cooking was noticed by her parents, which enrolled her in the Boston Cooking School.**

    What correction should be made to this sentence?

    (1) change *was* to *were*
    (2) change *parents* to *parent's*
    (3) replace *which* with *who*
    (4) change the spelling of *enrolled* to *enroled*
    (5) no correction is necessary

9. Sentence 5: **Upon Fannie's graduation, <u>they</u> asked her to stay on as an assistant director.**

    Which of the following is the best way to write the underlined portion of this sentence? If you think the original is the best way, choose option (1).

    (1) they   **(2)** the staff   **(3)** their   **(4)** there   **(5)** them

10. Sentence 6: **Within two years, she had become the school's director.**

    What correction should be made to this sentence?

    (1) change *years* to *year's*
    (2) change *she* to *her*
    (3) change *had become* to *has become*
    (4) change *school's* to *schools*
    (5) no correction is necessary

11. Sentence 7: **In 1902, she left and openned Miss Farmer's School of Cookery, a school that trained housewives.**

    What correction should be made to this sentence?

    (1) change the spelling of *left* to *leaved*
    (2) change the spelling of *openned* to *opened*
    (3) change *Farmer's* to *Farmers'*
    (4) replace *that* with *who*
    (5) change *housewives* to *housewive's*

12. Sentence 9: **In addition, she and her sister writed a regular column for ten years in *Woman's Home Companion*.**

    What correction should be made to this sentence?

    (1) change *she* to *her*
    (2) change *writed* to *wrote*
    (3) change *years* to *years'*
    (4) change *Woman's* to *Womans'*
    (5) no correction is necessary

13. Sentence 10: **Still popular among best-selling cookbooks today are her *Boston Cooking School Cookbook*, which is now known as *The Fannie Farmer Cookbook*.**

    What correction should be made to this sentence?

    (1) change *are* to *is*
    (2) change *which* to *who*
    (3) change *is* to *are*
    (4) change *known* to *knowed*
    (5) no correction is necessary

    Answers are on page 181.

2
SENTENCE STRUCTURE

In Chapter 1, you learned a lot about the parts of speech that make up our language. For example, you know what a verb is, and you know to watch out for certain trouble areas in using pronouns. As you saw in the very beginning of Chapter 1, the reason we study these parts of speech so carefully is that they help us to communicate in standard English sentences.

In this chapter, you will examine the uses and purposes of a complete sentence. You will also study a variety of ways to write and combine sentences. These skills will help you to recognize and correct errors on the multiple-choice part of the Writing Skills Test as well as to write well on the GED Writing Sample.

Three Characteristics of a Sentence

One of the first topics you reviewed in writing skills was the characteristics of a complete sentence. You saw that a sentence must contain a subject, the person or thing doing something or being described in a sentence. A sentence must also have a predicate, which contains the verb or verbs in a sentence and tells what the subject is or does. The subject and predicate are the two main parts of a complete sentence. Together they must express a complete thought.

A group of words that does not meet these requirements is a fragment. Can you identify the fragments in the following conversation?

(1) DAD: Where's John?

(2) SIS: Went to a job interview.

(3) DAD: Who drove him?

(4) SIS: His friend Jean.

(5) DAD: What did he wear?

(6) SIS: Your new gray suit.

(7) DAD: He'd better land this one!

The fragments are lines (2), (4), and (6). Have you ever had a conversation like this? When reading each line above, you could tell what was going on because of the lines before and after it. When you read line (2), *Went to a job interview*, you knew whom Sis was talking about because you also read Dad's line above.

However, what if each of these lines stood on its own—without any other lines to help you interpret its meaning? Would you still understand its meaning? The lines that have meaning on their own are complete sentences. The lines that do not make sense by themselves are fragments. For example, look at line (4).

His friend Jean.

What about Jean? This group of words has no predicate to tell you what the subject is or does. To make this fragment a complete sentence, the writer must add a predicate:

His friend Jean **drove him to the interview**.

Now look at line (2):

Went to a job interview.

Who went to a job interview? This group of words is a fragment because it doesn't have a subject to tell you who is performing the action in the sentence. The writer must add a subject to make a complete sentence:

John went to a job interview.

In a certain type of sentence, the subject may be hard to recognize. In a command or an instruction, the subject of the sentence is understood to be *you*. In the following sentence, the subject performing the action is the person being spoken to.

Go down the hall and turn left.

(You) go down the hall and turn left.

In addition to having a subject and predicate, a sentence must express a complete thought. What is the problem with the following sentence?

Caleb driving to the city.

In the sentence above, the verb is not complete. You could correct the sentence by writing *Caleb is driving to the city.*

Sentence fragments are often difficult to detect because they make sense when read with the sentences around them. When proofreading a passage or your own writing for sentence fragments, make sure each group of words has meaning when standing alone. You might want to check this by reading backward, sentence by sentence, in order to see each sentence in isolation.

EXERCISE 1: REWRITING FRAGMENTS
PART A

Directions: Write *S* in front of complete sentences and *F* in front of fragments. Rewrite each fragment as a complete sentence on a separate sheet of paper, making sure each has a subject and a predicate and expresses a complete thought.

Examples: _____*F*_____ An elderly clerk.

An elderly clerk gave me my change.

_____*S*_____ Turn on the TV to channel 8.

_____ **1.** The pickup truck.

_____ **2.** Joseph is a man with many dreams.

_____ **3.** Called your house last night.

_____ **4.** Anxious for some news, the inmate.

_____ **5.** Life, with its many disappointments.

_____ **6.** Go to bed.

_____ **7.** To pitch like Dwight Gooden and hit like Ryne Sandberg.

_____ **8.** He knows the answer.

_____ **9.** Movies shown at 5:00 P.M. daily.

_____ **10.** Add ½ teaspoon of cinnamon and stir the batter.

Possible answers are on page 181.

PART B

Directions: Rewrite the following paragraph, fixing all of the sentence fragments. You can fix these fragments by adding a missing subject or predicate, or by joining two fragments together.

> When President John F. Kennedy was inaugurated in 1960, he stated, "Ask not what your country can do for you; ask what you can do for your country." His philosophy did much for U.S. citizens and underdeveloped areas of the world. For example, the Peace Corps. This program sent volunteers. Into underdeveloped areas of the world. The volunteers educated the citizens of those countries in basic survival skills. The main goal was for the countries to become more self-sufficient. And also relations between the U.S. and these countries to be improved.

Possible answers are on page 182.

Sentence Combining

If you wanted to make one sentence out of these two simple sentences, how would you do it? Try writing both ideas in one sentence.

> Those nails are for the paneling.

> The others can be used for hanging pictures.

The most common way to combine sentences like these is to use the joining word *and*. In the combined sentence that follows, notice that a comma is necessary before the joining word—where the period was in the first sentence. The wording of the two original sentences is unchanged.

> Those nails are for the paneling, and the others can be used for hanging pictures.

The combined sentences you have just seen are made up of two independent clauses joined by a comma plus *and*. A *clause* is a group of words that contains a subject and a verb. An *independent clause* can stand on its own as a complete sentence: it has a subject and a predicate, and it expresses a complete thought.

The following joining words, or *coordinating conjunctions*, are used with a comma to combine independent clauses: *and, but, or, nor, for, so, yet*. Notice that the joining words have different meanings. The word *and* does not mean the same as *but* or *so*, for example.

In the two examples that follow, notice the difference in meaning because of the conjunctions used. The first sentence implies that Jacob really does not want to go out because it is raining, but he must. The second sentence implies that Jacob has to go out because it is raining.

It is raining, but Jacob has to go out.

It is raining, so Jacob has to go out.

The chart below shows the different coordinating conjunctions and their meaning in a sentence.

Coordinating Conjunction	Meaning
and	adds information
but yet	shows an opposite
or	shows a choice
nor	rejects both choices
for	links effect to cause
so	links cause to effect

EXERCISE 2: CONJUNCTIONS

Directions: Choose a logical conjunction from the chart above to connect each pair of sentences. Then, on a separate sheet of paper, rewrite them as one sentence. Be sure to punctuate each new sentence correctly.

Example: I don't want to work. I need a job.

I don't want to work, but I need a job.

1. We are planning a Fourth of July picnic. We hope all of you can attend.

2. He did not study for his driver's test. He passed it.

3. Al has always wanted his own business. He opened a restaurant.

4. You may have some strawberry pie. You may have some cherry pie.

5. I can do most of my own plumbing. I cannot do the electrical work.

6. Karen is not allowed any hard exercise. She is recovering from an operation.

Answers are on page 182.

Clues About Commas

Don't use a comma every time you see a coordinating conjunction such as *and* or *but.* So far you have learned that a comma is needed when two complete thoughts are joined. If a coordinating conjunction does *not* connect two complete thoughts, do not use a comma.

NO COMMA NEEDED: Sue and Bruce are married.
                      S   V

                   All of us went but Maureen.
                    S   V

                   They built a patio and enclosed it with shrubs.
                    S V   V

COMMA NEEDED: Sue is married, but Tina is not.
(two complete thoughts)   S V   S V

                   Most of the girls went, but Maureen stayed home.
                    S   V   S   V

                   They built a patio, but they did not build a deck.
                    S V   S   V

Can you see the difference between the two sets of sentences? The second set needs a comma because the conjunction is joining two complete thoughts; in each sentence there are two subject-verb pairs. In the first set of sentences, there is only one subject-verb pair.

EXERCISE 3: USING COMMAS CORRECTLY

Directions: Place commas where they are needed in the following sentences, according to the rule you have just learned. Some of the sentences are correct as written.

1. She took off her coat and hung it in the closet.

2. She took off her coat and she hung it in the closet.

3. Jorge called Marie but he did not call Clara.

4. Jorge called Marie but not Clara.

5. Our daughter has a learning disability but is doing well in school.

6. Our daughter has a learning disability but she is doing well in school.

7. We visited my Aunt Nancy for we had not seen her in a while.

8. The mayor was popular with both senior citizens and young people.

Answers are on page 182.

Run-ons and Comma Splices

"You should see Brooke, my fifteen-year-old daughter her hair is pink and seventeen different lengths it is hideous she has the wildest haircut I've ever seen."

If you let punctuation be your clue, you can count only one sentence in the quote above. *You* begins with a capital letter, and a period follows *seen*. However, how many complete thoughts does the sentence above contain, and what are they?

There are actually four complete thoughts, ending in *daughter, lengths, hideous,* and *seen*. The sentence is one long **run-on**. When two or more sentences are joined without correct punctuation or conjunctions, the result is a run-on—the words run on (and on and on). You can correct run-ons by dividing them into separate sentences or combining the ideas with proper punctuation and conjunctions. Here is a corrected version:

"You should see Brooke, my fifteen-year-old daughter. Her hair is pink and seventeen different lengths, and it is hideous. She has the wildest haircut I've ever seen."

Another type of error, a **comma splice**, results when two complete sentences are joined by a comma without a conjunction, as in this example:

"She did this right before our big family reunion, all of my relatives are going to think she is a creature from outer space."

A comma splice can be separated into two sentences, or a logical conjunction can be placed after the comma:

"She did this right before our big family reunion. All of my relatives are going to think she is a creature from outer space."

"She did this right before our big family reunion, so all of my relatives are going to think she is a creature from outer space."

EXERCISE 4: RUN-ONS AND COMMA SPLICES

Directions: Some of the following sentences are run-ons or comma splices. If a sentence is correct as written, write *C* in the space. Rewrite incorrect sentences on a separate sheet of paper. Either divide them into separate sentences or combine them correctly using a comma with *and, but, for, or, nor, so,* or *yet.*

——— 1. My pet peeve is waiting in long lines.

——— 2. Kyle broke his leg he was taken to the emergency room.

——— 3. Pass the donuts, I'm starving!

——— 4. Is a storm "watch" less serious than a storm "warning"?

——— 5. The make of her car is a Buick, the model is a Century.

——— 6. I'll have a ham on rye with mayonnaise, please.

_____ **7.** We attended the Special Olympics at my niece's school.

_____ **8.** Of course this is my sweater, I've had it for years.

_____ **9.** Dion won every swimming event in the meet we were proud of him.

_____ **10.** I'd rather have hay fever than food allergies, at least I can eat!

Answers are on page 182.

EXERCISE 5: RUN-ONS AND COMMA SPLICES

Directions: The following paragraph contains some run-ons and comma splices. Read each sentence carefully to determine if it is written correctly. On a separate sheet of paper, rewrite the paragraph, correcting all the run-ons and comma splices. Either separate the incorrect sentences into two sentences or combine them using a comma with *and, but, or, for, nor, so,* or *yet.*

My cousin Ernie loves solving brainteasers, doing magic tricks, and playing mathematical games. He subscribes to several magazines they are filled with puzzles. In one trick, Ernie challenges his friends to cut a hole in an index card that is big enough to put a person's head through! His friends always try, he watches and laughs. Then Ernie cuts the card into a long strand and places it over his head. Who knows, maybe someday he will be performing the card trick on TV he certainly works hard at his craft.

Possible answers are on page 182.

EXERCISE 6: SENTENCE STRUCTURE PRACTICE

Directions: The following paragraph may contain any type of error you have studied so far in writing skills. Make sure each sentence is complete and correct.

(1) Recently psychologists have been researching birth order, their research suggests that personality and intelligence are based partly on where a child ranks in the family. (2) One of their theories is that the first child receives more of the parents' attention than later children so first-borns tend to be more intellectual. (3) First-borns often pattern their behavior after they're parents and other adults. (4) Later children must share their parents with the oldest child they pattern their behavior after the older siblings and peers. (5) Some theories suggesting that the later children are happier than first-borns. (6) Several books have been published on the subject, but many people soon may be applying birth-order theories to their own families.

1. Sentence 1: **Recently psychologists have been researching birth <u>order, their</u> research suggests that personality and intelligence are based partly on where a child ranks in the family.**

Which of the following is the best way to write the underlined portion of this sentence? If you think the original is the best way, choose option (1).

(1) order, their
(2) order, or their
(3) order their
(4) order. Their
(5) order and their

2. Sentence 2: **One of their theories is that the first child receives more of the parents' attention than later children so first-borns tend to be more intellectual.**

   What correction should be made to this sentence?

   (1) change *is* to *are*
   (2) change *theories* to *theory's*
   (3) change *receives* to *received*
   (4) change *parents'* to *parent's*
   (5) insert a comma after *children*

3. Sentence 3: **First-borns often pattern their behavior after they're parents and other adults.**

   What correction should be made to this sentence?

   (1) change *pattern* to *patterned*
   (2) replace *their* with *they're*
   (3) replace *they're* with *their*
   (4) change *parents* to *parents'*
   (5) no correction is necessary

4. Sentence 4: **Later children must share their parents with the oldest <u>child they</u> pattern their behavior after the older siblings and peers.**

   Which of the following is the best way to write the underlined portion of this sentence? If you think the original is the best way, choose option (1).

   (1) child they
   (2) child, and they
   (3) child and they
   (4) child, and
   (5) child and, they

5. Sentence 5: **Some theories <u>suggesting</u> that the later children are happier than first-borns.**

   Which of the following is the best way to write the underlined portion of this sentence? If you think the original is the best way, choose option (1).

   (1) suggesting
   (2) were suggesting
   (3) suggest
   (4) suggested
   (5) will suggest

6. Sentence 6: **Several books have been published on the subject, but many people soon may be applying birth-order theories to their own families.**

   What correction should be made to this sentence?

   (1) change *published* to *publishing*
   (2) remove the comma after *subject*
   (3) replace *but* with *so*
   (4) change *may be* to *were*
   (5) no correction is necessary

   Answers are on page 182.

Using Longer Conjunctions

You have now learned one way to combine two independent clauses, by using a comma and a coordinating conjunction such as *and* or *but*. The following example shows another method. Note the punctuation and conjunction in the new sentence.

Rachel has a lot of friends in New Jersey.   She decided to move there.

Rachel has a lot of friends in New Jersey; **therefore,** she decided to move there.

Conjunctions such as *however* and *therefore* are called ***conjunctive adverbs***. Knowing this term is not important for the Writing Skills Test, but understanding this type of conjunction can help you on both sections of the test. Below is a list of some conjunctive adverbs and their meanings:

Conjunctive Adverb	Meaning
moreover furthermore in addition	adds related information (like *and*)
however nevertheless on the other hand	shows a contrast (like *but*)
therefore consequently	links cause to effect (like *so*) explains relationship between two ideas
otherwise	shows an alternative (like *or*)
for instance for example	gives specifics to illustrate a general idea
then	shows time order

When you are combining two independent clauses with this type of conjunction, the wording of the two clauses does not change. After the first clause comes a semicolon (;), then the conjunctive adverb, then a comma, then the second clause. The exception to the rule is that no comma is needed after *then*. Study the punctuation carefully in the following examples.

Barbara is from Iowa; **however,** she now lives in Illinois.
Barbara moved to Illinois; **then** she moved to New York.

When using this type of conjunction, you should always do two things:

1. **Choose the conjunction that has the correct meaning.** The chart above can help you learn what words to use and when to use them.

2. **Use the correct punctuation.** A semicolon comes *before* all conjunctive adverbs. A comma comes *after* all conjunctive adverbs except *then*.

EXERCISE 7: CONJUNCTIVE ADVERBS

Directions: Choose the correct conjunction to complete each sentence. Be sure the meaning of the conjunction relates the clauses logically.

1. He was qualified for the job; _____, he got it.

   (a) therefore   **(b)** however   **(c)** instead

2. The steak is very good; _____, you might prefer the chicken.

   (a) consequently   **(b)** on the other hand   **(c)** for example

3. The company is in financial trouble; _____, workers may be laid off.

   (a) nevertheless   **(b)** however   **(c)** as a result

4. Jason has been taking piano lessons for years; _____, he does not play well.

   (a) however   **(b)** consequently   **(c)** moreover

5. Jeri may run for councilperson; _____, she may someday become mayor.

   (a) otherwise   **(b)** furthermore   **(c)** for instance

Answers are on page 183.

EXERCISE 8: ERRORS WITH CONJUNCTIVE ADVERBS

Directions: Correct the errors in the following sentences by crossing out mistakes and inserting corrections. Check the punctuation carefully and make sure that the meaning of the conjunction logically links the two clauses. Some sentences may be correct as written.

Example: We saw several interesting sights during the tour; ~~nonetheless~~ *; therefore,* I enjoyed it very much.

1. The snowstorm worsened; nevertheless we postponed our trip.

2. Two of the students studied hard; therefore, they failed the test.

3. The dishwasher is broken, in addition the freezer won't stay cold.

4. Mrs. Jones felt ill; however, she called a doctor.

5. Jane has so many talents; otherwise, she sings in a professional choir, weaves detailed tapestries, and can play an excellent game of tennis.

Possible answers are on page 183.

EXERCISE 9: COMBINING SENTENCES

Directions: Combine each pair of sentences **two different ways**, using any correct sentence structure. Be sure to punctuate your new sentences correctly and to use logical conjunctions. Use the charts on pages 96 and 101 to help you.

1. The salesperson was very polite. She listened to my complaints.

2. The music was terrible. We decided to dance.

3. We bought the house in 1975. We sold it in 1980 for twice the price.

4. My friends give me advice. I do not always listen to them.

5. I could drive you to work in the morning. You could take the subway.

Possible answers are on page 183.

Joining Dependent and Independent Clauses

So far you have practiced combining independent clauses with two types of conjunctions. A third type of conjunction makes one clause "dependent" on the other and shows the relationship between the two clauses. Look at the two short sentences and the combined sentence in the following example. Notice that the wording of the original sentences has not changed.

Dirk ran on the ice. He fell.

Because Dirk ran on the ice, he fell.

The *dependent clause* is *Because Dirk ran on the ice*. This clause is dependent because it is not a complete thought on its own—it needs the independent clause that follows it. The conjunction *because* makes the clause dependent and shows the relationship between the two ideas.

The meanings of conjunctions like *because* are very important. On page 104 is a list of some common **subordinating conjunctions**, grouped according to meaning.

Conjunction	Meaning
before after while when whenever until	shows time relationship
because since so that	shows cause or effect
if unless	shows the condition under which something will happen
though although even though	shows a contrast
as though as if	shows similarity
where wherever	shows place

The clauses in a sentence using one of these conjunctions can be moved around. When the dependent clause comes first, a comma separates the two clauses. When the independent clause comes first, no comma is needed.

> After the fog lifted, the planes were no longer grounded.

> The planes were no longer grounded after the fog lifted.

Take care to choose a conjunction that logically relates the two ideas you want to combine. In the first of the following sentences, the conjunction used, *because*, makes the sentence very confusing. In the second sentence, *although* shows that the two ideas contrast.

> NONSENSE: Because I was hungry, I didn't bother to eat.

> MAKES SENSE: Although I was hungry, I didn't bother to eat.

EXERCISE 10: DEPENDENT CLAUSES
PART A

Directions: Using the list of conjunctions above, fill in the blank with an appropriate word. There are several possible answers in each case. Choose one that makes sense to you.

1. _____ Ray was afraid of water, he took swimming lessons.

2. _____ she already knows the words to the song, she can teach us.

3. I'm not going to the class reunion _____ my closest friends won't be there.

4. _____ we left the meeting, we went for pizza.

5. Celia stayed with her mother _____ the nurse returned.

Possible answers are on page 183.

PART B

Directions: Complete the following sentences with suitable dependent clauses, using the conjunction indicated. Be sure to punctuate the sentences correctly.

Example: (after) Margaret Kingsbury was born on Tuesday.

> Margaret Kingsbury was born on Tuesday *after* **her mother had put in a full day at the office.**

OR

> *After* **her mother had put in a full day at the office,** Margaret Kingsbury was born on Tuesday.

1. (since) we knew the food at the cafe was good

2. (before) the family bought a new mini-van

3. (whenever) Eliot has nightmares

4. (even though) I ordered a pepperoni pizza

5. (unless) Duane will paint the porch steps

Possible answers are on page 183.

PART C

Directions: Combine each pair of sentences by changing one of them into a dependent clause using one of the conjunctions listed on page 104. Be sure to place a comma after introductory dependent clauses.

Example: Russell attempted to bribe a police officer. Russell was arrested.

> **When he** attempted to bribe a police officer, **Russell was arrested.**

1. We arrived at the church late. We missed their wedding ceremony.

2. Bonnie said that she was not tired. She fell asleep at 7:00 P.M.

3. I left my umbrella at home. I was soaked from the unexpected thunderstorm.

4. Rose was angry with her babysitter. She said she would not hire the young girl again.

5. We drove into the parking lot. We noticed that the store was closed.

Answers are on page 183.

Sentence Combining on the GED Test

One kind of question on the Writing Skills Test will require you to change the structure of a sentence or to combine two sentences without changing the meaning. The original sentence or sentences will contain no error. To answer the question correctly, you will have to figure out which of the answer choices will result in a new sentence that has the same meaning as the original.

There are two types of these questions. Read through the following examples and explanations carefully to become familiar with each.

Sentence 1: **Though city law does not allow pets to run loose, unleashed dogs are frequently seen on the streets.**

If you rewrote Sentence 1 beginning with

City law does not allow pets to run loose;

the next word should be

(1) otherwise
(2) furthermore
(3) then
(4) nevertheless
(5) therefore

To find the correct answer, test each of the answer choices. Which of the following new sentences is correct?

Choice 1: City law does not allow pets to run loose; otherwise, unleashed dogs are frequently seen on the streets.

Choice 2: City law does not allow pets to run loose; furthermore, unleashed dogs are frequently seen on the streets.

Choice 3: City law does not allow pets to run loose; then unleashed dogs are frequently seen on the streets.

Choice 4: City law does not allow pets to run loose; nevertheless, unleashed dogs are frequently seen on the streets.

Choice 5: City law does not allow pets to run loose; therefore, unleashed dogs are frequently seen on the streets.

Choice 4 is correct. Use of the conjunction *nevertheless* shows the contrast between the two ideas in the original sentence. Can you see that none of the other choices make sense?

Sentences 2 and 3: **These dogs are hungry strays. They knock over garbage cans and scavenge in parks.**

The most effective combination of these sentences would include which of the following groups of words?

(1) Because these dogs
(2) Unless these dogs
(3) Although these dogs
(4) In order that these dogs
(5) Until these dogs

Once again, test each answer choice in a new sentence. The first two are done for you. On a piece of scratch paper, write out the other three. Which one is correct?

Choice 1: Because these dogs are hungry strays, they knock over garbage cans and scavenge in parks.

Choice 2: Unless these dogs are hungry strays, they knock over garbage cans and scavenge in parks.

Choice 1 is correct. The conjunction *because* shows the cause-and-effect relationship between the original sentences.

In the rest of the GED practice exercises, you'll see more questions like these.

EXERCISE 11: STRUCTURE AND USAGE

Directions: Read the following paragraph and look for errors in sentence structure and usage. The questions that follow will require you to correct errors as well as choose correct ways of rewriting portions of the paragraph.

(1) Some American consumers are able to save some of their earnings after the bills have been paid and the groceries have been purchased. (2) Many of these people find security in opening a savings account. (3) For others, saving is not as exciting as investing their extra cash. (4) While some bought bonds as a safe way of investing, other investors choose to buy stock in a corporation. (5) Ownership in a corporation is represented by the number of shares of stock a person owns, however, by buying stock, a person becomes an owner of the business. (6) When a corporation is successful, its stockholders reap the benefits. (7) They are paid a share of the increased profits in addition, the value of their stock increases. (8) If the business is not a success stockholders may see the value of their stock decrease. (9) If the value decreases enough, he may lose their entire investment. (10) Because investing money can be risky, a new investor should get some reliable advice.

1. Sentence 1: **Some American consumers are able to save some of their earnings after the bills have been paid and the groceries have been purchased.**

   Which of the following is the best way to write the underlined portion of this sentence? If you think the original is the best way, choose option (1).

   (1) earnings after the
   (2) earnings, after the
   (3) earnings; after the
   (4) earnings after, the
   (5) earnings; however, the

2. Sentences 2 and 3: **Many of these people find security in opening a savings account. For others, saving is not as exciting as investing their extra cash.**

   The most effective combination of these two sentences would include which of the following groups of words?

   (1) Because many of these people
   (2) When many of these people
   (3) Although many of these people
   (4) If many of these people
   (5) As though many of these people

3. Sentence 4: **While some bought bonds as a safe way of investing, other investors choose to buy stock in a corporation.**

What correction should be made to this sentence?

(1) replace *while* with *if*
(2) change *bought* to *buy*
(3) remove the comma after *investing*
(4) change *choose* to *chose*
(5) no correction is necessary

4. Sentence 5: **Ownership in a corporation is represented by the number of shares of stock a person <u>owns, however,</u> by buying stock, a person becomes an owner of the business.**

Which of the following is the best way to write the underlined portion of this sentence? If you think the original is the best way, choose option (1).

(1) owns, however, by
(2) owns; however, by
(3) owns, however by
(4) owns; therefore, by
(5) owns, therefore, by

5. Sentence 6: **When a corporation is successful, its stockholders reap the benefits.**

What correction should be made to this sentence?

(1) replace *When* with *Then*
(2) change *is* to *are*
(3) remove the comma after *successful*
(4) replace *its* with *it's*
(5) no correction is necessary

6. Sentence 7: **They are paid a share of the increased <u>profits in addition, the</u> value of their stock increases.**

Which of the following is the best way to write the underlined portion of this sentence? If you think the original is the best way, choose option (1).

(1) profits in addition, the
(2) profits, in addition the
(3) profits; in addition, the
(4) profits for example, the
(5) profits; for example, the

7. Sentence 8: **If the business is not a success stockholders may see the value of their stock decrease.**

What correction should be made to this sentence?

(1) replace *if* with *though*
(2) insert a comma after *success*
(3) change *stockholders* to *stockholders'*
(4) change *may see* to *are seeing*
(5) replace *their* with *his*

8. Sentence 9: **If the value decreases enough, he may lose their entire investment.**

What correction should be made to this sentence?

(1) remove the comma after *enough*
(2) replace *he* with *they*
(3) change *lose* to *lost*
(4) replace *their* with *his*
(5) no correction is necessary

9. Sentence 10: **Because investing money can be risky, a new investor should get some reliable advice.**

If you rewrote sentence 10 beginning with *Investing money can be risky*, the next word should be

(1) but
(2) nor
(3) yet
(4) as
(5) so

Answers are on page 184.

Sequence of Tenses

The following sentence is made up of two independent clauses, so it has two subjects and two verbs in it. Look at the verbs carefully. What mistake did the writer make?

The student reads the chapter, but he was unable to answer the test questions.

The verb *reads* is in the present tense, and *was* is in the past tense. Are you confused about when the action took place? Here is one way the sentence could be corrected, putting the first clause in the past, showing that the student has already read the chapter, and the second clause in the present, showing that right now the student can't answer the questions:

          past   present

The student **read** the chapter, but he **is** unable to answer the test questions.

Another possible correction puts the first clause in the past perfect and the second in the simple past. This combination of tenses shows that the action in the past perfect took place before the action in the simple past:

          past perfect   simple past

The student **had read** the chapter, but he **was** unable to answer the test questions.

Before you move on in this section, review the verb tenses and their explanations on pages 66–69. Understanding when each tense is used will help you combine different tenses correctly. Also study the following list of special helping verbs. Be careful to note which are used to indicate the past and which indicate present or future.

- If one clause is in the present tense, use one of the helping verbs from the "present or future" column in the other clause.

- If one clause is in the past tense, use one of the helping verbs from the "past" column in the other clause.

Past	Present or Future
could	can
should	shall
would	will
might	may
had to	must

In the following exercise, be careful to choose a logical tense as you choose each verb.

EXERCISE 12: CORRECT VERB SEQUENCE

Directions: In the following sentences, underline the correct verb in parentheses.

1. We had heard the bell, so we (were waiting, will wait) for class to begin.

2. If the nominating committee votes, Greg (became, will become) president.

3. When Connie applied for the job, she (should take, should have taken) her references along with her.

4. Everyone who attended the retirement dinner (was wearing, will wear) formal attire.

5. If Mary is smart, she (will call, called) her boss about the problem.

6. Eileen was really sorry that she (had slept, is sleeping) through the movie.

7. Members of the audience are cheering the dramatic ending because they (enjoy, have enjoyed) the play.

8. Will you make the beds while Bob (has swept, sweeps) the floor?

9. If we had sold the house, we (could have moved, can move) earlier.

10. If I miss work again, I (would lose, may lose) my job.

Answers are on page 184.

Dangling and Misplaced Modifiers

Another way to combine sentences is to use ***modifying phrases***, phrases that describe or add information. A correct sentence will always (1) make clear exactly what a modifying phrase modifies and (2) place the modifying phrase as close as possible to the word it modifies.

Look at the two combinations of the following pair of sentences. What is the difference between the correct and incorrect examples?

We heard the guard dog. The dog was growling loudly.

INCORRECT: Growling loudly, we heard the guard dog.

CORRECT: We heard the guard dog growling loudly.

In the incorrect sentence, the modifer *Growling loudly* is misplaced. The sentence implies that *we* were growling loudly, rather than the dog. In the correct sentence, the modifier *growling loudly* is placed next to the word it modifies, *dog*.

On a piece of scratch paper, rewrite the following sentence. Place the modifier as close as possible to the word it modifies.

The deer crossed in front of the driver with huge antlers.

The misplaced modifier is *with huge antlers*. It should be placed next to *deer*:

The deer with huge antlers crossed in front of the driver.

In addition to being misplaced, modifiers also may "dangle." A sentence with a ***dangling modifier*** contains no word for the modifier to modify. What is the difference between the correct and incorrect examples below?

INCORRECT: Stepping on the brakes too fast, the car slid.

CORRECT: When I stepped on the brakes too fast, the car slid.

The incorrect sentence contains a dangling modifier, *Stepping on the brakes too fast.* The sentence does not tell you *who* stepped on the brakes too fast. In the correct sentence, the dangling modifier has been changed to a dependent clause containing the subject *I.*

On a piece of scratch paper, rewrite the following sentence containing a dangling modifier. Make sure that your new sentence contains a word for the dangler to modify.

An accident was reported while watching the news.

The dangler is *while watching the news.* Here are two possible corrections to this sentence:

While watching the news, I heard an accident reported.

An accident was reported while I was watching the news.

EXERCISE 13: DANGLING AND MISPLACED MODIFIERS

Directions: Underline the modifying phrase in each of the following sentences. On a separate sheet of paper, rewrite each sentence that contains a dangling or misplaced modifier.

Example: <u>Wearing gloves</u>, the parrot perched on the hand of the trainer.

The parrot perched on the hand of the trainer wearing gloves.

1. Nailed to the wall, Rich saw the "No Smoking" sign.

2. The child called for his mother who wanted a toy.

3. While taking a shower, the telephone rang.

4. Driving to work, my papers blew out the window.

5. A bath felt good after working all day.

6. When traveling through Colorado, my luggage was lost on the train.

7. Wearing her wedding gown, we'll certainly be able to recognize the bride!

8. We heard the dog under the table whining for food.

Answers are on page 184.

Parallel Structure

In geometry, *parallel* lines are lines that are the same form. They are always the same distance apart, and they go in the same direction.

In sentences, two or more elements that have the same function must be written in the same form to be considered "parallel."

NOT PARALLEL: She prefers dancing, singing, and to act.

PARALLEL: She prefers dancing, singing, and acting.

Do you see the difference? Underline the three parallel parts in the second sentence above. In the first sentence, *to act* is not the same form as the two *ing* words it is joined to. To make the form parallel, change *to act* to *acting*.

Underline the incorrect part of the following sentence. On a piece of scratch paper, rewrite the sentence using parallel structure.

The model is tall, slim, and has attractive looks.

The corrected sentence would read like this: *The model is tall, slim, and attractive.*

EXERCISE 14: PARALLEL STRUCTURE
Part A
Directions: Cross out the word or phrase that is not parallel to the others. Replace it with an appropriate word or phrase.

Example: **(a)** knitting
(b) reading
(c) to ~~sew~~
(d) painting

_____*sewing*_____

1. **(a)** sad
   (b) happiness
   (c) afraid
   (d) lonely

   _____

2. **(a)** heart was thumping
   (b) ears were pounding
   (c) palms were perspiring
   (d) shaky knees

   _____

3. **(a)** being honest
   (b) courage
   (c) strength
   (d) pride

   _____

4. **(a)** set the table
   (b) cook the beans
   (c) pour the drinks
   (d) slicing the roast

   _____

5. **(a)** homemaker
   (b) mother
   (c) manager
   (d) is a married woman

   _____

Answers are on page 184.

PART B

Directions: In the blank, write the letter of the correct sentence from each pair.

_____ **1. (a)** Karla told Rita to get in the truck, start the engine, and that she should shift gears.
      (b) Karla told Rita to get in the truck, start the engine, and shift gears.

_____ **2. (a)** Thomas Edison invented the electric light bulb, and he started motion pictures, and the phonograph.
      (b) Thomas Edison invented the electric light bulb, the motion picture, and the phonograph.

_____ **3. (a)** His friends respect Tony because of his sincerity, honesty, and kindness.
      (b) His friends respect Tony because of his sincerity, honesty, and he is kind to people.

_____ **4. (a)** To have a good job, live alone, and enjoy herself are Vicki's goals.
      (b) To have a good job, be living alone, and enjoy herself are Vicki's goals.

_____ **5. (a)** I promise to be loving, cherish, and honor you.
      (b) I promise to love, cherish, and honor you.

Answers are on page 184.

EXERCISE 15: STRUCTURE AND USAGE

Directions: Read the following paragraph, checking for errors in:

- sequence of tenses
- misplaced and dangling modifiers
- parallel structure
- sentence structure and usage errors

Then answer the questions that follow.

(1) As the rest of our family gathered around to play trivia games, our youngest children felt left out of the fun, ages five and six. (2) Feeling sorry for them, new questions are being written by us that young children can answer. (3) We try to think of questions that they would find interesting and challenging but not to frustrate them. (4) Now when we play, we asked them to state the three colors of the American flag or recite the Pledge of Allegiance. (5) Also questions about the cartoons they watch. (6) We ask them about subjects they have learned about in school. (7) Other questions draw on information in the books we read to them. (8) Making up questions for the little children has become part of the game for the rest of us!

1. Sentence 1: **As the rest of our family gathered around to play trivia games, our youngest children felt left out of the fun, ages five and six.**

   Which of the following is the best way to write the underlined portion of this sentence? If you think the original is the best way, choose option (1).

   (1) our youngest children felt left out of the fun, ages five and six
   (2) their youngest children felt left out of the fun, ages five and six
   (3) our youngest children, ages five and six, felt left out of the fun
   (4) their youngest children, ages five and six, felt left out of the fun
   (5) our youngest, ages five and six, children felt left out of the fun

2. Sentence 2: **Feeling sorry for them, new questions are being written by us that young children can answer.**

   Which of the following is the best way to write the underlined portion of this sentence? If you think the original is the best way, choose option (1).

   (1) new questions are being written by us
   (2) new questions written by us
   (3) new questions have been written by us
   (4) we are writing new questions
   (5) they are writing new questions

3. Sentence 3: **We try to think of questions that they would find interesting and challenging but not to frustrate them.**

   Which of the following is the best way to write the underlined portion of this sentence? If you think the original is the best way, choose option (1).

   (1) to frustrate them
   (2) frustrating them
   (3) to frustrating them
   (4) frustrated
   (5) frustrating

4. Sentence 4: **Now when we play, we asked them to state the three colors of the American flag or recite the Pledge of Allegiance.**

   What correction should be made to this sentence?

   (1) change *play* to *played*
   (2) remove the comma after *play*
   (3) change *asked* to *ask*
   (4) change *recite* to *reciting*
   (5) no correction is necessary

5. Sentence 5: **Also questions about the cartoons they watch.**

   Which of the following is the best way to write the underlined portion of this sentence? If you think the original is the best way, choose option (1).

   (1) Also questions
   (2) We may also ask questions
   (3) They may also ask questions
   (4) We also asked questions
   (5) Also question them

6. Sentences 6 and 7: **We ask them about subjects they have learned about in school. Other questions draw on information in the books we read to them.**

   The most effective combination of these sentences would include which of the following groups of words?

   (1) subjects they have learned about in school and information
   (2) subjects they have learned about in school but draw on
   (3) subjects they have learned about in school; instead, we
   (4) If we ask them about subjects they have learned about in school
   (5) subjects they have learned about in school, not information

7. Sentence 8: **Making up questions for the little children** has become part of the game for the rest of us!

   Which of the following is the best way to write the underlined portion of this sentence? If you think the original is the best way, choose option (1).

   (1) Making up questions for the little children
   (2) For the little children, making up questions
   (3) Because we are making up questions for the little children
   (4) If we make up questions for the little children
   (5) Making up questions for the little children, we

Answers are on page 184.

3
MECHANICS

When we read, we rely on the signals of capitalization and punctuation to help us understand the writing. We also must be able to recognize the words by accurate spelling. We have all read, or tried to read, writing that contains so many mistakes that it is impossible to read—writing that, unfortunately, fails in its purpose: to communicate.

In this chapter, you will review skills that help make writing easier to read—capitalization, punctuation, and spelling. These skills will be tested in multiple-choice questions on Part 1 of the Writing Skills Test, and they will also help you write your essay correctly for Part 2. There are rules for capitalization and punctuation that are not covered in this book. The material you will see in this chapter focuses on those issues that may appear on the Writing Skills Test. If you would like more information on other issues, a grammar book will be a big help to you.

As you work through the rest of this book, work to improve your handwriting. Make capital letters big and make sure your punctuation marks are clear. Other people read your writing—write for them as well as for yourself.

Capitalization

Always capitalize *proper nouns*, or names. The naming process is similar for all nouns. When a child is born, we use the common noun *baby* or *infant*. Then the parents name the baby *Jennifer* or *Michael*, proper nouns. We name our pets; some people even name their cars (or at least call the car names when it doesn't start!).

As a society, we start organizations and businesses and name them. We build schools, visit historical sites, and live in towns and states. All of these particular people, places, and things have names that need capital letters. A good question to ask yourself when you are deciding whether to capitalize is "Am I naming someone or something?"

In each blank in the following chart, write a proper noun and be sure to capitalize it.

Common Nouns (General)	Proper Nouns (Specific)
woman	Bette Midler
man	George Washington
college	_____
street	_____
nation	_____
language	_____
holiday	_____
doctor	_____

The chart asks you to think consciously of specific names. Although several rules follow that explain in more detail some of the types of nouns that are capitalized, the rules still fall under the basic rule of "If it's a name, capitalize it."

Other Capitalization Rules

★ 1. **Capitalize a word used as a person's title.**

> Representing the state of Illinois is **Senator** Paul Simon.
>
> Our most experienced physician, **Doctor** Kundrat, will see you now.

Don't capitalize these words when they are used as general labels.

> The **senator** will meet with the press at 10:00.
>
> I went to see the **doctor** about a lingering cough.

★ 2. **Capitalize the specific names of places. Also capitalize words derived from the specific names of places.**

> My **Russian** boyfriend likes **French** dressing on his salad.
>
> **Washington Square** in **New York City** is the setting of a famous novel.
>
> Julian took **Highway 66** to **North Avenue**.

Don't capitalize general geographical terms.

> We drove **east** until we came to a four-lane highway.
>
> This **country** is the most beautiful I have ever seen.
>
> The **town square** was lit with colorful paper lanterns.

★ 3. **Capitalize names of special days and words used as part of a date.**

> My sister was born on **Independence Day**.
>
> The celebration was held on **Monday, January** 22nd.

Don't capitalize the names of seasons unless they are part of the specific name of an event or place.

> A fund-raiser for the group home will be held in the **spring**.
>
> The **Spring** Fling was a fund-raiser for the group home.

If you're not sure whether to capitalize something, the dictionary can help. For example, use your dictionary to look up *civil war*. You'll find a definition for the general term, using no capital letters. You may also find an entry for the specific war fought between the Union and the Confederacy in the 1860s—the Civil War—using capital letters.

EXERCISE 1: CAPITALIZATION RULES

Directions: Rewrite the following sentences, putting in capital letters where they belong and taking out those that are incorrect. The number of errors each sentence has is in parentheses.

1. The mayor of chestortown requested assistance from governor kelly. (3 errors)

2. My favorite time of Fall is thanksgiving. (2 errors)

3. Candy's doctor sent her to get a second opinion from doctor Schwartz. (1 error)

4. We will meet on wednesday, august 9, at lincoln center in memphis, tennessee. (6 errors)

5. Leading sunday services at st. gregory's cathedral will be father McMillan. (5 errors)

6. Drive North to baker avenue, then turn left at Kennedy highway. (4 errors)

7. My german lessons are helping me prepare for my european trip next Spring. (3 errors)

8. Marissa's birthday is christmas day, so her parents will surprise her with a party in january. (3 errors)

9. The ohio river is a beautiful river. (2 errors)

10. This Summer the band will be on the Road for a long tour. (2 errors)

Answers are on page 184.

Punctuation

As you know from all your work in writing, every sentence ends with a period, a question mark, or an exclamation point (!). Watch out for end punctuation that is missing or incorrect. As you learned in the sections about sentence fragments, the fact that a group of words ends with a period or a question mark does not mean it is a complete sentence.

INCORRECT:	Cleaned the garage.
CORRECT:	Peter cleaned the garage.
INCORRECT:	The man running the roulette wheel?
CORRECT:	Who is the man running the roulette wheel?

The Comma

You have already learned some comma rules in Chapter 2, "Sentence Structure." Now you will review those rules (the first two rules in the following list) as well as learn new ones. Keep in mind that commas are used for specific reasons. *Extra* commas are just as incorrect as missing ones!

Comma Rules

★ 1. **Use a comma with a coordinating conjunction to join two independent clauses.**

> Buying a new car can be exciting, but it can also be expensive.

Remember that an independent clause is a complete thought. If the second part of the sentence is not a complete thought, do *not* separate it from the first part with a comma.

> INCORRECT: Jill finished her exams, and went home for Christmas.

> CORRECT: Jill finished her exams and went home for Christmas.

★ 2. **Put a comma after introductory dependent clauses.**

> While she was waiting for a ride to work, Lavonna read the newspaper.

Remember that, if the dependent clause follows the independent clause, no comma is needed.

> INCORRECT: I would take a class, if I had time.
> CORRECT: I would take a class if I had time.

Now practice Rules 1 and 2. Insert commas wherever they are needed in the following sentences.

> After Jim gave permission Lana went out on his bike.

> I see my brothers whenever they are in town.

> Rex crawled under the bed and showed no interest in food.

> Tracy called the toddler but she could not coax him to come out.

You should have placed a comma after *permission* in the first sentence and after *toddler* in the fourth sentence. No commas are needed in the second and third sentences.

You can review this material further on pages 95–96 and 103–104.

★ 3. **Use commas to set off three types of phrases.**

(1) **Introductory or interrupting phrases:**

> **As usual,** no one wants to take out the garbage.

> Dora's job involves counseling parents, **for instance**.

> The goal, **of course,** is to score the most touchdowns.

The phrases in bold type above introduce or interrupt the main flow of the sentence. Notice that these phrases *never* contain the subject or verb of a sentence. They simply add an additional thought to the sentence.

(2) Modifying phrases:

Chattering happily, the children rode off to the picnic.

Our vacation was spent in New Mexico, my favorite state.

Alan Morse, the manager of our plant, is ill.

Notice that each of the above phrases set off by commas describes, or modifies, another word in the sentence.

(3) Adverb phrases:

We could, on the other hand, eat at McDonald's.

However, the team needs a better defense.

Mrs. Mugford, in addition, is a member of the lunch committee.

Notice that the adverb phrases above are not joining two complete sentences. Instead, they simply add some new meaning to the sentence. Can you see why the sentence below is incorrect?

INCORRECT: Nancy lost her glove, however, her son found it.

Simply using commas in this sentence is not correct because the adverb *however* is joining two complete sentences. As you learned in Chapter 2, this sentence should be punctuated like this:

CORRECT: Nancy lost her glove; however, her son found it.

Now practice Rule 3. Place commas wherever they are needed in the following sentences and cross them out if they are not needed. Be sure to place commas both before and after phrases that interrupt a sentence.

Mosquitoes I think are the worst part of camping.

Unlike her sister Mary asks men out frequently.

For heaven's sake stop making that terrible noise!

Joan, is leaving our firm, I'm sorry to say.

Afraid for her daughter Mrs. Donovan moved quickly toward her.

Nevertheless I'll need some additional income.

The huge blimp, sailed slowly overhead.

In the first sentence, commas are needed before *I* and after *think*. You should have placed commas after *sister* and *sake* in the second and third sentences. The comma after *Joan* in the fourth sentence should be crossed out. In the fifth sentence, add a comma after the modifying phrase *Afraid for her daughter*. In the sixth sentence, place a comma after the word *Nevertheless*. Finally, in the last sentence, take out the comma after *blimp*. Remember that you should never put a comma between a subject and a verb.

★ **4. Use commas to separate items in a** *series* **(a list of three or more items, actions, or descriptions).** Notice that each of the following series is in parallel structure.

> Children love to eat pizza, hot dogs, and peanut butter.
>
> Sid jogs, lifts weights, and plays handball.
>
> The young, tall, and talented athlete won the contest.

No comma comes before the first item in a series or after the last item.

INCORRECT: You'll find, potatoes, green beans, and lettuce, in that bag.

CORRECT: You'll find potatoes, green beans, and lettuce in that bag.

Do not use commas to separate only two items.

INCORRECT: George types, and takes dictation.

CORRECT: George types and takes dictation.

Now practice Rule 4. Place commas wherever they are needed in the following sentences.

> We traveled through Austria Germany Switzerland and Italy.
>
> The sleigh went over the river and through the woods.
>
> Dopey Sleepy and Doc were three of the seven dwarfs.
>
> My father did all the cooking cleaning and sewing.

In the first sentence, commas are needed after *Austria, Germany,* and *Switzerland.* The second sentence does not need any commas. In the third sentence, commas are needed after *Dopey* and *Sleepy.* In the fourth sentence, commas are needed after *cooking* and *cleaning.* Check your work carefully to make sure you did not add extra commas.

EXERCISE 2: USING COMMAS

Directions: Insert commas wherever they are needed in the body of the following letter. (You should insert nine commas.)

Dear Mom,
> Because I do not have enough money I will not be coming home for spring vacation. Unfortunately I need to stay here in Des Moines and work. I did not of course waste my money but I did not allow enough in my budget for an airline ticket. You will understand that I can't come I know. I'd really love to be home in March but I can't afford a ticket until June. Please call Sue Pam and Linda for me and relay the message.
>
> > Love always,
> > Dawn

Answers are on page 185.

Other Punctuation Marks

You have practiced using two other punctuation marks in this book, the semicolon and the apostrophe. Let's review these before you move on to Exercises 3 and 4, which require you to use all these types of punctuation correctly.

Semicolon

Use a semicolon to separate two independent clauses joined by a conjunctive adverb (*however, consequently, moreover, therefore,* etc.)

> I will check your files; however, your account seems to be in order.

Notice that this sentence structure also requires a comma following the conjunctive adverb.

You can review this sentence structure, including a list of conjunctive adverbs, on page 101.

Apostrophe

★ **1. Use an apostrophe to show possession.**

add $\boxed{'s}$ to all singular nouns
to plural nouns not ending in *s*

add $\boxed{'}$ to plural nouns ending in *s*

> I ran into a child's bicycle in the driveway.
>
> The children's bicycles are in the basement.
>
> My three brothers' rooms are always neat and clean.

★ **2. Use an apostrophe to replace missing letters in contractions.**

> They're going to lunch at the Ritz-Carlton.
>
> Lisa doesn't have time for a man like you.

You can review contraction-possessive pronoun confusion on pages 81–82 and subject-verb agreement with contractions on page 77.

EXERCISE 3: PUNCTUATION REVIEW

Directions: Each sentence below contains *one* error in punctuation. Find and correct each error.

Example: Kate finds that ~~its~~ *it's* very difficult to study at home, so she studies at the library.

1. To strip the paint from the woodwork, you will need, a gallon of stripper, old rags, a scraper, a paintbrush, steel wool, and a mask to protect you from the fumes.

2. Mr. Rider my insurance agent, called with information about a rate increase.

3. She hasn't returned the dresses to the store, because she lost the receipt.

4. I love to stay up late and watch old movies, however, I have difficulty getting up in the morning.

5. In spite of her parents protests, Charleen has moved in with her boyfriend.

Answers are on page 185.

EXERCISE 4: STRUCTURE, USAGE, AND MECHANICS

Directions: Read the following paragraph and answer the questions. You'll need to watch for all the types of errors you've studied in writing skills.

(1) Americans are moving to the Sun Belt, an area made up of southern and Western states. (2) Since World War II, many industries have relocated in States such as Nevada, Arizona, Colorado, Utah, and Florida. (3) As a result these states have steadily grown in population. (4) Industries' reasons for moving south and west include cheaper labor, lower taxes, milder weather, lower living costs, and a large market. (5) It's understandable that some industries prefer the climate of the Sun Belt to the long, cold winters of the northeastern and midwestern states the area called the Frost Belt. (6) Traditionally, older citizens have retired to states such as Arizona and Florida because of the climate. (7) Even younger Americans now are seeking the appealing weather and more relaxed lifestyles of the Sun Belt. (8) By the year 2000, the interests of the Sun Belt is expected to play a major part in national decision making as the states gain economic and political power.

1. Sentence 1: **Americans are moving to the Sun Belt, an area made up of southern and Western states.**

What correction should be made to this sentence?

(1) change *Sun Belt* to *sun belt*
(2) remove the comma after *Belt*
(3) change *southern* to *Southern*
(4) change *Western* to *western*
(5) change *states* to *States*

2. Sentence 2: **Since World War II, many industries have relocated in States such as Nevada, Arizona, Colorado, Utah, and Florida.**

What correction should be made to this sentence?

(1) remove the comma after *II*
(2) change *have* to *has*
(3) change *States* to *states*
(4) insert a comma after *as*
(5) no correction is necessary

3. Sentence 3: **As a result these states have steadily grown in population.**

What correction should be made to this sentence?

(1) insert a comma after *result*
(2) change *states* to *States*
(3) insert a comma after *states*
(4) change *have* to *had*
(5) change the spelling of *grown* to *growed*

4. Sentence 4: **Industries' reasons for moving south and west include cheaper labor, lower taxes, milder weather, lower living costs, and a large market.**

What correction should be made to this sentence?

(1) change *Industries'* to *Industries*
(2) change *south* to *South*
(3) change *west* to *West*
(4) insert a comma after *include*
(5) no correction is necessary

5. Sentence 5: **It's understandable that some industries prefer the climate of the Sun Belt to the long, cold winters of the northeastern and midwestern states the area called the Frost Belt.**

What correction should be made to this sentence?

(1) change *It's* to *Its*
(2) change *prefer* to *preferred*
(3) change *Sun Belt* to *sun belt*
(4) change *midwestern* to *Midwestern*
(5) insert a comma after *states*

6. Sentences 6 and 7: **Traditionally, older citizens have retired to states such as Arizona and Florida because of the climate. Even younger Americans now are seeking the appealing weather and more relaxed lifestyles of the Sun Belt.**

The most effective combination of these sentences would include which of the following groups of words?

(1) climate, so younger
(2) climate, but younger
(3) climate; for example, younger
(4) climate, or younger
(5) climate and now are seeking

7. Sentence 8: **By the year 2000, the interests of the Sun Belt is expected to play a major part in national decision making as the states gain economic and political power.**

What correction should be made to this sentence?

(1) remove the comma after *2000*
(2) change *interests* to *interests'*
(3) change *is* to *are*
(4) change *states* to *States*
(5) insert a comma after *economic*

Answers are on page 185.

Spelling

If we ol speld wurds lik tha sound, our riting mite look lik this!

Unfortunately, spelling English the way it sounds doesn't work very well most of the time, as you know. Don't despair.

Becoming a better speller is a goal of many adults. When we think of ourselves as "writers," we often think first of our spelling. In fact, many people think too much about spelling. There is much more to good writing than accurate spelling. Think of spelling as frosting on a cake. After hours of preparing and baking a delicious cake, we want the cake to be topped with frosting. Like frosting, accurate spelling reflects the writer's concern about the final product.

The GED Testing Service has provided you with a list of "frequently misspelled words" (see pages 128–131), words that the general public often misspells. This master list is the basis for the spelling errors you'll have to correct on the Writing Skills Test. The following pages are designed to help you study the words. The rules presented here apply to the words on the list, and almost all of the examples used in the practice exercises are from the list.

General Hints for Improving Your Spelling

1. **Use a dictionary.** There are many different kinds of dictionaries. A salesperson at a bookstore can help you choose a good one.

2. **Read.** You can learn much about spelling by reading material like newspapers, magazines, and books—you'll see common words used correctly over and over.

3. **Write.** You'll be able to practice what you've learned through writing and experimenting with new words.

4. **Record words that cause you difficulty in reading and writing.** Read over them and copy them a few times. Train yourself to spell them correctly.

5. **Make up memory tricks for words you find hard.** For example, *Wednesday* is pronounced "Wensday." Say to yourself WED-NES-DAY each time you write it. Which capital/capitol is a building? The capitol has a dome.

6. **Learn basic rules** that apply to many words on the master list and in everyday use. You'll find helpful spelling rules on pages 132–136.

7. **Don't overemphasize the importance of spelling.** There are a lot of other important topics to study as well. You don't have to be able to spell every word on the master list in order to pass the Writing Skills Test.

Getting to Know the Master List

The following hints will help you study the master list of commonly misspelled words on pages 128–131.

1. Make a few copies of the list so that you can underline, cut, check off, etc. Post the list where you will see the words often. Cut a copy of the list into many shorter lists. Divide and conquer!

2. Arrange for a friend or relative to dictate words to you. Try writing the word a few times as someone else reads it. If you are enrolled in a class, set up a time to meet with a classmate or a study group.

3. Remember, there are probably many words on the list that you *do* know how to spell. You may find that you're a better speller than you thought you were. Be positive! Check off the words you can spell; then attack the ones that are left.

4. Build your vocabulary. Most words on the list are common in daily life. There are, however, many words that you may not use in your own writing and speech. As you learn new words, try to use them. Knowing and practicing the meaning will help you keep the correct spelling fresh in your mind.

EXERCISE 5: THE MASTER LIST

Directions: Use the master spelling list on pages 128–131 to complete this exercise.

1. Find and list the nine entries that are capitalized.

2. There are many numbers on the list. Practice writing each of them. Then fill in the blanks with the missing word in the following sequences.

    (a) third, _____, fifth

    (b) eleventh, _____, thirteenth

    (c) seven, _____, nine

    (d) eleven, _____, thirteen, _____

3. Fill in the following blanks with amounts and measures from the list.

    (a) a coin worth twenty-five cents _____

    (b) a piece of paper worth one hundred cents _____

    (c) twelve of something make a _____

    (d) sixteen _____ make a pound

    (e) four quarts make a _____

4. Find and list the four entries that are written as two separate words.

5. There are seven words on the list that start with *q*. What letter usually follows *q* in a word?

6. Which two words contain apostrophes?

7. Find the other forms of the following words on the master list. Look carefully; different forms have different spellings that change their alphabetical order.

Example: dependent   independence   independent

(a) advise _____ _____

(b) argue _____ _____

(c) bury _____ _____

(d) know _____ _____ _____

(HINT: Look for one of the forms of *know* in the *a* listings.)

(e) decide _____ _____

(f) commit _____ _____

(g) marry _____ _____

(h) occur _____ _____

(i) please _____ _____

(j) possess _____ _____

(k) prefer _____ _____ _____

Answers are on page 185.

Master List of Frequently Misspelled Words

All misspelled words on the GED Test will be taken from the following master list. Other forms of most of these words, including plurals and forms requiring suffixes, also may be tested.

A	across	almost	appearance	associate
a lot	address	already	appetite	association
ability	addressed	although	application	attempt
absence	adequate	altogether	apply	attendance
absent	advantage	always	appreciate	attention
abundance	advantageous	amateur	appreciation	audience
accept	advertise	American	approach	August
acceptable	advertisement	among	appropriate	author
accident	advice	amount	approval	automobile
accommodate	advisable	analysis	approve	autumn
accompanied	advise	analyze	approximate	auxiliary
accomplish	advisor	angel	argue	available
accumulation	aerial	angle	arguing	avenue
accuse	affect	annual	argument	awful
accustomed	affectionate	another	arouse	awkward
ache	again	answer	arrange	B
achieve	against	antiseptic	arrangement	bachelor
achievement	aggravate	anxious	article	balance
acknowledge	aggressive	apologize	artificial	balloon
acquaintance	agree	apparatus	ascend	bargain
acquainted	aisle	apparent	assistance	basic
acquire	all right	appear	assistant	beautiful

because	cigarette	courage	disastrous	exceed
become	circumstance	courageous	discipline	excellent
before	citizen	course	discover	except
beginning	clothes	courteous	discriminate	exceptional
being	clothing	courtesy	disease	exercise
believe	coarse	criticism	dissatisfied	exhausted
benefit	coffee	criticize	dissection	exhaustion
benefited	collect	crystal	dissipate	exhilaration
between	college	curiosity	distance	existence
bicycle	column	cylinder	distinction	exorbitant
board	comedy	**D**	division	expense
bored	comfortable	daily	doctor	experience
borrow	commitment	daughter	dollar	experiment
bottle	committed	daybreak	doubt	explanation
bottom	committee	death	dozen	extreme
boundary	communicate	deceive	**E**	**F**
brake	company	December	earnest	facility
breadth	comparative	deception	easy	factory
breath	compel	decide	ecstasy	familiar
breathe	competent	decision	ecstatic	fascinate
brilliant	competition	decisive	education	fascinating
building	compliment	deed	effect	fatigue
bulletin	conceal	definite	efficiency	February
bureau	conceit	delicious	efficient	financial
burial	conceivable	dependent	eight	financier
buried	conceive	deposit	either	flourish
bury	concentration	derelict	eligibility	forcibly
bushes	conception	descend	eligible	forehead
business	condition	descent	eliminate	foreign
C	conference	describe	embarrass	formal
cafeteria	confident	description	embarrassment	former
calculator	congratulate	desert	emergency	fortunate
calendar	conquer	desirable	emphasis	fourteen
campaign	conscience	despair	emphasize	fourth
capital	conscientious	desperate	enclosure	frequent
capitol	conscious	dessert	encouraging	friend
captain	consequence	destruction	endeavor	frightening
career	consequently	determine	engineer	fundamental
careful	considerable	develop	English	further
careless	consistency	development	enormous	**G**
carriage	consistent	device	enough	gallon
carrying	continual	dictator	entrance	garden
category	continuous	died	envelope	gardener
ceiling	controlled	difference	environment	general
cemetery	controversy	different	equipment	genius
cereal	convenience	dilemma	equipped	government
certain	convenient	dinner	especially	governor
changeable	conversation	direction	essential	grammar
characteristic	corporal	disappear	evening	grateful
charity	corroborate	disappoint	evident	great
chief	council	disappointment	exaggerate	grievance
choose	counsel	disapproval	exaggeration	grievous
chose	counselor	disapprove	examine	grocery

guarantee	interrupt	marry	operate	please
guess	invitation	match	opinion	pleasure
guidance	irrelevant	material	opportune	pocket
H	irresistible	mathematics	opportunity	poison
half	irritable	measure	optimist	policeman
hammer	island	medicine	optimistic	political
handkerchief	its	million	origin	population
happiness	it's	miniature	original	portrayal
healthy	itself	minimum	oscillate	positive
heard	**J**	miracle	ought	possess
heavy	January	miscellaneous	ounce	possession
height	jealous	mischief	overcoat	possessive
heroes	journal	mischievous	**P**	possible
heroine	judgment	misspelled	paid	post office
hideous	**K**	mistake	pamphlet	potatoes
himself	kindergarten	momentous	panicky	practical
hoarse	kitchen	monkey	parallel	prairie
holiday	knew	monotonous	parallelism	precede
hopeless	knock	moral	particular	preceding
hospital	know	morale	partner	precise
humorous	knowledge	mortgage	pastime	predictable
hurried	**L**	mountain	patience	prefer
hurrying	labor	mournful	peace	preference
I	laboratory	muscle	peaceable	preferential
ignorance	laid	mysterious	pear	preferred
imaginary	language	mystery	peculiar	prejudice
imbecile	later	**N**	pencil	preparation
imitation	latter	narrative	people	prepare
immediately	laugh	natural	perceive	prescription
immigrant	leisure	necessary	perception	presence
incidental	length	needle	perfect	president
increase	lesson	negligence	perform	prevalent
independence	library	neighbor	performance	primitive
independent	license	neither	perhaps	principal
indispensable	light	newspaper	period	principle
inevitable	likelihood	newsstand	permanence	privilege
influence	likely	niece	permanent	probably
influential	literal	noticeable	perpendicular	procedure
initiate	literature	**O**	perseverance	proceed
innocence	livelihood	o'clock	persevere	produce
inoculate	loaf	obedient	persistent	professional
inquiry	loneliness	obstacle	persuade	professor
insistent	loose	occasion	personality	profitable
instead	lose	occasional	personal	prominent
instinct	losing	occur	personnel	promise
integrity	loyal	occurred	persuade	pronounce
intellectual	loyalty	occurrence	persuasion	pronunciation
intelligence	**M**	ocean	pertain	propeller
intercede	magazine	offer	picture	prophecy
interest	maintenance	often	piece	prophet
interfere	maneuver	omission	plain	prospect
interference	marriage	omit	playwright	psychology
interpreted	married	once	pleasant	pursue

pursuit
Q
quality
quantity
quarreling
quart
quarter
quiet
quite
R
raise
realistic
realize
reason
rebellion
recede
receipt
receive
recipe
recognize
recommend
recuperate
referred
rehearsal
reign
relevant
relieve
remedy
renovate
repeat
repetition
representative
requirements
resemblance
resistance
resource
respectability

responsibility
restaurant
rhythm
rhythmical
ridiculous
right
role
roll
roommate
S
sandwich
Saturday
scarcely
scene
schedule
science
scientific
scissors
season
secretary
seize
seminar
sense
separate
service
several
severely
shepherd
sheriff
shining
shoulder
shriek
siege
sight
signal
significance

significant
similar
similarity
sincerely
site
soldier
solemn
sophomore
soul
source
souvenir
special
specified
specimen
speech
stationary
stationery
statue
stockings
stomach
straight
strength
strenuous
stretch
striking
studying
substantial
succeed
successful
sudden
superintendent
suppress
surely
surprise
suspense
sweat

sweet
syllable
symmetrical
sympathy
synonym
T
technical
telegram
telephone
temperament
temperature
tenant
tendency
tenement
therefore
thorough
through
title
together
tomorrow
tongue
toward
tragedy
transferred
treasury
tremendous
tries
truly
twelfth
twelve
tyranny
U
undoubtedly
United States
university
unnecessary

unusual
useful
usual
V
vacuum
valley
valuable
variety
vegetable
vein
vengeance
versatile
vicinity
vicious
view
village
villain
visitor
voice
volume
W
waist
weak
wear
weather
Wednesday
week
weigh
weird
whether
which
while
whole
wholly
whose
wretched

EXERCISE 6: THE DICTIONARY

Directions: Below are some words on the list that may be unfamiliar to you. It is difficult to learn how to spell words that you may not use or hear very often (or at all). Use a dictionary to check the meanings and pronunciations of these words. Then use each one in a sentence that demonstrates its meaning.

auxiliary	negligence
ecstasy	perseverance
exorbitant	prevalent
flourish	suppress
hideous	tyranny

Possible answers are on page 185.

Helpful Spelling Rules

You have already studied rules for spelling noun plurals on pages 60–63 and rules for spelling verb forms on pages 70–72. You may want to review these sections now, since you'll need to know them for the exercises in this chapter. Knowing these rules for adding plural and verb endings will also help you learn the rules for adding suffixes, since they are very similar.

Compound Words

Compound words are formed by combining two or more words. When you form a compound word, never change the spelling of the original words.

The following are compound words from the master spelling list. Write them in the blanks.

day + break = daybreak   over + coat = _____

news + stand = _____   news + paper = _____

him + self = _____   it + self = _____

police + man = _____   room + mate = _____

Be careful of words that look like compound words but cannot be divided into two words:

almost	already	although	altogether
always	careful	mournful	pastime

Also remember the words you have found on the list that are written separately—*a lot, all right, post office.*

The IE/EI Rules

Learn the following rhyme to help you remember when you put *i* before *e*: "I before E except after C or when sounding like A as in *neighbor* and *weigh*."

Study the following rules and fill in two more examples of your own for each one.

★ **1. Most of the time, *i* comes before *e*.**

chief believe _____ _____

★ **2. After the letter *c*, *e* comes before *i*, except when *ci* together makes a *sh* sound as in *conscience*.**

receive perceive _____ _____

★ **3. When the sound is a long *a*, *e* comes before *i*.**

eight vein _____ _____

Now practice the rules by circling the error in each of the following groups:

1.	**2.**	**3.**	**4.**
(a) weird	**(a)** eight	**(a)** conceit	**(a)** peice
(b) breif	**(b)** seize	**(b)** ceiling	**(b)** belief
(c) foreign	**(c)** view	**(c)** believe	**(c)** reign
(d) leisure	**(d)** reciept	**(d)** receive	**(d)** thief
(e) mischief	**(e)** either	**(e)** seige	**(e)** priest

Answers: 1. b 2. d 3. e 4. a

Adding Prefixes

When a prefix is added to a word, the spelling of the prefix and the spelling of the base word always remain the same.

Here is a list of some prefixes used in words on the master spelling list and their meanings.

Prefix	Meaning	Examples
anti	against	antiseptic
auto	self	automobile
bene	good	benefit
co, com, con, cor	together	corroborate conversation
de	down	descend, descent
dis	not, away	disappear, disapprove
ex	out of	exceed
fore	front	forehead
im, in	in, into	immigrant, interrupt

Prefix	Meaning	Examples
in, ir	not	independent, irrelevant
mis	wrong	misspell, mistake
pre	before	prejudice
trans	across	transferred
un	not	undoubtedly, unnecessary, unusual

Practice adding common prefixes by filling in the blanks:

bi + cycle   = *bicycle*

dis + appoint   = _____

dis + satisfied   = _____

in + competent   = _____

in + convenient   = _____

ir + relevant   = _____

ir + resistible   = _____

un + acceptable   = _____

un + natural   = _____

Adding Suffixes

Most of the time, when a suffix is added to a base word, the spelling of the base word and the spelling of the suffix remain the same. However, the spelling of the base word is altered in some cases, according to the following rules.

★ 1. **If a word ends in a silent *e* and the suffix begins with a vowel, drop the silent *e*.**

appreciate + ation = appreciation

indispense + able = _____

coarse + est = _____

continue + ous = _____

Exceptions: Words that end in *ge* or *ce* must keep the final *e* to maintain the "soft" *g* (like *j*) and *c* (like *s*) sounds.

change + able = changeable

notice + able = _____

advantage + ous = _____

peace + able = _____

★ 2. **Keep a silent *e* at the end of the base word when adding a suffix that begins with a consonant.**

        care + ful = careful

        extreme + ly = _____

        advertise + ment = _____

Exceptions:

        argue + ment = argument

        true + ly = truly

        judge + ment = judgment

★ 3. **When adding a suffix to a word ending in *y* preceded by a consonant, change the *y* to *i* before adding the suffix. However, if the suffix begins with *i*, keep the *y*.**

        marry + age = marriage

        apply + ing = applying

        easy + er = _____

        bury + al = _____

        carry + ing = _____

        heavy + est = _____

If a base word ends in *y* preceded by a vowel, the spelling never changes when a suffix is added.

        employ + er = employer

        employ + ment = employment

★ 4. **The final consonant of a base word must be doubled if *all* of the following are true:**

- the base word ends in a single vowel and single consonant other than *h*, *w*, or *x*

- the accented syllable of the base word is on the last (or only) syllable

- the suffix begins with a vowel

Double the final consonant:

        prefer + ed = preferred

        permit + ing = _____

        transfer + ed = _____

Don't double the final consonant:

        benefit + ed = benefited

        counsel + or = _____

Sometimes the addition of a suffix shifts the accent to a different syllable. Don't double the final consonant unless the accent remains on the final syllable.

prefer + ence = **pre**ference (accent shifts)

oc**cur** + ence = oc**cur**rence (accent stays the same)

con**fer** + ence = _____

Tricky Vowels and Consonants

Below are some words that are often difficult to spell because of the placement or use of vowels. Some of the vowels are silent. Some sound like *e* instead of *a.* Some use *y* as a vowel. Look up the correct spelling of each word on the master spelling list; then write out the entire word for practice.

av__nue	be__utiful	b__ild
cafet__ria	conce__l	cr__stal
enco__raging	envelop__	g__idance
g__arantee	man__uver	misc__llaneo__s
persev__rance	pers__ade	sep__rate
specim__n	so__l	synon__m
t__ranny	tong__e	

Here are words that contain silent consonants. Look up the correct spelling of each word on the master spelling list; then write out the entire word for practice.

ans__er	autum__	colum__
campai__n	dou__t	ex__aust
ex__ibit	__new	__nock
__now	li__t	mor__gage
of__en	__sychology	recei__t
ri__t	r__ythmical	s__issors
si__t	solem__	strai__t

Watch out for combinations of letters that make different sounds. All the following words contain a consonant combination that makes an *f* sound. Look up the correct spelling of each on the master spelling list; then write out the entire word for practice.

enou__ __	lau__ __	pro__ __ecy
pro__ __et	so__ __omore	tele__ __one

For further work on combinations of letters, search the master list for words containing an *sh* sound and practice writing each one. There are several ways this sound can be spelled. To get you started, here are the first three words:

accompli__ __	accumula__ __on	affec__ __onate

EXERCISE 7: SPELLING LIST REVIEW

Directions: Be sure you have studied all the words on the master spelling list before you do this exercise. Place the letter of the word containing an error in the blank. If all the words are correct, write *f* in the blank.

_____ 1. (a) annually
(b) recipe
(c) shining
(d) bacheler
(e) college
(f) *no error*

_____ 2. (a) truely
(b) anxiously
(c) holidays
(d) mathematics
(e) temperature
(f) *no error*

_____ 3. (a) believed
(b) vicinity
(c) applies
(d) cheifly
(e) transferred
(f) *no error*

_____ 4. (a) scarcely
(b) procede
(c) incidentally
(d) judgment
(e) all right
(f) *no error*

_____ 5. (a) between
(b) employee
(c) loneliness
(d) unnecessarily
(e) restarant
(f) *no error*

_____ 6. (a) panicky
(b) critisize
(c) heroine
(d) February
(e) privilege
(f) *no error*

_____ 7. (a) knowledge
(b) obedient
(c) adviseable
(d) stomach
(e) significant
(f) *no error*

_____ 8. (a) burial
(b) obstacle
(c) pronunciation
(d) occuring
(e) technical
(f) *no error*

_____ 9. (a) exceptionaly
(b) possession
(c) appreciation
(d) leisure
(e) preferred
(f) *no error*

_____ 10. (a) persuading
(b) arguement
(c) commitment
(d) committee
(e) piece
(f) *no error*

Answers are on page 186.

Sound-Alike Words

Hear is a list of pears of words ewe knead too no.

Here is a list of pairs of words you need to know.

If you read both of these statements aloud, you will hear the same sounds. However, the words that sound alike, *Hear/Here, pears/pairs, ewe/you, knead/need, to, too,* and *two,* and *no/know,* have different meanings and spellings. Many pairs and groups of sound-alike words can be found on the master spelling list.

You have already studied some especially troublesome sound-alike words—the possessives and contractions. Review the material on pages 81–82 to refresh your memory.

Following are more pairs and groups of sound-alike words. Many of them sound exactly alike, such as *to, too,* and *two.* Others should not sound alike if you pronounce them carefully, such as *advice* and *advise.*

Read the explanations of the differences between the sound-alikes; then practice by filling in the blanks with the correct words.

accept (receive)
except (excluding; to leave out)

Everyone _____ Bryan will _____ an award.

advice (recommendation)
advise (recommend)

Samuel will _____ me, and I will follow his

_____ .

affect (act upon)
effect (result)

The medication will _____ me. I hope it doesn't cause any bad

side _____ s.

altogether (entirely)
all together (gathered in the same place)

I'm not _____ sure that the children were

_____ .

already (previously)
all ready (completely prepared)

We are _____ dressed and _____ for the party.

capital (city that is the official seat of a government)
capitol (building in which a state legislature works)
(*Capital* is also used in other ways: capital letters, capital in the bank.)

We visited the _____ building in Springfield, our state

_____ .

choose (pick)
chose (picked)

I'll _____ this dessert today. I _____ cake

yesterday.

coarse (rough)
course (plan of action; part of a meal; class)

When I took a woodworking _____, I learned to turn

_____ planks into fine furniture.

conscience (sense of right and wrong)
conscious (being aware)
conscientious (thorough, responsible)

Herb's _____ bothered him because he had not been

_____ of his daughter's problems. Normally he is a very

_____ father.

desert (dry region; pronounced DEH-zert)
desert (abandon; pronounced duh-ZERT)
dessert (last course of a meal)

Don't _____ your family in the hot, dry _____!

Save some pie or other type of _____ for me.

know (be aware of)
no (negative)

_____, I don't _____ the answer.

knew (was aware of)
new (not old)

I _____ I'd need a _____ coat before winter

came.

loose (not tight)
lose (misplace; fail to win)

The clasp on your key chain is _____. Tighten it, or you may

_____ your keys.

personal (individual)
personnel (relating to a group of workers)

Melinda had an appointment with the _____ director of her com-

pany. She arranged for a leave of absence for _____ reasons.

principal (main; head of a school)
principle (rules, facts, laws)

The _____ reason I called was to arrange a meeting with the
_____ of Jefferson School. I'd like to teach a course about the
_____s of physics.

quiet (silent)
quite (very)
quit (stop)

Please be _____. I'm _____ ill, so
_____ making so much noise.

to (preposition; word before a verb)
too (more than enough, very; also)
two (2)

I'd like _____ hamburgers. She went _____ the
store. Bud likes _____ swim. It's _____ cold in
here. I want _____ go on vacation, _____.

weak (not strong)
week (seven days)

After being hospitalized for a _____, Gloria felt very
_____.

weather (outdoor conditions)
whether (if)

She didn't know _____ she was going to the picnic. Rain was predicted in the _____ forecast.

EXERCISE 8: SOUND-ALIKE WORDS

Circle the error in each sentence; then write the correct word in the blank.

Example: The whole team worked hard all (weak) to build morale and break the

Olympic record. ____*week*____

1. The teachers knew that the principle's attitude was affected by the grievance they

   had filed. _____

2. If you choose to accept his advise and seek the job, you should apply at the per-

   sonnel office. _____

3. Tim knows that Shari is quite bored with the coarse. _____

4. The counselor's advice was not all together sound, so I chose to ignore her

   suggestions. _____

5. World peace is an issue we senators hear quite a lot about. Here inside the capitol

   we are conscience of world affairs. _____

6. He ate a whole pie for dessert. Now he's quiet affected by his

   actions. _____

7. I no the picnic will be tomorrow, whether the weather is good or

   not. _____

8. All of us except Charlie have all ready chosen to work for the reelection of the

   school board members. _____

Answers are on page 186.

EXERCISE 9: STRUCTURE, USAGE, SPELLING, AND MECHANICS

Directions: Read the following paragraph, looking for errors in capitalization, punctuation, spelling, and other types of errors you have studied in writing skills. Then answer the questions that follow.

(1) Every April, American taxpayers, surrounded by expense records, receipts, and canceled checks, cuddle up with their calculaters to figure out their yearly income taxes. (2) Taxpayers study their Internal Revenue Service instructions in order to fill out their tax forms accurately. (3) People want to pay the least possible amount of money but they must avoid mistakes and stay within the law. (4) Over the years, wealthy taxpayers have found several loopholes that seem unfair to others; consequently Americans have cried out annually for changes in the tax laws. (5) Private citizens also have criticized businesses for using loopholes in the laws to their advantage, the loopholes allow companies to pay fewer taxes and maintain higher profits. (6) As a result of years of discussion and debate over the tax dilemma, Congress passed the Tax Reform Act of 1986, which radically changed the way americans pay their income taxes. (7) One reason that the new law, in effect after 1988 was fairer is that it forced businesses to pay taxes on more of their profits. (8) Insted of adding exceptions and deductions, the new law eliminated hundreds of them. (9) Of course, taxpayers had to become competent in analyzing the new forms and learn the new rules for dependints, retirement benefits, and interest. (10) Taxpayers do not enjoy losing their personal income but they may part more easily with their hard-earned dollars if they think the tax laws are fair.

1. Sentence 1: **Every April, American taxpayers, surrounded by expense records, receipts, and canceled checks, cuddle up with their calculaters to figure out their yearly income taxes.**

   What correction should be made to this sentence?

   (1) change *April* to *april*
   (2) change *American* to *american*
   (3) change the spelling of *receipts* to *reciepts*
   (4) remove the comma after *checks*
   (5) change the spelling of *calculaters* to *calculators*

2. Sentence 2: **Taxpayers <u>study their</u> Internal Revenue Service instructions in order to fill out their tax forms accurately.**

   Which of the following is the best way to write the underlined portion of this sentence? If you think the original is the best way, choose option (1).

   (1) study their
   (2) studied their
   (3) will study their
   (4) study there
   (5) study his

3. Sentence 3: **People want to pay the least possible amount of money but they must avoid mistakes and stay within the law.**

   What correction should be made to this sentence?

   (1) change the spelling of *People* to *Poeple*
   (2) insert a comma after *money*
   (3) insert a comma after *but*
   (4) insert a comma after *mistakes*
   (5) no correction is necessary

4. Sentence 4: **Over the years, wealthy taxpayers have found several loopholes that seem unfair to others; consequently Americans have cried out annually for changes in the tax laws.**

   What correction should be made to this sentence?

   (1) remove the comma after *years*
   (2) change the spelling of *several* to *sevral*
   (3) insert a comma after *consequently*
   (4) change *Americans* to *americans*
   (5) change the spelling of *annually* to *annualy*

5. Sentence 5: **Private citizens also have criticized businesses for using loopholes in the laws to their advantage, the loopholes allow companies to pay fewer taxes and maintain higher profits.**

   Which of the following is the best way to write the underlined portion of this sentence? If you think the original is the best way, choose option (1).

   (1) their advantage, the
   (2) its advantage, the
   (3) their advantage. The
   (4) its advantage. The
   (5) their advantage the

6. Sentence 6: **As a result of years of discussion and debate over the tax dilemma, Congress passed the Tax Reform Act of 1986, which radically changed the way americans pay their income taxes.**

   What correction should be made to this sentence?

   (1) change the spelling of *dilemma* to *dilema*
   (2) remove the comma after *dilemma*
   (3) change *Congress* to *congress*
   (4) replace *which* with *who*
   (5) change *americans* to *Americans*

7. Sentence 7: **One reason that the new law, in effect after 1988 was fairer is that it forced businesses to pay taxes on more of their profits.**

   What correction should be made to this sentence?

   (1) change the spelling of *effect* to *affect*
   (2) insert a comma after *1988*
   (3) change the spelling of *businesses* to *buisnesses*
   (4) replace *their* with *they're*
   (5) no correction is necessary

8. Sentence 8: **Insted of adding exceptions and deductions, the new law eliminated hundreds of them.**

   What correction should be made to this sentence?

   (1) change the spelling of *Insted* to *Instead*
   (2) insert a comma after *exceptions*
   (3) remove the comma after *deductions*
   (4) change the spelling of *eliminated* to *elimanated*
   (5) no correction is necessary

9. Sentence 9: **Of course, taxpayers had to become competent in analyzing the new forms and learn the new rules for dependints, retirement benefits, and interest.**

   What correction should be made to this sentence?

   (1) change the spelling of *competent* to *competant*
   (2) change the spelling of *analyzing* to *analizing*
   (3) insert a comma after *forms*
   (4) change the spelling of *dependints* to *dependents*
   (5) insert a comma after *for*

10. Sentence 10: **Taxpayers do not enjoy losing their personal income but they may part more easily with their hard-earned dollars if they think the tax laws are fair.**

    What correction should be made to this sentence?

    (1) change the spelling of *losing* to *loosing*
    (2) change the spelling of *personal* to *personel*
    (3) insert a comma after *income*
    (4) change the spelling of *dollars* to *dollers*
    (5) insert a comma after *dollars*

Answers are on page 186.

4
PREPARING FOR THE GED WRITING SAMPLE

Usage, sentence structure, and mechanics are all crucial to communicating successfully with others in writing. However, these surface features of writing are not the whole story. A written composition may present accurate usage, contain no errors in mechanics, have well-structured, complete sentences, and *say nothing*. Good writing must *say something*—convey an explanation, present an opinion with logical and accurate support, or describe someone or something.

The writing process can be compared to an exercise workout: you go through a series of steps to reach the desired result. The five steps of the writing process are 1. Prewriting 2. Drafting 3. Revising 4. Editing 5. Publishing. A writing "workout" is an exercise program for our minds, helping us clarify our thoughts and get them on paper for our readers.

THE 45-MINUTE WORKOUT

Exercise for the Body

1. **Plan.** Arrange a time and place to exercise.

2. **Warm up** by stretching your muscles.

3. **Organize your exercises:** sit-ups, then jogging, etc.

4. **Use those muscles!** Keep moving! Don't give up!

5. **Cool down.** You've worked hard; relax your muscles.

Exercise for the Mind

1. **Prewriting.** Brainstorm for a topic, using mapping, clustering, organizing strategies.

2. **Drafting.** Write first draft based on prewriting activities.

3. **Revising.** Write second draft. Do a self-check based on what you like or dislike about the writing.

4. **Editing.** Check mechanics, spelling, punctuation, and grammar.

5. **Publishing.** Write for a purpose— family stories, the GED Essay Test.

As you can see, a good writing workout follows a series of steps. Throughout the rest of your work in writing skills, you'll practice these steps: prewriting, writing, revising, editing, and publishing. These writing steps will be very useful to you when you take the Writing Skills Test, so be sure to practice each one fully and carefully.

Warming Up to Writing

Think of the kinds of writing you already do. Underline any of these that you have written in your daily life. Add other kinds of writing you do.

1. *Lists*—grocery lists, meal planning or menu lists, errand lists, "Things to Do" lists, gift lists, _____

2. *Notes*—notes to family members, co-workers, children's teachers; notes inside of greeting cards; memos; postcards sent from vacation spots; _____ _____

3. *Letters*—friendly letters, business letters, letters of application for jobs, letters to the editors of newspapers or magazines, _____

4. *Diary or journal*—personal diary, daily written journal entries, notes to children in baby books, _____

5. Other types of writing that you do: _____

Building Material for Writing

Keeping informed and writing about your daily experiences, thoughts, and conversations will help you build your resources for writing.

1. *Keep a journal.* Write about whatever is on your mind or whatever happens to you. You'll have a record of your ideas and experiences.

2. *Think about discussions you have with others.* How do you verbally convince or persuade others? Try writing a few of your arguments in your journal or in letters.

3. *Read with a writer's point of view.* Look at how newspaper and magazine articles are written. Notice how the main ideas are developed, how paragraphs are organized, and what clues help you read and understand the articles.

4. *Try writing something you haven't before.*
   • If you always call relatives or friends, surprise them with a letter.
   • Write down stories you want to remember about your children or family; start a memory journal.

EXERCISE 1: WARMING UP

1. Write a note to someone or a journal entry of four or five sentences.

2. Think of a memorable day in your life and write a few lines describing the day or event.

3. Choose an article of at least five paragraphs in a newspaper or magazine. First read it to see what information you can learn from it. Then read it carefully once again to see how the information is ordered and structured. Jot down, in note form, what the main idea is.

Answers will vary.

Topic, Audience, and Purpose

The *topic* is the subject of your writing—what you are writing about. If you write a letter to a landlord, the topic may be "high rent," "longer lease," or "broken appliance." If you are writing an essay on marriage for a class or an organization, the topic may be "some reasons why most teenage marriages fail," "trust in a marriage," or "second marriages."

Once you have a topic, you need to determine your *purpose*. What point do you want to make? Why are you writing? Are you writing to tell a story? to describe? to inform? to persuade? If you are writing a letter of complaint to the credit department of a store, then your purpose is to state the problem, explain your opinion, and offer a solution. If you are writing an essay, you might describe a situation, inform about an issue, or state your opinion and support it.

Your purpose also depends on who is reading your writing—the *audience*. While diaries and journals are personal, most other types of writing are meant to be read. For example, you might write a letter of application to a personnel director, a note to the newspaper carrier, a report to a club or class, or an essay for an instructor to grade. An essay is usually meant for "general readership." It is written so that anyone reading it can understand it. Most of us write reports or essays with the idea that "someone out there" will be reading them. Keeping your readers in mind will help you make good word choices and use appropriate support for your ideas.

EXERCISE 2: TOPIC, AUDIENCE, AND PURPOSE

Directions: Read the following ending paragraph from a short letter and identify the writer, the topic, the purpose, and the reader (audience).

> For these reasons, I am asking that Erik be excused from your class next Friday. I hope that this absence will not hurt his progress in your history class. Please send homework with him.
>
> Thank you.

1. Who is the writer?

2. What is the topic?

3. What is the purpose?

4. Who is the reader?

Answers are on page 186.

Prewriting Paragraphs

There are many types of writing. However, being able to write a good paragraph is helpful in almost any kind of writing. Writing a good paragraph requires you to think clearly and organize your thoughts—the best writing practice you can get. Have you ever helped people move from one home to another? If they are packed and organized, the hard part is done before you come to carry boxes and furniture to the truck. Writing is the same way. If you plan and organize your ideas before you write, the writing itself is much easier and the end product is better.

Brainstorming for Paragraphs

You have taken a major step in the writing process. You have considered your topic, purpose, and audience. Now what? Once you have determined what point you want to make, you need to come up with ideas to put into your paragraph. This process is often called **brainstorming**.

To brainstorm, simply list rapidly all the ideas you can think of about your topic. Don't stop to edit or evaluate your ideas; don't worry about spelling or try to write complete sentences. A "whirlwind" of ideas should come to you as you think about the ways that you can support your topic. Write down all of your ideas—you want quantity now. You'll have time to think about quality later.

Here's an example of brainstorming:

Topic: garage sales

Topic sentence: It takes a lot of organization to get ready for a garage sale.

Brainstorm list:

    sorting and pricing items
    clean the garage
    watching my kids and keeping the dog in the yard
    cleaning out the closets and the basement before
    keeping the neighbor's kids out of my yard
    borrow tables
    taking out an ad in the newspaper
    friends always ask to sell their stuff
    I hate the cleanup afterward!
    making and posting signs

Some of these ideas are very useful. You can see that the writer wrote down every idea, even the problems with the neighbor's kids and dog. Not all of these ideas will be used in the paragraph, but all were part of the brainstorming process. Writing down everything helped keep the writer's thoughts and pencil flying.

EXERCISE 3: BRAINSTORMING

Directions: Choose *two* of the following topics. Make a brainstorm list of at least six items for each one. Don't worry about spelling, wording, or whether the ideas are relevant. Just write down all of your ideas. Spend at least five minutes on each topic.

Be sure to save your work! In fact, you will want to save all the work you do in this chapter as you will have many opportunities to work on it later.

1. fashion fads

2. my favorite television show

3. the worst job I ever had

Answers will vary.

Structure of a Paragraph

A paragraph is a group of sentences written about one topic or main idea. A paragraph has two very important components: a *topic sentence* and *supporting sentences*. The topic sentence states the main idea of the paragraph and often appears at the beginning. The supporting sentences back up and explain the main idea—giving evidence, examples, and reasons. A paragraph may also have a *concluding sentence*, which sums up or restates the main idea.

In the following example, notice that the first sentence is the topic sentence. It "sets the stage" for the paragraph. The supporting sentences explain the main idea, and the concluding sentence summarizes without repeating.

Karate lessons have really improved Jay's self-esteem. He is a small boy and not very athletically inclined, but after watching and loving the Karate Kid movies, he became interested in karate. He has taken lessons now for six months and feels very good about himself. As he advances in the classes, he gains confidence and seems to relate better to his friends. Jay is now more self-assured as he works toward his goal—a black belt!

Writing the Topic Sentence

The topic sentence is the most important sentence of a paragraph. It is often the first sentence of the paragraph, and it states the purpose of your piece of writing. Think of the topic sentence as an "umbrella" sentence. The supporting sentences should all belong under the main idea stated in the topic sentence.

Karate lessons have really improved Jay's self-esteem.

Topic sentence

Supporting sentences →
—saw K. Kid movies
—started lessons
—doing well in classes
—relates better to friends
—has a goal

Make sure your topic sentences state the subject of your paragraphs and the point you want to make. In the previous example, the subject of the paragraph is Jay's karate lessons. However, the writer also makes an important point in the topic sentence—that the lessons are improving Jay's self-esteem. When you are writing your own topic sentences, ask yourself these questions:

1. What is the topic?

2. What do I want to say about the topic?

EXERCISE 4: WRITING TOPIC SENTENCES
PART A

Directions: Write a topic sentence for a paragraph on each of the following topics. Make sure your topic sentence tells what point you would make about the topic. Remember, you need only write the topic sentence, not the whole paragraph.

1. birthday parties

2. the president of the United States

3. the kitchen in my new apartment

4. noise pollution

5. weather forecasting

Possible answers are on page 186.

PART B

Directions: Each of these paragraphs needs a good topic sentence. Read the supporting and concluding sentences; then write a topic sentence.

1. _____

The first record I ever bought was his "Fingertips," which he recorded when he was "Little Stevie Wonder." I've collected his singles and albums since the 1960s. His *Songs in the Key of Life* is my favorite and a classic. I watched the "We Are the World" video just to see Stevie. I saw the movie *Jungle Fever* just to hear his soundtrack. His music has brought me happiness for over thirty years.

2. _____

On sunny days, I have a lot of energy and feel good about myself. I'm usually easy to get along with when the sun shines. When it rains, I feel blue and do not want to work. I look forward to sledding with my children, so I'm happy when it snows. As you can see, if I never looked outside, I would be a more contented person.

3. _____

Buying tickets at the gate reminds me of the excitement I experienced at the yearly event. Sitting on the horse on the merry-go-round brings back many memories, and the music has not changed. The aromas of the fudge, popcorn, and cotton candy remind me of how I'd spend a month's allowance on food at the amusement park. Even now, when I get up my nerve and ride the roller coaster, I get sick. Some things never change!

Answers will vary.

Selecting and Organizing Ideas

Now that you have determined what stand you will take or what viewpoint you will present, worked on collecting ideas, and written your topic sentence, you need to select the ideas you will use. Can you use all of the ideas on your brainstorm list, or should you cross out some? You want to eliminate irrelevant ideas, ideas that do not support your topic sentence. For example, in the garage sale brainstorm on page 148, the item "I hate the cleanup afterward" is irrelevant because it does not support the topic sentence—"It takes a lot of organization to get ready for a garage sale." Go back and find at least two other items in the brainstorm list that do not support the topic sentence.

After you have eliminated irrelevant ideas, you have a list of ideas that you can use in a paragraph. But what order will you write them in? Every topic and every paragraph is different, so there's no one way to put ideas in order. You have to think carefully about what order of ideas will make your paragraph easy to understand. You can put things in time order, least-to-most-important order, or another order that works for your subject.

Here is the brainstorm list from page 148 with the irrelevant ideas eliminated. The remaining ideas are numbered in the order that the writer performs the tasks—time order.

2 sorting and pricing items

4 clean the garage

1 cleaning out the closets and the basement before

5 borrow tables

3 taking out an ad in the newspaper

6 making and posting signs

EXERCISE 5: SELECTING AND ORGANIZING IDEAS

Directions: Take out your brainstorm lists from Exercise 3, page 148. Eliminate irrelevant ideas from each list and number the ideas in logical order.

Be sure to save your work. You will need it in Exercise 6.

Answers will vary.

Writing a Rough Draft

You have worked through much of the process. You understand topic, purpose, and audience. You've brainstormed ideas. You've written topic sentences. You've chosen relevant ideas and put them in order. Now you're ready to create a paragraph—a first draft.

As you write, use your numbered brainstorm list as a guide. You don't have to follow it exactly, of course. But if you have done a good job of prewriting, you have already done most of the work—all that's left is turning the items on your list into supporting sentences and adding a concluding sentence.

Remember that you are writing a rough draft. Your paragraph does not have to be perfect on the first try. Just work on getting the ideas on paper. You can polish the writing and make corrections later. If you leave space between lines and wide margins, you'll be able to make changes more easily. As you write a draft, keep in mind the following features of a paragraph:

1. The first word is indented. Look at the first word of each paragraph in this book to see what *indented* means.

2. A paragraph has a topic sentence that tells a main idea.

3. A paragraph has several sentences that support the topic sentence.

EXERCISE 6: WRITING A ROUGH DRAFT

Directions: Choose *one* of your lists from Exercises 3 and 5. Write a rough draft of a paragraph. Be sure to save your work; you will need it in Exercise 8.

Answers will vary.

EXERCISE 7: PRACTICING THE WRITING PROCESS

Directions: Choose *two* of the following topics. For each,

- write a topic sentence that tells the main point you will make about the topic in a paragraph
- brainstorm ideas to support your topic sentence
- select and order the ideas you want to use in a paragraph
- write a rough draft of each paragraph

Be sure to save your work. You will be working on your paragraphs again in Exercise 8.

1. your favorite type of car

2. your least favorite musician or rock group

3. the quality of the schools in your area

4. a friend or relative whom you admire

Answers will vary.

Revising Your Rough Draft

Once you have drafted a paragraph, it's a good idea to take a break from it for a while—a couple of hours, if possible, so you can see it with a fresh eye when you revise. When you take it up again, think about what you wanted to say. Then read your paragraph as if you were the audience. Did you fully develop your main idea? Is your topic sentence clear and supported? Is there a closing sentence? Ask yourself these questions:

- What's good about my paragraph?
- What don't I like about my paragraph?
- What can I do to improve my paragraph?

This step in the writing process is called *revising*. The revision process is a "second chance." It is an opportunity to move words and sentences, add ideas, remove or rewrite irrelevant sentences, and clarify confusingly worded sentences. Rather than copying your paragraph over, use the spaces between the lines and the margins on each side to make changes. Don't worry about mechanical errors yet. You will have a chance to edit later.

To get an idea of what revising is all about, look at the following sample rough draft. It needs some work. What would you do to strengthen it?

Thanksgiving is a day to relax. The rest of our family usually sleeps late. Mom or Dad gets up at 6:00 A.M. to prepare the turkey, then the dutiful parent goes back to bed. Because our aunts, uncles, and cousins bring food, there are only last-minute preparations, so there is plenty of time to sit and talk or play cards. Little children run all over, making it difficult to have a quiet conversation. After a big meal at 1:00 and a long afternoon of visiting, we are all thankful for our time spent together.

Two changes that would strengthen the paragraph would be (1) reverse the second and third sentences and (2) eliminate or revise the sentence "Little children run all over, making it difficult to have a quiet conversation." This sentence does not support the topic sentence; it is an irrelevant idea.

EXERCISE 8: REVISING A ROUGH DRAFT

Directions: Choose *two* of the paragraphs you wrote in Exercises 6 and 7. Revise each one, making sure that your main idea is stated clearly and well supported.

Be sure to save your work. You will need it in Exercise 9.

Answers will vary.

Editing

Now that you have revised your paragraph, you will want to refine it by making corrections in usage, sentence structure, and mechanics. You have done a lot of editing in previous chapters, so you have some experience in looking for errors. In the example below, see how the writer has used markings to indicate corrections neatly and carefully.

About a week before the sale date, I call the ~~N~~ewspaper, and list the items
advertisement   *whole*
in an ~~advertizement~~. The ~~hole~~ family helps me clean the garage for the sale.

The day before the sale, I borrow tables and arrange all of the items.

EXERCISE 9: EDITING PRACTICE

Directions: Edit all the paragraphs you have written so far in this chapter, looking for errors in usage, sentence structure, and mechanics.

Answers will vary.

Four Types of Writing

Now that you have practiced the writing process, you are ready to put your skills to work for different purposes. The following pages present four types of writing and new skills to help you organize and develop each type.

Type of Writing	Purpose
Narrative	to narrate, or tell a story
Descriptive	to describe something
Informative	to inform or explain with facts
Persuasive	to persuade the reader to agree

Narrative Writing

The purpose of narrative writing is to tell a story, usually in time order. You have probably heard someone tell the punch line of a joke, then say, "Wait a minute! I left out a part!" If a joke or story is not told in the correct sequence, the listener or reader will not understand the story. Read the following paragraph and notice that the narrator, a police officer, relates in time order the events of a typical domestic call.

> One of the most difficult aspects of my job is answering the domestic dispute call. Many of these disputes involve violence, often a man beating a woman or children. When my partner and I arrive, we first check for weapons. Next we quickly decide which person is the aggressive one. We may then try to avoid arrest by counseling all members of the household. If necessary, my partner or I take one of the people outside to calm down. Because the victims are often too afraid to sign a complaint against the abusers, we may leave the home not knowing if the people living there are safe. For these reasons, the domestic call is one of the most frustrating for police officers.

Words that help you follow the sequence of ideas in a paragraph are *transitions*. The following words are helpful in narrative writing because they indicate time order.

after	before	then
during	finally	when
first	second	later
meanwhile	next	now

Scan the example paragraph about domestic dispute calls, underlining transition words that show time order.

You should have underlined *When, first, Next,* and *then*.

EXERCISE 10: PRACTICING NARRATIVE WRITING

Directions: Choose *one* of the following topics and write a narrative paragraph. Be sure your paragraph has a topic sentence and presents events in correct time order. Use transition words to help your reader follow the flow of your ideas.

1. Tell a story about an unusual experience in a supermarket. Write a true story or make one up.

2. Tell a story about an occasion you remember clearly from your childhood.

Answers will vary.

Descriptive Writing

Writing that draws a mental picture for the reader is descriptive writing. A writer may use all five senses, describing how something looks, smells, feels, tastes, and sounds. It's very important to include specific details in descriptive writing to ensure that the reader can "picture" what is described.

Here is a sample of descriptive writing. What is the problem with it?

> Rich and Heather have a new baby. She was born on November 10, and they named her Meghan. She is a pretty baby and is really large. They sent some pictures of her at a few days old. She sure is cute.

This paragraph is vague. We know that Meghan is pretty and large, but we have no idea what she actually looks like. Notice how the following improved paragraph gives us many more specific details.

> Meghan Brady Marmor appeared on November 10 as a nine-pound, round-faced, dark-eyed, gorgeous little girl. Her parents, Rich and Heather, proudly sent us pictures of their first daughter. Her wispy wheat-colored hair peeked out from a green hooded sleeper. Like most newborns, she has no neck, and her cheeks look as if they were formed from the soft material of a Cabbage Patch Doll. Because she is so big, she does not look like a fragile infant. Instead, she looks like a miniature toddler, very alert and ready to take on the world.

> **TIP:** When you write, avoid vague, overused words such as *very, nice, pretty, good, great, bad*, etc. Instead, use more specific words that tell the reader exactly what you mean. Try to avoid flowery and repetitive language.

EXERCISE 11: USING DESCRIPTIVE WRITING

Directions: Rewrite the following vague, dull sentences. Load them with interesting, specific details. Use your imagination!

Example: We bought a nice car.

> We finally bought a luxurious, full-sized family car, which is metallic gray with a dark blue interior and loaded with extras like cruise control, stereo and cassette player, and power locks and windows.

1. I got a great job.

2. That is a good dessert.

3. It's a funny movie.

4. Those are happy children.

5. He's a neat guy.

6. She gave a hard test.

Answers will vary.

EXERCISE 12: WRITING A DESCRIPTIVE PARAGRAPH

Directions: Choose *one* of the following situations and write a descriptive paragraph. Be sure to use specific details to draw a picture for the reader.

1. You're supposed to meet an old family friend at the airport. She has not seen you since you were five. Write a note describing yourself and what you'll be wearing so she will know you at the airport.

2. Joe, a co-worker, needs a ride home from work. You tell him to meet you at your car in the parking lot. Where is your car, and what does it look like?

Answers will vary.

Informative Writing

Informative writing presents facts. The writer's opinion is not included. A very common example of informative writing is the news story, which explains something to the reader. Other common examples of informative writing are recipes and instructions for assembling toys and furniture.

Many writers present information to (1) explain the causes of an effect or (2) explain the effects of a cause. Read the following paragraphs carefully to see how each is organized according to cause and effect. The first paragraph states an effect in the topic sentence (in bold type). The supporting sentences give causes.

There are several reasons why Nora decided to become a physical therapist. First, she was injured as a child and had to undergo months of therapy for an injured leg. While in high school, she volunteered in a children's hospital, and her major in college was premedicine. Consequently, her friend, a doctor, suggested that she take classes in physical therapy. Nora finally graduated and has a career as a therapist.

Identify the causes of Nora's becoming a physical therapist:

(1)   (2)   (3)   (4)

The following paragraph gives a *cause* in the topic sentence. The supporting sentences list the effects.

The Wilsons recently filed for divorce. As a result, the family home will be sold, and a property settlement must be decided. Mrs. Wilson, who has worked part-time for several years, may seek full-time employment. Since the separation, Mr. Wilson has moved into an apartment, while Mrs. Wilson and the children are living with her sister. The Wilsons' lives have certainly changed in the last two months.

Identify the effects of the Wilsons' divorce:

(1)   (2)   (3)   (4)   (5)

> **TIP:** Be careful not to confuse causes and effects in your writing. If you are asked to discuss the causes, check your writing to be sure you didn't also include effects.

Transition Words in a Cause-Effect Paragraph

In the two example cause-effect paragraphs, you may have noticed transition words that signaled both time order and cause-effect relationships. Review the list of time order transition words on page 154 and study the cause-effect transition words below. Then underline the transition words in the two paragraphs above.

as a result	because	consequently
for	for this reason	if . . . then
then	therefore	thus

EXERCISE 13: INFORMATIVE WRITING—CAUSE AND EFFECT

Directions: Choose *one* of the following topics and write a paragraph showing the causes or effects.

1. Write a paragraph explaining why you decided to prepare for the GED Test. (Your paragraph should discuss the *causes*.)

2. Write a paragraph explaining how studying for the GED Test has affected your life. (Your paragraph should discuss the *effects*.)

Answers will vary.

Persuasive Writing

Persuasive writing expresses an opinion. The writer's purpose is to "sell" a particular point of view or line of reasoning to the reader. A persuasive writer must be able to state an opinion, then focus on clear and logical reasons.

Stating an Opinion

Two writers were asked to write a paragraph in response to the following topic:

Should the town of Northpark approve a tax increase to pay for expanding the community college? State your opinion clearly and give solid reasons.

Which of the following opening paragraphs do you think is the more persuasive?

A tax increase to pay for expansion of the community college might be a good idea, but there are good reasons to vote against it, too. It's a very tough issue to decide.

A tax increase to pay for expansion of the community college now will help our town meet the demands of the future. Though it will be costly, an improved community college is an excellent idea.

The second one is much stronger because it states a clear point of view. The writer of the first paragraph would have a tough time convincing anyone to vote either for or against the tax increase! The writer of the second paragraph takes a firm position on the issue.

Giving Supporting Reasons

Once a writer has a good topic sentence for a persuasive paragraph, she needs some supporting reasons. *Why* would expansion of the community college benefit the community in the future? Look at the writer's brainstorm list on page 158. Cross out ideas that are *not* good reasons to support the writer's opinion.

Topic sentence: A tax increase to pay for expansion of the community college now will help our community meet the demands of the future.

Brainstorm list:

1. people won't have to go out of town for so many educational programs

2. most people won't vote for a tax increase

3. new industries coming into area will require new training programs

4. classes already overcrowded; enrollment rising

5. can always enroll in programs in nearby counties

You should have crossed out items 2 and 5. Item 5 is not relevant to the topic sentence, so including it in the paragraph would distract the reader from the writer's opinion. Item 2 argues against the writer's opinion instead of supporting it.

EXERCISE 14: WRITING PERSUASIVE PARAGRAPHS

Directions: Choose *one* of the following topics and write a persuasive paragraph. Be sure that your topic sentence states a clear position and that your supporting sentences are good reasons to back up your opinion.

1. When a man or woman runs for public office, his or her personal life often becomes front-page news. Sometimes a candidate's private life even affects his or her chances of winning an election. Does the public have a right to know about the private lives of political figures?

2. Although it has negative effects on the body, caffeine is found in many beverages consumed daily by both adults and children—soft drinks, tea, and coffee. Do you think people should be prevented from drinking beverages containing caffeine?

Answers will vary.

Comparison/Contrast Development

A useful technique for organizing ideas in many persuasive paragraphs is *comparison/contrast*. Look at how one writer handled the question "Which type of animal makes a better pet in the city, a dog or a cat?"

Topic sentence: A cat makes a better pet than a dog does for people who live in the city.

cats	dogs
use litter pan indoors	have to be walked outdoors
good company without being demanding	have to be played with frequently
don't need a lot of space	need large area to run

This chart, comparing the traits of cats and dogs, lists the writer's ideas in a useful form. The following paragraph is based on the ideas in the chart. You may notice the use of some transition words that signal comparison/contrast relationships between ideas. Underline these words as you read.

A cat makes a better pet than a dog does for people who live in the city. While a cat can use a convenient indoor litter pan, dogs have to be walked outdoors several times every day. Cats are good company, but they are not demanding. Dogs, on the other hand, need to be played with frequently, or they will be unhappy. Cats don't need a lot of space to run and play, but dogs need a large area to run in and take up a lot of space in a city apartment. A cat is the right choice for a city person who wants a pet's companionship.

You might have underlined *while, but,* and *on the other hand.*

> **TIP:** When you are comparing and contrasting two things, use a chart to list your ideas. Put related ideas about the two things across from each other, as the writer did in the above example.

EXERCISE 15: USING COMPARISON/CONTRAST TO PERSUADE

Directions: Choose *one* of the following topics and use comparison/contrast development to write a persuasive paragraph.

1. Choose two states or towns you are familiar with. Decide which of the two states or towns is a nicer place to live and write a paragraph persuading others that you have made the right choice.

2. Choose two television programs that come on the air at the same time and decide which you would rather watch. Write a paragraph convincing others to choose the same program you chose.

Answers will vary.

The Four Types of Writing

Notice that the methods of development you studied (time order, cause-effect, and comparison/contrast) can be helpful with all the types of writing. For example, time order can be very useful in informative writing when you are asked to give the steps in a process. Comparison/contrast can help you develop descriptive paragraphs if you have to describe more than one thing. And discussing the causes or effects of something may help you persuade readers to agree with you on an issue.

The following writing ideas and topics are listed under the headings of four types of writing: narrative, descriptive, informative, and persuasive. You may return to these suggested topics often in order to gain new ideas for journal writing, classroom assignments, and essay writing.

Narrative Writing
Tell a story about

(1) the best day of your life (or worst day)
(2) your first kiss
(3) your biggest mistake
(4) the first time you met _____ (spouse, close friend)
(5) your greatest accomplishment

Descriptive Writing
Use vivid description and specific language to describe

(1) a room in your home
(2) a beautiful view
(3) the fronts of two buildings
(4) a photograph, painting, or poster displayed in your home
(5) the physical appearance of a person you know well

Informative Writing
Explain carefully to your readers

(1) the importance of proper nutrition
(2) how to paint a room
(3) the steps in a simple recipe
(4) some tips for reducing utility costs in the home
(5) some simple fire safety rules

Persuasive Writing
State your opinion and give strong supporting reasons why your readers should agree with you about

(1) your annual raise
(2) an aspect of tobacco smoking or regulation of it
(3) prayer in the public schools
(4) drug testing
(5) nuclear arms reduction

Writing an Essay

You have been studying the writing process, the steps needed to develop a good paragraph. The same process is used for all types of writing. If you can write a good paragraph, you can apply that ability to longer pieces of writing.

There are many similarities between paragraphs and essays. The goals of writing a paragraph and an essay are the same:

- to discuss one main idea
- to provide plenty of support for the idea
- to stay on topic throughout the piece

The structure of an essay is also similar to that of a paragraph:

Paragraph	Essay
Topic sentence	Introductory paragraph
Supporting sentences	Body paragraphs
Concluding sentence	Concluding paragraph

As you read the following descriptions of the parts of an essay, think of a paragraph s-t-r-e-t-c-h-e-d.

- The *introductory paragraph* contains the *thesis statement*, which tells the reader the main idea, or purpose, of your essay. The introduction should also preview the major points you will be making to support your thesis statement.

- The main part of your essay is the *body*. As the supporting sentences of a paragraph support your topic sentence, the body paragraphs of an essay support your thesis statement. Each major supporting idea is developed in a paragraph. In your body paragraphs, you may want to use cause-effect, comparison/contrast, or sequence of events to organize your ideas.

- The *concluding paragraph* of an essay should contain a reworded version of the thesis statement to remind the reader of your main point. You can expand on your conclusion by asking yourself, "What do I want to suggest, recommend, or make sure my reader knows before I close my essay?"

Prewriting for an Essay

The way to get started on writing an essay is the same as getting started on a paragraph: write a statement that tells what point you are going to make in your writing; then brainstorm ideas to support your point. You can then use the ideas in your brainstorm list to write the body of your essay. Here's how one writer got started:

Thesis statement: Our elementary school needs more crossing guards.

Brainstorm list:

busy streets, more traffic
new mall on Oak St. four blocks away
Lincoln St./Davis Ave. is a dangerous intersection
Plum St./Morton St. dangerous too
some children leave school at noon for lunch
morning kindergartners leave at 11:30
afternoon kids come at 12:15
parents or senior citizens might be free at noon

Once you have written a thesis statement and brainstormed ideas to use in your body paragraphs, you can start organizing. Though there are many possibilities for organizing the ideas in any essay, outlining is one useful method.

TIP: When organizing ideas for an essay, make groups of ideas that you can turn into paragraphs when you draft the essay. Give each group a heading that you can turn into the topic sentence of the paragraph.

Read the following outline, based on the brainstorming list you just saw. The writer has grouped details and examples under main headings that tell how each paragraph will develop a single idea supporting the thesis statement.

Paragraph 1: Introduction
Thesis statement: Our elementary school needs more crossing guards.

Paragraph 2: two dangerous intersections a few blocks from school
    A. one at Lincoln St. and Davis Ave.
    B. another at Plum St. and Morton St.
    C. high-speed traffic through these intersections

Paragraph 3: many children leave and return to school at the noon hour
    A. the morning kindergartners leave at 11:30
    B. some students go home for lunch at 12:00 and return
    C. the afternoon kindergartners arrive at 12:15

Paragraph 4: increase in traffic this year due to the new shopping mall near the school
    A. new mall is on Oak St., four blocks from school
    B. busy streets, more traffic everywhere because of mall

Paragraph 5: Conclusion—For these reasons, I recommend that the principal request at least four more guards.
    A. parents or senior citizens might be free at noon
    B. school must make sure children are safe

Having finished the outline showing the organization of his essay ideas, the writer has completed a large part of the job. With the outline in hand, drafting the actual essay should be a straightforward task of turning the parts of the outline into sentences and paragraphs.

EXERCISE 16: PREWRITING FOR AN ESSAY

Directions: Choose *one* of the following topics and follow these steps in prewriting for an essay on that topic:

- Write a thesis statement that clearly states the main point of your essay.

- Brainstorm ideas to support your thesis statement. Keep in mind that you'll need plenty of ideas—enough to fill a whole essay of about five paragraphs.

- Read over your brainstorm list carefully. Cross out ideas that do not truly support your thesis statement.

- Organize your list into groups of related items that can be developed into well-unified paragraphs when the essay is written. Use an outline or any other method of organization you are comfortable with.

1. Think of a problem in your neighborhood or town, such as the need for organized neighborhood watches, a park or other recreational facility that needs improvement, etc. Prewrite an essay about the problem.

2. What has been the best period of your life, and why? Prewrite an essay describing the time of your life when you were happiest and explaining why you were happiest then. (You could choose to write about your life right now.)

    Be sure to save your work; you will need it in Exercise 17.

Answers will vary.

Drafting an Essay

With your paragraphs planned and outlined, you can draft your essay. All of the prewriting steps lead to the rough draft, which you don't have to get right the first time, since you will be revising and editing it. Leave wide margins and space between lines to make changes later.

> **TIP:** When writing a rough draft, keep your outline plan next to you. Use words and phrases from the plan as the basis for your sentences.

Begin to develop your own personal writing process as you practice writing these longer pieces. Many experienced writers complete the introduction and conclusion after they have written the body paragraphs. You are not breaking any rules of writing if you start with the body paragraphs, write a strong conclusion, then go back and add a general introduction to your thesis statement.

Next, you will read the rough draft of the essay on the crossing guard topic. The thesis statement is in bold type. As you read the rough draft, notice that the writer did not stick strictly to the outline; instead, he used it as a guide, changing wording in several places. You might notice places where the writer's thoughts are hard to follow. Underline these sections and try to think of changes that would improve them.

OUTLINE

Paragraph 1: Introduction
Thesis: Our elementary school needs more crossing guards.

Paragraph 2: two dangerous intersections
A. Lincoln and Davis
B. Plum and Morton
C. high-speed traffic

Paragraph 3: children leave and return at noon
A. morning kindergartners leave at 11:30
B. students go home for lunch and return
C. afternoon kindergartners arrive at 12:15

Paragraph 4: increase in traffic
A. new mall on Oak
B. more traffic

Paragraph 5: Conclusion—
For these reasons, I recommend that the principal request at least four more guards.
A. parents or senior citizens
B. school must ensure safety

Many parents of children attending Jefferson School are concerned about the safety of their children walking to and from school. Although older students act as crossing guards before and after school, they can't do the whole job. Unguarded intersections near the school, noon hour comings and goings, and the general increase in traffic from the new mall all make walking dangerous, especially for young children. **Our elementary school needs more crossing guards.**

We should hire guards to cover two very dangerous intersections located a few blocks from school. One is the intersection of Lincoln Street and Davis Avenue, where there is a "Yield" sign that drivers often miss. The other is at Plum Street and Morton Street, where there have been several accidents recently. An alert adult crossing guard is needed at each of the intersections whenever children are crossing.

Many children leave and return to school at the noon hour. When morning kindergartners are dismissed at 11:30, many five-year-olds walk home. There are no crossing guards on duty anywhere. At 12:00, many students go home for lunch and return around 12:45. The afternoon kindergartners arrive between noon and 12:15, so there are many children crossing unguarded intersections. Many parents drive their kids to school.

There has been an increase in traffic this year due to the new Oak Street Mall, four blocks from school. The traffic count is up in all areas of our neighborhood.

For these reasons, the principal should request that the school board hire at least four more crossing guards. Some parents are willing to volunteer temporarily, but we feel that the school district should provide the funds for ensuring the safety of the students over the long term.

Now that you have read the rough draft once, go back and study it again for a few moments. Notice how the introduction previews the arguments the author will raise in the body paragraphs: dangerous intersections, noon hour comings and goings, and increased traffic from the new mall. Then each of the body paragraphs takes up one of these arguments. Also notice that the conclusion contains a reworded version of the thesis statement.

EXERCISE 17: DRAFTING AN ESSAY

Directions: Write a rough draft of the essay you planned in Exercise 16. Use your plan as a guide, but make any improvements you can in organization as you write. You may also think of new ideas to add.

Be sure to save your draft. You will need it in Exercise 18.

Answers will vary.

Revising the Essay

Before you revise, take a break from the writing process. Leave the essay alone for a day or two—or at least several hours. You want to be able to look at your own writing as objectively as you can, so you will benefit by getting away from the essay for a while.

When you revise, read first as a reader. Read as if you are seeing the essay for the first time. What does it say to you? Then read as the writer. What can be rewritten or rearranged so that the ideas are clear and the purpose is supported? You can change the order of sentences or paragraphs, add or delete material, rewrite sentences, insert transition words, etc. At this stage, don't worry about looking for errors in usage, sentence structure, or mechanics. You'll come to that step last.

Checklist for Revising an Essay

1. Does the introduction preview my body paragraphs?

2. Does my thesis statement give my essay a clear purpose?

3. Are my ideas arranged logically in body paragraphs that support my thesis statement?

4. Will my reader be able to understand how my ideas fit together and support your thesis statement?

5. Are there any irrelevant ideas?

6. What's good about my essay?

7. What don't I like about my essay?

8. What can I do to improve my essay?

Now look at two ways the writer of the essay on crossing guards improved his writing in the revision stage. First look at the last sentence of the third paragraph of the essay.

> Many children leave and return to school at the noon hour. When morning kindergartners are dismissed at 11:30, many five-year-olds walk home. There are no crossing guards on duty anywhere. At 12:00, many students go home for lunch and return around 12:45. The afternoon kindergartners arrive between noon and 12:15, so there are many children crossing unguarded intersections. **Many parents drive their kids to school.**

The last sentence seems irrelevant because there is no transition between it and the rest of the paragraph. Here is a possible revision for the last sentence:

> Many parents drive their kids to school at noon, creating even more dangerous traffic in the area for the children who are walking.

Notice how the revised sentence makes the flow of the writer's thoughts clearer. The original wording did not show the relationship between the ideas.

Another problem spot in the essay is the fourth paragraph. The two sentences in the paragraph are not clearly related. In addition, the paragraph as a whole lacks strong supporting ideas. Here is the original version of the fourth paragraph, followed by a revised version:

> ~~There has been an increase in traffic this year due to the new Oak Street~~ Mall, four blocks from school. The traffic count is up in all areas of our neighborhood.

> This year the new Oak Street Mall, located four blocks from Jefferson School, opened for business. It has caused an increase in traffic throughout our neighborhood, but especially around the school. Much of the traffic going to and from the mall comes from the main highway, then down Oak Street. Since many of our students cross Oak Street, additional crossing guards are needed to cover more intersections along this busy street.

EXERCISE 18: REVISING AN ESSAY

Directions: Revise the essay you drafted in Exercise 17, page 164. Use the revising checklist on page 164 to guide you in looking for ways to improve your writing.

Be sure to save your work; you will be using it again in Exercise 19.

Answers will vary.

Editing Your Essay

Editing means checking for surface errors in your writing—misspelled words, comma splices, incorrectly capitalized words, etc. If the appearance of your paper distracts from your purpose, your reader will not be able to appreciate fully what you have written. Even minor errors can cause confusion for the reader and make your ideas hard to understand.

Learn to edit neatly. Cross out errors and print corrections above them or draw arrows into the margin and write the correction there. Use a caret (∧) to show where something should be inserted. Use a paragraph symbol (⁊) if you forgot to indent a paragraph or want to break one paragraph into two.

Last *S*pring I registered for some *c*college ~~coarses~~ *courses.* Then I was switched to the night shift at work,*so* I couldn't go.

Notice how the small marks help keep the paper neat.

> **TIP:** Many writers read their papers backward, word by word, to look for spelling errors. It's also helpful to read backward sentence by sentence while checking for fragments.

EXERCISE 19: EDITING YOUR ESSAY

Directions: Edit the essay you have been working on, checking for surface errors. The following questions should help remind you what to look for.

1. Are all the sentences complete thoughts?

2. Are your verbs correct? Are they consistent throughout your paragraphs?

3. Do pronouns refer correctly and clearly to their antecedents?

4. Have you combined ideas correctly, using the different types of conjunctions such as *and, therefore,* and *because*?

5. Have you used punctuation, especially commas and apostrophes, correctly?

6. Have you used capital letters correctly?

7. Are all the words spelled correctly? Use a dictionary to look up any you are unsure of.

Answers will vary.

Writing the GED Test Essay

Preparing for the GED essay is similar to training for a test of any skill. You must practice ahead of time so that when you are finally sitting at the testing site with your pen, scratch paper, writing booklet, and the topic in front of you, you will know what to do. The rest of this chapter provides you with plenty of explanations and practice exercises—your training program. As you practice, remember what you have already learned in this chapter about writing paragraphs and essays and apply that knowledge to the testing situation. Keep the writing process in mind: *prewriting, drafting, revising, editing,* and *publishing.*

Common Questions About the GED Essay

1. How much time will I have? How long should the essay be? Tell me the specifics!

The directions for Part 2 of the Writing Skills Test will present the essay topic and tell you to spend up to forty-five minutes writing an essay of about 200 words. The figure of 200 words is given *only as a guideline*; you will not be penalized if you write more words or fewer words—as long as you express your ideas well. The directions will also remind you to plan, revise, and edit your essay. You will need to use a ballpoint pen to write your answer in the test booklet. You'll be given scratch paper, but your notes will not be scored.

2. Why is there an essay on the GED Test?

Many educators and employers feel that writing is an important skill needed by every adult. In fact, some states require that seniors pass a writing test before they can receive a high school diploma. For the GED tests to truly represent a high school education, GED examinees also need to show that they can write. While the multiple-choice part of the test shows whether you can edit what another person has written, only by actually writing an essay can you show that you have learned to write.

3. What is the essay topic like?

You will be asked to present an opinion or explanation of an issue with which all adults are familiar. You will be expected to support your explanation with appropriate and specific reasons, details, and examples. The topic will be broad enough that many approaches to the essay will be possible, and no particular answer will be required or expected. In other words, there is no "right answer" on the GED Essay Test. You will see several examples of GED-type essay topics in this section.

4. How will the essays be scored?

Readers trained in standards developed by the GED Testing Service will read and score your essay on a scale of 1–6. The readers evaluate the essay for its overall effectiveness; in fact, your paper can contain some errors and still receive a high score. To score well, you should be able to plan an essay that effectively supports a central idea. You should also be able to use correct grammar and spelling most of the time.

5. What are the standards for the scores?

Here are descriptions of papers at each level of the scoring guide.

6 Papers show a clear organizational plan. Writers are able to support well-reasoned views with thorough, specific, and relevant detail. The papers are interestingly written and contain few errors.

5 Papers are well organized, and ideas are supported convincingly, but they are not as smoothly written as 6 papers. These essays are generally correct but contain some errors.

4 Papers show that writers organized their ideas and provided some support for their views. They contain more errors, but the errors do not prevent readers from understanding the essays.

3 Papers are somewhat organized or developed, but in a limited and unconvincing way. Use of standard English is weak, and essays fail to accomplish their writers' purposes.

2 Papers lack a clear purpose. They are disorganized, and little or no support is given for the writers' ideas. Errors in standard English are frequent and may prevent readers' understanding these essays.

1 Papers show no purpose or organization. Writers are unable to express themselves in correct English.

NOTE: Papers that are blank, illegible, or written on a topic other than the one assigned cannot be scored, and a Writing Skills Test composite score cannot be reported.

6. **What should I study in order to prepare for the essay?**

The best preparation is to write, write, and write. Spend your study time learning the writing process and how to put it to work in a test situation. Practice writing timed essays and plan how you will use your time when you take the test.

Making the Most of Your Time

One of the steps you should take in preparing for the GED essay is learning to adapt the writing process to the testing situation. You have practiced all the steps in the writing process before, but you need to have a strategy for using your time well when you take the test. Study the following description of how you might approach the essay. Think about how you could adapt this strategy to suit *your* writing style.

Prewrite (5-10 minutes): Study the topic, think about the choices you have and the different directions you might take, then jot down a thesis statement for your essay. Quickly brainstorm ideas to support your thesis statement. Organize your brainstorm list by numbering ideas, drawing arrows between ideas that belong together, or using any other workable method. You may even want to jot down a rough outline. Be sure you have a clear idea of how your ideas will be organized *before* you begin drafting your essay.

Draft (25-30 minutes): Neatly write a rough copy in ink, keeping in mind that you won't have time to recopy the essay. Leave wide margins so that you can go back and add ideas and make corrections. As you write, be sure to keep the overall organizational plan of your essay in mind.

Revise and edit (5-10 minutes): Read over your essay. Look for changes you can make that will make your ideas clearer to the reader, such as adding paragraph breaks or transition words. Make sure you have included a clear thesis statement in your introduction and that your supporting paragraphs are relevant and well organized. Then correct spelling, punctuation, and other mechanical errors.

Understanding the Topic

According to the GED Testing Service, "Examinees will be provided with a single topic which asks them to present an opinion or an explanation regarding a situation about which adults would be expected to have some general knowledge."

The topic will briefly identify an issue or situation. You will need to give an explanation of it, then back up your explanation with specific details, reasons, and examples.

Study this sample topic, which is similar to the type of topic you may see on the Writing Skills Test. Underline important words that tell you what to write about.

> Many of today's divorced parents are choosing joint custody of their children. The parents feel that the children benefit from being with each parent.
>
> What are the effects of joint custody on children of divorced parents? You may describe the positive effects, the negative effects, or both. Be sure to support your views with specific reasons and examples.

Many words in the topic are important. The term *joint custody* tells you what the subject of your essay must be. The word *effects* (both *positive effects* and *negative effects*) tells you more about your subject. Finally, you are told to use *specific reasons and examples*.

Notice that you are given three choices about the types of effects to describe in your essay:

1. describe the positive effects

2. describe the negative effects

3. describe both the positive and negative effects

Now that you have all this information from the topic, you can start thinking about how to approach the essay. Jot down a thesis statement you could use to tell your readers the main point of an essay on this topic. Make sure you have a couple of ideas in mind that could support your thesis statement.

Here is how one writer decided to write her essay:

Thesis statement: Joint custody has several positive effects on children, although no one usually thinks of them.

Supporting ideas: child gets to see each parent separately for a solid block of time; parents are happier and will share happiness with child; child gets to see and learn about two different lifestyles.

Notice that this writer chose to discuss *only positive effects*. You might have a different plan, and as a writer, you have this choice. However, with this topic, remember that you *must* discuss effects—not causes or anything else.

Take a look at another GED-type essay topic. Underline the key words that tell you what the topic is and what you are being asked to write.

> Some people feel very lucky to be born the sex that they are. Others feel that being a woman or being a man has too many drawbacks, and they may wish that they were born the opposite sex.
>
> Write a composition of about 200 words explaining the advantages or disadvantages or both of being the sex that you are. Support your ideas with specific examples.

With this topic, you are not being asked to discuss causes or effects. Instead, you are being asked to discuss *advantages* or *disadvantages* or *both*. These are key words that you should underline. Take a minute to think about how you might answer this topic. Then write a thesis statement that will tell your reader the main point of your essay.

Here is how one writer chose to write his essay:

Thesis statement: On the whole, the advantages of being a man outweigh the disadvantages.

Supporting ideas: physically able to do some things that women can't do; don't have to worry about sex discrimination as women do; I think being a father is easier than being a mother; I get a lot of satisfaction from being the main provider for my family

Remember that this is only *one* of *many* ways to respond to this topic. You may choose to write about disadvantages. You may also choose to talk about *both* the advantages and disadvantages. The important thing is that you support your ideas clearly. You'll learn more about supporting ideas later in the chapter.

In the following exercise, you'll see two other possible GED-type topics. These topics will suggest different types of ideas and different choices. Practice studying essay topics carefully so you can be flexible when you take the Writing Skills Test.

EXERCISE 20: UNDERSTANDING THE TOPIC

Directions: Study the following sample topics. First underline key words and phrases in each one. Then answer the questions following. By doing this, you will begin to understand what GED essay topics actually require of the writer.

TOPIC A

Some people think youth is the best part of life; others prefer the stability and privileges that come with age.

Write a composition of about 200 words discussing the advantages, disadvantages, or both of being your age. Be sure to support your views with specific reasons and examples.

1. What must be the *subject* of this essay topic?

2. What three choices does the topic give you?

3. Write a thesis statement that you could use in an essay on this topic. Then jot down at least two specific reasons or examples that would support your thesis statement.

TOPIC B

In spite of research proving the bad effects of tobacco, many people continue to puff or chew regularly on various forms of it, especially cigarettes.

In a composition of about 200 words, explain why people use tobacco. Be sure to support your views with specific reasons and examples.

4. What must be the subject of this essay topic?

5. This essay topic is asking you to explain a cause-effect relationship. Are you being asked to provide causes or effects in your essay?

6. Write a thesis statement that you could use in an essay on this topic. Then jot down at least two specific ideas that would support your thesis statement. (Make sure your thesis statement and your ideas reflect the correct cause-effect relationship.)

Answers are on page 186.

Ideas for Your Essay

Imagine that you open your essay booklet and find the following topic:

As citizens living in a democracy, we have the right to vote, yet voting records indicate that many of us do not go to the polls.

In a composition of about 200 words, explain why many citizens do not vote. Be sure to support your views with specific reasons and examples.

Perhaps you have never considered this topic before. You may never have even thought about why people don't vote. You may think, "I don't know why people don't vote. I have no ideas about this topic!"

Although you may not have thought about a topic before, the chances are good that you can come up with plenty of good ideas if you think in a productive way. The more practice you get writing with GED-type topics, the more comfortable you will be when you receive the actual test topic. You will have a *plan* for how you will think of ideas to include.

One effective way to generate ideas is to use *idea circles*. Here is how they work:

For the topic on page 171, you must identify reasons why people do not vote.

- Start at the inside circle. Do you vote? If you never vote, or you vote only part of the time, what stops you? Jot down these reasons.

- If you need more ideas, move to the next circle. Think of your family or other people you live with. If they didn't vote in the last election, why do you suppose they made that choice? Jot down whatever reasons you come up with.

- Moving to the next circle, what about your co-workers or friends—probably some of them do not vote. Why not? You may not know for sure what all their reasons are, but you probably have a pretty good idea of some of them. Jot these ideas down.

- Finally, if you feel you still need more ideas, you may want to think about what you have heard about society as a whole. Have you ever heard a newscaster say something like "Voter turnout is expected to be low today because freezing rain is in the forecast"? Or perhaps you read something in a newspaper or magazine that mentioned voting. What other reasons can you think of that explain why a lot of people don't vote? Sometimes just common sense can help you.

You can use this method of questioning yourself to generate ideas for almost any essay topic. Just imagine different groups of people, starting with yourself, and think about how the topic relates to each group. You don't even have to use all the circles—just go far enough so that you are comfortable with the ideas you have.

Of course, you may not need this technique to generate ideas. You may have a method of your own, such as simple brainstorming, that works just fine. However, if your mind just "goes blank" at the sight of a new writing topic, picturing these idea circles might help you get started on the GED Essay Test.

Here's an example showing how one writer used three of the circles to brainstorm ideas for the voting essay:

me—if I don't like any of the candidates, I don't bother to vote

my parents—never bother to vote

  don't seem interested in politics

  maybe feel that their votes won't make any difference

people in general—affected by weather, work schedules, child care

  may not be able to make time on that certain day

This writer has quite a lot of material that he can organize into an essay. He may not even want to use all of the ideas in the brainstorm list, depending on what he decides his main point should be.

Now take a look at how another writer took the *same topic* and came up with completely different ideas.

me—Last year I didn't vote because I moved and forgot to register

hard to know who to vote for—all politicians so much alike

my two best friends—too lazy

society as a whole—some never get around to registering, then can't vote even if they want to

may not realize how much politicians' work affects their lives

This writer has thought of a lot of reasons why people don't vote, and in her essay she may decide to use all or some of them. Notice that her ideas are quite different from those of the other writer, but both lists will make fine essays.

EXERCISE 21: USING THE IDEA CIRCLES

Directions: Use the idea circles to generate ideas on the following topics. Spend about five minutes brainstorming on each topic.

1. In the last twenty years, the roles of women have changed greatly. The changes in the roles of women affect all members of a family.

How have these changes in women's roles affected families? You may describe the positive effects, the negative effects, or both. Be sure to support your views with specific reasons and examples.

2. People who live in small towns or in the country often think that city living is glamorous and exciting, but city dwellers are just as likely to envy their suburban or country friends.

In a composition of about 200 words, discuss the advantages, disadvantages, or both of living in a big city *or* living in the country. Be sure to support your views with specific reasons and examples.

Answers will vary.

Using Examples

The instructions for the GED essay tell you to use *specific examples* to make your point. What does this mean, and where do you find examples? To see how useful examples can be, read the following paragraph.

Many people don't vote because of the weather. They also might not vote because it is hard to find time.

Now read this paragraph that includes some good examples:

Many people don't vote because of the weather. For example, if it is snowing and icy outside, a person may not go out to vote for fear he will get into a car accident. Another person just might not feel like going out on a rainy day. Other people don't vote because it's hard to find time. Between work and getting kids to and from school and dealing with traffic jams, many people just cannot fit another event into their busy schedules.

Can you see that the first paragraph made two very general statements? Although he gives two good reasons why people don't vote, the writer could use some examples that *show* the reader what he means. The second paragraph does just that. Instead of just giving the reason "weather," the writer gives an example of *how* weather can affect people's voting habits. Furthermore, this writer gives an example of *how* it can be hard to find time to vote. As a reader, you can really understand the writer's reasoning because he has given such clear examples.

When you are faced with a GED essay topic, remember to give examples that *show* the reader what you are talking about. Watch out for general statements in your writing and add an idea or two that can support those statements. If you have trouble thinking of examples, you might try using the "idea circles" again. This technique is useful whenever you find yourself stuck for an idea.

EXERCISE 22: USING SPECIFIC EXAMPLES

Directions: Add one or two specific examples to each of the following general statements made in a GED essay. Use the idea circles if you have trouble thinking of ideas. The first one is done as an example.

1. People don't vote because they are lazy.

For example, if I have to get up an hour early just to get to the polling place, I probably will sleep in instead.

In addition, smart voting requires a citizen to read a newspaper or pay attention to campaigns, and most people don't have the energy for this extra work.

2. Some people don't vote because they can't find an appealing candidate.

3. America does not have a good voter turnout because people don't believe that voting can improve their situation.

4. Many people fail to vote because elections are held too often.

Answers will vary.

Drafting Your Essay

Once you have a plan for what you will include in your essay, you'll need to communicate these ideas in essay form. Remember what you have already learned about writing a rough draft. In addition, use these hints:

Suggestions for Drafting a GED Test Essay

☑ 1. Write an introductory paragraph that contains your thesis statement and tells your reader what main points you will be making in your body paragraphs.

☑ 2. As you write, illustrate general statements with specific examples. You can draw from your personal experience, things you have read or seen on television, experiences of your friends and family members, etc. Use the idea circles if they have helped you in the past.

☑ 3. Leave wide margins around your writing so you'll have space to make corrections and add words after you have drafted your essay.

☑ 4. Write steadily. You will use your time better if you fully develop your major points than if you agonize over grammar and sentence structure. The readers who score your paper do not expect perfect papers.

☑ 5. Write a conclusion that contains a reworded version of your thesis statement and reminds your readers of your main points.

EXERCISE 23: DRAFTING A TEST ESSAY

Directions: Go back to your brainstorm lists from Exercise 21, page 173. Select the one you would like to continue to work with. Allow yourself 25 minutes of uninterrupted time and draft the essay. You may want to refer to the suggestions above as you write.

Be sure to save your work, since you'll need it in Exercise 24.

Answers will vary.

Revising and Editing a Test Essay

When you have finished drafting your test essay, check the time. You may not be able to make many changes. However, if you have a strategy planned, you can improve your paper in a short amount of time. By knowing your own writing strengths and weaknesses, you can prepare yourself to use those last few minutes well. A revising and editing checklist follows. Which tend to be *your* problem areas? Perhaps the most important revising and editing issues for you are not even on the checklist. Take a few minutes now to jot down some things you might want to be looking for in those final minutes. You won't be able to remember a lot of items, so choose ones that most apply to you.

Revising and Editing Checklist
Organization and Content

1. Does your introductory paragraph contain a thesis statement that tells the reader the main point of your essay?
2. Will the reader be able to see how each body paragraph develops an idea that supports the main point?
3. Did you illustrate general statements with specific reasons and examples?
4. Did you include a reworded version of your thesis statement in your concluding paragraph?

Proofreading

1. Check to make sure all your sentences are complete thoughts.
2. Make sure that commas are used correctly and not overused.
3. Check to be sure that connecting words like *and, but, because, then,* and *however* are used logically.
4. Check spelling by reading the essay backward.
5. Look for sound-alike words such as *their/there* and *its/it's* and make sure the spelling you chose is correct.
6. Check your verbs carefully, making sure you used tenses logically and formed them correctly. Check subject-verb agreement.

Improving the Essay

Now that you have an idea of what you will be looking for when you revise your test essay, look at an example of what one writer did in this situation. Here is another sample paragraph from the essay on the voting topic. The writer made some changes to improve the organization and content of the essay and also corrected some mechanical errors. Note the neat, clear markings he used to show the changes. Look carefully at each change to see how it improves the paragraph.

> Even someone who is interested in politics may not care much about
> voting ~~B~~ecause it's so hard to tell which candidates to vote for. Occasionally
> one candidate may stand out as really interested in improving the ~~comunity,~~ community
> or taking care of issues ~~that are important~~ *important* *like the arms race*. However, they usually seem pretty
> much the same, no matter what political party is backing them. They spend
> their time raising money *for fancy TV ads* and insulting their opponents. If voters knew what
> candidates ~~realy~~ *really* wanted to accomplish in office, they would be more likely to
> vote.

Now that you have given some thought to revising and editing in the testing situation, it's your turn to try it. Before you start the following exercise, be sure you have made a list of about five items that you want to be sure to check for in your GED Test essay. The items should be problem areas that you are likely to encounter in *your* writing. And keep in mind that your GED essay does not have to be a perfect paper. Your essay should simply be the best writing you can produce in forty-five minutes.

EXERCISE 24: REVISING AND EDITING A TEST ESSAY

Directions: Revise and edit the essay you drafted in Exercise 23, page 175. Spend about five minutes, no more than ten. Use your checklist to prioritize your time. Keep in mind that you don't have to produce a perfect paper. If you're not sure of the spelling of a word or perfect punctuation, that's OK.

Answers will vary.

Sample Topics for Practice

Here are some more essay topics that are similar to the ones that may be used as Part 2 of the Writing Skills Test. When you write essays based on these topics, use the skills you have been learning and manage your time carefully. Use the idea circles if they have been useful to you in the past. Remember that you should spend about forty-five minutes on your essay.

1. Equal rights and opportunities for women mean equal responsibilities. Some people feel that women should be drafted to serve in the military just as men are. Others feel that women should be exempt from required military service.

   Should women be drafted into the military? State your opinion and be sure to support it with specific reasons, details, and examples.

2. Leadership is a quality most of us admire. A president, governor, or mayor must be able to lead and inspire to be effective.

   Identify one or more personality traits that you feel leaders should have and explain the importance of the trait(s). Be sure to support your views with specific reasons and examples.

3. Personal qualities such as generosity, good humor, and selfishness are among the things that make us like or dislike a person.

   Identify a quality that you either admire or dislike in a person and explain why it affects you. Be specific and use examples to support your views.

4. Many people find that holidays are difficult times as well as joyous ones. Sad and lonely experiences may be as common for some people as parties and family gatherings are for others.

   Why do people often feel unhappy emotions during holidays? In answering this question, state your views clearly, and be sure to use specific examples and reasons.

5. In our society, the eight-hour work day and two-day weekend are considered very important. Even those of us who work the hours of three to eleven instead of nine to five, or who take off Monday and Wednesday instead of Saturday and Sunday, usually work about forty hours in a week. In contrast, workers 100 years ago often put in fourteen-hour days six days a week.

   What advantages does the forty-hour work week give us? Be specific, and use examples to support your views.

6. Frustration and anger are emotions that all people feel at one time or another. However, some people are able to recognize and control their feelings, while others resort to unkind actions and even violence when they are angry.

   Why are some people able to control themselves and their actions better than other people? Be specific with your ideas, and use good, clear examples to support them.

7. It has been said that reading can open up a whole new world for a person. Do you agree with this idea? State your opinion, and support it clearly with details and examples.

8. To the surprise of many, daytime and nighttime soap operas have always attracted large and faithful audiences. Soap opera fans say that these shows ease loneliness and help them cope with problems in their own lives. Critics of soap operas, however, see little value in such shows.

   Do you think soap operas can be valuable to people? State your opinion and support it with specific reasons, examples, and details.

TEST 1: WRITING SKILLS ANSWER KEY

CHAPTER 1: BASIC ENGLISH USAGE

Exercise 1: Subjects and Predicates
pages 58–59

1. (g) The first Academy Awards went to films made in 1927 and 1928.
2. (h) Julie Andrews won an award for her performance in *Mary Poppins* in 1964.
3. (c) Katharine Hepburn and Spencer Tracy acted together for the last time in 1967's *Guess Who's Coming to Dinner?*
4. (a) Dustin Hoffman and Tom Cruise costarred in *Rain Man*, "Best Film" of 1988.
5. (b) *Gone with the Wind, Stagecoach,* and *The Wizard of Oz* were nominated for "Best Film" in 1939.
6. (d) Awards for "Best Film," "Best Actor," "Best Actress," and "Best Director" were given to *Silence of the Lambs* in 1991.
7. (f) *Terminator 2* won the award for Special Effects in 1991.
8. (e) Clint Eastwood finally won an Academy Award for directing *Unforgiven* in 1992.

Exercise 2: Nouns and Subjects
pages 60–61
The nouns in each of the sentences are listed below, and the subject is in bold type. If you are confused about the subject in the following sentences, remember to ask yourself, "Who or what is doing something or being described in this sentence?"

1. **Bud**, bus, cab, concert
2. health, **Sheila**, Arizona
3. **Mary**, position, bank
4. **men**, drink, way, home
5. **children**, laundry, house
6. **pickle**

Exercise 3: Plural Nouns
page 63

1. countries	4	6. factories	4
2. homes	1	7. races	1
3. businesses	2	8. lives	5
4. alloys	3	9. women	7
5. cars	1	10. dishes	2

Exercise 4: Possessive Nouns
page 64
Corrections are in bold type.
1. My **cat's** favorite food never stays long in her dish.
2. Over the past two years, the **Wagners'** house has become worn around the doors and windows.
3. **Children's** pants and **toddlers'** playsuits are marked down at **Emily's** favorite shop.
4. The **president's** plan to restrict imports was abandoned due to several **allies'** protests.
5. For days after the **volcano's** eruption, ashes and dust in the atmosphere partially blocked the **sun's** rays.

Exercise 5: The Simple Tenses
pages 66–67

Verb	Time Clue
1. will walk	Next week
2. appears	Right now
3. planted	In March of 1975
4. will play	Tomorrow night
5. love	(statement is always true)

Exercise 6: The Continuing Tenses
page 68

Verb	Time Clue
1. is licking	At the moment
2. is barking	Now
3. will be cooking	By next month
4. will be picking	for the next two weeks
5. was sleeping	On yesterday's show

Exercise 7: The Perfect Tenses
page 69

Verb	Time Clue
1. will have walked	by bedtime
2. has curled	every day since her seventh birthday
3. had ordered	By 9:00 last night
4. has attended	so far
5. had worked	Before going into the army
6. will have mailed	By next October
7. has missed	In the last twenty-five years
8. had traveled	Before coming to Chicago last summer

Exercise 8: Regular Verb Review
page 71

Verb	Time Clue
1. was waiting	At the time of my arrival last week
2. will enter	Someday
3. sketches	every day
4. had plunged	By 8:00 this morning
5. have waited	this moment
6. will have lied	By the end of his term two years from now
7. shipped	Yesterday afternoon
8. will study or will be studying	For the next few months
9. feels or is feeling	Currently
10. seems	Today
11. has lived	Since the day she was born
12. decided	Last night

Exercise 9: Verbs
pages 74–76

1. (3) The first sentence in this paragraph is correct, and it is in the present tense. So, the passage as a whole must be in the present tense. Sentences 1–5 should be in the simple present, and Sentence 6 should be in the present continuing.
2. (2)
3. (1)
4. (5)
5. (2)
6. (3)

Exercise 10: Subject-Verb Agreement
page 78

Subject	Verb
1. racers	run
2. Letitia	visits
3. Time and money	were
4. secretary	Wasn't
5. mother	Has
6. A sandwich and a glass of juice	are
7. remains	lie

Exercise 11: More Subject-Verb Agreement
page 79

Subject	Verb
1. Mrs. Bundt	attends
2. Each	receives
3. Some	were
4. breakfast	keeps
5. anyone	wants
6. Most	are
7. tax	is
8. None	is

Exercise 12: Pronoun Form
page 81

1. **She** is going to the circus with **them**.
2. Give the pearls to **us**.
3. John and **his** friends left the meeting.
4. **We** read **her** paper with great delight.
5. Nancy was planning to bring her husband, so I brought **mine**.

Exercise 13: Possessive Pronouns and Contractions
page 82

1. **You're** not ready to move out of the house at age twelve.
2. **There's** no one here by that name, Officer.
3. I have given up hope that **your** father will ever stop telling bad jokes.
4. **Whose** coat is lying in the back corner of the bar?
5. **It's** not likely that Reginald will ever darken **its** door again.
6. **They're** going on a vacation to Alaska.

Exercise 14: Identifying Antecedents
page 83

Pronoun	Antecedent
3. they	Murray and Dee
4. who	eager friends
5. them	Murray, Dee, and Marissa
6. her	Marissa
7. it	crib
8. He	nursery worker
9. they	Murray and Dee
10. he	nursery worker
11. them	Murray and Dee

Exercise 15: Relative Pronouns
page 84

1. woman who
2. door that
3. Time, which
4. Dorothy, who
5. people that

Exercise 16: Agreement in Number
page 86
Part A

Antecedent	Pronoun
1. Japan	its
2. Muriel	her
3. twins	their
4. dog	its
5. company	its

Part B

Corrections are in bold type.

Over the last twenty years, Knoxville's population center, once clustered around **its** small downtown area, has shifted westward. However, **its** downtown area may become more important again in future years. Many of the city's older buildings are being restored, and its newer downtown buildings are lovely too.

Exercise 17: Clarifying Antecedents pages 87–88

The following sentences are *possible* revisions. The words in bold type replace the confusing pronoun or pronouns. Remember that your sentences can be different and still be correct. When checking your work, be sure that you have replaced all vague pronouns.

1. **X** I wrote to Ken and his sisters, but **Ken and his sisters** did not respond.
2. **X** **Experts on home remedies** say that drinking peppermint tea is good for an upset stomach.
3. **X** Herd the sheep away from the cattle and feed **the sheep.**
4. **X** Dion asked Tony if **Tony** thought **Dion** would win the contest.
5. **X** When the quarterback made the touchdown in the final seconds of the game, **the crowd** went wild in the stands.
6. **C**
7. **X** Darleen never wants to go out anymore, and she is not eating or sleeping well. This **behavior** worries her husband.
8. **X** Mr. Olivetti followed Dominick into **Dominick's** storeroom.
9. **C**

Exercise 18: Agreement in Person page 89

Corrections are in bold type.

Most of us think that having running water and electricity is normal. As a result, **we** might be surprised at the simple mud huts many Africans live in. Even when **we** are out of work here, we can get help from government agencies, including welfare or unemployment income. We may not all have lives of luxury, but **we** easily forget that people in many other countries feel lucky to earn only pennies per day.

Exercise 19: Sentence Structure pages 89–92

1. **(2)** The verb *is* must agree with the singular subject *One.*
2. **(4)** The object pronoun *them* must agree with its antecedent *paintings.*
3. **(3)** Pronouns in a passage should not shift from one person to another. *You* does not fit here because the writer is not talking directly to the reader.
4. **(4)** The verb *live* must agree with the plural subject *masterpieces.*
5. **(3)** If you substitute *who is* for *who's,* the sentence doesn't make sense. The possessive pronoun *whose* is correct.
6. **(5)** This verb should be in the past tense since the entire passage describes past events.
7. **(4)** *Began* is the correct simple past tense form of the irregular verb *begin. Begun* is the past participle.
8. **(3)** The relative pronoun *who* must be used when referring to people.
9. **(2)** Replace *they* with *the staff* to avoid a confusing pronoun reference.
10. **(5)** no correction is necessary
11. **(2)** When *ed* is added to most verbs, including *open,* the spelling of the base verb does not change.
12. **(2)** The past tense of *write* is *wrote. Writed* is not a correct verb form.
13. **(1)** The verb *is* must agree with the singular subject *Boston Cooking School Cookbook.*

CHAPTER 2: SENTENCE STRUCTURE

Exercise 1: Rewriting Fragments pages 94–95

Part A

The following are *possible* revisions of these fragments. Remember, your answers can be different and still be correct. When checking your answers, be sure your revised sentences contain a subject and predicate and express a complete thought.

1. **F** The pickup truck that I borrowed from George is now dented.
2. **S**
3. **F** Luis called your house last night.
4. **F** Anxious for some news, the inmate waited by the window for his lawyer.

5. **F** Life, with its many disappointments, is still worth living.

6. **S** (In a command or instruction, the subject is understood to be *you*.)

7. **F** You can't teach someone to pitch like Dwight Gooden and hit like Ryne Sandberg.

8. **S**

9. **F** Movies are shown at 5:00 P.M. daily.

10. **S** (In a command or instruction, the subject is understood to be *you*.)

Part B

Corrected sentences are in bold type. Remember, your revised sentences can be different and still be correct.

When President John F. Kennedy was inaugurated in 1960, he stated, "Ask not what your country can do for you; ask what you can do for your country." His philosophy did much for U.S. citizens and underdeveloped areas of the world. **For example, the Peace Corps sent volunteers into underdeveloped areas of the world.** The volunteers educated the citizens of those countries in basic survival skills. The main goal was for the countries to become more self-sufficient. **A second goal was to improve relations between the U.S. and these countries.**

Exercise 2: Conjunctions
pages 96–97

The correct conjunction and punctuation are in bold type. More than one conjunction may be correct in some sentences.

1. We are planning a Fourth of July picnic, **and** we hope all of you can attend.

2. He did not study for his driver's test, **but** he passed it.

3. Al has always wanted his own business, **so** he opened a restaurant.

4. You may have some strawberry pie, **or** you may have some cherry pie.

5. I can do most of my own plumbing, **but** I cannot do the electrical work.

6. Karen is not allowed any hard exercise, **for** she is recovering from an operation.

Exercise 3: Using Commas Correctly
page 97

Remember, a comma is needed only when two complete thoughts are joined by a coordinating conjunction such as *and* or *but*. If you use a comma, make sure the ideas you join have both a subject and a predicate.

1. She took off her coat and hung it in the closet.

2. She took off her coat, and she hung it in the closet.

3. Jorge called Marie, but he did not call Clara.

4. Jorge called Marie but not Clara.

5. Our daughter has a learning disability but is doing well in school.

6. Our daughter has a learning disability, but she is doing well in school.

7. We visited my Aunt Nancy, for we had not seen her in a while.

8. The mayor was popular with both senior citizens and young people.

Exercise 4: Run-ons and Comma Splices
pages 98–99

1. C

2. Kyle broke his leg, so he was taken to the emergency room.
   OR:
   Kyle broke his leg. He was taken to the emergency room.

3. Pass the donuts. I'm starving!

4. C

5. The make of her car is a Buick, and the model is a Century.
   OR:
   The make of her car is a Buick. The model is a Century.

6. C

7. C

8. Of course this is my sweater. I've had it for years.

9. Dion won every swimming event in the meet, so we were proud of him.
   OR:
   Dion won every swimming event in the meet. We were proud of him.

10. I'd rather have hay fever than food allergies. At least I can eat!

Exercise 5: Run-ons and Comma Splices
page 99

The sentences in bold type show possible ways to correct the run-ons and comma splices in this paragraph. They have been separated into two sentences or combined using a comma with *and, but, or, for, nor, so,* or *yet*.

My cousin Ernie loves solving brainteasers, doing magic tricks, and playing mathematical games. **He subscribes to several magazines. They are filled with puzzles.** In one trick, Ernie challenges his friends to cut a hole in an index card that is big enough to put a person's head through! **His friends always try, and he watches and laughs.** Then Ernie cuts the card into a long strand and places it over his head. **Who knows? Maybe someday he will be performing the card trick on TV. He certainly works hard at his craft.**

Exercise 6: Sentence Structure Practice
pages 99–100

1. (4) Comma splices can be corrected by making two complete sentences.

2. **(5)** When the conjunction *so* is used to combine two complete thoughts, you must place a comma before it.

3. **(3)** The possessive pronoun *their*, not its sound-alike contraction *they're*, is correct here.

4. **(2)** Run-ons can be corrected by joining the two complete thoughts with a conjunction (*and*) and a comma.

5. **(3)** The present-tense verb *suggest* is correct because the passage is in the present tense.

6. **(3)** The coordinating conjunction *so* links cause ("books have been published on the subject") to effect ("people soon may be applying birth-order theories to their families").

Exercise 7: Conjunctive Adverbs
page 102
The conjunctive adverb is in bold type.

1. **(a)** He was qualified for the job; **therefore**, he got it.

2. **(b)** The steak is very good; **on the other hand,** you might prefer the chicken.

3. **(c)** The company is in financial trouble; **as a result,** workers may be laid off.

4. **(a)** Jason has been taking piano lessons for years; **however**, he does not play well.

5. **(b)** Jeri may run for councilperson; **furthermore**, she may someday become mayor.

Exercise 8: Errors with Conjunctive Adverbs
page 102
The correct conjunctive adverb and punctuation are in bold type. More than one conjunctive adverb may be correct in some sentences.

1. The snowstorm worsened; **therefore,** we postponed our trip.

2. Two ot the students studied hard; **however,** they failed the test.

3. The dishwasher is broken; **in addition,** the freezer won't stay cold.

4. Mrs. Jones felt ill; **consequently,** she called a doctor.

5. Jane has so many talents; **for example,** she sings in a professional choir, weaves detailed tapestries, and can play an excellent game of tennis.

Exercise 9: Combining Sentences
page 103
The following are *possible* combinations of these sentences. Remember, your answers can be different and still be correct. When checking your answers, be sure that your punctuation is correct and that your conjunction is logical.

1. **(a)** The salesperson was very polite, so she listened to my complaints.
   (b) The salesperson was very polite; therefore, she listened to my complaints.

2. **(a)** The music was terrible, but we decided to dance.
   (b) The music was terrible; nevertheless, we decided to dance.

3. **(a)** We bought the house in 1975, and we sold it in 1980 for twice the price.
   (b) We bought the house in 1975; then we sold it in 1980 for twice the price.

4. **(a)** My friends give me advice, but I do not always listen to them.
   (b) My friends give me advice; however, I do not always listen to them.

5. **(a)** I could drive you to work in the morning, or you could take the subway.
   (b) I could drive you to work in the morning; otherwise, you could take the subway.

Exercise 10: Dependent Clauses
pages 104–105
Remember, your answers can be different from those in bold type and still be correct.

Part A

1. **Even though** Ray was afraid of water, he took swimming lessons.

2. **Since** she already knows the words to the song, she can teach us.

3. I'm not going to the class reunion **because** my closest friends won't be there.

4. **After** we left the meeting, we went for pizza.

5. Celia stayed with her mother **until** the nurse returned.

Part B
The dependent clause in each of the following sentences is in bold type.

1. **Since the tables were always full**, we knew the food at the cafe was good.

2. The family bought a new mini-van **before they went on vacation**.

3. **Whenever he reads science fiction books**, Eliot has nightmares.

4. I ordered a pepperoni pizza **even though I ate an hour ago**.

5. **Unless he finds another job**, Duane will paint the porch steps.

Part C
The subordinating conjunction in each sentence is in bold type.

1. **Because** we arrived at the church late, we missed their wedding ceremony.

2. **Even though** Bonnie said that she was not tired, she fell asleep at 7:00 P.M.

3. **Because** I left my umbrella at home, I was soaked from the unexpected thunderstorm.

4. **Since** Rose was angry with her babysitter, she said she would not hire the young girl again.

5. **When** we drove into the parking lot, we noticed that the store was closed.

Exercise 11: Structure and Usage pages 107–109

1. **(1)** No correction is necessary.

2. **(3)** The subordinating conjunction *although* shows the contrast in this sentence between "people who open savings accounts" and "people who invest."

3. **(2)** The passage as a whole is in the present tense, so change *bought* to *buy*.

4. **(4)** When combining two independent clauses with a conjunctive adverb, a semicolon should be placed before the conjunctive adverb and a comma placed after it. Also, be sure to choose the most logical conjunctive adverb. *Therefore* is correct because it links a cause to an effect.

5. **(5)** No correction is necessary.

6. **(3)** When combining two independent clauses with a conjunctive adverb, a semicolon should be placed before the conjunctive adverb and a comma placed after it.

7. **(2)** When a dependent clause comes first in a sentence, a comma must separate the two clauses.

8. **(2)** The passage as a whole refers to a group of people—stockholders. The plural subject pronoun *they* is correct.

9. **(5)** The coordinating conjunction *so* links cause to effect in this sentence.

Exercise 12: Correct Verb Sequence page 110

1. were waiting
2. will become
3. should have taken
4. was wearing
5. will call
6. had slept
7. have enjoyed
8. sweeps
9. could have moved
10. may lose

Exercise 13: Dangling and Misplaced Modifiers page 112

The modifying phrase in each of the following sentences is in bold type and is in its correct place—nearest to the word it modifies.

1. Rich saw the "No Smoking" sign **nailed to the wall**.

2. The child **who wanted a toy** called for his mother.

3. **While I was taking a shower**, the telephone rang.

4. My papers blew out the window **while I was driving to work**.

5. A bath felt good **after I had worked all day**.

6. **When I was traveling through Colorado**, my luggage was lost on the train.

7. We'll certainly be able to recognize the bride **wearing her wedding gown!**

8. We heard the dog **whining for food** under the table.

Exercise 14: Parallel Structure pages 113–114
Part A

1. **(b)** happy
2. **(d)** knees were shaking
3. **(a)** honesty
4. **(d)** slice the roast
5. **(d)** married woman

Part B

1. (b) 2. (b) 3. (a) 4. (a) 5. (b)

Exercise 15: Structure and Usage pages 114–116

1. **(3)** The modifier *ages five and six* should be placed next to *children*, the word it modifies.

2. **(4)** The dangling modifier in this sentence incorrectly implies that *new questions* were feeling sorry for the children.

3. **(5)** *Frustrating* is correct because it is parallel to *interesting* and *challenging*.

4. **(3)** The passage as a whole is in the present tense, so change *asked* to *ask*.

5. **(2)** This fragment is missing a subject and a verb. Choice (2) is correct because the subject pronoun *we* agrees with the rest of the passage and because the verb *ask* is in the present tense, as is the rest of the passage.

6. **(1)** The conjunction *and* joins two related ideas.

7. **(1)** No correction is necessary.

CHAPTER 3: MECHANICS
Exercise 1: Capitalization Rules page 119

1. The mayor of Chestortown requested assistance from Governor Kelly.

2. My favorite time of fall is Thanksgiving.

3. Candy's doctor sent her to get a second opinion from Doctor Schwartz.

4. We will meet on Wednesday, August 9, at Lincoln Center in Memphis, Tennessee.

5. Leading Sunday services at St. Gregory's Cathedral will be Father McMillan.

6. Drive north to Baker Avenue, then turn left at Kennedy Highway.

7. My German lessons are helping me prepare for my European trip next spring.

8. Marissa's birthday is Christmas Day, so her parents will surprise her with a party in January.

9. The Ohio River is a beautiful river.

10. This summer the band will be on the road for a long tour.

Exercise 2: Using Commas
page 122

Dear Mom,

   Because I do not have enough money, I will not be coming home for spring vacation. Unfortunately, I need to stay here in Des Moines and work. I did not, of course, waste my money, but I did not allow enough in my budget for an airline ticket. You will understand that I can't come, I know. I'd really love to be home in March, but I can't afford a ticket until June. Please call Sue, Pam, and Linda for me and relay the message.

Love always,
Dawn

Exercise 3: Punctuation Review
pages 123–124

1. To strip the paint from the woodwork, you will need a gallon of stripper, old rags, a scraper, a paintbrush, steel wool, and a mask to protect you from the fumes.

2. Mr. Rider, my insurance agent, called with information about a rate increase.

3. She hasn't returned the dresses to the store because she lost the receipt.

4. I love to stay up late and watch old movies; however, I have difficulty getting up in the morning.

5. In spite of her parents' protests, Charleen has moved in with her boyfriend.

Exercise 4: Structure, Usage, and Mechanics
pages 124–125

1. (4) Don't capitalize general directions.

2. (3) Don't capitalize general geographical terms.

3. (1) Use a comma to set off introductory phrases like *as a result.*

4. (5) No correction is necessary.

5. (5) Use a comma to set off a modifying phrase added at the end of a sentence.

6. (2) The coordinating conjunction *but* is correct because it shows the contrast between two ideas.

7. (3) The verb *are* agrees with the plural subject *interests.*

Exercise 5: The Master List
pages 127–128

1. American, August, December, English, February, January, Saturday, United States, Wednesday

2. (a) fourth
   (b) twelfth
   (c) eight
   (d) twelve, fourteen

3. (a) quarter
   (b) dollar
   (c) dozen
   (d) ounces
   (e) gallon

4. a lot, all right, post office, United States

5. u

6. it's, o'clock

7. (a) advisor, advisable
   (b) arguing, argument
   (c) burial, buried
   (d) acknowledge, knew, knowledge
   (e) decision, decisive
   (f) commitment, committed
   (g) marriage, married
   (h) occurred, occurrence
   (i) pleasant, pleasure
   (j) possession, possessive
   (k) preference, preferential, preferred

Exercise 6: The Dictionary
page 132

The following are *possible* sentences. Be sure your sentences have a subject and predicate and that they express a complete thought.

1. When the **auxiliary** system at the plant failed too, the engineers knew they had a real problem.

2. Pat enters a state of **ecstasy** whenever she eats a hot fudge sundae.

3. The cost of the ultrasuede coat was **exorbitant**.

4. Tulips **flourish** when they receive direct sunlight.

5. Timothy's monster mask for Halloween is **hideous**.

6. The cause of many household fires is pure **negligence**.

7. It takes great **perseverance** to finish a marathon race.

8. Heavy accents are **prevalent** in the deep South.

9. If the mayor and his wife **suppress** this information, they will be criticized sharply.

10. In response to unfair laws imposed by the British, Boston lawyer James Otis in 1763 said, "Taxation without representation is a form of **tyranny**."

Exercise 7: Spelling List Review
page 137
1. d **3.** d **5.** e **7.** c **9.** a
2. a **4.** b **6.** b **8.** d **10.** b

Exercise 8: Sound-Alike Words
page 141
The corrected word in each of the following sentences is in bold type.

1. The teachers knew that the **principal's** attitude was affected by the grievance they had filed.

2. If you choose to accept his **advice** and seek the job, you should apply at the personnel office.

3. Tim knows that Shari is quite bored with the **course**.

4. The counselor's advice was not **altogether** sound, so I chose to ignore her suggestions.

5. World peace is an issue we senators hear quite a lot about. Here inside the capitol we are **conscious** of world affairs.

6. He ate a whole pie for dessert. Now he's **quite** affected by his actions.

7. I **know** the picnic will be tomorrow, whether the weather is good or not.

8. All of us except Charlie have **already** chosen to work for the reelection of the school board members.

Exercise 9: Structure, Usage, Spelling, and Mechanics
pages 142–144

1. **(5)** The correct spelling is *calculators*.

2. **(1)** No correction is necessary.

3. **(2)** A comma is needed when a coordinating conjunction such as *but* connects two complete thoughts.

4. **(3)** When a conjunctive adverb joins two independent clauses, a comma is needed after the conjunction.

5. **(3)** This comma splice can be corrected by separating the two thoughts into two sentences.

6. **(5)** *Americans* is always capitalized because it is derived from the name of a specific place.

7. **(2)** Use a comma to set off an interrupting phrase in a sentence.

8. **(1)** The correct spelling is *Instead*.

9. **(4)** The correct spelling is *dependents*.

10. **(3)** A comma is needed when two complete thoughts are joined by a coordinating conjunction such as *but*.

CHAPTER 4: PREPARING FOR THE GED WRITING SAMPLE
Exercise 2: Topic, Audience, and Purpose
page 147

1. a parent

2. a child's absence from class

3. to ask that Erik be excused from class next Friday

4. a teacher

Exercise 4: Writing Topic Sentences
page 150
Part A
The following are *possible* topic sentences. Make sure your topic sentences state the subject of your paragraph and the point you would make about the subject.

1. My husband and I always tried to give our daughter memorable **birthday parties**.

2. Few people in the world have more power and responsibility than **the president of the United States.**

3. **The kitchen in my new apartment**, with its wood floors, flowered wallpaper, and small pantry, is nicer than any kitchen I've ever had.

4. Sometimes the ringing phones and computer printers in my office seem louder than any **noise pollution**.

5. Since **weather forecasting** is such an unpredictable science, I've stopped listening to forecasts.

Exercise 20: Understanding the Topic
pages 170–171

1. The subject of this essay must be your age.

2. You can discuss the advantages, disadvantages, or both of being your age.

3. Sample thesis statement: *There are far more advantages to being twenty-three years old than there are disadvantages.*
   - I am in extremely good health.
   - I don't yet have many of the responsibilities that will come later in life.

4. The subject of this essay must be why people use tobacco.

5. You are being asked to provide *causes*, or reasons why people smoke.

6. Sample thesis statement: *The reasons that people continue to risk their health by using tobacco are both personal and cultural.*
   - People think that smoking reduces stress.
   - People believe advertisements that suggest that cigarettes will make them more sophisticated, popular, and athletic.

Reading Skills for the GED

Developing strong reading and reasoning skills is key to your success on the GED Tests. This section focuses on skills that are used on all of the tests and particularly in the content areas of science, social studies, and literature and the arts. These skills are called *comprehension, application, analysis, synthesis,* and *evaluation.*

If these words sound unfamiliar to you, don't be concerned. The purpose of this section is to give you practice in four of these five skill areas. You encountered the synthesis level of critical thinking skills in the Writing Skills section of this book. Synthesis involves putting elements together to create a whole as in a piece of writing. In the Writing Skills section, you were asked to write an essay on a given subject that included an introduction, body, and conclusion.

Writing activities are included in the Science, Social Studies, and Literature and the Arts sections of this book. By writing paragraphs to answer the variety of questions asked, you will be strengthening your skills in synthesis.

The reading skills mentioned above can be understood as layers of a pyramid. Each higher-level skill rests on the skill that precedes it. Each skill is a stepping-stone to a higher one. Memory (knowledge), sometimes referred to as *recall,* is the foundation of the pyramid. At the memory level, you recall facts. *Memory* helps you answer the questions *who, what, when, where,* and *how.*

Other tests that you took in school may have focused heavily on memory-based questions in which you had to recall facts. On the GED Tests, however, you will have to manipulate, or work with, the information that you read and that you hold in your memory. The questions on the GED will test your ability to comprehend, apply, analyze, and evaluate what you read. The thinking skill pyramid is illustrated below.

PYRAMID OF THINKING SKILLS

Evaluation
Synthesis
Analysis
Application
Comprehension
Memory/Knowledge

The next two chapters will help you develop the critical thinking skills and interpret the types of illustrations you will see on the GED Tests.

1
CRITICAL THINKING SKILLS

Comprehension—
Understanding What You Read

When you *comprehend* something, you understand what you read. You show your understanding by being able to interpret or explain in your own words what something means. This skill involves putting one meaning into other words, identifying the main idea or key thought, and making inferences (sometimes referred to as *reading between the lines*).

When you *paraphrase*, you explain something so that another person can understand it. We are all familiar with slang—informal language used by a particular group. When you paraphrase slang spoken by a teenager to a member of an older generation, you do not repeat the message word for word; instead, you give the intended meaning. And that meaning does not last very long because slang words go out of style after a short period of time. Consider the example below, in which a teenager is speaking slang to an adult who may not comprehend the language of teenagers.

> *Teenager:* Your new shades are smooth.
> *Adult's literal translation:* Your new sunglasses have an even surface.
> *Intended meaning:* Your new sunglasses look good.

If you were paraphrasing the teen's statement, a word-for-word interpretation would not get the meaning across. You would have to explain *in other words* what the teen intended. Only by giving such an explanation could you show that you comprehended, or understood, what was said.

Idiomatic expressions, like slang, do not follow the rules of grammar, so it is difficult to translate them. However, we use them every day, and the English language would be much poorer without them. Common examples of idiomatic expressions are *get rid of, put up with, in the wink of an eye,* and *frog in my throat.* To understand the expression *frog in my throat,* we associate the sound of the person's voice with another concept familiar to us: the croaking sound made by a frog.

As you will find later, in the Literature and the Arts section, writers frequently use descriptive language and idiomatic expressions to make their writing more vibrant and vivid. You will often find yourself relying on your senses to understand what the writer is trying to say. The paragraph in the following exercise includes idiomatic expressions.

EXERCISE 1: UNDERSTANDING IDIOMATIC EXPRESSIONS

Directions: Read the following paragraph and paraphrase the numbered words or phrases by writing the intended meaning for each. The first one is done for you.

Carmen really needed to <u>brush up on</u> her Spanish. If she didn't <u>get cold</u>
                               (1)   (2)

<u>feet</u> and wasn't <u>broke</u> by the end of the month, she was going to Mexico. <u>Her</u>
(3)   (4)

<u>heart was set</u> on a trip, but she was <u>up to her ears in</u> work at the real estate
                               (5)

office. She had talked until she was <u>blue in the face</u> trying to persuade her
                               (6)

mother to <u>keep an eye on</u> the kids. As usual, Carmen had <u>bitten off more than</u>
        (7)   (8)

<u>she could chew</u>. How could she continue working just to <u>make ends meet</u> and
                                      (9)

plan for a trip? It <u>crossed her mind</u> just to <u>throw in the towel</u> and <u>hang around</u>
         (10)   (11)   (12)

<u>the house</u> during her vacation week.

1. *review*

2. _____

3. _____

4. _____

5. _____

6. _____

7. _____

8. _____

9. _____

10. _____

11. _____

12. _____

Answers are on page 238.

Identifying the Main Idea

    Another way you might show your comprehension of material is to **summarize**, or restate, the main idea. The main idea sums up what the writer is trying to get across. For example, if you answer the phone at work for an absent co-worker, and the caller gives you a long story about the reason for the call, you generally won't write down every word the caller says. You will summarize the message or simply write down the key thought or purpose of the call. You also might jot down key words or summarize main ideas when you take class notes.

    In a paragraph, the main idea is often stated first. Details that support the main idea are included in the sentences that follow. Occasionally, writers put the main idea in the middle or at the end of a paragraph. Then the author must ensure that enough supporting details are included before or after to "add up" to the main point the writer is trying to make. Read the following paragraph and identify the sentence that states the main idea.

Michael Jordan and Bo Jackson have gotten a lot more publicity these days than such trailblazers as the late U.S. Supreme Court justice Thurgood Marshall and the medical research pioneer Dr. Jane C. Wright. So historians at the Du Sable Museum of African American History in Chicago want to make sure that—besides athletes and entertainers—African-Americans' positive contributions to society are represented and respected. They aim to teach young African-Americans more about their own history and to show them that there are plenty of strong role models in different professions. To quote one recent visitor: "If they knew some of the things the pioneers of our people did, they'd have a better chance of being more successful in life." Through creative displays and educational tours, the museum succeeds in portraying these values.

The main idea here appears in the middle of the paragraph: "They aim to teach young African-Americans more about their own history and to show them that there are plenty of strong role models in different professions." Can you see how the sentences before it and the sentences that follow it all add up to the main idea?

And just as a paragraph has a main or central idea, a longer passage or article has a main idea. Read the following passage to identify the main idea. Where is it stated in the passage?

Weather is one of many variables that affect the nation's agricultural economy, and it is the most unpredictable. Northern farmers who hope for record harvests have frequently seen crops wiped out by droughts, seeds washed away by torrential rains, and early spring planting plans thwarted by frozen ground. You might think that a farmer's problems are solved by lots of sunshine, plentiful rain, and year-round warm temperatures. Well, think again! In recent years, orange growers in Florida have had their hopes dashed by unexpected subfreezing temperatures. These cold temperatures have resulted in reduced harvests.

The higher prices we must pay at the market for reduced crops cannot make up for the dollars lost because of Mother Nature's whims. The old adage that "we can only *talk* about the weather" accurately indicates just how powerless we are in controlling the forces of nature.

Which of the following sentences states the main idea of this passage?

(1) Man can't control the weather.
(2) Weather can have a serious effect on a nation's farm economy.
(3) A farmer's life can be very difficult.
(4) Man must strive to overcome all odds.
(5) The farmer is the backbone of the American economy.

The answer is **(2)**. The main idea of the passage is stated in the introductory sentence: "Weather is one of many variables that affect the nation's agricultural economy, and it is the most unpredictable." The passage goes on to explain how acts of nature affect the productivity of farmers. Choice (1) gives support for the main idea. Choices (3) and (4) are true statements that can be inferred after having read the passage. Choice (5) is not expressed at all in the passage.

Read the passage below to find the main idea. Where is it placed in the paragraph?

> In Africa, UNICEF (United Nations International Children's Emergency Fund) has helped provide emergency food supplies, water, and medicine for starving and malnourished children and adults in the nations of Angola, Ethiopia, Sudan, Zimbabwe and Somalia.
>
> UNICEF was also active in Latin America. In Mexico, it provided resources to help earthquake victims. It aided Colombians after a devastating volcanic eruption. In fact, UNICEF has worked hard on a number of international causes during the last decade.

The main idea is stated in the last sentence of the passage: "In fact, UNICEF has worked hard on a number of international causes during the last decade." The main idea is stated only after supporting details have built a case for it:

> In Africa, UNICEF . . .
> + In Mexico, it provided . . .
> + It aided Colombians . . .

UNICEF worked hard on a number of international causes.

In certain cases, an author may not directly state the main idea in a sentence or paragraph. Readers must always consider all of the important details to determine the main idea of a paragraph. Often they must make an inference or "read between the lines" to decide what the main idea is. Before readers come to any conclusion about the main idea, however, they must decide whether or not the main idea is stated. Read the passage below. Decide what the main idea is.

> The years pass and Abe Lincoln grows up, at 17 standing six feet, nearly four inches, long-armed with rare strength in his muscles. At 18 he could take an ax at the end of the handle and hold it out from his shoulders in a straight horizontal line, easy and steady. He could make his ax flash and bite into a sugar maple or a sycamore, one neighbor saying, "He can sink an ax deeper into wood than any man I ever saw."
>
> *The Prairie Years*, Carl Sandburg

The main idea—that Abe Lincoln was physically strong at a young age—must be inferred from the details provided. To determine the main idea, you have to find the key ideas:

> at 17 standing six feet, nearly four inches
> + long-armed with rare strength in his muscles
> + could take an ax at the end of the handle and hold it out from his shoulders in a straight horizontal line, easy and steady
> + can sink an ax deeper into wood than any man

Abe Lincoln was physically strong at a young age (or something similar).

Theme is another way that a writer can express a main idea. In one section on the Literature and the Arts Test, you will learn about a story's theme. An author does not directly state the theme in a story or novel. The reader must infer the main idea by putting together the details of plot, character, and setting that are shown in the story. The next exercise provides practice in reading between the lines to determine the main idea.

EXERCISE 2: READING BETWEEN THE LINES

Directions: Read the passage and answer the questions that follow.

The Priceless Gift

A young boy's dramatic adventure unfolds several years before the Soviet Union breaks up into the Commonwealth of Independent States. Picture a little Ukrainian boy coming to the United States with his parents. His parents decide to return to the Soviet Union, but he refuses to accompany them. Six years later, the boy, now twelve years old, receives a gift. The gift is something that native-born American children take for granted. It's a gift for a young boy who rode his bicycle to a relative's house and hid there for five days to avoid leaving the United States against his will. But this gift is wrapped in yards of legal red tape.

Before the boy earned the gift, he had to ignore the wishes of his parents and his native country. He had to learn to accept a whole new way of life without his parents and brother. He had to learn the English language and learn the ways of elementary school students in Chicago. He had to get used to grocery stores with plenty of food, unrestricted movement on the streets, and the option of celebrating religious holidays. He had to attempt to lead a normal life in spite of all the media attention. He knew the gift could not be bought with money; it was priceless.

1. The unstated main idea of the passage is that

   (1) teenage boys usually need to break with their parents
   (2) the boy earned the right to become a U.S. citizen
   (3) the boy was wrong to hide from his parents
   (4) the wrapped gift was delivered on the boy's birthday
   (5) the boy disliked Soviet schools

2. Which of the following details does *not* help you arrive at the main idea?

   (1) The boy was a twelve-year-old student in Chicago.
   (2) The gift was tied with yards of legal red tape.
   (3) Native-born Americans take this gift for granted.
   (4) The gift could not be bought with money.
   (5) The boy had to become used to living in the United States.

Answers are on page 238.

SKILL BUILDER: IDENTIFYING THE MAIN IDEA

1. Circle key words in a sentence. What words are absolutely necessary to get the message across?

2. Identify key ideas contained in a paragraph; key ideas are groups of key words. List what these ideas have in common; this is the main idea.

3. Notice headlines and titles; they usually contain key ideas.

Restating Information

When you paraphrase, or restate information, you use different words and phrases to express the same idea. Here are two examples of restated information:

Original

That author's enlightening new book gives deep insights into the nature of human relationships.

Restatement

There is a lot to be learned about personal relationships from this author's new book.

Previous experience with preschool education is more of a determinant of success in elementary education than socioeconomic status.

Going to preschool will have a positive effect on a child's elementary school education. This is a more important factor than whether the child comes from a rich or poor family.

On the GED Tests, you may be required to show how well you comprehend something by recognizing a restatement of a phrase, a sentence, or an idea.

EXERCISE 3: RESTATING IDEAS

Directions: Rewrite the following sentences in your own words.

1. One type of behavior is known as *stimulus-response*. According to this principle, an organism will respond in some way when acted on by a stimulus.

Restatement: _____

_____

2. It was no easy task to draw up a new constitution for the young United States. A split soon developed between the Federalists, who wanted a strong central government with authoritative control over the states, and the anti-Federalists, who were afraid the individual people and states would lose their freedoms under one central government.

Restatement: _____

_____

_____

3. A consumer would be foolhardy to assume that the mere assertion of a product's quality is proof enough. Consumers should not spend a great deal of money purchasing a new car without researching it in an authoritative source on car performance and standards.

Restatement: _____

_____

_____

4. All payments received will be applied first to the fees, if any, billed to your account by us, next to billed and unpaid finance charges, and then to billed and unpaid purchases and advances in the order determined by us.

Restatement: _____

_____

_____

5. The manufacturer warrants that if anything goes wrong with your television set within ninety days—and it's our fault—we will pay our authorized Servicenter only for the labor to repair it in that shop. Transportation to and from the Servicenter is your responsibility. After the ninety-day warranty expires, all labor charges are your responsibility.

Restatement: _____

_____

_____

Possible answers are on page 238.

Application—Applying What You Read

One of the most important outcomes of an education is the ability to apply what you have learned. For example, police cadets must be able to apply to test situations knowledge of the laws they have learned before they can be awarded their badges. Paramedics must be able to perform CPR (cardiopulmonary resuscitation) and other procedures before they can earn their certificates.

On the GED Tests, you will have to use information given to you and apply it in a problem-solving situation. The information that you will be given may be in the form of a definition, scientific theory, or principle. You will encounter application questions primarily in the areas of science and social studies; however, the Literature and the Arts Test will contain some as well.

To practice your skill in applying definitions, read the following passage about forms of drama and answer the questions that follow.

> The major forms of drama are the comedy and the tragedy. **Comedies** generally are light and amusing. They usually begin in humorously difficult situations and always end happily. Not all comedies are funny and light-hearted, although the majority are. Types of comedy include **slapstick**, a form of physical comedy that includes pratfalls and pie-in-the-face acts. **Farce** is a type of comedy that features exaggerated circumstances, improbable plots, and foolish action and dialogue.
> **Tragedies** often begin happily and always end in disaster. The main character is usually good but loses to an opponent in a conflict and is either ruined or killed. The major reason for the main character's failure is the tragic flaw—the human weakness that has made the tragic hero or heroine vulnerable.
> Somewhere between comedy and tragedy lies **melodrama**, a type of drama that relies on sentimentality, exaggerates emotion, and provides thrilling action.

Based on the information in the passage, answer the following questions.

1. The boisterous humor featured by comedians such as the Three Stooges, Jerry Lewis, and Charlie Chaplin would be classified *best* as

(1) comedy
(2) tragedy
(3) slapstick
(4) farce
(5) melodrama

2. A movie produced by Mel Brooks or Woody Allen and featuring actors such as Chevy Chase, Robin Williams, and Gene Wilder involved in outlandish circumstances would probably be classified *best* as

   (1) comedy
   (2) tragedy
   (3) slapstick
   (4) farce
   (5) melodrama

3. One of the most popular television programs of the last decade was "Cheers." This classic look at the human condition from the points of view of the lively characters in a Boston barroom would be described *best* as

   (1) comedy
   (2) tragedy
   (3) slapstick
   (4) farce
   (5) melodrama

4. Shows such as "Picket Fences," "All My Children," and "In the Heat of the Night" would fall into the category of

   (1) comedy
   (2) tragedy
   (3) slapstick
   (4) farce
   (5) melodrama

The answer to question 1 is **(3)**. Slapstick is defined in the passage as physical comedy characterized by pratfalls, pie-in-the-face acts, and other behavior demonstrated by the Three Stooges, Jerry Lewis, and Charlie Chaplin.

The answer to question 2 is **(4)**. The passage defines farce as a form of comedy featuring exaggerated circumstances and unbelievable plots. Actors such as Chevy Chase, Robin Williams, and Gene Wilder frequently perform in farces.

The answer to question 3 is **(1)**. The passage describes a comedy as light and amusing. "Cheers" featured humorous exchanges between Sam and the regulars of the barroom.

The answer to question 4 is **(5)**. The passage describes melodrama as a form of drama that relies on sentimentality, exaggerated emotion, and thrilling action. "In the Heat of the Night" is action-oriented, and "All My Children," a soap opera, and "Picket Fences," a drama, rely on sentimentality and exaggerated emotion.

Application in Social Studies and Science

The Social Studies and Science Tests will challenge your ability to apply given ideas in different situations using an item format similar to the one on the next page. In this type of item, certain categories are defined and specific situations are given. Some of the categories may seem very similar, so you will need to read each category *very carefully* to understand the differences among them.

EXERCISE 4: APPLICATION IN SOCIAL STUDIES

Directions: Read the definitions below and answer the questions that follow.

> **Propaganda** is information provided in such a way as to influence or slant the opinion or feelings of the audience that receives the message. Listed below are five techniques used by propagandists.
>
> **name-calling**—attaching an unfavorable name to an idea, a person, or a group so as to influence the attitude of the audience against the idea or position
>
> **glittering generalities**—high-sounding but general and vague terms used to influence positively the feelings of the audience toward a subject
>
> **bandwagoning**—advising people to do something because "everyone" does it, because it is popular, or because it is the "in" thing to do
>
> **transferring**—associating the respect, prestige, or power of one person or object with another person so that the audience is influenced favorably
>
> **card-stacking**—choosing only specific, favorable points that support a cause and ignoring the unfavorable points

1. In the 1992 presidential election, vice presidential candidate Albert Gore came to be known by his opponents as "Mr. Ozone" because of his efforts to educate the public about threats to the environment. Those who criticized him were employing the propaganda technique of

   (1) name-calling
   (2) glittering generalities
   (3) transferring
   (4) bandwagoning
   (5) card-stacking

2. A presidential candidate on the campaign stump who takes credit for increasing employment, lowering taxes, and improving trade relationships but ignores his foreign policy failures is guilty of engaging in

   (1) name-calling
   (2) glittering generalities
   (3) transferring
   (4) bandwagoning
   (5) card-stacking

3. After a tense night of police and gang clashes, fire has broken out in several stores on the street. Gang members begin to raid the supermarkets and appliance stores. More people on the streets join in the looting. As local residents are awakened and look out their windows, people in the streets call out, "Come on and grab what you can get. Hey, we're all getting free stuff. All the guys in the neighborhood are taking stuff. Get in on the free loot."

   What means of propaganda did the crowds use to justify their criminal acts?

   (1) name-calling
   (2) glittering generalities
   (3) transferring
   (4) bandwagoning
   (5) card-stacking

4. The local school council is proposing to adopt a measure to keep kids in school for an extra half hour each day. Parents and community leaders favor the idea, but the teachers aren't convinced. The president of the national teachers' association is known to oppose the plan. Staff teachers appeal to the council to drop the plan, arguing that if their national leader is against it, shouldn't they all fight it?

What propaganda technique is illustrated here?

   (1) name-calling
   (2) glittering generalities
   (3) transferring
   (4) bandwagoning
   (5) card-stacking

Answers are on page 238.

EXERCISE 5: APPLICATION IN SCIENCE

Directions: Read the definitions below and answer the questions that follow.

The human body is composed of several systems that keep it functioning. Though each system may be viewed separately, it is closely related to the others in the body—so much so that a problem in one system invariably affects another. Defined below are five of at least ten systems that make up the human body.

excretory system—the system that excretes or expels water and salts from the body; it includes the urinary system, in which the kidneys, ureters, urethra, and bladder play vital roles

endocrine system—the system made up of glands such as the pituitary, thyroid, and adrenal, which secrete body fluids, stimulating cells and regulating the body's development

lymphatic system—the system that circulates lymph (a pale fluid) to the body's tissues, bathing the cells; lymphocytes found in the system produce antibodies that help fight bacterial infections

digestive system—the system that processes and distributes nutrients from food; composed chiefly of the esophagus, stomach, liver, and large and small intestines

muscular system—the system composed of the three types of tissue that enable the body and its parts to move

1. AIDS (acquired immunodeficiency syndrome) is a disease that inhibits the body's ability to fight off infections. AIDS would interfere mainly with the proper functioning of which system?

   (1) excretory
   (2) endocrine
   (3) lymphatic
   (4) digestive
   (5) muscular

2. The skin (the body's largest organ) may be defined loosely as belonging to this system since, through perspiration, wastes are removed from the body.

(1) excretory
(2) endocrine
(3) lymphatic
(4) digestive
(5) muscular

3. The sudden growth spurt characteristic of adolescents may be attributed to the operation of which of the body's systems?

(1) excretory
(2) endocrine
(3) lymphatic
(4) digestive
(5) muscular

4. Saliva, needed by the body to perform the first step in the operation of one of the bodily systems, is an integral component of which system?

(1) excretory
(2) endocrine
(3) lymphatic
(4) digestive
(5) muscular

Answers are on page 238.

SKILL BUILDER: ANSWERING APPLICATION QUESTIONS

To answer application questions, use the process of elimination. Go through each category to rule out ones that do *not* fit the question. In this way, you should be able to find the correct choice.

Analysis—Analyzing What You Read

When you analyze something, you take it apart. You examine the elements to understand better what makes up its whole.

On the GED Tests you will be expected to analyze complete passages in the areas of social studies, science, and literature and the arts. You will look at specific ideas and pieces of information to understand better the point being made by a writer, graphic artist, or cartoonist.

The Social Studies and Science Tests will test your ability to

- distinguish facts from opinions and hypotheses
- recognize unstated assumptions
- draw conclusions

On the Literature and the Arts Test you will be required to identify

- elements or techniques of style and structure
- the techniques used to produce a particular effect
- the effects produced by the use of different techniques

Distinguishing Facts from Opinions and Hypotheses

Some of the material you will read on the GED Tests will be based on facts, opinions, or hypotheses. *Facts* can be proved to be true by using one or more of the five senses. Newspapers and magazine articles are based largely on facts.

Opinions are beliefs that may or may not be supported by facts. Opinions express feelings or ideas and are influenced greatly by one's background, values, and outlook on life. For example, editorials and columns in newspapers generally present a writer's opinions along with the facts.

Hypotheses are educated guesses that are made to explain a phenomenon or an event. Hypotheses may be proved or disproved by the passage of time or the acquiring of additional information. The statements below show how facts, opinions, and hypotheses differ.

- It is a fact that Pittsburgh has more bridges than any other major American city because of the meeting of two rivers—the Allegheny and the Monongahela—to form the Ohio. This fact can be proved by acquiring data on bridges in U.S. cities.

- It is an opinion that Pittsburgh is the most desirable place to live in the United States. This is a statement that is based on a person's values, background, and outlook on life.

- It is a hypothesis that Pittsburgh will experience a 15 percent decrease in population over the next five years because of the decline in smokestack industries there. More time and information will be needed to prove or disprove this hypothesis.

EXERCISE 6: FACTS, OPINIONS, AND HYPOTHESES

Directions: Read each group of statements below. Write *F* for the ones that express a fact, *O* for the ones that express an opinion, and *H* for the ones that express a hypothesis.

1. ____ **(a)** Our city is a great place to live.

   ____ **(b)** If the present trend continues, our city's population will reach 70,000 by the year 2000.

   ____ **(c)** The population of our city is 58,000.

2. ____ **(a)** Several million legal abortions have been performed.

   ____ **(b)** When birth control clinics are established at all inner-city high schools, the number of abortions in the city will decline by 50 percent.

   ____ **(c)** Antiabortion activists believe abortion is murder.

3. ____ **(a)** With her teaching methods, Mrs. Smith's class will experience an across-the-board increase in test scores by the year's end.

   ____ **(b)** Mrs. Smith is an outstanding teacher.

   ____ **(c)** The Board of Education has agreed to rehire Mrs. Smith for another year.

4. ____ **(a)** If you're patriotic, you'll buy only American-made cars.

   ____ **(b)** There continues to be a market for foreign-made cars.

   ____ **(c)** The number of Americans buying foreign-made cars will jump 20 percent when import quotas are lifted.

5. ____ **(a)** Marianne wallpapered the dining room herself.

   ____ **(b)** The wallpaper in the dining room will last two years longer than the wallpaper in the living room if Marianne uses premixed paste.

   ____ **(c)** Marianne should have hired a professional paperhanger to wallpaper the dining room.

Answers are on page 239.

EXERCISE 7: MORE ON FACTS, OPINIONS, AND HYPOTHESES

Directions: Read the passage and the statements that follow. Then write *F* if the statement is a fact stated in or supported by the passage, *O* if it is an opinion, and *H* if it is a hypothesis.

Hispanic influence is expanding in the United States of America. In fact, people of Hispanic origin are the second-fastest-growing minority in the United States, making up nearly 9 percent of the population. Demographers— people who study and report vital statistics on population groups—estimate that by the year 2020 Hispanic-Americans will become the nation's largest minority.

Where do they come from, and where do they live? Many Hispanic-Americans come from Mexico, frequently settling in San Antonio or Los Angeles. Those who come from Cuba often make Miami their home. New York and Chicago have large Hispanic populations from Puerto Rico.

Hispanic culture is expanding, too. After struggling for many years to achieve status, Hispanic-American culture is becoming more widely accepted in the United States. For instance, Hispanic artists and entertainers and Hispanic foods have become popular in many cities across the nation. Even more significant, however, is that Hispanic-Americans are being elected or appointed to political office and other important positions. Robert Martinez, the former governor of Florida, and Lauro Cavazos, formerly the Secretary of Education, for example, have earned respected leadership roles in government.

In 1993, President Bill Clinton named two Hispanics to his White House Cabinet: Henry Cisneros, Secretary of Housing and Urban Development (HUD), and Federico Peña, Secretary of Transportation. Although some people criticized Clinton for being influenced by activists who demanded more minorities, he said, "I can say with pride that I believe this Cabinet and these other appointees represent the best in America."

_____ **1.** By the year 2020, Hispanic-Americans will be the United States' largest minority.

_____ **2.** Hispanic-American artists owe their success to great struggles.

_____ **3.** Many Hispanic-Americans came from Cuba and Puerto Rico.

_____ **4.** President Clinton appointed two Hispanic-Americans to his 1993 Cabinet.

_____ **5.** The 1993 Cabinet appointees are the most effective leaders in America.

_____ **6.** Twenty years from now, Hispanic-Americans will live and work in every city in the United States.

_____ **7.** People who come here from Mexico help to advance our culture.

Answers are on page 239.

Hypotheses and the Scientific Method

Formulating a hypothesis is an important step in the scientific method. The scientific method is a system of investigation on which all scientific inquiry is based. Most science courses offer at least a bare summary of the procedure. It can be reduced to six steps:

1. Identify and state the problem.
2. Collect information.
3. Make a hypothesis.
4. Make a prediction on the basis of the hypothesis.
5. Make observations and perform experiments to test the hypothesis.
6. Draw a conclusion.

In step 1, the scientist identifies a problem that needs to be solved or a question that must be answered. Step 2 requires that the scientist gather as much information about the problem as possible. At step 3, the scientist makes an educated guess that might explain the reason for the problem or answer the question. The scientist then predicts what the outcome of the experiment or observation will be if the hypothesis is correct, step 4. During step 5, the scientist observes or experiments to test the hypothesis. According to step 6, if the results confirm the scientist's prediction, the hypothesis is correct. If they don't, the hypothesis must be changed or thrown out.

When the results of an experiment or observation can be explained by a hypothesis, a *theory* is formed. When a theory has few exceptions, it is called a *law*.

Let's look at a situation to which we might apply these six steps to solve a problem.

> We went to fish at our favorite lake, but the fishing was terrible. The water was very clear, and we didn't see any plants growing at the bottom of the lake at all. We were told a few weeks earlier that there had been a heavy die-off of fish. We called the Environmental Protection Agency. Agency officials said that they think the lake is a victim of acid rain. Water tests and an examination of frozen fish samples confirmed the belief that the high level of acidity in the lake had killed all life.

The situation described above can be investigated by following the six steps of the scientific method.

1. *Problem:* The fishing at our favorite lake was terrible.

2. *Information (observable facts):* The water was clear, there were no plants, and there was a recent die-off of fish.

3. *Hypothesis:* The lake may be a victim of acid rain.

4. *Prediction:* If the lake is acidic, a pattern will show up in water and fish samples.

5. *Experiment:* All tests prove positive for the characteristics of acid rain; our results agree with our prediction.

6. *Conclusion:* The lake has been affected by acid rain.

In following the scientific method, a scientist must be objective. The results of the experiment must not be influenced in any way by the scientist's hunches or beliefs. The results of the experiment must speak for themselves. For this reason, experiments involving the scientific method require the use of controls so that the outcome is not biased by the experimenter's expectations.

EXERCISE 8: HYPOTHESES AND THE SCIENTIFIC METHOD

Directions: Read the passage below. Then fill in the steps of the scientific method with the correct information from the passage.

The shipbuilding industry was a significant part of New England's economy. An important but hazardous mineral used in shipbuilding is asbestos. Asbestos is used widely for fireproofing and insulating. However, workers exposed to asbestos fibers for long periods of time are known to have a higher-than-average risk of getting lung cancer.

In the late 1950s, doctors were getting an unusual number of asbestos-related cancer cases. Two distinct forms of cancer were dominant—cancer of the abdominal lining and cancer of the bronchial tubes. Doctors who treated these diseases noticed that not all of the workers exposed to asbestos contracted bronchiogenic cancer. Physicians who compiled case histories for cancer patients found nothing in the records that would seem to cause one group of men over another to get the deadly disease.

A research team at one medical center, however, suspected that another factor—cigarette smoking—might increase a worker's chances of getting cancer of the bronchial tubes. They suggested that, if those suffering with this type of cancer were polled, the results would indicate that they were heavy cigarette smokers. When the team surveyed this group of cancer patients, it found that, indeed, a very high percentage were cigarette smokers.

1. *Problem:* _____

    _____

2. *Information (observable facts):* _____

    _____

3. *Hypothesis:* _____

    _____

4. *Prediction:* _____

    _____

5. *Observation (perform experiment):* _____

    _____

6. *Conclusion:* _____

    _____

Answers are on page 239.

EXERCISE 9: MORE ON HYPOTHESES AND THE SCIENTIFIC METHOD

Directions: Read the passage below. Then fill in the steps of the scientific method with the correct information from the passage.

We've long known that what vegetation grows in rain forests is determined partly by the climate there. However, recent scientific studies and computer simulations of rain forest weather reveal an interesting twist: the weather in tropical rain forests is determined partly by the vegetation that grows there.

Rain forests are being destroyed to grow food crops, to provide land for cattle grazing, and to provide settlement areas to ease population density. In the Amazon rain forests, evaporation from plants and soil accounts for half of all the water that falls. The removal of vegetation from the ecosystem may disrupt the water cycle, causing less water to be evaporated.

Some scientists believed that if they could perform a mathematical analysis of the climate and create the conditions of the South American rain forest, their results would show that removing plant growth would affect the weather, which would in turn affect future growth.

Using supercomputers and analyzing the climate, researchers were able to simulate the rain forest environment. Their projections showed that turning the South American rain forest into cattle pasture would reduce rainfall by 25 percent and increase average temperatures in the area by 5°F. This would also lengthen the dry season.

The result of this experiment was the knowledge that clearing away the rain forest would affect the weather, making it unlikely that forest plants could ever grow there again.

1. *Problem:* _____

   _____

2. *Information (observable facts):* _____

   _____

3. *Hypothesis:* _____

   _____

4. *Prediction:* _____

   _____

5. *Observation (experiment):* _____

   _____

6. *Conclusion:* _____

   _____

Answers are on page 239.

Drawing Conclusions Through Inductive and Deductive Reasoning

The scientific method is based on logical reasoning. When you draw conclusions that support evidence gathered in an investigation, you are following logic. Two methods of reasoning that are involved in logic are inductive reasoning and deductive reasoning.

Inductive reasoning involves drawing a conclusion by going from the specific to the general. In following induction, you observe the behavior or characteristics of members of a class or group and then apply this information to the unobserved members of the group. In other words, you *generalize* about the other members of the group. To see how a scientist follows inductive reasoning, read the following passage:

> Scientific evidence from field studies of golden eagles indicates that the pesticide DDT is threatening the existence of our birds of prey. Raptors such as hawks and eagles provide a service by controlling rodents that damage our food crops. Although DDT does not poison the birds directly, it can interfere with their metabolism, causing them to produce eggs with thinner shells that break easily. Also, the birds' ability to store toxic materials in the fatty tissues weakens the offspring, increasing mortality.
>
> A specific statement that can be made from this study is that DDT is threatening golden eagles (birds of prey).

Based on this observation, scientists can generalize that other birds of prey living in the same region as golden eagles are similarly threatened by DDT.

Deductive reasoning involves drawing a conclusion by applying a generalization to a specific example or case. In the case above, scientists who have found that our birds of prey are threatened by DDT may infer that bald eagles, red-tailed hawks, falcons, great horned owls, and other raptors in the area are also being threatened.

For a valid conclusion to be drawn, the generalization must be known, accepted, and true. If the generalization is faulty, it cannot be applied to a specific example.

EXERCISE 10: DEDUCTIVE REASONING

Directions: Read the generalization, then write *yes* for each conclusion that is valid based on the generalization, and *no* for each that is not.

Generalization: A stroke is a condition in which there is lessening or loss of consciousness, sensation, and motion caused by the rupture or obstruction of an artery of the brain.

Conclusions:

_____ **1.** A cerebral hemorrhage occurs when a defective brain artery bursts; therefore, a cerebral hemorrhage often can lead to a stroke.

_____ **2.** An embolism is the sudden blockage of a blood vessel by a mass or an air bubble in the blood; therefore, an embolism in the brain can lead to a stroke.

_____ **3.** A tumor is a mass of tissue that does not swell and that rises from tissue that already exists; therefore, brain tumors generally lead to a stroke.

_____ **4.** An aneurysm is a permanent, abnormal, blood-filled swelling of a vessel; therefore, the rupture of an aneurysm can cause a stroke.

_____ **5.** Phlebitis is the inflammation of a vein; varicose veins are abnormally swollen or dilated veins; therefore, phlebitis and varicose veins can lead to a stroke.

Answers are on page 240.

SKILL BUILDER: INDUCTIVE/DEDUCTIVE REASONING QUESTIONS

To answer these questions, ask yourself
- Is the generalization accepted by most people?
- Is it true, based on your experience and knowledge?
- Were a great number of subjects observed?
- Are you aware of any exceptions to the rule?

Faulty Reasoning and Unstated Assumptions

Writers and speakers may not always follow logic in expressing their views. Sometimes, they make statements or write essays that are based on information that is not true. They often do this to influence the opinions of their audience.

Propagandists are especially guilty of this practice. If an assumption is faulty, a writer's or speaker's entire argument can be faulty. One indication of an informed mind is the ability to recognize when a faulty assumption is being made. Read the statement below and consider the assumption being made.

All who receive welfare benefits under the AFDC (Aid to Families with Dependent Children) program should be forced to do community work if they want to keep their benefits.

An assumption that the speaker has made is that everyone who receives welfare benefits under AFDC is able to work. This is not necessarily the case for all recipients. In fact, according to statistics, most of the recipients are actually children who, of course, cannot go to work.

EXERCISE 11: FAULTY REASONING AND UNSTATED ASSUMPTIONS

Directions: Read the statements below to detect the assumption made by the writer. Then complete the statements that follow by filling in the blank with the appropriate word or words. *Note:* You may uncover underlying assumptions that are not included in the answer key.

1. All unwed mothers should be forced to complete high school before receiving any welfare benefits.

   The speaker assumes that all unwed mothers are _____

   _____.

2. All foreign-born doctors practicing in the United States should have their licenses reviewed annually and should undergo frequent competency exams.

   The speaker assumes that foreign-born doctors are less _____ than American-born doctors.

3. All polling places in the inner city should have pollwatchers to guard against vote fraud.

   The writer assumes that vote fraud is _____ in the inner city.

4. All cars over five years of age should undergo mandatory emissions tests.

   The speaker assumes that older cars tend to cause more _____ than newer cars.

5. In professional and collegiate sports, all athletes should undergo mandatory drug testing.

   The speaker assumes that professional and collegiate athletes are guilty of

   _____.

Answers are on page 240.

SKILL BUILDER: RECOGNIZING FAULTY REASONING AND UNSTATED ASSUMPTIONS

Be suspicious of blanket statements that include *all* people or things in a category. Such statements are often faulty since there are exceptions to every rule.

Analysis in Literature and the Arts

The Literature and the Arts Test will tap your skill in analyzing excerpts from fiction, nonfiction, and drama, as well as poetry. You will be required to identify techniques of style and to be able to understand how a writer's technique contributes to the overall effect of a piece of literature.

Style is the writer's way of using language to express an idea. Style varies among individual writers, as do their personalities. Style is established by the writer's choice of words and helps to create *tone*, the attitude an author conveys toward the subject and reader. An example of how tone is used is shown in the following statement:

Thanks a lot!

Spoken in one tone of voice, the statement can be taken as a compliment; however, if spoken in another tone, it can be taken as an insult, proving that it's not *what* you say but *how* you say it. You will learn more about style and tone in the Literature and the Arts section.

Read the following excerpt to determine the tone the writer is using. Is it serious, sentimental, or humorous? Could the passage be characterized as slapstick, tragedy, melodrama, or farce?

> . . . The ghost that got into our house on the night of November 17, 1915, raised such a hullabaloo of misunderstandings that I am sorry that I didn't just let it keep on walking, and go to bed. Its advent caused my mother to throw a shoe through a window of the house next door and ended up with my grandfather shooting a patrolman. I am sorry, therefore, that I ever paid any attention to the footsteps.
>
> from "The Night the Ghost Got In" by James Thurber

The tone may be described as humorous. The reader can infer the tone by the author's use of language. "The ghost . . . raised such a hullabaloo of misunderstandings . . ." lets us know that this is not the opening of a horror story about ghosts. The improbable actions triggered by the ghost's appearance include the mother's throwing a shoe through a neighbor's window and the grandfather's shooting a patrolman.

The passage could be characterized as farce, a form of comedy featuring exaggerated circumstances and unbelievable plots. A ghost getting into a house and causing the grandfather to shoot a patrolman would be unbelievable to many.

EXERCISE 12: STYLE AND TONE

Directions: Read the passage and answer the questions that follow.

> "Ah, Father, Father!" said Wilhelm. "It's always the same thing with you. Look how you lead me on. You always start out to help me with my problems, and be sympathetic and so forth. It gets my hopes up and I begin to be grateful. But before we're through I'm a hundred times more depressed than before. Why is that? You have no sympathy. You want to shift all the blame on to me. Maybe you're wise to do it." Wilhelm was beginning to lose himself. "All you seem to think about is your death. Well, I'm sorry. But I'm going to die too. And I'm your son. It isn't my fault in the first place. There ought to be a right

way to do this, and be fair to each other. But what I want to know is, why do you start up with me if you're not going to help me? What do you want to know about my problems for, Father? So you can lay the whole responsibility on me—so that you won't have to help me? D'you want me to comfort you for having such a son?" Wilhelm had a great knot of wrong tied tight within his chest, and tears approached his eyes but he didn't let them out. He looked shabby enough as it was. His voice was thick and hazy, and he was stammering and could not bring his awful feelings forth.

from *Seize the Day*, by Saul Bellow

1. The author's style suggests that Wilhelm is

    (1) talking too fast
    (2) suffering emotionally
    (3) getting ready for a fight
    (4) showing maturity and wisdom
    (5) acting responsibly

2. The overall tone of the excerpt is

    (1) nostalgic
    (2) mocking
    (3) tragic
    (4) angry
    (5) sentimental

3. In this excerpt, the author's style can be described as

    (1) formal
    (2) poetic
    (3) romantic
    (4) realistic
    (5) imaginative

4. The author portrays a father-and-son relationship that has a history of

    (1) conflict
    (2) physical violence
    (3) acceptance
    (4) understanding
    (5) mutual cooperation

5. Wilhelm may best be described as a man who

    (1) struggles with external and internal conflicts
    (2) lives in a world rich in fantasy
    (3) knows exactly what he wants and how to get it
    (4) turns his emotions on and off at will
    (5) hates his family

Answers are on page 240.

Evaluation—Evaluating What You Read

When you *evaluate* something, you make a judgment. You decide how well or poorly an idea or object meets certain standards. For example, when you evaluate a movie, you judge it according to the quality of its acting, directing, cinematography, sound track, and other standards. Standards by which a judgment is made are called *criteria*. Criteria may be either subjective or objective.

Objective criteria are standards that are not affected by an individual's personal tastes, beliefs, or opinions about what is being judged. *Subjective* criteria are standards that *are* affected by an individual's personal tastes, beliefs, or opinions.

For example, tests like true/false and multiple-choice exams, in which there is a single correct answer for each question, can be evaluated objectively. The correctness of the answer choice is not open to dispute; if the answer is debatable, then the question itself is not valid. On the other hand, an essay exam, one in which students have to interpret and answer questions using their own words, is open to subjective evaluation. The teacher who grades the test has to decide in his or her own mind whether or not the student answered the question adequately. For this reason, essay examinations are very difficult to grade, and instructors must establish clear-cut guidelines by which the exam is to be evaluated.

The following situation illustrates the difference between objective and subjective criteria. Read the paragraph and answer the questions that follow.

A young couple is purchasing their first home. They have two small school-age children. They must consider several factors in the decision to buy a home. They have drawn up a list of criteria by which to judge the prospective neighborhood for the home. In the space provided, write *O* if the standard is objective and *S* if it is subjective.

_____ **1.** the peacefulness of the community during the day

_____ **2.** the closeness, in walking distance, to the nearest school

_____ **3.** the attractiveness of the other homes on the block

_____ **4.** the community's tax rate compared to other communities

_____ **5.** the success of the community's recreational programs

_____ **6.** the performance of the school district on national standardized tests

_____ **7.** the quality of the municipal services the community offers

You should have identified the objective standards as numbers 2, 4, and 6. Each of these criteria can be evaluated by information that can be collected or measured objectively. The subjective criteria are numbered 1, 3, 5, and 7. These criteria are subjective because personal opinion, not objective facts, affects how a person views the community in this regard. What may be described as peaceful, attractive, successful, and of good quality varies from person to person. In fact, the husband and wife themselves may not even agree on these points.

EXERCISE 13: EVALUATING IDEAS

Directions: Read the following television commentary and answer the questions that follow.

They're fast, they're fun, they're not terribly difficult, and you could get a chance to win a lot of money or prizes. They're TV game shows, and they've been a staple of the daytime schedule since television began.

Game shows are remarkably good at offering something for everyone. Contestants can be famous for a day and get the thrill of competing. Studio and home audiences can share in the excitement and play along. Producers, whose hardest job is coming up with the idea for the game in the first place—and then selling it to a network or group of stations—can settle back and make money.

Mark Goodson, of Mark Goodson–Bill Todman Productions, has been the brains behind some of the most popular TV game shows, like "To Tell the Truth," "The Price Is Right," "Password," "Match Game," "Family Feud," and "Child's Play," where adults try to guess the secret word from clues given by six- to eight-year-olds.

Goodson says creating a game show is tricky. "You have to come up with a simple concept that is also novel and involving," he explains. There are other "rules" that must be followed as well. "Good game shows have at least three things in common," Goodson says. "First, there's an element of suspense, because we don't know who is going to win. Second, everyone can participate—even the audience can guess at the answers. And third, the viewers can identify with the contestants. They start thinking, 'I could do better than that guy.'"

Sometimes the viewers think they could do better than the show *host*. "People write in all the time asking to be the host of a game show," Goodman laughs. "That shows how successful we are in making it look simple. After all, they wouldn't [have asked] to replace Richard Burton in *Hamlet*, would they?" But hosting a game show isn't as easy as it looks, either. "The principal requirement is the hardest to explain," Goodman says. "It's a technical skill, an ability to be an emcee [master of ceremonies], like an ability to do acrobatics or play tennis. It's also important to be able to think on your feet, to be charming, and to have a good sense of humor. But that indescribable skill is the most important thing. . . ."

from "Game Shows: They're More Than Just 'Child's Play'"
by Dorothy Scheuer

1. The writer lists at least six adjectives as standards that game shows must meet. These standards are

(1) _____

(2) _____

(3) _____

(4) _____

(5) _____

(6) _____

2. Many of the criteria that successful game shows must follow are also necessary ingredients for successful

    A. poetry
    B. fiction—novels and short stories
    C. essays

    (1) A
    (2) B
    (3) C
    (4) A and B
    (5) B and C

3. Which of the following is also a requirement for a successful game show and is supported by the article?

    (1) the low budget compared to other TV programs
    (2) the time slot in which game shows are scheduled
    (3) the technical and personal abilities of the host
    (4) the age of the emcee
    (5) the number of markets in which the show airs

4. The article quotes Mark Goodson as saying "The principal requirement is the hardest to explain. It's a technical skill, an ability to be an emcee [master of ceremonies], like an ability to do acrobatics or play tennis. It's also important to be able to think on your feet, to be charming, and to have a good sense of humor. But that indescribable skill is the most important thing. . . ."

This quote suggests that the main requirement for hosting a game show

    (1) is based on objective and measurable characteristics
    (2) is based on subjective and nonmeasurable characteristics
    (3) is a God-given gift
    (4) is impossible to learn
    (5) does not come across effectively on the television screen

5. Which of the following statements is supported by the information in the article?

    (1) Practically anybody can host a game show.
    (2) Game shows have had a long history in television.
    (3) Game shows are not as profitable for producers as they are for contestants.
    (4) Game shows are relatively new in television.
    (5) The best game shows are difficult and challenging.

Answers are on page 240.

SKILL BUILDER: ANSWERING EVALUATION QUESTIONS
To answer evaluation questions:
1. Determine the standards or criteria for judging an idea.
2. Decide how closely the idea or object meets the established criteria.

Adequacy of Facts

Before you reach a decision or draw a conclusion, you need to evaluate the information that is available. You need to ask yourself, "Is there enough information to make this decision?" or "Is this decision supported adequately by the facts?"

When you don't have all the facts, you can't make an informed decision. Suppose you were interested in an issue in your community, such as "Should a low-rent apartment building be torn down to make room for a new high-rise building?" To be able to judge how you feel about the issue, you need to know all the facts. You need to know

1. How many people will be affected by tearing down the building?

2. What kinds of rents will be charged in the new building?

3. Will the construction company hire community residents to work on the project?

All of these facts (and others) will help you decide where you stand on the issue.

Similarly, when you answer questions on the GED Tests, you may need to determine whether there is enough information to support the writer's conclusion or point of view.

EXERCISE 14: ADEQUACY OF FACTS

Directions: Read the following commentary by a newspaper columnist about the construction of a high-rise building in the community. Then put an *F* next to the charges that the commentator has supported with facts and an *N* next to charges for which he has not cited any evidence.

A high-rise apartment building is being constructed in South Rochelle, but neither renters nor community businesses will benefit from this new venture. It will not increase much-needed rental properties because the building will consist solely of resident-owned condominiums. The developers, who have already shown their contempt for local residents, will certainly not try to involve local business in the project. Undoubtedly, they will go outside of the community for the labor and materials that they need.

This problem could have been prevented, but the newly elected mayor and her staff refused three different offers to meet with community organizations on this issue. The fat cats from the construction company must have lined the coffers of her campaign chest to influence the mayor to disregard the wishes of her constituents.

_____ **1.** The high-rise will not create more rental units in the community.

_____ **2.** The developers will not utilize community labor or businesses.

_____ **3.** The mayor refused to meet with community members.

_____ **4.** The construction company has lined the coffers of the mayor's campaign.

Answers are on page 240.

Roles of Values and Beliefs

When people make decisions, they are, in part, influenced by facts. But we all have deeply held values and personal beliefs that influence our decision making. Many of the literature selections that you read on the GED Tests will consist of commentaries—writers' opinions of various types of literary and artistic works. These commentaries are based on the writers' own values. In social studies and science-related issues, you will see that personal values have a big impact on decision making.

The following situation reflects a conflict between two different sets of values.

> Industrial waste from the Nelson Corporation is polluting the local lake. The corporation claims that if it has to spend a lot of money on water pollution cleanup, it will have to lay off several hundred community workers.

What values are in conflict here? If you think something like *interest in public health and safety vs. commitment to community employment*, you are correct. The following exercise examines the role of values and beliefs.

EXERCISE 15: THE ROLE OF VALUES AND BELIEFS

Directions: In each situation described below, there is a conflict between two competing sets of values. On the lines following each paragraph, write the two values that are in conflict.

1. Myrna wants to marry Sam, settle down, and have a family. However, she knows that while her family likes Sam personally, family members object to the marriage because Sam's religious background is different from their own.

   Myrna has to choose between _____ and

   _____ .

2. The government of New Zealand has a dilemma. On the one hand, its citizens demand that no ships with nuclear weapons dock in its ports. On the other hand, it is afraid of alienating its trading partner and military ally, the United States.

   The government of New Zealand must choose between _____

   and _____ .

3. One of the most controversial areas of scientific research is genetic engineering. Advocates of genetic engineering maintain that they will be able to prevent many genetically based birth defects such as Down's syndrome and sickle-cell anemia. Opponents of genetic engineering warn that this research tampers with nature and will lead to attempts to create a genetically "pure" master race.

   A scientist who is approached to do genetic research must choose between

   _____ and _____ .

Answers are on page 240.

Recognizing Organizational Patterns

Textbooks and reading passages in social studies and science are organized according to certain patterns. Also, literary works such as novels, short stories, plays, and forms of nonfiction are based on organizational patterns. Three common patterns used in writing are cause and effect, comparison and contrast, and sequence or time order.

Organizational patterns can be the framework for entire books as well as single paragraphs. For example, a chapter in U.S. history may be organized in a time-order pattern, and another may be organized to show causes and effects. Single paragraphs within those chapters may be organized in the same way. Often, there is a mixing of these three patterns within both single paragraphs and longer selections. However, generally you can see a predominant pattern within paragraphs of longer selections.

Cause and Effect

The *cause and effect* pattern shows a relationship between events. We connect causes with effects every day. For example, members of the baby boom generation, who had delayed starting their families, are now parents of school-age children. This change in the American family unit has caused an increase in school enrollment and has slowed the school closings that were characteristic of the 1970s and 1980s. Several results came from the single cause: increase in family size. Some are shown below.

Cause	Effect
1. increase in number of children	increase in enrollments
2. increase in school enrollments	greater need for teachers

What effect might come from the cause shown below? Write one.

Cause	Effect
3. greater need for teachers	_____
	_____
	_____

You may have written "higher salaries for teachers" since a low supply (in this case teachers) leads to higher salaries. You can probably think of other causes and effects stemming from this occurrence. For example, higher salaries for teachers (cause) might mean that more people will enter the field of education (effect). Also, more students becoming teachers (cause) results in increased enrollments in departments of education at universities (effect).

As demonstrated here, events can sometimes lead to a chain of cause-and-effect relationships. Understanding cause and effect helps us understand everyday events and plan our actions in accordance with them.

Usually, effects *follow* causes in time. However, sometimes an effect appears in a sentence *before* the cause, even though the effect follows the cause in time. The statement below is an example of this inverted relationship:

effect
Depression, which is twice as common in women as in men, is believed to

cause
come from biochemical changes.

Rewrite the sentence above with the cause coming before the effect.

_____

_____

You should have written something like *Biochemical changes are believed to cause depression, which is twice as common in women as in men.*

> ### SKILL BUILDER: RECOGNIZING CAUSE-AND-EFFECT RELATIONSHIPS
>
> The cause-and-effect relationship is frequently signaled by key words such as *because, since, therefore, as a result, consequently, accordingly, if . . . then, led to, brought about, the outcome was, the end result was,* and *was responsible for.*

EXERCISE 16: CAUSE AND EFFECT

Directions: Read the passage below. Then write the letter of each effect in the space next to its cause.

In 1961, during the cold war, the Peace Corps was established by President John Kennedy because he saw a need to expose U.S. citizens to citizens of developing Third World nations. The achievement of world peace and friendship were the intended goals of the humanitarian efforts of American volunteers.

The Peace Corps was such a success that in 1964 VISTA (Volunteers in Service to America) was founded to foster goodwill among different cultures *within* the United States. A decline in federal funding, however, contributed to the abandonment of VISTA in the early 1980s.

In 1993, President Clinton hoped to introduce a form of mandatory community service for young Americans, especially as a means of repaying millions of dollars worth of college loans.

Cause	Effect
____ 1. Kennedy's belief in a need to expose Americans to Third World nations	(a) beginning of VISTA in 1964
____ 2. the success of the Peace Corps	(b) discontinuation of VISTA in the 1980s
____ 3. a decline in federal funding	(c) would help to repay expensive tuition loans
____ 4. the concept of mandatory community service for all young Americans	(d) establishment of the Peace Corps in 1961

Answers are on page 241.

EXERCISE 17: ORGANIZING PARAGRAPHS

Directions: Read the effects below. Then write *yes* for the possible causes around which a paragraph could be organized and *no* for those that could not be a paragraph topic.

1. **Effect:** The population of the world has continued to grow rapidly.

    ____ (a) Birth control devices are not available in some parts of the world.

    ____ (b) Most of the world's population subsists on vegetables and grains.

    ____ (c) Mankind's ability to grow more food and fight disease has improved.

2. **Effect:** Gasoline prices increased 35 cents per gallon.

    ____ (a) New energy sources were uncovered.

    ____ (b) Refinery costs rose by 21 percent.

    ____ (c) The cost of crude oil remained the same.

3. **Effect:** Congress passed legislation to stop pollution of our major waterways.

    ____ (a) The quality of water tested in rivers near major cities was poor.

    ____ (b) Conservation groups in favor of the act sent petitions with thousands of signatures to their senators.

    ____ (c) The president, during a campaign speech, said that he favored an anti–water pollution act.

Answers are on page 241.

Comparison and Contrast

A writer uses the comparison/contrast pattern to explain or show the similarities and differences among ideas, people, or things. A writer who points out how two or more things are alike is making a *comparison*; one who points out how they are different is using *contrast*.

EXERCISE 18: COMPARISON AND CONTRAST

Directions: Read the following passage in which the writer compares and contrasts two modern presidents—Franklin D. Roosevelt and Ronald Reagan. Then fill in the blanks with the appropriate comparison and contrast phrases. The first two are done for you. As you are reading, keep in mind the following: does the writer compare these two presidents first or contrast them?

During the presidential campaign of 1980, Ronald Reagan lauded Franklin Delano Roosevelt as his political hero. On the face of it, this fact is hard to believe, given the sharp differences between the two.

President Roosevelt, a liberal Democrat, founded the social security system to provide a worry-free retirement for the nation's elderly. President Reagan, a conservative Republican, was criticized for trying to weaken the program. President Roosevelt's New Deal legislation provided for the regulation of banks and other financial institutions; under the Reagan administration, these institutions were greatly deregulated. President Roosevelt's administration set the minimum-wage law; President Reagan's administration favored abandoning it for teenagers. Labor organizations were encouraged under the Roosevelt administration and thrived; labor organizations were weakened and threatened under the Reagan administration.

Despite these differences, there are striking similarities between the two men. Roosevelt, an extremely popular leader, became president in the midst of economic despair. Reagan, an equally popular leader, became president when the country was suffering from a *malaise* and economic problems. Roosevelt was a persuasive politician and a strong communicator; Reagan's nickname was the "Great Communicator" because of his skill in handling the media. Both men were reelected to the presidency after huge landslides. The legislation of the New Deal affected the lives of many Americans, and as of the 1990s the effects of the "Reagan Revolution" seem likely to have a similar impact, for better or worse, on generations to come.

Roosevelt, a man from a wealthy background who became a champion of the "little people," is considered one of America's few great presidents. Will Ronald Reagan, a man from a modest background who became the "champion of big business," be accorded the same honor? Only time will tell.

Contrasting Words and Phrases (Differences)

Roosevelt	Reagan
1. *liberal Democrat*	1. *conservative Republican*
2. *founded social security*	2. *criticized for weakening it*
3. _____	3. _____
4. _____	4. _____
5. _____	5. _____
6. _____	6. _____
7. _____	7. _____

Comparative Words and Phrases (Similarities)

1. _Both were popular presidents._
2. _Both came to power after economic problems._
3. _____
4. _____
5. _____

Answers are on page 241.

SKILL BUILDER: IDENTIFYING COMPARISON AND CONTRAST PATTERNS

Words and phrases that signal comparisons include *like, likewise, also, similarly, on the one hand, in the same way* or *fashion,* and *compared to.*

Words and phrases that signal contrasts include *however, but, on the other hand, differently, on the contrary, while, although, yet, conversely, on the other side of the coin, versus, in contrast to,* and *either . . . or.*

EXERCISE 19: CONTRAST IN AN ESSAY

Directions: Read the following essay and list the four pairs of contrasting phrases contained in it. *Hint:* It helps to underline them as you read.

Television as a medium is a mixed blessing. Many people hold opposing views toward this powerful fixture in the American home. For some, it is a tasteful and exciting way to entertain; for others, an insult to standards of good taste. Television can be a captivating means to teach the young or a mindless, uninspiring babysitter. For some, the "tube" can bring important and accurate news of the moment, but for others it can spew trivia and "happy talk" that does not match the quality of newspapers and magazines.

While television commercials make a healthy contribution to society by helping consumers make intelligent buying decisions, commercials also plant seeds of dissatisfaction in viewers, making them crave what the advertisers sell.

1. _____ *vs.* _____

2. _____ *vs.* _____
   _____   _____

3. _____ *vs.* _____
   _____   _____

4. _____ *vs.* _____
   _____   _____

Answers are on page 241.

Sequence

Often, writers organize their works on the basis of *sequence*, sometimes known as *time order*. With this pattern of organization, events follow a series. Sequence is especially common in social studies when a writer describes historical events. It is also used widely in science writing to outline the steps in an experiment. Sequence is used as a pattern of organization in literature as well. In novels, short stories, and plays, plot events must follow a sequence. Often, this sequence has a cause-and-effect pattern.

SKILL BUILDER: RECOGNIZING SEQUENCE IN A PASSAGE

Some words and phrases that signal sequence include *on (a certain date— e.g., January 1), not long after, now, before, next, then, when, first, second,* and *third*.

EXERCISE 20: RECOGNIZING SEQUENCE

An *allegory* is a story in which the characters are symbolic; that is, they stand for abstract qualities. The plot events in an allegory reveal a truth or generalization about life. An example of a symbol would be a lion (concrete object) standing for courage (abstract quality).

Directions: Read the following summary of the famous short story "The Devil and Daniel Webster" by Stephen Vincent Benét. Then write *1* for the event that occurs first, *2* for the event that occurs second and so on.

The tale begins in New Hampshire during the time of Daniel Webster, a great lawyer and orator who aspired to be president of the United States. A local farmer, Jabez Stone, gets tired of poor crops and lack of prosperity. Enter the stranger, a lawyer, Mr. Scratch, who offers Stone a trade guaranteed to make him prosperous. Mr. Scratch then draws up a contract. Jabez Stone pricks his finger and signs with his blood. Afterward, every year for six years, the stranger visits Stone to remind him of the contract.

On the seventh year, the stranger comes to collect. Jabez Stone pleads for and receives a three-year extension. After the years pass, it is time for him to surrender the deed. Jabez Stone then goes to Daniel Webster to ask him to plead his case. When Daniel Webster visits Stone, the stranger appears.

The two argue strongly, but the stranger demands his due. Daniel Webster then asks for a trial including a courtroom, judge, and jury. Twelve men enter who have come from afar and who have the "fires of hell still upon them."

After Daniel Webster pleads the case all night, the defense rests. The jury finds for the defendant, Jabez Stone, and the judge and jury leave. Finally, the stranger signs a document promising never to bother Jabez Stone and is never seen in New Hampshire again.

_____ **1.** The stranger visits Jabez Stone to remind him of his contract.

_____ **2.** Twelve men with the "fires of hell still upon them" hear the case.

_____ **3.** Jabez Stone tires of his lack of prosperity.

_____ **4.** Daniel Webster argues with Mr. Scratch at Stone's house.

_____ **5.** Jabez Stone strikes a bargain with Mr. Scratch and signs in blood.

_____ **6.** Daniel Webster agrees to plead Jabez Stone's case.

_____ **7.** Mr. Scratch leaves New Hampshire and is never seen again.

_____ **8.** Mr. Scratch finally comes to collect from Jabez Stone.

_____ **9.** The jury rules in favor of Jabez Stone.

_____ **10.** Stone pleads for and gets a three-year extension.

Answers are on page 241.

EXERCISE 21: SYMBOLS IN ALLEGORY

Directions: Fill in the blanks with the correct answer from the plot summary of "The Devil and Daniel Webster."

1. The devil is _____.

2. Jabez Stone's selling his soul to the devil is demonstrated by Stone's agreement

to _____.

3. Jabez Stone's death sentence is represented by the devil coming to collect after

_____.

4. The twelve men who have come from hell are the _____

_____.

5. The fight between good and evil is shown by _____

arguing with _____.

Answers are on page 241.

2
INTERPRETING GRAPHS AND ILLUSTRATIONS

About one-third of the questions on the Science, Social Studies, and Mathematics Tests will be based on graphics. Many of the exercises later in this book are based on illustrations. Throughout this book and on the GED Test, you will need to understand how a writer uses pictorial information to support a point. The types of graphics that will appear on the test include graphs, maps, tables, and editorial cartoons.

To read and interpret graphic materials, you must pay close attention to all of the information that is given in both pictures and words. This means that you must look at how the material is labeled and the types of figures and numbers used. You may be asked to locate a particular number or fact, or you may be required to make an interpretation such as stating the main idea, reading between the lines, or drawing a conclusion.

Interpreting Graphs

A graph is a simple and clear way of presenting facts. Reading passages that include a lot of facts and figures can be difficult to understand, so writers often include graphs to help the reader understand the subject better. The types of graphs that are used to present information pictorially are pictographs, line graphs, bar graphs, and circle or pie graphs.

Pictographs

Pictographs are the simplest form of graphs. *Pictographs* use symbols to show how certain quantities of a thing compare. Some common symbols used in pictographs represent people, cars, houses, and dollars. Whole symbols and partial symbols may be used in a pictograph. Like all graphs, pictographs have a *title* that gives the main idea.

A *key* that shows the amount that each symbol stands for is always provided to help the reader interpret the graph. The pictograph on page 224 illustrates the growth of the world's population, estimated from the year A.D. 1.

WORLD POPULATION GROWTH A.D. 1 TO 1992

Source: *The World Almanac and Book of Facts, 1993 edition*

What was the world's population in 1650?

Look at the key. It indicates that the symbol of one person stands for 1 billion people. The symbol representing the population for the year 1650 is one-half of a person; therefore, the population of the world was approximately **half a billion (500,000,000) people**.

The greatest increase in the world's population occurred during which time period?

According to the pictograph,

- between A.D. 1 and 1650, world population grew from 200 million to 500 million;
- between 1650 and 1750, the world's population grew from 500 million to 725 million;
- from 1750 to 1850, population increased from 725 million to 1 billion people;
- from 1850 to 1950, the number of people in the world went from 1 billion to 3 billion;
- finally, between 1950 and 1992, the world's population grew from 3 billion to almost 5.5 billion.

Therefore, the greatest total increase in the number of people in the world occurred **between 1950 and 1992**.

Line Graphs

Line graphs are generally used to show a relationship among two or more things. They are used particularly to show a change in the quantity of something in relation to dates, years, or fixed amounts. Line graphs are especially helpful in showing trends at a glance. Look at the line graph below.

AVERAGE MONTHLY TEMPERATURES

Notice that the graph has a title, "Average Monthly Temperatures." This tells you the topic. The labels at the ends of the lines tell you that the cities San Francisco and Chicago are being compared.

The graph has numbers going up the left side of the graph (the *vertical axis*); these numbers are temperatures in degrees Fahrenheit. Also, the graph shows the twelve months of the year going across the bottom (the *horizontal axis*). The "picture" on the graph is created by connecting the points that stand for temperatures during each month of the year. As each point is connected, a line is formed; this is why such a graph is known as a *line graph.* Let's answer some questions based on this graph.

1. What is the temperature of San Francisco in July? Is it colder or warmer than Chicago's?

   To find the answer, place your finger at the point indicating July on the broken line representing San Francisco. Now look to the left at the vertical axis.

   The answer is 60 degrees Fahrenheit—the temperature for San Francisco in July.

   Follow the same procedure for Chicago. (The solid line represents Chicago.)

   The answer is about 72 degrees Fahrenheit; therefore, **it is colder in San Francisco than in Chicago at that same time of the year**. Notice that you may need to approximate values on line graphs—your answers may fall between the labeled points on the vertical axis.

2. Which city has the greater range in temperature; that is, which has the greater extreme from the lowest temperature to the highest?

   To find the answer, scan the graph to find the lowest point for each city. The lowest temperature would occur during January. Compare this temperature with the highest point for each city. The highest temperature would occur during July for Chicago and September for San Francisco.

The lowest average temperature in January for San Francisco is nearly 50 degrees; the highest average temperature in September is nearly 60 degrees. The lowest average temperature in January for Chicago is nearly 25 degrees; the highest average temperature in July is nearly 75 degrees. The extreme from 25 degrees to 75 degrees is greater than that from 50 degrees to 60 degrees. Therefore, **Chicago has the greater range in temperature**.

3. During which months do Chicago and San Francisco have almost the same average temperatures?

Scan the graph. Focus on the points where both lines come the closest and meet. The lines meet near the months of **May and September**.

EXERCISE 1: INTERPRETING LINE GRAPHS

Directions: Read the passage below and answer the questions based on the graph "Average Monthly Temperatures" on page 225.

1. For line graphs, a bell-shaped curve represents a normal distribution; in other words, the curve represents what one would expect as normal when a great number of instances are observed. When a great number of values are plotted as points on a graph, about half of the points will fall into the middle range of the graph and an equal number will fall at the extremes (the left and right ends of the graph). Of the two cities examined in the graph on page 225, Chicago's temperatures generally follow a bell-shaped curve. This fact suggests that

   A. San Francisco's average temperature distribution is not considered normal compared to that of most U.S. cities.

   B. Chicago's average temperature distribution is likely to be more representative of other U.S. cities than San Francisco's.

   C. Chicago's average temperature distribution is considered abnormal.

   D. San Francisco enjoys better weather than most other cities.
      (1) A
      (2) B
      (3) A and B
      (4) D
      (5) A and C

2. Which of the following cities is *most* likely to have an average temperature distribution more like Chicago's than San Francisco's?

   (1) Los Angeles
   (2) Miami
   (3) Detroit
   (4) Anchorage
   (5) New Orleans

Answers are on page 241.

EXERCISE 2: MORE ON INTERPRETING LINE GRAPHS

Directions: Study the graph below and answer the questions that follow.

PAPER INDUSTRY PROFITS/LOSSES

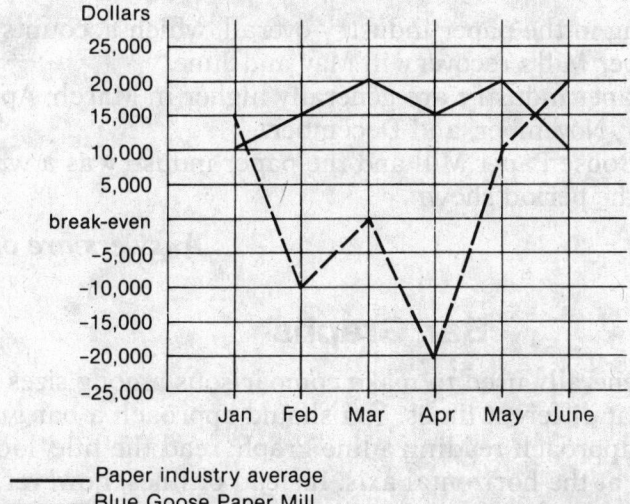

_____ Paper industry average
– – – – – Blue Goose Paper Mill

1. During how many months shown on the graph did the Blue Goose Paper Mill lose money?

   (1) none   **(2)** 1   **(3)** 2   **(4)** 3   **(5)** 4

2. In which month(s) did the Blue Goose Paper Mill exceed the industry average in profits?

   (1) January only
   (2) February, March, April, and May
   (3) June only
   (4) February and April
   (5) January and June

3. During the six-month period, the paper industry as a whole showed

   (1) profits and losses similar to that of the Blue Goose Paper Mill
   (2) average profits of between $10,000 and $20,000 per month
   (3) signs of a dangerous financial crisis
   (4) greater losses than the Blue Goose Paper Mill
   (5) better profits than in the previous six-month period

4. In which month was there the greatest difference between the industry's average profit/loss and that of the Blue Goose Paper Mill?

   (1) January
   (2) February
   (3) March
   (4) April
   (5) June

5. Which of the following statements best summarizes the data on the graph?

(1) The paper industry as a whole was profitable every month, but the Blue Goose Paper Mill showed wide variations from month to month.

(2) The Blue Goose Paper Mill will probably fold as a result of its heavy losses.

(3) Profits are rising in the paper industry overall, which accounts for the Blue Goose Paper Mill's recovery in May and June.

(4) Profits in the paper industry are generally higher in March, April, and May than in October, November, and December.

(5) Both the Blue Goose Paper Mill and the paper industry as a whole lost money during the period shown.

Answers are on page 241.

Bar Graphs

Bar graphs are generally used to make comparisons among sizes or quantities of similar items at different times. You should approach a bar graph the same way you would approach reading a line graph: read the title, look at the vertical axis, and look at the horizontal axis. Instead of lines, however, a bar graph uses bars or rectangular blocks running either vertically or horizontally. Sometimes a bar graph includes a key. The key is used when two or more sets of information are being compared as in Exercise 4 on pages 229–230.

Look at the bar graph below, "Number of Persons 65+: 1900–2050"

NUMBER OF PERSONS 65+:
1900–2050
(in millions)

Year (as of July 1)

Note: Increments in years on horizontal scale are uneven.

Based on data from U.S. Bureau of the Census

In what year is the percentage of persons 65 and over expected to double the figure shown for 1980?

Looking at the graph, you can see that the percentage of persons 65 years and older in 1980 was 25.7 percent of the population. If this figure is doubled, the percentage will be 51.4 percent. The year for which the percentage of persons 65+ reaches 51.4 is **2020** on the graph.

EXERCISE 3: INTERPRETING BAR GRAPHS

Directions: Answer the following question based on the preceding graph and the information provided below.

The growth of America's older population is expected to slow somewhat during the 1990s but is expected to increase rapidly after the year 2000. Which of the following implications can be drawn from these facts?

A. A relatively small number of babies were born during the Depression years of the 1930s; these people will be turning 65 in the 1990s.

B. A relatively large number of Americans born during the 1930s were killed in the Korean War.

C. A relatively large number of babies were born between the years 1940 and 1960; these people, called the *baby boom generation*, will be turning 65 between 2005 and 2025.

(1) A   **(2)** B   **(3)** C   **(4)** A and C   **(5)** B and C

Answer is on page 242.

EXERCISE 4: MORE ON READING BAR GRAPHS

Directions: Study the bar graph below and answer the questions that follow.

MARITAL STATUS OF PERSONS 65+: 1990

Based on data from U.S. Bureau of the Census

1. The figures in the bar graph tend to support the fact that

   (1) men 65 years or older were three times as likely to be married as women 65 years or older
   (2) women 65 years or older were twice as likely to be married as men 65 years or older
   (3) men 65 years or older were nearly twice as likely to be married as women 65 years or older
   (4) the percentages of older men and women who were likely to be married are equal
   (5) more women 65 years or older were married than men who were 65 years or older

2. From the percentages of older men and women who were widowed as of 1990, we can infer that

(1) older men who were married outlived their wives
(2) older women who were married outlived their husbands
(3) older men who were widowed represented the smallest segment of the older population
(4) the percentage of older women who were widowed was higher than the number of married, single, and divorced women combined
(5) the percentage of older men who were widowed was lower than the number of single and divorced men combined

3. Which of the following statements was true in 1990 according to the graph?

A. Nearly half of all older women were widows.
B. More than three-fourths of all older men were widowers.
C. More than three-fourths of all older men were married.
D. Half of all older women were married.

(1) A and B
(2) A and C
(3) B and D
(4) C and D
(5) D

Answers are on page 242.

Circle Graphs

Circle or *pie graphs* show important pieces of information as parts of a whole. Each slice is labeled and represents a percentage (part of the whole). All of the slices must add up to 100 percent. Sometimes a knowledge of basic arithmetic is necessary to answer questions based on a pie graph. A pie graph has a title that gives you the main topic. Like some bar graphs, some pie graphs also provide a key to help you understand what the information being shown means. Look at the pie graphs "Living Arrangements of Persons 65+: 1990."

LIVING ARRANGEMENTS OF PERSONS 65+: 1990

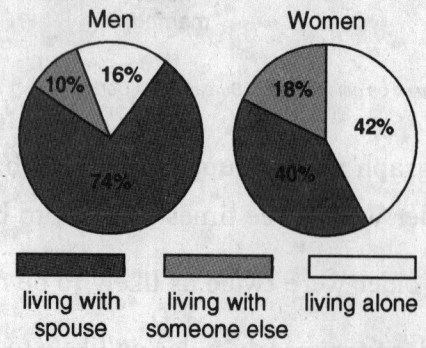

Based on data from U.S. Bureau of the Census

What percentage of men 65 years and older live in a family or group setting?

To answer this question, you must look at the pie graph labeled "Men" and look at the key. The key distinguishes among those men living with a spouse, those living with someone else, and those living alone. Add the percentage of men living with a spouse (74%) to those living with someone else (10%) to determine the total number living in a family or group setting—**84 percent.**

Do more older men than older women live in family settings?

Follow the same procedure with the pie graph labeled "Women." Add the percentage of those living with spouses (40%) to the percentage living with someone else (18%). Then compare the figure for men with the one for women (84% to 58%). The answer is **yes**; more men live in family or group settings than women—26 percent more.

EXERCISE 5: READING PIE GRAPHS

Directions: Compare the information in the bar graph titled "Marital Status of Persons 65+: 1990" on page 229 with the information in the pie graph "Living Arrangements of Persons 65+: 1990" on page 230, then answer the question below:

Generally, the facts in the pie graph "Living Arrangements of Persons 65+"

(1) dispute the figures contained in the "married" category of the graph "Marital Status of Persons 65+"
(2) have no relationship at all to the figures in the "married" category of the graph "Marital Status of Persons 65+"
(3) support the figures shown in the "married" category of the graph "Marital Status of Persons 65+"
(4) show that the divorced men and women whose numbers are illustrated in the bar graph are living alone
(5) demonstrate that all the people living in group facilities are widowed

Answer is on page 242.

Maps

Maps are another way of presenting pictorial information. Maps can provide a variety of information about a place. Like graphs, maps have a title that tells you what the focus of the map is. A *key* or *legend* explains the symbols that the map contains. Maps that require you to measure a distance have a scale of miles that you can use as a guide to find the distance between two points. Before you answer questions pertaining to a map, take time to study the map and the key that goes with it.

The map on page 232 is a demographic map. A *demographic* map shows the distribution of a certain segment of a population. The map on the next page shows the percentage change of the U.S. population 65 years or older between the years 1980 and 1990.

According to the map, how many states experienced the greatest percentage change in population from 1980 to 1990?

To answer this question, consult the key to find out which code stands for the greatest percentage change. The code with the greatest percentage change is 20 percent or more. Note the particular shading for that code and count the number of states that are filled in with exactly that shading. You will find that **six states** experienced 20 percent change in population or more. These states are California, Nevada, Arizona, Alaska, Florida, and New Hampshire.

POPULATION CHANGE, 1980–1990

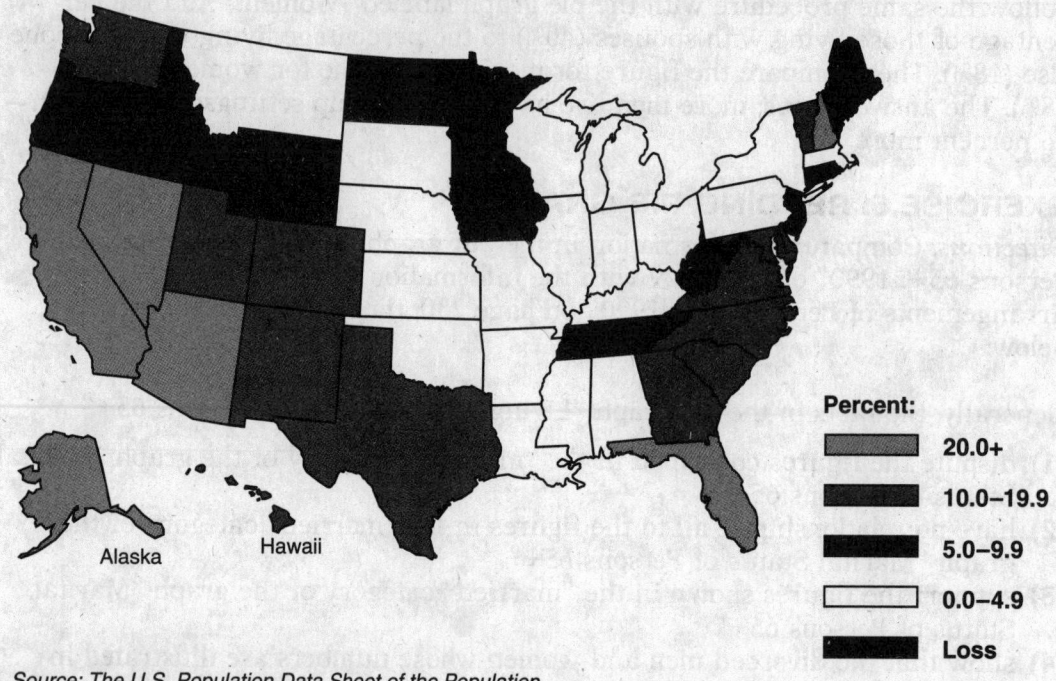

Alaska   Hawaii

Percent:	
	20.0+
	10.0–19.9
	5.0–9.9
	0.0–4.9
	Loss

Source: The U.S. Population Data Sheet of the Population Reference Bureau, Inc., Ninth Edition

EXERCISE 6: INTERPRETING MAPS

Directions: Look at the map above and answer the following questions.

1. The map could be used to support which of the following facts?

    (1) Florida's climate and lifestyle are more desirable than Alaska's.
    (2) The same number of states lost population as gained.
    (3) The smallest percentage of change occurred primarily in the north and central parts of the United States.
    (4) Alaska experienced an economic boom in the 1980s.
    (5) Hawaii and Alaska are farther away than any of the other states.

2. How many states experienced the moderate percentage growth of 5–9.9 percent?

    (1) eleven
    (2) four
    (3) twenty-two
    (4) eight
    (5) five

3. For the entire United States, the percentage change in population between 1980 and 1990 was 9.9 percent. How many states were above the national average in percentage change?

    (1) thirteen
    (2) seven
    (3) four
    (4) nineteen
    (5) six

4. Which statement can be inferred from the information given in the map?

  (1) Generally, the midwestern and central states have a fairly stable population.
  (2) Everyone who moves to a different state wants a warmer climate.
  (3) More states had 10–19.9 percent population growth than experienced less than 5 percent growth.
  (4) California farmers cannot grow the same kinds of crops in the Midwest as they can produce in their own state.
  (5) Fewer states gained population than lost population.

5. Which category of states among the five percentage groups on the population change map has no state bordering an ocean?

  (1) 5–9.9 percent
  (2) Loss
  (3) 0–4.9 percent
  (4) 10.0–19.9 percent
  (5) 20+ percent

Answers are on page 242.

Tables

A *table* is an organization of many facts into a small space. Tables are used to keep scores in games, list train schedules, assign work tasks, compare weather reports, and so on. A table has a title at the top. The separate columns and rows within it are also labeled so that you will know what information the table contains. Look at the table below.

**MARRIAGES AND DIVORCES
IN THE UNITED STATES
(Per 1,000 People)**

Year	Marriages	Divorces
1930	9.2	1.6
1940	12.1	2.0
1950	11.1	2.6
1960	8.5	2.2
1970	10.6	3.5
1980	10.6	5.2
1990	9.8	4.7

The title tells you that the table is about the number of marriages and divorces per 1,000 people in the United States. The row headings give the decades (beginning with 1930 and ending with 1990). The column headings give the number of marriages and the number of divorces. Study the table and answer the following questions.

During which decades was the number of marriages stable?

Stable means showing no change. If you scan the table to find the decades during which the number of marriages per 1,000 people remained unchanged, you will see that in the decades **1970 and 1980** the number of marriages per 1,000 people was 10.6.

Between which decades was there a decrease in both the number of marriages and the number of divorces per 1,000 people?

If you examine each ten-year interval, you will notice that **between 1950 and 1960** and **between 1980 and 1990** both the number of marriages and the number of divorces decreased. In the year 1950, the number of marriages was 11.1; it decreased to 8.5 by 1960. In the year 1950, the number of divorces was 2.6; it decreased to 2.2 by 1960. In the year 1980, the number of marriages was 10.6; it decreased to 9.8 by 1990. In the year 1980, the number of divorces was 5.2; it decreased to 4.7 by 1990.

EXERCISE 7: READING TABLES

Directions: Look at the table below and answer the questions that follow.

FORECAST OF POPULATION INCREASE, 1975–2000
(In Millions)

	Population		Increases, 1975–2000	
	1975	2000	Absolute	Percent
Anglo-America	242	295	53	22
Europe	474	540	66	14
former Soviet Union	254	314	60	24
Oceania	21	33	12	57
Subtotal	991	1,182	191	19
Latin America	328	610	282	86
Asia	2,407	3,800	1,393	58
Africa	420	830	410	98
Subtotal	3,155	5,240	2,085	66
World Total	4,146	6,422	2,276	55

1. According to the table, which area of the world will have the largest absolute increase in population between 1975 and 2000?

   (1) Anglo-America
   (2) former Soviet Union
   (3) Latin America
   (4) Asia
   (5) Africa

2. By what percentage is the population of the world projected to increase between 1975 and 2000?

   (1) 19
   (2) 2,276
   (3) 55
   (4) 191
   (5) 22

3. Which area of the world is projected to have the smallest percentage population increase between 1975 and 2000?

   (1) Anglo-America
   (2) Asia
   (3) Europe
   (4) Oceania
   (5) Africa

4. Which area of the world is projected to nearly double its population between 1975 and 2000?

   (1) Africa
   (2) former Soviet Union
   (3) Anglo-America
   (4) Asia
   (5) Europe

5. Which two areas expect the lowest percentage increase?

   (1) Oceania and Asia
   (2) former Soviet Union and Anglo-America
   (3) Latin America and Africa
   (4) Anglo-America and Europe
   (5) Asia and Africa

Answers are on page 243.

Editorial Cartoons

An *editorial cartoon* expresses the opinion of the cartoonist toward a political or social issue. Editorial cartoons often caricature (depict in cartoon figures) politicians or statesmen. The caricatures usually exaggerate a feature of the person being illustrated. For example, Ronald Reagan's dark hair, Jimmy Carter's toothy smile, and President Bill Clinton's full face and chin have been widely caricatured.

Political symbols are often used as well. For example, the donkey represents the Democratic party, an elephant represents the Republican party, a bearded man dressed in stars and stripes (Uncle Sam) represents the United States, a dove represents peace, and a hawk represents war. Cartoonists often use humor to express their opinions on important issues affecting our country and world.

Look at the political cartoon below. Notice that the cartoon is divided in half. The top half shows a line of unemployed people waiting to apply for benefits. Many of the people are complaining about the lack of jobs and criticizing the government and its leaders.

The bottom half of the cartoon, however, shows an empty polling place on election day. By placing the two illustrations together, the cartoonist is making a statement suggesting that, while citizens are quick to criticize the government, when it comes to making their voices heard at the ballot box they are silent— they don't show up to vote.

The exercise on page 237 will give you a chance to practice your skill in interpreting editorial cartoons.

EXERCISE 8: INTERPRETING EDITORIAL CARTOONS

Directions: Study the cartoon below and answer the questions that follow.

1. The cartoon appeared in 1992 during a long period of public dissatisfaction with American education. How do you think the cartoonist would like to influence our thinking about education?

   (1) We ought to work toward making American schools better by keeping Europeans and Asians out.
   (2) We ought to try to stimulate American students' interests in the same educational pursuits as their Asian and European counterparts.
   (3) We should emphasize athletics more in American schools because things such as tennis shoes and sports competitions are typically American.
   (4) European and Asian students should be urged to compete harder in sports.
   (5) European and Asian students should be encouraged to participate more in sports and entertainment.

2. The cartoonist is suggesting that

   (1) Asian, European, and American students think about similar problems
   (2) American and Asian students compete heavily with European students
   (3) the brains of students everywhere are about the same size
   (4) the minds of American students are centered on trivial interests compared to the minds of Asian and European students
   (5) Physics and biology are more important than chemistry and algebra

3. From your understanding of the cartoon, what inferences can you make about American culture?

   (1) We need a lot more Asian and European teachers to set standards.
   (2) Families ought to go to classes and try to learn together.
   (3) Our society needs to stress academics more than athletics.
   (4) European and American students are behind Asians in academic achievement.
   (5) Education will be at its best if we all cooperate and work together.

Answers are on page 243.

READING SKILLS FOR THE GED
ANSWER KEY

CHAPTER 1: CRITICAL THINKING SKILLS
Exercise 1: Understanding Idiomatic Expressions
page 190
Exact wording may vary.
1. review
2. become cautious
3. out of money
4. She really wanted to go
5. overwhelmed by the amount of
6. tired *or* out of breath
7. take care of
8. tried to do more than she could
9. meet her expenses
10. occurred to her
11. admit defeat
12. stay at home

Exercise 2: Reading Between the Lines
page 193
1. (2) Clues from the passage are "The gift is something that native-born American children take for granted"; "[he] hid there for five days to avoid leaving the United States against his will"; and "this gift is wrapped in yards of legal red tape."
2. (1) There are thousands of twelve-year-old elementary school boys in Chicago. However, this does not help you determine that he was seeking U.S. citizenship. Choices (2), (3), (4), and (5) do lead to that conclusion.

Exercise 3: Restating Ideas
pages 194–195
Answers will vary.
1. Another way to express the principle of stimulus-response is to say that if you touch or attack something, it will react.
2. The dispute over the Constitution developed between the Federalists, who wanted a strong central government, and the anti-Federalists, who feared it.
3. Don't buy a new car without checking it out in a car magazine or consumer guide.
4. When you make a payment on your credit card, the money pays off any amounts that you owe in fees and finance charges first. After those charges are fully paid, the remaining amount you paid goes toward the actual things you bought and charged.
5. The company promises that if anything goes wrong with your TV set within 90 days after you buy it, the manufacturer will pay for the cost of the labor (no mention is made of the parts) to repair it, provided that (1) the damage was not your fault and (2) you bring it in or send it in at your own expense.

Exercise 4: Application in Social Studies
pages 197–198
1. (1) The text defines name-calling as attaching an unfavorable name to an idea, a person, or a group so as to influence the attitude of the audience against an idea or position. People who opposed Vice President Gore's strong stand on environmental protection called him "Mr. Ozone."
2. (5) The text defines card-stacking as choosing only specific, favorable points that support a cause and ignoring unfavorable points. The candidate focuses on the favorable points of increased employment, lowered taxes, and improved trade relationships and ignores the unfavorable issue of foreign policy failures.
3. (4) The text defines bandwagoning as advising people to do something because "everyone" does it. Neighbors were being urged to join the gang's illegal looting because everybody else was doing it.
4. (3) The teachers who oppose the extended school day are trying to influence the local council by associating their own views with the prestige of the national association's president.

Exercise 5: Application in Science
pages 198–199
1. (3) Of the five systems described, only the lymphatic system produces lymphocytes, whose antibodies help fight bacterial infections.
2. (1) According to the definition, the excretory system excretes or expels water and salts from the body. Perspiration is a form of water; therefore, the skin loosely belongs to the excretory system.
3. (2) According to the definition, the endocrine system is made up of glands that secrete body fluids that regulate the body's development. A teen's growth spurt can be explained by hormones released by the endocrine system.
4. (4) According to the definition, the digestive system processes and distributes nutrients from food. The first step in processing food involves moistening by saliva.

Exercise 6: Facts, Opinions, and Hypotheses
page 201

1. (a) **O** The statement is based on personal values.
   (b) **H** More time and information are needed to prove the statement.
   (c) **F** The statement can be proved by obtaining census data.

2. (a) **F** The statement can be proved by acquiring data.
   (b) **H** Time and data are needed to prove this statement.
   (c) **O** The statement reflects the personal beliefs of a certain group.

3. (a) **H** Time and data are needed to prove this prediction.
   (b) **O** The statement expresses personal beliefs.
   (c) **F** The statement is a fact that can be proved.

4. (a) **O** The statement expresses a personal belief based on certain values.
   (b) **F** The statement is a fact that can be proved by obtaining data on foreign car purchases.
   (c) **H** Time and data about foreign car purchases are needed to prove or disprove the statement.

5. (a) **F** The statement can be proved.
   (b) **H** The passage of time will help to prove or disprove the statement.
   (c) **O** The statement expresses a personal belief; the word *should* indicates that an opinion is being expressed.

Exercise 7: More on Facts, Opinions, and Hypotheses
page 202

1. **H** The passage estimates that by 2020 Hispanic-Americans will become the nation's largest minority. This is a hypothesis that can be proved only with the passage of time.

2. **O** The statement that Hispanic-American artists owe their success to great struggles is not mentioned in the passage. This is an opinion, not something that can be proved or disproved.

3. **F** The passage states that Hispanic-Americans came from Cuba and Puerto Rico.

4. **F** The passage states that President Clinton appointed two Hispanics to his White House Cabinet.

5. **O** The statement that the 1993 Cabinet appointees are the most effective leaders in America is a personal opinion. Others may agree or disagree.

6. **H** The prediction that twenty years from now Hispanic-Americans will live and work in every city in the United States can be proved only when statistics are gathered twenty years from now.

7. **O** The statement that people who come here from Mexico help to advance our culture is an opinion since it's based on a person's beliefs. Other people may believe differently about the statement.

Exercise 8: Hypotheses and the Scientific Method
page 204
Exact wording may vary.

1. *Problem:* Certain workers in the shipbuilding industry were developing cancer of the bronchial tubes.

2. *Information:* Not all the workers exposed to asbestos fibers developed cancer of the bronchial tubes.

3. *Hypothesis:* Cigarette smoking might increase a worker's chances of getting cancer of the bronchial tubes.

4. *Prediction:* If patients suffering from cancer of the bronchial tubes were polled, the results would indicate that they were heavy cigarette smokers.

5. *Observation:* The poll revealed that a very high percentage of the cancer patients were smokers.

6. *Conclusion:* Asbestos workers who are heavy cigarette smokers are more likely to get cancer of the bronchial tubes than those who are not.

Exercise 9: More on Hypotheses and the Scientific Method
page 205
Exact wording may vary.

1. *Problem:* Rain forests are being destroyed.

2. *Information:* In the Amazon rain forest, evaporation from plants and soil accounts for half of all the water that falls there.

3. *Hypothesis:* The removal of plants from the ecosystem may disrupt the cycle, causing less water to be evaporated.

4. *Prediction:* If scientists could create the conditions of the rain forest, their results would show that removing plants would affect the weather and, in turn, future plant growth.

5. *Observation:* The experiment showed that clearing the rain forest land would reduce rainfall by 25 percent and increase average temperatures by 5°F.

6. *Conclusion:* Clearing away the rain forest would affect the weather, making future growth of rain forest plants unlikely.

Exercise 10: Deductive Reasoning
pages 206–207

1. yes A cerebral hemorrhage results from the bursting (rupture) of a brain artery.

2. yes An embolism results from the blockage (obstruction) of a blood vessel; if the embolism is found in an artery of the brain, it can lead to a stroke.

3. no A tumor is not a rupture or an obstruction of an artery of the brain.

4. yes An aneurysm is a blood-filled swelling of a vessel (artery). The rupture of an aneurysm can lead to a stroke.

5. no Phlebitis results from the swelling of a vein, not an artery of the brain.

Exercise 11: Faulty Reasoning and Unstated Assumptions
page 208
Exact wording may vary.

1. high school dropouts *or* high school age *or* teenagers

2. competent *or* qualified

3. widespread *or* common *or* rampant

4. air pollution

5. drug abuse *or* taking drugs

Exercise 12: Style and Tone
pages 209–210

1. (2) Wilhelm tells his father, "You always start out to help me with my problems, and be sympathetic. . . . It gets my hopes up and I begin to be grateful. But before we're through I'm a hundred times more depressed than before." The author uses this style of dialogue to show that Wilhelm is suffering emotionally.

2. (3) " 'It's always the same. . . . Look how you lead me on. . . . There ought to be a right way to do this, and be fair to each other. . . . why do you start up with me if you're not going to help me?' . . . Wilhelm had a great knot of wrong tied tight within his chest, and tears approached his eyes but he didn't let them out." These words suggest a tragic tone.

3. (4) The dialogue in this excerpt conveys a real-life situation.

4. (1) The son's desperate tone and the choice of words in the excerpt indicate that the relationship has had a history of conflict.

5. (1) Wilhelm has a knot "tied tight within his chest," he's stammering, and he's unable to express his real feelings. This suggests that he is struggling with external and internal conflicts— with himself and with his father.

Exercise 13: Evaluating Ideas
pages 212–213

1. The writer describes good game shows as simple, novel, involving, suspenseful, participatory, and fostering viewer identification.

2. (2) Of the three forms of literature shown, fiction—novels and short stories—shares many criteria with good game shows. The criteria that they share are novelty, involvement, suspense, and participation. Also, readers of novels and short stories must be able to identify with the characters.

3. (3) The article says that hosting a game show requires both technical and personal skills. The other choices are not mentioned in the article.

4. (2) The quote refers to characteristics that are hard to explain and describe, such as the ability to think on your feet, as well as having charm and a good sense of humor. All of these qualities may be described as subjective, nonmeasurable characteristics.

5. (2) The only statement that is supported by the article is that game shows have had a long history in television.

Exercise 14: Adequacy of Facts
page 214

1. F The writer has supported his view that the building will not open up any new rental units. He cites the fact that it will consist solely of resident-owned condominiums rather than rental units.

2. N The writer assumes that the development company will not use local workers or business, but he provides no evidence.

3. F The writer cites evidence that the mayor and her staff refused three times to meet with community groups.

4. N The writer assumes, but does not support his allegation, that the construction company has influenced the mayor with cash donations.

Exercise 15: The Role of Values and Beliefs
page 215
Exact wording may vary.

1. Myrna has to choose between her desire to marry Sam on the one hand and her loyalty to her own family on the other.

2. The government of New Zealand must choose between its opposition to nuclear war and weapons and its loyalty to a trading partner and military ally.

3. A scientist who is approached to do genetic research must choose between the chance of advances in preventing birth defects and the possible danger of contributing to the creation of a "genetically superior" master race.

Exercise 16: Cause and Effect
pages 217–218
1. (d)   **2.** (a)   **3.** (b)   **4.** (c)

Exercise 17: Organizing Paragraphs
page 218
1. (a) yes   **2. (a)** no   **3. (a)** yes
   (b) no   **(b)** yes   **(b)** yes
   (c) yes   **(c)** no   **(c)** yes

Exercise 18: Comparison and Contrast
pages 219–220
Differences

Roosevelt	*Reagan*
1. liberal Democrat	1. conservative Republican
2. founded social security	2. criticized for weakening it
3. passed laws to regulate financial institutions	3. passed laws to deregulate financial institutions
4. set minimum-wage law	4. favored abandoning the minimum-wage law for teenagers
5. encouraged labor unions	5. weakened and threatened labor unions
6. champion of "little people"	6. champion of "big business"
7. had a wealthy background	7. had a modest background

Similarities
1. Both were popular presidents.
2. Both came to power after economic problems.
3. Both were persuasive politicians and strong communicators.
4. Both were reelected to office after landslides.
5. Both oversaw legislation that greatly affected the lives of Americans.

Exercise 19: Contrast in an Essay
page 220
1. tasteful and exciting *vs.* insult to standards of good taste
2. captivating means to teach the young *vs.* mindless, uninspiring babysitter
3. can bring important, accurate news *vs.* can spew trivia and "happy talk"
4. commercials help consumers make intelligent buying decisions *vs.* plants seeds of dissatisfaction

Exercise 20: Recognizing Sequence
pages 221–222
1. 3   **3.** 1   **5.** 2   **7.** 10   **9.** 9
2. 8   **4.** 7   **6.** 6   **8.** 5   **10.** 4

Exercise 21: Symbols in Allegory
page 222
1. Mr. Scratch, the stranger
2. sign a contract with Mr. Scratch
3. the tenth year
4. jury
5. Daniel Webster, Mr. Scratch

CHAPTER 2: INTERPRETING GRAPHS AND ILLUSTRATIONS
Exercise 1: Interpreting Line Graphs
page 226
1. (3) The passage says that a bell-shaped curve represents a normal distribution of information. Chicago's average temperature distribution conforms to a bell-shaped curve, but San Francisco's does not. Therefore, San Francisco's average temperature distribution is not considered representative of most U.S. cities (choice A). Moreover, if Chicago's average temperature distribution is considered to be normal, it is more likely to be representative of other U.S. cities than is San Francisco (choice B).
2. (3) Among the cities listed, Detroit, located in the Midwest, is the city closest to Chicago. Therefore, its climate would be most like Chicago's. Los Angeles, Miami, and New Orleans have higher average temperatures. Anchorage, located in Alaska, would have a lower average temperature than Chicago.

Exercise 2: More on Interpreting Line Graphs
pages 227–228
1. (3) For February and April, the points for the Blue Goose Paper Mill are below the break-even point, indicating a loss for the Blue Goose Paper Mill.
2. (5) At the beginning of January and June, the points for the Blue Goose Paper Mill are above the points for the industry average.
3. (2) The points for the paper industry average are all between $10,000 and $20,000.
4. (4) The widest distance between the point for the industry average and the point for the Blue Goose Paper Mill for the same month is in April, when there was a difference of $35,000.
5. (1) This is the only statement you can prove by using the data on the graph. The paper industry average remains consistently between $10,000 and $20,000, and the Blue Goose Paper Mill shows several large increases and decreases.

Exercise 3: Interpreting Bar Graphs
page 229

(4) Two implications can be drawn from the two sets of facts: during the 1990s the growth of America's older population is expected to slow, and after the year 2000 it is expected to increase rapidly. The implications are (1) that the relatively small number of babies born during the Depression years explains the reduced number of older Americans in the 1990s, and (2) the large number of babies born between the years 1940 and 1960 explains the increased number of older Americans expected after the year 2000.

Exercise 4: More on Reading Bar Graphs
pages 229–230

1. **(3)** According to the graph, 41 percent of women 65 years of age and older were married and 77 percent of men 65 years of age and older were married. The latter figure represents nearly double the percentage of married women 65 years of age and older.

2. **(2)** The figures in the graph show that the percentage of older women who were widowed (49%) is greater than the percentage of older men who were widowed (14%); therefore, you can infer that older women who were married outlived their husbands.

3. **(2)** The graph shows that nearly half (49%) of all older women in 1990 were widows and that more than three-fourths (77%) of all older men were married.

Exercise 5: Reading Pie Graphs
page 231

(3) The figures in the bar graph show that, in 1990, 77 percent of men 65 years of age and older were married; the figures in the pie graph show that 74 percent of men 65 years of age and older were living with a spouse. Moreover, the figures in the bar graph show that, in 1990, 41 percent of women 65 years of age and older were married; the figures in the pie graph show that 40 percent of women 65 years of age and older were living with a spouse. Therefore, the figures in the pie graph generally support those found in the bar graph.

Exercise 6: Interpreting Maps
pages 232–233

1. **(3)** Look at the key code that stands for the smallest percentage of change (0–4.9 percent) and note where most of the states with this shading are located. Many of them are in the central and northern parts of the country.

2. **(4)** Find the code that represents the 5–9.9 percent change and count the number of states filled in with that shading. Eight states show 5–9.9 percent change: Maine, Rhode Island, Connecticut, New Jersey, Minnesota, Tennessee, Idaho, and Oregon.

3. **(4)** If the national average is 9.9 percent, then all states in the 10–19.9 percent category and all states in the 20+% category must be counted above the average. Nineteen states are above the national average in percent of population change: New Hampshire, Vermont, Delaware, Maryland, Virginia, North Carolina, South Carolina, Florida, Georgia, Texas, Colorado, New Mexico, Arizona, Utah, Nevada, Washington, California, Alaska, and Hawaii.

4. **(1)** The category 0–4.9 percent change indicates stability. This means that few people have moved in or moved out. These states are Massachusetts, New York, Pennsylvania, Ohio, Indiana, Illinois, Michigan, Wisconsin, Missouri, South Dakota, Nebraska, Kansas, Kentucky, Alabama, Mississippi, Arkansas, Louisiana, Oklahoma, and Montana.

5. **(2)** By checking the states that border coastlines and then looking at all the others, you can see that the group coded "Loss" does not have any ocean borders. These states include Iowa, North Dakota, District of Columbia, West Virginia, and Wyoming.

**Exercise 7: Reading Tables
pages 234–235**

1. **(4)** Looking down the column headed "Increases, Absolute," you will find that the highest number in the column is for Asia.

2. **(3)** The bottom row of the chart gives you the world total in all the categories. The forecasted total percentage increase is 55.

3. **(3)** Look down the column labeled "Percent" to find the lowest number. The smallest increase is 14 percent, on the line for Europe.

4. **(1)** Look at both columns under "Population." Under the year 2000, find the number that is almost double the 1975 number for the same country. Africa shows a 1975 population of 420 million. That number is nearly doubled, to 830 million, for the year 2000.

5. **(4)** Look down the "Percent" column for the lowest numbers: Anglo-America, 22 percent, and Europe, 14 percent.

**Exercise 8: Interpreting Editorial
Cartoons
page 237**

1. **(2)** Asian and European students have a reputation for doing well academically, while American students lag behind. The cartoonist is implying that we should try to get American students to think more about math and science.

2. **(4)** The cartoonist is contrasting what is going on in the minds of American students with what is going on in the minds of Asian and European students. The cartoon shows the brains of Asian and European students filled with important school subjects, while American students' brains are filled with thoughts of sports, food, and entertainment.

3. **(3)** Since Asian and European students often do better in school than American students, our society should stress academics more than sports.

Test 2: Social Studies

The GED Social Studies Test consists of multiple-choice questions. These questions require you to know some of the basic social studies concepts that will be covered in this book. However, the test emphasizes your ability to think about these concepts. You will not have to recall an isolated fact or date as on some other tests. Rather, you will read a passage or look at an illustration and answer questions based on it. To answer successfully, you will need to

▶ have an understanding of basic social studies concepts

▶ be able to interpret illustrations and reading passages

▶ be able to show that you can
  • understand what you read
  • apply information to a new situation
  • analyze relationships among ideas
  • make judgments about the material presented

Actually, you already use all of these different kinds of thinking skills in daily life. In this section, we will help you to apply these skills to social studies materials.

How many questions are on the test?

There are 64 multiple-choice questions, and you will be given 85 minutes to complete the test. About two-thirds of the questions will be based on reading passages of up to 250 words each, and one-third will be based on visuals—maps, charts, graphs, or political cartoons. (If you need practice in interpreting visual materials, you might want to review Chapter 2 on pages 223–237 of the Reading Skills section.) To get an idea of what the test is like, look at the Practice Test at the end of this book. This Practice Test is based on the real GED Test. In fact, all of the multiple-choice questions in this section are sample GED questions.

What's on the test?

The GED Social Studies Test can be broken down into the content areas it covers and the skills it tests. The following subjects make up the content of the test:

* Behavioral Science	20%
* U.S. History	25%
Political Science	20%
Economics	20%
* Geography	15%

* In Canada, 25% of the test is Canadian history, 15% is behavioral science, and 20% is geography.

These essential social studies concepts are covered in Chapters 1–5 of this section. However, keep in mind that a given question may draw from a number of these subjects. It's difficult to discuss society or people without touching on a number of topics. For example, a question on the U.S. Constitution may draw from material covered in both political science and history.

Also remember that you are being tested on your ability to think through certain ideas and concepts. You will be asked to do more than just find an answer that was given in a passage.

Thinking skills that you will be tested on include

Understanding Ideas	20%
Applying Ideas	30%
Analyzing Ideas	30%
Evaluating Ideas	20%

Chapter 1 of the Reading Skills section of this book (on pages 189–222) focuses on these thinking skills, and all of the activities and questions in this section will help you practice answering these types of questions. If you have not already worked through the Reading Skills section, you might want to go back and complete the exercises in that section. The more practice you have had in answering the four categories of questions, the better prepared you will be to answer questions in this section and on the actual test.

1
WHAT ARE THE BEHAVIORAL SCIENCES?

Behavioral science is the area in social studies that concerns how human beings behave as individuals and within groups and cultures. The Social Studies Test will include questions on three subjects in behavioral science: anthropology, sociology, and psychology.

Although each subject overlaps the others to some extent, this book examines each one individually. Each of the behavioral sciences focuses on a specific aspect of humankind. Anthropology addresses the question *Who are humans?* Sociology answers the question *To what groups do people belong?* and psychology deals with the complex question *How do people think and behave?*

Anthropology—Who Are Humans?

Have you ever wondered about the human race in general—about who we are, where we came from, how we are alike, and how we are different? *Anthropology* is the science that tries to answer these and many other questions about human origins and civilizations.

The word *anthropology* comes from two Greek words: *anthropos* meaning "man" and *logos* meaning "study of." Of course, the study of "man" includes all of humankind, men and women.

Anthropology has two branches: physical anthropology and cultural anthropology. *Physical anthropologists* study human ancestry to understand how humans have biologically adapted to a variety of environments found throughout the world.

Cultural anthropologists study how people live in groups and how they have developed the tools of culture such as language, religion, and technology in order to survive. *Culture* is the shared, learned behavior that people develop from group experiences.

Research in the field of anthropology has led to many surprising discoveries about humans and their adaptation to their environment. For example, in India in 1913, the "wolf children" were found. They were two ten-year-old boys who lived with three wolves. The boys would eat only raw food. They never smiled or talked. They avoided humans, but allowed a dog to eat with them. Even after they were captured by hunters, the children could not be taught any human behaviors and died a short time later.

A physical anthropologist might ask these questions about this phenomenon:

- How did humans survive among wolves?

- How did the boys' bodies adapt to the wolves' way of life?

- How were they accepted and raised by these animals?

A cultural anthropologist might ask:

• How could two boys learn to live with wolves?

• How did the human beings communicate with these animals?

Although each observes human behavior from different perspectives, both the physical and cultural anthropologist raise and answer questions that contribute to our overall knowledge about human beings in their varying environments.

EXERCISE 1: PHYSICAL AND CULTURAL ANTHROPOLOGY

Directions: Write *P* in front of the topic that a physical anthropologist would study and *C* in front of the topic a cultural anthropologist would study.

_____ **1.** fossils of bones of prehistoric people

_____ **2.** discovery of crude tools for digging

_____ **3.** hieroglyphics found on the walls of an Egyptian cave

_____ **4.** a people's preference for raw meat

_____ **5.** rites of manhood in African tribes

Answers are on page 343.

Culture

Culture consists of the knowledge, beliefs, and learned human behavior shared by a group of people. It includes the way we think, feel, and behave as we adapt to our environment. Humans can adapt to many environments that lower animals cannot. This is because we have the intelligence and creativity to develop culture.

In fact, humans *must* create culture in order to adapt and survive. For a culture to continue to exist, it must satisfy certain basic needs of its members. These needs, common to all cultures, are called *cultural universals*. Among them are food, shelter, language, family, belief system, economic system, and political system.

Customs

We study various cultures so that we may increase our understanding of other people throughout the world. We study their *customs*, the patterns of behavior shared by the members of a specific culture. The customs are based upon the values that each culture believes to be important. For example, eating with a knife and fork is an established custom in our society. In the United States, family, school, and church are the major institutions that transmit culture to young people.

Values, Ethnocentrism, and Cultural Relativity

Values are beliefs that direct and influence behavior. For example, a fundamental value in American life is the belief that all people are created equal. Values can include freedom, equality, fairness, and individualism.

While observing other cultures, anthropologists are careful not to judge the culture they study according to their own values. Judging another culture according to one's own values is called *ethnocentrism*. For example, an American who condemns child-rearing practices in Asia because they are different from ours is practicing ethnocentrism. Anthropologists attempt to study each culture realizing that each is different yet satisfying to its members.

The opposite of ethnocentrism is *cultural relativity*, judging each culture by using that particular culture's values. Recognizing differences among cultures increases our understanding of the varieties of ways in which people can adapt to the environment.

EXERCISE 2: ETHNOCENTRISM

Directions: Read the following humorous cultural study to see how others might view an aspect of American culture. Then answer the questions that follow.

THE SACRED RAC

An Indian anthropologist, Chandra Thapar, made a study of foreign cultures that had customs similar to those of his native land.

One culture in particular fascinated him because it reveres one animal as sacred, much as the people in India revere the cow.

The tribe Dr. Thapar studied is called the Asu and is found on the American continent north of the Tarahumara of Mexico. Though it seems to be a highly developed society of its type, it has an overwhelming preoccupation with the care and feeding of the rac—an animal much like a bull in size, strength, and temperament.

In the Asu tribe, it is almost a social obligation to own at least one if not more racs. Anyone not possessing at least one is held in low esteem by the community because he is too poor to maintain one of these beasts properly. Some members of the tribe, to display their wealth and social prestige, even own herds of racs.

Unfortunately the rac breed is not very healthy and usually does not live more than five to seven years. Each family invests large sums of money each year to keep its rac healthy.

There are rac specialists in each community, perhaps more than one if the community is particularly wealthy. These specialists, however, due to the long period of ritual training they must undergo and to the difficulty of obtaining the right selection of charms to treat the rac, demand costly offerings whenever a tribesman must treat his ailing rac.

At the age of sixteen in many Asu communities, many youths undergo a puberty rite in which the rac figures prominently. The youth must petition a high priest in a grand temple. He is then initiated into the ceremonies that surround the care of the rac and is permitted to keep a rac.

1. Who are the tribe called Asu? What clues helped you to decide?

   _____

   _____

2. What is the sacred "rac"? What clues helped you to make this inference?

   _____

   _____

3. What is the rite that is so important to the sixteen-year-olds?

   _____

   _____

Answers are on page 343.

EXERCISE 3: VALUES, ETHNOCENTRISM, AND CULTURAL RELATIVITY

Directions: Based on the passage "The Sacred Rac," choose the best answer for each statement or question that follows.

1. The passage is being used to illustrate the pitfalls of

   (1) ethnocentrism
   (2) cultural relativism
   (3) cultural diffusion
   (4) natural selection
   (5) cultural universal

2. This study of the customs of the Asu is intended to show

   (1) how strange human societies can become
   (2) that all cultures have the same customs and beliefs
   (3) that the Asu are normal and caring people
   (4) what the Asu society would look like to most other cultures
   (5) that Asu society is no better or worse than any other society

Answers are on page 343.

WRITING ACTIVITY 1

What differences in culture have you observed among Americans of ethnic groups other than your own? Choose one group and write two paragraphs describing a cultural difference in the area of dress, family relationships, child-rearing, or any other aspect with which you are familiar.

Sociology—To What Groups Do People Belong?

People belong to many different groups. You may be a parent, a spouse, a brother, or a sister. Unless you live alone and are a hermit, or you intensely dislike other human beings, you are a friend. You obviously are a student, because you are studying for the GED Test. All of these roles that you play indicate your membership in different groups.

Sociology studies how humans interact with other humans. We develop relationships and learn to behave in accordance with the beliefs and values of the society in which we live.

Sociologists define a *group* as two or more persons who communicate with each other. Merely being together, however, does not constitute a group relationship. All of the people on a bus or in a room are not considered a group unless they interact—unless they communicate with one another.

Types of Groups

Sociologists divide groups into two categories based upon the group's influence on the individual. *Primary groups* are most important and immediate to a person. Your family is the most primary of all groups. Most people have close, personal relationships with family members. From this group, you form your habits, beliefs, and attitudes. Though not quite as close as your family, personal friends with whom you share intimacies also are members of the primary group to which you belong.

Group relationships that are less personal and exert less influence on an individual are called *secondary groups*. The people you work with or the other students in your class are examples of secondary groups to which you belong. Your communication with co-workers and fellow students tends to be specific and brief. These relationships are usually temporary and impersonal. However, when you work as a team with the same people over a period of time, relationships with co-workers can begin to resemble those with close friends or family.

EXERCISE 4: PRIMARY AND SECONDARY GROUPS

Directions: Write *P* in the space if the situation describes a primary group and *S* if it describes a secondary group.

_____ 1. all the members of a fan club

_____ 2. students in math class

_____ 3. family

_____ 4. people in a town of 200

_____ 5. your daughter's closest playmates

Answers are on page 343.

WRITING ACTIVITY 2

Write two paragraphs describing the primary and secondary groups to which you belong. What makes these groups primary and secondary in your life?

Social Institutions

An institution is a system organized by society to provide for its members' basic needs. The major function of most institutions is to transmit to citizens their culture's customs and values. In advanced societies, institutions are of five major types: family, religious, economic, political, and educational. The most important of these is the family.

Socialization and the Family

The family is the first group to which we belong. The most important function of a family is reproduction of the species. For a society to survive, new members must be continually added. After a child is born, the family is responsible for protecting and caring for the child and teaching him or her the appropriate customs and behaviors. This teaching process is called *socialization*.

Humans must learn to be human. The wolf children described in the anthropology section were biologically human. However, they had never been socialized as humans and, as a result, never adjusted to human society. On occasion, newspapers and magazines report cases of people being raised without contact with other humans. An article by Jack Mabley from the *Chicago Tribune* recounts one such story.

EXERCISE 5: SOCIALIZATION AND THE FAMILY

Directions: Read the passage below and answer the questions that follow.

HE'S REBORN AFTER 51 YEARS IN AN ATTIC
by Jack Mabley

ALTON, IL—The neighbors thought the old man lived alone. But when he died, and they went through the house, they heard the noise in the attic.

They found this creature—a human being. Hairy, filthy, crawling on his hands and knees, eyes like gray marbles. They carried him out of the house, placed him upright in the back seat of a car, and drove him to Alton State Hospital.

He was taken to Holly Center, a building housing mentally retarded adults. They cleaned him up and started the long, arduous process of reclaiming this human soul.

I asked Peggy Barr, the Holly administrator, if they measured his IQ when he came. "No," she said. "There was nothing to measure. He was zero. No response. He was still crawling. To get him off the floor we tied him to a chair. He couldn't feed himself. Apparently he had been eating off the floor from a pan, like a dog. We had to start toilet training him. He was 51 years old, we found. We don't know how long he'd been in that attic. Maybe all his life. He'd never had any medical or dental attention. The doctors marveled that he'd survived at all. When we got him there was just no response. He couldn't distinguish between a table and a person. They were just objects he could dimly see.

"It was hard to get a response from him. Apparently his toys in the attic had been a coat hanger and a spoon. We'd hit them together, to see if he'd respond, and he did. Not immediately. But he'd hear the sound, and in a moment look around. He learned to recognize his name. Then he was walking by himself. Our greatest day came when he got up and very slowly, very tentatively, walked over to the window, pulled back the curtain, and looked out. We all felt like cheering."

1. Based on the information above, which of the following explains why the fifty-one-year-old man behaved as he did?

(1) his extreme isolation from other humans
(2) the fact that he was born mentally retarded
(3) the lack of medical attention
(4) repeated physical punishment by his family
(5) his fear of people

2. Which hypothesis might best explain why the fifty-one-year-old man survived among humans and the "wolf boys" could not?

(1) The "wolf boys" had a physical disease; the man did not.
(2) The man lived in a house; the boys were exposed to the elements.
(3) The man had a stronger constitution than the boys.
(4) The man had experienced some human contact during his early life; the boys had none.
(5) The man's diet was better than the boys' since they ate only meat.

Answers are on page 343.

Nuclear and Extended Families

The structure that the family takes depends upon the customs and values of the society. Traditionally, the family structure in the United States has been nuclear. A *nuclear* family is centered around a father, mother, and children. Other societies are based upon what is called an extended family structure. In the *extended* family, the nuclear family has been extended to include grandparents, great-grandparents, and sometimes other relatives. In the extended family structure, all adults are responsible for the care and upbringing of all of the children.

EXERCISE 6: NUCLEAR AND EXTENDED FAMILIES

Directions: Write *N* in the space if the situation below describes a nuclear family and *E* if it describes an extended family.

_____ **1.** In the countries of Japan, India, Iran, Turkey, and Africa, the family unit consists of three generations living together.

_____ **2.** The dominant culture of the United States dictates that in most cases only two generations—parents and their children—live together as a family unit.

_____ **3.** Chinese, Moslem, and Hindu cultures dictate that a newly married couple establish residence with the husband's family.

_____ **4.** The Hopi, Navajo, and Iroquois Indians require that a newly married couple establish residence with the wife's family.

_____ **5.** In general, the size of the family varies only in the number of siblings it contains.

Answers are on page 343.

The Changing American Family

Several trends in society have changed the nature of the American family. The divorce rate has increased significantly. Statistics show that more and more children come from single-parent homes. Also, economic pressures have encouraged and even forced some mothers to work to supplement or replace the income of the father. Since more educational and career opportunities have become available to women, some mothers have chosen to have careers in addition to raising children. Thus, the role of women in American society has changed dramatically during the past quarter century.

EXERCISE 7: THE CHANGING AMERICAN FAMILY

Directions: Based on the pictograph, choose the best answer for each of the following questions.

A CRYING NEED FOR HELP

WOMEN IN LABOR FORCE WITH CHILDREN UNDER SIX (Spouse present)

WOMEN IN LABOR FORCE WITH CHILDREN UNDER SIX (No spouse present)

1. Based on the information in the pictograph, the period that shows the greatest amount of increase of *married* women workers with children under six is

   (1) 1960–1965 **(2)** 1965–1970 **(3)** 1975–1980 **(4)** 1980–1985 **(5)** 1985–1990

2. Based on the graph, which of the following is a fact?

   (1) More single mothers are employed than mothers with spouses.
   (2) More than 26 million families require daycare.
   (3) There were nearly 3 million working mothers in 1960.
   (4) The daycare needs of America's families are being met.
   (5) Because more women are working, the divorce rate has skyrocketed.

3. Which of the following is the most likely explanation for the sharp increase in two-job families during the years 1975–1980?

   (1) fewer school-age children at home, permitting more women to work
   (2) less job discrimination against women
   (3) higher cost of living for families
   (4) increased acceptance of working mothers in society
   (5) lowered wages for male breadwinners

Answers are on page 344.

Social Structure

Many societies are divided into categories called social classes. Members of a *social class* possess similar levels of prestige. *Stratification* refers to the way that society is divided into classes. Placement of people into social classes is based upon society's values and behaviors.

· In the United States, the social classes are based upon economic values—how much one earns. The upper, middle, and lower classes are distinguished by the wealth and power of the individuals. The upper class is far more wealthy and powerful than the lower class.

Social class is an example of *ascribed* (automatically attained) *status* since one is born into it, but it is not permanent. As one moves upward from one level to a higher one, the new social class is considered an *achieved* (earned) *status*. Some societies prohibit this social mobility (change in status).

In India, for example, the social structure is called a caste system. One way to remember the meaning of *caste* is to compare it with the type of cast used for a broken limb. Neither permits movement. The caste system in India works the same way. People are born into one of the five levels (classes) of the caste system. They are prohibited from changing levels. Thus, the ascribed status will remain for the rest of that person's life, regardless of any attempt to rise above it. Like the three basic levels of social class in America, the five levels in India are based upon society's values and customs.

EXERCISE 8: SOCIAL STRATIFICATION

Directions: Read the statements below. Write *CL* in the space if it describes a class system and *CA* if it describes a caste system.

_____ **1.** promotes ambition and self-improvement

_____ **2.** encourages achieved status

_____ **3.** has strict social structure

_____ **4.** makes available many job choices

_____ **5.** is characterized by five levels

Answers are on page 344.

WRITING ACTIVITY 3

Controversy surrounds the issue of exactly how much social mobility exists in American society. The "American dream" is that anyone who works hard can succeed economically in this country. Is the American dream being realized? If not, why not? Write two or three paragraphs defending your position on this question. Be sure to include specific examples to support your position.

Psychology—How Do People Think and Behave?

Psychology, the study of human behavior, attempts to answer the questions that concern why human beings think and behave as they do. Three of the components psychologists study and analyze are thinking and learning processes, personality, and social environment.

The Thinking and Learning Process

Because people must learn to be human, learning is the basis for human behavior. According to the behaviorist school of psychology, *learning* is a permanent change in behavior that results from past experience.

Psychologists have identified many ways by which humans learn. Each of the ways represents an increasing level of sophistication by the learner. On the most basic level, people learn to respond to a stimulus (an event that causes a response or reaction). This is called *conditioning*. More sophisticated forms of learning involve reasoning and working out solutions to problems.

EXERCISE 9: TYPES OF LEARNING

Directions: Read the definitions and apply them to the four questions that follow.

classical conditioning—After a stimulus has been introduced several times, a person learns to respond in a certain way. Some reinforcement (either a reward or a punishment) is part of the conditioning process.

operant conditioning—Learning results from interacting with the environment. In operant conditioning there is no direct stimulus. People do things because they want to gain something or to avoid some outcome.

trial-and-error learning—A person solves a problem after trying several possibilities and finally arrives at the right answer or achieves the goal.

cognitive perception—Learning is the result of a logical thought process. The mind takes in information, reorganizes it, and adapts the information to fit a new situation.

maze learning—Learning requires a series of responses in order for the goal to be reached. The responses are often made by trial and error, but maze learning also requires that an individual follow a logical thought process in solving a problem.

1. An infant cries when she wakes up in a dark room. At the sound of the baby's voice, the father goes to the room, picks her up and turns on the light. The baby stops crying. The father continues this for several weeks. One night, he turns on the light before he picks up the baby. To his surprise, the baby stops crying. Thus, turning on the light has caused the same response as picking up the baby. This is an example of

   (1) classical conditioning
   (2) operant conditioning
   (3) trial-and-error learning
   (4) cognitive perception
   (5) maze learning

2. A child is told that birds fly. While playing outside, the child sees an airplane fly overhead. Based on his stored knowledge, the child tells his mother that he has seen a bird. His mother tells him, "No, dear, that's an airplane," and explains the differences between the two. The next time he sees an object flying, he will be able to know whether it is an airplane or a bird. This is an example of

    (1) classical conditioning
    (2) operant conditioning
    (3) trial-and-error learning
    (4) cognitive perception
    (5) maze learning

3. A pigeon receives food after it presses a bar in its cage. Thereafter, whenever the pigeon is hungry, it presses the bar. This is an example of

    (1) classical conditioning
    (2) operant conditioning
    (3) trial-and-error learning
    (4) cognitive perception
    (5) maze learning

4. If you are buying a pair of shoes for a child and no measuring tool is available, the child could try on shoes of several sizes until one pair fits. This is an example of

    (1) classical conditioning
    (2) operant conditioning
    (3) trial-and-error learning
    (4) cognitive perception
    (5) maze learning

Answers are on page 344.

EXERCISE 10: MODES OF LEARNING

Directions: Choose the best answer to complete the statement below.

Many experiments in classical conditioning mainly involve animals and humans at the very early stages in life. This suggests that

    (1) classical conditioning is useless in helping us learn about human behavior
    (2) classical conditioning is useful only for training animals like guide dogs for the blind
    (3) adults cannot be conditioned to do anything
    (4) after a certain stage in life, cognitive perception becomes a much more important component of how humans learn
    (5) it is against the law for adults to be involved in experimentation of any kind

Answer is on page 344.

Personality

To a great degree, our personality influences how we behave. *Personality* can be summed up as the traits a person exhibits in the way he or she behaves, adjusts, and relates to others and the environment.

Because no two people are exactly alike, it follows that no two personalities can be duplicates. There are, however, similarities in behaviors among people, and it is these similarities that psychologists study to better understand human behavior.

The study of personality is so complex that even psychologists do not all agree about how this facet of human behavior can be explained. Briefly described in this section are four theories that psychologists rely on to understand personality: psychoanalytic theory, superiority and compensation theory, anxiety theory, and self-actualization theory.

Psychoanalytic Theory

Developed by Sigmund Freud, the psychoanalytic theory was the first proposed theory of personality. According to Freud's theory, much of personality comes from unconscious instincts and desires. We are unaware of them because they are hidden from us. Freud labeled the three parts that make up the personality: the id, the ego, and the superego. The *id* is pleasure-seeking and can cause trouble in its drive to satisfy the needs of food, sex, and self-protection. The *ego* acts as a check on the id's search for pleasure. The *superego* represents the conscience. It stops us from doing things that satisfy the id but hurt society.

Freud also believed that personalities are developed during childhood. Childhood experiences influence our thoughts, feelings, and behaviors throughout our lives. Freud attributes some neurotic adult behavior to difficulty experienced during formative stages like toilet-training.

EXERCISE 11: PSYCHOANALYTIC THEORY

Directions: Read the situation and answer the questions that follow.

Otto likes to have a beer with the boys at the neighborhood bar every Friday after work. Greta, his wife, does not like him to drink because he has an ulcer and because he is abusive to her when he comes home drunk. One evening after work, Otto meets his drinking buddies and has a couple of drinks but takes care not to get "plastered." He leaves the bar early and on his way home feels guilty for stopping off. He buys Greta a bunch of roses from a roadside vendor.

1. What drive represents the id in this case?

   _____

   _____

   _____

2. What action represents the functioning ego?

   _____

   _____

   _____

3. What represents the superego?

_____

_____

_____

Answers are on page 344.

Superiority and Compensation Theory

Alfred Adler believed personality is shaped by a striving for superiority and that the failure of people to be as strong or as powerful as they would like to be can result in a feeling of inferiority.

According to Adler, awareness of one's weakness makes a person strive especially hard to overcome it. This explains why some people become experts in areas where they felt weak. An example is Teddy Roosevelt's drive for physical fitness after having been a sickly child. Like Freud, Adler attributes some adult problems to feelings of inadequacy in childhood.

Anxiety Theory

A third theory of personality, developed by Karen Horney, holds that people become anxious when they worry about not becoming who they want to be. To lessen the anxiety, they adopt behaviors or needs to help them adjust. This theory explains how adults develop neurotic needs—learned needs—to reduce anxiety. An example of a neurotic need is a woman's washing her hands several times a day, even when they are not dirty. According to Horney, this need was likely formed in childhood by a parent's overwhelming emphasis on the child's cleanliness.

Self-Actualization Theory

Still another theory to explain personality is the self-actualization theory developed by Abraham Maslow. According to Maslow, the human personality is motivated to satisfy certain needs in life. These needs are expressed in the form of a hierarchy—they are ranked in order of importance to people.

At the bottom of the pyramid are the *physiological* (survival) needs—food, shelter, and clothing. They are the most basic needs. Immediately above them are the *safety and security* needs—needs based on the desire for order and predictability. Third from the bottom is the need for *belongingness*—the need to develop social attachments. Next is the need for *esteem*—recognition and respect from others. The highest human need is the need to fulfill one's potential, to realize one's fullest capabilities—*self-actualization*.

Maslow believed that appeals to the higher-order needs are the most motivational for human beings. Failure to satisfy these needs is an important cause of frustration and unhappiness. The diagram illustrates Maslow's hierarchy.

MASLOW'S HIERARCHY OF HUMAN NEEDS

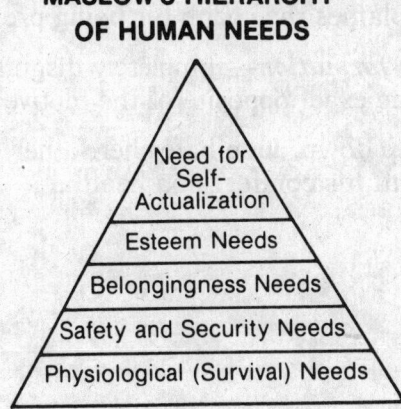

Need for Self-Actualization

Esteem Needs

Belongingness Needs

Safety and Security Needs

Physiological (Survival) Needs

EXERCISE 12: SELF-ACTUALIZATION THEORY

Directions: Choose the best answer for the following question.

Commercial advertisers base their television appeals on satisfying certain needs. For example, a popular toothpaste commercial implies that the particular brand will increase a person's popularity because of the brighter smile that results from using the product. Which need from Maslow's hierarchy does such a commercial appeal to?

(1) self-actualization
(2) belongingness
(3) esteem
(4) both 1 and 2
(5) both 2 and 3

Answer is on page 344.

Defense Mechanisms

Compensation was described as a part of Adler's theory of personality. A person compensates for a shortcoming by striving hard to overcome it. There are many other ways in which people seek to overcome a weakness or adjust to problems in their lives. *Defense mechanisms* are devices adopted to reduce frustration in achieving one's goals. Some of them include:

repression—keeping thoughts buried, that, if admitted, might arouse anxiety

Mary doesn't like dentists' drills, so she conveniently "forgets" her two o'clock dental appointment.

projection—hiding the source of the conflict by blaming others

Jim needs an "A" on the math test to pass the course. He'd like to cheat, but his conscience won't let him. Instead, he accuses innocent students of cheating.

displacement—substituting one object or goal with another

Ralph gets angry with his boss, but is afraid to tell him off. Instead, he comes home and picks a fight with his wife.

rationalization—assigning the reason for failure to reach a goal to something else. This is the most commonly used defense mechanism.

Hector wasn't good enough to make the basketball team's first string, so he blames the coach for being prejudiced against him.

reaction formation—completely disguising a motive by showing behavior that is the exact opposite of the motive

Deep down, June hates her father, but she appears to be overly concerned about his comfort and health.

EXERCISE 13: DEFENSE MECHANISMS

Directions: Reread the definitions on page 260 and choose the best answer for each of the following situations.

1. According to the "sour grapes" fable, a fox wanted a cluster of grapes that was out of his reach. Because he couldn't get the grapes, he turned away from them saying that they were sour and not worth having anyway. The defense mechanism described is

   (1) repression
   (2) projection
   (3) displacement
   (4) rationalization
   (5) reaction formation

2. Years after it happened, Tyrone still refuses to discuss a boating accident in which he was a passenger and in which his identical twin brother was killed. The defense mechanism described is

   (1) repression
   (2) projection
   (3) displacement
   (4) rationalization
   (5) reaction formation

3. Michael, angry because his team lost the football game, kicks his dog when it runs up to him. The defense mechanism described is

   (1) repression
   (2) projection
   (3) displacement
   (4) rationalization
   (5) reaction formation

Answers are on page 344.

Social Environment

People behave differently when they are alone from when they are in a group. Social environment greatly influences how humans behave. *Social psychologists* study the effects of groups on individuals. Social psychologists are concerned with two areas: social attitudes and group behavior.

Social attitudes involve the actions, beliefs, and feelings of people toward groups and classes of people. By studying attitudes, social psychologists are able to understand how people are attracted to one another and how they are repelled by one another.

Group behavior involves the different ways individuals behave in groups. An example of the influence of the group on individual behavior is the adolescent peer group. After a child reaches a certain age, his or her peer group becomes more important to him or her than the family. The peer group provides the child with a sense of identity and belonging. Parents must compete for influence with the peer group. Often, the parents lose. Children who resist the lure of the peer group often suffer rejection or ridicule.

Social psychologists have found that when people become members of certain types of groups, they become anonymous—they lose their individual identity—and become part of the crowd. This "loss of identity" enables them to do things that they would not ordinarily do as individuals. Two examples of groups in which people do things they would not ordinarily do are mobs and vigilante groups. A positive example of a group in which people lose their individual identities is a group of rescuers working together to help victims of an earthquake.

EXERCISE 14: SOCIAL ENVIRONMENT

Directions: Choose the best answer for the following question.

Which of the following best explains why individuals in groups often behave differently from when they are alone?

(1) People are easily influenced and are always looking for a cause.
(2) People in crowds never feel individually responsible for their actions.
(3) When caught up in a crowd, people lose their sense of who they really are.
(4) People want most to be accepted; therefore, they will do anything to gain the acceptance of the group.
(5) A group setting gives individuals the license to do whatever they have longed to do without being individually held accountable.

Answer is on page 344.

2
U.S. HISTORY—
WHAT IS OUR PAST?

Why study the past? We study the past because each of us is a result of those who came before. By understanding their triumphs and failures, we can better understand events that take place in our society today and better prepare ourselves for the future.

History is more than a collection of facts. It is largely a recording of cause-and-effect relationships. Historians study these connections between events.

This chapter is an overview and will highlight the most important events in U.S. history. In this chapter, you will follow historical events from the beginning of this country to the present. You will learn not only *what* happened but will be better able to understand *why* it happened.

A New Nation in a New World

No American holiday recognizes the contribution of the Norwegian Vikings, but 400 years before Columbus set sail, the Vikings landed on North America's shores at what is now Newfoundland. They were the first Europeans to reach North America.

Columbus Day, celebrated on the second Monday in October, honors a hero's mistake. Sailing from Spain in 1492 to search for gold and other treasures from the East, Columbus followed a "shortcut" and landed in North America on the island now made up of Haiti and the Dominican Republic. Thinking he was in India, he called the native Americans "Indians," a name that remains today.

Columbus's error, however, opened the doors for later exploration of the New World. Amerigo Vespucci, for whom America is named, and Ferdinand Magellan, who sailed around the world, were among our continent's most notable early explorers.

As Spain grew in wealth and power because of settlements in what is now Central and South America, France ventured north to Canada. England settled on the coastland between the areas claimed by Spain and France.

By the late 1500s and into the early 1600s, England and Spain fought for control of the southern territory of North America, which included what is now Florida. England's victory led to further colonization in an area that became the east coast of the United States.

As more and more English people came to the colonies to start a new life, England began to acquire more land. In the mid-1700s, England and France fought over the land in the north and central parts of North America. Again, England won and gained total control over the land from Georgia to Maine. This area became known as the thirteen colonies. See the map on the next page.

EXERCISE 1: DISCOVERY, EARLY EXPLORATION, AND COLONIZATION

Directions: Using the map, choose the best answer for each question or statement.

1. From the details in the map, it is clear that the New England state Maine was

   (1) not discovered by the English
   (2) owned and controlled by the French
   (3) owned and controlled by Spain
   (4) a part of Canada
   (5) originally part of Massachusetts (MA)

2. Which of the following can be proved by the map to be false?

   (1) Georgia was the last colony to become a state.
   (2) Pennsylvania was the most powerful colony.
   (3) In the 1700s, France gave up all interest in the New World.
   (4) England controlled much of the Eastern Seaboard.
   (5) The first colonists in New York were Dutch.

Answers are on page 344.

DID YOU KNOW THAT: The oldest European settlement in the New World is St. Augustine, Florida, settled by the Spanish in 1565?

The Thirteen English Colonies

Each of the thirteen colonies was governed by a council or governor who was appointed by the King of England. These leaders were to control the colonies in the name of the King. Because colonists came from many areas, they brought with them differing customs, religious beliefs, and dialects. This diversity of people made each colony unique and difficult to govern.

Coming to a strange land and trying to make a new start was difficult for the colonists. However, the Pilgrims at Plymouth Colony (Massachusetts) survived the first difficult year and in celebration observed the first Thanksgiving, during which they gave thanks for new opportunities and new freedoms.

In the new land, economic opportunities opened up because of the vast expanse of land available for farming. In the northern colonies, the abundance of natural resources permitted the development of industries such as shipbuilding and iron mining. Fur trading and fishing also were significant industries. Though individual ambition and effort were rewarded, the King ruled supreme and taxed the colonists for what he believed was his rightful share of earnings.

Although the colonists retained much of their cultural traditions and customs, they were forced to make changes as they adapted to a new environment. Thus, a new identity emerged for them. This sense of belonging was described by historian Thomas Wertenbaker in his book *The Shaping of Colonial Virginia.*

EXERCISE 2: THE THIRTEEN ENGLISH COLONIES

Directions: Read the following passage from Wertenbaker's book and choose the answer that best completes each statement.

The bulk of immigrants to Virginia were poor men seeking to better their condition in a new country. Many came as indentured workers who placed their signatures to contracts to work for four years in the tobacco fields in return for their passage across the Atlantic; other thousands paid their fare in advance and so entered the colony as freemen. . . . Most of them, indentured workers and freemen alike, sooner or later acquired small plantations and became members of the yeoman class. A few acquired wealth. Many went into trades to become carpenters, or bricklayers, or blacksmiths, or coopers, or saddlers, or wheelwrights. . . .

Among the thousands of Englishmen who left their homes to seek their fortunes in Virginia, there were no dukes, no earls, rarely a knight, or even a son of a knight. They were, most of them, ragged farm workers, deserters from the manor, ill-paid day laborers, yeomen who had been forced off their land . . . youthful tradesmen tempted by the cheapness of land or by the opportunities for commerce, now and then a lad who had taken a mug of doctored grog and awakened to find himself a prisoner aboard a tobacco ship. But Virginia claimed them all, moulded them into her own pattern, made them Virginians.

1. Indentured workers are

    (1) skilled craftspeople who began their own businesses
    (2) dentists who worked for free
    (3) people who agreed to work in return for a ticket to the New World
    (4) criminals who were sentenced to work in the tobacco fields
    (5) wealthy plantation owners who hired the workers for their fields

2. The purpose of this passage is to show that

    (1) the immigrants were no better off in Virginia than they had been in England
    (2) colonists who came to Virginia came of their own free will
    (3) Virginia was the best colony in which to settle for economic growth
    (4) regardless of their background, colonists who settled in Virginia developed a common bond
    (5) Virginia was a rich colony that had great political power

Answers are on page 345.

WRITING ACTIVITY 1

According to the information in this section, "Because colonists came from many areas, they brought with them differing customs, religious beliefs, and dialects. This diversity of people made each colony unique and difficult to govern." Does the fact that the United States is more diverse today than 200 years ago make the country difficult to govern? In two or three paragraphs, explain whether or not you think the country is difficult to govern because of the diversity of ethnic groups. Be sure to support your position with facts.

The Quest for Independence

Soon after the end of the French and Indian War in 1763, England needed to finance its huge war debt. As a result, the British Parliament and King George III passed the Stamp Act of 1765 and the Townshend Acts of 1767. The Stamp Act required all official documents in the colonies to bear a purchased British stamp. The Townshend Acts placed large duties on glass, lead, and tea. The colonists were outraged by these taxes and rebelled against them by dumping tea into Boston Harbor. This incident is usually referred to as the "Boston Tea Party." The English Parliament punished them by passing laws the colonists called the Intolerable Acts, which sought to further establish the authority of the Crown.

The colonists were quick to respond. In September 1774, at the First Continental Congress, representatives from all thirteen colonies demanded that the Intolerable Acts be repealed. Moreover, the colonists demanded to be treated fairly and given the same rights as all other English citizens. However, the King and Parliament refused.

Battles between British soldiers and colonists had already taken place by May 1775 when the Second Continental Congress was formed.

Inspired by colonist Thomas Paine's pamphlet "Common Sense," in which he explained why separation from England was necessary, Thomas Jefferson drafted the Declaration of Independence. This important document justified the need for a revolution by listing grievances that the colonists had against King George III. The declaration was approved by the Second Continental Congress on July 4, 1776.

Patriotism does not come without sacrifice. The Revolutionary War was a long and costly conflict for both sides. The fighting ended in 1781 when the British troops surrendered to the army of the Thirteen United States. Finally, in 1783, the Treaty of Paris was signed. In addition to gaining its independence, the new American nation was granted all the land west to the Mississippi River, north to the Great Lakes, and south to Florida.

DID YOU KNOW THAT: The first man to die in the fight for American independence was Crispus Attucks, a free African-American?

EXERCISE 3: THE REVOLUTIONARY WAR

Directions: Match the cause in the left column with its effect in the right column.

_____ **1.** the Townshend Acts

_____ **2.** the Intolerable Acts

_____ **3.** the Declaration of Independence

_____ **4.** king's refusal to compromise

_____ **5.** end of the Revolutionary War

a. First Continental Congress

b. Revolutionary War

c. Declaration of Independence

d. Boston Tea Party

e. signing of the Treaty of Paris

Answers are on page 345.

EXERCISE 4: THE QUEST FOR INDEPENDENCE

Directions: Choose the best answer for each of the following questions.

1. The purpose of the First Continental Congress was to

   (1) ask the British king for the colonies' independence
   (2) demand the repeal of the Intolerable Acts
   (3) form a militia to fight the British soldiers
   (4) write the Declaration of Independence
   (5) name George Washington as commander-in-chief of the militia

2. The fight of the American colonists against Great Britain can be compared with which event of the twentieth century?

   (1) the British invasion of the British-owned Falkland Islands causing a war with Argentina in 1982
   (2) India's rebellion against British domination in 1947
   (3) the resistance of Afghanistan rebels against the U.S.S.R.
   (4) the American support of the Contras in their fight against the Sandinistas
   (5) the attack on Pearl Harbor by the Japanese in 1941

Answers are on page 345.

DID YOU KNOW THAT: Three of the thirteen original states—Virginia, Massachusetts, and Pennsylvania—are officially called commonwealths as opposed to states, and that Kentucky is also a commonwealth?

The Beginning of American Government

To prevent the abuses the colonies suffered under the king, a central government was formed. It operated under the Articles of Confederation. Some of its powers under the Articles of Confederation are outlined here.

Powers of the States

The thirteen states had the power to

- levy taxes
- regulate business and commerce
- decide whether to support the decisions of the central government

Powers of the Central Government

The central government had the power to

- make treaties with other nations
- govern Indian affairs
- declare war
- develop a postal service

Within the framework of this new system of government, each of the thirteen states was determined to maintain its sovereignty. This posed a serious problem for the new nation because it limited the powers of the central government in dealing with major issues. These issues were: Who would regulate trade? Who should print money? Who should defend the new nation?

Realizing that the country might collapse if something was not done to address these issues, a convention to amend the Articles of Confederation was called in Philadelphia in May 1787. The result was the creation of the Constitution—the document by which we have been governed for the past 200 years.

EXERCISE 5: THE BEGINNING OF AMERICAN GOVERNMENT

Directions: Read the following statements. Write *T* before each true statement and *F* before each false statement.

_____ 1. The Articles of Confederation gave the central government the power to levy taxes.

_____ 2. After the Revolution, the power of the government was divided between the states and the central government.

_____ 3. As a document, the Articles of Confederation was inadequate in addressing issues that were common to the thirteen states.

_____ 4. The general feeling of the citizens was that the Articles of Confederation gave too much power to the central government.

_____ 5. The Articles of Confederation and the Constitution are two names for the same document.

Answers are on page 345.

The U.S. Constitution and Federalism

The challenge facing the Constitutional Convention was to develop a written document that would give the central government more power while allowing the states to retain their sovereignty. To accomplish this, the Constitution was written to create a federal system of government. Under *federalism*, a union is formed by the states, which gives supreme decision-making authority to a central government.

Although the Constitution established the framework for American democracy, its acceptance was no easy accomplishment. Several disputes arose between those who wanted a strong central government with authoritative control over the states (the Federalists) and those who feared that the individual states would lose their freedom under a strong central government (the anti-Federalists).

The Federalists were largely members of the merchant class who favored commercial and industrial expansion. The anti-Federalists were largely farmers who favored individual liberties and did not believe strongly in territorial expansion. Two historical figures whose policies reflected these opposing positions were Alexander Hamilton (a Federalist) and Thomas Jefferson (an anti-Federalist).

The disputes that arose out of the Constitutional Convention and their compromises are illustrated in the chart on the next page.

DISPUTES AND COMPROMISES AT THE CONSTITUTIONAL CONVENTION

Dispute:	Should the states be governed by a strong central government (Federalists' view) *or* Should the new government be based on the sovereignty of the states (anti-Federalists' view)?
Compromise:	1. President was to be elected by electoral college; the Senate, by the state legislatures (this was later changed by the Seventeenth Amendment, adopted in 1913); and House of Representatives, by the people. 2. Bill of Rights—first ten amendments were added to the Constitution later to guarantee individual rights.
Dispute:	Should the makeup of Congress be based on each state's population (large states' view) *or* Should all states have equal representation (small states' view)?
Compromise:	Bicameral legislature (two houses in Congress) 1. Members of House of Representatives were based on each state's population. 2. Senate would have two delegates from each state. (This was called the "Great Compromise.")
Dispute:	Should slaves be counted in the population (southern slave states' view) *or* Should slaves be excluded from the population count (northern industrialized states' view)?
Compromise:	1. Slave importation would be allowed until at least 1808. 2. Slaves would be counted as three-fifths of the population only for the purposes of representation and for assessing taxes; however, they were not permitted to vote.

EXERCISE 6: DISPUTES AND COMPROMISES

Directions: Based on the preceding chart, choose the best answer for each of the following questions.

1. Counting slaves as only three-fifths of the population was favorable to the northern states because it

   (1) limited the number of senators to represent the South
   (2) limited the South's number of seats for the House of Representatives
   (3) was based on the amount of property for taxing purposes
   (4) kept slavery from spreading
   (5) equalized the number of representatives for both the North and South

2. The anti-Federalists like Thomas Jefferson were motivated by certain concerns about government. Which of the following beliefs most likely shaped their opinions?

   (1) the likelihood that England would regain control over the colonies
   (2) the necessity for a strong central government to pull the new nation together
   (3) the greater likelihood of individual liberties being protected under local and state governments than under a national government
   (4) the feeling that slavery should be expanded throughout the states so that laws would be uniform for North and South
   (5) the belief that there was no need for a central government because each state could make its own laws

3. Most likely, a Federalist would have been a member of which of the following occupations?

   (1) a New York banker
   (2) a Virginia farmer
   (3) a Massachusetts commercial shipper
   (4) both (1) and (2)
   (5) both (1) and (3)

4. Today, many southern conservatives—Democrats and Republicans alike—are strong supporters of states' rights. These Americans would likely have been supporters of

   (1) anti-federalism
   (2) federalism
   (3) republicanism
   (4) democracy
   (5) colonialism

Answers are on page 345.

DID YOU KNOW THAT: Jefferson's vice president, Aaron Burr, killed his political rival, Federalist Alexander Hamilton, in a duel, and also tried to persuade the western states to secede from the Union?

WRITING ACTIVITY 2

The chart on page 269 cites the positions of southern and northern states about counting slaves as a part of the population. Write a paragraph telling why you think the South wanted slaves counted and the North did not.

Domestic and Foreign Policy

The years between 1701 and 1850 saw the United States expand geographically. Between 1791 and 1796, Vermont, Kentucky, and Tennessee were admitted to the Union under the administration of George Washington.

In 1802, under President Thomas Jefferson, Ohio was admitted to the Union, but the largest acquisition of land for the United States occurred with the Louisiana Purchase in 1803. By paying only $15 million for the territory, Jefferson doubled the size of the country. He subsequently appointed Lewis and Clark to explore the territory acquired. *Manifest Destiny*—the drive to extend the U.S. borders to the Pacific Ocean—became a rallying cry. The map on page 273 shows the territory acquired under the terms of the Louisiana Purchase.

The War of 1812

In 1812, the United States declared war against Great Britain. The war was declared in part because England allegedly interfered with U.S. trade with other European nations and because it aided the Indians in their uprisings in the West. As part of its strategy to cripple the U.S. economy, Britain imposed a blockade of U.S. ships going to France and forced American seamen to join its navy.

Despite successful military campaigns, the United States did not win the unpopular war, and in 1814 the war ended with the signing of the Treaty of Ghent. The Federalists, who were pro-British in foreign affairs, lost political strength and declined as an important voice in U.S. politics.

Westward expansion continued because of the victories over the Indians. Also, the United States began to industrialize and manufacture its own goods because of the shortages created by the British blockade during the war. As a result, a new sense of nationalism developed as the country turned its focus inward.

EXERCISE 7: THE WAR OF 1812

Directions: Choose the best answer for each of the following questions.

1. Which event contributed to the sense of nationalism in the United States after the War of 1812?

   (1) the spirit of Manifest Destiny that caught fire during the early 1800s
   (2) the need to manufacture its own goods because of the British naval blockade
   (3) the scapegoating of the Federalists as traitors
   (4) both 1 and 2
   (5) both 2 and 3

2. Which of the following could explain why the Federalists were pro-British and, therefore, did not support "Mr. Madison's War"?

   (1) The Federalists did not vote for President Madison and had a personal vendetta against him.
   (2) Madison declared war against Great Britain without consulting with the U.S. Congress.
   (3) The Federalists were mainly merchants and shipowners who feared that their trade with other European nations would suffer.
   (4) The Federalists did not believe that the United States had a navy strong enough to challenge the British.
   (5) The Federalists knew that taxes would have to be raised to support a war, and they were against higher taxes.

Answers are on page 345.

The Era of Good Feelings and the Monroe Doctrine

The strong sense of nationalism that developed after the War of 1812 was bolstered by President Monroe's proclamation to the world that European powers would no longer be allowed to colonize the Americas and the United States would remain neutral in European conflicts. Known as the *Monroe Doctrine*, this foreign policy statement marked the emergence of the United States as a world power.

Because of the western expansion into land acquired by the United States through the Louisiana Purchase and the continuing economic development in the East, the years under President Monroe were known as the Era of Good Feelings.

EXERCISE 8: THE ERA OF GOOD FEELINGS AND THE MONROE DOCTRINE

Directions: Choose the answer that best completes the following statement.

The situation that best represents an attempt to enforce the principles of the Monroe Doctrine would be

(1) the dispatch of American soldiers to Grenada to protect American medical students
(2) the U.S. bombing of Libya in retaliation for Libyan terrorist attacks against Americans
(3) the sending of arms to the Nicaraguan Contras in their guerilla war against the Sandinistas
(4) the American blockade of Cuba to prevent Soviet ships from entering the Western Hemisphere
(5) the sending of an American delegation to the Philippines to certify the results in the election between Corazon Aquino and Ferdinand Marcos

Answer is on page 345.

Jacksonian Democracy and the Mexican War

The Era of Good Feelings did not survive Monroe's term, for, after he left office, sectionalism became a problem for the nation. *Sectionalism* refers to the political, cultural, and economic differences among regions of the country—in this case the agricultural South and West and the industrial Northeast. The conflicting demands that each section put upon the government were the cause of great political turmoil.

The first U.S. president elected to office as a result of these factional differences was Andrew Jackson. A southerner and war hero, Jackson was considered to be a *populist*, a man who represented the interests of the common people. He believed that all people, not just the propertied few, should have a voice in deciding how the government should be run.

As the champion of the common people, Jackson opposed the establishment of a national bank, because he believed that it would only benefit the wealthy and because he feared the eastern merchants and industrialists would control it. Under Jacksonian democracy, farmers and craftspeople gained a louder voice in government than they had under previous administrations. Despite pressure to annex Texas, Jackson refused, fearing a war with Mexico.

President James Polk, Jackson's successor, had no such fear, and Congress, agreeing to the demands of the citizens of the territory, annexed Texas in 1845. Thus the expansionist fervor in the United States was renewed. When President Polk was unable to purchase the territory that included New Mexico and California, the United States declared war on Mexico as a result of a territorial dispute between the two countries.

The Treaty of Guadalupe Hidalgo that ended the war resulted in the Mexican Cession in 1848. The Mexican government gave to the United States the land that would later become California, Utah, Nevada, and parts of Colorado, New Mexico, Arizona, and Wyoming. Thus, the United States had set its continental boundaries. The following map shows the boundaries of the United States by 1853.

EXPANSION OF THE UNITED STATES, 1783–1853

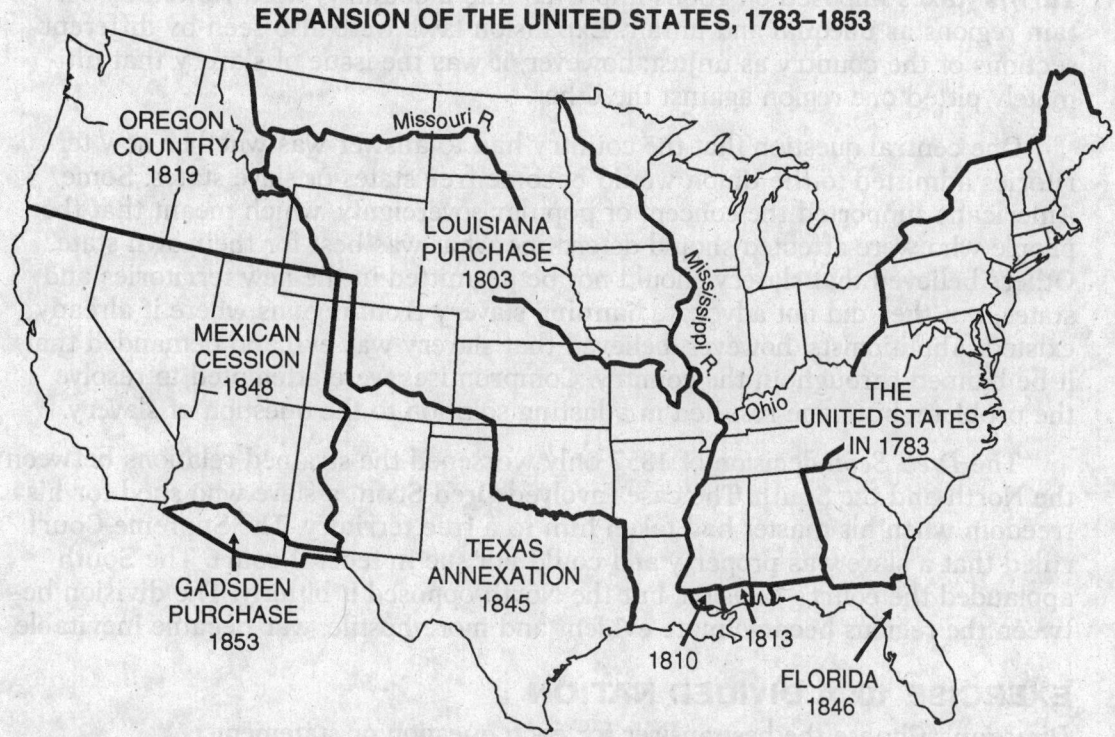

EXERCISE 9: JACKSONIAN DEMOCRACY AND THE MEXICAN WAR

Directions: Choose the best answer for each question or statement.

1. When Andrew Jackson, a southerner, was inaugurated, the shocked eastern establishment treated the invitees to his inauguration with contempt. Which twentieth-century president and his advisors were largely disliked by Washington society because he was considered an outsider?

    (1) John Kennedy
    (2) Gerald Ford
    (3) Jimmy Carter
    (4) Ronald Reagan
    (5) Dwight Eisenhower

2. The attitude toward Jackson described in the previous question is based on

    (1) racism
    (2) populism
    (3) colonialism
    (4) sectionalism
    (5) federalism

Answers are on page 345.

DID YOU KNOW THAT: Andrew Jackson lived with a bullet in his lung for forty years and that the bullet was a result of his being shot in a duel to defend his wife's honor?

Times of Internal Strife

By the 1850s, all the land that made up today's continental United States was under the control of the federal government. Sectionalism persisted, however, as citizens seemed more loyal to their own region than to the Union as a whole. *Tariffs* (taxes imposed on goods imported into a country) were viewed by certain regions as unequal and unfair. Expansion laws were also seen by different sections of the country as unjust; however, it was the issue of slavery that ultimately pitted one region against the other.

One central question that the country had to answer was whether new territories admitted to the Union would become free states or slave states. Some Americans supported the concept of popular sovereignty, which meant that the people who were affected should determine what was best for their own state. Others believed that slavery should not be permitted in the new territories and states, but they did not advocate banning slavery from regions where it already existed. Abolitionists, however, believed that slavery was evil and demanded that it be banned throughout the country. Compromises were attempted to resolve the problem, but none resulted in a lasting solution to the question of slavery.

The *Dred Scott* decision of 1857 only worsened the strained relations between the North and the South. The case involved Dred Scott, a slave who sued for his freedom when his master had taken him to a free territory. The Supreme Court ruled that a slave was property and could not sue in federal court. The South applauded the court's decision, but the North opposed it bitterly. The division between the regions became more evident and more hostile; war became inevitable.

EXERCISE 10: A DIVIDED NATION

Directions: Choose the best answer for each question or statement.

1. A referendum is a political procedure that allows voters to approve or disapprove of a measure proposed by the voters themselves or by the legislature. This method is most similar to which of the following proposed solutions to the issue of slavery?

   (1) abolitionism
   (2) compromise
   (3) popular sovereignty
   (4) secession
   (5) territorial balance

2. The passage cites the *Dred Scott* decision as a decisive event leading to the Civil War. The values upheld by the Supreme Court's decision were that

   (1) slavery was inhuman
   (2) states had more rights than people
   (3) new states could permit slavery
   (4) slavery could only be maintained in the South
   (5) human beings could be treated as property

Answers are on page 346.

The Nation Goes to War

In 1860, when Abraham Lincoln was elected president, he promised to restrict slavery to the states where it already existed. The Southern states, feeling that they were being treated unfairly, feared that they would eventually be dominated by the North. They voted to secede from the United States and to form their own government—the Confederate States of America.

South Carolina was first to secede in 1860, and by February 1861 Georgia, Florida, Alabama, Mississippi, Louisiana, and Texas seceded. Richmond, Virginia, was chosen as the Confederate capital and Jefferson Davis elected president of the Confederacy. In response, President Lincoln determined that the only way to preserve the Union was through the use of force. The South was disobeying the laws of the land. Lincoln believed that if the South did not follow the law, any state that chose to disagree with a national decision would feel that it could simply ignore the law. The Confederacy's firing on Fort Sumter in April 1861 opened the bloodiest war in the nation's history.

EXERCISE 11: THE VOTE ON SECESSION

Directions: Based on the following map, match the state in the left column with its description in the right column.

VOTE ON SECESSION IN THE SOUTH

☐ Overwhelmingly for secession

☐ Overwhelmingly against secession

_____ **1.** Virginia

a. As a "border state," it remained in the Union despite being a slave state.

_____ **2.** Texas

b. As a solid Southern slave state, it voted overwhelmingly to secede from the Union.

_____ **3.** Kentucky

c. This state split in two over the issue of secession, with the western part loyal to the Union.

_____ **4.** Mississippi

d. The entire state seceded from the Union even though only its eastern part voted to do so.

Answers are on page 346.

The Civil War

The nation could not exist half slave and half free, and the war that settled the question lasted four years. Most of the war was fought in the South. The North had the advantage of a larger army because of its greater population, an ability to manufacture goods needed for the war effort because of its industrialization, an excellent transportation system, and an abundance of natural resources.

The South, on the other hand, had the advantage of a greater familiarity with battle sites, as the war was fought on its soil, and great confidence in its outstanding military leaders.

In 1862, President Lincoln issued the **Emancipation Proclamation**. The document ordered the freeing of slaves in those slave states that were not border states loyal to the Union. As a result, the Union army's ranks grew by 180,000 former slaves who fought against the rebels.

The war ended on April 9, 1865, when Confederate General Robert E. Lee surrendered. However, the task ahead for President Lincoln and the citizens of the Union was enormous. The division between the North and the South had to be mended, and the devastated South had to be rebuilt. The South's readmission to the Union would prove to be difficult.

EXERCISE 12: NORTH VS. SOUTH

Directions: In the spaces below, write *N* if the description applies to the North and *S* if it applies to the South.

_____ **1.** outstanding field generals

_____ **2.** better transportation network

_____ **3.** greater population

_____ **4.** forces increased by former slaves

_____ **5.** greater familiarity with battle sites

Answers are on page 346.

EXERCISE 13: THE NATION GOES TO WAR

Directions: Choose the best answer for each of the following questions.

1. Which of the following *best* explains why Lincoln limited the Emancipation Proclamation to the Confederate states?

   (1) Confederate states would have the most to lose if slavery were weakened.
   (2) The Confederate states had a large number of loyal slaves who supported their cause.
   (3) President Lincoln did not want to alienate border states that held slaves but that were loyal to the Union.
   (4) He wanted to punish the Confederate states for leaving the Union.
   (5) The border slave states made a secret pact to join the Confederacy if he freed their slaves.

2. What effect did the Emancipation Proclamation have on the outcome of the war?

(1) It made the South more determined to win the war; therefore, the South won most of the battles that followed the proclamation.
(2) The South gained a reliable source of soldiers in the freed slaves.
(3) It officially ended the war, because the question of slavery for which the war was fought was no longer an issue.
(4) It made President Lincoln one of the most popular presidents in American history.
(5) It gave the Union army a military advantage because many former slaves fought on the side of the North.

Answers are on page 346.

DID YOU KNOW THAT: The military draft was started during the Civil War, or that President Lincoln suffered from frequent bouts of depression throughout his life?

Reconstruction

Lincoln's plan for reuniting the nation included allowing the South to regain citizenship rights and statehood. However, he did not live to see the plan, known as Reconstruction, carried out. While attending a play five days after the war was over, Abraham Lincoln was assassinated by a Confederate sympathizer.

He was succeeded by a Tennesseean, Andrew Johnson, who, though he supported the Union, was mistrusted by Congress as being pro-South. This mistrust contributed to Johnson's becoming the only U.S. president to be impeached—charged with official misconduct. However, the Senate failed by one vote to convict Johnson. Therefore, he was not removed from office.

By 1870, the Fourteenth Amendment was ratified, guaranteeing citizenship to blacks, and the Fifteenth Amendment the same year gave blacks the right to vote. Despite these gains, racial issues and their resulting problems would remain in the South for years.

EXERCISE 14: RECONSTRUCTION

Directions: Read the following passage and then choose the best answer for each question.

Strangers from the North who moved to the South after the Civil War to help the freed slaves find their place in society were called Carpetbaggers by the Southerners. These Northerners brought no more than they could carry in carpetbags—the first suitcases made from pieces of carpet. Many Southerners felt that they only came to profit from the opportunities that arose during the rebuilding of the South.

1. You can infer from the above information that the strangers were called Carpetbaggers because they

(1) were primarily salesmen
(2) did not intend to stay long
(3) were wealthy landowners
(4) were poor and illiterate
(5) did not like uncomfortable surroundings

2. History has shown that the Southerners' resentment of Carpetbaggers was justified in many cases. Which of the following is an example of corruption on the part of these Carpetbaggers?

(1) support of fraudulent bond schemes
(2) concern about the education of freed slaves
(3) attempt to register former slaves as voters
(4) contempt for former Confederate leaders of the South
(5) ability to buy land in the reconstructed South

Answers are on page 346.

DID YOU KNOW THAT: President Andrew Johnson was a tailor, and that when he died he was buried, as he requested, wrapped in the American flag and with his head resting on a copy of the U.S. Constitution?

The Rise of Industrial America

With the Industrial Revolution, America's position as a world power was cemented further. The *Industrial Revolution* was the change in the economy's character from a manual means of production to a mechanical one. Goods were mass-produced by machinery rather than crafted by hand. Because of this change in production methods, more products could be produced at lower costs.

Great Britain generally is credited as the place of origin of the Industrial Revolution. Advantages that Great Britain had were

- an abundance of mineral resources

- access to waterways for transporting products

- a compact size that encouraged consumerism within the country

- a ready market in the New World because of the demand for manufactured goods

- a large middle class that could afford commercially manufactured goods

- a comparatively free and literate society responsive to change

Although the Industrial Revolution began in Great Britain, the United States, with its abundant natural resources and growing population, became the world's industrial leader by the turn of the century. The number of factories in the United States grew, attracting people from rural areas who could earn more money working in factories than on farms. As a result, the population of the cities grew. With increased earnings, people could buy more goods and improve the quality of their lives. This consumer demand encouraged existing businesses to expand, new products to be created, and new industries to be developed.

EXERCISE 15: THE INDUSTRIAL REVOLUTION

Directions: Choose the best answer to each of the following questions.

1. Based on the preceding information, what can you infer about the relationship between a country's size and the development of industry at the beginning of the Industrial Revolution?

    (1) A small population adapted more easily to change than a larger one did.
    (2) A small area containing a large population gave manufacturers more opportunities to sell their goods.
    (3) The larger the population of a country, the more likely it was to resist change.
    (4) The smaller the population of a country, the less likely it was to purchase manufactured goods.
    (5) A large population spread over a large area presented more opportunity for industrialization.

2. Russia and Japan both had the potential at the turn of the century to become industrial giants. Japan succeeded eventually, but Russia still lags far behind. Which of the following would be a logical explanation for this difference between the two countries?

    (1) Japan has had an abundance of natural resources, while Russia has had relatively few.
    (2) Russia has had a long history of economic and social restraint, while Japan has encouraged technological and economic changes.
    (3) Russia has encouraged small groups of highly educated scientists and technicians, while Japan has not.
    (4) Japan has had a large and growing population, while Russia is a small country and is limited in its potential for growth.
    (5) Russia has had a system of serfdom under a tyrannical czar, while Japan has had a large proportion of poor peasants.

Answers are on page 346.

Growth of Big Business

Rapid and widespread industrialization led directly to the development of big business. As one company bought another related company, large corporations began to control the marketplace. This was true especially in the steel, railroad, and oil industries.

Working conditions for employees deteriorated as businesses ran unchecked by the government, and power became concentrated in the hands of a few powerful industrialists. The government practice of noninterference in the affairs of business is termed *laissez-faire* business policy.

EXERCISE 16: GROWTH OF BIG BUSINESS

Directions: Place a check before each of the following actions that represents economic activity *without* government intervention.

——— 1. The Federal Communications Commission (FCC) requires AT&T to divest—break up into smaller companies.

——— 2. A large company hires and pays unskilled workers whatever the market will bear and is not brought into court for violating the minimum wage law.

——— 3. The FCC requires a newspaper owner in Baltimore to sell one of its newspapers when it buys a local television station.

——— 4. A credit card company charges its customers whatever amount of interest it wants to.

——— 5. The USDA closes a dairy when it is found guilty of selling tainted butter.

Answers are on page 346.

Urbanization and Social Change

Urbanization is the shift of the population away from rural areas and to cities where most of the jobs are. Before industrialization, only one out of every six Americans lived in the cities.

By 1890, one-third of the population lived in the cities. Cities such as New York, Chicago, and Philadelphia had populations of more than one million people. These cities were railway centers that provided transportation for people, supplies, and manufactured goods.

Businesses and factories found an abundant labor supply in the cities. The tremendous number of immigrants who entered the United States from 1870 to 1900 flooded the job market. Their willingness to work long hours for less money forced native American workers to accept the same conditions.

Immigrants were often prevented from living in certain areas or from applying for certain jobs. Some Americans wanted to protect themselves from these "others." Yet people continued to come to the cities, bringing with them different cultures and backgrounds. Thus, cities became true melting pots of American society.

Urbanization changed the face of the country socially, economically, and politically. The following bar graph shows the gradual shift of the nation's population from rural to urban areas.

AMERICA BECOMES URBANIZED

EXERCISE 17: AMERICA BECOMES URBANIZED

Directions: Based on the bar graph above, answer the following questions.

1. What was the first decade in which more people lived in urban areas than in rural areas? _____

2. In what decade was the total population of the country approximately 50 million? _____

3. The population of the country in 1860 was approximately how many million people? _____

4. By 1930, the number of people living in urban areas was approximately how many million? _____

Answers are on page 346.

EXERCISE 18: URBANIZATION AND SOCIAL CHANGE

Directions: Choose the answer that best completes the statement below.

The figures in the bar graph support the fact that the United States reached half its present population of 248 million (based on the 1990 census) by

(1) 1890   (2) 1900   (3) 1910   (4) 1920   (5) 1930

Answer is on page 346.

WRITING ACTIVITY 3

Do Americans accept immigrants more readily today than in the nineteenth century? Write two or three paragraphs supporting your position. Be sure to include examples to support your point of view.

Labor and Progressivism

Health, safety, and comfort for laborers were largely ignored during the period of rapid industrialization. In response to these conditions, labor unions were organized to represent the needs of the workers when dealing with employers.

The Knights of Labor, formed in 1869, was the first attempt at a nationwide labor union. The American Federation of Labor (AFL) followed in 1881. By 1904, more than a million laborers joined the AFL led by Samuel Gompers.

In addition to labor, other groups and individuals emerged to fight the abuses of industrialization. The Progressive Era arose out of a reform movement whose goal was to eliminate political corruption and improve the quality of life for Americans. One great supporter of Progressivism was the president with whom the movement was closely associated—Theodore Roosevelt.

During the Progressive Era, the government abandoned its hands-off policy toward big business and initiated reforms that affect Americans today. Some of these reforms are highlighted in the following chart.

PROGRESSIVE REFORMS
Sherman Anti-Trust Act—outlawed monopolies
Hepburn Act—gave Interstate Commerce Commission increased authority to regulate the nation's railroads
Pure Food and Drug Act—set standards for production and sale of foods and drugs
United States Department of Agriculture (USDA)—began inspecting meat
Child labor laws—prohibited child labor
Minimum wage and worker's compensation laws—improved working conditions and wages

EXERCISE 19: THE PROGRESSIVE ERA

Directions: Read the passage below and choose the best answer.

The Sherman Anti-Trust Act outlawed price-fixing (the agreement between companies to set their prices), underproduction of goods, market sharing, and any other form of monopolizing among producers of a similar product. However, public utilities such as gas, electric power, and water companies are exempted from these restraints. These government-sanctioned monopolies are permitted to exist so that essential services are not duplicated and natural resources are not wasted.

According to the Sherman Anti-Trust Act, an example of an illegal monopoly is

(1) the existence of only one power company in a city, giving consumers no choice of whom to obtain service from
(2) a large commercial bank that has branches located throughout the city in direct competition with other banks
(3) a hamburger chain's restaurants, all of which belong to the same system of franchises
(4) oil manufacturers in a state that agree on a minimum price to set for gasoline
(5) a local telephone company that sets minimum and maximum rates for customers in a particular service area

Answer is on page 346.

EXERCISE 20: WOMEN'S SUFFRAGE

Directions: The two passages that follow represent two views of the women's suffrage movement—the movement to secure for women the right to vote. Read each passage and answer the questions that follow.

Although only a working woman, I have by hard work and close economy accumulated a small property that I find I have the privilege to pay taxes for, but have no right to vote for men that tax me. I also find that I am taxed for said property as much again as what many men are that have political influence. Last year I appealed against the enormous tax the assessor put on my property. But I could get no resolution because I have no political influence.

—Mrs. Callor, Jersey City, New Jersey

I intend to vote for woman suffrage in New Jersey because I believe that the time has come to extend that privilege and responsibility to the women of the state; but I shall vote, not as a leader of my party in the nation, but only upon my private conviction as a citizen of New Jersey called upon by the legislature of the state to express his conviction at the polls. I think that New Jersey will be greatly benefited by the change. My position with regard to the way in which this great question should be handled is well known. I believe that it should be settled by the states and not by the national government, and that in no circumstances should it be made a party question: and my view has grown stronger at every turn of the agitation.

—A press release by President Woodrow Wilson, October 6, 1915

1. Which statement summarizes the main idea of both passages?

   (1) It is time for women to be granted the right to vote.
   (2) Though it is a good idea, women are not yet ready to vote.
   (3) Only educated women who own property should vote.
   (4) Most women have always been treated as equals of men.
   (5) Most women would not vote even if given the right.

2. Who does President Wilson believe should make the decision regarding women's suffrage?

   (1) the Congress of the United States
   (2) the voters nationwide
   (3) the voters of each state
   (4) the U.S. Supreme Court
   (5) the women's suffrage movement

3. By Mrs. Callor's statement, you can tell that she has assumed that

   (1) women should not have the right to vote
   (2) she has no power because she cannot vote
   (3) she should not have to pay taxes
   (4) she should not have to work
   (5) President Wilson will help her

Answers are on page 346.

The United States as a World Power

From the time it had achieved its independence from England, the United States stayed out of the affairs of other countries. This policy of *isolationism* prevented the United States from forming alliances with other countries.

In 1867, the United States bought the territory of Alaska from Russia against the wishes of most Americans. The purchase turned out to be a good investment, however, because of Alaska's many natural resources. Also, because Alaska was the first land acquired that was outside the boundaries of the continental United States, the purchase marked the beginning of a new foreign policy. The United States was no longer an isolationist country.

Another motive for the United States to become less isolationist was the need to develop more markets for its manufactured goods. U.S. ships sailed the Pacific Ocean carrying goods to Japan and China. These ships often docked in many island ports along the way to buy supplies and to make repairs. By the late 1890s, the U.S. government had taken possession of a number of Pacific islands for their easy access and available resources. This marked America's emergence as an *imperialist* country—a nation that controls other territories or nations.

The Spanish-American War

America's emergence on the world scene was strengthened by the Spanish-American War. The United States supported rebels who revolted against Spain.

The battleship *Maine* was sent to Cuba to protect American citizens there. It exploded, killing 260 American sailors, and Spain was held responsible. The United States declared war against Spain in 1898 and won the war in four months. Under the terms of the peace treaty, the United States gained control of Guam, Puerto Rico, and the Philippines. These new territories and the islands in the Pacific increased the number of territories under American control.

EXERCISE 21: THE UNITED STATES BECOMES A WORLD POWER

Directions: Choose the best answer to each of the following questions.

1. Which of the following foreign policy actions today is a direct result of early American imperialist policy?

   (1) America's military support of Israel in the Middle East
   (2) the implicit support of apartheid in South Africa by some large American corporations
   (3) America's establishment of military bases in the Philippines' Subic Bay
   (4) the stationing of American troops in West Germany
   (5) America's patrolling of waters off the Libyan coast

2. From the end of the Civil War until the Spanish-American War in 1898, most Americans were isolationists. Which is the most likely cause of such widespread desire for withdrawal from international concerns?

   (1) the lack of information about events taking place in foreign lands
   (2) the desire to expand U.S. boundaries farther across the continent into Canada and Mexico
   (3) the disillusionment with foreign allies who had refused to take sides during the Civil War
   (4) the nation's preoccupation with reconstruction and industrialization after the Civil War
   (5) the resentment toward the new immigrants flooding the country

Answers are on page 347.

World War I

Conflicts over boundary lines and power struggles among European countries resulted in a war that, by its end, included twenty-seven nations. For this reason, it was called a world war.

The nations divided themselves into two rival groups—the Central Powers and the Allied Powers. The Central Powers included Germany, Austria-Hungary, Bulgaria, and Turkey. The Allied Powers included Great Britain, France, Russia, Belgium, and Italy.

The United States tried to remain neutral during the early years of the war that had begun in 1914. In 1917, however, in response to German attacks on ships carrying American citizens, the United States declared war.

The war resulted in many changes in the United States. Factories shifted their production to the manufacture of needed military weapons and supplies. Women and older children replaced draftees as factory workers. Shipyards built only naval vessels. To conserve food for the soldiers, the U.S. government restricted the consumption of meat and bread to particular days.

Strengthened by the United States' entrance in the war on their side, the Allies drove the Central Powers back to their own boundaries. When the Allies broke through the German lines, the Germans conceded defeat.

The Treaty of Versailles, signed in early 1919, officially ended the war. One condition of the treaty was that the League of Nations be established to maintain peace throughout the world. Congress did not want the United States to become involved in European affairs again, so the country did not join the League of Nations, contributing to the organization's decline. After the war, the United States returned to a policy of isolationism, and domestic issues became the focus of the postwar period.

EXERCISE 22: WORLD WAR I

Directions: Fill in the following blanks.

The United States became involved in the war in 1917 by joining the side of the

(1) _____. To rapidly increase the size of the U.S. Army, the Selective Service Act was passed. This act permitted the military to **(2)** _____ men

between the ages of 18 and 45. The **(3)** _____

ended the war in early 1919. Congress did not want the United States to join the

(4) _____. As a result of this sentiment, the United States

adopted its former foreign policy of **(5)** _____.

Answers are on page 347.

DID YOU KNOW THAT: President Woodrow Wilson was president of Princeton University before becoming president of the United States?

The Roaring Twenties

"Back to Normalcy" was the goal and slogan of President Warren G. Harding. The twenties, however, were anything but normal as Harding, relying on the poor advice of cabinet officers, became entangled in the financial oil lease scandal of Teapot Dome. The scandal disgraced the entire administration.

Also during the twenties, the Immigration Acts of 1921 and 1924 were enacted to preserve jobs for American workers. These acts strictly limited the number of immigrants that could enter the United States.

From Prosperity to Despair

Harding's successor, Calvin Coolidge, believed in few government regulations. He reduced government spending and lowered taxes. As a result, the people had more money to spend, and businesses were able to expand. This period in U.S. history was called the Golden Twenties because of the prosperity the nation enjoyed. The period was characterized by speculation (taking unwise risks in investments hoping to increase gains), bootlegging (the manufacture and purchase of illegal liquor, the sale of which was banned by the Eighteenth Amendment), and an emphasis on materialism.

Unfortunately, by the end of the decade, the Golden Twenties became tarnished as the stock market fell in 1929. Businesses failed and the unemployment rate soared while Herbert Hoover, elected president in 1928, continued the policies introduced by Coolidge. President Hoover believed in individual opportunity, free enterprise, and little government regulation. He maintained that if government left business alone, the country would quickly recover from the economic depression. By 1932, however, the number of unemployed workers reached 11 million. The U.S. economy required drastic measures in order to recover.

In 1932, the voters overwhelmingly elected Democrat Franklin D. Roosevelt president on his campaign promise to give Americans a "New Deal."

EXERCISE 23: THE ROARING TWENTIES

Directions: Using the graph below, answer the questions that follow.

This graph illustrates how effective the Immigration Acts of 1921 and 1924 were in controlling the number of immigrants entering the United States.

IMMIGRANTS ARRIVING IN THE U.S.

Millions

Decade	Value
1870 to 1879	2.8
1880 to 1889	5.2
1890 to 1899	3.7
1900 to 1909	8.2
1910 to 1919	6.3
1920 to 1929	4.3
1930 to 1939	0.7

Source: U.S. Department of Commerce, Bureau of the Census

1. The largest number of immigrants to enter the country occurred in which decade? _____

2. Which was the first full decade to be affected by the Immigration Act? _____

3. How many persons emigrated to the United States during that decade? _____

Answers are on page 347.

> **DID YOU KNOW THAT:** During the Depression, Americans in the Southwest ate armadillos (which taste like pork)? The armadillos were called "Hoover hogs."

The Thirties and Forties

The goals of the New Deal were to bring relief to people who were in need, to direct the recovery of the economic system, and to establish reforms that would prevent another depression from occurring.

Roosevelt's programs radically changed governmental policy. Within his first 100 days in office, he persuaded Congress to approve an unprecedented number of bills to address the nation's economic crisis. Many of the agencies created during the New Deal remain today. Most notable are the social security system and the Federal Housing Administration.

Roosevelt's actions reversed the economic and emotional climate of the country. Voters reelected him by the largest margin (up to that time) in U.S. history.

EXERCISE 24: THE NEW DEAL

Directions: Match the group in the left column with the New Deal legislation it would have most likely supported in the right column.

_____ **1.** sharecroppers

_____ **2.** unemployed laborers

_____ **3.** the elderly

_____ **4.** environmentalists

_____ **5.** bankers

a. National Industrial Recovery Act

b. Federal Deposit Insurance Corporation

c. Civilian Conservation Corps

d. Agricultural Adjustment Act

e. Social Security Act

Answers are on page 347.

> **DID YOU KNOW THAT:** Presidents Franklin D. Roosevelt and Theodore Roosevelt were cousins; that William Henry Harrison and Benjamin Harrison were grandfather and grandson; and that John Adams and John Quincy Adams were father and son?

World War II

Because of isolationist foreign policy and concern about the Depression, the United States chose to ignore the conflicts that were brewing in Europe and Asia. The struggle for power and territorial conquest brought Germany's dictator Adolf Hitler into conflict with Great Britain and France.

Japan, too, showed military aggression, especially toward China. Elsewhere in Europe, Spain was experiencing a bloody civil war, and Italy had invaded Ethiopia.

When Germany invaded Poland in 1939, Great Britain and France declared war. The United States tried to remain neutral, but its neutrality was being challenged and its security threatened. By 1940, Italy and Germany had joined the Axis forces, later to be joined by Japan in 1941.

On December 7, 1941, the Japanese Air Force attacked Pearl Harbor, an American naval base on the island of Hawaii. This attack on Americans forced the United States to declare war on Japan. The United States joined Great Britain, the Soviet Union, and France as the Allied Forces.

World War II was truly a global war. Battles were fought in Europe, North Africa, Asia, and on many Pacific Ocean islands. During the six years of the war, millions of lives were lost and millions of dollars were spent. One month before massive Allied military efforts forced Germany to surrender, President Franklin Roosevelt died.

Vice President Harry Truman succeeded him. Truman was determined to end the war with Japan very quickly. The dropping of atomic bombs on Hiroshima and Nagasaki brought a quick surrender from Japan on September 2, 1945.

In February 1945 President Roosevelt, Great Britain's Winston Churchill, and Russia's Joseph Stalin had met in the Soviet Union in the city of Yalta. Under the Yalta Agreement, Germany was divided into four zones under the control of Great Britain, the Soviet Union, France, and the United States, and the United Nations was established as a world organization to maintain world peace.

Although the war ended many years ago, its scars remain. In addition to the death of thousands of people and the radioactive fallout from the dropping of the atomic bombs in Japan, the extermination of six million Jews—known as the Holocaust—is a continual reminder of the war's atrocities.

EXERCISE 25: WORLD WAR II

Directions: Write *T* in the space if the statement is true and *F* if it is false.

——— **1.** Territorial aggression by the Axis Powers was a leading cause of World War II.

——— **2.** The Allied Powers included Germany, Italy, and Japan.

——— **3.** Japan's bombing of Pearl Harbor ended the United States' neutrality.

——— **4.** The Axis Powers included Great Britain, France, and the United States.

——— **5.** The United Nations is a league of nations determined to defend its members in the face of war.

Answers are on page 347.

EXERCISE 26: U.S. FOREIGN POLICY POSITIONS

Directions: Use the following definitions to answer the questions below.

Listed are five foreign policy positions followed by U.S. leaders during the 20th century.

isolationism—the policy of noninterference in world affairs

imperialism—the policy of one nation controlling other territories or nations

anti-imperialism—the policy of rejecting a nation's practice of controlling another territory

jingoism—extreme nationalism marked by frequent use of warlike rhetoric

internationalism—a policy of cooperation among different nations of the world

1. Lecturer and writer John Fiske believed in Charles Darwin's theory of natural selection. According to the theory, the strongest and best adjusted members of a group survive certain conditions. In his lectures, Fiske stated that it was the "white man's burden" to "civilize" underdeveloped countries of the world. Based on this view, Fiske would be described best as

   (1) an isolationist
   (2) an imperialist
   (3) an anti-imperialist
   (4) a jingoist
   (5) an internationalist

2. Two days after Japan attacked Pearl Harbor, FDR made the following statement: "In the past few years and most violently in the past few days, we have learned a terrible lesson. We must begin the great task that is before us by abandoning once and for all the illusion that we can ever again isolate ourselves from the rest of humanity." In the statement, Roosevelt is expressing the ideas of

   (1) an isolationist
   (2) an imperialist
   (3) an anti-imperialist
   (4) a jingoist
   (5) an internationalist

Answers are on page 347.

The Atomic Age

The end of the war marked the end of the cooperative relationship between the United States and the Soviet Union. President Truman, perceiving communism to be a serious threat to democracy, formulated the Truman Doctrine. With the **Truman Doctrine**, he announced that the United States would support free peoples who resist attempted control by armed minorities from within or by foreign powers from without. Thus, a U.S. policy of containment of communism was put into words.

EXERCISE 27: THE TRUMAN ERA

Directions: Place a check mark before each situation that represents an attempt to enforce the principles of the Truman Doctrine.

———— **1.** the sending of American troops to South Vietnam to preserve democracy and prevent an invasion from North Vietnam

———— **2.** the provision of financial and military aid to the Philippines to put down left-wing insurgents

———— **3.** the decision by the U.S. Congress to approve economic sanctions against South Africa

———— **4.** the American blockade of Cuba to prevent Soviet ships from entering the Western Hemisphere

———— **5.** U.S. support of the Polish Solidarity movement's rebellion against the communist government of Poland

Answers are on page 347.

DID YOU KNOW THAT: President Truman was a haberdasher (owner of a men's clothing store) before he became president?

The Korean War

At the end of World War II, the Soviet Union and the United States (who were allies at the time) agreed that the nation of Korea should be free from Japanese control. To protect this freedom, the Soviet Union occupied the northern half, while the United States occupied the southern half.

By 1950, however, a "cold war" between the two nations had developed, and neither country trusted the other. Each feared that the other would try to take control of Korea.

South Korea held public elections to determine its leadership, while a communist government was established in North Korea. Armies representing the North and the South were stationed along the border.

When a North Korean army crossed the border into the South, President Truman committed U.S. troops and asked for troop support from the United Nations.

President Truman claimed that the Korean conflict was a "U.N." war and never asked Congress for a formal declaration of war. Despite this, the United States suffered 137,000 casualties; the U.N.'s losses were 263,000. It was not until 1953, under newly elected president Dwight D. Eisenhower, that a treaty was signed. The original boundary between North and South Korea was reinstated. However, tensions between the two countries still exist today.

EXERCISE 28: THE KOREAN WAR

Directions: Choose the best answer for each of the following questions.

1. The undeclared war in Korea most closely resembled the situation of

    (1) World War I
    (2) World War II
    (3) the Spanish-American War
    (4) the Vietnam War
    (5) the Civil War

2. Which of the following is an opinion about the Korean War?

    (1) Dwight Eisenhower finally ended American military action in Korea.
    (2) The Soviet Union and the United States mistrusted each other's intentions in Korea.
    (3) The Korean conflict was an extension of American policy to contain communism.
    (4) Our government has no right to make soldiers fight in an undeclared war.
    (5) After the war, the boundary between the two countries was reinstated.

Answers are on page 347.

The Eisenhower Years

The end of the Korean War marked only the end of armed conflict. The United States and the Soviet Union, neither trusting the other, increased their military forces, and both developed the hydrogen bomb. This nuclear weapon was far more powerful than the atomic bomb. The mistrust between the two superpowers continued the *Cold War*—a war of words and beliefs—the Soviet Union pushing communism and the United States spreading its influence.

Also, during the 1950s, Senator Joseph McCarthy used the country's hatred and fear of communism to his political advantage. He accused hundreds of government officials, prominent businesspeople, and entertainers of being part of a communist plot to take over the country. Although he ruined many people, his charges were never proved. However, his reputation was so badly damaged that he lost all of his influence and power.

EXERCISE 29: THE EISENHOWER YEARS

Directions: Choose the best answer to the following question.

Under McCarthyism, hundreds of innocent Americans were wrongly accused of being communist sympathizers and suffered public humiliation and the loss of their jobs. Which earlier event created a similiar hysteria in the United States?

    (1) the Stock Market Crash of 1929
    (2) the Civil War
    (3) John Brown's raid at Harper's Ferry
    (4) the San Francisco earthquake of the 1920s
    (5) the Salem witchcraft trials

Answer is on page 347.

Space Exploration and Social Change

President Eisenhower's second term was marked by economic development and social change. Important technological advances encouraged America's involvement in the exploration of space. In 1957, the launching of the first man-made satellite (Sputnik) by the Soviet Union inaugurated the entry of the United States into the space race.

Also during the Eisenhower administration, the modern civil rights movement began as a direct result of the famous U.S. Supreme Court decision *Brown* v. *Topeka Board of Education*. In the case, the court ruled that "separate educational facilities are inherently unequal." This ruling was resisted in many school districts throughout the South. The most celebrated case occurred in Little Rock, Arkansas, when black students were refused entry to all-white Central High School. President Eisenhower sent federal troops to ensure the students' safety. Later, the Civil Rights Act of 1957 established the Civil Rights Commission to investigate illegal voting requirements based on race, national origin, or religion.

EXERCISE 30: SPACE EXPLORATION AND SOCIAL CHANGE

Directions: Choose the answer that best completes the following statement.

The *Brown* v. *Topeka Board of Education* decision is significant today because it

(1) sanctioned segregated schools
(2) allowed Eisenhower to set a precedent by sending out federal troops
(3) serves as the legal basis for school busing to achieve desegregation
(4) permitted blacks to attend private schools
(5) helped to increase Eisenhower's personal popularity

Answer is on page 347.

The Sixties

John F. Kennedy, the first Catholic and the youngest man to be *elected* president, brought great promise to the office. Kennedy's challenge to America is capsulized in the quote delivered at his inauguration: "Ask not what your country can do for you, ask what you can do for your country."

Youth rallied to his call as Kennedy established the Peace Corps and VISTA (Volunteers in Service to America) to share America's wealth and knowledge with underprivileged nations.

The U.S. space program helped symbolize Kennedy's vision of a "new frontier" as the Mercury Seven astronauts ushered in the era of U.S. manned space flights.

In 1961, the Soviet Union began supplying nuclear missiles to pro-Soviet Cuba, located just 90 miles off the Florida coast. President Kennedy established a naval blockade to prevent any Soviet ships from reaching Cuba. He demanded that the missile site already established be dismantled and the missiles be removed. Soviet Premier Khrushchev, not wanting to risk war, agreed to withdraw all of the missiles from Cuba.

On the domestic front, President Kennedy continued Eisenhower's policy of guaranteeing civil rights to the nation's black minority. In 1963, a civil rights commission found that voting rights of blacks were still being denied. Also that year, the Rev. Martin Luther King, Jr., led a series of nonviolent protests throughout the South, culminating in the historic march on Washington that August. President Kennedy's death by an assassin's bullet in November 1963 prevented many of his social programs from becoming a reality. The mantle of leadership passed to Kennedy's vice president, Texan Lyndon B. Johnson.

EXERCISE 31: KENNEDY'S NEW FRONTIER

Directions: Choose the answer that best completes each statement below.

1. The Soviet Union's attempt to establish a missile base in Cuba may be interpreted as a direct violation of

   (1) the Declaration of Independence
   (2) the Truman Doctrine
   (3) the Monroe Doctrine
   (4) the Strategic Arms Limitation Talks (SALT)
   (5) the U.S. Constitution

2. Based on the information in the passage, you can conclude that

   (1) the Soviet Union sought to control Cuba
   (2) the Soviet Union planned an attack on the United States from Cuba
   (3) Cuba and the United States enjoyed friendly relations
   (4) Cuba, a communist country, was an ally of the Soviet Union
   (5) Cuba planned to attack the United States

Answers are on page 347.

DID YOU KNOW THAT: President Kennedy's PT boat was cut in two by a Japanese destroyer during World War II, and he swam for fifteen hours guiding members of his crew to nonhostile land?

Johnson's Great Society

Lyndon Baines Johnson pursued the policy of fulfilling his predecessor's dreams, and, in the course, realized many of his own. A skillful politician, LBJ pushed bills through Congress in numbers that had not been seen since the New Deal. The social legislation he introduced became the basis for his "Great Society."

In 1964, he pushed through Congress the most significant achievement of his career—the Civil Rights Act. The law forbade racial discrimination in circumstances where federal funds were used.

Despite Johnson's domestic achievements in the area of civil rights, his foreign policy—particularly with regard to the Vietnam War—proved to be his undoing. Under Johnson, the Vietnam War, an inherited problem, was escalated in 1965. The number of American soldiers fighting in the undeclared war grew from 25,000 in 1963 to more than 500,000 American soldiers by 1968.

In the United States, public controversy over the war painfully divided the society. Supporters maintained that the war was necessary to contain communism and protect democracy in the Far East. Critics maintained that the war was essentially a civil war in which outsiders did not belong.

Antiwar protests occurred on college campuses across the nation. Draft resisters fled to Canada to avoid having to serve in the war. President Johnson continued to seek a military end to the war, but because of the division within the country, in 1968 he chose not to seek reelection to the presidency. His decision not to run opened the door to new leadership and a new direction for the American people.

EXERCISE 32: JOHNSON'S GREAT SOCIETY

Directions: Choose the answer that best completes the following statement.

Based on the preceding text, the Johnson administration's greatest single achievement was the

(1) active pursuit of world peace
(2) escalation of war in Vietnam
(3) successful containment of communism throughout the world
(4) successful passage of legislation to guarantee the rights of blacks and the disadvantaged
(5) withdrawal of troops from Vietnam

Answer is on page 348.

DID YOU KNOW THAT: Before he became a lawyer and politician, President Johnson was a schoolteacher?

The Nixon Era

In the extremely close presidential election of 1968, Republican Richard M. Nixon defeated Hubert Humphrey, Johnson's vice president. Many people attributed Humphrey's loss to his early support for the Vietnam War.

Nixon continued Johnson's earlier bombing strategy to force a surrender in Vietnam. He ordered troops into Cambodia, a military move that was unpopular with the American people. He did, however, gradually withdraw troops and negotiate a pullout by March 1973. The agreement to end the war included a cease-fire, U.S. withdrawal of all military troops, and a release of all prisoners captured during the war.

After the Vietnam pullout, Nixon was extremely popular among the American voters and was at the peak of his political career. To his credit, he enjoyed many achievements as a world statesman.

His policy of *détente* (the easing of tensions between nations) helped to establish the first SALT (Strategic Arms Limitation Talks) agreement. Both countries agreed to limit the number of missiles each could have. He was the first American president ever to visit the People's Republic of China, which he traveled to in 1972. In the Middle East, the United States had become a major peacekeeping influence. As a result of these successes, Nixon won the presidential election of 1972 with one of the largest margins in modern history.

Overshadowing all of these achievements in Nixon's career, however, was his involvement in the Watergate scandal that began in June 1972. The scandal involved the break-in of the Democratic Committee Headquarters, whose offices were located in the Watergate Hotel. Nixon's part in the attempted coverup led to his resignation in 1974. Thus, he became the first U.S. president to ever resign from office to escape the threat of impeachment proceedings. Vice President Gerald Ford succeeded Nixon and finished his term. Ford lost to Democrat Jimmy Carter in the 1976 election.

EXERCISE 33: THE NIXON ERA

Directions: Choose the best answer to each of the following questions.

1. Of President Nixon's foreign policy initiatives, for which will history likely credit him most?

   (1) ordering of troops into Cambodia
   (2) negotiating peace in the Middle East
   (3) reestablishing relations with the People's Republic of China
   (4) ordering the bombing of Hanoi
   (5) ending the Cold War with Russia

2. Which of the following opinions is best supported by the evidence presented in the passage?

   (1) Political spying is a common practice in American politics.
   (2) Nixon's military strategy brought about victory in Vietnam.
   (3) Nixon's aides broke the law for the good of the country.
   (4) A serious character flaw cost Nixon the presidency.
   (5) The President of the United States is not above the law.

Answers are on page 348.

Ending the 20th Century

Jimmy Carter, elected president in 1976, was considered a Washington "outsider" because he had never held a national political office. A peanut farmer and former governor of Georgia, Carter was seen by the public as a fresh change from the distrust of Washington government officials that was created by the Watergate scandal. One of Carter's chief goals was to regain the public's confidence in its leadership.

Carter may have been a new face, but the problems he confronted were the same old ones. Inflation, fueled by the increases in oil prices set by oil-exporting nations, rose steeply. In the meantime, the worsening situation in the Middle East added impetus to the effort of the United States to conserve energy.

In spite of the problems that beset his administration, Carter experienced some triumphs. He was instrumental in framing a peace treaty between Egypt and Israel; he was a driving force in establishing full diplomatic relations with mainland China; he signed a second SALT (Strategic Arms Limitation Talks) treaty with the Soviet Union; and he successfully returned control of the Panama Canal to Panama.

The event that many believe damaged Carter's image as an effective president was the takeover of the American embassy in Teheran, Iran, in which more than sixty Americans were held as hostages by militant Iranians. Most of the hostages remained in captivity for fifteen months despite an attempt to free them. They were finally released on the day of the inauguration of President Ronald Reagan.

EXERCISE 34: CARTER AND THE MIDDLE EAST

Directions: Choose the best answer for each of the following questions.

1. For which of the following actions will former President Jimmy Carter likely be remembered most favorably?

   (1) formally recognizing the African nation of Zimbabwe
   (2) allowing the shah of Iran to seek refuge in the United States
   (3) negotiating with Egypt and Israel for reconciliation between the two nations
   (4) framing a treaty to return the Canal Zone to Panama
   (5) coming to the White House on an anti-Washington platform

2. President Carter's part in relinquishing U.S. control of the Canal Zone to Panama would likely be described as a victory for

   (1) isolationism
   (2) imperialism
   (3) anti-imperialism
   (4) jingoism
   (5) conservatism

Answers are on page 348.

Reagan and the New Conservatism

At the age of sixty-nine, Ronald Reagan was the oldest man to be elected president of the United States. Before he became America's fortieth president, he had been a movie actor and governor of California. His conservative political philosophy and his ability to communicate with people made him a popular president.

Under Reagan, conservatism reigned as his administration sought to correct the problem of inflation, which he attributed to the overspending of the sixties. In an effort to reduce federal spending, many of the social programs implemented during the sixties were cut drastically. The Reagan administration expected the states, local governments, and private industry to replace those programs that were cut by the federal government.

The thrust of American foreign policy under Reagan was anticommunism. The administration supported the efforts of anticommunist rebels throughout the world. Much of the money saved by cutting domestic programs was redirected into the Defense Department. Both the increase in terrorist activity during the eighties and the Soviet military buildup were used to justify the Reagan administration's hard-line defense policies.

EXERCISE 35: REAGAN AND THE NEW CONSERVATISM

Directions: Choose the best answer for the following question.

Which of the following actions best exemplifies the main thrust of Reagan's foreign policy?

(1) giving aid to anticommunist rebels in Nicaragua, Afghanistan, and Angola
(2) setting up summit talks with Soviet leader Mikhail Gorbachev
(3) refusing to intervene in the Philippine elections of 1986 between dictator Ferdinand Marcos and Corazon Aquino
(4) arranging peace talks between Israel and the PLO (Palestine Liberation Organization)
(5) stationing U.S. troops in Lebanon

Answer is on page 348.

Bush and the "New World Order"

Vice president under Ronald Reagan for eight years, George Bush was elected president in 1988. Bush promised to carry on many of Reagan's conservative policies.

Political changes throughout the world during the Bush administration gave rise to Bush's phrase "a new world order." In 1989, communism collapsed in Eastern Europe. In February of 1991, the United States led worldwide efforts against Iraq in the Persian Gulf War. Later that same year, America's Cold War rival, the Soviet Union, disbanded as a result of economic and political turmoil.

Meanwhile, the U.S. economy dipped into recession in the early 1990s. The deepening recession seemed to defy attempts to resuscitate the economy and became a major issue in the 1992 presidential campaign.

Bush's strength was in foreign affairs. The American people began to feel he had ignored domestic policy. In the months before the 1992 election, the Gross National Product (GNP, the amount of all goods and services a nation produces in one year) dropped and the unemployment rate rose.

Bush's challengers focused on the economy, an issue that lost the Republicans their hold on the presidency. Ross Perot, the self-made millionaire and independent candidate, appealed to many Americans' discontent. Democrat William (Bill) Clinton, who promised tax cuts, creation of jobs, and health-care reform, won the election. Free from the threat of the Cold War, Americans had become more concerned about economic recovery than about the state of the rest of the world.

EXERCISE 36: BUSH'S "NEW WORLD ORDER"

Directions: Write *F* in the space if the statement is a fact and *O* if it is an opinion.

———— **1.** The fall of the Soviet Union shows that communism won't work anywhere.

———— **2.** Economic troubles in the United States can become a political issue.

———— **3.** Now that the Cold War is over, the CIA (Central Intelligence Agency) should disband.

———— **4.** During the Bush administration, momentous changes occurred worldwide.

———— **5.** Bush let the United States slip into recession.

Answers are on page 348.

Clinton—the First Baby-Boom President

The first of the baby-boom generation to hold the nation's highest office, Bill Clinton had run as a "New" Democrat. Clinton was seen as a moderate, moving away from the old image of a tax-and-spend big government. At age forty-six, he had already been governor of Arkansas for twelve years. Clinton projected himself as an outsider, a man of the people, and a force for change.

During the first 100 days of his tenure, a time period made famous by Franklin Roosevelt, Clinton found that campaign promises were difficult to keep. Reducing the federal deficit proved more complicated than he had expected. Because of Republican opposition, Clinton's first job-stimulus bill never reached a vote. In creating a budget proposal, he was accused of reverting to too much spending and too many new taxes. He also encountered controversy over his first nominee for attorney general, his attempt to drop the ban on homosexuals in the military, and the appointment of his wife, Hillary Rodham Clinton, to head the health-care task force.

His commitment to represent America's diversity through Cabinet appointments fared better. Well-qualified minorities and women played active roles in White House decisions. Tough-minded Janet Reno became the first woman attorney general, and highly regarded Ruth Bader Ginsberg was Clinton's first Supreme Court appointment.

Inexperienced in foreign policy, Clinton faced a number of major foreign-affairs crises. He continued Bush's military strategy in Iraq and, despite his preelection stand, upheld Bush's policy of denying asylum to Haitian refugees. Clinton granted a limited economic aid package to financially troubled Russia in hopes of preventing the return of hard-line communists. In urging military intervention in the ongoing Bosnian civil war, the president of four months ran into opposition from a reluctant Congress and a hesitant NATO.

EXERCISE 37: CLINTON—THE FIRST BABY-BOOM PRESIDENT

Directions: Choose the best answer for each of the following questions.

1. What do Bill Clinton's initial experiences in office suggest about the presidency?

   (1) Former governors make good presidents.
   (2) The presidency is more complex than candidates expect.
   (3) Presidents don't need to know much about foreign affairs.
   (4) There are few surprises for a newly elected president.
   (5) The presidency is overrated by the American people.

2. With which of the following statements would Bill Clinton most likely agree?

   (1) The Congress is easy to please.
   (2) Women have no real place in government.
   (3) Economic recovery is simply a matter of getting down to business.
   (4) The hardest part of being president is getting elected.
   (5) Thinking about tomorrow's problems is easier than creating today's solutions.

3. With which of the former presidents did Bill Clinton have the most in common?

(1) Jimmy Carter
(2) Ronald Reagan
(3) George Bush
(4) Franklin Roosevelt
(5) Richard Nixon

4. According to the passage, which of the following was Clinton's most successful action during his first few months in office?

(1) nominating Janet Reno attorney general
(2) proposing his first job-stimulus bill
(3) urging military intervention in Bosnia
(4) appointing the head of the health-care task force
(5) including new spending in the budget proposal

Answers are on page 348.

3
POLITICAL SCIENCE—
HOW ARE PEOPLE
GOVERNED?

Human beings are social animals; therefore, people must live in groups. To maintain order in society, governments with rules and laws are established to meet the needs of the individuals who make up society. Important functions of government include making decisions, resolving conflicts, and providing necessary services. *Political scientists* analyze the organization and management of government within a society.

Types of Political Systems

Several types of political systems exist in the world. The differences among political systems chiefly concern the way the government acquires and uses its authority.

Under a *dictatorship*, a single leader completely controls the political, social, and economic aspects of life in a country. The dictatorships of Adolf Hitler in Germany and Benito Mussolini in Italy are historical examples of one individual holding complete political power. Modern-day examples of dictatorships include Libya under Colonel Muammar Gadhafi and the Philippines when ruled by Ferdinand Marcos.

A *monarchy* is a political system in which the power to rule is held by a royal family. This power is passed within the family from one generation to the next. In the past, *absolute monarchies* were headed by a king or queen who had final say in governmental decision making. Today, however, monarchs are bound by the laws of a constitution and have limited authority, as is the case in Great Britain. Queen Elizabeth II of England is primarily a ceremonial leader; governmental decisions are made by a parliament headed by a prime minister.

In a *democracy*, the head of the government is chosen by the people he or she governs. The leader's decisions must meet the approval of the people.

Two types of democracies exist today—the pure democracy and the representative democracy. In a *pure democracy*, the people make the decisions directly. This is impractical with a large population, however, and is usually found only in small towns. The town meeting (still used in parts of New England) is an example of a pure democracy.

For large populations, such as that of the United States, a representative democracy is used. In a *representative democracy*, the people elect representatives to determine policies for the entire population. Thus, the representatives remain accountable to the people.

Sometimes nations are governed by a few leaders who form a group. Such a government by the few is called an *oligarchy*.

An oligarchy is similar to a dictatorship in that government officials are not elected by the people and often come to power after a revolution. A group of persons controlling a government after a revolutionary seizure of power is called a *junta* (*hoon-tuh*). Communist countries such as the former Soviet Union and the People's Republic of China are modern-day examples of oligarchies.

EXERCISE 1: METHODS OF OBTAINING POWER

Directions: Listed are five ways by which goverment leaders may assume power. Read the definitions and apply them to the questions that follow.

ancestry—The leader comes from a family that has led the country for many generations.

divine right—The leader claims to have been placed in his or her position by God.

conquest—The leader acquires territory through military domination.

revolution—The leader comes to power as a result of an overthrow of the earlier political system.

popular vote—The leader is chosen by the vote of the people he or she is to govern.

1. The French, inspired in part by the revolt of the thirteen colonies against England, replaced their monarchy with a republic. The new leader came to power by

   (1) ancestry
   (2) divine right
   (3) conquest
   (4) revolution
   (5) popular vote

2. Austria maintained its independence in the face of World War II until Hitler's army occupied the small nation and forced it to join the Third Reich. Hitler acquired power over Austria by

   (1) ancestry
   (2) divine right
   (3) conquest
   (4) revolution
   (5) popular vote

3. President Corazon Aquino of the Philippines outpolled former president Ferdinand Marcos in the election of 1986. Aquino won the presidency through

   (1) ancestry
   (2) divine right
   (3) conquest
   (4) revolution
   (5) popular vote

Answers are on page 348.

The U.S. Federal Government

The U.S. Constitution is based on the idea of federalism. Under *federalism*, the authority of the government is divided between the states and a central government. The central government is further divided into three branches: the *legislative*, which makes the laws; the *executive*, which carries out the laws; and the *judicial*, which interprets the laws. Under this separation of powers, no one part of government is able to dominate another. Each branch of government is able to exert its authority to prevent another branch from becoming too powerful.

The Legislative Branch: Maker of Laws

The legislative branch of the government is outlined in Article One of the Constitution. The U.S. legislature, called the U.S. Congress, is made up of two houses—the House of Representatives and the Senate. The House of Representatives is called the lower house, and the Senate is called the upper house.

In the House of Representatives, each state's number of representatives is based on its population in relationship to the population of the entire country. Smaller states have fewer representatives than larger states. To determine the correct number of representatives a state should have, a *census*, or counting of the population, occurs every ten years. In the Senate, each state is equally represented with two senators each.

Representatives are chosen by popular election and serve for two years. Senators are chosen by popular election also, although under the original Constitution they were chosen by the state legislatures. Senators serve six-year terms.

The U.S. Congress has the power to

- levy and collect taxes
- borrow money
- regulate commerce
- coin money
- declare war
- provide and maintain an army and navy

- approve treaties (Senate only)
- impeach the president (House only)
- introduce bills other than tax bills
- introduce a revenue or tax bill (House only)
- approve presidential appointments (Senate only)
- admit new states to the Union

These powers are called *enumerated* powers because they are listed in Article One of the U.S. Constitution. In addition to enumerated powers, the Constitution provides for powers that are not listed. The *elastic clause* enables the legislative branch to stretch its authority to meet the needs of specific situations that the Founding Fathers could not foresee.

EXERCISE 2: LEGISLATIVE REPRESENTATION

Directions: Choose the best answer for each of the questions below.

1. Which of the following states is likely to have the least number of representatives in the House?

    (1) Texas
    (2) New York
    (3) Rhode Island
    (4) California
    (5) Georgia

2. Although New Jersey is smaller in size than Wyoming and Nevada, it has a larger number of representatives. Based on this fact, which of the following can you infer to be true?

    (1) New Jersey has a dwindling population.
    (2) New Jersey is primarily an urban, industrial state.
    (3) New Jersey is a densely populated state.
    (4) Both (1) and (2)
    (5) Both (2) and (3)

3. Arizona, one of the fastest-growing Sunbelt states, is attracting residents from the industrial Northeast. Based on this fact, which of the following hypotheses could be true?

    (1) The number of senators for Arizona will need to be increased.
    (2) The number of representatives for Arizona will need to be adjusted to reflect the increase in population.
    (3) The number of representatives for the states in the Northeast that are losing residents will need to be adjusted.
    (4) Both (1) and (2)
    (5) Both (2) and (3)

Answers are on page 348.

EXERCISE 3: THE LEGISLATIVE BRANCH

Directions: Write *C* in the space if the action listed is an example of a power stated in the U.S. Constitution and listed on page 303. Write *E* in the space if it is an example of an application of the elastic clause, which allows Congress to stretch its authority to meet needs not mentioned in the Constitution.

_____ **1.** Congress approved economic sanctions against the apartheid regime of South Africa.

_____ **2.** Congress reformed the nation's tax structure in 1986.

_____ **3.** Congress admitted Hawaii as the fiftieth state of the Union.

_____ **4.** The Senate approved President Bush's appointment of Clarence Thomas as an Associate Justice of the U.S. Supreme Court.

_____ **5.** The 99th Congress introduced legislation to abolish the mandatory retirement age for workers.

Answers are on page 349.

The Executive Branch: Enforcer of the Laws

Article Two of the U.S. Constitution outlines the powers of the executive branch of the U.S. government. The executive branch consists of the president, vice president, and all of the agencies and departments that are necessary to administer and enforce the laws of the country. As described in Article Two of the U.S. Constitution, the president

- is commander-in-chief of the armed forces
- has power to grant reprieves and pardons for offenses against the United States
- may appoint judges to the U.S. Supreme Court and ambassadors with the approval of the Senate
- may nominate and appoint major executive officers
- may veto (refuse to approve) bills sent by Congress

Just as the legislative branch has powers not provided for in the Constitution, so too does the president. This vagueness of executive authority has allowed each president to shape the office to his own personality. "Strong" presidents, to some extent, have dominated the legislative branch and have relied less on the advice of their cabinets and direction from Congress. Strong presidents frequently use their veto power. "Weak" presidents, on the other hand, have made the office subordinate to the legislature, have relied more on their cabinets, and have been less authoritative. Generally speaking, however, the office of president has been one of increasing authority.

The president serves for four years and is limited to serving a maximum of two terms. The vice president serves if the president becomes disabled or dies in office before completing the term. The president and vice president are chosen by popular vote, but the electoral college later officially certifies the results of the popular election. The *electoral college* consists of a group of electors from each state who, a month after the general election, cast votes for the president and vice president. To be officially elected president, a candidate must receive a majority of the electoral votes. Originally established to serve as a check and balance against an unsound decision made by the voters, the electoral college today is a target of much criticism. Many politicians believe that the institution has outlived its usefulness and should be abolished.

In general, the candidate who receives the majority of a state's popular vote almost always receives the state's electoral votes. In only two instances in U.S. history has a candidate received the majority of the popular vote but lost the election because of the electoral vote. This occurred in the election of 1876 in which Rutherford B. Hayes was chosen as president even though his opponent, Samuel Tilden, received the majority of the popular vote. This also happened in the election of 1888, when Benjamin Harrison was elected president even though his opponent, Grover Cleveland, received the majority of the popular vote.

EXERCISE 4: THE EXECUTIVE BRANCH

Directions: Choose the best answer for each question below.

1. "Strong" presidents have been described as dominating the legislative branch and making the office of the presidency self-directing. "Weak" presidents have made the office more reliant on and subordinate to the legislature. Which of the following early presidents *best* fits the description above of a strong president?

    (1) President Madison, a statesman who declared war on Britain in 1812 only after popular demand called for it.
    (2) President John Adams, who believed that the governing representatives should be "the rich, the well-born, and the able."
    (3) President Thomas Jefferson, who opposed the Louisiana Purchase and the first Bank of the United States on the grounds that the Constitution did not provide for it.
    (4) President James Monroe, who advanced the idea of the Monroe Doctrine on the advice of his secretary of state, John Quincy Adams.
    (5) President Andrew Jackson, who made unprecedented use of his veto power and who relied little on Congress and his cabinet in making his decisions.

2. Based on what you read in the section on U.S. history, which of the following twentieth-century presidents may be best described as "weak" when he got embroiled in the Teapot Dome scandal by relying on the poor advice of his subordinates?

    (1) Theodore Roosevelt
    (2) Franklin D. Roosevelt
    (3) Woodrow Wilson
    (4) Harry Truman
    (5) Warren G. Harding

3. In the early years before political parties were established, the second highest vote-getter in a presidential election automatically became vice president. This was changed later when parties were founded and candidates for president and vice president ran together on a ticket. Which of the following is the *best* explanation as to why the policy for electing the vice president was changed?

    (1) The Constitution required that candidates for the offices of president and vice president be from the same party.
    (2) The country was better served when the candidates for president and vice president came from different regions of the country.
    (3) Before the system was changed, it was easier to cheat a candidate out of the presidency.
    (4) Too many unqualified candidates for the presidency were running for office; the new system guaranteed the candidates would be better qualified.
    (5) The new system prevented the vice president (who often had opposing political views) from obstructing the president's ability to govern.

Answers are on page 349.

WRITING ACTIVITY 1

The electoral college system was created as a way to check potentially "unsound" decisions made by the voting public. Should the president and vice president of the United States be elected by direct popular vote or by the electoral college system as is currently the case? Write one or two paragraphs defending your point of view.

The Judicial Branch: Interpreter of the Laws

Article Three of the Constitution describes the Supreme Court of the United States. The purpose of the Supreme Court is to rule on the constitutionality of certain laws passed by Congress, the president, and the states themselves. The authority to decide whether or not a law is in keeping with the spirit of the Constitution is called *judicial review*.

The Supreme Court is composed of nine justices appointed for life by the president. The head of the court is called the *chief justice*. The judicial branch of the federal government consists of the U.S. Supreme Court, the eleven Circuit Courts of Appeal distributed throughout the country, and approximately ninety federal District Courts.

Some of the powers vested in the Supreme Court are the powers to

- rule on cases involving a state and citizens of another state
- rule on controversies between two or more states
- rule on cases between citizens of different states
- rule on cases between a state and its citizens, and a foreign state and its citizens
- rule on conflicts arising on the high seas
- rule on conflicts over patents and copyrights

In carrying out its rulings, a decision is reached when a majority of the justices of the Supreme Court agree. When all nine justices are present and vote, a majority decision requires at least five votes.

EXERCISE 5: THE JUDICIAL BRANCH

Directions: Choose the best answer to complete each of the following statements.

1. Chief Justice Charles Evans Hughes wrote in 1907, "The Constitution is what the Judges say it is." This quote best defines the Supreme Court's power of

    (1) checks and balances
    (2) ignoring the decisions made by the legislative branch
    (3) being "above the law"
    (4) judicial review
    (5) judicial restraint

2. The purpose of the quote is to

    (1) define the role of the Supreme Court
    (2) show that the Supreme Court is the final authority on the Constitution's meaning
    (3) show how arrogant former Chief Justice Hughes was
    (4) both (1) and (2)
    (5) both (2) and (3)

Answers are on page 349.

EXERCISE 6: STATES' VS. INDIVIDUALS' RIGHTS

Throughout the history of the U.S. Supreme Court, the court has had to decide whether or not it should preserve and uphold the federal system (which included supporting the authority of the individual states) or uphold the rights of the individual. Supreme Court justices who lean toward upholding the rights of the states are described as exercising *judicial restraint*.

Directions: For each of these landmark cases, write *I* if it is a victory for the rights of the individual.

_____ **1.** the case of *Plessy* v. *Ferguson* (1896), in which the Supreme Court upheld a lower-court decision that ruled that separate but equal facilities for blacks and whites were correct and legal

_____ **2.** the case of *Roe* v. *Wade* (1973), in which the court ruled that states could not prohibit abortion under certain conditions during the first six months of pregnancy

_____ **3.** the case of *Dred Scott* v. *Sanford* (1857), in which the Supreme Court agreed with a lower court that freeing Dred Scott would be depriving his owner of personal property without due process of law

_____ **4.** the case of *Miranda* v. *Arizona* (1966), in which the court ruled that a person accused of a crime must be informed of his or her rights or any resulting confession would be invalid

_____ **5.** the case of *Brown* v. *Board of Education* (1954), in which the court ruled that separate facilities for the races were not equal and therefore were unconstitutional

Answers are on page 349.

WRITING ACTIVITY 2

One example of a president's use of implied powers is the replacement of retiring Supreme Court justices with judges sympathetic to the appointing president's political views. For example, Presidents Reagan and Bush, both conservatives, appointed conservative judges to the Supreme Court to fill vacancies. Do you think it is an abuse of presidential authority to appoint only judges who agree with the president's political philosophy? Write two or three paragraphs defending your point of view.

System of Checks and Balances

The framers of the Constitution understood that the powers of the three branches had to be balanced so that no one center of power dominated the other two. To prevent this from happening, the U.S. Constitution allows for certain actions by one branch to restrain the activities of another. One such restraint is the ability of the president to refuse approval of (veto) a bill sent from Congress.

However, Congress could still pass the bill into law by a majority vote of its members. This procedure is called *overriding a veto*. Finally, if the issue is brought to the Supreme Court, the court can still declare the law unconstitutional. This happens if the justices conclude that the law contradicts the principles of the Constitution. The following diagram shows how a bill is enacted into law.

THE ENACTMENT OF A LAW

HOUSE OF REPRESENTATIVES

BILL

1. Introduced
2. Numbered
3. Referred to Appropriate Committee

1. Comittee Hearing
2. Possibly Rewritten or Amended
3. Back to Body of Origin with Passage Recommended

1. Put on Calendar
2. Debated on Floor
3. May Be Amended
4. Voted Upon
5. If Passed, Goes to Other House

1. In Other House, Same Procedure as Before
2. If Passed, Usually Must Go to Conference Committee for Compromise

JOINT CONFERENCE COMMITTEE

1. Compromise Approved by Both Houses
2. Goes to President

1. Signed into Law
2. Allowed to Become Law Without Signature

OR

1. Vetoed
2. May Still Become Law if Approved by Two-thirds of Both Houses

SENATE

BILL

EXERCISE 7: THE ENACTMENT OF A LAW

Directions: Choose the best answer for the following question.

Which statement is best supported by the preceding chart?

(1) Bills justified by the elastic clause in the Constitution must be introduced directly by the president.
(2) Before being sent to the president, a bill must be approved in identical form by both houses of Congress.
(3) A filibuster on certain bills may not take place in either house.
(4) A bill introduced in the Senate may be changed by the House but not the other way around.
(5) The president must sign all bills for them to become law.

Answer is on page 349.

EXERCISE 8: FILIBUSTER

Directions: Read the passage below and answer the question that follows.

In 1957, Senator Strom Thurmond of South Carolina talked for more than twenty-four hours to delay the vote on the first civil rights law to be proposed since shortly after the Civil War. Thurmond's filibuster did not prevent passage of the bill, and the Civil Rights Act became law that year.

The best explanation of a filibuster is

(1) a twenty-four-hour delay of a vote to give legislators a chance to discuss a bill
(2) an opportunity to propose a bill on a topic that has been long ignored
(3) a monologue aimed at convincing legislators to vote for passage of a bill
(4) political lobbying to get others to vote either for or against a bill
(5) marathon talking for the purpose of preventing passage of a bill into law

Answer is on page 349.

EXERCISE 9: SYSTEM OF CHECKS AND BALANCES

Directions: In column I, write the branch of government that *exercises* the power described on the left. In column II, write the branch of government that is *checked* by the use of the power. The first one is done for you.

Power	I Who exercises power?	II Who is checked?
1. to appoint federal judges	(a) *executive*	(b) *judicial*
2. to impeach the president	(a) _____	(b) _____
3. to approve appointment of judges	(a) _____	(b) _____
4. to override a veto	(a) _____	(b) _____
5. to rule a law unconstitutional	(a) _____	(b) _____
6. to veto a bill	(a) _____	(b) _____

Answers are on page 349.

State and Local Governments

State Government

Article Four of the U.S. Constitution defines the role of the states. The structure of the state government resembles that of the federal government. The executive authority of the state is the governor. Like the president, the governor has veto power.

The legislative branch, which makes the laws, is composed of two houses in all states except Nebraska. Each state has its own court system, which includes trial courts, appellate courts, and a state supreme court. Also, each state has its own written constitution (most of which are based on the U.S. model).

The state constitution outlines the powers and duties of the various state officials and agencies. Like the federal governmental system on which they are based, the fifty states have a system of checks and balances among the three branches of government.

Most criminal codes and civil laws are established by state law. The state also establishes laws for contracts, chartering businesses, and marriage and divorce. Another responsibility of state government is to charter local governments. The powers of municipalities—villages, towns, and cities—are outlined and defined in a charter approved by the state.

EXERCISE 10: POWERS OF STATE GOVERNMENT

Directions: In the spaces provided, write *S* if the power belongs to the states, *F* if it belongs to the federal government, and *B* if it belongs to both.

_____ **1.** vetoing a bill by the chief executive

_____ **2.** passing laws that provide for the welfare of its citizens

_____ **3.** declaring war against a foreign country

_____ **4.** setting import quotas and duties

_____ **5.** establishing a legal age for drinking alcoholic beverages

_____ **6.** setting up guidelines for chartering a business

Answers are on page 349.

Local Government

While the structure and organization of the federal and state governments are similar, local governments can be quite different. Local governments are usually one of three types: mayor-council, council-manager, and commission.

Under the *mayor-council* form of municipal government, the mayor is the executive and is elected by the voters. The council is the legislature; each council member represents a ward or district established by legal boundaries.

Under the *council-manager* form of government, members of the council are elected by the people. The duties of the council are to make policies, set goals, and provide leadership. The council hires a manager to oversee the day-to-day operations of the government and carry out the policies set by the council.

Under the *commission* form of government, commissioners are elected by the people. Their job is to make policies and to run a specific department of the city or county. For example, one commissioner may be in charge of public safety (fire, police, civil defense), while another commissioner may be in charge of public works (water, sewers, roads).

All municipalities receive most of the money to operate from local taxes, fees, and service charges. The following graphs show the sources of income for cities and how they are allocated.

EXERCISE 11: CITY INCOME AND EXPENDITURES

Directions: Read the two graphs and fill in the blanks in the following sentences.

THE CITY DOLLAR
(23 largest cities)

Where It Comes From

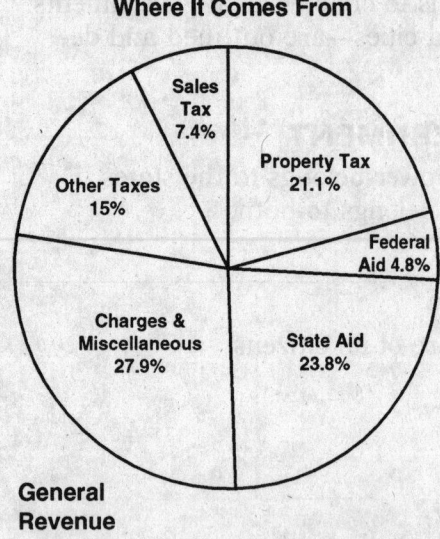

Sales Tax 7.4%
Property Tax 21.1%
Other Taxes 15%
Federal Aid 4.8%
Charges & Miscellaneous 27.9%
State Aid 23.8%

General Revenue

Where It Goes

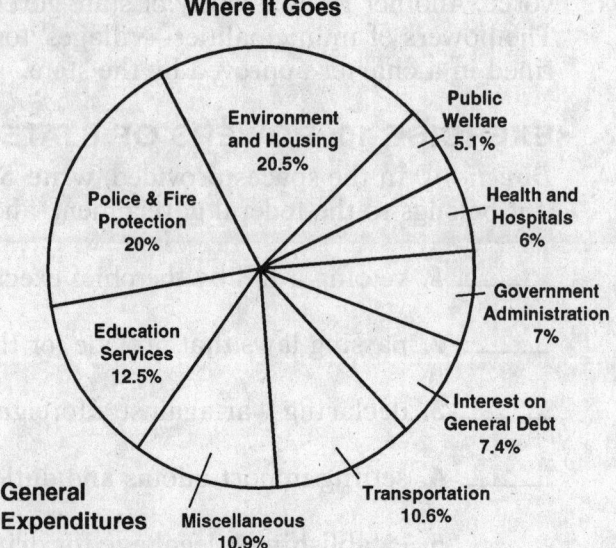

Environment and Housing 20.5%
Public Welfare 5.1%
Police & Fire Protection 20%
Health and Hospitals 6%
Government Administration 7%
Education Services 12.5%
Interest on General Debt 7.4%
Miscellaneous 10.9%
Transportation 10.6%

General Expenditures

1. The income that a government receives is called _____,

   and the money it spends is called _____.

2. In the graph, the largest source of income for the city is _____.

3. The largest percentage of the city dollar goes to _____.

Answers are on page 349.

EXERCISE 12: CITY BUDGETING

Directions: Choose the best answer for the following question.

If federal aid were cut to 3 percent and state aid remained the same, what options would the city have to make up for the loss in revenue?

(1) borrow money from a more prosperous state
(2) increase revenue by raising local taxes or fees
(3) decrease expenditures by cutting programs
(4) both (1) and (2)
(5) both (2) and (3)

Answer is on page 350.

WRITING ACTIVITY 3

What type of structure does your local government have? Write two to three paragraphs describing your municipal government's structure. State whether or not you think the form is effective and explain why. If you think it is not effective, tell what form you would replace it with.

The U.S. Political System

The voting public has been viewed as holding a range of positions on political issues. These political positions are illustrated as occupying one of five segments of a spectrum. The segments are generally referred to as political labels. To win an election, each political party must obtain the majority of the votes cast. Since most American voters occupy the middle of the spectrum, both political parties must appeal to this group of voters to win.

The following illustration shows the five political positions.

THE POLITICAL CONTINUUM

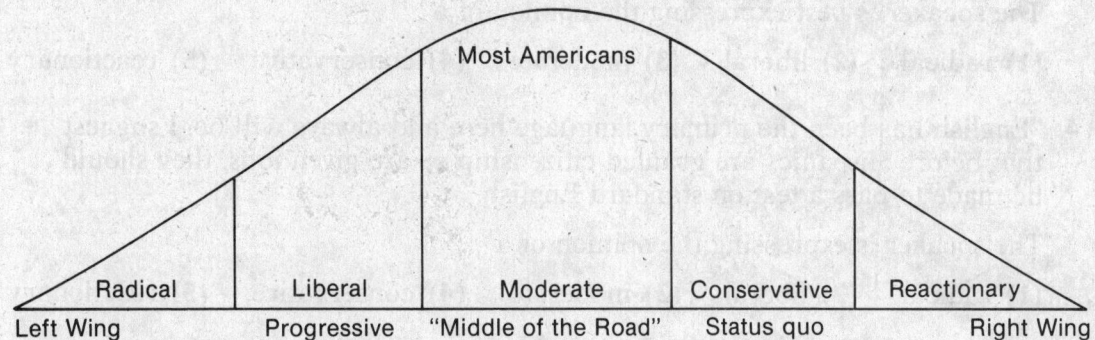

Radical	Liberal	Moderate	Conservative	Reactionary
Left Wing	Progressive	"Middle of the Road"	Status quo	Right Wing

radical: one who advocates sweeping changes in laws and methods of government with little delay

liberal: one who advocates political change in the name of progress, especially social improvement through governmental action

moderate: one who believes in avoiding extreme changes and measures in laws and government

conservative: one who advocates maintaining the existing social order and believes that change, if any, should be gradual

reactionary: one who resists change and usually advocates a return to an earlier social order or policy

EXERCISE 13: THE POLITICAL SPECTRUM

Directions: Read the passage and, using the definitions above, identify the political position of each of the quotes that follow the passage.

An issue in American life that has generated many positions and has divided the population is bilingualism. Many Americans are concerned that we are quickly becoming a bilingual country—the primary and secondary languages being English and Spanish. Americans have varying opinions about the increasing concessions made to our Spanish-speaking minority.

1. "We might as well accept the fact that Hispanic-Americans are here to stay and are significant contributors to our American way of life. Instead of criticizing them for speaking in their native tongue, the government should improve bilingual programs to make it easier for Hispanics to learn English."

The speaker is best expressing the opinion of a

   (1) radical   **(2)** liberal   **(3)** moderate   **(4)** conservative   **(5)** reactionary

2. "Let's not lose our heads. We don't need harsher laws, nor do we need to spend more money. The current strategies to bring Hispanics into the mainstream of American society by helping them to overcome language barriers are sufficient. We just need to work harder at them."

   The speaker is best expressing the opinion of a

   (1) radical   **(2)** liberal   **(3)** moderate   **(4)** conservative   **(5)** reactionary

3. "I'm tired of seeing my tax dollars spent to make it easier for people too lazy to learn the language. Every public sign written in Spanish should be taken down—my Italian parents didn't have it that easy back in the thirties. Then these people would have to learn English—they'd have to sink or swim."

   The speaker is best expressing the opinion of a

   (1) radical   **(2)** liberal   **(3)** moderate   **(4)** conservative   **(5)** reactionary

4. "English has been the primary language here and always will be. I suggest that before Hispanics are granted citizenship or are given jobs, they should be made to pass a test on standard English."

   The speaker is expressing the opinion of a

   (1) radical   **(2)** liberal   **(3)** moderate   **(4)** conservative   **(5)** reactionary

5. "Unless the laws that treat Mexicans as second-class citizens because of their inability to speak the language are changed immediately, starting tomorrow, Mexicans should stop picking lettuce, washing dishes, and sweeping floors—doing the dirty work at low pay that other Americans think they are above doing."

   The speaker is expressing the opinion of a

   (1) radical   **(2)** liberal   **(3)** moderate   **(4)** conservative   **(5)** reactionary

   Answers are on page 350.

WRITING ACTIVITY 4

Do you consider yourself a radical, liberal, moderate, conservative, or reactionary? Based on the definitions provided, write one or two paragraphs describing your political orientation.

Political Parties

A *political party* is a group whose goal is to influence public policy by getting its candidates elected to office. Although the U.S. Constitution makes no provision for political parties, they serve a useful function in our democracy. Political parties

- define the issues and propose possible solutions for governmental problems
- act as another check in our governmental system of checks and balances by monitoring the policies of the party in power
- enable citizens to become involved in the governmental apparatus
- help to keep the number of candidates running for public office manageable

For over a century, there have been two major political parties in the United States—the Democrats and the Republicans.

The differences between the Democratic and Republican parties tend to center around domestic, economic, and social issues as well as foreign policy. Most fundamentally, however, the two parties differ in their views of the role of government in solving problems.

In general, the Democratic party favors a strong federal government at the expense of the sovereign rights of the states; advocates government regulation of big business; endorses labor unions; and champions the rights of the disadvantaged and minorities.

The Republican party, on the other hand, favors stronger state authority at the expense of the federal government; advocates free enterprise; supports checks on labor unions; and believes in maintaining the status quo (keeping things as they are).

There are exceptions to these generalizations, of course, and in recent years, the distinctions between the two parties are becoming increasingly blurred.

EXERCISE 14: POLITICAL PARTIES

Directions: Write *D* in the space provided if the statement generally applies to the Democratic party's philosophy and *R* if it generally applies to the Republican party's philosophy.

_____ **1.** favors having state and local governments solve their own problems

_____ **2.** supports labor unions and the right of their members to strike

_____ **3.** represents the interests of big business

_____ **4.** advocates spending large amounts of money for welfare and other social services

_____ **5.** more often supports "guns" (defense spending) over "butter" (domestic spending)

Answers are on page 350.

WRITING ACTIVITY 5

Are you a Republican, Democrat, or an independent? Write two or three paragraphs describing your party affiliation or why you have none. List reasons why you are loyal to that party or political orientation.

Pressure Groups

Once public officials are elected, they are under constant pressure exerted by individuals, businesses, governmental agencies, and others who make up their constituency. *Pressure groups* are organized groups not associated with a political party, who actively seek to influence public opinion, policies, and actions. The attempt to influence legislation is called *lobbying*. Lobbyists constantly watch for bills that may affect the group or groups they represent.

For example, when the automobile emission-control law was being proposed, lobbyists for the automobile manufacturers worked hard to ensure that the law would be reasonable, not too costly, and not disruptive to automobile production.

Political Action Committees, known as PACs, seek to influence public officials directly. PACs contribute to legislators' campaign funds in the hope of obtaining favorable votes on legislation important to the committees.

Individuals, too, can influence their elected representatives by signing petitions, embarking on letter-writing campaigns, and staging public demonstrations against unpopular policies. Each of these methods is one more informal check in our governmental system of checks and balances.

WRITING ACTIVITY 6

Do you think special interest groups such as PACs have too much influence on legislators (and, indirectly, on the American political process)? Write two or three paragraphs defending your point of view.

The Electoral Process

Both the Democratic and Republican parties maintain national party headquarters and staffs. Every four years, a national convention is held to nominate a presidential candidate who must have won a majority of delegates in the primaries that precede the nominating convention. A political *primary* enables members of a party to express their preference for a candidate to run in the general election. In most primary elections, the candidate must receive a *plurality* (more votes than any other candidate) to win. Primaries may be open or closed. In an *open primary* voters need not declare their party affiliations. In a *closed primary* voters must declare whether they are Republicans or Democrats.

At the nominating convention, each state sends a designated number of delegates, who are local and state party representatives, to help select the party's nominee. At the end of a week-long forum in which the issues are discussed and speeches are delivered, the delegates vote to choose the party's nominee and to approve the party's platform. The *platform* is a formal declaration of the principles on which the party stands.

After the candidates from each party campaign for office, the general election is held. In the general election, the winner must receive a *majority* of the votes cast.

Once elected, public officials are responsible to a *constituency*—the people who elected them to office. The elected official is obligated to faithfully serve this group of people. For the president of the United States, of course, the constituency is the entire American population.

EXERCISE 15: ELECTING A PRESIDENT

Directions: Match each definition on the right with the correct term on the left.

_____ **1.** plurality   **a.** declaration of a party's stand on the issues

_____ **2.** primary   **b.** the people a public official represents

_____ **3.** platform   **c.** more than half of the votes cast in an election

_____ **4.** majority   **d.** party election to select a candidate to run in the general election

_____ **5.** constituency   **e.** more votes than any other candidate (but not more than half)

Answers are on page 350.

EXERCISE 16: THE DEMOCRATIC PRIMARY

Directions: Look at the cartoon and answer the questions that follow.

HUGH HAYNIE
Louisville Courier-Journal
©Los Angeles Times Syndicate

"Okay . . . are there any other Democratic presidential candidates who'd like t'be in the group picture?"

1. The cartoon supports the cartoonist's belief that

    (1) in presidential politics, the Democratic party is never to be taken seriously
    (2) anybody can run in the Democratic presidential primary
    (3) in the Democratic party, only familiar figures seek the nomination for the presidency
    (4) Democratic presidential candidates are well known for fighting among themselves
    (5) the Democratic party is seldom united during a presidential campaign

2. Based on the cartoon, the cartoonist would likely agree with which of the following opinions?

    (1) The Democratic party is more "democratic" than the Republican party.
    (2) The Democratic party is more popular than the Republican party.
    (3) The Republican party will win elections more often because it usually unites behind one candidate.
    (4) The Republican party should field as many presidential candidates as the Democratic party.
    (5) It is ridiculous for the Democratic party to allow such a large number of candidates to seek the office of president.

Answers are on page 350.

EXERCISE 17: THE ELECTORAL PROCESS

Directions: Choose the best answer for the following question.

Based on the definition of a closed primary, which of the following practices is generally true in order for the results to be valid?

(1) Republicans and Democrats alike can vote in any primary they choose.
(2) Voters should declare their party affiliations (Republican or Democrat) and vote in the respective primary.
(3) Voters need not declare whether or not they are Republican or Democrat when they vote in a primary.
(4) Voters should bypass the primary and only vote in the general election.
(5) Voters should not be eligible to vote in primaries; primaries are only for party regulars on the local and state levels.

Answer is on page 350.

The Impact of the Media

Another significant force in the modern American political process is the media. Television, radio, newspapers, and magazines are all part of the media. Television by far has the greatest influence on the American voter, as evidenced by the huge sums of campaign money spent on television. Close elections may be won or lost on the basis of a candidate's media campaign.

Some political observers believe that television is undermining the American democratic process since only those who have the money to finance huge publicity campaigns are able to run for office. This makes it nearly impossible for candidates who are not wealthy to run for office.

EXERCISE 18: THE IMPACT OF THE MEDIA

Directions: Read the passage and answer the question that follows.

Some people say that public opinion polls should not be taken close to an election because the results might influence the voters. For example, during the 1980 election in which President Carter lost to Ronald Reagan, the outcome was predicted by television networks before the polls closed. Informal surveys, *exit polls*, were being conducted outside the voting areas, and vote percentages for each candidate were projected from them.

Which of the following *best* explains how the televised poll results could have affected the election's outcome?

(1) Carter's supporters who had not yet voted did not bother to when they saw the lopsided results.
(2) When it became known that Carter was trailing Reagan, more of Carter's supporters rushed out to vote than would have otherwise.
(3) Backers of Reagan who had not yet voted did not think it necessary to vote since he was far ahead.
(4) Happy about the obvious victory, Reagan supporters came out in even greater numbers to vote.
(5) Voters who were previously undecided finally decided to join the winning team and vote for Reagan.

Answer is on page 350.

4
ECONOMICS—HOW ARE PEOPLE'S NEEDS MET?

"Man does not live by bread alone," it says in Deuteronomy, a book of the Bible. This means that there is more to human survival than meeting the needs of food, shelter, and clothing. However, economists might add, "But man lives by bread first of all." For before humans can satisfy their emotional and spiritual needs, they must first meet the physical needs of survival.

Economists study how a society meets its unlimited material needs with its limited resources. The limitation of resources requires that people make choices about what needs to satisfy.

Societies also must make choices. Every society must answer three basic questions when determining the type of economic system under which it will operate. These questions are:

- *What should be produced?* What do members of a society need and want?

- *How should it be produced?* Should each person make his or her own goods, or should businesses or government manufacture them for the entire society?

- *How should the product be distributed?* Should the products be given to everyone equally or only to those who can afford to buy them?

To answer these questions, each government must first identify its goals and values and then determine what resources are available to produce what the society needs.

Factors of Production

Economists have identified three vital factors of production: natural resources, capital, and labor.

Natural resources are the raw materials needed to produce goods. Trees must be available for the production of wood and paper products. Automobiles can be built only if ore can be mined to make the necessary steel.

Each society lacks some resources and, therefore, cannot produce certain goods. For example, the Dani tribe of New Guinea lives in a tropical climate on a remote mountain range. Their huts, weapons, and tools are built of wood because that is what natural resource is available. Nothing is made of metal because ore is not one of their natural resources.

A second factor of production is capital. *Capital*, as it is referred to here, is any equipment, factories, or machines that are used to produce other goods or to provide services. Capital also may be defined as money invested in an enterprise. A sewing machine used in the manufacture of dresses or shirts is an example of capital, as is an entire lumber mill that covers a square mile of land.

The third factor of production is labor. *Labor* is made up of the people who do the work. They run the assembly lines, plant the crops, build the buildings, drive the trucks, and sell the merchandise. For example, the seamstresses who cut and sew the patterns to make the dresses and shirts are considered to be labor.

History has shown that no matter how carefully and efficiently an economy manages the factors of production, they remain scarce as compared to the ever-increasing demands society makes upon them.

EXERCISE 1: FACTORS OF PRODUCTION

Directions: In each example, write *N* if the factor of production refers to natural resources, *C* if it refers to capital, and *L* if it refers to labor.

_____ 1. the seals, Arctic foxes, and walruses hunted by the Eskimos

_____ 2. the tools a plumber uses in practicing the trade

_____ 3. diamonds unearthed from the mines of South Africa

_____ 4. farmers who plant the spring corn crop

_____ 5. conveyor belts used in the packing houses to carry meat

Answers are on page 350.

WRITING ACTIVITY 1

Multinational corporations are corporations that cross national boundaries in their manufacturing and sales operations. In recent years, large American corporations have established operations in areas of the world where production costs and labor are cheaper than in the United States. Do you agree or disagree with this business practice? Whom do you think this affects? Does it affect them positively or negatively? Defend your point of view in two or three paragraphs.

Economics and Government

A nation's system of government often determines the type of economic system under which the nation will operate. For example, the U.S. system of government is founded on the principle of individual freedom. This belief in the importance of individual freedom contributed greatly to the establishment of capitalism as the economic form under which the American economy operates.

Capitalism

Capitalism is an economic system based on the private ownership of the resources of production. Investment decisions are made by the individual or corporation rather than by the government. The production, distribution, and prices of goods and services are determined by competition in a free market. The government intervenes only when necessary to protect the public interest.

Other governments place the importance of the collective (all the people) above the individual. This emphasis on the collective permitted the emergence of economic systems that are alternatives to capitalism. Two such types are socialism and communism.

Socialism

Under *socialism*, the most important industries and services are publicly and cooperatively owned. These industries, which may be steel production, banking and finance, public transportation, or health are controlled with the goal of providing equal opportunity for all.

In socialist economies, ownership of private property is permitted; however, owners of businesses together with the government decide what goods and services are produced, how they are produced, and who should get them. The economy of Sweden is a socialist economy.

Communism

A third economic order does not permit private ownership of property and the means of production at all. Under *communism*, the government, described as the community, owns the property and distributes the society's goods in accordance with the "common good." The government decides what goods and services are produced and who should get them. The economies of the People's Republic of China and Cuba operate under the principles of communism, as did the economy of the former Soviet Union.

None of these three economic systems exists in pure form. That is, no *completely* capitalist, socialist, or communist economy exists in the modern world. In its operation, each of the economic systems incorporates some aspect of another.

The term *mixed economy* is used to describe the U.S. economy, since some government regulation of private enterprise exists. For example, the Food and Drug Administration ensures that any new medicine or drug that is marketed in the United States has been properly tested before it is sold to the public.

EXERCISE 2: ECONOMIC SYSTEMS

Directions: Choose the best answer to complete each of the following statements.

1. The quote "From each according to his ability, to each according to his need" best describes the economic system of

   (a) capitalism
   (b) socialism
   (c) mixed economy

2. The quote "In the area of economics, the government that governs least governs best" best describes the economic system of

   (a) capitalism
   (b) socialism
   (c) communism

Answers are on page 350.

EXERCISE 3: ECONOMIC SYSTEMS AND GOVERNMENTS

Directions: The diagram below shows the continuum of economic systems. Look at the diagram and answer the questions that follow it.

THE CONTINUUM OF ECONOMIC SYSTEMS

MARKET — Capitalism — Socialism — Communism — COMMAND

1. According to the continuum of economic systems, which of the following conclusions may be drawn?

    (1) Communism is the best example of the market system.
    (2) Capitalism is the best example of the command system.
    (3) Socialism is the opposite of capitalism.
    (4) Capitalism is the opposite of communism.
    (5) Capitalism is better than any other system represented.

2. Which of the following situations *best* supports the statement "Each of the economic systems incorporates some aspect of the other"?

    (1) In socialist Sweden, SAAB, the automobile manufacturer, is owned and run by the government.
    (2) In Cuba, the government-controlled media schedules the broadcasting for all television and radio programs.
    (3) In the United States, a dairy manufacturer is told by a government agency what percentages of milk and cream a product sold as ice cream must contain.
    (4) In the People's Republic of China, all of the nation's farms are nationalized, and young people are forced to work them.
    (5) In the United States, major air carriers engage in a "price war" to attract passengers during the peak vacation season.

Answers are on page 351.

WRITING ACTIVITY 2

Great Britain has a national health-care system in which the costs for medical treatment are paid for by the government. In the United States, national health-care insurance has become an issue of heated political debate. Do you support such a program or not? Write an essay of two or three paragraphs defending your position for or against national health insurance paid by the government.

Supply and Demand

The foundation of American capitalism is supply and demand. *Supply* is the quantity of goods and services available for sale at all possible prices. *Demand* is the desire to buy the product or service and the ability to pay for it.

Producers or suppliers are in business to make a profit. Therefore, they supply goods and services at a price. They must charge prices high enough to cover their costs for production and earn a profit for themselves. Consumers who are willing and able to buy these goods and services create a demand.

The amount of production (supply) of an item and its price depend on the cost of production and the demand in the marketplace. In general, producers seek the highest possible prices to maximize their profits. Consumers seek the lowest possible prices to keep money in their pockets. These opposing goals of producers and consumers significantly affect prices in the marketplace.

Price and Supply—The Producer's View

In general, the higher the price, the greater the number of companies that supply a product or service. A high-priced item or service that yields a large profit will attract many producers who will compete with one another for a share of the market. This applies chiefly to manufactured goods and to services. Precious minerals and metals such as diamonds and gold command higher prices than more common minerals and metals because they are scarce and more cannot be made.

A good example of the relationship between price and supply is the running shoes phenomenon. When they were introduced to the buying public, running shoes bearing the trademarks of such companies as Nike and Reebok created great demand. Consumers—adults and teens—paid higher prices for the labels than they ordinarily might have for other brands. As a result, several competitors entered the market (increasing the supply) seeking to make money on the product. Each running shoe manufacturer fought to capture a share of the market.

When too many producers compete in the marketplace, however, supply exceeds demand because buyers cannot or will not buy all of the goods offered for sale. As a result, a surplus occurs and prices fall. Producers no longer reap the profits necessary for them to compete successfully. Some businesses streamline their operations, and others are forced out of business.

Price and Supply—The Consumer's View

From the consumer's viewpoint, the higher the price, the lower the demand; the lower the price, the greater the demand. If prices for running shoes became too high, consumers might stop buying them and revert to wearing offbrands. On the other hand, when prices for an item fall too low and consumer demand exceeds the producer's ability to provide the product, a shortage in supply occurs. As a result, prices rise higher, and in extreme cases, the product is rationed. Under rationing, the quantity of the item sold is restricted.

As shown in the graph on the left, as the price of running shoes goes up, the quantity supplied increases. In this graph, producers cannot supply running shoes at a price of $20. However, as the price increases to $30, about ten pairs of running shoes are available for purchase. According to this graph, what would happen to the supply if the price were $60?

You're right if you said that there would be about 80 pairs of running shoes available for purchase.

As shown in the graph on the right, as the price of running shoes goes down, the quantity demanded rises. At $60 each, the demand would be for ten pairs. If the price were lowered to $30, the demand would increase to about 45 pairs. According to this graph, if the price rose to $70 per pair, would demand increase or decrease?

Since the graph shows no values for $70 per pair, you can infer that there is no demand for running shoes at this price.

EXERCISE 4: SUPPLY AND DEMAND IN THE U.S. ECONOMY

Directions: Study the cartoon and answer the following questions.

1. One proposal to cover the costs of President Clinton's health-care package was to impose "sin taxes" and value-added taxes on tobacco and alcohol. Which of the following does the cartoonist suggest might result from these taxes?

   (1) high prices the consumer could not afford to pay
   (2) a greater demand for both tobacco and alcohol
   (3) a lower demand for health-care services
   (4) an increased demand for bartenders who can handle large amounts of money
   (5) a reduction in the number of people who can afford to pay their taxes

2. The cartoonist would most likely agree with which of the following statements?

   (1) Added taxes on alcohol and tobacco would be a fair way to raise money.
   (2) Excessive taxation is creating a nation of alcoholics.
   (3) Americans already feel the burden of paying high taxes.
   (4) Alcohol already costs too much.
   (5) Smoking should be banned in bars.

Answers are on page 351.

Supply and Equilibrium

To produce exactly the amount that consumers are willing to buy, producers must determine at what point supply equals demand. Economists call this point the *equilibrium*. Equilibrium occurs when the supply and demand curves intersect. This establishes the market price for a product or service.

When the price is greater than the equilibrium, demand falls and there is more of a product or service than people want to buy. This is called a *surplus*. When the price falls below the equilibrium, demand increases, exceeding supply, and a *shortage* in the product or service occurs.

The following graph illustrates the equilibrium.

EQUILIBRIUM FOR RUNNING SHOES

What is the price at which the supply of running shoes equals demand? The equilibrium point on the graph indicates that this is about $42.

EXERCISE 5: SUPPLY, DEMAND, AND EQUILIBRIUM

Directions: Study the graph and answer the following questions or statements.

1. According to the graph, the market price of these video-cassette recorders would be about

   (1) $500
   (2) $400
   (3) $300
   (4) $200
   (5) $100

SUPPLY, DEMAND, AND EQUILIBRIUM
Videocassette Recorders

2. If the market price for videocassette recorders fell to $150, what would be the likely result?

(1) Demand would decrease.
(2) Supply would remain the same.
(3) Demand would increase.
(4) Producers would not be able to satisfy demand.
(5) The supply would become scarce.

3. In recent years, Korea has developed the technology to manufacture and import to the United States electronic equipment such as videocassette recorders. If demand for VCRs were low, what impact would Korea's entrance into the market have on the sale of VCRs in the United States?

(1) Prices for VCRs would increase because the supply would be greater.
(2) Prices for VCRs would decrease because the supply would be greater.
(3) A surplus of VCRs might result.
(4) Both 1 and 2
(5) Both 2 and 3

Answers are on page 351.

Economic Growth

Economic growth is a major goal of an economic system. In a growing economy, there is an increasing capacity to produce more goods and services. During periods of great economic growth, consumers are increasingly able to buy these goods and services. An economy's growth must occur at a steady and controllable pace.

This process may be likened to blowing up a balloon. If a balloon is inflated too quickly, it may burst; if it is inflated too slowly, it may never reach its full capacity. Similarly, the American economy must grow evenly, or problems will occur. The following diagram illustrates what economists call the ***business cycle***.

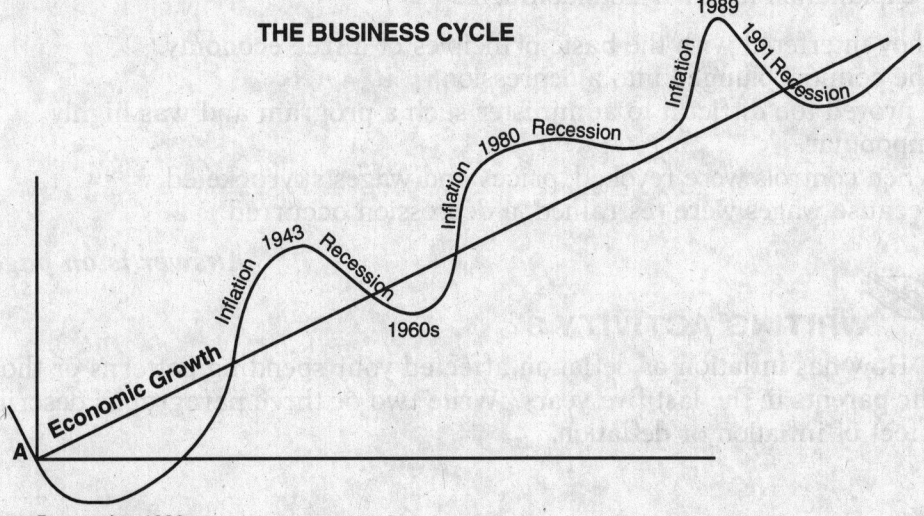

THE BUSINESS CYCLE

Line A is the goal of economic growth—what economists believe is a healthy level of producing goods and services. Comparing the blowing up of a balloon with the growth of the economy, the line represents the level at which air should be blown into the balloon. If too much air is blown into the balloon, it becomes overinflated. When not enough air is in the balloon, it is underinflated or deflated.

Inflation and Its Effects

When too much money and credit are available and too few goods are available to satisfy demand, the dollar loses its value and the prices of goods increase. The country begins a period of inflation. (Notice the upward slope of the line.)

For consumers to be able to keep pace with the rise in the cost of goods, their wages must increase. For producers to pay the increased wages, they must produce more goods and charge higher prices for them. This chainlike pattern in which wage increases feed on price increases is called an *inflationary spiral*. An "inflation psychology" sets in as consumers rush to make major purchases because they believe that prices will only increase.

For inflation to fall, demand must be decreased and credit restricted. However, one result of curbing high inflation is an economic recession. The United States experienced just this situation in the early 1980s when inflation raged out of control and the Federal Reserve System acted to control it.

Deflation and Its Effects

When too little money and credit are available, and more goods are available than necessary to satisfy demand, the dollar gains value and the prices of goods decrease. Under these circumstances, the economy enters a period of deflation. Because goods remain unsold, producers' profits fall. Falling profits lead to layoffs. Unless the situation is corrected, a recession occurs, and if the recession is prolonged, a depression can result. The United States experienced this condition during the Great Depression of the 1930s.

EXERCISE 6: ECONOMIC GROWTH

Directions: Choose the best answer for the following question.

During a period of severe inflation in 1973–1974, the Nixon administration implemented wage and price controls for a brief period. The controls were soon revoked, however, and did not break the inflationary spiral. Which is the most likely explanation for their abandonment?

(1) They interfered with the basic principles of a free economy.
(2) The country plunged into a depression.
(3) It proved too difficult to administer such a program and was highly unpopular.
(4) When controls were revoked, prices and wages skyrocketed.
(5) Because wages were restrained, a depression occurred.

Answer is on page 351.

WRITING ACTIVITY 3

How has inflation or deflation affected your spending patterns or those of your parents in the last five years? Write two or three paragraphs describing the effect of inflation or deflation.

Measurement of Economic Growth

Economic indicators are statistics that show economic experts how the economy is performing. Among the more commonly used economic statistics are stock market trading, unemployment percentages, number of housing starts, and the gross national product (GNP).

One of the most important measurements of economic growth, the *GNP* represents the total amount of all goods and services produced in one year.

Economists measure GNP in current dollars and again in constant dollars. *Current* dollars indicate the actual dollar value of goods. *Constant* dollars take into account the change in prices over the years because of inflation. In measuring the nation's GNP, economists measure current dollars against constant dollars during a given year. In recent years, economists have used 1987 as the base year with which to compare current GNP dollars. The following graph measures the GNP from 1977 to 1991.

EXERCISE 7: THE GNP AS A MEASURE OF ECONOMIC GROWTH

Directions: Study the graph and choose the *best* answer to complete each statement.

1. According to the graph, the constant-dollar GNP grew between the years

   (1) 1978 and 1980
   (2) 1980 and 1982
   (3) 1982 and 1989
   (4) 1988 and 1991
   (5) 1990 and 1991

GROSS NATIONAL PRODUCT (GNP) PER CAPITA 1977 TO 1991

Source: U.S. Bureau of the Census

2. The steep increase in the line that indicates GNP in current dollars may be attributed to

   (1) deflation
   (2) a recession
   (3) inflation
   (4) a depression
   (5) a booming economy

3. The GNP in constant dollars fell during the years 1979–1980, 1981–1982, and 1990–1991. These periods may best be described as

   (1) depressions
   (2) recessions
   (3) deflations
   (4) inflations
   (5) economic booms

Answers are on page 351.

Money and Monetary Policy

Money is the medium of exchange accepted by a society in payment for goods and services. The nation's money supply consists mainly of coins, bills, and checking and savings deposits.

The U.S. Federal Reserve Board is responsible for setting the nation's *monetary policy*—the regulation of the nation's supply of money and credit in order to keep the economy in balance. Through the nation's banking system, the Federal Reserve Board controls the availability of credit to consumers primarily in two ways—by determining the reserve ratio and by setting the discount rate.

The Reserve Ratio

Every lending institution—banks and savings and loan associations—must hold on to a certain amount of its deposits. This amount that cannot be lent out is called the *reserve ratio*. Most banks are members of the nation's Federal Reserve System (the Fed). By controlling the reserve ratio, the Fed determines the amount of money banks are able to lend.

Suppose, for example, Janet wants to borrow $5,000 to buy a new car, and Aaron wants to borrow $3,000 to fix a leaky roof. They go to the same bank and apply for a loan. The bank uses money from depositors to lend to customers such as Janet and Aaron.

Suppose further that the bank has $10,000 in deposits and the Fed has established the reserve ratio at 10 percent. That means that the bank must keep $1,000 in reserve (10 percent of $10,000). This leaves the bank $9,000 to lend. The bank has enough money to cover Janet's loan and Aaron's loan. Janet now has $5,000 more in purchasing power, so she can buy her car. Aaron now has $3,000 more in purchasing power, so he can fix his roof.

But what if the economy is in a period of inflation? The Fed might raise the reserve ratio to 25 percent. Now the bank must keep on deposit $2,500, leaving only $7,500 to lend. The bank can no longer loan money to both Janet and Aaron. The bank must make a decision. No matter who gets the loan, the other person's purchasing power will not increase. Thus, consumers' demand has been lowered indirectly. When this process is implemented nationwide, the impact on the economy is significant, chiefly because less money is available to lend.

The Discount Rate

A second way in which the Fed influences the nation's economy is through the discount rate. The *discount rate* is the rate of interest the Fed charges member banks to borrow money.

Banks make money by charging a higher interest rate on loans than they pay to those who deposit money into checking and savings accounts. Suppose, for example, that Jake deposits $100 in the bank at a 6 percent interest rate. If he leaves the funds on deposit for one year, he can collect $106 from the bank. This includes his $100 deposit plus the $6 in interest the bank owes him. During this time, however, the bank lends $100 to Samantha for a year. The bank charges her 15 percent interest. After one year, Samantha owes the bank $115. The bank then gives Jake his $106. The profit to the bank is $9. Obviously, the more money a bank has to lend, the more profit it can make.

To have more money to meet demand, banks often borrow from the Federal Reserve System. The bank then lends the money to its customers (borrowers) at a higher rate.

The Fed adjusts the discount rate to affect the supply of money. For example, if the discount rate is 5 percent, consumer banks might lend it out for 10 percent. If the discount rate were raised to 15 percent, consumer banks might charge 20 percent. Thus, you can see the impact a changing discount rate has on the availability of credit in the U.S. economy.

EXERCISE 8: MONEY AND MONETARY POLICY

Directions: Circle *T* if the statement is true or *F* if it is false.

T F **1.** The role of the Fed is to serve as a clearinghouse for all banks in one region.

T F **2.** Two ways in which the Federal Reserve influences the money supply are coining money and setting the prime rate.

T F **3.** Purchasing power is increased through the banking system by banks lending funds from deposited money after first setting aside required reserves.

T F **4.** Most banks belong to the Federal Reserve System.

T F **5.** The prime rate is the interest rate the Fed charges member banks to borrow money.

Answers are on page 351.

Government and Fiscal Policy

While the U.S. Federal Reserve Board directly influences the supply of money and credit in the economy, the government, through its fiscal policy, also indirectly affects the nation's economic condition.

In establishing *fiscal policy*, the president proposes an annual budget to the Congress. As Congress determines what programs are needed, it must also consider how these programs will be funded. Raising taxes is the simplest and most common answer.

Consumers and businesses pay these taxes to the government. The government, in turn, spends the money on programs designed to help the citizens and the country, such as interstate highways, the space program, and the military.

By deciding whether to raise or lower taxes and whether to increase or decrease spending, the government is controlling a major part of the money supply. For example, during inflationary times, the government might exercise fiscal policy by taking money out of the pockets of consumers by increasing taxes. During periods of deflation, the government might put more money in the hands of consumers by cutting spending and lowering taxes.

If the government spends less than it collects in taxes, a *budget surplus* results. If the government spends more than it collects, the condition is called *deficit spending*. A *balanced budget* results when the income from taxes equals the money spent on programs.

EXERCISE 9: FISCAL AND MONETARY POLICY

Directions: Circle the correct answer choice in parentheses.

1. During a recession, to put more money in circulation, the president and Congress should (increase/decrease) government spending while (raising/lowering) taxes.

2. During an inflationary period, the Fed should (increase/decrease) the money in circulation by (raising/lowering) the discount rate while (increasing/decreasing) the reserve ratio.

3. When the government spends more money than it receives in taxes, there is a (budget surplus/budget deficit).

Answers are on page 351.

5
GEOGRAPHY—WHERE DO PEOPLE LIVE?

Like the lower animals, humans are first, last, and always creatures of the land. However, humans differ from the lower animals in their ability to adapt to a variety of environments. This adaptability explains why there is no part of the globe that has not been visited by people and few regions where humans do not live.

Geographers study the physical features of the earth and the ways in which humans have adapted to these features.

In their investigation of the surfaces and regions of the earth, geographers rely on two basic tools. A *globe* is a spherical representation of the earth that shows the continents, countries, and waterways in their true proportions. Globes are not easily portable, however, so mapmakers draw *maps*, which are flat representations of the earth's regions.

Geographers generally use five kinds of maps:

topographical maps—show physical land features (hills, mountains, plains) of an area

population maps—illustrate the distribution of people throughout the world

world maps—illustrate the continents, oceans, seas, and rivers of the world

political maps—outline borders between countries or states and show trade relationships among countries

weather maps—show current or forecasted weather as well as the climate of a particular region

EXERCISE 1: MAPS

Directions: Complete the following statements about the five types of maps.

1. The regions of Asia that receive more than seventy-five inches of rain per year would be best illustrated on a

   (1) topographical map
   (2) population map
   (3) world map
   (4) political map
   (5) weather map

2. The best map for showing the borders of the fifty states in the United States would be a

   (1) topographical map
   (2) population map
   (3) world map
   (4) political map
   (5) weather map

3. A map that would show the highest elevation of the Wasatch Mountain Range in Utah would be a

   (1) topographical map
   (2) population map
   (3) world map
   (4) political map
   (5) weather map

Answers are on page 351.

Symbols and Legends

So that you can read a map, mapmakers provide symbols and a legend or key that tells what the symbols stand for.

For example, on a political map, a star usually indicates a state's or nation's capital. On a population map, the number of people who live in a given city is indicated by the size of the dot that locates the city. (Larger dots indicate cities with large populations; small dots indicate cities with small populations.)

On road maps, a scale of miles is often provided in the legend. A scale of miles is most commonly shown in inches. For example, the legend on a map scale might read "One inch equals 50 miles." An example of a scale is shown below.

You can measure distance with a ruler or with a strip of paper that has a straight edge. Lay a strip of paper against the map to make a straight line between the two points you are interested in. Mark off the two points on the paper's edge, and lay the paper strip against the scale of miles. The distance between the two points will be the number of miles from one place to another.

EXERCISE 2: MEASURING DISTANCE

Directions: Study the map and answer the questions that follow.

1. According to the map shown here, approximately how far is Denver from San Francisco? _____

2. Approximately how long is the state of Wyoming from north to south? _____

3. Approximately how far is the west coast of California from the easternmost boundary of Colorado? _____

Answers are on page 352.

Latitude and Longitude

The *equator*, an imaginary line that circles the earth's center, divides the earth into two *hemispheres*, or halves. The land and water above the equator lie in the Northern Hemisphere; the land and water below the equator are known as the Southern Hemisphere. North America, Central America, and a small part of South America lie in the Northern Hemisphere.

The distance from the equator is measured on maps and globes by degrees of latitude. Lines of *latitude* are parallel lines that measure distance north or south of the equator in degrees. These lines increase in 20-degree increments. The equator is located at 0 degrees latitude, the North Pole at 90 degrees north latitude, and the South Pole at 90 degrees south latitude. Most of the continental United States lies between 25 and 50 degrees north latitude.

Lines of *longitude* are lines that measure distances in degrees east and west of the *prime meridian*, an imaginary line running through Greenwich, England, that divides the world into the Eastern and Western Hemispheres. The prime meridian is located at 0 degrees longitude. There are 180 degrees east of the prime meridian and 180 degrees west of it, for a total of 360 degrees around the earth. Most of the United States, including Alaska and Hawaii, lies between 65 and 125 degrees west longitude.

The lines of latitude and longitude cross each other to form what is called a *grid*. To locate a particular place on a globe or map, you must find the point where two lines intersect. The number of degrees latitude and longitude indicate the location. For example, in the grid diagram below, the island of Madagascar, located off the southeast coast of Africa, is located at approximately 20 degrees south latitude and 45 degrees east longitude.

Based on the grid, what continent is found at 50 degrees north latitude and 0 degrees longitude?

You should have answered *Europe*. The point where the 50-degree-north line of latitude meets the 0-degree line of longitude is the continent of Europe; Europe is located directly north of Africa.

EXERCISE 3: THE LATITUDE AND LONGITUDE GRID

Directions: Choose the best answer for each of the following questions, which are based on the grid on page 335.

1. Which of the following is at 15 degrees north latitude and 20 degrees east longitude?

   (1) northern Europe
   (2) eastern South America
   (3) western Africa
   (4) southern Asia
   (5) central Africa

2. Which of the following countries is located nearest 30 degrees south latitude and 20 degrees east longitude?

   (1) Italy
   (2) Chile
   (3) Egypt
   (4) South Africa
   (5) England

Answers are on page 352.

Time Zones

A *time zone* is a geographical region within which the same standard time is used. To establish time zones for the entire world, geographers have divided the earth into 24 sections that are one hour long. Since the earth is 360 degrees, this means that 15 degrees (360 divided by 24) are equal to one hour of a day.

In the continental United States, there are four time zones: Eastern, Central, Mountain, and Pacific. As people travel west, they move into an earlier time zone for every 15 degrees they travel. For example, people completing a journey west through the Eastern time zone at 5:00 P.M. would have to change their watches to 4:00 P.M. as they entered the next time zone, Central time. The four time zones for the continental United States are shown in the following map.

TIME ZONES ACROSS NORTH AMERICA

EXERCISE 4: TIME ZONES

Directions: Choose the best answer for each question.

1. According to the map, what time is it in Los Angeles when it is midnight in Philadelphia, Pennsylvania?

   (1) 9:00 A.M.
   (2) 9:00 P.M.
   (3) 3:00 P.M.
   (4) 3:00 A.M.
   (5) 2:00 A.M.

2. What time is it in Denver when it is noon in Milwaukee?

   (1) 10:00 A.M.
   (2) 12:00 P.M.
   (3) 11:00 A.M.
   (4) 1:00 P.M.
   (5) 9:00 A.M.

3. The lines marking the four time zones are irregular. All of Indiana except a tiny section of northwest Indiana lies in the Eastern time zone. Which of the following is the most reasonable explanation for why northwest Indiana lies in the Central time zone?

   (1) The people in northwest Indiana voted to be included in the Central time zone.
   (2) The time zones must be evenly divided; in order to obtain an even division of time zones in the United States, part of Indiana was placed in the Central time zone.
   (3) Western Kentucky and western Tennessee, the states south of Indiana, are located in the Central time zone; therefore, northwest Indiana had to comply with the rule.
   (4) Northwest Indiana was once a part of northeast Illinois, which is why the region has a different time zone from the rest of the state.
   (5) Northwest Indiana is considered to be part of Chicago's metropolitan area; therefore, for economic reasons it lies in the same time zone as Chicago.

4. Which group would likely benefit the most from northwest Indiana's falling within the Central time zone?

   (1) people who travel to and from Chicago frequently
   (2) northwest Indiana's schoolchildren
   (3) merchants and businesspeople in northwest Indiana
   (4) both 1 and 3
   (5) both 2 and 3

Answers are on page 352.

Earth's Topography

The physical features of the earth also can affect a region's climate. In general, geographers divide the earth into flatlands (plains) and highlands (mountains, hills, and plateaus).

Plains typically are areas with little or no land elevation and few trees. *Hills* are elevations of less than 1,000 feet that have sides sloping up to flat or rounded tops. *Plateaus* are lower than hills, rise sharply above the level of the neighboring areas, and have elevations lower than 500 feet and broad, flat tops. *Mountains* are elevations of over 1,000 feet, usually with steep, rocky inclines on all sides and pointed or rounded tops.

Plains regions have a uniform climate characterized by hot, dry weather during the summer and very cold temperatures during the winter. Because plains are frequently treeless, there are no barriers against the cold air that sweeps across them during the winter. Hills and plateaus generally share the same climate characteristics of the plains near which they are located. Mountains often act as boundaries between different climate regions. The lower slopes of the mountains usually share the climate of the surrounding area, but the higher up one goes, the colder the air gets. Also, mountains are often snowcapped because the colder air above them is unable to hold moisture. It falls to the earth as snow.

Mapmakers illustrate the varying heights and shapes of land masses by using *contour lines*, lines that show elevations in numbers of feet or meters. The closer together the contour lines, the steeper the incline. The base line for determining the height of highlands is *sea level*. An example of a contour map follows.

CONTOUR MAP

200 feet
150 feet
100 feet
50 feet
Sea Level

What would this land form be classified as—a hill, plain, mountain, or plateau?

Because the land mass is lower than 1,000 feet and has a rounded top, it would be classified as a *hill.*

EXERCISE 5: U.S. TOPOGRAPHY

Directions: Choose the best answer for the statement and questions below.

1. Based on the information in the passage, it is reasonable to conclude that during the winter it is likely to be colder in

   (1) Wisconsin than in Minnesota
   (2) Nebraska than in New Jersey
   (3) Florida than in California
   (4) Washington than in Oregon
   (5) New York than in Connecticut

2. Based on its location, which of the following cities in the United States is at the highest altitude?

   (1) Detroit
   (2) Boston
   (3) Denver
   (4) Los Angeles
   (5) Memphis

3. Low-lying land is often subject to flooding because the area has no elevation. Land that lies below sea level acts as a bowl that collects water. As a result, an effective pumping system is needed to handle flooding. Which of the following cities best meets this description?

   (1) Las Vegas
   (2) New York City
   (3) New Orleans
   (4) Atlanta
   (5) Phoenix

Answers are on page 352.

EXERCISE 6: THE INDIAN PENINSULA

Directions: Study the map and answer the questions that follow.

THE INDIAN PENINSULA

Himalaya Mountains

Mt. Everest +29,028

Relief

■	Over 10,000 feet
▦	5,001–10,000 feet
▦	2,001–5,000 feet
▦	1,001–2,000 feet
□	Sea Level–1,000 feet

1. What is the highest point in the Himalaya Mountains?

(1) 6,000 feet
(2) 10,300 feet
(3) 19,861 feet
(4) 29,028 feet
(5) 33,411 feet

2. The majority of the land shown on the map may be generally described as being at an elevation of

(1) over 10,000 feet
(2) between 5,000 and 10,000 feet
(3) between 2,000 and 5,000 feet
(4) between 1,000 and 2,000 feet
(5) between sea level and 1,000 feet

Answers are on page 352.

WRITING ACTIVITY 1

In one or two paragraphs, describe the topography of the area in which you live. Do you live near mountains, hills, plains, or plateaus? Describe how the topography of your region affects the climate.

Population Distribution

Population demographics is the study of numbers and locations of people in a region. Climate and topography are two factors that affect where people live in the world.

Most of the world's population lives in the temperate zones because humans cannot survive very long in regions with extreme cold or intense heat. Also, regions with plains allow for a greater and more even distribution of population than regions that are mountainous. In mountainous regions, people tend to inhabit the land at the foot of the mountains or in the valleys.

EXERCISE 7: POPULATION DISTRIBUTION

Directions: Choose the best answer for each question below.

1. Which of the following western states is sparsely populated because of its extremes in temperature and altitudes as well as its rugged topography? (This state also has to import much of its food because the land is not good for farming.)

   (1) California
   (2) Washington
   (3) Oregon
   (4) Nevada
   (5) Colorado

2. Of the following states, which would most likely have the *least* even distribution of population because of its land features?

   (1) Georgia
   (2) New Jersey
   (3) Kansas
   (4) West Virginia
   (5) Michigan

Answers are on page 352.

Other Factors Affecting Population Distribution

Other factors can affect the population of an area. For instance, the location of jobs is one such factor. In the early history of the United States, agricultural areas were the major population centers because most of the jobs were in farming. With the beginning of the Industrial Revolution, the situation reversed, and cities, where the factories were, replaced rural areas as the nation's centers of population.

Another factor is the overall quality of life that a region provides. In the 1950s, for example, suburbs displaced big cities as the most popular places to live. The relative safety of the suburbs, their cleanliness, their better schools, and their wide-open spaces are all benefits that have attracted people and jobs away from the cities. While the population shift to the suburbs has provided Americans with an alternative lifestyle to city living, there have been problems.

Discrimination in the establishment of many suburbs has resulted in all-white or nearly all-white towns circling large minority-dominated cities. This pattern has been lamented often by social observers like writer Vance Packard. In his book *A Nation of Strangers*, Packard criticizes the uniformity of classes and colors that is characteristic of the suburbs.

EXERCISE 8: OTHER FACTORS AFFECTING POPULATION DISTRIBUTION

Directions: Read the following quote from Packard's book and choose the best answer for each question.

> Some social stratification (by income and ethnic background) is probably inevitable in any complex society. But we miss much of life's richness if we fail to take affirmative action against the current trend among developers to lay us all out with "our own kind" of people.

1. Which of the following statements supports the opinion expressed by Vance Packard?

   (1) The advantages of suburban living far outweigh the disadvantages.
   (2) Wealthy communities are safe because they can afford to pay for high levels of police protection, unlike big, poor cities.
   (3) Housing patterns based on income, class, and ethnic background are inevitable.
   (4) Children exposed to only one kind of people grow up crippled in their understanding of the world.
   (5) Big cities are to blame for driving white residents out, forcing them to live in the suburbs.

2. Vance Packard's argument could be used to support which of the following measures?

   (1) restrictive covenants—clauses in property deeds that keep certain people from buying homes in a community
   (2) separate suburbs established for specific ethnic and minority groups
   (3) the rehabilitation of the housing stock in the central areas of big cities
   (4) the practice of busing minority children from the big cities to the suburbs that have the best schools
   (5) the enforcement of fair-housing laws allowing for more ethnically diverse communities

Answers are on page 352.

TEST 2: SOCIAL STUDIES ANSWER KEY

CHAPTER 1: BEHAVIORAL SCIENCES

Exercise 1: Physical and Cultural Anthropology
page 248
Application

1. **P** Fossils or bones represent the physical aspect of human beings.

2. **C** Tools represent technology, a cultural aspect of human beings.

3. **C** Hieroglyphics (writings) on walls represent the cultural aspect.

4. **C** Eating habits represent the cultural aspect.

5. **C** Rites of manhood represent the cultural aspect.

Exercise 2: Ethnocentrism
pages 249–250
Analysis

Exact wording of responses may vary.

1. The tribe Asu represents the U.S.A., spelled backward. Clues are location on the American continent north of Mexico and highly developed society.

2. The sacred "rac" is the word *car* spelled backward. Some clues are: social obligation to own at least one rac (car); racs (cars) do not live more than five to seven years; there are rac (car) specialists in each community.

3. The rite that is so important to sixteen-year-olds is obtaining their driver's licenses.

Exercise 3: Values, Ethnocentrism, and Cultural Relativity
page 250
Application

1. (1) According to the essay preceding the passage, ethnocentrism is the judging of another culture by one's own values. Dr. Thapar is showing how Americans' reliance on the car appears to another culture.

Analysis

2. (4) The study of this aspect of American culture is intended to show how the role of the car in American society would appear to others not familiar with our culture.

Exercise 4: Primary and Secondary Groups
page 251
Application

1. **S** There need not be personal contact among members of a fan club.

2. **S** The math class is a secondary group because the interaction is brief and general.

3. **P** Your family is the most primary of all groups.

4. **S** You may know all of the townspeople, but you do not have a close relationship with each of them.

5. **P** Children who play together frequently develop a close bond—a feature of a primary group.

Exercise 5: Socialization and the Family
pages 252–253
Comprehension

1. (1) The passage suggests that the lack of socialization or extreme isolation from other humans is the cause of the man's behavior. None of the other choices is supported by the passage.

Analysis

2. (4) The hypothesis that the man experienced some human contact and the boys did not best explains why he survived among humans. Choice (1) is not stated. Choice (2) has nothing to do with their survival after human contact was made. Choices (3) and (5) are not supported.

Exercise 6: Nuclear and Extended Families
page 253
Application

1. **E** Three generations indicate that the parents, children, and grandparents live together; this describes an extended family.

2. **N** Two generations entail the parents and their children living together; this describes a nuclear family.

3. **E** According to the passage, an extended family includes relatives other than the husband, wife, and children, all of whom live together.

4. **E** According to the passage, an extended family includes relatives other than the husband, wife, and children, all of whom live together.

5. **N** A nuclear family may include no children, or it may include a few or many living together under one roof.

Exercise 7: The Changing American Family
page 254
Comprehension
1. (4) The increase for the years 1980–1985 is 1.2 million; the amount of increase for the others is less.

Evaluation
2. (3) This is the only fact supported by the graph. There were about 3 million (2.5 with spouses and .42 without spouses) working mothers in 1960. Choices (1) and (2) are not supported by the graph, and choices (4) and (5) are opinions.

Analysis
3. (3) The most likely explanation for the sharp increase in two-job families during the years 1975–1980 is inflation and the higher cost of living for families. The other choices are less supportable by the passage and pictograph.

Exercise 8: Social Stratification
page 255
Application
1. **CL** A class system enourages self-improvement and achievement.
2. **CL** Achieved status is permissible under the class system.
3. **CA** A caste system is strict and rigid.
4. **CL** Job choices are open in a class system.
5. **CA** The caste system is characterized by five levels.

Exercise 9: Types of Learning
pages 256–257
Application
1. (1) The baby learns to respond (stop crying) when it associates the light (stimulus) with being picked up and comforted (reward).
2. (4) The child makes a logical thought process and adapts information to distinguish between the bird and the airplane.
3. (2) The pigeon gains something (food) after it interacts with an element in its environment (presses a bar in its cage).
4. (3) Trying several alternatives to arrive at the right answer or solution to a problem (finding the right shoe size) demonstrates trial-and-error learning.

Exercise 10: Modes of Learning
page 257
Analysis
(4) The fact that experiments in classical conditioning are performed only on lower animals and very young children suggests that as humans get older, cognitive perception becomes much more important in their ability to learn. Choices (1) and (2) wrongly state that classical conditioning is not important in helping to understand human behavior. Choices (3) and (5) are not true.

Exercise 11: Psychoanalytic Theory
pages 258–259
Comprehension
1. Otto's habit of stopping off for a drink after work represents the **id**.
2. Otto's limiting himself to two drinks and his leaving the bar before he gets drunk represent his **ego**.
3. The guilt Otto experiences on his way home represents the **superego**.

Exercise 12: Self-Actualization Theory
page 260
Comprehension
(5) The need for personal popularity is directly related to one's need to belong and the need for recognition and respect from others.

Exercise 13: Defense Mechanisms
page 261
Application
1. (4) The fox makes an excuse (the grapes were sour anyway) for his failure to reach them. This is an example of rationalization.
2. (1) By refusing to discuss the boating accident that causes him anxiety, Tyrone is demonstrating repression.
3. (3) Michael directs his anger at his dog instead of directing it at the real cause of his team's loss. This demonstrates displacement.

Exercise 14: Social Environment
page 262
Analysis
(3) According to the passage, people lose their individual identities when they become part of a group. This means that they lose their sense of who they really are.

CHAPTER 2: U.S. HISTORY
Exercise 1: Discovery, Early Exploration, and Colonization
page 264
Comprehension
1. (5) Two places on the map are labeled MA (Massachusetts), but one has ME (Maine) written in it. This indicates that Maine was originally a part of Massachusetts.

Evaluation

2. (3) The map shows the area west of the 13 colonies to be disputed by France and Britain. Therefore, the map indicates that France still had interest in the New World. The other choices, whether true or untrue, cannot be supported by the information in the map.

Exercise 2: The Thirteen English Colonies
page 265
Comprehension

1. (3) The passage states that "indentured workers placed their signatures to contracts to work for four years in the tobacco fields in return for their passage across the Atlantic."

2. (4) The passage states that "Virginia claimed them all, moulded them into her own pattern, made them Virginians." This suggests that colonists who settled Virginia developed a common bond.

Exercise 3: The Revolutionary War
page 267
Analysis

1. d   2. a   3. b   4. c   5. e

Exercise 4: The Quest for Independence
page 267
Comprehension

1. (2) The passage states that the purpose of the First Continental Congress was to demand the repeal of the Intolerable Acts.

Application

2. (2) India's rebellion against British domination is the only event shown that can be compared to the American colonists' fight against the British. India was once a British colony until it revolted against British domination and gained its independence in 1947.

Exercise 5: The Beginning of American Government
page 268
Comprehension

1. F   2. T   3. T   4. F   5. F

Exercise 6: Disputes and Compromises
pages 269–270
Analysis

1. (2) Counting slaves as only three-fifths of the population was favorable to the northern states because it meant that the South would have fewer representatives in the House of Representatives.

Evaluation

2. (3) The passage and the chart indicate that the anti-Federalists feared strong, centralized control. You could conclude that this was because they believed that individual liberties were more likely to be protected under a local than a central authority.

Application

3. (5) The passage states that the Federalists were largely members of the merchant class who favored commercial and industrial expansion. A banker and shipper would fit this category.

4. (1) According to the passage, anti-Federalists were largely farmers who favored individual liberties and feared authoritative control by a central government. Similarly, today's southern conservatives of both parties favor state sovereignty over federal sovereignty.

Exercise 7: The War of 1812
page 271
Comprehension

1. (4) According to the passage, the events that contributed to the United States' sense of nationalism after the War of 1812 were the westward expansion (Manifest Destiny) and the increased need to manufacture its own goods because of the British naval blockade.

Analysis

2. (3) The Federalists, who were merchants and shipowners, feared that the war would interrupt their trade with other European nations.

Exercise 8: The Era of Good Feelings and the Monroe Doctrine
page 272
Application

(4) The only situation listed that represents an attempt to enforce the principles of the Monroe Doctrine is the American blockade of Cuba, in which the United States prevented foreign involvement in the Western Hemisphere.

Exercise 9: Jacksonian Democracy and the Mexican War
page 273
Application

1. (3) Jimmy Carter, a newcomer to Washington, is the only president listed who experienced a reception similar to Andrew Jackson's.

2. (4) Because easterners disliked southerners in each of these cases, the attitude may be described as one of sectionalism.

Exercise 10: A Divided Nation
page 274
Application

1. (3) Popular sovereignty permitted the people to approve or disapprove of a legislative action; therefore, of the choices given, popular sovereignty is the most similar to a referendum.

Evaluation

2. (5) When the Supreme Court ruled that Dred Scott could be returned to his master, it was upholding the practice of treating slaves as personal property.

Exercise 11: The Vote on Secession
page 275
Comprehension

1. (c) Virginia split in two over the issue of secession, with the western part (now known as West Virginia) loyal to the Union.

2. (d) Texas seceded from the Union despite the fact that only the eastern part of the state voted to do so.

3. (a) Kentucky was a border state that remained with the Union despite being a slave state.

4. (b) Mississippi is a solidly southern state that voted overwhelmingly to secede from the Union.

Exercise 12: North vs. South
page 276
Comprehension

1. S   2. N   3. N   4. N   5. S

Exercise 13: The Nation Goes to War
pages 276–277
Analysis

1. (3) Of the choices given, it is reasonable to assume that Lincoln did not issue an order for emancipation for the entire country out of loyalty to the four border states. Those states remained in the Union despite being slave states.

2. (5) The passage says, "As a result, the Union army's ranks grew by 180,000 former slaves who fought against the rebels." This was a considerable contribution to the Union's forces.

Exercise 14: Reconstruction
pages 277–278
Comprehension

1. (2) The passage suggests that the Carpetbaggers, who brought only what they could carry, did not intend to stay in the South.

2. (1) The only choice listed that is an example of corruption is the Carpetbaggers' support of fraudulent bond schemes.

Exercise 15: The Industrial Revolution
page 279
Analysis

1. (2) The passage cites Great Britain's advantages of "a compact size that encouraged consumerism within the country" and "a large middle class that could afford commercially manufactured goods."

Evaluation

2. (2) Choices (1), (3), (4), and (5) are not true. Russia has more natural resources than Japan; Japan has encouraged groups of scientists and technicians; Russia is much larger than Japan; and Japan does not have a large population of poor peasants.

Exercise 16: Growth of Big Business
page 280
Application

(2) and (4) The situations that represent economic activity without government intervention are (2) and (4). Choices (1), (3), and (5) all represent a government agency directing a business to do something.

Exercise 17: America Becomes Urbanized
page 281
Comprehension

1. 1920
2. 1880
3. 30 million
4. 70 million

Exercise 18: Urbanization and Social Change
page 281
Evaluation

(5) In 1930, the height of the bar for America's rural population is at about 52 million people; the bar for the urban population is at about 68 million people. The total population (rural and urban) was about 120 million, which is about half of the current population of 248 million.

Exercise 19: The Progressive Era
page 282
Application

(4) Agreement by oil manufacturers on a minimum price to set for gasoline is an example of price-fixing, an act outlawed by the Sherman Anti-Trust Act.

Exercise 20: Women's Suffrage
page 283
Comprehension

1. (1) Both readings reflect the belief that women should be given the right to vote.

2. (3) The passage states, "I believe it [this great question] should be settled by the states and not by the national government."

Analysis

3. (2) Mrs. Callor is complaining that while she works and pays taxes, she cannot vote for the men who decide what her taxes should be. Furthermore, she cannot get any results from her complaints about her taxes. In both cases, she is assuming that without the right to vote she is powerless.

Exercise 21: The United States Becomes a World Power
page 284
Analysis

1. (3) The Philippines were ceded to the United States under the terms of the treaty that ended the Spanish-American War; therefore, the U.S. establishment of military bases there is a result of a policy of expanding American control over other areas.

2. (4) The most likely explanation for America's isolationist position from the end of the Civil War until the Spanish-American War is that the country was preoccupied with healing its wounds and rebuilding the South after the Civil War.

Exercise 22: World War I
page 285
Comprehension

(1) Allies

(2) draft

(3) Treaty of Versailles

(4) League of Nations

(5) isolationism

Exercise 23: The Roaring Twenties
pages 286–287
Comprehension

1. 1900–1909

2. 1930–1939

3. 700,000 or 0.7 million

Exercise 24: The New Deal
page 287
Application

1. d   2. a   3. e   4. c   5. b

Exercise 25: World War II
page 288
Comprehension

1. T   2. F   3. T   4. F   5. F

Exercise 26: U.S. Foreign Policy Positions
page 289
Application

1. (2) An imperialist believes in controlling other territories or nations.

2. (5) An internationalist believes in cooperating with the nations of the world.

Exercise 27: The Truman Era
page 290
Application

(1) and **(2)** The situations that represent attempts to enforce the principles of the Truman Doctrine are (1), (2). Choice (3) has nothing to do with resisting communist takeover. Choice (4) involves the U.S.S.R.'s attempt to establish missile bases in Cuba, a country that had already become communist. Choice (5) involves U.S. support for a democratic movement against a communist government.

Exercise 28: The Korean War
page 291
Application

1. (4) The undeclared war in Vietnam most closely resembled the situation of the Korean War. Both were undeclared wars that resulted from the U.S. policy of trying to contain communism.

Analysis

2. (4) The belief that the U.S. government should not commit soldiers to an undeclared war represents an opinion and not a fact.

Exercise 29: The Eisenhower Years
page 291
Application

(5) The Salem witchcraft trials are the only historical event listed in which hysteria resulted in innocent people being wrongly accused and persecuted.

Exercise 30: Space Exploration and Social Change
page 292
Analysis

(3) The *Brown* v. *Topeka Board of Education* decision is significant today because it ruled that "separate but equal" educational facilities could no longer exist. This serves as the legal basis for school busing to achieve desegregation.

Exercise 31: Kennedy's New Frontier
page 293
Application

1. (3) The Soviet attempt to establish a missile base in Cuba may be interpreted as a direct violation of the principles of the Monroe Doctrine, which opposed foreign interference in the affairs of the Western Hemisphere.

Analysis

2. (4) From reading the passage, it may be assumed that Cuba, a communist nation, was an ally of the Soviet Union.

Exercise 32: Johnson's Great Society
page 294
Comprehension

(4) The passage states that the most significant achievement of former President Johnson was the passage of the Civil Rights Act.

Exercise 33: The Nixon Era
page 295
Evaluation

1. (3) Of former President Nixon's foreign policy initiatives, history will likely credit him most for reestablishing relations with the People's Republic of China. The other choices can be eliminated either because they are not true or are not achievements.

2. (5) The opinion best supported by the evidence presented in the passage is that "The president of the United States is not above the law." It was President Nixon's involvement in the coverup of the break-in and the subsequent threat of impeachment action that led to the first presidential resignation in U.S. history.

Exercise 34: Carter and the Middle East
page 296
Evaluation

1. (3) Of all the choices, Jimmy Carter will be remembered most favorably for his efforts to reconcile Egypt and Israel. Choices (1) and (5) are acts by Carter, but they lack the significance of the Mideast peace accords. Choices (2) and (4) were actions that were unpopular with large segments of the American people.

Application

2. (3) Anti-imperialists reject the policy of one nation controlling another nation or territory. Although the United States helped to build the Panama Canal, it is in territory that belongs to Panama. Therefore, anti-imperialists would favor the United States' relinquishing control of the canal.

Exercise 35: Reagan and the New Conservatism
page 297
Evaluation

(1) President Reagan's foreign policy is characterized generally as one of anticommunism. Giving support to anticommunist rebels in Nicaragua, Angola, and Afghanistan is an expression of this policy.

Exercise 36: Bush's "New World Order"
page 298
Analysis

1. O   2. F   3. O   4. F   5. O

Exercise 37: Clinton—The First Baby-Boom President
pages 299–300
Application

1. (2) According to the passage, Clinton "found that campaign promises were difficult to keep." His experience as governor, choice (1), did not necessarily make him a better president. Clinton's problems included foreign affairs (3) and often were a surprise (4).

Evaluation

2. (5) As a candidate, Clinton could think about tomorrow's problems without solving them, but as president, he had to act immediately on today's problems. Clinton's solutions did not always please the Congress (1) or lead easily to economic recovery (3). He appointed women to public office (2).

Application

3. (1) Like Carter, Clinton was a former Democratic governor who was regarded as a Washington "outsider." They both faced economic and political problems that had begun in a previous administration.

Evaluation

4. (1) The passage implies that Clinton's appointment of Janet Reno was well received. The other choices refer to unpopular or problem-ridden decisions.

CHAPTER 3: POLITICAL SCIENCE

Exercise 1: Methods of Obtaining Power
page 302
Application

1. (4) France's overthrow of the monarchy in favor of a republican form of government is an example of a revolution.

2. (3) Because Hitler overpowered Austria militarily, the method used to gain power is conquest.

3. (5) The people elected Corazon Aquino president of the Philippines; this is an example of a leader coming to power through popular vote.

Exercise 2: Legislative Representation
page 304
Application

1. (3) Rhode Island is the smallest state among those represented; therefore, it is likely to have the fewest representatives in the House.

Analysis

2. (5) Since the number of representatives a state has is based on its population, you can infer that New Jersey, in spite of its small size, is densely populated. Dense populations are characteristic of urban, industrialized states.

3. (5) Because the number of a state's representatives is based on its population, and because Arizona is gaining residents at the expense of states in the Northeast, the number of representatives for both Arizona and northeastern states will need to be adjusted.

Exercise 3: The Legislative Branch
page 304
Application

1. E The power to impose economic sanctions is not stated in the Constitution; therefore, the elastic clause applies.

2. C The power to pass tax laws is stated in the Constitution.

3. C The power to admit a state is stated in the Constitution.

4. C The power to approve presidential appointments is stated in the Constitution.

5. C The power to introduce legislation is stated in the Constitution.

Exercise 4: The Executive Branch
page 306
Application

1. (5) The passage states that strong presidents frequently use their veto power and attempt to dominate the legislature. The actions of Andrew Jackson best fit that description.

2. (5) Based on the information in the chapter on U.S. history, President Warren G. Harding may be described as a weak president; his reliance on the advice of his subordinates led to the Teapot Dome Scandal.

Analysis

3. (5) The vice president carries out many functions for the executive branch as a whole. Therefore, when the president and vice president are from differing political parties, the president's effectiveness and ability to govern can suffer.

Exercise 5: The Judicial Branch
page 307
Comprehension

1. (4) The practice of deciding on the constitutionality of a law (which the Supreme Court does) is called the power of judicial review.

2. (4) The quote both defines the role of the Supreme Court and affirms that the court is the final authority on the Constitution's meaning.

Exercise 6: States' vs. Individuals' Rights
page 308
Application

2. I In prohibiting states from outlawing abortions under certain conditions, the Supreme Court upheld the rights of the individual.

4. I In ruling that an accused must be informed of his or her rights, the Supreme Court supported the rights of the individual.

5. I In ruling that separate facilities for the races were not equal, the Supreme Court upheld the rights of the individual.

Exercise 7: The Enactment of a Law
page 309
Evaluation

(2) Choice (2) is supported by the part of the chart that shows that a bill must go to a conference committee for compromise. The chart does not indicate that a bill may be introduced directly by the president. A filibuster is an acceptable means by which a vote on a bill may be delayed. Bills introduced by *either* house may be amended as shown in the illustration. The chart shows that bills may become law without the president's signature if approved by two-thirds of both houses.

Exercise 8: Filibuster
page 310
Comprehension

(5) The passage says that "Senator Thurmond talked for more than 24 hours to delay the vote." This is the same as talking for the purpose of trying to prevent passage of a bill into law.

Exercise 9: System of Checks and Balances
page 310
Comprehension

1. (a) executive (b) judicial
2. (a) legislative (b) executive
3. (a) legislative (b) executive
4. (a) legislative (b) executive
5. (a) judicial (b) legislative
6. (a) executive (b) legislative

Exercise 10: Powers of State Government
page 311
Application

1. B 2. B 3. F 4. F 5. S 6. S

Exercise 11: City Income and Expenditures
page 312
Comprehension

1. revenue; expenditures
2. charges and miscellaneous
3. environment and housing

Exercise 12: City Budgeting
page 312
Analysis
(5) The only ways for a city to make up for lost revenue are to raise taxes or fees and to decrease expenditures. Borrowing from a more prosperous state is not a plausible alternative.

Exercise 13: The Political Spectrum
pages 313–314
Application
1. (2) Because the speaker advocates social improvement (improved bilingual programs) through governmental action, the speaker may be classified as a liberal.

2. (3) Because the speaker believes in avoiding extreme changes in laws and government ("we don't need harsher laws"), the speaker may be classified as a moderate.

3. (5) Because the speaker advocates a return to an earlier policy (the absence of public signs written in Spanish), the speaker may be classified as a reactionary.

4. (4) Because the speaker advocates maintaining the existing social order ("English has been the primary language here and always will be."), the speaker may be classified as a conservative.

5. (1) Because the speaker advocates swift, sweeping changes in laws, the speaker may be classified as a radical.

Exercise 14: Political Parties
page 315
Application
1. **R** Republicans generally favor stronger state and local authority.

2. **D** Democrats generally endorse the efforts of labor unions.

3. **R** Republicans advocate free enterprise (big business operating without restraint).

4. **D** Democrats support government expenditures for the disadvantaged and minorities.

5. **R** Republicans tend to favor defense spending at the expense of domestic spending.

Exercise 15: Electing a President
page 317
Comprehension
1. e   2. d   3. a   4. c   5. b

Exercise 16: The Democratic Primary
page 317
Evaluation
1. (2) The picture is crowded with several well-known cartoon figures. This suggests that anybody can run in the Democratic presidential primary.

2. (5) By making the Democratic presidential candidates cartoon characters, the cartoonist is ridiculing the Democratic party's practice of allowing large numbers of candidates to seek office.

Exercise 17: The Electoral Process
page 318
Evaluation
(2) Because the purpose of a closed primary is to give members of a party an opportunity to express their preference for a candidate to run in a general election, it follows that voters must declare their party affiliation; otherwise, the purpose of a primary election is defeated.

Exercise 18: The Impact of the Media
page 318
Analysis
(1) The best choice is (1), which is based on the hypothesis that the early announcements of Reagan's victory discouraged Carter's supporters from voting. Choice (2) is contrary to the facts in the passage because Carter lost overwhelmingly. Choices (3), (4), and (5) are not plausible reasons that motivate people to vote.

CHAPTER 4: ECONOMICS

Exercise 1: Factors of Production
page 320
Application
1. **N** Seals, Arctic foxes, and walruses are found in nature; Eskimos produce goods from them.

2. **C** A plumber's tools are equipment used to provide a service.

3. **N** Diamonds are raw materials found in nature.

4. **L** Farmers who plant crops are laborers.

5. **C** Conveyor belts are used in the production of other goods.

Exercise 2: Economic Systems
page 321
Comprehension
1. (b) The quote "From each according to his ability, to each according to his need" reflects the socialist goal of working together to provide equal opportunity for all.

2. (a) The quote "In the area of economics, the government that governs least governs best" reflects the capitalist feature of government's noninterference in business.

Exercise 3: Economic Systems and Governments
page 322
Comprehension

1. **(4)** Because capitalism and communism occupy the extremes of the continuum, you can conclude that they are opposites.

Application

2. **(3)** An aspect of a U.S. dairy manufacturer's operations (capitalist system) is dictated by a government agency's requirement (a feature of a socialist system).

Exercise 4: Supply and Demand in the U.S. Economy
page 325
Evaluation

1. **(1)** The bartender's bill, as a result of added taxes, is ridiculously high, suggesting that the overburdened taxpayer won't find any relief.

2. **(3)** The customer has just come from paying his income taxes and wants a drink to take his troubles away.

Exercise 5: Supply, Demand, and Equilibrium
pages 326–327
Comprehension

1. **(3)** The point where the lines intersect is at $300.

Analysis

2. **(3)** As the price decreases, the demand increases.

3. **(5)** With a greater supply brought about by the entrance of Korea into the market and a low demand for VCRs, the supply would exceed demand, resulting in a surplus.

Exercise 6: Economic Growth
page 328
Analysis

(3) The only plausible reason given for the abandonment of wage and price controls is that the program proved too difficult to administer and was highly unpopular. Choice (1) is incorrect because it was known before the controls were implemented that they would interfere with the basic principles of a free economy. Choice (2) is not true; choice (4) is a result of the revoking of the controls and not an explanation for their abandonment. Choice (5) is incorrect because even though wages were decreased, a depression did not occur.

Exercise 7: The GNP as a Measure of Economic Growth
page 329
Comprehension

1. **(3)** The span of years between 1982 and 1989 is the only period in which the slope of the line increases steadily.

Analysis

2. **(3)** Current dollars represent the current price of something. Inflation (an increase in prices) explains the steep increase in current dollar GNP shown on the graph.

3. **(2)** A falling constant dollar GNP indicates a period of poor economic growth, a recession. During the years 1979–1980, 1981–1982, and 1990–1991, the United States experienced recessions.

Exercise 8: Money and Monetary Policy
page 331
Comprehension

1. **F** According to the passage, the role of the Fed is to regulate the nation's supply of money and credit.

2. **F** The two primary ways in which the Federal Reserve influences the money supply are by setting the reserve ratio and the discount rate.

3. **T**

4. **T**

5. **F** The **discount rate** is the interest rate the Fed charges member banks to borrow; the prime rate, not mentioned in the passage, is the rate banks charge to their best customers.

Exercise 9: Fiscal and Monetary Policy
page 332
Comprehension

1. **decrease; lowering** To stimulate the economy during a recession, the government should decrease government spending while lowering taxes. Both actions put more money into the hands of consumers.

2. **decrease; raising; increasing** Inflation is an increase in the amount of money in circulation. To reduce inflation, the Fed reduces the amount of money in circulation by raising the discount rate. This makes it more costly for banks to borrow from the Fed. By increasing the reserve ratio, the Fed reduces the amount of money a bank can lend.

3. **budget deficit** When operating at a budget deficit, the government is spending more money than it takes in.

CHAPTER 5: GEOGRAPHY
Exercise 1: Maps
pages 333–334
Application

1. **(5)** A weather map shows the climate of a particular region, including its precipitation.

2. **(4)** A political map outlines the borders between states.

3. **(1)** A topographical map shows the physical land features of an area.

Exercise 2: Measuring Distance
page 334
Comprehension
1. about 900 miles
2. about 300 miles
3. about 1,100 miles

Exercise 3: The Latitude and Longitude Grid
page 336
Comprehension
1. (5) central Africa
2. (4) South Africa

Exercise 4: Time Zones
page 337
Application
1. (2) Los Angeles falls within the Pacific time zone, which is three hours earlier than the Eastern time zone, in which Philadelphia falls.
2. (3) Denver falls within the Mountain time zone, which is one hour earlier than the Central time zone, in which Milwaukee falls.

Analysis
3. (5) Northwest Indiana is economically tied to the Chicago metropolitan area; therefore, for economic reasons it falls within the Central time zone.
4. (4) Groups that benefit most from northwest Indiana's placement within the Central time zone are commuters who work in Chicago and live in northwest Indiana and the merchants and businesspeople in northwest Indiana who transact business with Chicagoans.

Exercise 5: U.S. Topography
page 339
Analysis
1. (2) Nebraska is located in the plains region—an area described in the text as having very cold temperatures during the winter.
2. (3) Denver (whose nickname is the "Mile High City") is located in the Rocky Mountains of Colorado. None of the other cities listed is located in a mountainous region.
3. (3) New Orleans is the only city represented that lies below sea level and experiences flooding because of its proximity to the Mississippi River. Las Vegas is located in a desert; Phoenix is located in a dry region of the country. Neither New York nor Atlanta is subject to flooding, as neither lies below sea level.

Exercise 6: The Indian Peninsula
page 340
Comprehension
1. (4) Mt. Everest, the highest mountain in the world, is also the highest point in the Himalaya Mountains at 29,028 feet above sea level.
2. (5) A glance at the map of the Indian Peninsula shows that the elevation for the majority of the land is between sea level and 1,000 feet. In the key, white space indicates this level of elevation.

Exercise 7: Population Distribution
page 341
Analysis
1. (4) Nevada, one of the least populous of the fifty states, is characterized by extremes in temperatures and altitude and rugged topography and has soil poorly equipped for farming. Because of climate and topography, neither California, Washington, Oregon, nor Colorado is as sparsely populated as Nevada.
2. (4) West Virginia is mainly mountainous, a characteristic that precludes an even distribution of the state's population.

Exercise 8: Other Factors Affecting Population Distribution
page 342
Evaluation
1. (4) The quote states, "We miss much of life's richness if we fail to take affirmative action against the current trend among developers to lay us all out with 'our own kind' of people." This opinion is similar to the opinion that children exposed to only one kind of people grow up crippled in their understanding of the world.
2. (5) Fair-housing laws that provide for more ethnically diverse communities are the only example of affirmative action that is related to changing housing patterns.

Test 3: Science

The GED Science Test consists of multiple-choice questions. These questions require you to know basic science concepts that will be covered in this section of the book. However, the test emphasizes your ability to think about these concepts. You will not be required to recall an isolated fact as you might have on some other tests. Rather, you will read a passage or look at an illustration and answer questions based on it. To answer successfully, you will need to

▶ have an understanding of basic science concepts

▶ be able to interpret illustrations and reading passages

▶ be able to show that you can
  - understand what you read
  - apply information to a new situation
  - analyze relationships among ideas
  - make judgments about the material presented

Actually, you already use all of these different kinds of thinking skills in daily life. In this section, we will help you to apply these skills to science materials.

How many questions are on the test?

There are 66 multiple-choice questions, and you will be given 95 minutes to complete the test. About two-thirds of the questions will be based on reading passages of up to 250 words each, and one-third will be based on visuals—diagrams, charts, or graphs. (If you need practice in interpreting visual materials, you might want to review Chapter 2 on pages 223–237 of the Reading Skills section.) To get an idea of what the test is like, look at the Practice Test at the end of this book. This Practice Test is based on the real GED Test. In fact, all of the multiple-choice questions in this section are sample GED questions.

What's on the test?

The GED Science Test can be broken down into the content areas it covers and the skills it tests. The following subjects make up the content of the test:

Life Sciences	50%
Biology	
Physical Sciences	50%
Earth Science	
Chemistry	
Physics	

These essential science areas are covered in Chapters 1–4 of this section. However, keep in mind that a given question may draw from a number of these subjects. It's difficult to discuss society or people without touching on a number of topics. For example, a question on air pollution may draw from material covered in both biology and chemistry.

Also remember that you are being tested on your ability to think through certain ideas and concepts. You will be asked to do more than just find an answer that was given in a passage.

Thinking skills that you will be tested on include

Understanding Ideas	20%
Applying Ideas	30%
Analyzing Ideas	30%
Evaluating Ideas	20%

Chapter 1 of the Reading Skills section of this book (on pages 189–222) focuses on these thinking skills, and all of the activities and questions in this section will help you practice answering these types of questions. If you have not already worked through the Reading Skills section, you might want to go back and complete the exercises in that section. The more practice you have had in answering the four categories of questions, the better prepared you will be to answer questions in this section and on the actual test.

1
BIOLOGY—THE STUDY OF LIVING THINGS

"How did life begin on Earth?" "Does life exist on Venus or Mars?" "Have UFOs (unidentified flying objects) ever brought alien beings to Earth?" Questions such as these fascinate people everywhere. In fact, all human beings seem to have a natural curiosity about life—both life on Earth and the possibility of life on other planets.

The scientific study of all life forms is known as *biology*. Biologists are interested in how living things grow, how they change over time, and how they interact with one another and with their environment. Of particular interest are the characteristics that all living things have in common. All living things react to stimuli, take in food and use it to grow, eliminate wastes, and reproduce. The starting point for any systematic study of biology is an examination of the basic unit of life, the cell.

The Cell, the Basis of Life

The *cell* is the smallest unit of living material capable of carrying on the activities of life. Like the bricks of a building, cells are the "building blocks" of an organism.

Cells were first observed in 1665 by Robert Hooke, who, with the aid of a crudely made microscope, examined a slice of cork. The tiny compartments he saw reminded him of the little rooms, or cells, of a monastery. By 1839 it had been proposed that all living things are made up of cells, and by 1855 it was theorized that cells can be produced only from existing cells. These breakthroughs supported the belief that life is a continuous process.

Cells vary widely in size and appearance. It is the number of cells in an organism, however, and not the size, that determines the size of an organism. The cells of an ant, a human being, and a whale are of equal size. The whale is larger because its genetic pattern dictates that a larger number of cells be produced.

An "average" cell measures about 10 micrometers (1/25,000 inch) in diameter. This means that a parade of 25,000 typical cells end to end would measure only one inch.

Types of Cells

Two kinds of cells are known to exist—plant cells and animal cells. One difference between the two is that the plant cell has a cell wall that protects it, and an animal cell does not. Also, plant cells contain *chloroplasts*, structures active in the food-making process, while animal cells do not.

Both plant and animal cells are surrounded by a delicate boundary, the **cell membrane**. The cell membrane

- preserves the cell by acting as a barrier between it and the outside environment
- helps the cell maintain its shape
- regulates molecular traffic passing into and out of the cell

The following illustration shows the differences between the plant cell and animal cell:

CELL STRUCTURE

Cell Structure

Within the cell membrane is **protoplasm**, a jellylike substance that forms the largest component of the cell. The protoplasm lying between the nuclear membrane and the cell membrane is called **cytoplasm**.

A highly specialized and complex structure, the cell has its own control center, transportation system, power plants, factories for making needed materials, and even a reproductive blueprint, or chemical recipe.

Most of the organelles (little organs) performing these functions are located within the cytoplasm. Resembling an intricate tunnel system, the **endoplasmic reticulum** serves as a network for transporting materials from one part of the cell to another or from the cell to the environment. The power plants of the cell are the **mitochondria**, the sites where the cell releases energy for cellular work. Mitochondria are abundant in highly active cells that produce energy for important life processes. For example, more than 1,000 mitochondria have been counted in a single liver cell.

Located in stacks of platelike membranes at one side of the nucleus is another organelle: the *Golgi apparatus*. The Golgi apparatus functions as a packaging plant. Proteins and carbohydrates are gathered together and enclosed in a membranous sac. In gland cells, the Golgi apparatus is responsible for releasing the gland's hormones into the body.

Of all the structures within the cell, the most important is the *nucleus*, the control center of the cell. The nucleus is surrounded by a double nuclear membrane. Pores in the nuclear membrane permit the passage of molecules between the cytoplasm and the nucleus. Within the *nucleus* are the *chromosomes* and the *nucleolus*. Each chromosome contains several hundred *genes*, which contain DNA, a molecular acid that carries instructions on how the organism should develop. While the chromosomes serve as a "chemical recipe" for the cell, the genes might be considered individual ingredients.

The nucleolus is rich in RNA, an acid that is essential in the chemical activity of the cell. The nucleolus contains sections of chromosomes that are believed to be important in the manufacture of protein.

EXERCISE 1: CELL STRUCTURE

Directions: Match the terms on the right with the mechanical function they perform on the left by writing the letter of the correct term in the space provided.

_____ **1.** power plant of cell; enables cell to breathe

_____ **2.** regulator of traffic passing into and out of cell

_____ **3.** control center for cell

_____ **4.** means of transportation for material within cell

_____ **5.** packager of proteins and carbohydrates

_____ **6.** factory where RNA ingredients are assembled and stored

(a) nucleus

(b) endoplasmic reticulum

(c) mitochondrion

(d) Golgi apparatus

(e) cell membrane

(f) nucleolus

Answers are on page 441.

EXERCISE 2: CELLS

Directions: Choose the best answer for each of the following questions.

1. The main purpose of the reading passage is to point out that

   (1) all living things are made of cells
   (2) the nucleus is the control center of the cell
   (3) there are differences between plant and animal cells
   (4) the cell is a highly organized, complex structure with subsystems of its own
   (5) the Golgi apparatus functions as a packaging plant in the cell

2. One of the many functions of cells in the stomach lining is to slowly release quantities of stomach acid into the stomach chamber. From the passage, we can infer that the part of the cell that is involved in this function is the

    (1) endoplasmic reticulum
    (2) Golgi apparatus
    (3) nucleus
    (4) nucleolus
    (5) chromosome

3. We can conclude from the passage that the largest number of mitochondria would be found in the cells of the

    (1) hair   **(2)** skin   **(3)** heart   **(4)** smooth muscles   **(5)** sense organs

4. In plant cells, chloroplasts are active in the chemical processes required to make food. Animal cells have no chloroplasts. Based on this, we can conclude that

    (1) plant cells are more complex than animal cells
    (2) plant cells and not animal cells generate chemical reactions
    (3) animal cells prey upon plant cells as a food source
    (4) animal cells are more complex than plant cells
    (5) animals must obtain food from outside sources

5. According to the passage, mitochondria are the power plants that produce energy for important life processes in the animal cell and are responsible for cellular respiration. What part of a plant cell serves a similar function?

    (1) cell wall
    (2) nucleus
    (3) nucleolus
    (4) chromosome
    (5) chloroplast

Answers are on page 441.

> **DID YOU KNOW THAT:** The single-celled organism *euglena* has both plant and animal features? It contains chlorophyll, which only plants have, and has no cell wall, a feature of an animal cell. Also, it moves—another characteristic of animals.

Cells and Active Transport

Every cell has a membrane that selectively permits the passage of certain molecules in and out of the cell.

The movement of molecules through the cell membrane without any effort on the cell's part is achieved by diffusion. *Diffusion* is the movement of molecules from an area of high concentration to an area of low concentration. Vibrating molecules are propelled away from one another after they collide. It is through this process that odors can fill a large room in a short period of time.

Diffusion is important in higher organisms. In the human body, for example, oxygen moves from the air sacs in the lungs through cell membranes and into the blood through diffusion.

A cell's cytoplasm contains many substances in varying degrees of concentration. These concentrations differ sharply from those in the fluid surrounding the cell. Such differences are so essential that the cell can die if the differences are not maintained. Given the opportunity, diffusion would quickly eliminate these critical differences. Therefore, the cell must be able to negate, and sometimes even reverse, the process of diffusion. This is accomplished by active transport. During *active transport*, the cell moves materials from an area of low concentration to an area of high concentration. This work requires energy.

EXERCISE 3: CELLS AND ACTIVE TRANSPORT

Directions: In the blank spaces below, supply the words that correctly complete each statement.

1. Diffusion is the movement of molecules from an area of

_____ concentration to an area of _____ concentration.

2. In active transport, materials are moved from an area of

_____ concentration to an area of _____ concentration.

3. Diffusion may be described as the _____ of active transport.

Answers are on page 441.

EXERCISE 4: DIFFUSION AND OSMOSIS

Directions: Choose the best answer for each of the following questions.

1. In the human body, the process of diffusion

   (1) allows for concentrations of materials where needed in the body, through stockpiling
   (2) regulates blood flow
   (3) allows an even distribution of substances throughout all cells of the body
   (4) comes into play in times of extreme illness
   (5) plays an insignificant role in the body's functioning

2. *Osmosis* may be described as a process by which water in a solution is able to move through the cell membrane from a *lower* concentration to a *higher* one in order to maintain balance on either side of the membrane. If the salt solution in blood plasma surrounding red blood cells is higher than the solution inside the cells, which is most likely to occur?

   A. Water will leave the cell and pass into the blood plasma.
   B. Water will leave the blood plasma and pass into the cell.
   C. The cell will shrink because of a loss of water.

   (1) A   (2) B   (3) C   (4) A and B   (5) A and C

Answers are on page 441.

Mitosis—Cell Division

One quality of an organism is that it has the capacity to grow. As a cell grows, its cell membrane becomes unable to provide oxygen and nutrients for the interior of the cell and wastes are unable to leave the cell. In addition, a nucleus can control only so much cytoplasm. Therefore, when a cell reaches its limit in size, it must divide, or undergo a process called mitosis.

Mitosis is the process by which cells reproduce themselves by division. In a multicellular organism, mitosis leads to tissue growth and maintenance. In a single-celled organism, mitosis results in two new genetically identical independent organisms. Mitosis can be divided into four stages or phases, as shown below.

Stage 1: Prophase

Just before prophase begins, genetic material in the nucleus is duplicated (doubled). Then, as prophase begins, the nuclear membrane and nucleolus disappear. The genetic material, which has not been easy to view, now becomes evident as long, threadlike bodies, the chromosomes. As prophase continues, centrioles appear at opposite ends of the cells and small fibers start to form between them.

Stage 2: Metaphase

During metaphase, the next phase in the sequence, the spindle fibers attach themselves to the genetic material at the center of the chromosomes (centromeres). The chromosomes are now quite thick and visible. They begin to line up at the equator of the cell.

Stage 3: Anaphase

During the third stage, anaphase, the centromeres divide, and the duplicate pairs of chromosomes separate. The separate pairs then repel each other and move toward the poles of the cell.

Stage 4: Telophase

When the chromosomes arrive at the poles, telophase begins. In telophase, the nuclei re-form, the chromosomes gradually become less visible, and the cell separates to form two new cells. The daughter cells are genetically and physically identical to the parent cell except for size.

In single-cell organisms, cell division results in two new individuals. In complex organisms made of more than one cell, the new daughter cells form a subsystem of the parent cell. In many organisms, cell reproduction is at its peak while the organism grows. As the organism ages, the process is limited to the replacement of old and damaged cells.

EXERCISE 5: MITOSIS

Directions: Match the phase of mitosis shown on the left with its description shown on the right.

_____ 1. prophase

_____ 2. metaphase

_____ 3. anaphase

_____ 4. telophase

(a) chromosomes become easily visible

(b) chromosomal material lines up at the center of the cell

(c) cell divides to form two new cells

(d) pairs of chromosomes move to opposite poles

Answers are on page 441.

Meiosis—Reproductive Cell Division

Each organism has a chromosome number that is characteristic of that organism. For example, all of the cells in the human body contain forty-six chromosomes except for the *gametes* (the reproductive cells). The reproductive cells (sperm and egg) cannot carry the same number of chromosomes as those of other parts of the body. If they did, the offspring that would result from the union of the egg and sperm would have twice the normal amount of genetic material after cell division. In animals, this would result in the termination of the embryo early in development. To prevent this, the sex cells undergo meiosis, a special division process.

Meiosis is a process in which a parent cell undergoes two special types of cell division that result in the production of four gametes (reproductive cells). Each gamete has half the number of chromosomes of the original parent cell. The two stages of meiosis are illustrated below.

MEIOSIS I

| Prophase I | Metaphase I | Anaphase I | | Telophase I |

As the preceding diagram shows, the chromosome pairs come together to exchange genes. This process is called crossing over. *Crossing over* ensures a recombination of genetic material. Later, the pairs separate and one of each pair moves to a new cell. During Telophase I, the cytoplasm divides and two daughter cells are formed. Each daughter cell is called a *haploid* cell, a cell that contains half the number of chromosomes of the original parent cell.

MEIOSIS II

| Prophase II | Metaphase II | Anaphase II | Telophase II (Four Haploid Cells) |

(*Note:* Only one daughter cell from Meiosis I is shown here.)

In Meiosis II, the chromosomal material combines, separates, and moves to new cells, resulting in four reproductive cells. In humans, when two haploid cells (a sperm and egg, each containing twenty-three chromosomes) unite in fertilization, they form a *diploid* cell, a cell containing forty-six chromosomes. The fertilized cell contains forty-six chromosomes, or twenty-three pairs—half from the mother and half from the father.

Genetics and Heredity

Heredity is the term used to describe the passing of traits from parents to off-spring. Every species has its own set of traits that it transmits to its offspring. *Genetics* is the study of how traits are passed on. *Geneticists*, the scientists who study heredity, have found that hereditary information of an organism is carried by the chromosomes of the cell nucleus.

Genes map out all our inherited traits. Every human receives two genes for each trait—one from the mother and one from the father. Genes may be dominant or recessive. The dominant gene will always appear in an offspring, if present. For example, since brown eye color is a dominant trait, 90 percent of human beings have brown eyes. If two dominant genes are inherited, the resulting trait will be a combination of the two inherited characteristics. For example, pink flowers result from the inheritance of a dominant gene for red and a dominant gene for white.

Sexual reproduction ensures that the offspring is composed of genetic material from both parents. This genetic material is thoroughly remixed with every fertilization so that, with the exception of identical twins, no two offspring of the same parents are similar genetically.

Gender and Mutations

Whether a mother gives birth to a boy or girl is determined by the "X" and "Y" chromosomes. A person receives two sex chromosomes—one from the father's sperm cell and one from the mother's egg cell. Egg cells contain a single "X" chromosome. Male sperm cells may contain either an "X" or a "Y" chromosome. If two "X" chromosomes unite, a female will result. If the sperm reaching the egg has a "Y" chromosome, a male will be produced. The sperm cells, then, carry the chromosome that determines the *gender* of offspring.

Sometimes a mistake occurs in the genetic makeup of a chromosome during cell duplication. This change in the genes is called a *mutation* and may be passed on to offspring. Many of these mutations are harmful. Two mutations in humans are Down's syndrome, which results in brain damage, and muscular dystrophy, a disease that causes muscles to waste away.

EXERCISE 8: GENETICS AND HEREDITY

Directions: Study the diagram and choose the best answer for the questions that follow.

HOW EYE COLOR IS INHERITED

G = Dominant Green Eye Gene

B = Dominant Brown Eye Gene

b = Recessive Blue Eye Gene

Parents

Bb   Gb

Offspring

Bb   GB   bb   Gb

1. According to the diagram, what percentage of this couple's children might have blue eyes?

(1) 75 percent
(2) 50 percent
(3) 0 percent
(4) 25 percent
(5) 100 percent

The following question is *not* based on the preceding diagram.

2. The Jones family has had four children, all girls. The fifth child born is a boy. This change is the result of

(1) conception classes taken by the parents
(2) the timing of the fertility cycles
(3) the father's contribution of a "Y" chromosome
(4) the mother's contribution of a "Y" chromosome
(5) the "law of averages" finally catching up

3. Which of the following can be supported by information in the preceding passage?

A. The father's chromosomes determine the sex of the offspring.

B. The father's genetic makeup determines eye and hair color.

C. Mutations are caused by mistakes in genetic makeup.

(1) A
(2) B
(3) C
(4) A and B
(5) A and C

Answers are on page 441.

DID YOU KNOW THAT: Some conditions in humans are sex-linked; that is, they are inherited through chromosomal genes carried by one of the sexes? For example, color blindness (the inability to distinguish colors such as red and green) is most often found in males. Hemophilia, the inability of the blood to clot properly, is another condition found almost exclusively in males.

WRITING ACTIVITY 1

In one form of genetic engineering, human parenting is made to be dependent on uniting individuals with certain traits, such as blond hair, blue eyes, above-average intelligence, etc. The theory is that the genes the offspring inherit will also carry these traits. Write an essay of two or three paragraphs expressing your opinion for or against this form of genetic engineering.

Growth, Energy, and Living Things

Some of the characteristics that distinguish living things from nonliving things are the capacities for growth, food consumption, and release of energy for cellular work. Important biological processes involved in these functions are the nitrogen cycle, photosynthesis, and cellular respiration.

The Nitrogen Cycle

Nitrogen, which makes up nearly 80 percent of Earth's atmosphere, is an essential ingredient for living tissues. Human beings and other animals depend on plants as a source of nitrogen. Plants cannot manufacture nitrogen themselves, so to obtain it they must depend on other organisms.

Free nitrogen, however, cannot be used by organisms, so it must combine with other elements to form *nitrates* that can be used. Plants absorb these nitrates to manufacture *amino acids*, which are essential components of protein needed by living cells. Amino acids are used to manufacture both proteins and nucleic acids that are absorbed by man.

The conversion of free nitrogen into a combined form is called *nitrogen fixing*. This is best achieved by certain bacteria—microorganisms and decomposers—that live in the soil. These microorganisms live in special sacs, called *nodules*, on the roots of legumes—plants such as alfalfa, peas, and beans. The microorganisms produce *nitrogenase*, an enzyme that is essential to nitrogen fixing.

Scientists believe that all of the nitrogen in Earth's atmosphere has been fixed and liberated many times. At any one time, probably only a few pounds of nitrogenase exist on our planet. This small amount, however, is enough to sustain all life on Earth.

EXERCISE 9: THE NITROGEN CYCLE

Directions: Choose the best answer for each of the following questions.

1. *Symbiosis* describes the relationship between two organisms that are different but that live together for their mutual benefit. The microorganisms that live in the nodules attached to legumes may be described as symbiotic. Another example of a symbiotic relationship would be

    (1) bacteria that can live only in the stomachs of hoofed animals and that help the animals digest food
    (2) bees that make their hives in caves, thereby providing a ready source of food for bears
    (3) soldier ants that live and work together in colonies
    (4) tapeworms that live in the intestines of humans
    (5) scavengers such as vultures that feed on the carcasses of dead animals

2. Which of the following foods, known for its high protein content, obtains this characteristic from the nitrogen-fixing process?

    (1) chicken   (2) beef   (3) peanuts   (4) wheat germ   (5) milk

3. Which of the following farming procedures best illustrates the process of nitrogen fixing?

(1) rotating a crop of cotton one year with a crop of beets
(2) irrigating the land with more modern methods
(3) using more advanced equipment to plow the land
(4) rotating the planting of cotton one year with a crop of soybeans
(5) using airplanes to spray the crops with insecticides

Answers are on page 442.

DID YOU KNOW THAT: Alfalfa, a popular nitrogen-fixing plant, is able to survive dry climates and long periods of drought and that its roots can penetrate seventeen feet into the ground to reach moist earth and water?

Photosynthesis

Plants can live without human beings, but human beings cannot live without plants. Plants provide the oxygen we need to breathe and the nutrients we need to thrive. Green plants are self-sufficient because they are able to make their own food, while humans and lower animals must obtain their food to live.

Photosynthesis is the food-making process by which green plants convert the light from the sun into usable chemical energy. Photosynthesis can be understood as a process involving several steps.

The first step is the capture of energy by the plant. In most plants the process of photosynthesis takes place within the *chloroplasts*, where chlorophyll molecules absorb light. *Chlorophyll* is the substance that gives plants their green color.

Using the energy that chlorophyll releases from sunlight, the plant splits water into its two components—oxygen and hydrogen. The oxygen is released to the atmosphere, and hydrogen recombines with carbon dioxide to produce carbohydrate molecules (a form of starch) in the plant.

EXERCISE 10: PHOTOSYNTHESIS

Directions: Choose the best answer for each of the following questions.

1. Which of the following may we conclude about plants and the process of photosynthesis?

A. Plants that do not possess chlorophyll must use a process other than photosynthesis to produce the energy they need.

B. Photosynthesis is used by plants to make energy because it is the simplest method available.

C. Plants that do not use the process of photosynthesis are parasites; they must obtain food from another source.

(1) A   (2) B   (3) C   (4) A and B   (5) A and C

Question 2 is based on the information in the following passage.

Some plants have leaves in which chlorophyll is lacking in some parts and is present in others. A coleus plant, with its brightly colored leaves, is one example. In an experiment in which the pigment (color) of the coleus leaf is removed, an iodine solution will identify places where starch is present by turning that part of the leaf brown.

2. Which of the following would you predict to happen to a coleus leaf in such an experiment?

(1) The areas that turn brown will be areas where the leaf was green originally.
(2) The leaf would not turn brown at all.
(3) The areas that turn brown are the areas where the leaf was not green.
(4) The entire leaf would turn brown.
(5) Only half the leaf would turn brown.

Answers are on page 442.

DID YOU KNOW THAT: Some algae (green plants that inhabit the ocean) are found at depths where light is nonexistent? Because light is necessary for photosynthesis, scientists are puzzled as to how these algae photosynthesize.

Cellular Respiration

Cellular respiration is the complex series of chemical reactions by which a cell releases the energy trapped inside glucose molecules. *Glucose*, a form of sugar, is the end product of the process of photosynthesis. The process of cellular respiration, then, is the reverse of photosynthesis.

During cellular respiration, cells (plant or animal) break down the glucose so that energy is released for cellular work. Because the energy cannot be free-floating in the cell, it is repackaged and stored.

Cellular respiration occurs in three stages, beginning with the breakdown of a molecule of glucose and ending with the energy needed for the cell to perform its work. Energy that is not used is released in the form of heat.

EXERCISE 11: CELLULAR RESPIRATION

Directions: Choose the best answer for each of the following questions.

1. The function of cellular respiration is to

(1) release water in the cell
(2) produce oxygen for the cell
(3) create energy from a cell fuel source
(4) consume carbon dioxide
(5) help in photosynthesis

2. From the information about cellular respiration, we can infer that

   (1) in plants, photosynthesis must always precede cellular respiration
   (2) no relationship exists between photosynthesis and cellular respiration
   (3) photosynthesis and respiration share many processes
   (4) cellular respiration occurs only in animal cells
   (5) plants do not perform cellular work

3. The rate of cellular respiration in humans can be measured by the amount of carbon dioxide exhaled. Which of the following would you expect to be true about the rate of cellular respiration for a group of students who are the same age, height, and weight?

   (1) Africans would have a higher rate of cellular respiration than Asians
   (2) boys would have a higher rate of cellular respiration than girls
   (3) girls would have a higher rate of cellular respiration than boys
   (4) athletes would tend to have higher rates of cellular respiration than nonathletes
   (5) nonathletes would have higher rates of cellular respiration than athletes

4. Which of the following procedures would be *most effective* in proving your hypothesis in the preceding example?

   (1) measuring the amounts of carbon dioxide exhaled by the students immediately after they wake up
   (2) measuring the amounts of carbon dioxide exhaled by every student after vigorous exercise
   (3) measuring the amounts of carbon dioxide exhaled by one student at rest and another student after vigorous exercise
   (4) measuring the amounts of carbon dioxide exhaled by half the students at rest and half the students after vigorous exercise
   (5) taking a reading of all of the students' blood pressures

Question 5 is based on the following passage.

> Glucose, a form of carbohydrate, is the body's main fuel source; however, it cannot get into the cells without insulin, a hormone secreted by the body. Diabetes mellitus is a condition in which the body either
>
> 1. does not produce enough insulin to break down glucose, or,
>
> 2. does not effectively use the insulin it produces to break down the glucose into a form cells can use.
>
> To correct this problem, some diabetics must take additional insulin.

5. By which of the following methods can *all* diabetics control the condition and avoid experiencing heart disease and blindness that can result from diabetes?

A. regulating their intake of glucose (sugars and carbohydrates)

B. increasing the levels of insulin in the body by taking insulin injections

C. maintaining a reasonable exercise regimen to keep weight down

   (1) A   **(2)** B   **(3)** C   **(4)** A and B   **(5)** A and C

Answers are on page 442.

Diversity of Life

The planet Earth is home to well over a million different kinds of living organisms. These organisms range from the lowest form—bacteria—to the highest form—*Homo sapiens*. Their habitats range from the ocean depths to mountain peaks, from subzero cold to boiling mud pots.

We take for granted this abundance and diversity of life until we are warned that one member of life's family faces extinction. Many years ago in the United States, the passenger pigeon became extinct. The same fate nearly happened to the whooping crane. Today, the panda (found mainly in China) is threatened with extinction.

Humanity, as the natural steward of Earth's life forms, has the important responsibility of overseeing this inventory of life. The job of categorizing the kinds of living things has been made easier by a system of classification.

Classification of Organisms

The classification system for living things moves from the general to the specific. Each downward step in the classification system provides more detail about the organism that is classified.

The *kingdom* is the broadest grouping. Within each kingdom, the organisms with the greatest similarities are grouped further into a *phylum*. Below the phylum is the *class*. The class is followed by an *order*, a *family*, a *genus*, and a species. The *species* is the final category of classification. The classification of the human (*Homo sapiens*) is illustrated in the following chart.

TAXONOMY OF HUMAN CLASSIFICATION

Category	Taxon	Characteristics
Kingdom	Animalia	Is multicellular, cannot make its own food, is able to move
Phylum	Chordata	Has a notochord (skeletal rod) and hollow nerve cord
Class	Mammalia	Has hair or fur, female secretes milk to nourish young
Order	Primate	Has flattened fingers for grasping, keen vision, poor sense of smell
Family	Hominidae	Walks on two feet, has flat face, eyes facing forward, color vision
Genus	Homo	Has long childhood, large brain, speech ability
Species	Sapiens	Has reduced body hair, high forehead, prominent chin

EXERCISE 12: CLASSIFICATION OF ORGANISMS

Directions: Read the definitions and apply them to the questions that follow.

Listed below, from lowest to highest, are the five kingdoms that all living organisms are classified into.

kingdom monera—simple one-celled, mobile organisms lacking organelles, some of which can produce their own food (example: bacteria)

kingdom protista—single-celled, mobile organisms having a more complex cell structure than monera (example: paramecia)

kingdom fungi—multicellular, lacks chlorophyll, cannot move, obtains food from other organisms (example: mushroom)

kingdom plantae—multicellular, has chlorophyll, produces its own food, has no mobility (example: moss)

kingdom animalia—multicellular, capable of moving by itself and obtaining its own food (example: bird)

1. Streptococcus is a single-celled organism that has no organelles and that occurs in a sequence of chains. It causes strep throat when it invades the throat. In which kingdom would it be classified?

   (1) monera   **(2)** protista   **(3)** fungi   **(4)** plantae   **(5)** animalia

2. Mold is a parasite that grows on bread, cheese, or other organic foods. It lacks chlorophyll and obtains nutrients from the host. In which kingdom would it be classified?

   (1) monera   **(2)** protista   **(3)** fungi   **(4)** plantae   **(5)** animalia

3. The amoeba is a one-celled organism with very few organelles. It changes its shape and moves with the aid of pseudopods, or "false feet." In which kingdom would it be classified?

   (1) monera   **(2)** protista   **(3)** fungi   **(4)** plantae   **(5)** animalia

Answers are on page 442.

DID YOU KNOW THAT: We are losing as many as one species per day and that the rate of extinction today is 400 times faster than in previous centuries?

Evolution and Natural Selection

Among all cultures of human beings, there is some explanation for the origin of humankind. In many cultures, the theory of Divine Creation is the most widely accepted explanation for the origin of Earth and its creatures. This belief holds that a supreme being created the world and its varied forms of life.

A scientific explanation that has wide currency is the theory of *evolution*. Proposed in 1859 by Charles Darwin in his book *On the Origin of Species*, the theory holds that all forms of life developed gradually (over 600 million years) from different and often much simpler ancestors. These forms of life adapted over the years to meet the demands of their environment. Thus, all lines of descent can be traced back to a common ancestral organism. As offspring differed from their parents, generations with characteristics that were less and less alike resulted. Ultimately, new species were formed from the diverse offspring because these new characteristics were inheritable.

The new characteristics of the offspring are explained by a process called natural selection. According to *natural selection*, the species that are best adapted to the conditions under which they live survive, and those that do not adapt perish. This theory is also known as the "survival of the fittest."

Darwin's theories were considered bizarre for his time. The creationist theory had held that all species had been created and remained unchanged since the beginning of time. It had widespread acceptance and, until Darwin's discovery, remained unchallenged. Darwin demonstrated that evolution is an ongoing process whose final outcome has not yet been determined.

EXERCISE 13: EVOLUTION AND NATURAL SELECTION

Directions: Choose the best answer for each question below.

1. An unusual member of the animal kingdom is the duckbill platypus—an animal that has many characteristics of birds, mammals, and reptiles. Found in Australia and Tasmania, the animal has a ducklike bill, has webbed and clawed feet, is covered with thick fur, and reproduces by laying eggs.

   Which of the following hypotheses related to Darwin's theory of evolution could be applied to the platypus?

   (1) The platypus is the result of the interbreeding of three distinct animal classes.
   (2) The platypus is the earliest living member of the mammalian family.
   (3) The platypus developed independently in a closed environment during the early history of mammals.
   (4) The platypus was not subject to the influences described in Darwin's theory.
   (5) Mammal life originated in Australia and Tasmania hundreds of millions of years ago.

Questions 2 and 3 refer to the following passage.

Mammals are placed in two groups—*placental* (having a placenta that nourishes the fetus) and *marsupial* (having a pouch in which the young are nourished and carried). Most of the world's marsupials are found on the continent of Australia and the islands nearby, where few placental mammals lived during the early history of the continents.

2. Which of the following hypotheses *best* suggests why marsupials are found primarily in and around Australia?

    A. Australia, a subcontinent, became isolated from the other six continents millions of years ago.

    B. Marsupials didn't have to compete with placental mammals for survival.

    C. Australia is the only continent that has the climate to support marsupials.

    (1) A   **(2)** B   **(3)** C   **(4)** A and B   **(5)** A and C

3. The presence of which of the following marsupials native to North America would dispute the belief that all marsupials originated in Australia?

    (1) koala
    (2) kangaroo
    (3) opossum
    (4) wombat
    (5) bandicoot

4. Based on the preceding information about how marsupials differ from placental mammals, we can infer that

    (1) marsupials are less biologically advanced than placental mammals
    (2) placental mammals are more primitive than marsupials
    (3) marsupials cannot survive in areas other than Australia and North America
    (4) marsupials are the oldest forms of life on Earth
    (5) marsupials descended from the reptiles

5. Which of the following mammals *best* exhibits a physical adaptation to environmental conditions?

    (1) cow
    (2) lion
    (3) mouse
    (4) seal
    (5) bear

Answers are on page 442.

DID YOU KNOW THAT: The oldest living thing in the United States is the General Sherman tree, an evergreen that grows in the Sequoia National Park? It is nearly 4,000 years old.

WRITING ACTIVITY 2

In 1925, a Tennessee science teacher, John Scopes, was tried in court for teaching the theory of evolution—the belief that humans and apes descended from common ancestors. At the time, a Tennessee statute forbade the teaching of any theory that contradicted the story of Divine Creation as depicted in the Bible. Should states have the authority to dictate what beliefs teachers should impart to their students? Write an essay of two or three paragraphs defending your point of view.

374 TEST 3: SCIENCE

Ecology and Ecosystems

The science of *ecology* involves the interrelationship of a living organism with its nonliving environment. Ecology is a young science. The word *ecology* comes from the Greek word *oikos*, meaning "house" or "dwelling." Ecology, then, is the study of how we live on the planet Earth. The ecologist studies the relationships between the component organisms and their environments. A self-supporting environment is called an *ecosystem*. The photosynthetic producers, the consumers, decomposers, and their environment constitute an ecosystem.

In a typical ecosystem, the primary producers are the green plants that derive their energy from the sun. A primary consumer would be a rabbit that feeds on the leaves of the green plant. A secondary consumer in this ecosystem would be a fox that preys on the rabbit. A tertiary, or third-level, consumer would be the buzzard that feeds on the carcass that the fox leaves behind. Finally, decomposers— the bacteria and fungi that feed on the scraps left by the buzzard—provide the nitrates necessary for the green plants, the first link in this chain.

The ecological balance of a community is delicate. The removal of one key element can destroy a system, sometimes permanently.

The following passage describes an imbalance in a particular ecosystem.

EXERCISE 14: ECOLOGY AND ECOSYSTEMS

Directions: Read the passage and in the blanks below write the correct element in the ecosystem described in the passage.

At the turn of the century, ranchers moved onto the grassy Kaibab Plateau in northern Arizona. They were attracted by the fine grazing areas and abundance of deer for hunting. Fearing that the mountain lion, another inhabitant of the region, would prey on the cattle and deer, the ranchers waged a campaign to eradicate the cat from the plateau. They were successful in their effort, and mountain lions disappeared within a few years.

Their success produced catastrophic ecological results, however. Increased numbers of deer, along with herds of cattle that grazed on the land, denuded it. Soon, heavy rains caused major erosion, and the land was reduced to a fraction of its usefulness. This problem has occurred repeatedly where humans have manipulated an ecosystem without considering the possible consequences.

1. primary producer _____

2. primary consumers _____ and _____

3. tertiary consumer _____

4. The destruction of the _____ led to the increase of grazing by

_____ and _____, which led to

_____ of the land and its eventual _____

by heavy rains.

Answers are on page 443.

DID YOU KNOW THAT: Scientists estimate that it takes between 500 and 600 years to make a one-inch layer of topsoil?

2
EARTH SCIENCE—THE STUDY OF EARTH

Some of the most dramatic scientific discoveries in recent years have taken place in the field of earth science. *Earth science* is the study of the planet Earth and its origin and development. It differs from the life sciences in that it focuses on nonliving rather than living things. Earth science is a very broad field that covers the subjects of astronomy, geology, meteorology, and oceanography.

Astronomy—The Study of Heavenly Bodies

The beginning of any study of Earth generally lies in astronomy, one of the oldest of all sciences. *Astronomers* study the size, movements, and composition of the heavenly bodies. By observing the stars, planets, comets, and other objects in space, astronomers hope to understand how our planet was created and how it evolved. A number of important theories have been advanced to explain the beginning of Earth and the universe in which it lies. Two related theories are the big bang theory and the pulsation theory.

The Big Bang and Pulsation Theories

The leading theory to explain the origin of the universe is the *big bang theory.* According to this theory, a "cosmic egg" made up of dust and gas containing all the matter in the universe exploded. This explosion occurred 15 to 20 billion years ago, creating the basic atoms, elements, and heavenly bodies of the universe. The big bang theory is widely accepted because it accounts for the apparent expansion of the universe and the background radiation found in outer space.

A further refinement of the big bang theory was the development of the *pulsation theory.* According to this theory, the universe will expand to a certain point and then begin to contract. This contraction will continue until the cosmic egg is again achieved, when another "big bang" will create expansion in the universe.

As scientists can never know for certain how the universe came to be, theories such as these help to explain their observations.

Stars and Galaxies

The big bang theory also explains how stars are formed. According to supporters of the theory, the energy from the bang was so powerful that matter lighter than air remained suspended in space (just as the energy from an explosion releases particles that remain in the atmosphere). Eventually, the force of gravity exerted itself, and the matter was drawn, along with helium and hydrogen gases, into dark, cloudlike formations. The gaseous matter became compressed, and the colliding of the compressed particles produced heat. A star developed when the temperature reached 15 million degrees centigrade—the temperature at which nuclear reactions begin.

The lifetime of a star ranges from a few hundred thousand years to billions of years. Most stars eventually use up their supply of hydrogen, contract to a smaller size, and then explode. The explosion results in clouds of dust and gas. Some stars eventually contract to black holes—stars of very small size that have gravitational fields so strong that not even light escapes from them.

Most stars exist within a very large formation called a *galaxy*. Hundreds of millions of galaxies are believed to exist in the universe. The stars of a galaxy may be so closely packed together that we can see them only as a blur of light rather than as individual stars.

Our galaxy, the Milky Way, is a spiral galaxy, as are 80 percent of all galaxies. The Milky Way is composed of at least 100 billion stars and enough matter, in the form of dust and gas, to create millions of additional suns. The following illustration shows the Milky Way Galaxy.

THE MILKY WAY GALAXY

Sun's Position

EXERCISE 1: THE BIG BANG THEORY

Directions: Choose the best answer for the following question.

Which of the following facts support the big bang theory's explanation of the creation of the universe?

(1) The universe is constantly expanding.
(2) The universe has no beginning or end.
(3) Background radiation is found throughout the universe.
(4) Both 1 and 2
(5) Both 1 and 3

Answer is on page 443.

EXERCISE 2: STARS AND GALAXIES

Directions: Number the steps of star formation in the correct sequence, with *1* representing the first step and *4* the last.

_____ Heat is produced by the colliding of molecules.

_____ Fifteen million degrees centigrade is reached, and visible light is emitted.

_____ Dust and gas move throughout the universe.

_____ Gas and dust become compressed because of gravitational forces.

Answers are on page 443.

DID YOU KNOW THAT: In 1987, astronomers reported observing starlight from a new galaxy and that they have evidence that planets are taking shape around stars other than our own?

The Sun and the Solar System

The Sun is the star at the center of our solar system, and, despite its importance to our world, it is really only an "average" star when compared to others in our galaxy. It is average in age (4 to 5 billion years old), size (860,000 miles in diameter or about 100 times Earth's diameter), and heat intensity (its surface temperature is about 6,000 degrees centigrade).

Other members of the solar system include the nine planets, seven of which have one or more satellites (moons), and 1,600 large asteroids located between Mars and Jupiter.

The inner planets (Mercury, Venus, Earth, and Mars) are small, with high densities and few satellites. The outer planets (Jupiter, Saturn, Uranus, and Neptune) are large gas giants and have many moons. Pluto is so far away that all we can tell is that it is not similar to other outer planets.

The planets are believed to have begun as clumps of matter within the dust cloud that formed the Sun. They were too small to achieve the conditions needed to become stars. Instead, they cooled and became the planets as we know them. Our space probes have reached all except the most distant outer planets, and it appears that Earth is the only inhabited body in our solar system.

The following illustration shows our solar system.

OUR SOLAR SYSTEM

EXERCISE 3: THE SOLAR SYSTEM

Directions: Choose the best answer for each question below.

1. The "Goldilocks problem" in astronomy (in which one of the eight planets other than Earth is too hot to support life and the other too cold to support life) applies to which two planets?

   (1) Pluto and Neptune
   (2) Mars and Saturn
   (3) Mercury and Venus
   (4) Venus and Mars
   (5) Jupiter and Uranus

2. The Earth's sister planets are Venus and Mars. Scientists most likely have designated these two as sister planets because

   (1) life has been proven to exist on Venus and Mars
   (2) all three planets share the same orbit
   (3) both planets show evidence of having had Earthlike climates sometime in the distant past
   (4) both planets are the two closest to the Sun
   (5) all three planets are the exact same age and size

Answers are on page 443.

EXERCISE 4: THE PLANETS

Directions: Based on the information in the table, complete each of the following statements by writing the name of the correct planet in the blank.

Planet	Length of Year	Rotates on Its Axis Every	Number of Satellites	Distance from Sun (miles)
Mercury	88 days	58 days	0	36 million
Venus	225 days	243 days	0	67 million
Earth	365.26 days	23.9 hours	1	93 million
Mars	686.98 days	24.6 hours	2	142 million

1. The length of the day is approximately the same on _____ and _____.

2. Of the planets listed, based on Earth years, you would age at the slowest rate on _____.

3. Of the planets listed, based on Earth years, you would age at the fastest rate on _____.

4. Of the planets listed, _____ rotates on its axis most slowly.

5. Mars takes a little more than three times longer to revolve around the Sun than _____.

Answers are on page 443.

EXERCISE 5: THE SUN AND SOLAR SYSTEM

Directions: Choose the best answer for the following question, based on the table on page 378.

There appears to be a relationship between the distance of these planets from the Sun and

    (1) the amount of time it takes for the planet to rotate on its axis
    (2) the number of satellites or moons it has
    (3) the time it takes the planet to revolve around the Sun
    (4) both 1 and 2
    (5) both 2 and 3

Answer is on page 443.

DID YOU KNOW THAT: Venus rotates backward with respect to the Sun, so that from Venus the Sun would appear to rise in the west and set in the east?

WRITING ACTIVITY 1

Solar energy is being considered seriously as an alternative form of energy in American life. To what extent is solar energy being explored and applied where you live? If it is not being applied, what are the likely reasons? Write a paragraph describing the role solar energy plays where you live.

Geology—The Study of Earth's Formation

Earthquakes! Floods! Volcanic eruptions! The occurrence of each of these natural disasters is evidence that, far from being the steady ground on which we stand, Earth is changing constantly.

Today's Earth is not the same as the Earth of a thousand years ago; nor will it be the same a thousand years from today. *Geologists* study the features of Earth and how they affect its development. In this century alone, geologists have made significant discoveries that have revolutionized the entire field of earth science. Probably the most significant of all findings made in recent history has been the formulation of the theory of plate tectonics, a theory that explains the development of mountains and ocean trenches and the occurrence of earthquakes and volcanic eruptions.

Continental Drift and Plate Tectonics

Scientists have long observed that accurately drawn maps of Africa and South America suggest that the two continents once fit together. Based on this observation, geologists formulated the *theory of continental drift.* According to the theory, all seven continents formed a supercontinent millions of years ago. It broke apart and split into the land masses that are recognized today as the seven continents.

Despite this appearance that the continents interlock like pieces of a puzzle, scientists could not explain why the continents drifted apart. The *theory of plate tectonics*, advanced in the 1960s, provided an explanation of the phenomenon.

According to the theory, Earth is made up of the crust, mantle, outer core, and inner core, as depicted in the following picture:

EARTH'S STRUCTURE

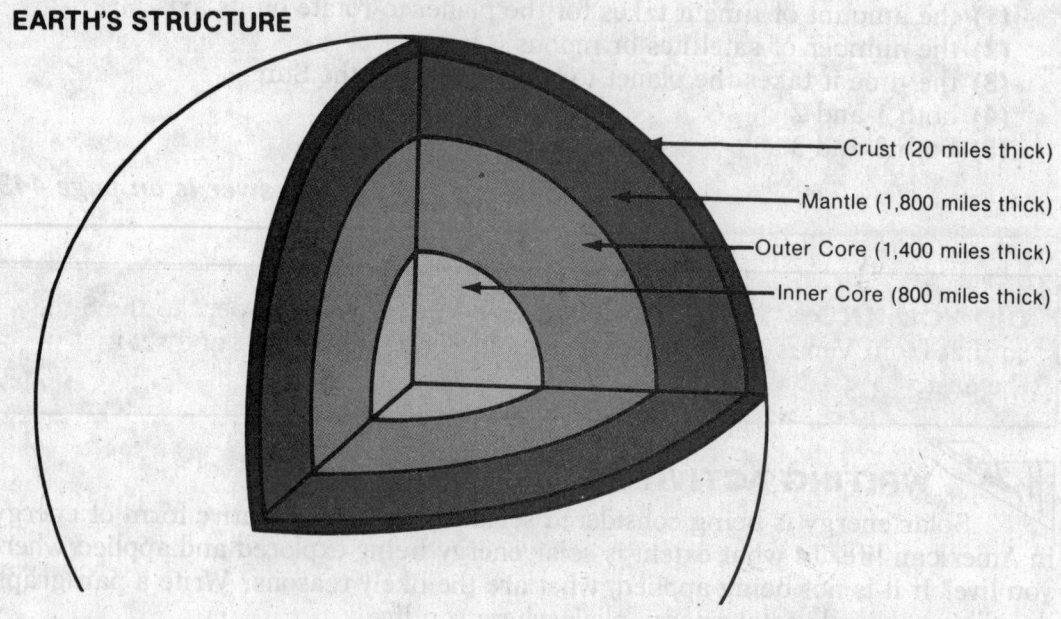

Crust (20 miles thick)
Mantle (1,800 miles thick)
Outer Core (1,400 miles thick)
Inner Core (800 miles thick)

The crust and upper mantle are made up of about twenty plates. These plates may be likened to plates floating on the surface of water in a vast sink. They move very slowly—approximately one-half to four inches per year. Attached to the surface of these plates are the continents and the ocean floor. As the plates slowly move, they carry the continents with them. Geologists believe that the plates move because currents of partially molten rock in the mantle carry them.

This motion of the plates appears to explain the formation of mountains and ocean trenches and the occurrence of earthquakes and volcanoes. For example, when two plates collide, one plate piles atop another, forming a mountain. When one plate is forced down into the mantle of another, a trench occurs. A volcano is created when the heat beneath the surface of Earth melts the plate material that was forced into the trench and sends the molten rock to the surface. An earthquake is formed by the shifting and breaking of the surface rocks when two plates slide past each other.

The vibrations caused by the slippage of plates are called *seismic waves*. The strength of these waves is measured by a device called a seismograph and then rated on the Richter scale. Earthquakes measuring more than 4.5 on the Richter scale are considered potentially dangerous.

EXERCISE 6: PLATE TECTONICS

Directions: Choose the best answer for the following question.

According to the passage, the theory of plate tectonics helps explain which of the following?

A. the Earth's gravitational pull

B. earthquakes, volcanoes, and mountains

C. the theory of continental drift

(1) A
(2) B
(3) C
(4) A and B
(5) B and C

Answer is on page 443.

EXERCISE 7: EARTHQUAKES

Directions: Choose the best answer for the question below, based on the following map.

U.S. EARTHQUAKE ZONES AND SEISMIC RISK

Potential for Damage

0—None
1—Minor
2—Moderate
3—Major

Which of the following statements about earthquakes is supported by the map?

(1) California is the only state in which residents might expect major earthquake damage.
(2) Texas and Florida are the only states that do not have to worry about earthquakes.
(3) The potential for moderate to major earthquake damage is greatest on the West Coast.
(4) Most of the continental United States is not affected by earthquakes.
(5) Earthquakes are the most dangerous phenomenon on Earth.

Answer is on page 443.

EXERCISE 8: CONTINENTAL DRIFT

Directions: Read the following passage and choose the best answer for each question.

Ascension Island is a small volcanic island located in the south Atlantic halfway between Africa and South America. It is a famous breeding ground for sea turtles. Giant green turtles each year swim 2,000 miles from the coast of South America to lay their eggs on Ascension Island. This phenomenon has puzzled scientists for years.

1. Which of the following geological hypotheses best explains the behavior of the giant sea turtles?

   A. Ascension Island is the only place in the world where turtle eggs can survive.

   B. Predators, like alligators that live on the coast of South America, eat turtle eggs, forcing the sea turtles to migrate.

   C. The turtles laid their eggs on Ascension Island millions of years ago before the continents of Africa and South America became separated.

   (1) A   **(2)** B   **(3)** C   **(4)** A and B   **(5)** B and C

2. The behavior of the sea turtles, the location of South America with respect to Africa, and the theory of continental drift all point to what possibility about the Atlantic Ocean?

   (1) It was once a river.
   (2) It has always been the size it is today.
   (3) It has moved from its original position on Earth.
   (4) It did not exist when giant sea turtles laid their eggs millions of years ago.
   (5) It was probably once a narrow sea between Africa and South America before the sea floor spread apart.

Answers are on page 443.

DID YOU KNOW THAT: The coastal areas of the continents surrounding the Pacific Ocean are collectively called the Ring of Fire because more than three-fourths of the world's earthquakes occur there?

Geologic Time

What is a long period of time to you? Without any reference point, your answer might vary from an hour to a century. If you were told to measure time in relation to your own life, you might consider fifty years to be a long time. In geology, however, fifty years is not very long, since geologic time extends back nearly five billion years, when geologists believe Earth was formed.

We owe our concept of *absolute time*—time not influenced by man's arbitrary reference points—to geology. Geologists are able to fix periods of time by studying the rocks found in Earth's crust. These rocks serve as records of time.

The rocks found in Earth's crust are of three types, described according to their origins. These rocks are igneous, metamorphic, and sedimentary. *Igneous* rocks are formed when molten rock (magma) hardens. Just below igneous rock are *metamorphic* rocks, which have been changed by high pressure and temperature within the crust. The rocks that undergo metamorphosis are mainly igneous rocks. *Sedimentary* rocks are deposited near Earth's surface by wind, water, and ice. In sedimentary rock, the oldest layers are on the bottom and the youngest are on the top.

Instruments for Measuring Time

We have determined which rocks are older than others, but how do we find out how old that is? Radiometric measurement is one tool that scientists use to measure absolute time. In *radiometric measurement*, geologists measure the rate of radioactive decay in the minerals found in the rock. Over the last century, scientists have learned that radioactive substances will change, or decay, into nonradioactive substances over a period of time. This method is valid for matter up to 50,000 years in age. Radiometric dating works well with samples of igneous and sedimentary rocks because it measures the radioactivity of minerals created when the rocks were formed. For metamorphic rock, however, the age of the original rock and the age of metamorphism are difficult to pinpoint.

In addition to radiometric dating, the principle of *faunal succession* is used to determine the age of sedimentary rock. With this method, geologists examine the types of animal fossils found in layers of sedimentary rock. Igneous and metamorphic rock rarely contain fossils. Scientists have found that certain layers of rock will contain certain kinds of fossils, no matter where in the world the rock is located. Moreover, scientists have found that certain fossils are always found at lower layers than others, indicating that a sequence exists to the evolution of organisms.

EXERCISE 9: MEASURING GEOLOGIC TIME

Directions: Choose the best answer for each of the following questions.

1. Based on the information in the preceding passage, which correctly describes the placement of the three types of rocks?

   (1) Igneous is located at the surface, metamorphic in the middle, and sedimentary on the bottom.
   (2) Sedimentary is located at the surface, metamorphic in the middle, and igneous at the bottom.
   (3) Metamorphic is located at the surface, sedimentary in the middle, and igneous at the bottom.
   (4) Igneous is located at the surface, sedimentary in the middle, and metamorphic at the bottom.
   (5) Sedimentary is located at the surface, igneous in the middle, and metamorphic at the bottom.

2. Dating metamorphic and igneous rocks presents problems for scientists because

A. they almost never contain fossils

B. for metamorphic rocks, the age of the original rock and date of metamorphism are more difficult to pinpoint

C. neither type of rock can be dated radiometrically

(1) A
(2) B
(3) C
(4) A and B
(5) A and C

3. Trilobite fossils are found at a depth of 18 meters in a rock bed, and coral fossils are found at 14 meters. Which of the following is likely to be true about each organism?

(1) Coral is older than trilobites.
(2) Coral and trilobites are the same age.
(3) Coral and trilobites share a common ancestry.
(4) Trilobites are more advanced than corals.
(5) Trilobites are older than corals.

Answers are on page 443.

Minerals and Rocks

Just as cells are the building blocks of living organisms, minerals are the building blocks of rocks. A *mineral* is a natural, inorganic solid with a specific composition and structure. All specimens of a given mineral share certain physical properties. Some physical properties of minerals are crystalline form, hardness, color, and cleavage (the way they break).

More than 95 percent of Earth's crust is made up of the minerals formed from the elements oxygen and silicon. The following chart shows the eight main elements, including their percent of the crust's weight and volume.

Element	Percent of Crust's Mass (weight)	Percent of Crust's Volume (space)
Oxygen	46.71	94.24
Silicon	27.69	0.51
Aluminum	8.07	0.44
Iron	5.05	0.37
Calcium	3.65	1.04
Sodium	2.75	1.21
Potassium	2.58	1.85
Magnesium	2.08	0.27

EXERCISE 10: MINERALS AND ROCKS

Directions: Choose the best answer for the questions below.

1. According to the information in the table, which element represents less of the crust's weight but occupies over three times the space of silicon, a major component of the crust?

    (1) sodium
    (2) calcium
    (3) potassium
    (4) magnesium
    (5) iron

2. Which of the following elements also represents less weight than silicon but takes up more space?

    (1) aluminum
    (2) oxygen
    (3) magnesium
    (4) sodium
    (5) iron

3. The implication from the facts in the preceding table is that the two elements that represent less weight than silicon but occupy more space

    (1) are denser than silicon
    (2) combine more often with oxygen than silicon
    (3) represent a greater percentage of the crust's weight
    (4) weigh less than oxygen
    (5) cannot be compressed as easily as silicon

4. Which of the following best explains why oxygen, a gas, is the largest component of Earth's crust?

    (1) Oxygen gives Earth's crust its lightness.
    (2) Oxygen is the most abundant element in the world.
    (3) Oxygen is found in plants, and plants are significant parts of Earth's crust.
    (4) Oxygen is needed to sustain all life on Earth.
    (5) Oxygen is capable of combining with most of the elements in Earth's crust.

Answers are on page 444.

DID YOU KNOW THAT: The softest mineral known to man is talc, from which talcum powder is made, and the hardest is the diamond? Diamonds are so hard that they can be cut only by another diamond.

The Changing Earth

Another process that contributes to the changing face of Earth is erosion. *Erosion* is the wearing away of Earth's surface. Erosion has occurred throughout time and will continue as long as dry land exists. You can see the process of erosion at work when you water your lawn. Under the pressure of a steady stream of water, loose soil is moved from a higher elevation to a lower one. The chief agents that cause erosion are gravity, wind, ice, and water.

The pull of *gravity* makes surface material move downward. Downslope movements may be rapid or very slow. They may involve only the surface material, or they may involve the bedrock underneath. Houses built on hills can contribute to soil movements because the weight of the homes may add to the gravitational force. For this reason, knowledge about erosional processes must be considered by homebuilders.

Wind contributes to the erosional process by carrying surface material from one location to another. Erosion occurs when rock particles wear away surface material much like the process involved in sandblasting, in which sand blown at high rates of speed wears away a brick's veneer.

Glaciers, huge sheets of ice that can move slowly over land, pick up and carry rocks and soil with them. When they pass through river valleys, they deepen them. Mountain glaciers, coupled with the downward force of gravity, create avalanches that can cause great erosional damage.

Of all the erosional agents, running water is the most powerful. Rivers, working with the force of gravity, are devastating in their erosional impact. The action of rivers flowing against the land has formed gorges as large as the Grand Canyon. As rivers erode land, they carry deposits with them. *Deltas* are formed at the mouths of rivers that empty into a lake or ocean. The soil that is carried along a river and deposited at its mouth is the richest and most fertile of all soils. The Nile and Mississippi rivers have formed deltas that are noted for their rich soil, making these regions highly desirable for agriculture.

EXERCISE 11: THE CHANGING EARTH

Directions: Choose the best answer for the following questions.

1. Which of the following procedures followed by a farmer is *not* related directly to preventing erosion?

   (1) planting grass in gullies to act as a filler
   (2) planting crops in alternate rows (strip farming)
   (3) contour plowing around a hill
   (4) planting new trees to replace those that die
   (5) planting more seeds than are necessary to yield a bountiful crop

2. The force of erosion is counteracted by the effects of changes in Earth's surface. Which of the following internal forces interrupt the external forces of erosion?

A. forces that cause volcanoes

B. forces that cause ocean trenches

C. forces that create mountains

(1) A
(2) B
(3) C
(4) A and B
(5) A and C

Answers are on page 444.

DID YOU KNOW THAT: Many lakes were formed by large holes dug by glaciers? These holes were later filled with water and became lakes.

WRITING ACTIVITY 2

What evidence of erosion can you see in the region where you live? Write two or three paragraphs describing how erosion has affected your community.

Oceanography—The Study of Earth's Oceans

Observed from space, Earth has been described as a big blue marble. The one feature that contributes to this description is water—it covers nearly 71 percent of Earth's surface. Water dominates our lives. For those who live near bodies of water, water provides recreation, food, and a means of transportation. Earth scientists who study large bodies of water are called *oceanographers*.

From their studies of the oceans, oceanographers have made many discoveries that help them to understand and explain phenomena they observe on Earth. For example, the theory of plate tectonics was further substantiated by the finding that a ridge encircling the globe lies under the ocean—the *oceanic ridge*. This ridge circles the globe like the seam of a baseball. Numerous openings have been photographed along the crest of this ridge. Evidence from the pictures provided the basis for the theory that magma forces itself up from the ridges, pushes the ocean plates apart, cools, and forms new rock that becomes part of the ocean plate.

The last twenty-five years have yielded many fascinating findings about the ocean, the last frontier on our planet. The advances in ocean technology, like those in space technology, are the chief reasons for our increased knowledge about the ocean. Inventions such as sonar (an underwater ranging device), deep-diving submarines, and remote-control cameras have aided in our exploration of the oceans.

The Oceans' Beginning

Oceanographers are not sure how Earth's oceans began. Many believe that the oceans were formed by the release of water bound up in rocks of Earth's interior. Evidence from some of the most ancient sedimentary rocks suggests that the original sediments forming the rocks were deposited in water.

While scientists are not certain about the beginning of Earth's oceans, they do know that the volume of water covering Earth is affected by the formation of glaciers and the melting of huge blocks of ice covering Earth's surface. The graph below illustrates the change in sea level during the past 20,000 years. (Glaciers covered much of Earth 20,000 years ago.)

EXERCISE 12: CHANGE IN SEA LEVEL

Directions: Choose the best answer for each of the following questions.

CHANGE IN SEA LEVEL
DURING THE PAST 20,000 YEARS

1. Based on the graph, Earth's sea level was at its lowest approximately

   (1) 1,000 years ago
   (2) 5,000 years ago
   (3) 10,000 years ago
   (4) 15,000 years ago
   (5) 18,000 years ago

2. Which of the following are best supported by the graph and the fact that the formation of glaciers significantly affects the level of Earth's oceans?

   A. The period when sea level was lowest was the period when glaciers were at their peak.

   B. The period when sea level was highest was the period after the glaciers had been melted for thousands of years.

   C. The period when sea level was at its lowest was the period when glaciers had been melted for thousands of years.

   D. The period when sea level was at its highest was the period when ice covered Earth.

   (1) A and B
   (2) A and C
   (3) B and C
   (4) A and D
   (5) B and D

Answers are on page 444.

EXERCISE 13: THE OCEANS' BEGINNING

Directions: Choose the best answer for the questions below.

DISTRIBUTION OF WATER ON EARTH

Type of Water	Relative % of abundance
Seawater	86.5
Lakes, rivers	0.03
Continental Ice	1.3
Water vapor in atmosphere	0.001
Water in sediments and sedimentary rocks	12.2
Total	100

1. Which of the following sources yields the smallest amount of water throughout Earth?

   (1) seawater
   (2) lakes and rivers
   (3) continental ice
   (4) water vapor in the atmosphere
   (5) water in sediments and sedimentary rocks

2. The presence of 12 percent of water in sediments and in sedimentary rocks lends support to the theory of

   (1) continental drift
   (2) plate tectonics
   (3) how Earth's sea level has risen over time
   (4) the origin of the oceans
   (5) faunal succession

Answers are on page 444.

DID YOU KNOW THAT: All the oceans except the North Pacific are divided in the center by an almost continuous system of mountains?

The Oceans' Tides

One phenomenon of the oceans that can be easily observed is the occurrence of tides. *Tides* result from the rising and falling of the ocean's surface caused by the gravitational pull of the Sun and the Moon on Earth. The Moon is the most dominant factor in causing tides because of its closeness to Earth.

When the Moon is directly overhead, the ocean beneath it tends to bulge up, causing a tide. On the opposite side of Earth, the oceans experience a lesser bulge. As Earth rotates once every twenty-four hours, it experiences two high tides and two low tides. The position of the Moon in relation to the Sun and Earth determines the period and height of the tides. *Spring tides* are tides of greater-than-average range. *Neap tides* are tides of smaller-than-average range. The illustration in the exercise below shows a spring tide and a neap tide.

EXERCISE 14: THE OCEANS' TIDES

Directions: Choose the best answer for the following questions.

SPRING AND NEAP TIDES

1. Spring tides are tides of greater-than-average range. During which two phases of the Moon is the gravitational pull of the Moon together with the Sun likely to be greatest, causing a spring tide?

   A. first quarter—when the Moon is to the right side of Earth

   B. full moon—when Earth is between the Sun and the Moon

   C. last quarter—when the Moon is to the left side of Earth, as shown

   D. new moon—when the Moon is between Earth and the Sun

   (1) A and B   **(2)** A and C   **(3)** A and D   **(4)** B and C   **(5)** B and D

2. Neap tides are tides of smaller-than-average range. During which two periods of the Moon is the gravitational pull of the Moon negated by the Sun, causing a neap tide?

A. first quarter—when the Moon is to the right side of Earth

B. full moon—when Earth is between the Sun and the Moon

C. last quarter—when the Moon is to the left side of Earth, as shown

D. new moon—when the Moon is between Earth and the Sun

(1) A and B
(2) A and C
(3) B and C
(4) B and D
(5) A and D

Questions 3 and 4 are based on the following explanation

Syzygy (siz'-e-je) is the term that describes a rare alignment of the Sun, Moon, and Earth that causes extraordinarily high tides. This phenomenon occurred during the period from December 30, 1986, to January 4, 1987. It aggravated the severe storms that occurred along the Atlantic Coast. Three coinciding events occurred during this five-day period.

A. The Moon's orbit was closest to Earth—about 223,000 miles instead of 240,000 miles.

B. The Moon was directly between Earth and the Sun, causing a new moon.

C. Earth's orbit was the closest to the Sun—91½ million miles, instead of the normal 93 million miles.

3. The occurrence of which of the preceding events best explains why the tide was higher than normal?

(1) A
(2) B
(3) C
(4) A and B
(5) A and C

4. Conditions under which the Moon's orbit is farthest from Earth, Earth is between the Sun and the Moon, and Earth's orbit is farthest from the Sun would likely result in

(1) the same effect as syzygy
(2) unusually low tides
(3) neap tides
(4) spring tides
(5) unusually high tides

Answers are on page 444.

> **DID YOU KNOW THAT:** There are areas in the world that have no tides, such as the Mediterranean Sea, the Baltic Sea, the Adriatic Sea, and the Gulf of Mexico?

WRITING ACTIVITY 3

Does water play a significant role in the region where you live? Write two or three paragraphs describing the importance of water in the areas of recreation, food, economics, transportation, and weather.

Meteorology—The Study of Earth's Atmosphere

Just as land and water constitute significant parts of Earth, so does the *atmosphere*—the invisible layer of air that envelops Earth. Scientists believe that it is primarily because of our atmosphere that life exists on Earth and not on neighboring planets such as Mars and Venus.

Meteorologists study Earth's atmosphere to understand and predict the weather. The atmosphere is not one distinct air mass that surrounds Earth; it is composed of several layers of air that begin at specific altitude ranges. Meteorologists have identified four layers of Earth's atmosphere. In ascending order (from lowest to highest) they are the troposphere, stratosphere, ionosphere, and exosphere. Each of these four layers serves a specific purpose in helping to sustain life on Earth.

The *troposphere* lies closest to Earth. It extends upward about seven to ten miles. Earth's weather occurs in this layer of the atmosphere, and it contains almost all of the clouds. The *tropopause* is the boundary where the troposphere ends and the stratosphere begins.

The *stratosphere* begins somewhere between seven and ten miles and extends upward about thirty miles. It is a uniform layer of air with little vertical air movement. Airplane travel in this layer is generally smooth and visibility always clear.

Beginning after the stratosphere, the *ionosphere* extends upward about 300 miles. The air in the ionosphere is extremely thin, and air particles are electrified. Through the ionosphere, radio waves are transmitted great distances around Earth.

The *exosphere* is the highest layer of the atmosphere. It is characterized by extreme heat during the day when the Sun's direct rays reach it and extreme cold at night when it is shielded from the Sun's direct rays.

EXERCISE 15: LAYERS OF EARTH'S ATMOSPHERE

Directions: Choose the best answer for each of the following questions after reading the passage below and studying the accompanying diagram.

At different altitudes of Earth's atmosphere we are able to observe different phenomena. Also, scientists are able to use different technologies to explore and understand Earth and the regions in outer space.

1. *Noctilucent* clouds, spectacular clouds that can be seen only at dusk, appear shortly after sunset. At which atmospheric level are these clouds visible?

   (1) exosphere
   (2) troposphere
   (3) stratosphere
   (4) ionosphere
   (5) tropopause

2. "D" layer radio waves that are transmitted around the world may be found at

   (1) the upper range of the stratosphere
   (2) the lower range of the stratosphere
   (3) the lower range of the ionosphere
   (4) the upper range of the ionosphere
   (5) the upper range of the troposphere

3. The illustration suggests that the peak of Mt. Everest

   A. is at times hidden by clouds

   B. extends beyond the tropopause

   C. lies in the troposphere

   (1) A
   (2) B
   (3) C
   (4) A and B
   (5) A and C

Atmospheric phenomena and observation tools

Answers are on page 444.

EXERCISE 16: OZONE IN THE ATMOSPHERE

Directions: Read the following passage and choose the best answer for each of the questions that follow.

Ozone, a corrosive, pungent, and toxic gas, occurs in the atmosphere when the Sun's ultraviolet rays cause ionization in oxygen atoms. Ozone is beneficial to us because it absorbs ultraviolet rays, preventing these lethal wavelengths from reaching Earth's surface. At lower levels in Earth's atmosphere, however, especially in large urban areas, ozone can be created from a chemical reaction involving solar heat and the exhaust from cars. The chief ingredient of smog, this form of ozone is harmful to humans and can cause difficulty in breathing.

1. The harmful form of ozone that can be seen as smog is formed in the

   (1) exosphere
   (2) troposphere
   (3) stratosphere
   (4) ionosphere
   (5) tropopause

2. At which time during the year does the ozone level present a particular health threat in urban areas for people with respiratory problems?

   (1) spring
   (2) summer
   (3) fall
   (4) winter
   (5) throughout the year

Answers are on page 444.

The Water Cycle

In predicting the weather, meteorologists must consider not just the air surrounding us but also how it interacts with the water that covers Earth's surface. The atmosphere and the *hydrosphere* (the watery portion of Earth) create the *water cycle*. This cycle helps to explain precipitation, an important element in our weather.

The Sun is a key link in the chain of events that makes up the water cycle. The Sun radiates heat, which daily evaporates millions of tons of water from Earth's oceans, lakes, rivers, and streams into the air. As moist air rises, it slowly cools. Finally, it cools so much that the humidity (the amount of water vapor the air is holding) reaches 100 percent. At this point, the water vapor condenses and clouds form. Depending on the temperature and other conditions, either rain or snow falls as precipitation when the clouds can't hold all of the water. The rain or snow eventually flows to the ocean, and the cycle is completed again. The illustration on the next page shows the water cycle.

THE WATER CYCLE

EXERCISE 17: THE WATER CYCLE

Directions: Number the steps of the water cycle in the correct sequence, with *1* representing the first step and *5* the last. The first one is done for you.

_____ Rain or snow returns water to the ocean.

_____ Condensation occurs, forming clouds.

___*1*___ The Sun radiates heat.

_____ Precipitation in the form of rain or snow occurs.

_____ Water evaporates into the atmosphere.

Answers are on page 444.

DID YOU KNOW THAT: The sky is blue because sunlight diffuses or scatters the rays of the colors found in the atmosphere's gases? Of all the colors in the rainbow, blue, purple, and violet have shorter rays than the other colors. So these three colors are diffused many more times and, therefore, dominate the sky.

EXERCISE 18: HUMIDITY

Directions: Read the passage and answer the questions that follow.

Humidity is the amount of water vapor in the air at a given time. At warm temperatures, the air can hold more moisture than it can hold at cold temperatures. *Relative humidity* is the amount of vapor the air is holding expressed as a percentage of the amount the air is capable of holding. For example, at 86 degrees Fahrenheit, the air can hold a maximum of 30.4 grams of water per cubic meter. If the air at the same temperature is holding only 15.2 grams of water, then the relative humidity is 50 percent. At the point when the air becomes saturated (exceeds the most water vapor it can hold), it releases water vapor in the form of dew or condensation.

1. If the air at 61 degrees is holding the maximum amount of moisture that it can, and the temperature suddenly drops to 45 degrees, what is likely to be the result?

   A. The humidity will remain unchanged.

   B. The air will become saturated with water vapor.

   C. Precipitation will be released in the form of rain.

   D. Precipitation will be released in the form of hail.

   (1) A
   (2) B
   (3) C
   (4) B and C
   (5) B and D

2. During subfreezing days in many parts of the country, the indoor relative humidity decreases when homes are heated. Furniture and skin dry out, and static electricity increases. For health reasons, doctors recommend the use of humidifiers. Which of the following best explains the lack of humidity in the air indoors?

   A. The amount of water vapor in the air goes down.

   B. The water vapor in the air evaporates.

   C. The water vapor present in the air at lower temperatures is less than the amount that heated indoor air can hold.

   (1) A
   (2) B
   (3) C
   (4) A and B
   (5) B and C

3. What indoor relative humidity range would probably be comfortable when the outside temperature and humidity levels are extremely low?

(1) 1 to 5 percent
(2) 10 to 15 percent
(3) 30 to 40 percent
(4) 75 to 80 percent
(5) 90 to 100 percent

Answers are on page 445.

DID YOU KNOW THAT: When the humidity is high, wood, skin, and hair absorb moisture and expand and that blond human hair increases its length by 2½ percent as the relative humidity increases from 0 to 100 percent?

Air Masses, Fronts, and Weather

Another key element in determining Earth's weather is an air mass. Basically, an air mass may be either warm or cold. Cold air masses tend to be unstable and turbulent and move faster than warm air masses. The clouds that are formed by cold air masses are *cumulus clouds*—puffy, cottonlike clouds. During warm weather, when cold air masses bring precipitation, it is likely to be in the form of thundershowers. Warm air masses are usually stable, and the wind that accompanies them is steady. Clouds that are formed by warm air masses are *stratus clouds*—low-lying, level clouds that in warm weather bring precipitation in the form of drizzle.

A *front* occurs when two air masses collide and a boundary between the two masses forms. The weather for the land below is affected. Fronts may be either weak or strong. Strong fronts generally bring precipitation.

When cold air acts like a plow and pushes warm air back, a *cold front* forms. If the cold air retreats, and the warm air pushes it away, a *warm front* occurs. Sometimes, the boundary between the two air masses does not move, and the front becomes stationary. *Stationary fronts* bring conditions similar to those brought by warm fronts. However, precipitation that results is usually milder and lasts longer.

An understanding of the behavior of air masses and fronts helps weather forecasters predict weather conditions for a particular region with reasonable accuracy.

EXERCISE 19: AIR MASSES, FRONTS, AND WEATHER

Directions: Choose the best answer for the following questions.

1. Which of the following changes in the weather can occur when a strong warm air mass displaces a cold air mass?

   (1) Cumulus clouds may form, winds become gusty, and thunderstorms may result.
   (2) Stratus clouds may form, winds may become steady, and drizzling occurs.
   (3) Stratus clouds may form, winds become turbulent, and thunderstorms may result.
   (4) Cumulus clouds may form, winds become steady, and thundershowers may result.
   (5) The sky remains cloudless, and no winds or precipitation occurs.

2. A region experiences a steady drizzle for two days straight after having had cool, clear weather for several days before. Which of the following fronts is likely to have caused these weather conditions?

   (1) A weak cold front has moved in.
   (2) A weak warm front has moved in.
   (3) A stationary front has moved in.
   (4) A stationary front is slowly departing.
   (5) A strong warm front has moved in.

3. Based on the preceding passage, which of the following has *no* relation to the action of fronts in causing weather changes?

   (1) the temperature of the air mass
   (2) the speed at which the air mass moves
   (3) the strength of the air mass
   (4) the stability of the winds that accompany the air mass
   (5) the direction in which the air mass moves

Answers are on page 445.

DID YOU KNOW THAT: The winds of hurricanes can reach 230 miles per hour and that the amount of energy a hurricane can release in a day if harnessed could supply electricity to the United States for about six months?

WRITING ACTIVITY 4
What is the general pattern of weather for the region where you live? In two or three paragraphs, describe the area where you live on the basis of its atmospheric conditions (pollution level), level of precipitation, humidity, and frequency in frontal activity.

3
CHEMISTRY—THE STUDY OF MATTER

Hardly a single moment occurs in our lives that is not affected by a chemical process. Our homes, schools, and places of employment are composed of glass, steel, plaster, insulation, and paint—items that are chemically based. Our cars run on a chemical—fuel. Much of our clothing is synthetic—composed of man-made chemical fibers. Our medicine is manufactured from chemicals developed in laboratories. Even many of our food products include chemical additives. *Chemistry* is the branch of science that concerns the composition, structure, and properties of matter as well as the changes it undergoes.

Matter is any substance that occupies space and has mass. Your chair, desk, and table are composed of matter. Even the air you breathe is composed of matter. Matter exists in four states—as solids, liquids, gases, and as plasma, an ionized gas of which the Sun is made. The starting point for a systematic study of chemistry generally begins with an examination of the basic unit of matter, the atom.

The Atom, the Basis of Matter

In biology, cells are the building blocks for living organisms; in chemistry, atoms are the building blocks for matter. The *atom* is the smallest particle of an element that has the properties of that element. An *element* is a substance that occurs in nature and that cannot be broken down into a simpler substance. Nearly 100 fundamental substances known as elements are known to occur in nature. A few elements have been produced synthetically by man.

Atoms also form molecules. A *molecule* is the smallest part of a compound that can exist by itself. A molecule consists of two or more atoms joined together chemically.

The belief that all elements are composed of atoms was first proposed in the early nineteenth century by John Dalton, an English chemist. At that time, only a few elements were known to exist. According to Dalton's theory, an atom cannot be made, destroyed, or divided, and atoms of the same element are alike. This became known as *atomic theory*. Atomic theory had to be modified later when physicists discovered that the nucleus of an atom can be split by bombarding it with neutrons, a process known as *nuclear fission*.

A Russian chemist, Dmitri Mendeleyev, constructed a table by which he calculated the atomic weights of the different elements. This table is known as the *periodic table*. The elements are identified by symbols taken largely from Latin names for the elements. Hydrogen is the lightest known element, so the weights of all the other elements are based on the weight (mass) of hydrogen. Hydrogen was given the atomic mass of 1 and assigned the atomic number 1. An atom of oxygen, an abundant gas on Earth, has a mass 16 times that of a hydrogen atom;

therefore, oxygen was given an atomic mass of 16. Oxygen is the eighth lightest element and is assigned the atomic number 8. Dalton's and Mendeleyev's discoveries were the most significant in the field of chemistry since that of Lavoisier, a French chemist who identified oxygen as the key element that supports combustion. An example of the periodic table is illustrated on page 404.

Atomic Structure

Scientists have learned a great deal about atoms since Dalton's time. For example, an atom is composed of a nucleus with electrons that surround it. The *nucleus*, located in the center of the atom, is made up of protons and neutrons. A *proton* is a positively charged particle. An element's atomic number is determined by the number of protons it has. Since hydrogen has only one proton in its nucleus, it has an atomic number of 1. A *neutron* has a mass nearly equal to a proton's but has no charge at all. The nucleus has a positive charge determined by the number of protons it contains. The nucleus provides the mass number for an element.

An *electron* is a negatively charged particle. Electrons occupy an orbit, or shell, that surrounds the nucleus. Each shell can hold only a fixed number of electrons. It is the number of shells that distinguishes one element from another. The greater the number of shells with orbiting electrons an element has, the greater its atomic number.

At one time, electrons were thought to orbit the nucleus like the planets orbit the Sun; however, this belief has not proved to be true. The following illustration shows the structure of an atom.

THE HELIUM ATOM

EXERCISE 1: ATOMIC STRUCTURE

Directions: Match the terms on the right with the correct description on the left by writing the correct letter of the term in the space provided.

_____ 1. the second lightest element; contains two protons in its nucleus

_____ 2. a negatively charged particle

_____ 3. the part of an atom that determines an element's mass

_____ 4. a particle that has no charge

_____ 5. a positively charged particle

_____ 6. an element containing eight protons in its nucleus

a. oxygen

b. neutron

c. proton

d. helium

e. electron

f. nucleus

Answers are on page 445.

EXERCISE 2: NUCLEAR ENERGY

Directions: Read the passage below and choose the best answer for each of the following questions. You may need to refer to the periodic table shown on page 404.

Nuclear energy may be released in two ways: by fission and by fusion. Nuclear *fission* involves the splitting of the nucleus of a heavy chemical element by bombardment with neutrons. Nuclear *fusion* involves the uniting of two nuclei of an element at high temperatures and pressure to form the nucleus of a new, heavier, element. In each process, nuclear energy is released.

1. Based on the information in the passage and the atomic masses shown in the periodic table, energy from nuclear fusion would be released when

    (1) uranium nuclei are fused to make plutonium
    (2) hydrogen nuclei are fused to make oxygen
    (3) oxygen nuclei are fused to make helium
    (4) hydrogen nuclei are fused to make helium
    (5) helium nuclei are fused to make hydrogen

2. Energy from nuclear fission would be released in the splitting of the nucleus of which element?

    A. plutonium

    B. hydrogen

    C. oxygen

    (1) A
    (2) B
    (3) C
    (4) A and B
    (5) A and C

Answers are on page 445.

EXERCISE 3: ISOTOPIC ELEMENTS

Directions: Read the passage and table below and choose the best answer for the statements that follow.

Sometimes the number of neutrons in the atom of an element varies. This can affect the mass number of an element. For example, the element carbon has six protons in its nucleus, but it can also have as few as six or as many as seven neutrons in its nucleus. An element that can vary in the number of neutrons in its nucleus is described as being *isotopic*. Thus, two isotopes of carbon exist—carbon 12 and carbon 13, and they have different chemical properties. Of the two, carbon 12 is the more common.

Element	Atomic Number	Mass Number
Hydrogen	1	1.01
Helium	2	4.00
Lithium	3	6.94
Beryllium	4	9.01
Boron	5	10.81

1. The only element in the preceding chart that could have an isotope of mass number 6 and whose two nuclei might be fused to form carbon 12 would be

    (1) hydrogen
    (2) helium
    (3) lithium
    (4) beryllium
    (5) boron

2. Deuterium and tritium are two isotopes that have mass numbers of 2 and 3 respectively. Of the two isotopes, tritium is especially radioactive. Based on the preceding chart, you could infer that these elements used in nuclear fusion are different forms of

    (1) hydrogen
    (2) helium
    (3) lithium
    (4) beryllium
    (5) boron

Answers are on page 445.

DID YOU KNOW THAT: The hydrogen bomb, created by the fusion of deuterium or tritium nuclei to form a helium atom, is far more explosive and destructive than an atomic bomb, created from the splitting of a uranium or plutonium atom?

WRITING ACTIVITY 1

As fossil fuels become scarce, our modern world is growing increasingly dependent on new energy sources. As a result, many energy producers have turned to nuclear energy as a source for generating electricity in heavily populated regions. The nuclear reactors that generate this energy pose considerable risks, as demonstrated by nuclear disasters such as those at Three Mile Island and Chernobyl. Are the risks to human life worth the benefits that nuclear energy provides? In two or three paragraphs, defend your position.

Elements and Periodicity

The periodic table organizes elements based on their atomic and physical properties. The table relates the properties of the elements to their atomic numbers. Elements in the same row (across) have the same number of shells containing a varying number of electrons. Elements in the same column (down) have the same number of electrons in their outermost shell.

In classifying elements according to physical properties, scientists consider color, odor, taste, density, boiling point, solubility (ability to dissolve), malleability (capability of being shaped by beating), and hardness. Out of these properties arose the three broad groupings that chemists have used to categorize all of the elements—metals, nonmetals, and metalloids.

Metals conduct heat and electricity well, melt at high temperatures, and have a high density and brilliant luster. Examples of these elements are sodium, gold, and aluminum.

Nonmetals melt at low temperatures, have low luster, are less dense than metals, and are poor conductors of heat and electricity. Examples of these elements are carbon, sulfur, and oxygen.

Metalloids have properties of metals and nonmetals. Antimony and arsenic are examples of metalloids.

According to the periodic law, as the atomic number increases for elements in a column, similar properties occur regularly and to a greater degree. For example, the metals with the atomic numbers 3, 11, and 19—lithium, sodium, and potassium—are all chemically active metals. In many cases, the greater the atomic number, the higher the degree of certain properties. While the second member of this group, sodium, is chemically active, rubidium, the fourth member, is so highly active that it bursts into flame upon exposure to air.

PERIODIC TABLE OF THE ELEMENTS

Key:
- (6) — Atomic Number
- **C** — Symbol (*man made)
- Name — Carbon
- 12 — Mass Number (number of protons and neutrons)

Period																		
1	(1) **H** Hydrogen 1																	(2) **He** Helium 4
2	(3) **Li** Lithium 7	(4) **Be** Beryllium 9											(5) **B** Boron 11	(6) **C** Carbon 12	(7) **N** Nitrogen 14	(8) **O** Oxygen 16	(9) **F** Fluorine 19	(10) **Ne** Neon 20
3	(11) **Na** Sodium 23	(12) **Mg** Magnesium 24											(13) **Al** Aluminum 27	(14) **Si** Silicon 28	(15) **P** Phosphorus 31	(16) **S** Sulfur 32	(17) **Cl** Chlorine 35	(18) **Ar** Argon 40
4	(19) **K** Potassium 39	(20) **Ca** Calcium 40	(21) **Sc** Scandium 45	(22) **Ti** Titanium 48	(23) **V** Vanadium 51	(24) **Cr** Chromium 52	(25) **Mn** Manganese 55	(26) **Fe** Iron 56	(27) **Co** Cobalt 59	(28) **Ni** Nickel 59	(29) **Cu** Copper 64	(30) **Zn** Zinc 65	(31) **Ga** Gallium 70	(32) **Ge** Germanium 73	(33) **As** Arsenic 75	(34) **Se** Selenium 79	(35) **Br** Bromine 80	(36) **Kr** Krypton 84
5	(37) **Rb** Rubidium 85	(38) **Sr** Strontium 88	(39) **Y** Yttrium 89	(40) **Zr** Zirconium 91	(41) **Nb** Niobium 93	(42) **Mo** Molybdenum 96	(43) **Tc*** Technetium 98	(44) **Ru** Ruthenium 101	(45) **Rh** Rhodium 103	(46) **Pd** Palladium 106	(47) **Ag** Silver 108	(48) **Cd** Cadmium 112	(49) **In** Indium 115	(50) **Sn** Tin 119	(51) **Sb** Antimony 122	(52) **Te** Tellurium 128	(53) **I** Iodine 127	(54) **Xe** Xenon 131
6	(55) **Cs** Cesium 133	(56) **Ba** Barium 137	(57) **La** Lanthanum 139	(72) **Hf** Hafnium 178	(73) **Ta** Tantalum 181	(74) **W** Tungsten 184	(75) **Re** Rhenium 186	(76) **Os** Osmium 190	(77) **Ir** Iridium 192	(78) **Pt** Platinum 195	(79) **Au** Gold 197	(80) **Hg** Mercury 201	(81) **Tl** Thallium 204	(82) **Pb** Lead 207	(83) **Bi** Bismuth 209	(84) **Po** Polonium 209	(85) **At** Astatine 210	(86) **Rn** Radon 222
7	(87) **Fr** Francium 223	(88) **Ra** Radium 226	(89) **Ac** Actinium 227	(104) **Rf*** Rutherfordium 261	(105) **Ha*** Hahnium 262	(106) **Unh*** Unnilhexium 263	(107) **Uns*** Unnilseptium 262	(108) **Uno*** Unniloctium	(109) **Une*** Unnilennium	(110) **Uun*** Ununnilium								

Rare Earth Elements

Lanthanide Series

(58) **Ce** Cerium 140	(59) **Pr** Praseodymium 141	(60) **Nd** Neodymium 144	(61) **Pm*** Promethium 145	(62) **Sm** Samarium 150	(63) **Eu** Europium 152	(64) **Gd** Gadolinium 157	(65) **Tb** Terbium 159	(66) **Dy** Dysprosium 163	(67) **Ho** Holmium 165	(68) **Er** Erbium 167	(69) **Tm** Thulium 169	(70) **Yb** Ytterbium 173	(71) **Lu** Lutetium 175

Actinide Series

(90) **Th** Thorium 232	(91) **Pa** Protactinium 231	(92) **U** Uranium 238	(93) **Np*** Neptunium 237	(94) **Pu*** Plutonium 244	(95) **Am*** Americium 243	(96) **Cm*** Curium 247	(97) **Bk*** Berkelium 247	(98) **Cf*** Californium 251	(99) **Es*** Einsteinium 252	(100) **Fm*** Fermium 257	(101) **Md*** Mendelevium 258	(102) **No*** Nobelium 259	(103) **Lr*** Lawrencium 260

EXERCISE 4: ELEMENTS AND PERIODICITY

Directions: Choose the best answer for each of the following questions.

1. The metals copper, silver, and gold are in the same family (column), having atomic numbers of 29, 47, and 79 respectively. According to the principle of periodic law, of the three metals, gold would have the highest degree of which *physical* property?

   (1) value
   (2) rarity
   (3) volatility
   (4) malleability
   (5) scarcity

2. Radon is in the same family as helium, neon, argon, krypton, and xenon. Which of the following facts would help you to determine that radon has a greater density than the other elements in the same family?

   A. Radon is found in the ground while the others are not.

   B. Radon has a higher atomic number than the other elements in its family.

   C. Radon poses potential health problems for people in areas where great concentrations are found in the ground.

   (1) A
   (2) B
   (3) C
   (4) A and B
   (5) B and C

Answers are on page 445.

DID YOU KNOW THAT: Silver has the greatest ability to conduct heat and electricity of any substance, but it is not used for this purpose because it is so expensive?

WRITING ACTIVITY 2

In recent years, the dangers radon gas poses to humans have been widely publicized in certain parts of the country. Radon poses such a potential health hazard that buyers of homes in certain areas where concentrations of the gas are high are advised to have readings done to measure the level of radon in the ground beneath the home's foundation.

Is radon or some other material in the ground perceived as a threat in the area in which you live? Whether or not such a threat is present in your area, write two or three paragraphs describing what you think the government should do about such dangers.

Elements and Chemical Reactions

You are involved in a variety of chemical reactions every day. Do you cook your food or heat your home with gas? Did you use a battery-powered object today? Have you cleaned your oven or bathroom fixtures with a cleaning agent? All of these activities and countless others, including those taking place within your body, are dependent upon chemical reactions.

Each chemical reaction has two components: a reactant and a product. A *reactant* is the substance or substances that enter into the reaction. The *product* is the substance or substances that result from the reaction. A chemical reaction may be either a *combination reaction*, in which two elements or substances are combined, or a *decomposition reaction*, in which an element or substance is broken down.

Chemical reactions are written in a shorthand called a *chemical equation*. A chemical formula uses symbols for elements and shows the number of atoms for each element of a substance. For example, the chemical reaction that produces water would be written:

$$2H_2 + O_2 \longrightarrow 2H_2O$$

When you read a chemical equation, the large number tells how many molecules (structures containing more than one atom) are present. When only a single molecule or atom is present, the number *1* is not written. The smaller subscript number tells how many atoms of an element are present in each molecule.

The equation for water says that two molecules of hydrogen gas (H_2) plus one molecule of oxygen gas (O_2) combine to form two molecules of water (H_2O). Notice that one molecule of hydrogen gas (H_2) contains two atoms of hydrogen, and one molecule of oxygen gas (O_2) contains two atoms of oxygen. Each molecule of water (H_2O) contains two atoms of hydrogen and one atom of oxygen.

The chemical reaction in which one atom of carbon unites with two atoms of oxygen to form carbon dioxide would be written:

$$C + O_2 \longrightarrow CO_2$$

This equation says that one molecule of carbon plus one molecule of oxygen (two atoms of oxygen) combine to form one molecule of carbon dioxide (CO_2).

All chemical reactions are governed by the *Law of Conservation of Matter*. This law holds that matter can neither be created nor destroyed in a chemical reaction. A chemical equation adheres to this law; it shows the same number of atoms on both sides of the arrow for each element involved in a reaction. For example, the following chemical reaction occurs when methane gas (CH_4) is burned with oxygen:

$$CH_4 + 2O_2 \longrightarrow CO_2 + 2H_2O$$

Methane gas burns with oxygen to form carbon dioxide and water vapor; specifically, one molecule of carbon dioxide and two molecules of water.

Notice that the reaction begins with one carbon atom (C) and ends with one carbon atom (C). The reaction begins with four hydrogen atoms (H_4) and ends with four hydrogen atoms ($2H_2$ or $2 \times 2 = 4$). The reaction begins with four oxygen atoms ($2O_2 = 2 \times 2 = 4$) and ends with 4 oxygen atoms ($O_2 + 2O = 4$).

When the number of atoms of each element is equal on both sides of the equation, we say that the equation is *balanced*.

EXERCISE 5: BALANCED EQUATIONS

Directions: Identify each of the following equations as either balanced or unbalanced by writing *B* or *U* in the space provided.

_____ **1.** $N_2 + O_2 \longrightarrow 2NO$

_____ **2.** $Fe + HCl \longrightarrow FeCl_3 + H_2$

_____ **3.** $2H + O \longrightarrow H_2O$

_____ **4.** $ZnCO_2 \longrightarrow ZnO + CO_2$

_____ **5.** $C + 2S \longrightarrow CS_2$

Answers are on page 445.

EXERCISE 6: CHEMICAL REACTIONS

Directions: Choose the best answer for each of the following questions.

1. When iron is exposed to moist air, it rusts. *Rust* is the common name for ferric oxide, formed by two iron atoms and three oxygen atoms. The correct chemical formula for rust would be:

   (1) Fe_3O_2
   (2) FeO
   (3) Fe_2O_3
   (4) Fe_2O_2
   (5) $2FeO_3$

2. The chemical reaction that gives soda pop (a carbonated beverage) its fizz results from dissolving a molecule of carbon dioxide into a molecule of water. Which of the following represents the chemical equation for the process?

   (1) $CO_3 + H_2O \longrightarrow H_2CO_4$
   (2) $CO_2 + H_2O \longrightarrow H_2CO_3$
   (3) $CO + H_2O \longrightarrow H_2CO_2$
   (4) $CO_2 + H_2O \longrightarrow H_2CO_2$
   (5) $CO + 2H_2O \longrightarrow H_4CO_2$

3. The reactants and products of a chemical reaction

   (1) always double in mass
   (2) must always balance
   (3) never equal each other in mass
   (4) always need a catalyst
   (5) must triple themselves to balance

Questions 4 and 5 refer to the following passage.

A *physical change* is a change that does not produce a new substance. For example, when you saw wood or dissolve salt in water you are not changing the chemical composition of the substances. However, a new substance *is* formed when a *chemical change* takes place. The result is a change in the chemical composition of a substance. Some common chemical changes include the burning of wood and the rusting of metal on a car.

In an experiment concerning physical and chemical changes, you add 10 g of copper sulfate to 100 ml of water. You heat the solution over a low flame and stir. After the solution cools, you place a piece of aluminum foil in the copper sulfate solution. After 24 hours, the solution has changed from deep blue to a very light blue, and the aluminum has acquired a deep copper coating.

4. Which of the following pieces of information would you need to prove that a chemical change had occurred?

   (1) whether the copper sulfate solution had been heated
   (2) whether the solution had been stirred
   (3) whether twenty-four hours had passed
   (4) whether the aluminum had acquired a copper coat
   (5) whether the aluminum was breakable

5. Which hypothesis best explains what happened in the experiment?

   (1) The experiment failed.
   (2) Aluminum and copper were incorrectly mixed.
   (3) The copper sulfate solution and aluminum produced a new substance.
   (4) The copper sulfate solution caused a temporary change in the appearance of the aluminum.
   (5) The aluminum caused the copper sulfate to turn blue.

Answers are on page 446.

DID YOU KNOW THAT: Yeast makes dough rise because yeast (a fungus) attacks the starch in the flour, changing it into sugar? The sugar changes to alcohol and carbon dioxide gas. Then the carbon dioxide bubbles up through the dough to make it rise.

Elements in Combination

Compounds are formed when two or more elements combine in a chemical reaction. The resulting product usually has different properties from either of the component elements. Compounds, when formed, can be broken down into simpler substances only by chemical action.

For example, water, the most commonly known compound, is composed of two atoms of hydrogen and one atom of oxygen. When water is subjected to extreme temperatures, it can be reduced to its component elements—hydrogen and oxygen—and its liquid characteristic is lost.

Mixtures are substances that are formed when two or more elements or compounds are mixed in different proportions. The resulting product retains the properties of the combining elements. In most mixtures the combining ingredients can be separated easily. For example, gunpowder is a mixture of charcoal (a form of carbon), sulfur, and potassium nitrate (a compound of potassium and nitrogen). When mixed, the three ingredients form gunpowder, a highly explosive substance. These three ingredients can be identified by their different colors in this mixture.

A *solution* is a mixture formed when a solid, liquid, or gaseous substance is dissolved in a liquid. The substance that is dissolved into the liquid is called the *solute*. The liquid in which the substance is dissolved is called the *solvent*. One of the characteristics that distinguishes a solution from a mixture is that a solution is homogeneous—the same throughout. An *aqueous* solution features water as the solvent. A *tincture* has alcohol as the solvent, such as the antiseptic tincture of iodine. Sometimes a solution is formed when a substance is dissolved in a gas or solid.

When metals are combined in varying proportions, they often form *alloys*. In an alloy, each metal dissolves into the other at high temperatures. Common examples of alloys are brass (copper and zinc), bronze (copper, tin, and other elements), and steel (iron, carbon, and other elements). An *amalgam* is formed when a metal is dissolved into mercury, a liquid metal. Amalgams are used chiefly in making tooth cements.

EXERCISE 7: TYPES OF SUBSTANCES

Directions: Listed below are five kinds of substances known to scientists. Read the definitions and apply them to the questions that follow.

compound—a substance that is composed of two or more elements, in specific proportions, but has properties different from the combining elements

mixture—a substance that is composed of two or more elements or other substances but that keeps the properties of the combining ingredients

solution—a homogeneous substance formed by dissolving a solid, liquid, or gas into a liquid

alloy—a substance formed by the combination of metals in which one metal dissolves into another at high temperatures

amalgam—an alloy that includes mercury and that is usually soft and may be liquid

1. Table salt—sodium chloride, one of the most common substances occurring in nature—is best classified as

   (1) a compound
   (2) a mixture
   (3) a solution
   (4) an alloy
   (5) an amalgam

2. Solder is a substance formed by the combination of tin and lead at low melting points. It is used in electronics for fusing metals. Solder may be best described as

   (1) a compound
   (2) a mixture
   (3) a solution
   (4) an alloy
   (5) an amalgam

3. Air is composed of nitrogen (78 percent), oxygen (21 percent), argon (0.93 percent), carbon dioxide (0.03 percent), and other gases (0.04 percent). Air may be *best* described as

   (1) a compound
   (2) a mixture
   (3) a solution
   (4) an alloy
   (5) an amalgam

4. Mercurochrome is a red, antiseptic liquid in which mercuric acetate, dibromin, and fluorescein are dissolved. Based on this composition, it may be best described as

   (1) a compound
   (2) a mixture
   (3) a solution
   (4) an alloy
   (5) an amalgam

Answers are on page 446.

EXERCISE 8: COMPOUNDS AND MIXTURES

Directions: Choose the best answer for the following question.

There is enough information in the preceding passage to support which of the following statements?

A. Compounds may contain mixtures but mixtures may not contain compounds.

B. Mixtures may contain compounds but compounds may not contain mixtures.

C. Solutions may contain compounds and mixtures.

   (1) A
   (2) B
   (3) C
   (4) A and B
   (5) B and C

Answer is on page 446.

DID YOU KNOW THAT: When copper combines with water it forms *verdigris*, a poisonous deposit that gives the gutters or rain troughs you see on old buildings their greenish color?

WRITING ACTIVITY 3

The defoliant Agent Orange, used to remove leaves from trees, contains the deadly chemical contaminant **dioxin**, a carbon compound. A link has been discovered between Agent Orange and the cancer found in some returning Vietnam veterans. The United Nations has attempted to ban all uses of chemical warfare. Do you agree with the UN's position on chemical warfare, or do you believe that "all is fair in war" and that a country can use whatever means it deems necessary to defeat its opponent? Take a position and write an essay of two or three paragraphs to support it.

Chemical Bonding

When compounds are made, a bond is formed between two or more elements. A **bond** is a force that holds together two atoms, two ions (electrically charged particles), two molecules, or a combination of these. Bonding may result from either the transfer or the sharing of electrons between atoms.

When electrons are transferred from one atom to another, an **ionic bond** is formed. In the following example, an ionic bond is formed when an electron from a sodium atom is transferred to the outermost shell of a chlorine atom. The result is the common compound table salt.

SODIUM AND CHLORINE ATOMS

Na   Cl

SODIUM CHLORIDE

Na⁺   Cl⁻

● = electron in Na

○ = electron in Cl

The Na electron has transferred over to the Cl atom.

In the preceding example, both sodium and chlorine are electrically neutral (have no charge); however, when the sodium atom loses its electron, it becomes positively charged. Opposite charges attract, forming a bond. Ionic compounds such as salt typically have high melting and boiling points, are flammable, conduct electricity when dissolved in water, and exist as solids at room temperatures.

When two or more different atoms of elements share electrons to form a molecule, a *covalent* bond is formed. In the following illustration, a covalent bond is formed when two atoms of hydrogen are bonded to one atom of oxygen to form the compound water.

WATER MOLECULE

○ = electrons bound only to oxygen atom

● = electrons shared by hydrogen and oxygen atoms

In covalent bonding, the outermost shell of the element with the greatest number of electrons is filled to capacity at eight electrons. Once the combining element achieves eight electrons in its outermost ring, it cannot combine with another element. Covalent compounds such as water typically have low melting and boiling points, are nonflammable, have poor conductivity, and exist as gases and liquids.

EXERCISE 9: COMPOUNDS AND CHEMICAL BONDING

Directions: Choose the best answer for each of the following questions.

1. The inert gases—helium, neon, argon, krypton, xenon, and radon—all have eight electrons in their outermost ring. These gases are called inert because their full outer electron shells keep them from engaging in chemical bonding. This fact explains their inability to

   A. form compounds

   B. undergo chemical reactions

   C. share or transfer electrons

   (1) A
   (2) B
   (3) C
   (4) A and B
   (5) A, B, and C

2. In ionic bonding, atoms are held together by

   (1) sharing electrons
   (2) transferring electrons
   (3) chemical attraction
   (4) temperature
   (5) magnetic fields

3. In covalent bonding, atoms are held together by

    (1) sharing electrons
    (2) transferring electrons
    (3) chemical attraction
    (4) temperature
    (5) magnetic fields

Answers are on page 446.

DID YOU KNOW THAT: Before helium was used to fill airships (blimps), hydrogen, a highly flammable gas, was used? The cause of the change was the *Hindenburg* disaster, in which hydrogen ignited and caused an explosion in which many people died. This prompted the use of helium to fill lighter-than-air vehicles. Helium, an inert gas, is nonflammable.

Acids, Bases, and Salts

Many compounds that result from ionic and covalent bonding are categorized as acids or bases. An *acid* is a covalent compound that produces hydrogen ions when dissolved in water. Acids have a sour taste. Common acids are acetic acid (the main component of vinegar), citric acid (found in citrus fruits), lactic acid (found in milk), and hydrochloric acid, a component of stomach acid used in digestion.

A *base* is a compound that forms hydroxide ions when dissolved in water. Bases are able to take a proton from an acid or to give up an unshared pair of electrons to an acid. Bases are described as alkaline because they dissolve in water and have a slippery feel. Many hydroxides are bases. Household cleaning agents such as ammonia, borax, lye, and detergents are common examples of bases.

When an acid combines with a base, a salt is formed and water is released because the metal found in the base replaces the hydrogen contained in the acid. Inorganic acids, bases, and inorganic salts can conduct electricity when dissolved in water.

Chemists apply the *litmus test* to a substance to determine whether or not it is an acid or base. Litmus paper is a colored paper that changes color when exposed to an acid or base. An acid turns blue litmus paper red, and a base turns red litmus paper blue.

EXERCISE 10: CHEMICAL FIRST AID

Directions: Read the passage below and choose the best answer for each of the following questions.

Many common household cleaning products are poisons; therefore, the labels of many products must contain an antidote to be administered in case the product is swallowed accidentally. These antidotes may be emetics (agents that cause the substance to be expelled from the body), neutralizers (agents that cancel out the effect of the substance swallowed), or diluents (agents that dilute the substance swallowed).

1. A person accidentally swallows ammonia. The first-aid instructions on the label tell you to administer two tablespoons of vinegar in two glasses of water or a glass of orange or lemon juice. The effect of this action would be that

   (1) the person would expel the ammonia
   (2) the ammonia would be changed into an acid
   (3) the ammonia would change into a salt by neutralization
   (4) the ammonia would be changed into a base
   (5) the ammonia would be diluted by the water and voided by the body

2. Which of the following antidotes would likely have a similar effect if vinegar or citrus juice were not available?

   (1) water
   (2) bread
   (3) milk
   (4) raw egg white
   (5) vegetable oil

3. If a person accidentally swallowed a toilet bowl cleaner that contained phenol, a corrosive acid, it would probably be *best* to first

   (1) induce vomiting immediately
   (2) administer milk of magnesia (magnesium hydroxide)
   (3) dilute the poison with plenty of water
   (4) dilute the poison with plenty of milk
   (5) administer plenty of lemon or orange juice

4. The antidote administered in the preceding case would be best described as

   (1) a diluent
   (2) an emetic
   (3) a reactant
   (4) a neutralizer
   (5) a catalyst

Answers are on page 446.

EXERCISE 11: ACIDS, BASES, AND SALTS

Directions: The questions are based on the following explanation and scale. Read the information and choose the best answer for each question.

The designation pH (*potential for Hydrogen-ion formation*) is a value by which certain substances are classified according to acidity or alkalinity. The pH scale ranges from 0 to 14, with the value 7 representing neutrality. The pH scale is illustrated below.

pH SCALE

increasing acidity   neutrality   increasing alkalinity

0   1   2   3   4   5   6   7   8   9   10   11   12   13   14

1. According to the pH scale, acetic acid, a very mild acid, would most likely be found between

   (1) 7 and 8
   (2) 0 and 1
   (3) 2 and 3
   (4) 4 and 5
   (5) 10 and 11

2. Oxalic acid, a strong, poisonous acid found in the leaves of rhubarb that is used as a bleaching agent, would most probably fall between

   (1) 9 and 10
   (2) 1 and 2
   (3) 5 and 6
   (4) 6 and 7
   (5) 13 and 14

3. Based on the pH scale, water would be found

   (1) between 0 and 1
   (2) between 3 and 4
   (3) at 7
   (4) at 14
   (5) between 5 and 6

4. Which of the following could be used to prove that a substance is an acid?

   A. The substance has a pH above 7.

   B. The substance is sour or caustic.

   C. It neutralizes a base to form a salt and water.

   (1) A
   (2) B
   (3) C
   (4) A and B
   (5) B and C

Answers are on page 446.

EXERCISE 12: A CAR BATTERY

Directions: Read the passage below and answer the questions.

Acids, bases, and inorganic salts (salts obtained from nonliving things) are effective conductors of electricity. The common car battery demonstrates an electric current generated by the chemical action between an acid and a metal.

In a car battery, pure lead (the negative post) and lead dioxide (the positive post) are submerged in sulfuric acid (the conductor). Distilled water is added periodically to maintain the proper level of the sulfuric acid. The pure lead loses two electrons when it reacts with the sulfuric acid—the acid changes the lead to lead dioxide. At the same time, the positive post containing lead dioxide gains two electrons and changes the sulfuric acid that it is submerged in to lead sulfate (a salt) and water. The current that makes the car start results from the flow of electrons from the lead dioxide to the lead through the sulfuric acid to the starter switch, all of which makes a complete circuit. A diagram of a car battery is shown below.

CAR BATTERY

1. An *electrolyte* is an inorganic compound that will conduct an electric current when dissolved in water. What is an electrolyte in the preceding example?

   A. lead dioxide

   B. sulfuric acid

   C. distilled water

   (1) A
   (2) B
   (3) C
   (4) A and B
   (5) B and C

2. A substance is *oxidized* when it loses electrons. In the preceding example, which of the following compounds is oxidized?

(1) lead
(2) lead dioxide
(3) lead sulfate
(4) water
(5) sulfuric acid

3. A substance is *reduced* when it gains electrons. In the preceding example, which of the following compounds is reduced?

(1) lead
(2) lead dioxide
(3) lead sulfate
(4) water
(5) sulfuric acid

4. The substances that oxidize and reduce other substances are called *oxidizing agents* and *reducing agents*. In the preceding example, the oxidizing and reducing agents, in correct order, are

(1) lead dioxide and water
(2) sulfuric acid and lead dioxide
(3) lead and sulfuric acid
(4) lead sulfate and lead dioxide
(5) sulfuric acid and water

5. Based on the preceding example, you can conclude that in a car battery, chemical energy is converted into electrical energy by

(1) nuclear fission
(2) nuclear fusion
(3) oxidation-reduction
(4) ionic bonding
(5) covalent bonding

6. Which of the following compounds would *not* adequately serve as an electrolyte?

(1) sodium chloride (salt)
(2) sulfuric acid
(3) citric acid
(4) sodium hydroxide
(5) hydrochloric acid

7. Which of the following can you conclude to be true when a battery is discharged and can no longer generate a current?

A. The sulfuric acid can no longer oxidize the lead.

B. The lead dioxide can no longer reduce the sulfuric acid.

C. The battery has run out of sulfuric acid.

(1) A
(2) B
(3) C
(4) A and B
(5) A and C

Answers are on page 447.

Reaction Rate, Catalysts, and Equilibrium

Chemical reactions occur at different rates determined by the conditions under which reactions occur. Sugar dissolves more quickly in hot water than in cold. White phosphorus bursts into flame when exposed to the air. Carbon monoxide from car exhaust remains in the atmosphere for up to two-and-a-half years before it is changed into carbon dioxide.

Reactions such as these may be speeded up or slowed down when another substance is introduced. A *catalyst* is a substance that increases the rate of a chemical reaction but itself remains chemically unchanged. Many finely divided metals act as catalysts. For example, today's cars are equipped with a catalytic converter, a device that contains finely divided platinum, a metal. The function of the converter is to change harmful carbon monoxide and unburned gasoline vapor into harmless carbon dioxide and water vapor and reduce the amount of nitrogen oxides released into the air. Platinum in this case is a catalyst because it speeds up the process but remains unchanged.

Some catalysts have a negative effect. A negative catalyst slows down the chemical reaction. Negative catalysts are often inhibitors, such as the chemicals used in undercoating a car to retard the rusting process.

A given set of reactants may react to form more than one product. Often, the by-products react to form the original reactants. When the rate of forward reaction balances the rate of reverse reaction, *chemical equilibrium* occurs. For example, the carbon monoxide in car exhaust enters the atmosphere and reacts with oxygen to form carbon dioxide. The carbon dioxide is broken down by sunlight into the original reactant—carbon monoxide. This reaction represents chemical equilibrium because the reaction reverses itself. Chemical reactions such as these create a cycle.

EXERCISE 13: REACTION RATE, CATALYSTS, AND EQUILIBRIUM

Directions: Choose the best answer for the following questions.

1. Lipase is an enzyme produced by the liver that helps in the digestion of fats by speeding up the rate at which lipids (fats) are changed into fatty acids and glycerol. Based on this description, we can conclude that an enzyme is

   (1) a product in a chemical reaction
   (2) a negative catalyst
   (3) a biological catalyst
   (4) both a product in a chemical reaction and a negative catalyst
   (5) both a product in a chemical reaction and a biological catalyst

2. Which of the following processes illustrates chemical equilibrium?

   A. bonding

   B. photosynthesis

   C. respiration

   (1) A
   (2) B
   (3) C
   (4) A and B together
   (5) B and C together

Answers are on page 447.

4
PHYSICS—THE STUDY OF HOW MATTER BEHAVES

"What makes the world go 'round?" is a question people have asked for thousands of years. In answer to this question, scientists long ago formulated laws that explain not only how Earth revolves around the Sun but also how other forms of matter behave in the physical world.

Physics is the branch of science that concerns the behavior of matter in our world—the forces that cause matter to behave as it does. Physics helps us to understand how things work.

The scope of physics is so broad that the other branches of science studied earlier in this book cannot be fully understood without some knowledge of its basic laws. For example, physics helps to explain how cellular molecules can move from a lower concentration in an organism to a higher one, how ocean tides occur, and how matter exists in the states of a solid, liquid, or gas.

The preceding examples from biology, earth science, and chemistry all illustrate some force at work on a body. A *force* shows the presence of energy in an environment. *Energy* is the capacity to do work. The area of physics that deals with forces, energy, and their effect on bodies is *mechanics*.

Mechanics

The study of mechanics was one of the first sciences developed. Ancient Greek philosopher and scientist Aristotle theorized that heavy bodies fall faster than light bodies. This theory was proved false in the early 17th century by Italian scientist and mathematician Galileo, who dropped items of different weights from the leaning tower of Pisa. The force acting upon the objects was not fully understood, however, until Sir Isaac Newton, an Englishman, formulated laws of gravity and motion that explained how different forces act on objects.

The Force of Gravity

Gravity is the most commonly experienced of all forces in nature. The presence of gravity was first proposed by Newton when he observed the motion of an apple falling from a tree. Based on the simple observation, he developed the *Law of Universal Gravitation*, which holds that every body having a mass exerts an attractive force on every other body having a mass in the universe. The strength of the force depends on the masses of the objects and the distance between them. (*Mass* is the measure of the amount of matter in an object.) Thus, the apple's falling to earth illustrates the gravitational pull (attraction) of the larger Earth on the smaller apple. The Law of Universal Gravitation also explains how the planets, attracted by the much larger Sun, remain in their orbits as they revolve around it.

Newton's Three Laws of Motion

Newton proposed other laws of motion to explain the relationship between force and motion. They are the Law of Inertia, the Law of Applied Force, and the Law of Action and Reaction.

According to the *Law of Inertia*, a body remains at rest or continues in a state of uniform motion unless a force acts on it. For example, when you drive a car and suddenly jam on the brakes, you continue to move forward. This is because your body's tendency is to remain in the same state of uniform motion (moving forward). The brakes were applied to the car, so its uniform motion was changed.

The *Law of Applied Force* holds that a body's change in speed and direction is proportional to the amount of force applied to it. For example, the vanes on a windmill, which move by the force of the wind, will accelerate according to the speed and direction of the wind that drives them.

Newton's third law, the *Law of Action and Reaction*, maintains that for every action there is an equal but opposite reaction force. For example, a gun's muzzle kicks backward when a bullet is discharged from it.

Newton's laws of motion help us to explain all known occurrences involving force in the field of mechanics.

EXERCISE 1: LAWS OF FORCE AND MOTION

Directions: In the space provided, write *G* if the example illustrates Newton's Law of Universal Gravitation, *I* if it applies to the Law of Inertia, *AF* if it applies to the Law of Applied Force, and *AR* if it applies to the Law of Action and Reaction.

_____ 1. A motorboat moves forward because its propeller rapidly throws water backward.

_____ 2. A jet, upon landing, lowers the flaps on its wings. The flaps create drag, a force that reduces lift and helps the plane to slow down.

_____ 3. A rocket is propelled upward by the powerful downward discharge of exhaust gases.

_____ 4. A bullet discharged into the air eventually falls to the ground.

_____ 5. A pendulum in a grandfather clock, once set in motion, continues to swing, thereby regulating the clock's movement.

Answers are on page 447.

EXERCISE 2: THE FORCE OF GRAVITY

Directions: Read the paragraph below and answer the question that follows.

An astronaut weighs in before blast-off. He weighs only a fraction of his original weight when he steps on a scale on the moon. Journeying to Jupiter, he finds that his weight has increased several times over his original weight. These changes in weight may be explained *best* by

(1) the amount of force each planet produced as the astronaut weighed himself
(2) the distance from the Sun of the planetary bodies on which he weighed himself
(3) changes in the atmospheric pressure on the different heavenly bodies
(4) the amount of calories consumed during the flight
(5) the duration of time that elapsed between weigh-ins

Answer is on page 447.

EXERCISE 3: MECHANICS, FORCE, AND MOTION

Directions: Read the passage below and answer the questions that follow.

In an experiment, a *vacuum* is created when all air is removed from a tube. A coin and bits of confetti are released in the vacuum at the same time. They fall at the same rate and reach the bottom at the same time.

1. The results of this experiment prove that

A. in a vacuum, the rate of acceleration is the same for all objects regardless of weight

B. outside a vacuum, air resistance is what makes different objects fall at different rates

C. gravity has no effect at all on objects that fall in a vacuum

(1) A
(2) B
(3) C
(4) A and B
(5) B and C

2. The experiment described above serves to support

(1) Aristotle's theory of falling objects
(2) Galileo's findings about falling objects
(3) Newton's Law of Inertia
(4) Newton's Law of Applied Force
(5) Newton's Law of Action and Reaction

Answers are on page 448.

DID YOU KNOW THAT: Of all the forces present in our physical world, gravity is considered by scientists to be the weakest?

Work, Energy, and Power

Everyone knows what work is. Work is the labor put forth to do a job. Whether it is typing a letter, sawing wood, or providing a needed service, most of us are familiar with work.

In physics, work has a different meaning. **Work** occurs when a force succeeds in moving an object it acts upon. For example, a person who lifts a fifty-pound weight one foot off the floor is performing work. For work to be performed, the movement of the object must be in the same direction as the force—in this case vertical. Work may be expressed as any force unit times any distance unit and may be written as follows:

$$W = F \times D$$

The amount of work done is the amount of force multiplied by the distance moved. In the preceding example, fifty foot-pounds of work is done when fifty pounds are lifted one foot:

$$50 \text{ lb} \times 1 \text{ ft} = 50 \text{ ft lb}$$

Energy is required to do work. In the example above, muscular energy is illustrated in the form of a body that is capable of doing work. Energy may be classified as either kinetic or potential energy. **Kinetic energy** is energy possessed by a body in motion. The form of energy shown by a moving train is kinetic energy. **Potential energy** is energy that is stored or is available for use by a body. For example, coal has potential energy that is released only when it is burned. A boulder positioned on a hilltop has potential energy before it is released. When the boulder is pushed, its potential energy becomes kinetic.

Power is the rate at which work is done. Power is generally measured in horsepower, which is equal to 550 foot-pounds per second or 33,000 foot-pounds per minute.

The Law of Conservation of Energy

In chemistry, the Law of Conservation of Matter governs all chemical reactions. The law holds that matter can be neither created nor destroyed in a chemical reaction. The same principle applies to the expenditure of energy. The **Law of Conservation of Energy** holds that all the energy of the universe is conserved. The capacity for energy to do work can be changed from one kind to another, but it cannot be lost. This principle can be illustrated in the following example of energy generated from a waterfall:

Water possesses *potential energy*. When water moves rapidly in a downward motion, drawn by the pull of gravity, the potential energy is changed into *kinetic energy*. Kinetic energy from a waterfall can be harnessed to power a turbine, a rotary engine, creating *rotational energy*. This rotational energy is sufficient to generate *electrical energy*, which in turn is converted into *light* and *heat* energy, which we use in our home. As this chain shows, the initial potential energy was not lost but was changed into five different forms.

EXERCISE 4: FORMS OF ENERGY

Directions: In the space provided, write *K* if the example demonstrates kinetic energy and *P* if it demonstrates potential energy.

_____ **1.** a strong west wind blowing across a region

_____ **2.** a stick of unlit dynamite

_____ **3.** a tightly coiled spring

_____ **4.** a moving car

_____ **5.** a steaming kettle

Answers are on page 448.

EXERCISE 5: TYPES OF ENERGY

Directions: Defined below are five types of energy that can perform work. Read the definitions and apply them to the questions that follow.

nuclear energy—energy obtained from splitting an atom or fusing more than one atom

chemical energy—energy obtained from the reaction of two or more substances combining with one another

electrical energy—energy obtained from an electric current

solar energy—energy obtained from the Sun's heat

steam energy—energy derived from steam pressure

1. Energy that is radiated to Earth and is the means of sustaining all forms of life is

    (1) nuclear energy
    (2) chemical energy
    (3) electrical energy
    (4) solar energy
    (5) steam energy

2. Energy that results from the fission of uranium-235 nuclei that is used to generate electrical power is

    (1) nuclear energy
    (2) chemical energy
    (3) electrical energy
    (4) solar energy
    (5) steam energy

3. Energy that results from the ignition of a gas and air mixture and that powers a car is

    (1) nuclear energy
    (2) chemical energy
    (3) electrical energy
    (4) solar energy
    (5) steam energy

Answers are on page 448.

Simple Machines

Many jobs require that greater amounts of energy be expended at a faster rate than human muscle power can provide. A *machine* is a device that transmits or multiplies force. A machine operates on the principle of a little force being applied through a great distance and a great resistance being overcome through a short distance.

A *lever* is a simple machine used to perform work by lifting a great weight. A lever is just a bar that is free to pivot on its support (called a *fulcrum*). Through the use of a lever, for example, a one-thousand-pound weight can be lifted with relatively little effort (force).

THE LEVER—A SIMPLE MACHINE

The illustration above shows that it would take 100 pounds of force for a person to lift a 1,000-pound weight positioned 1 foot from the fulcrum when the lever bar is 10 feet long. This may be expressed as follows:

$$1,000 \text{ lb} \times 1 \text{ ft} = 100 \text{ lb} \times 10 \text{ ft}$$

In this case, a relatively small force (100 lb) applied at a great distance from the object (10 ft) is able to overcome great resistance (1,000 lb). According to this principle, the greater the distance between the fulcrum and the applied force, the less force required to perform the work.

The wheelbarrow and the crowbar are two simple machines that operate on the principle of the lever. Other simple machines include the pulley and the inclined plane. All machines are classified as being either simple or complex. Complex machines are made of more than one simple machine.

EXERCISE 6: SIMPLE MACHINES

Directions: Choose the best answer for the following questions.

1. According to the principle that a little force applied through a great distance can overcome great resistance, which is likely to happen if the lever bar in the preceding illustration is increased to 20 feet in length and the weight remains at the end of the bar?

   (1) The effort to lift the weight would increase to 150 pounds of applied force.
   (2) The effort to lift the weight would remain at 100 pounds of applied force.
   (3) The effort would be decreased by half, to 50 pounds of applied force.
   (4) The resistance of the weight would double.
   (5) The resistance of the weight would triple.

2. Which of the following variables has *no* direct bearing on the lever's effectiveness in performing work?

  (1) the length of the bar
  (2) the distance from the fulcrum of the object being lifted
  (3) the shape of the fulcrum
  (4) the weight of the load
  (5) the distance of the object being lifted from the point where the force is applied

Answers are on page 448.

The Nature of Heat and Energy

One of the world's most valuable commodities is invisible. It cannot be held in our hands or manufactured in a factory. Yet it is necessary to all living things. It warms our homes, cooks our food, and helps to generate electricity through nuclear fission. This valuable commodity is heat.

In the early nineteenth century, heat was thought to be a fluid substance that moved from a hot to a cold object. Today, however, we know that heat is the result of the random motion of molecules. It is nothing more than energy itself. One theory of physics that has contributed greatly to our understanding of the phenomenon of heat is kinetic theory, a basic theory that explains how different states of matter can exist.

The Kinetic Theory of Matter

According to the *kinetic theory of matter*, matter exists in three states—as solids, liquids, or gases. A fourth state, *plasma*, is an ionized gas; the Sun is made up of plasma. The form, or phase, of matter is determined by the motion of the molecules within it.

Solids are composed of atoms or molecules in limited motion. These atoms or molecules are in direct contact with one another, allowing for little or no space available for random movement. The attractive forces of the particles keep the solid intact and give the solid its definite shape and structure.

In *liquids*, individual atoms or molecules are able to move past one another into new positions, giving this form of matter its fluidity. Cohesive forces hold liquids intact.

Gases are substances in which the individual atoms or molecules are in constant random motion. The motion, or kinetic energy, increases along with an increase in temperature. Molecules are unable to hold together, and this property gives gases the ability to flow or spread out to fill the container in which they are placed.

Heat, Temperature, and the States of Matter

The state of matter depends on its heat content. *Temperature* is a measure of heat intensity. The change from one state of matter to another involves the addition or subtraction of a certain amount of heat per gram of substance. For example, at 32 degrees Fahrenheit, water, a liquid, changes to ice, a solid. When the temperature is raised above 32 degrees Fahrenheit, the ice changes to water, a liquid. At temperatures at or above 212 degrees Fahrenheit, the boiling point of water, it changes to steam, a gaseous state. Impurities in water affect its freezing point.

Certain materials expand when their temperature is raised and shrink when it is lowered. Liquids expand more noticeably than solids, but gases expand even more. The mercury thermometer employs this principle. Mercury, an element that expands uniformly over a wide range of temperatures, is placed in a bulb attached to a glass tube. Changes in temperature become apparent as the mercury expands and contracts.

Temperature can be measured in degrees centigrade or degrees Fahrenheit. On the centigrade (or Celsius) scale, 0 degrees represents the freezing point of water, and 100 degrees is the boiling point. On the Fahrenheit scale, 32 degrees represents the freezing point of water, and 212 degrees is the boiling point. While temperature is measured in degrees by thermometer, heat is measured by the calorie or British Thermal Unit (BTU). A *calorie* is the amount of heat needed to raise one gram of water one degree centigrade. The BTU is the amount of heat required to raise one pound of water 1 degree Fahrenheit.

EXERCISE 7: KINETIC THEORY OF MATTER

Directions: In the space provided, write *T* if the statement is true or *F* if it is false.

_____ **1.** There is more rigid molecular structure in a solid than in a gas.

_____ **2.** Molecules in a gas are close together and exhibit little motion.

_____ **3.** An increase in temperature decreases the molecular motion of a gas.

_____ **4.** Molecules moving past each other in a liquid give it fluidity.

_____ **5.** The presence or absence of heat has no connection with the state of matter of a substance.

Answers are on page 448.

EXERCISE 8: KINETIC THEORY AND MOTION

Directions: Choose the best answer for the following questions.

1. In an experiment, a drop of blue ink is placed on the surface of a glass of water. In a few minutes, the drop of ink is dispersed throughout the water, turning it light blue. The results of the experiment prove that

  (1) ink molecules have less density than water molecules
  (2) a new compound is formed by the combination of ink and water
  (3) heat causes the ink molecules to disperse
  (4) molecules of ink and molecules of water are in constant motion
  (5) the molecules of ink are in motion, but the molecules of water are not

2. If the water were heated, and the ink were not, which of the following would likely be the effect?

   (1) The movement of the water molecules would be slowed, and it would take longer for the color to change.

   (2) The movement of the ink molecules would be speeded up, and the water would change color more quickly.

   (3) The movement of the water molecules would be speeded up, causing the ink molecules to be dispersed more quickly.

   (4) The movement of the ink molecules would be slowed, and the water would change color more slowly.

   (5) Heating would have no effect on the rate of change.

Answers are on page 448.

EXERCISE 9: THE THERMOSTAT

Directions: Read the passage below and answer the questions that follow.

> A *thermostat* is a device for regulating the temperature of a heating or cooling system. In a thermostat, a strip of steel and a strip of brass, both of equal length, are welded together in the shape of a question mark. When heated, brass expands nearly 50 percent more than steel. As the metals expand and contract with the application and removal of heat, the tail end of the thermostat trips an electrical switch that turns a furnace or an air conditioner on or off. The temperature at which the thermostat is set determines the point at which the system goes on or off, based on a change in temperature.

1. The principle under which a thermostat operates is the same under which

   (1) ink disperses throughout a liquid

   (2) a gas expands to fill the container in which it is held

   (3) the level of mercury rises or falls in a glass tube

   (4) a chemical reaction occurs when two substances combine

   (5) a pendulum swings when set into motion

2. In operating an air conditioner, the thermostat is set for 70° so that when the temperature rises above 70° the air conditioner goes on. Which of the following is likely to occur when the temperature inside remains below seventy?

   (1) The brass strip will expand and turn the heating system on.

   (2) The steel strip will contract and turn the air conditioner on.

   (3) The brass strip will expand and turn the air conditioner on.

   (4) The brass strip will contract and turn the air conditioner off.

   (5) The thermostat will not trigger the air conditioner to go on.

Answers are on page 448.

EXERCISE 10: HEAT AND TEMPERATURE

Directions: Read the passage below and answer the question that follows.

Different materials expand at different degrees of temperature change and in different percentages of their length, volume, or surface. In the preceding example, brass expands lengthwise 50 percent more than steel when heat is applied. Buckling can occur when a material such as asphalt used for road surfaces reacts to changes in temperature, causing potholes. This is one of the reasons for the widespread use of reinforced concrete (concrete with a steel framework) on road surfaces rather than asphalt and the use of reinforced concrete in high-rise apartment construction.

The widespread use of reinforced concrete in construction suggests that

A. concrete and steel expand and contract at nearly the same temperatures

B. reinforced concrete expands at temperatures much higher than ordinary asphalt and does not buckle

C. reinforced concrete does not expand and contract at all

(1) A   **(2)** B   **(3)** C   **(4)** A and B   **(5)** B and C

Answer is on page 448.

DID YOU KNOW THAT: A steel bridge one mile long changes in length by more than four feet when there is a change in temperature from 40 degrees below zero in winter to 100 degrees in summer?

The Nature of Waves

You may not realize how important waves and wave action are to your life. Consider the following example. After a long day at work, you come home to a darkened apartment. You turn on the lights and put your favorite tape on the stereo. After washing up, you go to the refrigerator, take out the leftovers, and reheat them in your microwave oven. When dinner is over, you wash the dishes, turn off the stereo, and turn on the television for an evening of entertainment. After a couple of hours in front of the set, you go to bed, where you fall asleep to the gentle motion of your waterbed.

Each of the preceding activities is dependent on the existence of waves. A *wave* is a periodic or harmonic disturbance in space or through a medium (water, for instance) by which energy is transmitted. Water, sound, and light all travel in waves.

In the preceding example, the illumination the lamp provides comes from light waves (a form of electromagnetic waves); the music emanating from the stereo comes from sound waves; the powers to preserve your food and warm it come from electromagnetic waves; the power that transmits signals to your TV set comes from radio waves (another form of electromagnetic waves); and the energy that gives your waterbed its soothing motion comes from water waves.

Types and Properties of Waves

Waves transmit energy in different ways, and all phases of matter transmit waves. An example of a solid transmitting wave energy is an earthquake that takes place when rocks are under pressure and snap or slide into new positions. Waves that are felt and seen in water are examples of a liquid transmitting wave energy. Gases also transmit wave energy, as in an explosion, when heat, sound, and light waves are generated.

Two basic types of waves exist—longitudinal waves and transverse waves. A *longitudinal* wave is one in which the particles of the medium move back and forth in the same direction as the wave itself moves. An example of a longitudinal wave is a sound wave that occurs when a tuning fork is tapped, as shown below.

LONGITUDINAL WAVE

When a tuning fork is tapped, the prongs move from right to left in a rapid periodic motion. A sound wave is produced, and it moves parallel (right and left) to the moving prong.

A *transverse* wave is one in which the particles of the medium move at right angles to the direction of the wave's movement. An example of a transverse wave is one that occurs when a pebble is tossed into a still pond. Light travels in transverse waves. An example of a transverse wave is shown below.

stone

wave front

TRANSVERSE WAVE

When a stone is dropped into a pond, the waves produced appear to move outward. These waves move at right angles to the dropped stone.

Waves have two components, a crest and a trough. A *crest* is the point of highest displacement in a wave, and the *trough* is the point of lowest displacement. Crests and troughs are easily visible in water waves. The following illustration shows the crest and trough of a wave.

Two specific characteristics of a wave are length and frequency. **Wavelength** is defined as the distance between two successive wave crests or two successive wave troughs. Wave *frequency* is the number of wave crests that pass a given point per second. Therefore, the shorter the wavelength, the higher the wave frequency. In fact, a wave's speed equals the wavelength times the wave frequency. Wavelength is illustrated in the diagram below.

SOUND WAVE

Sound Waves

Sound waves, as illustrated above, are longitudinal waves. A musical pitch, or tone, is heard when there is a definite frequency to a wave. The lower the frequency, the lower the tone. For example, the frequency of a bass speaker in a stereo is lower than a tweeter, or high-frequency speaker, because the low-pitched sound of the bass results from a lower number of vibrations per second.

A sound wave is a wave of compression. It begins at a source—in the case above, a horn speaker. The speaker vibrates, compressing the air in front of it, and, like a spring, pushes it away. As the wave passes, the air molecules are forced together. The sensation of hearing results when these waves strike the eardrum.

Sound waves can travel through solids, liquids, and gases. In fact, the human body can be a medium for sound waves. Ultrasonic waves, very high-pitched waves, are used in medicine today. These waves are transmitted through an expectant mother's abdomen to pinpoint the location, condition, and even sex of a fetus by reading vibrations that occur within the womb.

EXERCISE 11: WAVE TYPES

Directions: In the space provided, write *L* if the example is an example of a longitudinal wave and *T* if it is an example of a transverse wave.

———— **1.** a wave that can be seen when a loose rope held end to end is jerked at one end

———— **2.** a noise caused by the detonation of an atomic bomb

———— **3.** the hum created when an arrow is released from a bow

———— **4.** waves created on the surface of boiling soup

———— **5.** waves that appear on the surface of the ocean

Answers are on page 449.

EXERCISE 12: PROPERTIES OF WAVES

Directions: Look at the illustration below and answer the question that follows.

According to the illustration above, which points could be used to measure wavelength?

(1) T and Y
(2) X and Y
(3) Z and Y
(4) V and W
(5) T, X, and U

Answer is on page 449.

DID YOU KNOW THAT: Sound travels through air more slowly than it does through water, wood, or steel? Air molecules are not as closely packed together as water, wood, or steel molecules. Therefore, the sound waves lose much of their energy when passing through air.

The Nature of Light

Light is so ordinary to us that we take it for granted, yet light is so vital a part of life that neither plants nor animals could exist without it. Light produces heat, color, and the conditions that make vision possible. In fact, ancient scientists believed that light and vision were practically the same and that all light originated in the eye when contact was made with observed objects. Today, of course, we know this is not true.

Physicists define *light* as a form of electromagnetic energy that stimulates sensitive cells of the retina of the human eye to cause perception of vision. Electromagnetic energy can be expressed in wavelength ranges along a continuum, or spectrum. Light occupies the center of a spectrum that ranges from the low end (gamma rays) to the high end (radio waves). The other rays that occupy the electromagnetic spectrum are x-rays, ultraviolet rays, and infrared rays. Ultraviolet rays are invisible and are chiefly responsible for sunburn and tan. Heat-emitting objects such as the sun, an electric heater, and a radiator send out infrared rays that can be detected only by certain sensitive instruments. An illustration of the electromagnetic spectrum is shown on page 432.

The visible rays of the spectrum are recognized by the human eye as color. In order, these colors are red, orange, yellow, green, blue, indigo (deep blue), and violet. The shortest wavelengths that we can see are those we call violet; the longest ones we call red.

Two theories about the nature of light exist: the wave theory and the particle theory. These theories seem to oppose each other, but really just focus on different properties of light. According to the *wave theory of light*, light is a luminous energy emitted by a light source and travels through space as a transverse wave. According to the *particle theory of light*, light energy is both radiated (transmitted) and absorbed as tiny packets, or bundles, and not as continuous waves. Atoms and molecules are able to emit or absorb light energy in specific amounts.

EXERCISE 13: ANCIENT THEORY OF LIGHT

Directions: The ancients believed that light and vision were the same and that light originated in the eye. Write *S* in the space if the statement would support the ancients' beliefs and *D* if the statement would disprove the theory.

_____ 1. Glowing bodies are clearly perceived in total darkness by the human eye.

_____ 2. Extremely bright light can cause blindness in humans.

_____ 3. Nocturnal animals such as bats, opossums, and raccoons see better at night than during the day; their eyes are more keenly suited to darkness than to light.

_____ 4. Light exists despite the inability of the blind to observe it.

_____ 5. Although they can no longer see it, people who have lost their sense of sight nevertheless know that light exists.

Answers are on page 449.

EXERCISE 14: THE PHOTOELECTRIC PRINCIPLE

Directions: Read the passage below and answer the question that follows.

The electric eye, or photoelectric cell, is a mechanism used to open and close a garage door when a beam of light is activated or broken. The principle of the electric eye is based on the photoelectric effect. The photoelectric effect occurs when a beam of light strikes certain metals, causing electrons to be knocked out of the metal, producing an electric current. This is how it happens: Light falling on the inside of a bulb coated with an active substance causes electrons to be emitted. The electrons are attracted to a positively charged electrode positioned in the center of the bulb like a filament. An electric current results when the electrons (negatively charged particles) are attracted to the positively charged particles of the electrode. It is observed that electrons will be knocked loose only when a certain light energy is reached. The current can then be controlled by changes in light intensity. It appears that electrons are able to absorb only a certain amount of light at one time. When light shines on the electric eye, a current is established and the door moves. When the beam of light is broken, the door stops.

The principle of the electric eye acts to

A. support the wave theory of light that light comes only from a luminous source

B. dispute the belief that all light exists only as a continuous wave

C. support the particle theory of light, which states that light energy is transmitted in packets and bundles and not as waves

(1) A   (2) B   (3) C   (4) A and B   (5) B and C

Answer is on page 449.

EXERCISE 15: THE PHOTOELECTRIC EFFECT

Directions: Write *Yes* in the space provided if the example demonstrates the use of the photoelectric effect described in Exercise 14 and *No* if it doesn't.

_____ 1. a light sensor in an outdoor light that causes the light to come on when dusk approaches and turn itself off when daylight begins

_____ 2. an automatic door at a supermarket that opens when the rubber tread is stepped on

_____ 3. an ultrasonic remote control device that turns a televison set on or off when a button is touched

_____ 4. the sound of a film is controlled by markings on the side of a filmstrip that establish a current when exposed to the projector's lamp

_____ 5. an elevator door remains open when a beam is broken by a hand placed in front of it

Answers are on page 449.

Properties of Light Waves

Waves of light can be affected in at least five different ways: by reflection, refraction, diffraction, interference, and polarization. **Reflection** of light rays occurs when light waves strike a surface and bounce back or are returned at an angle. An example is light bouncing off a mirror. The angle of light and the type of reflecting surface produce different types of reflection.

Refraction occurs when light rays appear to bend as they pass from one medium to another. For example, when a straw is held upright in a glass of water, it looks broken. This is because light rays travel faster in air than in water. The light ray changes its path and bends when it passes through water.

Diffraction results when light waves bend according to their wavelengths as they pass near the edge of an obstacle or through a small opening. Longer waves bend more than shorter ones. For example, holding a phonograph record edgewise toward a white light will produce an iridescent (rainbow) pattern on the record's surface. This occurs because the wavelengths of light are bent, or diffracted, by the grooves (obstacles) on the record's surface.

Interference of light rays occurs when two or more light waves come together, interfering with each other. When light waves interfere, an alternating pattern of lightness and darkness occurs because the rays displace each other and cancel each other out. For example, if you hold your thumb and index finger together and look through the opening at a bright light, you will see alternating patterns of light and darkness—interference.

Polarization of light waves occurs when they are caused to vibrate on one plane, usually horizontal or vertical. A *polarizer* is a material that will block all light except waves that vibrate in a particular plane. A light wave that travels at a vertical angle can be prevented from traveling at a horizontal angle by a polarizer. Reflection alone is capable of polarizing light. The ability of light waves to be polarized suggests that light waves are transverse waves and not longitudinal waves as sound waves are. Longitudinal waves cannot be polarized.

EXERCISE 16: PROPERTIES OF LIGHT WAVES

Directions: Defined below are five changes that light waves can undergo. Read the definitions and apply them to the questions that follow.

reflection—the angular return of a light wave that occurs when it strikes a shiny surface

refraction—the apparent bending of light waves as they pass from one medium to another

diffraction—the bending of light waves according to their wavelengths as they pass near the edge of an obstacle or through a small opening

interference—the altering of brightness of light rays that occurs when they interfere with each other, causing reinforcement and cancellation

polarization—the restriction of light waves to a particular plane, horizontal or vertical

1. A coin lying at the bottom of a pool is located at a different point from where the eye perceives it to be. The light rays from the coin bend as they pass from water to air. This demonstrates

   (1) reflection **(2)** refraction **(3)** diffraction **(4)** interference **(5)** polarization

2. Rays of light striking a polished piece of chrome appear to bounce off its surface. This demonstrates

   (1) reflection **(2)** refraction **(3)** diffraction **(4)** interference **(5)** polarization

Answers are on page 449.

EXERCISE 17: WAVE PROPERTIES

Directions: Read the passage below and choose the best answer for the following question.

On bright sunny days, sunlight is reflected from a concrete road surface and from a large body of water. This light is polarized horizontally. When we look at these surfaces without wearing sunglasses or polarized glasses, we experience glare from the reflection. Wearing polarized sunglasses prevents the reflected light from striking our eyes and causing glare. Which of the following best describes the action of the polarized glasses?

(1) The lenses are polarized horizontally, cutting off the reflected light rays.
(2) The lenses are polarized vertically, cutting off the reflected light rays.
(3) The lenses act as a mirror, reflecting all light.
(4) The lenses act as a refractor, bending the light rays.
(5) The lenses absorb the light rays.

Answer is on page 449.

DID YOU KNOW THAT: Stars appear to twinkle because the light rays from the stars are bent several times by layers of moving air before they reach our atmosphere.

The Nature of Electricity

Electricity is another invisible but vital form of energy that we often take for granted. Without electricity, however, our lives would be paralyzed. To appreciate our near total dependence on this form of energy, we need only to consider what happens when a power failure occurs overnight.

Our clock radios don't function, so we oversleep. Unless we're wearing a watch, we don't know the correct time. Refrigerated food that doesn't spoil can't be cooked if we depend on a microwave oven or an electric stove. Trains powered by electric rails can't run, elevators in high-rises get stuck, and business comes to a standstill because typewriters, computers, and other office machines powered by electricity cannot operate. If the power outage continues into the night, we use flashlights, if we have them, or rely on candles and kerosene lamps to find our way around.

The more urbanized we become, the more dependent on electricity we are. Nuclear energy, despite its potential hazards, has emerged in recent years as an important source for generating the electrical power we need. Physicists define *electricity* as a form of energy that results from the flow of loose electrons—electrons weakly bound to atoms. Electricity is closely related to magnetism; therefore, the attractive force of magnetism must be discussed in order to understand electrical energy better.

Magnetism and Electrical Charges

Magnetism has been known to humankind for a long period of time. The ancient Greeks discovered that a rock called *magnetite* was able to attract iron, and the Chinese experimented and found that a piece of free-hanging magnetite would always align itself in a northerly-southerly direction. These early discoveries led to the invention of the compass to help direct ships.

You have probably observed that a magnet dipped into a pile of iron filings will attract the metal to each end. These points of attraction at opposite ends of a magnet are called its *poles*. Magnets have a north and a south pole, also called a positive and a negative pole. The opposite poles of two different magnets (a north pole and a south pole) will attract each other. Correspondingly, similar poles (two north or south poles) will repel each other. The space around magnets is called a *magnetic field*. Only a few natural and manmade materials can be magnetized—iron, steel, nickel, cobalt, and some alloys. A magnet, with its poles and lines of force, is illustrated below.

MAGNET AND LINES OF FORCE

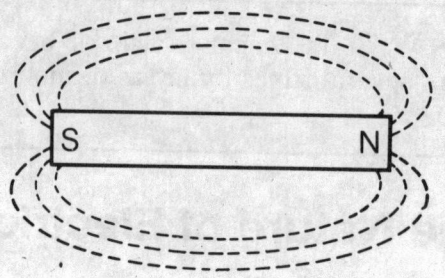

Magnetic Lines of Force

Every magnetic substance contains domains, groups of molecules with attractive forces. Before a substance is magnetized, these domains are arranged randomly so that the field of one domain is canceled out by the field of another. When the substance is magnetized, the domains line up parallel to the lines of force, with all north poles facing the same direction. This makes a permanent magnet out of a material in which the domains are too weak to disarrange themselves. The illustration on page 437 shows the difference between a magnetized and an unmagnetized substance.

In most elements, the atoms possess a slight magnetic field because of their spinning electrons. However, the fields cancel each other out because the atoms rotate and spin in different directions. In a magnet, whole groups of atoms line up in one direction and increase each other's magnetic effect rather than cancel it out. These magnetic concentrations are called *magnetic domains*.

Static Electricity and Magnetism

If you have ever shocked yourself in dry weather after walking across a carpet and touching an object, you have experienced static electricity. ***Static electricity*** is a stationary electrical charge caused by the friction of two objects, one positively charged and the other negatively charged.

Static electricity operates on the same principle as magnetism. The rubbing of the carpet by your shoes causes your body to become electrified. The shock you feel is caused by your negatively charged body being neutralized by the positive charge of the object you touch. Upon contact, your body is no longer charged. Static electricity is stored and does not move. The charged object must be brought into contact with another object that has an opposite charge for electrical shock to occur.

MAGNETIZED AND UNMAGNETIZED IRON ATOMS

Unmagnetized Iron Atoms

N ☐ ■ S—Domain

Magnetized Iron Atoms

N Pole   S Pole

EXERCISE 18: ELECTRICITY AND MAGNETISM

Directions: Choose the best answer for the questions below. The first question is based on the following paragraph.

> Earth itself is surrounded by a magnetic field. This may be because of strong electric currents in Earth's core and the rotation of Earth. The north magnetic pole is located in Canada; the south magnetic pole is in nearly the opposite location. The strong magnetic attraction of these poles tends to align the needle of a compass in a northerly-southerly direction.

1. Based on the preceding passage, a compass will tell direction because

   (1) the whole Earth acts as a magnet
   (2) the Chinese discovered the magnetic poles
   (3) the Greeks discovered the magnetic poles
   (4) large iron deposits are located in Canada
   (5) the magnetic attraction of Earth is increasing

2. Which of the following would be attracted to either pole of a magnet?

    (1) a piece of aluminum
    (2) a piece of brass
    (3) a piece of tin
    (4) an unmagnetized piece of cobalt
    (5) a magnetized piece of cobalt

Answers are on page 449.

EXERCISE 19: LIKE AND UNLIKE CHARGES

Directions: Read the following passage and answer the questions.

    In an experiment, a rod made of hard rubber is rubbed vigorously with a piece of fur. After being rubbed, the rod will pick up bits of paper. Similarly, a glass rod rubbed with silk will pick up bits of paper. Both rods are said to be electrically charged and carry opposite charges.

1. Which of the following would you predict to happen based on what you know about electrically charged objects?

    (1) Two rubber rods rubbed with fur will attract each other.
    (2) Two glass rods rubbed with silk will attract each other.
    (3) A glass rod rubbed with silk and a rubber rod rubbed with fur will repel each other.
    (4) A glass rod rubbed with silk and a rubber rod rubbed with fur will attract each other.
    (5) A glass rod rubbed with fur and a rubber rod rubbed with silk will attract each other.

2. Which of the following statements could *not* be true based on the results of the preceding experiment?

    (1) The glass rod is negatively charged, and the rubber rod is positively charged.
    (2) The glass rod is positively charged, and the rubber rod is negatively charged.
    (3) Both rods carry the same electrical charge.
    (4) Both rods have different electrical charges.
    (5) Both rods have been magnetized.

3. Which of the following would be true in the above experiment?

    A. The fur would attract the rubber rod.

    B. The fur would repel the rubber rod.

    C. The silk would attract the glass rod.

    D. The silk would repel the glass rod.

    (1) A   **(2)** B   **(3)** C   **(4)** A and C   **(5)** A and D

Answers are on page 449.

DID YOU KNOW THAT: A permanent magnet made of cobalt, nickel, and aluminum (alnico) can hold up to sixty times its own weight? A one-pound magnet can lift a sixty-pound child suspended in a steel harness.

Electric Currents

Can you imagine one of our modern electric appliances being run by static electricity? It would take forever just to toast a slice of bread! A charge would have to be built up on the toaster by rubbing it, and it would discharge immediately upon touch.

Early scientists who experimented with electric charges found that charges could move easily through certain materials called *conductors*. As you learned in the chemistry section, metal was found to be a good conductor of electricity, as were salt solutions, acids, and hot gases. Other materials such as rubber were found not to conduct charges at all. These materials are called *insulators*.

An *electric current* is created by an electric charge in motion. In a solid conductor, such as wire, the current is a stream of moving electrons. In a liquid or gas, the current may be positively and negatively charged atoms—ions.

An electric current flowing through a solid conductor can be compared to the flow of water through the pipes in your plumbing system. An electric current moves slowly—about a hundredth of an inch per second. Although our lights come on instantly when a switch is turned on, it is not because the electrons race through the wires; it is because the wires are always filled with electrons just as a water pipe is always filled with water.

Electromagnets

An *electromagnet* is a core of soft magnetic material surrounded by a coil of wire. An electric current is passed through the wire to magnetize the core when a switch is flicked or a button pushed. The device then has the power to attract iron objects. When the switch is turned off, the attraction is broken.

Electromagnets are used in radios and an ordinary doorbell. In the doorbell, when the bell is pushed, the core is magnetized and attracts the clapper, causing the bell to sound. An electromagnet has obvious advantages over a permanent magnet in that an electromagnet can be turned on or off at will, and its attractive force can be increased by changing the amount of electricity sent to the coil. Modern electromagnets can lift up to 50,000 pounds of scrap iron and steel. They are used extensively in loading and transportation.

EXERCISE 20: CONDUCTORS AND INSULATORS

Directions: In the blanks below, write *C* if the material is a conductor of electricity and *I* if it is an insulator.

_____ **1.** leather　　　　_____ **6.** glass

_____ **2.** porcelain　　　_____ **7.** salt water

_____ **3.** silver　　　　 _____ **8.** distilled water

_____ **4.** copper　　　　_____ **9.** sulfuric acid

_____ **5.** wood　　　　　_____ **10.** plastic

Answers are on page 449.

EXERCISE 21: ELECTROMAGNETS

Directions: Choose the best answer for the following question.

A radio with a strong electromagnet would *not* be placed near the navigation instruments on a plane or ship because

(1) the radio wouldn't work because of electrical interference
(2) the radio couldn't be heard clearly because of static
(3) the accuracy of the compass would be affected by the magnetic field established by the radio's electromagnet
(4) the radio's electromagnet would cause all the navigation instruments to malfunction
(5) the radio would draw too much electrical energy, causing the electrical system of the ship or plane to discharge

Answer is on page 449.

DID YOU KNOW THAT: An electric eel can generate enough electricity to knock down a full-grown horse or drive a small motor? A large electric eel can discharge up to 600 volts of electricity.

TEST 3: SCIENCE ANSWER KEY

CHAPTER 1: BIOLOGY

Exercise 1: Cell Structure
page 357
Comprehension
1. c   2. e   3. a   4. b   5. d   6. f

Exercise 2: Cells
pages 357–358
Comprehension
1. (4) Choices (1), (2), (3), and (5) are not the main idea. They are details that support the key idea that the cell is a highly organized, complex structure.

Analysis
2. (1) The passage states that the endoplasmic reticulum serves as a network for transporting materials from one part of the cell to another or from the cell to the environment.

3. (3) According to the passage, mitochondria are abundant in highly active cells that produce energy for important life processes. The heart, which pumps blood throughout the body, is the most active of the choices listed.

4. (5) Chloroplasts are important in the food-making process for plants. Since animal cells have no chloroplasts, you can infer that animals must obtain their own food.

Application
5. (5) The organelle present in plants but not in animals that produces energy for important life processes is the chloroplast.

Exercise 3: Cells and Active Transport
page 359
Comprehension
1. high/low
2. low/high
3. reverse *or* opposite

Exercise 4: Diffusion and Osmosis
page 359
Analysis
1. (3) According to the passage, diffusion is the passage of molecules from an area of high concentration to an area of low concentration. This process allows for an even distribution of substances throughout all the cells of the body.

2. (5) In osmosis, water moves from a *lower* concentration to a *higher* one. The salt solution in the blood plasma is higher; therefore, the cell will lose water. If it loses water, it will shrink.

Exercise 5: Mitosis
page 361
Comprehension
1. a   2. b   3. d   4. c

Exercise 6: Meiosis
page 363
Comprehension
4, 1, 3, 2

Exercise 7: Cell Division
page 363
Comprehension
1. (3) Because of the exchange and recombination of chromosomal material, the method of reproduction that allows for the most variety is sexual reproduction.

Analysis
2. (1) The purpose of meiosis is to reduce the number of chromosomes in reproductive cells so that when sperm and egg unite, they create the proper number of chromosomes for the species. You can infer that without meiosis, offspring would have twice the assigned number of chromosomes.

Comprehension
3. (2) An egg cell is a reproductive cell. Only reproductive cells have a haploid number of chromosomes.

Analysis
4. (3) Because cancerous cells spread to invade healthy cells, you can conclude that cancer cells divide more unpredictably than normal cells.

Exercise 8: Genetics and Heredity
pages 364–365
Comprehension
1. (4) The diagram shows only one child out of four that does not have a dominant green eye gene or a dominant brown eye gene. This is the only child that will have blue eyes; therefore, the chances are that 25 percent of the children will have blue eyes.

Analysis
2. (3) The "Y" chromosome that determines a child's sex is carried by the father.

Evaluation
3. (5) Both A and C are supported by information in the reading. Choice B is not true.

Exercise 9: The Nitrogen Cycle
pages 366–367
Analysis
1. (1) The only case that shows a mutually beneficial relationship between two different organisms is that of bacteria that live in the stomachs of hoofed animals and at the same time help the animals digest food.

Comprehension
2. (3) Nitrogen fixing is described as the process by which legumes form nitrates in the soil. Peanuts are the only legume among the choices listed.

Application
3. (4) Soybeans are legumes and are important in the nitrogen-fixing process. The introduction of soybeans into the crop rotation process improves the possibility of replenishing the supply of nitrogen.

Exercise 10: Photosynthesis
pages 367–368
Analysis
1. (5) Plants that do not possess chlorophyll must use a process other than photosynthesis to obtain the energy they need. One such process is parasitism, in which one organism feeds off another.

2. (1) Green pigment indicates the presence of chlorophyll. The areas of the coleus leaf that were green originally contained starch, which is produced through photosynthesis. Therefore, the starch turns brown when iodine is applied.

Exercise 11: Cellular Respiration
pages 368–369
Comprehension
1. (3) According to the passage, cellular respiration is the series of chemical reactions by which a cell releases the energy trapped inside glucose molecules.

Analysis
2. (1) Glucose molecules must be present for cellular respiration to occur. Since glucose molecules are the end product of photosynthesis in plants, you can infer that photosynthesis must precede cellular respiration.

Application
3. (4) The more active a person is, the more energy he or she expends and the more carbon dioxide he or she exhales. Athletes are more active than most people; therefore, they would have higher rates of cellular respiration.

Evaluation
4. (4) The rate of cellular respiration is affected by whether or not a person is at rest or is physically active. Choices (3) and (4) include both criteria; however, in choice (4) the greater number of students tested provides more reliable data.

Analysis
5. (5) The passage describes two types of diabetics—those whose bodies do not produce enough insulin and those whose bodies cannot effectively use the insulin produced. The passage states further that *some* diabetics must take additional insulin. Since not all diabetics are required to increase their insulin intake, the only precautions that would apply to *both* categories of diabetics is regulating their glucose intake and maintaining a reasonable exercise regimen.

Exercise 12: Classification of Organisms
page 371
Application
1. (1) Streptococcus is a single-celled organism of the bacteria family and fits in the kingdom monera.

2. (3) Mold lacks chlorophyll and obtains food from another organism. It is classified in the kingdom fungi.

3. (2) An amoeba is a single-celled organism that can move and has a more complex cell structure than monerans. It is classified in the kingdom protista.

Exercise 13: Evolution and Natural Selection
pages 372–373
Application
1. (3) According to the passage, certain forms of life adapted to meet the demands of the environment. The fact that the duckbill platypus is found only in and around Australia supports the hypothesis that the platypus developed independently in a closed environment during the early history of mammals.

2. (4) That Australia became isolated from the other six continents millions of years ago (choice A), and that marsupials didn't have to compete with placental mammals (choice B), are two facts that together help to explain why marsupials are found primarily around Australia. Choice C is not true, since marsupials survive in zoos throughout the world.

3. (3) The opossum is the only marsupial listed that is native to North America.

Analysis

4. **(1)** Choice (1) is the best answer because choices (3), (4), and (5) are not true. Choice (2) is not true because the highest forms of animal life are placental mammals.

Evaluation

5. **(4)** Of the choices listed, the seal is the only mammal listed whose body is adapted for living in water—an environment that is not typically one that mammals live in.

Exercise 14: Ecology and Ecosystems
page 374
Application

1. grass
2. cattle and deer
3. mountain lion

Analysis

4. The destruction of the **mountain lion** led to the increase of grazing by **deer** and **cattle**, which led to **denuding** of the land and its eventual **erosion** by heavy rains.

CHAPTER 2: EARTH SCIENCE

Exercise 1: The Big Bang Theory
page 376
Comprehension

(5) The passage states that the big bang theory accounts for both the expansion of the universe and the presence of background radiation.

Exercise 2: Stars and Galaxies
page 377
Comprehension
3, 4, 1, 2

Exercise 3: The Solar System
page 378
Application

1. **(4)** According to the story of Goldilocks and the Three Bears, Goldilocks tried one bowl of porridge that was too cold, another that was too hot, and a third that was just right. This corresponds to Mars being too cold, Venus too hot, and Earth just right to support life.

Analysis

2. **(3)** Choice (1) is not true. Earth is the only planet known to support life. You can see from the illustration of the solar system that choices (2) and (4) are not true. The exact age of the planets cannot be determined, choice (5). Choice (3) is the only reasonable explanation.

Exercise 4: The Planets
page 378
Comprehension

1. Earth, Mars
2. Mars
3. Mercury
4. Venus
5. Venus

Exercise 5: The Sun and Solar System
page 379
Analysis

(5) Based on the facts in the chart, the farther away from the Sun these planets are, the greater number of moons they have and the longer they take to revolve around the Sun.

Exercise 6: Plate Tectonics
page 381
Comprehension

(5) In the passage, the occurrence of earthquakes, volcanoes, and mountains and the theory of continental drift are explained by the theory of plate tectonics.

Exercise 7: Earthquakes
page 381
Evaluation

(3) The map shows the potential for most moderate and major earthquake damage occurring on the West Coast. Choices (1), (2), and (4) are directly contradicted by the map. Choice (5) is an opinion, not a fact.

Exercise 8: Continental Drift
page 382
Analysis

1. **(3)** This choice reflects an understanding of continental drift. Choice (A) is untrue, and choice (B) is not a good explanation.

2. **(5)** This is the best choice because it takes into account both the theory of continental drift and the behavior of sea turtles.

Exercise 9: Measuring Geologic Time
pages 383–384
Comprehension

1. **(5)** The text states that sedimentary rocks are deposited near Earth's surface and that metamorphic rock is located just below igneous rock.

2. **(4)** According to the passage, metamorphic and igneous rock rarely contain fossils, and it is difficult to determine the age of original rock in metamorphic rocks. Igneous rock is capable of being dated radiometrically although metamorphic rock is not.

Analysis

3. **(5)** The trilobite rocks are likely to be older than the coral because the greater the depth at which a fossil is found, the older it is likely to be.

Exercise 10: Minerals and Rocks
page 385
Analysis
1. **(3)** Potassium, which makes up 1.85 percent of Earth's crust, is the only element that occupies three times more space than does silicon.

2. **(4)** The other choices given either weigh more or take up less space than silicon.

Comprehension
3. **(5)** If an element weighs more than another but takes up less space, it is highly compressible, a property of silicon.

Analysis
4. **(5)** The fact that oxygen combines with most of Earth's elements explains why it constitutes such a great part of Earth's crust. Choices (1), (2), and (3) are not true. Choice (4) has no relation to the issue of the composition of Earth's crust.

Exercise 11: The Changing Earth
pages 386–387
Application
1. **(5)** Choice (5) is a procedure most farmers follow to increase their chances of a bountiful harvest and has nothing to do with preventing erosion.

Comprehension
2. **(5)** Forces that cause volcanoes and mountains both result in an uplifting of Earth's surface; ocean trenches do not.

Exercise 12: Change in Sea Level
pages 388–389
Comprehension
1. **(5)** According to the graph, nearly 18,000 years ago the depth of the oceans was at almost 400 feet below sea level, its lowest level.

Evaluation
2. **(1)** Glaciers covered the earth 20,000 years ago, and sea level was at its lowest—400 feet. Today, glaciers no longer cover Earth, and sea level is at its highest according to the graph.

Exercise 13: The Oceans' Beginning
page 389
Comprehension
1. **(4)** At 0.001 percent, water vapor in the atmosphere yields the lowest amount of water on Earth.

Analysis
2. **(4)** According to the text, many scientists believe that oceans were formed by the release of water bound up in Earth's interior.

Exercise 14: The Oceans' Tides
pages 390–391
Analysis
1. **(5)** According to the illustration, the Moon is in a direct line with the Sun and receives the Sun's greatest attractive force. The periods when this occurs are at full moon and new moon.

2. **(2)** According to the illustration, the Moon is at a right angle to the Sun and the rays are indirect, striking only a portion of the Moon's surface. This corresponds to the periods of first quarter moon and last quarter moon.

3. **(5)** The two conditions that are more pronounced during unusually high tide are the Moon's closeness to Earth and Earth's closeness to the Sun. These two conditions increase the gravitational pull of the Moon and the Sun on Earth.

Application
4. **(2)** The opposite condition of syzygy results in unusually low tides because the gravitational pull of the Moon and the Sun on Earth is at its weakest.

Exercise 15: Layers of Earth's Atmosphere
page 393
Comprehension
1. **(4)** The ionosphere extends from 30 miles to 300 miles in Earth's atmosphere. Noctilucent clouds are found at heights above 50 miles.

2. **(3)** "D" radio waves are found at the same level as noctilucent clouds—in the lower ionosphere.

3. **(5)** Clouds (located in the troposphere) shown at the same level as Mt. Everest's peak suggest that the peak may be hidden by clouds.

Exercise 16: Ozone in the Atmosphere
page 394
Analysis
1. **(2)** Smog is visible and, therefore, lies in the troposphere, the level of the atmosphere closest to Earth.

2. **(2)** Ozone is formed by heat and the exhaust from cars. The heat during hot summer days contributes to the formation of ozone.

Exercise 17: The Water Cycle
page 395
Comprehension
5, 3, 1, 4, 2

Exercise 18: Humidity
pages 396–397
Analysis

1. **(4)** According to the passage, warm air holds more moisture than cold air; therefore, when the temperature drops, the colder air cannot hold the amount of moisture that the warmer air held. As a result, the saturation point is reached and excess humidity is released as rain.

2. **(3)** At a given time, water vapor in the air is constant. Cold air can hold less moisture than warm air. When air is heated, it has the capacity to hold more water. If moisture is not added to the air, the humidity level goes down.

3. **(3)** Choices (1) and (2) are too low for comfort; choices (4) and (5) too high for comfort.

Exercise 19: Air Masses, Fronts, and Weather
page 398
Comprehension

1. **(2)** According to the passage, warm fronts bring low-lying clouds, steady winds, and drizzling rain.

2. **(3)** According to the passage, a stationary front lingers and brings conditions similar to those of a warm front.

Evaluation

3. **(5)** The passage discusses all of the properties affecting fronts except the direction in which the air mass moves.

CHAPTER 3: CHEMISTRY

Exercise 1: Atomic Structure
page 401
Understanding Ideas

1. d 2. e 3. f 4. b 5. c 6. a

Exercise 2: Nuclear Energy
page 401
Application

1. **(4)** The passage states that fusion involves the uniting of two nuclei of a chemical element at high temperatures and pressures to form a new element. Hydrogen, the lightest element, is the only one listed whose nuclei when fused can form the second lightest element—helium.

2. **(1)** The passage states that fission involves the splitting of the nucleus of a heavy element. Plutonium is not a gas and, therefore, is the only heavy element shown.

Exercise 3: Isotopic Elements
page 402
Application

1. **(3)** According to the chart, lithium's atomic mass is 6.94. Of all the elements shown, it would be the most likely to have an isotope of 6. If two lithium isotopes are fused, the atomic mass of the new element would be 12—the atomic mass of carbon 12.

2. **(1)** According to the passage, an isotope is a form of an element that varies in the number of neutrons in its nucleus. The only element represented that is capable of doubling or tripling its mass to achieve a final mass of 2 or 3 would be hydrogen, with an atomic mass of 1.01.

Exercise 4: Elements And Periodicity
page 405
Application

1. **(4)** The passage states that as the atomic number increases for elements in a column, similar chemical properties occur regularly and to a greater degree. The only *physical* property that gold would have a higher degree of would be malleability because it is a soft and workable metal. Choices (1), (2), and (5) are not physical properties. Choice (3) is not true of gold or the other metals.

Evaluation

2. **(4)** The fact that radon is found in the ground (choice A) suggests that it is denser and weighs more than the others. Also, the fact that it has a higher atomic number (choice B) indicates that its properties, including weight and density, are greater than those of other elements in its family.

Exercise 5: Balanced Equations
page 407
Comprehension

1. **B**—The reaction begins and ends with two atoms of nitrogen (N) and two atoms of oxygen (O).

2. **U**—The reaction begins with one atom of iron (Fe), one atom of hydrogen (H), and one atom of chlorine (Cl). However, it ends with one atom of iron, two atoms of hydrogen, and three atoms of chlorine. Therefore, it is not balanced.

3. **B**—The reaction begins and ends with two atoms of hydrogen (H) and one atom of oxygen (O).

4. **U**—The reaction begins with one atom of zinc (Zn), one atom of carbon (C), and two atoms of oxygen (O). It ends with one atom of zinc, one atom of carbon, and three atoms of oxygen.

5. **B**—The reaction begins and ends with one atom of carbon (C) and two atoms of sulfur (S).

Exercise 6: Chemical Reactions
pages 407–408
Analysis
1. (3) None of the other formulas indicate two iron atoms and three oxygen atoms.

2. (2) None of the others are balanced equations indicating one molecule of carbon dioxide (CO_2) and one molecule of water (H_2O). Choice (4) starts with carbon dioxide and water but does not result in a balanced equation.

Comprehension
3. (2) According to the passage, a chemical equation is balanced when it follows the Law of Conservation of Matter, which states that matter can neither be created nor destroyed in a chemical reaction.

Evaluation
4. (4) The fact that there is a copper coating on the aluminum is the only evidence cited that can prove that a chemical change has taken place.

Analysis
5. (3) The appearance of a new substance is best explained by the occurrence of a chemical change.

Exercise 7: Types of Substances
pages 409–410
Application
1. (1) Salt is a compound composed of elements sodium and chlorine and has properties different from each.

2. (4) Solder is an alloy composed of two metals—tin and lead—with one dissolved into the other.

3. (2) Air is a mixture composed of at least four gases. Each gas retains its own distinct properties.

4. (3) Mercurochrome is a solution composed of three compounds dissolved in a liquid.

Exercise 8: Compounds and Mixtures
page 410
Evaluation
(2) Compounds are substances that are composed of two or more elements in which the elements lose their original properties, so only statement B is correct. In a mixture, the combining elements do not lose their original properties. Therefore, by definition, a compound cannot contain a mixture (statement A). Statement C can be eliminated because a solution is a mixture; it does not contain mixtures.

Exercise 9: Compounds and Chemical Bonding
pages 412–413
Comprehension
1. (5) The inert gases are incapable of forming compounds, undergoing chemical reactions, and sharing or transferring electrons, all of which involve some form of chemical bonding.

2. (2) The passage says that ionic bonding is achieved by the transfer of electrons.

3. (1) The passage says that a covalent bond is one in which atoms are held together by sharing electrons.

Exercise 10: Chemical First Aid
page 414
Analysis
1. (3) The passage on page 413 says that when an acid combines with a base a salt is formed. In this case, the base is ammonia, and the acid is vinegar, orange juice, or lemon juice.

2. (3) Milk is the only substance listed that contains acid—lactic acid.

3. (2) The acid must be neutralized—changed into a salt and water. A base such as milk of magnesia is the only antidote listed that can neutralize the acid phenol.

4. (4) The action of the milk of magnesia would neutralize the acid, changing it into a salt and water.

Exercise 11: Acids, Bases, and Salts
page 415
Analysis
1. (4) Acetic acid, a mild acid contained in vinegar, would be found at the acidic end of the pH scale closest to neutrality—between the values 4 and 5. Choices (1) and (5) represent alkalinity, not acidity, and choices (2) and (3) represent high acidity.

2. (2) Oxalic acid, described as a strong, poisonous acid, would be found at the lower end of the pH scale nearest increasing acidity—between 1 and 2. Choice (1) represents low alkalinity, choice (3) low acidity, choice (4) low acidity approaching neutrality, and choice (5) high alkalinity.

3. (3) Water is neither acidic nor alkaline; therefore, it would be neutral on the pH scale.

Evaluation

4. (5) A substance is an acid if it tastes sour (choice B) or neutralizes a base (choice C). An acid has a pH reading under 7, so choice A is eliminated.

Exercise 12: A Car Battery
pages 416–417
Application

1. (2) In the example, sulfuric acid, a conductor of electricity, is dissolved in water.

2. (1) The passage says that the lead loses two electrons when it reacts with sulfuric acid; therefore, lead is oxidized.

3. (2) The passage says that lead dioxide gains two electrons, so it is the substance that is reduced.

4. (2) Sulfuric acid is an oxidizing agent because it causes the lead in the battery to lose electrons. The lead dioxide is a reducing agent because it causes the sulfuric acid to gain electrons.

5. (3) Oxidation-reduction is a process in which one substance loses electrons and the other gains electrons to convert chemical energy into electrical energy. The other choices do not reflect this process. Nuclear fission and nuclear fusion, choices (1) and (2), involve the splitting and the uniting of the nuclei of atoms. Ionic bonding and covalent bonding, choices (4) and (5), are processes that create compounds by either the transferring or sharing of electrons.

Analysis

6. (3) Citric acid (obtained from fruits) is the only organic compound listed. Organic compounds do not conduct electrical currents.

7. (4) A battery is completely discharged when the sulfuric acid is no longer capable of oxidizing lead, and the lead dioxide is no longer able to reduce the sulfuric acid; thus the oxidation-reduction process that causes an electric current to flow cannot occur.

Exercise 13: Reaction Rate, Catalysts, and Equilibrium
page 418
Analysis

1. (3) A catalyst is an agent that speeds up a chemical reaction but that is not affected by the reaction itself. Lipase speeds up the rate at which fats are changed into fatty acids. Because lipase is found in the body, it may be described as a biological catalyst. A negative catalyst (choice B) inhibits, or slows down, a chemical reaction.

Application

2. (5) According to the passage, chemical equilibrium occurs when the rate of forward reaction balances the rate of reverse reaction. In photosynthesis (B), plants take in water and carbon dioxide from the air to make starch with the sun's help. The by-product oxygen is released. The reverse of this process is respiration (C), the taking in of oxygen by animals and the combining of oxygen with starch to form carbon dioxide and water, which the plants use for photosynthesis. Thus, the forward reaction of photosynthesis is balanced by the reverse reaction of respiration, resulting in chemical equilibrium.

CHAPTER 4: PHYSICS
Exercise 1: Laws of Force and Motion
page 420
Application
1. AR **2.** AF **3.** AR **4.** G **5.** I
Exercise 2: The Force of Gravity
page 421
Comprehension

(1) Weight is a function of the attractive force of one object on another. According to the passage, the strength of the force depends on the masses of the objects. Since Jupiter is larger than Earth, the attractive force must be greater. This would result in an increase in the astronaut's weight relative to his weight on Earth.

Exercise 3: Mechanics, Force, and Motion
page 421
Evaluation

1. **(4)** Air does not exist in a vacuum. Both the coin and the confetti fall at the same rate even though the coin is heavier. This proves that weight has less to do with the rate of acceleration of falling objects than air resistance. Outside a vacuum, the coin would fall faster than the confetti, which would flutter because of the air resistance. Choice C is incorrect because *all* falling objects are affected by the force of gravity.

2. **(2)** By dropping items of different weights from the leaning tower of Pisa, Galileo proved that falling objects fell at the same rate of speed.

Exercise 4: Forms of Energy
page 423
Application

1. K   2. P   3. P   4. K   5. K

Exercise 5: Types of Energy
page 423
Application

1. **(4)** The Sun radiates energy to Earth; its warmth and light sustain all life on Earth.

2. **(1)** Nuclear energy results from the splitting of an atom of a heavy chemical element such as U-235.

3. **(2)** Gas and air are mixtures. When they are ignited, combustion, a chemical process, occurs.

Exercise 6: Simple Machines
pages 424–425
Analysis

1. **(3)** According to the passage, the greater the distance between the fulcrum and the applied force, the less the force required to perform the work. If the distance is increased to 20 feet, then the effort would be halved:
$100 \div 2 = 50$ pounds of applied force.

Evaluation

2. **(3)** The shape of the fulcrum is the only variable not cited in the passage that would have any bearing on the lever's effectiveness.

Exercise 7: Kinetic Theory of Matter
page 426
Comprehension

1. T   2. F   3. F   4. T   5. F

Exercise 8: Kinetic Theory and Motion
pages 426–427
Evaluation

1. **(4)** The dispersion of the ink throughout the water, turning it light blue, proves that the molecules of ink and water are in constant motion and intermingle. Choices (1) and (2) cannot be proved by observation alone. Choice (3) is incorrect because the variable of heat is not introduced. Choice (5) is incorrect since all liquids are fluid because their molecules are able to move past each other.

Analysis

2. **(3)** According to the passage, heat causes molecules to speed up and materials to expand. Choice (3) is the only one that correctly shows an effect of heating the water.

Exercise 9: The Thermostat
page 427
Application

1. **(3)** The passage states that certain materials expand when their temperatures are raised and shrink when they are lowered. The expansion and contraction of the brass strip in the thermostat is similar to the rising and falling of mercury in a thermometer.

Analysis

2. **(5)** If the thermostat is set for 70°, this means that when the room temperature rises above seventy degrees, the air conditioner will come on; when the temperature reaches seventy degrees, the air conditioner will go off. If the temperature remains below seventy degrees, the thermostat will not trigger the air conditioner to go on.

Exercise 10: Heat and Temperature
page 428
Analysis

(4) Reinforced concrete could not maintain its durability if the two materials, concrete and steel, expanded and contracted at different temperatures—so choice A is correct. Also, because reinforced concrete does not buckle as asphalt does, you can infer that reinforced concrete must expand at a higher temperature than asphalt—so choice B is correct. Choice C is not true since steel is known to expand and contract.

Exercise 11: Wave Types
page 430
Application
1. T   2. L   3. L   4. T   5. T

Exercise 12: Properties of Waves
page 431
Comprehension
(3) The passage states that wavelength is the distance between two successive wave crests or troughs. Points Z and Y are two successive wave crests.

Exercise 13: Ancient Theory of Light
page 432
Evaluation
1. S   2. D   3. D   4. D   5. D

Exercise 14: The Photoelectric Principle
pages 432–433
Evaluation
(5) The passage states that an active substance emits electrons when light falls on it. Light intensity determines the strength of the current generated by the emission of electrons. This suggests that light energy is transmitted in packets or bundles and disputes the belief that light exists only as a continuous wave.

Exercise 15: The Photoelectric Effect
page 433
Evaluation
1. Yes   2. No   3. No   4. Yes   5. Yes

Exercise 16: Properties of Light Waves
page 434
Application
1. (2) Refraction is the bending of light waves as they pass from one medium to another—in this case, from water to air.
2. (1) Reflection is the return of a light wave when it strikes a shiny surface.

Exercise 17: Wave Properties
page 435
Comprehension
(2) Polarization is the restriction of light waves to a particular plane, horizontal or vertical. In this case, the lenses are polarized vertically, restricting the penetration of the horizontally polarized light from the water and concrete surfaces.

Exercise 18: Electricity and Magnetism
pages 437–438
Analysis
1. (1) According to the information in the text, the strong magnetic attraction coming from Earth's core tends to align the compass' needle in a northerly-southerly direction.

Comprehension
2. (4) A magnetized object will attract either end of an unmagnetized object made of iron, steel, nickel, or cobalt, but will attract only the opposite pole of another magnetized object. Aluminum, brass, and tin cannot be attracted.

Exercise 19: Like and Unlike Charges
page 438
Analysis
1. (4) An electrically charged rubber rod and glass rod will attract each other because they carry opposite charges.

Evaluation
2. (3) The experiment states that the rods carry opposite charges. Therefore, they cannot carry the same charge.
3. (4) In order for fur to magnetize a rubber rod and silk to electrify a glass rod, an attractive force between the respective materials must exist.

Exercise 20: Conductors and Insulators
page 440
Application
1. I   3. C   5. I   7. C   9. C
2. I   4. C   6. I   8. I   10. I

Exercise 21: Electromagnets
page 440
Analysis
(3) The only plausible reason listed for a radio's not being placed near navigational instruments is that the radio's electromagnet would exert an attractive force on the compass of a ship or plane, thus throwing it off course. Choices (1) and (2) have nothing to do with navigational instruments. Choices (4) and (5) are neither plausible nor true.

Test 4:
Literature and the Arts

The GED Literature and the Arts Test consists of prose passages of about 200 to 400 words, poetry passages of about 8 to 25 lines, and drama excerpts. Each passage is followed by multiple-choice questions. These questions require you to interpret selections from popular literature, classical literature, and commentaries about literature and the arts. (All of these types of literature are covered in this book.) To answer successfully, you will need to

▶ understand what you read

▶ apply information to a new situation

▶ analyze elements of style and structure in passages

Actually, you already use many of these different kinds of reading and thinking skills in daily life. In this section, we will help you learn to apply these skills to literature and commentaries on the arts.

How many questions are on the test?

There are 45 multiple-choice questions, and you will be given 65 minutes to complete the test. Each passage on the literature test is preceded by a purpose question. This question is *not* a title for the passage. Rather, it is intended to help you focus your reading of the piece. To get an idea of what the test is like, look at the Practice Test at the end of this book. The Practice Test is based on the real GED Test. In fact, all of the multiple-choice questions in this section are sample GED questions.

What's on the test?

The GED Literature and the Arts Test can be broken down into the content areas it covers and the skills it tests. The following subjects make up the content of the test:

Popular Literature	50%
Classical Literature	25%
Commentaries about Literature and the Arts	25%

These content areas are covered in Chapters 1–4 of this section. There you will find selections of fiction, poetry, drama, nonfiction, and articles about literature and the arts.

Also remember that you are being tested on your ability to think through certain ideas and concepts. You will be asked to do more than just find a statement or quotation that was given in a passage.

Thinking skills that you will be tested on include:

Understanding Ideas	60%
(Literal and Inferential Comprehension)	
Applying Ideas	15%
Analyzing Ideas	25%

Chapter 1 of the Reading Skills section of this book (on pages 189–222) focuses on these thinking skills, and all of the activities and questions in this section will help you to practice answering these types of questions. If you have not already worked through the Reading Skills section, you might want to go back and complete the exercises in that section. The more practice you have had in answering the three categories of questions, the better prepared you will be to answer questions in this section and on the actual test.

1
INTERPRETING PROSE FICTION

The fiction passages presented on the Literature and the Arts Test are taken from either novels or short stories. Both novels and short stories usually present imaginary people and events that imitate life. Novels and short stories are written in *prose*—ordinary spoken language—and share common literary devices and techniques. These devices and techniques will be explored in this section.

By reading fiction, you can enjoy stories about interesting people and situations and gain a greater understanding of life. Your understanding of literature will also aid you as a moviegoer and television viewer, for many characteristics of literature can be applied to films and TV.

Although many elements in fiction are common to both the novel and the short story, there are basic differences between the two forms.

The Novel and the Short Story

The *novel* is a long, book-length story. Often, the novelist writes a story that involves several characters and events in their lives. A skillful novelist brings together characters, their adventures, and their struggles, and weaves them into one main plot.

The *short story* is also a work that deals with imaginary characters, locations, or events, but the story is much shorter than a novel. Moreover, a short story usually focuses on fewer characters and on one event. By narrowing the focus, the short-story writer achieves a single effect.

Edgar Allan Poe, one of America's earliest and best short-story writers, believed that a short story should be read in one sitting. Of course, how long that is depends upon how long you choose to sit and read, but the idea is that a short story should be read in hours, not days or weeks—the length of time it might take to read a novel.

A good short-story writer gets to the point and quickly develops believable characters and events. Like an artist who must create within the limited confines of a canvas, the writer has limited space in which to create a work of art. When you read a piece of fiction, think about its creation. Focus on how the writer expresses ideas as well as on the ideas themselves.

Although novels and short stories are developed around fictional characters, the events that occur may sometimes be based on fact. This is especially true in historical novels. For example, *Gone with the Wind*, one of the most popular novels of this century, describes events in the American Civil War. Novelist Margaret Mitchell used facts about the war, such as the battles, their locations, and the leaders of the North and South. However, Scarlett O'Hara, Rhett Butler, and the plantation home Tara were made up by Mitchell.

Basic Elements of Fiction

The basic elements of fiction are illustrated in the puzzle below. These elements and other literary terms will be explained in this section. As you progress through this section, this diagram will help you to understand the parts (elements) that make up the whole (novel or short story).

BASIC ELEMENTS OF FICTION
The Novel and Short Story

Setting
When and where the story takes place

Plot
What happens in the story

Characterization
Who is in the story

Theme
What the story means

Style and Language
What makes the writing unique

Point of View
Who tells the story

Tone
What the author's attitude is

Setting: When and Where the Story Takes Place

The *setting* of a short story or novel is the time and place in which the action occurs. Time of day or year, conditions, and atmosphere are all part of the setting. Some authors are very direct about revealing their settings. They state early in a work exactly when and where the story is happening:

- He rode into St. Louis at high noon in August 1875.

- 11:00 A.M.—San Francisco, July 1984—at Democratic Convention headquarters.

- The vehicle completed its orbit before landing on the lunar surface. It was A.D. 2021.

Inferring Time and Place

In many stories, the time and place are not directly stated. The reader needs to read between the lines, or look for clues, to identify a specific time and place.

Read the following paragraph to infer setting. Underline all the clues that suggest *time* (when the action takes place) and *location* (where the action takes place).

James saddled the pony and led the new pet around to the side of the porch. He stopped and tied the reins to the tractor so that he could attach a big red bow to the bridle.

Yesterday, he'd bought the saddle, reins and bridle, and the bow at the department store over in Helena. He'd planned well for this surprise.

The sun had barely risen when Angie, barefoot and still dressed in her nightgown, ran out of the old screen door and heard her father say, "Happy tenth birthday, honey!"

1. Does the action take place in a city or on a farm? _____

   What details act as clues? _____

2. Does the action take place in the 1860s or 1960s? _____

   What details act as clues? _____

3. Does the action take place in the early morning or the late evening? _____

   What details act as clues? _____

4. Does the action take place in Montana or in New Jersey? _____

   What details act as clues? _____

   _____

The action takes place on a farm. You can infer this from the words *tractor* and *barn*. Other helpful clues are "saddled the pony" and "over in Helena." (James had to travel to a city to buy the gifts.) Your second answer should be *1960s*. Tractors and department stores did not exist in the 1860s, so you can assume that the time is sometime during the 1900s. Your third answer should be *early morning*. You can infer time of day by these details: "The sun had barely risen" and "Angie, barefoot and still dressed in her nightgown." The location of the story is Montana; Helena is in Montana. If you had not known already that Helena is in Montana, an atlas or map of the United States could have helped you determine this.

EXERCISE 1: IDENTIFYING SETTING

Directions: Read the passage below and answer the questions that follow.

WHERE ARE YUN-JA AND CHONG-IL?

Yun-ja floated on the blue swells, her face toward the dazzling sun. At first the water had chilled her, but now it felt agreeable, almost responding to her touch. Ripples slapped about her ears, and a breeze brushed the wet tip of her nose. Sailboats eased out of the corner of her eye and into the distance. She heard the drone of powerboats, the laughter of children, and the babble of English, Spanish, and other tongues blending indistinguishably like faraway sounds in a dream. Her only reaction to all this was an occasional blink. She felt drugged by the sun.

Yun-ja straightened herself in the water and looked for Chong-il. There he was, sitting under the beach umbrella with his head tilted back, drinking something. From her distant vantage point, twenty-seven-year-old Chong-il looked as small as a Boy Scout. He reminded her of a houseboy she had seen in a photo of some American soldiers during the Korean War.

—Excerpted from "A Certain Beginning" by Kim Chi-won

1. At the beginning of the excerpt, where is Yun-ja and what is she doing?

   _____

   What details act as clues? _____

2. Yun-ja is Korean. Is she in a place frequented only by Koreans or a place popular with people from other countries?

   _____

   What details act as clues? _____

3. Where is Chong-il and what is he doing?

   _____

   What details act as clues? _____

4. Is the action taking place in the present, the distant future, or the long-ago past?

   _____

   What details act as clues? _____

5. Is the action taking place during the day or during the evening?

   _____

   What details act as clues? _____

Answers are on page 547.

Atmosphere as Part of Setting

An important part of setting is *atmosphere*—the sensations and emotions associated with details of the physical setting.

For example, if a story opens with a nighttime setting, a thunderstorm, a castle, and a man approaching the door, the author is creating an atmosphere of mystery or suspense. On the other hand, if a story opens with early morning as the setting and children playing happily in a playground, the atmosphere is different, maybe one of hope. Of course, something shocking could happen, thus changing the atmosphere of the entire story.

EXERCISE 2: ATMOSPHERE AS PART OF SETTING

Directions: Read the passage below and answer the questions that follow.

HOW DOES THIS MAN FEEL?

I've got to hide, he told himself. His chest heaved as he waited, crouching in a dark corner of the vestibule. He was tired of running and dodging. Either he had to find a place to hide, or he had to surrender. A police car swished by through the rain, its siren rising sharply. They're looking for me all over. . . . He crept to the door and squinted through the fogged plate glass. He stiffened as the siren rose and died in the distance.

Yes, he had to hide, but where?

He gritted his teeth. Then a sudden movement in the street caught his attention. . . .

—Excerpted from "The Man Who Lived Underground" by Richard Wright

1. Is the atmosphere of the passage one of fear, optimism, or happiness?

_____

2. Which details help you determine the atmosphere?

_____

_____

Answers are on page 547.

BASIC ELEMENT OF FICTION: SETTING

Time—refers to *when* actions occur, from time of day to time period in history

Place—refers to *where* actions occur, from a specific place, such as a room in a house, to a general place, such as a community, city, or country

Characterization: Who Is in the Story

Characters are the fictional people in a novel or short story. *Characterization* is the method by which a writer creates fictional people who seem lifelike and believable. Writers may use any of these different methods to create character:

- describing the character and his or her actions
- revealing the character's speech patterns
- revealing what other characters say about the character
- revealing the character's unspoken thoughts

EXERCISE 3: INFERRING CHARACTER

Directions: Read the passage below and choose the best answer to each question that follows.

WHAT KIND OF MAN IS SLIM?

A tall man stood in the doorway. He held a crushed Stetson hat under his arm while he combed his long, black, damp hair straight back. Like the others he wore blue jeans and a short denim jacket. When he had finished combing his hair he moved into the room, and he moved with a majesty only achieved by royalty and master craftsmen. He was a jerkline skinner, the prince of the ranch, capable of driving ten, sixteen, even twenty mules with a single line to the leaders. He was capable of killing a fly on the wheeler's butt with a bull whip without touching the mule. There was a gravity in his manner and a quiet so profound that all talk stopped when he spoke. His authority was so great that his word was taken on any subject, be it politics or love. This was Slim, the jerkline skinner. His hatchet face was ageless. He might have been thirty-five or fifty. His ear heard more than was said to him, and his slow speech had overtones not of thought, but of understanding beyond thought. His hands, large and lean, were as delicate in their action as those of a temple dancer.

—Excerpted from *Of Mice and Men* by John Steinbeck

1. The description that best conveys Slim's personality is

   (1) "He was a jerkline skinner."
   (2) "His hands, large and lean, were as delicate in their action as those of a temple dancer."
   (3) "His hatchet face was ageless."
   (4) "he wore blue jeans and a short denim jacket."
   (5) "His authority was so great that his word was taken on any subject."

2. In this excerpt, we learn about Slim's character primarily from

   (1) Slim's actual speech
   (2) other characters' statements about Slim
   (3) Slim's unspoken thoughts
   (4) descriptions of Slim
   (5) scenes showing Slim in action

Answers are on page 547.

Dialogue as an Element of Characterization

In the previous exercise, you learned about a character by reading an extended description of him. Another way an author reveals character is through dialogue. *Dialogue* is conversation among characters in a story. Quoting what a character says allows authors to reveal a character's attitudes, feelings, and true personality in the character's own words rather than through descriptions alone.

In novels and short stories, quotation marks are placed around each speaker's exact words. Usually an author will provide transitions like *he said* and *she replied* to indicate when a character is speaking. For example: Joan said, "Help!"

The following sentences illustrate the difference between a restatement of a person's words and a speaker's exact words:

> *Restatement:* She told me that she would call me for an appointment.

> *Exact words:* "I will call you for an appointment," she said.

In longer conversations, *he said* and *she asked* may not be used in each sentence. Notice that the speakers are identified only once in this passage:

> "May I help you?" inquired the eager car salesman.

> "I'm looking for a used car, but I can't spend much money," Jill replied.

> "I'm sure we can find something in your price range! Step over here, please. I'll show you our newer models. We have some beauties. . . ."

> "Uh, I don't have much money—only a few hundred dollars."

> "Well, . . . step this way to some of our older, economy cars."

Now read this passage, in which the speakers are not identified. Paragraph indenting and quotation marks show you when a new speaker is talking:

> "We were out at Suburban Gardens Mall last night and tried a new Oriental restaurant."

> "Really? Was it nice?"

> "Yes! It was beautiful. We sat at a hibachi table, and a chef prepared our seafood right in front of us."

> "Did the kids like it?"

> "Not at first. I had to explain to them that they couldn't order burgers after they finished their egg rolls. My kids have been to so many drive-through fast-food joints that they don't know how to act in a fancy ethnic restaurant."

Who are the two characters in this dialogue? Briefly describe each.

The two characters are probably neighbors, co-workers, or friends. They are familiar with the Suburban Gardens Mall and take their children to drive-through restaurants. Therefore, it is likely that they live in the suburbs. The references to children make it clear that both characters are parents.

EXERCISE 4: IDENTIFYING CHARACTERS THROUGH DIALOGUE

Directions: Read the passage below and answer the questions that follow.

WHO'S TALKING TO WHOM?

"Oh, the shame of it—a whole family of skinny children. And your father—he's so skinny, he's disappearing."

"Don't worry about him, Mama. Doctors are saying that skinny people live longer. Papa's going to live a long time."

"So! I knew I didn't have too many years left. Do you know how I got all this fat? Eating your leftovers. Aiaa, I'm getting so old. Soon you will have no more mother."

"Mama, you've been saying that all my life."

"This time it's true. I'm almost eighty."

"I thought you were only seventy-six."

"My papers are wrong. I'm eighty."

"But I thought your papers are wrong, and you're seventy-two, seventy-three in Chinese years."

"My papers are wrong, and I'm eighty, eighty-one in Chinese years. Seventy. Eighty. What do numbers matter? I'm dropping dead any day now. The aunt down the street was resting on her porch steps, dinner all cooked, waiting for her husband and son to come home and eat it. She closed her eyes for a moment and died. Isn't that a wonderful way to go?"

"But our family lives to be ninety-nine."

"That's your father's family. My mother and father died very young. My youngest sister was an orphan at ten. Our parents were not even fifty."

"Then you should feel grateful you've lived so many extra years."

Excerpted from *The Woman Warrior* by Maxine Hong Kingston

1. What is the relationship of the two speakers in the excerpt?

_____

2. Which character speaks first?

_____

3. Which character thinks that being skinny is healthier than being fat?

_____

4. Which character is blamed for making someone fat?

_____

5. Briefly describe what you think the two characters are like. Base your description on details included in the conversation.

_____

_____

Answers are on page 547.

BASIC ELEMENT OF FICTION: CHARACTERIZATION

You can understand what characters are like by looking for these elements:

- how characters are described
- what characters say to and about each other
- what characters think
- what characters do

Plot: What Happens in the Story

The events that occur in a story make up the *plot*. The plot events occur in some time order, or sequence.

To see how events might follow a logical sequence, arrange the plot events below in order. Place the number *1* in the blank before the first event, *2* in front of the second event, and so on. Notice the cause-and-effect relationship between events: one event leads to another, which leads to another, and so on.

_____ **a.** Then, a small crafts shop was for sale, so we decided to make our move.

_____ **b.** For years, my sisters and I discussed owning our own business.

_____ **c.** We contacted a real estate agent about purchasing the shop.

_____ **d.** With pride, we stood with our families outside of our new shop as the workmen hoisted the sign that read "Pins and Needles."

_____ **e.** First, I read articles about developing a "cottage industry" as we considered opening a store in one of our homes.

The first event, the desire to open a shop, is described in b. Sentence e follows; the sisters think about using one of their homes for a shop. Next, sentence a explains that a crafts shop went on the market. A real estate agent was then contacted (sentence c). Sentence d is the conclusion. The families see the dream come true.

Flashback as an Element of Plot

An author may choose to present events out of order, allowing the reader to piece the events together. One such popular technique is called *flashback*. For example, a novel or film may open with a voice saying, "It all began fifteen years ago when the couple met. . . ." The story then shifts to another scene, fifteen years ago. The events progress in order until, by the end of the story, the characters have returned to the time and place of the opening scene. If you have ever watched television soap operas, you have witnessed this type of scene.

Parts of a Plot

The events that make up a plot may be grouped and labeled according to their function in a story. The diagram illustrates the basic parts of a plot: exposition, conflict, climax, and resolution.

Exposition refers to background information that "sets the stage" for a story. *Conflict*, or friction between opposing characters or forces, is the basis of every plot.

Most stories and novels are centered around one of the following conflicts:

- *Individual vs. self*—inner struggles characters suffer while trying to decide what to do—change jobs, get divorced, have children, tell someone the truth about something.

- *Individual vs. another*—disagreements between characters.

- *Individual vs. society*—struggles against the rules, conventions, or pressures of living with other humans.

- *Individual vs. nature and other forces*—struggles against forces beyond a character's control, such as an earthquake or other natural disaster, or an abstraction like evil.

Another element of plot is *climax*, the point of highest intensity in the plot. The climax of a story occurs when the conflict comes to a head. For example, the climax of many westerns occurs when the hero and villain meet face-to-face in a gun duel. The climax does not always occur at the very end of the story, but it usually occurs in the last part. All of the events and conflicts involving characters must be evident before they can lead to the climax. Mystery stories have very obvious climaxes. All of the clues come together to provide the answer to "Whodunit?"

Following the climax, all of the loose ends are tied together, and readers learn the outcome of the conflict, or *resolution*. The *resolution* of the story is usually its ending.

Bear in mind that novels and stories do not have to follow the traditional plot pattern just described. For example, many stories have open endings in which conflicts are not resolved. And many stories include *subplots*—"stories within stories" that involve conflicts of their own. Nevertheless, it is helpful to know the parts of the traditional plot, because most stories include some form of exposition, conflict, climax, and resolution.

EXERCISE 5: IDENTIFYING DETAILS OF SETTING, PLOT, AND CONFLICT

Directions: Read the passage below and answer the questions that follow.

WHO ARE RALPH AND JACK AND WHAT IS HAPPENING TO THEM?

Ralph cleared his throat.

"Well then."

All at once he found he could talk fluently and explain what he had to say. He passed a hand through his fair hair and spoke.

5 "We're on an island. We've been on the mountain top and seen water all round. We saw no houses, no smoke, no footprints, no boats, no people. We're on an uninhabited island with no other people on it."

Jack broke in.

"All the same you need an army—for hunting. Hunting pigs—"

10 "Yes. There are pigs on the island."

All three of them tried to convey the sense of the pink live thing struggling in the creepers.

"We saw—"

"Squealing—"

15 "It broke away—"

"Before I could kill it—but—next time!"

Jack slammed his knife into a trunk and looked round challengingly.

The meeting settled down again.

"So you see," said Ralph, "we need hunters to get us meat. And another
20 thing."

He lifted the shell on his knees and looked round the sun-slashed faces.

"There aren't any grownups. We shall have to look after ourselves."

The meeting hummed and was silent.

—Excerpted from *Lord of the Flies* by William Golding

1. Which line supports the fact that the plot involves children?

_____

2. Which lines establish the location?

_____

3. What was the "pink live thing struggling in the creepers"?

_____

4. Who is leading the meeting?

_____

5. Name at least two conflicts that are evident here.

_____

_____

6. Put the plot events below in the order in which they happen by writing the number *1* for the event that happened first, *2* for the event that occurred second, and so on.

_____ Jack thrusts his knife into a tree trunk.

_____ Three boys tell of the "pink live thing."

_____ Ralph begins the meeting by telling the boys where they are.

_____ The boys react to the fact that they're without adults.

_____ Ralph states that there are pigs (food) on the island.

Answers are on page 547.

BASIC ELEMENT OF FICTION: PLOT
Traditional plots follow this pattern and sequence:

1. **exposition**, or background information
2. **conflict**, or friction between opposing forces
3. **climax**, or point of highest tension
4. **resolution**, or the outcome of the conflict

WRITING ACTIVITY 1

Lord of the Flies is a novel about British school boys stranded on an island after a plane crash. No adults survive, so the boys are on their own. Golding presents the negative side of human nature, and the novel concerns evil overcoming good. Even without reading the book, you can probably predict some of the conflicts, or problems, that might arise in this situation.

First, list three problems facing the marooned boys. Then resolve the conflicts by writing one paragraph for each problem, suggesting possible solutions.

Point of View: Who Tells the Story

When you read fiction, ask yourself, Through whose eyes, or *point of view*, is the story being told? An author can choose from a variety of ways to tell a story. For example, if you were to write a story about a basketball game, you might choose from the following points of view:

1. *The coach's*—"The fourth quarter began. My team was twelve points down. I had to make a decision—fast!"

2. *The fan's*—"Here I paid big bucks for these tickets, and my team is getting killed! I should have known. . . .''

3. *The guard of the team that's leading*—"Twelve points. We're in good shape! I'll just work the ball around a bit, kill time, and wait for the best shots."

4. *A player sitting on the bench*—"Boy, if I could just convince Coach to let me in. Just once, I'd like to turn a game around. Just once, I'd like to be a hero."

The point of view from which a story is told is important because the reader has to identify with, or "get into the skin of," the character. For this reason, most authors tell their story through the eyes of the **main character**—the character whom the action affects most. Only the thoughts of the main character are revealed when the author chooses this point of view.

A writer, having decided who is to tell, or **narrate**, the story, may relate the events in first person or third person. In **first-person narration**, the word *I* is used, and the narrator speaks directly to the reader. The four points of view above are first-person narration. In his famous novel *The Adventures of Huckleberry Finn*, Mark Twain created Huck Finn as the narrator to tell the story. Huck is the main character, and the story is told through his eyes, using the first-person *I* method.

In **third-person narration**, the story is told by an "outsider"—someone who is not involved in the action—and the main character is referred to as *he* or *she*. There are several different approaches to the third-person point of view, depending on how much the author wants readers—and the main character—to know.

The passage on page 466 is from an Ernest Hemingway short story, "The Short Happy Life of Francis Macomber." In the passage, Macomber hunts and shoots a lion, and Hemingway captures the moment by describing the hunter's activities and the lion's thoughts as the animal is shot. You can tell that the story is told in the third person, because Hemingway uses *he* to refer to both Macomber and the lion. However, the story is unusual in that Hemingway tells us what the lion, rather than the hunter, is thinking.

EXERCISE 6: DETERMINING POINT OF VIEW

Directions: Underline each noun (e.g., *Macomber*) or pronoun (e.g., *he, his,* or *them*) that represents a person or people. Circle each noun or pronoun that refers to the lion. The first three are done for you.

HOW DOES THE LION FEEL?

Macomber stepped out of the curved opening at the side of the front seat, onto the step and down onto the ground. The lion still stood looking majestically and coolly toward this object that his eyes only showed in silhouette, bulging like some super-rhino. There was no man smell carried toward him and he watched the object [jeep], moving his great head a little from side to side. Then watching the object, not afraid, but hesitating before going down the bank to drink with such a thing opposite him, he saw a man figure detach itself from it and he turned his heavy head and swung away toward the cover of the trees as he heard a cracking crash and felt the slam of a .30–06 220-grain solid bullet that bit his flank and ripped in sudden hot scalding nausea through his stomach. He trotted, heavy, big-footed, swinging wounded full-bellied, through the trees toward the tall grass and cover, and the crash came again to go past him ripping the air apart. Then it crashed again and he felt the blow as it hit his lower ribs and ripped on through, blood sudden hot and frothy in his mouth, and he galloped toward the high grass where he could crouch and not be seen and make them bring the crashing thing close enough so he could make a rush and get the man that held it.

Answers are on page 547.

BASIC ELEMENT OF FICTION: POINT OF VIEW

First-person narration—a speaker identified as *I* talks directly to readers
Third-person narration—an unidentified outsider refers to characters as *he* and *she.*

WRITING ACTIVITY 2

Choose one of the four points of view described in the example of the basketball game on page 465. Write a paragraph to finish the story. If you prefer, choose a different point of view for the game. Become the referee, the spouse or child of a player, a sportswriter, even the basketball court, backboard, or ball! Use *I* and write in dialogue what the narrator would see, feel, and think.

Theme: What the Story Means

Behind all of the action in a story or movie is the writer's or director's purpose. The creator of a work wants it to have meaning for the audience. The main idea, or theme, may be an insight into life, a viewpoint about a social issue, a new view of an old problem, or positive or negative looks into human nature.

In successfully written fiction, as in effective films, the theme is rarely stated directly. Instead, it is implied or suggested. The reader or viewer is expected to interpret the meaning from all elements presented.

For example, since the early 1950s, many science fiction writers and film-makers have given us stories about aliens landing on our planet. A typical plot involves the aliens trying to take over Earth. One human being usually leads a rebellion against them. The theme is fear of the unknown.

BASIC ELEMENT OF FICTION: THEME
- The main idea, or central meaning, of a story
- Often involves an insight into people's lives, or human nature

---

EXERCISE 7: INFERRING THEME

Directions: Read the passage below and choose the best answer to each question that follows.

WHAT CONCERNS MISS STRANGEWORTH?

After thinking for a minute, she decided that she would like to write another letter, perhaps to go to Mrs. Harper, to follow up the ones she had already mailed. She selected a green sheet this time and wrote quickly: HAVE YOU FOUND OUT YET WHAT THEY WERE ALL LAUGHING ABOUT AFTER YOU LEFT THE BRIDGE CLUB ON THURSDAY? OR IS THE WIFE REALLY ALWAYS THE LAST ONE TO KNOW?

Miss Strangeworth never concerned herself with facts; her letters all dealt with the more negotiable stuff of suspicion. Mr. Lewis would never have imagined for a minute that his grandson might be lifting petty cash from the store register if he had not had one of Miss Strangeworth's letters. Miss Chandler, the librarian, and Linda Stewart's parents would have gone unsuspectingly ahead with their lives, never aware of possible evil lurking nearby, if Miss Strangeworth had not sent letters opening their eyes. Miss Strangeworth would have been genuinely shocked if there *had* been anything between Linda Stewart and the Harris boy, but as long as evil existed unchecked in the world, it was Miss Strangeworth's duty to keep her town alert to it.

—Excerpted from "The Possibility of Evil" by Shirley Jackson

1. The plot concerns Miss Strangeworth's

   (1) preventing others from hearing damaging rumors
   (2) blackmailing others for money
   (3) caring about those around her
   (4) suspecting her husband and Linda Stewart
   (5) sending anonymous warnings to others

2. The conflict of this passage is Miss Strangeworth vs.

   (1) nature
   (2) Mrs. Harper
   (3) herself
   (4) society
   (5) imaginary evil

3. The theme of the passage is best stated in which of these ways?

   (1) It is a citizen's duty to judge the behavior of others.
   (2) What people don't know won't hurt them.
   (3) Regardless of their intentions, some people create pain for others.
   (4) Knowing all the facts is not important when making accusations.
   (5) One should not join organizations if one has something to hide.

Answers are on page 548.

EXERCISE 8: REVIEW OF FIVE FICTION ELEMENTS

Directions: Read the passage below and answer the questions that follow.

HOW DOES IVAN ILYCH FEEL?

Ivan Ilych saw that he was dying, and he was in continual despair.

In the depth of his heart he knew he was dying, but not only was he not accustomed to the thought, he simply did not and could not grasp it. . . .

He could not understand it, and tried to drive this false, incorrect, morbid thought away and to replace it by other proper and healthy thoughts. But that thought, and not the thought only but the reality itself, seemed to come and confront him.

And to replace that thought he called up a succession of others, hoping to find in them some support. He tried to get back into the former current of thoughts that had once screened the thought of death from him. But strange to say, all that had formerly shut off, hidden, and destroyed his consciousness of death no longer had that effect. Ivan Ilych now spent most of his time in attempting to re-establish that old current. He would say to himself: "I will take up my duties again—after all I used to live by them." And banishing all doubts he would go to the law courts, enter into conversation with his colleagues, and sit carelessly as was his wont, scanning the crowd with a thoughtful look and leaning both his emaciated arms on the arms of his oak chair; bending over as usual to a colleague and drawing his papers nearer he would interchange whispers with him, and then suddenly raising his eyes and sitting erect would pronounce certain words and open the proceedings. But suddenly in the midst of those proceedings the pain in his side, regardless of the stage the proceedings had reached, would begin its own gnawing work. Ivan Ilych would turn his attention to it and try to drive the thought of it away, but without success. *It* would come and stand before him and look at him, and he would be petrified and the light would die out from his eyes, and he would begin to ask himself whether *It* alone was true. And his colleagues and subordinates would see with surprise and distress that he, the brilliant and subtle judge, was becoming confused and making mistakes.

—Excerpted from "The Death of Ivan Ilych" by Leo Tolstoy

1. The major conflict developed in the passage is Ivan Ilych's struggle to

(1) restore his health
(2) regain his old job as a judge
(3) come to terms with death
(4) win an important legal case
(5) overcome mental illness

2. The story is told in which of the following points of view?

(1) first person, by Ivan Ilych himself
(2) first person, by Ivan Ilych's colleagues and subordinates
(3) first person, by Leo Tolstoy, the author
(4) third person, by an unnamed outsider
(5) third person, by Ivan Ilych's physician

3. The author develops the character of Ivan Ilych mainly by

(1) revealing what Ilych says to other people
(2) disclosing what Ilych secretly thinks
(3) showing how Ilych interacts with other characters
(4) describing what Ilych looks like
(5) summarizing what other characters think of Ilych

4. Which of the following statements best sums up the theme of the passage?

(1) One cannot comprehend his or her impending death.
(2) People can overcome their fear of death by concentrating on their work.
(3) A positive mental outlook can help a person cope with a terminal illness.
(4) One must expect seriously ill people to become confused and make mistakes.
(5) Healthy people do not understand what it is like to be seriously ill.

5. The setting for the action in the last paragraph is

(1) a crowded courtroom
(2) the waiting room of a doctor's office
(3) the lobby of a medical building
(4) a private room in a hospital
(5) an ambulance's interior

Answers are on page 548.

Tone and Style

Tone: What the Author's Attitude Is

The *tone* of a novel or short story is the overall attitude that an author conveys toward his or her subject. When listening to a person speak, you can infer the person's attitude by the sound of his or her voice. The tone tells you whether the person means to be sarcastic or serious or funny. When reading, you must infer the author's tone.

An author's choice of words and phrasing reflects his or her attitude. What tone is presented in the paragraph below? Write a few words that describe the tone of this passage.

Our first-born son, "Matt the Mouth," was a wild, oversized, constantly hungry toddler. As he grew, he seemed to dwarf all other children around him. His first word was *cake*, and his first step was taken toward the refrigerator! How that kid loved to eat!

You might have written *funny, humorous, comical, light, nostalgic,* or *mocking*. The author is a parent looking back on a son whose eating habits were memorable. The tone is not one of sadness or resentment, but one of fond yet humorous memories of "Matt the Mouth."

> **BASIC ELEMENT OF FICTION: TONE**
> To determine the tone of a passage, ask yourself the following questions:
> • What subject is the author describing?
> • How does the author feel about the subject?
> • What language or descriptive details reveal the author's attitude?

EXERCISE 9: TONE AND CHARACTERIZATION

Directions: Read the passage below and answer the questions that follow.

WHAT IS THE AUTHOR'S TONE?

Her doctor had told Julian's mother that she must lose twenty pounds on account of her blood pressure, so on Wednesday nights Julian had to take her downtown on the bus for a reducing class at the Y. The reducing class was designed for working girls over fifty, who weighed 165 to 200 pounds. His mother was one of the slimmer ones, but she said ladies did not tell their age or weight. She would not ride the buses by herself at night since they had been integrated, and because the reducing class was one of her few pleasures, necessary for her health, and *free*, she said Julian could at least put himself out to take her, considering all she did for him. Julian did not like to consider all she did for him, but every Wednesday night he braced himself and took her.

—Excerpted from "Everything That Rises Must Converge"
by Flannery O'Connor

1. Julian's mother may best be described as a woman who

    (1) subscribes to old-fashioned values and beliefs
    (2) is easy to please
    (3) takes advantage of every opportunity to improve herself
    (4) believes in the equality of all people
    (5) is without an identity of her own

2. "[S]he said Julian could at least put himself out to take her [to her class], considering all she did for him. Julian did not like to consider all she did for him, but every Wednesday night he braced himself and took her." If the author read these lines, how would her voice sound?

    (1) gentle and tolerant
    (2) angry and bitter
    (3) tragic and depressed
    (4) sarcastic and funny
    (5) sweet and resigned

3. The author's attitude is most likely that people like Julian's mother are

    (1) to be laughed at or ridiculed
    (2) to be respected for their high ideals
    (3) to be tolerated and sympathized with
    (4) absolutely wrong in their outlook on life
    (5) morally superior to all other people

Answers are on page 548.

Style and Language: What Makes the Writing Unique

A writer of fiction is a craftsperson. The tools of the trade are words. The effectiveness and success of a piece of literature depend upon the quality of words the writer uses.

Style refers to the author's unique use of the language—the choice and arrangement of words. An author's style may contain long, complex sentences, it may contain everyday spoken language, or it may contain dialect.

Which of the following statements do you consider to be more formal?

a. Joan said she would drop by after she got a bite to eat.
b. Joan stated that she would visit us after her lunch.

Sentence b is stated formally. Sentence a presents the same information worded casually.

Dialect as an Element of Style

Dialect is the pattern of speech characteristic to a certain region. In the United States, we can sometimes tell if people are from the Deep South or New England just by their accents. Regional expressions, word choices, and pronunciations contribute to dialect.

Writers of fiction may have their characters speak in dialects. Mark Twain, for instance, used dialect throughout *The Adventures of Huckleberry Finn* to make the characters more real and believable. Below are two examples of how the dialect of an area and time period are used in novels. The first example is from Nathaniel Hawthorne's *The Scarlet Letter*. The characters are Puritans living around Boston in the 1600s:

> "Pearl! Little Pearl!" cried he, after a moment's pause; then, suppressing his voice, "Hester! Hester Prynne! Are you there?"
>
> "Yes; it is Hester Prynne!" she replied, in a tone of surprise; and the minister heard her footsteps approaching from the sidewalk, along which she had been passing, "It is I, and my little Pearl."
>
> "Whence come you, Hester?" asked the minister. "What sent you hither?"
>
> "I have been watching at a deathbed," answered Hester Prynne—"at Governor Winthrop's deathbed, and have taken his measure for a robe, and am now going homeward to my dwelling."

Notice words such as *whence* ("from where") and *hither* ("here").

The next passage is from Zora Neale Hurston's 1937 novel *Their Eyes Were Watching God*. It is written in a dialect that was spoken by some rural southern African-Americans of the time. As the novel opens, a group of neighbors are gossiping about Janie, a woman who has just returned to the neighborhood she moved away from some time before.

> "What she doin' coming back here in dem overhalls? Can't she find no dress to put on?—Where's dat blue satin dress she left here in?—Where all dat money her husband took and died and left her?—What dat ole forty year ole 'oman doin' wid her hair swingin' down her bak lak some young gal?—Where she left dat young lad of a boy she went off here wid?"

Types of Styles

Authors who publish many works often become known and appreciated for their styles as well as their themes and characters. Hemingway, for example, was trained in writing as a newspaper reporter. He is known for a terse writing style because his ideas are expressed in few words.

On the other hand, Charles Dickens is known for a narrative style characterized by long sentences and vivid descriptions. Edgar Allan Poe used short sentences; the repetition of words; and many dashes, exclamation points, and italics to add emotion and suspense to his stories. He opens "The Tell-Tale Heart" with:

"True!—nervous—very, very dreadfully nervous I had been and am! but why *will* you say that I am mad?"

In her novel *The Bell Jar*, Sylvia Plath, who was known primarily as a poet, used poetic style and images that appealed to the senses. The following exercise is an example of that style.

EXERCISE 10: IDENTIFYING AN AUTHOR'S STYLE

Directions: Read the passage below. Underline all descriptions and images that appeal to your senses: sight, smell, taste, touch, and especially hearing.

WHAT IMAGES DOES THE WRITER CALL TO MIND?

The soprano screak of carriage wheels punished my ear. Sun, seeping through the blinds, filled the bedroom with a sulphurous light. I didn't know how long I had slept, but I felt one big twitch of exhaustion.

The twin bed next to mine was empty and unmade.

At seven I had heard my mother get up, slip into her clothes and tiptoe out of the room. Then the buzz of the orange squeezer sounded from downstairs, and the smell of coffee and bacon filtered under my door. Then the sink water ran from the tap and dishes clinked as my mother dried them and put them back in the cupboard.

Then the front door opened and shut. Then the car door opened and shut, and the motor went broom-broom and, edging off with a crunch of gravel, faded into the distance.

Answers are on page 548.

WRITING ACTIVITY 3

Rewrite one of the dialect passages on page 471. For *The Scarlet Letter* passage, rewrite the speeches in present-day English. For the passage from *Their Eyes Were Watching God*, change the dialect into modern written English, formalizing the grammar.

Descriptive Language as an Element of Style

Look again at the passage in Exercise 10. Did the screak of wheels actually "punish" the narrator's ear? Was the bed really "unmade"—an unassembled frame and pieces of lumber? When you say you're going to "make" your bed, do you mean you're going to build a bed, using wood, hammer, and nails? Of course not! You mean you're going to rearrange the pillow, blankets, and bedspread to make the bed look neat and tidy. *Figures of speech* like these are not meant to be taken literally. They are expressive ways of describing.

EXERCISE 11: DESCRIPTIVE LANGUAGE

Directions: Match the expression on the left with its meaning on the right by writing the appropriate letter in the space provided.

_____ **1.** She tried to *iron out* her problems.

a. exhausted

_____ **2.** I've complained until I'm *blue in the face*, but no one seems to care.

b. extremely quick

_____ **3.** I still have a lot of packing to do, but I think I'm finally *on top of it!*

c. in control of the situation

_____ **4.** The running back is *like greased lightning.*

d. solve

Answers are on page 548.

Figures of Speech as an Element of Style

You hear figures of speech in spoken English every day. In fiction writing, figurative language is used to create vivid pictures and original descriptions.

There are many kinds of figures of speech. In literature, especially in poetry, you can find specific figures of speech called *similes, metaphors,* and *personification.* A brief explanation of each will help you recognize the use of this type of descriptive language.

A *simile* (sim'-ih-lee) is a comparison that shows a likeness between two unlike things. A simile is introduced by the words *like, than,* or *as.*

Her hair was like woven straw.   She is colder than ice.

Bill is as strong as an ox.

A *metaphor* (met'-uh-for) is a comparison that does not contain *like, than,* or *as.* A metaphor implies that one thing is something else.

The path was a ribbon of moonlight.   All the world is a stage.

Personification (per-sahn-ih-fih-kay'-shun) attributes some human activity or quality to an animal or thing.

The sun smiled down on me.   The leaves awoke and greeted the season.

EXERCISE 12: IDENTIFYING FIGURES OF SPEECH

Directions: As you read the passage below, underline similes, metaphors, and examples of personification. Then choose the best answer to each question that follows the passage.

WHO IS GRANDMA KIRK AND WHAT IS SHE LIKE?

Grandma Kirk was a whisper of a woman—four feet eleven and weighing only ninety pounds—but the strength and determination with which she attacked chickens were admirable (and comical).

5 She would casually approach the chicken-yard like a fox moving in for the kill. Swooping down on a trusting, unsuspecting hen, Grandma would become a cyclone. With two or three crafty twists of her wrist, she would break the hen's neck and would nimbly thrust her prey over a chopping stump for the beheading.

Her ax, a bloody character that seemed to lie in wait for hens, would sever 10 the head. As the hen's body departed from its head, Grandma's strength would give way, and the headless chicken would be released to dance around the yard like a savage in an ancient tribal rite.

Unnerved, Grandma would chase the unruly dancing corpse, grab it, and thrust it into a tub of boiling water. She would then patiently pluck, feather by 15 feather, until the naked bird was ready for roasting pan and family feast.

I think of my grandmother's effort, time, and spirit each time I shop at the local suburban supermarket with its plastic-wrapped parcel of fowl labeled "Combo-Pak." My microwave oven lazily sits waiting for the quick preparation, brief cooking process, and "instant" meal. My family thinks every chicken is 20 equipped with three breasts, four thighs, six legs, and organs wrapped in white paper.

1. "Grandma Kirk was a whisper of a woman" refers to her

    (1) sneaky approach
    (2) quiet manner
    (3) small stature
    (4) pride
    (5) speech pattern

2. The sentence "Her ax, a bloody character that seemed to lie in wait for hens, would sever the head" (lines 9–10) creates an image that makes the ax seem

    (1) old
    (2) rusted
    (3) bent
    (4) alive
    (5) useless

3. The tone of this passage is one of

    (1) nostalgia
    (2) distaste
    (3) suspicion
    (4) dread
    (5) mystery

4. The narrator is contrasting Grandma Kirk's killing chickens with

    (1) fox hunting in the wild
    (2) a cyclone's destruction of a village
    (3) modern shopping and cooking practices
    (4) primitive ritual tribal dances
    (5) chopping wood for the winter

5. With which of the following statements would the author of the passage be the most likely to agree?

    (1) In general, food is tastier today than it was a few generations ago.
    (2) Grandma Kirk was a brutal person.
    (3) Supermarkets and microwaves are unnecessary conveniences.
    (4) Years ago, women were not allowed to do physical labor.
    (5) Life today is much easier than it was in our grandparents' day.

Answers are on page 548.

How to Read Fiction on Your Own

You have learned about the basic elements of fiction illustrated in the puzzle on page 454. In both the novel and the short story, the elements contribute to the whole. While your examination of each element of fiction contributes to your understanding, it is the *whole*, not its *parts*, that creates a work of art. Use the tips that follow to guide your reading of literature.

TIPS ON READING FICTION

As you read a story, ask yourself:

- What is the setting?
- What is the atmosphere?
- Who are the characters?
- Are they named or described?
- What is the plot?
- What is the conflict?
- From whose point of view is the story told?
- What are clues to the theme?
- What is the author's style like?
- What is the author's tone?

EXERCISE 13: INTERPRETING A SHORT STORY

Directions: A complete short story (much longer than the passages on the GED Test) follows. Read the story and answer the questions that follow.

WHAT IS THE AUTHOR SAYING ABOUT WAR?

The long June twilight faded into night. Dublin lay enveloped in darkness, but for the dim light of the moon, that shone through fleecy clouds, casting a pale light as of approaching dawn over the streets and the dark waters of the Liffey. Around the beleaguered Four Courts the heavy guns roared. Here and
5   there through the city machine guns and rifles broke the silence of the night, spasmodically, like dogs barking on lone farms. Republicans and Free Staters were waging civil war.

On a rooftop near O'Connell Bridge, a Republican sniper lay watching. Beside him lay his rifle and over his shoulders were slung a pair of field-
10   glasses. His face was the face of a student—thin and ascetic, but his eyes had the cold gleam of the fanatic. They were deep and thoughtful, the eyes of a man who is used to looking at death.

He was eating a sandwich hungrily. He had eaten nothing since morning. He had been too excited to eat. He finished the sandwich, and taking a flask
15   of whiskey from his pocket, he took a short draught. Then he returned the flask to his pocket. He paused for a moment, considering whether he should risk a smoke. It was dangerous. The flash might be seen in the darkness and there were enemies watching. He decided to take the risk. Placing a cigarette between his lips, he struck a match, inhaled the smoke hurriedly and put out
20   the light. Almost immediately, a bullet flattened itself against the parapet of the roof. The sniper took another whiff and put out the cigarette. Then he swore softly and crawled away to the left.

Cautiously he raised himself and peered over the parapet. There was a flash and a bullet whizzed over his head. He dropped immediately. He had
25   seen the flash. It came from the opposite side of the street.

He rolled over the roof to a chimney stack in the rear, and slowly drew himself up behind it, until his eyes were level with the top of the parapet. There was nothing to be seen—just the dim outline of the opposite housetop against the blue sky. His enemy was under cover.

30   Just then an armoured car came across the bridge and advanced slowly up the street. It stopped on the opposite side of the street fifty yards ahead. The sniper could hear the dull panting of the motor. His heart beat faster. It was an enemy car. He wanted to fire, but he knew it was useless. His bullets would never pierce the steel that covered the grey monster.

35   Then round the corner of a side street came an old woman, her head covered by a tattered shawl. She began to talk to the man in the turret of the car. She was pointing to the roof where the sniper lay. An informer.

The turret opened. A man's head and shoulders appeared, looking towards the sniper. The sniper raised his rifle and fired. The head fell heavily on
40   the turret wall. The woman darted toward the side street. The sniper fired again. The woman whirled round and fell with a shriek into the gutter.

Suddenly from the opposite roof a shot rang out and the sniper dropped his rifle with a curse. The rifle clattered to the roof. The sniper thought the noise would wake the dead. He stooped to pick the rifle up. He couldn't lift it.
45 His forearm was dead. "I'm hit," he muttered.

Dropping flat on to the roof, he crawled back to the parapet. With his left hand he felt the injured right forearm. The blood was oozing through the sleeve of his coat. There was no pain—just a deadened sensation, as if the arm had been cut off.

50 Quickly he drew his knife from his pocket, opened it on the breastwork of the parapet and ripped open the sleeve. There was a small hole where the bullet had entered. On the other side there was no hole. The bullet had lodged in the bone. It must have fractured it. He bent the arm below the wound. The arm bent back easily. He ground his teeth to overcome the pain.

55 Then, taking out his field dressing, he ripped open the packet with his knife. He broke the neck of the iodine bottle and let the bitter fluid drip into the wound. A paroxysm of pain swept through him. He placed the cotton wadding over the wound and wrapped the dressing over it. He tied the end with his teeth.

60 Then he lay still against the parapet, and closing his eyes, he made an effort of will to overcome the pain.

In the street beneath all was still. The armoured car had retired speedily over the bridge, with the machine gunner's head hanging lifeless over the turret. The woman's corpse lay still in the gutter.

65 The sniper lay for a long time nursing his wounded arm and planning escape. Morning must not find him wounded on the roof. The enemy on the opposite roof covered his escape. He must kill that enemy and he could not use his rifle. He had only a revolver to do it. Then he thought of a plan.

Taking off his cap, he placed it over the muzzle of his rifle. Then he
70 pushed the rifle slowly upwards over the parapet, until the cap was visible from the opposite side of the street. Almost immediately there was a report, and a bullet pierced the center of the cap. The sniper slanted the rifle forward. The cap slipped down into the street. Then, catching the rifle in the middle, the sniper dropped his left hand over the roof and let it hang, lifelessly. After
75 a few moments he let the rifle drop to the street. Then he sank to the roof, dragging his hand with him.

Crawling quickly to the left, he peered up at the corner of the roof. His ruse had succeeded. The other sniper, seeing the cap and rifle fall, thought that he had killed his man. He was now standing before a row of chimney
80 pots, looking across, with his head clearly silhouetted against the western sky.

The Republican sniper smiled and lifted his revolver above the edge of the parapet. The distance was about fifty yards—a hard shot in the dim light, and his right arm was paining him like a thousand devils. He took a steady aim. His
85 hand trembled with eagerness. Pressing his lips together, he took a deep breath through his nostrils and fired. He was almost deafened with the report and his arm shook with the recoil.

Then, when the smoke cleared, he peered across and uttered a cry of joy. His enemy had been hit. He was reeling over the parapet in his death agony.
90 He struggled to keep his feet, but he was slowly falling forward, as if in a dream. The rifle fell from his grasp, hit the parapet, fell over, bounded off the pole of a barber's shop beneath and then cluttered on to the pavement.

Then the dying man on the roof crumpled up and fell forward. The body turned over and over in space and hit the ground with a dull thud. Then it lay
95 still.

The sniper looked at his enemy falling and he shuddered. The lust of battle died in him. He became bitten by remorse. The sweat stood out in beads on his forehead. Weakened by his wound and the long summer day of fasting and watching on the roof, he revolted from the sight of the shattered
100 mass of his dead enemy. His teeth chattered. He began to gibber to himself, cursing the war, cursing himself, cursing everybody.

He looked at the smoking revolver in his hand and with an oath he hurled it to the roof at his feet. The revolver went off with the concussion, and the bullet whizzed past the sniper's head. He was frightened back to his senses by
105 the shock. His nerves steadied. The cloud of fear scattered from his mind and he laughed.

Taking the whiskey flask from his pocket, he emptied it at a draught. He felt reckless under the influence of the spirits. He decided to leave the roof and look for his company commander to report. Everywhere around was
110 quiet. There was not much danger in going through the streets. He picked up his revolver and put it in his pocket. Then he crawled down through the skylight to the house underneath.

When the sniper reached the laneway on the street level, he felt a sudden curiosity as to the identity of the enemy sniper whom he had killed. He
115 decided that he was a good shot whoever he was. He wondered if he knew him. Perhaps he had been in his own company before the split in the army. He decided to risk going over to have a look at him. He peered around the corner into O'Connell Street. In the upper part of the street there was heavy firing, but around here all was quiet.

120 The sniper darted across the street. A machine gun tore up the ground around him with a hail of bullets, but he escaped. He threw himself face downwards beside the corpse. The machine gun stopped.

Then the sniper turned over the dead body and looked into his brother's face.

—"The Sniper" by Liam O'Flaherty

1. Underline the seven words and phrases below that correctly describe the setting and background for "The Sniper."

rooftop, August, civil war, Dublin, Paris, rural hillside, noon, Ireland, June, city, night, World War II

2. Which word below best describes the overall atmosphere of "The Sniper"?

(1) thrilling **(2)** nostalgic **(3)** lighthearted **(4)** depressing **(5)** tense

3. Match the description on the left with the character on the right. One choice on the right will be used twice.

_____ **(1)** "whirled round and fell with a shriek into the gutter"

_____ **(2)** "The head fell heavily on the turret wall."

_____ **(3)** "seeing the cap and rifle fall, thought that he had killed his man"

_____ **(4)** "paused for a moment, considering whether he should risk a smoke"

a. the sniper

b. the enemy

c. the informer

4. Arrange these events in the order in which they happen in the story by writing *1* in the space before the event that occurred first, *2* before the event that occurred second, and so on.

_____ **a.** The sniper is shot in the arm by his enemy.

_____ **b.** The sniper shoots an old woman, an informer.

_____ **c.** The sniper turns over his victim.

_____ **d.** The sniper drinks whiskey and leaves the roof.

_____ **e.** The sniper eats a sandwich.

5. Does the author reveal all of his characters' thoughts or just the sniper's?

Why? _____

6. Is the point of view first-person narration or third-person narration?

_____

7. The tone of the story may best be described as

(1) matter-of-fact
(2) lighthearted
(3) exaggerated
(4) disrespectful
(5) sarcastic

8. In the spaces below, write *s* if the figure of speech is a simile, *m* if it is a metaphor, or *p* if it represents personification. (See pages 473–474 for definitions of *simile*, *metaphor*, and *personification*.)

_____ **1.** "like dogs barking on lone farms"

_____ **2.** "the steel that covered the grey monster"

_____ **3.** "dull panting of the motor"

_____ **4.** "Morning must not find him"

_____ **5.** "like a thousand devils"

9. Figures of speech such as "grey monster" (line 34) and "like a thousand devils" (line 84) reveal the author's attitude toward

   (1) guns
   (2) soldiers
   (3) brothers
   (4) war
   (5) informers

10. The climax of the plot occurs when the sniper

   (1) sees the armoured car leave
   (2) shoots the old woman
   (3) shoots the enemy on the roof
   (4) climbs down from the roof
   (5) turns over his brother

11. The excerpt "he revolted from the sight of the shattered mass of his dead enemy. His teeth chattered. He began to gibber to himself, cursing the war, cursing himself, cursing everybody" (lines 99–101) illustrates the conflict between the sniper and

   (1) the old woman
   (2) the enemy
   (3) the Republican Army
   (4) himself
   (5) nature

12. The description "The lust of battle died in him. He became bitten by remorse" (lines 96–97) reveal that the

   (1) sniper thinks the enemy may be his brother
   (2) sniper feels guilty about killing his enemy
   (3) sniper fears that he will be shot by another enemy
   (4) sniper could now leave the rooftop
   (5) enemy deserved his fate

13. What is the theme of "The Sniper"?

   (1) A good soldier never feels guilty about killing.
   (2) A sniper must be ready to die for his country.
   (3) The character of a sniper is different from that of other soldiers.
   (4) A civil war is the worst kind of war.
   (5) War often brings out the negative side of human nature.

Answers are on page 549.

WRITING ACTIVITY 4

Choose two of the topics below and write a paragraph on each.

1. What did the sniper do next? Write one more paragraph that could be added to the story.

2. The author was seriously wounded in World War I. How do you think that affected his attitude toward war and influenced his writing? Write a paragraph that expresses your opinion.

3. Write a short story from the enemy's point of view. (Use *I*—first-person narration.) Give your reactions to the sniper's killing of the old woman, the trick used by the sniper, and other major events in the plot.

About Prose Fiction: Commentary

You have learned techniques to help you approach and analyze literature in order to gain an understanding of what you read. You have read samples of fiction and answered questions in order to test your ability to interpret prose fiction.

Sometimes, however, it is useful to read literary criticism *about* fiction. **Criticism** is the art of evaluating and analyzing a work of art or literature. A **critic** is a person who expresses an opinion about or who comments on a work of art or literature. Critics are also known as **reviewers**, persons who review works of literature or art.

Writers of literary criticism analyze a particular work by discussing the elements introduced earlier in this section—setting, plot, characterization, theme, tone, and style and language. Critics read works of fiction, poetry, drama, and nonfiction. They ask such questions as "How did the author create the story?" and "Was the author successful in achieving her goal?"

A critic may write general commentary about fiction and nonfiction in a newspaper or magazine column that appears regularly. A critic may also write reviews of movies, television programs, theater performances, art exhibits, live or recorded musical performances, or dance.

Nearly one-fourth of the questions on the Literature and the Arts Test will deal with commentary. **Commentary** is writing *about* literature and the arts—published comments, reviews, and criticism. You will study commentary in greater depth in the nonfiction section of this book.

EXERCISE 14: COMMENTARY ABOUT FICTION

Directions: Below is a review of a novel. The review is brief and, as many book reviews do, tells a little about the author and his or her career, major events in the plot of the book, and the reviewer's opinion of the book. Read the review and answer the questions that follow.

History Repeats Itself
by Anne Whitehouse
A Review of *The Last Room* by Elean Thomas
Virago/Trafalgar Square, paper, $13.95

The Last Room, the Jamaican writer Elean Thomas's first novel, is about two generations of mothers and daughters. Valerie Barton, nicknamed Putus ("meaning sweet and special"), is the only child and bright hope of her parents. As her mother says, "You wi be the one who bruk dem slavery chain fi-ever." But Putus's father dies, her mother remarries, and the girl is sent away. Befriended by an older man, she becomes pregnant. Young and naive, she does not realize at first that her condition means the death of her hopes. History repeats itself when Putus leaves her own daughter, Icylane, behind in Jamaica to join a man in England whom she will marry. Eighteen years pass. The story continues through Icy, now a civil servant, who goes to England to seek out the mother who abandoned her and who is said to be ill. Throughout the novel, Ms. Thomas makes generous use of dialect, and a glossary of Jamaican terms is provided. Her storytelling only falters with the somewhat disconcerting break between the stories of Putus and Icy; one wants to follow Putus's life as a young woman instead of returning to her decades later, when she has only the remnants of her anger and pride. Nevertheless, *The Last Room* is an affecting novel about hope and disillusionment, expectation and failure.

1. What is the reviewer's opinion of the story?

   (1) Its dialect is confusing.
   (2) The focus should be on Putus.
   (3) Icy is the book's best character.
   (4) The characters should remain in Jamaica.
   (5) The story falters because it's set in England.

2. Which statement best sums up the reviewer's opinion of the author?

   (1) She is a good storyteller.
   (2) She is a beginning writer.
   (3) Her writing is confusing.
   (4) She doesn't know Jamaica.
   (5) She doesn't know England.

3. Which of the following categories does *The Last Room* most likely fall into?

   (1) humorous writing
   (2) detective-mystery
   (3) science fiction
   (4) real-life drama
   (5) light romance

Answers are on page 549.

2
INTERPRETING POETRY

Poetry expresses ideas and emotions in a tightly controlled and structured way. Simply put, poetry is the best words in their best order.

Poetry is compressed. *Imagery* (word pictures that appeal to the five senses) and figures of speech enable the poet to convey ideas in just a few words.

Some poems are written in rhyme, the repetition of a sound at the end of two or more words, like *say* and *hay*. Sound and rhythm, the "beat," arouse feelings and evoke thoughts. All of these characteristics of poetry make it a distinct form of literature.

This chapter will help you to read and appreciate poetry. You will read many poems and examine their use of language, shape, sound, and meaning.

On the Literature and the Arts Test, you will be expected to demonstrate your understanding of a poem's meaning. You should be able to read a poem, spend a few minutes interpreting it, and answer the questions about the theme.

Interpreting Two Poems

The following poems are about human relationships. The first poem is nostalgic—the poet is remembering. The second poem is highly emotional. It is a sonnet, a structured poem that expresses a single emotion or idea.

EXERCISE 1: INTERPRETING TWO POEMS
Directions: Read each poem aloud and answer the questions that follow.

WHAT ARE THE POETS SAYING AND HOW ARE THEY SAYING IT?

Oh, When I Was in Love with You

Oh, when I was in love with you,
    Then I was clean and brave,
And miles around the wonder grew
    How well did I behave.

And now the fancy passes by,
    And nothing will remain,
And miles around they'll say that I
    Am quite myself again.

            —A. E. Housman

Sonnet 43

How do I love thee? Let me count the ways.
I love thee to the depth and breadth and height
My soul can reach, when feeling out of sight
For the ends of Being and ideal Grace.
I love thee to the level of every day's
Most quiet need, by sun and candlelight.
I love thee freely, as men strive for Right;
I love thee purely, as they turn from Praise.
I love thee with the passion put to use
In my old griefs, and with my childhood's faith.
I love thee with a love I seemed to lose
With my lost saints—I love thee with the breath,
Smiles, tears, of all my life!—and, if God choose,
I shall but love thee better after death.

—Elizabeth Barrett Browning

1. The theme of both poems involves

    (1) separation
    (2) love that is not returned
    (3) beauty
    (4) romantic love
    (5) love for one's fellow human being

2. A technique common to both poems is the use of

    (1) personification
    (2) imagery
    (3) rhyme
    (4) simile
    (5) metaphor

Answers are on page 549.

Poems as Riddles

In some ways, reading a poem is much like solving a riddle. The following poem presents a riddle to solve. Read the poem and answer the questions that follow.

Southbound on the Freeway

A tourist came in from Orbitville,
parked in the air, and said:

The creatures of this star
are made of metal and glass.

Through the transparent parts
you can see their guts.

Their feet are round and roll
on diagrams—or long

measuring tapes—dark
with white lines.

They have four eyes.
The two in the back are red.

Sometimes you can see a 5-eyed
one, with a red eye turning

on the top of his head.
He must be special—

the others respect him,
and go slow,

when he passes, winding
among them from behind.

They all hiss as they glide,
like inches, down the marked

tapes. Those soft shapes,
shadowy inside

the hard bodies—are they
their guts or their brains?

—May Swenson

1. Who is the tourist? (Two clues are "from Orbitville" and "parked in the air.")

_____

2. Who are the "creatures of this star"?

_____

3. What are their "feet"?

_____

4. What are "measuring tapes"?

_____

5. Who is the "5-eyed / one, with a red eye"?

_____

6. What observation does the visitor make about this "5-eyed" creature?

_____

7. What are the "soft shapes, / shadowy inside / the hard bodies"?

_____

Were you able to solve the riddle? Did you imagine a UFO looking down at the "creatures of this star"? The creatures are cars; their feet are tires; the measuring tapes are the roads. The five-eyed one is a police car. The tourist observes how the other cars behave when a police car is in traffic: "the others respect him, / and go slow, / when he passes, winding / among them from behind."

The poem captures a certain point of view that is much different from that of a driver in a car. You can now imagine what it must be like to see our driving habits from the viewpoint of someone looking down. If you have ever seen traffic out of an airplane window, then you have a better idea of this viewpoint.

TIPS ON READING POETRY

1. Read the title as a clue to the meaning.

2. Read the whole poem to get the general ideas and mood.

3. Ask yourself, What is this about? What is the poet saying? What does the poem mean? What is the theme?

4. Reread the poem using the punctuation as a guide. (Stop where there's a period or other end mark, not at the end of a line.)

5. Notice how lines are grouped together and if lines are repeated. What is the poet stressing by repeating words and lines?

6. Notice the language used and unusual word choices, comparisons, imagery, and figures of speech.

7. Read the poem aloud so you can hear it, especially if words rhyme.

8. Summarize in your own words what the poem is saying to understand the poem's tone and theme.

The Shape of Poetry

The structure and form of poetry distinguish it from other types of literature. Many poets choose a highly structured format, in which they shape their ideas using rhyme, rhythm, and stanzas. A *stanza* is a group of lines that work together to express an idea. Just as a new paragraph signals that a new idea is beginning in an article, so a new stanza signals that a new idea is being introduced in a poem. Often, stanzas are separated by a blank space.

The following poem by Dorothy Parker contains two stanzas:

On Being a Woman

stanza 1
> Why is it, when I am in Rome,
> I'd give an eye to be at home
> But when on native earth I be,
>   My soul is sick for Italy?

stanza 2
> And why with you, my love, my lord,
>   Am I spectacularly bored,
> Yet do you up and leave me—then
> I scream to have you back again?

When you sing a song, you may sing a verse, a chorus, the second verse, the same chorus, the third verse, a chorus, etc. A *verse* is any piece of poetry that is arranged in a pattern. Many songs were poems before they were set to music. An example is "The Battle Hymn of the Republic," by Julia Ward Howe.

The term *free verse* refers to verses without a regular rhythmic pattern and usually without rhyme. Much of today's poetry is free verse. Most of the poems in this section are written in free verse.

Capitalization and Punctuation

In poetry, a comma or a dash means "pause." A period means "stop." If the poem contains capitalization and punctuation, it should be read in sentences, not just one line at a time. Sometimes the reader may have to run two or more lines together. For example, in the poem "History," which follows, lines 2–4 are read "morning sunlight lengthened in spears across the linoleum floor."

The use of capital letters in poetry can vary. Sometimes a poet capitalizes each line. Sometimes a poet capitalizes a word for emphasis. Refer to the poems in this section to see how each poet uses capitalization and punctuation.

EXERCISE 2: THE SHAPE OF POETRY

Directions: Read aloud the poem below and answer the questions that follow. Notice the capitalization and punctuation as you read.

HISTORY

Grandma lit the stove.
Morning sunlight
Lengthened in spears
Across the linoleum floor.
Wrapped in a shawl,
Her eyes small
With sleep,
She sliced papas,
Pounded chiles
With a stone
Brought from Guadalajara.

After
Grandpa left for work,
She hosed down
The walk her sons paved
And in the shade
Of a chinaberry,
Unearthed her
Secret cigar box
Of bright coins
And bills, counted them
In English,
Then in Spanish,
And buried them elsewhere.
Later, back
From the market,
Where no one saw her,
She pulled out
Pepper and beet, spines
Of asparagus
From her blouse,
Tiny chocolates
From under a paisley bandana,
And smiled.

That was the '50s,
And Grandma in her 50s,
A face streaked
From cutting grapes
And boxing plums.
I remember her insides
Were washed of tapeworm,
Her arms swelled into knobs
Of small growths—
Her second son
Dropped from a ladder
And was dust.
And yet I do not know
The sorrows
That sent her praying
In the dark of a closet,
The tear that fell
At night
When she touched
Loose skin
Of belly and breasts.
I do not know why
Her face shines
Or what goes beyond this shine,
Only the stories
That pulled her
From Taxco to San Joaquin,
Delano to Westside,
The places
In which we all begin.

—Gary Soto

1. There are eleven lines in the first stanza. How many *sentences* are there? (Notice periods.)

_____

2. List at least three details from the third stanza that describe Grandma's earlier years:

(1) _____

(2) _____

(3) _____

3. In which stanza is she happier? Give the clue word that indicates this mood.

_____

4. Who is the narrator in this poem?

_____

5. What work did Grandma do? List two clues.

_____

Answers are on page 549.

The Sound of Poetry

Poets rely on many devices to communicate their messages to readers. Three common poetic devices are rhyme, rhythm, and alliteration.

Babies and toddlers may be introduced to the literature of their native language through nursery rhymes. **Rhyme** is the repetition, in two or more words, of the stressed vowel sound and of the syllables that follow that sound.

Hickory-dickory-*dock*, the mouse ran up the *clock*.

Jack and *Jill* went up the *hill*.

Some of the poems in this section rhyme: "Sonnet 43," page 484; "Oh, When I Was in Love with You," page 483; "maggie and milly and molly and may," page 489; "Memory," page 493; "Design," pages 496–497. Refer to these poems to see the use of rhyme. Read the poems aloud if necessary.

Just as word choices produce a desired effect in poetry, so does the beat, or rhythm, of a poem. In poetry, **rhythm** is the rise and fall of stressed words and syllables. If the rhythm is regular, or ordered strictly, the poem is said to have **meter**.

The repetition of consonant sounds, usually at the beginning of words, is **alliteration**. "Peter Piper picked a peck of pickled peppers" is an example of alliteration. Nursery rhymes contain much alliteration, and advertising slogans and jingles incorporate this technique frequently.

E. E. Cummings was a poet known for experimenting with the structure of poems. Cummings seldom used traditional capitalization and punctuation in his poetry. In addition, some of his poems present unique syllable divisions. Cummings creatively used language as he explored new forms for poetry. An example of his poetry is in Exercise 3.

EXERCISE 3: THE SOUND OF POETRY

Directions: The poem below presents insights into the characters of four girls. Read the poem and answer the questions that follow. Notice (1) the absence of capitalization in names, (2) the rhythm, (3) alliteration of the letters *s*, *b*, and *m.*

maggie and milly and molly and may

maggie and milly and molly and may
went down to the beach (to play one day)

and maggie discovered a shell that sang
so sweetly she couldn't remember her troubles, and

5 milly befriended a stranded star
whose rays five languid fingers were;

and molly was chased by a horrible thing
which raced sideways while blowing bubbles: and

may came home with a smooth round stone
10 as small as a world and as large as alone.

For whatever we lose (like a you or a me)
it's always ourselves we find in the sea

1. List at least three different examples of alliteration:

   (1) _____

   (2) _____

   (3) _____

2. Cummings uses rhyme in this poem. In lines 5–6 *star* and *were* do not rhyme perfectly, but they do share a similar sound. Which pairs of lines do not rhyme at all?

   _____

3. From a quick reading, you might say that the poem is not structured. Yet there is alliteration, two-line stanzas, rhyme, and rhythm. Read the poem aloud. How many "beats" per line do you hear?

   _____

4. Lines 11–12, which read "For whatever we lose (like a you or a me) / it's always ourselves we find in the sea," contain the theme of the poem. In these lines, the author is expressing which of the following ideas?

   (1) The sea is a source of life and death.
   (2) The sea is the best place for a person to reflect about life.
   (3) Everybody does not have the same respect for the sea.
   (4) The sea and its surroundings can give people a fresh view on life.
   (5) The sea represents all of our moods.

Answers are on page 549.

Words That Stand for Sounds

Most poetry is written to be read aloud. As the poet writes the words, he or she is aware of the sound of the poem. Many poets use "sound words" to enhance the imagery and message of their poetry. The term **onomatopoeia** (ahn'-uh-mah'-tuh-pee'-uh) refers to the use of words whose sounds imitate their meanings. Sound-imitating words include *buzz, screech, boom,* and *crash. Whisper* is also a sound word.

Carl Sandburg wrote the following poem in 1920. Notice the poet's use of the sound words to describe jazz—a new music at the time. Jazz originated in New Orleans, and Sandburg makes reference to its birthplace by mentioning the Mississippi River in the fourth stanza. Notice how the "mood" of the poem changes as does the mood of a jazz tune. Count the number of times you see a word beginning with the letter *s*. Sandburg uses the sounds "s" and "sh" throughout his poem.

EXERCISE 4: WORDS THAT STAND FOR SOUNDS

Directions: Read aloud the poem below and answer the questions that follow.

WHAT JAZZ SOUNDS CAN YOU HEAR?

Jazz Fantasia

Drum on your drums, batter on your banjos, sob on the long cool winding saxophones. Go to it, O jazzmen.

Sling your knuckles on the bottoms of the happy tin pans, let your trombones ooze, and go husha-husha-hush with the slippery sandpaper.

Moan like an autumn wind high in the lonesome treetops, moan soft like you wanted somebody terrible, cry like a racing car slipping away from a motorcycle-cop bang-bang! you jazzmen, bang altogether drums, traps, banjos, horns, tin cans—make two people fight on the top of a stairway and scratch each other's eyes in a clinch tumbling down the stairs.

Can the rough stuff. . . . Now a Mississippi steamboat pushes up the night river with a hoo-hoo-hoo-oo . . . and the green lanterns calling to the high soft white stars . . . a red moon rides on the humps of the low river hills. . . . Go to it, O jazzmen.

1. Sandburg uses alliteration to establish a rhythm in the first stanza. Which words illustrate alliteration?

   (1) *long* and *cool*
   (2) *sob* and *winding*
   (3) *to* and *it*
   (4) *O* and *jazzmen*
   (5) *batter* and *banjos*

2. One descriptive device that Sandburg uses in the third stanza is both a simile *and* an example of personification. Which of the following descriptions represents both of these?

   (1) "high in the lonesome treetops"
   (2) "like a racing car slipping away from a motorcycle-cop"
   (3) "Moan like an autumn wind"
   (4) "make two people fight on the top of a stairway"
   (5) "bang altogether drums, traps, banjos, horns, tin cans"

3. The fiction passage most similar in technique to "Jazz Fantasia" would be the excerpt from

(1) "The Man Who Lived Underground"
(2) *Of Mice and Men*
(3) "The Possibility of Evil"
(4) *The Bell Jar*
(5) *Lord of the Flies*

Answers are on page 550.

Interpreting Meaning

When you interpret a poem, you rephrase it, putting the poem into your own thoughts and words. You may simply change words around to make a statement more understandable to you. You may guess at the poet's main purpose and ask yourself, "Why is the poet using this comparison?" or "Why does the poet say this?"

Read the following poem, "My Papa's Waltz," by Theodore Roethke. Then read it again, a stanza at a time. On the lines provided next to each stanza, write a sentence or two summarizing the stanza in your own words. After you write *your* interpretation, read the interpretation provided at the end of the poem. You may agree with the interpretation, or you may not. Remember, there is no single correct interpretation.

My Papa's Waltz   **Interpretation**

The whisky on your breath
Could make a small boy dizzy;
But I hung on like death:
Such waltzing was not easy.

We romped until the pans
Slid from the kitchen shelf;
My mother's countenance
Could not unfrown itself.

The hand that held my wrist
Was battered on one knuckle;
At every step you missed
My right ear scraped a buckle.

You beat time on my head
With a palm caked hard by dirt,
Then waltzed me off to bed
Still clinging to your shirt.

Interpretation of stanza 1:   A man is remembering his father. His father must have been drinking before he began dancing with his son.

Interpretation of stanza 2:   The son remembers dancing wildly around the kitchen while his mother watched disapprovingly.

Interpretation of stanza 3:   The son remembers being tall enough to notice the battered knuckle of his father and to remember the pain of his ear scraping against his father's belt buckle each time his father stumbled.

Interpretation of stanza 4:   His father was dirty from working hard; his hands were still dirty as they danced. The son held on to his father as they waltzed.

This poem might be interpreted in different ways. Use the answers above as guidelines for checking your own.

EXERCISE 5: INFERRING MEANING

Directions: In the blanks below the poem, indicate the line numbers and key words that support the inferences. The first one has been done for you.

Strength

```
     That strong right hand that
     once balanced our
     young sons near the sky,
     once tossed bales of
5    straw each August,
     once pitched no-hitters
     after Sunday picnics,
     once tenderly stroked
     my once-auburn hair . . .
10   That hand
     now crudely arches to grasp
     a bamboo cane and
     now trembles as you reverently
     bow your feeble body in prayer
15   and give thanks for the years
     of that strong right hand.
```

Inferences	Line numbers	Key words
1. The man is a father.	2,3	our young sons
2. The man prays.		
3. The man was a farmer.		
4. The man is now elderly.		
5. The man was athletic.		

Answers are on page 550.

Inferring Mood

Mood is very important in poetry. When a poet creates a poem, the words chosen help present an overall feeling. The mood may be humorous and light, or it may be somber and serious. Underline the word below that best describes the mood of the poem "My Papa's Waltz," on page 491.

brooding   ecstatic   affectionate   light-hearted

You probably underlined *brooding* since the writer was brooding over the fear of waltzing with his father.

Within a poem, the mood sometimes changes. Read the following song from the musical *Cats*. As you read, identify the mood of each part. Circle the word that most accurately describes the mood of the lines.

Memory

Midnight, not a sound from the pavement.
Has the moon lost her memory?
She is smiling alone.
In the lamp light the withered leaves
        collect at my feet
And the wind begins to moan.

1. (a) optimistic
(b) lonely
(c) eager

_____

Memory. All alone in the moonlight
I can smile at the old days.
I was beautiful then.
I remember the time
        I knew what happiness was,
Let the memory live again. . . .

2. (a) nostalgic
(b) humorous
(c) afraid

_____

Daylight. I must wait for the sunrise
I must think of a new life
And I mustn't give in.
When the dawn comes
        tonight will be a memory, too
And a new day will begin. . . .

3. (a) depressed
(b) sarcastic
(c) hopeful

_____

Touch me. It's so easy to leave me
All alone with the memory
Of my days in the sun.
If you touch me you'll understand
        what happiness is.
Look, a new day has begun.

4. (a) regretful
(b) content
(c) confused

_____

The first part of the song refers to the moon smiling alone and the wind moaning. The word *lonely* (b) most accurately describes the mood. For 2, you should have chosen (a), *nostalgic*, because the cat is smiling and remembering. For the third part, *hopeful* (c) describes the cat anticipating daylight and a new day. The last part sounds final. A new day has begun. *Content* (b) describes the mood. Of course, other word choices that weren't given above may apply, but you should see four different moods in this song.

EXERCISE 6: INTERPRETING A POEM

Directions: Circle the number of the choice that best answers each question.

WHO IS THE NARRATOR OF THE POEM?

The Negro Speaks of Rivers

I've known rivers:
I've known rivers ancient as the world and
    older than the flow of human blood in
    human veins.

My soul has grown deep like the rivers.

I bathed in the Euphrates when dawns
    were young.
I built my hut near the Congo and it lulled
    me to sleep.
I looked upon the Nile and raised the
    pyramids above it.
I heard the singing of the Mississippi when
    Abe Lincoln went down to New Orleans,
    and I've seen its muddy bosom turn all
    golden in the sunset.
I've known rivers:
Ancient, dusky rivers.

My soul has grown deep like the rivers.

—Langston Hughes

1. "My soul" in the poem refers to the soul of

   (1) the poet himself
   (2) the rivers
   (3) all people of African descent
   (4) Abe Lincoln
   (5) all people

2. The mood of the lines "I heard the singing of the Mississippi when / Abe Lincoln went down to New Orleans, / and I've seen its muddy bosom turn all / golden in the sunset" is one of

   (1) awe
   (2) fear
   (3) dread
   (4) joy
   (5) sorrow

3. Throughout the poem, the poet refers to rivers. He does this to

   (1) emphasize the beauty of rivers
   (2) show rivers as ever-present in African-American history
   (3) share his love for rivers
   (4) give the poem a feeling of tranquillity
   (5) tell why his soul is like a river

Answers are on page 550.

The Language of Poetry

You were introduced to descriptive language in the fiction section of this book. While figures of speech contribute greatly to style in short stories and novels, poetry relies even more heavily on this special language. This is because of the compression of ideas that a poem requires. In this section, you will review some of the devices introduced in the fiction section and analyze how they are used in poems to arouse the mind and emotions.

Imagery

When you use your imagination, you are forming *images*, or pictures, in your mind. A poet relies on readers' ability to create pictures in their minds from the words on a page. For this reason, the poet must choose the perfect word to convey a thought. When a poem appeals to your senses and enables you to imagine a scene, the poem is rich in *imagery*. The following line is an example of imagery:

The noisy raindrops hit the car's hood like thousands of thumbtacks.

Can you "see" the raindrops and "hear" the metallic sound made as they hit the car's hood?

Personification

Recall that *personification* is a form of imagery in which human activities or qualities are attributed to an animal or a thing. In other words, a nonhuman thing comes "alive" as it is given human abilities.

Carl Sandburg used personification to immortalize a city in his famous poem "Chicago." Notice that he addresses the city as a person. Here are the opening lines:

Chicago
Hog Butcher for the World,
Tool Maker, Stacker of Wheat,
Player with Railroads and the Nation's Freight Handler;
Stormy, husky, brawling,
City of the Big Shoulders:

The names he calls the city in the first three lines refer to commerce and industry Chicago was known for. Chicago is personified—made human—when the poet calls it by name.

In the following poem, underline all examples of personification. In what ways is the town human?

Steel Town

August skies accept
your belch of refuse
and ashes are excreted
high above new grass that
timidly borders
your concrete veins,
pulsating to sustain the hectic tempo
of days that too soon expire.
Your structure ages, breathing lessens,
and you remain
a body
with no soul.

You should have underlined the following words as examples of personification: *belch, excreted, timidly, veins, pulsating, expire, ages, breathing,* and *body with no soul.* The poet writes as if the town possesses the human abilities to live and die.

EXERCISE 7: THE LANGUAGE OF POETRY

Directions: Write *imagery* if a line evokes an image or *personification* if it attributes a human quality to an inanimate object.

Line 1: Midnight, not a sound from the pavement.   _____

Line 2: Has the moon lost her memory?   _____

Line 3: She [the moon] is smiling alone.   _____

Line 4: In the lamp light the withered leaves collect at my feet   _____

Line 5: And the wind begins to moan.   _____

Answers are on page 550.

Simile and Metaphor

As described in the fiction section, a *simile* is a comparison of two unlike things. A simile includes the word *like, than,* or *as.* Poet Robert Frost uses similes in the following poem, "Design." Underline the four similes.

Design

I found a dimpled spider, fat and white,
On a white heal-all,[1] holding up a moth
Like a white piece of rigid satin cloth—
Assorted characters of death and blight
Mixed ready to begin the morning right,
Like the ingredients of a witches' broth—
A snow-drop spider, a flower like a froth,

[1]A *heal-all* is a type of plant.

And dead wings carried like a paper kite.
What had that flower to do with being white,
The wayside blue and innocent heal-all?
What brought the kindred spider to that height,
Then steered the white moth thither in the night?
What but design of darkness to appall?—
If design govern in a thing so small.

You should have underlined these similes: "a moth / Like a white piece of rigid satin cloth"; "Like the ingredients of a witches' broth"; "a flower like a froth"; and "dead wings carried like a paper kite."

Recall that a **metaphor** is an implied or suggested comparison between two things. A metaphor does not contain *like, than,* or *as.* With a metaphor, one thing *is* the second thing to which it is being compared.

The day was an unwritten journal page waiting to be filled.

This metaphor presents an image of a blank paper—the day—ready for activities. The day *is* an unwritten journal page.

In this opening stanza of "An Indian Summer Day on the Prairie," by Vachel Lindsay, there are three metaphors. What three comparisons are made?

The sun is a huntress young,
The sun is a red, red joy,
The sun is an Indian girl,
Of the tribe of the Illinois.

The poet compares the sun to a huntress, joy, and an Indian girl. The reader gets a different image of the sun and an idea of the prairie setting.

Note the comparison made in this opening stanza of "Dreams" by Langston Hughes:

Hold fast to dreams
For if dreams die
Life is a broken-winged bird
That cannot fly.

The metaphor of "Life is a broken-winged bird" draws an unusual but very vivid image.

EXERCISE 8: REVIEW OF FIGURATIVE LANGUAGE AND THEME

Directions: Read the poem and answer the questions that follow.

HOW DOES THE SPEAKER VALUE BEAUTY?

Barter

Life has loveliness to sell,
    All beautiful and splendid things,
Blue waves whitened on a cliff,
    Soaring fire that sways and sings,
And children's faces looking up,
Holding wonder like a cup.

Life has loveliness to sell,
    Music like a curve of gold,
Scent of pine trees in the rain,
    Eyes that love you, arms that hold,
And for your spirit's still delight,
Holy thoughts that star the night.

Spend all you have for loveliness,
    Buy it and never count the cost;
For one white singing hour of peace
    Count many a year of strife well lost,
And for a breath of ecstasy
Give all you have been, or could be.

—Sara Teasdale

1. Which of the following lines from the poem is a simile?

   (1) "Life has loveliness to sell"
   (2) "Soaring fire that sways and sings"
   (3) "Holding wonder like a cup"
   (4) "Eyes that love you, arms that hold"
   (5) "Buy it and never count the cost"

2. What does the poet compare music to?

   (1) the scent of pine trees
   (2) the rain
   (3) eyes that love
   (4) arms that hold
   (5) a curve of gold

3. Which of the following lines from the poem is a metaphor?

   (1) "All beautiful and splendid things"
   (2) "Blue waves whitened on a cliff"
   (3) "Spend all you have for loveliness"
   (4) "Holy thoughts that star the night"
   (5) "Count many a year of strife well lost"

Answers are on page 550.

EXERCISE 9: INTERPRETING A POEM

Directions: Read the poem below and answer the questions that follow.

WHAT IS SILVER IN THE POEM?

Wind and Silver

Greatly shining,
The Autumn moon floats in the thin sky;
And the fish-ponds shake their backs and flash their dragon scales
As she passes over them.

—Amy Lowell

1. The fish-ponds are personified. What living creature are the ponds
compared to?

_____

2. There is a second instance of personification in the poem. What object is
compared to a woman?

_____

Answers are on page 550.

EXERCISE 10: PRACTICE IN INTERPRETING A POEM

Directions: Read the following poem and answer the questions that follow.

WHAT IS THE POET SAYING ABOUT DEATH?

Because I Could Not Stop for Death

Because I could not stop for Death,
He kindly stopped for me;
The carriage held but just ourselves
And Immortality.

We slowly drove, he knew no haste,
And I had put away
My labor, and my leisure too,
For his civility.

We passed the school where children played
At wrestling in a ring;
We passed the fields of gazing grain,
We passed the setting sun.

We paused before a house that seemed
A swelling of the ground;
The roof was scarcely visible,
The cornice but a mound.

Since then 'tis centuries; but each
Feels shorter than the day
I first surmised the horses' heads
Were toward eternity.

—Emily Dickinson

1. Match the stanza on the left with the images on the right by writing the correct letter in the space provided.

_____	Stanza 1	**a.**	images of a school yard, farm, land, dusk
_____	Stanza 2	**b.**	the narrator riding in a carriage with two others
_____	Stanza 3	**c.**	a slow ride as the narrator accepts her fate
_____	Stanza 4	**d.**	the narrator remembering the day of the carriage ride, hundreds of years before
_____	Stanza 5	**e.**	the carriage pausing at a gravesite

2. The poet capitalizes the words *Death* and *Immortality* to illustrate that

   (1) death is a major theme
   (2) they are the chief concerns of a person's life
   (3) they are characters in the poem
   (4) the two words are opponents, one fighting the other
   (5) they are two unexplainable concepts that people must deal with

3. The lines that begin the poem, "Because I could not stop for Death,/ He kindly stopped for me . . ."

   (1) prove that Death is of the male gender
   (2) give human qualities to an abstract state
   (3) show that Death can be postponed if one puts up a fight
   (4) indicate that the suffering poet was relieved of her pain
   (5) imply that the writer of the poem is a woman

4. The title and lines 1–2 imply that the speaker of the poem

   (1) was very ill
   (2) drove the carriage
   (3) stopped at a school yard
   (4) fought death to the last
   (5) died unexpectedly

5. From the last stanza, one can infer that the speaker in the poem

   (1) knows when she is going to die
   (2) feels time moves too slowly
   (3) never looks back at the past
   (4) enjoys carriage rides
   (5) believes in eternal life

Answers are on page 550.

EXERCISE 11: MORE PRACTICE IN INTERPRETING A POEM

Directions: Read the following poem and choose the best answer to each question that follows.

WHO IS THE MAN FROM WASHINGTON AND WHAT IS THE POET SAYING ABOUT HIM?

The Man from Washington

The end came easy for most of us.
Packed away in our crude beginnings
in some far corner of a flat world,
we didn't expect much more
than firewood and buffalo robes
to keep us warm. The man came down,
a slouching dwarf with rainwater eyes,
and spoke to us. He promised
that life would go on as usual,
that treaties would be signed, and everyone—
man, woman, and child—would be innoculated
against a world in which we had no part,
a world of wealth, promise, and fabulous disease.

—James Welch

1. The speaker of the poem is a

    (1) man from Washington
    (2) politician
    (3) white settler
    (4) Native American
    (5) slave

2. The mood of this poem could best be described as one of

    (1) alienation
    (2) hopefulness
    (3) anticipation
    (4) fear
    (5) nostalgia

3. The theme that is reflected in this poem is the

    (1) welcoming of the Puritans by Native Americans
    (2) signing of the treaties between the U.S. government and Native Americans
    (3) mass execution of soldiers in Custer's Last Stand
    (4) destruction of the Native Americans' way of life
    (5) slaughter of the buffalo

Answers are on page 550.

About Poetry: Commentary

On the Literature and the Arts Test, you may be expected to read and answer questions about a review or criticism of poetry.

Below is a sample review of a poetry collection. The review is written by a literary critic whose purpose is to evaluate a volume of poetry. You might see a review of poetry in a literary magazine or the literature section of a news magazine or newspaper.

WHAT IS THE CRITIC'S OPINION?

Whispered Secrets by Ann Fox Chandonnet, Denise Lassaw, Eleanor Limmer, and Joanne Townsend
Sedna Press, $10
Reviewed by Stephen C. Levi

Whispered Secrets was a book long in coming and well worth the wait. In fact, it is unexpectedly refreshing. Allow this reviewer to explain. Sedna Press, as the foreword explains, takes its name from the Eskimo goddess Sedna whose father severed her fingers and then allowed her to sink into the sea. There she created all of the marine life on which the Eskimos lived as well as all storms at sea. She was thus both creator and destroyer.

With such a publishing imprint and four women poets, I was prepared for another manhating, how-I-hurt collection of poetry by bitter women. I was pleasantly surprised. As a unit, the poems form a spear of opinion thrusting forward with a single theme: a woman's personal ownership of herself achieved through self-knowledge and coming to terms with herself and her surroundings. More basically put, the poems carry the message that wealth of spirit comes from knowledge of oneself and understanding that the slings and arrows of outrageous fortune are often gifts which make us stronger.

Further, the four women present their point of view separately. Each poet adds her own special direction of philosophical travel yet, at the same time, collimates [runs parallel] with the bent of the other three. In the end, the collection holds together well and delivers the message clearly.

EXERCISE 12: COMMENTARY ON POETRY

Directions: Choose the best answer for each of the questions.

1. Which of the following statements would the reviewer agree with?

   (1) Women's poetry is almost always objective.
   (2) Hardships can help us face up to our lives.
   (3) Publishers need to have interesting imprints.
   (4) Women poets should always write in groups.
   (5) The goddess Sedna is not a subject for a poem.

2. The reviewer states, "*Whispered Secrets* was a book long in coming and well worth the wait." What is another way of saying the same thing?

   (1) The time put into the book shows in the excellence of the writing.
   (2) The writers took much too long to write the book.
   (3) Readers had to wait a long time to read the book.
   (4) The book would be better if it had come out earlier.
   (5) Waiting for the book made people expect too much.

Answers are on page 551.

3
INTERPRETING DRAMA

Around 1950, the television entered the American living room; as a result, life in America has never been the same. The average American watches several hours of television each day, from movies to soap operas to sitcoms (situation comedies). Turn on your TV at this moment, and on at least one channel you will see drama.

What Is Drama?

Drama is the form of literature designed to be performed in the theater by actors taking on the roles of characters. In many cases, drama closely imitates life because the actors confront real-life situations and come to grips with real-life problems. As you study this chapter, do not think of drama as an unfamiliar form of literature and art. Think of how much you already know about drama from life and from TV.

The requirements for interpreting drama on the GED Test are similar to the requirements for interpreting prose fiction and poetry. For example, on the test, you may be asked to read an excerpt from a play and interpret the meaning or tone of the character's speech.

It is not difficult to read a play, even if you are not accustomed to reading drama. However, as you read a play, you must be able to "see" the action. You must use your imagination and picture the action taking place. You need to read carefully to infer setting, characterization, and theme, just as you do when you read prose and poetry.

Read the following exchange of conversation (dialogue) and try to visualize the action. The words in parentheses—stage directions—are not meant to be read aloud. They are directions to the actors and explanations of "what's happening" as the actors speak.

WHAT DO YOU *HEAR*? WHAT DO YOU *SEE*?

[*The scene begins in a community college parking lot. Glen parks his car as Rob walks by.*]

GLEN: [*Locking his car and putting his keys in his pocket*] Hi! [*Waving to Rob*] Well, this is it, huh?

ROB: Yeah, why else would I be up at 7:30 on a Saturday morning?

GLEN: [*As he joins Rob to walk up the hill to the administration building*] I've done all the right things. I went to bed at ten o'clock, ate a good breakfast, and got here a little early. Now all I have to do is pass this test!

ROB: Not me, man. I partied until one o'clock. I'm too nervous to eat, and I don't think I'm gonna pass. I decided to come anyway, try the test, and see what happens. [*He opens the door for Glen as they enter the building.*] Let's grab a cup of coffee and try to relax. We have a little while before checking in.

503

GLEN: [*Shaking his head*] Y'know, I've waited ten years to come back to school. [*Getting coffee and sitting down.*] I went to most of the classes, did some studying at home, and finally got enough nerve to register for this test. I just can't believe that by the end of the day I could have earned my GED certificate.

ROB: [*Raising his coffee cup in a toast*] Cheers! Good luck!

GLEN: [*Toasting*] Same to you. See you in real estate class this summer, huh?

ROB: [*Rising from his chair*] Yeah, let's go get 'em. [*They walk toward the testing area.*]

What happened in the scene between Rob and Glen? Could you picture the setting, the two men, and the general theme of this scene? To check your understanding, fill in the blanks with the appropriate words.

Glen and Rob are arriving at a _____ to take their

_____ . _____ is well prepared for the test,

while _____ is less confident. They decide to have

_____ and try to _____ before checking in.

They wish each other _____ and plan to see each other in

_____ . _____ has a better chance of passing

the test.

You could have filled the blanks with these answers: community college, GED Tests, Glen, Rob, coffee, relax, luck, real estate class or the summer, Glen. Most of these answers are stated directly in the reading. If you answered that Glen had a better chance of passing, you *inferred* this information from the fact that Rob had attended a party until one o'clock and Glen had taken his studying very seriously.

If you can imagine where the characters would be taking the test, how they would feel and act, and what the achievement means to them, you can relate to the situation.

How Drama Differs from Other Forms of Literature

Although drama has much in common with the two other forms of literature you have studied—poetry and fiction—each of the three forms of literature treats its subject differently. Illustrated below are differences in the way each form of literature treats the same subject—a marriage proposal.

Prose: The young couple, John and Mary, went for a midnight boat ride on the Mississippi River. John gave Mary a diamond ring, and she accepted his proposal of marriage.

Poetry:	Lovers in the moonlight Aboard the Delta Miss Exchanged a ring and promises And sealed them with a kiss.
Drama:	[*John and Mary board the* Delta Miss *for a midnight cruise.*]
JOHN:	[*Embracing Mary*] I love you. [*He gives her a package.*]
MARY:	[*Surprised*] What's this?
JOHN:	It's a symbol of our future together—if you agree to marry me next month.
MARY:	[*Opening the package and seeing a diamond ring*] Oh, John!
JOHN:	[*Slipping the ring on her finger*] Don't ever take it off.
MARY:	No . . . [*flustered*] I mean yes! I mean *no* I won't take it off . . . *Yes*, I'll marry you. [*They kiss.*]

EXERCISE 1: HOW DRAMA DIFFERS

Directions: Reread the three versions of the marriage proposal. Then choose the best answer for each of the following questions.

1. In which of the three versions do the characters seem to come to life?

   (a) prose   **(b)** poetry   **(c)** drama

2. Which version contains concise images and is written in verse?

   (a) prose   **(b)** poetry   **(c)** drama

3. Which example seems the most like real life?

   (a) prose   **(b)** poetry   **(c)** drama

4. Which example relates the exact words and actions of characters?

   (a) prose   **(b)** poetry   **(c)** drama

5. Which version presents a summary of action in sentences?

   (a) prose   **(b)** poetry   **(c)** drama

Answers are on page 551.

Dialogue

In a play, as in other forms of literature, *dialogue* is conversation between characters. When reading dialogue in a novel or short story, it is sometimes difficult to keep track of who is talking, because the speakers are not always identified. In reading drama, however, there are clues to help you keep track of who is speaking.

Clue #1:   The speakers are identified in each line that is delivered.

In the scene at the beginning of this section, the clues *GLEN* and *ROB* indicate who is talking. The names and the use of the colon (:) let you know who's speaking.

When only two people are speaking, it is easy to follow, but when three or more characters get involved, you must read more carefully and be aware of which speaker is responding to which other characters.

Clue #2: Punctuation marks are used to begin and end a character's speech.

In the writing skills section of this book, you reviewed punctuation. Notice the end marks, especially for questions (?) and exclamations (!). Punctuation is used in drama to show volume of voice and emotion. Dashes (—) and ellipses (. . .) are also used to show pauses. Dashes are used to show a break in thought, while ellipses indicate that there is a pause in the action or that one character is being interrupted by another character.

Clue #3: Line spacing between lines of dialogue indicates who's speaking.

A more obvious and visual clue that indicates when a different speaker is talking is the "white space" between lines of dialogue.

EXERCISE 2: DIALOGUE AND PUNCTUATION

Directions: Read the dialogue below, noticing the punctuation. Then answer the questions that follow.

[*The scene begins in a nineteenth-century parlor as Catherine, Edward and Victoria's daughter, enters with tea.*]

CATHERINE: Would you like some tea and . . .

EDWARD: Not now—Can't you see we're talking?

VICTORIA: *You're* talking—I'm not!

EDWARD: Oh—a little irritable, are we?

VICTORIA: No—just bored—with you. . .

CATHERINE: [*Mumbling*] I'm leaving. [*She exits.*]

In the space below, write the name of the character that correctly completes each statement.

1. Catherine interrupts _____.

2. _____ asks two questions.

3. _____ is rude to Catherine.

4. Victoria is upset with _____.

Answers are on page 551.

EXERCISE 3: INFERRING MOOD FROM DIALOGUE

Directions: Choose the best answer to the question that follows.

The mood of this scene may *best* be described as

(1) tense   **(2)** happy   **(3)** suspenseful   **(4)** nostalgic   **(5)** humorous

Answer is on page 551.

Stage Directions

Stage directions are used to assist the actors and director in interpreting the writer's intentions and purpose and to help the reader follow the imagined actions. In the brief scene above, the stage directions are "[*The scene begins in a nineteenth-century parlor as Catherine, Edward and Victoria's daughter, enters with tea.*]"; "[*Mumbling*]"; and "[*She exits.*]."

Notice that the playwright inserts the directions within and between the dialogue. In the scene above, the stage directions tell the reader who Catherine is and why she leaves.

There are two play excerpts on the next few pages. The first excerpt relies on your understanding of dialogue, while the second requires you to follow the action as well as the words.

Interpreting a Scene

The scene below has been included to give you practice in reading plays. The more comfortable you are with following the format of a play, the better your understanding of it will be. Read the following play scene and try to imagine the characters, setting, mood, and action. The scene presents facts about the history of drama. If you're studying with a group or a class, perhaps your instructor would like to assign parts as you read the dialogue aloud.

WHO ARE THE CHARACTERS AND WHAT IS TAKING PLACE?

[*The scene is a drama class where students are learning about the history of drama. The teacher is seated on her desktop, referring to her notes as her students ask questions.*]

MISS ANDERSON: You need to take some notes on this, so listen carefully and interrupt me if you have a relevant question . . .

PETE: Anyone have a pen I can borrow? . . . [*Ann, tapping him on the shoulder, hands him one.*] Thanks.

MISS ANDERSON: That's not what I would call a relevant question, Pete. OK . . . Western drama began in Greece about 500 B.C. at the festivals of Dionysus, the god of wine. In early Greek drama, there were few individual actors; instead, a chorus was used to "chant" and recite passages. The spectators sat on the hillside, looking down upon the performance. Later, arenas and the Colosseum were built. There were no costumes or makeup, but robes and masks were worn. These festival plays often lasted three days.

PETE: What a party!

MISS ANDERSON: Well . . . yes, it was a party atmosphere.

LINDA: Were there any stars or famous actors of the time?

MISS ANDERSON: The first actor is believed to be Thespis.

LINDA: Is that why actors are called thespians?

MISS ANDERSON: Yes. If drama students, actors, or crew members earn so many hours of credit in drama, they can join the International Thespian Society.

LARRY: Did they use swords and stuff on stage then, or is that just in movies?

MISS ANDERSON: Later, in Roman theater, there was much violence. It's believed that in the days of gladiators some people were actually killed on stage.

PETE: I can see it now. "This play is rated *R*. Death scenes not for people under seventeen!" [*Laughter from class*]

MISS ANDERSON: Let's go on, please. As drama advanced, the raised stage was developed. The audience sat in front of or around it. In the Middle Ages, plays centered around religion, and traveling actors performed plays on pageant wagons that traveled from village to village throughout Europe.

PETE: Is that where the expression "Let's get this show on the road!" comes from? [*Groans from the teacher and class*]

MISS ANDERSON: Very funny, Pete. By the late 1500s, the Elizabethan era in England gave us William Shakespeare. Drama would never be the same. It became much better.

RICK: Excuse me, what's the big deal about Shakespeare? I can't read or understand his stuff unless a teacher is standing in front of the class "translating" for me. Then I like and understand it.

MISS ANDERSON: Today it *is* necessary to translate Shakespeare because he wrote in the English spoken during his time. But once you study Shakespeare, you'll see that his themes about human nature still apply to us today. In fact, the musical *West Side Story* is based on Shakespeare's play *Romeo and Juliet*. Many of today's soap operas about conflicts between two families reflect some of Shakespeare's themes. Imagine a play such as *Romeo and Juliet*, which includes many characters, an exciting plot, an everlasting theme about love, and all of it written in verse form!

RICK: OK, I'm impressed.

MISS ANDERSON: Also, keep in mind that Juliet and all of the women were played by men.

RICK AND PETE: [*together*] WHAT!?

MISS ANDERSON: That's right. Theater was quite bawdy—obscene. Women were not allowed to act in or to attend many plays, so all of the women's roles were played by boys or men.

PETE: [*Standing and "acting"*] "Romeo, Romeo, wherefore art thou, Romeo?"

RICK: Oh, Juliet. You need a shave. You have to look good for the next scene. [*Laughter from the class*]

MISS ANDERSON: Let's go on, guys. In the next 200 years, theater would evolve to allow the wearing of elaborate costumes and the use of movable scenery, lighting, and indoor theaters. Women were allowed in the audience, then finally in the productions as actresses.

PETE: I have only two lines left on my page. This history of drama is longer than I thought.

MISS ANDERSON: The first American theater was built in 1716, so I have a lot to tell you about American drama—tomorrow. I will conclude by saying Western drama today is a "mixed bag." It's a product of all that has come before us—classical Greek, Roman, Shakespearean, and experimental. Plays are performed daily in our city theaters, in community playhouses, and on TV. Directors and actors try new approaches and forms . . . [*Bell rings*] Go home and watch TV, and you'll see drama in some form.

PETE: [*Turning*] Here's your pen, Ann. Now, that's my kind of homework assignment! See ya tomorrow, Miss A!

The stage directions that open this scene tell the reader *where* the action takes place and *who* is involved. They set the scene. They establish the *setting*, the drama class. Also, the stage directions set the *mood*. As in prose and poetry, the mood is set early in a work to help determine the attitude the playwright expects from the audience.

The stage directions here include "[*The teacher is seated on her desktop, referring to her notes as her students ask questions.*]"

As in prose literature and poetry, the reader must *infer* character, plot, setting, mood, and theme.

EXERCISE 4: IDENTIFYING CHARACTERS

Directions: Match the character on the right with the appropriate action or description on the left. Base your answers on the classroom scene you just read.

_____ 1. likable "class clown"   **a.** Miss Anderson

_____ 2. asks about early actors   **b.** Pete

_____ 3. asks about violence on stage   **c.** Linda

_____ 4. character who doesn't speak   **d.** Larry

_____ 5. asks about studying Shakespeare **e.** Ann

_____ 6. leads the discussion   **f.** Rick

Answers are on page 551.

EXERCISE 5: HISTORY OF DRAMA

Directions: Choose the best answer for each question that follows.

1. All of the following facts were presented in the scene *except*:

(1) Only in the last few hundred years have women been in theater.
(2) Actors are known as thespians.
(3) During the Middle Ages, plays centered around religion.
(4) William Shakespeare's plays are seldom performed today.
(5) The Greeks performed without costumes or makeup.

2. The mood of the scene may be best described as

(1) informal **(2)** serious **(3)** suspenseful **(4)** blissful **(5)** threatening

3. Miss Anderson's approach may be described as

(1) strict (2) unenthusiastic (3) haphazard (4) casual (5) formal

4. Based on her explanations, we can infer that Miss Anderson

(1) has no knowledge of Greek theater
(2) has great admiration for Shakespeare
(3) is angered by Pete's interruptions
(4) sees no link between drama of the past and drama of today
(5) does not like teaching literature at all

5. The purpose of this scene is to

(1) compare and contrast different types of plays
(2) explain why Shakespeare is so important to drama
(3) distinguish between comedy and tragedy
(4) trace the development of Western drama from past to present
(5) show how Miss Anderson handles a difficult situation

Answers are on page 551.

WRITING ACTIVITY 1

Create your own play scene based on a classroom or work experience. Use the speakers' names followed by a colon (:). Insert your own stage directions in brackets. Use four or five exchanges of dialogue to practice with the play format.

From Idea to Production

The ancient Greeks sat on a hillside to watch plays; today we turn on our television sets or attend live productions. We escape for a while as we are entertained by situations that often are more exciting than our own lives.

To appreciate a play or TV drama fully, it helps to know how drama is created and produced. A play is created by a writer (playwright or dramatist). Usually, it is written to be performed, rather than to communicate directly to *readers*. It takes the work of many different people with different talents and skills to put on a performance. Costumers, set designers, makeup artists, and many others contribute.

The diagram below illustrates the process by which a play—an idea in the writer's head—becomes the reality of a live production.

Writer → Producer → Director → Actors / Technical Crews → Performance → Reception by Audience (and Critics)

When playwrights or screenplay writers create a script, they visualize their final work as a performance. The producer, who finances the production, chooses a director who will effectively present the raw material—the script. The director casts actors and actresses who fit the characters the writers have created.

Structure of Drama

Like poetry and fiction, drama has structure. A play is composed of *acts*—the major divisions of a dramatic work. Acts are composed of scenes. *Scenes* show an action that occurs in one place among characters.

A *prologue* begins classical drama. Because there was no scenery in early drama, the audience needed to know when and where the story was taking place and what circumstances caused the action. An actor would come on stage and introduce the play by explaining the setting and some of the plot.

The *epilogue* ends classical drama. At the end of the play, an actor would come on stage and deliver a summary poem or speech. Although the prologue and epilogue are not as common in drama today, some television dramas and movies use them to help the audience understand the plot.

Shakespeare developed and refined the structure of drama as we know it today. He presented his plots in five acts. These acts are subdivided into numbered scenes. The diagram below shows the relationship between the acts and the corresponding elements of a traditional plot.

Elements of Drama

Plot, setting, character, and theme are all devices that were introduced and explained in the prose and poetry sections. These elements also apply to drama.

As you can see from the diagram above, the plot in drama is tightly structured. As in a short story, there is *exposition* that orients the audience to the dramatic situation and setting.

The *rising action* is made up of all of the events that create suspense and arouse the audience's interest. We wonder, "What will happen next?" "What will the main character do?" All of these events and conflicts lead to the *climax*, the point of highest intensity in the play.

The *falling action* may be brief. The conclusion or *resolution* is the logical outcome of the plot. As in fiction, the resolution ties up all of the loose ends of the plot.

Characterization

Since characters in plays are intended to be brought to life by actors before a live audience, they are not developed in exactly the same ways as characters in novels and stories. How can you interpret character? One way is by listening to the character's dialogue and watching his or her facial expressions and mannerisms. Another way to interpret character is to be aware of the motivation for the character's actions.

Dialogue and Nonverbal Communication

A writer of fiction need not rely solely on dialogue for the reader to *understand* why characters behave the way they do. The novelist or short story writer can *tell* us how a character thinks and feels and why the character feels that way.

In drama, however, personalities are revealed by what characters say. Thus, dialogue carries greater responsibility for getting the author's point across in drama than in fiction.

Another difference between interpreting character in drama and in prose fiction is that in drama, character is revealed by the actor's **nonverbal communication**—mannerisms, tone of voice, facial expression, and costume. For example, you might be able to infer a character's job by the costume he wears. Or you might infer a character's unspoken thoughts by her tone of voice and facial expressions.

Motivation

In drama, a character's behavior is based on his or her **motivation**—the reasons for the character's actions. You might ask, "Why is a character acting this way?" until you learn the nature of the character.

Actors who perform the roles of characters ask themselves, "What is my motivation?" "What are my character's reasons for acting this way?" For example, if a film actress is cast as a police officer, she may spend weeks working with police departments and observing the behavior and tasks of police officers in order to understand her character's motivation more completely. The actress attempts to "become" the character.

Below is an excerpt of a play about the relationship between a mother and daughter. They are having a discussion in which much is revealed about their personalities, backgrounds, and conflicts. In order to infer mood, character, and form, you must rely on your understanding of dialogue.

EXERCISE 6: UNDERSTANDING CHARACTER

Directions: Read the passage below and answer the questions that follow.

WHAT ARE THE CHARACTERS' PERSONALITIES?

MAMA: Nothing I ever did was good enough for you, and I want to know why.

JESSIE: That's not true.

MAMA: And I want to know why you've lived here this long feeling the way you do.

JESSIE: You have no earthly idea how I feel.

MAMA: Well how could I? You're real far back there, Jessie.

JESSIE: Back where?

MAMA: What's it like over there, where you are? Do people always say the right thing or get whatever they want, or what?

JESSIE: What are you talking about?

MAMA: Why do you read the newspaper? Why don't you wear that sweater I made for you? Do you remember how I used to look, or am I just any old woman now? When you have a fit do you see stars, or what? How did you fall off the horse, really? Why did Cecil leave you? Where did you put my old glasses?

JESSIE: They're in the bottom drawer of your dresser in an old Milk of Magnesia box. Cecil left because he made me choose between him and smoking.

MAMA: Jessie, I know he wasn't that dumb.

JESSIE: I never understood why he hated it so much when it's so good. Smoking is the only thing I know that's always just what you think it's going to be. Just like it was the last time and right there when you want it and real quiet.

MAMA: Your fits made him sick, and you know it.

JESSIE: Say seizures, not fits. Seizures.

MAMA: It's the same thing. A seizure in the hospital is a fit at home.

JESSIE: They didn't bother him at all. Except he did feel responsible for it. It was his idea to go horseback riding that day. It was his idea I could do *anything* if I just made up my mind to. I fell off the horse because I didn't know how to hold on. Cecil left for pretty much the same reason.

—Excerpted from *'night, Mother* by Marsha Norman

1. The relationship between the mother and daughter seems to suffer from

(1) Jessie's dependence on Mama
(2) Mama's dependence on Jessie
(3) a lack of communication
(4) Jessie's resentment of her mother
(5) Mama's hatred of Cecil, Jessie's husband

2. Mama may best be described as

(1) understanding
(2) vengeful
(3) supportive
(4) critical
(5) selfish

3. Jessie seems to like smoking because

(1) its effect is something she can depend on
(2) it irritates her mother
(3) it makes her feel as strong as Cecil
(4) she started at a young age
(5) it calms her nerves

4. Jessie may best be described as

   (1) conniving
   (2) responsible
   (3) out of touch with reality
   (4) at odds with her mother
   (5) hopeless

5. The mood that this excerpt conveys is one of

   (1) despair   **(2)** happiness   **(3)** suspense   **(4)** tension   **(5)** doubt

Answers are on page 551.

EXERCISE 7: SUPPORTING FACTS AND INFERENCES

Directions: Below is a list of facts and inferences made about Jessie's character. In the spaces provided, write the key words from the passage that support each fact or inference.

1. Jessie has epilepsy. _____

2. Jessie is separated from Cecil. _____

_____

3. Jessie smokes. _____

4. Jessie is confused about what her mother wants to know. _____

_____

5. Mama doesn't believe Jessie's story of how she fell off the horse. _____

_____

Answers are on page 552.

EXERCISE 8: INTERPRETING A SCENE FROM A PLAY

Directions: Read the passage below and answer the questions that follow.

WHAT PROBLEM IS BEING DISCUSSED BY ALICE AND GENE?

ALICE: I'm doing a lot for my kids. I don't expect them to pay me back at the other end. [*Gene wanders around, thinking, scuffing the grass.*] I'm sure we could find a full-time housekeeper. He can afford it.

GENE: He'd never agree.

ALICE: It's that or finding a home. [*Gene frowns.*] Sidney's folks like where they are. Also, we might as well face it, his mind's going. Sooner or later, we'll have to think about powers of attorney, perhaps committing him to an institution.

GENE: It's all so ugly.

ALICE: [*smiling*] Yes, my gentle Gene, a lot of life is.

GENE: Now, look, don't go trying to make me out some soft-hearted . . . [*He can't find the word.*] I know life is ugly.

ALICE: Yes, I think you know it. You've lived through a great deal of ugliness. But you work like a Trojan to deny it, to make it not so. [*After a moment, not arguing*] He kicked me out. He said he never wanted to see me again. He broke Mother's heart over that for years. He was mean, unloving. He beat you when you were a kid. . . . You've hated and feared him all your adult life. . . .

GENE: [*cutting in*] Still he's my father, and a man. And what's happening to him appalls me as a man.

ALICE: We have a practical problem here.

GENE: It's not as simple as all that.

ALICE: To me it is. I don't understand this mystical haze you're casting over it. I'm going to talk to him tomorrow, after the session with the lawyer, about a housekeeper. [*Gene reacts but says nothing.*] Just let me handle it. He can visit us, and we can take turns coming to visit him. Now, I'll do the dirty work. Only when he turns to you, don't give in.

GENE: I can't tell you how ashamed I feel . . . not to say with open arms, "Poppa, come live with me . . . I love you, Poppa, and I want to take care of you." . . . I need to love him. I've always wanted to love him. [*He drops his arms and wanders off.*]

—Excerpted from *I Never Sang for My Father* by Robert Anderson

1. The relationship between Alice and Gene is

   (1) husband and wife
   (2) nurse and doctor
   (3) sister and brother
   (4) close friends
   (5) mother and son

2. Alice would agree with which of the following statements?

   (1) All children should care for their elderly parents.
   (2) Nursing homes are for people who have no children.
   (3) The best situation for the elderly is staying in their own houses.
   (4) Children should get powers of attorney before placing parents in institutions.
   (5) Elderly parents should not expect their children to take care of them.

3. Alice's attitude toward her father is one of

   (1) devotion
   (2) resentment
   (3) undying love
   (4) indifference
   (5) respect

4. Alice is upset by Gene's

   (1) denial of his father's abusive treatment of Gene
   (2) refusal to love and care for his own father
   (3) lack of concern for his father now that his father is old
   (4) carefree attitude toward the situation
   (5) indifference to the feelings of all other family members

5. Gene exhibits all of the following emotions except

   (1) depression
   (2) relief
   (3) disgust
   (4) shame
   (5) frustration

6. The fact that Alice is making the final decision in this situation is shown by the line

   (1) "We have a practical problem here."
   (2) "I'm sure we could find a full-time housekeeper. He can afford it."
   (3) "Sooner or later, we'll have to think about powers of attorney. . . ."
   (4) "Just let me handle it. He can visit us, and we can take turns coming to visit him. Now, I'll do the dirty work."
   (5) "I don't understand this mystical haze you're casting over it."

7. Gene's last speech reveals Gene's

   (1) acceptance of his father's love
   (2) anger with Alice's negative attitude
   (3) eagerness to visit his father and offer to care for him
   (4) guilt that he doesn't love his father
   (5) inability to make decisions that affect his future

Answers are on page 552.

About Drama: Commentary

On the Literature and the Arts Test, you may be required to answer questions about commentary on a film or play. Below is a film review.

EXERCISE 9: INTERPRETING A FILM REVIEW

Directions: Read the review below and answer the questions that follow.

HOW DOES *THE LAST TYCOON* PORTRAY HOLLYWOOD?

Film Review of *The Last Tycoon*

F. Scott Fitzgerald, author of *The Great Gatsby*, has been called the "Poet of the Jazz Age," the 1920s. But he also had something important to say about Hollywood's Golden Age, the 1930s—and he said it in his last book, *The Last Tycoon*. He showed Hollywood as a kind of company town and the heads of studios as absolute rulers. Critic Edmund Wilson has called *The Last Tycoon* the best book ever written about moviemaking.

Somehow, director Elia Kazan and Harold Pinter (who wrote the screenplay) have managed to turn *The Last Tycoon* into a fascinating low-key film. It couldn't have been easy. Fitzgerald died in 1940, leaving only six finished chapters of *The Last Tycoon*. He left notes for some possible endings, and the one Pinter and Kazan chose may not please everybody.

The time is 1933, the place a big Hollywood studio like MGM. Monroe Stahr (Robert De Niro) is the studio production head. Fitzgerald meant Stahr to be based on the late Irving Thalberg, MGM's creative "Boy Wonder." Like

15 Thalberg, Stahr is a human dynamo. He controls every stage of filmmaking. He shows actors how to act, screenwriters how to write, and the studio boss (Robert Mitchum) how to run things.

But Stahr himself is a flawed human being. He sees life as a movie and people as shadows. He even tries to "cast" Kathleen (Ingrid Boulting), the girl

20 he loves, as a reincarnation of his dead wife. But real life keeps getting into the act. People refuse to stay in the roles he has chosen for them. The writers he thinks of as children are ready to strike. His boss resents his arrogance and looks for a way to get rid of him.

The Last Tycoon won't please Hollywood Boosters, but Fitzgerald fans

25 should like it. It pays respect to his work and to his last troubled years as a screenwriter in Hollywood.

1. Lines 7–9, "Elia Kazan and Harold Pinter have managed to turn *The Last Tycoon* into a fascinating low-key film," illustrate the writer's attitude toward Kazan and Pinter, which is one of

(1) ridicule
(2) admiration
(3) envy
(4) indifference
(5) disgust

2. Lines 18–19, "He sees life as a movie and people as shadows," is a figure of speech that

(1) gives an inanimate object human qualities
(2) compares two unlike things
(3) suggests one thing is exactly the same thing as another
(4) hints at an unexpected turn of events
(5) completely exaggerates the quality of a thing

3. Lines 18–19 also offer support for the statement that Stahr

(1) is a man with character flaws
(2) is like Irving Thalberg, the "Boy Wonder"
(3) is energetic and thoughtful
(4) treats writers as children
(5) heads all aspects of production

4. "*The Last Tycoon* won't please Hollywood Boosters" implies that the film will

(1) be unpopular with most film critics
(2) be successful as a money-making film
(3) not win Academy Awards
(4) offend Fitzgerald's survivors
(5) offend the producers of Hollywood films

Answers are on page 552.

WRITING ACTIVITY 2

Be the critic—write your own film review. The next time you watch a movie, use the following form to critique the film.

Evaluate the acting, directing, plot, and entertainment value (or lack of it). Indicate in your review who this film would appeal to most. Be sure to provide specific examples from the movie that support your judgment. Try to see the movie through the eyes of a film critic.

The Artists
Read the credits. Know *who* made the film.

1. Director: _____

2. Actors/Actresses: (stars) _____

_____

(supporting) _____

_____

3. Writer and performer of musical score: _____

_____

The Film Itself

4. In a paragraph or two, what is the plot of the movie?_____

_____

_____

5. Are the actors' and actresses' portrayals believable?_____

6. What do you like about the film?_____

_____

7. What do you dislike about the film and would like to see improved?_____

_____

_____

8. What is the film's message or theme?_____

9. Who would this film likely appeal to the most?_____

10. Rate the film on a scale of 0 to 5. (0 for poor, 5 for excellent)_____

4
INTERPRETING NONFICTION

Do you read nonfiction? If you read a daily newspaper, you read nonfiction. If you read articles in *People, Newsweek, Sports Illustrated, Ebony,* or *Better Homes and Gardens,* you read nonfiction. If you read articles or books explaining how to diet, strip furniture, or buy a car, you read nonfiction.

Nonfiction is literature that is *not* fiction and is based on fact. The nonfiction author writes about actual people, events, and ideas. The author's purpose may be to inform, instruct, entertain, record, examine, persuade, or analyze. Read the following excerpt about the teen years taken from a nonfiction book about parenting. Then answer the questions that follow the passage. As you read, ask yourself:

- What is the author's purpose for writing the piece?
- What details does he include to support his theory?

WHY DO TEENS REBEL?

I am now convinced that most theories about the "stress and strain of adolescence" have focused incorrectly on such factors as the adolescent's physical changes, his emerging sexuality, his new social demands, his struggle between being a child and an adult, and so on. This period is difficult for children and parents largely because the adolescent becomes so independent of his parents that he can no longer be easily controlled by their rewards and punishments. And since most parents rely so heavily on rewards and punishment, adolescents react with much independent, resistive, rebellious, hostile behavior.

Parents assume that adolescent rebellion and hostility are inevitably a function of this stage of development. I think this is not valid—it is more that the *adolescent becomes more able to resist and rebel.* He is no longer controlled by his parents' rewards because he does not need them so much; and he is immune to threats of punishment because there is little they can do to give him pain or strong discomfort. The typical adolescent behaves as he does because he has acquired enough strength and resources to satisfy his own needs and enough of his own power so that he need not fear the power of his parents.

An adolescent, therefore, does not rebel against his *parents.* He rebels against their *power.* If parents would rely less on power and more on non-power methods to influence their children *from infancy on,* there would be little for the child to rebel against when he becomes an adolescent. The use of power to change the behavior of children, then, has this severe limitation: parents inevitably run out of power, and sooner than they think.

—Excerpted from *Parent Effectiveness Training* by Dr. Thomas Gordon

Place a check mark (✓) before each statement with which the author would likely agree.

———— **1.** There has been too much focus on parenting techniques and not enough on the teen's development.

———— **2.** The main factor of the rebellious period is the adolescent's independence of parental control.

———— **3.** Parents should not assume that a teenager's rebellious behavior is inevitable.

———— **4.** A teenager no longer needs his or her parents' love.

———— **5.** Parents should use power to discipline their children.

———— **6.** Most theories about the "terrible teens" have missed the main point.

———— **7.** Parents' use of power over children is counterproductive. Although power works for children, it causes problems during adolescence.

———— **8.** A teenager is rebelling more against the power than the parents.

The author's purpose is clear. By using phrases such as "I am now convinced . . ." and "I think this is not valid," the author is giving his opinion. He is rejecting most other theories about the "terrible teens" and rebellion.

You should have checked off statements 2, 3, 6, 7, and 8. The others (1, 4, 5) are not the views of the author according to the passage.

What is the author's main point? Reread the first two sentences of the last paragraph. These sentences clearly tell the author's purpose—to state why teens rebel.

In this section, you will read a variety of nonfiction excerpts. As in the previous fiction, poetry, and drama sections, you will be asked to interpret meaning, style, tone, and language.

Types of Nonfiction

Nonfiction appears in several forms and covers every conceivable subject. To organize such a wide range of material, libraries use the Dewey decimal system or the Library of Congress system in categorizing their books. Under the Dewey decimal system, main classes of books and other publications are given a three-digit number. For example, nonfiction books that fall within the category of literature are found in the 800s. Under the Library of Congress system, classes of books are given an alphabetical prefix. For example, books that fall under the heading of literature are assigned the letter *P.*

Forms of nonfiction include biographies, autobiographies, articles, essays, and speeches. A description and example from each category is represented in this section.

Biography—About People

Most people like to read about other people's lives; consequently, biography is a popular form of nonfiction. A *biography* is a factual book or sketch that records the life of an individual. Biographies are written about historical figures, politicians, sports figures, current and past celebrities, and any other people who might have attracted the public's eye.

Biographers report major events in a person's life and interpret their meaning. A biography is often meant to entertain as well as to educate; you can certainly learn from the experiences of others. Traditionally, biographies were written after someone's death, as a tribute. But today, more and more biographies are written about people who are still alive.

Most major writers and literary figures are subjects of biographies, because critics and readers want to know more about the personal lives of writers and how those events relate to their writings. The passage below is a biographical sketch of a famous essayist.

EXERCISE 1: THE BIOGRAPHY

Directions: Read the biographical sketch below and answer the questions that follow.

WHO WAS HENRY DAVID THOREAU?

Henry David Thoreau was born in Concord, Massachusetts, in 1817. He graduated from Harvard in 1837. The week he graduated, he heard a speech by Ralph Waldo Emerson and became a follower of the famous essayist and poet. Thoreau tried teaching but resigned after objections to his refusal to use corporal punishment; teachers were expected to hit students. In 1839, Thoreau, on a vacation from teaching, journeyed down the Concord River with his brother. The trip resulted in his first book, *A Week on the Concord and Merrimack Rivers*. He and his brother also opened a private school, where he introduced the idea of field trips to study nature.

Philosopher and writer Ralph Waldo Emerson encouraged Thoreau to keep a daily journal and to write poetry and essays. On July 4, 1845, Thoreau began his famous "experiment in living" at Walden Pond. He lived in a cabin in the woods.

He wrote, "I went to the woods because I wished to live deliberately. . . ." The journal entries he wrote while living at Walden Pond were later published and became an American nonfiction classic, *Walden*.

Known as an individualist and nonconformist, someone who did not always go along with the rest of society, Thoreau also wrote the essay "On the Duty of Civil Disobedience." [See pages 529–530.] The essay was written as a result of his one-day imprisonment for refusing to pay a poll tax that helped fund the United States' war with Mexico. He also opposed slavery and did much in 1859 to publicize abolitionist John Brown as a martyr. Thoreau died of tuberculosis in Concord in 1862.

His works, especially "On the Duty of Civil Disobedience," were later read by Mahatma Gandhi of India and Martin Luther King, Jr. Thoreau's ideas of civil disobedience and passive resistance were practiced by both Gandhi and King in their protests against their respective governments. Today, Thoreau is viewed as one of the great thinkers and writers in American history.

1. The biographical sketch of Thoreau does all of the following except

    (1) tell when he lived
    (2) describe some of his beliefs
    (3) name his most important literary works
    (4) criticize his writing style
    (5) summarize his contributions to society

2. It is significant that Thoreau moved to Walden Pond on July 4, 1845, because

    (1) it was his summer vacation from teaching
    (2) he wanted to attract worldwide attention to his cause
    (3) the pond was beautiful in July
    (4) he was hiding from the law
    (5) it was the anniversary of the nation's independence

3. In *Walden*, Thoreau writes: "I went to the woods because I wished to live deliberately, to front only the essential facts of life, and see if I could not learn what it had to teach, and not, when I came to die, discover that I had not lived." If you were to follow Thoreau's advice, you would

    (1) live and work in New York City
    (2) get involved in national politics
    (3) live away from civilization
    (4) take time out to ponder the meaning and beauty of life
    (5) become a stockbroker and make as much money as possible

4. According to the biographical sketch, Thoreau's most influential work is

    (1) the essay "On the Duty of Civil Disobedience"
    (2) the book *A Week on the Concord and Merrimack Rivers*
    (3) the book *Walden*
    (4) his journals
    (5) his poetry

5. Civil disobedience may best be described as

    (1) disregarding all laws passed by one's government
    (2) nonviolent resistance to unjust laws
    (3) breaking any law that one does not like
    (4) living one's life as a free spirit
    (5) a violent attempt to overthrow one's government

6. In the conclusion of *Walden*, Thoreau writes, "If a man does not keep pace with his companions, perhaps it is because he hears a different drummer. Let him step to the music which he hears, however measured or far away." This statement reveals Thoreau's belief in

    (1) laws
    (2) individualism
    (3) conformity
    (4) friendship
    (5) patriotism

Answers are on page 552.

WRITING ACTIVITY 1

Choose one of Thoreau's quotations from questions 3 and 6 in Exercise 1. In a paragraph or two, explain its meaning in your own words.

Oral History—Word of Mouth

Not all biographical works document the life of a famous or distinguished individual. Studs Terkel's book *Hard Times* records facts and impressions about the lives of many different "common people" who were affected by the Great Depression of the 1930s. He interviewed people about their memories of the Depression and recorded their responses as oral history. In the following excerpt from the oral history, he interviews Cesar Chavez, who was, at the time of the interview, the head of the United Farm Workers of America. Chavez recalls what it was like for his family to leave a farm that they owned and become migrant workers.

Many times, nonfiction authors interview their sources, then summarize the interview in their own words. Here, Terkel reports both his questions to Chavez and Chavez's responses.

EXERCISE 2: ORAL HISTORY

Directions: Read the passage below and answer the questions that follow.

WHAT DOES CHAVEZ REMEMBER ABOUT THE DEPRESSION?

[Chavez] We had been poor, but we knew every night there was a bed *there* and that *this* was our room. There was a kitchen. It was sort of a settled life, and we had chickens and hogs, eggs and all those things. But that all of a sudden changed. When you're small, you can't figure these things out. You know something's not right and you don't like it, but you don't question it and you don't let that get you down. You sort of just continue to move.

But this had quite an impact on my father. He had been used to owning the land and all of a sudden there was no more land. What I heard . . . what I made out of conversations between my mother and my father—things like, we'll work this season and then we'll get enough money and we'll go and buy a piece of land in Arizona. Things like that. Became like a habit. He never gave up hope that some day he would come back and get a little piece of land.

I can understand very, very well this feeling. These conversations were sort of melancholy. I guess my brothers and my sisters could also see this very sad look on my father's face.

[Terkel] *That piece of land he wanted . . . ?*

[Chavez] No, never. It never happened. He stopped talking about that some years ago. The drive for land, it's a very powerful drive.

When we moved to California, we would work after school. Sometimes we wouldn't go. "Following the crops," we missed much school. Trying to get enough money to stay alive the following winter, the whole family picking apricots, walnuts, prunes. We were pretty new, we had never been migratory workers.

Write *T* if a statement is true or *F* if it is false.

—— **1.** There were at least five people in Chavez's family.

—— **2.** Chavez is very bitter about his experience.

—— **3.** Chavez's parents were hopeful people.

—— **4.** According to Chavez, children keep going along even when they do not understand what's happening.

—— **5.** Chavez's parents had always been migrant workers.

—— **6.** Being a migrant worker affected Chavez's opportunity to get a good education.

—— **7.** The Great Depression did not greatly affect Chavez's family.

—— **8.** Chavez has trouble remembering much about the Depression.

Answers are on page 553.

WRITING ACTIVITY 2

TV interviews are popular. Programs like "60 Minutes," "Nightline," and "The Oprah Winfrey Show," to name a few, rely on the interview process. Interview an older person whom you know who lived through the Depression. Ask at least five questions, and write up the results of your interview in a question-and-answer format.

Autobiography—About You

Only *you* can write your autobiography, the story of your own life. ***Autobiography*** is a *self*-biography. Many writers of autobiographies are not professional writers but notable individuals telling their own story. Autobiographies are also known as *memoirs*.

Notable autobiographies include *The Diary of Anne Frank*, a diary of a young Jewish girl who hid from the Nazis in World War II; *Out of Africa*, the autobiography of Isak Dinesen, which was the basis for the film of the same title; and *The Autobiography of Malcolm X*, which served as the basis for Spike Lee's film about Malcolm X.

Like authors of fiction, authors of nonfiction exhibit particular styles. Autobiographies, especially, tend to be written in a less formal style because the writers are revealing the personal details of their lives. In the passage on page 525, Dick Gregory, writer, comedian, and social activist, uses many sentence fragments—quick images to set the mood. Notice his style and the effects he achieves.

EXERCISE 3: AUTOBIOGRAPHY

Directions: Read the passage below and answer the questions that follow.

HOW DOES DICK GREGORY FEEL ABOUT SCHOOL?

The teacher thought I was stupid. Couldn't spell, couldn't read, couldn't do arithmetic. Just stupid. Teachers were never interested in finding out that you couldn't concentrate because you were so hungry, because you hadn't had any breakfast. All you could think about was noontime, would it ever come? Maybe you could sneak into the cloakroom and steal a bite of some kid's lunch out of a coat pocket. A bite of something. Paste. You can't really make a meal of paste, or put it on bread for a sandwich, but sometimes I'd scoop a few spoonfuls out of the paste jar in the back of the room. Pregnant people get strange tastes. I was pregnant with poverty. Pregnant with dirt and pregnant with smells that made people turn away, pregnant with cold and pregnant with shoes that were never bought for me, pregnant with five other people in my bed and no Daddy in the next room, and pregnant with hunger. Paste doesn't taste too bad when you're hungry.

The teacher thought I was a troublemaker. All she saw from the front of the room was a little black boy who squirmed in his idiot's seat and made noises and poked the kids around him. I guess she couldn't see a kid who made noises because he wanted someone to know he was there.

—Excerpted from "Not Poor, Just Broke" in *Nigger—An Autobiography*

1. The author uses the word *pregnant* to mean

   (1) overdue with
   (2) carrying the burden of
   (3) separated from
   (4) expecting a baby
   (5) looking forward to

2. From the author's point of view, the teacher was all of the following *except*

   (1) unaware of his hunger
   (2) insensitive to his real needs
   (3) aware of his disruptive behavior
   (4) uninterested in him
   (5) understanding of his problems

3. The use of the word *pregnant* is effective because the word

   (1) expresses a feeling of expectation
   (2) appeals to mothers
   (3) creates a vivid image in the reader's mind
   (4) is used in a different way than is expected
   (5) contributes to the writer's use of alliteration as a device

4. Cesar Chavez and Dick Gregory were alike in that both men

   (1) lived in fatherless homes
   (2) had their early education interrupted
   (3) had no brothers or sisters
   (4) made names for themselves despite their childhood poverty
   (5) had no faith at all in adults

5. The title of the chapter from which the excerpt comes is, "Not Poor, Just Broke." This title suggests that Gregory

(1) wasn't poor; he'd just spent his lunch money
(2) was used to poverty, so it didn't bother him
(3) supposes that being poor is the same thing as being broke
(4) believes being broke is better than being poor
(5) thinks those who are called poor by others don't necessarily consider themselves to be poor

Answers are on page 553.

Journals and Letters

Have you ever kept a diary or journal? Both are daily records of personal activities, events, or reflections. Many people keep records of their lives for themselves or for their children. When people write their autobiographies, they may refer to their diaries or journals as sources of material.

Ralph Waldo Emerson referred to his journals as his "savings banks" in which he deposited his thoughts. Later, he drew out those thoughts and wrote some of his famous speeches, essays, and poems. Below is an entry from one of his journals.

EXERCISE 4: JOURNAL ENTRIES

Directions: Read the passage below and answer the questions that follow.

WHAT IS EMERSON'S ATTITUDE TOWARD LIFE?

November 11, 1842 [age thirty-nine]

Do not be too timid and squeamish about your actions. All life is an experiment. The more experiments you make the better. What if they are a little coarse, and you may get your coat soiled or torn? What if you do fail, and get fairly rolled in the dirt once or twice? Up again you shall never be so afraid of a tumble.

1. Based on the quotation above, with which of the following statements about life might Emerson agree?

(1) Life is one big bowl of cherries.
(2) Life is a precious gift not to be wasted.
(3) Life is one big rat race.
(4) Life isn't fair.
(5) Life is a risk; to risk is to be alive.

2. Which of the following occupations is the best expression of Emerson's beliefs?

(1) philosopher
(2) writer
(3) astronaut
(4) physician
(5) historian

Answers are on page 553.

Article—Just the Facts, Please

An *article* is a short nonfiction piece, often appearing in a newspaper or magazine. The writer presents facts, usually in an objective manner. *Feature articles* are special attractions that cover topics that have high reader interest. An article may instruct readers in how to do something, or it simply may be entertaining.

The following article about the Vietnam Veterans Parade presents facts in an objective way; the writer's opinions are not included in the article. Read the article and answer the questions that follow.

On Friday, June 13, 1986, approximately 200,000 marchers participated in Chicago's Vietnam Veterans Parade. Along the 2.8-mile route, an estimated 500,000 spectators gathered. For almost five hours, they cheered, hugged, and even walked along with the veterans and the veterans' families.

The parade was the major activity of the four-day reunion for those serving in the controversial war of the 1960s and 1970s. Gen. William Westmoreland, former U.S. wartime commander, was Grand Marshal of the parade. Politicians, older veterans, and ethnic organizations also marched. The parade ended in Grant Park, where the half-size replica of the Vietnam War Memorial was on display. The purpose of the parade was to recognize the veterans for their service in the war.

The tone of this article is *objective*, and the purpose is to convey the facts. What five facts are related in the article above? Answer the questions by filling in the blanks below with the correct words.

1. Who? _____

2. What? _____

3. When? _____

4. Where? _____

5. Why? _____

You should have answered *Who?*—Vietnam veterans; *What?*—Chicago Vietnam Veterans parade; *When?*—June 13, 1986; *Where?*—Chicago; *Why?*—to recognize the veterans for their service in the war. This article is an objective reporting of facts.

Now read the next article on the same subject and answer the questions that follow. This article is said to be a *subjective* account because the writer's opinions are included.

EXERCISE 5: THE ARTICLE AS NONFICTION

Directions: Read the article below and answer the questions that follow.

WHAT IS THE AUTHOR'S VIEW OF THE VIETNAM PARADE?

June 13, 1986—They came from all over America—200,000 heroes strong, with their families. Some veterans were clad in their old uniforms, others in battle fatigues. They marched, those that could, near their buddies in wheelchairs or on crutches. Others rode in VA buses. Some marched with their children, babies born during the war. A few ex-POWs waved at TV cameras. One marcher carried a sign, "Honor the warriors and not the war." And Chicago came out for them—years later than we should've—but we came—for the Vietnam War Vets who were deprived of the "Welcome Home" and "Thank You" they deserved in the 1970s.

The crowd of about 500,000 sat on curbs, ran along, and helped throw tons of confetti on the troops that were led by Gen. William Westmoreland, their commander in Vietnam. On Friday the 13th, thirteen years after the U.S. troops pulled out of Vietnam, the veterans' luck ran high. The much-deserved five-hour parade was part of the four-day observance. It ended in Grant Park, where the marchers and spectators viewed the half-size replica of the Vietnam Memorial of Washington, D.C.

There they paused. There they were quiet. They had marched for themselves, for their families, for those men and women not yet home—the MIAs—for the names on the Wall—for those who weren't there to march. To the veterans who marched, welcome home and thank you.

1. The opening line of the article immediately suggests that the writer

   (1) is a flag-waving patriot
   (2) opposed the Vietnam War
   (3) was a veteran of the war
   (4) felt that the parade was an unnecessary gesture
   (5) holds great admiration for the veterans

2. The author emphasizes the date, Friday the 13th, and the fact that the parade occurred thirteen years after the withdrawal of troops in order to

   (1) show that she is highly superstitious
   (2) indicate that the parade's success had everything possible against it
   (3) prove that the Vietnam veterans have been plagued by bad luck since the days of the war
   (4) show contrast between the success of the parade and the outcome normally associated with the number thirteen
   (5) impress the reader with her memory of important dates

Answers are on page 553.

NEWSPAPER NONFICTION

A good way to prepare for the GED Test is to read a major daily newspaper regularly. Besides practicing your reading and comprehension skills, you can enjoy interesting nonfiction in the form of articles and editorials.

Of the pieces that you just read about the Vietnam Veterans Parade, the first is very similar to what you would find on the front page or in other news sections of the paper. The second piece is similar to what you would find either in a featured writer's weekly column or on the editorial page of the paper because it expresses either one person's opinion or the opinion of the publisher.

As you read your newspaper, use the index to guide you to the articles and learn the differences between objective and subjective reporting.

Essay—One Person's View

An *essay* is a nonfiction work in which an author presents a personal viewpoint on a subject. Traditionally, an essay is a formal piece of writing, an expository piece that "exposes" and analyzes a subject.

Below is an excerpt from a well-known formal essay, "On the Duty of Civil Disobedience," by Henry David Thoreau. As you read it, recall Thoreau's background from page 521. Remember that the essay was written after Thoreau was jailed for refusing to pay a poll tax that he viewed as support for the Mexican War. The essay is personal in that Thoreau uses *I* to explain his views; it is serious in tone, and the vocabulary is somewhat more difficult than today's prose. The ideas put forth in this excerpt of the long essay were shared by civil rights leaders of the 1960s and 1970s, the Nazi-resisters of the 1930s and 1940s, and many other people who chose to disobey unfair rules or laws.

EXERCISE 6: THE FORMAL ESSAY

Directions: Read the passage below and answer the questions that follow.

WHAT IS THE PURPOSE OF GOVERNMENT?

I heartily accept the motto,—"That government is best which governs least;" and I should like to see it acted up to more rapidly and systematically. Carried out, it finally amounts to this, which also I believe,—"That government is best which governs not at all;" and when men are prepared for it, that will be the kind of government which they will have. Government is at best but an expedient; but most governments are usually, and all governments are sometimes, inexpedient. The objections which have been brought against a standing army, and they are many and weighty, and deserve to prevail, may also at last be brought against a standing government. The standing army is only an arm of the standing government. The government itself, which is only the mode which the people have chosen to execute their will, is equally liable to be abused and perverted before the people can act through it. Witness the present Mexican war, the work of comparatively a few individuals using the standing government as their tool; for, in the outset, the people would not have consented to this measure.

This American government,—what is it but a tradition, though a recent one, endeavoring to transmit itself unimpaired to posterity, but each instant losing some of its integrity? It has not the vitality and force of a single living man; for a single man can bend it to his will. It is a sort of wooden gun to the people themselves; and, if ever they should use it in earnest as a real one against each other, it will surely split. . . .

1. The title of the essay implies that a citizen

   (1) is disloyal for disobeying laws
   (2) should serve in the army
   (3) should appreciate U.S. citizenship
   (4) is obligated to break an unjust law
   (5) must vote in all elections

2. In the line "The government itself, which is only the mode which the people have chosen to execute their will," the word *execute* is used to mean

   (1) capital punishment of criminals
   (2) kill during a war
   (3) carry out; perform
   (4) ignore the wishes of
   (5) create; originate

3. Thoreau's view of the army is that the army exists

   (1) for each individual's use
   (2) for the government to use as it wishes
   (3) as a necessary part of democracy
   (4) as the symbol of individual heroism
   (5) independently of the government

4. Thoreau's interpretation of "government" is that the government

   (1) is the people themselves
   (2) is made up of knowledgeable leaders
   (3) is a tool of the standing army
   (4) should give fewer freedoms to its citizens
   (5) encourages individual liberty

5. Emerson said of Thoreau, "No truer American existed than Thoreau." Emerson admired Thoreau's

   (1) undying patriotism
   (2) faith in the justice system
   (3) military mind
   (4) belief in individual liberty
   (5) legislative ability

Answers are on page 553.

EXERCISE 7: REVIEW OF THOREAU

Directions: After reading the biography of Thoreau (p. 521) and the excerpt above, review your knowledge of Thoreau's beliefs. Place a check mark (✓) in front of the actions you think Thoreau would support today.

_____ **1.** antiwar protests

_____ **2.** the military draft

_____ **3.** civil rights demonstrations

_____ **4.** the women's movement

_____ **5.** the end of apartheid in South Africa

_____ **6.** literary censorship

Answers are on page 554.

WRITING ACTIVITY 3

Is it ever right to break a law? If so, under what conditions? Write two or three paragraphs using examples to support your answer.

EXERCISE 8: COMPARING AND CONTRASTING STYLES

As you learned in the section on fiction, *style* refers to the author's unique use of language to express an idea. It is the writer's style that distinguishes a formal from an informal essay. Below are two essays about computers. One is written with a light approach—a conversation between a customer and an airline worker. The other is a discussion of the danger of computers in the workplace. Note the differences in style and approach.

Directions: Read each passage below and answer the questions that follow.

Passage 1

HOW DOES THE WRITER FEEL ABOUT COMPUTERS?

The most frightening words in the English language are, "Our computer is down." You hear it more and more as you go about trying to conduct your business.

The other day I was at the airport attempting to buy a ticket to Washington and the attendant said, "I'm sorry, I can't sell you a ticket. Our computer is down."

"What do you mean your computer is down? Is it depressed?"

"No, it can't be depressed. That's why it's down."

"So if your computer is down just write me out a ticket."

"I can't write you out a ticket. The computer is the only one allowed to issue tickets for the plane." I looked down the counter, and every passenger agent was just standing there drinking coffee and staring into a blank screen.

"What do all you people do?"

"We give the computer the information about your trip, and then it tells us whether you can fly with us or not."

"So when it goes down, you go down with it."

"That's very good, sir. I haven't heard it put that way before."

"How long will the computer be down?" I wanted to know.

"I have no idea. Sometimes it's down for ten minutes, sometimes for two hours. There is no way we can find out without asking the computer, and since it's down it won't answer us."

"Don't you have a backup computer when the main computer goes down?"

"I doubt it. Do you know what one of these things costs?"

"Let's forget the computer. What about your planes? They're still flying aren't they?"

"I couldn't tell without asking the computer, and as I told you—"

"I know, it's down."

—Excerpted from "The Computer Is Down" by Art Buchwald

1. All of the following elements of style are found in this passage *except*

   (1) exaggerated circumstances
   (2) first-person narration
   (3) long explanatory paragraphs
   (4) dialogue
   (5) sarcasm

2. "There is no way we can find out without asking the computer, and since it's down it won't answer us." This statement reveals the airline agent's

   (1) irritation with the customer
   (2) creativity
   (3) ability to deal with crises
   (4) total dependence on the computer
   (5) seniority of position

3. The line that best summarizes the main idea of this passage is

   (1) "What do you mean your computer is down?"
   (2) "So if your computer is down just write me out a ticket."
   (3) "So when it goes down, you go down with it."
   (4) "How long will the computer be down?"
   (5) "Let's forget the computer. What about your planes?"

Passage 2

WHAT IS THIS WRITER'S OPINION OF COMPUTERS?

The millions of people on the bottom levels of electronic hierarchies [computer networks that connect managers with workers] are increasingly likely to spend their days in an isolated no-man's-land, subservient to intelligent information systems that report their progress to unseen supervisors far away. Because computers measure quantity better than quality, such systems tend to reward employees who work faster more than those who work better. There's a sharp rise in loneliness and disconnection as individuals blindly forge ahead. Service people on the telephone or at a cash register curtly terminate attempts at idle conversation because their performance is being electronically monitored. Once judged on their ability to communicate with customers or troubleshoot unexpected situations, they're now evaluated by the number of transactions they complete in a shift or the number of keystrokes required to draft a document. In these "electronic sweatshops," the computers are running the people, not the other way around.

"I think people are going to feel an increased fragmentation of self. They won't be able to hold the pieces together," human resources consultant Philip Nicholson says. "How do you keep a coherent space if you're going in and out of spaces that don't exist?" A graduate of the law-psychiatry program at Stanford University Law School, Nicholson has advocated preventive psychiatry since a Vietnam-era Air Force stint spent designing programs to alleviate drug abuse and race relations problems. He likens the psychic numbing of electronic information overload to symptoms of post-traumatic stress syndrome. In office wars, people become overwhelmed by the sheer amount of information available, internalize the diversity of the world outside, and fear losing control over their own lives.

"You operate from a position of chronic performance anxiety and background stress," Nicholson says. "In fact, I think it fosters a kind of mass self-hypnosis. When you're working on the computer, it's you and the screen and your mind. That's exactly what happens when you go into a hypnotic trance."

—Excerpted from "The Dark Side of the Boom" by Mary S. Glucksman

4. The tone of this passage, as compared to Passage 1, is more

   (1) humorous
   (2) satirical
   (3) conversational
   (4) serious
   (5) informal

5. When the author calls highly computerized offices "electronic sweatshops," she is

   (1) commenting on the amount of heat generated by electronic equipment
   (2) complaining that computers generate fear in the workplace by causing layoffs
   (3) praising computers for making entry-level employees work harder
   (4) saying that computers make workers "sweat it out," or worry excessively
   (5) comparing today's electronic office to the dehumanizing factory of yesterday

6. The main idea, or point, of the excerpt is that electronic offices are

(1) the wave of the future
(2) an improvement over old-time offices
(3) causing psychological problems in workers
(4) increasing American productivity
(5) helping people develop their ability to troubleshoot

7. The major purpose of quoting human resources consultant Philip Nicholson is to

(1) make the article more convincing by including the opinions of an expert
(2) enliven the article by offering a real-life, concrete example
(3) balance the article by presenting a different point of view about computers
(4) develop the ideas in the article in a variety of ways
(5) tie in problems suffered by vets with problems suffered by office workers

8. Both authors would agree with which of the following statements?

(1) We would be better off without any computers.
(2) The airline industry would be safer without computers.
(3) Computers are a necessary part of human life.
(4) People should control computers rather than letting computers control them.
(5) The government should control all computers.

Answers are on page 554.

Speech—Telling It Like It Is

As you can see from what you've read, essays embrace a variety of tones, styles, language, and themes. While an essay is a *written* communication of an opinion or a point of view, a **speech** is a *spoken* communication about a topic.

A speech is similar to the essay in its organization. The speaker should have an interesting introduction, support for the main idea, and a strong conclusion.

Notable speeches include Abraham Lincoln's "Gettysburg Address," John F. Kennedy's "Inaugural Address," and Martin Luther King, Jr.'s "I Have a Dream." King's speech has been publicized, taped, and widely recognized as instrumental in the civil rights movement.

Because speeches are considered to be nonfiction, they can be analyzed by examining tone, style, message, and purpose. The following speech was delivered in 1805 by Sagoyewatha (Red Jacket), chief of the Seneca people and spokesperson for the Iroquois League, a confederation of six Native American nations. This speech was his answer to requests that the Native Americans be baptized into Christianity. As you read, ask yourself these questions: What is the great water? The island? The Book? The Great Spirit?

EXERCISE 9: INTERPRETING A SPEECH

Directions: Read the passage below and answer the questions that follow.

WHY DOES SAGOYEWATHA REJECT THE WHITE PEOPLE'S RELIGION?

Your forefathers crossed the great water and landed on this island. Their numbers were small. They found friends and not enemies. They told us they had fled from their own country for fear of wicked men and had come here to enjoy their religion. They asked for a small seat. We took pity on them, granted their request, and they sat down among us. We gave them corn and meat; they gave us poison in return.

Brother, our seats were once large and yours were small. You have now become a great people, and we have scarcely a place left to spread our blankets. You have got our country, but are not satisfied; you want to force your religion upon us.

Brother, continue to listen. You say that you are sent to instruct us how to worship the Great Spirit agreeably to His mind; and, if we do not take hold of the religion which you white people teach we shall be unhappy hereafter. You say that you are right and we are lost. How do we know this to be true? We understand that your religion is written in a Book. If it was intended for us, as well as you, why has not the Great Spirit given to us, and not only to us, but why did He not give to our forefathers the knowledge of that Book, with the means of understanding it rightly? We only know what you tell us about it. How shall we know when to believe, being so often deceived by the white people?

Brother, you say there is but one way to worship and serve the Great Spirit. If there is but one religion, why do you white people differ so much about it? Why do not all agree, as you can all read the Book?

1. In the lines, "Brother, our seats were once large and yours were small. You have now become a great people, and we have scarcely a place left to spread our blankets," the word *great* refers to white people's

   (1) generosity
   (2) kindness
   (3) increased population
   (4) evil intentions
   (5) honesty

2. The statement quoted in question 1 refers to the Native Americans' loss of

   (1) food   (2) land   (3) blankets   (4) religion   (5) buffalo

3. The statement "They told us they had fled from their own country for fear of wicked men and had come here to enjoy their religion" makes the Native Americans' situation ironic because it refers to the

   (1) English citizens' seeking religious freedom in America
   (2) way the white people had been treated by the Native Americans
   (3) beginning of the Revolutionary War
   (4) settlers' rejecting all religions
   (5) worship of the Great Spirit

4. Sagoyewatha's tone expresses

    (1) faith in the white people
    (2) distrust of the white people
    (3) loyalty to American government
    (4) lack of faith in the Great Spirit
    (5) willingness to convert to Christianity

5. Sagoyewatha demonstrates that he is skeptical about the assertion that there is only one true religion. He points out that

    (1) all white people cannot even agree about the Book
    (2) the Indians cannot read the Book
    (3) the Great Spirit wrote the Book for Indians only
    (4) the Native Americans fear baptism
    (5) the Native Americans will have to move closer to churches

Answers are on page 554.

EXERCISE 10: MORE PRACTICE INTERPRETING SPEECHES

Directions: The following passage is from John F. Kennedy's "Inaugural Address." Read the excerpt and answer the questions that follow.

WHAT DOES THE PRESIDENT ASK OF HIS FELLOW CITIZENS?

In your hands, my fellow citizens, more than mine, will rest the final success or failure of our course. Since this country was founded, each generation of Americans has been summoned to give testimony to its national loyalty. The graves of young Americans who answered the call to service surround the globe.

Now the trumpet summons us again—not as a call to bear arms, though arms we need; not as a call to battle, though embattled we are; but a call to bear the burden of a long twilight struggle, year in and year out, "rejoicing in hope, patient in tribulation," a struggle against the common enemies of man: tyranny, poverty, disease and war itself.

Can we forge against these enemies a grand and global alliance, North and South, East and West, that can assure a more fruitful life for all mankind? Will you join me in this historic effort?

In the long history of the world, only a few generations have been granted the role of defending freedom in its hour of maximum danger. I do not shrink from this responsibility; I welcome it. I do not believe that any of us would exchange places with any other people or any other generation. The energy, the faith, the devotion which we bring to this endeavor will light our country and all who serve it, and the glow from that fire can truly light the world.

And so, my fellow Americans, ask not what your country can do for you; ask what you can do for your country.

My fellow citizens of the world, ask not what America will do for you, but what together we can do for the freedom of man.

1. The tone of the speech can best be characterized as

    (1) sarcastic
    (2) light-hearted
    (3) angry
    (4) uplifting
    (5) sad

2. One of the purposes of the speech is to motivate listeners to

    (1) preserve the right to bear arms
    (2) enlist in the armed services
    (3) serve their country
    (4) take an oath swearing to their national loyalty
    (5) prepare themselves for battle

3. In the speech, Kennedy paints a picture of the United States as a nation that is

    (1) on the brink of world war
    (2) longing to return to the past
    (3) the leading defender of freedom
    (4) struggling to survive
    (5) weakened by citizens whose major interest is self-gain

4. The speech is characterized by all of the following stylistic devices *except*

    (1) a standard, predictable rhythm and the use of rhyme
    (2) the use of the personal pronouns *we* and *us* to build rapport with listeners
    (3) catchy turns of phrase in which subjects and objects are inverted
    (4) the repetition of key words
    (5) questions that invite readers to answer "yes" silently

Answers are on page 554.

Commentary

Commentary is a form of nonfiction in which the writer comments about literature and the arts: film, television, dance, music, art, and theater. A person who writes commentary—a critic—evaluates a work of art and assesses the work's strengths and weaknesses.

You have already seen an example of commentary at the end of each of the fiction, poetry, and drama sections. As a result of reading these commentaries, you already know that a review often discusses the work of art and the artist and presents the critic's opinion of both.

The Style and Language of Commentary

Because a critic or reviewer is both describing and analyzing a work of art, the style and language of commentary is often highly descriptive.

The reader of commentary must be able to analyze style as well as tone to evaluate the reviewer's judgment about a work of art.

Reading on Two Levels

To understand criticism, you must be able to read on two levels. First, you must understand facts about both the work of art and its creator. Then, you have to understand the critic's opinions. Below are the opening lines of a review of a popular nonfiction book.

> Father of the Year
> by Barbara E. Anderson
> A review of *Fatherhood* by Bill Cosby
>
> Every father must read Bill Cosby's *Fatherhood*! Cosby's comedic treatment of such an important role in society entertains while it instructs fathers how to become better at such a formidable job.
>
> Over the years, many of us have bought his albums and have been delighted by his presence in many commercials. For the past few years, Americans have planned their evenings around the popular "Cosby Show," so it should be no surprise that his book is at the top of the best-seller list.

The following facts are covered in the review:

- Title of book being reviewed: *Fatherhood*
- Author of book: Bill Cosby
- Reviewer: Barbara Anderson

In addition to the facts about *Fatherhood*, the reviewer offers her opinion of the book. Choose the number of the answer that best completes the three questions below.

1. Anderson's opinion about *Fatherhood* might *best* be described as

   (1) unfavorable   **(2)** lukewarm   **(3)** very favorable

2. A reliable clue to Anderson's opinion about the book might be

   (1) her knowledge about Cosby's television exposure
   (2) the title of her review
   (3) her reference to his albums and popular show

3. Anderson's tone might *best* be described as

   (1) academic   **(2)** enthusiastic   **(3)** humorous

In answering question 1, you should have circled choice (3). Phrases in the review that indicate Anderson's favorable opinion of *Fatherhood* are "Every father must read Bill Cosby's *Fatherhood*"; "Cosby's comedic treatment of such an important role . . . entertains while it instructs"; and "it should be no surprise that his book is at the top of the best-seller list."

In answer to question 2, you should have circled choice (2), since the title of the review, "Father of the Year," best indicates the reviewer's favorable opinion of the book.

In answer to question 3, you should have circled choice (2). The reviewer's statement "Every father must read Bill Cosby's *Fatherhood*" indicates enthusiastic support for the book.

TIPS FOR READING LITERARY CRITICISM

When you read literary criticism, ask yourself these questions:

1. What does the critic say about the author or the author's abilities?

2. What does the critic like about the literary work? What does the critic dislike about the work? Look for words that communicate the critic's feelings about the work.

3. What statements are based on facts about the work? What statements are based on the critic's opinion or personal reaction to the work?

4. Does the critic recommend the work? Does the critic recognize the literary value of the work?

EXERCISE 11: INTERPRETING A BOOK REVIEW

Read the following review of a novel and answer the questions that follow.

A Review of *Looking for Bobby* by Gloria Norris, Knopf, $15.95

The narrator of this often funny novel, Marianne, is a Mississippi woman just awakening to the fact that although her husband is rich and handsome and practically perfect, their marriage was a mistake. She runs off to New York City, hoping to find her first cousin Bobby. Once when they were children and she was lost on a fox hunting trip, Bobby found her and said, "Even if you were a thousand miles away, I would still be close to you and know what you're thinking. No matter what happens, when we grow up, I'll always be there right by you. All you ever have to do is think about me and I'll be close." The descriptions of Marianne's courtship and marriage, her talkative mother-in-law, and the New Orleans scenes are all wonderful. But problems mount, even for a sympathetic reader, when Marianne, in New York, learns that Bobby has switched from selling stocks to directing a play off-Broadway. A producer's lunch at Sardi's is preposterous, and Bobby and his much discussed charisma become equally unbelievable. Nothing that he does makes him appear to the reader as magnetic as he seems to everyone in the book. Then, thanks to Bobby, Marianne gets into show business and becomes a successful agent. She also bumps into him in Mexico and learns his secret. What she finds out about his past isn't all that surprising—a good therapist ought to be able to straighten him out in a couple of weeks. Norris, who has had several short stories published, is skillful at creating eccentric, oversized characters, but they are a lot more fun in the Deep South than when she wedges them into the tritely portrayed showbiz worlds of New York or Hollywood.

Directions: Write a (+) in the blank if the following statement is a positive opinion, (−) if the statement is a negative opinion, and (*F*) if the statement is only a fact about the novel's plot.

_____ 1. "The narrator of this often funny novel, Marianne, is a Mississippi woman. . . ."

_____ 2. "She runs off to New York City, hoping to find her first cousin Bobby."

_____ 3. "The descriptions of Marianne's courtship and marriage, her talkative mother-in-law, and the New Orleans scenes are all wonderful."

———— **4.** "But problems mount, even for a sympathetic reader, when Marianne, in New York, learns that Bobby has switched from selling stocks to directing a play off-Broadway."

———— **5.** "A producer's lunch at Sardi's is preposterous, and Bobby and his much described charisma become equally unbelievable."

———— **6.** "Nothing that he does makes him appear to the reader as magnetic as he seems to everyone in the book."

———— **7.** "She also bumps into him in Mexico and learns his secret."

Answers are on page 554.

EXERCISE 12: INTERPRETING A REVIEW OF A NOVEL

Directions: Choose the best answer to each question below.

1. The critic's least favorite character in the book is

 (1) Marianne
 (2) Marianne's husband
 (3) Bobby
 (4) the mother-in-law
 (5) the producer

2. The critic says, "Norris, who has had several short stories published, is skillful at creating eccentric, oversized characters. . . ." In this quotation, the term *oversized* means

 (1) large; overweight
 (2) too many characters for the length of the book
 (3) inappropriate; out of place
 (4) bossy; overbearing; rude
 (5) memorable; unique

3. The critic would agree with which of the following statements?

 (1) Norris should write short stories, not novels.
 (2) A major flaw in the novel is the way the New York scenes are written.
 (3) The most exciting scenes in the novel are set in Mexico.
 (4) *Looking for Bobby* is an exceptionally well-written novel.
 (5) The character of Marianne should be better developed.

4. The reviewer states, "But problems mount, even for a sympathetic reader. . . ." The word *but* indicates

 (1) that the author of the review is not a sympathetic reader
 (2) a shift from praise to criticism of the book
 (3) the reviewer's contempt for the author of the book
 (4) the author's sympathy for Marianne
 (5) a new complication in the plot events

Answers are on page 554.

Satire in Nonfiction

Satire is a literary form that uses ridicule and irony to expose people's faults or behavior. Often utilizing exaggerated characters or circumstances, satire is used in both fiction and nonfiction.

The following piece of commentary is a review of a nonfiction book that was written to poke fun at a department of the U.S. government. The book, written in the form of a catalog, is a satire. The reviewer uses direct quotations from the book to help make his opinion clear to the reader.

EXERCISE 13: REVIEW OF A SATIRE

Directions: Read the following review and answer the questions that follow. Be sure to distinguish facts about the book from the reviewer's opinion about it.

WHAT IS THE REVIEWER'S OPINION
ABOUT THIS SATIRE ON PENTAGON SPENDING?

Review of *The Pentagon Catalog: Ordinary Products at Extraordinary Prices*,
compiled by Christopher Cerf and Henry Beard
Reviewed by Clarence Petersen, *Chicago Tribune*

"Buy this catalog for only $4.95," begins the irresistible offer on the cover, "and get this $2,043 nut for FREE!" And there, beautifully mounted on the cover, is a shiny hex nut of genuine steel construction, with center hole, threads, six equal sides and beveled edges. I screwed mine onto the rear axle of my bicycle, and you can imagine what this has done for the resale value of an ordinary Schwinn 10-speed. This is a funny book indeed, taken from real life, as well as from congressional investigations, news reports and expert testimony presented on "Donahue," which together have driven Cap Weinberger right up the wall. It offers a slim, durable flat washer for only $387, a deluxe, lightweight toilet seat for only $640.09, a space-age coffeemaker for only $7,622 and a P-3 Orion luncheon refrigerator for only $12,000. "And remember," the catalog promises, "When you buy from us, you're backed by this unique pledge: If you find that any of the products listed in this catalog are offered for sale by a retail outlet or mail-order company at a higher price, bring us that price and we will top it. *We will not be oversold!*"

1. All of the following are sources of information contained in this nonfiction book *except*

    (1) real life
    (2) expert testimony on a television talk show
    (3) news reports
    (4) mail-order catalogs
    (5) congressional investigations

2. The critic thinks the authors of the book are

    (1) too sarcastic
    (2) very funny
    (3) uninformed
    (4) unfair
    (5) too serious

3. The book satirizes, or pokes fun at,

   (1) Pentagon spending
   (2) TV talk shows
   (3) catalogs
   (4) the president
   (5) the high price of hardware

4. The tone of the book and the style in which it is written are similar to

   (1) a television talk show host
   (2) a formal speech; a lecture
   (3) a forceful advertisement; a sales pitch
   (4) the military's approach in recruiting
   (5) a soft sell approach to marketing a product

5. The reviewer relies heavily on quotations from the book to

   (1) show that he read it
   (2) illustrate how ridiculous it is
   (3) support his opposition to Pentagon spending
   (4) help his readers get a feeling for the book's humor
   (5) encourage the readers to order from the catalog

Answers are on page 555.

Interpreting Other Forms of Commentary

The following three reviews are commentaries on music, art, and television. As you read each review, look for specific qualities of the work that each critic is evaluating. Ask yourself:

- What facts about the work itself does the critic include?

- Does the critic like or dislike this work? Why?

- What does the critic say about the background of the artist?

- What is the critic's style? How does he or she present the message?

EXERCISE 14: INTERPRETING MUSICAL COMMENTARY

Directions: Read the music review below and answer the questions that follow.

**WHO IS WYNTON MARSALIS, AND WHAT DOES
THIS CRITIC THINK OF HIM?**

Review of *Hot House Flowers* by Wynton Marsalis
(A Four Star Review) ★★★★

    Jazz history can be traced through the arrival of precociously talented trumpet players who revolutionize the way jazz is perceived, both by the public and by the musicians who play it. King Oliver, Louis Armstrong, Roy Eldridge, Dizzy Gillespie, Clifford Brown, Miles Davis, Lee Morgan and Lester Bowie, among others, came on the scene and turned everything upside down by forging new directions or simply making obvious something that had been overlooked. Though he has only made three albums as a leader, Wynton Marsalis has already joined this elite, at least by reputation.

Part of what distinguishes Marsalis is that he has seemingly assimilated jazz history at the tender age of twenty-three. At this point only his beautiful tone and impressive technique are his own, for he has chosen to work, for the most part, in familiar styles. Therein may lie the key to his genius. Marsalis has avoided the trap so many young players fall into of trying to be different just for the sake of being different. Marsalis obviously relishes drawing comparisons to Miles Davis of the fifties on "Melancholis." His specialty is acknowledging such a debt, then playing in such a way as to make it totally an expression of himself. The fact that Wynton Marsalis is also an accomplished classical player may explain in part his understanding of how a tradition can be nurtured rather than just copied.

1. This review reveals the critic's

    (1) dislike of young musicians
    (2) admiration and appreciation of Marsalis
    (3) bias against older, familiar jazz styles
    (4) lack of knowledge about classical jazz musicians
    (5) belief that classical music is better than jazz

2. According to the critic, Marsalis is unique because of his

    (1) application of his own technique to traditional jazz
    (2) mastery of a variety of instruments
    (3) long, established career
    (4) ability to play gospel as well as jazz
    (5) many television performances

3. Besides being a jazz musician, Marsalis also plays

    (1) country
    (2) rock
    (3) gospel
    (4) classical
    (5) rhythm and blues

4. The reviewer states, "a tradition can be nurtured rather than just copied." This statement supports the critic's belief that a musician should

    (1) ignore other musicians in his rise to fame
    (2) improve, not just repeat, the art
    (3) reject all musicians of the past
    (4) experiment with all types of music
    (5) record the music of previous artists

Answers are on page 555.

EXERCISE 15: INTERPRETING A PAINTING

Directions: Read the art review below and answer the questions that follow.

WHAT DOES THE CRITIC SEE IN WYETH'S WORK?

A Review of Artist Andrew Wyeth and His Work
by Frieda Davenport

We can take photographs to "freeze moments" in our memories. We do not consider ourselves artists, for we use the camera to capture the memory for us. When we see a painting which freezes a moment and gives meaning to it, we know art.

Andrew Wyeth, one of the most popular American artists of our time, has the ability to capture moments on canvas. His temperas and watercolors present natural colors—earth tones of browns, greys, and muted shades of pink. He uses white as no other artist has.

Wyeth's subjects and landscapes are rural. His compositions reflect a thoughtful simplicity as if he has created "impressionistic" photographs. Not only is a landscape captured but a subject against a horizon, old farmhouses, bruised buckets, torn lace curtains, and window frames.

To learn about Wyeth is to see one of his paintings—*Christina's World* (1948)—his most well-known work. Christina, an actual friend of his, is in a crawling position with her back to the observer. She leans into, perhaps yearning for, a farmhouse on the horizon. Centered on the painting and on the horizon is an out-shed, a barn, which is to the left of the house.

The three focal points—the girl, the barn, and the farmhouse—are "balanced" on a grassy, barren field. The "plainness" is characteristic of Wyeth. Each time we look at the painting, we are drawn to Christina, the "center" of the painting and of her world.

Wyeth is often categorized as an American Realist, but to label artists is to limit our views of their accomplishments. The simplicity of Wyeth's work discourages complexity of thought, and we are left to thoroughly enjoy the moment that he creates for us.

1. The review discusses all of the following *except*

   (1) the popularity of the artist
   (2) the types of paints and techniques used
   (3) the artist's preference in colors
   (4) a specific painting
   (5) the price of one of Wyeth's paintings

2. The critic is most impressed with Wyeth's

   (1) development of new techniques
   (2) use of earth tones
   (3) fame and fortune
   (4) ability to capture a specific moment
   (5) use of "balance" in the paintings

3. The quality that the critic likes most in *Christina's World* is Wyeth's

(1) accuracy
(2) colors
(3) simplicity
(4) complexity
(5) portrayal of the 1940s

Answers are on page 555.

Interpreting a Television Review

Most of the reviews you have been reading deal with a specific work. The critic reacts to one book, film, or work of art. However, criticism may discuss trends or characteristics of one type of art.

The following television review presents views not only about a specific show but about the nature of TV programming. As you read, look for statements of facts and statements of opinion. Remember that most reviews are persuasive essays. The critic's purpose is illustrated with details and examples. Notice this critic's style, tone, and use of language.

EXERCISE 16: INTERPRETING A TELEVISION REVIEW

Directions: Read the television review below and answer the questions that follow.

HOW DOES THE REVIEWER RATE THE "ALL-TIME BEST" SITCOMS?

"M*A*S*H"

Where "Lucy" created a new comic form for TV, and "All in the Family" used social issues for comic fodder, "M*A*S*H" did what only the greatest— the classic—comedies do: mix hilarity and tragedy, often in equal measure. "M*A*S*H" made us laugh till we cried. And though its anti-war message occasionally got heavy-handed, it was never at the expense of laughter or character. Like all great sitcoms, it succeeded mainly by exploring, indeed celebrating, the chemistry between the characters. The last episode of "M*A*S*H" was the most-watched program in TV history for good reason. Yes, the final episode of "Cheers" may yet rival it, but "M*A*S*H" has an underriding urgency to its comedy—it's about life, death, war, and the redeeming grace of humor—that makes it, in our eyes, the best sitcom in history.

1. If you were retitling the review, which of the following titles would you choose?

(1) Keeping It All in the Family
(2) How "Lucy" Changed Our Viewing
(3) Watching the Last of the Best
(4) Is TV Getting Better or Worse?
(5) Laughing and Crying with a Classic

2. The comment "And though its anti-war message occasionally got heavy-handed" suggests the reviewer's belief that

(1) sitcoms like "M*A*S*H" might sometimes be about war
(2) the sitcom's characters were sometimes interesting
(3) sometimes the show was about hand-to-hand combat
(4) sometimes the message against war was too obvious
(5) the sitcom's characters sometimes got into fights

3. The reviewer would agree that a sitcom that hopes to become the best in history must

(1) contain very powerful anti-war messages
(2) have strong relationships among characters
(3) closely follow the comic form of the "Lucy" show
(4) use "All in the Family" as a writing blueprint
(5) use humor to cover up the tragedy in a story

4. The reviewer's statement that "'M*A*S*H' has an underriding urgency to its comedy" means

(1) stunts with horses were used in the show
(2) the humor in the show was always fast-paced
(3) there was always a deeper reason for the humor
(4) shows were always written at the last minute
(5) there was always someone facing danger

5. You are eager to write a good TV sitcom. After reading the review, which of the following "rules" would you observe?

(1) Being funny is more important than developing good characters.
(2) Good one-liners can make or break a show.
(3) Social issues do not belong on television.
(4) War should be dealt with in a serious way.
(5) Mix humor and tragedy in balanced amounts.

6. What is the tone of the review?

(1) appreciative
(2) questioning
(3) uncomplimentary
(4) irresolute
(5) sarcastic

Answers are on page 555.

TEST 4: LITERATURE AND THE ARTS ANSWER KEY

CHAPTER 1: INTERPRETING PROSE FICTION

Exercise 1: Identifying Setting
page 456
Inferential

1. Yun-ja is in the water, swimming. The clues are "floated on the blue swells," "the water chilled her," and "ripples slapped about her ears."
2. She is in a public place frequented by people from many different countries, as evidenced by the fact that she can hear "the babble of English, Spanish, and other tongues. . . ."
3. Chong-il is relaxing on the beach. Note the clue that reads, "There he [Chong-il] was, sitting under the beach umbrella . . . drinking something."
4. The story is set in the present. The clue is "She heard the drone of powerboats. . . ."
5. The action takes place during the day. The clue is the reference to "the dazzling sun."

Exercise 2: Atmosphere as Part of Setting
page 457
Inferential

1. The atmosphere of the passage is one of fear.
2. The words that indicate fear are *crouching, running, dodging, hide,* and *stiffened.*

Exercise 3: Inferring Character
page 458
Literal

1. (5) Only choice (5) describes Slim's personality; the other choices are physical descriptions.
2. (4) The descriptions of Slim are the only information we have about his character.

Exercise 4: Identifying Characters Through Dialogue
pages 460–461
Literal

1. mother and adult child
2. the mother
3. the adult child
4. the adult child
5. The mother is an elderly Chinese woman who likes to complain. The adult child is a level-headed person who appears to be used to the mother's complaining.

Exercise 5: Identifying Details of Setting, Plot, and Conflict
pages 463-464
Literal

1. Line 22: "There aren't any grownups. We shall have to look after ourselves."
2. Lines 5–7: "We're on an island. . . ."
3. a pig; line 10 states, "There are pigs on the island."
4. Ralph; The line "we need hunters to get us meat" (line 19) and the author's statement that Ralph "looked round the sun-slashed faces" (line 21) suggest that Ralph is leading the meeting.

Inferential

5. Individual vs. nature; the boys have to adapt to the island. Individual vs. society; the boys have to deal with each other without grownups. Individual vs. another; Ralph and Jack are in conflict.

Literal

6. 4, 3, 1, 5, 2

Exercise 6: Determining Point of View
page 466
Application

The words you should have underlined are in italic type and the circled words appear in bold type.

Macomber stepped out of the curved opening at the side of the front seat onto the step and down onto the ground. The **lion** still stood looking majestically and coolly toward this object that **his** eyes only showed in silhouette, bulging like some super-rhino. There was no man smell carried toward **him** and **he** watched the object [jeep], moving **his** great head a little from side to side. Then watching the object, not afraid, but hesitating before going down the bank to drink with such a thing opposite **him**, **he** saw a *man figure* detach *itself* from it and **he** turned **his** heavy head and swung away toward the cover of the trees as **he** heard a cracking crash and felt the slam of a .30–06 220-grain solid bullet that bit **his** flank and ripped in sudden hot scalding nausea through **his** stomach. **He** trotted, heavy, big-footed, swinging wounded full-bellied, through the trees toward the tall grass and cover, and the crash came again to go past **him** ripping the air apart. Then it crashed again and **he** felt the blow as it hit **his** lower ribs and ripped on through, blood sudden hot and frothy in **his** mouth, and **he** galloped toward the high grass where **he** could crouch and not be seen and make *them* bring the crashing thing close enough so **he** could make a rush and get the *man* that held it.

Exercise 7: Inferring Theme
page 467
Inferential

1. **(5)** All of the incidents concern Miss Strangeworth's sending anonymous letters.

2. **(5)** The excerpt concerns Miss Strangeworth's fighting "possible evil lurking nearby."

3. **(3)** While Miss Strangeworth's motives may have seemed good to her, her actions hurt innocent people.

Exercise 8: Review of Five Fiction Elements
pages 468–469
Inferential

1. **(3)** The first two sentences state that "Ivan Ilych saw that he was dying, and he was in continual despair. In the depth of his heart he knew he was dying, but not only was he not accustomed to the thought, he simply did not and could not grasp it."

2. **(4)** Note the use of the word *he* to refer to Ivan Ilych. The third-person narrator is never named and does not take part in the action.

3. **(2)** Most of the passage consists of Ilych's thoughts about death and his desperate attempts to erase the thoughts from his mind.

4. **(1)** As the second sentence states, "[Ilych] simply did not and could not grasp it [his impending death]."

5. **(1)** Paragraph four states that Ilych would "go to the law courts."

Exercise 9: Tone and Characterization
page 470
Analysis

1. **(1)** The passage states that Julian's mother "said ladies did not tell their age or weight" (lines 5–6) and that "she would not ride buses by herself at night since they had been integrated" (lines 6–7). This suggests that Julian's mother subscribes to old-fashioned values.

2. **(4)** The last two sentences point to a funny and sarcastic tone of voice.

3. **(3)** The author seems to feel that people like Julian's mother require tolerance and sympathy.

Exercise 10: Identifying an Author's Style
page 472
Analysis

The descriptions and images that appeal to the senses appear in italic type.

The *soprano screak of carriage wheels punished my ear.* Sun, *seeping through the blinds, filled the bedroom* with a *sulphurous light.* I didn't know how long I had slept, but I *felt one big twitch of exhaustion.*

The twin bed next to mine was empty and unmade.

At seven I had *heard my mother get up, slip into her clothes* and *tiptoe out of the room.* Then the *buzz of the orange squeezer sounded* from downstairs, and the *smell of coffee and bacon filtered under my door.* Then the *sink water ran from the tap and dishes clinked* as my mother dried them and put them back in the cupboard.

Then the *front door opened and shut.* Then the *car door opened and shut,* and the *motor went broom-broom* and, edging off with a *crunch of gravel, faded into the distance.*

Exercise 11: Descriptive Language
page 473
Application

1. d   2. a   3. c   4. b

Exercise 12: Identifying Figures of Speech
pages 474–475
Analysis

Words underlined include: *a whisper of a woman* (metaphor)
like a fox moving in for the kill (simile)
Grandma would become a cyclone. (metaphor)
Her ax, a bloody character that seemed to lie in wait for hens, would sever the head. (personification)
like a savage in an ancient tribal rite (simile)
My microwave oven lazily sits waiting (personification)

Analysis

1. **(3)** "Whisper of a woman" is a metaphor referring to her size.

2. **(4)** Personification is used to make the ax seem human.

Inferential

3. **(1)** The author is looking back with nostalgia.

4. **(3)** Grandma's killing of a chicken is contrasted to present-day shopping habits and microwave meals.

5. **(5)** The last paragraph expresses this sentiment.

**Exercise 13: Interpreting a
Short Story
pages 476–480**
Literal
1. rooftop, civil war, Dublin, Ireland,
   June, city, night

Analysis
2. **(5)** Because of the subject of the
   story, war, the atmosphere may be
   best described as tense.

Literal
3. c, b, b, a

Analysis
4. 3, 2, 5, 4, 1

Inferential
5. The author lets us know the thoughts
   of only the sniper to create an
   atmosphere of suspense.

Analysis
6. Third person; the references *he* and
   they indicate third-person narration
7. **(1)** The author reports the incidents
   in a controlled and unemotional
   manner.

Application
8. s, m, p, p, s

Inferential
9. **(4)** The figures of speech "grey
   monster" and "like a thousand
   devils" suggest the author's
   attitude toward the horror of war.

Analysis
10. **(3)** The point of highest intensity in
    the story is when the sniper kills
    the enemy.

Inferential
11. **(4)** The lines reflect the sniper's inner
    struggle.
12. **(2)** To show remorse means to express
    guilt.

Analysis
13. **(5)** The author explores human
    behavior by showing the sniper's
    character. Because of the sniper's
    "lust for battle," he kills his
    brother.

**Exercise 14: Commentary
About Fiction
page 482**
Literal
1. **(2)** The review states that "one wants
   to follow Putus's life as a young
   woman instead of returning to her
   decades later. . . ."

Inferential
2. **(1)** The last sentence of the review
   makes it clear that the reviewer
   admires the writer's story-telling
   abilities.

Application
3. **(4)** The review of the book indicates
   that it fits only the real-life drama
   category.

**CHAPTER 2: INTERPRETING
POETRY**
**Exercise 1: Interpreting Two Poems
pages 483–484**
Inferential
1. **(4)** Romantic love is mentioned in both
   poems; it is referred to repeatedly
   in Sonnet 43.

Analysis
2. **(3)** Both poems include rhyme.
   Rhyming words in "Oh, When I
   Was in Love with You" include *you*
   and *grew*; *brave* and *behave*, and
   remain and *again*; rhyming words
   in Sonnet 43 include *height* and
   sight.

**Exercise 2: The Shape of Poetry
pages 487–488**
Literal
1. There are three sentences; a period
   ends each sentence.
2. The third stanza refers to Grandma's
   life as a younger woman. She had been
   (1) a migrant "cutting grapes and
   boxing plums." (2) She had had
   tapeworm and diseased skin. (3) Her
   son had died. (4) She had been sad
   and had traveled to various locations
   to work in the fields.

Inferential
3. The first stanza tells of her later years,
   of a happier life. At the end of the
   second stanza, Grandma smiles. *Smiled*
   is the clue word that indicates the
   mood of contentment.
4. The narrator is the grandchild of a
   Hispanic migrant farm worker.
5. Grandma was a migrant farm worker.
   The clues are "cutting grapes and
   boxing plums" and "that pulled her
   from Taxco to San Joaquin, Delano
   to Westside."

**Exercise 3: The Sound of Poetry
page 489**
Analysis
1. Some different examples of alliteration
   are:
   (1) "maggie and milly and molly and
       may"
   (2) "a shell that sang / so sweetly
       she . . ."
   (3) "blowing bubbles"
   (4) "smooth round stone / as
       small . . ."
   (You may have found others)
2. Lines 3 and 4 and 7 and 8 do not rhyme
   at all.
3. There are four "beats" per line.

Inferential

4. (4) The author is saying that when we "lose" ourselves at the beach, it's because we become interested in something outside ourselves: the water, the fish, the shells, the sand, etc. This gives us a new view on life.

Exercise 4: Words that Stand for Sounds
pages 490–491
Analysis

1. (5) *b*atter and *b*anjos; alliteration is a repetition of a beginning consonant sound.

2. (3) The word *like* makes a comparison between two things—moan and autumn wind. The sound of the autumn wind is given a human quality.

Application

3. (4) In *The Bell Jar*, Plath uses sound words such as *screak, buzz, clinked,* and *broom-broom*. Examples of alliteration are *soprano screak* and *sun seeping*.

Exercise 5: Inferring Meaning
page 492
Inferential

2. Inference: The man prays./ Line numbers: 13–15/ Key words: *reverently, prayer, give thanks*

3. Inference: The man was a farmer./ Line numbers: 4, 5/ Key words: *tossed bales of straw each August*

4. Inference: The man is now elderly./ Line numbers: 11–12/ Key words: *now crudely arches to grasp a bamboo cane.*/ Line number: 14/ Key words: *bow your feeble body in prayer*

5. Inference: The man was athletic./ Line number: 6/ Key words: *once pitched no-hitters*

Exercise 6: Interpreting a Poem
page 494
Inference

1. (3) The title of the poem, "The Negro Speaks of Rivers," is a clue to the narrator's identity. "My soul" refers to a person of African descent, speaking for the race.

Analysis

2. (4) This is a positive image and probably refers to Lincoln's freeing the slaves. He "heard" the "singing" of the river, and the bosom of the river "turned golden."

3. (2) The poem mentions four great rivers of the world that are associated with African and African-American people: the Euphrates, the Congo, the Nile, and the Mississippi.

Exercise 7: The Language of Poetry
page 496
Analysis

Line 1: *imagery*
Line 2: *personification*
Line 3: *personification*
Line 4: *imagery*
Line 5: *personification*

Exercise 8: Review of Figurative Language and Theme
page 498
Analysis

1. (3) "Holding wonder like a cup"; *like* is a word that identifies a simile.

2. (5) In line 8, the speaker compares music to "a curve of gold."

3. (4) Thoughts are compared to stars.

Exercise 9: Interpreting a Poem
page 499
Analysis

1. fish
2. the moon

Exercise 10: More Practice in Interpreting a Poem
pages 499–500
Literal

1. b, c, a, e, d

Analysis

2. (3) Death and Immortality are characters who ride in the carriage with the narrator.

3. (2) The lines "Because I could not stop for Death, He kindly stopped for me" are an example of personification—giving human qualities to an abstraction.

Inferential

4. (5) The title of the poem and lines 1–2 imply that the narrator of the poem was full of life and died unexpectedly.

5. (5) From the last stanza, we can infer that the poet believes that the narrator was taken from earth but lives on.

Exercise 11: More Practice in Interpreting a Poem
page 501
Inferential

1. (4) The narrator of the poem "The Man from Washington" is a Native American. Clue words to this are: *firewood and buffalo robes, rainwater eyes, treaties signed, a world in which we had no part.*

Analysis

2. (1) The mood of the poem is one of alienation. Clue words are *would be innoculated against a world in which we had no part, a world of wealth, promise, and fabulous disease.*

3. (4) The theme of this poem concerns the loss of self-determination and the way of life for the Native American.

Exercise 12: Commentary on Poetry
page 502
Inferential

1. (2) The reviewer (quoting Shakespeare's *Hamlet*) states "that 'the slings and arrows of outrageous fortune' are often gifts which make us stronger."

2. (1) This is a simpler rewording of the cliché.

CHAPTER 3: INTERPRETING DRAMA

Exercise 1: How Drama Differs
page 505
Analysis

1. (c) Drama shows the words and actions of characters in a real-life setting.

2. (b) The poetry version is written in verse with concise images.

3. (c) We can "see" the setting, the characters and how they react to each other.

4. (c) In drama, character is revealed through dialogue and action.

5. (a) The prose version summarizes the action and is written in simple sentence form.

Exercise 2: Dialogue and Punctuation
page 506
Literal

1. Edward and Victoria; the ellipses indicate that Catherine interrupts Edward's speech.

2. Edward; both of Edward's speeches are questions.

3. Edward; Edward is bothered by Catherine's interruption.

4. Edward; Victoria's tone and responses to Edward indicate that she is upset with him.

Exercise 3: Inferring Mood from Dialogue
page 506
Analysis

(1) The rudeness of Edward toward Catherine, Victoria's responses to Edward, and Catherine's abrupt departure all indicate that the mood of the scene is tense.

Exercise 4: Identifying Characters
page 509
Literal

1. b　**2.** c　**3.** d　**4.** e　**5.** f　**6.** a

Exercise 5: History of Drama
pages 509–510
Literal

1. (4) Choices (1), (2), (3), and (5) are stated in the scene. Choice (4) is contrary to the information provided in the scene.

Analysis

2. (1) The setting—Miss Anderson seated on her desktop—and her students' humorous responses indicate that the mood is informal.

3. (4) Miss Anderson's manner and tone in responding to Pete's antics indicate that her approach is casual.

Inferential

4. (2) Miss Anderson's discussion of Shakespeare, especially her remark "and all of it written in verse form," indicates great admiration for Shakespeare.

5. (4) The stage directions that introduce the play state "The scene is a drama class where students are learning about the history of drama." Also, in her dialogue, Miss Anderson describes the origin and progression of Western drama.

Exercise 6: Understanding Character
pages 512–514
Inferential

1. (3) In the scene, Jessie's mother asks her a series of questions, including where Jessie put her glasses. Mama's initial statement, "I want to know why," and Jessie's response, "You have no earthly idea of how I feel," suggest that a lack of communication exists between mother and daughter. None of the other choices are supported adequately by the dialogue in the scene.

2. (4) The scene contains several lines of dialogue in which Mama criticizes Jessie for being ungrateful and distant. Also, Mama blames Jessie for Cecil's leaving.

3. (1) A line of Jessie's dialogue states, "smoking is the only thing I know that's always just what you think it's going to be. Just like it was the last time and right there when you want it and real quiet." This line suggests that Jessie likes smoking because its effect is something she can depend on.

4. (4) Because the dialogue between Jessie and her mother is angry and bitter, we can infer that Jessie is at odds with her mother.

Analysis

5. (4) The angry, accusing tone shown by Jessie's mother and Jessie's responses to her mother suggest a mood of tension.

Exercise 7: Supporting Facts and Inferences
page 514
Inferential

1. Support for the inference that Jessie has epilepsy are the lines of dialogue that refer to "seizures" and "fits." Mama asks Jessie, "When you have a fit do you see stars, or what?" and "Your fits made him sick."

2. Support for the inference that Jessie is separated from Cecil are the following lines: "Why did Cecil leave you?" "Cecil left me because he made me choose between him and smoking." "Cecil left for pretty much the same reason."

3. Support for the fact that Jessie smokes are the lines: "Cecil left me because he made me choose between him and smoking." Also "Smoking is the only thing I know . . ."

4. The inference that Jessie is confused about what her mother wants to know is supported by the lines of dialogue: "Back where?" "What are you talking about?"

5. Support for the inference that Mama doesn't believe Jessie's story about the accident is the line of dialogue, "How did you fall off the horse, really?"

Exercise 8: Interpreting a Scene from a Play
pages 514–516
Inferential

1. (3) Alice's second line of dialogue, in which she suggests finding a home for her senile father (like her husband Sidney did for his parents) and the discussion about powers of attorney imply that she and Gene are sister and brother. Another clue to their relationship comes later in the scene: "He broke Mother's heart over that for years."

Application

2. (5) Alice's first line of dialogue, in which she says "I'm doing a lot for my kids. I don't expect them to pay me back at the other end," suggests that she believes elderly parents should not expect their children to take care of them.

Inferential

3. (2) Alice says in the scene, "He kicked me out. He said he never wanted to see me again. He broke Mother's heart over that for years. He was mean, unloving." These lines of dialogue suggest resentment toward her father.

4. (1) In the scene, Alice says, "You've lived through a great deal of ugliness. But you work like a Trojan to deny it, to make it not so."

5. (2) Based on Gene's dialogue, he is not relieved; he is ashamed that he can't ask his father to live with him.

Literal

6. (4) Alice's last line of dialogue in the exchange tells Gene to let her handle it and not to give in.

7. (4) Gene's line, "I can't tell you how ashamed I feel . . . not to say with open arms, 'Poppa, come live with me. . . . I love you, Poppa, and I want to take care of you,'" indicates that he feels guilty for not loving his father.

Exercise 9: Interpreting a Film Review
pages 516–517
Analysis

1. (2) The fact that the novel *The Last Tycoon* was unfinished and that Pinter and Kazan nevertheless were able to turn the book into a "fascinating low-key film" implies an attitude of admiration.

2. (2) The figure of speech, "He sees life as a movie and people as shadows," is a simile; it uses the word *as* to compare two unlike things. It suggests that life is like a movie and people are like shadows.

Literal

3. (1) The passage states directly that "Stahr himself is a flawed human being."

Inferential

4. (5) Because "Hollywood Boosters" are supporters of Hollywood, and these supporters are likely to be movie producers, the implication is that the film will offend the producers of Hollywood films.

CHAPTER 4: INTERPRETING NONFICTION

Exercise 1: The Biography
pages 521–522
Literal

1. (4) The passage does not comment on Thoreau's writing style.

Analysis

2. **(5)** The significance of Thoreau's move to Walden Pond on July 4 is that the date is the anniversary of the nation's independence. On that date, Thoreau was declaring his own independence.

Application

3. **(4)** While secluded in the woods, Thoreau reflected on the meaning and beauty of life. The other choices have nothing to do with considering the meaning of life.

Literal

4. **(1)** The passage states that the essay "On the Duty of Civil Disobedience" influenced the works of Gandhi and Martin Luther King, Jr.

Inferential

5. **(2)** The passage states that Thoreau was imprisoned for refusing to pay a poll tax that supported the Mexican War. Thoreau's action is an example of nonviolent resistance to an unjust law.

6. **(2)** The quote reflects the ideal of individualism. No other choice listed is supported by the quote.

Exercise 2: Oral History
pages 523–524
Literal

1. **T** The passage refers to Chavez's parents and brothers and sisters.

2. **F** The passage relates sadness and hope and Chavez's belief that "you don't let [things] get you down."

3. **T** The passage states that his father never gave up hope.

4. **T** The passage says that when you're small, you don't question things; you continue to move.

5. **F** The last sentence of the passage says that "we had never been migratory workers."

6. **T** The passage states that " 'following the crops,' we missed much school."

7. **F** The entire passage describes the effect the Depression had on Chavez's family.

8. **F** The facts presented in the passage show that the speaker remembers many things about the Depression's impact on his family.

Exercise 3: Autobiography
pages 525–526
Inferential

1. **(2)** The word *pregnant* is connected with many unpleasant experiences that the writer faced, suggesting a burden he was carrying.

2. **(5)** The passage describes the teacher as being unaware, insensitive, and uninterested in the author. She is not described as being understanding.

Analysis

3. **(4)** The use of the word *pregnant* to mean "burdened with" is an example of the writer's unique mode of expression.

4. **(4)** The only similarity between Chavez's and Gregory's childhood is that both made successful lives despite their childhood poverty. Choices (1), (2), (3), and (5) are not true of *both* men's childhoods.

5. **(5)** The title suggests that people do not always think of themselves the way others might think of them. The other choices are not supported by the passage.

Exercise 4: Journal Entries
page 526
Inferential

1. **(5)** The quote refers to experimenting with life. Experimenting involves taking a risk. The other choices are not supported by the advice in the quote.

Application

2. **(3)** An astronaut's occupation involves a greater degree of physical risk than the other choices provided.

Exercise 5: The Article as Nonfiction
page 528
Inferential

1. **(5)** The reference to the veterans as heroes suggests that the writer holds great admiration for the marchers.

Analysis

2. **(4)** The writer emphasizes the number thirteen to point out the positive outcome despite the parade's association with an unlucky number. The other choices are not supported by the information in the passage.

Exercise 6: The Formal Essay
pages 529–530
Inferential

1. **(4)** The word *duty* implies an obligation; therefore, the title suggests that a person is obligated to break an unjust law.

2. **(3)** The government represents the people and is the means by which a people carry out their desires. The other choices do not help to define government in this sense.

3. **(2)** The essay states that "The standing army is only an arm of the standing government."

4. (1) According to the essay, "The government . . . is only the mode which the people have chosen to execute their will."

5. (4) Emerson, who also believed in nonconformity, admired Thoreau's belief in individual liberty.

Exercise 7: Review of Thoreau
page 531
Application

1, 3, 4, and 5 Thoreau would have supported 1, 3, 4, and 5 because they further social justice and individual freedoms. Choices 2 and 6 limit individual freedoms; therefore, Thoreau would not have supported them.

Exercise 8: Comparing and Contrasting Styles
pages 531–534
Analysis

1. (3) The short essay is characterized by all of the choices given except long, explanatory paragraphs.

Inferential

2. (4) The statement and the entire thrust of the passage show the agent's total dependence on the computer.

Literal

3. (3) The agent is completely paralyzed by the situation in which the computer is down.

Analysis

4. (4) Passage 2 lacks the humor of Passage 1.

Inferential

5. (5) *Sweatshop* originally referred to nineteenth- and early twentieth-century factories in which workers labored long hours for low pay in unhealthy work conditions.

6. (3) Throughout the excerpt, the author talks about psychological problems caused by electronic offices—for example, "a rise in loneliness and disconnection" and "fragmentation of self."

Analysis

7. (1) The author briefly describes Nicholas's educational background and experience to let readers know that he is a reliable and expert source of opinion.

Application

8. (4) Both passages illustrate our dependence on and trust in computers. Both writers feel we should retain control over computers.

Exercise 9: Interpreting a Speech
pages 535–536
Inferential

1. (3) Because Sagoyewatha says that "we have scarcely a place left to spread our blankets," he is referring to the growth in numbers of the white population.

Literal

2. (2) *Place* is a clue to the land that Sagoyewatha speaks about.

Inferential

3. (1) The irony is that, while white people left their homeland to seek freedom of religion, they did not respect the Native Americans' choice to worship freely.

Analysis

4. (2) The speech refers to acts of betrayal by the white man; the tone is one of distrust.

Literal

5. (1) The speech concludes with the opinion that, though whites practice one religion, they do not all worship in the same way.

Exercise 10: More Practice Interpreting Speeches
pages 536–537
Analysis

1. (4) As the first speech of his presidency, Kennedy wants to inspire listeners.

2. (3) The most persuasive call to serve the public is in the second to the last paragraph: "ask not what your country can do for you; ask what you can do for your country."

Literal

3. (3) In paragraph 4, Kennedy says that "only a few generations have been granted the role of defending freedom in its hour of maximum danger."

Analysis

4. (1) The speech does not rhyme or display a standardized rhythmic pattern.

Exercise 11: Interpreting a Book Review
pages 539–540
Analysis

1. + **2.** F **3.** + **4.** − **5.** − **6.** − **7.** F

Exercise 12: Interpreting a Review of a Novel
page 540
Inferential

1. (3) The critic says, "Bobby and his much described charisma become equally unbelievable" and "Nothing that he does makes him appear to the reader as magnetic as he seems to everyone in the book."

Analysis

2. (5) The only choice that reflects on the author's skillfulness in creating characters are the words *memorable* and *unique*.

Application

3. (2) The statements "A producer's lunch at Sardi's is preposterous" and "tritely portrayed show-biz worlds of New York or Hollywood" reflect the critic's view that New York scenes are flawed.

Analysis

4. (2) Prior to this comment, the reviewer has said only positive things about the book. This quote indicates a shift to critical comments.

Exercise 13: Review of a Satire pages 541–542

Literal

1. (4) "Mail-order catalogs" is the only choice listed that is not a source for information contained in the book.

2. (2) The review states, "This is a funny book indeed. . . ."

3. (1) The topic of the book is Pentagon spending.

Application

4. (3) The book begins with a forceful sales pitch.

Analysis

5. (4) The reviewer uses lots of quotes from the book to give his audience an appreciation of the book's humor.

Exercise 14: Interpreting Musical Commentary pages 542–543

Inferential

1. (2) The reviewer describes Marsalis as belonging to an elite—a superior group. This statement indicates admiration for the musician.

Literal

2. (1) The review refers to Marsalis's "beautiful tone and impressive technique."

3. (4) The passage states that Marsalis also plays classical music.

Application

4. (2) *To nurture* means "to further one's development." This suggests that the critic supports Marsalis's improvement of the tradition.

Exercise 15: Interpreting a Painting pages 544–545

Literal

1. (5) The only topic not discussed in the review is the cost of Wyeth's paintings.

2. (4) The review begins by discussing Wyeth's ability to capture a specific moment.

Inferential

3. (3) The passage refers to Wyeth's simplicity twice—"a thoughtful simplicity" and "The simplicity of Wyeth's work discourages complexity of thought. . . ."

Exercise 16: Interpreting a Television Review pages 545–546

Inferential

1. (5) The reviewer says of "the classic" "M*A*S*H" it "made us laugh till we cried."

2. (4) Choice 4 is the only accurate reworking of the quoted line.

Application

3. (2) The reviewer states, "Like all great sitcoms ["M*A*S*H"] succeeded mainly by exploring, indeed celebrating, the chemistry between the characters."

Inferential

4. (3) This would seem to be the only correct explanation of the term.

Application

5. (5) The reviewer writes " 'M*A*S*H' did what only the greatest—the classic—comedies do: mix hilarity and tragedy, often in equal measure."

Analysis

6. (1) The reviewer showed his admiration for all the sitcoms discussed.

Test 5: Mathematics

The GED Mathematics Test consists of multiple-choice questions. Almost all of the questions will be either word problems or based on some graph or other illustration. These math items will test not only your ability to do arithmetic, algebra, and geometry but also your problem-solving skills. To answer successfully, you will need to

▶ estimate an answer

▶ go through several steps to solve a problem

▶ select only the information needed to solve the problem

▶ determine that not enough information is given to get an answer

Actually, you already use these skills in your work with math on the job or at home. In this section, we will give you lots of practice in basic math skills as well as these crucial problem-solving areas.

How many questions are on the test?

There are 56 problems, and you will be given 90 minutes to complete the test. About one-third of the items will be based on diagrams, charts, or graphs. Some of the questions will appear in item sets—a passage or drawing that is followed by 2 or more problems. Some of the problems will not require any computation. Instead, you will have to determine how a problem could be set up to solve it.

To get an idea of what the test is like, look at the Practice Test at the end of this book. This Practice Test is based on the real GED Test.

What's on the test?

The GED Mathematics Test can be broken down into the content areas it covers and the skills it tests. The following subjects make up the content of the test:

Arithmetic	50%
Measurement	
Number Relationships	
Data Analysis	
Algebra	30%
Geometry	20%

The ten chapters in this section will provide you with explanations, examples, and exercises in all of these content areas. Some of the material will be familiar and even seem easy. You will still want to sharpen your skills in those areas. Other areas will be new and difficult and will require concentrated study and repeated practice to learn.

What can help me prepare for the test?

To be successful, you must constantly practice and test each skill as you learn it. Remember, this is a book to work with, not just to read. Learning mathematics is like learning to play the piano; you can read a book about it or watch someone else do it. But until you actually practice it yourself, you won't know how to play a piano or solve a math problem.

The following are some specific suggestions to help you:

1. To learn a new skill, go over the example problems carefully. Try to do the example problems yourself.

2. Learn the rules that are summarized in the boxes in each section. Then try to say the rules out loud and explain how to use them.

3. Check each exercise with the answer key starting on page 712. You need to know right away if you are grasping the skills.

4. Use all of the problem-solving strategies that are provided in this section. In particular, you will find that drawing a picture with the information and estimating an answer will often help you understand a problem that seems confusing.

5. Do your practice work in pencil. Carefully write down all the information that you need to solve a problem.

Getting Rid of "Math Anxiety"

Many people feel that they are just "not good in math." If this is true of you, listed below are some ideas that will help.

1. Accept the fact that while you have some math anxiety, most other people do too.

2. Math requires logic, but often intuition comes first. Don't be afraid to use the ideas that pop into your mind.

3. You can be creative. Solving a problem in a way that's different from what is given in the book is fine too.

4. Estimating answers is helpful with many problems.

5. Use all the tools at hand—your fingers, paper, pencil, pictures—whatever works for you.

6. Have confidence in yourself and your ability to learn math concepts and try new approaches.

1
WHOLE NUMBERS AND PROBLEM SOLVING

Most of the problems on the Mathematics Test are word problems. In this chapter and throughout the math section, you will practice and learn techniques for working with word problems.

Basic to solving all word problems is a good, strong foundation in math facts, mainly the multiplication tables and the addition facts. If you are unsure of any of these facts, now is the time to review and memorize those that give you trouble. Just as you can remember the phone numbers, addresses, and other important numbers in your life, you can remember these facts. Your ability to work with decimals, fractions, and other math skills depends on how quickly and accurately you can do these computations.

Before starting work on problem solving, let's review the basic operations of addition, subtraction, multiplication, and division.

Review of Math Operations

The examples below will help you refresh your memory about the basics of addition, subtraction, multiplication, and division. An *estimate* for each problem is also shown in bold type. In some situations, an estimated (approximate) answer can serve as the final answer. At other times, estimates are used to check the reasonableness of exact answers, including calculator computations.

Example 1 shows how you must *regroup* (*carry*) in some addition problems.

Example 1:

$$
\begin{array}{r}
\overset{2\;2}{}\;\; \\
4\;8\;6 \\
\overset{1}{}\;\;3\;9 \\
1\;7\;2\;5 \\
+\quad\;\;8\;9 \\
\hline
2\;3\;3\;9
\end{array}
$$

← regroup to the next column to the left

Estimate:

$$
\begin{array}{r}
5\;0\;0 \\
5\;0 \\
1\;7\;0\;0 \\
1\;0\;0 \\
\hline
2\;3\;5\;0
\end{array}
$$

Example 2 illustrates *regrouping* (*borrowing*) in subtraction.

Example 2:

$$
\begin{array}{r}
\overset{3\;\;10\;\;7\;\;16}{\cancel{4}\;\cancel{0}\;\cancel{8}\;\cancel{6}} \\
-\quad\;9\;5\;7 \\
\hline
3\;1\;2\;9
\end{array}
$$

← regroup from the next available unit to the left

Estimate:

$$
\begin{array}{r}
4\;0\;0\;0 \\
-\;1\;0\;0\;0 \\
\hline
3\;0\;0\;0
\end{array}
$$

Example 3 shows both *regrouping* and *indenting* in multiplication.

Example 3:

$$
\begin{array}{r}
\overset{2\;1}{}\;\; \\
4\;8 \\
\times\quad 3\;2 \\
\hline
9\;6 \\
1\;4\;4\;\;\; \\
\hline
1\;5\;3\;6
\end{array}
$$

← regroup to the next column to the left

← indent rows one column at a time

Estimate: $50 \times 30 = 1500$

For most people, division is the most complicated operation. Example 4 shows the basic steps.

Example 4: 3049 ÷ 6

STEP 1. Divide by the number that follows the division sign (÷). Divide into the first number that you can. Since 6 won't divide into 3, divide into 30.

$$\overset{5}{6)\overline{3049}}$$

divisor → dividend

STEP 2. Multiply and subtract. Bring down the next number. If you can't divide into it, write a zero in the answer before you bring down the next number.

$$\overset{50}{6)\overline{3049}} \\ -30 \\ \overline{04}$$

STEP 3. Divide 6 into 49. Multiply. Subtract. Write the *remainder* as a part of your answer.

$$\overset{508\ r1}{6)\overline{3049}} \\ -30 \\ \overline{49} \\ -48 \\ \overline{1}$$

Estimate: 3000 ÷ 6 = 500

▶ **TIP:** There is no *one* correct estimate. Work with numbers that you are comfortable with. Estimates can vary.

Now practice a mixed group of problems to test your understanding of math facts.

EXERCISE 1: WHOLE NUMBERS

Directions: Solve each problem. Find an estimate and an exact answer for each problem. Compare the two answers in each problem. Are they close?

1.
```
  9873
   412
   509
+   48
```

2.
```
  3000
-   56
```

3.
```
  1276
-   99
```

4.
```
   87
×  95
```

5.
```
   268
×   47
```

6. 9)5643

7. 15)4021

8. 72)36,072

Answers are on page 712.

Problem-Solving Skills

In this section, we will discuss a six-step approach for solving word problems. Since most of the problems on the Mathematics Test are word problems, you should be sure to master these skills. When you do a word problem, read it carefully. Sometimes, you will need to read a problem more than once.

The six steps on page 561 will help you understand and solve math word problems.

STEP 1: QUESTION Understand what the *question* is asking.

STEP 2: NECESSARY INFORMATION Select important *information* to use in solving the problem and organize it.

STEP 3: OPERATION Choose the correct arithmetic *operations* (addition, subtraction, multiplication, division).

STEP 4: ESTIMATION Estimate an answer. For some problems, an estimate is all you will need.

STEP 5: CALCULATION Calculate the operations *accurately*.

STEP 6: EVALUATION Reread the problem and evaluate your solution to make sure it answers the question *sensibly*. Use your estimate to check whether your answer makes sense.

Step 1: Question

First, read the entire problem and determine exactly what the question is asking. Below are three sample problems with the question in italic type.

Example 1: In 1930, the attendance at the World Series games was 312,619. At the 1960 World Series games, the attendance was 349,813. *How many more people attended the World Series in 1960 than in 1930?*

Example 2: Two pancakes contain 120 calories. *How many calories did Fred consume* if he had a stack of 6 pancakes for breakfast?

Example 3: *Find the area of a triangle* whose base is 4 inches and whose height is 6 inches.

Your first thought when you solve a problem should be "What am I looking for?" As shown in the three examples, the question can be at the beginning, in the middle, or at the end of a problem.

Step 2: Necessary Information

Every word problem contains a lot of information. You must decide which information is necessary to solve the problem. Keeping the question in mind, go through the problem and select the numbers with their unit labels (for example, choose 5 *apples*, not just the number 5). Be sure you choose only the numbers you need to solve the problem.

The examples below illustrate selecting only the information that is necessary to answer the question.

Example 1: Ellis has been renting an apartment for two years. The first year, his rent was $320 per month. At the beginning of the second year, his landlord raised the monthly rent to $355. How much more was the monthly rent the second year than the first year?

The question: How much more was the monthly rent the second year than the first year?

Needed information: $320 first-year rent, $355 second-year rent

Example 2: An estate of $16,920 was divided between a widow and her three children. The widow received one-half of the estate. The rest was divided equally among the children. What was each child's share?

The question: What was each child's share?

Needed information: $16,920 estate, 3 children, $\frac{1}{2}$ estate for widow

▶ **TIP:** Notice that the information "one-half of the estate" was given in words. Be sure to select *all* information—words and numbers—that you need.

Special Problems

On the Mathematics Test, you will run into two areas of difficulty with selecting the necessary information:

1. extra information
2. not enough information is given

Example 1: For the company picnic, only 20 out of the 30 employees paid the $6 fee. How much did the company collect?

In this problem, the fact that there are 30 employees is not needed to answer the question. You need only 20 × $6 = $120.

Example 2: At the 20%-off sale, Tom bought 6 ties. How much did he pay?

Here, you are given the numbers 20% and 6 ties. However, you are not given the original price of the ties. Since you do not have the information you need, the correct answer is "not enough information is given."

▶ **TIP:** On the GED Test, some problems have "not enough information is given" as a possible answer choice. Be sure you read the problem thoroughly before you choose this as your answer.

EXERCISE 2: UNDERSTANDING THE QUESTION AND SELECTING INFORMATION

Directions: Read the problems below and underline the question. In the space, write *all* of the information you would need to solve the problems. Be sure to write numbers and the labels that go with the numbers. If there is not enough information to solve a problem, write *N* for "not enough information is given." *Do not solve the problems.*

1. Dave worked 8 hours at his regular rate and 2 hours of overtime. If he makes $10.00 per hour and $15.00 for each hour of overtime, how much did Dave make altogether?

   Information: _____

2. Mercedes put $150 down and paid $48 a month for 30 months for new furniture. How much did her monthly payments total?

   Information: _____

3. When Esther shipped 3 boxes to her mother, she was charged $1.05 per pound. Two of the boxes weighed 12 pounds 3 ounces and 5 pounds 7 ounces. How much was she charged?

   Information: _____

4. Over the years, Bensenville received $2.7 million from the state for highway construction, education, and public health. If Bensenville spends $800,000 on education, how much does it spend on public health?

Information: _____

5. Only 7,000 people are registered voters out of an adult population of 12,000. If 3,000 voters are women, how many voters are men?

Information: _____

Answers are on page 712.

Step 3: Operation

Once you are ready to solve a problem, remember that there are only four arithmetic operations from which to choose: addition, subtraction, multiplication, and division. Each problem will contain key words or concepts that will help you decide what to do.

Many times, your intuition will help you determine which operation to choose. This intuition comes from both personal experience and your understanding of math concepts from school.

The following chart will help you decide which operation to use.

When combining amounts	add
When finding the difference between two amounts	subtract
When given one unit of something and asked to find several	multiply
When asked to find a fraction of a quantity	multiply
When given the amount for several and asked for one	divide
When splitting, cutting, sharing, etc.	divide

Notice that there are clue words in the first three examples below that help you decide what to do.

Example 1: During one week, the U.S. Motor Company produced 4821 passenger cars, 7216 trucks, and 596 station wagons. *Altogether*, how many vehicles did the company produce that week?

Question: How many vehicles did the company produce?

Information: 4821 cars, 7216 trucks, 596 station wagons

Operation: "Altogether, how many"—addition

Example 2: The local village borrowed $2,250,000 and has repaid $955,000 of its debt. How much of the debt still *remains unpaid*?

Question: How much debt remains?

Information: $2,250,000; $955,000

Operation: "How much remains"—subtraction

Example 3: How much money will each of 68 stockholders receive if $98,600 is *divided equally* among them?

Question: How much money will each receive?

Information: 68 stockholders; $98,600

Operation: "divided equally"—division

If no clue words appear in the problem, look for the math concept involved in the problem. Use your understanding of the problem to help you choose whether to add, subtract, multiply, or divide.

Example 4: Allan's yearly salary is $20,304. What is his monthly salary?

Question: What is his monthly salary?

Information: $20,304; 1 year

Operation: No key words. However, *monthly* means "each month." There are 12 months in one year. Thus, we choose to divide by 12 to find the salary each month.

EXERCISE 3: CHOOSING THE OPERATION

Directions: Read each problem and decide whether to add, subtract, multiply, or divide. Write the name of the operation only. *Do not solve the problems.*

1. When Myron drove 300 miles on 15 gallons of gas, he tried to figure out how many miles he got per gallon. On the average, how many miles did he get per gallon?

2. Sandy lost 34 pounds on her diet. If her weight is now 123, what was her original weight?

3. Brownsville has 23,340 people, and Sylvan has 23,346. How many more people live in Sylvan than in Brownsville?

4. One package is 100 pounds, and the other is 150 pounds. The weight of the second package is how many times that of the first?

5. Sal's mother sent him to the store to buy 5 feet of ribbon. The clerk wants to know how many inches he needs. How many inches are in 5 feet?

Answers are on page 712.

Step 4: Estimation

After choosing the operation, estimate an answer. Sometimes, an estimate can be the final answer. At other times, use the estimate to check whether your answer makes sense.

Example 1: If you drive 448 miles in 7 hours, what is your average rate of speed?

Question: What is the average speed?

Information: 448 miles; 7 hours

Operation: "average"—divide

Estimation: $420 \div 7 = 60$ miles per hour

Example 2: An auto mechanic receives a salary of $525 each week. Find the auto mechanic's earnings for 4 weeks.

Question: How much does the mechanic earn in 4 weeks?

Information: $525 each week; 4 weeks

Operation: No clue words. The problem gives the salary for one week and asks you to find the amount of several (4)—multiply.

Estimation: $500 × 4 = $2000

Step 5: Calculation

After estimating the answer, solve the problem. Do the computations carefully and accurately. Let's go through the five problem-solving steps for the next two examples:

Example 1: If you drive 448 miles in 7 hours, what is your average rate of speed?

Question: What is the average speed?

Information: 448 miles; 7 hours

Operation: "average"—divide

Estimation: 420 ÷ 7 = 60 miles per hour

Calculation:

$$
\begin{array}{r}
64 \\
7\overline{)448} \\
-42 \\
\hline
28 \\
-28 \\
\hline
0
\end{array}
$$

Example 2: An auto mechanic receives a salary of $525 each week. Find the auto mechanic's earnings for 4 weeks.

Question: How much does the mechanic earn in 4 weeks?

Information: $525 each week; 4 weeks

Operation: No clue words. The problem gives the salary for one week and asks you to find the amount of several (4)—multiply.

Estimation: $500 × 4 = $2000

Calculation:

$$
\begin{array}{r}
\$525 \\
\times \quad 4 \\
\hline
\$2100
\end{array}
$$

Step 6: Evaluation

The final step in solving any problem is to evaluate your answer. Does your solution answer the question? Is your answer a sensible one? Is your calculation close to your estimate?

Look at Example 2 above. Suppose you had misunderstood the problem and had divided instead of multiplying:

$$\$525 \div 4 = \$131.25$$

This *wrong* answer tells you that the mechanic earned $131.25 in 4 weeks. Would it make sense for the mechanic to earn *less* in a month than in a week? No. By seeing whether your answer makes sense, you may be able to catch a mistake.

The following problems will give you a chance to practice the 6-step approach to problem solving.

EXERCISE 4: PROBLEM SOLVING

Directions: Solve the problems. For each problem, draw a chart like this and fill it in as you do the problem.

Question:	Calculation:
Necessary Information:	
Operation:	
Estimation:	
Evaluation—Does the answer make sense?	

1. You are leaving for a three-day minivacation. The odometer on your car reads 49,752 miles. You plan to drive 162 miles the first day, 229 miles the second day, and 375 miles the third day. How many miles do you plan to drive?

2. A contest prize of $12,855 is shared equally by 15 people. What amount does each person receive?

3. How much larger is Canada than the United States? Canada is 3,851,809 square miles, and the United States is 3,675,633 square miles.

4. A buyer for a motel purchased 97 color TVs at $325 each. What is the total cost of the 97 TVs?

5. Marlene pays $2492 each quarter for estimated tax. What total amount does she pay in one year if a quarter year is three months?

6. When Mr. MacDonald died, he left his 588 acre farm to be divided equally among his three children. How many acres did each child inherit?

7. Jose makes $1300 a month. He pays $345 for a month's rent and $90 per week for food. How much does he have left each month after paying for rent and food?

Answers are on page 712.

Multi-Step Problems

Many of the problems you see on the Mathematics Test will take more than one calculation to solve. As with the problems you've already done, use the 6-step process, but identify all the steps you need to take. Make sure that you do all calculations.

Example: The yearly rainfall for four consecutive years in Rockton was 22 inches, 28 inches, 31 inches, and 19 inches. Find the average rainfall over the four-year period.

Question: What is the average rainfall?

Information: 22 in, 28 in, 31 in, and 19 in; 4 years

Operation: STEP 1: To get the total rainfall—add.
STEP 2: To get the average rainfall—divide.

Estimation:

STEP 1	STEP 2
20 in	$100 \div 4 = 25$
30 in	
30 in	
+ 20 in	
100 in	

Calculation:

STEP 1	STEP 2
22 in	25
28 in	4) 100
31 in	8
+ 19 in	20
100 in	20
	0

Does it make sense? It makes sense that the average is within the range of 19–31 inches. And your estimate and calculation are not only close; they're an exact match!

▶ **TIP:** With multi-step problems, after you have finished your calculations, go back and see if your answer to the question makes sense. If you have forgotten a step, this can help you catch yourself and finish the problem correctly.

Using Charts and Diagrams

You have heard the saying "A picture is worth a thousand words." A picture that accompanies a problem can help you "see" how to solve word problems. Sometimes a word problem gives several numbers that could be organized into a chart. Also, drawing a diagram might help you picture the information in a problem so you can "see" what to do. Let's look at a few examples.

Example 1: To better insulate his house, Miguel had to put new weather stripping around the large window in his family room. The window frame measured 5 feet wide and 4 feet high. How many feet of weather stripping did he need for that window?

First draw a diagram of the window. Remember, a window has four sides!

Since Miguel wants to put the weather stripping around the whole window, label all four sides. The diagram helps you see that you have to add all the sides. Miguel needs 18 feet of weather stripping: $5 + 5 + 4 + 4 = 18$.

Example 2: A warehouse clerk had a checking account balance of $425.15 before making a deposit of $185.75. The clerk then wrote two checks, one for $43.50 and another for $260.10. Find the current checkbook balance.

Make a box to list the clerk's assets, which include the deposit and account balance. In the second box, list the two checks she wrote. The last box is the current balance, which is the difference between the assets and checks written.

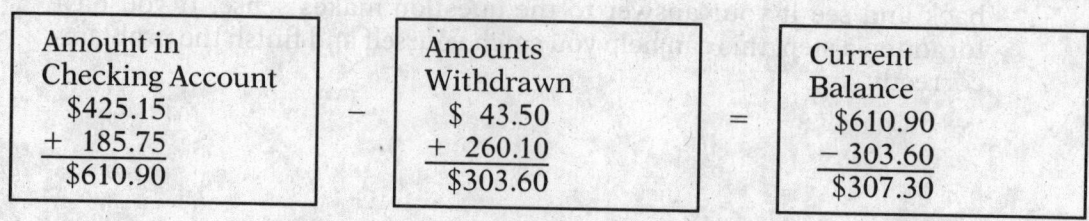

Restating the Problem

The two previous examples show that it helps to restate the problem by organizing the information into charts or diagrams. Another way of restating a problem is to try to put the problem into your own words. Sometimes this means you might actually talk to yourself. As you do this, jot down notes on paper to help you organize your thoughts.

Example: A teacher drives 7 miles one way to school. How many miles does the teacher drive to and from school during one five-day workweek?

After reading the problem, say out loud (or just in your mind) what the problem says. "A teacher drives 7 miles to work. (That means she must drive 7 miles home each day, too.)"

"She works 5 days. (That means she drives 14 miles each day for 5 days.)"
"How many miles does she drive?" $14 \times 5 = 70$ She drives 70 miles in 5 days.

Personalizing a Problem

If you have trouble restating a problem, reread it several times. Think about how you might solve a similar problem in your own life. Many of the problems on the GED Test will involve questions about practical, everyday situations.

Example: The total cost of a computer system is $4830. A down payment of $1500 is made, and the balance is paid in 18 equal monthly payments. Find the monthly payments.

As you read this problem, recall the times you have purchased something and put down a deposit, planning to pay the rest later. You subtracted the deposit from the purchase price to find out how much you still owe.

$$
\begin{array}{rl}
\$4830 & \text{purchase price} \\
-\ 1500 & \text{deposit} \\
\hline
\$3330 & \text{amount owed}
\end{array}
$$

According to the problem, you can pay the amount owed in 18 equal payments. So you have to divide by 18 to find out how much you will pay each month.

$3330 \div 18 = \$185$ per month

Setup Problems

Some problems on the GED will require you to choose a way to solve the problems. These are called *setup problems* because they show a way that a problem could be set up before an answer is found.

Example 1: Tracy will type a 600-word paper and then a 150-word letter. If she types 60 words a minute, how many minutes will it take her to do this work?

(1) $600 \times 150 \times 60$ **(2)** $600 + 150 \times 60$ **(3)** $\dfrac{600 + 150}{60}$ **(4)** $\dfrac{60}{600 + 150}$
(5) not enough information is given

To approach a setup problem, you represent the mathematical relations with numbers and symbols for operations. This kind of statement is called an **arithmetic expression**. In the example above, you want to find how many minutes *both* documents will take to type.

total words $= 600 + 150$

words per minute $= 60$

minutes to type $= \dfrac{\text{total words}}{\text{words per minute}} = \dfrac{600 + 150}{60}$

Your answer will be (3). This answer choice indicates that to get a solution you must add the number of words together and then divide the sum by 60.

► **TIP:** In the solution on page 569, the *fraction bar* means "divided by." This representation of division is often used in setup problems.

Sometimes you will have to use *parentheses* to separate one part of an arithmetic expression from another.

Example 2: $(200 \times 2) - (40 + 2)$

In the arithmetic expression above, you would solve the problems within the parentheses first and then carry out the operation between the parentheses. This could be solved by

$$\underbrace{(200 \times 2)}_{400} - \underbrace{(40 + 2)}_{42} = 358$$

WRITING ARITHMETIC EXPRESSIONS

1. Write the individual steps of multi-step problems (within parentheses if necessary).

2. Division can be indicated by the division sign ($\div$) or by a fraction bar.

3. Unless otherwise indicated, the order in which an arithmetic expression should be solved is
   a. parentheses or tops of fraction bars first
   b. multiplication or division next
   c. addition or subtraction last

EXERCISE 5: WORD PROBLEMS

Directions: Solve each problem.

1. You just inherited an apartment building. If your income from the building is $5160 per month, what is the building's yearly income?

   (1) $430
   (2) $5,160
   (3) $15,480
   (4) $61,920
   (5) not enough information is given

2. There were 395 people who registered for a tour around the country. If a bus can hold 72 people, how many buses will be needed to accommodate everyone?

   (1) 5
   (2) 6
   (3) 7
   (4) 10
   (5) 50

3. A garment factory completed an order for 500 pairs of pants and was paid $5500. It received $9130 for a second order of the same kind of pants. How many pairs of pants were in the second order?

(1) 363
(2) 500
(3) 830
(4) 913
(5) 3630

Questions 4–6 refer to the information below.

High School Student Enrollment

Year	Lincoln	Mead	Sandburg	Austin	Edison
1983	1686	1982	2234	1648	1846
1993	1420	1650	1847	1296	1318

The local high school district has experienced a recent decline in enrollment. The chart above compares enrollment figures between 1983 and 1993 for the five high schools in the district.

4. Which high school had the greatest decline in enrollment?

(1) Lincoln
(2) Mead
(3) Sandburg
(4) Austin
(5) Edison

5. What was the total decline in the district during the ten-year period?

(1) 1865
(2) 2865
(3) 7531
(4) 9396
(5) not enough information is given

6. What was the average decline per school in the district?

(1) 373
(2) 1865
(3) 1879
(4) 7531
(5) 9396

7. Four workers for Transmachine, Inc., must produce 1298 parts in a week's time. If the first worker produces 350 parts, the second worker 375 parts, and the third worker 417 parts, how many parts remain for the fourth worker?

(1)   39
(2) 156
(3) 324
(4) 610
(5) 2440

8. Melanie bought a new car. The final price was $12,800. In addition, she purchased the following options: $282 for an AM/FM radio, $252 for power steering, and $156 for rustproofing. The dealer gave her a $500 rebate for the purchase of the new car. If Melanie made a down payment of $3150, what would be her monthly payments if she takes 48 months to pay the remaining balance?

   (1) $186
   (2) $205
   (3) $225
   (4) $267
   (5) $310

9. The manager of a men's shop can buy 80 men's suits for $4800. Each sports jacket will cost the store $23. The manager decides to order 80 men's suits and 25 sports jackets. Which expression shows how to find the total cost of the order?

   (1) (25 × $23)
   (2) (25 + $23) + $4800
   (3) (25 × $23) × $4800
   (4) (25 × $23) + $4800
   (5) $4800 − (25 × $23)

10. A charity organization collected $348,284 in a recent fund-raising drive. Of the amount collected, some was put aside to pay expenses. The remaining money was divided equally among six local charities. What amount did each charity receive?

    (1) $58,041
    (2) $58,047
    (3) $58,053
    (4) $348,284
    (5) not enough information is given

Answers are on page 713.

2
DECIMALS

Maxine's normal temperature is 98.6°. When she had the flu, it rose to 102.4°.

Elena has a new job working as a receptionist. She is paid $6.55 an hour and makes $245.63 a week.

Numbers like 98.6, 102.4, 6.55, and 245.63 are *decimals*. These everyday decimals are already familiar to you. To fully understand and use decimals, it is important to learn about place values first.

Using Decimals

In our number system, we have ten digits: 0, 1, 2, 3, 4, 5, 6, 7, 8, 9. We use these digits to write every number. The place that a digit occupies in a number tells us the value of the digit. This means that each digit has a *place value*.

We can use the chart below to read the place value of numbers. The whole numbers are to the left of the *decimal point*. The decimals, which are parts of a whole, are to the right of the decimal point. Decimals are also called *decimal fractions*. The places to the right of the decimal point are called *decimal places*. Notice that the names of the decimal places end in *th*.

Billions	Hundred Millions	Ten Millions	Millions	Hundred Thousands	Ten Thousands	Thousands	Hundreds	Tens	AND Ones	Tenths	Hundredths	Thousandths	Ten-Thousandths	Hundred-Thousandths	Millionths
							3	2	6.7	5					

▶ **TIP:** We use the decimal point to separate the whole-number places and the decimal places. The point is read as "and."

Let's consider the number 326.75 from the chart. We can say that

3 is in the hundreds place. Now fill in the blanks below.

2 is in the _____ place.

6 is in the _____ place.

7 is in the _____ place.

5 is in the _____ place.

In the number 326.75, 3 is in the hundreds place, 2 is in the tens place, 6 is in the ones place, 7 is in the tenths place, and 5 is in the hundredths place.

The number 326.75 has two decimal places. The number is read as "326 and 75-hundredths." The .75 is read as "75-hundredths" because we give the entire decimal the name of the last decimal place it occupies. This is also why we read $326.75 as "326 dollars and 75 cents."

READING DECIMALS

1. Read the whole part first.
2. Say "and" for the decimal point.
3. Read the decimal part.
4. Say the place name of the last digit.

▶ **TIP:** If there is no whole number, start at step 3. For instance, .008 is read as eight-thousandths.

Zeros in Decimals

The zero is very important in writing and reading decimal numbers. To see how important zeros are, read the names of each of the mixed decimals below. *Mixed decimals* combine whole numbers with decimal fractions.

12.5   12.05   12.005

The first number is read as "12 and 5-tenths," the second as "12 and 5-hundredths," and the third as "12 and 5-thousandths." You can see that the only digits used to write these numbers are 0, 1, 2, and 5. The actual value of the number depends on the place value of each digit. The zeros in the second two numbers "hold" the number 5 in a specific decimal place—the hundredths place in 12.05 and the thousandths place in 12.005.

EXERCISE 1: READING DECIMALS

Directions: Circle the number on each line that matches the written value. Remember that the word *and* stands for the decimal point.

1. five-hundredths   500   .05   .5

2. six and two-tenths   6.2   .62   .062

3. one hundred and two-thousandths   102.00   100.2   100.002

4. one thousand thirty-two   1032   1.032   .1032

5. four hundred and twenty-five thousandths   400.25   400.025   .0425

6. Write the following in number form:
   (a) seven-tenths
   (b) six and thirty-two thousandths
   (c) two thousand and eight-hundredths
   (d) three hundred five and fifty-six thousandths
   (e) sixty-five ten-thousandths

Answers are on page 713.

Comparing and Ordering Decimals

Sometimes we need to compare decimals to see which one is larger. This is when adding zeros *after* the last decimal digit is most useful. It is easier to compare two numbers that have the same number of decimal places.

Adding zeros to the right of the last decimal digit does not change the value of a number. For example, 12.5, 12.50, and 12.500 all have the same value.

To compare .14 and .126, first add a zero to .14 to make it .140. Now both .126 and .140 are expressed in thousandths and have the same number of decimal places:

$$.14 = .140$$
$$.126 = .126$$

You can now see that 126-thousandths is smaller than 140-thousandths because 126 is less than 140.

Example: Put 4.8, 4.12, 4.2, and 4.1003 in order from the *smallest to the largest*.

STEP 1. Write in zeros so that each number has the same number of decimal places. Then number the mixed decimals in order from the *smallest* to the *largest*.

4.8	= 4.8000	4th
4.12	= 4.1200	2nd
4.2	= 4.2000	3rd
4.1003	= 4.1003	1st

STEP 2. Using your ranking system, put the *original numbers* in order from smallest to largest.

1st	4.1003
2nd	4.12
3rd	4.2
4th	4.8

EXERCISE 2: COMPARING DECIMALS

Directions: Solve each problem.

1. Select the *larger* number in each pair.

   (a) .005; .05 **(b)** 4.10; 4.01 **(c)** .7; .68 **(d)** .5; .51 **(e)** 1.033; 1.03

2. Arrange each set of numbers in size order with the *largest* number first.

   (a) 1.95; 2.105; 2.15 **(b)** .0035; .0503; .005

3. Put these weights in order from the *lightest to the heaviest*.

   14.3 lb   14.03 lb   14.003 lb   14.3033 lb

4. Sarah has to pile these crates in order from the *heaviest on the bottom to the lightest on the top*. What would be the correct order in which to pile the crates? (List them from bottom to top.)

4.67 lb   4.0067 lb   4.067 lb

Answers are on page 713.

Rounding Decimals

We might solve a problem involving money and get an answer like $25.128. Since our money is expressed in hundredths, we must round off the answer to dollars and cents. Following are the steps we use to round off the answer.

Example 1: Round off $25.128 to the nearest cent.

STEP 1. Underline the place value to which you are rounding. $25.1<u>2</u>8

STEP 2. Identify the digit to the right of the place to which you are rounding. $25.1<u>2</u>8 ← number to the right

STEP 3. a) If this digit is 5 or more, increase the digit in the place to which you are rounding by 1 and drop the digits to the right.

$25.128 ← 5 or more
+   1
―――――――
$25.13

   b) If this digit is less than 5, keep the same digit in the place to which you are rounding and drop the digits to the right.

Example 2: Round 10.0239 to the nearest thousandth.

10.023<u>9</u> rounds to 10.024

Example 3 shows an application of rounding decimals.

Example 3: A bank computes the interest on Sonya's savings account and finds it to be $37.7034. Round off this interest to the nearest cent.

Solution: $37.70<u>3</u>4 rounds to $37.70

EXERCISE 3: ROUNDING DECIMALS

Directions: Solve each problem.

1. A $\frac{3}{8}$ inch drill bit has a diameter of .375 inches. What is the size of the drill bit to the nearest hundredth inch?

2. Today's interest rate is 7.58 percent. What is the interest rate to the nearest tenth of a percent?

3. At the gas station, the pump says the gas costs $1.298 per gallon. In dollars and cents, how much will you pay per gallon?

4. A blueprint shows that a sidewalk should be 17.124 feet long. What is the length to the nearest hundredth of a foot?

5. The width of a boat is 8.275 feet. What is the width to the nearest tenth of a foot?

6. The value of π, a number useful in geometric measurement, is 3.14159. Round off this value to the nearest hundredth.

7. Juanita's temperature was 101.68 degrees. What was her temperature to the nearest degree?

Answers are on page 714.

Adding and Subtracting Decimals

A cashier who adds up your bill is adding decimals. One who makes change is subtracting decimals. This is done the same way as with whole numbers. There are three basic rules to follow:

> **ADDING AND SUBTRACTING DECIMALS**
>
> 1. Line up the decimal points.
> 2. Add or subtract the numbers.
> 3. Bring the decimal point straight down.

Example 1: Add 4.5 and 38.68.

Read this space as a zero. ——————————— Line up the decimal points.

$$
\begin{array}{r}
4.5 \\
+\ 38.68 \\
\hline
43.18
\end{array}
$$

▶ **TIP:** If necessary, add zeros to the right of the decimal point to fill in place values. This will help you keep the rows lined up but won't change the value of the numbers.

Example 2: Add 2.1, .48, 38, and .005.

Filled-in zeros will help you line up the columns.

$$
\begin{array}{cc}
2.1 & 2.100 \\
.48 & .480 \\
38. & 38.000 \\
.005 & +\ \ \ .005 \\
\hline
& 40.585
\end{array}
$$

When you subtract decimals, you may have to fill in zeros to get enough decimal places.

Example 3: Subtract .0856 from 12.1.

$$
\begin{array}{r}
12.1 \\
-\ \ .0856
\end{array}
\qquad
\begin{array}{r}
^{0\ 9\ 9\ 1} \\
12.1000 \\
-\ \ .0856 \\
\hline
12.0144
\end{array}
$$

Filled-in zeros are necessary.

Example 4: Jake gave the cashier $20 to pay for the lunch check of $7.48. How much change did Jake get back?

$$
\begin{array}{r}
\$20.00 \\
-\ \ 7.48
\end{array}
\qquad
\begin{array}{r}
^{1\ 9\ \ 9\ 10} \\
\$20.00 \\
-\ \ 7.48 \\
\hline
\$12.52
\end{array}
$$

▶ **TIP:** Notice that whole numbers like 20 have an "imaginary" decimal point at the end. You can put in this point when you need it.

EXERCISE 4: ADDING AND SUBTRACTING DECIMALS

Directions: Solve each problem.

1. Add 12.4 and 132.647.

2. Add 5.9, 2.46, 6, 3.07, and .48.

3. Subtract 5.2 from 43.

4. Find the difference between 85.2 and 6.9.

5. Find the distance around the field shown. All distances are in meters.

6. Can you balance a checkbook? At the beginning of the week, your balance was $472.24. During the week, you wrote checks for $42.87, $5.93, $10, $17.48, and $38.40. What is your new balance?

7. At the start of a trip, your mileage meter read 25,176.3; at the end of the trip, it read 28,054.1. How far did you travel?

8. Sam bought a sandwich for $4.75, a cup of soup for $.95, and a drink for $.75. How much change did he receive from a ten-dollar bill?

   (1) $2.45
   (2) $2.95
   (3) $3.55
   (4) $4.50
   (5) $5.25

9. Although Jill's temperature is usually 98.6°, it rose to 104.2° when she had a fever. Her medication brought her fever down to 102.8°. By how many degrees did the medication bring it down?

   (1) 0.6
   (2) 1.4
   (3) 1.6
   (4) 2.0
   (5) 2.2

10. A piece of wood was 1.03 inches long. Jill needed to cut some off. First she cut off .2 inch. Then she cut off .15 inch. Which of the expressions below shows how much she cut off?

   (1) (1.03 + .2) + .15
   (2) 1.03 − .2
   (3) 1.03 − .15
   (4) .2 + .15
   (5) .2 − .15

Part of a service order is shown below. Use the information given to answer questions 11 and 12.

LAKE MARINE SERVICE				Date: 8/12	Name: Kim Yang	
Qty.	**Part**	**Amount**		**Work Performed**	**Labor Charge**	
1	Gear lube	17	50	1. Winterize	70	00
1	Grease	4	95	2. Weld skeg	90	00
1	Oil	6	00	3. Repair ladder	n	c
1	Gas	13	44			
3	Antifreeze	60	75	**Total Labor**	160	00
				Total Parts		
				Tax	2	63
	Total			**Invoice Total**		

11. Find the total cost of the parts.

12. What is the invoice total for Mr. Yang's boat?

Answers are on page 714.

Multiplying and Dividing Decimals

Decimals are multiplied the same way as whole numbers, and then the decimal point is placed in the answer. There are three rules for multiplying decimals.

> **MULTIPLYING DECIMALS**
>
> 1. Multiply the two numbers as whole numbers, ignoring the decimal points.
>
> 2. Find the total number of decimal places in the numbers being multiplied.
>
> 3. Count the total number of decimal places in the answer, starting from the right, and place the point there.

Example 1: Multiply 3.2 and 4.05.

$$
\begin{array}{r}
4.05 \\
\times\ 3.2 \\
\hline
810 \\
12\ 15 \\
\hline
12.960
\end{array}
$$

two decimal places
one decimal place

$12.960 = 12.96$ total of three decimal places (You can drop the last zero.)

Example 2: $28 \times .06$

$$
\begin{array}{r}
28 \\
\times\ .06 \\
\hline
1.68
\end{array}
$$

no decimal places
two decimal places
total of two decimal places

Example 3 shows putting zeros at the beginning of the answer to have enough decimal places.

Example 3: .043 × .0056

```
     .0056   4 decimal places
 ×   .043    3 decimal places
     168
     224
     2408   You need a total of 7 decimal places.
```

In this case, put three zeros at the beginning of the number:

.0002408

▶ **TIP:** Notice that it is easier to multiply if you put the larger number on top.

Dividing Decimals

How many $.59 hamburgers can you buy for $8.00? To answer this question, you have to divide decimals.

There are two basic types of decimal division: (1) division of decimals by whole numbers and (2) division of decimals by decimals. Let's look at examples of each type.

Dividing By A Whole Number

DIVIDING DECIMALS BY WHOLE NUMBERS

1. Divide as though both numbers were whole numbers.
2. Divide by the number that follows the division sign (÷).
3. Place the decimal point in the answer directly above the decimal point in the dividend.

Example 1 shows how to divide a decimal by a whole number.

Example 1: 36.48 ÷ 4

Place decimal point directly above the decimal point in the dividend.

```
       9.12
   4) 36.48
    − 36
       04
      −  4
         08
        − 8
          0
```

As Example 2 shows, some whole-number problems require you to add a decimal point and zeros.

Example 2: 12 ÷ 25

Place decimal point directly above and zeros below.

```
       .48
   25) 12.00
       10 0
        2 00
        2 00
           0
```

Example 3 shows a problem that often causes difficulty. If the first whole number in the divisor doesn't divide into the first number after a decimal point, you *must* put in a zero before continuing your division.

Example 3: .35 ÷ 7

Put in the zero after the decimal point.

```
      .05
   7) .35
```

Dividing By A Decimal

To divide a decimal by a decimal, you have to change the divisor into a whole number. Because you do this, you also have to move the decimal point in the dividend the same number of places.

Example 1: 4.864 ÷ .32

Place the decimal point directly above the decimal point in the dividend.

Move the decimal point two places to the right.

Move the decimal point two places to the right.

```
           15.2
   .32) 4.86 4
         − 3 2
           1 66
         − 1 60
             6 4
           − 6 4
              0
```

Sometimes, you will have to add zeros to move the decimal point.

Example 2: 25 ÷ .125

Move the decimal point three places to the right.

Add three zeros and move the decimal point three places to the right.

```
            200.
   .125 ) 25.000
         − 25 0
            00
           − 0
             0
           − 0
             0
```

DIVIDING A DECIMAL BY A DECIMAL

1. Move the decimal point in the divisor all the way to the right.

2. Move the decimal point in the dividend the same number of places to the right.

3. Place the decimal point in the answer directly above the decimal point in the dividend.

4. Divide as though both numbers were whole numbers.

▶ **TIP:** The easy way to multiply or divide by multiples of ten (10, 100, 1000, etc.) is simply to move the decimal point. When you multiply, you move the decimal point to the right, and when you divide, you it to the left. In either case, the decimal point moves as many places as there are zeros in the multiple of ten. (As the examples show, you add zeros when necessary.)

For example: $.13 \times 1000 = 130$ $9.5 \div 100 = .095$

3 zeros 3 places   2 zeros 2 places

EXERCISE 5: MULTIPLYING AND DIVIDING DECIMALS

Directions: Solve each problem.

1. Multiply $.342 \times 1.5$.

2. Multiply $46 \times .00034$.

3. Multiply $.8 \times .03$.

4. Multiply $\$6.50 \times 3.5$.

5. Divide 6.005 by .05.

6. $.012 \div 3$

7. Divide 2.8 by .04.

8. Divide 56 by .08.

9. $.38 \times 10$

10. $472 \times 10,000$

11. $.0972 \times 100$

12. $.617 \div 10$

13. $456.12 \div 100$

14. $57 \div 1000$

15. Monica pays $7.85 each month for newspaper home delivery. Which expression shows how much she pays for the newspaper over a year's time?

   (1) $7.85 \times 4 \times 12$
   (2) $(7.85 + 4) \times 12$
   (3) 7.85×12
   (4) 7.85×52
   (5) 7.85×365

16. One stamp costs $.29. How much does a roll of 100 stamps cost?

   (1) $14.50
   (2) $20.00
   (3) $25.00
   (4) $29.00
   (5) $31.00

17. Finishing Touch Decorators can paint 1.5 rooms in an hour. Working 10 hours each day, how many days will it take them to paint a 75-room building?

    (1) 3
    (2) 4
    (3) 5
    (4) 8
    (5) 10

18. At the store, Mike bought a 3.5-pound package of chicken at $1.19 a pound and 2 gallons of milk at $2.30 a gallon. Which expression shows what Mike paid?

    (1) $(3.5 + 1.19) + (2 + 2.30)$

    (2) $(3.5 + 2) + (1.19 + 2.30)$

    (3) $(3.5 \times 1.19) + (2 \times 2.30)$

    (4) $2.5(1.19 + 2.30)$

    (5) $2(1.19 + 2.30)$

Answers are on page 714.

Estimating for Problem Solving

Estimating is a handy tool to use in solving decimal problems. If a problem involves decimals, reread the problem and replace the mixed decimals with whole numbers. This will help you see how to solve the problem. After choosing the correct operations to use, work the problem with the original decimal numbers if an exact answer is necessary.

Example 1: What is the cost of 12.8 gallons of gasoline at $1.19 per gallon?

Estimation: What is the cost of 13 gallons of gasoline at $1 per gallon? Using whole numbers helps us see we should multiply 1×13, which equals 13. Our answer in the original problem should be about $13. The actual answer rounds off to $15.23.

Example 2: Approximately how much did Emil spend on his recent shopping spree? This is what he bought: a blazer, $49.95; slacks, $24.95; shirt, $18.69; tie, $9.75; belt, $12.25; shoes, $34.95.

Estimation: To estimate the answer, round off the numbers.

	Estimate
$49.95 to	50
$24.95 to	25
$18.69 to	20
$ 9.75 to	10
$12.25 to	10
$34.95 to	35
Total	$150

Emil spent approximately $150. The actual amount is $150.54. If Emil wanted to know about how much he spent, an estimate would give him a close enough answer.

Estimating can help you see how to do a problem, provide you with an approximate answer, allow you to choose a multiple-choice answer, or help you double-check your work.

EXERCISE 6: ESTIMATING

Directions: Estimate the answers to the following problems.

1. Dino drove his truck the following distances during the week: Monday, 4.8 miles; Tuesday, 12.3 miles; Wednesday, 74.5 miles; Thursday, 10 miles; and Friday, 8.1 miles. Approximately how far did he travel?

   estimation _____

2. Liz had $50 in her purse. She spent $24.75 on cosmetics and $2.50 on a magazine. Approximately how much did she have left from her $50?

   estimation _____

3. If a bushel of apples cost $8.95, what will ten bushels cost?

   estimation _____

4. How many streamers, each 1.75 feet long, can be cut from a roll of crepe paper 36 feet long?

   estimation _____

Answers are on page 715.

EXERCISE 7: DECIMAL WORD PROBLEMS

Directions: Use estimation to help you solve the problems. Sometimes you may need to find the exact amount.

1. You are building a bookcase with shelves that are 3.2 feet long. How many complete shelves can be cut from a 12-foot board?

   (1) 2
   (2) 3
   (3) 4
   (4) 5
   (5) not enough information is given

2. Mr. Stansky earns a part-time salary of $425 every four weeks. During the past four weeks he also received commissions of $485.75, $399.87, $642.15, and $724.52. What was his total income for the past 4-week period?

   (1) $535.46
   (2) $669.32
   (3) $2252.29
   (4) $2256.42
   (5) $2677.29

3. On a bicycle road trip, Otis rode 2492 miles in 140 hours. What was his average speed in miles per hour, to the nearest tenth?

   (1) .178
   (2) 1.78
   (3) 17.8
   (4) 178
   (5) 1780

4. The carat is a unit of measure used to weigh precious stones. It equals 3.086 grains. How many grains does a 2.8-carat diamond weigh?

(1)   3.086
(2)   5.886
(3)   8.6408
(4)   86.408
(5) 8640.8

Questions 5 and 6 are based on the table below.

As an assistant accountant for a computer company, you must calculate each employee's gross earnings, total of deductions, and net pay by using the following table.

Employee No.	Regular Pay	Overtime Pay	Gross Earnings	Social Security Tax (FICA)	Federal Income Tax (FIT)	Total of Deductions	Net Pay
24	237.25	117		26.48	71.26		
35	339.45	71.25		26.93	82.14		
17	265.72	168.75		27.03	86.90		

5. Find the net pay for employee 17 after deductions are taken out.

(1) $113.93
(2) $320.54
(3) $434.47
(4) $548.40
(5) not enough information is given

6. How much did employee 24 make per hour?

(1) $5.93
(2) $6.42
(3) $8.85
(4) $354.25
(5) not enough information is given

7. A Tercel can be bought for $3500 down and monthly payments of $207.25 for 48 months. What is the total cost of the Tercel?

(1) $5,987
(2) $9,948
(3) $13,448
(4) $17,795
(5) not enough information is given

8. If large eggs are on sale for $.69 per dozen, what does one egg sell for to the nearest cent?

   (1) $ .06
   (2) $ .07
   (3) $ .08
   (4) $6
   (5) $7

9. The odometer of your sports car read 7353.2 miles at the start of a trip. When you returned, it read 8747.6 miles, and you had used 86.4 gallons of gasoline. How many miles per gallon did you get? (Round off to the nearest tenth.)

   (1)   1.6
   (2)   16.1
   (3)   16.2
   (4)   18.6
   (5) 1394.4

10. One evening, a waiter received the following tips: $4.25, $3.80, $5.75, $10, $6, $3.70, $4.90. What was his average tip for the evening?

   (1) $3.22
   (2) $5.40
   (3) $5.49
   (4) $38.40
   (5) not enough information is given

Answers are on page 715.

3
FRACTIONS

We encounter fractions in all aspects of life without even thinking about it. "Let me borrow half a dollar." "Cut the pie into eighths so everyone gets a piece." "It's a quarter past seven; I'd better hurry, or I'll be late." "She bought $3\frac{7}{8}$ yards of material."

Forms of Fractions

Fractions represent a part of a whole. The top number is called the **numerator**, and the bottom number is called the **denominator**.

$\dfrac{5}{8}$ **numerator**
tells how many parts you have

denominator
tells how many parts a whole is divided into

 This circle is divided into 8 parts. $\frac{5}{8}$ of this circle is shaded. $\frac{3}{8}$ is not.

There are many types of fractions that you will use in your work:

Proper fractions: The numerator is smaller than the denominator. $\frac{1}{2}, \frac{2}{5}, \frac{1}{7}, \frac{3}{9}$

Improper fractions: The numerator is the same as or larger than the denominator. $\frac{5}{4}, \frac{3}{2}, \frac{7}{3}, \frac{5}{5}$

Like fractions: Fractions have the same denominator. $\frac{1}{8}, \frac{3}{8}, \frac{6}{8}, \frac{9}{8}$

Unlike fractions: Fractions have different denominators. $\frac{1}{4}, \frac{7}{8}, \frac{3}{5}, \frac{9}{2}$

Mixed numbers: The combination of a whole number and a proper fraction. $2\frac{1}{3}, 3\frac{1}{4}, 6\frac{1}{5}$

EXERCISE 1: TYPES OF FRACTIONS

Directions: Based on the information on page 587, name each group of fractions below.

1. $\frac{2}{3}$, $\frac{5}{3}$, $\frac{1}{3}$, $\frac{7}{3}$ _____

2. $1\frac{3}{4}$, $7\frac{1}{5}$, $2\frac{1}{8}$ _____

3. $\frac{9}{3}$, $\frac{10}{5}$, $\frac{4}{2}$, $\frac{6}{6}$ _____

4. $\frac{1}{5}$, $\frac{3}{7}$, $\frac{7}{8}$, $\frac{1}{3}$ _____

5. $\frac{1}{2}$, $\frac{1}{4}$, $\frac{2}{5}$, $\frac{3}{7}$ _____

Answers are on page 715.

Raising and Reducing Fractions

To use fractions easily, you must be able to *raise* a fraction to higher terms or to *reduce* a fraction to lower terms. In either case, you are changing both the numerator and the denominator of the fraction. When you do either, you are finding an *equivalent fraction*—a fraction that has the same value. For example, a half-dollar has the same value as two quarters. As equivalent fractions, these can be written as $\frac{1}{2} = \frac{2}{4}$. This relationship can also be shown in pictures.

$$\frac{1}{2} = \frac{2}{4}$$

TO RAISE A FRACTION TO HIGHER TERMS

Multiply both the numerator and the denominator by the same number. You will obtain an equivalent fraction.

Example 1: $\frac{5 \ (\times 2)}{8 \ (\times 2)} = \frac{10}{16}$

TO REDUCE A FRACTION TO LOWER TERMS

Divide both the numerator and the denominator by the same number. You will obtain an equivalent fraction. (*Hint:* Look for a number that divides evenly into both.)

Example 2: $\frac{12 \ (\div 4)}{16 \ (\div 4)} = \frac{3}{4}$

A fraction is in the ***lowest terms*** if there is no whole number that will divide evenly into both the numerator and denominator. For example, $\frac{3}{8}$ is already in lowest terms because there is no whole number other than 1 that divides evenly into 3 and 8. Fraction answers should always be reduced to lowest terms. In fact, all fraction answers for the Mathematics Test will be given in lowest terms.

EXERCISE 2: RAISING AND REDUCING FRACTIONS

Directions: Solve each problem.

1. Raise each fraction to higher terms as indicated.

(a) $\dfrac{3\ (\times 3)}{8\ (\times 3)} = \dfrac{}{24}$ (b) $\dfrac{3\ (\times 5)}{4\ (\times 5)} = \dfrac{}{20}$ (c) $\dfrac{1\ (\times 6)}{6\ (\times 6)} = \dfrac{}{36}$

(d) $\dfrac{3}{7} = \dfrac{}{21}$ (e) $\dfrac{6}{7} = \dfrac{}{28}$ (f) $\dfrac{2}{5} = \dfrac{}{30}$

2. Reduce each fraction to lower terms as indicated.

(a) $\dfrac{12\ (\div 4)}{16\ (\div 4)} = \dfrac{}{4}$ (b) $\dfrac{21\ (\div 7)}{28\ (\div 7)} = \dfrac{}{4}$ (c) $\dfrac{2\ (\div 2)}{6\ (\div 2)} = \dfrac{}{3}$

(d) $\dfrac{40}{50} = \dfrac{}{5}$ (e) $\dfrac{24}{36} = \dfrac{}{3}$ (f) $\dfrac{30}{42} = \dfrac{}{7}$

3. Reduce each of the following fractions to the lowest terms.

(a) $\frac{6}{8}$ (b) $\frac{15}{20}$ (c) $\frac{9}{27}$ (d) $\frac{4}{12}$ (e) $\frac{25}{30}$

Answers are on page 715.

Relating Fractions and Decimals

In many arithmetic problems, you will work with both fractions and decimals. Each fraction can be expressed as a decimal, and vice versa. That's because decimals and fractions each represent parts of a whole.

You can think of decimals as fractions with denominators in powers of 10: 10, 100, 1000, and so on.

For example: one decimal place $= \dfrac{}{10}$

two decimal places $= \dfrac{}{100}$

three decimal places $= \dfrac{}{1000}$

Therefore, $.1 = \frac{1}{10}$ and $.03 = \frac{3}{100}$. Let's review the methods of changing from decimals to fractions and fractions to decimals.

Example 1: Change .75 to a fraction.

STEP 1. Write the number 75 without a decimal point as a numerator. $\dfrac{75}{}$

STEP 2. Write 100, the value of the last decimal place, as a denominator. $\dfrac{75}{100}$ This can be reduced to $\frac{3}{4}$.

Example 2: Change .039 to a fraction.

$.039 = \dfrac{39}{1000}$ ← number without decimal point
← three decimal places are thousandths

CHANGING A DECIMAL TO A FRACTION

1. Write the number without the decimal point. This is your numerator.

2. Make the denominator the value of the last place value in the decimal.

To change a fraction to a decimal, divide the numerator by the denominator. You can do this because a fraction bar also indicates division. In other words, $\frac{5}{8}$ can mean $5 \div 8$ or $8\overline{)5}$.

Example 1:

$$\frac{5}{8} = \begin{array}{r} .625 \\ 8\overline{)5.000} \\ \underline{-\ 4\ 8} \\ 20 \\ \underline{-\ 16} \\ 40 \\ \underline{-\ 40} \\ 0 \end{array}$$

Example 2:

$$\frac{2}{3} = \begin{array}{r} .66\frac{2}{3} \\ 3\overline{)2.00} \\ \underline{-\ 1\ 8} \\ 20 \\ \underline{-\ 18} \\ 2 \end{array}$$

▶ **TIP:** Example 2 is a repeating decimal. After two decimal places, you can bring up the remainder to be part of a fraction. If necessary, you can round off decimals; for example, $.66\frac{2}{3} = .67$.

CHANGING A FRACTION TO A DECIMAL

Divide the numerator by the denominator. After two decimal places, make a fractional remainder.

You now know three meanings for fractions: $\frac{5}{8}$ means

                    5 ÷ 8

5 out of 8 parts   5 out of 8 pieces   5 divided by 8

EXERCISE 3: CHANGING FRACTIONS AND DECIMALS

Directions: Solve each problem.

1. Change the following decimals to fractions. Reduce if necessary.

    (a) $.05 = \frac{}{100}$ **(b)** $.450 = \frac{}{1000}$ **(c)** $.07 = \frac{}{100}$

    (d) $.32$ **(e)** $.005$ **(f)** 3.1

2. Change the following fractions to decimals. Write a fractional remainder after two decimal places.

    (a) $\frac{3}{8}$ **(b)** $\frac{1}{5}$ **(c)** $\frac{4}{9}$ **(d)** $\frac{4}{3}$ **(e)** $\frac{5}{3}$ **(f)** $\frac{5}{6}$

Answers are on page 716.

Relating Mixed Numbers and Improper Fractions

In your work with fractions, you will have to make another type of change. This involves changing mixed numbers to improper fractions, and vice versa.

Example 1: Change $3\frac{7}{8}$ to an improper fraction.

STEP 1. Multiply the whole number by the denominator. $(3 \times 8) = 24$

STEP 2. Add that to the numerator of the fraction. $24 + 7 = 31$

STEP 3. Write the sum over the original denominator. $3\frac{7}{8} = \frac{31}{8}$

CHANGING A MIXED NUMBER TO AN IMPROPER FRACTION

1. Multiply the whole number by the denominator. Add that to the numerator of the fraction.

2. Write the sum over the original denominator.

The other skill you need is to be able to change an improper fraction to a mixed number.

Example 2: Change $\frac{11}{5}$ to a mixed number.

STEP 1. Divide the denominator into the numerator.

$$\frac{11}{5} = 5\overline{)11} \quad \begin{array}{r} 2 \\ \hline -10 \\ \hline 1 \end{array}$$

STEP 2. Put the remainder over the denominator.

$$\frac{11}{5} = 5\overline{)11} \quad \begin{array}{r} 2\frac{1}{5} \\ \hline -10 \\ \hline 1 \end{array}$$

CHANGING AN IMPROPER FRACTION TO A MIXED NUMBER

1. Divide the denominator into the numerator to get the whole-number part of the answer.

2. Put the remainder over the denominator to get the fractional part of the mixed number.

EXERCISE 4: CHANGING IMPROPER FRACTIONS AND MIXED NUMBERS

Directions: Solve each problem.

1. Change the following to improper fractions.

(a) $1\frac{5}{9}$ (b) $12\frac{1}{4}$ (c) $3\frac{2}{5}$ (d) $3\frac{1}{4}$ (e) $2\frac{1}{2}$ (f) $6\frac{2}{3}$

2. Change the following to whole or mixed numbers.

(a) $\frac{4}{3}$ (b) $\frac{16}{7}$ (c) $\frac{9}{9}$ (d) $\frac{9}{8}$ (e) $\frac{17}{5}$ (f) $\frac{3}{2}$

Answers are on page 716.

Comparing Numbers

On the GED Test, you may have to compare whole numbers, fractions, or decimals. In arithmetic, we often use a number line to help us "see" the relationships among numbers.

The Number Line

The number line is similar to a ruler except that it has no beginning or end. We indicate this by putting arrows at both ends of the line. We can say that all numbers are represented on this line even though it would be impossible to try to label all of them.

Whole numbers as well as mixed numbers can be represented on the number line.

Note that the numbers get larger as you go to the right on the line.

As the illustration shows, the same points can indicate either fractions or decimals. For example, $1\frac{1}{2}$ has the same value as 1.5.

We can use the number line to compare numbers and show their order. If we are given two numbers, then one of three statements must be true:

    1. The two numbers are equal.

    2. The first is larger than the second.

    3. The first is smaller than the second.

There are symbols to indicate these relationships:

Symbol	Meaning	Example
$=$	is equal to	$4 = 4$
$>$	is greater than	$7 > 3$
$<$	is less than	$2 < 9$

▶ **TIP:** The arrow always points to the smaller number.

Comparing Decimals

When you compare decimals, make sure you have the same number of decimal places in each number. Attach as many zeros as needed after the last number in the decimal. Remember that adding zeros to the end of a decimal number does *not* change its value.

Example: Compare .064 and .06.

.064 has 3 decimal places   .064   both now have 3 decimal places

.06 has 2 decimal places   .060

Now both numbers are expressed in thousandths. Because 64 > 60, .064 > .060. So .064 > .06.

Comparing Fractions

To compare fractions, we must make sure that they have the same denominator. This is called the ***common denominator***. For instance, we can compare $\frac{3}{16}$ and $\frac{11}{16}$. We know $\frac{11}{16} > \frac{3}{16}$ because 11 is greater than 3. If the fractions that you are comparing have different denominators, you must find a common denominator.

Example 1: Which is larger, $\frac{5}{8}$ or $\frac{1}{2}$?

STEP 1. Look at the larger denominator. If it is evenly divisible by the smaller denominator, use the larger one as the common denominator. $\frac{5}{8}$ $\frac{1}{2}$

STEP 2. Write both fractions with the same denominator. Change one fraction to higher terms. $\frac{5}{8} = \frac{5}{8}$

$\frac{1}{2} \frac{(\times 4)}{(\times 4)} = \frac{4}{8}$

STEP 3. Compare and determine which is larger. $\frac{5}{8} > \frac{4}{8}$, so

$\frac{5}{8} > \frac{1}{2}$

In some cases, the smaller denominator will not divide into the larger. You can multiply them together if they are small enough to get a reasonable common denominator.

Example 2: Which is larger, $\frac{2}{3}$ or $\frac{3}{4}$?

STEP 1. Multiply the denominators to get a common denominator. $3 \times 4 = 12$

STEP 2. Give them both the same denominator. In this case, it will be 12. Multiply $\frac{2}{3}$ by 4 and $\frac{3}{4}$ by 3. $\frac{2}{3} \frac{(\times 4)}{(\times 4)} = \frac{8}{12}$

$\frac{3}{4} \frac{(\times 3)}{(\times 3)} = \frac{9}{12}$

STEP 3. Compare the fractions. $\frac{9}{12} > \frac{8}{12}$, so

$\frac{3}{4}$ is larger than $\frac{2}{3}$.

In other cases, the common denominator you get by multiplying might be too large to work with. In this case, find multiples of both denominators. Use the smallest multiple they have in common as the common denominator.

Example 3: Which is larger, $\frac{5}{12}$ or $\frac{3}{10}$?

STEP 1. Find multiples of both denominators. The smallest multiple of both will be the common denominator.

12: 12, 24, 36, 48, 60
10: 10, 20, 30, 40, 50, 60

STEP 2. Raise both fractions to higher terms. Divide the denominators into 60 to find which numbers to multiply the fractions by: $60 \div 12 = 5$ and $60 \div 10 = 6$.

$\frac{5}{12} \frac{(\times 5)}{(\times 5)} = \frac{25}{60}$

$\frac{3}{10} \frac{(\times 6)}{(\times 6)} = \frac{18}{60}$

STEP 3. Compare the fractions.

$\frac{25}{60} > \frac{18}{60}$, so

$\frac{5}{12}$ is greater than $\frac{3}{10}$.

TO FIND A COMMON DENOMINATOR

Look at the larger denominator.

1. Is it divisible by the other denominator? If so, use the larger number as the common denominator.

2. If not, try multiplying the denominators together.

3. If multiplying results in a very large common denominator, try multiples of both denominators until you find a common multiple.

Comparing Fractions and Decimals

We can compare fractions and decimals, but we must first change the decimal to a fraction or the fraction to a decimal.

Example: Compare $\frac{7}{8}$ and .75.

STEP 1. Change $\frac{7}{8}$ to a decimal.

$\frac{7}{8} = 8\overline{)7.000}$ .875

STEP 2. Write .75 with 3 decimal places because .875 has 3 decimal places.

.75 = .750

.875 > .750, so

STEP 3. Compare.

$\frac{7}{8}$ is greater than .75.

▶ TIP: You can also compare by changing a decimal to a fraction. For instance, .75 is $\frac{75}{100}$ or $\frac{3}{4}$. Both fractions would then have to have the same denominator: $\frac{6}{8}$ and $\frac{7}{8}$.

EXERCISE 5: COMPARING NUMBERS

Directions: Solve each problem.

1. Which of the following is larger?

(a) $\frac{7}{8}$ or $\frac{3}{5}$ (b) $\frac{2}{3}$ or $\frac{4}{9}$ (c) $\frac{3}{10}$ or $\frac{3}{4}$

2. Compare using the symbol $>$, $<$, or $=$. For example, $6 \boxed{<} 9$.

(a) $3 \boxed{} 8$

(b) $6 \boxed{} 0$

(c) $\frac{3}{8} \boxed{} \frac{1}{8}$

(d) $\frac{3}{4} \boxed{} \frac{2}{3}$

(e) $2\frac{3}{8} \boxed{} \frac{5}{2}$

(f) $\frac{5}{6} \boxed{} \frac{8}{9}$

(g) $.3 \boxed{} \frac{1}{4}$

(h) $\frac{1}{2} \boxed{} \frac{6}{12}$

(i) $\frac{9}{9} \boxed{} \frac{2}{2}$

(j) $.07 \boxed{} .0873$

(k) $\frac{3}{5} \boxed{} .6$

Answers are on page 717.

Operations with Fractions

Adding and Subtracting Fractions

When you are asked to add or subtract fractions or mixed numbers, you must be sure that the fractions have common denominators. If they don't, then rewrite the fractions with common denominators before adding or subtracting.

Example 1: Add $\frac{3}{8}$ and $\frac{1}{8}$.

STEP 1. Since the denominators are the same, add the numerators.

STEP 2. Reduce the answer.

$$\begin{array}{r} \frac{3}{8} \\ + \frac{1}{8} \\ \hline \frac{4}{8} \, (\div 4) = \frac{1}{2} \end{array}$$

Example 2: Add $\frac{1}{10}$ and $\frac{3}{5}$.

STEP 1. Find the common denominator and equivalent fractions.

STEP 2. Add the numerators.

$$\begin{array}{r} \frac{1}{10} = \frac{1}{10} \\ + \frac{3}{5} \, (\times 2) = \frac{6}{10} \\ \hline \frac{7}{10} \end{array}$$

Example 3: $\frac{2}{3} + \frac{1}{6} + \frac{3}{4}$

STEP 1. Find the common denominator for all numbers.

STEP 2. Add the numerators and put them over the denominator.

STEP 3. Change the improper fraction to a mixed number.

$$\begin{array}{r} \frac{2}{3} = \frac{8}{12} \\ \frac{1}{6} = \frac{2}{12} \\ + \frac{3}{4} = \frac{9}{12} \\ \hline \frac{19}{12} = 1\frac{7}{12} \end{array}$$

TO ADD FRACTIONS

1. Be sure all fractions have common denominators.

2. Add the numerators.

3. Put the total over the common denominator and be sure the answer is in lowest terms.

You follow the same method for adding mixed numbers. Add the fractions first in case you need to combine your fraction total with the whole numbers.

Example 4: Jorge bought $1\frac{3}{4}$ pounds of chicken and $6\frac{2}{3}$ pounds of ground beef for the picnic. How much did he buy altogether?

STEP 1. Find the common denominator: 12.

STEP 2. Add the fractions. Simplify the improper fraction $\frac{17}{12}$ to the mixed number $1\frac{5}{12}$.

STEP 3. Add $1\frac{5}{12}$ to 7 to get $8\frac{5}{12}$.

$$1\frac{3}{4} = 1\frac{9}{12}$$
$$+\ 6\frac{2}{3} = 6\frac{8}{12}$$
$$\overline{}$$
$$7\frac{17}{12} = 7 + 1\frac{5}{12} = 8\frac{5}{12}$$

TO ADD MIXED NUMBERS

1. Be sure fractional parts have common denominators.

2. Add the fractional parts. Simplify to a mixed number if necessary.

3. Add the whole numbers.

4. Be sure your answer is in lowest terms.

The process of subtracting fractions is similar to adding fractions.

Example 5: $\frac{7}{16} - \frac{3}{16}$

$$\frac{7}{16}$$
$$-\ \frac{3}{16}$$
$$\overline{}$$
$$\frac{4}{16} = \frac{1}{4}$$

Example 6: Take $\frac{3}{8}$ from $\frac{11}{12}$.

$$\frac{11}{12} = \frac{22}{24}$$
$$-\ \frac{3}{8} = \frac{9}{24}$$
$$\overline{}$$
$$\frac{13}{24}$$

TO SUBTRACT FRACTIONS

1. Be sure the fractions have common denominators.

2. Subtract the numerators.

3. Put the difference over the common denominator.

4. Be sure the answer is in lowest terms.

One difference between adding and subtracting mixed numbers is that you might have to regroup to be able to subtract.

Example 7: Miriam needs to lose $9\frac{1}{4}$ pounds. She has already lost $5\frac{3}{4}$ pounds. How much does she have left to lose?

STEP 1. When you write the problem, you see that you can't take $\frac{3}{4}$ from $\frac{1}{4}$. You must regroup 1 from 9. Since 1 can also be written as $\frac{4}{4}$, rewrite the 9 as $8\frac{4}{4}$.

$$9\frac{1}{4} = 8\frac{4}{4} + \frac{1}{4} = 8\frac{5}{4}$$
$$- 5\frac{3}{4} \qquad\qquad = 5\frac{3}{4}$$
$$\overline{\qquad\qquad\qquad 3\frac{2}{4} = 3\frac{1}{2}} \text{ pounds}$$

STEP 2. Add the numerators to get $\frac{5}{4}$.

STEP 3. Subtract the fractions and whole numbers. Reduce the fraction.

▶ **TIP:** To decide how to rewrite a 1 that you regroup, look at the denominator of the fraction being subtracted. For example, if you are subtracting $\frac{3}{8}$, write the 1 as $\frac{8}{8}$, or if you are subtracting $\frac{5}{6}$, write the 1 as $\frac{6}{6}$.

TO SUBTRACT MIXED NUMBERS

1. Whether or not you need to regroup, be sure that the fractions have common denominators.

2. Subtract the fraction. If you have to regroup 1 from a whole number, convert it to an improper fraction with the same denominator and add it to the original fraction (if there is one).

3. Subtract the whole number.

EXERCISE 6: ADDING AND SUBTRACTING FRACTIONS

Directions: Solve each problem.

1. $\frac{1}{9}$ $+ \frac{5}{9}$

2. $\frac{2}{3}$ $+ \frac{1}{4}$

3. $\frac{3}{8}$ $+ \frac{1}{12}$

4. $\frac{5}{6}$ $+ \frac{1}{6}$

5. $1\frac{5}{12}$ $+ 6\frac{4}{12}$

6. $4\frac{1}{5}$ $+ 3\frac{2}{7}$

7. $4\frac{2}{9}$ $+ 5\frac{1}{9}$

8. $3\frac{7}{8}$ $2\frac{5}{6}$ $+ 3\frac{1}{3}$

9. $\frac{9}{10}$ $- \frac{3}{10}$

10. $\frac{5}{8}$ $- \frac{1}{2}$

11. $\frac{4}{5}$ $- \frac{1}{2}$

12. $\frac{12}{18}$ $- \frac{5}{18}$

13. $4\frac{3}{4}$ $- 2\frac{7}{8}$

14. $25\frac{1}{6}$ $- 11\frac{1}{2}$

15. 10 $- 3\frac{2}{17}$

16. 20 $- \frac{4}{5}$

Answers are on page 717.

Multiplying Fractions

Unlike adding and subtracting fractions, there is no need for common denominators when you multiply and divide. In some cases, you will just multiply straight across, multiplying numerator by numerator and denominator by denominator.

Example 1: $\frac{3}{4} \times \frac{1}{2} = \frac{3}{8}$

Other problems can be solved more easily by *canceling*—reducing a numerator and a denominator divisible by the same factor.

Example 2: $\frac{6}{15} \times \frac{5}{12}$

STEP 1. The 15 and the 5 can be divided by 5.

$$\frac{6}{\overset{}{\underset{3}{\cancel{15}}}} \times \frac{\overset{1}{\cancel{5}}}{12}$$

STEP 2. The 6 and the 12 can be divided by 6.

$$\frac{\overset{1}{\cancel{6}}}{\underset{3}{\cancel{15}}} \times \frac{\overset{1}{\cancel{5}}}{\underset{2}{\cancel{12}}}$$

STEP 3. Multiply straight across. If necessary, reduce the answer. $\frac{1}{3} \times \frac{1}{2} = \frac{1}{6}$

TO MULTIPLY FRACTIONS

1. Reduce numerators and denominators by canceling.

2. Multiply straight across.

3. Be sure your answer is reduced to lowest terms.

You can also cancel with three fractions. Sometimes you have to "jump" over the middle number.

Example 3: $\frac{3}{8} \times \frac{4}{7} \times \frac{5}{9}$

STEP 1. Divide both the 3 and the 9 by 3.

$$\frac{\overset{1}{\cancel{3}}}{8} \times \frac{4}{7} \times \frac{5}{\underset{3}{\cancel{9}}}$$

STEP 2. Divide both the 4 and the 8 by 4.

$$\frac{\overset{1}{\cancel{3}}}{\underset{2}{\cancel{8}}} \times \frac{\overset{1}{\cancel{4}}}{7} \times \frac{5}{\underset{3}{\cancel{9}}} = \frac{5}{42}$$

STEP 3. Multiply straight across.

Example 4 shows a case that involves multiplying mixed numbers.

Example 4: Sarah usually jogs $2\frac{1}{3}$ miles daily. She jogged the full distance on 3 days and $\frac{1}{2}$ the distance on another day. How many miles did she jog in all?

STEP 1. Change all mixed numbers to improper fractions.

$$2\frac{1}{3} \times 3\frac{1}{2} = \frac{7}{3} \times \frac{7}{2}$$

STEP 2. Multiply and change the improper fraction back to mixed numbers.

$$\frac{7}{3} \times \frac{7}{2} = \frac{49}{6} = 8\frac{1}{6}$$

TO MULTIPLY MIXED NUMBERS

1. Change mixed numbers to improper fractions.

2. Reduce numbers divisible by the same number by canceling.

3. Multiply straight across.

4. Be sure your answer is reduced to lowest terms.

▶ **TIP:** Sometimes you may have to multiply a whole number by a fraction or a mixed number. Rewrite the whole number over 1 and then multiply as usual. For example, 4 can be written as $\frac{4}{1}$, so

$$\frac{1}{2} \times 4 = \frac{1}{\cancel{2}_1} \times \frac{\cancel{4}^2}{1} = 2.$$

EXERCISE 7: MULTIPLYING FRACTIONS

Directions: Solve each problem.

1. $\frac{6}{15} \times \frac{5}{12}$

2. $8 \times \frac{3}{4}$

3. $\frac{3}{8} \times \frac{2}{15} \times \frac{6}{7}$

4. $8\frac{1}{6} \times 4$

5. $\frac{5}{9} \times \frac{2}{5}$

6. $2\frac{1}{2} \times 2\frac{1}{3}$

7. $2\frac{3}{4} \times \frac{6}{7}$

8. $1\frac{3}{10} \times 5$

9. $3\frac{3}{8} \times 1\frac{3}{9}$

Answers are on page 718.

Dividing Fractions

Division is the opposite operation of multiplication. For instance, when we divide a number by 2, we are actually multiplying by $\frac{1}{2}$.

$$12 \div 2 = \frac{\cancel{12}^6}{1} \times \frac{1}{\cancel{2}_1} = \frac{6}{1} = 6$$

The fraction $\frac{1}{2}$ is called the ***reciprocal*** of 2. Two numbers whose product is 1 are reciprocals. Because $5 \times \frac{1}{5} = 1$, the numbers 5 and $\frac{1}{5}$ are reciprocals. To find the reciprocal of a number, you merely invert it, which means you turn it over.

To divide a fraction, follow the method shown below.

Example 1: Divide $\frac{7}{8}$ by $\frac{3}{4}$.

STEP 1. Multiply the first fraction by the reciprocal of the second.

$$\frac{7}{8} \div \frac{3}{4} = \frac{7}{8} \times \frac{4}{3}$$

STEP 2. Multiply across and change the improper fraction to a mixed number.

$$\frac{7}{\cancel{8}_2} \times \frac{\cancel{4}^1}{3} = \frac{7}{6} = 1\frac{1}{6}$$

To divide a mixed number, first change any mixed numbers to improper fractions.

Example 2: What is $4\frac{2}{3} \div 1\frac{1}{2}$?

STEP 1. Change both mixed numbers to improper fractions.

$$\frac{14}{3} \div \frac{3}{2}$$

STEP 2. Multiply the first fraction by the reciprocal of the second and change improper fractions back to mixed numbers.

$$\frac{14}{3} \times \frac{2}{3} = \frac{28}{9} = 3\frac{1}{9}$$

TO DIVIDE FRACTIONS OR MIXED NUMBERS

1. Change mixed numbers to improper fractions.

2. Multiply the first fraction by the reciprocal of the second.

3. Change any improper fractions back to mixed numbers.

EXERCISE 8: DIVIDING FRACTIONS

Directions: Solve each problem.

1. $\frac{4}{10} \div \frac{2}{3}$ 3. $\frac{3}{7} \div \frac{6}{35}$ 5. $1\frac{3}{8} \div 11$

2. $\frac{2}{5} \div 4$ 4. $3\frac{2}{3} \div 1\frac{1}{2}$ 6. $9 \div 2\frac{1}{2}$

Answers are on page 718.

Simplifying Fraction Problems

The best way to simplify fraction word problems is to *restate* the problem using whole numbers. Many times the fractions scare us off and make it difficult to figure out what to do. Let's look at a few examples of restating fraction problems.

▶ **TIP:** You can always look for key words or basic concepts that indicate the operation to use. A frequently used key word in fraction problems is *of*. A problem may ask you to find "$\frac{1}{2}$ of" something or "$\frac{2}{3}$ of" something. When you find a "part of" something, you multiply.

Example: An upholstery cleaner schedules $1\frac{1}{2}$-hour appointments for each couch to be cleaned. If he works $7\frac{1}{2}$ hours, how many couches will he clean?

Restated replacing fractions with whole numbers: "A cleaner schedules 2-hour appointments for each couch. If he works 8 hours, how many couches will he clean?"

Solution: After restating the problem, it seems more obvious that it is a division problem—the cleaner is splitting his day into smaller segments. Therefore, we would choose to use division in the original problem.

$$7\frac{1}{2} \div 1\frac{1}{2} = \frac{15}{2} \div \frac{3}{2} \qquad \frac{\overset{5}{\cancel{15}}}{\underset{1}{\cancel{2}}} \times \frac{\overset{1}{\cancel{2}}}{\underset{1}{\cancel{3}}} = 5$$

The cleaner will clean 5 couches.

▶ **TIP:** Be sure that the amount that is being divided up comes first in a division problem. In the example above, the $7\frac{1}{2}$-hour period was being divided into $1\frac{1}{2}$-hour segments.

Item Sets

Some problems on the Mathematics Test will be presented as item sets. An item set refers to a lot of information given in a paragraph or two or in an illustration. Then several questions based on that information (usually 3–5) will follow.

▶ **TIP:** The key to solving questions based on item sets is choosing only the information needed to answer that particular question.

The next group of problems follows the item set format. These problems require you to use your skills with whole numbers, decimals, and fractions.

EXERCISE 9: ITEM SETS

Directions: Write the information needed for each problem and then solve the problem.

Questions 1–3 are based on the problem below.

José wants to build bookshelves in his den. He needs 8 shelves, each $5\frac{1}{4}$ feet long. He must buy the lumber for the shelves in 6-foot lengths and then cut the $5\frac{1}{4}$-foot pieces from those lengths. The cost of the lumber is $98\frac{1}{2}$ cents per linear foot.

1. How much will the lumber cost for all of the shelves?

   Information needed:_____

   (1) $5.91 **(2)** $47.28 **(3)** $591 **(4)** $788 **(5)** $1379

2. How many linear feet of lumber will he waste by cutting?

   Information needed:_____

   (1) $\frac{3}{4}$ foot **(2)** $4\frac{1}{2}$ feet **(3)** 6 feet **(4)** 8 feet **(5)** 10 feet

3. The cost of varnishing all of the shelves will amount to an additional $12. José can buy prevarnished shelves of the correct length ($5\frac{1}{4}$ feet) for $13.95 each. How much will he save by doing the cutting and varnishing himself?

   Information needed:_____

   (1) $52.32 **(2)** $59.28 **(3)** $64.32 **(4)** $99.60 **(5)** $111.60

Questions 4–6 are based on the picture below.

The owner of a campground is planning to add two new roads, Birch Trail and Pine Way. The campground area is $\frac{7}{8}$ mile wide and $\frac{19}{20}$ mile deep.

4. What is the length of Pine Way?

   Information needed:_____

   (1) $\frac{1}{8}$ mile **(2)** $\frac{7}{20}$ mile **(3)** $\frac{19}{40}$ mile **(4)** $1\frac{11}{40}$ miles **(5)** $1\frac{2}{3}$ miles

5. What is the total length of the two new roads?

Information needed:_____

   (1) $\frac{19}{40}$ mile   **(2)** $\frac{13}{20}$ mile   **(3)** $\frac{21}{23}$ mile   **(4)** $1\frac{1}{8}$ miles   **(5)** $1\frac{1}{4}$ miles

6. How wide is Elm Lane?

Information needed:_____

   (1) $\frac{1}{5}$ mile   **(2)** $\frac{2}{5}$ mile   **(3)** $\frac{19}{40}$ mile   **(4)** $\frac{19}{20}$ mile

   (5) not enough information is given

Questions 7–9 are based on the problem below.

     Al Watt gets paid an hourly wage for the first 40 hours he works. He gets $1\frac{1}{2}$ times his hourly wage for any overtime hours past the original 40 hours. The chart below shows his time sheet for the second week in April.

Name	Employee #	Hourly Wage	Hours
Al Watt	08395	$7.86	$43\frac{1}{3}$

7. What is Al's hourly wage per hour of overtime?

Information needed:_____

   (1) $3.93   **(2)** $5.24   **(3)** $11.79   **(4)** $15.72
   (5) not enough information is given

8. What is Al's total pay for the third week in April?

Information needed:_____

   (1) $314.40   **(2)** $340.60   **(3)** $353.70   **(4)** $510.90
   (5) not enough information is given

9. Which expression represents Al's total pay for the second week in April?

Information needed:_____

   (1) $7.86 × 40   **(2)** $11.79 × $\frac{10}{3}$ **(3)** ($7.86 × 40) × ($11.79 × $3\frac{1}{3}$)

   (4) ($7.86 × 40) + ($11.79 × $\frac{10}{3}$)   **(5)** not enough information is given

Answers are on page 718.

The following practice problems are GED-type problems that require you to use your skills with fractions as well as problem solving.

EXERCISE 10: FRACTION REVIEW

Directions: Solve each problem.

1. An $8\frac{3}{8}$-foot post was set $2\frac{3}{4}$ feet into the ground. What is the exact length of the post above ground?

   (1) $5\frac{5}{8}$ ft

   (2) $5\frac{7}{8}$ ft

   (3) 6 ft

   (4) $11\frac{1}{8}$ ft

   (5) not enough information is given

2. If a share of oil stock costs $\$36\frac{1}{4}$, how much do 24 shares cost?

   (1) \$1.51

   (2) $\$16\frac{7}{8}$

   (3) $\$60\frac{7}{8}$

   (4) \$864

   (5) \$870

3. A car averages $22\frac{1}{2}$ miles per gallon of gasoline on a trip. Which of the following shows how many gallons of gasoline the car uses on a 720-mile trip?

   (1) $22\frac{1}{2} + 720$

   (2) $22\frac{1}{2} - 720$

   (3) $720 \div 22\frac{1}{2}$

   (4) $720 \times 22\frac{1}{2}$

   (5) $22\frac{1}{2} \div 720$

4. A dosage of medicine is $\frac{2}{3}$ milliliter. How many dosages can be given from a bottle containing 20 milliliters?

   (1) $13\frac{1}{3}$

   (2) $19\frac{1}{3}$

   (3) 20

   (4) 30

   (5) not enough information is given

5. Find the total weight of 2 cartons including the weight of both the cartons and the contents of the cartons. Each carton contains $16\frac{3}{4}$ pounds of potatoes.

   (1) $8\frac{3}{8}$ lb

   (2) $16\frac{3}{4}$ lb

   (3) $33\frac{1}{2}$ lb

   (4) $18\frac{3}{4}$ lb

   (5) not enough information is given

6. Find the missing length *l* in the drawing below.

(1) $4\frac{3}{4}$ in

(2) $5\frac{3}{4}$ in

(3) 6 in

(4) $8\frac{1}{8}$ in

(5) not enough information is given

7. The price of round-trip airfare to Dallas is $285. How much will it cost a family of four if the husband pays full fare, the wife pays $\frac{2}{3}$ of full fare, and the two children each pay $\frac{1}{2}$ of the regular price?

(1) $475

(2) $570

(3) $617.50

(4) $760

(5) $1140

8. Mr. Cortez owns a $10\frac{1}{2}$-acre tract of land, and he plans to subdivide this tract into $\frac{1}{4}$-acre lots. He must first set aside $\frac{1}{6}$ of the total land for roads. How many lots will this tract yield?

(1) $1\frac{3}{4}$

(2) $8\frac{3}{4}$

(3) 35

(4) $41\frac{1}{3}$

(5) 42

9. A carpenter wanted three pieces of wood each $1\frac{5}{8}$ feet long. If he planned to cut them from a 6-foot piece of wood, how much of the piece would be left?

(1) $1\frac{1}{8}$ ft

(2) 3 ft

(3) $4\frac{3}{8}$ ft

(4) $4\frac{7}{8}$ ft

(5) not enough information is given

10. A politician wants to get his message to $\frac{2}{3}$ of the population of 48,000 in Springfield. However, his advertising campaign reaches only $\frac{3}{4}$ of the number he intended. How many people does he actually reach?

(1) 16,000

(2) 24,000

(3) 36,000

(4) 68,000

(5) 72,000

Answers are on page 718.

4
RATIO AND PROPORTION

Let's move from fractions to ratio and proportion. The word *ratio* basically means fraction, and we can use fractions to set up most ratios that compare two quantities; together, these two ratios are called a *proportion*. A proportion shows that two fractions are equal to each other. In this chapter, we will use proportions to solve many types of problems. In the next chapter, we will use proportions to solve percent word problems.

Ratio

A *ratio* is a mathematical way of comparing two quantities. Some everyday uses of ratio are "Six out of every eight students saw the concert," "I drove 55 miles per hour on the expressway," and "The mixture contains 2 cups of flour for every cup of water."

If the ratio compares two quantities with different units, it is called a *rate*. For example, 55 *miles* per *hour* is a rate. Whether we call the comparison a ratio or a rate, it can be written as a fraction, as a comparison using the word *to*, or as a comparison using a colon. You can set up a ratio whenever you are comparing two numbers.

Example 1: Write a ratio for: Six out of eight students saw the concert.

The ratio is: 6 to 8 OR 6:8 OR $\frac{6}{8}$

$\frac{6}{8}$ can be reduced to $\frac{3}{4}$

▶ **TIP:** The smaller the numbers are, the easier it is to understand the comparison, so it is a good idea to reduce the ratio to lowest terms.

Example 2: "I drove 55 miles per hour."

The rate is: 55 miles to 1 hour OR 55:1 OR $\frac{55}{1}$

The word *per* often tells you to set up a ratio. This ratio is a rate because it compares two different units: *miles* to *hours*.

▶ **TIP:** In a ratio, unlike a fraction, the number 1 is kept in the denominator.

Sometimes it is necessary to change the form of one of the numbers to make a comparison.

Example 3: Eggs cost 72 cents per dozen. What is the cost per egg?

$72:12 = \frac{72}{12} = \frac{6}{1}$

First you had to write 12 for a dozen eggs. When the ratio is reduced, it is 6 to 1, which means each egg costs 6 cents.

EXERCISE 1: RATIO

Directions: Write each comparison as a ratio or a rate in fraction form. Be sure to reduce each fraction completely.

1. 3 miles to 8 miles

2. 30 minutes to 1 hour

3. 27 feet to 18 feet

4. 3 pounds of meat for 4 people

5. 300 miles on 15 gallons of gas

6. 88 feet in 8 seconds

7. $42.21 earned in 7 hours

8. $80 for 12 boards

Answers are on page 719.

Application of Ratio

The real value of ratio on the GED Test is its application to real-life problem solving. For example, "Which is the better buy?" is a question frequently posed by shoppers. These problems can be solved by using ratios to compare the cost per unit of weight for each item.

Example: There are three sizes of Wow Chow on the grocer's shelves. Which is the best buy?

To find the per-unit cost for each item, calculate the ratio of cost to weight. This is represented by the ratio $\frac{cost}{weight}$.

(a) $\frac{\$1.89}{3\,lb} = \frac{\$.63}{1\,lb}$ OR $.63 per lb

(b) $\frac{\$2.95}{5\,lb} = \frac{\$.59}{1\,lb}$ OR $.59 per lb

(c) $\frac{\$11.40}{20\,lb} = \frac{\$.57}{1\,lb}$ OR $.57 per lb

Notice that each ratio was reduced. The 20-lb bag costs 57 cents per pound, the 5-lb bag costs 59 cents per pound, while the 3-lb bag costs 63 cents per pound. The 20-lb bag is the best buy. Now all you would need to decide is how much dog food you *really* want to buy.

Next, let's look at a few application problems involving ratios and rates.

EXERCISE 2: APPLICATION OF RATIOS

Directions: Solve each problem.

Questions 1–3 are based on the information in the table below. Write each ratio as a fraction to compare the expenses.

PAINTERS' WEEKLY WORK EXPENSES				TOTAL
Tools $25	Supplies $120	Transportation $40	Telephone $15	$200

1. Compare the cost of supplies to total expenses.

2. The total expenses are how many times greater than the expense for transportation?

3. Find the ratio of supplies to tools.

4. A company has assets of $6,800,000 and liabilities of $1,700,000. What is the company's ratio of liabilities to assets?

5. In a tennis club of 750 members, 250 members are women. What is the ratio of female members to total membership?

6. You own 300 shares of Consolidated Merchants stock and receive a dividend of $729. What is the dividend per share?

Questions 7 and 8 are based on the information below.

The Miranda family purchased a 250-pound side of beef and had it packaged. They paid $365 for the side of beef. During the packaging, 75 lb of beef were discarded as waste.

7. How many pounds of beef were packaged?

8. What was the cost per pound for the packaged beef?

Answers are on page 719.

Proportion

A ***proportion*** is a statement that two ratios (fractions) are equal. The arithmetic statement $\frac{7}{8} = \frac{14}{16}$ is an example of a proportion. In words, it means "7 is to 8 as 14 is to 16." A proportion is true if the ***cross products*** are equal. Cross products are the numbers that are at opposite corners of the equivalent fractions.

Example 1:

$$\frac{7}{8} = \frac{14}{16}$$

$$7 \times 16 = 8 \times 14 \qquad \textit{7 × 16 and 8 × 14 are cross products.}$$

$$\underbrace{112} = \underbrace{112}$$

A useful type of proportion is one in which one of the ratios is not completely known. The missing number is represented by a letter. Example 2 shows how to solve for the letter.

Example 2: If 3 apples cost 50 cents, find the cost of 15 apples at the same rate. You can write a proportion to represent this.

STEP 1. Set up the proportion where c represents the unknown cost of the apples.

$$\frac{3 \text{ apples}}{\$.50} = \frac{15 \text{ apples}}{c}$$

$$\frac{3}{.50} = \frac{15}{c}$$

STEP 2. Cross multiply the two given numbers.

$$15 \times .50 = \$7.50$$

STEP 3. Divide that answer by the number that is left.

$$\$7.50 \div 3 = \$2.50$$
$$c = \$2.50$$

Therefore, if 3 apples cost 50 cents, 15 apples cost $2.50.

We know this is true because the cross products are equal.

$$\frac{3}{\$.50} = \frac{15}{\$2.50}$$

$$3 \times \$2.50 = 15 \times \$.50$$

$$\$7.50 = \$7.50$$

▶ **TIP:** When setting up a proportion, be sure to set up both fractions in the same way. In this case, we put *apples* over *money* in both fractions. It helps to begin by writing the labels *apples* and *c* on each fraction to make sure they are both written the same way.

TO SOLVE A PROPORTION

1. Cross multiply two given numbers.

2. Divide that answer by the number that is left in the proportion.

You can also represent the operations to solve a proportion in the following way.

1. Write the proportion.

$$\frac{b}{8} = \frac{5}{20}$$

2. Write the multiplication above a fraction bar. Remember that a fraction bar also means "divided by."

$$8 \times 5$$

3. Write the remaining number under the fraction bar.

$$\frac{8 \times 5}{20}$$

4. Solve by multiplying the top and dividing by the bottom.

$$\frac{40}{20} = 2$$

EXERCISE 3: SOLVING PROPORTIONS

Directions: Solve the following proportions for the missing element in each.

1. $\frac{2}{5} = \frac{m}{10}$ 2. $\frac{x}{7} = \frac{3}{21}$ 3. $\frac{5}{y} = \frac{15}{20}$ 4. $\frac{6}{4} = \frac{12}{z}$ 5. $\frac{x}{12} = \frac{30}{24}$

Answers are on page 719.

Application of Proportion

As you will see throughout the math section of this book, proportion has a great many applications. If a problem compares two types of quantities and asks for a missing factor, you should consider using a proportion to solve the problem.

Example 1: A 25-acre field yields 350 bushels of wheat. At that rate, how many bushels will a 60-acre field yield?

STEP 1. Set up the proportion, keeping acres on the top and bushels on the bottom.

$$\frac{25 \text{ acres}}{350 \text{ bushels}} = \frac{60 \text{ acres}}{b}$$

$$\frac{25}{350} = \frac{60}{b}$$

STEP 2. Cross multiply and divide by the remaining number.

$$\frac{350 \times 60}{25} = \frac{21,000}{25} = 840 \text{ bushels}$$

Therefore, a 60-acre field will yield 840 bushels of wheat.

The most challenging part of setting up a proportion is putting the numbers in the right part of the proportion. Try setting up a proportion to solve the problem below.

Example 2: If a baseball player hits 10 home runs in the first 45 games, at the same rate how many home runs can he expect to hit during the 162-game season?

STEP 1. Gather the given information and identify the unknown quantity.

10 home runs in 45 games.
h home runs in 162 games.

STEP 2. Write a proportion, keeping the labels in the same part of both ratios.

$$\frac{10 \text{ home runs}}{45 \text{ games}} = \frac{h}{162 \text{ games}}$$

STEP 3. Solve.

$$\frac{162 \times 10}{45} = \frac{1620}{45} = 36$$

The player can expect to hit 36 home runs in 162 games.

EXERCISE 4: APPLICATION OF PROPORTION

Directions: Solve each problem.

1. A car travels 96 miles on 8 gallons of gas. How far can the car travel on a full tank of gas that holds 20 gallons?

2. The picture to the right is to be enlarged. If the width of the enlargement will be 8 inches, how high will it be?

7 in

?

5 in

8 in

3. At Foster's Department Store, the ratio of managers to salespeople is 2:9. If Foster's currently has 180 salespeople, how many managers are there?

4. On the scale drawing to the right, $\frac{1}{8}$ inch = 1 foot. If the length of a room on the scale drawing is $2\frac{1}{4}$ inches, how long is the actual room?

$2\frac{1}{4}$

Key: $\frac{1}{8}$ in = 1 ft

5. Two pancakes contain 120 calories. Ellen had a stack of 7 pancakes. How many calories did she have?

Answers are on page 719.

5
PERCENTS

One of the most common and practical applications of math is the study of percents. We are confronted with percents when we buy on installment, pay taxes, get a loan, get discounts on purchases, read major-league baseball standings, or even listen to the weather report.

You might hear on the radio or TV that mortgage loans are at 7.5%. The interest rate on credit cards is 16%. You can finance your new car at 6.9%. The state sales tax is 7%. Crawford's Department Store has 20% off on winter coats this week. Percents are everywhere!

What Are Percents?

Percents, like decimals and fractions, are ways of writing parts of a whole. A percent is a part of a whole that has been divided into 100 equal pieces. Therefore, **percent** means "per hundred."

A percent is written as a number with the sign %. For example, the number 50% means the same as $\frac{50}{100}$ or .50. When you work with percents, you may have to change them to an equivalent decimal or fraction. The chart below shows the relationship among percents, fractions, and decimals. You should memorize this list because these relationships are used over and over again.

Percent	Fraction	Decimal
1%	$\frac{1}{100}$	.01
5%	$\frac{5}{100} = \frac{1}{20}$	.05
10%	$\frac{10}{100} = \frac{1}{10}$	.10
25%	$\frac{25}{100} = \frac{1}{4}$	.25
$33\frac{1}{3}\%$	$\frac{33\frac{1}{3}}{100} = \frac{1}{3}$	$.33\frac{1}{3}$
50%	$\frac{50}{100} = \frac{1}{2}$	.50
$66\frac{2}{3}\%$	$\frac{66\frac{2}{3}}{100} = \frac{2}{3}$	$.66\frac{2}{3}$
75%	$\frac{75}{100} = \frac{3}{4}$	.75
100%	$\frac{100}{100} = 1$	1.00

▶ **TIP:** Since 100% is one whole, then anything less than 100% is less than one whole. For example, 75% of a quantity is a part of that quantity.

Changing to Fractions and Decimals

Many problems require a change back and forth from fractions to decimals to percents. To change a percent to a fraction or decimal, remember what % means: percent means "per hundred."

$$\% \text{ means } "\times \tfrac{1}{100}," \text{ and } \% \text{ means } "\times .01."$$

Example 1: Change 13% to an equivalent fraction and to an equivalent decimal.

To a fraction: $13 \times \frac{1}{100} = \frac{13}{1} \times \frac{1}{100} = \frac{13}{100}$

To a decimal: $13 \times .01 = .13$

▶ **TIP:** You will notice that multiplying by .01 moves the decimal point 2 places to the left. $13\% = .13. = .13$

Example 2: Change the following to an equivalent fraction and an equivalent decimal. Be sure to reduce fractions to lowest terms.

80% *To a fraction:* $80 \times \frac{1}{100} = \frac{\overset{4}{\cancel{80}}}{1} \times \frac{1}{\underset{5}{\cancel{100}}} = \frac{4}{5}$

To a decimal: $80 \times .01 = .80$ or $.8$

$33\frac{1}{3}\%$ *To a fraction:* $33\frac{1}{3} \times \frac{1}{100} = \frac{\overset{1}{\cancel{100}}}{3} \times \frac{1}{\underset{1}{\cancel{100}}} = \frac{1}{3}$

To a decimal: $33\frac{1}{3} \times .01 = .33\frac{1}{3}$

150% *To a mixed number:* $150 \times \frac{1}{100} = \frac{\overset{3}{\cancel{150}}}{1} \times \frac{1}{\underset{2}{\cancel{100}}} = \frac{3}{2} = 1\frac{1}{2}$

To a decimal: $150 \times .01 = 1.50$ or 1.5

Some percents can be written like this: .6%. This means "six-tenths of one percent" and is less than 1%.

Example 3: Write .6% as a fraction and as a decimal.

As a fraction: First, write the decimal part as a fraction. Then, multiply by $\frac{1}{100}$. $.6 = \frac{6}{10} = \frac{3}{5}$

$\frac{3}{5} \times \frac{1}{100} = \frac{3}{500}$

As a decimal: Just write the decimal part and multiply by .01. $.6 \times .01 = .006$

▶ **TIP:** Always read a decimal carefully for its meaning. Anything over 100% is *more than one whole*. For example, 200% is the same as 2 times a whole. Thus, 200% of 6 is 12.

Any proper fraction or decimal followed by % means *less than 1%*. For example, $\frac{3}{4}\%$ means "three-quarters of one percent," and .75% means "seventy-five hundredths of one percent," *not* 75%.

EXERCISE 1: CHANGING TO FRACTIONS AND DECIMALS

Directions: Change each percent to an equivalent fraction *and* an equivalent decimal.

1. 87%   **4.** $66\frac{2}{3}\%$ **7.** 18%

2. 40%   **5.** 200%   **8.** .8%

3. 2%   **6.** 12.5%   **9.** $\frac{1}{2}\%$

Answers are on page 720.

Changing to Percents

In some problems, you are given a fraction or a decimal, and you need to change it to a percent. You can do this by dividing by one-hundredth.

- To change a fraction to a percent, multiply by 100 and attach a % sign.

- To change a decimal to a percent, multiply by 100 and attach a % sign.

Example 1: Change $\frac{7}{8}$ to a percent.

$$\frac{7}{8} \times 100 = \frac{7}{8} \times \frac{100}{1} = \frac{700}{8} = 87\frac{1}{2} = 87\frac{1}{2}\%$$

Example 2: Change .3 to a percent.

$$.3 \times 100 = 30 = 30\%$$

Example 3: Change the mixed number 2.04 to an equivalent percent.

$$\frac{2.04}{1} \times \frac{100}{1} = \frac{204}{1} = 204 = 204\%$$

EXERCISE 2: CHANGING TO PERCENTS

Directions: Change the following numbers to equivalent percents.

1. $\frac{3}{5}$ **4.** .0025   **7.** $\frac{9}{10}$

2. .70   **5.** $\frac{3}{8}$ **8.** .625

3. $\frac{1}{3}$ **6.** 4.5   **9.** $2\frac{1}{4}$

Answers are on page 720.

Solving Percent Problems

As you've seen, a percent can be written as a fraction. The percent 25% can be written as $\frac{25}{100}$. From your study of ratio, you also know that $\frac{25}{100}$ means "25 out of 100." Because of this relationship among percents, fractions, and ratios, you can use an interesting method to solve percent word problems.

Using Proportions

A percent word problem can be solved by setting up a proportion. We call this the "PART over WHOLE" method. The proportion below shows how to set up one of these problems.

$$\frac{\text{PART}}{\text{WHOLE}} = \frac{\% \,(\text{PART})}{100\% \,(\text{WHOLE})}$$

You may also see it shown this way:

part	%
whole	100

In the example of 25%, the proportion would look like this:

part → $\dfrac{25}{100}$ ← whole   = $\dfrac{25\%}{100\%}$ ← percent (part) / always 100%

This proportion shows that the relationship of a part to a whole is the same as the relationship of a percent to 100%. To solve a percent word problem, you must read the problem carefully and first decide whether you are looking for the *percent, part*, or *whole*. Use an *n* for the number you are trying to find. Remember, the 100 on the bottom right *never* changes.

To illustrate the use of this method in solving percent problems, we will work through three examples.

Example 1: Find 40% of 120.

Solution: We are looking for a missing PART.

the missing part → $\dfrac{n}{120}$ ← whole   = $\dfrac{40}{100}$ ← percent part / always 100

Cross multiply: 120 × 40 = 4800

Divide: 4800 ÷ 100 = 48

The missing number is 48. 40% of 120 is 48.

▶ **TIP:** Sometimes, to find a percent, it may be easier just to change the percent to a decimal or fraction and multiply. For example, to find 40% of 120: 120 × .40 = 48, and 120 × $\frac{2}{5}$ = 48.

Example 2: 18 is what percent of 72?

Solution: We are looking for the PERCENT.

part → $\dfrac{18}{72}$ ← whole   = $\dfrac{n}{100}$ ← the missing percent / always 100

Cross multiply: 18 × 100 = 1800

Divide: 1800 ÷ 72 = 25

The number is 25%. 18 is 25% of 72.

Example 3: 120% of what number is 60?

Solution: We are looking for the WHOLE.

part → $\dfrac{60}{n}$ = $\dfrac{120}{100}$ ← percent

the missing whole ↗   ↘ always 100

Cross multiply: $60 \times 100 = 6000$

Divide: $6000 \div 120 = 50$

The missing number is 50. 120% of 50 is 60.

Notice that in Example 3 the part (60) is larger than the whole (50). This is because the percent is 120%, which is more than 100%.

SOLVING A PERCENT PROBLEM

1. Decide if you are looking for the part, whole, or percent. Use *n* in place of the missing number.

2. Set up the proportion and put any given numbers and the *n* in the right place.

$$\frac{\text{Part}}{\text{Whole}} = \frac{\text{Percent (\%)}}{100}$$

3. Cross multiply.

4. Divide.

EXERCISE 3: PERCENT PROBLEMS

Directions: Write down which you are looking for: part, whole, or percent. Then solve each problem.

1. Find 4% of 30.

2. What percent of 56 is 14?

3. 10 is 2.5% of what number?

4. 7% of what amount is 14?

5. What percent of $340 is $30.60?

6. $\frac{1}{2}$% of 62 is what number?

7. What is 120% of 45?

8. 210 is what percent of 600?

9. 16% of what number is 18?

10. 20 is what percent of 5?

Answers are on page 720.

Percent Word Problems

As you know, percents are a part of the math that people do every day—at work, while shopping, or in personal money matters. On pages 617–619, you will study special types of percent problems—finding interest, discounts, and repayments of loans. In general, percent word problems are multi-step problems. You know, of course, that you always multiply and then divide after you have set up a proportion. However, you may also have to perform some addition or subtraction to get a final answer.

The tricky part of percent word problems is to identify what is being asked for. These problems require more careful reading than those in Exercise 3.

Example 1: To pass her science test, Amy must get 75% of the problems correct. Out of 80 questions, how many must she get right to pass?

Given: 75%—the percent
80—the whole test

Look for: n—the number to get right (the part)

The proportion for this problem reads:

$$\frac{n}{80} = \frac{75}{100}$$

part → n → percent; whole → 80; always 100

Example 2: Erica is charged 21% in finance charges for the unpaid balance on her credit cards. If her bank tells her she owes $42 in finance charges, what is her unpaid balance?

The proportion for this problem is:

$$\frac{42}{n} = \frac{21}{100}$$

finance charge → 42; balance → n; percent; always 100

Example 3 is a case that needs more than one step to find the answer.

Example 3: A car depreciates (loses value) 20% the first year it is owned. If Elena's car cost her $12,480 when it was new, what was it worth after the first year?

STEP 1. Find the amount of depreciation.

$$\frac{n}{12,480} \times \frac{20}{100}$$

Cross multiply: 12,480 × 20 = 249,600

Divide: 249,600 ÷ 100 = $2496 depreciation

STEP 2. Find the value of the car after 1 year.

Subtract: $12,480 − $2496 = $9984

EXERCISE 4: PERCENT WORD PROBLEMS

Directions: Solve each problem.

Questions 1–3 refer to the information below.

Jesse takes home $2100 a month. He saves 12% of his earnings, and he spends $420 a month for rent.

1. How much does Jesse save each month?

2. Jesse's rent is what percent of his take-home pay?

3. Jesse's employer has offered him a 5% raise for next year. What will be his monthly take-home pay next year?

4. On her test, Rachel got 26 out of 40 questions right. What percent did she get wrong?

5. Mrs. Rogers put 15% down on her new car. If the down payment was $1800, how much did the car cost?

6. A political campaign conducted a poll to determine how the candidate was doing. The results were as follows. What percent of the voters was undecided?

Allen	Gault	Undecided
200	120	180

7. Employees at Todd's Musicmart get a 20% discount on all purchases. If Hosea buys three cassettes at $7.49 each, what will he have to pay after his employee discount?

Answers are on page 720.

Interest Problems

If you borrow or invest money, you will be dealing with an ***interest rate*** that is expressed as a percent. Interest rates are calculated on an annual basis. Thus, if the loan is longer or shorter than one year, the amount of interest per year must be multiplied by the length of time.

The length of time of the loan must always be expressed as one year or a part of a year. If the time is given in months, write the months as a fraction comparing the given number of months to 12 months.

For example, 9 months $= \frac{9 \text{ months}}{12 \text{ months}} = \frac{3}{4}$ year

If the time is given in days, change it to a fraction of a year by comparing the given number of days to 360 (approximately the number of days in a year).

For example, 120 days $= \frac{120 \text{ days}}{360 \text{ days}} = \frac{1}{3}$ year

Example 1: To expand one of its factory-outlet stores, a towel manufacturer secures a $2\frac{1}{2}$-year loan for $35,000 at an annual interest rate of 7%. How much interest will the manufacturer pay on the loan?

STEP 1. Find the interest for 1 year. $\qquad \frac{n}{35,000} = \frac{7}{100}$

STEP 2. Cross multiply and divide. $\qquad \frac{35,000 \times 7}{100} = 2450$

STEP 3. Find the interest for $2\frac{1}{2}$ years. $\qquad 2450 \times 2\frac{1}{2} = \$6125$

Example 2: Mrs. Barnes borrowed $4000 for 3 years. Find the amount she repaid if the annual rate of interest was 9%.

STEP 1. Find the interest for 1 year.

$$\frac{n}{4000} = \frac{9}{100}$$

$$\frac{9 \times 4000}{100} = \frac{36,000}{100} = 360$$

STEP 2. Find the interest for 3 years.

$$360 \times 3 = 1080$$

STEP 3. Find the amount she repaid.

$$4000 + 1080 = \$5080$$

▶ **TIP:** Some interest problems require you to find only the interest, and others require you to find the total amount of the loan or investment. The total is the amount that you borrowed plus the interest. You must read problems carefully to make sure you understand whether you are being asked for the *interest* or the *amount to pay back* as in Example 2.

Example 3: Marcy borrowed $18,000 for 90 days to buy inventory for her gift shop at an annual rate of 12%. How much interest did she pay?

STEP 1. Find the interest for 1 year.

$$\frac{n}{18,000} = \frac{12}{100}$$

$$\frac{18,000 \times 12}{100} = \frac{216,000}{100} = 2160$$

STEP 2. Find the interest for $\frac{1}{4}$ year.

$$2160 \times \frac{1}{4} = \$540$$

SOLVING INTEREST PROBLEMS

1. Set up a proportion and solve it for the interest.

$$\frac{\text{Interest}}{\text{Original Amount}} = \frac{\text{Percent}}{100}$$

2. To find the total interest, multiply the interest by the length of time of the loan.

3. To find the total amount of the loan or investment, add the original amount to the total interest.

In some cases, you may have to find an amount other than the interest. You can still use the proportional method to find the percent of interest (rate).

Example 4: The yearly income from an investment of $2400 is $192. What is the annual rate of interest?

STEP 1. Write the proportion.

$$\frac{192}{2400} = \frac{n}{100}$$

STEP 2. Solve for the percent.

$$\frac{192 \times 100}{2400} = 8\%$$

▶ **TIP:** A common way to find interest is to use the formula $I = prt$, where p = principal, r = rate, and t = time.

EXERCISE 5: INTEREST PROBLEMS

Directions: Solve each problem.

1. A building contractor borrowed $60,000 for 9 months at an annual interest rate of 8%. What is the interest due on the loan?

(1) $2400 **(2)** $3600 **(3)** $3900 **(4)** $64,800 **(5)** $72,000

2. To take advantage of a closeout sale, a motel owner borrows $31,000 to buy 124 color television sets. The loan is for 90 days at an annual interest rate of 12.5%. Find the total amount to be repaid.

   (1) $968.75   **(2)** $3,875   **(3)** $31,968.75   **(4)** $34,875
   (5) not enough information is provided

3. Which expression shows how you find the interest on $1500 at $8\frac{1}{2}$% for one year?

   (1) $\dfrac{1500 \times 8\frac{1}{2}}{100}$ **(2)** $\dfrac{1500 \times 100}{8\frac{1}{2}}$ **(3)** $\dfrac{1500}{100 \div 8\frac{1}{2}}$ **(4)** $\dfrac{100}{1500 \times 8\frac{1}{2}}$ **(5)** $\dfrac{100}{1500 \div 8\frac{1}{2}}$

4. Alex borrowed some money for one year at a rate of 8%. If he paid $360 in interest that year, how much did he borrow?

   (1) $28.80   **(2)** $288   **(3)** $2,880   **(4)** $4,500   **(5)** $36,000

5. Ted has already saved $12,000, which he plans to use in building a summer cottage. The lot he wants costs $8500. The builder estimates that it will cost $32,000 to build the house, and Ted expects that there will be additional expenses of $2500. Ted will borrow the additional money he needs from the American Bank. At 10.5%, how much interest will he owe at the end of the first year?

   (1) $3255   **(2)** $4816   **(3)** $31,000   **(4)** $34,255   **(5)** $347,200

Answers are on page 721.

EXERCISE 6: PERCENT REVIEW

Directions: Solve each problem.

1. During a recent shopping spree, Tom and Ali bought some new accessories for their apartment. Ali chose a crocheted throw pillow at $24.95, and Tom purchased a rural landscape painting for $135. How much did they actually spend if they paid 7% sales tax on their purchases?

   (1) $11.20
   (2) $12.00
   (3) $148.75
   (4) $159.95
   (5) $171.15

2. Paint that regularly sells for $15.90 per gallon is on sale at a 20% discount. Which expression shows how to find the price of the paint after the discount?

   (1) $15.90 × .20(15.90)
   (2) $15.90 + .20(15.90)
   (3) $15.90 − .20(15.90)
   (4) $15.90 ÷ .20(15.90)
   (5) $15.90 − .20

3. You buy a new car for $12,800 and make a down payment of $2500. If you finance the remainder at 8% annually for three years, how much will you actually pay for the car?

   (1) $10,300
   (2) $12,190
   (3) $9,400
   (4) $12,772
   (5) $15,272

4. A car dealer is offering a rebate of $750 on any new-car purchase. If the purchase price of a car is $2000 more than it was last year, what is the rate of discount offered by the rebate?

   (1) 7.5%
   (2) 10%
   (3) 13.3%
   (4) 75%
   (5) not enough information is given

5. A real estate agent received a $4\frac{1}{2}\%$ commission on the sale of a condominium. The condominium sold for $48,900. How much did the agent receive?

(1) $1,956
(2) $2,200.50
(3) $19,560
(4) $22,005
(5) not enough information is given

Questions 6–11 refer to the chart below.

Margaret's net earnings (take-home pay) for last year were $24,000. Her expenses for the year were

Food	$3900
Rent	6000
Utilities	2400
Medical	600
Insurance	1500
Car	3800
Clothing	1000
Dues	300
Phone	300
Entertainment	1200
Savings	2400
Miscellaneous	600

6. What percent of her total net income did Margaret spend on rent?

(1) $\frac{1}{4}$ (2) 2.5 (3) 4 (4) 25 (5) 40

7. What is the ratio of savings to total income?

(1) $\frac{1}{24}$ (2) $\frac{1}{10}$ (3) $\frac{10}{1}$ (4) $\frac{24}{1}$ (5) $\frac{21,600}{1}$

8. Entertainment and savings account for what percent of Margaret's expenditures?

(1) 5 (2) 10 (3) 15 (4) 50 (5) 75

9. Assume that insurance costs are expected to rise 6.5% next year. How much will Margaret pay for insurance then?

(1) $6.50 (2) $65.00 (3) $97.50 (4) $1565 (5) $1597.50

10. Margaret's property taxes rose 7% last year. How much of her take-home pay went to property taxes?

(1) $168 (2) $1200 (3) $4800 (4) $6168
(5) not enough information is given

11. Margaret's take-home pay is 67% of her gross pay, which amounts to $35,821. Which expression shows how you would find her take-home pay?

(1) (35,821 + 67) ÷ 100
(2) (35,821 × 67) ÷ 100
(3) (35,821 × 100) ÷ 67
(4) (35,821 + 100) ÷ 67
(5) (35,821 + 100) + 67

Answers are on page 722.

6
MEASUREMENT

What is measurement? What do we do when we measure the length of a room or take the weight of a package? To measure any physical object, we assign both a number and a unit of measurement to it. For instance, a room is 23 feet long, and a package weighs 2 pounds 3 ounces. Units of measurement connect our real world to our number system.

Standard Measurement

The units of measurement below are the ones used most often in the United States. They are often referred to as the *standard* or *American* units of measure.

Units of Length
12 inches (in)	= 1 foot (ft)
3 feet	= 1 yard (yd)
36 inches	= 1 yard
5280 feet	= 1 mile (mi)

Units of Capacity
4 quarts (qt)	= 1 gallon (gal)
2 pints (pt)	= 1 quart
2 cups (c)	= 1 pint
8 ounces (oz)	= 1 cup

Units of Weight
2000 pounds (lb)	= 1 ton (T)
16 ounces	= 1 pound

Units of Time
12 months (mo)	= 1 year (yr)
52 weeks (wk)	= 1 year
365 days (da)	= 1 year
7 days	= 1 week
24 hours (hr)	= 1 day
60 minutes (min)	= 1 hour
60 seconds (sec)	= 1 minute

Converting Units

In solving measurement problems, it is often convenient to change the units of measure. This is called making a *conversion*. There are two types of conversions. One is a conversion from a large unit to a smaller unit. For example, a weight given in pounds might be converted to ounces. The other is a conversion to a larger unit, such as changing feet (small unit) to yards (larger unit). The following table will be useful in converting units.

CONVERTING UNITS		
To change a large unit to a smaller unit	Multiply $\times$	This is because we want *more* of the smaller unit.
To change a small unit to a larger unit	Divide $\div$	This is because we want *fewer* of the larger unit.

▶ **TIP:** The diagram below will remind you what to do. For this diagram to work, you always put the larger unit on the left and keep the arrows and signs in the same places.

$$\times$$

larger ⤸⤵ smaller

$$\div$$

This process could be represented with feet and inches. Example 1 changes feet (larger) to inches (smaller).

Example 1: Change 7 feet to inches.

Because we are changing from feet (a large unit) to inches (a smaller unit), we multiply. (Recall: 12 inches = 1 foot.)

$$\begin{array}{r} 12 \text{ inches} \\ \times \ 7 \\ \hline 84 \text{ inches} \end{array}$$

Example 2: Change 6 tons to pounds.

Because we are changing from a large unit to a smaller unit, we multiply. (Recall: 2000 pounds = 1 ton.)

$$\begin{array}{r} 2000 \text{ pounds} \\ \times \ 6 \\ \hline 12{,}000 \text{ pounds} \end{array}$$

Example 3: Change 48 ounces to pints.

Because we are changing from a smaller unit (ounces) to a larger unit (pints), we divide. (Recall: 8 ounces = 1 cup, and 2 cups = 1 pint.)

Before dividing to find the number of pints, we must find the number of ounces in a pint.

First, multiply 8 ounces by 2 cups to get 16 ounces in a pint. $8 \times 2 = 16$

Then, divide 48 ounces by 16 ounces. $48 \div 16 = 3$

There are 3 pints in 48 ounces.

Example 4: Change 20 ounces to pounds.

Because we are changing from a smaller unit to a larger unit, we divide by the number of ounces in a pound.

$$\begin{array}{r} 1 \\ 16\overline{)20} \\ -\ 16 \\ \hline 4 \end{array}$$

The answer is 1 pound with 4 ounces left over, which is written as 1 lb 4 oz.

The next example is a practical application of converting measurement.

Example 5: A tailor needs 18 inches of seam tape that costs $1.08 per yard. How much does he pay for the material?

We must convert from inches to yards because the price is given in yards.

Question: How much does he pay?

Information: 18 inches; $1.08 per yard

Operation: Change 18 inches to yards by dividing the number of inches in a yard. Then multiply $1.08 by the number of yards.

Estimation: .50 × $1 = $.50

Calculation:

$$\begin{array}{r} .5 \\ 36\overline{)18.0} \\ -\ 18\ 0 \\ \hline 0 \end{array} \qquad \begin{array}{r} \$1.08 \\ \times \quad .5 \\ \hline \$.540 \text{ or } \$.54 \end{array}$$

Evaluation: If 18 inches are half a yard, it makes sense that the tape costs half of the price of a yard. Now let's try a few problems with conversion.

EXERCISE 1: CONVERSIONS

Directions: Make the conversions in the following problems.

1. 5 yards = _____ feet

2. 40 ounces = _____ pounds

3. 96 hours = _____ days

4. 20 quarts = _____ gallons

5. 2 quarts = _____ ounces

6. 2 days = _____ minutes

7. 3 pints = _____ quarts

8. If Pike's Peak is 14,110 feet high, what is its elevation in miles (to the nearest tenth)?

9. If a half-gallon of milk costs 96 cents, what is the cost of an 8-ounce glass of milk?

10. One shrub is to be placed every 15 feet along an expressway. How many shrubs are to be planted along a 2-mile stretch of the expressway?

Answers are on page 722.

Basic Operations with Measurements

We often need to add, subtract, multiply, or divide measurements. Let's review these skills.

Example 1: Add 3 pounds 8 ounces to 15 ounces.

```
   3 lb  8 oz    Be sure to add ounces to ounces.
+       15 oz
   3 lb 23 oz    Because 23 ounces is more than 16 ounces (1 pound),
                 simplify it by dividing by 16.

        1 r 7 = 1 lb 7 oz
   16) 23
      − 16
         7
```

3 pounds 23 ounces = 3 pounds + 1 pound 7 ounces = 4 pounds 7 ounces

Example 2: Take 5 pounds 7 ounces from 8 pounds 12 ounces.

```
   8 lb 12 oz    Subtract ounces from ounces.
−  5 lb  7 oz    Then subtract pounds from pounds.
   3 lb  5 oz
```

Example 3: Subtract 2 yards 2 feet from 6 yards 1 foot.

```
    5   4
    6 yd 1 ft    Regroup 1 yard = 3 feet from the 6 yards. Add the 3 feet to the 1 foot.
−   2 yd 2 ft    Then subtract feet from feet and yards from yards.
    3 yd 2 ft
```

Example 4: Multiply 4 feet 8 inches by 3.

    4 ft 8 in   Multiply 3 by 8 inches, then multiply 3 by 4 feet.
    ×   3
    12 ft 24 in ◄ Since 12 inches = 1 foot, simplify the answer.

12 ft 24 in = 12 ft + 2 ft = 14 ft

In some cases, as in Example 5, you will have to change units to the same form before you can do any calculating.

Example 5: Multiply 8 feet by 2 yards.

First change yards to feet, so we are multiplying   2 × 3 = 6 feet
like units. (1 yd = 3 ft)   Now multiply

    8 feet
    × 6 feet
    48 square feet
Note: feet × feet = square feet

Example 6: Divide 2 quarts 5 ounces by 3.

        0 qt   23 oz = 1 pt 7 oz
    3) 2 qt   5 oz
    − 0
        2 qt = 64 oz ◄ 3 will not go into 2 quarts. Change 2 quarts to 64 ounces.
             69 oz ◄ Add 64 ounces to 5 ounces. Then divide by three.
           − 69 oz
               0

BASIC OPERATIONS WITH MEASUREMENTS	
ADDITION	1. Add like units.
	2. Write the answer in simplest form.
SUBTRACTION	1. Subtract like units.
	2. Regroup units when necessary.
	3. Write the answer in simplest form.
MULTIPLICATION	1. Multiply like units if units are involved.
	2. Write the answer in simplest form.
DIVISION	1. Divide into the larger unit first.
	2. Change the remainder to the smaller unit and add that to any other smaller units.
	3. Then divide into the smaller unit.
	4. Be sure your answer is in simplest form.

EXERCISE 2: BASIC OPERATIONS WITH MEASUREMENTS

Directions: In the following practice problems, add, subtract, multiply, or divide as indicated. Be sure the final answer is in simplest form. For example, an answer of 15 inches should be changed to 1 foot 3 inches.

1. 9 feet 4 inches − 2 feet 9 inches

2. 1 hour 20 minutes + 3 hours

3. 130 pounds − 8 pounds 4 ounces

4. 5.3 inches × 7

5. 22 feet 6 inches ÷ 3

6. 5 hours 20 minutes ÷ 8

7. What is the difference in weight of two boxes of cereal, one weighing 1 pound 4 ounces and the other weighing 13 ounces?

8. If you divide a 6-foot 8-inch board into four equal lengths, how long will each piece be?

9. Each of 45 delegates to the convention will be given a badge made of a 4-inch piece of ribbon. At 65 cents per yard, how much will the ribbon cost to make the badges?

    (1) $1.80
    (2) $2.40
    (3) $3.25
    (4) $3.60
    (5) $6.50

10. At a price of $415 per ounce, which of the following represents the value of 1 pound 3 ounces of gold?

    (1) 3($415)
    (2) 16($415)
    (3) 3 + 16 + $415
    (4) 19($415)
    (5) $\frac{\$415}{19}$

11. Shane has a part-time job at the local hardware store. He earns $5 per hour. Last week he worked the following times: Monday, 2 hours 30 minutes; Wednesday, 3 hours; Friday, 4 hours 45 minutes; Saturday 7 hours 15 minutes; and Sunday, 4 hours. How much was he paid last week?

    (1) $ 28
    (2) $ 66
    (3) $ 72
    (4) $ 86
    (5) $107.50

Answers are on page 723.

The Metric System

The *metric system* is an international measuring system used to simplify trade and commerce among nations. The basic unit of measure of length is the *meter*. One meter is a little longer than a yard. The basic unit of weight is the *gram*. A paper clip weighs approximately one gram. A more practical comparison to our American system is the kilogram, which is about 2 pounds. The basic liquid measure is a *liter*. A liter has slightly more capacity than a quart.

All units are derived from the basic units of meter (length), gram (weight), and liter (liquid). Prefixes are added to the basic unit to indicate the amount of each unit. For example, the prefix *centi* means one-hundredth; therefore, one centimeter is one-hundredth of a meter, one centigram is one-hundredth of a gram, and one centiliter is one-hundredth of a liter.

Prefix	Meaning
kilo	1000
hecto	100
deca	10
BASIC UNIT	
deci	$\frac{1}{10}$ (.1)
centi	$\frac{1}{100}$ (.01)
milli	$\frac{1}{1000}$ (.001)

The diagram below relates the metric prefixes to the decimal system that you already know.

The charts below show the most common units of metric measure.

LENGTH

1 kilometer (km) = 1000 m

1 meter (m) = 1 m

1 centimeter (cm) = .01 m

1 millimeter (mm) = .001 m

WEIGHT

1 kilogram (kg) = 1000 g

1 gram (g) = 1 g

1 milligram (mg) = $\frac{1}{1000}$ g (.001 g)

CAPACITY

1 kiloliter (kl) = 1000 l

1 liter (l) = 1 l

1 milliliter (ml) = $\frac{1}{1000}$ l (.001 l)

Conversion in the Metric System

Conversions between units involve moving the decimal point to the right or left.

As with standard measurement, it is important to remember how to convert. The diagram below represents the conversions.

$$\text{larger} \underset{\text{left }(\div)}{\overset{\text{right }(\times)}{\rightleftharpoons}} \text{smaller}$$

The diagram below represents the prefixes from larger to smaller.

| kilo | hecto | deca | unit | deci | centi | milli |

Example 1: Change 420 meters to kilometers.

STEP 1. Recognize that meters to kilometers is going from a smaller unit to a larger. (1000 meters = 1 kilometer) Draw the arrow to show that.

kilometers $\overset{}{\longleftarrow}$ meters
left ($\div$)

STEP 2. Since kilo means "thousand," move 3 places.

km hm dam m dm cm mm
420 = .420

Example 2: Convert 4.2 kilograms to grams.

kg hg dag g dg cg mg
3 moves right

4.2 kg = 4.200 g = 4200 g
3 moves right

Example 3: Convert 4 meters 48 centimeters to centimeters.

First, change 4 meters to centimeters.

km hm dam m dm cm mm
2 moves right

4 m = 4.00 cm = 400 cm

Then, add.

400 cm + 48 cm = 448 cm

TO CHANGE METRIC UNITS

1. List the units from largest to smallest.
2. Put a mark at the starting unit.
3. Move by units to the new unit and count the moves right or left.
4. Move the decimal point the same number of places in the same direction.

The following is an example of metric problem solving.

Example 4: On an airplane trip from Chicago to London, you are told that the luggage limit is 20 kilograms. There is an extra charge of $2.80 for every kilogram over that limit. If your luggage weighs 23,000 grams, what additional charge can you expect?

STEP 1. First, change 23,000 grams to kilograms. Then, subtract to find out how much you are over the limit.

kg hg dag g dg cg mg

3 moves left

23,000 g = 23000 kg = 23 kg

23 kg − 20 kg = 3 kg

STEP 2. Since there are 3 extra kilograms, multiply to find the additional charge.

3 × $2.80 = $8.40

EXERCISE 3: METRIC MEASUREMENT

Directions: Convert to the units shown.

1. 500 meters to centimeters

2. 7423 milligrams to grams

3. 50.3 centimeters to millimeters

4. .027 kilograms to grams

5. 1 kiloliter 47 liters to liters

6. 6 meters 42 centimeters to meters

7. Find the length of the shaft illustrated below in meters.

400 cm   1285 cm

15 cm   15 cm

8. The recommended dosage of vitamin C is 857 *milligrams* per day. How many *grams* of vitamin C will Max take in one week if he takes the recommended dosage?

9. Terry competed in a 1000-meter speed-skating race; how many kilometers did he skate?

10. If the speed limit sign in Canada reads 80 kilometers per hour and the speed limit sign in some areas of the United States reads 55 miles per hour, which country allows the motorist to drive at a faster speed? (1 kilometer = .621 mile)

SPEED LIMIT 80 KPH   SPEED LIMIT 55 MPH

11. Which expression can be used to find the cost of .75 kilogram of cheese at the price of $6.40 per kilogram?

(1) $\frac{\$6.40}{.75}$

(2) .75 × $6.40

(3) $\frac{\$6.40}{2}$

(4) .75 + $6.40

(5) $6.40 − .75

12. A yard is approximately .91 meter. A football field is 100 yards long. What is the length of a football field in meters?

(1) 30
(2) 49.5
(3) 91
(4) 100
(5) 109

Answers are on page 723.

Special Topics in Measurement

The next several topics will present some tips for solving specific practical problems. We'll look at money problems, time problems, scale drawings, and meter reading. We'll follow these discussions with a variety of problems from these topics.

Money Problems

Some of the ways we handle money include paying bills, making purchases, writing a budget, and writing bills and receipts. Let's look at a few problems that require calculations involving money.

To do these calculations, you will be using the formula $c = nr$. A *formula* uses letters to represent rules for finding different quantities or measurements. When you work with formulas, you can substitute different numbers for the letters. You will be learning more about using formulas in Chapter 8.

To find the total cost (c), multiply the number of units (n) by the cost per unit (r). This is written as $c = nr$. (Two letters next to each other in a formula indicate that the two quantities have to be multiplied.) For example, you buy 4 tires at $98 each. To find the total cost of the tires, you must multiply $4 \times \$98 = \$392$.

Example: Margaret bought the following groceries on May 15: $1\frac{1}{2}$ dozen apples at $1.69 per dozen, 2 dozen eggs at 84¢ per dozen, 2 boxes of bran flakes at $3.15 each, 1 pound of margarine at $1.58 per pound, and 3 cans of soup at 79¢ per can. How much change did Margaret receive from a twenty-dollar bill?

STEP 1. Use the formula $c = nr$ to find the total cost of each item she bought. Then add to find the total cost of the purchases.

Apples:	$1\frac{1}{2} \times 1.69 =$	
	$1.5 \times 1.69 =$	
	$2.535 =$	$2.54
Eggs:	$2 \times .84 =$	1.68
Bran flakes:	$2 \times 3.15 =$	6.30
Margarine:	$1 \times 1.58 =$	1.58
Soup:	$3 \times .79 =$	+ 2.37
	Total	$14.47

STEP 2. Subtract to find the change from $20.

$20.00
$- \underline{\quad 14.47}$
$ 5.53

▶ **TIP:** Always round money to the hundredths place. In general, we round upward as opposed to downward. For instance, suppose you want one item and the price is 3 items for $1.24. If you divide $1.24 by 3, you get about $.413. The actual price you would pay for one item is 42¢ even though .413 would normally round to .41.

EXERCISE 4: MONEY PROBLEMS

Directions: Solve each problem.

Question 1 is based on the sales slip below.

Corey's Fashions 579 Mall Drive Elk Grove, Illinois 60007			
Qty.	**Description**	**Unit Price**	**Amount**
1	Dress	$49.95	
2	Shirts	$14.95	
3	Pairs of hose	$ 4.95	
		Subtotal	
		Tax (7%)	
Pay this amount		**Total**	

1. Lola works at Corey's Fashions. Her customer made the purchases shown on the sales slip. How much money should Lola collect from this customer?

   (1) $6.63 **(2)** $66.33 **(3)** $94.70 **(4)** $101.33 **(5)** $196.03

2. Mr. Barnes stocked his garden supply stores with 2 tons of sand in 50-pound bags for $138 per ton. If he sells the entire order of bags of sand for $5.95 per bag, what will be his profit?

   (1) $3.19 **(2)** $69 **(3)** $200 **(4)** $276 **(5)** $470.40

3. You need 48 feet of molding to finish decorating the family room. What is the cost of the molding if each 1-yard length costs 98 cents?

   (1) $3.92 **(2)** $15.68 **(3)** $47.04 **(4)** $392.00 **(5)** $470.00

4. If one serving of ice cream is $1\frac{1}{2}$ cups, how many servings can be made from 3 quarts?

   (1) 2 **(2)** 3 **(3)** 4 **(4)** 8 **(5)** 16

5. Happy Bran cereal costs $1.79 for a 1-pound 9-ounce box; Wheatos cereal in a 12-ounce box costs $1.49; Friendly Flakes costs $2.19 for a 1-pound 13-ounce box; and Sugar Snaps is $2.39 for 1 pound 4 ounces. Which cereal is the most economical purchase?

   (1) Happy Bran **(2)** Wheatos **(3)** Friendly Flakes **(4)** Sugar Snaps **(5)** They are all the same.

6. A famous-brand multisymptom cold reliever costs $6.48 for 36 capsules. The generic equivalent costs $4.32 for 36 capsules. How much money do you save per dose using the generic medicine if each dose is 2 capsules?

   (1) 6¢ **(2)** 12¢ **(3)** 18¢ **(4)** $1.08 **(5)** $2.16

7. First-class postage is $.29 for up to 1 ounce and $.23 for each additional ounce. Which of the following represents the cost of sending a 4-ounce envelope by first class?

   (1) 4($.29)

   (2) 4($.23)

   (3) ($.29 + $.23)

   (4) $.29 + 3($.23)

   (5) $\dfrac{(\$.29 + \$.23)}{2}$

Answers are on page 724.

Time Problems

Many jobs require you to punch in on a time clock when you arrive at work and punch out when you leave. The time card will record a starting time and an ending time.

TIME CLOCK

A.M. means "hours between midnight and noon."

P.M. means "hours between noon and midnight."

Numbers on the left of the colon are hours.

3:30

Numbers on the right of the colon are minutes.

Example 1: Tina worked overtime on Thursday. She started at 7:30 A.M. and ended at 6:45 P.M. How long did she work?

STEP 1. Find her morning hours.

$$\begin{array}{r}
{\scriptstyle 11\ 60} \\
\cancel{12:00} \\
-\ \ \ 7:30 \\
\hline
4:30 \text{ or 4 hr 30 min}
\end{array}$$
← Borrow 60 minutes from the hours

STEP 2. Find her afternoon hours.

Noon to 6:45 is 6 hours 45 minutes.

STEP 3. Add the total hours.

$$\begin{array}{r}
4:30 \\
+\ \ 6:45 \\
\hline
10:75 = 11:15
\end{array}$$
— Because 75 minutes is more than 60 minutes (one hour), we simplify that to 1 hour and 15 minutes and add it to 10 hours.

11:15 can be written as *11 hr 15 min* or $11\frac{15}{60} = 11\frac{1}{4}$ *hr.*

HOW TO CALCULATE TIME

1. Find the number of morning hours.

2. Find the number of evening hours.

3. Add the morning hours and evening hours. Be sure to simplify your answer.

Example 2: Kelly's time card showed a starting time of 8:10 A.M. and an ending time of 6:40 P.M. If she gets paid $5.25 per hour straight time and $7.50 per hour overtime (any time more than the straight eight-hour shift), how much did she make that day?

STEP 1. Calculate the work hours. 8:10 A.M. to noon $3\frac{5}{6}$ hours

noon to 6:40 P.M. $+ 6\frac{2}{3}$ hours

total $10\frac{1}{2}$ hours

STEP 2. Calculate the overtime hours.

$10\frac{1}{2} - 8 = 2\frac{1}{2}$ hours overtime

8 hours at $5.25	$42.00
$2\frac{1}{2}$ hours at $7.50	+ 18.75
Total pay	$60.75

If you know rate and time, you can find distance by using the formula distance (d) equals the rate or speed (r) times the amount of time (t) traveled. This relationship is represented as $d = rt$.

▶ TIP: Time must be in hours or parts of an hour because the rate is in miles per hour.

For instance, what if you travel 6 hours at 55 miles per hour? To get the distance traveled, you would multiply $6 \times 55 = 330$. The distance traveled is 330 miles.

On the other hand, you often know the distance to be traveled but have to figure out the length of time required for a trip. Suppose you must travel 726 miles and the legal speed limit is 55 mph. You know the distance and the rate; to find the time, you'll have to divide:

$$726 \div 55 = 13\frac{1}{5} \text{ hours}$$

EXERCISE 5: TIME PROBLEMS

Directions: Solve each problem.

1. The sign on a parking meter states, "12 minutes for a nickel; maximum deposit 75 cents." How many hours can you legally park for the maximum deposit?

   (1) $1\frac{1}{4}$ **(2)** 3 **(3)** $6\frac{1}{4}$ **(4)** $7\frac{1}{2}$ **(5)** 15

2. Roger works the lunch shift from 10:00 A.M. to 2:30 P.M. Monday through Friday each week at $8.00 per hour. Which expression shows how much he earns every four weeks?

   (1) $4\frac{1}{2} + 8 + 5 + 4$

   (2) $(4\frac{1}{2} \times 8) + (5 \times 4)$

   (3) $4\frac{1}{2} \times 8 \times 5 \times 4$

   (4) $4\frac{1}{2}(8 + 5 + 4)$

   (5) $4\frac{1}{2} \times 8$

3. Sonya and Olaf leave home at 8:30 A.M. to begin their driving tour of Wisconsin. At 3:45 P.M., they decide to stop for the day. If they drive a steady 50 miles per hour, how many miles do they drive that day?

   (1) 362.5 **(2)** 387.5 **(3)** 437.5 **(4)** 426.5 **(5)** 600.0

Questions 4–6 refer to the time card below:

MARSHALL MANUFACTURING					
NAME: Tom Wolper SS# 000-45-0000					
Date From To	5/20 8:00 A.M. 4:00 P.M.	5/21 8:00 A.M. 5:30 P.M.	5/22 8:00 A.M. 6:45 P.M.	5/23 8:00 A.M. 4:00 P.M.	5/24 8:00 A.M. 4:30 P.M.
Total Regular Hours _____ at $7.85 Overtime Hours _____ at $12.00 (over 40 hours)					

4. According to his time card, Tom Wolper worked the week of 5/20 to 5/24. How many overtime hours (any time more than the straight eight-hour shift) did he work that week?

   (1) $3\frac{3}{4}$ **(2)** 4 **(3)** $4\frac{1}{4}$ **(4)** $4\frac{1}{2}$ **(5)** $4\frac{3}{4}$

5. What is Tom's full pay before deductions? (Include regular hours and overtime hours.)

   (1) $57 **(2)** $314 **(3)** $351 **(4)** $371 **(5)** $537

6. If state withholding tax is 1%, federal withholding tax is 25%, and social security tax (FICA) is 7%, how much will Tom's take-home pay be after these deductions?

   (1) $122.43 **(2)** $155.82 **(3)** $215.18 **(4)** $248.57 **(5)** $493.43

7. An airplane travels 960 miles per hour. Which expression tells how far it travels in twenty minutes?

   (1) 960×20 **(2)** $960 \times \frac{1}{3}$ **(3)** $\frac{960}{20}$ **(4)** $\frac{3}{960}$ **(5)** $\frac{\frac{1}{3}}{960}$

8. A tornado traveled 75 miles in $2\frac{1}{2}$ hours. Which expression shows how fast the tornado is traveling?

   (1) $2\frac{1}{2} \times 75$

   (2) $75 + 2\frac{1}{2}$

   (3) $75 - 2\frac{1}{2}$

   (4) $2\frac{1}{2} \div 75$

   (5) $75 \div 2\frac{1}{2}$

Answers are on page 724.

Reading and Interpreting Scales and Meters

You often have to read a scale or meter to get information. For instance, a map is a scale drawing you use when you travel. You read a thermometer when you're sick and read an electric meter to check your electric bill. On the next few pages, we'll take a look at some scales and meters.

READING SCALES AND METERS

Follow these tips when you solve problems with scales or meters.

1. Read the labels on the meter carefully.

2. If instructions are included, refer to the meter as you read them.

3. Write down the information you get as you read the meter.

4. Ignore extra information that is not needed for the problem.

Scale Drawings

A map is a drawing of land area. When a map is drawn to scale (in proportion to the land it represents), a *key* is given so you may calculate distances on the map. A key has the information about the ratio for that particular drawing. You can use the scale to set up a proportion to find a distance.

Let's look at the local map below. Answer the following questions while referring to the map. Notice the scale of miles at the top of the map.

Example 1: If the distance from Halsey to Rock Falls on the map is 2.5 inches, what is the actual distance between Halsey and Rock Falls?

The ratio is 1 inch to 100 miles. If the distance on the map between Halsey and Rock Falls is 2.5 inches, we can set up the following proportion to solve the problem. Notice that we are using a proportion to compare two things (inches to miles).

$$\frac{1 \text{ in}}{100 \text{ mi}} = \frac{2.5 \text{ in}}{n \text{ mi}}$$

Cross multiply: $100 \times 2.5 = 250$

Divide: $250 \div 1 = 250$

The actual distance between Halsey and Rock Falls is 250 miles. (This makes sense because each inch is 100 miles. Since we have more than 2 inches, there are more than 200 miles.)

Example 2: To go by road from Lyle to Halsey, you must go through Billings, Dix, and Rock Falls. How much farther is it from Lyle to Halsey than from Billings to Rock Falls?

STEP 1.	Calculate the distance from Lyle to Halsey. Then calculate the distance from Billings to Rock Falls.	.5 in + 4 in + 3 in + 2.5 in = 10 in 4 in + 3 in = 7 in
STEP 2.	Subtract to find the difference.	10 in − 7 in = 3 in
STEP 3.	Set up and solve a proportion to compare inches to miles. Cross multiply and divide.	$\dfrac{1 \text{ in}}{100 \text{ mi}} = \dfrac{3 \text{ in}}{n \text{ mi}}$ $\dfrac{100 \times 3}{1} = 300$

It is 300 miles farther from Lyle to Halsey.

Reading Meters

Meters are devices used to measure time, speed, distance, and energy used. You might recognize some meters such as a speedometer, barometer, or thermometer. Meters give us information to solve problems. It's important that you read a meter accurately. Always notice the labels on the meter and read the instructions for use if they are given.

On the next few pages, we'll look at some problems that require meter reading.

The Electric Meter

Appliances such as refrigerators, fans, radios, TVs, and dishwashers require electricity. The electric meter is the instrument that measures the amount of electricity used in kilowatt-hours (kwh).

The numbers above the dial indicate one complete round around the dial. Notice that the numbers may go in different directions around the dial.

Dial (1) measures the number of 1000 kwh.

Dial (2) measures the number of 100 kwh.

Dial (3) measures the number of 10 kwh.

Dial (4) measures the number of 1 kwh.

(1) (2) (3) (4)

Example: Read the meter above.

Start reading the dials with the left dial. If the pointer is between two numbers, read the *smaller* of the two numbers. Reading the meter above, you get ⬚ 2176 ⬚ .

Dial (1)	2	2 × 1000 = 2000
Dial (2)	1	1 × 100 = 100
Dial (3)	7	7 × 10 = 70
Dial (4)	6	6 × 1 = 6
Total kwh used:		2176

EXERCISE 6: SCALES AND METERS

Directions: Solve each problem.

1. The scale on a map is 1 inch = 180 miles. How far apart on this map are two cities if the distance between them is 450 miles?

    (1) 1 in   **(2)** $1\frac{1}{2}$ in   **(3)** 2 in   **(4)** $2\frac{1}{2}$ in   **(5)** $3\frac{1}{2}$ in

2. What is the scale for a map in which 2000 miles is represented by 10 inches?

    (1) 1 in = 2 mi   **(2)** 1 in = 20 mi   **(3)** 1 in = 200 mi   **(4)** 1 in = $\frac{1}{2}$ mi
    (5) 1 in = 100 mi

3. Emma's last reading on her electric meter was 3843 kwh. Her new reading is indicated on the meter shown below. If the charge is 12.5¢ per kwh, what is Emma's new electric bill?

KILOWATT-HOURS

    (1) $113.63   **(2)** $909   **(3)** $2,020   **(4)** $2,562.50   **(5)** $11,362.50

4. Daryl wanted to check his gas bill, shown below. From the information given, find his total current bill.

Your Acct. # 12345678	Meter Number 00386	
METER READINGS Current 3380 Previous 3207 100 cu ft 173		
Gas Supply Charge ($.3065 per 100 cu ft)		
Monthly Customer Charge		$ 2.00
Distribution Charge		$19.16
	Subtotal	
	Utility Tax (5%)	
	Total Current Bill	

    (1) $3.71   **(2)** $53.02   **(3)** $74.19   **(4)** $77.89   **(5)** $203.87

Answers are on page 725.

7
GRAPHS, STATISTICS, AND PROBABILITY

Graphs, charts, and statistical tables help us organize information. When you are presented with material that has been organized for you, you must carefully study the details such as the title, subtitle, column and row headings, key (if shown), and type of information given. We call this interpreting the *data*. Statistics is the study of data. With statistics, you organize the data and then draw a conclusion based on them.

Mean and Median

Two common types of statistical problems ask you to find the mean or median of a set of data. The *mean* is the average of the numbers. To find the average, you add the data and then divide by the number of pieces of data.

For instance, Brenda bowled 132, 147, and 108 at the bowling alley last night. To find her mean (average) score, you add:

$$132 + 147 + 108 = 387$$

and then divide by 3 (the number of scores):

$$387 \div 3 = 129$$

Therefore, her average or *mean* bowling score is 129.

The *median* of a set of data is found by arranging the numbers from smallest to largest and then choosing the middle number in the arrangement. That middle number is the median. You would arrange Brenda's three bowling scores to read 108, 132, 147. The middle score is 132, so the median is 132.

TO FIND THE AVERAGE OR MEAN

1. Add the numbers.
2. Divide by the number of numbers.

TO FIND THE MEDIAN

1. Put the numbers in order from lowest to highest.
2. Choose the middle number. (If there are two middle numbers, find the average of the two numbers.)

Example 1: Mr. Parker wants to know his average monthly gas bill. The chart below lists his gas expenses for the last six months of the year. What is his average monthly gas bill?

July	$148.70
August	385.60
September	195.20
October	208.40
November	186.75
December	220.88

Add all six months; the total is $1345.53. Then divide by 6 (the number of months) and get $224.255. Round off the amount to an average of $224.26.

If you want to find Mr. Parker's median gas bill, arrange the amounts in order from smallest to largest. Since there is no middle number, you must find the average of the two middle numbers. The median is $201.80.

STEP 1.	STEP 2.	STEP 3.
148.70	195.20	$201.80
186.75	+ 208.40	2) $403.60
195.20 } Middle	403.60	
208.40 } Middle		
220.88		
385.60		

Example 2: To get information on the number of evening diners at her Shamrock Inn, Shannon accumulated the following information for the first 17 days of March. What is the median of the number of diners?

35, 37, 43, 28, 32, 38, 45, 21, 26, 27, 44, 46, 29, 39, 42, 86, 117

The median is 38, while the average (mean) is 43.24.

In this case, the median of 38 is a better representation of the normal amount of diners. The average is thrown off by the large crowds on the 17th day, St. Patrick's Day. The median is often used when the mean does not give a true picture because of a few unusually high or low scores.

EXERCISE 1: MEAN AND MEDIAN

Directions: Solve each problem.

1. Your seven salesclerks reported the sales figures at the right during the week of April 19. To the nearest cent, what was the average of the sales figures?

Tom	$4300
Astrid	$5600
Ben	$1875
Josephine	$4250
Wilbur	$2876
Inez	$4108
Zoe	$2983

Questions 2–4 are based on the information below. Round your answer to the nearest whole number.

The scorekeeper for the Union Town basketball team recorded the results of the last six games.

Date	Opponent	Union Town vs. Opponent
12/4	Hinkley	48 to 37
12/6	Barton	45 to 63
12/10	Angel Park	53 to 42
12/12	Eagle Rock	72 to 24
12/18	Bennett	68 to 44
12/20	Alton	74 to 51

2. What is the average number of points scored by the opponent?

3. What is the median score scored by Union Town?

4. What is the average score of Union Town?

5. The prices of identical winter jackets at five local stores are $48.95, $39.95, $44.80, $52.25, and $42.88. What is the median price of that jacket?

Answers are on page 725.

Graphs

Graphs and charts are useful ways of simplifying complicated information by putting it in picture form. We can often understand an entire situation with only a quick look at a graph. By organizing data visually, graphs and charts help us interpret, compare, and analyze numbers. In this section, we'll look specifically at circle graphs, bar graphs, and line graphs.

Circle Graphs

The circle in a *circle graph* represents a whole quantity. For instance, a circle could represent the whole population of the United States or an entire family income. Each circle is then subdivided into sections that represent parts of the whole.

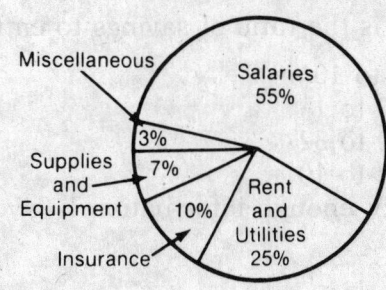

HAMPTON PRODUCTS BUSINESS EXPENSES

The circle at the right represents all of the business expenses of Hampton Products, a small family business. If you add all the sections in the circle, the total is 100%.

Example 1: If Hampton Products' business expenses totaled $125,000 last year, how much were the expenses for rent and utilities? We see from the graph that rent and utilities account for 25% of the total. We need to find 25% of $125,000.

$$\frac{n}{125,000} = \frac{25}{100}$$

$$\frac{125,000 \times 25}{100} = \$31,250$$

Example 2: What is the ratio of insurance costs to the total budget? Set up a ratio of insurance to total.

$$\frac{10\%}{100\%} = \frac{10}{100} = \frac{1}{10}$$

The ratio is 1 to 10. Another way of saying this is $1 out of every $10 spent is used for insurance.

EXERCISE 2: CIRCLE GRAPHS

Directions: Solve each problem.

1. Using the circle graph below and this chart, find the average yearly amount spent on salaries in the three years 1991–1993.

HAMPTON PRODUCTS	
Year	**Total Expenses**
1991	$ 92,000
1992	$156,000
1993	$125,000

HAMPTON PRODUCTS BUSINESS EXPENSES

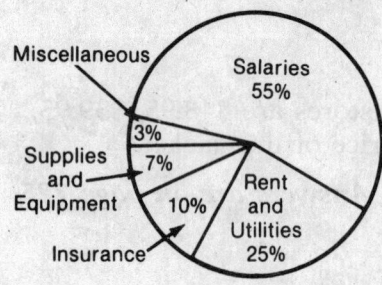

Questions 2–5 are based on the graph below and to the right.

2. How much is spent for car expenses each year?

3. What is the average *monthly* expense for rent?

4. How much is spent on clothing during the year?

   (1) $320 **(2)** $480 **(3)** $800 **(4)** $3200
   (5) not enough information is given

5. What is the ratio of savings to entire income?

   (1) 1 to 10
   (2) 10 to 1
   (3) 10 to 32
   (4) 32 to 10
   (5) not enough information is given

DISTRIBUTION OF A YEARLY INCOME OF $32,000

Answers are on page 725.

Bar Graphs

A **bar graph** is an excellent way of comparing amounts. This bar graph shows the distance five experimental cars traveled on one gallon of gas. You can see that Car Z had the highest gas mileage and that Car T traveled 30 miles on a gallon of gas.

MILES PER GALLON OF GASOLINE

In the bar graph below, compare income with expenses for a particular year.

EXERCISE 3: BAR GRAPHS

Directions: Use the following graph to answer the questions.

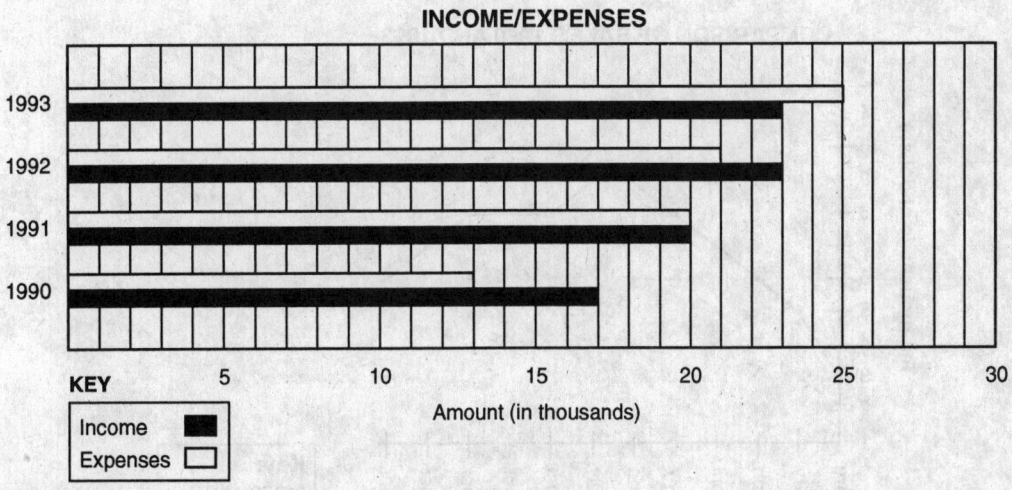

INCOME/EXPENSES

1. What was the income in 1990?

2. What was the average of expenses for the years 1990–1993?

3. In what year did expenses exceed income?

   (1) 1990 **(2)** 1991 **(3)** 1992 **(4)** 1993
   (5) not enough information is given

4. In 1992, what was the difference between income and expenses?

   (1) $200 **(2)** $2,000 **(3)** $20,000 **(4)** $21,000 **(5)** $23,000

Answers are on page 725.

Line Graphs

Line graphs are used to show trends or patterns. On a line graph, each point relates two values. One is the value on the vertical (↕) axis at the left side, and the other is the value on the horizontal (↔) axis at the bottom.

As you look at the line graph at the right, notice the following:

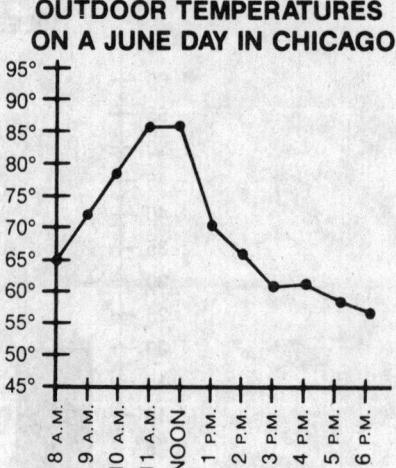

OUTDOOR TEMPERATURES ON A JUNE DAY IN CHICAGO

1. The title tells what the graph is about.

2. The vertical scale is labeled on the left side of the graph. Each line is an increase of 5°. The horizontal scale is labeled on the bottom of the graph. Each line is an increase of 1 hour.

3. The line shows the following trend: the temperature rose until 11:00 A.M., then remained steady until noon. Then the temperature fell.

You can also use a line graph to compare two different trends. Below is an example of this. One trend is shown with a solid line; the other is shown with a broken line. When a graph uses two or more lines, you can compare information from the lines.

EXERCISE 4: LINE GRAPHS

Directions: Use the graph below to answer the questions.

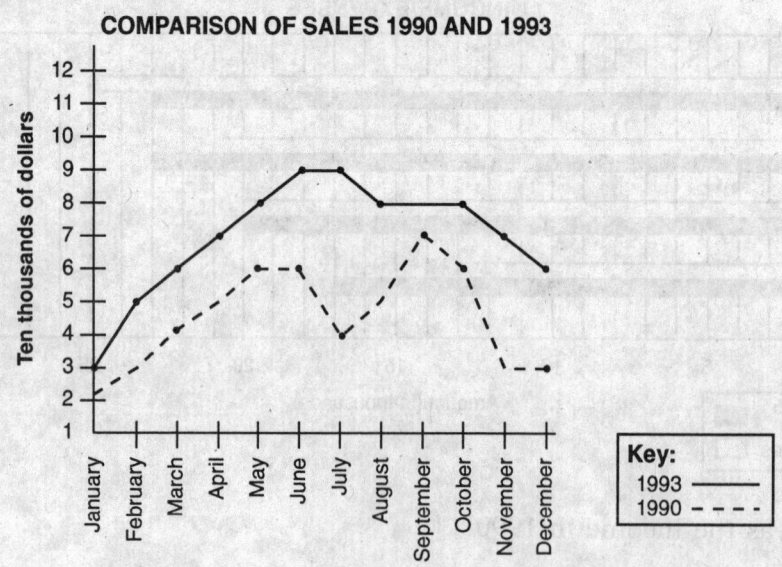

COMPARISON OF SALES 1990 AND 1993

Key:
1993 ———
1990 - - - -

1. The title tells us that the graph compares _____ in _____ (year) and _____ (year).

2. The vertical scale is labeled in _____.

3. The horizontal scale is labeled in _____.

4. In June of 1990, sales were about _____.

5. In June of 1993, sales were about _____.

6. The graph shows that both 1990 and 1993 had seasonal highs and lows. In general, 1993 produced considerably _____ sales all year long.

Answers are on page 726.

EXERCISE 5: MIXED GRAPH PRACTICE

Directions: Solve each problem. Questions 1–5 are based on the circle graph below.

1. What is the ratio of savings to earnings?

2. If you make $12,000 per year, what is your monthly take-home pay?

3. If you make $25,000 per year, what is your annual contribution to social security?

4. If you wanted to have take-home pay of $20,000, how much would your actual earnings have to be?

DISTRIBUTION OF EARNINGS

5. One year, Mike earned $24,000. The deductions from his paycheck were federal tax, FICA, and state tax. What was his yearly take-home pay?

Questions 6–12 refer to the bar graph below.

6. What is the difference in height between the Empire State Building and the Sears Tower?

7. If a 107-foot TV antenna were erected at the top of the Sears Tower, what would be the total height of the tower?

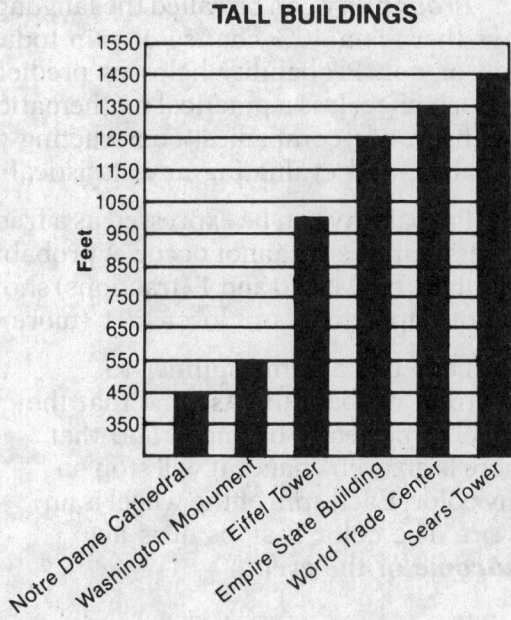

8. The World Trade Center is how many times as tall as the Washington Monument?

9. The height of Notre Dame Cathedral is approximately what percent of the height of the Sears Tower?

10. What is the average height of these six structures?

11. What is the median height of these six structures?

12. If each floor is about 13 feet tall, about how many floors are in the Sears Tower?

Questions 13–15 refer to the line graph below.

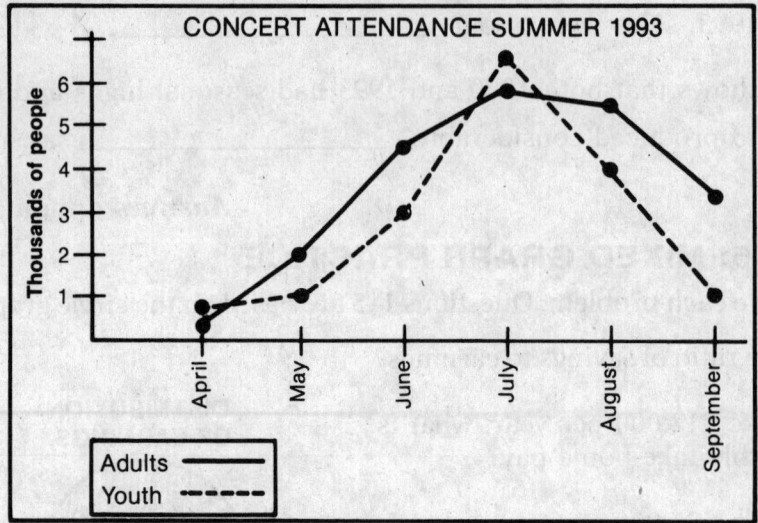

13. How many people attended concerts in June?

14. In which months was youth attendance higher than that for adults?

15. If adult tickets were $8.50 and youth tickets were $5.75, what were the receipts for the concerts held in August?

Answers are on page 726.

Probability

Probability can be called the language of uncertainty. The weather reporter says there is a 40% chance of rain today, but we still don't know if it's going to rain or not. Probability helps us predict the future based on analyzing past performance. It is a practical mathematical tool used in developing mortality rates for insurance companies, constructing polls to assess public opinion during elections, and evaluating any statistical data.

Probability can be expressed as a fraction, ratio, or percent. A probability of 0 means an event cannot occur. A probability of 1 means an event is sure to happen. Numbers between 0 and 1 (fractions) show whether the event is closer to 0 (closer to not happening) or closer to 1 (more likely to happen).

Let's use a game spinner to illustrate probability. Assume that the wheel is perfectly balanced and that there is an even chance it will stop on any color. Each spin of the wheel is an ***event***. The color it stops at is an ***outcome*** of the event.

There are four possible outcomes when you spin this wheel: red, blue, green, and orange. A successful event occurs when you spin the wheel and get the color you want. The probability of success is the ratio of the number of successes of an event to the number of possible outcomes of that event. You can express probability in the following fraction or ratio form. Remember, this can also be a percent.

$$\text{Probability} = \frac{\text{Number of Successful Outcomes}}{\text{Number of Possible Outcomes}}$$

Using the spinning wheel, the probability of stopping at red would be $\frac{1}{4}$. While there are four possible outcomes (red, blue, green, or orange), there is only one successful outcome (red). The probability of $\frac{1}{4}$ can also be written as 25%, so you can say there is a 25% chance of landing on red.

Again, using the spinning wheel on page 644, find the probability of landing on *either* red *or* green. Now there are two possible outcomes that would be successful. The probability is:

$$\frac{2}{4} \quad \begin{array}{l} \text{number of successes} \\ \text{number of possibilities} \end{array}$$

You can reduce $\frac{2}{4}$ to $\frac{1}{2}$. Thus, the probability of landing on red or green is $\frac{1}{2}$, or 50%.

Probability of 0 or 1

A probability of 0 or 0% means an event will *not* take place. Using the same spinning wheel, the probability of landing on purple is 0, because the number of successful outcomes of purple on this wheel is 0. So we would have $\frac{0}{4} = 0$. There is 0% chance of landing on purple.

A probability of 1 or 100% means an event is *certain* to happen. Let's use the spinning wheel to find the probability of landing on red, green, blue, or orange. The number of successful outcomes is 4, and the number of possible outcomes is 4. Now we have $\frac{4}{4} = 1$.

EXERCISE 6: PROBABILITY

Directions: Solve each problem.

1. If a single card is picked from a deck of 52 playing cards, what is the probability that it is the ace of spades?

2. From the same deck of 52 cards, what is the probability of drawing a heart? Give your answer as a percent. (*Hint:* There are 13 cards in each suit.)

3. In a deck of 52 cards, what is the probability of drawing a king? Give your answer as a fraction.

For questions 4–10, consider the roll of a single die; a single die has six faces as shown:

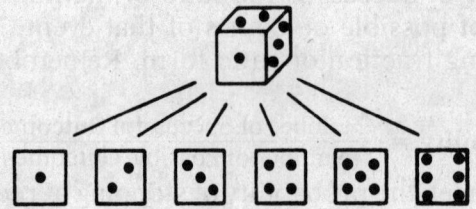

4. What is the probability of rolling a 5?

   (1) $\frac{1}{6}$ **(2)** $\frac{1}{5}$ **(3)** $\frac{1}{3}$ **(4)** $\frac{1}{2}$ **(5)** $\frac{5}{6}$

5. What is the probability of rolling either a 3 or a 4?

   (1) $16\frac{2}{3}\%$ **(2)** 25% **(3)** 30% **(4)** $33\frac{1}{3}\%$ **(5)** 40%

6. What is the probability of rolling an even number?

   (1) $16\frac{2}{3}\%$ **(2)** 20% **(3)** 30% **(4)** $33\frac{1}{3}\%$ **(5)** 50%

7. What is the probability of rolling a number greater than 6?

   (1) 0 **(2)** $\frac{1}{6}$ **(3)** $\frac{1}{3}$ **(4)** $\frac{1}{2}$ **(5)** 1

8. What is the probability of rolling a number less than 5?

   (1) 0% **(2)** 30% **(3)** $33\frac{1}{3}\%$ **(4)** 40% **(5)** $66\frac{2}{3}\%$

9. What is the probability of rolling a number less than 7?

   (1) 0% **(2)** 25% **(3)** 60% **(4)** 70% **(5)** 100%

10. What is the probability that you will read this page in March instead of another month?

    (1) $\frac{1}{25}$ **(2)** $\frac{1}{12}$ **(3)** $\frac{1}{4}$ **(4)** $\frac{1}{3}$ **(5)** not enough information is given

11. What is the probability that your social security number will end in 8?

    (1) $\frac{1}{12}$ **(2)** $\frac{1}{10}$ **(3)** $\frac{1}{8}$ **(4)** $\frac{4}{5}$ **(5)** not enough information is given

12. You flip a coin nine times, and each time it lands on heads. What is the probability it will land on heads the tenth time you flip it?

    (1) $\frac{1}{9}$ **(2)** $\frac{1}{10}$ **(3)** $\frac{1}{2}$ **(4)** $\frac{9}{10}$ **(5)** not enough information is given

13. In every shipment of clay pots, a number of them will be broken. In a recent shipment, 240 out of 960 were cracked. At the same rate, what is the probability of getting pots that are *not* cracked?

    (1) $\frac{1}{24}$ **(2)** $\frac{1}{4}$ **(3)** $\frac{1}{2}$ **(4)** $\frac{3}{4}$ **(5)** not enough information is given

Answers are on page 726.

Dependent Probability

Suppose a box contains two green balls and three red balls. If one ball is drawn from the box, the probability of drawing a green ball is $\frac{2}{5}$ and the probability of drawing a red ball is $\frac{3}{5}$. If you do not replace the ball drawn, there are now only four balls in the box. The probability for the drawing of the next ball now depends on which ball you drew the first time.

Possibility 1: You Drew a Green Ball

If you drew a *green* ball on the first draw, the box now contains one green ball and three red balls. In this situation, the probability of next drawing a green ball is now $\frac{1}{4}$ and the probability of drawing a red ball is $\frac{3}{4}$.

Possibility 2: You Drew a Red Ball

If you drew a *red* ball on the first draw, the box now contains two green balls and two red balls. The probability of drawing a green ball is now $\frac{2}{4}$ or $\frac{1}{2}$, and the probability of drawing a red ball is now $\frac{2}{4}$ or $\frac{1}{2}$.

We see that the second draw *depends* on the first draw. This is an example of ***dependent probability***.

EXERCISE 7: DEPENDENT PROBABILITY

Directions: Solve each problem.

Questions 1–4 are based on the following situation. Express your answers as fractions. Draw a picture if necessary to help you find the probabilities.

Two cards are drawn in succession from a deck of 52 playing cards without the first card being replaced.

1. Find the probability that the first card drawn is an ace.

2. If the first card drawn was an ace, what is the probability that the second draw is also an ace?

3. What is the probability that the second card drawn is an ace if the first card drawn was not an ace?

4. Suppose the first card drawn is a spade. What is the probability that the second card drawn is a spade?

Questions 5–7 are based on the following situation. Express your answers as fractions.

A committee is to be chosen at random from a group of seven men and three women. The names of the ten people are placed on slips of paper and put in a hat.

5. What is the probability that the first name drawn from the hat will be a woman's?

6. If the first name drawn is a man's, what is the probability that the second name drawn will also be a man's?

7. What is the probability that the third name drawn will be a woman's if the first two draws were also women's names?

Questions 8–10 are based on the following situation. Express your answers as fractions.

A change purse contains 3 nickels, 4 dimes, and 2 quarters.

8. What is the probability that the first coin taken from the purse will be a quarter?

9. If the first coin taken from the purse was a nickel, what is the probability that the next coin will be a quarter?

10. What is the probability that the third coin taken from the purse will be a nickel if the first two coins were also nickels?

Answers are on page 726.

8
NUMERATION

Numeration is the study of number relationships. In this chapter, we'll review powers, roots, and the order of operations. We'll also look at the use of formulas and substitution. We'll conclude the study of arithmetic with a look at number patterns, properties of numbers, ordering of numbers, and scientific notation.

Powers and Roots

Powers

When a number is multiplied by itself, we say that it is **squared**. We show that with a small 2 placed to the upper right of the number. For example, $7^2 = 7 \times 7 = 49$. This means seven squared is 7 times 7, which is 49.

In the expression 7^2, the two is called the **power** or **exponent**, and the seven is called the **base**. It is best to think of the exponent as an instruction. The exponent tells you what to do with the base. When the exponent is 2, the base is squared, and we multiply the base by itself.

Examples: $3^2 = 3 \times 3 = 9$ $\qquad$ $9^2 = 9 \times 9 = 81$

$\qquad\qquad$ $10^2 = 10 \times 10 = 100$ $\qquad$ $\left(\frac{1}{3}\right)^2 = \frac{1}{3} \times \frac{1}{3} = \frac{1}{9}$

Sometimes the exponent is a number other than 2. The exponent tells how many times to multiply the base by itself. For example:

$3^4 = 3 \times 3 \times 3 \times 3 = 81$

$5^3 = 5 \times 5 \times 5 = 125$

$10^6 = 10 \times 10 \times 10 \times 10 \times 10 \times 10 = 1,000,000$

$\left(\frac{1}{2}\right)^3 = \frac{1}{2} \times \frac{1}{2} \times \frac{1}{2} = \frac{1}{8}$

Here are three special rules you should know.

SPECIAL RULES ABOUT POWERS

1. The number 1 to any power is 1. $1^5 = 1 \times 1 \times 1 \times 1 \times 1 = 1$

2. Any number to the first power is that number. $6^1 = 6$

3. Any number to the zero power is 1. $14^0 = 1$

When we multiply a number by itself, we get a ***perfect square***. For instance, $6^2 = 36$; 36 is a perfect square. Some perfect squares that are helpful to know are listed here.

$1^2 = 1$	$6^2 = 36$	$11^2 = 121$	$20^2 = 400$
$2^2 = 4$	$7^2 = 49$	$12^2 = 144$	$30^2 = 900$
$3^2 = 9$	$8^2 = 64$	$13^2 = 169$	$40^2 = 1600$
$4^2 = 16$	$9^2 = 81$	$14^2 = 196$	$50^2 = 2500$
$5^2 = 25$	$10^2 = 100$	$15^2 = 225$	$100^2 = 10,000$

EXERCISE 1: POWERS

Directions: For each number below, multiply the base by itself the number of times indicated by its exponent.

1. 5^2

2. $\left(\frac{1}{2}\right)^2$

3. 9^3

4. $\left(\frac{3}{4}\right)^3$

5. $(.3)^2$

6. 1^{10}

7. 2^4

8. $(1.2)^2$

9. 4^0

10. 10^4

11. 25^2

12. $(.2)^3$

13. $\left(\frac{2}{3}\right)^2$

14. 3^3

15. 0^2

Answers are on page 727.

Square Roots

The operation opposite of squaring a number is finding the ***square root*** of a number. For instance, $5^2 = 25$, so $\sqrt{25} = 5$. The $\sqrt{}$ symbol is called the ***radical symbol***, and it means to find the square root of the number underneath the radical. $\sqrt{36}$ is read, "the square root of 36." Being familiar with perfect squares makes many square roots relatively easy to find. For instance, $\sqrt{100} = 10$ because $10^2 = 100$. $\sqrt{49} = 7$ and $\sqrt{4} = 2$.

If you need to find the square root of a number that is not a perfect square, you can simplify the square root. For instance, $\sqrt{75}$ can be expressed as

$$\sqrt{25 \cdot 3} = \sqrt{25} \cdot \sqrt{3} = 5\sqrt{3}.$$

You choose 25 and 3 because 25 is a perfect square, and you can find its square root.

EXERCISE 2: SIMPLIFYING SQUARE ROOTS

Directions: Simplify the following square roots.

1. $\sqrt{18}$ 2. $\sqrt{48}$ 3. $\sqrt{8}$ 4. $\sqrt{72}$ 5. $\sqrt{27}$

Answers are on page 727.

Approximating Square Roots

Calculators and tables of square roots can help us find the square roots of unfamiliar numbers. If a table or calculator is not available, **approximation** is helpful. For example, let's find the square root of 75. To find $\sqrt{75}$, we look at the perfect squares closest to 75. Those are 64 and 81.

$\sqrt{64} = 8$
$\sqrt{75}$
$\sqrt{81} = 9$ $\left\{$ Notice that $\sqrt{75}$ is between $\sqrt{64}$ and $\sqrt{81}$.

Therefore, $\sqrt{75}$ is between 8 and 9. Because 75 is closer to 81 than to 64, $\sqrt{75}$ is closer to 9. Approximate the answer to be 8.7.

Now let's approximate $\sqrt{40}$.

$\sqrt{36} = 6$
$\sqrt{40}$
$\sqrt{49} = 7$ $\left\{$ 40 is closer to 36 than 49.
(42 or 43 is about halfway.)

You can approximate $\sqrt{40} \approx 6.3$ (6.2 and 6.4 are also good approximations.)

EXERCISE 3: SQUARE ROOTS

Directions: This is a mixture of square root problems. When finding the square root of a perfect square, give the exact answer. When finding a square root that is not a perfect square, give either an approximate answer or a simplified answer.

1. $\sqrt{81}$ 4. $\sqrt{9}$ 7. $\sqrt{10}$ 10. $\sqrt{90}$ 13. $\sqrt{32}$

2. $\sqrt{1}$ 5. $\sqrt{144}$ 8. $\sqrt{16}$ 11. $\sqrt{225}$ 14. $\sqrt{64}$

3. $\sqrt{28}$ 6. $\sqrt{52}$ 9. $\sqrt{121}$ 12. $\sqrt{400}$ 15. $\sqrt{0}$

Answers are on page 727.

Order of Operations

Accurate calculations depend on careful use of addition, subtraction, multiplication, and division. These are our four main arithmetic operations. Throughout this section, you have been working with arithmetic expressions that combine these operations. The following is a series of steps called *the order of operations.*

THE ORDER OF OPERATIONS

First: Perform all powers and roots as they appear from left to right.

Second: Perform all multiplication and division as they appear from left to right.

Third: Perform all addition and subtraction as they appear from left to right.

Example 1: $4 + 3 \times 2 + 7$

STEP 1. Multiply first. $4 + \underline{3 \times 2} + 7$

STEP 2. Add. $4 + \quad 6 \quad + 7 = 17$

Example 2:

$$15 - 3 \times 4 + 7 \times 2 - 5$$
$$15 - 12 + 14 - 5$$
$$3 + 14 - 5$$
$$17 - 5$$
$$12$$

Example 3:

$$16 - 4 \times 2 + 16 \div 8$$
$$16 - 8 + 2$$
$$8 + 2$$
$$10$$

▶ **TIP:** If you do not follow the order of operations, you will *not* get the right answer. For example, in the problem $8 + 2 \times 2$, you should get $8 + 4$ or 12. If you simply worked from left to right, you would *incorrectly* get $8 + 2$ or $10 \times 2 = 20$.

EXERCISE 4: ORDER OF OPERATIONS

Directions: Simplify the following expressions.

1. $7 - 5 + 3 - 5$

2. $8 \times 3 + 5$

3. $8 + 3 \times 5$

4. $6 + 21 \div 3 - 5$

5. $40 \div 2 - 5 \times 3$

6. $3 + 5^2$

7. $15 - 3 + 2^3$

8. $4 + 3^3 + 3 \times 2 - 2^2$

Answers are on page 727.

Parentheses

You will always follow the preceding order of operations when you evaluate an arithmetic expression. However, if a pair of parentheses ( ) is used in the expression, do the work within the parentheses first.

Now our order of operations is

First: Do all work inside parentheses or above and below a fraction bar.

Second: Evaluate powers and square roots.

Third: Multiply and divide.

Fourth: Add and subtract.

Examples:

$4 \times (3 + 5) = 4 \times (8) = 32$ Work inside parentheses first.

$(8^2 + 3) \times (5 + 4) = (64 + 3) \times (5 + 4)$ Work inside parentheses first.

$= (67) \times (9)$

$= 603$

$\dfrac{10 - 4}{4 - 2} = \dfrac{6}{2}$ Work above and below the fraction bar.

$= 3$ A fraction bar means divide.

EXERCISE 5: MORE ORDER OF OPERATIONS

Directions: Simplify the following expressions.

1. $2 + 3^2 \times (4 + 5)$

2. $(12 - 5) + (14 - 6)$

3. $49 - (28 - 19)$

4. $8 + 6 \times (10 - 2^2)$

Answers are on page 727.

Formulas

Letters of the alphabet are often used to represent numbers that you need to find. For instance, you may remember the distance formula $d = rt$. The letters d, r, and t are used to represent numbers for distance (d), rate (r), and time (t). Letters used this way are called **unknowns** or **variables**. This use of letters helps us express general relationships about numbers.

Formulas are a way of showing these general relationships. Some common formulas that help us are the area of a circle ($A = \pi r^2$), the perimeter of a rectangle ($P = 2l + 2w$), and the Pythagorean theorem ($c^2 = a^2 + b^2$). The GED Mathematics Test will include a page of formulas that will help you solve some problems on the test. As you read a particular problem, *you* will have to decide which formula will help you solve it. You should become familiar with the formulas on page 711.

Evaluating Formulas

When you replace letters with numbers in a formula, you **substitute** numbers for letters.

When you perform mathematical operations on the substituted values, you are **evaluating** a formula.

In evaluating formulas, it is very important to follow this order of operations:

1. Solve any expressions in parentheses or above or below a fraction bar.

2. Evaluate powers and roots.

3. Multiply and divide.

4. Add and subtract.

Example 1: The formula for the perimeter (distance around) of a rectangle is $P = 2l + 2w$. Substitute 6 for l (the length) and 5 for w (the width).

STEP 1. Substitute in the formula. $\quad P = 2l + 2w$

$$P = 2(6) + 2(5)$$

STEP 2. Multiply. $\qquad\qquad\qquad P = 12 + 10$

STEP 3. Add. $\qquad\qquad\qquad\qquad P = 22$

Example 2: Find the volume of a rectangular box whose length is 7 inches, width is 5 inches, and height is 3 inches.

STEP 1. Find the appropriate formula on the formulas page. $\qquad\qquad\qquad V = lwh$

STEP 2. Substitute the values given. $\qquad\qquad\qquad V = (7)(5)(3)$

STEP 3. Multiply. Notice that the parentheses indicate multiplication. $\qquad\qquad\qquad V = 105$ cubic inches

EXERCISE 6: EVALUATING FORMULAS

Directions: Select the appropriate formula from the formulas page. Substitute the numbers in the problem and evaluate the formulas. The units of your answers are given in parentheses.

1. Find the area of a square if one side (s) is 12 inches. (square inches)

2. Find the volume of a cube if one side (s) is 5 inches. (cubic inches)

3. Find the simple interest if the principal (p) is $800 at ($r$) 12% annually for 3 years (t). (dollars)

4. Find the area of a circle where $\pi \cong$ 3.14 and the radius (r) is 3 inches. (square inches)

5. Find the distance (d) traveled if you are going 38 miles per hour (r) for 2 hours (t). (miles)

6. Find the volume of a cylinder if $\pi \cong 3.14$, the radius (r) is 6 inches, and the height (h) is 10 inches. (cubic inches)

7. Find the area of a triangle where the base (b) is 12 centimeters and the height (h) is 9 centimeters. (square centimeters)

8. Find the perimeter of a rectangle if the length (l) is 14 feet and the width (w) is 2 yards. (feet)

Answers are on page 727.

Scientific Notation

Our number system is based on multiples of ten. ***Scientific notation*** uses this idea of a base of 10 to give us a shortened method of writing extremely large or extremely small numbers. The notation is used a lot in science, but we are seeing it more often in everyday life as we use calculators and computers.

We can also express fractional powers of ten using negative exponents. The negative sign is used to indicate the reciprocal. (The reciprocal of 10 is $\frac{1}{10}$.) For instance, $10^{-1} = \frac{1}{10} = .1$.

Let's look at some powers of ten using positive and negative exponents:

$$10^0 = 1$$

$$10^1 = 10 \qquad\qquad 10^{-1} = \frac{1}{10} = .1$$

$$10^2 = 100 \qquad\qquad 10^{-2} = \frac{1}{10^2} = \frac{1}{100} \text{ or } .01$$

$$10^3 = 1000 \qquad\qquad 10^{-3} = \frac{1}{10^3} = \frac{1}{1000} \text{ or } .001$$

$$10^4 = 10{,}000 \qquad\qquad 10^{-4} = \frac{1}{10^4} = \frac{1}{10{,}000} \text{ or } .0001$$

WRITING A NUMBER IN SCIENTIFIC NOTATION

1. Represent the number as a number or a mixed decimal between 1 and 10.

2. Write a multiplication sign and represent the number's value to the correct power of 10.

You can use scientific notation to write some numbers in shortened form. Simply count the number of positions that the decimal point must be moved to determine the power of 10 to use. The power of 10 is positive for whole numbers and negative for decimals.

Example 1: Express 86,200,000 in scientific notation. (The original decimal point is understood to be at the end of the number.)

STEP 1. Represent the number as a mixed decimal between 1 and 10. Insert the decimal point between 8 and 62 to get 8.62. $\qquad 86{,}200{,}000 = 8.62 \times 10^?$

STEP 2. Count the number of places the decimal point moved to get from 86,200,000 to 8.62. Since the point moved 7 places to the left, the power of 10 is 7. $\qquad 86{,}200{,}000 = 8.62 \times 10^7$

7 places left

Example 2: Express .00098 in scientific notation.

STEP 1. Represent the number as a mixed decimal between 1 and 10. Insert the decimal point between 9 and 8 to get 9.8.

$$.00098 = 9.8 \times 10^{-4}$$
4 places right

STEP 2. Count the number of places the decimal point moved to get from .00098 to 9.8. Since the point moved 4 places to the right, the power of 10 is −4.

EXERCISE 7: SCIENTIFIC NOTATION

Directions: Express each of the numbers below in scientific notation.

1. .0082
2. 500
3. 38,200
4. .58

Each number below is written in scientific notation. Find the actual value.

5. 1.624×10^3
6. 3.12×10^{-1}
7. 8.24×10^0
8. 7.13×10^3

Answers are on page 727.

9
GEOMETRY

Geometry is the study of shapes and the relationships among them. The geometry that you are required to know for the Mathematics Test is fundamental and practical. You will not be asked to "prove" theorems as you would in a formal geometry class. Instead, you will review the basic concepts in geometry and apply them to everyday situations.

Angles

An *angle* is formed when two lines intersect. The point of intersection is called the *vertex* of the angle. On the angle here, point S is the vertex. The two sides are ST and SR.

An angle is named with a small angle symbol $\angle$ and three points—two on the ends of the angle and one at the vertex: $\angle RST$. Sometimes, we just name an angle by its vertex, such as $\angle S$.

An angle is measured in *degrees*. The symbol for degrees is a familiar one from weather reports, such as in 72°.

One complete revolution around a point is 360°. One-fourth of a revolution is 90°. A 90° angle, called a *right angle*, is often used in construction. You can often recognize a right angle because of the small square drawn in the vertex. When two intersecting lines meet at right angles, we say they are *perpendicular lines*. The symbol for perpendicular lines is $\perp$.

Special Pairs of Angles

The Mathematics Test will give information about angles and then ask you to use your understanding of their relationships. Let's look at some rules that apply to certain pairs of angles.

Complementary angles are two angles whose sum is 90°. That means the two angles together make a right angle. A 60° angle and a 30° angle are complements of each other because their sum is 90°.

Example 1: What is the complement of a 53° angle?

Solution: 90° − 53° = 37°

Supplementary angles are two angles whose sum is 180°. When the two angles are placed side by side, their sides form a straight line. A 110° angle is the supplement of a 70° angle because their sum is 180°.

Example 2: What is the supplement of a 30° angle?

Solution: 180° − 30° = 150°

Vertical angles are formed when two lines intersect. The pair of angles opposite each other are equal. In the picture at right, ∠ABC and ∠DBE are vertical angles. Therefore, ∠ABC is equal to ∠DBE. We write this as ∠ABC = ∠DBE. ∠ABD and ∠CBE are also vertical angles; therefore, ∠ABD = ∠CBE. Sometimes, as in Example 3, you may be given a pair of intersecting lines and the measurement of one angle. From that one angle, you can find the measure of the other angles.

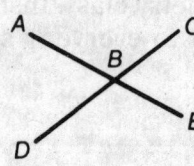

Example 3: Find the measure of ∠EFG.

Solution: ∠EFG and ∠HFJ are vertical angles and, therefore, equal.
   ∠EFG = 130°

Example 4: Find the measure of ∠GFJ.

STEP 1. Notice that ∠GFJ is the supplement to ∠EFG. Together, they are on a straight line that equals 180°.

STEP 2. Subtract the angle you know from 180°.

   180° − 130° = 50°

   ∠GFJ = 50°

Sometimes, angles are merely parts of a picture in a problem. Knowing these angle relationships (complementary, supplementary, and vertical) can help you solve the problem if you look for a pair of angles formed by intersecting lines.

Example 5: Find the measure of the angle indicated.

The ladder forms a supplementary angle with the ground. To find the missing angle, subtract 45° from 180°.

Solution: 180° − 45° = 135°

EXERCISE 1: PAIRS OF ANGLES

Directions: Solve each problem.

Use the picture below to answer questions 1–3.

1. Find the measure of ∠DBC.

2. Find the measure of ∠ABE.

3. Find the measure of ∠EBC.

4. Two pieces of a puzzle fit together to form a right angle. If one piece has an angle of 52°, what is the angle of the complementary piece?

5. A carpenter is putting an oak chair rail around a dining room wall. He wants to make sure it fits nicely and looks straight. What is the measure of the angle that will supplement 75° to make a straight, snug fit?

Answers are on page 727.

Triangles

Triangles are the basis of land measurement. Surveyors use triangles to measure a small plot of ground, an entire state or county, or a large body of water. Triangles are used in science, navigation, and building construction. Carpenters use right triangles when no T squares or carpenters' squares are available. Astronomers use triangles to find out how far stars are from Earth. We also find important uses for triangles in maps, scale drawings, and architectural plans.

What Are Triangles?

On the Mathemetics Test, you will find measurement problems concerning triangles. Let's review the basic information about triangles and see how it applies to the type of problem that appears on the GED Test.

A *triangle* is a closed three-sided figure. The point where the sides meet is called a *vertex*. At each vertex, we find an angle. The figure on the right is called *triangle ABC*, written $\triangle ABC$. It has three angles: $\angle A$, $\angle B$, $\angle C$. The triangle has three sides labeled *a*, *b*, and *c*. We can name a side by using a single letter or by using the letters representing the angles at the endpoints. For example, another name for side *a* is BC, for side *b* is AC, and for side *c* is AB.

The three angles of every triangle add up to 180°. So we say $\angle A + \angle B + \angle C = 180°$. Use this fact to find the measure of the third angle of a triangle when the measure of the first two angles is known, as in the following example.

Example: Find $\angle C$ in the triangle below.

STEP 1. First, add the measures of the two known angles.

$40° + 100° = 140°$

STEP 2. Then, subtract the sum from 180°.

$180° - 140° = 40°$

▶ **TIP:** When you see a three-sided figure in a drawing, look for a special triangular relationship.

EXERCISE 2: ANGLES IN TRIANGLES

Directions: Find the measurement of the missing angle in each of the following triangles.

1.

2.

3.

4.

Answers are on page 728.

Types of Triangles

Triangles may be named according to the length of their sides. A triangle may be referred to as *scalene, isosceles,* or *equilateral.*

- A *scalene* triangle has no equal sides and no equal angles. In the figure at right, △*ABC* is scalene. Side *AB* is not equal to side *BC* or to side *AC*.

- An *isosceles* triangle has two equal sides and two equal angles. In △*DEF* in the figure at right, *DF* is the **base** of the triangle, *DE* and *EF* are the **legs** of the triangle, ∠*D* and ∠*F* are the **base angles**, and ∠*E* is the **vertex angle**. Because *DE* = *EF*, the triangle is isosceles. The two base angles are equal; ∠*D* = ∠*F*.

- An *equilateral* triangle has three equal sides and three equal angles. Because the three angles of the triangle must add up to 180°, each angle must be 60°. △*PQR* is equilateral because *PQ* = *QR* = *PR*. It is also true that ∠*P* = ∠*Q* = ∠*R*. (An equilateral triangle is sometimes referred to as an *equiangular* triangle.)

- A right triangle is a special type of triangle that is often used in geometry problems. A *right triangle* has one right angle of 90°. We can recognize right triangles because the right angle looks like a corner. The small box in the corner indicates a right triangle. In △*XYZ* at right, ∠*X* is the right angle. The side opposite the right angle (*YZ*) is called the *hypotenuse*.

EXERCISE 3: TYPES OF TRIANGLES

Directions: Solve each problem.

1. Name each triangle as either a scalene, isosceles, equilateral, or right triangle.

    (a)   **(b)**   **(c)**   **(d)**   **(e)**

2. In triangle *RST*, ∠*R* = 70° and ∠*S* = 20°. What kind of triangle is △*RST*?

3. In isosceles triangle *ABC*, the base angles are each 52°. Find the measure of the third angle.

4. A right triangle contains a 60° angle. What is the measure of the third angle?

Answers are on page 728.

Similar Triangles

Similar triangles are figures that have the same shape. We often use similar figures to find hard-to-measure lengths, such as the distance across a lake or the height of a building. ***Similar triangles*** are two triangles whose ***corresponding angles*** are equal and whose ***corresponding sides*** are in proportion.

Look at △*ABC* and △*DEF*. They are similar triangles because they have the same shape. We can see that corresponding angles are equal. ∠*A* = ∠*D*, ∠*B* = ∠*E*, and ∠*C* = ∠*F*. Therefore, the two triangles are not the same size, but their sides are in proportion. We write this relationship as

$$\frac{AB}{DE} = \frac{BC}{EF} = \frac{AC}{DF}$$

Example 1: On a sunny day, the village inspector used similar triangles to find the height of a flagpole without climbing it. She found that her 6-foot-tall coworker cast a 10-foot shadow at the same time the flagpole cast a 40-foot shadow. How tall is the flagpole?

STEP 1. Notice that the coworker and the flagpole are at right angles to the ground. Set up a proportion.

$$\frac{\text{flagpole}}{\text{coworker}} = \frac{\text{flagpole's shadow}}{\text{coworker's shadow}}$$

STEP 2. Fill in the numbers from the problem. Let *f* stand for the flagpole.

$$\frac{f}{6} = \frac{40}{10}$$

STEP 3. Cross multiply and divide.

$$f = \frac{6 \times 40}{10} = \frac{240}{10} = 24 \text{ ft}$$

Another type of problem involving similar triangles is a surveying problem.

Example 2: The figure below shows a method of measuring the width of a river. If measurements are taken along the riverbank as shown, how wide is the river?

STEP 1. Look to see if there are two similar triangles. $\angle B = \angle E$ because they are both right angles, and both angles at point C are the same because they are vertical angles. Since two pairs of angles are the same, the triangles must be similar.

STEP 2. Redraw the triangles by turning them in the same direction. Label the sides.

STEP 3. Set up a proportion with the sides of the angles.

$$\frac{AB}{DE} = \frac{CB}{CE} \qquad \frac{22}{DE} = \frac{24}{120}$$

STEP 4. Cross multiply and divide.

$$DE = \frac{120 \times 22}{24} = \frac{2640}{24} = 110 \text{ ft}$$

▶ **TIP:** Always look for similar triangles when you are comparing two triangles.

SOLVING SIMILAR TRIANGLE PROBLEMS

1. Look for two triangles that have the same shape. Be sure the triangles are similar. Corresponding angles must be equal.

2. Redraw the triangles if necessary to show the corresponding sides and angles.

3. Set up and solve a proportion to find the missing length.

EXERCISE 4: SIMILAR TRIANGLES

Directions: Solve each problem.

1. $\triangle ABC$ is similar to $\triangle DEF$. Find DF.

2. An oak tree along a parkway casts an 18-foot shadow at the same time an 8-foot traffic light casts a 12-foot shadow. Find the height of the tree.

3. Suppose we need to find the distance d across a pond but are unable to swim to the other side and measure the distance directly. We can still find the distance. Find a marker on one side of the pond. On the other side of the pond, place a stake in the ground directly across from the marker. Measure a given distance c on a line perpendicular to the line determined by the marker and the stake. Then form two triangles as in the sketch below.

   (a) With these measures, what would you do first to determine the distance, d?

   (b) Find the distance across the pond if $a = 2$ feet, $b = 6$ feet, and $c = 50$ feet.

4. To find the height of a tower, Melissa held a yardstick perpendicular to the ground. She measured the shadow cast by the tower and the shadow cast by the yardstick. The tower's shadow was 42 feet, and the yardstick's shadow was 4 feet. How tall is the tower?

Answers are on page 728.

The Pythagorean Theorem

Although the **Pythagorean theorem** was developed by the Greek mathematician Pythagoras in about 500 B.C., it is still widely used today. Since the rule applies only to right triangles, the problem has to include a 90° angle or the right angle symbol (∟) for the Pythagorean theorem to apply. In a right triangle, the side opposite the right angle is called the *hypotenuse*, and the other two sides are called the *legs* of the triangle.

The Pythagorean theorem states that in a right triangle the square of the hypotenuse equals the sum of the squares of the legs. According to the diagram, the Pythagorean theorem is written as $c^2 = a^2 + b^2$. This is put in terms of the right triangle with legs a and b and hypotenuse c.

▶ **TIP:** To use the rule effectively, you need to be familiar with the use of squares and square roots. Refer to pages 649–651 for a review of squares and square roots.

Example 1: Find the length of the hypotenuse of a right triangle with legs 6 inches and 8 inches.

First, draw a right triangle and label its sides. Next, substitute the number values in the Pythagorean theorem and simplify the equation.

STEP 1. Write the Pythagorean theorem.

$$c^2 = a^2 + b^2$$

STEP 2. Substitute the numbers for a and b (the legs of the triangle).

$$c^2 = 6^2 + 8^2$$

STEP 3. Square the numbers.

$$c^2 = 36 + 64$$

STEP 4. Add the numbers.

$$c^2 = 100$$

STEP 5. Take the square root.

$$c = \sqrt{100} = 10 \text{ in}$$

Example 2 asks us to find the length of a leg when the hypotenuse and one leg are given. We still use the Pythagorean theorem. However, to find a leg rather than the hypotenuse, we subtract instead of add before taking the square root.

Example 2: The hypotenuse of a right triangle is 13 feet. If one leg is 12 feet, what is the length of the other leg?

First sketch a right triangle with a corner to show the right angle and then label its parts. Remember, the hypotenuse is the side opposite the right angle.

STEP 1. Write the Pythagorean theorem.

$$c^2 = a^2 + b^2$$

STEP 2. Substitute the numbers for c and b.

$$13^2 = a^2 + 12^2$$

STEP 3. Square the numbers.

$$169 = a^2 + 144$$

STEP 4. Subtract the numbers when looking for a leg.

$$169 - 144 = a^2$$
$$25 = a^2$$

STEP 5. Take the square root.

$$a = \sqrt{25} = 5 \text{ ft}$$

To solve the next problem, you first have to recognize a right triangle relationship in a familiar figure.

Example 3: A painter is concerned about setting up his equipment too near the street. He leans a 50-foot ladder against the top of a 48-foot building. How far is the bottom of the ladder from the foot of the building?

First sketch a picture of the problem and label the parts. A building makes a right angle with the ground. The leaning ladder completes a triangle. Substitute the values in the Pythagorean theorem and simplify the equation.

STEP 1. Write the Pythagorean theorem.

$$c^2 = a^2 + b^2$$

STEP 2. Substitute the numbers for c and b.

$$50^2 = a^2 + 48^2$$

STEP 3. Square the numbers.

$$2500 = a^2 + 2304$$

STEP 4. Subtract the numbers when looking for a leg.

$$2500 - 2304 = a^2$$

STEP 5. Take the square root.

$$\sqrt{196} = a \qquad 14 \text{ ft} = a$$

▶ **TIP:** Always make a sketch when working a geometry problem. If the sketch is a right triangle, consider using the Pythagorean theorem.

SOLVING PYTHAGOREAN THEOREM PROBLEMS

1. Sketch the information in the problem and label the parts.

2. Identify the right angle and then the hypotenuse.

3. Substitute the values into the formula $c^2 = a^2 + b^2$.

4. Square the values.

5. Add if you are looking for the hypotenuse or subtract if you are looking for a leg.

6. Take the square root.

EXERCISE 5: THE PYTHAGOREAN THEOREM

Directions: Solve each problem.

1. In a right triangle whose legs are a and b and whose hypotenuse is c, find the length of the missing side when

   (a) $a = 9, b = 12$ **(b)** $b = 4, c = 5$ **(c)** $a = 10, b = 24$

2. The screen on Alberto's TV has the measurements shown. Find the measure of the diagonal for Alberto's TV.

3. Can 20 inches, 21 inches, and 29 inches be the sides of a right triangle?

4. At summer camp, the swimming course runs the length (*l*) of a small lake. To determine the length of the course, the camp counselors measure the two "dry" legs of a right triangle. What is the length in meters of the swimming course in the figure below?

(1) 75
(2) 90
(3) 100
(4) 120
(5) 144

5. A television antenna is 24 feet tall and is held in place by three guy wires (braces) fastened at the top of the antenna and to hooks 7 feet from the base of the tower. If the antenna is installed on a flat roof, how many feet of guy wire are used?

(1) 40
(2) 50
(3) 60
(4) 65
(5) 75

6. A ladder that is 13 feet long is placed against a house. The foot of the ladder is 5 feet from the base of the house. How many feet above the ground does the ladder touch the building?

(1) 10
(2) 12
(3) 15
(4) 16
(5) 20

Answers are on page 728.

Plane Figures

Rectangles and squares are used extensively in the construction of buildings. Floor tile, tabletops, windowpanes, doors, books, and picture frames are a few of the items that often are rectangular or square. The GED Mathematics Test will ask you to recognize these shapes and to solve problems based on them.

Types of Figures

A *rectangle* is a closed four-sided figure. The points where the four sides meet are called *vertices*. At each vertex there is a right angle (90°).

1. The sum of the four angles is 360°.
2. Opposite sides are equal.
3. Opposite sides are parallel.
4. All four angles are equal (90°).

A *parallelogram* is a closed four-sided figure. It has four angles (not necessarily right angles).

> 1. The sum of the four angles is 360°.
> 2. Opposite sides are equal.
> 3. Opposite sides are parallel.
> 4. Opposite angles are equal.

A *square* is a four-sided figure with four right angles.

> 1. All four sides are equal.
> 2. All four angles are equal; each is 90°.
> 3. Opposite sides are parallel.

Circles

Many objects around us are circular: clock faces, wheels, bottle caps, rings, and the pupils of eyes. What makes a circle a circle? In geometry, we define a *circle* as a set of points all the same distance from a center point.

That distance from the center to the circle is called the *radius*. A radius can be drawn from any point on the circle to the center. A *diameter* is a straight line that goes through the center of the circle and has its endpoints on the circle. A diameter is twice as long as a radius.

Measurement of Figures

Perimeter

Perimeter is the distance around a figure. Measuring for a fence around a yard, putting a baseboard around a room, or setting up a baseball diamond are some uses of perimeter. You will find formulas for perimeter on the formulas page of the GED Mathematics Test.

▶ **TIP:** Keep in mind that the perimeter of a figure is the distance all the way around the figure, so you can also *add* all the sides of the figure.

The perimeter of a square is $P = 4s$ where P is the perimeter and s is one side. Since all four sides of a square are equal, multiply one side by 4 to get the total distance around the square.

Example 1: Find the perimeter of this square.

7 yd

$P = 4s$
$P = 4 \times 7 = 28$ yd

The perimeter of a rectangle is $P = 2l + 2w$ where P is the perimeter, l is the length, and w is the width. Since opposite sides of a rectangle are equal, double the length and double the width, then add to find the total distance around the rectangle.

Example 2: Find the
perimeter of this
rectangle.

$P = 2l + 2w$
$P = (2 \times 7) + (2 \times 3) = 20$ ft

The perimeter of a triangle is $P = a + b + c$ where P equals the perimeter and a, b, and c are the lengths of the three sides. To find the perimeter, add the lengths of the three sides.

Example 3: Find the
perimeter of this triangle.

$P = a + b + c$
$P = 4 + 7 + 9 = 20$ in

The *circumference* of a circle is the perimeter of (or distance around) a circle. The formula is $C = \pi d$ where C is the circumference, pi or $\pi \cong 3.14$, and d is the diameter. The circumference is equal to approximately 3.14 times the diameter. You could also use $\frac{22}{7}$ for π if the diameter or radius is given as a fraction or when the problem would be easier to solve with $\frac{22}{7}$.

Example 4: Find the
circumference of this
circle.

$C = \pi d$
$C = \frac{22}{7} \times 42 = 132$ in

EXERCISE 6: PERIMETER

Directions: Solve each problem.

1. A baseball diamond is a square with distances between the bases as shown. How far will the batter run if he hits a home run?

2. Find, in feet, the amount of framing needed to frame a picture $8\frac{1}{2}$ in by 11 in.

3. How much binding is needed around a triangular sail for the toy sailboat shown below?

4. A farmer wants to fence a rectangular pasture 400 yards by 224 yards. The cost of fencing is $5.75 per eight-foot section. What will his cost be?

5. Find the perimeter of the figure shown below.

6. How many feet of fencing are needed to fence the yard below?

7. To jog 6 miles, how many times must you jog around a city block that is $\frac{1}{4}$ mile long by $\frac{1}{8}$ mile wide?

8. Find the perimeter of the ice-skating rink with the given dimensions. (*Hint*: Think of the rink as made up of a rectangle and 2 half-circles.)

Answers are on page 729.

Area

    Area is the amount of surface over a certain region. It can be used to describe the size of farmland, floor space, or a tabletop. Area is measured in square units such as square inches or square feet. Imagine a square one inch on each side. This is a square inch.

    When we are asked to find the area in square inches, we are actually finding the number of squares one inch by one inch that could fit on the surface we are measuring. For example, the rectangle to the right contains 8 square inches of area.

    Remember that the formulas page of the GED Test will provide the formulas for the area of the square, the rectangle, and the triangle. All of the formulas appear on page 711 of this book.

▶ **TIP:** Answers in area problems are given in square units, such as square inches or square meters.

    The area of a square is $A = s^2$ where A is the area and s is one side. The area equals the side times the side. Given a square with a side of 7 inches, the area equals 7 in × 7 in = 49 square inches.

    The area of a rectangle is $A = lw$ where A is the area, l is the length, and w is the width. The area equals the length times the width.

Example 1: How much surface area is the rectangular top of a desk 3 feet by 5 feet?

Solution: The area is $A = lw = 3$ ft × 5 ft = 15 square feet or 15 ft^2

    The area of a triangle is $A = \frac{1}{2}bh$ where A is the area, b is the base, and h is the height. To find the area of a triangle, multiply the base by the height and find $\frac{1}{2}$ of that amount.

Example 2: Find the area of a triangle with a base of 6 inches and height of 9 inches.

STEP 1. Multiply the base by the height.

$A = \frac{1}{2}bh$

$A = \frac{1}{2}(6 \cdot 9) = \frac{1}{2}(54)$

STEP 2. Divide that by 2 to find $\frac{1}{2}$.

$A = \frac{1}{2}(54) = 27$ square inches
or 27 in^2

The area of a circle is $A = \pi r^2$ where A is the area, π is approximately 3.14 or $\frac{22}{7}$, and r is the radius.

Example 3: Find the area of a circle whose diameter is 12 inches.

STEP 1. Find the radius.

$12 \div 2 = 6$

STEP 2. Substitute numbers in the formula and do the calculation.

$A = \pi r^2$

$A = 3.14(6)^2$

$A = 3.14(36)$

$A = 113.04$ sq in or 113.04 in^2

12 in

EXERCISE 7: AREA

Directions: Solve each problem. For questions 1–3, find the area of the figures.

1.
14.3 m
9 m

2.

10 in
10 in
5.3 in
5.3 in
(This shape combines a square and a rectangle.)

3.
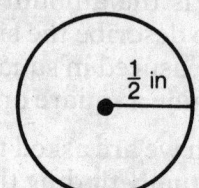
$\frac{1}{2}$ in
(Use $\frac{22}{7}$ for π.)

4. How many square yards of carpet are needed for a room 30 feet by 15 feet? (1 sq yd = 9 sq ft)

5. At $1.15 per square foot, find the rental cost for an office 20 feet by 15 feet.

6. How many square feet is the largest circular rug that can be put on the floor of a room 10 feet by 12 feet?

Questions 7–10 are based on the following information and diagram.

The diagram below shows the backyard at the Smith house. In the yard are an 18-foot-diameter swimming pool, an 8-foot square garden, and a 10-foot-by-20-foot patio deck. The rest of the yard is grass-covered.

7. How large is the patio?

8. What percentage (to the nearest 1 percent) of the yard is covered by the pool?

9. How many square yards (to the nearest hundredth) of outdoor carpeting are needed to cover the patio?

10. To the nearest whole number, how many times larger is the pool than the garden?

Answers are on page 729.

Volume

Volume is the amount of space that a solid, or a three-dimensional figure, contains. Examples of solids are a rectangular box, a cylinder, and a cube.

Volume is measured in *cubic units* such as cubic feet, cubic inches, or cubic yards. For example, a cubic inch is a cube with edges of 1 inch each.

The formulas page of the GED Mathematics Test gives formulas for the volume of a cube, a rectangular container, and a cylinder. Let's look at each formula.

The volume of a *cube* is $V = s^3$ where V is the volume and s is the edge of the cube. A die and a square box are examples of cubes. Each edge of the cube has the same length. Thus, the volume of a cube is equal to the edge cubed, or edge times edge times edge.

Example 1: Find the volume of the cube at the right:

$$V = s^3$$
$$= 2 \times 2 \times 2$$
$$= 8 \text{ cu in or } 8 \text{ in}^3$$

2 in

The volume of a *rectangular container* is $V = lwh$ where V is the volume, l is the length, w is the width, and h is the height. The volume is equal to the length times the width times the height.

Example 2: What is the volume of the container at the right?

$V = lwh$
$= 18 \times 15 \times 6$
$= 1620 \text{ cm}^3 \text{ or } 1620 \text{ cu cm}$

The volume of a *cylinder* is $V = \pi r^2 h$ where V is the volume, r is the radius of the circular base, and h is the height of the cylinder. π is approximately 3.14 or $\frac{22}{7}$.

Example 3: Find the volume of the container at the right.

$V = \pi r^2 h$
$= 3.14(3)^2(5)$
$= 141.3 \text{ cu in or } 141.3 \text{ in}^3$

▶ **TIP:** On the GED Mathematics Test, you may be asked to find the perimeter (or circumference), area, or volume of a figure. However, you may not be told directly *which* measurement you are to find. Keep in mind that the perimeter is what goes around a figure, the area is what covers a figure, and the volume is the capacity of an object. Once you have determined what you are looking for, you can select the right formula from the formulas page.

EXERCISE 8: VOLUME

Directions: Solve each problem.

1. Find the volume of a freezer chest that is 6 feet long, 4 feet deep, and 3 feet wide.

2. How many gallons of water will fill a fish tank that is 18 inches by 12 inches by 48 inches? (There are 231 cubic inches per gallon.) Round your answer to the nearest gallon.

3. How much topsoil is needed to cover a garden 25 feet by 40 feet to a depth of 6 inches?

4. The edge of a small cube is 2 inches, and the edge of a larger cube is 4 inches. What is the ratio of the volume of the small cube to the volume of the larger cube?

5. The farmer's silo has the dimensions shown at the right. What is the volume of the silo? (Use $\frac{22}{7}$ for π.)

42 ft

28 ft

Answers are on page 730.

EXERCISE 9: REVIEW OF GEOMETRY

Directions: Solve each problem. Refer to the formulas on page 711 when necessary.

1. How many feet of weather stripping are needed to frame the two windows with the dimensions indicated?

   (1) 12 **(2)** 15 **(3)** 33 **(4)** 396 **(5)** 4752

2. The Family Food Co. is redesigning its bran flakes box as shown. Find the capacity of the new box in cubic inches.

   (1) 22 **(2)** 92 **(3)** 115 **(4)** 230 **(5)** 460

3. Family Foods is also redesigning its soup can. Which of the following can be used to find the capacity of the new soup can?

   (1) $(3.14)(1.5)^2(4)$
   (2) $(3.14)(3)(4)$
   (3) $(3.14)(1.5)^2$
   (4) $(3.14)(3)^2$
   (5) not enough information is given

4. The diagonal of a rectangle is 17 inches. If the length of the rectangle is 15 inches, what is the width of the rectangle in inches?

   (1) 4 **(2)** 8 **(3)** 16 **(4)** 32 **(5)** 64

5. A local radio station broadcasts over a 21-mile radius. How many square miles does this cover? (Use $\frac{22}{7}$ for π.)

   (1) 66 **(2)** 441 **(3)** 1386 **(4)** 1764 **(5)** 5542

6. Ramon needs to carpet a room. Carpeting costs $11.50 per square yard. Disregarding waste, how much will it cost to carpet the room in the diagram?

   (1) $159.25
   (2) $207
   (3) $1380
   (4) $1601.38
   (5) not enough information is given

7. Mary planted a triangular flower bed with the dimensions shown at right. What is the area (in square feet) of the garden?

   (1) 37 **(2)** 45 **(3)** 60 **(4)** 120 **(5)** 150

8. An observer on the shore sees a ship anchored off the coast. To find the distance to the ship, he makes the measurements shown in the figure. How far is it from the shoreline to the ship? (Note that d represents the distance from ship to shore.)

(1) 65 m   **(2)** 210 m   **(3)** 400 m   **(4)** 500 m   **(5)** 10,000 m

9. A right triangle contains a 60° angle. What is the measure of the third angle?

(1) 30°   **(2)** 120°   **(3)** 150°   **(4)** 210°   **(5)** not enough information is given

Use the information below to answer questions 10–12.

Ellen was curious about the height of a radio tower near her house. On a sunny day, her brother Bill stood next to the tower. Both Bill and the tower cast a shadow. The figure at right represents Bill and the tower.

10. Which expression below correctly represents the height of the tower, t?

(1) $t = \dfrac{s \times b}{a}$ **(2)** $t = a + b + c$ **(3)** $t = s - r$ **(4)** $t = \dfrac{a \times b}{s}$ **(5)** $t = s + a$

11. If Bill is 5 feet tall and casts a 12-foot shadow while the tower casts a 42-foot shadow, how many feet tall is the tower?

(1) $17\frac{1}{2}$ **(2)** 20   **(3)** 30   **(4)** 35   **(5)** 60

12. If Bill is 6 feet tall and casts an 8-foot shadow, what is the distance from the top of his head to the tip of his shadow?

(1) 7 feet   **(2)** 10 feet   **(3)** 14 feet   **(4)** 50 feet   **(5)** 100 feet

13. How much larger is the supplement of a 57° angle than the complement of a 75° angle?

(1) 18°   **(2)** 105°   **(3)** 108°   **(4)** 123°   **(5)** 228°

14. A delivery truck has a cargo area that is 8 feet by 8 feet by 12 feet. Approximately how many square boxes 2 feet on a side can be loaded into the cargo area?

(1) 48   **(2)** 96   **(3)** 160   **(4)** 768   **(5)** not enough information is given

15. A circular pond has a circumference of 628 feet. What is the distance in feet from the center to the edge of the pond?

(1) 100   **(2)** 157   **(3)** 200   **(4)** 314   **(5)** 628

Answers are on page 730.

10
ALGEBRA

Algebra, an extension of arithmetic, is an organized system of rules that help us solve problems. Think of algebra as a game. When you first sit down to play, you read the rules and try to understand how to use them.

Every game has its own vocabulary that is defined in the rules. As you actually begin to play the game, you find yourself using the vocabulary of the game and following the rules. The more you play the game, the easier it is to remember both the vocabulary and the rules. Let's start our study of algebra with a look at its special vocabulary.

The Language of Algebra

Algebra uses letters of the alphabet to represent numbers or unknown quantities. These letters are called *variables*. These values are variable because they change from problem to problem. The letters can be capital letters, lowercase letters, or even Greek letters. Some examples are x, t, B, R, and P. *Constants* are fixed numbers. The value of a constant is known and does not change from problem to problem. Some constants are 8, 75, 0, π, and $\sqrt{3}$.

In algebra, we still work with the four operations of addition, subtraction, multiplication, and division. Look at the chart below to see the symbols that are used for these four operations.

TABLE OF OPERATIONS			
Operation	Symbol	Example	Meaning
Addition	+	$5 + x$	5 plus x
Subtraction	−	$8 - x$ $y - 8$	8 minus x y minus 8
Multiplication	· (dot) ( ) parentheses no symbol	$5 \cdot 3$ $10(2)$ xy	5 times 3 10 times 2 x times y
Division	÷ —— (fraction bar)	$x \div y$ $\frac{x}{12}$ $\frac{3}{x}$	x divided by y x divided by 12 3 divided by x

Whenever a number and a variable are multiplied together, the number part is called the **coefficient** of the variable. In the expression $7x$, the coefficient of x is 7. The variable x is multiplied by 7.

▶ **TIP:** Whenever the variable is written without a number in front of it, the coefficient is understood to be 1. Therefore, y means $1y$, and the coefficient is 1.

Algebraic Expressions

An **algebraic expression** connects variables to variables or variables to constants using the operation signs. For example, $a + 4$, $5 - 3y$, and $\frac{m + n}{4}$ are all algebraic expressions. In the expression $x + 5$, x is the variable that represents the unknown, and 5 is the constant value. The operation is addition.

Algebraic expressions contain **terms**. A term can be a number, a variable, or the multiplication or division of numbers with variables. Some examples of terms are

5 (a number) $7y$ (the product of a number and a variable)

y (a variable) $\frac{y}{3}$ (the quotient of a variable and a number)

In an algebraic expression, terms are separated by + and − signs. The sign before the term belongs to the term.

Examples:

is an expression that contains two terms: $5x$ and $+4y$.

is an expression that contains three terms: $8x^2$, $-4x$, and $+7$.

is an expression that contains two terms: $\frac{x}{5}$ and -2.

▶ **TIP:** Keep the plus or minus sign with the term, as in -2 above. You will learn more about negative numbers on pages 690–696.

EXERCISE 1: TERMS

Directions: Name the terms in the following expressions

1. $4 + x$ **2.** $8x + 7y - 5$ **3.** $2x^2 - \frac{3}{x}$ **4.** $8ab + 12$

Answers are on page 731.

Equations

An algebraic *equation* sets one expression equal to another expression or a value.

$$x + 7 \quad = \quad 10 \qquad\qquad x + 3 \quad = \quad 2x - 9$$

expression   equals   value   expression   equals   expression

---

AN ALGEBRAIC EQUATION ALWAYS HAS THREE PARTS:

1. left-side expression
2. an equal sign (=)
3. right-side expression

The equation $x + 7 = 10$ says that some number (x) added to 7 equals 10. We know that 3 added to 7 equals 10, so 3 is the *solution* of the equation. The solution is the value of the variable that makes the statement true. You *solve* an equation when you find the solution for the variable. On the Mathematics Test, you may have to translate a word problem into an equation. You will also write and interpret your own equations.

Example: $2x + 5 = 17$

This expression means that *a number multiplied by 2 and added to 5 equals 17.* Do you know what the number is? You're right if you said 6, because $2(6) + 5 = 17$.

EXERCISE 2: EQUATIONS

Directions: Write in words what each expression means. Use the words *a number* for any letter as shown in the example above.

1. $5 + 7y = 19$ **2.** $9y = 27$ **3.** $a - 5 = 23$ **4.** $\frac{10}{y} - 5 = 0$ **5.** $\frac{y}{8} = 9$

Answers are on page 731.

Solving One-Step Equations

Among the most important uses of algebra are the solution of equations and the use of equations to solve word problems.

Eyeballing the Solution

Solving an equation means finding the value of the variable that makes the equation true. Some equations will be fairly easy to solve because you know your math facts. If you can just look at the equation and see the answer, you are "eyeballing" the equation.

For example, $x + 3 = 10$ is an algebraic equation. What value of x will make this true? You would choose $x = 7$ because you know $7 + 3 = 10$. Another example is $3x = 15$. What value of x makes this equation true? The answer is 5 because you know $3(5) = 15$.

EXERCISE 3: EYEBALLING

Directions: Solve the following equations by "eyeballing" them. Ask yourself, "What number would make this equation true?" Then choose that number to represent the variable (letter) shown in the problem.

1. $x - 2 = 0$ **3.** $4 + x = 9$ **5.** $x - 5 = 8$ **7.** $5a = 10$

2. $\frac{x}{5} = 2$ **4.** $x + 3 = 8$ **6.** $3x = 9$ **8.** $\frac{36}{x} = 9$

Answers are on page 731.

Algebraic Solutions

Let's look at algebraic methods of solving one-step equations. Before you start solving equations, you must understand a couple of mathematical ideas. First of all, an equation is a perfect balance between what is on the left side of the equal sign and what is on the right side of the equal sign.

$x + 3$ $=$ 10
Left side   Right side
of equation   Balances   of equation

If you make any changes on the left side, you must make the *same* changes on the right side. For instance, if you add 7 to the left side, you must add 7 to the right side for the 2 sides to remain equal. Then you know the result will be true.

Second, your goal in solving an equation is to get the variable all by itself on one side of an equation. Concentrate on the variable. In the equation $x + 3 = 10$, concentrate on the x. Notice that the x is being added to 3. This will tell you how to solve the equation.

▶ **TIP:** Keep the equation in balance and concentrate on the variable.

To solve an equation, perform the opposite operation (called the *inverse* operation). Addition and subtraction are opposites, and multiplication and division are opposites. In the equation $x + 3 = 10$, you see that x is being added to three. The opposite of "adding three" is "subtracting three." If you subtract three from both sides, you will get x all by itself.

Example 1: $x + 3 = 10$

STEP 1. Look at x. It is added to 3. $x + 3 = 10$

STEP 2. Subtract 3 from both sides. $x + \underline{3 - 3} = \underline{10 - 3}$
                                                    0 7

STEP 3. Solve the equation. $x = 7$

WHEN SOLVING AN EQUATION, REMEMBER:

1. Keep the equation in balance.

2. Concentrate on the variable.

3. Perform the opposite operation.

Example 2: $7x = 21$

STEP 1. Look at x. It is multiplied by 7. $7x = 21$

STEP 2. Divide by 7 on both sides. The $\frac{\cancel{7}x}{\cancel{7}} = \frac{\cancel{21}^3}{\cancel{7}}$
7s on the left side "cancel out."

STEP 3. Solve the equation. $x = 3$

Check the answers to each problem by substituting the answer in the original equation. For example, when we solved $7x = 21$, we got $x = 3$. Check that answer by substituting 3 for x in the original problem.

$7x = 21$

$7(3) = 21$ Substitute 3 for x.

$21 = 21$ This is a true statement, so $x = 3$ is the solution for $7x = 21$.

Example 3: $8 = \frac{x}{5}$

STEP 1. Look at x. It is divided by 5. $8 = \frac{x}{5}$

STEP 2. Multiply both sides by 5. $5 \cdot 8 = \frac{x}{\cancel{5}} \cdot \cancel{5}^1$

          $5 \cdot 8 = x$

STEP 3. Solve the equation. $40 = x$

EXERCISE 4: ONE-STEP EQUATIONS

Directions: Solve for x. Check your answers.

1. $3 + x = 7$ **3.** $2x = 6$ **5.** $5x = 75$ **7.** $x - 3 = 12$

2. $\frac{x}{3} = 12$ **4.** $x - 8 = 0$ **6.** $\frac{x}{4} = 16$ **8.** $\frac{1}{2}x = 14$

Answers are on page 731.

Solving Algebra Word Problems

To use algebra to solve mathematical problems, you have to translate the problem into algebraic language. Let a letter of the alphabet, a variable, represent the unknown quantity. The letters x, y, and z are most often used as variables.

A few English phrases are used repeatedly in algebra problems. Become familiar with the phrases and their algebraic expressions in the chart on page 680.

TRANSLATING EXPRESSIONS

1. First assign a variable to the unknown quantity.

2. Use that variable to write an expression for any other unknown quantity.

3. Identify the phrases that indicate the mathematical operation.

4. Use the operation to write the expression.

Translate: "The square of a number decreased by the number."

1. Let x be the number.
2. The square of a number is x^2.
3. *Decreased by* means "subtract."
4. Write $x^2 - x$.

TRANSLATION CHART		
English Phrase	Operation	Algebraic Expression
the *sum* of two numbers	+ (add)	$x + y$
five *more than* a number		$x + 5$
a number *increased by* 4		$x + 4$
a number *added to another* number		$x + y$
nine *plus* a number		$9 + x$
the *difference* between two numbers	− (subtract)	$x - y$
seven *decreased by* a number	(Be sure the number subtracted follows the minus sign.)	$7 - x$
a number *reduced by* 4		$x - 4$
three *less than* a number		$x - 3$
six *subtracted* from a number		$x - 6$
six *minus* a number		$6 - x$
the *product* of two numbers	multiply	xy
six *times* a number	( )	$(6)(x)$
twice a number	or $\cdot$	$2 \cdot x$
two-thirds *of* a number	or no sign	$\left(\frac{2}{3}\right)x$ or $\frac{2x}{3}$
double a number		$2x$
one number *multiplied* by another number		xy
the *quotient* of two numbers	divide	$\frac{x}{y}$ $x \div y$
a number *divided by* three	(Be sure the number you are dividing by is below the fraction bar or follows the division symbol.)	$\frac{x}{3}$
seven *divided by* a number		$\frac{7}{x}$
half a number		$\frac{x}{2}$ or $\frac{1}{2}x$
a number *squared*	raise to the second power	x^2
a number *cubed*	raise to the third power	y^3
the *square root* of a number	square root	$\sqrt{x}$

Using the chart as a guide to the examples below, translate the following English phrases into algebraic expressions.

Examples:

four more than a number

$$4 \quad + \quad x \qquad = 4 + x$$

six decreased by half a number

$$6 \quad - \quad \tfrac{1}{2}x \qquad = 6 - \tfrac{1}{2}x \text{ or } 6 - \tfrac{x}{2}$$

twelve divided by a number squared

$$12 \quad \div \quad x^2 \qquad = \dfrac{12}{x^2}$$

twice the sum of a number and 4

$$2 \qquad (x + 4) \qquad = 2(x + 4)$$

the sum of twice a number and 4

$$+ \qquad 2x \qquad 4 \qquad = 2x + 4$$

EXERCISE 5: TRANSLATING ENGLISH TO ALGEBRA

Directions: Translate the English phrases to algebraic expressions using x and y to stand for the unknown numbers.

1. six minus a number

2. the product of fourteen and a number

3. the difference between two numbers, divided by 3

4. the sum of a number squared and another number squared

5. four times the sum of ten and a number

6. seven less than twice a number

7. the square of a number increased by twelve

8. a number cubed divided by 4

9. the sum of two numbers less 4

10. five times a number divided by twice the same number

Answers are on page 731.

Translating Equations

We can now practice translating an entire sentence into an algebraic equation. Remember, an equation has three parts: left-side expression, equal sign, and right-side expression.

Many key words or phrases indicate "equal." Become familiar with the list below:

equals	is	was
is equal to	are	were
equal to	gives	leaves
the same as	the sum is	makes
the result is	the difference is	yields
the product is	the quotient is	the answer is

TRANSLATING EQUATIONS

1. Assign a variable to the unknown quantity.
2. Write two expressions for the values.
3. Use an equal sign between the expressions.

Example 1: Three times a number is one more than twice the number.
$$3x = 1 + 2x \text{ or } 3x = 1 + 2x$$

Example 2: Four more than a number equals 15.
$$x + 4 = 15 \text{ or } x + 4 = 15$$

Example 3: Twice a number reduced by six is equal to 9.
$$2x - 6 = 9 \text{ or } 2x - 6 = 9$$

Example 4: To promote holiday sales, a magazine offers one-year subscriptions for $7 and additional gift subscriptions for $5 each. With a one-year subscription, how many gift subscriptions can you get if you have $42 to spend altogether?

You would let x represent the number of $5 gift subscriptions. Then 5 times x is the cost of the additional subscriptions. The basic statement is

original subscription price plus additional subscription cost is 42
$$7 + 5x = 42 \text{ or } 7 + 5x = 42$$

In Example 4, the variable was identified first. Then, algebraic expressions and the operation were written. Finally, these values were translated into an algebraic equation.

▶ **TIP:** To identify the variable in a word problem, isolate the term or element that you don't know. Then assign a letter to that term.

EXERCISE 6: TRANSLATING SENTENCES TO EQUATIONS

Directions: Translate each sentence to an equivalent algebraic equation as shown above.

1. One-fourth of a number equals 18.

2. Two less than a number is 40.

3. Three times a number increased by 1 is 25.

4. Nine increased by half a number gives a result of 13.

5. The product of six and a number makes 35.

6. The difference between two numbers is 8.

7. Eighteen more than twice a number is 22.

8. A number divided by four yields a quotient of 18.

9. Twice a number, reduced by 3, is equal to 5 times the same number increased by 9.

In questions 10–14 select the equation that could be used to find the unknown in the problem.

10. A man had x dollars. After paying a bill of $48, he had $75 left.

    (1) $x + 48 = 75$ **(2)** $48 - x = 75$ **(3)** $x - 48 = 75$ **(4)** $75 - 48 = x$

11. A golfer had x number of golf balls. After playing eighteen holes of golf, he lost 5 balls and had 19 left. How many balls did he have before he played the eighteen holes of golf?

    (1) $x - 5 = 19$ **(2)** $\frac{x}{5} = 19$ **(3)** $x - 18 = 19$ **(4)** $x + 5 = 19$

12. In a wrestling meet, Mike scored 5 points, which represented one-seventh of his team's final score. What was the final score, x?

    (1) $x + \frac{1}{7} = 5$ **(2)** $x - 5 = \frac{1}{2}$ **(3)** $x - 5 = 7$ **(4)** $\frac{x}{7} = 5$

13. A plumber charges $22 for a house call plus $12 per hour for the time worked. If the charge is $64, how many hours, h, did he work?

    (1) $12 + h + 22 = 64$ **(2)** $12h = 64$ **(3)** $22 + 12h = 64$ **(4)** $\frac{h}{12} + 22 = 64$

14. Sue will not tell her age, x. But in six years, her age will be $\frac{7}{6}$ as much as it is now. How can her age be written?

    (1) $x + 6 = \frac{7}{6}x$ **(2)** $x - \frac{7}{6}x = 1$ **(3)** $\frac{x}{6} = \frac{7}{6}x$ **(4)** $\frac{7}{6}x = 6$

Answers are on page 731.

Solving One-Step Algebra Word Problems

    This next exercise combines practice in translating, setting up, and solving one-step algebra problems. Let's look at an example before you begin the exercise.

Example: Sue has x dollars, and Tom has $\frac{2}{3}$ as much money as Sue. If Tom has $48, how much does Sue have?

STEP 1. Translate and set up.
    Tom has $48.

    $\frac{2}{3}$ of Sue's money is $48 $\frac{2}{3}x = 48$

STEP 2. Solve the equation. Divide both sides by $\frac{2}{3}$.

$$\frac{2}{3}x = 48$$

$$\frac{2}{3}x \div \frac{2}{3} = 48 \div \frac{2}{3}$$

$$x = 48 \times \frac{3}{2}$$

$$x = \$72$$

EXERCISE 7: SOLVING ONE-STEP ALGEBRA WORD PROBLEMS

Directions: Solve each problem.

1. If seven less than a number is 8, find the number.

2. Baseballs cost $2.25 each. How many baseballs can you buy for $40.50?

3. Jack saved one-eighth of his allowance. If he saved $2.50, how much is his allowance?

4. Amanda sold her stereo set for $120 less than she paid for it. If she sold the stereo set for $72, what did she originally pay for it?

5. After $5\frac{1}{2}$ feet were cut off a wooden beam, $6\frac{1}{2}$ feet were left. What was the original length of the beam?

6. After José gained 14 pounds, he weighed 172 pounds. What was his original weight?

7. Twelve years from now, Lucille will be 48 years old. How old is she now?

8. By purchasing a fleet of cars for its salespeople, Tower Manufacturing gets a discount of $927 on each car purchased. This is 16% of the regular price. Find the regular price.

Answers are on page 731.

Solving Multi-Step Problems

Many algebraic expressions contain two or more terms. For instance, $2x - 7$ has two terms, and $3x - 9y + 7z$ has three terms. It is best to write algebraic expressions in the simplest form possible. We will cover several steps in simplifying algebraic expressions so that you can solve more complicated algebra word problems.

Simplifying Algebraic Expressions

To simplify an algebraic expression, combine like terms and remove all symbols of grouping such as parentheses and brackets.

Simplifying by Combining Like Terms

Like terms are terms that contain the same variables to the same power.

Examples of like terms: $4x$ $7x$ $12x$ $2xy$ xy $17xy$ $9x^2$ $4x^2$ x^2

Examples of unlike terms: $3x$ $4y$ -2 $2xy$ $3x$ $4y$ $3x^2$ $2x$ -5

We can combine like terms to simplify an expression.

Example 1: $3x + 5x = 8x$ (Just add the coefficients—the numbers.)

Example 2: $7y^2 - 5y^2 = 2y^2$ (You can also subtract coefficients.)

Example 3: $3x^2 + 6y + 2x^2 - 4y = 5x^2 + 2y$

First, combine x^2 terms.   Then, combine y terms.

$$
\begin{array}{r} 3x^2 \\ + \ 2x^2 \\ \hline 5x^2 \end{array}
\qquad\qquad
\begin{array}{r} + \ 6y \\ - \ 4y \\ \hline + \ 2y \end{array}
$$

Example 4: $2x - 3y - 5y + 2 + 4x - 6 = 6x - 8y - 4$

Combine x terms.   Combine y terms.   Combine numbers.

$2x + 4x = 6x$ $-3y - 5y = -8y$ $-6 + 2 = -4$

▶ **TIP:** Notice that in Example 4, three of the terms had answers with a minus sign. These are called *negative numbers* and will be discussed on pages 690–691. If the signs of numbers are the same (+ or −), combine the numbers and just attach the sign (+6 and +3 = +9; −6 and −3 = −9). If the signs are different, find the *difference* between the numbers and attach the sign of the *larger* number (−6 + 2 = −4).

EXERCISE 8: COMBINING LIKE TERMS

Directions: Simplify the following expressions by combining like terms.

1. $3x + 12x$

2. $7y - 4y$

3. $2x + 3y + 6y + 7x$

4. $7x^2 + 3x + 4x - 2x$

5. $8x - 3 + 5x$

6. $3x^2 + 14 + 7x + 2x^2 - 5$

7. $4a + 3b - 2a - 3b + a$

8. $x + 2y - y$

9. $9a^2 + 4a + a + 3a^2$

10. $5xy + 7x - 3y - x + 4xy$

Answers are on page 732.

Removing Grouping Symbols

Sometimes algebraic expressions are grouped together. Grouping symbols can be parentheses or brackets. These symbols draw your attention first when you simplify an expression.

Example 1: $3(2x - 4)$

Multiply 3 by $2x$ and 3 by (-4).

$3(2x - 4) = 3(2x) - 3(4) = 6x - 12$

If a plus sign or no sign is in front of parentheses, the terms do not change when you remove the parentheses.

Example 2: $6x + (2x - 7) = 6x + 2x - 7 = 8x - 7$

A minus sign in front of a set of parentheses changes the sign inside to the opposite sign. With a minus and a number, you change the signs, multiply the numbers, and combine like terms.

Changed sign

Example 3: $3x - 2(6x - 4) = 3x - 12x + 8 = -9x + 8$

REMOVING GROUPING SYMBOLS

1. Remove the parentheses or brackets.

2. Distribute the multiplication over every term in the parentheses.

EXERCISE 9: REMOVING GROUPING SYMBOLS

Directions: Simplify the following expressions by removing grouping symbols.

1. $5(3x + 2)$

2. $4(7x - 8)$

3. $6x + 2(12x - 7)$

4. $2(x - 1)$

5. $3(2x + 4 - 3y)$

6. $-6(5x - 12)$

7. $x - 2(9 + 6x)$

8. $2(x - y)$

Answers are on page 732.

Solving Multi-Step Equations

We study multi-step equations because we will use them to solve some algebra word problems on the GED Mathematics Test. To solve multi-step equations, we must take a step-by-step approach as shown below. Always plan to start with step 1 and progress through the following steps in order. But keep in mind that some equations will not need every step.

STEP 1. Simplify expressions on both sides of the equation.

STEP 2. Get all the variables on the left side of the equation using addition or subtraction from the right side.

STEP 3. Concentrate on the variable and *undo addition and subtraction* using the opposite operation.

STEP 4. Concentrate on the variable and *undo multiplication and division* using the opposite operation.

Example 1: $3x + 7 = 13$

STEP 1. Already simplified

STEP 2. Variable already on left side

STEP 3. $\quad 3x + \underbrace{7 - 7}_{0} = 13 - 7$

$\quad\quad\quad\quad 3x = 6$

STEP 4. $\quad\quad\quad\quad \dfrac{3x}{3} = \dfrac{6}{3}$

$\quad\quad\quad\quad\quad x = 2$

Example 2: $3(x - 2) + 18 = 6 + 2(x + 6)$

STEP 1. $\quad\quad\quad 3x - 6 + 18 = 6 + 2x + 12$

$\quad\quad\quad\quad\quad 3x + 12 = 2x + 18$

STEP 2. $\quad\quad \underbrace{3x - 2x}_{x} + 12 = \underbrace{2x - 2x}_{0} + 18$

$\quad\quad\quad\quad\quad x + 12 = 18$

STEP 3. $\quad\quad x + \underbrace{12 - 12}_{0} = 18 - 12$

$\quad\quad\quad\quad\quad\quad x = 6$

EXERCISE 10: SOLVING MULTI-STEP EQUATIONS

Directions: Solve the following equations.

1. $3x + 9 = 15$

2. $2x - 26 = 2$

3. $\frac{x}{3} + 4 = 9$

4. $\frac{4x}{3} - 14 = 14$

5. $8(x - 4) = 0$

6. $2(5x - 11) + 12x = 0$

Answers are on page 732.

Translating in Multi-Step Problems

To set up a multi-step problem, we have to translate from English to algebra.

Remember to check your answer to see if it satisfies the original problem.

Example: Tony worked 35 hours last week and only a few hours this week. He makes $9 per hour, and his paycheck for the two weeks is $477 before deductions. How many hours did he work this week?

STEP 1. Let x be the number of hours he worked this week.

STEP 2. $x + 35$ is the total number of hours worked during both weeks.

$9(x + 35)$ is the amount of money he is paid for working

$x + 35$ hours at $9 per hour.

STEP 3. $9(x + 35) = 477$ (The amount of money he is paid equals $477.)

STEP 4. $\quad\quad 9(x + 35) = 477$

$\quad\quad\quad 9x + 315 = 477$

$\quad 9x + \underbrace{315 - 315}_{0} = 477 - 315$

$\quad\quad\quad\quad\quad 9x = 162$

$\quad\quad\quad\quad\quad \dfrac{9x}{9} = \dfrac{162}{9}$

$\quad\quad\quad\quad\quad\quad x = 18 \text{ hours this week}$

EXERCISE 11: SETTING UP AND SOLVING MULTI-STEP EQUATIONS

Directions: Solve each problem.

Questions 1 and 2 are based on the following information.

Oscar went on a ski trip for 3 days and 3 nights. His chalet cost him $32 a night, and he paid for a lift ticket each day. His total bill was $123. Find the cost of the daily lift ticket, x.

1. Which equation best describes the problem?

    (1) $x + 96 = 123$
    (2) $3x + 32 = 123$
    (3) $x + 32 = 123$
    (4) $3(x + 32) = 123$
    (5) not enough information is given

2. What is the cost of the daily lift ticket?

    (1) $ 9
    (2) $27
    (3) $30.33
    (4) $41
    (5) $91

Questions 3 and 4 are based on the following information.

The perimeter of a triangle is 56 inches. If one side is 24 inches and the other two sides have the same measure, find the length, x, of one of these two sides.

3. Which equation best describes the problem above?

    (1) $x + 24 = 56$
    (2) $2x + 56 = 24$
    (3) $2x - 24 = 56$
    (4) $2x + 24 = 56$
    (5) $x - 24 = 56$

4. What is the length of one of the two equal sides?

    (1) 16
    (2) 32
    (3) 40
    (4) 80
    (5) 160

Questions 5 and 6 are based on the following information.

Nick's age is six years less than twice Tom's age, x. The sum of their two ages is 42. Find Tom's age.

5. Which equation best describes the problem above?

    (1) $2x - 6 = 42$
    (2) $x - 6 = 42$
    (3) $x + 2x = 42$
    (4) $(2x - 6) + x = 42$
    (5) not enough information is given

6. What is Tom's age?

    (1) 14
    (2) 16
    (3) 18
    (4) 24
    (5) not enough information is given

Questions 7 and 8 are based on the following information.

Eric purchased a new car for $10,200. He made a $4800 down payment and agreed to pay the balance in 36 equal monthly payments. How much will he pay each month?

7. Which equation best describes the problem above? Let x be the amount of the monthly payment.

    (1) $36x = 10,200$
    (2) $36x = 4800$
    (3) $36x - 4800 = 10,200$
    (4) $4800 - 36x = 10,200$
    (5) $4800 + 36x = 10,200$

8. How much will Eric pay each month?

    (1) $133.33
    (2) $150.00
    (3) $283.33
    (4) $416.67
    (5) $450.00

Questions 9 and 10 are based on the following information.

Twice as many adult tickets for a soccer game were sold as children's tickets. Also, some of the tickets were given free of charge to contest winners. The attendance at the game was 8324 people. How many tickets of each type were sold?

9. Which equation best describes the problem above? Let x be the number of children's tickets sold.

(1) $x + 2x = 8324$
(2) $x - 2x = 8324$
(3) $2(x + 2) = 8324$
(4) $2(x - 2) = 8324$
(5) not enough information is given

10. How many adult tickets were sold?

(1) 2770
(2) 2775
(3) 2780
(4) 4155
(5) not enough information is given

Answers are on page 732.

Signed Numbers

Number Line

The **number line**, shown below, represents all of the real numbers that we use. In algebra, we use zero and the numbers greater than zero, called the **positive numbers**, but we also use the numbers less than zero, called the **negative numbers**. Signed numbers include all positive numbers, zero, and all negative numbers.

Negative numbers Zero Positive numbers

Positive numbers have a plus sign in front of them, like +7, or no sign in front, like 8. Negative numbers have a minus sign in front of them, like −2 (read as "negative two"). The graph of a signed number is a dot on the number line. On the number line below, we see the graph of −3.5, −1, and 3.

We can use the number line to show the relationship among signed numbers. A number to the right of another number is greater than (>) the other number. A number to the left of another number is less than (<) the other number.

▶ **TIP:** The symbols < and > always point to the smaller number.

 $$1 > -3$$

1 is greater than −3 because it is to the right of −3 on the number line.

 $$-2.5 > -6$$

−2.5 is greater than −6 because it is to the right of −6.

 $$-3\frac{1}{2} < -\frac{1}{2}$$

$-3\frac{1}{2}$ is less than $-\frac{1}{2}$ because it is to the left of $-\frac{1}{2}$.

EXERCISE 12: NUMBER LINE

Directions: Identify the relationships between the numbers graphed below.

1.

3.

2.

4.

Answers are on page 732.

Absolute Values

The *absolute value* is the distance on the number line between zero and the number. Since distance is always a positive value, the absolute value of a number is always positive or zero. The symbol for absolute value is $|\quad|$.

$|7| = 7$ The absolute value of 7 is 7.

$|-2| = 2$ The absolute value of -2 is 2.

▶ **TIP:** The absolute value of a positive number is the same positive number. The absolute value of a negative number is the same number but with a positive sign. The absolute value of zero is zero.

EXERCISE 13: SIGNED NUMBERS

Directions: Solve each problem. For questions 1–5, represent the quantities with either positive or negative numbers.

1. a loss of $12

2. a temperature 15° below zero Fahrenheit

3. a three-yard loss on the second down of a football game

4. a credit of $75 on your credit card

5. a stock rise of $4\frac{1}{2}$ points for the week

For questions 6–11, place the correct symbol, $<$ or $>$, between the pairs of numbers.

6. 7   11

7. -9 -4

8. -3 1

9. 0 -4

10. -6 2.4

11. $-\frac{1}{4}$ $-\frac{1}{2}$

For questions 12–15, find the values.

12. $|9|$

13. $\left|-\frac{1}{2}\right|$

14. $\left|2\frac{1}{3}\right|$

15. $|-3|$

Answers are on page 732.

Operations with Signed Numbers

Signed numbers can be added, subtracted, multiplied, and divided. Let's use a personal financial situation to understand these operations with signed numbers.

Todd has a part-time job while attending the technical institute. In the month of April, he earns $132, $120, $180, $49, $68, and $75. (These are all positive values.) His total earnings are $624. When we combine all the positive numbers, we get a larger positive number.

During the month of April, Todd pays the following bills: car insurance, $185; gas, $78; lunches, $60; and room and board, $250. (These are all negative values.) His total expenses are $573. When we combine all his bills, we get a larger negative number (which can be written −$573).

To find out how much money Todd has left at the end of April, we have to find the difference between his income (the positive total) and his expenses (the negative total). If his income is larger, he'll have a positive amount left (profit). If his expenses are larger than his income, he'll be in a negative situation. (He'll owe money.) The difference between +624 and −573 is +51. Todd has a profit of $51.

Combining Signed Numbers

The first two rules about combining signed numbers are the same as what we just used to understand Todd's financial situation.

> If the numbers being combined are *all positive* or *all negative*, add the numbers and keep the same sign.

Both positive   Both negative

$+8 + 7 = +15$ $-8 - 7 = -15$

> If two numbers being combined are *opposite* in sign, subtract the numbers and use the sign from the number with the larger absolute value.

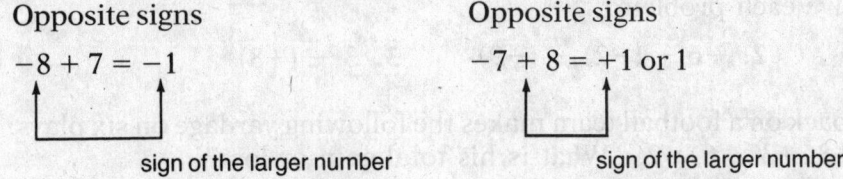

Opposite signs   Opposite signs

$-8 + 7 = -1$ $-7 + 8 = +1$ or 1

sign of the larger number   sign of the larger number

The next problem contains several numbers. Some of them are positive, and some of them are negative. We'll use both rules to come up with the answer.

Example: $-6 + 1 + 14 - 2 - 8 + 6 - 9$

First, combine the positive numbers. $1 + 14 + 6 = 21$

Then, combine the negative numbers. $-6 - 2 - 8 - 9 = -25$

The difference between 21 and −25 is 4.

The absolute value of −25 (the negative number) is larger, so the answer is −4.

EXERCISE 14: COMBINING SIGNED NUMBERS

Directions: Solve each problem.

1. $7 + 8$	**4.** $6 - 8$	**7.** $140 - 236$	**10.** $-5 - 7 - 1 - 6$
2. $-3 + 2$	**5.** $-3 - 2$	**8.** $-12 + 6 + 3$	**11.** $5.2 - 6.7 + 5.3$
3. $-9 - 8$	**6.** $-127 + 94$	**9.** $16 + 23 - 4$	**12.** $-4.5 - 3.2$

Answers are on page 732.

Eliminating Double Signs

Sometimes, we encounter a number that has two signs in front of it. We always want to *eliminate* double signs. There are two rules for doing this:

ELIMINATING DOUBLE SIGNS

1. If the double signs are the same, replace them with +.

   Examples: $+ (+3) = +3$

   $- (-8) = +8$

   $-4 - (-12) = -4 \underbrace{- (-12)}_{\text{same}} = -4 + 12 = +8$

   (*Note:* a minus sign [−] changes the sign of the negative following number to a positive number [+] as in the last two examples above.)

2. If the double signs are opposite, replace them with −.

   Examples: $+ (-4) = -4$

   $- (+2) = -2$

   $5 + (-7) = \underbrace{5 + (-7)}_{\text{opposite}} = 5 - 7 = -2$

EXERCISE 15: ELIMINATING DOUBLE SIGNS

Directions: Solve each problem.

1. $-6 - (-2)$ **2.** $-6 + (-2) - (-9)$ **3.** $3 - (+8)$

4. A running back on a football team makes the following yardage on six plays: $+23, -4, +8, +3, -6, -2$. What is his total gain or loss?

5. What is his average yardage per play in question 5?

6. What is the drop in temperature if the thermometer goes from 12°F to −7°F?

7. At Arlington Park Race Track, Larry had $140 to begin the day. On the first race, he won $56; on the second race, he lost $14; on the third race, he lost $32; on the fourth race, he lost $18; on the fifth race, he won $26. How much money did he have at the end of the 5 races?

Answers are on page 732.

Multiplying and Dividing Signed Numbers

Let's return to Todd and his finances to understand the multiplication and division of signed numbers. If Todd earns $3 per hour and works 7 hours, then he earns 7 × $3, or $21. A positive number $3 times a positive number 7 is 7 × 3 = 21.

If Todd had to pay $3 per day for the past seven days, how much *more* money did he have seven days *ago*? He had $21 *more* dollars 7 days ago than he does now. (−7)(−3) = 21 equals a positive number, $21.

Suppose Todd spends $3 each day for lunch. How much does he spend in 7 days? The money *spent* (−3) times the number of days (7) equals −$21. The rules below for multiplying and dividing signed numbers will help you solve problems like those related to Todd's financial situation.

1. If the two numbers being multiplied or divided *have the same sign*

   a. Multiply or divide.

   b. Make the answer *positive*.

Both positive	*Both negative*
8(7) = 56	−8(−7) = 56
26 ÷ 2 = 13	−32 ÷ −16 = 2

2. If the two numbers being multiplied or divided are *opposite* in sign

   a. Multiply or divide.

   b. Make the answer *negative*.

Opposite in sign	*Opposite in sign*
−7(8) = −56	8(−7) = −56
$\dfrac{-48}{12} = -4$	$\dfrac{-56}{7} = -8$

MULTIPLYING AND DIVIDING SIGNED NUMBERS

1. When you are multiplying or dividing two numbers with the *same* sign, the answer is *positive*.

2. When you are multiplying or dividing two numbers with *opposite* signs, the answer is *negative*.

When multiplying a string of signed numbers, you may count the number of negative signs to determine whether the answer is positive or negative.

a. Even number of negative signs: answer is positive.

b. Odd number of negative signs: answer is negative.

Example 1: (−3) (−2) (−1) (−5) = 30   (4 negative signs, EVEN: answer is +)

$$(+6) \quad (+5)$$

$$(+30)$$

Example 2: $(-1)(-5)(-4) = -20$ (3 negative signs, ODD: answer is −)

(5)

-20

EXERCISE 16: MULTIPLYING AND DIVIDING SIGNED NUMBERS

Directions: Solve each problem.

1. $(8)(5)$ 4. $-22(4)$ 7. $(-6)(-7)(-2)$ 10. $\dfrac{-48}{-16}$

2. $12(-12)$ 5. $-15(-15)$ 8. $-8(5)(0)$ 11. $\dfrac{56}{-14}$

3. $-5(6)$ 6. $(-9)(-4)$ 9. $-25/5$ 12. $\dfrac{-50}{-10}$

13. The stock fell $\frac{3}{8}$ point for each day for four consecutive days. What was the total drop for the stock?

14. A-One Sales bought 9 car telephones at a cost of $2476 each. How much does the company owe for the telephones? (Express the answer as a negative number.)

Answers are on page 733.

Inequalities

The relationship between two things is not always equal, so we cannot always use an equation to solve a problem. If the relationship is not equal, we can use *inequalities* such as < (is less than) or > (is greater than) to solve the problem. For example, $x + 3 > 10$ is an algebraic inequality. What value of x would make this a true statement? Several values of x would make this statement true. The letter x could be 8 because $8 + 3 > 10$. It could be 25 because $25 + 3 > 10$. In fact, x could be any number larger than 7. Our solution is $x > 7$.

When you solve any inequality, the set of possible solutions is often infinite. You must be aware of the boundary of the solution. In this case, the boundary is 7; x cannot be 7, but it can be any number larger than 7.

Solving Inequalities

The algebraic methods for solving an inequality are much the same as for algebraic equations.

SOLVING INEQUALITIES

1. Keep the inequality in balance. Whatever operation you perform on one side of the inequality, perform on the other.

2. Concentrate on the variable. Your goal is to get the variable on one side of the equation.

3. Perform the opposite operation. First, do addition or subtraction; then, do multiplication or division.

Example 1: $x + 3 > 10$
Look at x. It is added to 3. Subtract 3 from both sides.
The inequality is solved (x is all by itself on the left
side of the inequality).

$$x + 3 > 10$$
$$\underbrace{x + 3 - 3}_{0} > 10 - 3$$
$$x > 7$$

Check: Choose any number greater than 7. Let's
choose 9.

$$x + 3 > 10$$
$$9 + 3 > 10$$
$$12 > 10$$

There is one major rule that you must keep in mind when solving an inequality.

> When you multiply or divide both sides of an inequality by a negative number,
> it changes the direction of the inequality sign.

For example, we know that
$8 < 12$.

$$8 < 12$$

If we multiply both sides by
-2, we get $8(-2)$, which is
-16, and $12(-2)$, which is
-24. You know that -16 is
greater than -24. So the
answer is

$$8(-2) > 12(-2)$$

Notice that the arrow changed
direction from less than to greater
than.

$$-16 > -24$$

Example 2: $-4x < 12$

$$-4x < 12$$

Divide both sides by -4.
Notice that you are dividing
by a *negative number*, so
change the direction of the
inequality sign.

$$\frac{-4x}{-4} > \frac{12}{-4}$$
$$x > -3$$

Check: Choose any number
greater than -3.
Let's choose 0.

$$-4x < 12$$
$$-4(0) < 12$$
$$0 < 12$$

Sometimes, you may see the signs $\leq$ and $\geq$. These mean "less than or equal
to" and "more than or equal to," respectively. So, if an answer is $x \geq 3$, this means
that the answer is 3 or a number larger than 3.

EXERCISE 17: ONE-STEP INEQUALITIES

Directions: Solve for x. Check your answers.

1. $x - 3 > -5$
2. $5 + x < 7$
3. $-3 + x < -10$
4. $\frac{x}{-3} < 12$
5. $x - 5 \geq -1$
6. $-4x > 8$
7. $x - 7 \leq 0$
8. $70 > 5x$
9. $-4x > -16$

Answers are on page 733.

Factoring

Some problems require factoring algebraic expressions. To *factor* means to find and separate numbers that have been multiplied. An example from arithmetic helps to explain factoring. There are two ways to multiply to get the number 15: $3 \times 5 = 15$ and $15 \times 1 = 15$. We can say that 3 and 5 are factors of 15 and that 1 and 15 are also factors of 15. The factors are the numbers that were multiplied.

Factoring is the process of looking for the factors in a multiplication problem. This process can be used to solve some types of equations and to simplify some expressions. As with arithmetic, an algebraic expression is the answer to a multiplication problem. We must determine what expressions were multiplied to get that answer.

Multiplying Algebraic Expressions

Algebraic expressions can be multiplied together. An algebraic expression may consist of a number (coefficient), a letter (variable), and an exponent. Remember, an exponent is a small raised number to the right of the variable.

When we multiply variables with exponents, the base must be the same. For example, x^2, x^3, and x^5 all have the same base, x. However, x^2 and y^3 have different bases; they are x and y.

MULTIPLYING VARIABLES WITH EXPONENTS

1. Keep the same base.
2. Add the exponents.

Examples: $x^2 \cdot x^3 = x^{2+3} = x^5$ $x^2 y^3 \cdot x^4 y^5 = x^{2+4} \cdot y^{3+5} = x^6 y^8$

$y^4 \cdot y^7 = y^{4+7} = y^{11}$ $x \cdot x^3 = x^1 \cdot x^3 = x^{1+3} = x^4$

▶ **TIP:** The last example shows that the letter x alone is understood to have an exponent of 1. Although no number is written in front of the variables above, the number 1 is understood to be there. The examples below show what you do when there are coefficients in front of the variables.

ONE TERM TIMES ONE TERM

1. Multiply the coefficients.
2. Multiply the variables—keep the same base and add the exponents.

Examples: $4x \cdot 7x^2 = 4 \cdot 7 \cdot x^1 \cdot x^2 = 28x^{1+2} = 28x^3$

$-3y^2 \cdot 5xy = -3 \cdot 5 \cdot x^1 \cdot y^2 \cdot y^1 = -15x \cdot y^{2+1} = -15xy^3$

ONE TERM TIMES AN EXPRESSION OF TWO OR MORE TERMS

Distribute the multiplication over the expression by multiplying each term.

Examples:

$$5x(2x + 3) = 5x \cdot 2x + 5x \cdot 3$$
$$= 10x^2 + 15x$$

$$-x(2x^2 + 3x - 7) = -x \cdot 2x^2 - x \cdot 3x - x(-7)$$
$$= -2x^3 - 3x^2 + 7x$$

EXERCISE 18: MULTIPLYING ALGEBRAIC EXPRESSIONS

Directions: Solve each problem.

1. $8x \cdot 3x^2$

2. $7xy(-4x)$

3. $(-6ab^2)(3a^2)$

4. $(-5x^2y)(3xy^2)$

5. $2x(x^2 + 1)$

6. $3y(2y^2 - 4y - 7)$

Answers are on page 733.

Finding the Greatest Common Factor

The expression $2x + 10$ has two terms, $2x$ and 10. To factor $2x + 10$, look for the largest number that is a factor of both $2x$ and 10. $2x = 2 \cdot x$ $10 = 5 \cdot 2$

Therefore, 2 is a common factor of both $2x$ and 10. In factored form, we write $2x + 10 = 2(x + 5)$.

Example 1: Factor $7x^2 + 14x$

STEP 1. Look for the common factors.
7 and x are common factors in both terms.

$$7x^2 \quad + \quad 14x$$
$$\boxed{7} \cdot \boxed{x} \cdot x + 2 \cdot \boxed{7} \cdot \boxed{x}$$

STEP 2. Write the common factors in front of the rest of the expression.

$$7x(x + 2)$$

To check this factored expression, multiply $7x$ by $x + 2$ to be sure the result is $7x^2 + 14x$. $7x(x + 2) = 7x^2 + 14x$

Example 2: Factor $65y^3 - 35y^2 + 15y$

The greatest common factor for the terms of this expression is $5y$.

$$65y^3 - 35y^2 + 15y =$$
$$\boxed{5y} \cdot 13y^2 + \boxed{5y} \cdot -7y + \boxed{5y} \cdot 3 =$$
$$5y(13y^2 - 7y + 3)$$

Example 3: Factor $3x^2 + x$

The greatest common factor for the terms of this expression is x.

Note that 1 is a factor of x; x means "1 times x." So if you can't factor a variable any other way, show it as 1 times the variable.

$$3x^2 + x =$$
$$3x(x) + 1(x) =$$
$$x(3x + 1)$$

EXERCISE 19: THE GREATEST COMMON FACTOR

Directions: Write each expression in factored form.

1. $21x^3 - 14x^2$

2. $100a^4 - 16a^2$

3. $121p^5 - 33p^4$

4. $8x^2 - 4$

5. $9x^3y^2 + 36x^2y^3$

6. $100x^5 - 50x^3 + 100x^2$

7. $5x^4 + 25x^3 - 20x^2$

8. $9x^3 - 9x$

Answers are on page 733.

Factoring by Grouping

In an expression of four or more terms, we can use the method of factoring by grouping to factor the expression. We generally separate the four terms of the expression into pairs of terms. Then we factor out the common factor from each pair. If possible, factor the common factor from the results.

Example 1: $x^2 + 5x + 2x + 10$

STEP 1. Separate into pairs of terms. $\boxed{x^2 + 5x} + \boxed{2x + 10}$

STEP 2. Factor each pair. $x(x + 5) + 2(x + 5)$

STEP 3. Put the common factor $(x + 5)$ in front. $(x + 5)(x + 2)$

Example 2: $2y^2 - 8y + 3y - 12$

STEP 1. $\boxed{2y^2 - 8y} + \boxed{3y - 12}$

STEP 2. $2y(y - 4) + 3(y - 4)$

STEP 3. $(y - 4)(2y + 3)$

FACTORING BY GROUPING

1. Separate the four terms into pairs that have common factors.

2. Factor out the common factor from each pair of terms.

3. Put the common factor in front of the other factors.

EXERCISE 20: FACTORING BY GROUPING

Directions: Use grouping to factor the following expressions.

1. $x^2 + 4x + 3x + 12$

2. $x^2 - 2x + 5x - 10$

3. $8y^2 + 6yz + 12yz + 9z^2$

4. $2xy^2 - 8y^2 + x - 4$

Answers are on page 733.

Graphing

In Chapter 7, we saw how graphs can be used to display data visually. Graphs can also be used to represent an equation.

Rectangular Coordinates

To understand the graph of an equation, we must first learn how points are plotted on a grid. The grid is called a **rectangular coordinate plane**. A horizontal number line called the **x-axis** and a vertical number line called the **y-axis** intersect at a point called the **origin**.

Each point that is graphed is identified by an **ordered pair** of numbers (x,y). The first number in the ordered pair is called the **x-coordinate**, and the second number is called the **y-coordinate**. The order of the coordinates is very important. The x-coordinate is always given first in the ordered pair, and the y-coordinate is always given second.

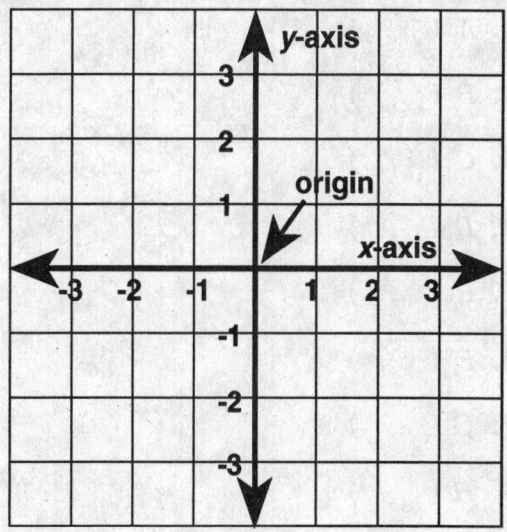

PLOTTING A POINT WITH THE COORDINATES (x, y)

1. Start at the origin (0,0).

2. If x is positive, move x units to the right.
   If x is negative, move x units to the left.
   If x is 0, make no move.

3. If y is positive, move y units upward.
   If y is negative, move y units downward.
   If y is 0, make no move.

4. Place a point at the location and label it with the positive or negative numbers of the ordered pair (x,y).

Example 1: Plot the point (3,4).

Start at the origin.

x is 3 → move 3 units right.

y is 4 → move 4 units up.

Example 2: Plot the point (−3,5).

Start at the origin.

x is −3 → move 3 units left.

y is 5 → move 5 units up.

EXERCISE 21: ORDERED PAIRS

Directions: Label the ordered pairs given below.

1. *A* (,   )

2. *B* (,   )

3. *C* (,   )

4. *D* (,   )

5. *E* (,   )

6. *F* (,   )

7. *G* (,   )

8. *H* (,   )

9. *I* (,   )

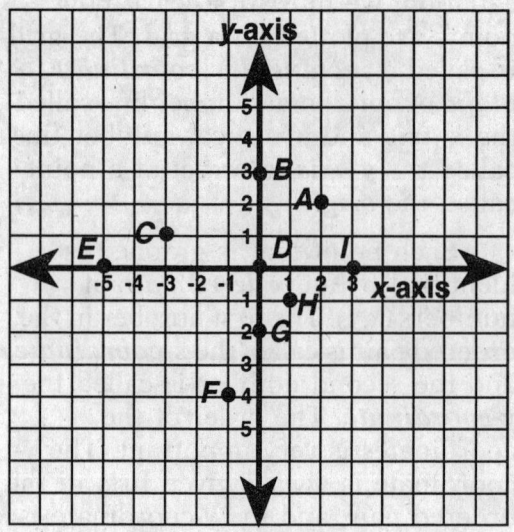

Answers are on page 734.

Distance Between Two Points

There are two methods of finding the distance between two points on a graph. If the two points are on the same horizontal line or the same vertical line, we can simply count the units between the two points.

Counting

To find the distance between point *C* and point *A* as shown at right, count the units from *C* to *A*. The distance is 10 units.

To find the distance between point *A* and point *B* as shown at right, count the units from *A* to *B*. The distance is 7 units.

Using a Formula

The second method of finding the distance between two points uses the formula $d = \sqrt{(x_2 - x_1)^2 + (y_2 - y_1)^2}$ for the two points. You will not need to memorize this formula; it will be on the formulas page of the Mathematics Test. We can use this formula to find the distance between *any* two points, whether or not they are on the same horizontal or vertical line.

In the formula, x_1 is the x-coordinate of one graphed point and x_2 is the x-coordinate of the other. Similarly, y_1 is the y-coordinate of the first graphed point and y_2 is the y-coordinate of the other. So, in the coordinates $(4,2)$ and $(3,-3)$

$$x_1 = 4 \qquad y_1 = 2$$
$$\text{and}$$
$$x_2 = 3 \qquad y_2 = -3$$

Using the figure at right, look at the next examples, which use the distance formula to find the distance between two points.

Example 1: Find the distance from A to B.

Point A is $(-4,5)$. Let that be (x_1,y_1). So $x_1 = -4$ and $y_1 = 5$. Point B is $(2,3)$. Let that be (x_2,y_2). So $x_2 = 2$ and $y_2 = 3$.

$$d = \sqrt{(x_2 - x_1)^2 + (y_2 - y_1)^2}$$
$$= \sqrt{(2 - (-4))^2 + (3 - 5)^2}$$
$$= \sqrt{6^2 + (-2)^2}$$
$$= \sqrt{36 + 4}$$
$$d = \sqrt{40}$$

Simplify $\sqrt{40}$ to $\sqrt{4 \cdot 10} = 2\sqrt{10}$

Example 2: Find the distance from D to E.

Let $(x_1,y_1) = (0,0)$ and $(x_2,y_2) = (3,-4)$.

$$d = \sqrt{(x_2 - x_1)^2 + (y_2 - y_1)^2}$$
$$= \sqrt{(3 - 0)^2 + (-4 - 0)^2}$$
$$= \sqrt{3^2 + (-4)^2}$$
$$= \sqrt{9 + 16}$$
$$= \sqrt{25}$$
$$d = 5$$

▶ **TIP:** Use the distance formula only if the points are not on a horizontal or vertical line. If the points are on the same horizontal or vertical line, simply count the units between them.

EXERCISE 22: DISTANCE BY COUNTING

Directions: Find the distance
between the following points.

1. *A* to *B* _____

2. *C* to *D* _____

3. *C* to *F* _____

4. *E* to *B* _____

5. *D* to *E* _____

Answers are on page 734.

EXERCISE 23: DISTANCE BETWEEN TWO POINTS

Directions: Use the graph below to find the distances indicated.

1. *I* to *J*

2. *C* to *D*

3. *E* to *F*

4. *G* to *H*

5. *x*-axis to *B*

Answers are on page 734.

The Slope of a Line

An equation whose graph is a straight line has a special number associated with the line. This number is called the **slope** of the line. The slope is actually the ratio of the change in *y*-values to the change in *x*-values as we go from point to point on the line.

Look at the graph of the line $2x - 3y = 6$.

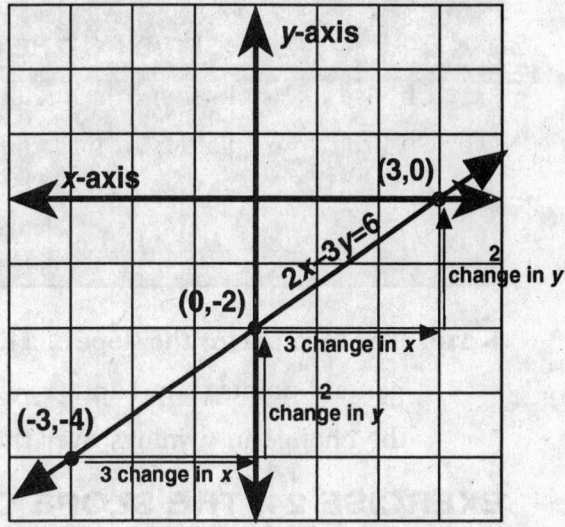

As we go from $(-3,-4)$ to $(0,-2)$, there is a 2-unit change in the y values at the same time there is a 3-unit change in the x values.

The slope then is

$$\frac{\text{change in } y}{\text{change in } x} = \frac{2}{3}$$

Example 1: Find the slope of the line that contains the points $(-6,-3)$ and $(-2,-1)$.

Change in y: $-3 - (-1) = -3 + 1 = -2$

Change in x: $-6 - (-2) = -6 + 2 = -4$

Slope $= \dfrac{\text{change in } y}{\text{change in } x} = \dfrac{-2}{-4} = \dfrac{1}{2}$

The slope is $\frac{1}{2}$. The line has a positive slope and slants upward.

Example 2: Find the slope of the line graphed below.

Change in $y = 6 - 0 = 6$

Change in $x = 0 - 2 = -2$

Slope $= \dfrac{6}{-2} = -3$

The slope is -3. The line has a negative slope and slants downward.

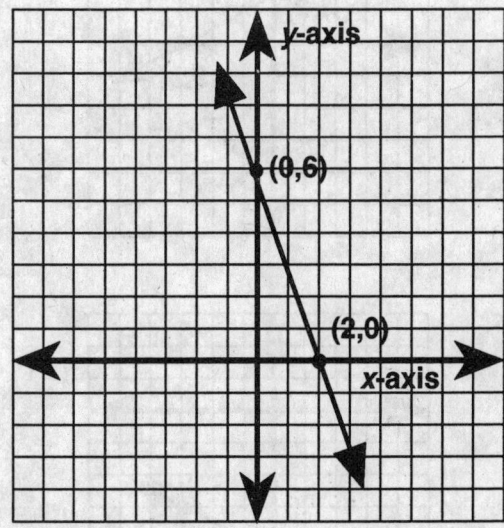

If the slope is a positive number, it represents a line that slants upward from left to right. A line that slants downward is said to have a negative slope. A line that is parallel to the x-axis has a slope of zero. A line that is parallel to the y-axis has no slope.

> ## FINDING THE SLOPE OF A LINE
>
> 1. Choose two points on the line.
> 2. Subtract the y values to find the change in y.
> 3. Subtract the x values to find the change in x.
> 4. Write the slope as the ratio: $\dfrac{\text{change in } y}{\text{change in } x}$

▶ **TIP:** The formula for the slope of a line is given on the formulas page. For two general points (x_1, y_1) and (x_2, y_2), the slope is $\dfrac{y_2 - y_1}{x_2 - x_1}$. This says the slope is the change in y values over the change in x values.

EXERCISE 24: THE SLOPE OF A LINE

Directions: Solve each problem. For questions 1–4, find the slope of the line that contains the two given points.

1. (0,0) and (3,4)   **3.** (−9,3) and (9,3)

2. (−5,−1) and (6,0)   **4.** (−1,−2) and (−2,−1)

For questions 5–8, find the slope of the graphed lines.

5.

7.

6.

8.

Answers are on page 734.

EXERCISE 25: ALGEBRA REVIEW

Directions: Solve each problem.

1. If a $1400 computer decreases in value $120 per year, which expression shows the value at the end of x years?

   (1) $1400 - (120 + x)$
   (2) $1400 - 120x$
   (3) $1400 - x$
   (4) $1400 + 120x$
   (5) $1400 + x$

2. Joe spent one-third of his monthly salary. After he used $70 more, he had spent half of his salary. Choose the equation that represents this information.

   (1) $3x + 70 = 2x$
   (2) $\frac{1}{3}x = 70 \div \frac{1}{2}x$
   (3) $\frac{1}{3}x - 70 = \frac{1}{2}x$
   (4) $\frac{1}{3}x + \frac{1}{2}x = 70$
   (5) $\frac{1}{3}x + 70 = \frac{1}{2}x$

3. Steve, the local handyman, has a board 42 inches long. He wishes to cut it into three pieces so that one piece is six inches longer than the shortest piece and the third piece is twice as long as the shortest piece. How long should the shortest piece be?

   (1) $4\frac{2}{3}$ in

   (2) $5\frac{1}{4}$ in

   (3) 9 in

   (4) $11\frac{1}{3}$ in

   (5) 12 in

4. The perimeter of a rectangle is 78 meters. The length of the rectangle is 5 meters more than the width. If x is the width of the rectangle, which equation below best describes these relationships?

   (1) $x^2 + 5x = 78$
   (2) $2x + 2(x + 5) = 78$
   (3) $2x + 5 = 78$
   (4) $x + 5 = 78$
   (5) not enough information is given

5. On a cold winter morning, the temperature at 3:00 A.M. was −12°, but it went up 25° by 11:00 A.M. At noon it had risen another 7°. What was the temperature at noon?

   (1) 13°
   (2) 20°
   (3) 30°
   (4) 32°
   (5) 44°

6. If six times a number is subtracted from ten times a number, the result is six less than twice the number. Find the number.

   (1) −3
   (2) $-\frac{4}{3}$
   (3) −1
   (4) $\frac{4}{5}$
   (5) 1

7. If an object is thrown straight up with an initial velocity of 128 feet per second, its height after t seconds is $h = 128t - 16t^2$. Find the height of the object after three seconds.

   (1) 240 ft
   (2) 336 ft
   (3) 1104 ft
   (4) 1120 ft
   (5) 3312 ft

8. Find the value of x in the equation $3x + 2(4 - x) = x - (3x + 1) - 3$.

   (1) −4
   (2) −2.5
   (3) −2
   (4) −1
   (5) 4

9. Find the value of x in the inequality $x + 5 < 13$.

   (1) $x > 8$
   (2) $x > \frac{1}{8}$
   (3) $x < 8$
   (4) $x < \frac{1}{8}$
   (5) $x < 0$

10. On a business trip, Margo traveled to her destination at an average speed of 55 mph. Coming home, her average speed was 45 mph, and the trip took two hours longer. How many hours did she travel altogether?

    (1) 9
    (2) 11
    (3) 20
    (4) 405
    (5) 495

11. A football team gained 17 yards and then lost 4 yards on each of the next two plays. On the 4th play, it passed for a gain of 28 yards. What is its total yardage for the four plays?

    (1) 29
    (2) 37
    (3) 41
    (4) 45
    (5) not enough information is given

12. Frank's car gets 24 miles per gallon of gasoline. Which expression below best shows how to find how many gallons he needs for a trip of 672 miles?

    (1) $\frac{24}{x} = 672$

    (2) $\frac{x}{24} = 672$

    (3) $24x = 672$

    (4) $x + 24 = 672$

    (5) $672 - x = 24$

13. Yesterday, you spent twice as much money as you did today. Altogether you spent $48. How much did you spend yesterday?

    (1) $12
    (2) $16
    (3) $24
    (4) $32
    (5) not enough information is given

14. After Pauly bought some cotton material, she found that she had only $\frac{3}{4}$ of what she needed. How many more yards does she need to buy?

    (1) $\frac{1}{4}$

    (2) $\frac{3}{4}$

    (3) 3

    (4) 4

    (5) not enough information is given

15. Find the distance between line *A* and line *B*.

(1) −16
(2) −8
(3) 8
(4) 12
(5) 16

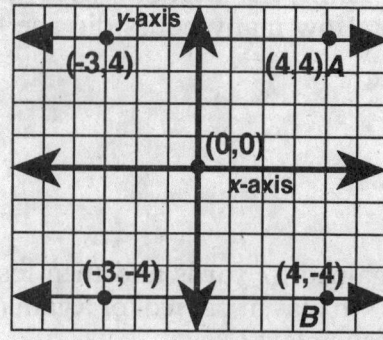

For questions 16 and 17, use the following information.

Foods That Add Calories	
1 slice of cheesecake	+478 calories
1 chocolate sundae	+560 calories
1 soda pop (12 oz)	+105 calories
1 orange juice (8 oz)	+ 96 calories
1 apple (medium)	+ 70 calories
3 chocolate chip cookies	+160 calories

Activities That Take Off Calories	
1 set of tennis	−200 calories
1 hour of swimming	−480 calories
1 mile of walking	−172 calories
1 hour of dancing	−264 calories
1 hour cross-country skiing	−430 calories

16. This afternoon, Fred had a chocolate sundae before playing three sets of tennis. After tennis, he had a glass of orange juice and six cookies. How many calories has he used or gained during the afternoon?

(1) −40 (2) +216 (3) +376 (4) +616 (5) +1416

17. How many miles would you need to walk to work off a slice of cheesecake and two 12-ounce bottles of soda pop?

(1) 2.4 (2) 2.8 (3) 3.4 (4) 4 (5) not enough information is given

18. The slope of the line that contains the points (−4,3) and (5,2) is

(1) $-\frac{1}{9}$ (2) $\frac{1}{9}$ (3) $\frac{1}{5}$ (4) 5 (5) 9

Answers are on page 734.

FORMULAS

Description	Formula
AREA (A) of a:	
square	$A = s^2$ where s = side
rectangle	$A = lw$ where l = length, w = width
parallelogram	$A = bh$ where b = base, h = height
triangle	$A = \frac{1}{2}bh$ where b = base, h = height
circle	$A = \pi r^2$ where $\pi \cong 3.14$, r = radius
PERIMETER (P) of a:	
square	$P = 4s$ where s = side
rectangle	$P = 2l + 2w$ where l = length, w = width
triangle	$P = a + b + c$ where a, b, and c are the sides
circle—circumference (C)	$C = \pi d$ where $\pi \cong 3.14$, d = diameter
VOLUME (V) of a:	
cube	$V = s^3$ where s = side
rectangular container	$V = lwh$ where l = length, w = width, h = height
cylinder	$V = \pi r^2 h$ where $\pi \cong 3.14$, r = radius, h = height
Pythagorean theorem	$c^2 = a^2 + b^2$ where c = hypotenuse, a and b are legs of a right triangle
distance (d) between two points in a plane	$d = \sqrt{(x_2 - x_1)^2 + (y_2 - y_1)^2}$ where (x_1, y_1) and (x_2, y_2) are two points in a plane
slope of a line (m)	$m = \frac{y_2 - y_1}{x_2 - x_1}$ where (x_1, y_1) and (x_2, y_2) are two points in a plane
mean	$mean = \dfrac{x_1 + x_2 + \ldots + x_n}{n}$ where the xs are the values for which a mean is desired and n = number of values in the series
median	$median$ = the point in an ordered set of numbers at which half of the numbers are above and half of the numbers are below this value.
simple interest (i)	$i = prt$ where p = principal, r = rate, t = time
distance (d) as function of rate and time	$d = rt$ where r = rate, t = time
total cost (c)	$c = nr$ where n = number of units, r = cost per unit

TEST 5: MATHEMATICS ANSWER KEY

CHAPTER 1: WHOLE NUMBERS AND PROBLEM SOLVING

Exercise 1: Whole Numbers
page 560

Exact anwers:

1. 10,842

```
    1 1 2
    9873
     412
     509
  +   48
  ─────────
  10,842
```

2. 2944

```
    29 9 10
    3̶0̶0̶0̶
  -    56
  ─────────
     2944
```

3. 1177

```
    1 16 16
    1 2̶7̶6̶
  -     99
  ─────────
     1 1 7 7
```

4. 8265

```
        6
        3
       87
     × 95
  ─────────
      435
      783
  ─────────
     8265
```

5. 12,596

```
       2 3
       4 5
      268
     × 47
  ─────────
    1 876
   10 72
  ─────────
   12,596
```

6. 627

```
         627
    9) 5643
       54
       ──
        24
        18
        ──
        63
        63
        ──
         0
```

7. 268 r1

```
         268 r1
    15) 4021
        30
        ──
        102
         90
        ───
        121
        120
        ───
          1
```

8. 501

```
          501
    72) 36,072
        36 0
        ────
          72
          72
          ──
           0
```

Exercise 2: Understanding the Question and Selecting Information
pages 562–563

1. *Question:* How much did Dave make altogether?
   Information: 8 hours and 2 hours overtime; $10.00 per hour and $15.00 per hour for overtime.

2. *Question:* How much did her monthly payments total?
   Information: $48; 30 months. You don't need her down payment.

3. *Question:* How much was she charged?
   Information: N; you do not have enough information because you don't know how much the third box weighs.

4. *Question:* How much does Bensenville spend on public health?
   Information: N; you do not have enough information because you don't know how much Bensenville spends on highway construction.

5. *Question:* How many voters are men?
   Information: 7,000 registered voters; 3,000 women. You don't need to know the total population of 12,000 to answer the question.

Exercise 3: Choosing the Operation
page 564

1. **Divide;** you have to find an average.
2. **Add;** add the new weight and the amount she lost to find her original weight.
3. **Subtract;** you have to find a difference.
4. **Divide;** to find how many times heavier one package is, you divide.
5. **Multiply;** there will be more inches than feet, so you multiply.

Exercise 4: Problem Solving
page 566

1. *Question:* How many miles do you plan to drive?
   Information: 162 miles, 229 miles, 375 miles
   Operation: You need to find the combined amount of miles driven—add.
   Estimation: 150 + 200 + 400 = 750
   Calculation: 162 + 229 + 375 = 766 miles
   Evaluation: It makes sense that the total mileage is more than any one distance. Also, the answer is close to the estimate.

2. *Question:* What amount does each person receive?
   Information: $12,855; 15 people
   Operation: "shared"—divide
   Estimation: $15,000 ÷ 15 = $1000
   Calculation: 12,855 ÷ 15 = $857
   Evaluation: It makes sense that the answer is around but less than the estimate of $1000.

3. *Question:* How much larger is Canada than the United States?
Information: 3,851,809 square miles (Canada); 3,675,633 square miles (U.S.)
Operation: "How much larger"—subtract
Estimation: 3,900,000 − 3,700,000 = 200,000
Calculation: 3,851,809 − 3,675,633 = 176,176 square miles
Evaluation: The answer should be much smaller than the two numbers and close to the estimate.

4. *Question:* What is the cost of 97 TVs?
Information: $325 each; 97 TVs
Operation: from the cost of one to many: multiply
Estimation: $325 × 100 = $32,500
Calculation: 97 × $325 = $31,525
Evaluation: The answer should be almost 100 times $325.

5. *Question:* How much does Marlene pay in estimated tax per year?
Information: $2492 paid each quarter and 4 quarters in a year
Operation: you need to find the amount for all 4 quarters—multiply.
Estimation: $2500 × 4 = $10,000
Calculation: $2492 × 4 = $9968
Evaluation: The answer should be much larger than quarterly tax and close to the estimate.

6. *Question:* How many acres did each child inherit?
Information: 588 acres altogether and 3 children
Operation: The clue word *divided* is provided in the question.
Estimation: 600 ÷ 3 = 200
Calculation: 588 ÷ 3 = 196
Evaluation: The answer should be about a third smaller than the total number of acres.

7. *Question:* How much does he have left each month after paying for rent and food?
Information: $1300 a month in earnings, $345 a month for rent, $90 a week or $360 a month in food.
Operation: How much does he have left means subtract.
Estimation: $1300 − 300 − 400 = $600
Calculation: $1300 − 345 − 360 = $595
Evaluation: The answer should be much smaller than $1300 dollars.

Exercise 5: Word Problems
pages 570–572

1. **(4) $61,920**

$$
\begin{array}{r}
\$5160 \\
\times \quad 12 \\
\hline
10\,320 \\
51\,60 \\
\hline
\$61,920
\end{array}
$$

2. **(2) 6**

$$
\begin{array}{r}
5\text{ r}35 \\
72)\overline{395} \\
360 \\
\hline
35
\end{array}
$$

Because the answer is 5 r35, you will need 6 buses to accommodate the people.

3. **(3) 830**

STEP 1	STEP 2
$ 11 per pair	830 pairs

$$
\begin{array}{r}
500)\overline{5500} \\
500 \\
\hline
500 \\
500 \\
\hline
0
\end{array}
\qquad
\begin{array}{r}
11)\overline{9130} \\
88 \\
\hline
33 \\
33 \\
\hline
00
\end{array}
$$

4. **(5) Edison**

$$
\begin{array}{r}
1846 \\
- 1318 \\
\hline
528
\end{array}
$$

5. **(1) 1865**

STEP 1	STEP 2	STEP 3
1686	1420	9396
1982	1650	− 7531
2234	1847	1865
1648	1296	
+ 1846	+ 1318	
9396	7531	

6. **(1) 373**

$$
\begin{array}{r}
373 \\
5)\overline{1865} \\
15 \\
\hline
36 \\
35 \\
\hline
15 \\
15 \\
\hline
0
\end{array}
$$

7. **(2) 156**

STEP 1	STEP 2
350	1298
375	− 1142
+ 417	156
1142	

8. **(2) $205**

STEP 1	STEP 2	STEP 3	STEP 4
$12,800	$13,490	$12,990	$205
282	− 500	− 3 150	48)9840
252	$12,990	$9 840	96
+ 156			240
$13,490			240
			0

9. **(4) (25 × $23) + $4800** The cost of the jackets is 25 × $23. Add the cost of the suits: (25 × $23) + $4800.

10. **(5) not enough information is given** The problem does not tell how much was put aside to pay expenses.

CHAPTER 2: DECIMALS
Exercise 1: Reading Decimals
page 574

1. .05
2. 6.2
3. 100.002
4. 1032
5. 400.025
6. (a) .7
   (b) 6.032
   (c) 2000.08
   (d) 305.056
   (e) .0065

Exercise 2: Comparing Decimals
page 575

1. (a) .05 (b) 4.10 (c) .7 (d) .51
   (e) 1.033
2. (a) 2.15; 2.105; 1.95
   (b) .0503; .005; .0035
3. 14.003; 14.03; 14.3; 14.3033
4. 4.67; 4.067; 4.0067

Exercise 3: Rounding Decimals
page 576
1. .375 rounds to **.38**
2. 7.58 round to **7.6**
3. $1.298 rounds to **$1.30**
4. 17.124 rounds to **17.12**
5. 8.275 rounds to **8.3**
6. 3.14159 rounds to **3.14**
7. 101.68 rounds to **102**

Exercise 4: Adding and Subtracting Decimals
pages 578–579

1. **145.047**
$$
\begin{array}{r}
12.4 \\
+\,132.647 \\
\hline
145.047
\end{array}
$$

2. **17.91**
$$
\begin{array}{r}
5.9 \\
2.46 \\
6 \\
3.07 \\
+\;.48 \\
\hline
17.91
\end{array}
$$

3. **37.8**
$$
\begin{array}{r}
43.0 \\
-\;5.2 \\
\hline
37.8
\end{array}
$$

4. **78.3**
$$
\begin{array}{r}
85.2 \\
-\;6.9 \\
\hline
78.3
\end{array}
$$

5. **968.749 meters**
$$
\begin{array}{r}
237.42 \\
150.045 \\
186.21 \\
298.674 \\
+\;96.4 \\
\hline
968.749 \text{ meters}
\end{array}
$$

6. **$357.56**

STEP 1
$$
\begin{array}{r}
\$42.87 \\
5.93 \\
10.00 \\
17.48 \\
+\;38.40 \\
\hline
\$114.68
\end{array}
$$

STEP 2
$$
\begin{array}{r}
\$472.24 \\
-\,114.68 \\
\hline
\$357.56
\end{array}
$$

7. **2877.8 miles**
$$
\begin{array}{r}
28,054.1 \\
-\,25,176.3 \\
\hline
2\,877.8 \text{ miles}
\end{array}
$$

8. **(3) $3.55**

STEP 1
$$
\begin{array}{r}
\$4.75 \\
.95 \\
.75 \\
\hline
\$6.45
\end{array}
$$

STEP 2
$$
\begin{array}{r}
\$10.00 \\
-\;6.45 \\
\hline
\$3.55
\end{array}
$$

9. **(2) 1.4**
$$
\begin{array}{r}
104.2° \\
-\,102.8° \\
\hline
1.4°
\end{array}
$$
98.6° is unnecessary information.

10. **(4) .2 + .15** This is the only expression given that you could solve to find out how much wood she cut off.

11. **$102.64**
$$
\begin{array}{r}
\$17.50 \\
4.95 \\
6.00 \\
13.44 \\
+\;60.75 \\
\hline
\$102.64
\end{array}
$$

12. **$265.27**
$$
\begin{array}{r}
\$160 \\
102.64 \\
+\;2.63 \\
\hline
\$265.27
\end{array}
$$

Exercise 5: Multiplying and Dividing Decimals
pages 582–583

1. **.513**
$$
\begin{array}{r}
.342 \\
\times\;1.5 \\
\hline
1710 \\
342 \\
\hline
.5130 = .513
\end{array}
$$

2. **.01564**
$$
\begin{array}{r}
.00034 \\
\times\;46 \\
\hline
00204 \\
00136 \\
\hline
0.01564
\end{array}
$$

3. **.024**
$$
\begin{array}{r}
.03 \\
\times\;.8 \\
\hline
.024
\end{array}
$$

4. **$22.75**
$$
\begin{array}{r}
\$6.50 \\
\times\;3.5 \\
\hline
3\,250 \\
19\,50 \\
\hline
\$22.750 = \$22.75
\end{array}
$$

5. **120.1**
$$
.05\overline{)6.005}
$$
quotient 120.1
$$
\begin{array}{r}
5 \\
\hline
1\,0 \\
1\,0 \\
\hline
0 \\
0 \\
\hline
05 \\
5 \\
\hline
0
\end{array}
$$

6. **.004**
$$
3\overline{)\,.012}
$$
quotient .004
$$
\begin{array}{r}
0 \\
\hline
01 \\
0 \\
\hline
12 \\
12 \\
\hline
0
\end{array}
$$

7. **70**
$$
.04\overline{)2.80}
$$
quotient 70
$$
\begin{array}{r}
2\,8 \\
\hline
00 \\
0 \\
\hline
0
\end{array}
$$

8. **7 00**
$$
.08\overline{)56.00}
$$
quotient 700
$$
\begin{array}{r}
56 \\
\hline
000 \\
00 \\
\hline
0
\end{array}
$$

9. $.38 \times 10 = $ **3.8**
10. $472 \times 10,000 = $ **4,720,000**
11. $.0972 \times 100 = $ **9.72**
12. $.617 \div 10 = $ **.0617**
13. $456.12 \div 100 = $ **4.5612**
14. $57 \div 1000 = $ **.057**
15. **(3)** 7.85×12
16. **(4) $29.00**
$$.29 \times 100 = 29 = \$29.00$$
17. **(3) 5**

STEP 1. 1.5 rooms per hour × 10 hours = 15 rooms per day

STEP 2. 75 rooms ÷ 15 rooms per day = 5 days

18. **(3)** $(3.5 \times 1.19) + (2 \times 2.30)$

Exercise 6: Estimating
page 584
1. *estimate:* $5 + 12 + 75 + 10 + 8 =$ **110 miles**
2. *estimate:* $\$50 - 25 = 25$
   $\$25 - 2.50 =$ **$22.50**
3. *estimate:* $\$9 \times 10 =$ **$90**
4. *estimate:* $36 \div 2 =$ **18**

Exercise 7: Decimal Word Problems
pages 584–586

1. **(2) 3**

$$
\begin{array}{r}
3.75 \\
3.2\,\overline{)12.0\ 00} \\
9\ 6 \\
\overline{2\ 4\ 0} \\
2\ 2\ 4 \\
\overline{1\ 6\ 0} \\
1\ 6\ 0 \\
\overline{0}
\end{array}
$$

   3.75 shelves can be cut, but only 3 *complete* shelves can be cut.

2. **(5) $2677.29**

$$
\begin{array}{r}
\$425.00 \\
485.75 \\
399.87 \\
642.15 \\
+\ 724.52 \\
\hline
\$2677.29
\end{array}
$$

3. **(3) 17.8**

$$
\begin{array}{r}
17.8 \\
140\,\overline{)2492.0} \\
140 \\
\overline{1092} \\
980 \\
\overline{1120} \\
1120 \\
\overline{0}
\end{array}
$$

4. **(3) 8.6408**

$$
\begin{array}{r}
3.086 \\
\times\ \ 2.8 \\
\hline
2\ 4\ 688 \\
6\ 1\ 72 \\
\hline
8.6\ 408
\end{array}
$$

5. **(2) $320.54**

Gross Earnings:	Total Deductions:	Net Pay:
$265.72	$27.03	$434.47
+ 168.75	+ 86.90	− 113.93
$434.47	$113.93	$320.54

6. **(5) not enough information is given**
   You cannot calculate the answer because the problem does not contain the number of hours that employee 24 worked.

7. **(3) $13,448**

   Total Monthly Payments:

$$
\begin{array}{r}
\$207.25 \\
\times\ \ \ \ 48 \\
\hline
1658\ 00 \\
8290\ 0 \\
\hline
9948.00
\end{array}
$$

   Total Cost:

$$
\begin{array}{r}
\$\ 3\ 500 \\
+\ 9\ 948 \\
\hline
\$13,448
\end{array}
$$

8. **(1) $.06**

   .0575 rounds to .06

$$
\begin{array}{r}
12\,\overline{).6900} \\
0 \\
\overline{69} \\
60 \\
\overline{90} \\
84 \\
\overline{60} \\
60 \\
\overline{0}
\end{array}
$$

9. **(2) 16.1**

   Miles Traveled:

$$
\begin{array}{r}
8747.6 \\
-\ 7353.2 \\
\hline
1394.4
\end{array}
$$

   Miles per Gallon:

   16.13 rounds to 16.1

$$
\begin{array}{r}
86.4\,\overline{)1394.4\ 00} \\
864 \\
\overline{530\ 4} \\
518\ 4 \\
\overline{12\ 0\ 0} \\
8\ 6\ 4 \\
\overline{3\ 3\ 60} \\
2\ 5\ 92 \\
\overline{7\ 68}
\end{array}
$$

10. **(3) $5.49**

STEP 1	STEP 2
4.25	5.485 rounds to $5.49
3.80	
5.75	
10.00	
6.00	
3.70	
+ 4.90	
38.40	

$$
\begin{array}{r}
7\,\overline{)38.400} \\
35 \\
\overline{3\ 4} \\
2\ 8 \\
\overline{60} \\
56 \\
\overline{40} \\
35 \\
\overline{5}
\end{array}
$$

CHAPTER 3 FRACTIONS
Exercise 1: Types of Fractions
page 588
1. like fractions and improper fractions
2. mixed numbers
3. improper fractions and unlike fractions
4. unlike fractions and proper fractions
5. proper fractions and unlike fractions

Exercise 2: Raising and Reducing Fractions
page 589
1. (a) $\dfrac{9}{24}$

   (b) $\dfrac{15}{20}$

   (c) $\dfrac{6}{36}$

   (d) $\dfrac{3}{7}\dfrac{(\times 3)}{(\times 3)} = \dfrac{\mathbf{9}}{\mathbf{21}}$

   (e) $\dfrac{6}{7}\dfrac{(\times 4)}{(\times 4)} = \dfrac{\mathbf{24}}{\mathbf{28}}$

   (f) $\dfrac{2}{5}\dfrac{(\times 6)}{(\times 6)} = \dfrac{\mathbf{12}}{\mathbf{30}}$

2. (a) $\frac{3}{4}$

(b) $\frac{3}{4}$

(c) $\frac{1}{3}$

(d) $\frac{40}{50}\begin{smallmatrix}(\div 10)\\(\div 10)\end{smallmatrix} = \frac{4}{5}$

(e) $\frac{24}{36}\begin{smallmatrix}(\div 12)\\(\div 12)\end{smallmatrix} = \frac{2}{3}$

(f) $\frac{30}{42}\begin{smallmatrix}(\div 6)\\(\div 6)\end{smallmatrix} = \frac{5}{7}$

3. (a) $\frac{6}{8}\begin{smallmatrix}(\div 2)\\(\div 2)\end{smallmatrix} = \frac{3}{4}$

(b) $\frac{15}{20}\begin{smallmatrix}(\div 5)\\(\div 5)\end{smallmatrix} = \frac{3}{4}$

(c) $\frac{9}{27}\begin{smallmatrix}(\div 9)\\(\div 9)\end{smallmatrix} = \frac{1}{3}$

(d) $\frac{4}{12}\begin{smallmatrix}(\div 4)\\(\div 4)\end{smallmatrix} = \frac{1}{3}$

(e) $\frac{25}{30}\begin{smallmatrix}(\div 5)\\(\div 5)\end{smallmatrix} = \frac{5}{6}$

Exercise 3: Changing Fractions and Decimals
page 590

1. (a) $\frac{5}{100}\begin{smallmatrix}(\div 5)\\(\div 5)\end{smallmatrix} = \frac{1}{20}$

(b) $\frac{450}{1000}\begin{smallmatrix}(\div 50)\\(\div 50)\end{smallmatrix} = \frac{9}{20}$

(c) $\frac{7}{100}$

(d) $.32 = \frac{32}{100}\begin{smallmatrix}(\div 4)\\(\div 4)\end{smallmatrix} = \frac{8}{25}$

(e) $.005 = \frac{5}{1000}\begin{smallmatrix}(\div 5)\\(\div 5)\end{smallmatrix} = \frac{1}{200}$

(f) $3.1 = 3\frac{1}{10}$

2. (a) $\begin{array}{r} .37 \\ 8\overline{)3.00} \\ 2\ 4 \\ \hline 60 \\ 56 \\ \hline 4 \end{array}$ = $.37\frac{4}{8}$ = $.37\frac{1}{2}$

(b) $\begin{array}{r} .20 \\ 5\overline{)1.00} \\ 1\ 0 \\ \hline 00 \\ 0 \\ \hline 0 \end{array}$ = $.2$

(c) $\begin{array}{r} .44 \\ 9\overline{)4.00} \\ 3\ 6 \\ \hline 40 \\ 36 \\ \hline 4 \end{array}$ = $.44\frac{4}{9}$

(d) $\begin{array}{r} 1.33 \\ 3\overline{)4.00} \\ 3 \\ \hline 1\ 0 \\ 9 \\ \hline 10 \\ 9 \\ \hline 1 \end{array}$ = $1.33\frac{1}{3}$

(e) $\begin{array}{r} 1.66 \\ 3\overline{)5.00} \\ 3 \\ \hline 2\ 0 \\ 1\ 8 \\ \hline 20 \\ 18 \\ \hline 2 \end{array}$ = $1.66\frac{2}{3}$

(f) $\begin{array}{r} .83 \\ 6\overline{)5.00} \\ 4\ 8 \\ \hline 20 \\ 18 \\ \hline 2 \end{array}$ = $.83\frac{2}{6}$ = $.83\frac{1}{3}$

Exercise 4: Changing Improper Fractions and Mixed Numbers
page 591

1. (a) $1\frac{5}{9} = \frac{(1 \times 9) + 5}{9} = \frac{9 + 5}{9} = \frac{14}{9}$

(b) $12\frac{1}{4} = \frac{(12 \times 4) + 1}{4} = \frac{48 + 1}{4} = \frac{49}{4}$

(c) $3\frac{2}{5} = \frac{(3 \times 5) + 2}{5} = \frac{15 + 2}{5} = \frac{17}{5}$

(d) $3\frac{1}{4} = \frac{(3 \times 4) + 1}{4} = \frac{12 + 1}{4} = \frac{13}{4}$

(e) $2\frac{1}{2} = \frac{(2 \times 2) + 1}{2} = \frac{4 + 1}{2} = \frac{5}{2}$

(f) $6\frac{2}{3} = \frac{(6 \times 3) + 2}{3} = \frac{18 + 2}{3} = \frac{20}{3}$

2. (a) $\frac{4}{3} = \begin{array}{r} 1 \\ 3\overline{)4} \\ 3 \\ \hline 1 \end{array} = 1\frac{1}{3}$

(b) $\frac{16}{7} = \begin{array}{r} 2 \\ 7\overline{)16} \\ 14 \\ \hline 2 \end{array} = 2\frac{2}{7}$

(c) $\frac{9}{9} = \begin{array}{r} 1 \\ 9\overline{)9} \\ 9 \\ \hline 0 \end{array} = 1$

(d) $\frac{9}{8} = \begin{array}{r} 1 \\ 8\overline{)9} \\ 8 \\ \hline 1 \end{array} = 1\frac{1}{8}$

(e) $\frac{17}{5} = \begin{array}{r} 3 \\ 5\overline{)17} \\ 15 \\ \hline 2 \end{array} = 3\frac{2}{5}$

(f) $\frac{3}{2} = \begin{array}{r} 1 \\ 2\overline{)3} \\ 2 \\ \hline 1 \end{array} = 1\frac{1}{2}$

Exercise 5: Comparing Numbers page 595

1. (a) $\frac{7}{8} > \frac{3}{5}$ $\frac{7}{8} \frac{(\times 5)}{(\times 5)} = \frac{35}{40}$
$\frac{3}{5} \frac{(\times 8)}{(\times 8)} = \frac{24}{40}$

(b) $\frac{2}{3} > \frac{4}{9}$ $\frac{2}{3} \frac{(\times 3)}{(\times 3)} = \frac{6}{9}$
$\frac{4}{9} = \frac{4}{9}$

(c) $\frac{3}{4} > \frac{3}{10}$ $\frac{3}{10} \frac{(\times 4)}{(\times 4)} = \frac{12}{40}$
$\frac{3}{4} \frac{(\times 10)}{(\times 10)} = \frac{30}{40}$

2. (a) $3 < 8$

(b) $6 > 0$

(c) $\frac{3}{8} > \frac{1}{8}$

(d) $\frac{3}{4} = \frac{9}{12}$
$\frac{2}{3} = \frac{8}{12}$
$\frac{3}{4} > \frac{2}{3}$

(e) $2\frac{3}{8} = \frac{19}{8}$
$\frac{5}{2} = \frac{20}{8}$
$2\frac{3}{8} < \frac{5}{2}$

(f) $\frac{5}{6} = \frac{15}{18}$
$\frac{8}{9} = \frac{16}{18}$
$\frac{5}{6} < \frac{8}{9}$

(g) $.3 = .30$
$\frac{1}{4} = .25$
$.3 > \frac{1}{4}$

(h) $\frac{1}{2} = \frac{6}{12}$
$\frac{6}{12} = \frac{6}{12}$
$\frac{1}{2} = \frac{6}{12}$

(i) $\frac{9}{9} = 1$
$\frac{2}{2} = 1$
$\frac{9}{9} = \frac{2}{2}$

(j) $.07 = .0700$
$.0873 = .0873$
$.07 < .0873$

(k) $\frac{3}{5} = .6$
$.6 = .6$
$\frac{3}{5} = .6$

Exercise 6: Adding and Subtracting Fractions page 597

1. $\frac{2}{3}$ $\frac{\frac{1}{9}}{+\frac{5}{9}}$
$\frac{6}{9} = \frac{2}{3}$

2. $\frac{11}{12}$ $\frac{2}{3} = \frac{8}{12}$
$+\frac{1}{4} = \frac{3}{12}$
$\frac{11}{12}$

3. $\frac{11}{24}$ $\frac{3}{8} = \frac{9}{24}$
$+\frac{1}{12} = \frac{2}{24}$
$\frac{11}{24}$

4. 1 $\frac{5}{6}$
$+\frac{1}{6}$
$\frac{6}{6} = 1$

5. $7\frac{3}{4}$ $1\frac{5}{12}$
$+6\frac{4}{12}$
$7\frac{9}{12} = 7\frac{3}{4}$

6. $7\frac{17}{35}$ $4\frac{1}{5} = 4\frac{7}{35}$
$+3\frac{2}{7} = 3\frac{10}{35}$
$7\frac{17}{35}$

7. $9\frac{1}{3}$ $4\frac{2}{9}$
$+5\frac{1}{9}$
$9\frac{3}{9} = 9\frac{1}{3}$

8. $10\frac{1}{24}$ $3\frac{7}{8} = 3\frac{21}{24}$
$2\frac{5}{6} = 2\frac{20}{24}$
$+3\frac{1}{3} = 3\frac{8}{24}$
$8\frac{49}{24} = 8 + 2\frac{1}{24} = 10\frac{1}{24}$

9. $\frac{3}{5}$ $\frac{9}{10}$
$-\frac{3}{10}$
$\frac{6}{10} = \frac{3}{5}$

10. $\frac{1}{8}$ $\frac{5}{8} = \frac{5}{8}$
$-\frac{1}{2} = \frac{4}{8}$
$\frac{1}{8}$

11. $\frac{3}{10}$ $\frac{4}{5} = \frac{8}{10}$
$-\frac{1}{2} = \frac{5}{10}$
$\frac{3}{10}$

12. $\frac{7}{18}$ $\frac{12}{18}$
$-\frac{5}{18}$
$\frac{7}{18}$

13. $1\frac{7}{8}$ $4\frac{3}{4} = 4\frac{6}{8} = 3\frac{14}{8}$
$-2\frac{7}{8} = 2\frac{7}{8} = 2\frac{7}{8}$
$1\frac{7}{8}$

14. $13\frac{2}{3}$ $25\frac{1}{6} = 25\frac{1}{6} = 24\frac{7}{6}$
$-11\frac{1}{2} = 11\frac{3}{6} = 11\frac{3}{6}$
$13\frac{4}{6} = 13\frac{2}{3}$

15. $6\frac{15}{17}$ $10 = 9\frac{17}{17}$
$-\ 3\frac{2}{17} = 3\frac{2}{17}$
$\overline{\qquad 6\frac{15}{17}}$

16. $19\frac{1}{5}$ $20 = 19\frac{5}{5}$
$-\ \frac{4}{5} = \frac{4}{5}$
$\overline{\qquad 19\frac{1}{5}}$

Exercise 7: Multiplying Fractions
page 599

1. $\frac{6}{15} \times \frac{5}{12} = \frac{1}{6}$
2. $8 \times \frac{3}{4} = \frac{8}{1} \times \frac{3}{4} = \frac{6}{1} = 6$
3. $\frac{3}{8} \times \frac{2}{15} \times \frac{6}{7} = \frac{6}{140} = \frac{3}{70}$
4. $8\frac{1}{6} \times 4 = \frac{49}{6} \times \frac{4}{1} = \frac{98}{3} = 32\frac{2}{3}$
5. $\frac{5}{9} \times \frac{2}{5} = \frac{2}{9}$
6. $2\frac{1}{2} \times 2\frac{1}{3} = \frac{5}{2} \times \frac{7}{3} = \frac{35}{6} = 5\frac{5}{6}$
7. $2\frac{3}{4} \times \frac{6}{7} = \frac{11}{4} \times \frac{6}{7} = \frac{33}{14} = 2\frac{5}{14}$
8. $1\frac{3}{10} \times 5 = \frac{13}{10} \times \frac{5}{1} = \frac{13}{2} = 6\frac{1}{2}$
9. $3\frac{3}{8} \times 1\frac{3}{9} = \frac{27}{8} \times \frac{12}{9} = \frac{9}{2} = 4\frac{1}{2}$

Exercise 8: Dividing Fractions
page 600

1. $\frac{4}{10} \div \frac{2}{3} = \frac{4}{10} \times \frac{3}{2} = \frac{6}{10} = \frac{3}{5}$
2. $\frac{2}{5} \div 4 = \frac{2}{5} \times \frac{1}{4} = \frac{1}{10}$
3. $\frac{3}{7} \div \frac{6}{35} = \frac{3}{7} \times \frac{35}{6} = \frac{5}{2} = 2\frac{1}{2}$
4. $3\frac{2}{3} \div 1\frac{1}{2} = \frac{11}{3} \times \frac{2}{3} = \frac{22}{9} = 2\frac{4}{9}$
5. $1\frac{3}{8} \div 11 = \frac{11}{8} \times \frac{1}{11} = \frac{1}{8}$
6. $9 \div 2\frac{1}{2} = \frac{9}{1} \times \frac{2}{5} = \frac{18}{5} = 3\frac{3}{5}$

Exercise 9: Item Sets
pages 601–602

1. **(2) $47.28**
   Information: $.98\frac{1}{2}$, 6 feet; 8 shelves

   Cost to make 1 shelf:
   $.98\frac{1}{2} \times 6 = \frac{1.97}{2} \times \frac{6}{1} = \$5.91$
   Cost of 8 shelves: $5.91 \times 8 = \$47.28$

2. **(3) 6 feet**
   Information: 6-ft lengths; $5\frac{1}{4}$-ft length; 8 pieces
   Amount cut off each: $6 - 5\frac{1}{4} = \frac{3}{4}$ ft
   Total amount of waste:
   $8 \times \frac{3}{4} = \frac{8}{1} \times \frac{3}{4} = 6$ feet

3. **(1) $52.32**
   Information: 8 shelves; $13.95 prevarnished; $12 varnishing; $47.28 (cost of shelves from question 1)
   Cost of prevarnished shelves:
   $8 \times \$13.95 = \$111.60$
   Cost to self-varnish: $12 + \$47.28 = \$59.28$
   Difference: $111.60 - \$59.28 = \$52.32$

4. **(3) $\frac{19}{40}$ mile**
   Information: $\frac{7}{8}$ mile; $\frac{2}{5}$ mile (from map)
   Length of Pine Way: $\frac{7}{8} - \frac{2}{5} = \frac{35}{40} - \frac{16}{40} = \frac{19}{40}$ mile

5. **(4) $1\frac{1}{8}$ miles**
   Information: $\frac{19}{20}$ and $\frac{3}{10}$ for Birch Trail (from map); $\frac{19}{40}$ for Pine Way (from question 4)
   Length of Birch Trail: $\frac{19}{20} - \frac{3}{10} = \frac{19}{20} - \frac{6}{20} = \frac{13}{20}$

   Total of both roads: $\frac{13}{20} + \frac{19}{40} = \frac{26}{40} + \frac{19}{40} = \frac{45}{40} = 1\frac{5}{40} = 1\frac{1}{8}$ miles

6. **(5) not enough information is given**
   You need to know the width of Camping Area A, but this is not given.

7. **(3) $11.79**
   Information: $1\frac{1}{2}$ times; $7.86
   $\$7.86 \times 1\frac{1}{2} = \frac{7.86}{1} \times \frac{3}{2} = \$11.79$

8. **(5) not enough information is given**
   There is no information on the number of hours in the third week; this chart is for the *second* week in April.

9. **(4) ($7.86 × 40) + ($11.79 × $\frac{10}{3}$)**

   Information: 40 hr at $7.86; $11.79 overtime rate (from question 7)
   Number of hours of overtime:
   $43\frac{1}{3} - 40 = 3\frac{1}{3}$ hours
   Represent amount at hourly wage: $7.86 × 40

   Represent amount at overtime rate: $11.79 $\times 3\frac{1}{3} = \$11.79 \times \frac{10}{3}$
   Represent total wages:
   ($7.86 × 40) + ($11.79 × $\frac{10}{3}$)

Exercise 10: Fraction Review
pages 603–604

1. **(1) $5\frac{5}{8}$ ft**

   $8\frac{3}{8} = 8\frac{3}{8} = 7\frac{11}{8}$
   $-\ 2\frac{3}{4} = 2\frac{6}{8} = 2\frac{6}{8}$
   $\overline{\qquad\qquad 5\frac{5}{8}$ feet}

2. **(5) $870**
   $36\frac{1}{4} \times 24$
   $\frac{145}{4} \times \frac{24}{1} = \$870$

3. **(3) $720 \div 22\frac{1}{2}$**
   This expression shows the number of miles divided by miles per gallon. This would give you total gallons.

4. **(4) 30**
   $20 \div \frac{2}{3}$
   $\frac{20}{1} \times \frac{3}{2} = 30$ doses

5. **(5) not enough information is given**
You cannot figure this out because you do not know the weight of the cartons.

6. **(2) $5\frac{3}{4}$ in**

Total of two given widths: $2\frac{3}{8} \times 2 =$
$\frac{19}{8} \times \frac{2}{1} = \frac{38}{8} = 4\frac{6}{8} = 4\frac{3}{4}$

Subtract that from length: $10\frac{1}{2} - 4\frac{3}{4} =$
$10\frac{2}{4} - 4\frac{3}{4} = 9\frac{6}{4} - 4\frac{3}{4} = 5\frac{3}{4}$ in

7. **(4) $760**

Wife's fare: $285 \times \frac{2}{3} = \frac{285}{1} \times \frac{2}{3} =$ $190

Childrens fare: $2 \times \frac{285}{2} = 285

Total fares: $285 + $190 + $285 = $760

8. **(3) 35**

Find the $\frac{1}{6}$ for roads: $10\frac{1}{2} \times \frac{1}{6} =$
$\frac{21}{2} \times \frac{1}{6} = \frac{21}{12} =$
$1\frac{9}{12} = 1\frac{3}{4}$ acres

Remaining acreage for lots:
$10\frac{1}{2} = 10\frac{2}{4} = 9\frac{6}{4}$
$- \quad 1\frac{3}{4} = \quad 1\frac{3}{4} = 1\frac{3}{4}$
_____
$8\frac{3}{4}$ acres

Number of lots: $8\frac{3}{4} \div \frac{1}{4} =$
$\frac{35}{4} \times \frac{4}{1} = 35$ lots

9. **(1) $1\frac{1}{8}$**

Total amount of wood needed:
$3 \times 1\frac{5}{8} =$
$\frac{3}{1} \times \frac{13}{8} = \frac{39}{8} = 4\frac{7}{8}$ ft

Amount left: $6 = 5\frac{8}{8}$
$- 4\frac{7}{8} = 4\frac{7}{8}$
_____
$1\frac{1}{8}$ ft

10. **(2) 24,000**

First, find $\frac{3}{4}$ of $\frac{2}{3}$:
$\frac{2}{3} \times \frac{3}{4} = \frac{3}{6} = \frac{1}{2}$

Then, find how many people got the message:
$\frac{48,000}{1} \times \frac{1}{2} = 24,000$

CHAPTER 4: RATIO AND PROPORTION

Exercise 1: Ratio
page 606

1. $\frac{3 \text{ miles}}{8 \text{ miles}} = \frac{3}{8}$

2. First, change 1 hour to 60 minutes to make a comparison of like units.
$\frac{30 \text{ minutes}}{1 \text{ hour}} = \frac{30 \text{ minutes}}{60 \text{ minutes}} = \frac{1}{2}$

3. $\frac{27 \text{ feet}}{18 \text{ feet}} = \frac{3}{2}$

4. $\frac{3 \text{ pounds}}{4 \text{ people}} = \frac{3}{4}$

5. $\frac{300 \text{ miles}}{15 \text{ gallons}} = \frac{20}{1}$

6. $\frac{88 \text{ feet}}{8 \text{ seconds}} = \frac{11}{1}$

7. $\frac{\$42.21}{7 \text{ hours}} = \frac{6.03}{1}$

8. $\frac{\$80}{12 \text{ boards}} = \frac{20}{3}$

Exercise 2: Application of Ratios
page 607

1. $\frac{\text{cost of supplies}}{\text{total expenses}} = \frac{\$120}{\$200} \div \frac{40}{40} = \frac{3}{5}$

2. $\frac{\text{total}}{\text{transportation}} = \frac{\$200}{\$40} \div \frac{40}{40} = \frac{5}{1}$

3. $\frac{\text{supplies}}{\text{tools}} = \frac{\$120}{\$25} \div \frac{5}{5} = \frac{24}{5}$

4. $\frac{\text{liabilities}}{\text{assets}} = \frac{\$1,700,000}{\$6,800,000} = \frac{17}{68} \div \frac{17}{17} = \frac{1}{4}$

5. $\frac{\text{women}}{\text{total}} = \frac{250}{750} \div \frac{250}{250} = \frac{1}{3}$

6. $\frac{\text{dividend}}{\text{shares}} = \frac{\$729}{300} = \$2.43 \text{ per share}$

7. $\begin{array}{r} 250 \text{ lb of beef} \\ - \quad 75 \text{ lb of waste} \\ \hline \mathbf{175 \text{ lb of packaged beef}} \end{array}$

8. $\frac{\text{cost}}{\text{lb of packaged beef}} = \frac{\$365}{175}$
$365 \div 175 = 2.085 = \$2.09 \text{ per lb}$

Exercise 3: Solving Proportions
page 609

1. $m = 4$ $\qquad \frac{2}{5} = \frac{m}{10}$
$\frac{2 \times 10}{5} = 4$

2. $x = 1$ $\qquad \frac{x}{7} = \frac{3}{21}$
$\frac{7 \times 3}{21} = \frac{21}{21} = 1$

3. $y = 6\frac{2}{3}$ $\qquad \frac{5}{y} = \frac{15}{20}$
$\frac{20 \times 5}{15} = \frac{100}{15} = 6\frac{2}{3}$

4. $z = 8$ $\qquad \frac{6}{4} = \frac{12}{z}$
$\frac{12 \times 4}{6} = \frac{48}{6} = 8$

5. $x = 15$ $\qquad \frac{x}{12} = \frac{30}{24}$
$\frac{30 \times 12}{24} = \frac{360}{24} = 15$

Exercise 4: Application of Proportion
page 610

1. **240 miles**
$\frac{96 \text{ miles}}{8 \text{ gallons}} = \frac{m \text{ (number of miles)}}{20 \text{ gallons}}$
$\frac{96 \times 20}{8} = \frac{1920}{8} = 240 \text{ miles}$

2. **$11\frac{1}{5}$ inches tall**
$\frac{5 \text{ inches wide}}{7 \text{ inches tall}} = \frac{8 \text{ inches wide}}{i \text{ (number of inches)}}$
$\frac{7 \times 8}{5} = \frac{56}{5} = 11\frac{1}{5} \text{ inches tall}$

3. **40 managers**
$\frac{2 \text{ managers}}{9 \text{ salespeople}} = \frac{m \text{ (managers)}}{180 \text{ salespeople}}$
$\frac{180 \times 2}{9} = \frac{360}{9} = 40 \text{ managers}$

4. 18 feet

$$\frac{\frac{1}{8} \text{ inch}}{1 \text{ foot}} = \frac{2\frac{1}{4} \text{ inches}}{f \text{ (feet)}}$$

$$\frac{2\frac{1}{4} \times 1}{\frac{1}{8}} = \frac{2\frac{1}{4}}{\frac{1}{8}} = 2\frac{1}{4} \div \frac{1}{8} = \frac{9}{4} \times \frac{8}{1} = 18 \text{ feet}$$

5. 420 calories

$$\frac{2 \text{ pancakes}}{120 \text{ calories}} = \frac{7 \text{ pancakes}}{c \text{ (calories)}}$$

$$\frac{120 \times 7}{2} = \frac{840}{2} = 420 \text{ calories}$$

CHAPTER 5: PERCENTS
Exercise 1: Changing to Fractions and Decimals
page 613

1. $\frac{87}{100}$ $87 \times \frac{1}{100} = \frac{87}{1} \times \frac{1}{100} = \frac{87}{100}$
   .87 $87 \times .01 = .87$

2. $\frac{2}{5}$ $40 \times \frac{1}{100} = \frac{40}{1} \times \frac{1}{100} = \frac{2}{5}$
   .4 $40 \times .01 = .40 = .4$

3. $\frac{1}{50}$ $2 \times \frac{1}{100} = \frac{2}{1} \times \frac{1}{100} = \frac{1}{50}$
   .02 $2 \times .01 = .02$

4. $\frac{2}{3}$ $66\frac{2}{3} \times \frac{1}{100} = \frac{200}{3} \times \frac{1}{100} = \frac{2}{3}$
   $.66\frac{2}{3}$ $66\frac{2}{3} \times .01 = .66\frac{2}{3}$

5. 2 $200 \times \frac{1}{100} = \frac{200}{1} \times \frac{1}{100} = 2$
   2   $200 \times .01 = 2$

6. $\frac{1}{8}$ $12.5 \times \frac{1}{100} = 12\frac{1}{2} \times \frac{1}{100} =$
   $\frac{25}{2} \times \frac{1}{100} = \frac{1}{8}$
   .125 $12.5 \times .01 = .125$

7. $\frac{9}{50}$ $18 \times \frac{1}{100} = \frac{18}{1} \times \frac{1}{100} = \frac{9}{50}$
   .18 $18 \times .01 = .18$

8. $\frac{1}{125}$ $.8 \times \frac{1}{100} = \frac{8}{10} \times \frac{1}{100} = \frac{2}{250} = \frac{1}{125}$
   .008 $.8 \times .01 = .008$

9. $\frac{1}{200}$ $\frac{1}{2} \times \frac{1}{100} = \frac{1}{200}$
   .005 $\frac{1}{2} \times .01 = .5 \times .01 = .005$

Exercise 2: Changing to Percents
page 613

1. $\frac{3}{5} \times \frac{100}{1} = \frac{300}{5} = 60\%$

2. $.70 \times 100 = 70\%$

3. $\frac{1}{3} \times \frac{100}{1} = \frac{100}{3} = 33\frac{1}{3}\%$

4. $.0025 \times 100 = .25\%$

5. $\frac{3}{8} \times \frac{100}{1} = \frac{300}{8} = 37\frac{1}{2}\%$

6. $4.5 \times 100 = 450\%$

7. $\frac{9}{10} \times \frac{100}{1} = \frac{900}{1} = 90\%$

8. $.625 \times 100 = 62.5\%$

9. $2\frac{1}{4} \times 100 = \frac{9}{4} \times \frac{100}{1} = \frac{900}{4} = 225\%$

Exercise 3: Percent Problems
page 615

1. **1.2**   You are looking for the part:
   $$\frac{n}{30} = \frac{4}{100}$$
   Cross multiply: $30 \times 4 = 120$
   Divide: $120 \div 100 = 1.2$

2. **25%**   You are looking for the percent:
   $$\frac{14}{56} = \frac{n}{100}$$
   Cross multiply: $14 \times 100 = 1400$
   Divide: $1400 \div 56 = 25\%$

3. **400**   You are looking for the whole:
   $$\frac{10}{n} = \frac{2.5}{100}$$
   Cross multiply: $10 \times 100 = 1000$
   Divide: $1000 \div 2.5 = 400$

4. **200**   You are looking for the whole:
   $$\frac{14}{n} = \frac{7}{100}$$
   Cross multiply: $14 \times 100 = 1400$
   Divide: $1400 \div 7 = 200$

5. **9%**   You are looking for the percent:
   $$\frac{30.60}{340} = \frac{n}{100}$$
   Cross multiply:
   $30.60 \times 100 = 3060$
   Divide: $3060 \div 340 = 9$

6. **.31**   You are looking for the part:
   $$\frac{n}{62} = \frac{\frac{1}{2}}{100}$$
   Cross multiply: $62 \times \frac{1}{2} = 31$
   Divide: $31 \div 100 = .31$

7. **54**   You are looking for the part:
   $$\frac{n}{45} = \frac{120}{100}$$
   Cross multiply: $120 \times 45 = 5400$
   Divide: $5400 \div 100 = 54$

8. **35%**   You are looking for the percent:
   $$\frac{210}{600} = \frac{n}{100}$$
   Cross multiply:
   $210 \times 100 = 21,000$
   Divide: $21,000 \div 600 = 35\%$

9. **112.5**   You are looking for the whole:
   $$\frac{18}{n} = \frac{16}{100}$$
   Cross multiply: $18 \times 100 = 1800$
   Divide: $1800 \div 16 = 112.5$

10. **400%**   You are looking for the percent:
    $$\frac{20}{5} = \frac{n}{100}$$
    Cross multiply: $20 \times 100 = 2000$
    Divide: $2000 \div 5 = 400$

Exercise 4: Percent Word Problems
pages 616–617

1. **$252**
   You are looking for the part Jesse saves each month.
   $$\frac{n}{2100} = \frac{12}{100}$$
   Cross multiply: $2100 \times 12 = 25,200$
   Divide: $25,200 \div 100 = \$252$

2. 20%

You are looking for the percent of his income that goes for rent.

$$\frac{420}{2100} = \frac{n}{100}$$

Cross multiply: 420 × 100 = 42,000
Divide: 42,000 ÷ 2100 = 20%

3. $2205

First, find the amount of his raise:

$$\frac{n}{2100} = \frac{5}{100}$$

Cross multiply: 2100 × 5 = 10,500
Divide: 10,500 ÷ 100 = $105
Then, add his raise to his old monthly income:
$2100 + $105 = $2205

4. 35% wrong

You are looking for the percent she got wrong. First, find the percent correct:

$$\frac{26}{40} = \frac{n}{100}$$

Cross multiply: 26 × 100 = 2600
Divide: 2600 ÷ 40 = 65% correct
Then, find the percent she got wrong:
100% − 65% = 35% wrong

5. $12,000

You are looking for the whole cost of the car.

$$\frac{1800}{n} = \frac{15}{100}$$

Cross multiply: 1800 × 100 = 180,000
Divide: 180,000 ÷ 15 = $12,000

6. 36% undecided

First, find the total number of voters:
200 + 120 + 180 = 500
Then, find the percent undecided:

$$\frac{180}{500} = \frac{n}{100}$$

Cross multiply: 180 × 100 = 18,000
Divide: 18,000 ÷ 500 = 36% undecided

7. $17.98

First, find the total cost of the cassettes:
$7.49 × 3 = $22.47
Then, find Hosea's discount:

$$\frac{n}{22.47} = \frac{20}{100}$$

Cross multiply: 22.47 × 20 = 449.40
Divide: 449.40 ÷ 100 = $4.49
Find Hosea's final cost.
$22.47 − $4.49 = $17.98

Exercise 5: Interest Problems
pages 618–619

1. (2) $3,600

First, find the interest for 1 year:

$$\frac{n}{60,000} = \frac{8}{100}$$

Cross multiply: 60,000 × 8 = 480,000
Divide: 480,000 ÷ 100 = $4800
Then, find the interest for 9 months:

9 months = $\frac{9}{12} = \frac{3}{4}$ year

$\frac{4800}{1} \times \frac{3}{4}$ = $3600 for 9 months

2. (3) $31,968.75

First, find the interest on the loan for 1 year:

$$\frac{n}{31,000} = \frac{12.5}{100}$$

Cross multiply:
31,000 × 12.5 = 387,500
Divide: 387,500 ÷ 100 = $3875 for 1 year
Then, find the interest for 90 days:

$\frac{90}{360} = \frac{1}{4}$ year

$3875 × $\frac{1}{4}$ = $968.75 for 90 days
Finally, find the total amount to be repaid:
$31,000 + 968.75 = $31,968.75

3. (1) $\dfrac{1500 \times 8\frac{1}{2}}{100}$

This represents how to solve the proportion

$$\frac{n}{1500} = \frac{8\frac{1}{2}}{100}$$

Cross multiply: 1500 × $8\frac{1}{2}$

Divide: (1500 × $8\frac{1}{2}$) ÷ 100 or

$$\frac{1500 \times 8\frac{1}{2}}{100}$$

4. (4) $4,500

Find the whole to find how much he borrowed:

$$\frac{360}{n} = \frac{8}{100}$$

Cross multiply: 360 × 100 = 36,000
Divide: 36,000 ÷ 8 = $4500

5. (1) $3255

First, find the total Ted needs:
$32,000 + $8500 + $2500 = $43,000
Then, find the amount he needs to borrow:
$43,000 − $12,000 saved = $31,000
Finally, find the interest for 1 year:

$$\frac{n}{31,000} = \frac{10.5}{100}$$

Cross multiply:
31,000 × 10.5 = 325,500
Divide: 325,500 ÷ 100 = $3255 interest

Exercise 6: Percent Review
pages 619–620

1. (5) $171.15
First, add the purchases:
$135.00 + $24.95 = $159.95
Then, find the tax:
$$\frac{n}{159.95} = \frac{7}{100}$$
Cross multiply: 159.95 × 7 = 1119.65
Divide: 1119.65 ÷ 100 = 11.1965 =
$11.20 tax
Then, find the total:
$159.95 + $11.20 = $171.15

2. (3) $15.90 − .20(15.90)
This represents the original cost
($15.90) less the 20% discount for the
sale.

3. (5) $15,272
First, find the amount to be financed:
$12,800 − $2500 = $10,300
Then, find one year's interest:
$$\frac{n}{10,300} = \frac{8}{100}$$
Cross multiply: 10,300 × 8 = 82,400
Divide: 82,400 ÷ 100 = $824
Then, find three years' interest:
$824 × 3 = $2472
Finally, find the total, including the
sale price of the car and the interest:
$12,800 + $2472 = $15,272
Note that you were asked to find the
total cost of the car, not the total cost
of the interest.

4. (5) not enough information is given
You are not told the current cost of
the car, so you cannot find the
discount rate.

5. (2) $2,200.50
Find the commission, which is a part
of the sales price.
$$\frac{n}{48,900} = \frac{4\frac{1}{2}}{100}$$
Cross multiply: 48,900 × $\frac{9}{2}$ = 220,050
Divide: 220,050 ÷ 100 = $2200.50

6. (4) 25
$$\frac{rent}{net\ income} = \frac{6000}{24,000} = \frac{1}{4}$$
$$4\overline{)1.00}\ \ \ \frac{.25}{} = 25\%$$

7. (2) $\frac{1}{10}$
$$\frac{savings}{income} = \frac{2400}{24,000} = \frac{1}{10}$$

8. (3) 15
First, find the total spent on
entertainment ($1200) and savings
($2400):
$1200 + $2400 = $3600
Then, find the percent this is of the
total expenses:
$$\frac{3600}{24,000} = \frac{n}{100}$$
Cross multiply:
3600 × 100 = 360,000
Divide: 360,000 ÷ 24,000 = 15

9. (5) $1597.50
First, find 6.5% of Margaret's
insurance:
$$\frac{n}{1500} = \frac{6.5}{100}$$
Cross multiply: 1500 × 6.5 = 9750
Divide: 9750 ÷ 100 = 97.50
Then, add this to her original
insurance payments:
$1500.00 + $97.50 = $1597.50

10. (5) not enough information is given
You cannot find an answer to this
question. Although you are told that
her property taxes rose 7%, you do
not know how much her property
taxes originally were.

11. (2) (35,821 × 67) ÷ 100
This represents the solution to the
following proportion to find net pay:
$$\frac{n}{35,821} = \frac{67}{100}$$
Cross multiply and divide:
(35,821 × 67) ÷ 100

CHAPTER 6:
MEASUREMENT
Exercise 1: Conversions
page 623

1. Convert from a large unit (yards) to a
smaller unit (feet). Multiply 5 by the
number of feet in a yard (3 ft = 1 yd):
3 × 5 = **15 feet**

2. Convert from a small unit (ounces) to a
larger unit (pounds). Divide 40 by the
number of ounces in a pound (16 oz =
1 lb):
40 ÷ 16 = 2.5 or **$2\frac{1}{2}$ pounds**

3. Convert from a small unit (hours) to a
larger unit (days). Divide 96 by the
number of hours in a day (24 hr = 1 day):
96 ÷ 24 = **4 days**

4. Convert from a small unit (quarts) to a
larger unit (gallons). Divide 20 by the
number of quarts in a gallon (4 qt = 1
gal):
20 ÷ 4 = **5 gallons**

5. Convert from a large unit (quarts) to a
smaller unit (ounces). Multiply 2 by the
number of ounces in a quart (32 oz = 1
qt):
32 × 2 = **64 ounces**

6. Convert from a large unit (days) to a
smaller unit (minutes). First, find the
number of minutes in one day (1 day =
24 hr, and 1 hr = 60 min):
24 × 60 = 1440
Then, multiply that total by 2 for 2 days:
1440 × 2 = **2880 minutes**

7. Convert a small unit (pints) to a larger
unit (quarts). Divide 3 by the number of
pints in a quart (2 pts = 1 qt):
3 ÷ 2 = **1.5 quarts**

8. Convert a small unit (feet) to a larger unit (miles). Divide 14,110 by the number of feet in a mile (5280 ft = 1 mi):
14,110 ÷ 5280 = 2.67 = **2.7 miles** (to the nearest tenth)

9. First, find how many ounces are in a half-gallon. Since a half-gallon is two quarts, multiply 2 by 32 ounces (1 quart):
32 × 2 = 64 oz in a half-gallon
Then, divide by 8 to find how many 8-ounce glasses there are in 64 ounces:
64 ÷ 8 = 8 eight-ounce glasses
Divide 96 cents by 8 to find out how much each eight-ounce glass costs:
96 ÷ 8 = 12
Each eight-ounce glass of milk costs 12 cents.

10. First, find how many feet are in 2 miles: Change 2 miles (a larger unit) to feet (a smaller unit). Multiply 2 by the number of feet in a mile (1 mi = 5280 ft):
5280 × 2 = 10,560
Then, divide that by 15 feet to find the number of shrubs needed:
10,560 ÷ 15 = **704 shrubs**

Exercise 2: Basic Operations with Measurement
page 625

1. **6 ft 7 in**

$$\begin{array}{r} 9\text{ ft }4\text{ in} \\ -\ 2\text{ ft }9\text{ in} \end{array} = \begin{array}{r} 8\text{ ft }16\text{ in} \\ -\ 2\text{ ft }\ 9\text{ in} \\ \hline 6\text{ ft }\ 7\text{ in} \end{array}$$

2. **4 hr 20 min**

$$\begin{array}{r} 1\text{ hr }20\text{ min} \\ +\ 3\text{ hr} \\ \hline 4\text{ hr }20\text{ min} \end{array}$$

3. **121 lb 12 oz**

$$\begin{array}{r} 130\text{ lb} \\ -\ \ 8\text{ lb }4\text{ oz} \end{array} = \begin{array}{r} 129\text{ lb }16\text{ oz} \\ -\ \ \ 8\text{ lb }\ \ 4\text{ oz} \\ \hline 121\text{ lb }12\text{ oz} \end{array}$$

4. **37.1 in or 3 ft 1.1 in**

$$\begin{array}{r} 5.3\text{ in} \\ \times\ \ \ \ 7 \\ \hline 37.1\text{ in} \end{array}$$

5. **7 ft 6 in**

$$\begin{array}{r} 7\text{ ft} \qquad 6\text{ in} \\ 3\overline{)22\text{ ft}} \qquad 6\text{ in} \\ \underline{21\text{ ft}} \\ 1 = \underline{+\ 12\text{ in}} \\ 18\text{ in} \\ \underline{18\text{ in}} \\ 0 \end{array}$$

6. **40 min**

$$\begin{array}{r} 0\text{ hr} \qquad 40\text{ min} \\ 8\overline{)5\text{ hr}} \qquad 20\text{ min} \\ \underline{0} \\ 5\text{ hr} = \underline{+\ 300\text{ min}} \\ 320 \\ \underline{320} \\ 0 \end{array}$$

7. **7 oz**

$$\begin{array}{r} 1\text{ lb }4\text{ oz} \\ -\ \ \ \ 13\text{ oz} \end{array} = \begin{array}{r} 20\text{ oz} \\ -\ 13\text{ oz} \\ \hline 7\text{ oz} \end{array}$$

8. **1 ft 8 in**

$$\begin{array}{r} 1\text{ ft} \qquad 8\text{ in} \\ 4\overline{)6\text{ ft}} \qquad 8\text{ in} \\ \underline{4\text{ ft}} \\ 2\text{ ft} = \underline{+\ 24\text{ in}} \\ 32\text{ in} \\ \underline{32\text{ in}} \\ 0 \end{array}$$

9. **(3) $3.25**
First, find the number of inches needed:
45 × 4 = 180 in
Then, find the number of yards in 180 inches (36 in = 1 yd):
180 ÷ 36 = 5 yd
Then, find the cost of 5 yards:
5 × $.65 = $3.25

10. **(4) 19($415)**
1 lb 3 oz = 16 oz + 3 oz = 19 oz

11. **(5) $107.50**
First, find the total number of hours:

$$\begin{array}{r} 2\text{ hr }30\text{ min} \\ 3\text{ hr} \\ 4\text{ hr }45\text{ min} \\ 7\text{ hr }15\text{ min} \\ +\ 4\text{ hr} \\ \hline 20\text{ hr }90\text{ min} = 21\text{ hr }30\text{ min} = 21\tfrac{1}{2}\text{ hr} \end{array}$$

Then, find the total pay:

$$21\tfrac{1}{2}\text{ hr} \times \$5 = \frac{43}{2} \times \frac{5}{1} = \$107.50$$

Exercise 3: Metric Measurement
page 628
This chart will help you follow the solutions below:

kilo hecto deca	basic unit	deci centi milli

1. 500 meters to centimeters: Move the decimal point 2 places right.
500.00 m = **50,000 cm**
2. 7423 milligrams to grams: Move the decimal point 3 places left.
7423 mg = **7.423 g**
3. 50.3 centimeters to millimeters: Move the decimal point 1 place right.
50.3 cm = **503 mm**
4. .027 kilograms to grams: Move the decimal point 3 places right.
.027 kg = **27 g**
5. First, 1 kiloliter to liter: Move the decimal point 3 places right.
1.000 kl = 1000 l
Second, add 47 liters to 1000 liters = **1047 liters**
6. First, 42 centimeters to meters: Move the decimal point 2 places left.
42 cm = .42 m
Second, add 6 meters + .42 meters = **6.42 m**

7. First, add

$$400 \text{ cm} + 15 \text{ cm} + 1285 \text{ cm} + 15 \text{ cm}$$
$$= 1715 \text{ cm}$$

Second, 1715 centimeters to meters:
Move the decimal point 2 places left.

$$1715 \text{ cm} = \textbf{17.15 m}$$

8. First, one week = 7 days

$$857 \text{ mg} \times 7 = 5999 \text{ mg}$$

Second, 5999 milligrams to grams: Move the decimal point 3 places left.

$$5999 \text{ mg} = \textbf{5.999 g}$$

9. 1000 meters to kilometers: Move the decimal point 3 places left.

$$1000 \text{ m} = 1.000 = \textbf{1 km}$$

10. $\dfrac{1 \text{ km}}{.621 \text{ mi}} = \dfrac{80 \text{ km}}{n}$

$$\dfrac{.621 \times 80}{1} = 49.68 \text{ mph in Canada}$$

The U.S. allows 55 mph, and Canada allows 49.68 mph.
The U.S. allows a faster speed.

11. **(2)** $.75 \times \$6.40$

12. **(3) 91**

$$.91 \times 100 = 91$$

Exercise 4: Money Problems
pages 630–631

1. **(4) $101.33**

First: $\$49.95 + \$29.90 + \$14.85 = \$94.70$ subtotal
Second: $\$94.70 \times .07 = \$6.63$ tax
Third: $\$94.70 + \$6.63 = \$101.33$ total

2. **(3) $200**

First, find the number of pounds in two tons.

$$\dfrac{1 \text{ T}}{2000 \text{ lb}} = \dfrac{2 \text{ T}}{n \text{ lb}}$$

$$\dfrac{2000 \times 2}{1} = 4000 \text{ lb}$$

Then, find the total number of bags:
$4000 \text{ lb} \div 50 \text{ lb} = 80 \text{ bags}$
Then, find the profit:
$\$5.95 \times 80 = \$476$ income
$2 \times \$138 = \$276$ expenses
$\$476 - \$276 = \$200$ profit

3. **(2) $15.68**

First, find the number of yards in 48 feet:

$$\dfrac{1 \text{ yd}}{3 \text{ ft}} = \dfrac{n \text{ yd}}{48 \text{ ft}}$$

$$\dfrac{1 \times 48}{3} = \dfrac{48}{3} = 16 \text{ yd}$$

Then, find the total cost:
$16 \times \$.98 = \$15.68$

4. **(4)** $8 \dfrac{1 \text{ qt}}{4 \text{ c}} = \dfrac{3 \text{ qt}}{n \text{ c}}$

$$\dfrac{4 \times 3}{1} = \dfrac{12}{1} = 12 \text{ cups}$$

$$12 \div 1\tfrac{1}{2} = 8 \text{ servings}$$

5. **(1) Happy Bran**

Happy Bran:

$$\dfrac{\$1.79}{25 \text{ oz}} = \dfrac{n}{1 \text{ oz}}$$

$$\dfrac{1.79 \times 1}{25} = \$.0716 = \$.07$$

Wheatos:

$$\dfrac{\$1.49}{12 \text{ oz}} = \dfrac{n}{1 \text{ oz}}$$

$$\dfrac{1.49 \times 1}{12} = \$.1242 = \$.12$$

Friendly Flakes:

$$\dfrac{\$2.19}{29 \text{ oz}} = \dfrac{n}{1 \text{ oz}}$$

$$\dfrac{2.19 \times 1}{29} = \$.0755 = \$.08$$

Sugar Snaps:

$$\dfrac{\$2.39}{20 \text{ oz}} = \dfrac{n}{1 \text{ oz}}$$

$$\dfrac{2.39 \times 1}{20} = \$.1195 = \$.12$$

6. **(2) 12¢**

$$\dfrac{\$6.48}{36} = \$.18 \text{ per capsule}$$

$$\$.18 \times 2 = \$.36 \text{ per dose}$$

$$\dfrac{\$4.32}{36} = \$.12 \text{ per capsule}$$

$$\$.12 \times 2 = \$.24 \text{ per dose}$$

$$\$.36 - \$.24 = \$.12$$

7. **(4)** $\$.29 + 3(\$.23)$

Exercise 5: Time Problems
pages 632–633

1. **(2) 3**

$75¢ \div 5¢ = 15¢$
$15 \times 12 \text{ min} = 180 \text{ min}$

$$\dfrac{1 \text{ hr}}{60 \text{ min}} = \dfrac{n}{180 \text{ min}} \qquad \dfrac{180 \times 1}{60} = 3 \text{ hr}$$

2. **(3)** $4\tfrac{1}{2} \times 8 \times 5 \times 4$

First:
10 A.M. to noon = 2 hr
noon to 2:30 P.M. = $+ 2\tfrac{1}{2}$ hr
$\overline{ 4\tfrac{1}{2} \text{ hr each day}}$

Second: Multiply $4\tfrac{1}{2}$ hours per day by $\$8$ per hour by 5 days per week by 4 weeks.

3. **(1) 362.5**

8:30 A.M. to noon = $3\tfrac{1}{2}$ hrs
noon to 3:45 P.M. = $+ 3\tfrac{3}{4}$ hrs
$\overline{}$
Total time $ 7\tfrac{1}{4}$ hrs
$7\tfrac{1}{4}$ hrs $\times 50 = 362.5$ miles

4. (5) $4\frac{3}{4}$

5/20	8 hr
5/21	$9\frac{1}{2}$ hr
5/22	$10\frac{3}{4}$ hr
5/23	8 hr
5/24	+ $8\frac{1}{2}$ hr
Total	$44\frac{3}{4}$ hr

$44\frac{3}{4} - 40 = 4\frac{3}{4}$ hr overtime

5. (4) $371

$40 \times \$7.85 = \$314$
$4\frac{3}{4} \times \$12 = + \ 57$
Total $\qquad \$371$

6. (4) $248.57

$1\% + 25\% + 7\% = 33\%$
$33\% \times \$371 = \$122.43$ deductions
$\$371 - \$122.43 = \$248.57$ take-home pay

7. (2) $960 \times \frac{1}{3}$

$d = rt \qquad (20 \text{ min} = \frac{1}{3} \text{ hr})$
$= 960\left(\frac{1}{3}\right)$ or $960 \times \frac{1}{3}$

8. (5) $75 \div 2\frac{1}{2}$

75 miles $\div 2\frac{1}{2}$ hr

Exercise 6: Scales and Meters
page 636

1. (4) $2\frac{1}{2}$ in

$\dfrac{1 \text{ in}}{180 \text{ mi}} = \dfrac{n \text{ in}}{450 \text{ mi}}$

$\dfrac{1 \times 450}{180} = 2\frac{1}{2}$ in

2. (3) 1 in = 200 mi

$\dfrac{2000 \text{ mi}}{10 \text{ in}} = \dfrac{n \text{ mi}}{1 \text{ in}}$

$\dfrac{2000 \times 1}{10} = 200$ miles

3. (1) $113.63

New reading	4752 kwh
Old reading	− 3843 kwh
difference	909 kwh

$\dfrac{\$.125}{1 \text{ kwh}} = \dfrac{n \text{ dollars}}{909 \text{ kwh}}$

$\dfrac{\$.125 \times 909}{1} = \$113.625$ or $\$113.63$

4. (4) $77.89

First, find the cost of 100 cu ft:
$\$.3065 \times 173 = 53.0245 = \$53.02$
Then, find the subtotal:
$\$53.02 + \$19.16 + \$2.00 =$
$\$74.18$ subtotal
Find the 5% tax and add it to the subtotal:
$\$74.18 \times .05 = 3.709 = \$3.71$
$\$74.18 + \$3.71 = \$77.89$ total

CHAPTER 7: GRAPHS, STATISTICS, AND PROBABILITY
Exercise 1: Mean and Median
pages 638–639

1. $3,713.14
$4300 + 5600 + 1875 + 4250 + 2876 + 4108 + 2983 = 25,992$
$25,992 \div 7 = 3,713.142 = \$3,713.14$

2. 44 points
$37 + 63 + 42 + 24 + 44 + 51 = 261$
$261 \div 6 = 43.5 = 44$ points

3. 61 points
Find the middle numbers:

45 48 | 53 68 | 72 74

Find the average: $53 + 68 = 121$
$\qquad\qquad\qquad 121 \div 2 = 60.5,$
$\qquad\qquad\qquad$ or 61 points

4. 60 points
$48 + 45 + 53 + 72 + 68 + 74 = 360$
$360 \div 6 = 60$ points

5. $44.80
Arrange from smallest to largest and find the middle number:

$39.95 $42.88 | $44.80 | $48.95 $52.25

Exercise 2: Circle Graphs
page 640

1. $68,383.33
Find the total expenses for 3 years:
$92,000 + 156,000 + 125,000 = 373,000$
Find the average for one year:
$373,000 \div 3 = \$124,333.33$
Find 55% of this:
$\$124,333.33 \times .55 = \$68,383.33$

2. $4800
$\dfrac{n}{32,000} \times \dfrac{15}{100} = \dfrac{32,000 \times 15}{100} = \$4800$

3. $666.67
First, find the yearly expenses for rent:
$\dfrac{n}{32,000} \times \dfrac{25}{100} = \dfrac{32,000 \times 25}{100} = \$8000$
Then, find the monthly expenses for rent:
$\$8000 \div 12 = \$666.67$

4. (5) not enough information is given
Nothing is said about clothing on the graph.

5. (1) 1 to 10
$\dfrac{\text{savings}}{\text{total}} = \dfrac{10\%}{100\%} = \dfrac{10}{100} = \dfrac{1}{10}$

Exercise 3: Bar Graphs
page 641

1. $17,000

2. $19,750
First, find the total:
$13,000 + 20,000 + 21,000 + 25,000 = \$79,000$
Then, find the average:
$\$79,000 \div 4 = \$19,750$

3. (4) 1993

4. (2) $2,000
$\$23,000 - \$21,000 = \$2,000$

Exercise 4: Line Graphs
pages 642–643
1. sales; 1990; 1993
2. ten thousands of dollars
3. months of the year
4. $60,000
5. $90,000
6. higher

Exercise 5: Mixed Graph Practice
pages 643–644
1. $\frac{3}{100}$

$$\frac{\text{savings}}{\text{earnings}} = \frac{3\%}{100\%} = \frac{3}{100}$$

2. $600

First, find the yearly take-home pay:
$$\frac{n}{12,000} = \frac{60}{100} \qquad \frac{12,000 \times 60}{100} = 7200$$
Then, find the monthly pay:
$7200 \div 12 = 600

3. $1750
$$\frac{n}{25,000} = \frac{7}{100} \qquad \frac{25,000 \times 7}{100} = $1750$$

4. $33,333.33
$$\frac{20,000}{n} = \frac{60}{100} \qquad \frac{20,000 \times 100}{60} = $33,333.33$$

5. $15,120

First, find the total deductions:
27% + 7% + 3% = 37%
$$\frac{n}{24,000} = \frac{37}{100} \qquad \frac{24,000 \times 37}{100} = $8880$$
Now, subtract to find Mike's take-home pay.

$24,000 - 8880 = $15,120$

6. **200 ft** $\quad 1450 - 1250 = 200$ ft
7. **1557 ft** $\quad 1450 + 107 = 1557$ ft
8. **2.45 times as tall**
$$\frac{\text{World Trade Center}}{\text{Washington Monument}} = \frac{1350}{550} = 2.45$$

9. **31%**
$$\frac{\text{Notre Dame Cathedral}}{\text{Sears Tower}} = \frac{450}{1450} = \text{approximately } 31\%$$

10. **$1008\frac{1}{3}$ ft**
450 + 550 + 1000 + 1250 + 1350 + 1450 = 6050
$6050 \div 6 = 1008\frac{1}{3}$ ft

11. **1125 ft**
1000 + 1250 = 2250
2250 ÷ 2 = 1125 ft

12. **111 floors**
1450 ÷ 13 = 111.5 or 111 floors

13. **7500 people**
4500 + 3000 = 7500 people

14. April and July

15. **$69,750**
Youth: 4000 at $5.75 = $23,000
Adults: 5500 at $8.50 = $\underline{46,750}$
$$$69,750

Exercise 6: Probability
pages 645–646
1. $\frac{1}{52}$ $\quad \frac{1 \text{ ace of spades}}{52 \text{ cards}} = \frac{1}{52}$

2. 25% $\quad \frac{13 \text{ hearts}}{52 \text{ cards}} = \frac{1}{4} = 25\%$

3. $\frac{1}{13}$ $\quad \frac{4 \text{ kings}}{52 \text{ cards}} = \frac{1}{13}$

4. (1) $\frac{1}{6}$ $\quad \frac{1 \text{ possibility}}{6 \text{ faces}} = \frac{1}{6}$

5. (4) $33\frac{1}{3}\%$
$$\frac{2 \text{ possibilities}}{6 \text{ faces}} = \frac{1}{3} = 33\frac{1}{3}\%$$

6. (5) 50%
$$\frac{3 \text{ possibilities}}{6 \text{ faces}} = \frac{3}{6} = 50\%$$

7. (1) 0 $\quad$ This is not possible.

8. (5) $66\frac{2}{3}\%$
$$\frac{4 \text{ possibilities}}{6 \text{ faces}} = \frac{2}{3} = 66\frac{2}{3}\%$$

9. (5) 100%

10. (2) $\frac{1}{12}$ $\quad \frac{\text{March}}{12 \text{ months}} = \frac{1}{12}$

11. (2) $\frac{1}{10}$ $\quad \frac{1 \text{ digit}}{\text{the numbers } 0-9} = \frac{1}{10}$

12. (3) $\frac{1}{2}$ $\quad \frac{1 \text{ head}}{2 \text{ possibilities}} = \frac{1}{2}$

13. (4) $\frac{3}{4}$
$960 - 240 = 720 \qquad \frac{720 \text{ good pots}}{960 \text{ pots}} = \frac{3}{4}$

Exercise 7: Dependent Probability
pages 647–648
1. $\frac{1}{13}$ $\quad \frac{4 \text{ aces}}{52 \text{ cards}} = \frac{1}{13}$

2. $\frac{1}{17}$ $\quad \frac{3 \text{ aces}}{51 \text{ cards}} = \frac{1}{17}$

3. $\frac{4}{51}$ $\quad \frac{4 \text{ aces}}{51 \text{ cards}} = \frac{4}{51}$

4. $\frac{4}{17}$ $\quad \frac{12 \text{ spades}}{51 \text{ cards}} = \frac{12}{51} = \frac{4}{17}$

5. $\frac{3}{10}$ $\quad \frac{3 \text{ women}}{10 \text{ people}} = \frac{3}{10}$

6. $\frac{2}{3}$ $\quad \frac{6 \text{ men}}{9 \text{ people}} = \frac{6}{9} = \frac{2}{3}$

7. $\frac{1}{8}$ $\quad \frac{1 \text{ woman}}{8 \text{ people}} = \frac{1}{8}$

8. $\frac{2}{9}$ $\quad \frac{2 \text{ quarters}}{9 \text{ coins}} = \frac{2}{9}$

9. $\frac{1}{4}$ $\quad \frac{2 \text{ quarters}}{8 \text{ coins}} = \frac{1}{4}$

10. $\frac{1}{7}$ $\quad \frac{1 \text{ nickel}}{7 \text{ coins}} = \frac{1}{7}$

CHAPTER 8: NUMERATION
Exercise 1: Powers
page 650
1. **25** $5 \times 5 = 25$
2. $\frac{1}{4}$ $\frac{1}{2} \times \frac{1}{2} = \frac{1}{4}$
3. **729** $9 \times 9 \times 9 = 729$
4. $\frac{27}{64}$ $\frac{3}{4} \times \frac{3}{4} \times \frac{3}{4} = \frac{27}{64}$
5. **.09** $.3 \times .3 = .09$
6. **1** 1 to any power is 1.
7. **16** $2 \times 2 \times 2 \times 2 = 16$
8. **1.44** $1.2 \times 1.2 = 1.44$
9. **1** Any number to the 0 power is 1.
10. **10,000** $10 \times 10 \times 10 \times 10 = 10,000$
11. **625** $25 \times 25 = 625$
12. **.008** $(.2)(.2)(.2) = .008$
13. $\frac{4}{9}$ $\left(\frac{2}{3}\right)\left(\frac{2}{3}\right) = \frac{4}{9}$
14. **27** $3 \times 3 \times 3 = 27$
15. **0** $0 \times 0 = 0$

Exercise 2: Simplifying Square Roots
page 650
1. $3\sqrt{2}$ $\sqrt{18} = \sqrt{9 \cdot 2} = 3\sqrt{2}$
2. $4\sqrt{3}$ $\sqrt{48} = \sqrt{16 \cdot 3} = 4\sqrt{3}$
3. $2\sqrt{2}$ $\sqrt{8} = \sqrt{4 \cdot 2} = 2\sqrt{2}$
4. $6\sqrt{2}$ $\sqrt{72} = \sqrt{36 \cdot 2} = 6\sqrt{2}$
5. $3\sqrt{3}$ $\sqrt{27} = \sqrt{9 \cdot 3} = 3\sqrt{3}$

Exercise 3: Square Roots
page 651
1. 9
2. 1
3. 5.3 (approx.); $\sqrt{4 \cdot 7} = 2\sqrt{7}$ (simplified)
4. 3
5. 12
6. 7.2 (approx.); $\sqrt{4 \cdot 13} = 2\sqrt{13}$ (simplified)
7. 3.2 (approx.)
8. 4
9. 11
10. 9.5 (approx.); $\sqrt{9 \cdot 10} = 3\sqrt{10}$ (simplified)
11. 15
12. 20
13. 5.7 (approx.); $\sqrt{16 \cdot 2} = 4\sqrt{2}$ (simplified)
14. 8
15. 0

Exercise 4: Order of Operations
page 652
1. **0** $\dfrac{7-5}{2} + 3 - 5 = 0$
2. **29** $8 \times 3 + 5 = 24 + 5 = 29$
3. **23** $8 + 3 \times 5 = 8 + 15 = 23$
4. **8** $6 + 21 \div 3 - 5 = 6 + 7 - 5 = 8$
5. **5** $40 \div 2 - 5 \times 3 = 20 - 15 = 5$

6. **28** $3 + 5^2 = 3 + 25 = 28$
7. **20** $15 - 3 + 2^3 = 15 - 3 + 8 = 20$
8. **33** $4 + 3^3 + 3 \times 2 - 2^2 = 4 + 27 + 3 \times 2 - 4 = 4 + 27 + 6 - 4 = 33$

Exercise 5: More Order of Operations
page 653
1. **83** $2 + 3^2 \times (4 + 5) = 2 + (9 \times 9) = 83$
2. **15** $(12 - 5) + (14 - 6) = 7 + 8 = 15$
3. **40** $49 - (28 - 19) = 49 - 9 = 40$
4. **44** $8 + 6 \times (10 - 2^2) = 8 + 6 \times (10 - 4) = 8 + 6 \times 6 = 8 + 36 = 44$

Exercise 6: Evaluating Formulas
page 654
1. **144 sq in** $A = s^2$ $A = 12^2 = 144$
2. **125 cu in** $V = s^3$ $V = 5^3 = 125$
3. **$288** $i = prt$ $i = (800)(.12)(3) = \$288$
4. **28.26 sq in** $A = \pi r^2$ $A = (3.14)(3^2)$ $A = (3.14)(9) = 28.26$
5. **76 miles** $d = rt$ $d = (38)(2) = 76$
6. **1130.4 cu in** $V = \pi r^2 h$ $V = (3.14)(6^2)(10)$ $V = (3.14)(36)(10) = 1130.4$
7. **54 sq cm** $A = \frac{1}{2}bh$ $A = \dfrac{(12)(9)}{2} = \dfrac{108}{2} = 54$
8. **40 ft** $P = 2l + 2w$ Change 2 yards to 6 feet: $P = 2(14) + 2(6)$ $P = 28 + 12 = 40$

Exercise 7: Scientific Notation
page 656
1. 8.2×10^{-3}
2. 5×10^2
3. 3.82×10^4
4. 5.8×10^{-1}
5. $1.624 \times 1000 = \mathbf{1624}$
6. $3.12 \times .10 = \mathbf{.312}$
7. $8.24 \times 1 = \mathbf{8.24}$
8. $7.13 \times 1000 = \mathbf{7130}$

CHAPTER 9: GEOMETRY
Exercise 1: Pairs of Angles
pages 658–659
1. **38°** because $\angle DBC$ and $\angle ABD$ are supplementary angles. $180° - 142° = 38°$
2. **38°** because $\angle ABE$ and $\angle DBC$ are vertical angles.
3. **142°** because $\angle EBC$ and $\angle ABD$ are vertical angles.
4. **38°** $90° - 52° = 38°$
5. **105°** $180° - 75° = 105°$

Exercise 2: Angles in Triangles
page 660

1. $\angle B = 70°$
Add the two known angles:
$70° + 40° = 110°$
Subtract that sum from 180°:
$180° - 110° = 70°$

2. $\angle Q = 125°$
Add the two known angles:
$30° + 25° = 55°$
Subtract that sum from 180°:
$180° - 55° = 125°$

3. $\angle X = 90°$
Add the two known angles:
$30° + 60° = 90°$
Subtract that sum from 180°:
$180° - 90° = 90°$

4. $\angle E = 60°$
Add the two known angles:
$60° + 60° = 120°$
Subtract that sum from 180°:
$180° - 120° = 60°$

Exercise 3: Types of Triangles
pages 660–661

1. (a) **Scalene triangle**—because all three sides have different lengths
(b) **Right triangle**—because the triangle has one right angle
(c) **Isosceles triangle**—because two sides and two angles of the triangle are equal
(d) **Equilateral triangle**—because all three sides of the triangle are equal
(e) **Right triangle**—because $\angle C$ is a right angle

2. $\triangle RST$ **is a right triangle.**
Add the two given angles:
$70° + 20° = 90°$
Subtract from the number of degrees in a triangle:
$180° - 90° = 90°$

3. 76°
Find the total of the base angles:
$52° \times 2 = 104°$
Subtract from the total degrees in a triangle:
$180° - 104° = 76°$

4. 30°
Find the total of the known angles—you are told that this is a right triangle (one angle of 90°) and that there is a 60° angle.
$90° + 60° = 150°$
Subtract from the total degrees in a triangle:
$180° - 150° = 30°$

Exercise 4: Similar Triangles
pages 662–663

1. 9 in $\dfrac{DF}{AC} = \dfrac{DE}{AB}$

$\dfrac{DF}{15} = \dfrac{6}{10}$

$\dfrac{15 \times 6}{10} = \dfrac{90}{10} = 9$ in

2. 12 ft
$\dfrac{t}{8} = \dfrac{18}{12}$

$t = \dfrac{18 \times 8}{12} = \dfrac{144}{12} = 12$ ft

3. (a) First recognize two similar triangles and draw them. Set up a proportion:

$\dfrac{d}{b} = \dfrac{c}{a}$

(b) 150 ft

$\dfrac{d}{6} = \dfrac{50}{2}$

$d = \dfrac{50 \times 6}{2} = \dfrac{300}{2} = 150$ ft

4. $31\frac{1}{2}$ **ft**

(Remember: a yardstick is 3 feet long.)

$\dfrac{t}{3} = \dfrac{42}{4} = \dfrac{42 \times 3}{4} = \dfrac{126}{4} = 31\frac{1}{2}$ ft

Exercise 5: The Pythagorean Theorem
pages 665–666

1. (a) $c = 15$ $c^2 = a^2 + b^2$
$c^2 = 9^2 + 12^2$
$c^2 = 81 + 144$
$c^2 = 225$
$c = \sqrt{225} = 15$

(b) $3 = a$ $c^2 = a^2 + b^2$
$5^2 = a^2 + 4^2$
$25 = a^2 + 16$
$25 - 16 = a^2$
$9 = a^2$
$\sqrt{9} = a$
$3 = a$

(c) $c = 26$ $c^2 = a^2 + b^2$
$c^2 = 10^2 + 24^2$
$c^2 = 100 + 576 = 676$
$c = \sqrt{676} = 26$

2. $c = 25$ **in** $c^2 = a^2 + b^2$
$c^2 = 15^2 + 20^2$
$c^2 = 225 + 400 = 625$
$c = \sqrt{625} = 25$

3. Yes, the triangle is a right triangle.
Side 1 is 20 in; $20^2 = 400$ $a^2 = 400$
Side 2 is 21 in; $21^2 = 441$ $b^2 = 441$
Side 3 is 29 in; $29^2 = 841$ $c^2 = 841$
$a^2 + b^2 = c^2$
$400 + 441 = 841$

4. (3) 100 $c^2 = a^2 + b^2$
$c^2 = 60^2 + 80^2$
$c^2 = 3600 + 6400 = 10,000$
$c = \sqrt{10,000} = 100$ meters

5. (5) 75

First draw a sketch of the problem. A television antenna is perpendicular to the flat roof. There are three guy wires, but draw only one and then multiply the answer by 3 to find out how much wire is used on the antenna.

$$c^2 = a^2 + b^2$$
$$c^2 = 7^2 + 24^2$$
$$c^2 = 49 + 576 = 625$$
$$c = \sqrt{625} = 25$$
$$3 \times 25 = 75 \text{ feet of wire}$$

6. (2) 12

First draw a sketch of the problem.

$$c^2 = a^2 + b^2$$
$$13^2 = a^2 + 5^2$$
$$169 = a^2 + 25$$
$$169 - 25 = a^2$$
$$144 = a^2$$
$$\sqrt{144} = a$$
$$12 = a$$

Exercise 6: Perimeter
pages 668–669

1. 360 ft $P = 4s$
$$P = 4 \times 90 = 360 \text{ ft}$$

2. $3\frac{1}{4}$ ft

First, find the number of inches:
$$P = 2l + 2w$$
$$P = 2\left(8\tfrac{1}{2}\right) + 2(11) = 2\left(\tfrac{17}{2}\right) + 22$$
$$P = 17 + 22 = 39 \text{ inches}$$
Then, change inches to feet:
$$39 \div 12 = 3\tfrac{3}{12} = 3\tfrac{1}{4} \text{ feet}$$

3. 49.9 in $P = a + b + c$
$$P = 16.5 + 12.4 + 21 = 49.9 \text{ in}$$

4. $2691

First, find the total perimeter:
$$P = 2l + 2w$$
$$= 2(400) + 2(224)$$
$$= 800 + 448 = 1248 \text{ yd}$$
Then, convert to feet:
$$1248 \times 3 = 3744 \text{ ft}$$
Then, find the number of 8-foot sections:
$$3744 \div 8 = 468 \text{ sections}$$
Finally, find the total cost:
$$468 \times 5\tfrac{3}{4} = \tfrac{468}{1} \times \tfrac{23}{4} = 117 \times 23 = \$2691$$

5. 70 m

First, find the lengths of the sides that are not labeled:
$$20 - 15.3 = 4.7$$
$$10.8 + 4.2 = 15.0$$
Then, add all of the sides together:
$$20 + 4.2 + 4.7 + 10.8 + 15.3 + 15 = 70 \text{ m}$$

6. 194 ft

Find the perimeter:
$$P = 2l + 2w$$
$$= 2(70) + 2(48) = 236$$
Subtract the length of the house:
$$236 - 42 = 194 \text{ feet}$$

7. 8 times

First, find the perimeter of the block:
$$P = 2l + 2w$$
$$= 2\left(\tfrac{1}{4}\right) + 2\left(\tfrac{1}{8}\right)$$
$$= \tfrac{2}{4} + \tfrac{2}{8} = \tfrac{4}{8} + \tfrac{2}{8} = \tfrac{6}{8} = \tfrac{3}{4} \text{ mile}$$

Then, find how many times around the block equals 6 miles:
$$6 \div \tfrac{3}{4} = \tfrac{6}{1} \times \tfrac{4}{3} = \tfrac{24}{3} = 8 \text{ times}$$

8. 97.68 m

The perimeter of the rink includes two sides of 30 meters and the circumference of two half-circles (or one full circle). Find the circumference of the circle:
$$C = \pi d$$
$$= 3.14(12) = 37.68 \text{ meters}$$
Add the given sides to the circumference:
$$30 + 30 + 37.68 = 97.68 \text{ meters}$$

Exercise 7: Area
pages 670–671

1. 128.7 m² $A = lw$
$$= 14.3 \times 9$$
$$= 128.7 \text{ m}^2$$

2. 75.09 sq in

This figure consists of two shapes.
Square: $A = s^2$
$$= 4.7 \times 4.7$$
$$= 22.09 \text{ sq in}$$
Rectangle: $A = lw$
$$= 5.3 \times 10$$
$$= 53 \text{ sq in}$$
Add together for total area:
$$53 + 22.09 = 75.09 \text{ sq in}$$

3. $\frac{11}{14}$ sq in $A = \pi r^2$
$$= \tfrac{22}{7} \times \left(\tfrac{1}{2}\right)^2$$
$$= \tfrac{22}{7} \times \tfrac{1}{4}$$
$$= \tfrac{11}{7} \times \tfrac{1}{2} = \tfrac{11}{14} \text{ sq in}$$

4. 50 sq yd

First, find the area of the room:
$$30 \times 15 = 450 \text{ sq ft}$$
Then, divide by 9 to get the number of square yards:
$$450 \div 9 = 50 \text{ sq yd}$$

5. $345

First, find the area of the room:
$$15 \times 20 = 300 \text{ sq ft}$$
Then, find the cost of the office:
$$300 \times \$1.15 = \$345$$

6. 78.5 sq ft

The largest possible diameter for this rug is 10 feet, so the radius is 5 feet.

The area is: $A = \pi r^2$
$$= 3.14 (5^2)$$
$$= 78.5 \text{ sq ft}$$

7. 200 sq ft
$A = lw$
$= 20 \times 10$
$= 200$

8. 10%
Find the area of the pool:
$A = \pi r^2$
$= 3.14 \times 9^2 = 254.34$ sq ft
Find the area of the yard:
$A = lw$
$= 45 \times 58 = 2610$ sq ft
Round the area of the pool and make a ratio:

$$\frac{\text{area of pool}}{\text{area of yard}} = \frac{254}{2610}$$

$$\frac{254}{2610} = \frac{n}{100} = \frac{254 \times 100}{2610}$$

$$\frac{25,400}{2610} = 9.7; \text{ rounds to } 10\%$$

9. 22.22 sq yd
First, find the area of the patio:
$A = lw = 20 \times 10 = 200$ sq ft
Then, divide by 9 (number of square feet in a square yard):
$200 \div 9 = 22.22$ sq yd

10. 4 times larger
First, find the area of the pool:
$A = \pi r^2 = 3.14 \times 9^2 = 254.34$
Then, find the area of the garden:
$A = s^2 = 8^2 = 64$

Then find $\dfrac{\text{pool}}{\text{garden}}$
$\dfrac{254}{64} = 3.97 = 4$ times larger

Exercise 8: Volume
page 672

1. 72 cu ft $\quad V = lwh$
$= (6)(3)(4)$
$= 72$ cu ft

2. 45 gallons
Find the volume of the fish tank:
$V = (18)(12)(48)$
$= 10,368$ cu in
Find how many gallons will fit in this tank:
$10,368 \div 231 = 44.9 = 45$ gallons

3. 500 cu ft
Convert 6 inches to $\frac{1}{2}$ foot:
$V = (25)(40)(\frac{1}{2})$
$= 500$ cu ft

4. $\frac{1}{8}$

Find the volume of each cube:
$V = 2^3 = 8$ cu in
$V = 4^3 = 64$ cu in
Compare the two with a ratio:
$\dfrac{\text{small cube}}{\text{large cube}} = \dfrac{8}{64} = \dfrac{1}{8}$

5. 25,872 cu ft
$V = \pi r^2 h$
$= \frac{22}{7}(14^2)(42)$
$= 22(196)(6) = 25,872$ cu ft

Exercise 9: Review of Geometry
pages 673–674

1. (3) 33
First, find the perimeter of each window.
Window A:
$2l + 2w = 2(36) + 2(54) = 180$ in
Window B:
$2l + 2w = 2(60) + 2(48) = \underline{216 \text{ in}}$
$\qquad\qquad\qquad$ Total $= 396$ in
Then, find how many feet this is:
$396 \div 12 = 33$ feet

2. (4) 230 $\quad V = lwh$
$= 11\frac{1}{2} \times 8 \times 2\frac{1}{2}$
$= \frac{23}{2} \times \frac{8}{1} \times \frac{5}{2}$
$= 23 \times 2 \times 5 = 230$ cu in

3. (1) $(3.14)(1.5)^2(4)$
This represents substitution in the formula $V = \pi r^2 h$. The radius, r, which is $\frac{1}{2}$ the diameter (3), is 1.5.

4. (2) 8 $\qquad c^2 = a^2 + b^2$
$17^2 = 15^2 + b^2$
$289 = 225 + b^2$
$289 - 225 = b^2$
$64 = b^2$
8 in $= b$

5. (3) 1386 $\quad A = \pi r^2$
$= (\frac{22}{7})(21)^2$
$= (\frac{22}{7})(\frac{21 \times 21}{1})$
$= (22)(63) = 1386$ sq mi

6. (5) not enough information is given
To find this, you would need the radius of the half-circle. The radius is not given.

7. (3) 60 $\quad A = \frac{1}{2}bh$
$= \frac{1}{2}(15)(8) = 60$ sq ft

8. (3) 400 m $\quad \dfrac{d}{40} = \dfrac{250}{25}$
$d = \dfrac{250 \times 40}{25} = 400$ meters

9. (1) 30° $\qquad 90° + 60° = 150°$
$180° - 150° = 30°$

10. (1) $t = \dfrac{s \times b}{a}$

This represents the solution to the proportion that can be used to find a side of a similar triangle.

$\dfrac{t}{b} = \dfrac{s}{a}$
$t = \dfrac{s \times b}{a}$

11. (1) $17\frac{1}{2}$ $\quad \dfrac{\text{height}}{\text{shadow}} = \dfrac{\text{height}}{\text{shadow}}$
$\dfrac{5}{12} = \dfrac{n}{42}$
$\dfrac{42 \times 5}{12} = \dfrac{210}{12} = 17\frac{1}{2}$

12. (2) 10 feet $\quad c^2 = a^2 + b^2$
$c^2 = 8^2 + 6^2 = 100$
$c = 10$ feet

13. (3) 108°
Find the angles being compared:
$180° - 57° = 123°$
$90° - 75° = 15°$
Find the difference:
$123° - 15° = 108°$

14. **(2) 96**

Cargo area = lwh
$= 8 \times 8 \times 12 = 768$ cu ft

Boxes = $s^3 = 2^3 = 8$ cu ft

Find how many boxes will fit:
$768 \div 8 = 96$ boxes

15. **(1) 100**

$C = \pi d$
$628 = 3.14d$
$\dfrac{628}{3.14} = d$
$200 = d$
$100 = \dfrac{1}{2}d$ or r

CHAPTER 10: ALGEBRA

Exercise 1: Terms
page 676

1. 4 and $+x$
2. $8x$ and $+7y$ and -5
3. $2x^2$ and $-\dfrac{3}{x}$
4. $8ab$ and $+12$

Exercise 2: Equations
page 677

1. 5 added to 7 times a number (y) equals 19.
2. 9 times a number (y) is 27.
3. A number (a) minus 5 equals 23.
4. 10 divided by a number (y) minus 5 equals 0.
5. A number (y) divided by 8 equals 9.

Exercise 3: Eyeballing
page 678

1. 2   3. 5   5. 13   7. 2
2. 10   4. 5   6. 3   8. 4

Exercise 4: One-Step Equations
page 679

1. $x = 4$

$3 + x = 7$
$3 - 3 + x = 7 - 3$
$\quad 0$
$\qquad x = 4$

2. $x = 36$

$\dfrac{x}{3} = 12$
$\dfrac{3}{1} \cdot \dfrac{x}{3} = 12 \cdot 3$
$x = 36$

3. $x = 3$

$2x = 6$
$\dfrac{2x}{2} = \dfrac{6}{2}$
$x = 3$

4. $x = 8$

$x - 8 = 0$
$x \underbrace{- 8 + 8}_{0} = 0 + 8$
$\qquad x = 8$

5. $x = 15$

$5x = 75$
$\dfrac{5x}{5} = \dfrac{75}{5}$
$x = 15$

6. $x = 64$

$\dfrac{x}{4} = 16$
$\dfrac{4}{1} \cdot \dfrac{x}{4} = 16 \cdot 4$
$x = 64$

7. $x = 15$

$x - 3 = 12$
$x \underbrace{-3 + 3}_{0} = 12 + 3$
$\qquad x = 15$

8. $x = 28$

$\dfrac{1}{2}x = 14$
$\dfrac{2}{1} \cdot \dfrac{1}{2}x = 14 \cdot 2$
$x = 28$

Exercise 5: Translating English to Algebra
page 681

1. $6 - x$
2. $14x$
3. $\dfrac{x - y}{3}$
4. $x^2 + y^2$
5. $4(x + 10)$
6. $2x - 7$
7. $x^2 + 12$
8. $\dfrac{x^3}{4}$
9. $(x + y) - 4$
10. $\dfrac{5x}{2x}$

Exercise 6: Translating Sentences to Equations
pages 682–683

1. $\dfrac{1}{4}x = 18$ or $\dfrac{x}{4} = 18$
2. $x - 2 = 40$
3. $3x + 1 = 25$
4. $9 + \dfrac{1}{2}x = 13$
   or $9 + \dfrac{x}{2} = 13$
5. $6x = 35$
6. $x - y = 8$
7. $18 + 2x = 22$
8. $\dfrac{x}{4} = 18$
9. $2x - 3 = 5x + 9$
10. **(3)** $x - 48 = 75$
11. **(1)** $x - 5 = 19$
12. **(4)** $\dfrac{x}{7} = 5$
13. **(3)** $22 + 12h = 64$
14. **(1)** $x + 6 = \dfrac{7}{6}x$

Exercise 7: Solving One-Step Algebra Word Problems
page 684

1. $x = 15$

$x - 7 = 8$
$x \underbrace{- 7 + 7}_{0} = 8 + 7$
$\qquad x = 15$

2. **18 baseballs**

$2.25x = 40.50$
$\dfrac{2.25}{2.25}x = \dfrac{40.50}{2.25} = 18$

3. $x = \$20$

$\dfrac{1}{8}x = 2.50$
$\dfrac{8}{1} \cdot \dfrac{1}{8}x = 2.50 \cdot 8$
$x = \$20$

4. $x = \$192$

$72 = x - 120$
$72 + 120 = x \underbrace{- 120 + 120}_{0}$
$\$192 = x$

5. $x = 12$ ft

$x - 5\dfrac{1}{2} = 6\dfrac{1}{2}$
$x \underbrace{- 5\dfrac{1}{2} + 5\dfrac{1}{2}}_{0} = 6\dfrac{1}{2} + 5\dfrac{1}{2}$
$\qquad x = 12$

6. $x = 158$ lbs

$$x + 14 = 172$$
$$\underbrace{x + 14 - 14}_{0} = 172 - 14$$
$$x = 158$$

7. $x = 36$ years

$$x + 12 = 48$$
$$x + 12 - 12 = 48 - 12$$
$$0$$
$$x = 36$$

8. $x = \$5793.75$

$$927 = .16x$$
$$\frac{927}{.16} = \frac{.16x}{.16}$$
$$927 \div .16 = x$$
$$\$5793.75 = x$$

Exercise 8: Combining Like Terms
page 685

1. $15x$ **6.** $5x^2 + 7x + 9$
2. $3y$ **7.** $3a$
3. $9x + 9y$ **8.** $x + y$
4. $7x^2 + 5x$ **9.** $12a^2 + 5a$
5. $13x - 3$ **10.** $9xy + 6x - 3y$

Exercise 9: Removing Grouping Symbols
page 686

1. $5(3x + 2) = 15x + 10$
2. $4(7x - 8) = 28x - 32$
3. $6x + 2(12x - 7) = 6x + 24x - 14$
$$= 30x - 14$$
4. $2(x - 1) = 2x - 2$
5. $3(2x + 4 - 3y) = 6x + 12 - 9y$
6. $-6(5x - 12) = -30x + 72$
7. $x - 2(9 + 6x) = x - 18 - 12x$
$$= -11x - 18$$
8. $2(x - y) = 2x - 2y$

Exercise 10: Solving Multi-Step Equations
page 687

1. $x = 2$

$$3x + 9 = 15$$
$$3x + 9 - 9 = 15 - 9$$
$$3x = 6$$
$$x = 2$$

2. $x = 14$

$$2x - 26 = 2$$
$$2x - 26 + 26 = 2 + 26$$
$$2x = 28$$
$$x = 14$$

3. $x = 15$

$$\frac{x}{3} + 4 = 9$$
$$\frac{x}{3} + 4 - 4 = 9 - 4$$
$$\frac{x}{3} = 5$$
$$x = 15$$

4. $x = 21$

$$\frac{4x}{3} - 14 = 14$$
$$\frac{4x}{3} - 14 + 14 = 14 + 14$$
$$\frac{4x}{3} = 28$$
$$4x = 84$$
$$x = 21$$

5. $x = 4$

$$8(x - 4) = 0$$
$$8x - 32 = 0$$
$$8x - 32 + 32 = 0 + 32$$
$$8x = 32$$
$$x = 4$$

6. $x = 1$

$$2(5x - 11) + 12x = 0$$
$$10x - 22 + 12x = 0$$
$$22x - 22 + 22 = 0 + 22$$
$$22x = 22$$
$$x = 1$$

Exercise 11: Setting Up and Solving Multi-Step Equations
pages 688–690

1. (4) $3(x + 32) = 123$
2. (1) $\$9$
3. (4) $2x + 24 = 56$
4. (1) 16
5. (4) $(2x - 6) + x = 42$
6. (2) 16
7. (5) $4800 + 36x = 10,200$
8. (2) $\$150.00$
9. (5) **not enough information is given**
You do not know how many attendees were contest winners.
10. (5) not enough information is given

Exercise 12: Number Line
page 692

1. $1\frac{1}{2} > -1$ **3.** $-2 > -3$
2. $-4 < -2\frac{1}{2}$ **4.** $-6 < 0$

Exercise 13: Signed Numbers
page 692

1. $-\$12$ **9.** $0 > -4$
2. $-15°F$ **10.** $-6 < 2.4$
3. -3 yd   **11.** $-\frac{1}{4} > -\frac{1}{2}$
4. $+\$75$
5. $+4\frac{1}{2}$ pt   **12.** 9
                        13. $\frac{1}{2}$
6. $7 < 11$
7. $-9 < -4$ **14.** $2\frac{1}{3}$
8. $-3 < 1$ **15.** 3

Exercise 14: Combining Signed Numbers
page 694

1. 15   **4.** -2 **7.** -96 **10.** -19
2. -1 **5.** -5 **8.** -3 **11.** 3.8
3. -17 **6.** -33 **9.** 35   **12.** -7.7

Exercise 15: Eliminating Double Signs
page 694

1. $-6 - (-2) = -6 + 2 = -4$
2. $-6 + (-2) - (-9) =$
$$-6 - 2 + 9 = 1$$
3. $3 - (+8) = 3 - 8 = -5$
4. **total gain of 22 yd**

$$
\begin{array}{rr}
+23 & -4 \\
+8 & -6 \\
\underline{+3} & \underline{-2} \\
34 & -12 \\
\end{array}
$$
$$+34 - 12 = +22$$

5. $3\frac{2}{3}$ yd $22 \div 6 = 3\frac{2}{3}$

6. $19°$ $12 - (-7) = 12 + 7 = 19$

7. **$158**

$$
\begin{array}{rr}
+140 & -14 \\
+56 & -32 \\
\underline{+26} & \underline{-18} \\
+222 & -64 \\
\end{array}
$$
$$+222 + (-64) = +158$$

Exercise 16: Multiplying and Dividing Signed Numbers
page 696

1. 40   5. 225   9. -5
2. -144 6. 36   10. 3
3. -30 7. -84 11. -4
4. -88 8. 0   12. 5
13. $-1\frac{1}{2}$ or a drop of $1\frac{1}{2}$ pt

$$\left(-\frac{3}{8}\right)(4) = -\frac{12}{8} = -1\frac{1}{2}$$

14. $-\$22,284$

$$(-\$2476)(9) = -\$22,284$$

Exercise 17: One-Step Inequalities
page 697

1. $x > -2$ $x - 3 > -5$
$x - 3 + 3 > -5 + 3$
$x > -2$
2. $x < 2$ $5 + x < 7$
$5 - 5 + x < 7 - 5$
$x < 2$
3. $x < -7$ $-3 + x < -10$
$-3 + 3 + x < -10 + 3$
$x < -7$
4. $x > -36$ $\dfrac{x}{-3} < 12$
$-3 \cdot \dfrac{x}{-3} > 12 \cdot (-3)$
$x > -36$
Note change in direction.
5. $x \geq 4$ $x - 5 \geq -1$
$x - 5 + 5 \geq -1 + 5$
$x \geq 4$
6. $x < -2$ $-4x > 8$
$\dfrac{-4x}{-4} < \dfrac{8}{-4}$
$x < -2$
Note change in direction.
7. $x \leq 7$ $x - 7 \leq 0$
$x - 7 + 7 \leq 0 + 7$
$x \leq 7$
8. $14 > x$ $70 > 5x$
$\dfrac{70}{5} > \dfrac{5x}{5}$
$14 > x$
9. $x < 4$ $-4x > -16$
$\dfrac{-4x}{-4} < \dfrac{-16}{-4}$
$x < 4$
Note change in direction.

Exercise 18: Multiplying Algebraic Expressions
page 699

1. $24x^3$ $8x \cdot 3x^2 =$
$8 \cdot 3 \cdot x \cdot x^2 = 24x^3$
2. $-28x^2y$ $7xy(-4x) =$
$7 \cdot (-4) \cdot x \cdot x \cdot y = -28x^2y$
3. $-18a^3b^2$ $(-6ab^2)(3a^2) =$
$-6 \cdot 3 \cdot a \cdot a^2 \cdot b^2 =$
$-18a^3b^2$
4. $-15x^3y^3$ $(-5x^2y)(3xy^2) =$
$-5 \cdot 3 \cdot x^2 \cdot x \cdot y \cdot y^2 =$
$-15x^3y^3$

5. $2x^3 + 2x$ $2x(x^2 + 1) =$
$2x \cdot x^2 + 2x \cdot 1 =$
$2x^3 + 2x$
6. $6y^3 - 12y^2 - 21y$
$3y(2y^2 - 4y - 7) =$
$3y(2y^2) + 3y(-4y) + 3y(-7) =$
$6y^3 - 12y^2 - 21y$

Exercise 19: The Greatest Common Factor
page 700

1. $7x^2(3x - 2)$
$21x^3 - 14x^2 =$
$7x^2(3x) + 7x^2(-2) =$
$7x^2(3x - 2)$
2. $4a^2(25a^2 - 4)$
$100a^4 - 16a^2 =$
$4a^2(25a^2) + 4a^2(-4) =$
$4a^2(25a^2 - 4)$
3. $11p^4(11p - 3)$
$121p^5 - 33p^4 =$
$11p^4(11p) + 11p^4(-3) =$
$11p^4(11p - 3)$
4. $4(2x^2 - 1)$
$8x^2 - 4 =$
$4(2x^2) + 4(-1) =$
$4(2x^2 - 1)$
5. $9x^2y^2(x + 4y)$
$9x^3y^2 + 36x^2y^3 =$
$9x^2y^2(x) + 9x^2y^2(4y) =$
$9x^2y^2(x + 4y)$
6. $50x^2(2x^3 - x + 2)$
$100x^5 - 50x^3 + 100x^2 =$
$50x^2(2x^3) + 50x^2(-x) + 50x^2(2) =$
$50x^2(2x^3 - x + 2)$
7. $5x^2(x^2 + 5x - 4)$
$5x^4 + 25x^3 - 20x^2 =$
$5x^2(x^2) + 5x^2(5x) + 5x^2(-4) =$
$5x^2(x^2 + 5x - 4)$
8. $9x(x^2 - 1)$
$9x^3 - 9x =$
$9x(x^2) + 9x(-1) =$
$9x(x^2 - 1)$

Exercise 20: Factoring by Grouping
page 700

1. $(x + 4)(x + 3)$
$x^2 + 4x + 3x + 12$
$x(x + 4) + 3(x + 4)$
$(x + 4)(x + 3)$
2. $(x - 2)(x + 5)$
$x^2 - 2x + 5x - 10$
$x(x - 2) + 5(x - 2)$
$(x - 2)(x + 5)$
3. $(4y + 3z)(2y + 3z)$
$8y^2 + 6yz + 12yz + 9z^2$
$2y(4y + 3z) + 3z(4y + 3z)$
$(4y + 3z)(2y + 3z)$
4. $(x - 4)(2y^2 + 1)$
$2xy^2 - 8y^2 + x - 4$
$2y^2(x - 4) + 1(x - 4)$
$(x - 4)(2y^2 + 1)$
Notice 1 is the common factor of the second pair of terms.

Exercise 21: Ordered Pairs
page 702
1. $A(2,2)$ 4. $D(0,0)$ 7. $G(0,-2)$
2. $B(0,3)$ 5. $E(-5,0)$ 8. $H(1,-1)$
3. $C(-3,1)$ 6. $F(-1,-4)$ 9. $I(3,0)$

Exercise 22: Distance by Counting
page 704
1. 9   2. 9   3. 3   4. 5   5. 6

Exercise 23: Distance Between
Two Points
page 704

1. **5** $(x_1, y_1) = (0, -2)$
$(x_2, y_2) = (4, -5)$
$d = \sqrt{(4-0)^2 + (-5-(-2))^2}$
$= \sqrt{4^2 + (-3)^2}$
$= \sqrt{16 + 9}$
$= \sqrt{25} = 5$

2. **13** $(x_1, y_1) = (6,3)$
$(x_2, y_2) = (-6,-2)$
$d = \sqrt{(-6-6)^2 + (-2-3)^2}$
$= \sqrt{(-12)^2 + (-5)^2}$
$= \sqrt{144 + 25}$
$= \sqrt{169} = 13$

3. **6** E and F are on the same vertical line.
Count the units from $(1,4)$ to $(1,-2)$;
$d = 6$

4. **$5\sqrt{2}$** $(x_1, y_1) = (-2,3)$
$(x_2, y_2) = (-1,-4)$
$d = \sqrt{(-1-(-2))^2 + (-4-3)^2}$
$= \sqrt{(-1+2)^2 + (-7)^2}$
$= \sqrt{1^2 + (-7)^2}$
$= \sqrt{1 + 49}$
$= \sqrt{50} = \sqrt{25 \cdot 2} = 5\sqrt{2}$

5. **6**   The distance can be counted;
$d = 6$

Exercise 24: The Slope of a Line
page 706

1. $\frac{4}{3}$ $\frac{4-0}{3-0} = \frac{4}{3}$

2. $\frac{1}{11}$ $\frac{0-(-1)}{6-(-5)} = \frac{1}{11} = \frac{1}{11}$

3. **0** $\frac{3-3}{9-(-9)} = \frac{0}{18} = 0$

4. **-1** $\frac{-1-(-2)}{-2-(-1)} = \frac{-1+2}{-2+1} = \frac{1}{-1} = -1$

5. **1** $\frac{2-3}{-1-0} = \frac{-1}{-1} = 1$

6. $\frac{1}{2}$ $\frac{-6-(-3)}{-3-3} = \frac{-3}{-6} = \frac{1}{2}$

7. **0**   The line is parallel to the x-axis; the
slope is 0.

8. $\frac{3}{7}$ $\frac{5-8}{0-7} = \frac{-3}{-7} = \frac{3}{7}$

Exercise 25: Algebra Review
pages 707–710

1. **(2)** $1400 - 120x$
Let $120x = $ depreciation in x years
$1400 - 120x = $ value at end of x years

2. **(5)** $\frac{1}{3}x + 70 = \frac{1}{2}x$

Let $x = $ monthly salary
$\frac{1}{3}x = \frac{1}{3}$ salary and $\frac{1}{2}x = \frac{1}{2}$ salary
$\frac{1}{3}x + 70 = \frac{1}{2}x$

3. **(3) 9 in**   Let $x = $ shortest piece
$x + 6 = $ second piece
$2x = $ third piece
$x + (x + 6) + 2x = 42$
$4x + 6 = 42$
$4x + 6 - 6 = 42 - 6$
$4x = 36$
$x = 9$

4. **(2)** $2x + 2(x + 5) = 78$
Let $x = $ width
$x + 5 = $ length
$P = 2l + 2w$
$78 = 2(x + 5) + 2x$

5. **(2) 20°** $-12 + 25 + 7 = -12 + 32 = 20$

6. **(1)** -3 Let $x = $ the number
$10x - 6x = 2x - 6$
$10x - 6x - 2x = 2x - 2x - 6$
$2x = -6$
$x = \frac{-6}{2} = -3$

7. **(1) 240 ft** $h = 128t - 16t^2$
$= 128(3) - 16(3)^2$
$= 384 - 16(9)$
$= 384 - 144 = 240$

8. **(1)** -4
$3x + 2(4 - x) = x - (3x + 1) - 3$
$3x + 8 - 2x = x - 3x - 1 - 3$
$x + 8 = -2x - 4$
$x + 2x + 8 = -2x + 2x - 4$
$3x + 8 = -4$
$3x + 8 - 8 = -4 - 8$
$3x = -12$
$x = -4$

9. **(3)** $x < 8$
$x + 5 < 13$
$x + 5 - 5 < 13 - 5$
$x < 8$

10. (3) 20
Let x = number of hours at 55 mph
$x + 2$ = 2 more hours
$$55x = 45(x + 2)$$
$$55x = 45x + 90$$
$$55x - 45x = 45x - 45x + 90$$
$$10x = 90$$
$$x = 9$$
$$x + x + 2 = 9 + 9 + 2 = 20 \text{ hr}$$

11. (2) 37 yd $+17 - 4 - 4 + 28 =$
$+45 - 8 = +37$

12. (3) $24x = 672$
Let x = number of gallons
miles per gallon $\times$ gallons = miles
$24x = 672$

13. (4) $32 x = today
$2x$ = yesterday
$$x + 2x = 48$$
$$3x = 48$$
$$\frac{3x}{3} = \frac{48}{3}$$
$$x = 16 \quad 2x = 32$$

14. (5) not enough information is given
You are not able to set up an equation because you do not know how much she originally needed.

15. (3) 8 x-axis to (4,4) is 4
x-axis to (4,−4) is 4
$4 + 4 = 8$

16. (3) +376
chocolate sundae = +560 calories
three sets of tennis =
$3(-200) = -600$
one glass of orange juice = +96
six cookies = 2(160) = +320
$+560 - 600 + 96 + 320 =$
$976 - 600 = +376$

17. (4) 4
slice of cheesecake = 478
2 12-oz bottles of soda =
$2(105) = 210$
$478 + 210 = 688$ calories
$688 \div 172 = 4$ miles

18. (1) $-\dfrac{1}{9}$
$$m = \frac{y_2 - y_1}{x_2 - x_1}$$
$$= \frac{2 - 3}{5 - (-4)} = \frac{2 - 3}{5 + 4}$$
$$= \frac{-1}{9} = -\frac{1}{9}$$

Post-Tests

Since you began your study in this book, you have been moving closer to your goal—the actual GED Tests. To find out how ready you are, you should take the Post-Tests on the following pages. These tests will indicate how well you understood the subjects you studied in each of the five test areas presented earlier in this book. These Post-Tests will give you an idea of what the real ones are like. They are based on the real GED Tests with the same kinds and number of questions.

We recommend the following approach to the Post-Tests.

1. Take only one Post-Test at a time. Try to finish the test within the allotted time so that you can see how you will do on the actual GED Tests. If you are not done within that time period, mark where you were when the time was up and finish the test. You want to finish the entire Post-Test so that you can make use of the Evaluation Charts.

Time Allowed for Each Test		
Writing Skills	Part 1	75 minutes
	Part 2	45 minutes
Social Studies		85 minutes
Science		95 minutes
Literature and the Arts		65 minutes
Mathematics		90 minutes

2. After you have finished each of the Post-Tests, check the answers in the answer key and fill in the Evaluation Charts. The answer keys and Evaluation Charts follow each test. Be sure to read the explanations for all of the questions that you missed.

3. If the Evaluation Charts indicate that you still need work in a certain area, refer to the review pages given in the charts.

4. Although these are Post-Tests, you should give them your best effort. If an item seems difficult, mark it and come back later. Always answer every question—even if you have to make an "educated guess." Sometimes you may know more than you give yourself credit for. Also, on the real GED Tests a blank counts as a wrong answer. It's always wise to answer every question as best you can.

POST-TEST 1: WRITING SKILLS
Part 1: Conventions of English

The following items are based on paragraphs that contain numbered sentences. Some of the sentences may contain errors in sentence structure, usage, or mechanics. A few sentences, however, may be correct as written. Read the paragraph and then answer the items based on it. For each item, choose the answer that would result in the most effective writing of the sentence or sentences. The best answer must be consistent with the meaning and tone of the rest of the paragraph.

When you are finished with the test, check your answers and turn to the Evaluation Charts on pages 753 and 755. Use the charts to evaluate whether or not you are ready to take the final Practice Test and, if not, in what areas you need more work.

POST-TEST 1: WRITING SKILLS ANSWER GRID

1 ① ② ③ ④ ⑤	15 ① ② ③ ④ ⑤	29 ① ② ③ ④ ⑤	43 ① ② ③ ④ ⑤
2 ① ② ③ ④ ⑤	16 ① ② ③ ④ ⑤	30 ① ② ③ ④ ⑤	44 ① ② ③ ④ ⑤
3 ① ② ③ ④ ⑤	17 ① ② ③ ④ ⑤	31 ① ② ③ ④ ⑤	45 ① ② ③ ④ ⑤
4 ① ② ③ ④ ⑤	18 ① ② ③ ④ ⑤	32 ① ② ③ ④ ⑤	46 ① ② ③ ④ ⑤
5 ① ② ③ ④ ⑤	19 ① ② ③ ④ ⑤	33 ① ② ③ ④ ⑤	47 ① ② ③ ④ ⑤
6 ① ② ③ ④ ⑤	20 ① ② ③ ④ ⑤	34 ① ② ③ ④ ⑤	48 ① ② ③ ④ ⑤
7 ① ② ③ ④ ⑤	21 ① ② ③ ④ ⑤	35 ① ② ③ ④ ⑤	49 ① ② ③ ④ ⑤
8 ① ② ③ ④ ⑤	22 ① ② ③ ④ ⑤	36 ① ② ③ ④ ⑤	50 ① ② ③ ④ ⑤
9 ① ② ③ ④ ⑤	23 ① ② ③ ④ ⑤	37 ① ② ③ ④ ⑤	51 ① ② ③ ④ ⑤
10 ① ② ③ ④ ⑤	24 ① ② ③ ④ ⑤	38 ① ② ③ ④ ⑤	52 ① ② ③ ④ ⑤
11 ① ② ③ ④ ⑤	25 ① ② ③ ④ ⑤	39 ① ② ③ ④ ⑤	53 ① ② ③ ④ ⑤
12 ① ② ③ ④ ⑤	26 ① ② ③ ④ ⑤	40 ① ② ③ ④ ⑤	54 ① ② ③ ④ ⑤
13 ① ② ③ ④ ⑤	27 ① ② ③ ④ ⑤	41 ① ② ③ ④ ⑤	55 ① ② ③ ④ ⑤
14 ① ② ③ ④ ⑤	28 ① ② ③ ④ ⑤	42 ① ② ③ ④ ⑤	

Choose the best answer to each question that follows.

Questions 1–11 refer to the following passage.

(1) Many people own and operate microwave ovens, but they were not really aware of exactly how a microwave oven cooks their food. (2) A magnetron tube in the oven convert electrical energy to microwave energy and directs that energy to a fanlike stirrer. (3) The stirrer evenly channels into the oven the short radio waves who penetrate food and cause the molecules in the food to vibrate. (4) This vibration or friction creating the heat that cooks the food. (5) Glass, paper, and most types of china are used in microwave cooking becuase the microwaves can pass through these containers; however, the microwaves do not pass through metal. (6) The microwaves penetrated the food to a depth of ¾ to 1½ inches. (7) As cooking continues, the heat spreads to the interior of the food. (8) When the microwaves stop, the friction action continues, slows, and it stops.

(9) Most microwave ovens have settings such as warm, defrost, simmer medium-high, and high so that a person can choose the speed at which the food cooks. (10) The time needed to cook food depends on the amount of food being cooked. (11) One hot dog may cook in one minute, while four hot dogs take about two minutes, and six hot dogs take about four minutes. (12) Microwave ovens vary in features, and size, but owners can safely and effectively use this household appliance by following instructions carefully.

1. Sentence 1: **Many people own and operate microwave ovens, but they were not really aware of exactly how a microwave oven cooks their food.**

   What correction should be made to this sentence?

   (1) change *own* to *owns*
   (2) remove the comma after *ovens*
   (3) replace *they* with *he or she*
   (4) replace *were* with *are*
   (5) replace *their* with *they're*

2. Sentence 2: **A magnetron tube in the oven convert electrical energy to microwave energy and directs that energy to a fanlike stirrer.**

   What correction should be made to this sentence?

   (1) insert a comma after *oven*
   (2) change *convert* to *converts*
   (3) insert a comma after *microwave energy*
   (4) change *directs* to *direct*
   (5) no correction is necessary

3. Sentence 3: **The stirrer evenly channels into the oven the short radio waves who penetrate food and cause the molecules in the food to vibrate.**

   What correction should be made to this sentence?

   (1) insert a comma after *oven*
   (2) change *waves* to *waves'*
   (3) replace *who* with *that*
   (4) insert a comma after *food*
   (5) no correction is necessary

4. Sentence 4: **This vibration or friction <u>creating</u> the heat that cooks the food.**

   Which of the following is the best way to write the underlined portion of this sentence? If you think the original is the best way, choose option (1).

   (1) creating
   (2) may create
   (3) creates
   (4) then creating
   (5) create

5. Sentence 5: **Glass, paper, and most types of china are used in microwave cooking becuase the microwaves can pass through these containers; however, the microwaves do not pass through metal.**

What correction should be made to this sentence?

(1) remove the comma after *Glass*
(2) replace *china* with *China*
(3) replace *are* with *is*
(4) change the spelling of *becuase* to *because*
(5) replace *containers; however* with *containers, however*

6. Sentence 6: **The microwaves <u>penetrated</u> the food to a depth of ¾ to 1½ inches.**

Which of the following is the best way to write the underlined portion of this sentence? If you think the original is the best way, choose option (1).

(1) penetrated
(2) penetrates
(3) penetrate
(4) had penetrated
(5) will penetrate

7. Sentence 7: **As cooking continues, the heat spreads to the interior of the food.**

What correction should be made to this sentence?

(1) change *continues* to *continuing*
(2) remove the comma after *continues*
(3) change *spreads* to *spread*
(4) insert a comma after *interior*
(5) no correction is necessary

8. Sentence 8: **When the microwaves stop, the friction action continues, slows, and <u>it stops</u>.**

Which of the following is the best way to write the underlined portion of this sentence? If you think the original is the best way, choose option (1).

(1) it stops
(2) they stop
(3) stops
(4) to stop
(5) stopped

9. Sentence 9: **Most microwave ovens have settings such as warm, defrost, simmer medium-high, and high so that a person can choose the speed at which the food cooks.**

What correction should be made to this sentence?

(1) change *have* to *has*
(2) insert a comma after *simmer*
(3) replace *a person* with *you*
(4) change *choose* to *chose*
(5) change *cooks* to *cooking*

10. Sentences 10 and 11: **The time needed to cook food depends on the amount of food being cooked. One hot dog may cook in one minute, while four hot dogs take about two minutes, and six hot dogs take about four minutes.**

The most effective combination of sentences 10 and 11 would include which of the following groups of words?

(1) cooked, one hot dog
(2) cooked, but one hot dog
(3) cooked; however, one hot dog
(4) cooked; for example, one hot dog
(5) cooked although one hot dog

11. Sentence 12: **Microwave ovens vary in features, and size, but owners can safely and effectively use this household appliance by following instructions carefully.**

What correction should be made to this sentence?

(1) change *vary* to *varies*
(2) remove the comma after *features*
(3) remove the comma after *size*
(4) insert a comma after *safely*
(5) change the spelling of *carefully* to *carfully*

Questions 12–23 refer to the following passage.

(1) Americans have been jogging for several years, and most of us were aware of the many physical and psychological benefits of running or walking outdoors. (2) For many people, however, hectic schedules make it difficult to find the time to go out and run around the neighborhood. (3) Some people do not want to be seen perspiring and jiggling along their neighbors sidewalks, and others are afraid to jog after sundown, the only time they have to exercise. (4) A good alternative to outdoor jogging are staying inside one's room, apartment, or house and running in place. (5) Although some joggers enjoy the privacy of this form of exercise, its main advantage is convenience. (6) A person who does not relish the idea of jogging outdoors in the heat of summer or the cold of Winter can find a spot on the floor and run in place. (7) Experts state that they should jog for at least fifteen minutes and run more vigorously than they would outside. (8) Knees and feet should be raised high off the floor the runner must be careful of wearing the carpet thin! (9) Wearing good running shoes and running on a thick carpet or folded throw rug may reduce stress on feet and ankles. (10) Indoor runners can releive the boredom by watching television, listening to music, or including children in the exercise time. (11) If parents have to stay home alone with small children who need supervision, indoor jogging be a good way for them to keep fit.

(12) Indoor runners may not breath fresh air or appreciate nature, but those who would otherwise be sitting in front of their televisions are better off jogging.

12. Sentence 1: **Americans have been jogging for several years, and most of us were aware of the many physical and psychological benefits of running or walking outdoors.**

What correction should be made to this sentence?

(1) replace *years* with *year's*
(2) remove the comma after *years*
(3) change *were* to *are*
(4) change the spelling of *benefits* to *bennefits*
(5) no correction is necessary

13. Sentence 2: **For many people, however, hectic schedules make it difficult to find the time to go out and run around the neighborhood.**

Which of the following is the best way to write the underlined portion of this sentence? If you think the original is the best way, choose option (1).

(1) people, however, hectic
(2) people. However, hectic
(3) people; however, hectic
(4) people however, hectic
(5) people however hectic

14. Sentence 3: **Some people do not want to be seen perspiring and jiggling along their neighbors sidewalks, and others are afraid to jog after sundown, the only time they have to exercise.**

What correction should be made to this sentence?

(1) change *do* to *does*
(2) replace *their* with *there*
(3) replace *neighbors* with *neighbors'*
(4) remove the comma after *sidewalks*
(5) change the spelling of *exercise* to *exercize*

15. Sentence 4: **A good alternative to outdoor jogging are staying inside one's room, apartment, or house and running in place.**

    What correction should be made to this sentence?

    (1) change *are* to *is*
    (2) replace *one's* with *ones*
    (3) remove the comma after *room*
    (4) insert a comma after *house*
    (5) no correction is necessary

16. Sentence 5: **Although some joggers enjoy the privacy of this form of exercise, its main advantage is convenience.**

    If you rewrote sentence 5 beginning with

    While the main advantage of this form of exercise is convenience,

    the next word should be

    (1) so
    (2) although
    (3) enjoy
    (4) before
    (5) some

17. Sentence 6: **A person who does not relish the idea of jogging outdoors in the heat of summer or the cold of Winter can find a spot on the floor and run in place.**

    What correction should be made to this sentence?

    (1) replace *who* with *which*
    (2) insert a comma after *outdoors*
    (3) change *summer* to *Summer*
    (4) change *Winter* to *winter*
    (5) insert a comma after *floor*

18. Sentence 7: **Experts state that <u>they</u> should jog for at least fifteen minutes and run more vigorously than they would outside.**

    Which of the following is the best way to write the underlined portion of this sentence? If you think the original is the best way, choose option (1).

    (1) they
    (2) the experts
    (3) you
    (4) a person
    (5) indoor joggers

19. Sentence 8: **Knees and feet should be raised high off the <u>floor the</u> runner must be careful of wearing the carpet thin!**

    Which of the following is the best way to write the underlined portion of this sentence? If you think the original is the best way, choose option (1).

    (1) floor the
    (2) floor, the
    (3) floor, and the
    (4) floor; and the
    (5) floor, to the

20. Sentence 9: **Wearing good running shoes and running on a thick carpet or folded throw rug may reduce stress on feet and ankles.**

    If you rewrote sentence 9 beginning with

    To reduce stress on feet and ankles,

    the next word should be

    (1) wearing
    (2) joggers
    (3) running
    (4) should
    (5) to

21. Sentence 10: **Indoor runners can releive the boredom by watching television, listening to music, or including children in the exercise time.**

What correction should be made to this sentence?

(1) replace *runners* with *runners'*
(2) change the spelling of *releive* to *relieve*
(3) replace *listening* with *they can listen*
(4) change *including* to *include*
(5) no correction is necessary

22. Sentence 11: **If parents have to stay home alone with small children who need supervision, indoor jogging be a good way for them to keep fit.**

What correction should be made to this sentence?

(1) change *have* to *has*
(2) insert a comma after *alone*
(3) remove the comma after *supervision*
(4) replace *who* with *which*
(5) change *be* to *is*

23. Sentence 12: **Indoor runners may not breath fresh air or appreciate nature, but those who would otherwise be sitting in front of their televisions are better off jogging.**

What correction should be made to this sentence?

(1) change the spelling of *breath* to *breathe*
(2) change the spelling of *appreciate* to *apreciate*
(3) remove the comma after *nature*
(4) replace *but* with *or*
(5) no correction is necessary

Questions 24–34 refer to the following passage.

(1) Mars, a small rocky planet is about half the size of Earth. (2) Transmitted by an unmanned Mariner IV space probe, we on Earth first saw close-range photos of Mars in 1965. (3) In view was cratered landscapes, deserts, and mountains. (4) The highest mountain on Earth, Mt. Everest, is 5.5 miles high, one mountain on Mars reaches a height of 15 miles. (5) In 1976, Vikings I and II orbited and landed on Mars, produsing more high-quality, close-up photographs. (6) The additional photos will reveal huge mountains, deep holes, and sandy dunes on Mars. (7) Another feature revealed by the photos was large cracks in the surface of the planet one crack is larger than our Grand Canyon. (8) Dried-up riverbeds suggested that water once may have flowed on the Planet. (9) Also noticeable in the photos was that Mars looked red. (10) Looking for the source of the red color, scientists tested samples of Mars atmosphere and soil. (11) In the future, scientists will continue to study this planet that may tell us more about Earth's origins, development, and what may be ahead.

24. Sentence 1: **Mars, a small rocky planet is about half the size of Earth.**

What correction should be made to this sentence?

(1) remove the comma after *Mars*
(2) insert a comma after *planet*
(3) change *is* to *are*
(4) change *Earth* to *earth*
(5) no correction is necessary

25. Sentence 2: **Transmitted by an unmanned Mariner IV space probe, <u>we on Earth first saw close-range photos of Mars in 1965.</u>**

Which of the following is the best way to write the underlined portion of this sentence? If you think the original is the best way, choose option (1).

(1) we on Earth first saw close-range photos of Mars in 1965
(2) Mars was first seen by us on Earth in close-range photos in 1965
(3) Mars was first seen close-range by us in photos on Earth in 1965
(4) Mariner IV photos of us on Mars were first seen in 1965
(5) the first close-range photos of Mars were seen by us on Earth in 1965

26. Sentence 3: **In view <u>was</u> cratered landscapes, deserts, and mountains.**

Which of the following is the best way to write the underlined portion of this sentence? If you think the original is the best way, choose option (1).

(1) was
(2) were
(3) are
(4) is
(5) have been

27. Sentence 4: **The highest mountain on Earth, Mt. Everest, is 5.5 miles <u>high, one</u> mountain on Mars reaches a height of 15 miles.**

Which of the following is the best way to write the underlined portion of this sentence? If you think the original is the best way, choose option (1).

(1) high, one
(2) high, so one
(3) high; in contrast, one
(4) high; consequently, one
(5) high one

28. Sentence 5: **In 1976, Vikings I and II orbited and landed on Mars, produsing more high-quality, close-up photographs.**

What correction should be made to this sentence?

(1) replace *Vikings* with *vikings*
(2) change the spelling of *orbited* to *orbitted*
(3) change *landed* to *land*
(4) change the spelling of *produsing* to *producing*
(5) no correction is necessary

29. Sentence 6: **The additional photos will reveal huge mountains, deep holes, and sandy dunes on Mars.**

What correction should be made to this sentence?

(1) replace *photos* with *photo's*
(2) change *will reveal* to *revealed*
(3) replace *mountains* with *Mountains*
(4) insert a comma after *dunes*
(5) no correction is necessary

30. Sentence 7: **Another feature revealed by the photos was large cracks in the surface of the <u>planet one</u> crack is larger than our Grand Canyon.**

Which of the following is the best way to write the underlined portion of this sentence? If you think the original is the best way, choose option (1).

(1) planet one
(2) planet, one
(3) planet. One
(4) planet and one
(5) planet; however, one

31. Sentence 8: **Dried-up riverbeds suggested that water once may have flowed on the Planet.**

What correction should be made to this sentence?

(1) change *riverbeds* to *Riverbeds*
(2) change *suggested* to *suggests*
(3) change *flowed* to *flown*
(4) change *Planet* to *planet*
(5) no correction is necessary

32. Sentence 9: **Also noticeable in the photos was that Mars looked red.**

If you rewrote sentence 9 beginning with

The fact that Mars looked red

the next word should be

(1) was
(2) being
(3) noticeable
(4) and
(5) photos

33. Sentence 10: **Looking for the source of the red color, scientists tested samples of Mars atmosphere and soil.**

What correction should be made to this sentence?

(1) remove the comma after *color*
(2) replace *scientists* with *scientist's*
(3) replace *Mars* with *Mars's*
(4) add a comma after *atmosphere*
(5) no correction is necessary

34. Sentence 11: **In the future, scientists will continue to study this planet that may tell us more about Earth's origins, development, and <u>what may be ahead.</u>**

Which of the following is the best way to write the underlined portion of this sentence? If you think the original is the best way, choose option (1).

(1) what may be ahead
(2) what may lie ahead
(3) days ahead
(4) years ahead
(5) future

Questions 35–44 refer to the following.

(1) Consumers are constantly warned about the dangers of eating foods that may contribute to obesity, cavities, diabetes, heart disease, stress, or cancer. (2) We were told to avoid junk food, but that term means different things to different people. (3) To some people, junk food is fast food. (4) Other people think junk food is any food available in vending machines, such as potato chips, candy, cookies, ice cream bars, and soda pop. (5) Many of us are not quiet sure why we should not eat hot dogs, but we know they are also on the list of junk foods. (6) Lack of nutritional value, as well as negative health effects, are characteristic of junk food, say nutritionists. (7) Especially bad for us are sugar, salt, refined flour, and chemical additives. (8) Additives artificially improve the color, flavor, and shelf life of foods. (9) Refined sugar, which can be found in about one-fourth of the foods we eat, can affect us badly; in fact, though giving a boost of energy, stress can be caused by too much sugar. (10) So if our lunchboxes contains a sandwich made of cold cuts and slices of processed cheese on white bread, potato chips, and packaged pudding, nutrition is lacking. (11) Wanting quick and easy-to-prepare meals, you may be sacrificing nutrition for convenience. (12) By learning more about junk food and it's damaging effects, we may be healthier for years to come.

35. Sentence 1: **Consumers are constantly warned about the dangers of eating foods that may contribute to obesity, cavities, diabetes, heart disease, stress, or cancer.**

What correction should be made to this sentence?

(1) insert a comma after *warned*
(2) insert a comma after *to*
(3) remove the comma after *obesity*
(4) change *disease* to *disese*
(5) no correction is necessary

36. Sentence 2: **We were told to avoid junk food, but that term means different things to different people.**

What correction should be made to this sentence?

(1) change *were* to *are*
(2) insert a comma after *told*
(3) remove the comma after *food*
(4) replace *but* with *so*
(5) change the spelling of *different* to *differant*

37. Sentences 3 and 4: **To some people, junk food is fast food. Other people think junk food is any food available in vending machines, such as potato chips, candy, cookies, ice cream bars, and soda pop.**

The most effective combination of sentences 3 and 4 would include which of the following groups of words?

(1) fast food, but other people
(2) fast food or any food available
(3) fast food in vending machines
(4) junk food is available
(5) fast food; therefore, other people

38. Sentence 5: **Many of us are not quiet sure why we should not eat hot dogs, but we know they are also on the list of junk foods.**

What correction should be made to this sentence?

(1) replace *us* with *them*
(2) replace *quiet* with *quite*
(3) replace *hot dogs* with *Hot Dogs*
(4) remove the comma after *dogs*
(5) replace *they are* with *it is*

39. Sentence 6: **Lack of nutritional value, as well as negative health effects, <u>are</u> characteristic of junk food, say nutritionists.**

    Which of the following is the best way to write the underlined portion of this sentence? If you think the original is the best way, choose option (1).

    (1) are
    (2) is
    (3) were
    (4) was
    (5) being

40. Sentences 7 and 8: **Especially bad for us are sugar, salt, refined flour, and chemical additives. Additives artificially improve the color, flavor, and shelf life of foods.**

    The most effective combination of sentences 7 and 8 would include which of the following groups of words?

    (1) additives; in fact, all these ingredients
    (2) additives that artificially improve
    (3) additives artificially improve
    (4) additives, or they
    (5) additives' artificial color

41. Sentence 9: **Refined sugar, which can be found in about one-fourth of the foods we eat, can affect us badly; in fact, though giving a boost of energy, <u>stress can be caused by too much sugar.</u>**

    Which of the following is the best way to write the underlined portion of this sentence? If you think the original is the best way, choose option (1).

    (1) stress can be caused by too much sugar
    (2) too much sugar can cause stress
    (3) too much stress can be caused by sugar
    (4) stress is a result of eating too much sugar
    (5) sugar can cause too much stress

42. Sentence 10: **So if our lunchboxes contains a sandwich made of cold cuts and slices of processed cheese on white bread, potato chips, and packaged pudding, nutrition is lacking.**

    What correction should be made to this sentence?

    (1) replace *our* with *your*
    (2) change *contains* to *contain*
    (3) remove the comma after *bread*
    (4) remove the comma after *pudding*
    (5) no correction is necessary

43. Sentence 11: **Wanting quick and easy-to-prepare meals, you may be sacrificing nutrition for convenience.**

What correction should be made to this sentence?

(1) change the spelling of *prepare* to *prepair*
(2) remove the comma after *meals*
(3) replace *you* with *we*
(4) insert a comma after *nutrition*
(5) change the spelling of *convenience* to *conveniance*

44. Sentence 12: **By learning more about junk food and it's damaging effects, we may be healthier for years to come.**

What correction should be made to this sentence?

(1) insert a comma after *food*
(2) replace *it's* with *its*
(3) replace *effects* with *affects*
(4) change the spelling of *healthier* to *healthyer*
(5) no correction is necessary

Questions 45–55 refer to the following passage.

(1) Leasing a car can be a useful alternative to the high price tag of ownership. (2) In the last decade, the price of automobiles have risen greatly, and you can expect to spend over $15,000 for a car that cost $7,000 ten years ago. (3) An alternative to the high cost of new cars is buying a used car, but consumers have found that inflation also has effected the price of used cars. (4) Leasing a car can be a wise economic decision just as leasing a home has some advantages over buying. (5) Recently, the concept of leasing a car grew more popular. (6) Before leasing a car, you should shop around to see the variety of cars and lease agreements available. (7) You may have to pay a security deposit before you can sign a lease agreement, the monthly payments are usually lower than a typical monthly loan payment on a new car. (8) Some leasing business's allow you to apply all of your payments to the eventual purchase of the car, much like renting with an option to buy a home. (9) Other companies simply rent by the month and do not wish to sell its rental cars. (10) You should study carefully any leasing agreement before signing it. (11) Issues to consider before signing include responsibility for maintenance and insurance. (12) Before completing the deal, the car should be examined by all potential drivers.

45. Sentence 1: **Leasing a car can be a useful alternative to the high price tag of ownership.**

What correction should be made to this sentence?

(1) change *can be* to *was*
(2) change the spelling of *useful* to *usefull*
(3) insert a comma after *alternative*
(4) insert a comma after *tag*
(5) no correction is necessary

46. Sentence 2: **In the last decade, the price of automobiles have risen greatly, and you can expect to spend over $15,000 for a car that cost $7,000 ten years ago.**

Which of the following is the best way to write the underlined portion of this sentence? If you think the original is the best way, choose option (1).

(1) have risen
(2) has risen
(3) have rose
(4) has rose
(5) has rised

47. Sentence 3: **An alternative to the high cost of new cars is buying a used car, but consumers have found that inflation also has effected the price of used cars.**

What correction should be made to this sentence?

(1) change *is* to *are*
(2) remove the comma after *car*
(3) replace *found* with *finded*
(4) replace *effected* with *affected*
(5) no correction is necessary

48. Sentence 4: **Leasing a car can be a wise economic decision just as leasing a home has some advantages over buying.**

If you rewrote sentence 4 beginning with

Leasing a home has some advantages over buying; similarly,

the next word should be

(1) leasing
(2) cars
(3) can
(4) a
(5) just

49. Sentence 5: **Recently, the concept of leasing a car grew more popular.**

Which of the following is the best way to write the underlined portion of this sentence? If you think the original is the best way, choose option (1).

(1) grew
(2) has grew
(3) has grown
(4) will grow
(5) grows

50. Sentence 6: **Before leasing a car, you should shop around to see the variety of cars and lease agreements available.**

Which of the following is the best way to write the underlined portion of this sentence? If you think the original is the best way, choose option (1).

(1) you should shop
(2) one should shop
(3) you shop
(4) you should have shopped
(5) he or she should shop

51. Sentence 7: **You may have to pay a security deposit before you can sign a lease agreement, the monthly payments are usually lower than a typical monthly loan payment on a new car.**

Which of the following is the best way to write the underlined portion of this sentence? If you think the original is the best way, choose option (1).

(1) agreement, the
(2) agreement the
(3) agreement but the
(4) agreement, but the
(5) agreement and the

52. Sentence 8: **Some leasing business's allow you to apply all of your payments to the eventual purchase of the car, much like renting with an option to buy a home.**

What correction should be made to this sentence?

(1) replace *business's* with *businesses*
(2) change *allow* to *allows*
(3) replace *you* with *one*
(4) replace *your* with *you're*
(5) no correction is necessary

53. Sentence 9: **Other companies simply rent by the month and do not wish to sell its rental cars.**

What correction should be made to this sentence?

(1) change the spelling of *companies* to *companys*
(2) replace *month* with *Month*
(3) add a comma after *month*
(4) change *do* to *does*
(5) replace *its* with *their*

54. Sentences 10 and 11: **You should study carefully any leasing agreement before signing it. Issues to consider before signing include responsibility for maintenance and insurance.**

The most effective combination of sentences 10 and 11 would include which of the following groups of words?

(1) signing issues such as
(2) signing it and considering issues
(3) signing it and considering responsibility
(4) signing it to be responsible
(5) signing it, considering such issues as

55. Sentence 12: **Before completing the deal, the car should be examined by all potential drivers.**

Which of the following is the best way to write the underlined portion of this sentence? If you think the original is the best way, choose option (1).

(1) Before completing the deal
(2) Before the deal is completed
(3) Before the deal has been completed
(4) Before you complete the deal
(5) Before completing your deal

Answers begin on page 752.

Part 2: The Essay

Directions: This part of the test is designed to find out how well you write. The test has one question that asks you to present an opinion on an issue or explain something. In preparing your answer for this question, you should take the following steps:

1. Read all of the information accompanying the question.

2. Plan your answer carefully before you write.

3. Use scratch paper to make any notes.

4. Write your answer on a separate sheet of paper.

5. Read carefully what you have written and make any changes that will improve your writing.

6. Check your paragraphing, sentence structure, spelling, punctuation, capitalization, and usage and make any necessary corrections.

Take 45 minutes to plan and write on the assigned topic. Write legibly and use a ballpoint pen.

Topic

The invention of the television brought about many changes in American life. It provided us with a whole new way of receiving information, and it quickly became a new form of entertainment.

Write a composition of about 200 words describing the effects of television on American life. You may describe the positive effects, the negative effects, or both. Be specific and use examples to support your view.

Information on evaluating your essay is on page 755.

POST-TEST 1: WRITING SKILLS ANSWER KEY

Part 1: Conventions of English

1. **(4)** The verb *are* is consistent with the present tense of this sentence.

2. **(2)** The verb form *converts* agrees with the singular subject *tube*.

3. **(3)** The relative pronoun *who* is never used to refer to things. The relative pronoun *that* can refer to either things or people.

4. **(3)** The original sentence is a fragment because *creating* requires a helping verb. The verb form *creates* does not.

5. **(4)** The correct spelling is *because*.

6. **(3)** *Penetrate* agrees with the rest of the passage, which is written in the present tense.

7. **(5)** No correction is necessary.

8. **(3)** Each of the parts of the series should have parallel structure: *continues, slows, stops*.

9. **(2)** Always separate the items in a series with commas.

10. **(4)** The new sentence would read, "The time needed to cook food depends on the amount of food being cooked; for example, one hot dog may cook . . ."

11. **(2)** No comma is needed to separate only two items.

12. **(3)** The verb *are* is consistent with the present tense of the sentence and of the passage as a whole.

13. **(1)** There is no error.

14. **(3)** The plural possessive *neighbors'* shows that several neighbors have sidewalks.

15. **(1)** The verb *is* agrees with the singular subject *alternative*.

16. **(5)** The new sentence would read, "While the main advantage of this form of exercise is convenience, some joggers enjoy its privacy."

17. **(4)** The names of seasons are not capitalized.

18. **(5)** In the original sentence, *they* incorrectly refers to *experts*. Substituting *indoor joggers* makes the meaning clear.

19. **(3)** The original sentence is a run-on. Using the conjunction *and* joins the two independent clauses correctly.

20. **(2)** The new sentence would read, "To reduce stress on feet and ankles, joggers should wear good running shoes and run on a thick carpet or folded throw rug."

21. **(2)** The spelling of *relieve* follows the general "I before E" rule.

22. **(5)** The correct present-tense form of *be* for the singular subject *indoor jogging* is *is*.

23. **(1)** *Breathe* is a verb, the action of taking air into the lungs. *Breath* is a noun.

24. **(2)** The phrase *a small rocky planet* is a renaming phrase and should be set off by commas.

25. **(5)** The modifying phrase *Transmitted by an unmanned Mariner IV space probe* is misplaced. It describes the first photos, not we on Earth.

26. **(2)** The plural compound subject *landscapes, deserts, and mountains* requires the verb *were*.

27. **(3)** The original sentence contains a comma splice. This choice joins the two independent clauses correctly.

28. **(4)** Even though *producing* sounds like it contains an *s*, it is spelled with a *c*.

29. **(2)** The past tense *revealed* should be used to be consistent with the rest of the passage.

30. **(3)** This run-on can be corrected by dividing the independent clauses into two separate sentences.

31. **(4)** *Planet* is not a specific name and should not be capitalized.

32. **(1)** The new sentence would read, "The fact that Mars looked red was also noticeable in the photos."

33. **(3)** The possessive *Mars's* shows that the atmosphere and soil were of Mars.

34. **(5)** The noun *future* is in parallel form with *origins* and *development*.

35. **(5)** No correction is necessary.

36. **(1)** Use the verb *are*, present tense, to be consistent with the rest of the passage.

37. **(1)** The new sentence would read, "To some people, junk food is fast food, but other people think junk food is any food available in vending machines, such as potato chips, candy, cookies, ice cream bars, and soda pop."

38. **(2)** *Quiet* means "still"; *quite* means "very."

39. (2) The singular subject *value* requires the verb *is*. The phrase *as well as negative health effects* is not part of the subject.

40. (2) The new sentence would read, "Especially bad for us are sugar, salt, refined flour, and chemical additives that artificially improve the color, flavor, and shelf life of foods."

41. (2) The modifier *though giving a boost of energy* should describe *too much sugar*, not *stress*.

42. (2) The verb *contain* agrees with the plural subject *lunchboxes*.

43. (3) Throughout the passage, the pronouns *we*, *us*, and *our* are used.

44. (2) The correct possessive pronoun is *its*.

45. (5) No correction is necessary.

46. (2) The verb *has risen* agrees with the singular subject *price*.

47. (4) *Affected*, meaning "influenced," is the correct verb.

48. (1) The new sentence would read, "Leasing a home has some advantages over buying; similarly, leasing a car can be a wise economic decision."

49. (3) The word *recently* shows that the present perfect tense is needed.

50. (1) There is no error.

51. (4) The original sentence contains a comma splice. This choice joins the two complete thoughts correctly.

52. (1) The plural form, *businesses*, not the possessive, is needed.

53. (5) The possessive pronoun *their* is plural and correctly refers to *companies*.

54. (5) The new sentence would read, "You should study carefully any leasing agreement before signing it, considering such issues as responsibility for maintenance and insurance."

55. (4) The original sentence implies that the car will be completing the deal. The modifier, *Before completing the deal*, dangles. Changing it to an independent clause with the subject *you* makes the meaning clear.

Use the answer key on pages 752–753 to check your answers to the Post-Test. Then find the item number of each question you missed and circle it on the chart below to determine the writing content areas in which you need more practice. Pay particular attention to areas where you missed half or more of the questions. The page numbers for the content areas are listed below on the chart. For those questions that you missed, review the pages indicated.

POST-TEST 1: WRITING SKILLS EVALUATION CHART

Content Area	Item Number	Review Pages
Nouns	14, 33, 52	60–64
Verbs	6, 22, 29, 36, 49	65–76
Subject-Verb Agreement	2, 15, 26, 39, 42, 46	76–79
Pronoun Reference	3, 18, 43, 53	82–92
Sentence Fragments	4	93–95
Sentence Combining	10, 16, 19, 20, 27, 30, 32, 37, 40, 48, 51, 54	95–107
Sequence of Tenses	1, 12	109–110
Misplaced/Dangling Modifiers	25, 41, 55	111–112
Parallel Structure	8, 34	112–116
Capitalization	17, 31	117–119
Punctuation	9, 11, 13, 24	119–125
Spelling	5, 21, 23, 28, 38, 44, 47	126–141
No Error	7, 35, 45, 50	

Important Note

On the actual GED Writing Skills Test, you will be given one score, which is a composite of your scores from Part 1 and Part 2 of the test. This score is determined by grading your essay holistically, giving it a score, then combining this score with your score from Part 1 in a proportion determined by the GED Testing Service.

Because you are not able to score your essay holistically, it is not possible for you to determine a valid composite score for your performance on this Writing Skills Test. Instead, it is wise to look at your performance on each part of the test separately. In this way, you will be able to determine whether you need additional work in one part of the test or the other.

The following chart gives you a general idea of how you might do on Part 1 of the GED Writing Skills Test, given your performance on Part 1 of this Post-Test and your performance on Part 1 of the Practice Test that starts on page 832.

Fewer than 20 items correct:

You are probably not ready to take the GED Writing Skills Test. Even with a good score on Part 2, you are unlikely to receive a passing composite score. Work through the Writing Skills section of this book again, or consult Contemporary's *GED Test 1: Writing Skills* for further instruction.

20–35 items correct:

With a good score on Part 2 of this Post-Test, you are probably ready to take the GED Writing Skills Test. To prepare further, look at the evaluation chart on page 753 and determine the areas in which you need more work.

More than 35 items correct:

You have done very well on Part 1 of this Post-Test, and you are certainly ready to take the GED Writing Skills Test if you also do well on Part 2 of this test (see page 755). You may want to review the explanations for items you missed in order to be as well prepared as possible.

Part 2: The Essay

If possible, give your essay to an instructor to evaluate. That person's opinion of your writing will be useful in deciding what further work you need to write a good essay.

If, however, you are unable to show your work to someone else, you can try to evaluate your own essay. If you can answer *yes* to the five questions in the Essay Evaluation Checklist, your essay would *probably* earn an upper half score (4, 5, or 6) on Part 2 of the Writing Skills Test. If you receive any *no* answers on your evaluation checklist, you should read your essay carefully to see how it could be improved and review Chapter 4 of the Writing Skills section.

Essay Evaluation Checklist

YES   NO

____ ____ **1.** Does the essay answer the question asked?

____ ____ **2.** Does the main point of the essay stand out clearly?

____ ____ **3.** Does each paragraph contain specific examples and details that help prove the main point?

____ ____ **4.** Can you follow how the writer has arranged and linked ideas in sentences and paragraphs?

____ ____ **5.** Is the writer's control of grammar and usage effective enough so that you were able to read the essay easily and smoothly?

756 POST-TESTS

POST-TEST 2: SOCIAL STUDIES

This Social Studies Post-Test will give you an opportunity to evaluate your readiness for the actual GED Social Studies Test.

This test contains 64 questions. Some of the questions are based on short reading passages, and some of them require you to interpret a chart, map, graph, or an editorial cartoon.

You should take appproximately 85 minutes to complete this test. At the end of 85 minutes, stop and mark your place. Then finish the test. This will give you an idea of whether or not you can finish the real GED Test in the time allotted. Try to answer as many questions as you can. A blank will count as a wrong answer, so make a reasonable guess for the answers to questions you are not sure of.

When you are finished with the test, check your answers and turn to the Evaluation Chart on page 778. Use the chart to evaluate whether or not you are ready to take the final Practice Test and, if not, in what areas you need more work.

POST-TEST 2: SOCIAL STUDIES ANSWER GRID

(Answer grid with questions 1–64, each with options 1 2 3 4 5)

Choose the best answer to each question that follows.

Questions 1 and 2 are based on the following passage.

. . . The Monroe Doctrine of 1823 was largely an expression of the vibrant post–1812 nationalism suffusing the United States. . . . While giving vent to a spirit of patriotism, it simultaneously deepened the illusion of isolation. Many unthinking Americans falsely concluded, then and later, that we were in fact isolated from European dangers simply because we wanted to be, and because, in a nationalistic outburst, we had publicly proclaimed that we were going to be.

1. In the passage, the phrase "illusion of isolation" refers to the

   (1) guarantee that the United States will not become involved in European affairs
   (2) false belief that the United States can stay out of European affairs
   (3) promise that the United States will fight for its allies worldwide
   (4) mistaken belief that Americans want the United States to be a world power
   (5) view that the United States and Europe will be allies in all future crises

2. The passage about the Monroe Doctrine addresses only *one* of *two* aspects of the proclamation—neutrality in European affairs. Which of the following describes the other aspect of the doctrine not mentioned in the quote?

   (1) containment of communism in the Americas
   (2) prohibition against further European intervention in the Americas
   (3) announcement of American imperialist intentions throughout the world
   (4) declaration of American support of all free peoples resisting domination
   (5) a drive to extend the U.S. borders to the Pacific Ocean

Questions 3 and 4 are based on the following map and definitions.

plains—extensive areas with little or no change in elevation

hills—elevations of 500 to 1,000 ft. that have sides sloping up to flat or rounded tops

plateaus—elevations of less than 500 ft. with sides that rise sharply to broad flat tops

trenches—steep-sided valleys usually associated with plateaus

mountains—elevations of over 1,000 ft., usually with steep rocky inclines on all sides and a pointed or rounded top

3. Based on the land elevations indicated on the map, the dominant topographical feature consists of

(1) plateaus
(2) plains
(3) hills
(4) mountains
(5) trenches

4. The topography shown on this map would most likely apply to which of the following states?

(1) Ohio
(2) Mississippi
(3) Kentucky
(4) West Virginia
(5) Iowa

5. "The price of the 'melting pot' theory is self-annihilation. While the foreign groups are permitted to contribute to the life of a nation, they do so by losing their own existence." The author of this quote holds the position that immigrants

(1) must give up their own customs and traditions in order to become Americans
(2) are more likely to die in America than in their native lands
(3) are really not welcome in the United States
(4) must give up all of their wealth in order to gain permission to live in America
(5) are openly accepted into American life

Questions 6 and 7 are based on the following passage.

More than thirty years ago, anthropologist Jane Goodall went to Africa to begin her study of chimpanzees. She has since witnessed chimps working together to kill baboons and pigs, and she has seen them use sticks to find and eat termites.

6. These behaviors can lead to the conclusion that chimpanzees

(1) are cruel and vicious animals
(2) have the instinctive behavior to kill
(3) are capable of making tools and cooperating with one another
(4) are a selfish and greedy species
(5) have exactly the same behaviors as humans

7. Jane Goodall believes her studies have given scientists some clues about human behavior because chimpanzees

(1) and humans have similar cultures
(2) and humans both live in a variety of environments
(3) are the most intelligent species in the world
(4) can be taught the behavior of humans
(5) and humans are believed to have evolved from a common ancestor

Question 8 is based on the following passage.

Walk into a factory in the year 2000 and chances are you'll see teams of robots at work. The number of robots performing heavy and routine chores in manufacturing is expected to increase to 200,000—10 times the number there were in 1979. That increase will probably lower the demand for factory workers. The BLS (Bureau of Labor Statistics) expects that manufacturing will claim only one tenth of the 16 million new jobs that will be created by 1995. Some experts predict that the portion of U.S. workers in manufacturing, 17.4 percent in 1991, will decline to 10 percent by the year 2000.

8. The impact that the increased use of robots will have on the job market is likely to be

(1) an increase in the number of people employed in factories
(2) a lowered demand for factory workers
(3) a reduced number of people who will rely on goods manufactured in factories
(4) increased individual salaries to make up for employment changes
(5) a decrease in the number of people employed in service industries

Questions 9 and 10 are based on the following passage.

Quite often, underdeveloped or developing countries are referred to collectively as the *Third World*. The term originated in France in the 1950s as a comparison to the third estate, or class, of the population. The third class in France was made up of commoners who had little material wealth and who wanted more. So, the Third World has little of the world's wealth and seeks more of its share. To get more, social scientists agree that the Third World will have to strive for

- good communication systems
- good transportation networks
- a healthy and employable population
- political stability
- adequate raw materials, especially fuels for power and manufacturing

9. Which of the following would most likely fit the description of a Third World nation?

(1) Japan
(2) West Germany
(3) Great Britain
(4) Australia
(5) Zimbabwe

10. The islands of the South Pacific enjoy a mild climate, a disease-free environment, long-running governments, and even modern telephones, televisions, and airports. But they are small, widely dispersed, and lacking in the production of goods essential to their economic development. So, their biggest drawback to development is their not having

(1) good communication systems
(2) good transportation networks
(3) a healthy and employable population
(4) political stability
(5) adequate raw materials, especially fuels for power and manufacturing

Questions 11 and 12 are based on the following graph.

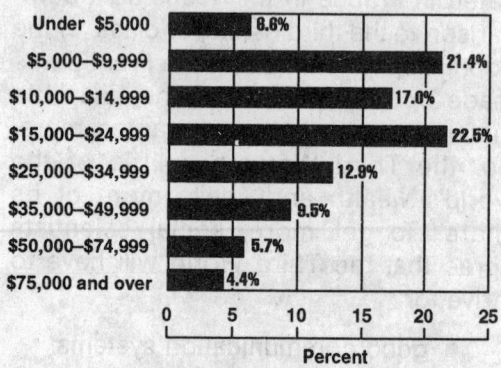

PERCENT DISTRIBUTION BY INCOME: 1991

Families with head 65+

Income	Percent
Under $5,000	6.6%
$5,000–$9,999	21.4%
$10,000–$14,999	17.0%
$15,000–$24,999	22.5%
$25,000–$34,999	12.9%
$35,000–$49,999	9.5%
$50,000–$74,999	5.7%
$75,000 and over	4.4%

Source: U.S. Bureau of the Census

11. Based on the facts in the graph, which of the following can you conclude about families headed by individuals 65 years or older?

(1) A greater percentage are very poor than are very wealthy.
(2) Twice as many had incomes of $15,000 or more than had incomes of less than $10,000.
(3) The percentages of very poor and very wealthy are equal.
(4) Elderly women are more likely to be poor than elderly men.
(5) There are more households comprised of single senior citizens than couples.

12. If the official poverty level was designated to be $7,905 for elderly couples in 1990 and $6,268 for individuals, which of the following is supported by the information in the graph?

(1) 6.6 percent of all families 65+ live below the poverty level.
(2) 28 percent of all families 65+ live below the poverty level.
(3) 21.4 percent of all families 65+ live below the poverty level.
(4) The total percentage of families 65+ living below the poverty level cannot be determined from the graph.
(5) The percentage of families 65+ who live below the poverty level can be determined only for individuals and not for couples.

---

13. In the Dani culture of New Guinea, pigs are raised by the children and considered a sign of wealth among the community members. In India, cows are sacred and are symbols of worship. The importance of animals in these two countries is based on

(1) cultural universals
(2) cultural relativity
(3) ethnocentrism
(4) values and customs
(5) cultural diffusion

14. In 1974 and again in 1986, the U.S. Congress established committees to investigate alleged wrongdoings by the president and his staff. This congressional action is an example of

(1) amending the Constitution
(2) overriding a veto
(3) passing a bill
(4) applying checks and balances
(5) approving a treaty

Questions 15 and 16 are based on the following passage.

During the early 1980s, the IRS had 87,000 employees. By 1990, that number had risen to 116,425, an increase of 33 percent. But the number of taxpayers' returns has climbed from 137.4 million to 201.7 million, a jump of 46 percent. The IRS has attempted to handle the rising workload by reducing by 20 percent the staff members who handle taxpayer inquiries, process returns and get refunds in the mail. The personnel remaining in these jobs have had to pick up the slack and have faced unrealistic work quotas. Overwhelming workloads led to large-scale foul-ups. Clearly, massive tax reform is needed on several fronts. The income tax must be simplified and made as fair as possible for all. But on top of that, the IRS must clean up its own house so that it can do its work with accuracy and precision. Until the code is simplified and until the computer works, more help must be hired.

15. Which of the following is an opinion suggested, but not directly stated, by the author of the editorial?

(1) More than 116,000 IRS workers processed more than 200,000 tax returns in 1990.

(2) The number of tax returns to be processed rose by 46 percent from the early 1980s to 1990.

(3) Workloads should be lightened to avoid major mistakes in tax processing.

(4) Twenty percent of the IRS's staff were reassigned in an attempt to remedy problems.

(5) Remaining personnel have had to face unrealistic workloads.

16. What does the writer believe to be the cause of the major foul-ups by the IRS?

(1) computer errors
(2) heavy workloads
(3) complicated tax forms
(4) unskilled workers
(5) unfair tax laws

---

17. In recent years, the top two manufacturers of soft drinks, Coca-Cola and PepsiCo, each sought to purchase the number three and four soft drink producers, Dr. Pepper and Seven-Up. However, the Federal Trade Commission prevented the takeover. The FTC refused the companies' attempts because the takeovers would

(1) interfere with free competition in the soft drink industry among its four largest manufacturers

(2) create a monopoly, concentrating merchandising power in the hands of a single company

(3) reduce the quality and variety of the product offered

(4) drive the prices up, forcing consumers to buy fewer soft drinks

(5) force the other smaller, independent bottlers to merge with one of the two giants

Questions 18 and 19 are based on the following map.

COLONIAL AMERICA
IN 1763

MA
(ME)

VT

NH

MA

NY

CT

RI

PA

NJ

NEW
FRANCE

MD

DE

VA

NC

SC

GA

—— Proclamation
Line of 1763

England

French/English
disputed territory

Spanish/English
disputed territory

18. Vermont, admitted to the Union in 1791, was the subject of a territorial dispute during colonial times. Based on the map, which bordering states can you conclude were rivals for the Vermont territory before it obtained statehood?

(1) Maine and New Hampshire
(2) New Hampshire and Rhode Island
(3) New York and Rhode Island
(4) Connecticut and New York
(5) New York and New Hampshire

19. The Proclamation Line of 1763 resulted from a treaty between France and England for control of colonial America. What was the intended effect of the Line of Proclamation?

(1) to separate the country geographically into east and west
(2) to grant freedom to portions of the thirteen colonies lying east of the line
(3) to establish a mountain pass connecting the northeast with the southeast
(4) to separate French from English territory in the New World
(5) to prevent colonists from escaping into New France

20. The United States has put quotas (limits) on the number of automobiles that foreign countries can export to America. Which one of the following explanations would be an acceptable justification for the quotas?

(1) American manufacturers must be protected from unfair competition.
(2) Automobiles are the highest-costing products to export.
(3) More cars are exported than any other product.
(4) The dollar amount of trade between other car-manufacturing countries and the United States is very low.
(5) There is no demand for foreign cars by American consumers.

21. In an attempt to try to reduce the trade deficit, the United States should limit its trade with which one of the following trade partners from which it imports more than it exports?

(1) Eastern Europe
(2) Latin America
(3) Australia and Oceania
(4) Spain
(5) Japan

Questions 22 and 23 are based on the following passage.

So many issues now receiving attention in the media and in the political arena are really family issues—drug abuse, teen suicide, teen pregnancy, the crisis in education. If we can redirect our discussions of these issues to an exploration of what can be done early in a child's life to help families create a healthy environment in which to grow and develop, we can lessen both the likelihood and the extent of many subsequent personal and societal crises.

We place great stock in the importance and effectiveness of preventive measures, and research and practical experience are behind us. We know, for example, the following:

Children who do not receive regular preventive health care from an early age are likely to suffer from undetected health problems and disabilities.

Children without supportive adult care are likely to lack confidence, feel alienated and distrustful, and suffer from learning and behavioral problems.

Children who are not stimulated and encouraged to develop through activities appropriate to their age are likely to experience problems in school.

22. A child grows and develops within the environment in which he or she is raised. This learning process is known as

(1) heredity
(2) socialization
(3) conditioning
(4) programming
(5) trial-and-error learning

23. Which one of the following statements would likely be inconsistent with the author's beliefs?

(1) Attitudes and behaviors of adults result from childhood experiences.
(2) Families can be affected by a variety of governmental programs and policies.
(3) Many problems in society can be solved by providing a healthy family environment.
(4) Schools are the only place children can be taught discipline and proper attitudes.
(5) Children from good family environments are less likely to find themselves in trouble.

Question 24 is based on the following.

"The conjunction of an immense military establishment and a large arms industry . . . new in American experience, exercises a total influence . . . felt in every city, every state house, every office of the federal government. . . . In the councils of government, we must guard against the acquisition of unwarranted influence by the military-industrial complex."

General Dwight Eisenhower,
34th President of the United States,
Farewell Address, 1961

24. Which of the following opinions is supported by this statement?

(1) An overgrown military establishment could pose a threat to democracy.
(2) Industrial influence on the military has made our government more democratic.
(3) Only the military-industrial complex can safeguard our liberties.
(4) The military should be allowed more influence in government affairs.
(5) Civilian control of the military should never be allowed.

Questions 25 and 26 are based on the graph and information below.

FEDERAL DEFICIT
(In Billions of Dollars Per Fiscal Year)

Source: Office of Management and Budget

In 1985, the Congress passed a law known as the Gramm-Rudman-Hollings Act. Its purpose was to achieve a balanced budget by 1991 by yearly cuts in the budget deficit. The graph shows the planned implementation of the law.

25. A budget deficit refers to the

    (1) taxes collected in a given year
    (2) money spent on domestic programs
    (3) funds allocated to pay the national debt
    (4) money the government has left over for special projects
    (5) money spent that exceeds the amount received in taxes

26. Assuming the graph is accurate, which of the following should have resulted from the Gramm-Rudman-Hollings legislation?

    (1) The Congress would have spent more money than it received in taxes.
    (2) Government programs would have been established to control private enterprise.
    (3) The national debt gradually would have been reduced.
    (4) The Gramm-Rudman-Hollings Act would have been repealed.
    (5) The business cycle would no longer be part of the American economy.

Questions 27 and 28 are based on the graph below.

27. According to the graph, what would be the market price of the tires?

    (1) $20
    (2) $40
    (3) $60
    (4) $80
    (5) $100

28. What would a producer probably do to increase demand if the price of the tires rose above the market price shown on the graph?

    (1) increase production
    (2) put 800 tires on the market to sell
    (3) raise the price even more
    (4) lower the cost of the tires
    (5) reduce the quality of the tires but keep the prices the same

Questions 29–31 are based on the following definitions.

Economic systems may be categorized in several different ways. Defined below are five categories of economic systems that operate throughout the world.

pure communism—an economic system in which there is no government control with each individual working for the good of all

Marxian socialism—an economic system in which the government owns all the means of production and controls all aspects of the citizens' economic life

democratic socialism—an economic system in which the government owns the basic industries such as steel, textiles, and energy while permitting some private enterprise and greater consumer freedom

American capitalism—an economic system in which individuals rather than government own the means of production and, along with consumer demand, determine what will be produced

pure capitalism—an economic system in which there is no government regulation or influence, with each individual working for his or her own success

29. Which economic system maintains that decisions about the production and distribution of goods must be determined by a central authority?

    (1) pure communism
    (2) Marxian socialism
    (3) democratic socialism
    (4) American capitalism
    (5) pure capitalism

30. Biologist Charles Darwin believed that the species that was better able to adapt would continue to exist—survival of the fittest. Under which one of the following economic and social policies did the belief in and application of survival of the fittest thrive?

    (1) Franklin Roosevelt's New Deal and government-funded work programs
    (2) Teddy Roosevelt's progressivism and regulation of big business activities
    (3) Herbert Hoover's conservatism and noninterference in the affairs of business
    (4) Dwight Eisenhower's policies of moderation
    (5) Lyndon Johnson's Great Society and generous spending for social programs

31. An economic system is designed to meet the needs of the people by establishing production priorities and allocating the limited resources. In which one of the following economic systems would there be the most coordinated use of production facilities while still permitting individual consumer choice?

    (1) pure communism
    (2) Marxian socialism
    (3) democratic socialism
    (4) American capitalism
    (5) pure capitalism

Questions 32 and 33 are based on the following passage.

Virginia Louisa Minor was the first woman in Missouri to take a public stand in favor of women's suffrage. Her husband, Francis Minor, was a lawyer, and he was the first person to argue that women were enfranchised by the equal protection clause of the Fourteenth Amendment. In 1872 Mrs. Minor and her husband filed suit against a St. Louis registrar who had refused to allow her to register. The lower court held against the Minors, who then appealed to the Supreme Court of the United States. In 1875 the court handed down a unanimous decision holding that suffrage was not coextensive with citizenship and that the political rights of women were to be decided by the states. The opinion did say, "If the law is wrong, it ought to be changed," but added that "the power for that is not with us." After this ruling the National Woman Suffrage Association felt it had no alternative but to propose an amendment to the U.S. Constitution.

32. Which one of the following conclusions best summarizes the Supreme Court's decision in this case?

(1) Women should not have the right to vote because they do not own property.

(2) The government is a male domain, and women have no place in it.

(3) Virginia Minor did not meet the age or residency requirements to register to vote.

(4) The Equal Rights Amendment was being considered by the state legislature.

(5) The Supreme Court cannot interfere with the states' right to determine voter requirements.

33. A *precedent* is a legal decision that may serve as a reason or justification for a later case. Using the Minor case as such, what would the U.S. Supreme Court decide in a case appealed by a seventeen-year-old male citizen who claims that under the state criminal code he is considered an adult and, therefore, should be treated as an adult and given the right to vote? The U.S. Supreme Court would probably

(1) permit seventeen-year-olds to vote to make the laws more consistent

(2) deny the appeal because the law must be changed by the state

(3) refuse to hear the case because the issue was previously decided

(4) allow only seventeen-year-old males to vote since women were already denied the vote

(5) require the states to amend their law to allow seventeen-year-olds to vote

34. A presidential primary election is *chiefly* different from a general election in that

(1) a presidential primary is usually of local interest only

(2) a person does not have to be a registered voter to vote in a primary

(3) a primary election does not determine who will be the president of the United States

(4) a primary election determines the number of electoral college votes a particular candidate gets

(5) a primary election must have only two opposing candidates on the ballot

Questions 35 and 36 refer to the following illustration.

**VIOLENT CRIMES:
THE FUNNEL EFFECT**

Of every 100 violent crimes*:

48 are reported to police

21 result in an arrest

11 result in cases filed for prosecution

8 result in convictions

2 result in incarceratoins

*Violent crimes include murder, rape, robbery, assault.

Source: National Crime Survey, Bureau of Justice Statistics

35. The term "funnel effect" refers to the

(1) idea that all crimes are put into the same criminal justice system
(2) belief that every criminal gets caught and is punished
(3) concept that most suspects who go through the criminal justice process are actually guilty
(4) idea that only a very few suspects arrested for committing a crime are actually punished
(5) belief that crime is under control in the United States

36. Which one of the following statements about the criminal justice system is *not* based on the illustration?

(1) Over half of violent crimes go unreported.
(2) Less than one-fourth result in an arrest.
(3) Most violent crimes occur in instances in which the victim knows the criminal.
(4) The states' criminal justice system has a low conviction rate.
(5) About 10 percent of the violent crimes are actually prosecuted.

Questions 37 and 38 refer to the following passage.

WE, THEREFORE, the Representatives of the UNITED STATES of AMERICA, in General Congress, Assembled, appealing to the Supreme Judge of the world for the rectitude of our intentions, do, in the Name, and by Authority of the good People of these Colonies, solemnly publish and declare, That these United Colonies are, and of Right ought to be, FREE AND INDEPENDENT STATES. . . .

37. This statement was proclaimed by members of which group?

(1) Constitutional Convention
(2) Boston Tea Party
(3) Pilgrims
(4) Second Continental Congress
(5) the first House of Representatives

38. Which of the following statements supports the author's opinion?

(1) All people should be free from government control.
(2) The United States should be free from outside control.
(3) All wealthy countries have the right to control the weaker countries of the world.
(4) The people shall have the right to vote for their leaders.
(5) The United States needs a strong federal government.

39. The fact that the U.S. Constitution can be amended is the basis for the conclusion that the authors

(1) made many mistakes in the original writing
(2) did not really know what they wanted to say
(3) took into account future changes in the needs and values of the people
(4) were required by the Supreme Court to include this power
(5) considered all possible circumstances and situations and included them in the original Constitution

Questions 40 and 41 refer to the following passage.

Despite the attention afforded female astronauts or Supreme Court justices, statistics show that women's occupations have remained "remarkably traditional."

So writes Nancy Barrett in "The American Woman 1987: A Report in Depth." Women still "are overwhelmingly concentrated in low-paying female occupations," according to Barrett. "In 1985, 70 percent of all full-time employed women were working in occupations in which more than three-quarters of the employees were female. Among those occupations were receptionist, child-care worker, bank teller, data-entry keyer, and cashier. More than one-third of all employed women work in clerical jobs.

"Where they have moved into formerly male domains, they remain on the bottom rungs of the job ladder or are tracked into predominantly female 'ghettos'—relatively low-paying subcategories of jobs with higher-paying occupations dominated by men," Barrett says.

According to 1991 Bureau of Labor statistics, the situation had improved only slightly in six years. The number of women in professional and administrative positions had increased only a few percentage points.

40. With which one of the following conclusions would Barrett likely agree?

(1) Women are not given the same job opportunities as men.
(2) The quality of men's work is superior to that of women's.
(3) Working women seek lower-paying jobs.
(4) Most female college graduates work in the medical field.
(5) Women prefer raising families to developing careers.

41. The majority of women who are employed full-time

(1) receive salaries equal to those of men
(2) have a college education
(3) work in predominantly female occupations
(4) fill executive and administrative positions
(5) prefer clerical work

42. In the 1930s, England and France followed a policy of appeasement toward German territorial expansion. Germany took over all of Czechoslovakia and threatened Poland and Austria. Many experts in international relations claim that appeasing German expansionism led to World War II.

Based on this description, you could infer that appeasement is

(1) refusing to allow European nations to interfere in American affairs
(2) taking in unlimited numbers of immigrants from other countries
(3) the right to use land that belongs to someone else
(4) compromising in the face of aggression
(5) German domination of international politics

Questions 43 and 44 are based on the following map.

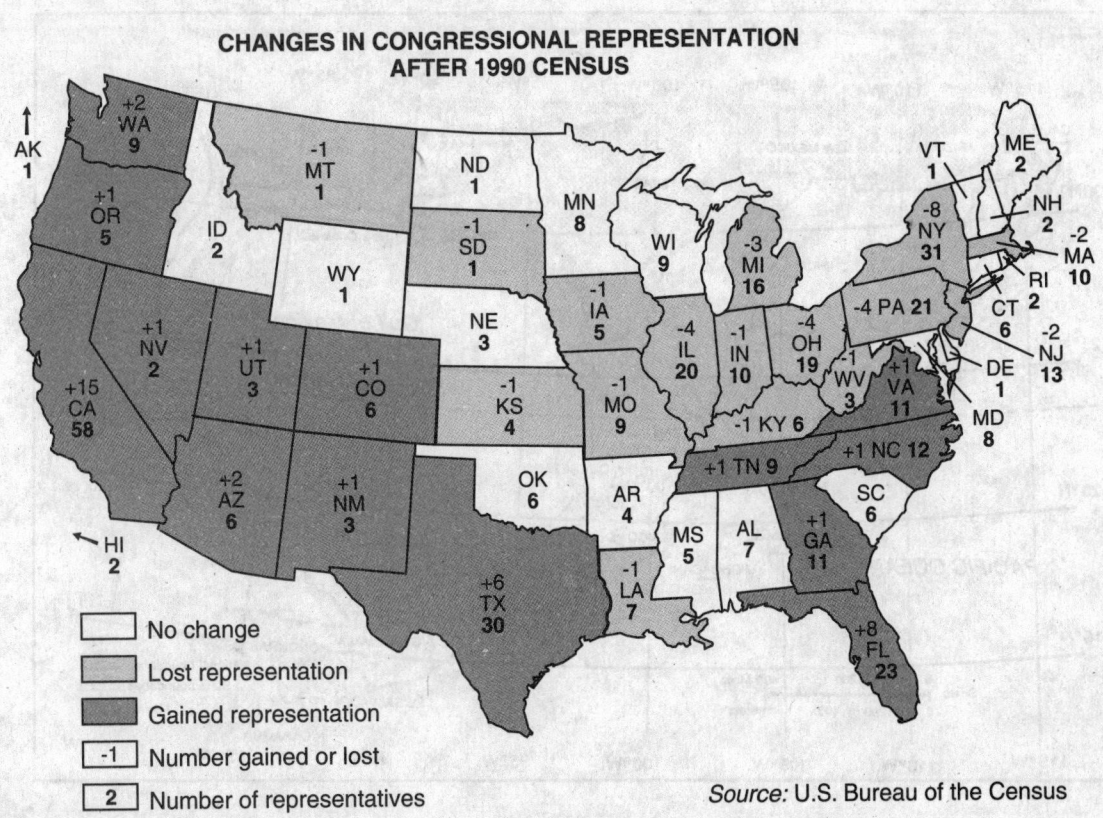

**CHANGES IN CONGRESSIONAL REPRESENTATION
AFTER 1990 CENSUS**

AK
1

+2
WA
9

-1
MT
1

ND
1

MN
8

VT
1

ME
2

NH
2

-8
NY
31

-2
MA
10

+1
OR
5

ID
2

WY
1

-1
SD
1

WI
9

-3
MI
16

RI
2

-4 PA 21

CT
6

-2
NJ
13

+1
NV
2

+1
UT
3

+1
CO
6

NE
3

-1
IA
5

-4
IL
20

-1
IN
10

-4
OH
19

-1
WV
3

+1
VA
11

DE
1

+15
CA
58

-1
KS
4

-1
MO
9

-1 KY 6

MD
8

+2
AZ
6

+1
NM
3

OK
6

AR
4

+1 TN 9

+1 NC 12

HI
2

+6
TX
30

-1
LA
7

MS
5

AL
7

+1
GA
11

SC
6

+8
FL
23

☐ No change

▨ Lost representation

▨ Gained representation

| -1 | Number gained or lost

| 2 | Number of representatives

Source: U.S. Bureau of the Census

43. Which one of the following statements is supported by the information in the map?

(1) More states lost representatives than gained them.

(2) New York has more representatives than any other state.

(3) More states experienced no change in representation than gained representatives.

(4) States that lost representatives are concentrated in the South.

(5) States that gained representatives are concentrated in the North.

44. A candidate for president needs a majority of electoral votes to be elected. Which group of states would have the largest number of electoral votes?

(1) Nebraska, North Carolina, California

(2) Texas, Ohio, Minnesota

(3) Pennsylvania, Tennessee, Oregon

(4) Wisconsin, Mississippi, Connecticut

(5) Florida, Virginia, New York

Questions 45–47 are based on the map below.

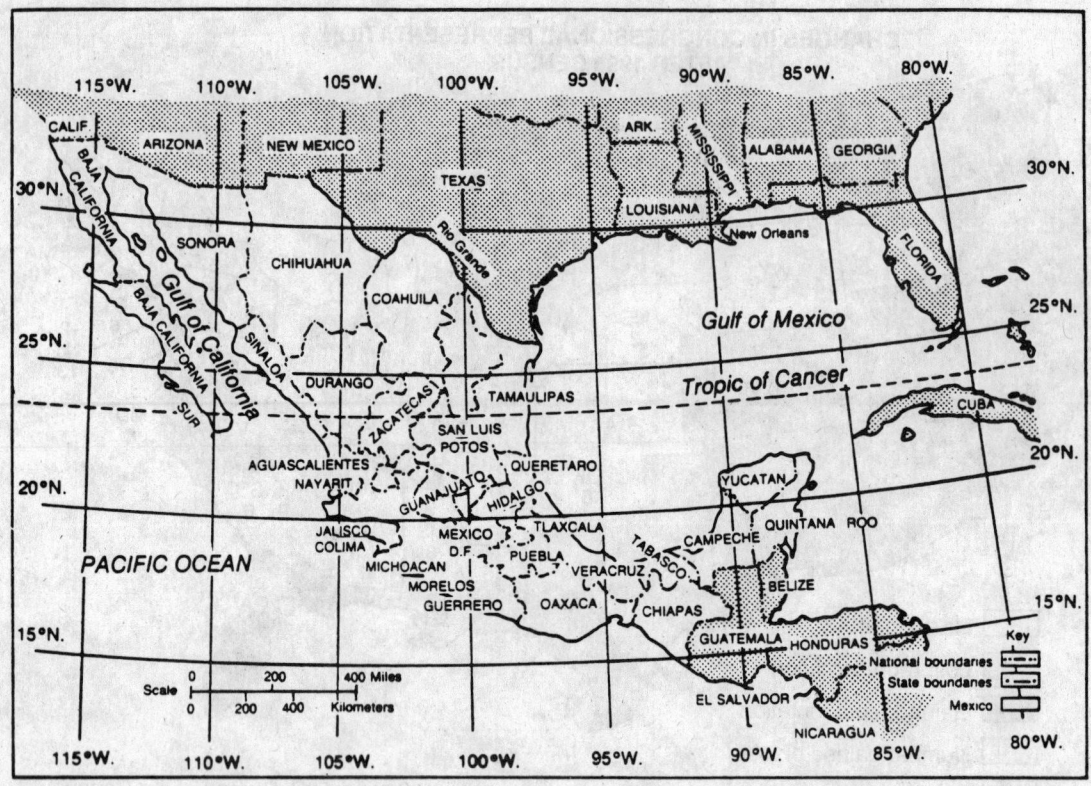

45. Durango, Mexico, is located at 25 degrees north and 105 degrees west. A pilot traveling from Durango to the country of Guatemala would have to follow which instructions as he leaves Durango and travels?

(1) 15 degrees north and 90 degrees west
(2) 10 degrees north and 15 degrees east
(3) 10 degrees south and 90 degrees west
(4) 10 degrees north and 15 degrees west
(5) 10 degrees south and 15 degrees east

46. This map would be most useful in

(1) identifying political boundaries
(2) developing a highway map
(3) identifying topographical formations
(4) recognizing historical landmarks
(5) identifying population centers

47. Looking from west to east on the map, for every 15 degrees an hour is added. If it is 9:00 P.M. in eastern Arizona, what time would it be on the eastern coast of Florida?

(1) 11:00 P.M.
(2) 10:00 P.M.
(3) 9:00 P.M.
(4) 8:00 P.M.
(5) 7:00 P.M.

Questions 48–50 are based on the following passage.

Never in history have the interests of all the people been so united in a single economic problem. . . . Danger to one is danger to all. . . .

What do the people of America want more than anything else? To my mind, they want two things: work, with all the moral and spiritual values that go with it; and with work, a reasonable measure of security. . . .

Our Republican leaders tell us economic laws—sacred, inviolable, unchangeable—cause panics which no one could prevent. But while they prate [talk] of economic laws, men and women are starving. We must lay hold of the fact that economic laws are not made by nature. They are made by human beings. . . .

48. Based on this quote, you can infer that the speaker would *not* support which of the following?

    (1) laissez-faire business policies
    (2) progressive social legislation
    (3) government-funded public works programs
    (4) government-funded welfare programs
    (5) wage-price controls

49. The statement "economic laws are made by human beings" implies that

    (1) Americans are the only people to have an economic system
    (2) Republican leaders said that man could not control economics
    (3) economic laws are based upon moral and spiritual values not controlled by man
    (4) nations throughout the world can select and control their own economic system
    (5) laws of economics are "sacred, invaluable, unchangeable"

50. The preceding quote could accurately be attributed to

    (1) Harry S Truman
    (2) Franklin D. Roosevelt
    (3) Herbert C. Hoover
    (4) Dwight D. Eisenhower
    (5) Ronald W. Reagan

---

51. Ethnocentrism refers to the practice of judging another culture by one's own standards and beliefs. Which of the following represents ethnocentric behavior?

    (1) a student who tutors an immigrant in English
    (2) a tourist who lectures his foreign hosts on the "uncivilized" nature of their marriage customs
    (3) a Peace Corps volunteer who helps dig wells in Central Africa
    (4) a Russian Jewish immigrant who insists that his children learn English and Hebrew
    (5) a Hispanic community group that demands that public aid forms be published in English and Spanish

52. Liberals believe that the problems of the country should be solved by a strong federal government. They support funding for social programs, limiting military spending, and negotiation as the basis for American foreign policy. Which one of the following federal programs would liberals in America be likely to oppose?

    (1) guaranteed government loans to college students
    (2) a national health insurance program
    (3) stricter pollution laws
    (4) Star Wars space defense system
    (5) job training for the handicapped

Questions 53–55 are based on the following cartoon.

53. Which of the following best describes the man in the cartoon?

 (1) an average citizen
 (2) an elected official
 (3) a political poll taker
 (4) a political candidate
 (5) a behavioral scientist

54. What information is the man trying to get from the woman?

 (1) how her feelings about the present election compare with her feelings about the 1988 election
 (2) what it takes to make her happy
 (3) why she is happy the election is over
 (4) why she was unhappy about the 1988 election
 (5) how she voted in the 1992 and 1988 elections

55. The cartoonist is expressing which of the following opinions?

 (1) Americans should feel happier about elections.
 (2) Poll takers don't know when to quit asking questions.
 (3) Political polls are getting too personal.
 (4) Ordinary people don't care enough about political analysis.
 (5) Public opinion polls don't do any good.

56. In 1993, the Army recommended that the Pentagon consider shutting down undersized and outdated Fort Riley. But the base was not included on the Pentagon's list of possible closings. After all, Fort Riley was located in Kansas, the home state of a powerful senator. The information in this passage supports which of the following conclusions?

 (1) Politics can influence military decisions.

 (2) Military decisions are based solely on standards of efficiency.

 (3) The Army is not in favor of any more base closings.

 (4) Politics has no effect on military decisions.

 (5) Fort Riley will be closed in spite of the Pentagon's decision.

Questions 57 and 58 are based on the following table.

COMPARISON OF AVERAGE TEMPERATURE AND RAINFALL IN EASTERN ASIA AND EASTERN NORTH AMERICA

Shanghai (Lat. 31°11'N.)

	Jan.	Feb.	Mar.	Apr.	May	Jun.	Jul.	Aug.	Sep.	Oct.	Nov.	Dec.	Year
Temperature (in Fahrenheit)	37.8°	39.4°	46.0°	56.1°	65.5°	73.4°	80.4°	80.2°	73.0°	63.5°	52.0°	42.1°	59.1°
Rainfall (in inches)	2.0	2.3	3.5	3.7	3.5	7.2	6.0	5.7	4.4	3.2	2.1	1.4	45.0

Charleston, S.C. (Lat. 32°47'N.)

	Jan.	Feb.	Mar.	Apr.	May	Jun.	Jul.	Aug.	Sep.	Oct.	Nov.	Dec.	Year
Temperature (in Fahrenheit)	49.8°	51.2°	57.5°	63.9°	72.1°	78.1°	80.6°	80.0°	76.2°	67.0°	57.8°	51.0°	65.4°
Rainfall (in inches)	3.1	3.3	3.4	2.9	3.4	4.8	7.1	6.6	5.0	3.6	2.4	2.9	48.5

57. Using the table as a basis, which one of the following conclusions is *most* valid?

(1) On a day-to-day basis, the weather in both cities is the same.

(2) The summer months in Shanghai and Charleston show the least variation in temperature.

(3) Heavy rainfall makes Shanghai uninhabitable.

(4) While it is winter in Charleston, it is summer in Shanghai.

(5) Eastern Asia and eastern North America experience the same jet stream patterns.

58. Which one of the following statements is an *opinion* rather than a fact?

(1) Weather conditions in Charleston are better than those in Shanghai.

(2) Charleston, S.C., has a greater amount of annual rainfall than does Shanghai.

(3) Both cities are north of the equator.

(4) The greatest amount of rainfall in both cities occurs in the summer months.

(5) January is the coldest month in Charleston and Shanghai.

59. In 1972, eighteen-year-olds were given the right to vote through which one of the following methods?

(1) a Supreme Court decision

(2) a law passed by Congress

(3) an amendment to the Constitution

(4) an executive order from the president

(5) a consensus vote of the fifty states

60. "Government should do for the people only what the people cannot do for themselves" best describes the philosophy of which of the following forms of government?

(1) dictatorship

(2) authoritarianism

(3) democracy

(4) totalitarianism

(5) monarchy

Questions 61 and 62 are based on the following cartoon.

61. According to the cartoon, what effect does the abortion debate have on Illinois legislators?

(1) It makes them angry.
(2) It makes them nervous.
(3) It makes them think about philosophy.
(4) It makes them feel confused.
(5) It makes them think about other important issues.

62. The cartoon supports which of the following conclusions about Illinois legislators?

(1) They don't believe the abortion debate is a valid political issue.
(2) They have already taken sides on the abortion issue.
(3) They enjoy controversial issues.
(4) They want to avoid making a decision about such a controversial issue.
(5) They are willing to protest against procrastination.

63. Political parties in America are a significant part of the electoral process. If the political parties no longer existed

(1) democratic elections would no longer be held
(2) the number of candidates would probably be unlimited
(3) election campaigns would be unnecessary
(4) elected officials would not have a constituency
(5) issues would be more clearly defined and identifiable

64. Sociologists define "classical conditioning" as behavior that is maintained after a stimulus has been introduced several times. Which of the following is an application of classical conditioning in child rearing?

(1) getting the child to consistently associate the time that "Sesame Street" ends with naptime
(2) becoming irritable with a child who will not be toilet trained
(3) giving a child a bicycle for his seventh birthday
(4) keeping a child with chicken pox away from school
(5) giving young girls gifts of cars and trucks instead of dolls

Answers begin on page 775.

POST-TEST 2: SOCIAL STUDIES ANSWER KEY

1. **(2)** An illusion is a false belief. The passage says that "Americans falsely concluded . . . that we were in fact isolated from European dangers simply because we wanted to be. . . ."

2. **(2)** The only choice listed that represents the other aspect of the Monroe Doctrine is the prohibition against further European colonization in the Americas.

3. **(4)** Mountains are land elevations of over 1,000 feet. Most of the land shown is over 1,000 feet above sea level.

4. **(4)** West Virginia is the only mountainous state listed among the choices.

5. **(1)** Giving up one's customs and traditions is a restatement of the quote from the passage "losing their own existence."

6. **(3)** Working together to kill other animals and using sticks to find and eat termites are examples of cooperating with each other and making tools.

7. **(5)** The study of chimpanzees is important to understanding human behavior because it is believed that both species have a common ancestor.

8. **(2)** The passage states that the portion of U.S. workers in manufacturing is predicted to fall to 10 percent by the year 2000.

9. **(5)** Of the choices listed, only Zimbabwe meets the criteria of having little material wealth and wanting more. The other choices represent industrialized nations.

10. **(5)** The passage states that the South Pacific islands lack the production of goods essential for their economic development.

11. **(2)** The combined total percentage of families headed by persons 65+ earning less than $10,000 is 28 percent; the combined total for those earning more than $15,000 is 55 percent.

12. **(4)** The information on the graph is not broken down into these two categories—those earning less than $6,268 and those earning less than $7,905.

13. **(4)** Values and customs determine what practices a culture follows.

14. **(4)** Congressional investigations into the actions of the president are an example of the checks and balances built into the Constitution.

15. **(3)** Choice (3), which contains the word *should*, represents an opinion. Choices (1), (2), (4), and (5) are facts stated in the passage.

16. **(2)** The passage refers to a rising workload and a reduction of staff as well as to overwhelming workloads.

17. **(1)** The takeover would result in the two major soft drink manufacturers controlling the third- and fourth-largest companies.

18. **(5)** New York and New Hampshire are states that border Vermont; therefore, you can conclude that a territorial dispute involved these two states.

19. **(4)** The Proclamation Line divided New France from the English colonies; the other choices are not supported by the map.

20. **(1)** Quotas would limit the number of foreign cars that could be placed on the market to compete with American-made automobiles.

21. **(5)** Currently, Japan is the only area or nation given that exports more to the United States than it imports from the United States.

22. **(2)** The process by which an individual learns the ways of the culture is called *socialization*.

23. **(4)** The author clearly believes that many institutions in society, especially the family, play a key role in children's development.

24. **(1)** This is the only statement that reflects Eisenhower's concern about "an immense military establishment and a large arms industry."

25. **(5)** A budget deficit occurs when the government spends more money than it receives in taxes.

26. **(3)** The goal of the Gramm-Rudman-Hollings Act was to eliminate further budget deficits through gradual reductions in government spending.

27. **(2)** The market price is $40 because that is the equilibrium point (the point at which the demand and supply curves intersect).

28. **(4)** The producers would lower the price of the tires to encourage consumers to buy the tires.

29. **(2)** Marxian socialism is the only economic system in which these decisions are made by the government.

30. **(3)** Herbert Hoover's policies of government noninterference in business encouraged the strongest businesses to survive, sometimes at the expense of the weakest.

31. **(3)** Democratic socialism permits individual consumers choice while maintaining government control over the means of production.

32. **(5)** The Supreme Court decided that the states had the right to determine voter requirements, and therefore the laws of the state would have to be changed.

33. **(2)** Based upon precedent, the state law would have to be changed to allow seventeen-year-olds to vote. Choice (5) is incorrect because the Supreme Court cannot require a state to amend its laws.

34. **(3)** In a general election, the president of the United States is elected; a primary election determines which candidate from each party will run in the general election.

35. **(4)** Of all the crimes committed and reported to the police, only about 2 percent result in incarceration.

36. **(3)** The illustration does not indicate that most violent crimes occur in instances in which the victim knows the criminal.

37. **(4)** The Second Continental Congress met in order to declare the colonies' independence from England.

38. **(2)** The authors of the Declaration of Independence believed that the colonies should be free and independent states.

39. **(3)** An article for amending the Constitution was included so that the document could be altered to reflect the needs and values of the people in the future.

40. **(1)** Barrett believes that women do not have the same job opportunities as men, and she cites statistics that show that in 1985, 70 percent of all full-time employed women were working in occupations in which more than three-quarters were female.

41. **(3)** Women who are employed full-time tend to be in the traditionally female-oriented occupations of receptionist, child-care worker, bank teller, data-entry keyer, and cashier.

42. **(4)** The passage points out that England and France followed a policy of appeasement in the face of Germany's aggression. This means that appeasement is compromise in the face of aggression.

43. **(3)** A greater number of states are white on the map; this indicates that those states experienced no change in congressional representation.

44. **(1)** Of the states shown, Nebraska, North Carolina, and California would have the largest total number since they are the most populous.

45. **(5)** To travel from Durango to Guatemala, one would have to travel 10 degrees south then 15 degrees east.

46. **(1)** This map identifies the political boundaries within and surrounding Mexico.

47. **(1)** Traveling east from Arizona to the eastern coast of Florida, you go from 110 degrees west to 80 degrees west, resulting in a gain of two hours. Therefore, it would be 11:00 P.M. in Florida.

48. **(1)** *Laissez-faire* means letting business operate on its own without government interference. The speaker's words suggest that it is government's responsibility to help its citizens cope with economic hardships.

49. **(4)** Each nation has an economic system that best reflects the values of the people in that culture.

50. **(2)** Franklin D. Roosevelt, a Democrat, was best known for the federal programs his administration began that helped provide jobs and security for Americans during the Great Depression.

51. **(2)** To call the practices of another culture "uncivilized" is judgmental and therefore ethnocentric.

52. **(4)** The "Star Wars" space defense system is a military program that would be opposed by liberals.

53. (3) The questions the man asks and the clipboard he carries identify him as a political poll taker rather than any of the other choices.

54. (1) The man's first question is clearly about a recent election. His second question asks the woman to compare her degree of happiness to how she felt in 1988, another election year.

55. (2) By having the woman respond "Aaah" to the second question, the cartoonist is saying that the poll taker has asked one question too many.

56. (1) The passage supports the conclusion that the Pentagon omitted Fort Riley from its list of closings because the base was located in the home state of a powerful senator. Closing the base would hurt the state's economy and offend the senator, a politician with influence.

57. (2) The temperatures for the months of June, July, August, and September show the least variation.

58. (1) It is an opinion to say that one city has better weather conditions than another since the term *better* is relative.

59. (3) The Twenty-sixth Amendment to the Constitution gives eighteen-year-olds the right to vote.

60. (3) In a democracy, the government is there to help the people, but the people do most things for themselves.

61. (2) The figure representing the legislature is pulling at his collar, sweating, and gulping—all signs of nervousness. There are no visible signs that suggest the other choices.

62. (4) By delaying action on the abortion debate, the legislature hopes that the issue will go away before they have to make a decision about it. Only the pro-life and pro-choice protestors appear to have clearly taken sides (2). The legislature is avoiding controversy and is in favor of procrastination, or putting off the vote.

63. (2) Without political parties to reduce the number of candidates, any number of candidates could run for public office.

64. (1) The only example of a conditioned response is the child who learns to associate taking a nap with the end of "Sesame Street."

Use the answer key on pages 775–777 to check your answers to the Post-Test. Then find the item number of each question you missed and circle it on the chart below to determine the reading skill and content areas in which you need more practice. Pay particular attention to areas where you missed half or more of the questions. The reading skills are covered on pages 187–243. The page numbers for the content areas are listed below on the chart. Knowledge of reading skill and content area–based questions is absolutely essential for success on the GED Social Studies Test. The numbers in boldface are questions based on graphics. For those questions that you missed, review the skill pages indicated.

POST-TEST 2: SOCIAL STUDIES EVALUATION CHART

Skill Area/ Content Area	Comprehension (pages 189–195)	Application (pages 195–199)	Analysis (pages 200–210)	Evaluation (pages 211–222)
Behavioral Sciences (pages 247–262)	22, 41	13, 51, 64	6, 40	5, 7, 23
U.S. History (pages 263–300)	1, 37	24	2, **18**, 42, 50	**19**, 38, 39
Political Science (pages 301–318)	34, **35**, **55**, **57**, **58**	14, 52, 56, 60, **61**	15, 16, 32, 59	33, **36**, **62**, 63
Economics (pages 319–332)	**25**, **27**, 49	21, 29, 30, 31	**11**, 17, **26**, **28**	8, **12**, 20, 48
Geography (pages 333–342)	**3**, 44	4, 9, **45**, **46**, **47**	10, **54**	**43**, **53**

POST-TEST 3: SCIENCE

This Science Post-Test will give you the opportunity to evaluate your readiness for the actual GED Science Test.

This test contains 66 questions. Some of the questions are based on short reading passages, and some require you to interpret a chart or diagram.

You should take approximately 95 minutes to complete this test. At the end of 95 minutes, stop and mark your place. Then finish the test. This will give you an idea of whether or not you can finish the real GED Test in the time allotted. Try to answer as many questions as you can. A blank will count as a wrong answer, so make a reasonable guess for answers to questions you are not sure of.

When you are finished with the test, check your answers and turn to the Evaluation Chart on page 799. Use the chart to evaluate whether or not you are ready to take the final Practice Test and, if not, in what areas you need more work.

POST-TEST 3: SCIENCE ANSWER GRID

1 ① ② ③ ④ ⑤   18 ① ② ③ ④ ⑤   35 ① ② ③ ④ ⑤   51 ① ② ③ ④ ⑤
2 ① ② ③ ④ ⑤   19 ① ② ③ ④ ⑤   36 ① ② ③ ④ ⑤   52 ① ② ③ ④ ⑤
3 ① ② ③ ④ ⑤   20 ① ② ③ ④ ⑤   37 ① ② ③ ④ ⑤   53 ① ② ③ ④ ⑤
4 ① ② ③ ④ ⑤   21 ① ② ③ ④ ⑤   38 ① ② ③ ④ ⑤   54 ① ② ③ ④ ⑤
5 ① ② ③ ④ ⑤   22 ① ② ③ ④ ⑤   39 ① ② ③ ④ ⑤   55 ① ② ③ ④ ⑤
6 ① ② ③ ④ ⑤   23 ① ② ③ ④ ⑤   40 ① ② ③ ④ ⑤   56 ① ② ③ ④ ⑤
7 ① ② ③ ④ ⑤   24 ① ② ③ ④ ⑤   41 ① ② ③ ④ ⑤   57 ① ② ③ ④ ⑤
8 ① ② ③ ④ ⑤   25 ① ② ③ ④ ⑤   42 ① ② ③ ④ ⑤   58 ① ② ③ ④ ⑤
9 ① ② ③ ④ ⑤   26 ① ② ③ ④ ⑤   43 ① ② ③ ④ ⑤   59 ① ② ③ ④ ⑤
10 ① ② ③ ④ ⑤   27 ① ② ③ ④ ⑤   44 ① ② ③ ④ ⑤   60 ① ② ③ ④ ⑤
11 ① ② ③ ④ ⑤   28 ① ② ③ ④ ⑤   45 ① ② ③ ④ ⑤   61 ① ② ③ ④ ⑤
12 ① ② ③ ④ ⑤   29 ① ② ③ ④ ⑤   46 ① ② ③ ④ ⑤   62 ① ② ③ ④ ⑤
13 ① ② ③ ④ ⑤   30 ① ② ③ ④ ⑤   47 ① ② ③ ④ ⑤   63 ① ② ③ ④ ⑤
14 ① ② ③ ④ ⑤   31 ① ② ③ ④ ⑤   48 ① ② ③ ④ ⑤   64 ① ② ③ ④ ⑤
15 ① ② ③ ④ ⑤   32 ① ② ③ ④ ⑤   49 ① ② ③ ④ ⑤   65 ① ② ③ ④ ⑤
16 ① ② ③ ④ ⑤   33 ① ② ③ ④ ⑤   50 ① ② ③ ④ ⑤   66 ① ② ③ ④ ⑤
17 ① ② ③ ④ ⑤   34 ① ② ③ ④ ⑤

Choose the best answer to each question that follows.

Questions 1–4 are based on the following passage.

Cancer is one of the leading causes of death in our society. *Cancer* is a disease in which a cell in the body loses its sensitivity to factors that regulate cell growth and division. The cell begins to multiply without restriction, creating a growing mass called a *tumor*, which interferes with the structure and functioning of the organ in which it is located.

Frequently, cancer cells become *metastatic*, meaning that they travel, settling in a number of places and giving rise to secondary tumors. Much of medical research is devoted to finding ways of preventing, controlling, and curing cancer.

1. The passage above indicates that cancer cells usually

   (1) are of only one type
   (2) may be eradicated by radiation
   (3) are not restricted to one body area
   (4) are caused by viruses
   (5) look just like normal cells

2. Because of the metastatic trait of cancer cells, we can judge a cancer treatment to be effective only if

   (1) the entire body has been proven free of tumors over a period of time
   (2) the highest possible levels of treatment have been used
   (3) the original-source tumor has been identified
   (4) no new cancer cells are found in two weeks
   (5) the complete tumor is removed

3. Based on the information in the passage, you can conclude that

   (1) some specific body sites are more susceptible to cancer than others
   (2) the cure for cancer will be found in the near future
   (3) understanding the factors that affect cell growth is critical to finding a cure for cancer
   (4) secondary tumors are of greater danger than the original tumor
   (5) cancer is known only in our society

4. We would be correct in rejecting any proposed cure for cancer that

    (1) did not alter cancer cells' ability to metastasize
    (2) was based on research that was done on a variety of experimental subjects
    (3) was done for a period of time, with frequent checks and controls
    (4) was based on radiation therapy
    (5) was based on a drug therapy approach

Questions 5–8 are based on the following passage.

Although most animals and some plants detect and respond to sound vibrations, the precise sensitivity that we call *hearing* is rare in the living world. It is highly developed only in birds and mammals, and the same operational system applies in all vertebrate auditory systems.

Sound waves cause a liquid within the organism's auditory apparatus to vibrate. These vibrations are picked up by receptors that transmit signals to nerve cells. These cells then communicate the sound to the brain. Humans can hear vibrational frequencies of 20 to 20,000 cycles per second; cats respond to frequencies of up to 50,000 cycles per second; and porpoises and bats pick up frequencies of 100,000 cycles per second.

5. According to the passage, we can infer that one nonhearing organism is the

    (1) eagle
    (2) orangutan
    (3) opossum
    (4) cricket
    (5) whale

6. According to the information in the passage, auditory systems are based on the principle of

    (1) acoustical waves striking the bones of the outer ear
    (2) sound waves vibrating solid masses
    (3) sound waves setting a liquid in motion
    (4) sound waves bouncing off the eardrum
    (5) sound waves traveling through the ear canal

7. The passage supports the statement that

    (1) humans have the best hearing of all animals
    (2) cats and porpoises are especially adapted to hearing low frequencies
    (3) ears are damaged by high frequencies
    (4) some frequencies are beyond the hearing range of humans
    (5) invertebrates have better "hearing" systems than vertebrates

8. If subjected to sound frequencies of 25,000 to 100,000 cycles per second, which of the following animals would be least affected?

    (1) a porpoise
    (2) a house cat
    (3) a cheetah
    (4) a bat
    (5) a human being

Questions 9–12 are based on the following passage.

Fat can be defined loosely as a source for energy storage in the human body. The human anatomy is designed to carry food reserves to ensure the body's survival when food becomes scarce. However, in our slim-conscious society, many people go to great lengths to keep fat from accumulating on their bodies, sometimes with harmful effects.

Fat is more efficient in storing energy than carbohydrates for several reasons. One, fat is a highly concentrated energy source. Two, fat weighs less than the same energy amount of carbohydrates. Three, fat is much more efficient to carry as an energy source because it does not hold water as do carbohydrates. For example, an average 70 kg human male normally has about 11 kg of fat in his body. This fat represents enough stored energy to keep him alive for a month without eating. The same amount of energy stored as starch would double his body weight.

9. According to the passage, humans store energy in the form of fat because

   (1) fat keeps our bodies from drying out
   (2) fat is difficult to burn off
   (3) fat is used as a protective covering
   (4) body definition requires fat acquisition
   (5) it is nature's way of providing an auxiliary food source

10. If humans stored energy as carbohydrates instead of fat, they would

   (1) be in a constant search for food
   (2) eliminate many potential food sources
   (3) weigh much more than normal
   (4) maintain the same body structure
   (5) require a much higher liquid intake

11. The passage supports the opinion that

   (1) being obese is healthier than being underweight
   (2) reserves of fat serve no purpose in the human body
   (3) excessive dieting can be detrimental to one's health
   (4) fats lead to high cholesterol levels
   (5) one's physical appearance is more important than the storage of fat

12. The passage indicates that fat makes up approximately what fraction of body weight in a normal person?

   (1) none
   (2) $\frac{1}{7}$
   (3) $\frac{1}{2}$
   (4) $\frac{2}{3}$
   (5) $\frac{3}{4}$

Questions 13–15 are based on the following diagram.

ECOSYSTEM

Tertiary Consumer

Secondary Consumer

Primary Consumer

Primary Producer

Decomposer

← **Number of Individuals** →

Snake

Toad

Insect

Green Plants

Bacteria

13. According to the ecosystem diagram above, which member is the most populous?

(1) snakes
(2) toads
(3) insects
(4) green plants
(5) bacteria

14. The illustration best proves which well-known fact about the animal world?

(1) Amphibians are the largest group known.
(2) Insects form the largest group.
(3) Mammals form the largest group.
(4) Birds form the largest group.
(5) Reptiles are nearly extinct, as they represent the smallest group shown.

15. The South American boa constrictor, which eats amphibians, would be categorized in this ecosystem as a

(1) decomposer
(2) primary producer
(3) primary consumer
(4) secondary consumer
(5) tertiary consumer

Questions 16–19 are based on the following diagram.

PEA PLANTS

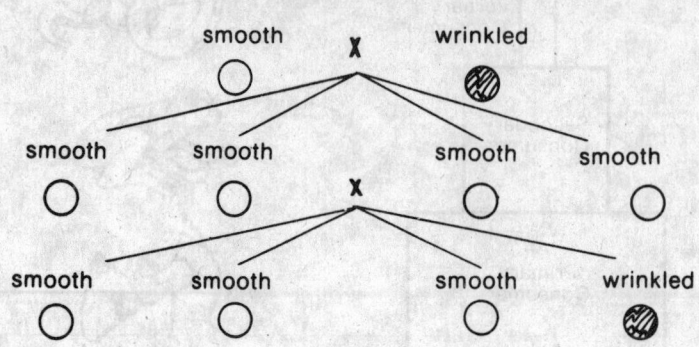

16. The diagram above shows the results when a smooth pea plant is crossed with a wrinkled pea plant. From the information in the diagram, you could conclude that the smooth trait is

(1) mutated
(2) recessive
(3) dominant
(4) hidden
(5) incomplete

17. From the information in the diagram, you could conclude that the wrinkled trait is

(1) mutated
(2) recessive
(3) dominant
(4) hidden
(5) incomplete

18. A geneticist would agree that the evidence shown in the example of the pea plants

(1) has no relationship to human transmission of traits
(2) is true only in the plant world
(3) is helpful in showing us how traits are transmitted from parents to offspring
(4) is too dated to have application in today's world
(5) is based purely on chance

19. Based on the diagram, when the middle two smooth peas are crossed, the percentage of the offspring that is likely to be wrinkled is

(1) 33 percent
(2) 50 percent
(3) 25 percent
(4) 10 percent
(5) 75 percent

Questions 20–25 are based on the following information.

One way in which organisms are classified is by how they obtain their food for energy use. Listed and defined below are five categories that describe the food-getting habits of organisms.

herbivore—an organism that feeds directly on plant matter

carnivore—an organism that feeds on the flesh of other organisms

omnivore—an organism that includes both plant and animal matter in its diet

parasite—an organism that obtains its nourishment by attaching itself to another organism, called a *host*

decomposer—an organism that usually lives in soil and obtains food by breaking down the wastes and remains of other organisms

20. A giant manatee that spends its day in a Florida river consuming water hyacinths would be categorized as a(n)

    (1) herbivore
    (2) carnivore
    (3) omnivore
    (4) parasite
    (5) decomposer

21. A consumer of fast-food fare such as a hamburger and french fries would be categorized as a(n)

    (1) herbivore
    (2) carnivore
    (3) omnivore
    (4) parasite
    (5) decomposer

22. A flea that attaches itself to a dog's skin and feeds on its blood would be categorized as a(n)

    (1) herbivore
    (2) carnivore
    (3) omnivore
    (4) parasite
    (5) decomposer

23. The Kodiak bear of Alaska feeds on various food items during the year. If the bear eats salmon in the fall, berries in the summer, and small animals year-round, the bear would be categorized as a(n)

    (1) herbivore
    (2) carnivore
    (3) omnivore
    (4) parasite
    (5) decomposer

24. The harpy eagle of Central America subsists exclusively on monkeys, sloths, and other small mammals. Based on this information, you would judge the harpy eagle to be a(n)

    (1) herbivore
    (2) carnivore
    (3) omnivore
    (4) parasite
    (5) decomposer

25. Based on the information above, the relationship between a biting mosquito and its human victim would be

    (1) prey-predator
    (2) organism-decomposer
    (3) parasite-host
    (4) herbivore-carnivore
    (5) omnivore-carnivore

Questions 26 and 27 are based on the following passage.

Insectivorous (insect-eating) plants are among the most fascinating members of the plant kingdom. They combine the characteristics of a plant with those of an animal. These plants have highly specialized leaves that capture and digest insects. The proteins of the digested insect supply the plant with nitrogen, which is usually unavailable in the poor soils in which these plants grow.

The Venus's flytrap of North and South Carolina is an example of an insectivorous plant. The leaves of this plant are hinged along the middle and swing upward and inward. An insect landing on the leaf triggers a sensitive motor mechanism that closes the leaf blades. The captured insect is then slowly digested by enzymes secreted by cells in the leaves.

26. According to the passage, what would probably result if insectivorous plants grew in richer soils?

(1) They would grow to a much larger size.
(2) It would be possible for the plants to take larger insects.
(3) They would be able to obtain nitrogen from sources other than insects.
(4) The plants would bloom more often.
(5) The plants would be able to grow deeper roots.

27. Insectivorous plants such as the Venus's flytrap demonstrate best which of the following scientific principles?

(1) the law of action and reaction
(2) the law of conservation of energy
(3) the theory of natural selection
(4) the law of periodicity
(5) the theory of evolution

Questions 28–30 are based on the following passage.

A plant stem's two main functions are to support the leaves and to transport materials between roots and leaves. As a stem develops, it possesses three types of permanent tissues: surface tissue, ground tissue, and vascular tissue. The surface and ground tissues support and give structure to the plant. The vascular tissues are the transport systems of the plant. The vascular tissues usually exist in one of three patterns and are known as the *phloem* and *xylem*.

Both the xylem and phloem are made up of several different types of cells that make up transport tubes for needed nutrients. In general, xylem nutrients, or "sap," travel from the roots to the rest of the plant. Phloem sap is derived from photosynthesizing leaves and from there is carried throughout the plant.

28. You can predict that a cut made through the stem of a plant would

(1) cause the plant to bud
(2) not affect the xylem and phloem
(3) destroy a plant's material transportation systems
(4) rejuvenate (restore) a plant
(5) not be critical to a plant's survival

29. Which generalization can we make about the transport functions of xylem and phloem?

(1) Xylem sap flows "from the bottom up"; phloem sap flows "from the top down."
(2) Phloem sap flows "from the bottom up"; xylem sap flows "from the top down."
(3) Both xylem and phloem handle two-way sap transport.
(4) The transport functions of the xylem and phloem are secondary to those of the pith and cortex.
(5) The transport functions of the xylem and phloem are exactly the same in all cases.

30. By injecting a nutrient dye into the root of a plant, we would be able to study

    (1) phloem sap transport
    (2) all vascular tissues
    (3) xylem sap transport
    (4) pith and cortex cells
    (5) total plant photosynthesis

Questions 31–36 are based on the following definitions.

Plants can propagate, or reproduce themselves, by one of five different methods. Listed and described below are five parts of plants out of which new plants are known to grow.

bud—a protuberance of a plant that can be cut off and planted, resulting in a new plant

runner—a horizontal offshoot from a plant that runs above or below ground and that can develop root systems to start new plants

bulb—an underground fleshy bud that multiplies and whose leaves store food; bulbs can be separated to grow a new plant

seed—a grain or ripened ovule of a mature plant that, when planted in moist soil, sprouts a new plant

stem cutting—a section of a plant that, when placed in a moist environment, develops roots and grows into a new plant

31. New peonies, perennial plants that produce showy flowers, can be propagated from the parent plant by dividing corms that grow undergound. This reproductive form described most closely resembles a

    (1) bud
    (2) runner
    (3) bulb
    (4) seed
    (5) stem cutting

32. Strawberries produce stolons that crawl along the ground and produce new plants when the tips of the stolons take root. This form of vegetative propagation is a

    (1) bud
    (2) runner
    (3) bulb
    (4) seed
    (5) stem cutting

33. Ferns grow from spores, one-celled structures that grow in cases on the undersides of the leaves. When the cases split, the spores fall to the ground, resulting in new plants when the soil conditions are right. A spore is most like a

    (1) bud
    (2) runner
    (3) bulb
    (4) seed
    (5) stem cutting

34. Potatoes have eyes that, when cut out from the fleshy tuber, can be planted to grow a new plant. This form of propagation is a

    (1) bud
    (2) runner
    (3) bulb
    (4) seed
    (5) stem cutting

35. We can propagate certain varieties of fruit trees by grafting—joining recently cut parts from two different trees. The method of vegetative propagation that this is most similar to is

    (1) bud
    (2) runner
    (3) bulb
    (4) seed
    (5) stem cutting

36. Potato plants are usually grown from buds, not seeds. The most likely explanation for this is that

    (1) seeds germinate only in Idaho soil
    (2) buds are more likely to duplicate the qualities of the parent plant
    (3) buds are not as subject to blight as seeds are
    (4) potatoes cannot be grown from seeds
    (5) buds represent a form of asexual reproduction and seeds represent sexual reproduction

Questions 37–41 are based on the diagram and the information below.

Mechanical energy is classified in two ways: energy waiting to be used and energy causing action. When an object is at rest at a place from which it can move, it is said to have potential energy, such as the rock illustrated in the diagram. An idling car has this stored energy, as does a ball in one's hand or a cocked pistol. The higher the rock sits on the hill, the greater potential energy it has.

The other type of energy is kinetic energy, or the energy of motion. Once an object is upset from its position and set into motion—the accelerator of a car is depressed, a ball thrown, or a pistol fired—the potential energy is converted to kinetic energy.

37. The purpose of this passage is to describe

    (1) the two types of mechanical energy
    (2) how kinetic energy becomes potential energy
    (3) the relationship of mass and kinetic energy
    (4) how height can be changed into power
    (5) the dissipation of energy

38. In the diagram, the rock in the resting position at the top of the hill is said to have

    (1) mechanical force
    (2) mechanical advantage
    (3) no energy
    (4) kinetic energy
    (5) potential energy

39. The energy of motion is called

    (1) kinesthetic energy
    (2) fuel-burning energy
    (3) kinetic energy
    (4) hydraulic energy
    (5) potential energy

40. In order for an object to have kinetic energy, there must be

    (1) elevation
    (2) motion
    (3) a storage mechanism
    (4) a starting gun
    (5) conversion

41. A pendulum at the top of its swing represents

    (1) potential energy
    (2) kinetic energy
    (3) no energy
    (4) hydraulic energy
    (5) mechanical energy

Questions 42–44 are based on the following passage.

The orderly pattern of the atoms in a crystal influences many properties apart from its external appearance. One of these properties is cleavage. *Cleavage* refers to the ability of a crystal to split in a certain direction along its surface. The direction of the cleavage is always parallel to a possible crystal face. Cleavage planes are dependent on the atomic structure, and they pass between sheets of atoms in well-defined directions.

How easily a mineral cleaves and the effect of the cleavage vary from one mineral to another. A crystal whose cleavage results in exceptionally smooth surfaces is said to show *eminent cleavage*; other types of cleavages are classified as *distinct* or *poor*. All crystalline gemstones undergo cleavage before they can be mounted in a setting. This cutting process may also be easy or difficult. A diamond cleaves easily despite its great hardness and may be cut into many different forms.

42. The passage indicates that the type of cleavage that a crystal exhibits is dependent upon the crystal's

(1) direction of cleavage
(2) eminent cleavage
(3) molecular makeup
(4) arrangement of atoms
(5) elemental mass

43. According to the passage, we can conclude that

(1) all crystals demonstrate good cleavage
(2) some crystals may not be used for gemstones because of poor cleavage
(3) eminent cleavage is inherent in all crystals of the quartz family
(4) cleavage of diamonds is a random property and differs from stone to stone
(5) cleavage improvement depends upon the location of mineral excavation

44. Based upon the knowledge that cleavage is characteristic of crystals, which of the following gems would *not* have this property?

(1) ruby
(2) emerald
(3) pearl
(4) diamond
(5) sapphire

Questions 45 and 46 are based on the following passage.

Off the coast of Chile and Peru, ocean currents and winds cause a rising of cold, nutrient-laden water. This enrichment of the ocean's surface layer results in an abundant plankton crop, which in turn supports large fish and seabird populations.

El Niño is the name for a set of oceanographic conditions that occurs every five to eight years, causing disturbances in Earth's biological and weather systems. El Niño (Spanish for "Christ child") gets its name from the fact that it usually happens around Christmas.

El Niño occurs when trade winds that drive the currents weaken and fail. In the ocean, the supply of nutrients is cut off, and rather sterile warm water kills off the plankton. The fish and seabirds starve.

Dramatic changes also take place in the world's weather. As the trade winds subside, the wind patterns around the globe are disrupted. For example, the normally cool European continent may experience prolonged periods of torrid temperatures as its normal wind patterns change. El Niño's effects may be felt for as long as two years at a time.

45. According to the passage, a resumption of the trade winds off the coast of South America would likely result in

(1) a major anchovy and tuna migration
(2) an end to El Niño
(3) further weather disruptions
(4) continued high European temperatures
(5) a condition known as El Aguaje

46. A spokesman states, "El Niño will have no effect on world food prices." The speaker is probably in error because

(1) food consumption goes up during El Niño
(2) food production increases because of El Niño
(3) new food sources are constantly being found
(4) the loss of fish as well as variable weather conditions reduce the availability of food
(5) the Northern Hemisphere makes up the Southern Hemisphere's food losses

Questions 47–49 are based on the following passage.

Quasars are recent additions to our body of knowledge about the physical universe. *Quasars* (quasistellar objects) are astronomical objects that are starlike in appearance and emit nonthermal radiation, usually more ultraviolet and infrared radiations than stars.

Quasars were first discovered in the early 1960s when telescopes picked up mysterious radio-wave emission sources that, at the time, couldn't be explained. Since then, thousands of radio-emitting and radio-quiet quasars have been located.

One interesting feature of quasars is that their energy output can change by great amounts in a short period of time. To date, scientists have not been able to account for these energy changes.

47. The information in the passage supports the belief that

(1) we really know nothing about our physical universe
(2) scientists hold the key to all knowledge about outer space
(3) scientists are baffled by new discoveries in outer space
(4) often, significant discoveries are made by accident
(5) at some point we will know all there is to know about our physical universe

48. The information in the passage supports the opinion that

(1) quasars are a threat to life on Earth
(2) the radio emissions of quasars are signs of communication from aliens
(3) quasars are restricted to the Milky Way galaxy
(4) there is still much to learn about the behavior of quasars
(5) the nearest quasar is 4.2 light-years away from Earth

49. Forms of life similar to those on Earth could not sustain themselves near quasars because of

(1) the distance of quasars from Earth
(2) the changes in the energy that quasars emit
(3) the blinding light that quasars emit
(4) the nearness of quasars to black holes
(5) an overabundance of radio waves in space

Questions 50–52 are based on the following illustration and caption.

CHEMICAL CELL

The model above illustrates the components of a chemical cell in A and its operation in B.

50. When a zinc rod and a copper rod are connected by a wire and immersed in a hydrochloric acid solution, an electrical current is generated. Unless it is disconnected, the circuit will continue until

(1) the hydrochloric acid evaporates
(2) the glass jar breaks
(3) the zinc rod disintegrates
(4) the copper rod disintegrates
(5) the wire breaks

51. An electrolyte is a substance that when dissolved in a liquid will conduct an electric current. The electrolyte in this battery is the

(1) zinc rod
(2) glass jar
(3) wire
(4) water
(5) hydrochloric acid

52. A substance is oxidized when it loses electrons and reduced when it gains electrons. Which of the following is true in the above experiment?

(1) The zinc rod loses electrons and is oxidized.
(2) The zinc rod gains electrons and is reduced.
(3) The copper rod loses electrons and is reduced.
(4) The hydrochloric acid reduces the copper.
(5) The hydrochloric acid oxidizes the copper.

Questions 53 and 54 are based on the following passage.

The science of producing and transmitting sound waves in materials has become widespread with many practical applications. *Ultrasonics*, as this science is called, was first developed during World War II as a method of detecting enemy submarines. Today ultrasonics has many applications. When the waves used are of a low amplitude, ultrasonics can be used to map the ocean's depths, detect flaws in materials, locate cancers in the human body, and scan fetuses for deformities.

Higher-amplitude waves are used in cleaning, in manufacturing materials, and in fatigue tests for metals. The destruction of bacteria and the use of tightly focused ultrasound as a surgical knife are biological applications of high-amplitude waves.

53. The passage indicates that the uses of ultrasonics are dependent upon the

   (1) frequency of the sound waves
   (2) amplitude of sound waves used
   (3) type of ultrasonic generator employed
   (4) medium to be investigated
   (5) wattage available to the user

54. According to the passage, a low-amplitude ultrasonic scanning of the human body would be able to

   (1) give a clear picture of interior body details
   (2) remove cancerous materials without radiation
   (3) remove bacteria painlessly
   (4) serve as an antiviral agent in infectious cases
   (5) aid the body's immune system

Questions 55 and 56 are based on the following passage.

Nuclear scientists have determined that a fourth state of matter exists: plasma. The state of plasma is reached when matter acquires a temperature so high that some of the molecules and atoms are broken down into ions and electrons. Stellar and interstellar matters are mostly forms of plasma.

On Earth, plasma exists in the ionosphere, in flames, and in chemical and nuclear explosions. Matter in a controlled thermonuclear reactor also exists in a plasma state.

Plasma is most like a gas. However, it differs from un-ionized gas in that it is a good conductor of electricity and heat.

Scientists hope to understand the occurrence of plasma in nature and to harness it as an inexpensive energy source.

55. Based upon the passage, we can infer that
   (1) plasma is a by-product of human research
   (2) plasma exists in nuclear reactions only
   (3) the plasmatic state of matter exists when a hydrogen bomb is detonated
   (4) the dangers of plasma research are not worth the risk to human life
   (5) fusion power would never be shared with developing countries

56. Based on the passage, the cost of developing thermonuclear power can be defended because

   (1) it is applicable to all technologies
   (2) plasma is the source of power that can be used without special equipment
   (3) it provides cheap power
   (4) it is almost perfected already
   (5) current nuclear power is too dangerous

Questions 57–59 are based on the following passage.

Chemists have determined that elements with atomic numbers greater than 92 are all radioactive. In general, their half-lives are much shorter than the age of the universe. This means that they no longer exist in nature and have all been artificially produced by scientists in nuclear reactions.

Elements 93 through 105 in the periodic table have been created and named, and scientists have claimed discovery of elements 106 and 107. The transuranium elements, as they are called, become less stable as the atomic number and mass increase. For example, element number 93, neptunium, has a half-life of two million years, while element number 104, kurchatovium, has a half-life of seventy seconds.

The transuranium elements are the heaviest elements that exist and are readily fissionable when subjected to a nuclear bombardment. Chemists studying these elements and the periodic table predict that stable elements may be found around atomic numbers 114 or 126.

57. According to the passage, we would predict that the half-life of element number 105 would be

(1) measured in days or weeks
(2) less than seventy seconds
(3) incalculable (not capable of being determined)
(4) greater than the other transuranium elements
(5) greater than two million years

58. From the information listed, we can conclude that

(1) all newly discovered elements will probably be radioactive
(2) scientists are in extreme danger in carrying out transuranium research
(3) half-lives of newly discovered elements will all be very long
(4) there is an end limit to the discovery of new elements
(5) new elements will be named after the planets

59. Based on the information in the passage, which of the following relationships appears to be true?

(1) The greater the atomic number, the higher the half-life.
(2) The greater the atomic number, the lower the half-life.
(3) The greater the radioactivity, the greater the half-life.
(4) The greater the half-life, the greater the radioactivity.
(5) The greater the atomic number, the greater the element's stability.

Questions 60 and 61 are based on the following passage.

Although water is the most common hydrogen-oxygen compound, hydrogen and oxygen form another compound called *hydrogen peroxide*, H_2O_2. Hydrogen peroxide was first obtained by treating barium peroxide with an acid. Very small quantities of hydrogen peroxide are present in dew, rain, and snow because of the action of ultraviolet light upon oxygen and water vapor.

Hydrogen peroxide has many different applications, depending upon its concentration. A 3 percent solution is used in the home as a mild antiseptic and germicide. A 30 percent solution is used in industry as a bleaching agent because of the permanency of the whiteness it produces. Concentrations of 90 percent are used as oxidizing agents in rockets and high explosives.

60. According to the information in the passage, we could predict that adding water to an industrial-strength hydrogen peroxide solution could result in

   (1) an explosion
   (2) a new substance
   (3) an antiseptic
   (4) a rocket fuel
   (5) a bleaching agent

61. The main idea of the passage is that hydrogen peroxide has

   (1) the same characteristics as water
   (2) different uses in different concentrations
   (3) all of the molecular characteristics of a peroxide
   (4) characteristics atypical of a peroxide
   (5) the chemical characteristics of barium

Questions 62–64 are based on the following illustration.

62. According to the scale above, a substance that registers 2.5 on the pH scale would be categorized as a(n)

   (1) base
   (2) neutral substance
   (3) alkali
   (4) acid
   (5) hydroxide

63. According to the scale, a substance that registers 7 on the pH scale would be categorized as a(n)

   (1) base
   (2) neutral substance
   (3) alkali
   (4) acid
   (5) hydroxide

64. Compost is a mixture that consists of decayed organic matter and is used for fertilizing and conditioning soil. Coffee grounds are often used as a compost for such plants as evergreens and rhododendrons. Based on this fact, and the information in the pH scale, you can infer that these plants

    (1) are deficient in iron
    (2) thrive in alkaline soil
    (3) thrive in clay-like soil
    (4) thrive in acidic soil
    (5) are members of the coffee family

Questions 65 and 66 are based on the following definitions and illustration.

reflection—angular return of a light wave

refraction—apparent bending of light waves through different mediums

diffraction—bending of light waves near an obstacle

interference—altering of brightness of light waves

polarization—restriction of light waves to one plane

RAYS OF LIGHT

A   B

65. A certain type of lens changes the direction of light rays from A to B. This illustrates the property of

    (1) deflection
    (2) diffraction
    (3) reflection
    (4) refraction
    (5) polarization

66. In the illustration, which rays are being screened out?
    A. vertical rays
    B. diagonal rays
    C. horizontal rays

    (1) A
    (2) B
    (3) C
    (4) A and B
    (5) B and C

Answers begin on page 797.

POST-TEST 3: SCIENCE ANSWER KEY

1. **(3)** Cancer cells metastasize and travel to various regions in the body.

2. **(1)** Since cancer can spread so widely, only long-term scans of the body that indicate an absence of cancer can indicate that the cancer has been cured.

3. **(3)** Until the mechanisms of cell growth are known completely, the variables that cause cancer cannot be identified.

4. **(1)** A cure for cancer would likely include preventing cancer from metastasizing or spreading to other sites in the body.

5. **(4)** The cricket is an insect—the only animal form listed for whom hearing is not possible.

6. **(3)** The passage says that vibrations in a liquid are translated into signals, which serve as the basis for auditory systems.

7. **(4)** Human hearing range extends to only 20,000 cycles per second, thus making higher frequency levels inaudible.

8. **(5)** Human beings are not capable of hearing frequencies of 25,000 cycles per second and more.

9. **(5)** The passage says that the human anatomy is designed to carry food reserves to ensure the body's survival when food becomes scarce.

10. **(3)** The passage states that the storage of carbohydrates would double a person's body weight.

11. **(3)** The passage states that in our society, people go to great lengths to keep fat from accumulating, sometimes with harmful effects. This suggests that excessive dieting can be detrimental to one's health.

12. **(2)** You can estimate that 11 out of 70 kg of weight is approximately $^{10}/_{70}$, or $^1/_7$.

13. **(5)** The label at the bottom of the ecosystem pyramid shows the number of individuals in that category. The longest bar is for the category labeled **bacteria**.

14. **(2)** Of the animals listed, insects form the largest group.

15. **(5)** A boa constrictor is a snake that eats amphibians. The chart shows snakes that eat toads (a kind of amphibian) as tertiary consumers.

16. **(3)** Since the number of offspring having smooth skins outnumbers the number with wrinkled skins, you can conclude that the trait for smooth skin is dominant.

17. **(2)** Since only one of the offspring is wrinkled, you can infer that the trait is recessive.

18. **(3)** By studying heredity in pea plants, geneticists have learned how plants and animals transmit traits to their offspring.

19. **(3)** One-fourth, or 25 percent, of the pea plants are wrinkled.

20. **(1)** Water hyacinths are plants; an animal that lives on plants is classified as a herbivore.

21. **(3)** A hamburger is beef—the flesh of a steer—and french fried potatoes belong to the vegetable family.

22. **(4)** The definitions classify a parasite, such as a flea, as an organism that feeds itself by attaching itself to another organism, such as a dog.

23. **(3)** An animal that feeds on plant and animal matter is categorized as an omnivore.

24. **(2)** Because the harpy eagle subsists on monkeys, sloths, and other small mammals, it is categorized as a carnivore.

25. **(3)** The mosquito lives on humans' blood; therefore, the relationship would be described as parasite-host.

26. **(3)** From the information given, the only choice that can be made is that the plants may become less dependent on insects for nitrogen.

27. **(3)** The Venus's flytrap demonstrates the theory of natural selection. In a nitrogen-deficient environment, the plant developed specialized leaves to trap insects from which it obtains nitrogen to survive.

28. **(3)** A cut made through the stem of a plant would kill the plant by severing its food transport system.

29. **(1)** Xylem absorbs nutrients through the roots and transports the nutrients upward. Phloem nutrients created from the process of photosynthesis are sent from the leaves down to the rest of the plant.

30. **(3)** The dye would be absorbed by the xylem at the root level and would be distributed throughout the plant.

31. **(3)** A corm is similar to a bulb, which grows underground and stores food for the plant's usage. Corms and bulbs multiply and can be divided to start new plants.

32. **(2)** A strawberry plant produces stolons, or runners, that trail along the surface of the soil, take root, and start new plants.

33. **(4)** A spore is most similar to a seed— a grain or ripened ovule that sprouts when planted in moist soil.

34. **(1)** A bud from a potato can be planted and can develop into a new plant.

35. **(5)** Sap running from both cuts creates a moist environment that enables the parts to grow together. This is most similar to the process described as stem cutting.

36. **(2)** The only plausible explanation for the effectiveness of a potato bud over a potato seed is the possibility that a bud is more likely to duplicate the qualities of the parent plant than a seed is.

37. **(1)** The entire passage describes the differences between the two forms of mechanical energy.

38. **(5)** The rock is not in motion, so it has potential energy.

39. **(3)** Kinetic energy is defined in the passage as energy in motion.

40. **(2)** The second paragraph of the passage states that in order for an object to have kinetic energy, there must be motion.

41. **(1)** A pendulum at the top of its swing represents potential energy because it pauses to change direction and is not in motion. As it begins to swing again, the energy becomes kinetic.

42. **(4)** According to the passage, cleavage is dependent on the atomic structure of crystal.

43. **(2)** A crystal must have good cleavage in order to be cut into a gemstone.

44. **(3)** Although considered by many to be a gemstone, a pearl is not a crystal and would not have the property of cleavage.

45. **(2)** A resumption of the trade winds would reverse the condition that caused El Niño.

46. **(4)** El Niño affects fishing and agricultural harvests, leading to reduced food supplies.

47. **(4)** According to the passage, quasars were discovered when astronomers picked up mysterious wave emissions from planetary objects. This fact suggests that the discovery of quasars was an accident.

48. **(4)** Since much of the information about quasars is hypothetical, there is still much to be learned about them.

49. **(2)** Life is dependent upon a steady, stable flow of energy. Energy flowing from quasars is described as being changeable. Therefore, life could not be sustained near quasars.

50. **(3)** Illustration B shows the zinc rod being used up by the electrical current in the chemical cell.

51. **(5)** The electrolyte is the hydrochloric acid, which conducts the current.

52. **(1)** A substance is oxidized when it loses electrons. In the experiment, the negatively charged zinc rod is oxidized.

53. **(2)** The uses of ultrasonics are divided into two broad categories as defined by wave amplitude— low-amplitude and high-amplitude ultrasonics.

54. **(1)** The passage states that low-amplitude ultrasonics can be used to pinpoint the location of potential deformities in the unborn.

55. **(3)** The passage says that plasma exists in nuclear explosions; the detonation of a hydrogen bomb is an example of a nuclear explosion.

56. **(3)** The passage states that scientists hope to harness plasma as an inexpensive energy source.

57. **(2)** The passage says that element 104 has a half-life of seventy seconds. The half-life decreases as the atomic number increases; therefore, element 105 would have a shorter half-life.

58. (1) Since all transuranium elements are radioactive, we can assume that newly discovered elements will also be radioactive.

59. (2) According to the information in the passage, the transuranium elements become less stable as their atomic numbers increase. This means that the greater the atomic number, the lower the half-life.

60. (3) Diluting an industrial hydrogen peroxide solution with water could reduce it to a concentration level suitable for use as an antiseptic.

61. (2) Hydrogen peroxide is used in one concentration as an oxidizing agent for rocket fuels, in another as a bleach, and in a third concentration as an antiseptic.

62. (4) An acid registers below 7 on the pH scale.

63. (2) The number 7 represents neutrality on the pH scale.

64. (4) On the pH scale, coffee has a reading of 5, indicating that it is an acid. Therefore, you can infer that evergreens and rhododendrons thrive in acidic soil.

65. (5) Polarization of light rays is the restriction of reflected rays to one plane.

66. (5) Horizontal and diagonal rays are being screened out, and vertical rays are allowed to penetrate the lens.

Use the answer key on pages 797–799 to check your answers to the Post-Test. Then find the item number of each question you missed and circle it on the chart below to determine the reading skill and content areas in which you need more practice. Pay particular attention to areas where you missed half or more of the questions. The reading skills are covered on pages 187–243. The page numbers for the content areas are listed below on the chart. Knowledge of reading skill and content area–based questions is absolutely essential for success on the GED Science Test. The numbers in boldface are questions based on graphics. For those questions that you missed, review the skill pages indicated.

POST-TEST 3: SCIENCE EVALUATION CHART

Skill Area/ Content Area	Comprehension (pages 189–195)	Application (pages 195–199)	Analysis (pages 200–210)	Evaluation (pages 211–222)
Biology (pages 355–374)	1, 6, 9, 10, 12, **13**, 19	8, **15**, 20, 21, 22, 23, 24, 25, 27, 30, 31, 32, 33, 34, 35	3, 5, **16**, **17**, 26, 28, 29, 36	2, 4, 7, 11, **14**, **18**
Earth Science (pages 375–398)			45, 49	46, 47, 48
Chemistry (pages 399–418)	51, **52**, 53, 54, 61	**62**, **63**	**50**, 57, 58, 60, 64	59
Physics (pages 419–440)	**37**, **39**, 42	**38**, **41**, 44, **65**	40, 43, 55, **66**	56

POST-TEST 4:
LITERATURE AND THE ARTS

The Literature and the Arts Post-Test will give you the opportunity to evaluate your readiness for the actual GED Literature and the Arts Test.

This test contains 45 questions. Most of the questions are based on excerpts from novels, short stories, plays, and speeches; some questions are based on a complete poem, essay, or review.

You should take approximately 65 minutes to complete this test. At the end of 65 minutes, stop and mark your place. Then finish the test. This will give you an idea of whether or not you can finish the real GED Test in the time allotted. Try to answer as many questions as you can. A blank will count as a wrong answer, so make a reasonable guess for answers to questions you are not sure of.

When you are finished with the test, check your answers and turn to the Evaluation Chart on page 813. Use the chart to evaluate whether or not you are ready to take the final Practice Test and, if not, in what areas you need more work.

POST-TEST 4: LITERATURE AND THE ARTS ANSWER GRID

1 ① ② ③ ④ ⑤	13 ① ② ③ ④ ⑤	25 ① ② ③ ④ ⑤	36 ① ② ③ ④ ⑤
2 ① ② ③ ④ ⑤	14 ① ② ③ ④ ⑤	26 ① ② ③ ④ ⑤	37 ① ② ③ ④ ⑤
3 ① ② ③ ④ ⑤	15 ① ② ③ ④ ⑤	27 ① ② ③ ④ ⑤	38 ① ② ③ ④ ⑤
4 ① ② ③ ④ ⑤	16 ① ② ③ ④ ⑤	28 ① ② ③ ④ ⑤	39 ① ② ③ ④ ⑤
5 ① ② ③ ④ ⑤	17 ① ② ③ ④ ⑤	29 ① ② ③ ④ ⑤	40 ① ② ③ ④ ⑤
6 ① ② ③ ④ ⑤	18 ① ② ③ ④ ⑤	30 ① ② ③ ④ ⑤	41 ① ② ③ ④ ⑤
7 ① ② ③ ④ ⑤	19 ① ② ③ ④ ⑤	31 ① ② ③ ④ ⑤	42 ① ② ③ ④ ⑤
8 ① ② ③ ④ ⑤	20 ① ② ③ ④ ⑤	32 ① ② ③ ④ ⑤	43 ① ② ③ ④ ⑤
9 ① ② ③ ④ ⑤	21 ① ② ③ ④ ⑤	33 ① ② ③ ④ ⑤	44 ① ② ③ ④ ⑤
10 ① ② ③ ④ ⑤	22 ① ② ③ ④ ⑤	34 ① ② ③ ④ ⑤	45 ① ② ③ ④ ⑤
11 ① ② ③ ④ ⑤	23 ① ② ③ ④ ⑤	35 ① ② ③ ④ ⑤	
12 ① ② ③ ④ ⑤	24 ① ② ③ ④ ⑤		

Read each excerpt and choose the best answer to each question that follows.

Questions 1–5 refer to the following excerpt from a short story.

WHAT MADE THE TEACHER CRY?

The day Mr. DePalma came out into the cold and asked us to line up in front of him was the day that President Kennedy was shot. Mr.
5 DePalma, a short, muscular man with slicked-down black hair, was the science teacher, P.E. coach, and disciplinarian at P. S. 13. He was the teacher to whose homeroom you
10 got assigned if you were a trouble-maker, and the man called out to break up playground fights, and to escort violently angry teenagers to the office. And Mr. DePalma was the
15 man who called your parents in for a "conference."

That day, he stood in front of two rows of mostly black and Puerto Rican kids, brittle from their
20 efforts to "keep moving" on a No-vember day that was turning bitter cold. Mr. DePalma, to our complete shock, was crying. Not just silent adult tears, but really sobbing.
25 There were a few titters from the back of the line where I stood shivering.

"Listen," Mr. DePalma raised his arms over his head as if he were
30 about to conduct an orchestra. His voice broke, and he covered his face with his hands. His barrel chest was heaving. Someone giggled behind me.
35 "Listen," he repeated, "some-thing awful has happened." A strange gurgling came from his throat, and he turned around and spat on the cement behind him.

40 "Gross," someone said, and there was a lot of laughter.
"The President is dead, you idi-ots. I should have known that wouldn't mean anything to a bunch
45 of losers like you kids. Go home."

—Judith Ortíz-Cofer, excerpted from "American History," 1992

1. Where does the action of the story take place?

   (1) in the gym of a community center
   (2) on the front steps of a federal courtroom
   (3) on the playground of a public school
   (4) in the yard of a federal prison
   (5) in front of a detention home

2. Mr. DePalma might best be described as

   (1) softhearted
   (2) funny
   (3) conceited
   (4) strict
   (5) bookish

3. Mr. DePalma cried because he was

   (1) hurt that people were making fun of him
   (2) upset about the death of the president
   (3) in pain after a fight with a violent young man
   (4) sick to his stomach and unable to breathe
   (5) frightened that war was about to be declared

4. How does Mr. DePalma feel about the speaker and her friends?

   (1) indifferent
   (2) proud
   (3) fearful
   (4) affectionate
   (5) disgusted

5. The author develops the character of Mr. DePalma in all of the following ways except

(1) revealing what Mr. DePalma says to other characters
(2) disclosing what Mr. DePalma secretly thinks
(3) showing how Mr. DePalma interacts with others
(4) describing what Mr. DePalma looks like
(5) having the narrator (speaker) summarize what Mr. DePalma is like

Questions 6–11 refer to the following excerpt from a play.

WHAT HAS HAPPENED TO D.J.?

DOCTOR [*Reads from folder*]: "An anonymous soldier standing in front of him, the barrel of his AK-47 as big as a railroad tun-
5 nel, his finger on the trigger slowly pressing it."

D.J.: That's the one.

DOCTOR: Who is that anonymous soldier?

10 D.J.: You know who that is.

DOCTOR: No, I don't.

D.J.: Ain't you done your home-work? [*Pointing to folder*]

DOCTOR: My memory is shaky. . . .
15 Please?

D.J.: That's the dude who should have killed me.

DOCTOR: "Should have"?

D.J.: Would have.

20 DOCTOR: What happened?

D.J.: He misfired.

DOCTOR: And?

D.J.: And that's it.

DOCTOR: That's what?

25 D.J.: That's it, man. What do you want—a flag that pops out of his rifle and says "Bang"?

DOCTOR: They say you then beat him to death with the butt of
30 your weapon. . . . In combat, near—Dakto.

D.J.: That's what they say.

DOCTOR: That is what they say.

D.J.: So I have heard.

35 DOCTOR: What else have you heard?

D.J.: That I showed "conspicuous gallantry."

DOCTOR: You're quoting to me?

40 D.J.: That is what they say, at ban-quets given in my honor.

DOCTOR: It's part of the citation. Is it not?

D.J. [*Quoting; far-away look*]: Con-
45 spicuous gallantry, above and beyond the call of duty. . . . [*With Texas accent*] "Ouah hearts and ouah hopes are turned to peace . . . as we as-
50 semble heah . . . in the East Room . . . this morning . . ."

DOCTOR: Lyndon B. Johnson?

D.J.: You got it.

DOCTOR: What did you feel?

55 D.J.: Nothing.

DOCTOR: But when he hung the medal around your neck, you were crying.

D.J.: See, you *done* your homework!

—Tom Cole, excerpted from
Medal of Honor Rag, 1977

6. D.J. had received a medal for his part in

(1) World War II
(2) the Korean conflict
(3) the Vietnam War
(4) riots at Kent State University
(5) American invasion of Grenada

7. The action of this excerpt centers around

- **(1)** a police inquiry into the actions of D.J.
- **(2)** a doctor attempting to learn more about a patient
- **(3)** an interview for a military promotion
- **(4)** an inquiry about drug use in the military
- **(5)** a newspaper interview about a soldier

8. Lines 14, 15, and 18, "My memory is shaky. . . . Please?" and "Should have?" suggest that the doctor is

- **(1)** probing for more information
- **(2)** very confused about D.J.
- **(3)** old and incompetent
- **(4)** young and inexperienced
- **(5)** not very interested in D.J.'s feelings

9. D.J.'s attitude toward the doctor can be described best as

- **(1)** playful and coy
- **(2)** respectful and appreciative
- **(3)** extremely hostile and violent
- **(4)** cooperative and cordial
- **(5)** guarded and sarcastic

10. Which of the following *best* characterizes the tone of this excerpt?

- **(1)** friendly exchanges between the doctor and D.J.
- **(2)** sarcastic comments made by the doctor
- **(3)** humorous responses given by D.J.
- **(4)** short, rapid-fire exchanges between D.J. and the doctor
- **(5)** angry outbursts by the doctor

11. Based on the excerpt, this play would most likely fall within the category of

- **(1)** farce, an exaggerated form of comedy
- **(2)** situation comedy
- **(3)** slapstick, or highly physical comedy
- **(4)** melodrama
- **(5)** allegory, or highly symbolic drama

Questions 12–19 refer to the following poem.

WHAT CONFLICT TAKES PLACE ON THE LAWNS?

Suburban Prophecy

On Saturday, the power-mowers' whine
Begins the morning. Over this neighborhood
Rises the keening, petulant voice, begin
Green oily teeth to chatter and munch the cud.

5 Monsters, crawling the carpets of the world,
Still send from underground against your blades
The roots of things battalions green and curled
And tender, that will match your blades with blades
Till the revolted throats shall strangle on
10 The tickle of their dead, till straws shall break
Crankshafts like camels, and the sun go down
On dinosaurs in swamps. A night attack
Follows and by the time the Sabbath dawns
All armored beasts are eaten by their lawns.

—Howard Nemerov, 1977

12. In the first stanza, the poet uses words such as *whine, voice, teeth, chatter,* and *munch* to suggest that the power-mowers are

- **(1)** alive
- **(2)** green
- **(3)** in need of repair
- **(4)** like cows
- **(5)** very powerful

13. The imagery in the first stanza most appeals to the reader's sense of

    (1) sight
    (2) touch
    (3) hearing
    (4) taste
    (5) smell

14. The phrase "your blades" in line 8 refers to

    (1) grass
    (2) roots
    (3) gardeners
    (4) lawnmowers
    (5) monsters

15. The action of the poem takes place in the time period of

    (1) an afternoon
    (2) a morning
    (3) twenty-four hours
    (4) a week
    (5) one sunset; a few hours

16. The events and imagery of the second stanza create an atmosphere in which

    (1) the lawns are overrun with crabgrass
    (2) suburbanites use their lawnmowers against each other
    (3) the people pushing the mowers are completely exhausted
    (4) the smell of freshly cut grass lingers in the air
    (5) lawns and lawnmowers are battling

17. Throughout the poem, Nemerov creates an interesting image of lawnmowers by comparing them to

    (1) other machines
    (2) people
    (3) animals
    (4) plants
    (5) swamps

18. The poet is ridiculing

    (1) suburbanites who turn into monsters
    (2) suburbanites who keep perfect lawns
    (3) lawnmowers and other modern machines
    (4) realtors who sell houses without lawns
    (5) neighbors who borrow from each other

19. In one description, Nemerov makes a comparison using the word *like* (a simile) and uses repetition of a beginning consonant (alliteration). Which of the following descriptions represents both of these techniques?

    (1) "crawling the carpets of the world"
    (2) "Green oily teeth to chatter and munch the cud"
    (3) "Crankshafts like camels"
    (4) "and the sun go down / on dinosaurs in swamps"
    (5) "All armored beasts are eaten by their lawns"

Questions 20–25 refer to the following essay.

WHAT IS HARRIS'S IDEA OF REALISM?

Narrow "Realism" Misses the Point of Real Vision

One of the half-dozen most difficult words in the world to define or to understand is *realism*; and yet people use it all the time to make

5 judgments about many things, including the arts.

What does a man really mean when he says he likes realistic painting? He means, in most cases, that

10 he likes a picture to represent objects the way the eye sees them. But the eye does not see reality.

When we look at a chair, we do not see the real chair, but an optical

15 illusion. The real chair is a mass of particles moving at incredible speeds with ceaseless energy.

When we look at a person, we see the face, the limbs, the clothes.

20 Are these the real person? Nobody would deny that it is the character, the spirit, the emotional structure beneath the bone that makes the real person.

25 A telescope sees big things more "realistically" than the eye; a microscope sees little things more "realistically" than the eye. If we do not expect the scientist to look at

30 the world with our naive realism, why should we expect the artist to do so?

What we call reality is merely the surface of things, the appear-

35 ance of objects. There is no truth to be found in this, and both the scientist and the artist seek a truth not visible to the naked eye.

Actually, we do not even believe

40 in our own realism; we do not believe that the Earth is flat, as it seems to be; we do not believe that the man who looks kind is kind, as he seems to be. We ourselves apply

45 more critical, more sophisticated, and (to use a dirty word) more intellectual yardsticks to everyday things around us.

The artist goes us one further.

50 He accepts *nothing* as it seems to be, for it is his task to throw a searchlight on the caverns and labyrinths of life. Now, his searchlight may be weak, or soiled, or focused

55 in the wrong way, and the art he gives us will then be dim or defective.

But whether he is a good or bad artist, we cannot ask him to look at

60 the world the way we do, for then he would see nothing more than we do. If anything, history shows that the mass of mankind spend their todays in trying to catch up to the artists of

65 yesteryear. We have just barely begun to come to an appreciation of [William] Blake's visions.

There is an amusing story about realism and [Pablo] Picasso.

70 A sailor once complained to him that his paintings were not realistic, and then took out a tiny snapshot of his child for the painter to see. Picasso squinted seriously at the

75 snapshot and handed it back to the father, merely saying, "Small, isn't she?"

—Sydney J. Harris, 1982

20. According to the author, the main problem with defining realism in art is that

(1) everything is real
(2) we cannot see what is real
(3) artists dislike the term
(4) science is real, but art is not
(5) only art of this century is realistic

21. The author sees the artist as someone who

    (1) looks deeper into life than the rest of us

    (2) sees everything as real

    (3) tries to see the world as the majority of us do

    (4) searches for the most realistic presentation

    (5) ignores the opinions of critics and does as he or she pleases

22. The story about Picasso illustrates that realistic, if taken literally, means that

    (1) a photograph is realistic art

    (2) photography is not art

    (3) the sailor's daughter was actually the size in the photo

    (4) the sailor did not have a daughter

    (5) the artist will always reject the work of others

23. If you saw a four-star action-packed movie and said you liked the film because it was realistic, you described the movie that way because it was

    (1) real to everyone

    (2) lifelike, according to the way you see life

    (3) set in a believable location

    (4) based on someone's life story

    (5) easy to understand

24. In the essay, Harris draws comparisons between the artist and the scientist. This technique is effective because both the artist and the scientist

    (1) use quite different skills

    (2) follow the scientific method of inquiry

    (3) exercise the same skills

    (4) suffer from a lack of respect

    (5) work in fields that have a longer history than most other fields

25. For gifted artists whose works are more widely appreciated after their deaths, Harris would likely have agreed that

    (1) their art wasn't real enough to the average person in the street

    (2) they hadn't perfected their craft during their lifetime

    (3) they were too far behind the public in the minds of the critics

    (4) they were visionaries who saw far beyond what the public was able to understand

    (5) their work was too abstract for anybody to appreciate

Questions 26–30 refer to the following excerpt from a novel.

WHO IS CAROL MILFORD?

On a hill by the Mississippi where Chippewas camped two generations ago, a girl stood in relief against the cornflower blue of
5 Northern sky. She saw no Indians now; she saw flour-mills and the blinking windows of skyscrapers in Minneapolis and St. Paul. Nor was she thinking of squaws and por-
10 tages, and the Yankee fur-traders whose shadows were all about her. She was meditating upon walnut fudge, the plays of Brieux, the reasons why heels run over, and the
15 fact that the chemistry instructor had stared at the new coiffure which concealed her ears.

A breeze which had crossed a thousand miles of wheatlands bel-
20 lied her taffeta skirt in a line so graceful, so full of animation and moving beauty, that the heart of a chance watcher on the lower road tightened to wistfulness over her
25 quality of suspended freedom. She lifted her arms, she leaned back against the wind, her skirt dipped and flared, a lock blew wild. A girl on a hilltop; credulous, plastic,
30 young; drinking the air as she longed to drink life. The eternal aching comedy of expectant youth.

It is Carol Milford, fleeing for an hour from Blodgett College.
35 The days of pioneering, of lassies in sunbonnets, and bears killed with axes in piney clearings, are deader now than Camelot; and a rebellious girl is the spirit of that bewil-
40 dered empire called the American Middlewest.

—Sinclair Lewis, excerpted from *Main Street*, 1920

26. Carol Milford is
    (1) an Indian squaw
    (2) a pioneer
    (3) a college student
    (4) a princess
    (5) a chemistry instructor

27. The setting of this passage is the state of
    (1) Mississippi
    (2) Iowa
    (3) Illinois
    (4) New York
    (5) Minnesota

28. The author's style is characterized by
    (1) concise wording
    (2) descriptive images
    (3) the use of suspense
    (4) exciting plot events
    (5) short sentences

29. The author uses the character of Carol Milford to represent
    (1) traditional women
    (2) female teachers
    (3) the future of immigrants
    (4) the spirit of the Midwest
    (5) the shallowness of young girls

30. The writing style of this passage would probably *not* be effective in a(n)
    (1) biography
    (2) textbook
    (3) poem
    (4) short story
    (5) opening scene of a play

Questions 31–38 refer to the following speech.

WHAT IS THE SPEAKER'S GOAL?

FRIENDS AND FELLOW CITIZENS—I stand before you to-night under indictment for the alleged crime of having voted at the last
5 presidential election, without having a lawful right to vote. It shall be my work this evening to prove to you that in thus voting, I not only committed no crime, but, instead, simply
10 exercised my *citizen's rights*, guaranteed to me and all United States citizens by the National Constitution, beyond the power of any State to deny.
15 The preamble of the Federal Constitution says:

"We, the people of the United States, in order to form a more perfect union, establish justice, insure
20 *domestic* tranquillity, provide for the common defense, promote the general welfare, and secure the blessings of liberty to ourselves and our posterity, do ordain and establish
25 this Constitution for the United States of America."

It was we, the people; not we, the white male citizens; nor yet we, the male citizens; but we, the whole
30 people, who formed the Union. And we formed it, not to give the blessings of liberty, but to secure them; not to the half of ourselves and the half of our posterity, but to the
35 whole people—women as well as men. And it is a downright mockery to talk to women of their enjoyment of the blessings of liberty while they are denied the use of the only
40 means of securing them provided by this democratic-republican government—the ballot.

—Susan B. Anthony, excerpted from "On Woman's Right to Suffrage," 1873

31. The speaker emphasizes the term "citizen's rights" (line 10) because she believes that

(1) no citizens have any rights in this country
(2) all men have the right to vote
(3) as a woman, she should be allowed to vote
(4) only Native Americans are truly citizens
(5) no one really cares about the meaning of citizenship

32. The speaker quotes from the Preamble of the Constitution to illustrate

(1) the principles on which voting laws should be based
(2) that men wrote the Constitution
(3) the contrast between the rights of men and women
(4) the basis of the women's rights movement
(5) that voting is not mentioned in the document

33. What the speaker believes to be "downright mockery" is to

(1) speak to women in public places
(2) treat women as if they were really free
(3) insist that women respect the Constitution
(4) place women on trial for crimes
(5) live by the principles set forth in the Constitution

34. The speaker uses the term "this democratic-republican government" (lines 41–42) to refer to

(1) America's two-party system
(2) the advantage that Democrats have over Republicans
(3) the liberty of men and lack of freedom of women
(4) a system that is led by males
(5) a system in which the people govern

35. The theme of this passage is that

(1) black men as well as white men should be allowed to vote
(2) both men and women should be allowed to vote
(3) the U.S. Constitution is out-of-date
(4) only those who founded the Union should be allowed to vote
(5) only women should be allowed to vote

36. The speaker's tone can best be described as

(1) polite and reserved
(2) weak and without support
(3) rude and abusive
(4) confident and forceful
(5) radical and too emotional

37. The speaker's use of the term "alleged crime" (lines 3–4) reveals that she

(1) has been found guilty by a jury
(2) finds humor in her arrest
(3) does not believe she has committed a crime
(4) does not respect the U.S. Constitution
(5) has a long history of criminal activity

38. Because of her beliefs expressed in this passage, the speaker would support which of the following?

(1) a nuclear test ban treaty
(2) an amendment outlawing capital punishment
(3) anti-handgun legislation
(4) the Equal Rights Amendment
(5) a right to life amendment

Questions 39–45 refer to the following review of a musical.

WHAT IS THE CRITIC'S OPINION OF *SMILE*?

"Beauty Marks"
Review of *Smile*
Music by Marvin Hamlisch
Book and Lyrics by Howard Ashman

This season's first four new American musicals all closed the week they opened, continuing a daunting three-year run of almost
5 unrelieved financial failure for what used to be Broadway's mainstay. Staged with varying degrees of artistry, the ill-fated shows shared one disabling presumption: musicals
10 must be "about" something beyond melody and romance. . . . All suffocated under the weight of their ambition.

One might expect the same fate to befall *Smile*, adapted from a 1975
15 Michael Ritchie film that satirized beauty pageants. The narrative, centering on girls who are strangers, inevitably lacks complex
20 relationships and love interest. Moreover, it is difficult to write a parody much funnier than the real Miss America proceedings. And it is hard to keep audiences interested in
25 the climax—which entrant will win—after repeatedly telling them it shouldn't matter. Curiously, *Smile* works. It is a swift-paced, skillfully performed and thoroughly profes-
30 sional entertainment that balances amusement at the shallow ambitions of the characters with respect for the depth of their feelings. Composer Marvin Hamlisch (*A Chorus
35 Line*) and Author-Lyricist Howard Ashman (*Little Shop of Horrors*) have written touching songs for the stars, Anne Marie Bobby as a sweet, awkward A student who realizes she

40 is out of her element at the pageant
and Jodi Benson as a wanderer who
is prematurely wise in the ways of
selling herself, including a talent-
show "dramatic reading" that turns
45 into a strip-tease. *Smile* may not be
a landmark, but it is a pleasure.

—William A. Henry III,
Time, December 8, 1986

39. According to the critic, musicals
were, at the time,

(1) as popular as ever
(2) unsuccessful on Broadway
(3) gaining popularity each year
(4) successful only when the
subjects were serious
(5) not as popular as films

40. Lines 11–13 state that "All
suffocated under the weight of
their ambition." The critic
includes this descriptive language
to suggest that

(1) there was not time to breathe
between scenes
(2) the directors and actors were
not experienced
(3) the musicals relied too much
on light humor
(4) producers were too concerned
with winning awards
(5) the musicals tried to make a
statement as well as entertain

41. The critic states that the musical
"balances amusement at the
shallow ambitions of the
characters with respect for the
depth of their feelings" (lines
30–33). This expresses a contrast
between the audience's

(1) feelings about Miss America
and patriotism
(2) depth of understanding of the
two main characters
(3) mixed emotions about the
characters' struggles
(4) favorable opinion of *Smile*
(5) impatience with the
characters and weak plot

42. The critic believes the music is

(1) too humorous for the theme
(2) shallow and without purpose
(3) appropriate for the characters
(4) outstanding and destined to
be popular
(5) inappropriate for the topic

43. Which of the following statements
best describes the critic's opinion
of *Smile*?

(1) Although *Smile* is not a great
musical, it is enjoyable.
(2) *Smile* is an example of why
musicals are no longer
popular.
(3) *Smile* unjustly criticizes the
Miss America pageant.
(4) Since *Smile* is about women,
it will surely be popular.
(5) *Smile* is the best musical of
the year.

44. According to the experience of
Broadway shows for three years
running, the type of production
that would have been most likely
to fail would be a

(1) comedy about marriage
(2) drama about Nazi Germany
(3) satire on college life
(4) musical about a person's
personal triumph
(5) one-woman concert

45. The statement "Curiously, *Smile*
works" reveals the critic's

(1) total disgust
(2) dislike of the musical
(3) lack of faith in the audience
(4) surprise at the
musical's success
(5) belief that all musicals are
worth watching

Answers begin on page 811.

POST-TEST 4: LITERATURE AND THE ARTS ANSWER KEY

1. (3) The first paragraph makes reference to "P.S. 13" (a public school), teachers, homeroom, and parent-teacher conferences. In the second paragraph, references to the cold let readers know that the action takes place outdoors, probably on a playground.

2. (4) In the first paragraph, Mr. DePalma is described as a "disciplinarian" (line 8) and "the man who called . . . parents in for a 'conference' " (lines 14–16).

3. (2) In paragraphs 3 and 4, Mr. DePalma is choked by sobs as he tries to tell the students that President Kennedy has been assassinated.

4. (5) In the last paragraph, Mr. DePalma says, "I should have known that [Kennedy's death] wouldn't mean anything to a bunch of losers like you kids."

5. (2) Because the story is told in the first person by a former student, rather than Mr. DePalma or an outside narrator, Mr. DePalma's unspoken thoughts cannot be disclosed.

6. (3) Clues in the passage that refer to the Vietnam War are "Dakto" and Lyndon B. Johnson, who was president during the latter years of the Vietnam War.

7. (2) The doctor refers to a folder and asks D.J. questions in order to learn more about D.J. This suggests a doctor-patient relationship.

8. (1) The doctor wants D.J. to give more details and explanations.

9. (5) D.J. does not volunteer information; the doctor has to ask for it. D.J. also makes sarcastic remarks such as "Ain't you done your homework?"

10. (4) The exchanges between the doctor and D.J. are short and to the point. Choices (1), (2), (3), and (5) cannot be supported by the excerpt.

11. (4) The serious circumstances under which the questioning takes place suggest that the play would be a melodrama and not a form of comedy or an allegory.

12. (1) The poet uses characteristics of living things.

13. (3) Sound words such as *whine, keening, petulant voice,* and *munch* appeal to hearing.

14. (4) The poem is about lawnmowers. The phrase "Monsters . . . send from underground against your blades" implies that blades of grass fight the blades of lawnmowers.

15. (3) The time referred to in the poem is Saturday morning until the dawn of Sabbath (Sunday).

16. (5) References in the poem that suggest war or battle are *battalions, blades, strangle, attack,* and *armored beasts.*

17. (3) Phrases that suggest the imagery of animals include "munch the cud," "crankshafts like camels," "dinosaurs in swamps," and "armored beasts."

18. (2) Suburbanites are often ridiculed for the care they lavish upon their lawns. The poem pokes fun by suggesting the lawns will someday fight back.

19. (3) A simile is a comparison between two unlike things using the word *like.* Alliteration is the repetition of a beginning consonant. The phrase "Crankshafts like camels" represents both.

20. (2) The essay states that "the eye does not see reality." This means that we cannot see what is real.

21. (1) The passage says that it is the task of the artist "to throw a searchlight on the caverns and labyrinths of life" and that "we cannot ask him to look at the world the way we do." These lines indicate that the artist is someone who looks deeply into life.

22. (3) Picasso describes the sailor's daughter as being small to show that if reality is the way things appear to be, then in real life the daughter would be as small as she is in the picture.

23. (2) The passage says that reality is judged by how an individual sees things in life.

24. (1) The comparison between the artist and the scientist is effective because each is perceived as representing different skills. The artist is perceived to be dreamy and impractical, and the scientist is perceived to be logical and practical.

25. (4) The passage says that "the mass of mankind spend their todays in trying to catch up to the artists of yesteryear." This suggests that artists see far beyond what the public is able to understand.

26. (3) The excerpt included references to a chemistry instructor and Carol's "fleeing for an hour from Blodgett College."

27. (5) Minneapolis and St. Paul are in Minnesota.

28. (2) The first sentence of the excerpt uses words to paint a picture. The rest of the passage describes the setting and character.

29. (4) The last sentence states that "a rebellious girl is the spirit" of the Midwest.

30. (2) Textbook writing is generally factual and objective, not excessively descriptive.

31. (3) According to Susan B. Anthony, *citizen* includes men and women.

32. (1) Anthony quotes the Preamble to the Constitution to support her purpose: to show why she felt she should have been able to vote.

33. (2) Anthony states "to talk to women of their enjoyment of . . . liberty while they are denied . . . the ballot" is "downright mockery." This suggests that a gap exists between what is practiced and what is proclaimed.

34. (5) The term refers to the U.S. government—of, by, and for the people.

35. (2) The entire speech is based on the argument that women should not be denied the right to vote.

36. (4) From the words used, Anthony's speech expresses confidence and forcefulness.

37. (3) The word *alleged* means "supposed." Anthony does not feel she has broken a law.

38. (4) The only choice shown that is closely related to Susan Anthony's suffragist movement is the Equal Rights Amendment—an amendment that was drafted to end discrimination on the basis of sex.

39. (2) According to the review, musicals had failed on Broadway for three years.

40. (5) The critic's words suggest that the musicals tried to do too much by being entertaining and making a social statement at the same time.

41. (3) The words *amusement* and *respect* suggest competing feelings, which can be described as mixed emotions.

42. (3) The critic says the songwriters "have written touching songs for the stars." This suggests that the music is appropriate for the characters.

43. (1) The last sentence states that "*Smile* may not be a landmark, but it is a pleasure." This suggests that the musical is enjoyable although it is not great.

44. (4) The review begins by reporting the failures of Broadway musicals. Therefore, of the choices listed, choice (4), a musical about a person's personal triumph, would have been likely to fail.

45. (4) Considering the fate of the other musicals on Broadway that year and the problems with *Smile*, the musical is suprisingly enjoyable according to the critic.

Use the answer key on pages 811–812 to check your answers to the Post-Test. Then find the item number of each question you missed and circle it on the chart below to determine the reading skill and content areas in which you need more practice. Pay particular attention to areas where you missed half or more of the questions. The reading skills are covered on pages 187–243. The page numbers for the content areas are listed below on the chart. Knowledge of reading skill and content area–based questions is absolutely essential for success on the GED Literature and the Arts Test. For those questions that you missed, review the skill pages indicated.

POST-TEST 4: LITERATURE AND THE ARTS EVALUATION CHART

Skill Area/ Content Area	Comprehension (pages 189–195)	Application (pages 195–199)	Analysis (pages 200–210)
Prose Fiction (pages 453–482)	1, 2, 3, 4, 26, 27	30	5, 28, 29
Poetry (pages 483–502)	14, 15, 18		12, 13, 16, 17, 19
Drama (pages 503–518)	6, 7, 8, 9	11	10
Nonfiction Prose (pages 519–536)	20, 21, 22, 25, 31, 33, 34, 37	23, 38	24, 32, 35, 36
Commentaries (pages 537–546)	39, 40, 42, 43, 45	44	41

POST-TEST 5: MATHEMATICS

This Mathematics Post-Test will give you the opportunity to evaluate your readiness for the actual GED Mathematics Test.

The test contains 56 questions and should take approximately 90 minutes to complete. At the end of 90 minutes, stop and mark your place. Then finish the test. This will give you an idea of whether or not you can finish the real GED Test in the time allotted. Try to answer as many questions as you can. A blank will count as a wrong answer, so make a reasonable guess for answers to questions you are not sure of.

When you are finished with the test, check your answers and turn to the Evaluation Chart on page 830. Use the chart to evaluate whether or not you are ready to take the final Practice Test and, if not, in what areas you need more work.

You may find the formulas on page 815 useful for some of the problems.

POST-TEST 5: MATHEMATICS ANSWER GRID

1 ① ② ③ ④ ⑤	15 ① ② ③ ④ ⑤	29 ① ② ③ ④ ⑤	43 ① ② ③ ④ ⑤
2 ① ② ③ ④ ⑤	16 ① ② ③ ④ ⑤	30 ① ② ③ ④ ⑤	44 ① ② ③ ④ ⑤
3 ① ② ③ ④ ⑤	17 ① ② ③ ④ ⑤	31 ① ② ③ ④ ⑤	45 ① ② ③ ④ ⑤
4 ① ② ③ ④ ⑤	18 ① ② ③ ④ ⑤	32 ① ② ③ ④ ⑤	46 ① ② ③ ④ ⑤
5 ① ② ③ ④ ⑤	19 ① ② ③ ④ ⑤	33 ① ② ③ ④ ⑤	47 ① ② ③ ④ ⑤
6 ① ② ③ ④ ⑤	20 ① ② ③ ④ ⑤	34 ① ② ③ ④ ⑤	48 ① ② ③ ④ ⑤
7 ① ② ③ ④ ⑤	21 ① ② ③ ④ ⑤	35 ① ② ③ ④ ⑤	49 ① ② ③ ④ ⑤
8 ① ② ③ ④ ⑤	22 ① ② ③ ④ ⑤	36 ① ② ③ ④ ⑤	50 ① ② ③ ④ ⑤
9 ① ② ③ ④ ⑤	23 ① ② ③ ④ ⑤	37 ① ② ③ ④ ⑤	51 ① ② ③ ④ ⑤
10 ① ② ③ ④ ⑤	24 ① ② ③ ④ ⑤	38 ① ② ③ ④ ⑤	52 ① ② ③ ④ ⑤
11 ① ② ③ ④ ⑤	25 ① ② ③ ④ ⑤	39 ① ② ③ ④ ⑤	53 ① ② ③ ④ ⑤
12 ① ② ③ ④ ⑤	26 ① ② ③ ④ ⑤	40 ① ② ③ ④ ⑤	54 ① ② ③ ④ ⑤
13 ① ② ③ ④ ⑤	27 ① ② ③ ④ ⑤	41 ① ② ③ ④ ⑤	55 ① ② ③ ④ ⑤
14 ① ② ③ ④ ⑤	28 ① ② ③ ④ ⑤	42 ① ② ③ ④ ⑤	56 ① ② ③ ④ ⑤

FORMULAS

Description	Formula
AREA (A) of a:	
square	$A = s^2$ where s = side
rectangle	$A = lw$ where l = length, w = width
parallelogram	$A = bh$ where b = base, h = height
triangle	$A = \frac{1}{2}bh$ where b = base, h = height
circle	$A = \pi r^2$ where $\pi \cong 3.14$, r = radius
PERIMETER (P) of a:	
square	$P = 4s$ where s = side
rectangle	$P = 2l + 2w$ where l = length, w = width
triangle	$P = a + b + c$ where a, b, and c are the sides
circle—circumference (C)	$C = \pi d$ where $\pi \cong 3.14$, d = diameter
VOLUME (V) of a:	
cube	$V = s^3$ where s = side
rectangular container	$V = lwh$ where l = length, w = width, h = height
cylinder	$V = \pi r^2 h$ where $\pi \cong 3.14$, r = radius, h = height
Pythagorean theorem	$c^2 = a^2 + b^2$ where c = hypotenuse, a and b are legs of a right triangle
distance (d) between two points in a plane	$d = \sqrt{(x_2 - x_1)^2 + (y_2 - y_1)^2}$ where (x_1, y_1) and (x_2, y_2) are two points in a plane
slope of a line (m)	$m = \frac{y_2 - y_1}{x_2 - x_1}$ where (x_1, y_1) and (x_2, y_2) are two points in a plane
mean	$mean = \frac{x_1 + x_2 + \ldots + x_n}{n}$ where the xs are the values for which a mean is desired and n = number of values in the series
median	$median$ = the point in an ordered set of numbers at which half of the numbers are above and half of the numbers are below this value.
simple interest (i)	$i = prt$ where p = principal, r = rate, t = time
distance (d) as function of rate and time	$d = rt$ where r = rate, t = time
total cost (c)	$c = nr$ where n = number of units, r = cost per unit

Solve each problem.

1. If Tom pays $10.56 every two months for his newspaper home delivery, how much does he pay in one year?

   (1) $9.36
   (2) $10.56
   (3) $36.72
   (4) $63.36
   (5) $126.72

2. Wesley willed his estate to Margaret, Betty Jo, and Johnny. He gave Margaret $2000. Betty Jo got $2\frac{1}{2}$ times as much as Margaret. Johnny got $3\frac{1}{2}$ times as much as Margaret. What was the total value of the estate?

   (1) $8000
   (2) $12,000
   (3) $14,000
   (4) $122,000
   (5)   not enough information is given

3. Of the following, which is the nearest in value to 8?

   (1) 8.1
   (2) 8.001
   (3) 7.998
   (4) 8.01
   (5) 7.09

4. José has 2 boards. One board is $2\frac{3}{4}$ feet and the other is $2\frac{1}{3}$ feet. To make them equal, how many *inches* must he cut from the longer piece?

   (1) $\frac{1}{3}$

   (2) $\frac{5}{12}$

   (3) $\frac{1}{2}$

   (4) 2

   (5) 5

5. Valentina needs $3\frac{1}{2}$ yards of nylon at $2.40 per yard. Excluding tax, how much change should she get back from a $20 bill?

   (1) $2.40
   (2) $5.90
   (3) $8.40
   (4) $11.60
   (5) $11.95

Questions 6 and 7 are based on the information below.

John worked as a waiter on Friday nights to supplement his income. He kept a list of the tips he received for 8 weeks and the number of hours he worked each Friday night.

WEEK	1	2	3	4	5	6	7	8
TIPS	$48	$65.25	$20	$73	$60	$62.50	$70.25	$53
HOURS	6	6	3	6	4	5	6	4

6. To the nearest dollar, what was the average amount of John's weekly tips?

(1) $50
(2) $57
(3) $60
(4) $227
(5) $452

7. In addition to his tips, John was paid $2 per hour by his employer. How much did he actually earn per hour, including his wages and his tips, during week 5?

(1) $2
(2) $4
(3) $8
(4) $17
(5) $68

Questions 8 and 9 are based on the drawing below.

8. Find the missing length (l) in inches.

(1) $2\frac{3}{4}$

(2) $3\frac{1}{4}$

(3) $4\frac{1}{4}$

(4) $9\frac{3}{4}$

(5) not enough information is given

9. How many inches of molding would be needed to frame the figure above?

(1) $16\frac{7}{8}$

(2) $26\frac{5}{8}$

(3) $33\frac{3}{4}$

(4) 37

(5) not enough information is given

10. School District #105 has 450 employees. There are 35 administrators, 40 clerical staff, and 15 custodians. If the remainder are instructors, what is the ratio of instructors to the total number of employees?

(1) $\frac{1}{5}$

(2) $\frac{1}{4}$

(3) $\frac{4}{5}$

(4) $\frac{5}{4}$

(5) $\frac{4}{1}$

11. A semiprofessional baseball player hits 9 home runs in the first 12 games of the season. At the same rate, how many can he expect to hit in the entire 28-game season?

(1) 18
(2) 20
(3) 21
(4) 22
(5) 27

12. On a scale drawing, $\frac{1}{2}$ inch = 10 miles. If the length of a road on this scale is 4 inches, which of the following could be used to find the length of the road?

(1) $10 \times 4 \times \frac{1}{2}$

(2) $10 \times 4 \times 2$

(3) $(10 + 4)2$

(4) $(10 + 4) \div 2$

(5) $(10 + 4) \div \frac{1}{2}$

13. Brenda earns $1840 a month. Her employer deducts 18% for federal income tax, 7% for social security tax, and 3% for state income tax. What is her *take-home pay* for the month?

(1) $515.20
(2) $1320.80
(3) $1324.80
(4) $2355.20
(5) not enough information is given

14. A salesman at Daniel's Jewelers is paid $350 per week plus 15% commission on sales. If he sells jewelry items for $42, $126, $785, and $384 during the week, which expression below best describes his pay for the week?

(1) 350 + 15(1337)
(2) 350 + .05(1337)
(3) .05 + 350(1337)
(4) .05 + 350 + 1337
(5) 350 + .15(1337)

15. Mrs. Caille is buying a school jacket for her son. She wants his name stitched on the front and his favorite school activity printed on the back. The basic cost of a jacket is $32.95 plus $2.50 to stitch his name on the front. It will cost an additional $.80 per letter to print the activity on the back. What other information does Mrs. Caille need to figure the cost of the jacket?

A. the basic cost of the jacket
B. the number of letters in her son's name
C. the cost of having his name stitched
D. the number of letters in his activity

(1) A
(2) B
(3) C
(4) D
(5) A and C

16. Susan bought 12 yards of terry cloth. How many towels, each 24 inches long, can be cut from this length of material?

(1) 2
(2) 4
(3) 6
(4) 18
(5) 108

17. At six candy bars for 89¢, what will 2 dozen candy bars cost?

(1) $.45
(2) $2.76
(3) $3.56
(4) $5.34
(5) $10.68

18. The scale on a map is 1 inch equals 65 miles. How many miles apart are two towns that are $2\frac{1}{2}$ inches apart on the map?

    (1) 97.5
    (2) 135
    (3) 145
    (4) 150
    (5) 162.5

19. If Sarah and her 2 roommates share their apartment rent evenly, what is Sarah's portion of their $300 per month rent?

    (1) $50
    (2) $100
    (3) $150
    (4) $175
    (5) $275

Questions 20–22 are based on the information below.

BARNES FAMILY BUDGET – 1993

Total Income – $25,000

20. Housing costs include home mortgage payments and utilities. How much were the housing costs in 1993 for the Barnes family?

    (1) $725
    (2) $2250
    (3) $5000
    (4) $7250
    (5) not enough information is given

21. If the money is spent equally, how much is allocated to each person in the Barnes family for clothing in 1993?

    (1) $500
    (2) $800
    (3) $1000
    (4) $2000
    (5) not enough information is given

22. If the Barnes family's income rose 10% in 1994 and the family followed the same budget, how much money was put into savings in 1994?

    (1) $250
    (2) $330
    (3) $2500
    (4) $3300
    (5) not enough information is given

Questions 23 and 24 are based on the graph below.

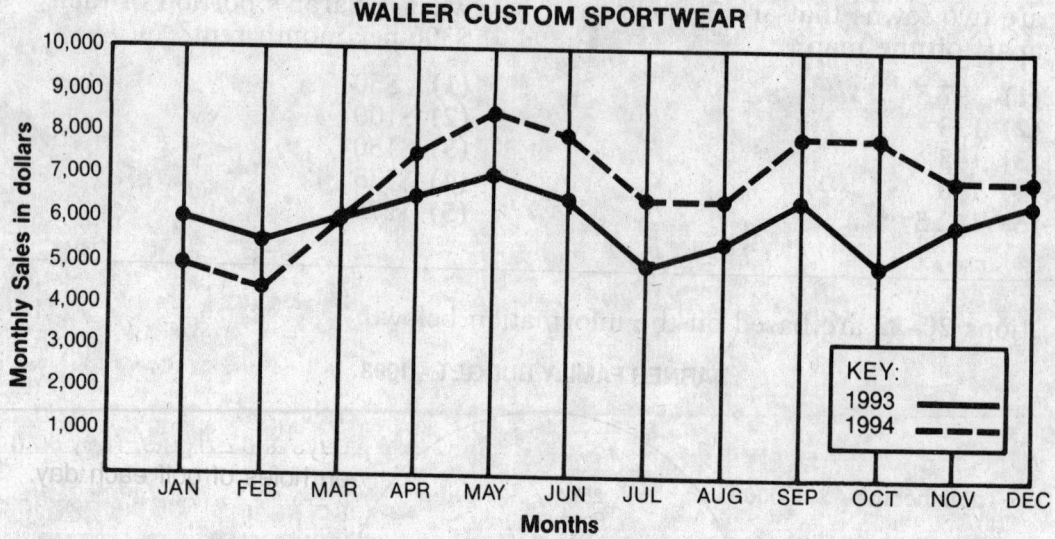

WALLER CUSTOM SPORTWEAR

KEY:
1993 ———
1994 - - - -

23. In which month were the sales for 1993 and the sales for 1994 the closest?

(1) JAN
(2) FEB
(3) MAR
(4) AUG
(5) DEC

24. The statement that best describes the graph is

(1) average monthly sales were about the same in both years
(2) average monthly sales doubled in 1994
(3) average sales were higher in 1993
(4) average sales were higher in 1994
(5) sales were always higher in the summer than in the rest of the year

25. The ten finalists in the local beauty pageant include 3 blonds, 4 brunettes, 1 redhead, and 2 black-haired women. What is the probability that the winner will be a brunette?

(1) $\frac{1}{9}$
(2) $\frac{1}{10}$
(3) $\frac{2}{5}$
(4) $\frac{4}{9}$
(5) $\frac{2}{3}$

26. Arrange the following numbers in order from the *smallest value to the greatest*: 1^5, 2^3, 4^1, and 6.

(1) 6, 4^1, 1^5, 2^3
(2) 1^5, 4^1, 6, 2^3
(3) 1^5, 2^3, 4^1, 6
(4) 6, 4^1, 2^3, 1^5
(5) 2^3, 4^1, 6, 1^5

27. Many calculators express very large or very small numbers in scientific notation. If the number 4.32×10^4 appears in the display of a calculator, what is the value of this number?

(1) .0432
(2) 4.0032
(3) 432
(4) 43,200
(5) 4,320,000

28. Evaluate the expression
$3z + 3(x + y)$, if $x = 6, y = 2$, and
$z = 5$.

(1) 13
(2) 20
(3) 24
(4) 31
(5) 39

29. Choose the point that is closest to
the value $-\frac{3}{4}$.

(1) A
(2) B
(3) C
(4) D
(5) E

30. On the highway, Albert always
drives at 55 mph. Colleen always
drives at 65 mph. If they start
together, driving in the same
direction, which expression below
tells how far apart they will be at
the end of a 4-hour drive?

(1) $4(65 + 55)$
(2) $4 \times 65 - 55$
(3) $65 - 55 \times 4$
(4) $\frac{65 + 55}{4}$
(5) $4(65 - 55)$

31. A store had received a supply of 8
dozen calculators, which it sold
for $9.99 each. If the store sold all
but 2 dozen of the calculators,
approximately how much money
did it make?

(1) $72
(2) $100
(3) $172
(4) $720
(5) $1000

32. Katy's age is 14 years less than
Sarah's age, x. The sum of their
two ages is 22. Choose the
equation that can be solved to find
the girls' ages.

(1) $2x - 14 = 22$
(2) $2(x - 14) = 22$
(3) $2x - 14 + x = 22$
(4) $x^2 - 14 = 22$
(5) not enough information is
given

Questions 33 and 34 are based on the
information below.

Manny and Judy went on a golfing
vacation for 2 days and 2 nights. They both
played eighteen holes of golf each day.
Eighteen holes of golf cost $18 per person.
The total bill for the weekend including golf
and their hotel room (including meals) was
$182.

33. Which equation best describes the
situation above?

(1) $x + 18 = 182$
(2) $2x + 18 = 182$
(3) $2x + 36 = 182$
(4) $2(x + 36) = 182$
(5) $x + 36 = 182$

34. What is the daily room rate
(including meals)?

(1) $55
(2) $73
(3) $82
(4) $146
(5) $164

35. Find the value of x in the equation
$\frac{2x}{3} = 12$.

(1)   2
(2)   4
(3)   9
(4)   18
(5)   108

36. What is the point of intersection of the line $x + y = 5$ with the line $y = -2$?

   (1) (2,3)
   (2) (7,−2)
   (3) (−2,7)
   (4) (−2,3)
   (5) (3,−2)

37. Emily was notified by her bank that she is overdrawn $187. If the bank charged her account $15 for correcting the overdraft and she deposited $350, what would be her new balance in the account?

   (1) $148
   (2) $178
   (3) $522
   (4) $552
   (5) not enough information is given

38. In the equation $x^2 + 7x = 0$, the equation will be true if x is

   (1) only −7
   (2) only 7
   (3) only 0
   (4) 0 or −7
   (5) 0 or 7

39. A social club has 20 members. There are 6 more men than women in the club. How many men and women are in the club?

   (1) 6 women and 14 men
   (2) 14 women and 6 men
   (3) 7 women and 13 men
   (4) 13 women and 6 men
   (5) not enough information is given

40. One winter day in the Rocky Mountains, the thermometer read 12°F at 9:00 A.M. The temperature dropped $3\frac{1}{2}$ degrees per hour for the next four hours, then rose one degree during the next hour. What was the temperature at the end of that hour?

   (1) −1°
   (2) 0°
   (3) 1°
   (4) 6°
   (5) 15°

41. Which of the following shows how the expression $4x^2 - 36x$ should be factored?

   (1) $4(x^2 - 36)$
   (2) $4x(x - 36)$
   (3) $4x(x - 9x)$
   (4) $4x(x - 9)$
   (5) $4x(x^2 - 9)$

42. In the expression $x + 2 > 13$, which of the following could be the value of x?

   (1) 2
   (2) 9
   (3) 11
   (4) 13
   (5) not enough information is given

43. In the figure below, find the distance between point A and point B.

   (1) −4
   (2) 0
   (3) 2
   (4) 4
   (5) 8

WEEKLY MUTUAL FUND REPORT

Company	High	Low	Close	Change
Faith Investments	13.16	12.91	13.61	+.38
Hatton Group	15.13	14.77	15.13	+.14
Mary Link Services	12.01	11.94	11.97	−.09
Selected Funds	14.56	14.29	14.56	+.09
American Mutuals	17.26	16.94	17.26	+.08

44. The weekly investment report above shows each company's stocks with its high bid, low bid, closing bid prices, and the net change from last week's closing bid. What is the average net change for all five companies listed?

   (1) .02
   (2) .06
   (3) .6
   (4) .12
   (5) 1.2

45. Which statement best describes the relationship between lines M and N?

   (1) Line M and line N both have positive slopes.
   (2) Line M and line N both have negative slopes.
   (3) Line M has a positive slope, and line N has a negative slope.
   (4) Line M has a negative slope, and line N has a positive slope.
   (5) There is not enough information to calculate the slopes of line N and line M.

46. Opposite sides of the figure below are parallel. Find the measure of angle x in the parallelogram shown here.

(1) 35°
(2) 55°
(3) 90°
(4) 180°
(5) 235°

47. According to the map below, how many miles is it from Jackson to Pierce?

(1) 3
(2) 8
(3) 9
(4) 15
(5) 21

48. Two angles of a triangle are equal, and the third angle is 38°. Which expression below describes the relationship among the three angles if one of the equal angles is x?

(1) $x + 38° = 90°$
(2) $2x + 38° = 90°$
(3) $x + 38° = 180°$
(4) $2x + 38° = 180°$
(5) $2x + 38° = 360°$

49. To estimate the height of the tall evergreen on his farmland, Doug used the measurements of a small pine tree and the lengths of the shadows of the evergreen and the pine tree. What is the height in feet of the evergreen?

(1) 49
(2) $71\frac{1}{2}$
(3) 75
(4) 100
(5) 105

50. According to the Pythagorean theorem, the length of the side *BD* can be found by solving which of the expressions below the figure?

(1) $5^2 + 3^2 = BD^2$
(2) $3^2 + BD^2 = 5^2$
(3) $5^2 + BD^2 = 3^2$
(4) $\sqrt{5^2 + 3^2} = BD^2$

(5) not enough information is given

51. Britton wants to cut material for a flag she is making. The diagram below shows 4 triangular sections. Each triangle will be cut from a different cloth. She must be sure that each angle has the correct measure. If $\angle AEC$ is 110°, what is the measure of $\angle CED$?

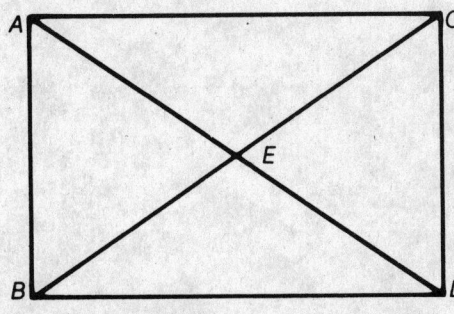

(1) 35°
(2) 55°
(3) 70°
(4) 125°
(5) 250°

52. How many square inches larger is the area of $\triangle ABC$ than $\triangle CDE$ shown in the figure?

(1) 9
(2) 24
(3) 30
(4) 54
(5) 78

53. How many inches long is the radius of the largest circle that can fit inside a rectangle 18 inches long and 12 inches wide?

(1) 3
(2) 6
(3) 9
(4) 12
(5) 18

54. The Lytle family plans to install indoor-outdoor carpeting to cover their patio with the dimensions shown below. At $8.00 per *square yard*, how much will it cost them to do this?

(1) $28
(2) $160
(3) $180
(4) $1440
(5) not enough information is given

55. The pirates buried their treasure chest in the ground. The dimensions of the chest were 3 feet high by 2 feet wide by 4 feet long. They had to dig a hole 2 feet deeper than the height of the chest to sink it low enough. How many cubic feet of dirt were dug out of the ground to make the hole for the chest?

(1)   9
(2) 11
(3) 24
(4) 40
(5) 120

56. A circle has a diameter of 14 inches. Which of the following could be used to find the area of the circle?

(1) $\frac{22}{7} \cdot 14^2$

(2) $\frac{22}{7} \cdot 7^2$

(3) $\frac{22}{7} \cdot 14$

(4) $\frac{22}{7} \cdot 7$

(5) $\frac{22}{7} \cdot 28$

Answers begin on page 827.

POST-TEST 5: MATHEMATICS ANSWER KEY

1. (4) $63.36
Find the number of 2-month payments in a year:
12 ÷ 2 = 6
Find how much Tom pays in a year:
10.56 × 6 = $63.36

2. (3) $14,000
Find each part of the estate:
Margaret = $2000
Betty Jo = $2000 × $2\frac{1}{2}$ = $5000
Johnny = $2000 × $3\frac{1}{2}$ = $7000
Add to get the total estate:
$2000 + $5000 + $7000 = $14,000

3. (2) 8.001
Give all the same number of decimal places:
8.100; 8.001; 7.998; 8.010; 7.090
8.001 is the closest to 8.

4. (5) 5
Find the difference between the two boards:
$2\frac{3}{4}$ = $2\frac{9}{12}$
$-2\frac{1}{3}$ = $2\frac{4}{12}$
$\frac{5}{12}$ ft = 5 in

5. (4) $11.60
Find the cost of the nylon:
$2.40 × $3\frac{1}{2}$ = $8.40
Subtract to determine the amount of change:
$20.00 − $8.40 = $11.60

6. (2) $57
Find the average:
$48 + $65.25 + $20 + $73 + $60 + $62.50 + $70.25 + $53 = $452
$452 ÷ 8 = $56.50 to the nearest dollar is $57

7. (4) $17
Find John's salary in week 5:
4 hr × $2 = $8
Add that to his tips:
$60 + $8 = $68
Divide by the number of hours:
$68 ÷ 4 = $17

8. (1) $2\frac{3}{4}$
Add the given sides that are parallel to the top:
$8\frac{1}{4}$ + $1\frac{1}{2}$ = $9\frac{3}{4}$
Subtract from the length of the top side:
$12\frac{1}{2}$ − $9\frac{3}{4}$ = $2\frac{3}{4}$

9. (5) not enough information is given
Since you cannot find the two interior sides, you cannot find the perimeter of the drawing.

10. (3) $\frac{4}{5}$
Find the number of instructors:
35 + 40 + 15 = 90 noninstructors
450 − 90 = 360 instructors
Write the ratio of instructors to employees:
$\frac{360}{450}$ ÷ $\frac{90}{90}$ = $\frac{4}{5}$

11. (3) 21
$\frac{9 \text{ home runs}}{12 \text{ games}} = \frac{x \text{ home runs}}{28 \text{ games}}$
$x = \frac{28 \times 9}{12} = 21$

12. (2) 10 × 4 × 2
$\frac{\frac{1}{2}\text{ in}}{10 \text{ mi}} = \frac{4 \text{ in}}{x \text{ mi}}$
$x = \frac{10 \times 4}{\frac{1}{2}} = 10 \times 4 ÷ \frac{1}{2}$ or 10 × 4 × 2

13. (3) $1324.80
Find the total percent of tax deductions:
18% + 7% + 3% = 28%
Find the amount deducted:
$\frac{x}{\$1840} = \frac{28}{100}$
$x = \frac{28 \times \$1840}{100} = \$515.20$
Subtract to find Brenda's take-home pay:
$1840 − $515.20 = $1324.80

14. (5) $350 + .15($1337)
First find the total in sales:
$42 + $126 + $785 + $384 = $1337
Identify the expression for the salesman's salary plus 15% commission on sales:
$350 + .15($1337)

15. (4) D only
Since she already knows the basic cost of the jacket (A) and the cost of getting his name stitched on the coat (C), she needs the number of letters in his activity to multiply by $.80.

16. (4) 18
Find the number of inches in 12 yards:
12 × 36 = 432 in
Divide to find how many 24-inch towels can be cut:
432 ÷ 24 = 18

17. (3) $3.56

2 dozen candy bars = 24 candy bars

$$\frac{6 \text{ candy bars}}{\$.89} = \frac{24 \text{ candy bars}}{x}$$

$$x = \frac{24 \times \$.89}{6} = \$3.56$$

18. (5) 162.5

$$\frac{1}{65} = \frac{2\frac{1}{2}}{x}$$

$$x = 2\frac{1}{2} \times 65$$

$$x = 162.5$$

19. (2) $100

Divide the rent by the number of people sharing the apartment:
$300 ÷ 3 = $100

20. (4) $7250

Find the total in housing costs:
20% + 9% = 29%
Find 29% of total income:

$$\frac{x}{\$25,000} = \frac{29}{100}$$

$$x = \frac{\$25,000 \times 29}{100} = \$7250$$

21. (5) not enough information is given

You do not know how many people are in the Barnes family.

22. (4) $3300

Find 10% of the income:

$$\frac{x}{\$25,000} = \frac{10}{100}$$

$$x = \frac{\$25,000 \times 10}{100}$$

$$= \frac{\$250,000}{100} = \$2500$$

Find the total income for 1994:
$25,000 + $2500 = $27,500
Find 12% to be put into savings:

$$\frac{x}{\$27,500} = \frac{12}{100}$$

$$x = \frac{\$27,500 \times 12}{100} = \$3300$$

23. (3) MAR

In the month of March, sales are the same.

24. (4) average sales were higher in 1994

The graph shows the overall sales were higher in 1994 than in 1993.

25. (3) $\frac{2}{5}$

$$\frac{4 \text{ brunettes}}{10 \text{ finalists}} = \frac{2}{5}$$

26. (2) 1^5, 4^1, 6, 2^3

$1^5 = 1 \times 1 \times 1 \times 1 \times 1 = 1$
$4^1 = 4$
$6 = 6$
$2^3 = 2 \times 2 \times 2 = 8$

27. (4) 43,200

$4.32 \times 10^4 = 4.3200 = 43,200$

28. (5) 39

$3z + 3(x + y) =$
$3(5) + 3(6 + 2) = 15 + 24 = 39$

29. (3) C

$-\frac{3}{4}$ is between 0 and −1.

30. (5) 4(65 − 55)

Using $d = rt$, this expression shows the difference in their distances assuming the same amount of time but different rates of speed.

31. (4) $720

Find how many dozen calculators were sold:
8 dozen − 2 dozen = 6 dozen
Approximate the total sales:
72(6 dozen) × $10(approximately $9.99) = $720

32. (1) $2x − 14 = 22$

Let x = Sarah's age
$x − 14$ = Katy's age
The sum of the ages is
$x + x − 14 = 22$ or
$2x − 14 = 22$

33. (4) $2(x + 36) = 182$

Let x = room rate
Golf cost 2 × 18 = $36 per day
Two days cost $2(x + \$36)$

34. (1) $55

$2(x + \$36) = \$182$
$2x + \$72 = \$182$
$2x = \$110$
$x = \$55$

35. (4) 18

$$\frac{2x}{3} = 12$$

$2x = 12 \cdot 3$
$2x = 36$
$x = 18$

36. (2) (7,−2)

Substitute −2 for y.
$x + y = 5$
$x + (−2) = 5$
$x + 2 − 2 = 5 + 2$
$x = 7$
$x = 7$ and $y = −2$ so the point of intersection is (7,−2)

37. (1) $148

−$187 overdrawn
− $15 charge
−$202 + $350 = $148

38. (4) 0 or −7

$x^2 + 7x = 0$
For 0: $0^2 + 7(0) = 0$
For −7: $(−7)^2 + 7(−7) =$
$49 − 49 = 0$

39. (3) 7 women and 13 men

Let x = number of women
$x + 6$ = number of men
$x + x + 6 = 20$
$2x = 20 − 6$
$2x = 14$
$x = 7$ women
$x + 6 = 13$ men

40. (1) −1°

$-3\frac{1}{2}° \times 4 = −14°$
$12° − 14° = −2°$ at the end of 4 hours
$−2° + 1° = −1°$ at the end of 5 hours

41. (4) $4x(x − 9)$

$$4x^2 − 36x =$$

$\boxed{4 \cdot x} \cdot x − 9 \cdot \boxed{4 \cdot x} =$
$4x(x − 9)$

42. (4) 13

$x + 2 > 13$
$x + 2 - 2 > 13 - 2$
$x > 11$

Since x must be greater than 11, the only possible value of those given is 13.

43. (5) 8

Since both points are on the horizontal line $y = 2$, you can count the units:
-4 to $0 = 4$; 0 to $4 = 4$
$4 + 4 = 8$

44. (4) .12

Find the total:
$+.38 + .14 - .09 + .09 + .08 = .60$
Find the average:
$.60 \div 5 = .12$

45. (1) Line M and line N both have positive slopes.

46. (2) 55°

Subtract to find the supplement of 125° since x is equal to that supplementary angle:
$180° - 125° = 55°$

47. (3) 9

$$c^2 = a^2 + b^2$$
$$15^2 = 12^2 + b^2$$
$$225 = 144 + b^2$$
$$225 - 144 = b^2$$
$$81 = b^2$$
$$9 = b$$

48. (4) $2x + 38° = 180°$

The angles of a triangle equal 180°. Two equal angles ($2x$) plus 38° equal 180°.

49. (4) 100

Set up a proportion:

$$\frac{height}{70 \text{ ft shadow}} = \frac{5 \text{ ft}}{3\frac{1}{2} \text{ ft shadow}}$$

$$h = \frac{70 \times 5}{3\frac{1}{2}}$$

$$h = \frac{350}{1} \div \frac{7}{2} = \frac{350}{1} \times \frac{2}{7} = 100$$

50. (2) $3^2 + BD^2 = 5^2$

Side BD is one side of a right triangle, $\triangle BCD$. Substitute the given values in the Pythagorean theorem as follows:
$$a^2 + b^2 = c^2$$
$$3^2 + BD^2 = 5^2$$

51. (3) 70°

$\angle CED$ is the supplement of $\angle AEC$.
$180° - 110° = 70°$

52. (3) 30

Set up a proportion to find side BC:

$$\frac{x}{12} = \frac{6}{8}$$

$$x = \frac{6 \times 12}{8} = 9$$

Find the area of both triangles:

$$\triangle ABC = \frac{1}{2} \cdot \frac{9 \cdot 12}{1} = 54 \text{ sq in}$$

$$\triangle CDE = \frac{1}{2} \cdot \frac{6 \cdot 8}{1} = 24 \text{ sq in}$$

Find the difference:
$54 - 24 = 30$ sq in

53. (2) 6

The width of the rectangle would be the diameter of the circle, $d = 12$.

Radius $= \frac{1}{2}d$

$$r = \frac{1}{2} \cdot \frac{12}{1} = 6 \text{ in}$$

54. (2) $160

Find the area of the patio:
$A = lw$
$A = 18 \times 10 = 180$ sq ft
Find the number of square yards (there are 9 square feet in a square yard):
$180 \div 9 = 20$ sq yd
Find the total cost:
$20 \times \$8 = \$160$

55. (4) 40

Find the depth of the hole (height):
$3 + 2 = $ height
Find the volume of dirt:
$V = lwh$
$V = (4)(2)(5)$
$V = 40$ cu ft

56. (2) $\frac{22}{7} \cdot 7^2$

Choose the correct formula for area:
$A = \pi r^2$ where $\pi \approx \frac{22}{7}$
$A = \frac{22}{7} \cdot r^2$
Since the diameter is 14, the radius is 7.
$A = \frac{22}{7} \cdot 7^2$

Use the answer key on pages 827–829 to check your answers to the Post-Test. Then find the item number of each question you missed and circle it on the chart below to determine the mathematics skill and content areas in which you need more practice. Pay particular attention to areas where you missed half or more of the questions. The page numbers for the content areas are listed below on the chart. The numbers in boldface are questions based on graphics. For those questions that you missed, review the pages indicated.

POST-TEST 5: MATHEMATICS EVALUATION CHART

Skill Area/ Content Area	Item Number	Review Pages
Whole Numbers & Problem Solving	**7**, 15, 19, **21**, 30, 31, 37	559–572
Decimals	1, **6**	573–586
Fractions	2, 4, 5	587–604
Ratio & Proportion	10, 11, 17	605–610
Percent	13, 14, **20**, **22**	611–620
Measurement	12, 16, **18**	621–636
Graphs, Statistics, & Probability	**23**, **24**, 25	637–648
Numeration	3, 26, 27	649–656
Geometry	**8**, **9**, **46**, **47**, 48, **49**, **50**, **51**, **52**, **53**, **54**, 55, 56	657–674
Algebra	28, **29**, 32, 33, 34, 35, 36, 38, 39, 40, 41, 42, **43**, **44**, 45	675–710

Practice Tests

Realizing that practice makes perfect, we've added Practice Tests as final indicators of your readiness for the real GED Test. These tests are just like the Post-Tests in terms of format, level of difficulty, and percentages found on the real test. After you have completed the Practice Tests, you will be able to finally determine whether you are ready to take the GED Test and, if not, what areas you need to review. As with the Post-Tests, Evaluation Charts are included to help you judge your performance. We recommend the following approach to the Practice Tests.

1. Take only one Practice Test at a time. Try to finish the test within the allotted time so that you can see how you will do on the actual GED Tests. If you are not done within that time period, mark where you were when the time was up and finish the test. You want to finish the entire Practice Test so that you can make use of the Evaluation Charts.

Time Allowed for Each Test

Writing Skills	Part 1	75 minutes
	Part 2	45 minutes
Social Studies		85 minutes
Science		95 minutes
Literature and the Arts		65 minutes
Mathematics		90 minutes

2. After you have finished each of the Practice Tests, check the answers in the answer key and fill in the Evaluation Charts. The answer keys and Evaluation Charts follow each test. Be sure to read the explanations for all of the questions that you missed.

3. If the Evaluation Charts indicate that you still need work in a certain area, refer to the review pages given in the charts.

4. When you have finished all of the tests, checked your answers, and filled out the Evaluation Charts, transfer your test scores from the Evaluation Charts to the GED Readiness Worksheet on page 927. Use the Worksheet to determine whether you are ready for the actual GED Tests.

5. Although these are Practice Tests, you should give them your best effort. If an item seems difficult, mark it and come back later. Always answer every question—even if you have to make an "educated guess." Sometimes you may know more than you give yourself credit for. Also, on the real GED Tests a blank counts as a wrong answer. It's always wise to answer every question as best you can.

Good luck on the Practice Tests and on the GED!

PRACTICE TEST 1: WRITING SKILLS
Part 1: Conventions of English

The following items are based on paragraphs that contain numbered sentences. Some of the sentences may contain errors in sentence structure, usage, or mechanics. A few sentences, however, may be correct as written. Read the paragraph and then answer the items based on it. For each item, choose the answer that would result in the most effective writing of the sentence or sentences. The best answer must be consistent with the meaning and tone of the rest of the paragraph.

When you are finished with the test, check your answers and turn to the Evaluation Charts on page 848. Use the charts to evaluate whether or not you are ready to take the actual GED Test and, if not, in what areas you need more work.

PRACTICE TEST 1: WRITING SKILLS ANSWER GRID

1 ① ② ③ ④ ⑤	15 ① ② ③ ④ ⑤	29 ① ② ③ ④ ⑤	43 ① ② ③ ④ ⑤
2 ① ② ③ ④ ⑤	16 ① ② ③ ④ ⑤	30 ① ② ③ ④ ⑤	44 ① ② ③ ④ ⑤
3 ① ② ③ ④ ⑤	17 ① ② ③ ④ ⑤	31 ① ② ③ ④ ⑤	45 ① ② ③ ④ ⑤
4 ① ② ③ ④ ⑤	18 ① ② ③ ④ ⑤	32 ① ② ③ ④ ⑤	46 ① ② ③ ④ ⑤
5 ① ② ③ ④ ⑤	19 ① ② ③ ④ ⑤	33 ① ② ③ ④ ⑤	47 ① ② ③ ④ ⑤
6 ① ② ③ ④ ⑤	20 ① ② ③ ④ ⑤	34 ① ② ③ ④ ⑤	48 ① ② ③ ④ ⑤
7 ① ② ③ ④ ⑤	21 ① ② ③ ④ ⑤	35 ① ② ③ ④ ⑤	49 ① ② ③ ④ ⑤
8 ① ② ③ ④ ⑤	22 ① ② ③ ④ ⑤	36 ① ② ③ ④ ⑤	50 ① ② ③ ④ ⑤
9 ① ② ③ ④ ⑤	23 ① ② ③ ④ ⑤	37 ① ② ③ ④ ⑤	51 ① ② ③ ④ ⑤
10 ① ② ③ ④ ⑤	24 ① ② ③ ④ ⑤	38 ① ② ③ ④ ⑤	52 ① ② ③ ④ ⑤
11 ① ② ③ ④ ⑤	25 ① ② ③ ④ ⑤	39 ① ② ③ ④ ⑤	53 ① ② ③ ④ ⑤
12 ① ② ③ ④ ⑤	26 ① ② ③ ④ ⑤	40 ① ② ③ ④ ⑤	54 ① ② ③ ④ ⑤
13 ① ② ③ ④ ⑤	27 ① ② ③ ④ ⑤	41 ① ② ③ ④ ⑤	55 ① ② ③ ④ ⑤
14 ① ② ③ ④ ⑤	28 ① ② ③ ④ ⑤	42 ① ② ③ ④ ⑤	

Choose the best answer to each question that follows.

Questions 1–9 refer to the following passage.

(1) Is you stressed out by work or school or life in general? (2) One popular way to cope with stress the practice of meditation. (3) Many people spend ten minutes meditating quietly. (4) Meditating lets them get back to their day feeling refreshed and energetic. (5) First, sit comfortably in a chair with your back straight but not stiff. (6) Relax, place your hands in your lap, and your feet flat on the floor. (7) Close your eyes feel your abdomen expand when you breathe in and collapse when you breathe out. (8) If the worries of the day keep intruding, don't fight it off. (9) Just let them go gently, out of your mind. (10) Concentrating on your breathing. (11) Once you got the hang of it, ten minutes of meditating can leave you feeling as rested as a night's sleep.

1. Sentence 1: **Is you stressed out by work or school or life in general?**

   What correction should be made to this sentence?

   (1) change *Is* to *Are*
   (2) insert a comma after *work*
   (3) change *school* to *School*
   (4) change the spelling of *general* to *genral*
   (5) change the question mark to a period

2. Sentence 2: **One popular way to cope with stress the practice of meditation.**

   Which of the following is the best way to write the underlined portion of this sentence? If you think the original is the best way, choose option (1).

   (1) with stress the practice of
   (2) with stress is to practice
   (3) with stress, the practice of
   (4) with stress, practice
   (5) with stress. The practice of

3. Sentences 3 and 4: **Many people spend ten minutes meditating quietly. Meditating lets them get back to their day feeling refreshed and energetic.**

   The most effective combination of sentences 3 and 4 would include which of the following groups of words?

   (1) After meditating quietly for ten minutes,
   (2) Before meditating quietly for ten minutes,
   (3) Meditating quietly for ten minutes, therefore,
   (4) To spend ten minutes meditating quietly,
   (5) While meditating quietly for ten minutes,

4. Sentence 6: **Relax, place your hands in your lap, and your feet flat on the floor.**

   Which of the following is the best way to write the underlined portion of this sentence? If you think the original is the best way, choose option (1).

   (1) lap, and your feet
   (2) lap, and you're feet
   (3) lap, and put your feet
   (4) lap and your feet
   (5) lap; and your feet

5. Sentence 7: **Close your eyes feel your abdomen expand when you breathe in and collapse when you breathe out.**

   What correction should be made to this sentence?

   (1) change *Close* to *Closed*
   (2) insert a semicolon after *eyes*
   (3) insert a comma after *eyes*
   (4) change *expand* to *expands*
   (5) insert a comma after *in*

6. Sentence 8: **If the worries of the day keep intruding, don't fight it off.**

   What correction should be made to this sentence?

   (1) change *If* to *Because*
   (2) insert a comma after *day*
   (3) change *keep* to *keeps*
   (4) change *don't* to *dont*
   (5) change *it* to *them*

7. Sentence 9: **Just let them go gently, out of your mind.**

   Which of the following is the best way to write the underlined portion of this sentence? If you think the original is the best way, choose option (1).

   (1) let them go gently,
   (2) lets them go gently,
   (3) let it go gently,
   (4) let them goes gently,
   (5) let them go gently

8. Sentence 10: **Concentrating on your breathing.**

   What correction should be made to this sentence?

   (1) change *Concentrating* to *Concentrate*
   (2) change the spelling of *Concentrating* to *Consentrating*
   (3) insert a comma after *Concentrating*
   (4) change *your* to *you're*
   (5) no correction is necessary

9. Sentence 11: **Once you got the hang of it, ten minutes of meditating can leave you feeling as rested as a night's sleep.**

   What correction should be made to this sentence?

   (1) change *you* to *you'll*
   (2) change *got* to *get*
   (3) change *it* to *them*
   (4) change *leave* to *left*
   (5) change the spelling of *night's* to *nite's*

Questions 10–19 refer to the following passage.

(1) Vultures have the worst reputation of all birds but make an important contribution to our world. (2) They cleans up dead bodies. (3) Road kills and other animal carcasses can infectious diseases. (4) When vultures eat this meat, they protect humans and other animals from getting infected. (5) Some vultures even have eaten bones. (6) The lammergeier vulture which can be found in Africa and Eurasia drops bones from a great height onto a rocky surface. (7) The bones land with enough force to split open, and then the vulture consumes it. (8) These Trash Collectors of the skies do their work efficiently. (9) They find carcasses through sharp eyesight, alertness, and they work as a team. (10) A vulture swoops down, and it's a signal to other vultures that a meal is on the table. (11) They sped toward the scene on their massive wings and devour even a large animal in minutes.

10. Sentence 1: **Vultures have the worst reputation of all birds but make an important contribution to our world.**

Which of the following is the best way to write the underlined portion of this sentence? If you think the original is the best way, choose option (1).

(1) reputation of all birds but
(2) reputation, of all birds, but
(3) reputation of all birds and
(4) reputation. Of all birds but
(5) reputation of all birds so

11. Sentence 2: **They cleans up dead bodies.**

What correction should be made to this sentence?

(1) change *They* to *He*
(2) change *cleans* to *clean*
(3) insert a comma after *up*
(4) change the spelling of *bodies* to *bodys*
(5) no correction is necessary

12. Sentence 3: **Road kills and other animal carcasses can infectious diseases.**

Which of the following is the best way to write the underlined portion of this sentence? If you think the original is the best way, choose option (1).

(1) carcasses can
(2) carcass can
(3) carcasses can carry
(4) carcasses. They can carry
(5) carcasses can carries

13. Sentence 5: **Some vultures even have eaten bones.**

What correction should be made to this sentence?

(1) change *vultures* to *vulture*
(2) insert a comma after *vultures*
(3) change *have eaten* to *eat*
(4) change *have eaten* to *ate*
(5) change *have eaten* to *eats*

14. Sentence 6: **The lammergeier vulture which can be found in Africa and Eurasia drops bones from a great height onto a rocky surface.**

Which of the following is the best way to write the underlined portion of this sentence? If you think the original is the best way, choose option (1).

(1) vulture which can be found in Africa and Eurasia
(2) vultures which can be found in Africa and Eurasia
(3) vulture, which can be found in Africa and Eurasia,
(4) vulture what can be found in Africa and Eurasia
(5) vulture which can be found in africa and eurasia

15. Sentence 7: **The bones land with enough force to split open, and then the vulture consumes it.**

    What correction should be made to this sentence?

    (1) change *land* to *lands*
    (2) insert a comma after *land*
    (3) change *vulture* to *vultures*
    (4) change *it* to *them*
    (5) no correction is necessary

16. Sentence 8: **These Trash Collectors of the skies do their work efficiently.**

    What correction should be made to this sentence?

    (1) change *These* to *This*
    (2) change *Trash Collectors* to *trash collectors*
    (3) insert a comma after *skies*
    (4) change *their* to *there*
    (5) change the spelling of *efficiently* to *eficiently*

17. Sentence 9: **They find carcasses through sharp <u>eyesight, alertness, and they work as a team.</u>**

    Which of the following is the best way to write the underlined portion of this sentence? If you think the original is the best way, choose option (1).

    (1) eyesight, alertness, and they work as a team
    (2) eyesight alertness, and they work as a team
    (3) eyesight, alertness, and it works as a team
    (4) eyesight, alertness, and they work like a team
    (5) eyesight, alertness, and teamwork

18. Sentence 10: **A vulture swoops down, and it's a signal to other vultures that a meal is on the table.**

    If you rewrote sentence 10 beginning with

    Swooping down,

    the next words should be

    (1) a vulture
    (2) a signal
    (3) other vultures
    (4) a meal
    (5) on the table

19. Sentence 11: **They sped toward the scene on their massive wings and devour even a large animal in minutes.**

    What correction should be made to this sentence?

    (1) change *They* to *It*
    (2) change *sped* to *speed*
    (3) change the spelling of *scene* to *seen*
    (4) change *on* to *under*
    (5) change *their* to *they're*

Questions 20–28 refer to the following passage.

(1) Times are tough it's harder than ever to live within your income. (2) A lot of people are looking for ways to live more cheaply than he or she used to. (3) Even people who used to have money, are trading in their BMWs for sensible, high-mileage compact cars. (4) One of the best ways to save money is to stop buying on credit. (5) The interest is so high. (6) You might also have skipped one meat-based meal each week. (7) Pasta, rice, and to eat other grains are much cheaper than meat. (8) Avoid buying everything from food to clothes to compact discs on impulse, you'll be surprised at how much you save. (9) Finally, don't throw things out until their really worn out. (10) Americans threw away almost 1,500 pounds of garbage per person per year. (11) Getting a few more wearings out of those jeans and re-using grocery bags is good for both your wallet and the environment.

20. Sentence 1: **Times are tough it's harder than ever to live within your income.**

    Which of the following is the best way to write the underlined portion of this sentence? If you think the original is the best way, choose option (1).

    (1) are tough it's
    (2) is tough it's
    (3) are tough, it's
    (4) are tough, and it's
    (5) are tough its

21. Sentence 2: **A lot of people are looking for ways to live more cheaply than he or she used to.**

    What correction should be made to this sentence?

    (1) change the spelling of *people* to *poeple*
    (2) change *are* to *is*
    (3) change *are looking* to *looked*
    (4) change *ways* to *way*
    (5) change *he or she* to *they*

22. Sentence 3: **Even people who used to have money, are trading in their BMWs for sensible, high-mileage compact cars.**

    What correction should be made to this sentence?

    (1) change *who* to *what*
    (2) change the spelling of *sensible* to *sensable*
    (3) remove the comma after *money*
    (4) change *are* to *is*
    (5) change *their* to *they're*

23. Sentences 4 and 5: **One of the best ways to save money is to stop buying on credit. The interest is so high.**

    The most effective combination of sentences 4 and 5 would include which of the following groups of words?

    (1) credit, even if the interest
    (2) credit because the interest
    (3) credit, although the interest
    (4) credit; however, the interest
    (5) credit, and the interest

24. Sentence 6: <u>**You might also have skipped**</u> **one meat-based meal each week.**

    Which of the following is the best way to write the underlined portion of this sentence? If you think the original is the best way, choose option (1).

    (1) You might also have skipped
    (2) One might also have skipped
    (3) You might also, have skipped
    (4) You might also skip
    (5) You might also skips

25. Sentence 7: **Pasta, rice, and to eat other grains are much cheaper than meat.**

    What correction should be made to this sentence?

    (1) remove the comma after *pasta*
    (2) remove *to eat*
    (3) change *to eat* to *eating*
    (4) change *are* to *is*
    (5) change *than* to *then*

26. Sentence 8: **Avoid buying everything from food to clothes to compact discs on** <u>**impulse, you'll be surprised**</u> **at how much you save.**

    Which of the following is the best way to write the underlined portion of this sentence? If you think the original is the best way, choose option (1).

    (1) impulse, you'll be surprised
    (2) impulse you'll be surprised
    (3) impulse. You'll be surprised
    (4) impulse, youll be surprised
    (5) impulse, you'll be surprized

27. Sentence 9: **Finally, don't throw things out until their really worn out.**

    What correction should be made to this sentence?

    (1) change *don't* to *dont*
    (2) change *throw* to *threw*
    (3) insert a comma after *out*
    (4) change *their* to *they're*
    (5) change *their* to *there*

28. Sentence 10: **Americans throwed away almost 1,500 pounds of garbage per person per year.**

    What correction should be made to this sentence?

    (1) change *Americans* to *americans*
    (2) change *throwed* to *threw*
    (3) change the spelling of *almost* to *allmost*
    (4) change *garbage* to *Garbage*
    (5) no correction is necessary

Questions 29–37 refer to the following passage.

(1) The average person catches four colds a year and miss about seven days of work, according to a medical study. (2) Young children get colds more often and spread them more rapidly. (3) So it's not surprising that the parents of young children take more sick days than anyone else. (4) Not only do they have to stay home to take care of their sick kids, but they're also likely to get sick from their kids. (5) The best way to stay healthy, is to avoid exposure to cold germs. (6) Colds are usualy passed on by hand-to-hand contact. (7) This could include shaking hands with a sick person which has just rubbed his eyes or even using the phone of a sniffling co-worker. (8) While a cold virus can't penetrate skin, it can penetrate mucous membranes in your mouth, nose, and eyes. (9) All colds are caused by germs. (10) That myth you're mother told you about the dangers of catching cold from sitting in a draft or getting your feet wet is just a myth. (11) If one is unlucky enough to come down with a cold, your best cures are resting, eating right, and avoiding stress.

29. Sentence 1: **The average person catches four colds a year and miss about seven days of work, according to a medical study.**

What correction should be made to this sentence?

(1) change *catches* to *catch*
(2) change the spelling of *four* to *for*
(3) change *miss* to *misses*
(4) change *days* to *days'*
(5) no correction is necessary

30. Sentences 2 and 3: **Young children get colds more often and spread them more rapidly. So it's not surprising that the parents of young children take more sick days than anyone else.**

The most effective combination of sentences 2 and 3 would include which of the following groups of words?

(1) If young children
(2) Since young children
(3) Although young children
(4) But young children
(5) While young children

31. Sentence 5: **The best way to stay healthy, is to avoid exposure to cold germs.**

Which of the following is the best way to write the underlined portion of this sentence? If you think the original is the best way, choose option (1).

(1) to stay healthy, is
(2) too stay healthy, is
(3) to stay helthy, is
(4) to stay healthy is
(5) to stay healthy, are

32. Sentence 6: **Colds are usualy passed on by hand-to-hand contact.**

What correction should be made to this sentence?

(1) change *are* to *is*
(2) change the spelling of *usualy* to *usually*
(3) insert a comma after *usualy*
(4) insert a comma after *on*
(5) no correction is necessary

33. Sentence 7: **This could include shaking hands with a sick <u>person which has just rubbed his eyes</u> or even using the phone of a sniffling co-worker.**

   Which of the following is the best way to write the underlined portion of this sentence? If you think the original is the best way, choose option (1).

   (1) person which has just rubbed his eyes
   (2) person, which has just rubbed his eyes
   (3) person who has just rubbed his eyes
   (4) person which will rub his eyes
   (5) person which has just rubbed their eyes

34. Sentence 8: **While a cold virus can't penetrate skin, it can penetrate mucous membranes in your mouth, nose, and eyes.**

   If you rewrote sentence 8 beginning with

   A cold virus can't penetrate skin,

   the next word should be

   (1) since
   (2) therefore
   (3) and
   (4) but
   (5) so

35. Sentence 9: **All colds are caused by germs.**

   What correction should be made to this sentence?

   (1) change *All* to *Every*
   (2) change *colds* to *Colds*
   (3) insert a comma after *colds*
   (4) change *are* to *were*
   (5) no correction is necessary

36. Sentence 10: **That <u>myth you're mother told you</u> about the dangers of catching cold from sitting in a draft or getting your feet wet is just a myth.**

   Which of the following is the best way to write the underlined portion of this sentence? If you think the original is the best way, choose option (1).

   (1) myth you're mother told you
   (2) myth, you're mother told you
   (3) myth your mother told you
   (4) myth you're Mother told you
   (5) myth you're mother will tell you

37. Sentence 11: **If one is unlucky enough to come down with a cold, your best cures are resting, eating right, and avoiding stress.**

   What correction should be made to this sentence?

   (1) change *If* to *Because*
   (2) change *one is* to *you are*
   (3) change *your* to *you're*
   (4) change *cures* to *cure*
   (5) change *avoiding* to *to avoid*

Questions 38–46 refer to the following passage.

(1) Did you know their are people who work as garbologists? (2) Study garbage to learn more about our society and how to help the environment. (3) They have learned that almost none of the garbage buried in landfills breaks down into useful soil. (4) Garbologists have found 40-year-old hot dogs and old newpapers that are still readable. (5) Paper is the single biggest part of any landfill. (6) It accounts for almost half of the garbage thrown away. (7) A year's subscription, to the *New York Times*, takes up as much space as 19,000 crushed aluminum cans. (8) Potato peels take up more room in landfills than any other fresh food. (9) Garbologists have found that most people eat both Health Foods and junk foods. (10) When they find the remains of lettuce and high-fiber bread, he knows the Twinkies wrappers aren't far behind. (11) The contents of landfills varies depending on the geographic region and local income level.

38. Sentence 1: **Did you know their are people who work as garbologists?**

What correction should be made to this sentence?

(1) change *Did* to *Does*
(2) change *know* to *knew*
(3) change *their* to *there*
(4) change *are* to *were*
(5) change *garbologists* to *Garbologists*

39. Sentence 2: **Study garbage to learn more about our society and how to help the environment.**

Which of the following is the best way to write the underlined portion of this sentence? If you think the original is the best way, choose option (1).

(1) Study garbage
(2) You study garbage
(3) We study garbage
(4) I study garbage
(5) They study garbage

40. Sentence 3: **They have learned that almost none of the garbage buried in landfills breaks down into useful soil.**

Which of the following is the best way to write the underlined portion of this sentence? If you think the original is the best way, choose option (1).

(1) They have learned
(2) They will learn
(3) One has learned
(4) They has learned
(5) They will be learning

41. Sentence 4: **Garbologists have found 40-year-old hot dogs and old newpapers that are still readable.**

What correction should be made to this sentence?

(1) change *have* to *has*
(2) change the spelling of *newpapers* to *newspapers*
(3) insert a comma after *newpapers*
(4) change *are* to *is*
(5) no correction is necessary

42. Sentences 5 and 6: **Paper is the single biggest part of any landfill. It accounts for almost half of the garbage thrown away.**

If you rewrote sentences 5 and 6 beginning with

The single biggest part of any landfill,

the next word should be

(1) accounting
(2) paper
(3) almost
(4) half
(5) garbage

43. Sentence 7: **A year's <u>subscription, to the *New York Times*, takes up</u> as much space as 19,000 crushed aluminum cans.**

Which of the following is the best way to write the underlined portion of this sentence? If you think the original is the best way, choose option (1).

(1) subscription, to *The New York Times*, takes
(2) subscription, to *The New York Times*, take
(3) subscription, to *the new york times*, takes
(4) subscription to *The New York Times* takes
(5) subscription, to *The New York Times*, took

44. Sentence 9: **Garbologists have found that most people eat both Health Foods and junk foods.**

What correction should be made to this sentence?

(1) change *have* to *has*
(2) insert a comma after *found*
(3) change *eat* to *were eating*
(4) change *Health Foods* to *health foods*
(5) change *junk foods* to *Junk Foods*

45. Sentence 10: **When they find the remains of lettuce and high-fiber bread, he knows the Twinkies wrappers aren't far behind.**

What correction should be made to this sentence?

(1) change *When* to *Until*
(2) change *they find* to *he finds*
(3) remove the comma after *bread*
(4) change *he knows* to *they know*
(5) change *aren't* to *weren't*

46. Sentence 11: **The contents of landfills varies depending on the geographic region and local income level.**

What correction should be made to this sentence?

(1) change *geographic region* to *Geographic Region*
(2) change *varies* to *veries*
(3) change *depending* to *depends*
(4) change *varies* to *vary*
(5) insert a comma before *and*

Questions 47–55 refer to the following passage.

(1) Is you're job a pain in the neck? (2) If you works at a computer all day, it may be a pain in the wrists. (3) Millions of americans suffer from something called repetitive stress injuries. (4) For example, suppose you keystroke day after day. (5) Eventually your wrists may start to hurt because the small muscles are repeating the exact same movement again and again. (6) The pain can be intense enough to keep you from keyboarding for weeks. (7) There were ways to protect against repetitive stress. (8) Stand up every half hour or so and shake out your arms, and hands. (9) Make the tightest fists you can and rotate them to work your mussels in different directions. (10) Better yet, if your keyboard has a tilt adjustment, adjusting it to the same height as your elbows while you work. (11) That way your wrists won't have to tilt, and his muscles won't be subjected to repetitive stress.

47. Sentence 1: **Is you're job a pain in the neck?**

What correction should be made to this sentence?

(1) change *Is* to *Are*
(2) change *you're* to *your*
(3) insert a comma after *job*
(4) change *job* to *jobs*
(5) no correction is necessary

48. Sentence 2: **If you works at a computer all day, it may be a pain in the wrists.**

Which of the following is the best way to write the underlined portion of this sentence? If you think the original is the best way, choose option (1).

(1) If you works
(2) Although you works
(3) If one works
(4) If you work
(5) If you worked

49. Sentence 3: **Millions of americans suffer from something called repetitive stress injuries.**

What correction should be made to this sentence?

(1) change the spelling of *millions* to *millyuns*
(2) change *americans* to *Americans*
(3) change *suffer* to *suffers*
(4) insert a comma after *something*
(5) no correction is necessary

50. Sentences 4 and 5: **For example, suppose you keystroke day after day. Eventually your wrists may start to hurt because the small muscles are repeating the exact same movement again and again.**

The most effective combination of sentences 4 and 5 would contain which of the following groups of words?

(1) If you keystroke day after day,
(2) Before you keystroke day after day,
(3) Despite keystroking day after day,
(4) Then you keystroke day after day,
(5) Unless you keystroke day after day,

51. Sentence 7: **There were ways to protect against repetitive stress.**

What correction should be made to this sentence?

(1) change *There* to *Their*
(2) change *were* to *are*
(3) change *ways* to *way*
(4) insert a comma after *protect*
(5) change the spelling of *against* to *aganst*

52. Sentence 8: **Stand up every half hour or <u>so and shake out your arms,</u> and hands.**

Which of the following is the best way to write the underlined portion of this sentence? If you think the original is the best way, choose option (1).

(1) so and shake out your arms,
(2) so, and shake out your arms,
(3) so but shake out your arms,
(4) so and shake out you're arms,
(5) so and shake out your arms

53. Sentence 9: **Make the tightest fists you can and rotate them to work your mussels in different directions.**

What correction should be made to this sentence?

(1) change *Make* to *Makes*
(2) change *rotate* to *rotated*
(3) change *them* to *it*
(4) change the spelling of *mussels* to *muscles*
(5) change the spelling of *different* to *differnt*

54. Sentence 10: **Better yet, if your keyboard has a tilt adjustment, adjusting it to the same height as your elbows while you work.**

What correction should be made to this sentence?

(1) change *has* to *had*
(2) change *adjusting* to *adjust*
(3) change *keyboard* to *keybord*
(4) change *work* to *worked*
(5) no correction is necessary

55. Sentence 11: **That way your wrists won't have to tilt, <u>and his muscles won't be subjected to</u> repetitive stress.**

Which of the following is the best way to write the underlined portion of this sentence? If you think the original is the best way, choose option (1).

(1) and his muscles won't
(2) if his muscles won't
(3) and your muscles won't
(4) and his muscles wouldn't
(5) and his muscles wont

Answers begin on page 846.

Part 2: The Essay

Directions: This part of the test is designed to find out how well you write. The test has one question that asks you to present an opinion on an issue or explain something. In preparing your answer for this question, you should take the following steps:

1. Read all of the information accompanying the question.

2. Plan your answer carefully before you write.

3. Use scratch paper to make any notes.

4. Write your answer on a separate sheet of paper.

5. Read carefully what you have written and make any changes that will improve your writing.

6. Check your paragraphing, sentence structure, spelling, punctuation, capitalization, and usage and make any necessary corrections.

Take forty-five minutes to plan and write on the assigned topic. Write legibly and use a ballpoint pen.

Topic

Movies are increasingly available on videocassettes for use on a VCR, and many people have less and less reason to go to movie theaters. These changes are profoundly affecting the entire motion picture industry, which is losing money as never before.

Write a composition of about 200 words describing the effects of these changes on your life. You may write about the positive and negative aspects of the video revolution, as well as the way you prefer to watch movies and why. Be specific and use examples to support your view.

Information on evaluating your essay is on page 848.

PRACTICE TEST 1: WRITING SKILLS ANSWER KEY

Part 1: Conventions of English

1. **(1)** Even though this sentence is inverted, the verb still agrees with the subject, *you*. So it should be *Are*.

2. **(2)** This sentence needs a verb (*is*) to make it complete.

3. **(1)** The original sentences have a time order relationship. Starting the new sentence with *After* best expresses this relationship.

4. **(3)** The three parts of the sentence that are separated by commas should all be in the same form, so the second one needs to have a verb added: *Relax, place, . . . and put. . . .*

5. **(2)** The original sentence contains two independent thoughts run together. A semicolon separates them.

6. **(5)** The antecedent is *worries*, so the pronoun should be plural: *them*.

7. **(5)** The prepositional phrase *out of your mind* should not be separated from the main sentence with a comma.

8. **(1)** The original sentence is a fragment. Change the verb to *Concentrate*.

9. **(2)** To agree with the rest of the paragraph, the verb form should be in the present tense: *get*.

10. **(1)** This sentence is correct as written.

11. **(2)** The pronoun *they*, referring to the vultures, is plural, but the verb *cleans* is singular. Change *cleans* to *clean* to make the subject agree with the verb in number.

12. **(3)** The sentence needs a verb. The verb must agree with the subject (*road kills and . . . carcasses*) in number. That plural verb is *carry*.

13. **(3)** The passage is written in the present tense, but the original verb here is a present perfect verb. Option (3), *eat*, is present tense.

14. **(3)** The nonrestrictive clause *which can be found in Africa and Eurasia* must be set off with commas.

15. **(4)** The object refers to *bones*, so the pronoun should be *them*.

16. **(2)** The term *trash collectors* is a common noun, not a proper name, so it should not be capitalized.

17. **(5)** The three parts of the sentence that are separated by commas should all be nouns. *Teamwork* is a noun, but *they work as a team* is a clause.

18. **(1)** The phrase *Swooping down* modifies the sentence's subject, so the subject must be *a vulture*. The word modified by such a phrase should always be placed as close to the modifying phrase as possible.

19. **(2)** *Sped* is a past tense verb form. For consistency with the rest of the paragraph, the verb should be present tense: *speed*.

20. **(4)** This sentence is complex, with two subject-verb combinations: *Times are* and *it's* (*it is*). The two parts should be separated with the conjunction *and* and a comma.

21. **(5)** The pronoun refers to *people*, so it should be plural: *they*.

22. **(3)** Never separate the main parts of a sentence, the subject and predicate, with a comma.

23. **(2)** The original sentences have a cause-and-effect relationship. This is best expressed by *because*.

24. **(4)** To agree with the rest of the paragraph, the verb form should be in the present tense: *skip*.

25. **(2)** The three parts of the sentence that are separated by commas should all be in the same single-item form: *Pasta, rice, and grains*. In the original sentence, the third item is in the form of an infinitive phrase (*to eat other grains*).

26. **(3)** The original sentence contains two complete thoughts run together. Choice (3) correctly divides the two complete thoughts into separate sentences.

27. **(4)** Test the contraction *they're* by replacing it with *they are*. This makes sense. The possessive pronoun *their* does not.

28. **(2)** The correct past tense form of this irregular verb is *threw*.

29. **(3)** The subject is singular (*person*). So the verb must be singular to agree with it: *misses*.

30. **(2)** The original sentences have a cause-and-effect relationship. Starting the new sentence with *Since* expresses this relationship. (*Because* would also work.) The new sentence might read, "Since young children get colds more often and spread them more rapidly, it's not surprising that their parents take more sick days than anyone else."

31. **(4)** Never separate the main parts of a sentence, the subject and predicate, with a comma.

32. **(2)** You may need to memorize the spelling of this tricky word.

33. **(3)** Always use the relative pronoun *who* to refer to a person. *Which* is the correct relative pronoun for a thing.

34. **(4)** The main part of the sentence is an exception to the fact stated in the introductory clause. The conjunction *but* expresses this relationship. The new sentence would read, "A cold virus can't penetrate skin, but it can penetrate mucous membranes in your mouth, nose, and eyes."

35. **(5)** This sentence is correct as written.

36. **(3)** Substitute the words *you are* for the contraction *you're*. *You are mother* doesn't make sense, so the contraction must be wrong. Change it to the possessive pronoun *your*.

37. **(2)** To agree with the rest of the paragraph, the pronoun should be in the second person: *you*, not *one*. You takes a plural verb, so change the verb from *is* to *are*.

38. **(3)** The possessive pronoun *their* has nothing to modify in this sentence. The correct word is the adverb *there*.

39. **(5)** To agree with the rest of the paragraph, the subject of this sentence should be the third person plural: *They*. This pronoun refers to the garbologists.

40. **(1)** This sentence is correct as written.

41. **(2)** You may need to memorize the spelling of this word.

42. **(2)** The subject of the first sentence is *paper*. The subject of the second sentence is a pronoun that refers to *paper*. Therefore, when the first sentence is turned into an introductory clause modifying the subject, that subject is still *paper*.

43. **(4)** "To the *New York Times*" is a prepositional phrase. Prepositional phrases should not be set off by commas.

44. **(4)** The term *health foods* is a common noun, not a proper noun, so it should not be capitalized.

45. **(4)** The subject of the sentence must agree with the subject of the introductory clause, *they*. The plural form also makes this sentence agree with the rest of the passage.

46. **(4)** *Contents* is a plural noun, so the verb should be *vary* to agree in number with the subject.

47. **(2)** *You're* is a contraction for *you are*. However, *you are job* makes no sense. Change the contraction to the possessive pronoun *your*.

48. **(4)** *You* is the subject, so for agreement, it requires the verb *work*. The second person *you* is also consistent with the rest of the paragraph.

49. **(2)** *Americans* is a proper noun, so it should be capitalized.

50. **(1)** The original sentences have a cause-and-effect relationship. Starting the new sentence with *If* expresses this relationship. The new sentence would read, "If you keystroke day after day, eventually your wrists may start to hurt because the small muscles are repeating the exact same movement again and again."

51. **(2)** To agree with the rest of the paragraph, this sentence should be in the present tense: *are*. *Were* is a past tense verb.

52. **(5)** *Arms and hands* is part of a compound predicate. It should not be interrupted by a comma.

53. **(4)** You may need to memorize the spelling of this word.

54. **(2)** *Adjusting* is a participle, not a verb, so Sentence 10 is a fragment, since there is no verb in the main clause. Change *adjusting* to *adjust* to make this fragment a complete sentence.

55. **(3)** The rest of the sentence (and the paragraph) is written in the second person: *your* wrists. For consistency, change the third-person *his* to *your*.

Use the answer key on pages 846–847 to check your answers to the Practice Test. Then find the item number of each question you missed and circle it on the chart below to determine the writing content areas in which you need more practice. Pay particular attention to areas where you missed half or more of the questions. The page numbers for the content areas are listed below on the chart. For those questions that you missed, review the pages indicated on the chart.

PRACTICE TEST 1: WRITING SKILLS EVALUATION CHART

Content Area	Item Number	Review Pages
Nouns, Pronouns	27, 36, 37, 38, 47, 55	60–64, 80–92
Verbs	2, 12, 28	65–76
Subject-Verb Agreement	1, 11, 29, 46, 48	76–79
Pronoun Reference	6, 15, 21, 33, 45	82–92
Sentence Fragments	5, 8, 20, 26, 39, 54	93–98
Sentence Combining	3, 23, 30, 34, 42, 50	95–107
Sequence of Tenses	9, 13, 19, 24, 51	109–110
Misplaced/Dangling Modifiers	18	111–112
Parallel Structure	17, 25	112–116
Capitalization	16, 44, 49	117–119
Punctuation	4, 7, 14, 22, 31, 43, 52	119–125
Spelling	32, 41, 53	126–141
No Error	10, 35, 40	

Part 2: The Essay

If possible, give your essay to an instructor to evaluate. That person's opinion of your writing will be useful in deciding what further work you need to write a good essay.

If, however, you are unable to show your work to someone else, you can try to evaluate your own essay. If you can answer *yes* to the five questions in the Essay Evaluation Checklist, your essay would *probably* earn an upper half score (4, 5, or 6) on Part 2 of the Writing Skills Test. If you receive any *no* answers on your evaluation checklist, you should read your essay carefully to see how it could be improved and review Chapter 4 of the Writing Skills section.

Essay Evaluation Checklist

YES NO

____ ____ **1.** Does the essay answer the question asked?

____ ____ **2.** Does the main point of the essay stand out clearly?

____ ____ **3.** Does each paragraph contain specific examples and details that help prove the main point?

____ ____ **4.** Can you follow how the writer has arranged and linked ideas in sentences and paragraphs?

____ ____ **5.** Is the writer's control of grammar and usage effective enough so that you were able to read the essay easily and smoothly?

PRACTICE TEST 2: SOCIAL STUDIES

This Social Studies Practice Test will give you an opportunity to evaluate your readiness for the actual GED Social Studies Test.

This test contains 64 questions. Some of the questions are based on short reading passages, and some of them require you to interpret a chart, map, graph, or an editorial cartoon.

You should take appproximately 85 minutes to complete this test. At the end of 85 minutes, stop and mark your place. Then finish the test. This will give you an idea of whether or not you can finish the real GED Test in the time allotted. Try to answer as many questions as you can. A blank will count as a wrong answer, so make a reasonable guess for the answers to questions you are not sure of.

When you are finished with the test, check your answers and turn to the Evaluation Chart on page 874 and the GED Readiness Worksheet on page 927. Use the chart and worksheet to evaluate whether or not you are ready to take the actual GED Test and, if not, in what areas you need more work.

PRACTICE TEST 2: SOCIAL STUDIES ANSWER GRID

(answer grid, questions 1–64, each with options 1 2 3 4 5)

Choose the best answer to each question that follows.

Questions 1 and 2 are based on the following pie charts.

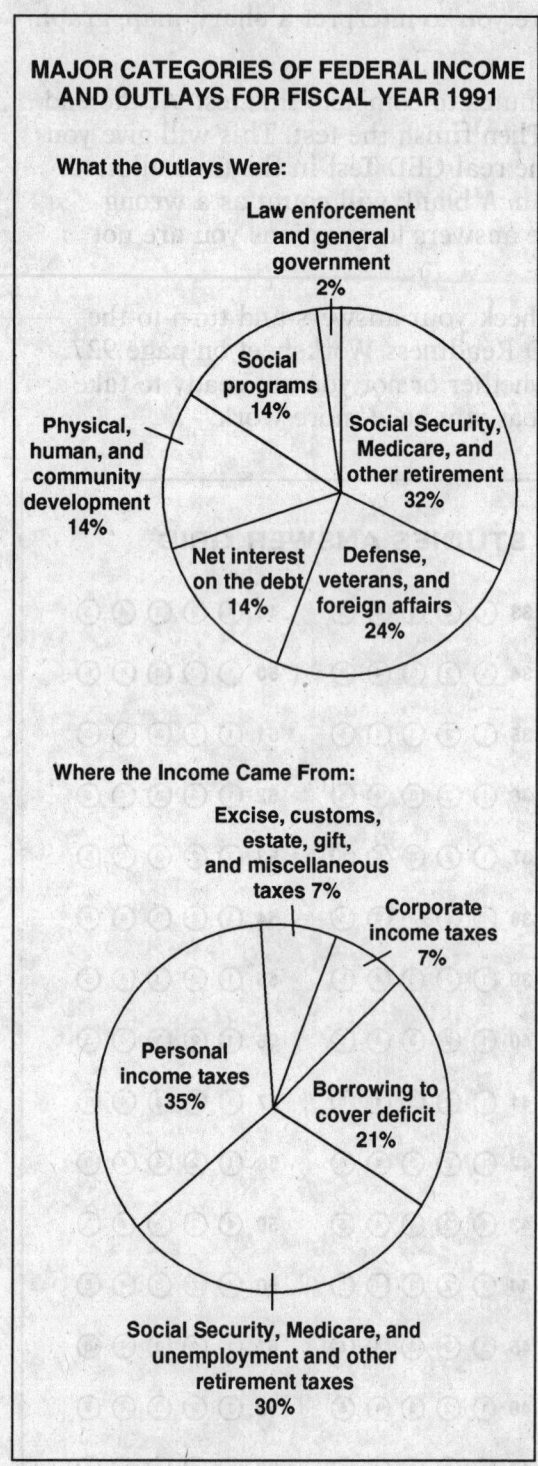

MAJOR CATEGORIES OF FEDERAL INCOME AND OUTLAYS FOR FISCAL YEAR 1991

What the Outlays Were:

Law enforcement and general government 2%

Social programs 14%

Social Security, Medicare, and other retirement 32%

Physical, human, and community development 14%

Net interest on the debt 14%

Defense, veterans, and foreign affairs 24%

Where the Income Came From:

Excise, customs, estate, gift, and miscellaneous taxes 7%

Corporate income taxes 7%

Personal income taxes 35%

Borrowing to cover deficit 21%

Social Security, Medicare, and unemployment and other retirement taxes 30%

1. Based on these charts, from which of the following sources does the federal government derive most of its income?

    (1) a variety of taxes on individuals
    (2) business taxes
    (3) income tax alone
    (4) taxes on goods
    (5) trade with other countries

2. According to the pie charts, which of the following was true about federal spending in 1991?

    (1) More was spent on social programs than on physical, human, and community development.
    (2) More was spent on social security, Medicare, and other retirement benefits than was taken in through taxes.
    (3) More was spent on deficit interest than was taken in through borrowing.
    (4) Seven percent of borrowed money was actually spent on paying off the deficit.
    (5) Defense spending accounted for the largest expenditure.

Questions 3 and 4 are based on the following passage.

Humans share two methods of learning with the other animals. One is *individual situational learning*, in which individuals learn from their own experience. For example, both a person and an animal learn that standing out in the rain will make them wet. The second shared method is *social situational learning*, in which behavior is learned from other members of a social group through observation. Kittens learn to catch mice by imitating their mothers, and children learn to play tag by watching other children. A third method of learning is uniquely human. *Cultural learning* relies on concepts and values to guide behavior. For example, mothers tell children to share their toys, and people learn that certain behaviors are thought of as right or wrong. No other animal has been observed to learn in this manner.

3. Which of the following is an example of cultural learning?

   (1) avoiding fire
   (2) saying thank you after receiving a gift
   (3) making a snowman
   (4) standing in line in the supermarket
   (5) doodling

4. Which of the following is a conclusion that the author draws?

   (1) Cultural learning is uniquely human.
   (2) Cultural learning is based on concepts and values.
   (3) Mothers teach children to share.
   (4) People learn that some behavior is right and some is wrong.
   (5) No other animals learn about concepts and values.

Questions 5–7 are based on the following passage.

The Bill of Rights, which most Americans take for granted, was not unanimously accepted by the thirteen original colonies. Federalist delegates to the Constitutional Convention in 1787 didn't think that a Bill of Rights was needed. They argued that most of the states already provided enough protection for citizens. Anti-Federalists believed that a national Bill of Rights was important to protect the people from an overly powerful central government. The argument lasted for four years, with a three-fourths approval vote by the states in 1791. One hundred and fifty years later, Massachusetts, Georgia, and Connecticut finally ratified the Bill of Rights.

5. The Federalists' argument was based on which of the following assumptions?

   (1) A central government might override states' rights.
   (2) The states were powerful enough to protect the rights of their citizens.
   (3) Citizens' rights were unimportant.
   (4) Citizens' rights were too important to be ignored.
   (5) A Bill of Rights would take too long to be ratified.

6. Which of the following conclusions is supported by the information in the passage?

(1) The Bill of Rights wasn't really necessary.

(2) The Bill of Rights was never ratified by the original states.

(3) The Founding Fathers had differing views about the role of the central government.

(4) Members of the Constitutional Congress all agreed about political issues.

(5) The federal government is too powerful.

7. According to the passage, the Bill of Rights became law by approval of the states in which of the following years?

(1) 1776

(2) 1787

(3) 1791

(4) 1900

(5) 1939

Question 8 is based on the following cartoon.

© 1986 WASSERMAN—BOSTON GLOBE

8. The cartoonist is expressing which of the following opinions?

(1) Working women should be given maternity leave.

(2) Businesses would rather treat working women like men than like women.

(3) Women should be at home instead of at work.

(4) Business women should be wives.

(5) Workers and management can never come to an agreement.

Questions 9–12 are based on the following passage.

"Yesterday, December 7, 1941—a date which will live in infamy—the United States of America was suddenly and deliberately attacked by naval and air forces of the Empire of Japan.

The United States was at peace with that nation and, at the solicitation of Japan, was still in conversation with the government and its emperor looking toward the maintenance of peace in the Pacific.

. . . . It will be recorded that the distance of Hawaii from Japan makes it obvious that the attack was deliberately planned many days or even weeks ago. During the intervening time, the Japanese government has deliberately sought to deceive the United States by false statements and expressions of hope for continued peace.

. . . . As commander in chief of the Army and Navy, I have directed that all measures be taken for our defense.

. . . . No matter how long it may take us to overcome this premeditated invasion, the American people in their righteous might will win through to absolute victory.

I believe I interpret the will of the Congress and of the people when I assert that we will not only defend ourselves to the uttermost but will make very certain that this form of treachery will never endanger us again."

—from President Franklin Roosevelt's message to Congress after the invasion of Pearl Harbor

9. According to the passage, which of the following is true about President Roosevelt?

(1) He wanted to avoid war at all costs.
(2) He felt that Japan was in the right.
(3) He had not expected to go to war with Japan.
(4) He had little faith in the American people.
(5) He was willing to ignore the attack on Pearl Harbor.

10. Roosevelt was offended by Japan's action because he placed a high value on which of the following?

(1) freedom of speech
(2) honesty
(3) military strength
(4) patriotism
(5) good planning

11. According to the passage, Japan's action led to

(1) American isolationism
(2) America's entrance into World War II
(3) Roosevelt's conflict with Congress
(4) Hawaii's admittance to the Union
(5) a peace treaty between the United States and Japan

12. According to this message, Roosevelt made which of the following assumptions?

(1) Congress was unwilling to declare war.
(2) Americans would sympathize with Japan.
(3) Americans would support going to war with Japan.
(4) Japan's army and navy were stronger than America's.
(5) Japan would be willing to return to peace negotiations.

13. Clearing of forest lands for timber and pasture has been blamed for soil erosion. Cattle grazing on newly cleared land tends to leave the earth bare. The small root systems of shrubs and weeds can't anchor the soil, so topsoil is blown or washed away. Which of the following is most likely to result in prevention of soil erosion?

(1) bringing in sheep instead of cattle
(2) letting nature take its course
(3) watering the land intensively
(4) immediate replanting of trees and grasses
(5) clearing more forest land

Questions 14 and 15 are based on the following table.

14. According to the table below, which circuit court handles the highest number of burglary, robbery, and auto theft cases?

(1) the First
(2) the Fourth
(3) the Sixth
(4) the Seventh
(5) the Tenth

15. Which of the following statements is supported by the information in the table?

(1) The sentence imposed for each type of crime is standardized throughout the court system.
(2) The sentence imposed for each type of crime varies from court to court.
(3) The sentence imposed for each type of crime depends on the number of cases handled in that court.
(4) Burglary is the same as robbery.
(5) Auto theft is the most recurrent crime.

MEDIAN SENTENCE IMPOSED BY JUDICIAL COURTS
(In Years)

Circuit	Burglary Median	Burglary Number of Cases	Robbery Median	Robbery Number of Cases	Class 2 Auto Theft Median	Class 2 Auto Theft Number of Cases
1st	4.0	51	5.5	6	7.0	3
2nd	4.0	29	0.0	0	3.0	2
3rd	4.0	65	3.5	8	3.0	18
4th	4.0	82	4.0	1	4.0	8
5th	4.0	46	3.0	2	4.0	4
6th	4.0	130	4.0	17	6.0	3
7th	4.0	71	4.8	6	3.5	3
8th	3.5	32	0.0	0	3.0	1
9th	4.0	35	6.0	1	3.5	2
10th	4.0	97	3.8	116	4.0	6

Questions 16–19 are based on the following information.

To sociologists, crowds are groups of people who get together temporarily with a common focus. There are five general types of crowds.

casual crowd—people who share a brief interest on an unplanned basis and have little to do with one another
conventional crowd—people who gather as a result of deliberate and formal planning but have little to do with one another
expressive crowd—people who gather informally to share an emotional or entertaining experience
acting crowd—people who, after gathering for any reason, commit violent and destructive acts
protest crowd—people who intentionally gather to perform actions to promote a political goal

16. A group of people gather on a city street to watch a firefighter rescue a child from a burning building. This is an example of

    (1) a casual crowd
    (2) a conventional crowd
    (3) an expressive crowd
    (4) an acting crowd
    (5) a protest crowd

17. A group of people gather in front of City Hall with picket signs. They want to stop the rezoning of a residential area. This is an example of

    (1) a casual crowd
    (2) a conventional crowd
    (3) an expressive crowd
    (4) an acting crowd
    (5) a protest crowd

18. A group of people gather in a large tent to hear a traveling preacher. This is an example of

    (1) a casual crowd
    (2) a conventional crowd
    (3) an expressive crowd
    (4) an acting crowd
    (5) a protest crowd

19. A group of people who had gathered to watch a hockey game became upset by a ruling. The people began to throw things into the rink and then started climbing over the barricades and attacking the players. This is an example of

    (1) a casual crowd
    (2) a conventional crowd
    (3) an expressive crowd
    (4) an acting crowd
    (5) a protest crowd

20. Psychologists believe that social play is an important part of a child's development. One study shows that riddling builds language and logic skills. In addition to telling traditional riddles, a child will often experiment by creating new riddles based on already-learned patterns. This information supports the conclusion that

(1) verbal play is more than simply a way for children to amuse each other

(2) a child who does not create riddles will not develop properly

(3) a child who tells only traditional riddles does not understand the underlying pattern

(4) psychologists are wrong to place importance on social play

(5) language and logic skills cannot be learned from social play

Question 21 is based on the following graph.

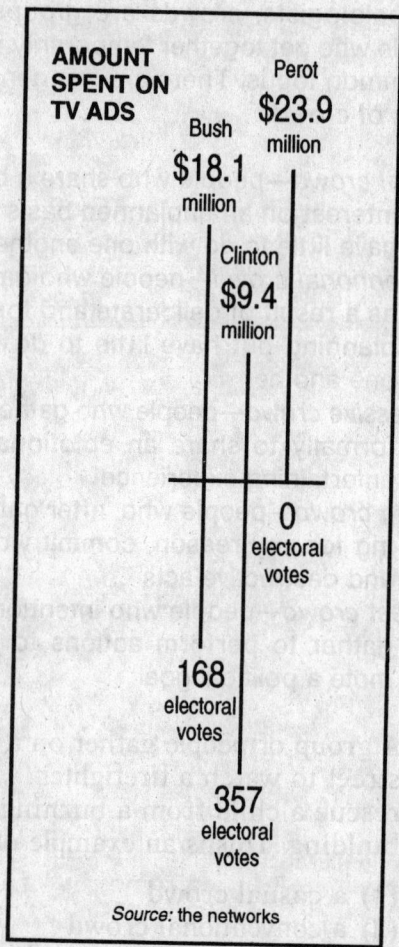

Source: the networks

21. The main idea of this graph is that

(1) the more a candidate spends on ads, the better the chances of getting elected

(2) presidential candidates spend too much on their campaign ads

(3) the Democratic party is opposed to spending excessively on political campaigns

(4) spending a lot on political ads does not guarantee election

(5) political ads have no effect on an election

Questions 22–25 are based on the following information.

The president of the United States is often advised by members of his Cabinet, most of whom are heads or secretaries of one of fourteen executive government departments. The executive departments help regulate and serve many aspects of American life. For example, funeral services for ex-military personnel are provided by the National Cemetery System, an agency administered by the Department of Veterans Affairs. The general services provided by five of the executive departments are as follows:

Department of Agriculture—responsible for improving farms and farm income and reducing poverty, hunger, and malnutrition

Department of Commerce—responsible for encouraging international trade and economic growth and preventing unfair trade

Department of the Interior—responsible for the conservation of public lands and natural resources, including wildlife and historic places

Department of State—responsible for formulating and carrying out foreign policy and protecting American overseas interests

Department of Transportation—responsible for the planning and safety of highways, mass transit, railroads, aviation, and waterways

22. An agency builds merchant ships for the federal government and provides aid to private shipbuilders. Which Cabinet member heads this agency's department?

   (1) secretary of commerce
   (2) secretary of agriculture
   (3) secretary of the interior
   (4) secretary of state
   (5) secretary of transportation

23. An agency helps the establishment and development of businesses owned by minorities. Which Cabinet member heads this agency's department?

   (1) secretary of commerce
   (2) secretary of agriculture
   (3) secretary of the interior
   (4) secretary of state
   (5) secretary of transportation

24. An agency administers the standardization, grading, and classing of over six hundred farm products. Which Cabinet member heads this agency's department?

   (1) secretary of commerce
   (2) secretary of agriculture
   (3) secretary of the interior
   (4) secretary of state
   (5) secretary of transportation

25. An agency protects and maintains the nation's system of national parks and recreation areas. Which Cabinet member heads this agency's department?

   (1) secretary of commerce
   (2) secretary of agriculture
   (3) secretary of the interior
   (4) secretary of state
   (5) secretary of transportation

26. A monarchy that had been under native rule since 1795, the Hawaiian Islands began to attract American missionaries during the late nineteenth century. In addition to the opportunity to save souls, Hawaii offered new agricultural and military resources. Despite anti-imperialist objections, Hawaii became an American territory in 1898. Which of the following assumptions prompted the first missionaries to go to the Hawaiian islands?

   (1) The native monarchy was failing.
   (2) Americans would soon develop a taste for tropical fruit.
   (3) Native Hawaiians would welcome the opportunity to become the fiftieth American state.
   (4) Native Hawaiians would welcome the opportunity to become Christians.
   (5) The American government would welcome new sites for military bases.

27. One factor in the law of supply and demand is the ratio of sellers to buyers. The more sellers of a product, the greater the choices a buyer has. This principle of supply and demand has a special effect on the real estate market. When there have been more houses on the market for a long period than there have been buyers, which of the following is likely to happen?

   (1) A buyer will offer more than the seller's asking price.
   (2) A seller will refuse to consider an offer lower than the stated asking price.
   (3) A seller will accept an offer lower than the asking price.
   (4) More people will put up their homes for sale.
   (5) Potential buyers will wait until house prices go down.

28. *Acculturation* refers to the process by which members of one culture adopt the customs and tastes of the culture into which they have moved. But firsthand contact between two cultures can also influence the dominant culture. Chinese-Americans have adopted many American ways. Which of the following is the best example of how Americans have adapted to Chinese culture?

   (1) trade with Hong Kong
   (2) Nixon's diplomatic trip to China
   (3) the use of Chinese lanterns at pool parties
   (4) the use of bicycles as inner-city transportation
   (5) the acceptance of Chinese cuisine as a popular American food

Questions 29 and 30 are based on the following graph.

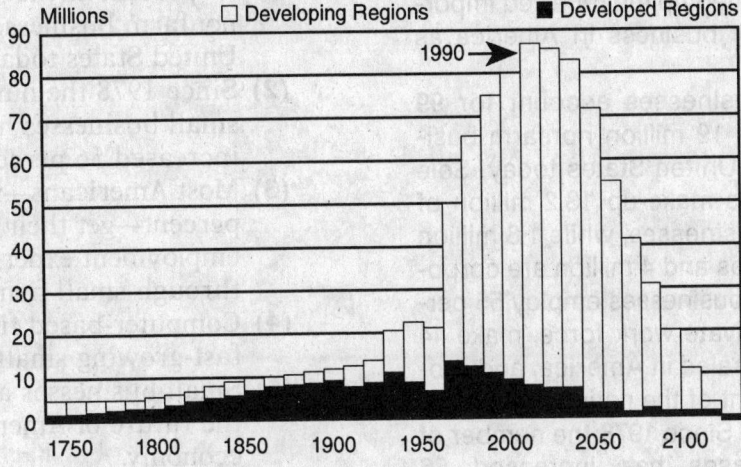

WORLD POPULATION: AVERAGE ANNUAL INCREASE FOR EACH DECADE, 1750–2100 (PROJECTED)

Millions | ☐ Developing Regions ■ Developed Regions

1990 →

90
80
70
60
50
40
30
20
10
0

1750 1800 1850 1900 1950 2000 2050 2100

Source: "World Population in Transition," *Population Bulletin*, by Thomas W. Merrick and PRB Staff

29. According to the graph, which of the following is true about the population of developed and developing regions of the world?

(1) The populations of both developed and developing regions have already reached their peak.

(2) The population of developed regions will drop in the future while the population of developing regions will continue to grow.

(3) A sharp rise in world population will not begin until the year 2000.

(4) The population of developed regions and developing regions grow and decline at about the same rate.

(5) The population of developed regions will continue to grow, while the population of developing regions will drop in the future.

30. Which of the following is the most probable cause of the change in the population in developing regions between 1950 and 1990?

(1) Developing regions began using effective forms of birth control.

(2) Residents of developing nations migrated in large numbers to developed regions.

(3) Improved health care and agricultural practices had been adopted by developing regions.

(4) The pregnancy rate in developed regions began to drop.

(5) Women in developing regions realized the economic value of having large families.

Questions 31–33 are based on the following passage.

The writers of *The Universal Almanac* have summed up the renewed importance of small business in America as follows:

"Small businesses account for 99 percent of the 19 million nonfarm businesses in the United States today. Sole proprietorships make up 13.2 million of these small businesses, while 1.8 million are partnerships and 4 million are corporations. Small businesses employ 55 percent of the private work force, make 44 percent of all sales in America, and produce 38 percent of the nation's gross national product. Since 1978 the number of small businesses has increased 56 percent.

"Most Americans—nearly 67 percent—get their first employment experience through small firms. Small businesses lead the way in the creation of new jobs in the American economy. Between 1981 and 1986, small businesses with fewer than 500 employees created 62 percent of the 8.9 million new jobs in the country. Between September 1987 and 1988 alone, 2.3 million new jobs were generated in small-business-dominated industries.

"Among the fastest-growing small businesses today are eating and drinking establishments, trucking firms, doctors' offices, computer and data services, and amusements and recreation services."

Small businesses are clearly the future of America's economy. The role they play is too important to be ignored. Anyone who starts a small business today is guaranteed financial success.

31. According to the passage, which of the following is the most important economic function of small businesses?

(1) hiring high school students
(2) creating new jobs
(3) providing fast food
(4) adding to the GNP
(5) competing with large corporations

32. Which of the following is an opinion expressed in this passage?

(1) Small businesses account for 99 percent of the 19 million nonfarm businesses in the United States today.
(2) Since 1978 the number of small businesses has increased 56 percent.
(3) Most Americans—nearly 67 percent—get their first employment experience through small firms.
(4) Computer-based firms are fast-growing small businesses.
(5) Small businesses are clearly the future of America's economy.

33. Which of the following is wrong with the logic of the conclusion "Anyone who starts a small business today is guaranteed financial success"?

(1) It falsely assumes that small businesses are economically important.
(2) It ignores the role of large companies.
(3) It falsely equates any small business with the small businesses that have actually succeeded.
(4) It falsely assumes that America needs more small businesses.
(5) It ignores the problem of small business insurance.

Questions 34–36 are based on the following passage.

The first post office mail deliveries to the American West went by steamship to Panama, crossed to the Pacific by rail, and then traveled again by ship to San Francisco. The process took at least a month, and letters arrived in huge, unsorted bundles.

Official overland delivery began in 1858, with John Butterfield's stagecoach company bringing the mail over a 2,800-mile route in only twenty-four days. The short-lived Pony Express further reduced the time to ten days. But the effort had its dangers. The ad for riders read, "Wanted: Young, skinny, wiry fellows not over 18. Must be expert riders, willing to risk death daily. Orphans preferred."

The completion of the transcontinental railroad in 1869 changed mail delivery to the West forever. Letters and packages began to arrive in cities and small towns alike, quickly and presorted.

34. Which of the following was the major obstacle to efficient mail delivery in the early days of the American West?

    (1) lack of willing riders
    (2) unreliability of stagecoaches
    (3) the distance to be covered
    (4) the post office red tape
    (5) the sorting process

35. California residents requested improved overland mail delivery in 1856. They took this action because they placed a high value on which of the following?

    (1) support of the government
    (2) communication with friends and family
    (3) employment of orphans
    (4) the hardships of frontier life
    (5) railroad travel

36. The major change in mail service to the West is comparable to which of the following?

    (1) the gradual settlement of the Midwestern states
    (2) the increase in postal rates between the 1960s and 1990s
    (3) the development of small telephone companies because of demonopolization of AT&T
    (4) the growing competition between personal computer companies
    (5) the improvement of international telephone communication because of the laying of the transatlantic cable

37. In April 1993, the passage of President Clinton's short-term job-stimulus package was prevented by Republicans' filibustering. The rule of unlimited debate allows a senator to keep the floor by filibustering, or talking long enough to force the withdrawal of the bill under discussion. By engaging in a filibuster, the Republicans made it clear that they

    (1) could talk longer than the Democrats
    (2) objected to the contents of the bill
    (3) wanted the bill to pass
    (4) wanted to embarrass President Clinton
    (5) believed that America had enough jobs

Questions 38–40 are based on the following cartoon.

Situation Room at Rand McNally--1992 Edition

38. Which of the following best states the main idea of this cartoon?

  (1) Improved technology is causing problems for mapmakers.
  (2) Mapmaking is simpler now than ever before.
  (3) The changes in national politics are difficult for mapmakers to keep up with.
  (4) Maps do not reflect changes in political boundaries.
  (5) Rand McNally is involved in a war.

39. The cartoon supports the statement that major changes are occurring in which of the following areas?

  (1) Canada and the United States
  (2) Western Europe
  (3) Latin America
  (4) the Middle East
  (5) Eastern Europe

40. Which of the following *best* expresses the artist's opinion about mapmakers?

  (1) Making accurate maps today is as complicated as going to war.
  (2) Mapmakers depend too much on secondhand reports.
  (3) Mapmakers don't try hard enough to keep up with world changes.
  (4) Mapmakers should be more concerned about political geography.
  (5) Mapmakers take their job too seriously.

Questions 41–43 are based on the following information.

Lobbyists work to affect foreign policy and to influence domestic issues. There are five general types of lobbyists:

economic lobby groups—representatives of American businesses and industries who attempt to influence domestic and international policy in their own favor

ethnic lobby groups—associations based on common national or cultural background

foreign government lobby groups—representatives of foreign countries who attempt to influence legislation in favor of their own nation's business and national interests

public-interest lobby groups—representatives working to protect the welfare of most or all of the American public

single-issue lobby groups—representatives working to promote legislation that affects only one issue, usually not related to economics

41. A group works to promote laws that protect the environment. This is an example of a(n)

(1) economic lobby
(2) ethnic lobby
(3) foreign government lobby
(4) public-interest lobby
(5) single-issue lobby

42. A group works to promote legislation that outlaws abortions. This is an example of a(n)

(1) economic lobby
(2) ethnic lobby
(3) foreign government lobby
(4) public-interest lobby
(5) single-issue lobby

43. A group works to promote legislation that allows off-shore oil exploration and drilling. This is an example of a(n)

(1) economic lobby
(2) ethnic lobby
(3) foreign government lobby
(4) public-interest lobby
(5) single-issue lobby

44. The term *melting pot* was coined by Israel Zangwell in 1907 to express the idea that immigrants from many countries came to America to form one nation. Zangwell had a vision of people sharing their traditions to become one united people. Fifty years later, Jesse Jackson said that the United States was more like a "vegetable soup." Jackson expressed a vision of the American people in which

(1) many types of people live together but do not give up their distinct identities
(2) all Americans look and act alike
(3) Americans would never be able to live together in peace
(4) Americans are more concerned with food than with cultural ideas
(5) people from other cultures are no longer accepted as true Americans

Question 45 is based on the following graph.

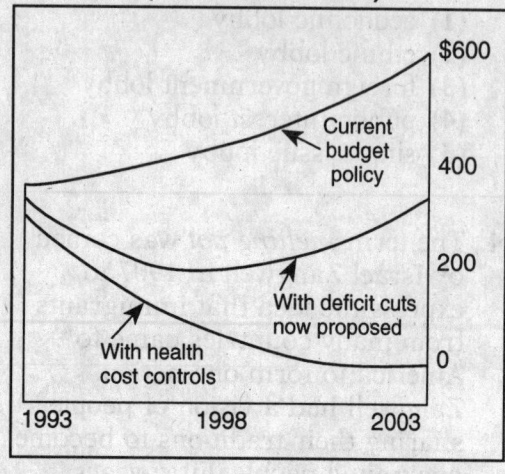

PROJECTED FEDERAL DEFICIT
(in billions of dollars)

45. According to the graph, health cost controls will result in

(1) a continued rise in the federal deficit
(2) a higher federal deficit than would occur with the current budget policy
(3) the same decrease in the federal deficit as would occur with the deficit cuts now proposed
(4) a dramatic decrease in the federal deficit
(5) little or no change in the federal deficit

Questions 46 and 47 are based on the map below.

AMERICA'S NATIONAL PARK SYSTEM

In 1872, the U.S. government began to set aside and conserve unusually scenic and natural areas as national parks. The most recent parks were established in Alaska and Nevada between 1980 and 1986. The map shows the general location of America's national parks.

46. According to the map, where are the majority of national parks located?

(1) in the Northeast
(2) in the Southeast
(3) in the West
(4) in Alaska and Hawaii
(5) in most of the states

47. Which of the following best accounts for the locations of many of the national parks?

(1) These areas were still undeveloped for residential or agricultural use.
(2) These areas couldn't be used for anything else.
(3) These areas were difficult to reach.
(4) These areas were rich in natural resources such as oil, gold, and timber.
(5) These areas could be bought cheaply by the government.

48. As cities grew in the twentieth century, so did their social problems. Overcrowding, traffic jams, crime, pollution, and unemployment became commonplace. Faced with decaying downtowns and "white flight" to the suburbs, city planners began to incorporate social programs in their plans for economic and physical urban renewal. Efforts to rehabilitate low-income inner-city neighborhoods are based on which of the following assumptions?

(1) Downtown areas are not worth saving.
(2) Suburbanites can be tempted back into the cities.
(3) Low-income families won't be willing to move to the suburbs.
(4) Government intervention can correct and prevent social problems.
(5) Low-income neighborhoods won't cost much to improve.

49. Acid rain is a toxic by-product of coal and oil-burning industries, power plants, and automobile exhaust. Because of the natural water cycle, acid rain can travel as far as 2,500 miles from its source. This information supports which of the following conclusions?

(1) Acid rain cannot be considered a localized pollution problem.
(2) Acid rain is a natural phenomenon.
(3) The effects of acid rain can easily be contained to industrial areas.
(4) Acid rain is limited to cities.
(5) Rural areas are free from the effects of acid rain.

Questions 50 and 51 are based on the following table.

EFFECTIVE FEDERAL MINIMUM HOURLY WAGE RATES, 1950–1992

In effect	Minimum rate for nonfarm workers	Percent of avg. earnings[1]	Minimum rate for farm workers[2]
1950	$0.75	54%	N.A.
1956	1.00	52	N.A.
1961	1.15	50	N.A.
1963	1.25	51	N.A.
1967	1.40	50	$1.00
1968	1.60	54	1.15
1974	2.00	46	1.60
1975	2.10	45	1.80
1976	2.30	46	2.00
1978	2.65	44	2.65
1979	2.90	45	2.90
1980	3.10	44	3.10
1981	3.35	43	3.35
1989	3.35	32	3.35
1991	4.25[3]	39	4.25[3]

Note: N.A. = not applicable. 1. Percent of gross average hourly earnings of production workers in manufacturing. 2. Not included until 1966. 3. In effect June 1, 1992. Source: U.S. Dept. of Labor.

50. The information in the table supports the conclusion that

(1) The minimum wage doubled between the mid-seventies and the early nineties.
(2) Wages for farm workers always lag behind wages for nonfarm workers.
(3) The minimum wage in the fifties was too low.
(4) The minimum wage will not increase until 1999.
(5) More people than ever before are earning the minimum wage.

51. Which of the following is the most probable cause of the increase in the minimum wage?

(1) the increase in the number of women in the workforce
(2) the increase in the national debt
(3) a recognition of the importance of unskilled workers
(4) an attempt to decrease unemployment
(5) a continued rise in the cost of living

Questions 52–54 are based on the following information.

Any new business faces many challenges and obstacles. There are five major barriers to new businesses entering into economic competition:

previous patent on a product—A patent guarantees the right of its owner to be the sole producer of a product for seventeen years. If a patent for a product already exists even if it has not been put on the market, the inventor of a similar product cannot manufacture the product until the previous patent expires or is purchased from the patent holder.

government licensing—federal, state, and local governments can restrict the number of similar businesses in an area by issuing a limited number of licenses

control of raw materials—limited access to materials needed to produce a product

limited market size—a market needs to be large enough to provide enough consumers for the product or service

large capital outlay—the amount of money needed to begin and sustain operation of a business, including equipment, raw materials, and wages

52. A new restaurant in town wanted to begin serving alcoholic drinks with dinner to attract a broader clientele. But the owners discovered that the city issued only a certain number of liquor permits, and none would be available until an existing business gave up its permit. This situation describes which barrier to competition?

   (1) patent on a product
   (2) government licensing
   (3) control of raw materials
   (4) limited market size
   (5) large capital outlay

53. A recent college graduate came up with a totally new design for a kitchen product. Her research showed that no one else had thought of the same design even though there would be a good market for it. But because of her large college debt and her lack of business experience, the bank would not grant her a loan to begin manufacturing the product on her own. Which barrier to competition is the young inventor facing?

   (1) patent on a product
   (2) government licensing
   (3) control of raw materials
   (4) limited market size
   (5) large capital outlay

54. A couple who had run a video rental store moved to a new neighborhood. They wanted to open a similar store in their new area, but they found that two video stores were already operating there. Which barrier to competition is the couple facing?

   (1) patent on a product
   (2) government licensing
   (3) control of raw materials
   (4) limited market size
   (5) large capital outlay

55. Bill Clinton's first nomination for attorney general, Zoe Baird, was rejected because she once had hired undocumented workers as household help without paying taxes on their wages. Congress later approved the appointment of Janet Reno, the first woman to hold this important position. These events support which of the following conclusions about the American people?

(1) They did not want a woman as attorney general.
(2) They wanted the attorney general to obey the laws.
(3) They did not trust the president's judgment.
(4) They believed that undocumented workers should not be discriminated against.
(5) They preferred Baird to Reno.

56. Post-traumatic stress disorder is a random recurrence of a horrifying event in the mind of the person who experienced it. PTSD victims also suffer from depression, nightmares, memory loss, or delayed feelings of isolation, guilt, and rage. Which of the following might be a cause of this disorder?

(1) watching a violent movie
(2) being in a massive traffic accident
(3) witnessing a fire
(4) hearing that a friend has been murdered
(5) reading about a rape in the newspaper

Question 57 is based on the following political cartoon.

JORGENSEN

"WE BELIEVE PRESIDENT-ELECT CLINTON'S CABINET APPOINTMENTS DO NOT REFLECT AMERICA'S DIVERSITY... THEY'RE ALL HUMANS!"

© 1992 JORGENSEN—EXTRA NEWSPAPER FEATURES

57. The artist intended this cartoon as a comment on the demands for political appointments by

(1) animal-rights activists
(2) space aliens
(3) Republicans
(4) Democrats
(5) minority groups

Questions 58 and 59 are based on the following passage.

"Aristotle said it was the reward of an active life lived with sweet reason. Sigmund Freud said it was mostly a matter of work and love. Charles Shultz, the cartoonist-philosopher, claimed it was really a warm puppy. So just what is this thing called happiness? For centuries, people were too busy pursuing it to spend much time analyzing it. Now a pioneering band of researchers has finally bagged the elusive quarry—or at least taken its measure. . . . And their answer to the age-old mystery is that it all depends.

"Happiness, that is, depends on what makes you feel happy, which is why psychologists often call it 'subjective well-being.' But from studies of various age and population groups in the United States and abroad, they have reached some objective conclusions on the makings of happiness. What comes up consistently at the top of the charts is not, as many might expect, success, youth, good looks or any of those enviable assets. The clear winner is relationships. Close ones. Followed by a happy marriage. Next comes religious faith, of almost any kind. 'Supportive, intimate connections with other people seem tremendously important,' says psychologist David Myers, whose book *The Pursuit of Happiness* is one of the cluster of recent publications in the field."

58. According to the passage, what is the *primary* cause of happiness?

(1) success
(2) youth
(3) good looks
(4) close relationships
(5) religious faith

59. The information in the passage supports which of the following conclusions about the definition of happiness?

(1) Happiness was best defined by early philosophers.
(2) Happiness is easy to define.
(3) There is no one clear definition of happiness.
(4) There is only one clear definition of happiness.
(5) Psychologists have finally defined happiness.

Questions 60–62 are based on the following map.

Allies Reply to Saddam, 1991

After Saddam Hussein violated international agreements by sending Iraqi troops into Kuwait and missiles into other neighboring countries, the Allies responded with military action.

Source: U.S. News & World Report

60. Which part of the Allied action is detailed on the map?

(1) the ground war in the desert
(2) the air campaign in the Baghdad area
(3) the battle on the Kuwait-Iraq border
(4) the Allied bases in Saudi Arabia
(5) the movement of Allied troops into Iraq

61. The information on the map supports which statement about the Allied attack?

(1) Its purpose was to destroy oil refineries.
(2) It was unable to penetrate Iraqi defenses.
(3) It was focused on Iraq's military centers.
(4) It underestimated Iraq's military strength.
(5) It was poorly planned and unorganized.

62. The strategy of this attack was based on which of the following assumptions?

(1) The action would totally destroy Iraq's economy.
(2) Saddam Hussein would be killed during the attack.
(3) Saddam Hussein would be forced to renew his offensive.
(4) Residents of Baghdad would join forces with the Allies.
(5) Destruction of major military centers would help bring a quick end to the conflict.

63. *La Linea* is the Hispanic name for America's 1,950-mile southern border. It draws thousands of jobless migrants from Mexico's interior. To them, La Linea represents much more than a national boundary. The crossing of the muddy waters of the Tijuana River and Rio Grande River by these families is similar to which of the following?

(1) the crossing of the Atlantic by Columbus

(2) the crossing of the Atlantic by enslaved Africans

(3) the ocean crossings by the ancestors of Irish, Polish, and Chinese-Americans

(4) the crossing of the Delaware River by Washington's troops

(5) the crossing of the English Channel by American soldiers

64. Women's roles differ widely from culture to culture. The Yanomamo female is dominated by her husband and brothers. Her life is spent doing endless labor on tasks thought too menial for men. The independent Ibo woman is much luckier. She has economic freedom and enjoys high social status. Which of the following best states the opinion of the passage?

(1) Neither the Ibo nor the Yanomamo understand women's rights.

(2) Women have to fight against their cultural roles.

(3) The Yanomamo women are treated properly.

(4) Ibo women are luckier than Yanomamo women.

(5) Women's roles vary from culture to culture.

Answers begin on page 871.

PRACTICE TEST 2: SOCIAL STUDIES ANSWER KEY

1. (1) The chart for income shows that 30 percent comes from social security and other personal taxes, 35 percent comes from income tax, and 7 percent comes from other taxes that apply to individuals.

2. (2) The amount taken in for social security, etc., was 30 percent, but the amount expended was 32 percent. None of the other choices are supported by the figures shown.

3. (2) Expressing thanks is an act of politeness, a learned value. Choices (1) and (5) are examples of individual situational learning. Choices (3) and (4) are learned through observation.

4. (1) Choice (2) is a definition of cultural learning. Choices (3) and (4) are examples of cultural learning by humans. Choice (5) is a fact about the other animals. They are all supporting statements that lead to the conclusion that only humans use cultural learning.

5. (2) The Federalists assumed that the Federal government had no power over what had already been decided by the states. Choice (1) refers to the Anti-Federalist position.

6. (3) The Founding Fathers were split into two groups over the Bill of Rights. The split was based on their ideas about the rights and powers of a central government.

7. (3) The passage states that a three-fourths approval vote occurred in 1791, making the Bill of Rights law. None of the other dates affected its acceptance as law.

8. (2) By having the employer suggest that the women need wives instead of benefits, the artist is saying the employer wants the women to be more like men. None of the other choices apply to the cartoonist's drawing.

9. (3) Roosevelt's expectation that war with Japan would not happen is found in paragraph 2, "looking toward the maintenance of peace in the Pacific."

10. (2) Roosevelt emphasized that Japan had "deliberately sought to deceive the United States." Although he placed importance on the other choices, it was this betrayal that offended the president.

11. (2) Based on the date of the message and Roosevelt's call to military action, the result of the invasion of Pearl Harbor was America's entrance into the war. None of the other choices would have resulted from the Japanese invasion.

12. (3) Roosevelt believed the American public was willing to defend themselves and so would support going to war. He expected no opposition from Congress (1) nor any Japanese renegotiation (5).

13. (4) Replanting of trees whose roots would hold the soil would be a practical solution. Sheep (1) would be even more destructive than cattle. The natural process (2), further watering (3), or clearing (5) would result in further soil erosion.

14. (5) The highest total for all three sentencing rates can be found on the table for the tenth circuit court.

15. (2) The table shows that the median years of sentences changes from court to court, rather than being standardized (1). None of the other choices is supported by the table.

16. (1) The group described came together by accident and have only a brief interest in the rescue in common.

17. (5) The group described have come together with an intentional political purpose.

18. (3) The group described have gathered informally, each person coming as a result of personal interest. But the intent is to share a spiritual experience.

19. (4) The group described began as an expressive crowd, sharing an entertaining experience. But emotions got out of hand and turned the crowd into an acting group.

20. **(1)** According to the passage, riddling, a form of verbal play, helps children develop language and logic skills in addition to being an amusement, so choice (5) is wrong. Pyschologists are right to see social play as important, so choice (4) is incorrect. There is no evidence for choices (2) or (3).

21. **(4)** The graph shows how much each of the three 1992 presidential candidates spent on TV ads and the number of electoral votes they received. It demonstrates that there is no direct relationship between the amount of money spent and the number of electoral votes attained, since Perot spent the most and got the fewest electoral votes.

22. **(5)** The secretary of transportation would oversee an agency that dealt with maritime vessels.

23. **(1)** The secretary of commerce would oversee an agency that helped promote new businesses.

24. **(2)** Anything to do with farm products would belong to an agency under the secretary of agriculture.

25. **(3)** Because national parks are public lands, this agency would be governed by the secretary of the interior.

26. **(4)** Missionaries originally went to the island to "save souls," so they expected that the Christian religion would be welcome. None of the other choices would have been assumptions that influenced the missionaries' decision.

27. **(3)** With more houses on the market, the seller would realize that a buyer could choose another house and so would likely accept a lower offer. Choices (1) and (2) apply to a situation in which there are more buyers than sellers. With many homes on the market, homeowners would be discouraged from putting their houses up for sale. Choice (5) indicates a buyer who knows little about the housing market.

28. **(5)** Chinese food is popular as shown by the number of Chinese restaurants. Choices (1) and (2) are not examples of acculturation. Chinese lanterns are a fad, not a cultural adaptation. Bicycles are not used as often as alternative means of transportation in inner cities as they could be.

29. **(1)** The highest point of population for both developed countries and developing countries occurs at or before 1990. After that period, both figures are projected to decline.

30. **(3)** The graph shows that the population of developing nations increased sharply between 1950 and 1990. Improved health care and nutrition would mean that more babies would be carried to term, more children would live to be adults, and more adults would live to bear children, thus increasing the population. Improved birth control would be more likely to influence a decrease rather than an increase in population. The same is true of migration from developing to developed regions. The pregnancy rate in developed regions would not affect developing regions.

31. **(2)** The passage emphasizes the economic importance of new jobs generated by small businesses. None of the other choices are as important to the economy.

32. **(5)** Speculation about the future is an opinion. The other choices are established facts backed up with figures.

33. **(3)** There is no evidence that any specific small business will be a financial success. In fact, the contrary is true. Small businesses have a high failure rate. The evidence supports only the conclusion that small business in general is important in the economy.

34. **(3)** Mail had to travel 2,800 miles to reach the West. The other choices might have been minor problems but were much less important than the distance to be traveled.

35. **(2)** Improved delivery would mean better communication. The other choices would not influence a decision about mail delivery.

36. **(5)** The transatlantic cable linked two distant places through improved technology. None of the other changes improved communication or involved a major technological advance.

37. **(2)** By forcing the withdrawal of the bill, Republicans showed their disapproval of it, which is the opposite of choice (3). Choice (1) might be true, but there is no evidence of how long Democrats could talk if they wanted to. There is no evidence that choices (4) or (5) are true.

38. (3) The mapmakers are tracing rapidly changing political events in order to update the map.

39. (5) The only countries mentioned in the cartoon are in Eastern Europe.

40. (1) The artist compares mapmaking to war by using the setting of a "situation room," a term for a place used for planning military strategies.

41. (4) Protection of the environment is in the public interest.

42. (5) This group is concerned with a single law.

43. (1) Off-shore drilling and exploration are economic issues and could benefit specific businesses.

44. (1) Vegetable soup is made up of a variety of ingredients that retain their own characteristics and are not blended together into a single taste, choice (2), or at odds with each other, choice (3).

45. (4) The line for the effect of health control costs dips down to 0 by the year 2003. The other lines both show a continued federal deficit.

46. (3) Only a few of the marked areas are in the Northeast (1) or Southeast (2). The map shows an uneven distribution of parks, with most marked areas in the West and a few in Hawaii and Alaska (4).

47. (1) By 1872, much of the East and Midwest was already settled while large areas in the West were still unspoiled and unclaimed even though they were rich in natural resources.

48. (4) By renovating inner-city neighborhoods, modern city planners assume they can eliminate the sources of many social problems. This assumption is also applied to downtown areas, choice (1), but is definitely not cheap, choice (5).

49. (1) The passage states that acid rain spreads miles from its source, so it is not a local problem. People cannot control the natural water cycle, so acid rain is difficult to contain to specific areas.

50. (1) The figures for the minimum wage in 1974 and 1975 are $2.00 and $2.10, and in 1991 the figure is $4.25, just over twice the amount. By 1978, farm wages equaled nonfarm wages. There are no figures to support the other choices.

51. (5) The government realizes that a rise in the cost of living requires higher wages in order for workers to keep up. Increases in the type of people in the work force or the amount of government spending would not affect wages.

52. (2) The owners are limited by the number of licenses available. Until they can get one, they cannot compete with other businesses that serve alcohol.

53. (5) The inventor cannot raise the necessary cash to make her product even though she has no problem with a patent or market size.

54. (4) The other two video stores are already serving the market and would limit the number of customers available to the couple.

55. (2) Baird had broken a law. As a candidate for the highest legal position in the land, she would set a poor example for the American people. Another woman was appointed, so (1) is incorrect. The other choices have no support.

56. (2) The traffic accident is the only horrifying event that the person actually experienced. The other events are reports or observations.

57. (5) The characters' demands refer to "America's diversity," a phrase that is used to include all minority groups.

58. (4) According to the passage, relationships are top on the list of the makings of happiness. Faith comes in third. The others are not included as causes of happiness.

59. (3) The first paragraph gives several definitions of happiness but ends with the statement that happiness "all depends." The information does not support the other conclusions.

60. (2) The symbol in the map legend specifies the targets of air strikes.

874 PRACTICE TESTS

61. **(3)** The targets indicated on the map are mainly missile sites, air bases, and weapons-research complexes. The Allied attack did get through Iraq's defenses and showed no evidence of underestimating Iraq or of being disorganized.

62. **(5)** By focusing on destruction of military centers, the Allies could expect that Iraq's defense would be weakened to the point of surrender.

63. **(3)** Immigrants who crossed the oceans to America came in search of better jobs and a better life for their families; these are the same goals as those of migrant Mexicans. Columbus crossed the water for economic reasons. Enslaved Africans came to America involuntarily. The other two choices refer to military events.

64. **(4)** The author is making a judgment by saying the Ibo women are luckier. Such a description of the contrast is opinion, not fact. The author's opinions about women's rights and what women should do are not expressed. Choice (5) is a fact, not an opinion.

Use the answer key on pages 871–874 to check your answers to the Practice Test. Then find the item number of each question you missed and circle it on the chart below to determine the reading skill and content areas in which you need more practice. Pay particular attention to areas where you missed half or more of the questions. The reading skills are covered on pages 187–243. The page numbers for the content areas are listed below on the chart. Knowledge of reading skill and content area–based questions is absolutely essential for success on the GED Social Studies Test. The numbers in boldface are questions based on graphics. For those questions that you missed, review the pages indicated.

PRACTICE TEST 2: SOCIAL STUDIES EVALUATION CHART

Skill Area/ Content Area	Comprehension (pages 189–195)	Application (pages 195–199)	Analysis (pages 200–210)	Evaluation (pages 211–222)
Behavioral Sciences (pages 247–262)	3, 4	16, 17, 18, 19, 28	**8**, 56, 58, 64	20, 59
U.S. History (pages 263–300)	7, 9, 34, **60**	36, 44	5, 11, 12, 26, 48, **62**	6, 10, 35, **61**
Political Science (pages 301–318)	14, 37, **57**	22, 23, 24, 25	**21**, 41, 42, 43	**15**, 55
Economics (pages 319–332)	**2**, 31	52, 53, 54	27, 32, **45**, **51**	1, 33, **50**
Geography (pages 333–342)	**29**, **38**, **46**	13, 63	**30**, **40**, **47**	**39**, 49

PRACTICE TEST 3: SCIENCE

This Science Practice Test will give you the opportunity to evaluate your readiness for the actual GED Science Test.

This test contains 66 questions. Some of the questions are based on short reading passages, and some require you to interpret a chart or diagram.

You should take approximately 95 minutes to complete this test. At the end of 95 minutes, stop and mark your place. Then finish the test. This will give you an idea of whether or not you can finish the real GED Test in the time allotted. Try to answer as many questions as you can. A blank will count as a wrong answer, so make a reasonable guess for answers to questions you are not sure of.

When you are finished with the test, check your answers and turn to the Evaluation Chart on page 897 and the GED Readiness Worksheet on page 927. Use the chart and worksheet to evaluate whether or not you are ready to take the actual GED Test and, if not, in what areas you need more work.

PRACTICE TEST 3: SCIENCE ANSWER GRID

1 ① ② ③ ④ ⑤	18 ① ② ③ ④ ⑤	35 ① ② ③ ④ ⑤	51 ① ② ③ ④ ⑤
2 ① ② ③ ④ ⑤	19 ① ② ③ ④ ⑤	36 ① ② ③ ④ ⑤	52 ① ② ③ ④ ⑤
3 ① ② ③ ④ ⑤	20 ① ② ③ ④ ⑤	37 ① ② ③ ④ ⑤	53 ① ② ③ ④ ⑤
4 ① ② ③ ④ ⑤	21 ① ② ③ ④ ⑤	38 ① ② ③ ④ ⑤	54 ① ② ③ ④ ⑤
5 ① ② ③ ④ ⑤	22 ① ② ③ ④ ⑤	39 ① ② ③ ④ ⑤	55 ① ② ③ ④ ⑤
6 ① ② ③ ④ ⑤	23 ① ② ③ ④ ⑤	40 ① ② ③ ④ ⑤	56 ① ② ③ ④ ⑤
7 ① ② ③ ④ ⑤	24 ① ② ③ ④ ⑤	41 ① ② ③ ④ ⑤	57 ① ② ③ ④ ⑤
8 ① ② ③ ④ ⑤	25 ① ② ③ ④ ⑤	42 ① ② ③ ④ ⑤	58 ① ② ③ ④ ⑤
9 ① ② ③ ④ ⑤	26 ① ② ③ ④ ⑤	43 ① ② ③ ④ ⑤	59 ① ② ③ ④ ⑤
10 ① ② ③ ④ ⑤	27 ① ② ③ ④ ⑤	44 ① ② ③ ④ ⑤	60 ① ② ③ ④ ⑤
11 ① ② ③ ④ ⑤	28 ① ② ③ ④ ⑤	45 ① ② ③ ④ ⑤	61 ① ② ③ ④ ⑤
12 ① ② ③ ④ ⑤	29 ① ② ③ ④ ⑤	46 ① ② ③ ④ ⑤	62 ① ② ③ ④ ⑤
13 ① ② ③ ④ ⑤	30 ① ② ③ ④ ⑤	47 ① ② ③ ④ ⑤	63 ① ② ③ ④ ⑤
14 ① ② ③ ④ ⑤	31 ① ② ③ ④ ⑤	48 ① ② ③ ④ ⑤	64 ① ② ③ ④ ⑤
15 ① ② ③ ④ ⑤	32 ① ② ③ ④ ⑤	49 ① ② ③ ④ ⑤	65 ① ② ③ ④ ⑤
16 ① ② ③ ④ ⑤	33 ① ② ③ ④ ⑤	50 ① ② ③ ④ ⑤	66 ① ② ③ ④ ⑤
17 ① ② ③ ④ ⑤	34 ① ② ③ ④ ⑤		

Choose the best answer to each question that follows.

1. Which of the following facts is the *best evidence* that helium gas is lighter than air?

(1) Helium will not burn when exposed to flame in the presence of oxygen.
(2) By volume, helium makes up only 0.0005 percent of air.
(3) Helium atoms do not combine with other air atoms.
(4) Helium-filled balloons rise in air.
(5) Helium has the lowest boiling point of all known elements.

2. Tides, caused by the moon's gravity, create a frictional force that is gradually slowing down Earth's rotation speed. One million years from now, scientists may discover that, compared to today, Earth's

(1) day is longer
(2) day is shorter
(3) year is longer
(4) year is shorter
(5) day has stayed the same

3. To fight the effects of acid rain, scientists in many countries dump large quantities of calcium carbonate into polluted lakes. You can infer from this action that calcium carbonate is

(1) an acid
(2) a base
(3) a neutral substance
(4) a powdered substance
(5) not harmful to fish

4. The source of energy responsible for life on Earth is

(1) the moon
(2) the Sun
(3) the wind
(4) water
(5) plant life

Questions 5 and 6 refer to the following passage.

When a green plant cell is exposed to sunlight, a chemical reaction called photosynthesis takes place. During photosynthesis, carbon dioxide gas (CO_2) reacts with water (H_2O) to produce three compounds: a type of sugar called glucose ($C_6H_{12}O_6$), oxygen gas (O_2), and water. The chemical equation for photosynthesis is written as follows:

$$6CO_2 + 12H_2O \rightarrow C_6H_{12}O_6 + 6O_2 + 6H_2O$$

5. In the equation for photosynthesis, how many molecules of oxygen gas are produced in the formation of one molecule of glucose?

(1) one
(2) two
(3) six
(4) seven
(5) twelve

6. Which of the following must be present in order for photosynthesis to take place?

(1) glucose
(2) oxygen
(3) nitrogen
(4) water
(5) soil

7. An advertisement for a new diet drink claims that an eight-ounce serving

   A. contains only 240 calories
   B. contains two ounces of protein
   C. tastes better than other leading brands
   D. costs only 14 cents per ounce

Which of the above claims is (are) based on opinion?

   (1) A
   (2) B
   (3) C
   (4) D
   (5) C and D

8. Precipitation is the process by which atmospheric water vapor returns to Earth's surface in one form or another. Each of the following is an example of precipitation *except*

   (1) rain
   (2) sleet
   (3) dust
   (4) snow
   (5) hail

9. Self-preservation is a natural reaction shown by an animal for the purpose of avoiding serious harm. Which of the following is the best example of self-preservation?

   (1) a young man decides to quit smoking
   (2) a salmon swims back to the place of its birth to lay eggs
   (3) a bee spreads pollen as it flies from flower to flower
   (4) a dog barks when it sees its owner
   (5) a mouse runs when it sees a cat

Questions 10–14 are based on the following passage.

Organisms vary greatly in complexity. Single-celled organisms, such as bacteria, are much less complex than multicellular organisms such as flowers. In bacteria, all functions needed to sustain life are carried out by the one cell. In a flower, each life function is carried out by a group of cells working as a unit. Flowers, like other complex organisms, show several levels of structural organization. Here are five of the most common levels:

organelle—An organized structure found in a cell's cytoplasm. Each organelle takes part in carrying out some cellular function. Plant cells, for example, contain chloroplasts that absorb and use light energy to make the cell's food.

cell—The basic structural and functional unit of life. A cell uses energy, moves, grows, responds to changes in its environment, and reproduces. In a multicellular organism, a cell performs a specific function. For example, a human nerve cell relays messages to different parts of the body.

tissue—A group of structurally similar cells that are organized to perform the same activity. In a plant cell, vascular tissue carries water and nutrients to all parts of the cell.

organ—A structural unit composed of several tissues that work together to perform a specific function. The heart is an example of a human organ whose function is to pump blood throughout the body.

organ system—An association of several organs that work together to perform one or more functions. The muscular system, made up of groups of muscles, is an example of a human organ system.

10. In a plant, the epidermis is a special layer of cells that covers and helps protect roots, stems, leaves, flowers, and seeds. This layer of specialized cells is best classified as a(n)

(1) organelle
(2) cell
(3) tissue
(4) organ
(5) organ system

11. Mitochondria are rod-shaped structures in a cell's cytoplasm. Mitochondria are the centers of cellular respiration and are a type of

(1) organelle
(2) cell
(3) tissue
(4) organ
(5) organ system

12. When Derek reached forty-three years of age, his pancreas no longer produced sufficient insulin, a hormone that controls sugar levels in the blood. As a result, Derek was diagnosed as having diabetes, a condition that often can be controlled through proper diet. Because it is made up of several types of specialized tissues, the pancreas is best classified as a(n)

(1) organelle
(2) cell
(3) tissue
(4) organ
(5) organ system

13. As soon as you put food in your mouth, saliva breaks the food down into a form your cells can use. This process is further carried out in your stomach and small intestine. Your mouth, stomach, and small intestine work together as a(n)

(1) organelle
(2) cell
(3) tissue
(4) organ
(5) organ system

14. An amoeba is a microscopic organism that has a complete life cycle. As a single-celled organism, an amoeba reproduces by fission, dividing itself into two new amoebas. The highest level of organization exemplified by an amoeba is that of a(n)

(1) organelle
(2) cell
(3) tissue
(4) organ
(5) organ system

15. Which of the following shows that sunlight can be changed to heat energy?

A. a magnifying glass can focus a beam of sunlight
B. you feel warmer in sunlight than in shade
C. the surface of a car gets hot when sitting in direct sunlight
D. sunlight reflects off a mirror without noticeably warming the mirror

(1) A and B
(2) A and C
(3) A and D
(4) B and C
(5) B and D

Questions 16–20 refer to the following passage.

Celery has long been used in Asian countries to help in the treatment of high blood pressure. Recently, researchers at the University of Chicago have found a possible explanation for this medical benefit of celery. They discovered that celery contains a chemical called 3-n-butyl phthalide. They believe that this phthalide compound causes muscles that line blood vessels to relax, allowing the vessels to widen, lowering blood pressure.

In an experiment with rats, these researchers found that a dose of the phthalide compound equivalent to four stalks of celery for humans lowered blood pressure by 13 percent. The hope is that further studies may lead to the development of a safer, more effective drug treatment of high blood pressure than is now available.

The statements in questions 16–20 can be classified into one of the five categories defined below:

an experiment—a procedure used to investigate a problem

a finding—an experimental result obtained or a conclusion reached as part of the investigation

a hypothesis—a reasonable, but not proved, explanation of an observed fact

a prediction—an opinion about something that may occur in the future

a nonessential fact—a fact that does not help the researcher understand the problem being investigated

16. Researchers believe that eating celery helps lower blood pressure by causing muscles that line blood vessels to relax.

    This is best classified as a(n)

    (1) experiment
    (2) finding
    (3) hypothesis
    (4) prediction
    (5) nonessential fact

17. Celery is a biennial plant, living for two years before it produces seeds and dies. You should classify this statement as a(n)

    (1) experiment
    (2) finding
    (3) hypothesis
    (4) prediction
    (5) nonessential fact

18. Researchers gave rats a dose of 3-n-butyl phthalide and measured changes in the rats' blood pressure.

    This statement is best classified as a(n)

    (1) experiment
    (2) finding
    (3) hypothesis
    (4) prediction
    (5) nonessential fact

19. With further research, scientists may find that other stalky vegetables such as carrots also help lower blood pressure.

    This statement is best classified as a(n)

    (1) experiment
    (2) finding
    (3) hypothesis
    (4) prediction
    (5) nonessential fact

20. Researchers discovered that the chemical 3-n-butyl phthalide can lower the blood pressure of rats.

    You should classify this statement as a(n)

    (1) experiment
    (2) finding
    (3) hypothesis
    (4) prediction
    (5) nonessential fact

Questions 21–25 are based on the following passage.

In recent years, scientists have discovered that Earth's temperature is slowly increasing. In fact, scientists believe that today's average temperature is several degrees higher than the average at the beginning of the industrial revolution in the late 1700s. This warming is thought to be caused by a phenomenon known as the greenhouse effect.

In a greenhouse, sunlight passes through a glass roof and provides energy to the plants growing inside. The glass prevents heat in the greenhouse from escaping. Similarly, sunlight passes through our atmosphere and warms Earth's surface. Much of the surface heat is prevented from escaping because it is absorbed by greenhouse gases in the atmosphere. As long as the average level of greenhouse gases does not increase, Earth's temperature stays in a comfortable range.

Two main greenhouse gases are carbon dioxide and carbon monoxide. Since the industrial revolution, humans have increased the amount of atmospheric carbon dioxide by burning fossil fuels (wood, coal, and oil) both for the production of electricity and for home heating. By driving cars, humans have increased the amount of atmospheric carbon monoxide, present in car exhaust.

Scientists point out that further increases in Earth's average temperature could result in the melting of the polar ice caps and in the changing of weather patterns worldwide.

21. Which of the following is the best definition of a greenhouse gas?

(1) any gas that is commonly present in automobile exhaust
(2) any gas that absorbs heat radiating off of Earth's surface
(3) any gas that reflects sunlight
(4) any gas that is commonly present in a greenhouse
(5) any gas that is given off by the burning of fossil fuels

22. Which of the following best demonstrates the greenhouse principle?

(1) a kettle-type barbecue grill
(2) a heated aquarium
(3) a car with rolled-up windows
(4) a solar battery–powered calculator
(5) a microwave oven

23. Which of the following would most likely result from a gradual increase in Earth's average temperature?

(1) a gradual decrease in the length of a day
(2) a gradual increase in the length of a year
(3) a lowering of ocean levels
(4) a gradual increase in the number of active volcanos
(5) a gradual rise in ocean levels

24. Each of the following contributes to the greenhouse effect *except*

(1) a forest fire
(2) a bus that runs on diesel fuel
(3) soil bacteria that release carbon dioxide gas
(4) a gas-powered lawn mower
(5) a hydroelectric power plant

25. Scientists predict that if something is not done to stop the increase in atmospheric greenhouse gases, the average temperature of Earth may increase 6°F to 10°F in the next fifty years. Which of the following actions would be *most effective* toward helping solve the greenhouse effect?

(1) reducing human dependence on all types of fossil fuels
(2) raising the gas tax on cars
(3) restricting the use of fireplaces to wintertime only
(4) developing efficient electric cars to replace gasoline-powered cars
(5) recording changes in Earth's average temperature during the next fifty years

Questions 26 and 27 refer to the following table.

```
COMPOSITION OF PURE DRY AIR
```

Gas	Symbol or Formula	Percent by Volume
Nitrogen	N_2	78.1%
Oxygen	O_2	20.9%
Argon	Ar	0.9%
Carbon dioxide	CO_2	0.03%
Neon	Ne	
Helium	He	
Krypton	Kr	very
Xenon	Ze	small
Hydrogen	H_2	amounts
Nitrous Oxide	N_2O	
Methane	CH_4	

26. According to the table, the third most abundant gas in pure dry air is

(1) helium
(2) carbon dioxide
(3) krypton
(4) oxygen
(5) argon

27. Which of the following can be determined from information given on the table above?

A. the difference in percent of helium and oxygen present in pure dry air
B. the volume of oxygen present in a one cubic foot sample of pure dry air
C. the difference in the percent of argon and carbon dioxide present in pure dry air
D. the volume of water vapor present in 100 percent humid air

(1) A and B
(2) A and C
(3) B and C
(4) B and D
(5) C and D

Questions 28 and 29 refer to the following passage.

Temperature and pressure affect the amount of gas that can be dissolved in a liquid. An increase in temperature decreases the amount of dissolved gas. An increase in pressure increases the amount of dissolved gas.

28. Soda pop has a fizz because of dissolved carbon dioxide gas. If a cold bottle of soda is left open on a kitchen counter, which of the following will occur?

(1) The amount of dissolved carbon dioxide gas will remain the same.
(2) The amount of dissolved carbon dioxide gas will increase.
(3) The amount of dissolved carbon dioxide gas will decrease.
(4) The temperature of the soda will decrease.
(5) The pressure that the soda exerts on the bottle will increase.

29. In a stream, fish tend to swim in shaded areas along the river bank or in regions of deep water. The reason for this is most likely that water in these places

(1) contains the largest number of insects close to the surface
(2) has the least amount of dissolved carbon dioxide gas
(3) has the greatest amount of dissolved carbon dioxide gas
(4) has the least amount of dissolved oxygen gas
(5) has the greatest amount of dissolved oxygen gas

Questions 30–33 are based on the following passage.

What does an aluminum rowboat have in common with a helium-filled balloon? Both the rowboat and balloon exhibit buoyancy—the tendency of an object to float in liquid or to rise in gas.

The rowboat and balloon each have two forces acting on them: a downward gravitational force (equal to the object's weight) and an upward buoyancy force. The buoyancy force is equal to the weight of liquid or gas that the object displaces (takes the place of).

- A rowboat floats in water because the upward buoyancy force exactly balances the downward gravitational force. A 500-pound rowboat sinks just to the point where it displaces 500 pounds of water.
- A rock sinks in water because the gravitational force is greater than the buoyancy force.
- A helium-filled balloon rises in air because it displaces a volume of air that weighs more than the weight of the helium gas–filled balloon—in other words, the upward buoyancy force is greater than the downward gravitational force.

30. According to the passage, buoyancy refers to the tendency of an object to

A. have weight
B. float in liquid
C. move when pushed
D. rise in air

(1) A
(2) A and C
(3) B
(4) B and D
(5) A, B, C, and D

31. An iceberg floats with about 11 percent of its ice above the water's surface. From the passage we know that the weight of the water displaced by the iceberg is

(1) 11 percent greater than the weight of the iceberg
(2) 11 percent less than the weight of the iceberg
(3) equal to the weight of that part of the iceberg rising above the surface
(4) equal to the weight of that part of the iceberg lying below the surface
(5) equal to the weight of the iceberg

32. Each of the following objects is designed to employ the buoyancy principle *except* a

(1) submarine
(2) life preserver
(3) hot-air balloon
(4) kite
(5) canoe

33. When Erin swims, she notices that if she takes a deep breath, she floats. If she exhales all the air in her lungs, she sinks. Which of the following is the best explanation of Erin's discovery? After exhaling, but not before, Erin displaces an amount of water that

(1) weighs less than her body
(2) weighs more than her body
(3) is equal to her body weight
(4) has more volume than her body volume
(5) has less volume than her body volume

Questions 34 and 35 refer to the following drawing.

NORMAL DAYTIME CONDITIONS

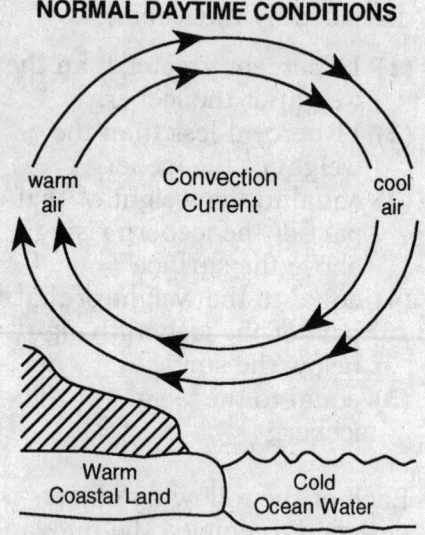

34. The best definition of a convection current is movement of

    (1) air caused by elevation differences
    (2) air caused by differences in distance from the ocean
    (3) air caused by temperature differences
    (4) water caused by the presence of land
    (5) water caused by elevation differences

35. In normal nighttime conditions, the wind next to Earth's surface blows toward the water from the land. From this fact, you can deduce that usually at night

    (1) ocean currents are not as strong as during the day
    (2) ocean temperature changes more quickly than land temperature
    (3) the sun is not warming either the land nor the ocean
    (4) the temperature of the land is higher than that of the ocean
    (5) the temperature of the land is lower than that of the ocean

Questions 36 and 37 refer to the following passage.

Respiration takes place in the body cells and provides a source of energy. During respiration, oxygen (O_2) reacts with the sugar glucose ($C_6H_{12}O_6$). The products of this reaction are carbon dioxide (CO_2), water (H_2O), and energy. The chemical equation for respiration is written as follows:

$$C_6H_{12}O_6 + 6O_2 \rightarrow 6CO_2 + 6H_2O + \text{energy}$$

36. For each molecule of oxygen (O_2) that is used during respiration, how many molecules of carbon dioxide (CO_2) are produced?

    (1) one
    (2) two
    (3) four
    (4) six
    (5) twelve

37. Which of the following is most likely considered a waste product of cellular respiration?

    (1) glucose
    (2) oxygen
    (3) carbon dioxide
    (4) nitrogen
    (5) energy

Questions 38–40 refer to the following information.

An electric circuit can be either a series circuit or a parallel circuit. In a series circuit there is only one path for the electric current to take. A break anywhere in this circuit stops all of the current flow.

In a parallel circuit, there is more than one electric current path. A break in one part of the circuit does not stop current from flowing in a second (or third) path.

SERIES CIRCUIT

If bulb A burns out, bulb B also goes out.

PARALLEL CIRCUIT

If bulb C burns out, bulb D stays lit.

38. Four wall sockets are wired in series with an emergency shutoff switch. If the shutoff switch is opened, what happens to the wall sockets?

(1) Only the socket closest to the switch goes out.
(2) All four wall sockets go out.
(3) All four wall sockets stay on.
(4) Two wall sockets go out, one on each side of the switch.
(5) Only the socket farthest from the switch goes out.

39. What is most likely the main advantage of buying a string of Christmas tree lights that are wired in a parallel circuit rather than in a series circuit?

(1) Parallel circuits cost less to make.
(2) Different colored lights can be used in a parallel circuit.
(3) A parallel circuit uses less electricity.
(4) A burned-out bulb is found more easily in a parallel circuit.
(5) The bulbs are closer together in a parallel circuit.

40. Which statement is true about the circuit drawn below?

(1) If bulb B burns out, bulb A and bulb C will stay lit.
(2) If bulb C burns out, bulb A and bulb B will go off.
(3) If bulb A burns out, bulb B will go off, but bulb C will stay lit.
(4) If bulb B burns out, bulb A and bulb C will go off.
(5) If bulb A burns out, bulb B will stay lit, but bulb C will go off.

Questions 41–44 are based on the following passage.

AIDS (acquired immunodeficiency syndrome) is a serious, contagious disease for which there is no cure as yet. AIDS is a disease of the human immune system, the system that enables the body to destroy germs that cause infections and illness. With an AIDS-weakened immune system, a patient may develop life-threatening infections and cancers that usually don't affect healthy people.

AIDS is caused by a virus known as HIV, the human immunodeficiency virus. Once infected, a person is called "HIV positive." The first symptoms of AIDS include weight loss, swollen lymph nodes, body weakness, persistent cough, and chronic yeast infections of the mouth or genital areas. Other symptoms include pneumonia and a type of cancer characterized by the presence of purplish spots.

An HIV-positive person may show no symptoms of AIDS for years after he or she becomes infected. And, without showing symptoms, that person may be unaware that he or she is infected. However, *an HIV-positive person is infectious and can transmit the HIV virus to other people*. The HIV virus is spread from the blood of an infected person to the blood of an uninfected one. Because blood cells are present in sexual fluids, the HIV virus can spread from one person to another during sexual activity.

AIDS is spread in one of three main ways:
• by having unsafe sex with an infected person
• by sharing a needle with an infected drug user
• from an infected mother to the fetus during pregnancy, or to the baby during delivery or breast feeding

Although AIDS is not curable, AIDS is preventable. People can protect themselves from AIDS by engaging in safe sex and by staying away from drugs.

41. AIDS is a disease of the

   (1) reproductive system
   (2) digestive system
   (3) nervous system
   (4) skeletal system
   (5) immune system

42. Which of the following is true about all HIV-positive people?

   All HIV-positive people

   (1) show AIDS symptoms
   (2) caught AIDS from drug use
   (3) can transmit AIDS
   (4) are single adults
   (5) know they have AIDS

43. You can infer from the passage that each of the following activities is classified as high risk for catching AIDS *except*

   A. sharing needles for drug use
   B. having multiple sex partners
   C. swimming in a community pool
   D. playing with an HIV-positive child

   (1) A
   (2) A and B
   (3) A and C
   (4) C and D
   (5) D

44. An increase in the number of reported HIV-positive people is occurring in the U.S. This increase is most likely due to each of the following reasons *except*

   (1) an increasing awareness by doctors of the symptoms of AIDS
   (2) an increasing effort to educate U.S. citizens about the AIDS problem
   (3) an increase in the spread of AIDS
   (4) an increase in testing to determine who has the HIV virus
   (5) an influx of HIV-positive people into the United States from foreign countries

45. Two important processes performed for plants by leaves are photosynthesis and transpiration. During photosynthesis, leaves produce glucose, a form of sugar. During transpiration, plants release water by evaporation from the leaf surfaces. What is the most likely reason that a desert plant has few or no leaves?

(1) to increase photosynthesis
(2) to decrease photosynthesis
(3) to keep photosynthesis at a constant level, day and night
(4) to increase transpiration
(5) to decrease transpiration

Questions 46–48 are based on the following drawing and passage.

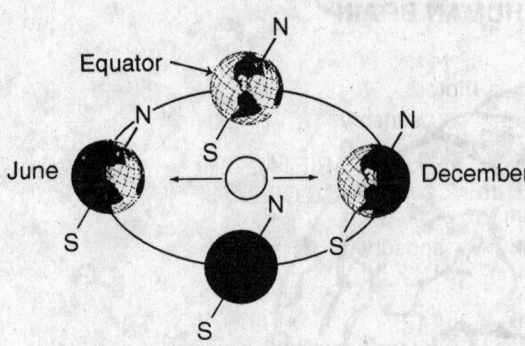

Earth's rotation axis is tilted with respect to the direction of the Sun's rays. This tilt remains constant as Earth rotates on its axis and as it moves around the Sun. The tilt leads to two important consequences for Earth:
• Summer occurs in the hemisphere that is tilted toward the Sun, while winter occurs in the hemisphere that is tilted away from the Sun.
• The hemisphere that is tilted toward the Sun has longer days and shorter nights than the hemisphere that is tilted away from the Sun.

46. During summer in the northern hemisphere, the North Pole experiences

(1) twenty-four hours of darkness each day
(2) twenty-four hours of daylight each day
(3) twelve hours of daylight each day
(4) twelve hours of darkness each day
(5) eighteen hours of daylight each day

47. During December, which location will have most nearly twelve hours of daylight and twelve hours of darkness?

A town that is located

(1) close to the North Pole
(2) close to the South Pole
(3) halfway between the equator and North Pole
(4) halfway between the equator and the South Pole
(5) close to the equator

48. Which of the following would be true if Earth's rotation axis did not tilt?

A. Days and nights would be the same length everywhere on Earth.
B. There would be no hours of darkness on points along the equator.
C. Earth would have no seasons.
D. Each part of Earth would have the same daily temperature pattern.

(1) A
(2) A and C
(3) A and D
(4) B
(5) B and C

49. Malaria is a disease caused by *parasitic protozoans,* one-celled animals that feed upon the cells of the host—the body of the person they invade. Malaria can be spread by the bite of the *Anopheles* mosquito. Knowing this, you can deduce that protozoans that cause malaria are present in the host's

(1) lungs
(2) stomach
(3) bone tissue
(4) liver
(5) blood

50. Which of the following is the best evidence that light travels at a greater speed than sound?

(1) Humans have separate sense organs for vision and hearing.
(2) Light travels through outer space, but sound doesn't.
(3) Light passes easily through thick glass, but sound doesn't.
(4) You see lightning before you hear thunder.
(5) The frequency of visible light is much greater than that of sound.

Questions 51–54 refer to the following drawing and passage.

CEREBRUM OF THE HUMAN BRAIN

The largest region of the human brain is the cerebrum, or forebrain. The cerebrum consists of two halves, or hemispheres, joined through the center by a bundle of nerve fibers known as the corpus callosum. Each hemisphere is made up of four parts, or lobes, that control specific motor (voluntary movement) and sensory (sensation) functions.

Scientists have long known that the left hemisphere (shown above) controls the right side of the human body and the right hemisphere controls the left side. In recent years, scientists have also discovered that each hemisphere is specialized for specific learning activities. The left hemisphere seems best suited for written language, scientific skills, math, and logical reasoning. The right hemisphere seems more specialized for art, music, insight, and imagination.

51. An elderly woman suffered a stroke—a restriction of blood flow to the brain. If the stroke caused the right side of her body to become temporarily paralyzed, she most likely experienced a decreased blood flow to

(1) the left side of her body
(2) the right side of her body
(3) the front of her brain
(4) the left side of her brain
(5) the right side of her brain

52. Which two of the following people are most likely to be referred to as "left-brained"—showing skills most often associated with the left side of the human brain?

A. a mathematician
B. a portrait painter
C. a chess player
D. a storyteller

(1) A and B
(2) A and C
(3) B and C
(4) B and D
(5) C and D

53. Which area of the brain controls feeling on the left side of a person's face?

(1) the right occipital lobe
(2) the left parietal lobe
(3) the left temporal lobe
(4) the right frontal lobe
(5) the right parietal lobe

54. Which facts below represent the best evidence that brain size is not the main cause for differences in intelligence?

A. An adult's brain is larger than a baby's brain.
B. A human being's brain is larger than a cat's.
C. All adult human brains are about the same size.
D. An elephant's brain is larger than a human being's.

(1) A and B
(2) A and D
(3) B and C
(4) B and D
(5) C and D

Questions 55 and 56 refer to the graph below.

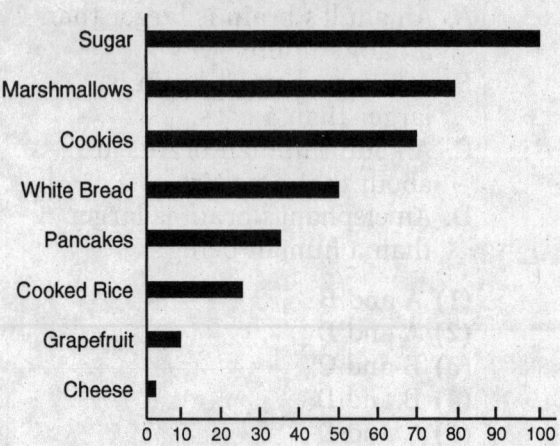

PERCENT OF CARBOHYDRATES IN SELECTED FOODS

55. Which of the following foods has a carbohydrate content of 50 percent or more?

    A. grapefruit
    B. rice
    C. marshmallows

    (1) A
    (2) B
    (3) C
    (4) A and C
    (5) B and C

56. Which statement is best supported by information given on the graph?

    (1) Cooking increases the carbohydrate content of food.
    (2) Sugar is not a form of carbohydrate.
    (3) The carbohydrate content of food increases as its sugar content increases.
    (4) A food that does not contain sugar has zero carbohydrate content.
    (5) All foods contain some amount of sugar.

57. Many people feel that while it is all right to raise animals such as cows for slaughter, it is not all right to kill more intelligent animals such as whales or chimpanzees. What value concerning intelligence is reflected by this position?

    (1) Food production for human consumption is more important than animal rights.
    (2) Humans should have a higher regard for animals of high intelligence than for animals of low intelligence.
    (3) Animals should not be harmed when used for medical research.
    (4) The only justification for killing an animal is for use as a source of food.
    (5) Animals that are physically similar to people ought to be treated differently than animals that aren't.

Question 58 is based on the following graph.

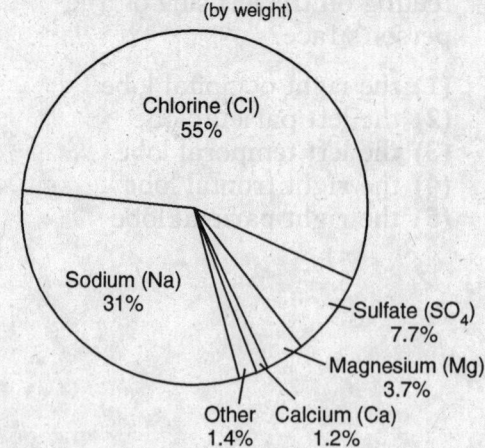

MAIN SUBSTANCES IN SEA WATER
(by weight)

58. From information given on the graph, you can deduce that the main substance dissolved in sea water is

    (1) magnesium oxide (MgO)
    (2) sulfuric acid (H_2SO_4)
    (3) calcium chloride ($CaCl_2$)
    (4) potassium chloride (KCl)
    (5) sodium chloride ($NaCl$)

Question 59 refers to the following drawing.

BAR MAGNET

S   N

CUT IN HALF

S   N   S   N

59. You can infer from the drawing above that

(1) a bar magnet has more than one north pole and one south pole
(2) cutting a bar magnet in half produces two weaker bar magnets
(3) cutting a bar magnet in half produces two shorter bar magnets
(4) cutting a bar magnet in half doubles the magnetic strength available
(5) to produce two bar magnets, a larger bar magnet must be cut exactly in half

Question 60 is based on the following drawing.

← Olive Oil

← Water

← Mercury

60. You can infer from the drawing above that the density of water

A. is less than the density of olive oil
B. is less than the density of mercury
C. is greater than the density of ice
D. is greater than the density of olive oil

(1) A and B
(2) B
(3) B and D
(4) C and D
(5) D

Questions 61 and 62 are based on the following drawing.

REFRACTION OF WHITE LIGHT BY A GLASS PRISM

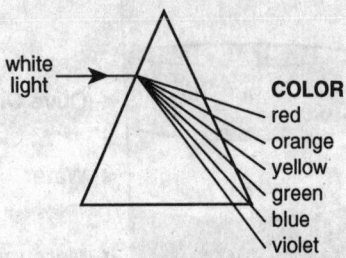

61. The refraction of white light through a glass prism shows that

(1) white light travels in a straight line as it passes through a glass prism
(2) white light consists of several types of colored light
(3) white light cannot pass through glass without being separated into its color components
(4) glass absorbs white light but allows colored light to pass through
(5) red light refracts more than violet light when passing through a glass prism

62. What is the *best evidence* that sunlight is a form of white light (light that looks white but consists of many colors)?

(1) a clear blue sky
(2) white moonlight
(3) a color television
(4) a rainbow
(5) a color photograph

Questions 63 and 64 are based on the following drawing and information.

MUSCLES THAT CONTROL EYE MOVEMENT

Each eye muscle controls eye movement by contracting (shortening) and pulling the eye.

63. As you look at a picture, the lateral rectus muscle in your right eye allows your eye to

(1) sweep from the top of the picture to the bottom
(2) sweep from the bottom of the picture to the top
(3) sweep from right to left across the picture
(4) sweep from left to right across the picture
(5) close the eyelid to rest the eye when it is tired

64. If a woman has a detached superior rectus muscle in her left eye, what symptom will she most likely show?

(1) an inability to raise her left eye
(2) an inability to see through her left eye
(3) an inability to shut her left eye
(4) an inability to blink with her left eye
(5) an inability to move her left eye from right to left

Question 65 is based on the drawing below.

PROPANE MOLECULE

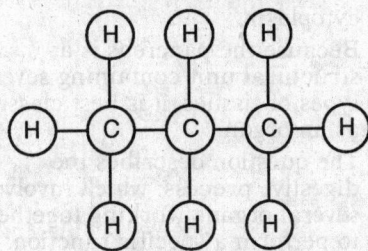

65. The drawing above shows the molecular structure of propane. Each H stands for one hydrogen atom and each C stands for one carbon atom. The formula for a propane molecule is written as

(1) 3C8H
(2) $3C_8H$
(3) C_3H_8
(4) C_8H_3
(5) C_8H_8

Question 66 is based on the drawing below.

SIMPLE REFLEX ARC

66. A reflex reaction, such as pulling your hand back from a hot stove, does not immediately involve the brain. The nerve impulse that controls the reaction takes place in a simple reflex arc as shown above. In a simple reflex arc, an interneuron

(1) starts the nerve impulse at the sensory receptor
(2) transmits the nerve impulse to a motor neuron
(3) transmits the nerve impulse to the brain
(4) transmits the nerve impulse to the spinal cord
(5) transmits the nerve impulse to the muscles that react

Answers begin on page 894.

PRACTICE TEST 3: SCIENCE ANSWER KEY

1. (4) Although all five choices are facts, only choice (4), that helium-filled balloons rise, involves a relationship between the relative weights of helium gas and air.

2. (1) Earth's rotation (spin on its axis) speed determines the length of its day. As the rotation speed slows, the length of an Earth day will lengthen.

3. (2) A base neutralizes an acid. Choice (1) would increase acidity. Choice (3) is incorrect because a neutral substance such as water would have no effect. Neither choice (4) nor (5) can be inferred from the action of the scientists.

4. (2) All life on Earth is possible because of sunlight, which is the primary source of energy for all activity (including life) on Earth's surface.

5. (3) The products of the reaction are shown on the right side of the arrow. The formula $6O_2$ shows that six molecules of oxygen gas (O_2) are formed.

6. (4) Besides sunlight, both carbon dioxide and water must be present for photosynthesis to take place. Only water is given as one of the choices. Glucose, choice (1), is a product of photosynthesis; oxygen, choice (2), is a by-product of the process; and nitrogen gas, choice (3), does not exist in a free state.

7. (3) Only choice (3) is an opinion. Choices (A) and (B) can be checked by chemical analysis. Choice (D) can be checked by going to a store that sells the drink.

8. (3) Dust is the only choice that is not a form of water.

9. (5) Of all the examples, only choice (5), a mouse running when it sees a cat, represents a natural reaction intended to avoid harm. Choice (1) is based on an intelligent decision, not on a natural reaction. None of the other choices is an example of self-preservation.

10. (3) The epidermis is a layer of cells, each of which is organized to perform the same activity, leading to its classification as a tissue.

11. (1) Mitochondria are organelles, structures found within a cell's cytoplasm.

12. (4) Because the pancreas is a structural unit containing several types of tissues, it is best classifed as an organ.

13. (5) The question describes the digestive process, which involves several organs working together to perform a specific function.

14. (2) An amoeba is a single-celled organism that carries on all the major life processes.

15. (4) Choices (A) and (D) are facts but neither shows that sunlight can be changed to heat energy.

16. (3) This statement is a hypothesis because it gives a reasonable but untested explanation of why celery helps lower blood pressure.

17. (5) The life cycle of celery has nothing to do with the attempt to determine the medicinal characteristics of celery.

18. (1) Giving rats the phthalide compound was part of the experiment described in the passage.

19. (4) This is a prediction because it is an opinion about something that might happen in the future.

20. (2) Any experimental result or discovery is classified as a finding.

21. (2) A greenhouse gas is defined by its ability to absorb heat that radiates from Earth's surface, preventing it from radiating into space.

22. (3) A car with its windows rolled up is almost identical to a greenhouse. The glass lets light energy in but prevents heat energy from escaping.

23. (5) As Earth's temperature rises, the polar ice caps will likely melt. The water from the melting ice will cause a rise in ocean levels.

24. (5) A hydroelectric plant converts the energy of flowing water to electricity. No greenhouse gases are emitted in the process.

25. (1) Reducing our dependence on all types of fossil fuels would reduce the atmospheric greenhouse gases released.

26. **(5)** Nitrogen is most abundant, followed by oxygen, and argon is the third most abundant.

27. **(3)** Choice (A) is incorrect because the percent of helium is not listed. Choice (D) is not correct because the table refers to pure dry air only.

28. **(3)** The amount of carbon dioxide gas will decrease as the temperature of the pop increases. The soda will then taste flat.

29. **(5)** Cold water has a greater amount of dissolved oxygen gas than warm water, which explains why fish tend to swim in shaded areas or in deep water, where the temperature is lower.

30. **(4)** Choices (B) and (D), an object's tendency to float in water or rise in air, demonstrate the principle of buoyancy, as described in the first paragraph of the passage.

31. **(5)** The weight of water displaced by any floating object is equal to the weight of the whole object, regardless of how much of the object is floating above the water level.

32. **(4)** A kite rises in air because of the pressure of the wind against its surface, not because of buoyancy.

33. **(1)** After exhaling, Erin sinks, which means that her weight is greater than the buoyancy force. Therefore, the weight of the water she displaces is less than her body weight.

34. **(3)** As the drawing shows, a convection current is air movement caused by temperature differences. Water convection currents occur in the ocean.

35. **(5)** In normal nighttime conditions, the land is colder than the ocean. As a result, the air over the ocean rises and causes a breeze to flow from the land.

36. **(1)** The chemical equation shows that six molecules of O_2 are used up while six molecules of CO_2 are created. The same number are created that are used up: one used up, one created.

37. **(3)** The energy and water that are created by cellular respiration are used by the body. The CO_2 (carbon dioxide) is expelled by the lungs as a waste product.

38. **(2)** Since the switch and wall sockets are wired in series, if one goes out they all go out. Opening the switch breaks the circuit, and all sockets go out.

39. **(4)** If the bulbs are wired in a parallel circuit, the burned-out bulb does not affect the other good bulbs, making the burned-out one easy to find.

40. **(3)** Only choice (3) is true. Lights A and B are part of the same series circuit, and if one goes out, so will the other. Light C, though, will stay lit no matter what happens to lights A and B.

41. **(5)** The first paragraph of the passage states that AIDS is a disease of the human immune system.

42. **(3)** All HIV-positive people can transmit AIDS, and this makes the spread of AIDS difficult to stop. Many HIV-positive people don't know they are infected, and they infect others.

43. **(4)** As far as is known, no one has ever caught AIDS in a community swimming pool or from playing with an HIV-positive child. Choices (A) and (B) are the two most high-risk activities known.

44. **(2)** Increasing efforts to educate citizens about AIDS can only help in the worldwide effort to conquer this dreaded disease.

45. **(5)** Cacti and other desert plants can survive in the desert only by conserving water. As a result, desert plants have evolved little or no leaf surface through which transpiration can take place.

46. **(2)** During summer months, the North Pole is tilted toward the sun and receives sunlight twenty-four hours each day.

47. **(5)** Actually, a town that is located just south of the equator will have twelve hours of daylight and twelve hours of darkness during December. During June, a town that is just north of the equator will have equal day and night hours.

48. **(2)** As the passage states, the tilt of Earth's axis is responsible for differences in day and night hours and for seasonal differences.

49. **(5)** A mosquito can transmit the blood of one person to the blood of a second person. Therefore, you can correctly conclude that malaria is transmitted by the blood.

50. **(4)** An electrical discharge in a cloud causes both thunder and lightning. You see the lightning before you hear the thunder because light travels faster than sound.

51. (4) According to the passage, the left side of the brain controls the right side of the body. Problems on the right side of the body indicate a decreased blood flow to the left side of the brain.

52. (2) Of the four choices listed, mathematician and chess player are the two whose skills most depend on math and logical reasoning—"left-brain" skills.

53. (5) The left side of the face is controlled by the right side of the brain. The parietal lobe controls facial sensations.

54. (5) Choices (A) and (B) would seem to indicate that a larger brain implies greater intelligence. Choices (C) and (D) suggest that brain size is not a determining factor for differences in intelligence.

55. (3) Marshmallows have a carbohydrate content of about 80 percent; the other choices contain less than 50 percent of carbohydrates.

56. (3) The list when read from bottom to top indicates that as the sugar content increases, the carbohydrate content increases.

57. (2) Many people feel that more intelligent species should be preserved from slaughter, possibly because of their value in research on intelligence.

58. (5) The two major substances in sea water are chlorine (Cl) and sodium (Na), the two elements that make up sodium chloride (NaCl), most often called table salt.

59. (3) You can infer only that two shorter magnets are created. However, you can't tell from the drawing what the strength of these magnets are.

60. (3) When liquids don't freely mix, the one with the greatest density sinks to the bottom. The liquid with least density floats on top.

61. (2) Each color component of white light refracts (changes direction) a different amount as it enters and leaves the prism. This is how a prism separates white light into its color components.

62. (4) A rainbow forms because suspended rain drops act as tiny prisms and cause sunlight (natural white light) to separate into its color components.

63. (4) When the lateral rectus contracts it pulls the front of the eye to the right, sweeping the eye from left to right across the picture.

64. (1) The superior rectus contracts to pull the eye upward. If this muscle is detached (or severely weakened) the woman would be unable to raise the eye.

65. (3) The correct way to show three carbon atoms and eight hydrogen atoms is with the formula C_3H_8.

66. (2) As the drawing shows, the interneuron receives the nerve impulse from the sensory neuron and transmits the impulse to the motor neuron.

Use the answer key on pages 894–896 to check your answers to the Practice Test. Then find the item number of each question you missed and circle it on the chart below to determine the reading skill and content areas in which you need more practice. Pay particular attention to areas where you missed half or more of the questions. The reading skills are covered on pages 187–243. The page numbers for the content areas are listed below on the chart. Knowledge of reading skill and content area–based questions is absolutely essential for success on the GED Science Test. The numbers in boldface are questions based on graphics. For those questions that you missed, review the pages indicated.

PRACTICE TEST 3: SCIENCE EVALUATION CHART

Skill Area/ Content Area	Comprehension (pages 189–195)	Application (pages 195–199)	Analysis (pages 200–210)	Evaluation (pages 211–222)
Biology (pages 355–374)	41, 42, 43, **53**, **55**, 63	9, 10, 11, 12, 13, 14, 16, 17, 18, 19, 20, 52	45, 49, **51**, **64**, **66**	44, **54**, **56**, 57
Earth Science (pages 375–398)	21, **34**, **46**	8, 22, 24, **47**	2, 23, **35**, 48	25, 27
Chemistry (pages 399–418)	5, **26**, **27**, 36, **65**	3, 28	6, 7, 29, 37, **58**	1
Physics (pages 419–440)	4, 30, **59**, **60**, **61**	31, 32, **38**	15, **39**, **40**	33, 50, **62**

PRACTICE TEST 4: LITERATURE AND THE ARTS

The Literature and the Arts Practice Test will give you the opportunity to evaluate your readiness for the actual GED Literature and the Arts Test.

This test contains 45 questions. Most of the questions are based on excerpts from novels, short stories, plays, and speeches; some questions are based on a complete poem, essay, or review.

You should take approximately 65 minutes to complete this test. At the end of 65 minutes, stop and mark your place. Then finish the test. This will give you an idea of whether or not you can finish the real GED Test in the time allotted. Try to answer as many questions as you can. A blank will count as a wrong answer, so make a reasonable guess for answers to questions you are not sure of.

When you are finished with the test, check your answers and turn to the Evaluation Chart on page 913 and the GED Readiness Worksheet on page 927. Use the chart and worksheet to evaluate whether or not you are ready to take the actual GED Test and, if not, in what areas you need more work.

PRACTICE TEST 4: LITERATURE AND THE ARTS ANSWER GRID

1 ① ② ③ ④ ⑤	13 ① ② ③ ④ ⑤	25 ① ② ③ ④ ⑤	36 ① ② ③ ④ ⑤
2 ① ② ③ ④ ⑤	14 ① ② ③ ④ ⑤	26 ① ② ③ ④ ⑤	37 ① ② ③ ④ ⑤
3 ① ② ③ ④ ⑤	15 ① ② ③ ④ ⑤	27 ① ② ③ ④ ⑤	38 ① ② ③ ④ ⑤
4 ① ② ③ ④ ⑤	16 ① ② ③ ④ ⑤	28 ① ② ③ ④ ⑤	39 ① ② ③ ④ ⑤
5 ① ② ③ ④ ⑤	17 ① ② ③ ④ ⑤	29 ① ② ③ ④ ⑤	40 ① ② ③ ④ ⑤
6 ① ② ③ ④ ⑤	18 ① ② ③ ④ ⑤	30 ① ② ③ ④ ⑤	41 ① ② ③ ④ ⑤
7 ① ② ③ ④ ⑤	19 ① ② ③ ④ ⑤	31 ① ② ③ ④ ⑤	42 ① ② ③ ④ ⑤
8 ① ② ③ ④ ⑤	20 ① ② ③ ④ ⑤	32 ① ② ③ ④ ⑤	43 ① ② ③ ④ ⑤
9 ① ② ③ ④ ⑤	21 ① ② ③ ④ ⑤	33 ① ② ③ ④ ⑤	44 ① ② ③ ④ ⑤
10 ① ② ③ ④ ⑤	22 ① ② ③ ④ ⑤	34 ① ② ③ ④ ⑤	45 ① ② ③ ④ ⑤
11 ① ② ③ ④ ⑤	23 ① ② ③ ④ ⑤	35 ① ② ③ ④ ⑤	
12 ① ② ③ ④ ⑤	24 ① ② ③ ④ ⑤		

Read each excerpt and choose the best answer to each question that follows.

Questions 1–6 refer to the following excerpt from an autobiography.

HAS SHE CHANGED?

For four days I waited on the curious in the Store, and let them look me over. I was that rarity, a
5 Stamps girl who had gone to the fabled California and returned. I could be forgiven a few siditty airs. In fact, a pretension to worldliness was expected of me, and I was too happy to disappoint.
10 When Momma wasn't around, I stood with one hand on my hip and my head cocked to one side and spoke of the wonders of the West and the joy of being free. Any lis-
15 tener could have asked me: if things were so grand in San Francisco, what had brought me back to a dusty mote of Arkansas? No one asked, because they all needed to
20 believe that a land existed some- where, even beyond the Northern Star, where Negroes were treated as people and whites were not the all- powerful ogres of their experience.
25 For the first time the farmers acknowledged my maturity. They didn't order me back and forth along the shelves but found subtler ways to make their wants known.
30 "You all have any long-grain rice, Sister?"
The hundred-pound sack of rice sat squidged down in full view.
"Yes, ma'am, I believe we do."
35 "Well then, I'll thank you for two pounds."
"Two pounds? Yes, ma'am."
I had seen the formality of black adult equals all my youth but had

40 never considered that a time would come when I, too, could participate. The customs are as formalized as an eighteenth-century minuet, and a child at the race's knee learns the
45 moves and twirls by osmosis and observation.

Values among Southern rural blacks are not quite the same as those existing elsewhere. Age has
50 more worth than wealth, and reli- gious piety more value than beauty.

There were no sly looks over my fatherless child. No cutting in- sinuations kept me shut away from
55 the community. Knowing how closely my grandmother's friends hewed to the Bible, I was surprised not to be asked to confess my evil ways and repent. Instead, I was
60 seen in the sad light which had been shared and was to be shared by black girls in every state in the coun- try. I was young, yes, unmarried, yes—but I was a mother, and that
65 placed me nearer to the people.

I was flattered to receive such acceptance from my betters (se- niors) and strove mightily to show myself worthy.

—Maya Angelou, excerpted from *Gather Together in My Name*, 1974

1. The young woman in the excerpt has just returned from living in

(1) San Francisco, California
(2) Greensboro, North Carolina
(3) Northern Star, Mississippi
(4) Stamps, Arkansas
(5) New York City, New York

2. When the woman returned home, she pretended to be

(1) rich
(2) religious
(3) sophisticated
(4) married
(5) famous

3. The town where the excerpt takes place can best be described as

(1) wealthy and exclusive
(2) rural and small
(3) mysterious and threatening
(4) exciting and bustling
(5) cold and impersonal

4. Which of the following words best describes how the townspeople feel about the woman?

(1) ashamed
(2) angry
(3) resentful
(4) accepting
(5) proud

5. In lines 30–37, the author quotes a conversation between herself and a townsperson to

(1) help readers picture how badly store clerks were treated
(2) let readers know what kinds of food were popular in the town
(3) show what kind of job she held when she returned home
(4) poke fun at the way the people in the town spoke
(5) give an example of the townspeople's idea of good manners

6. Imagine that you're taking a poll. Which of the following individuals would you expect to top the town's Most Admired People list?

(1) an Oscar-winning actor
(2) the head of the nation's largest corporation
(3) a local religious leader
(4) the wealthiest person in the county
(5) the winner of a state beauty pageant

Questions 7–11 refer to the following excerpt from an article.

IS HER FUTURE IN BASEBALL?

"I'm going to be the first woman playing in the major leagues." The speaker is my daughter, Casey, age 10. She is convinced of her future as
5 a first baseman for the Red Sox. "Baseperson sounds stupid," she tells me, looking at me evenly. "If a woman has the same athletic skills as a man, why shouldn't she play
10 baseball in the major leagues?" This much has changed in 14 years.

We sit in the stands, mother and daughter. There have been hundreds of women sportswriters since
15 I was in Boston. I would like to be able to say that Casey and I talk baseball stats but the truth is her father, a scholar of Red Sox history, has infected her with his love of the
20 game. As a 10-year-old girl, she understands the mechanisms: She has a feel for the individual players, a sense of their capabilities and the benighted baseball fate of her be-
25 loved team.

She has thoughts about the 1993 Red Sox and is filled with judgments on the skills of Ivan Calderon, Roger Clemens and Frank Viola.
30 Baseball cards clog her room. At spring training batting practice, as always, young fans push baseballs at the players, begging for autographs. "Mr. Clemens!" "Mr. Cal-
35 deron!" "Mr. Dawson, pul-leese." I look down at the crowd of kids. Half of them are girls. This is new. During a game against the Minnesota Twins, I noticed that the bat boy was
40 a girl.

—Marie Brenner,
excerpted from "Girls of Summer,"
New York Times, April 5, 1993

7. Casey, the ten-year-old girl, would like to become a

(1) sportswriter
(2) sports announcer
(3) baseball historian
(4) bat girl
(5) first baseman

8. Casey is a collector of

(1) sports stars' autographs
(2) signed baseballs
(3) baseball cards
(4) sports statistics
(5) books about sports

9. The excerpt is mainly about how

(1) females are becoming more and more involved in professional sports
(2) a father helped his daughter develop an intense interest in sports
(3) the daughter of a female sportswriter shares her love of sports
(4) girls make up a large part of the audience for a typical Red Sox game
(5) major league baseball is making an effort to attract female fans

10. The purpose of the last sentence is to

(1) make the article more interesting by giving specific details
(2) prove that the team does not discriminate against females
(3) give an example of how the Red Sox are preparing for the future
(4) support the idea that females are taking a more active role in sports
(5) convince girls to become participants in major league baseball

11. Which of the following statements would the author of the excerpt be most likely to make?

(1) "A woman's place is at home plate."
(2) "It's a man's world."
(3) "The more things change, the more they stay the same."
(4) "Anything men can do, women can do better."
(5) "Girls don't have the same interests as boys."

Questions 12–16 refer to the following excerpt from a short story.

WHO'S LISTENING?

In the living room the voice-clock sang, *Tick-tock, seven o'clock, time to get up, time to get up, seven o'clock*! as if it were afraid that no-
5 body would. The morning house lay empty. The clock ticked on, repeating and repeating its sounds into the emptiness. *Seven-nine, breakfast time, seven-nine!*
10 In the kitchen the breakfast stove gave a hissing sigh and ejected from its warm interior eight pieces of perfectly browned toast, eight eggs sunnyside up, sixteen
15 slices of bacon, two coffees, and two cool glasses of milk.
"Today is August 4, 2026," said a second voice from the kitchen ceiling, "in the city of Allendale, Cal-
20 ifornia." It repeated the date three times for memory's sake. "Today is Mr. Featherstone's birthday. Today is the anniversary of Tilita's marriage. Insurance is payable, as are
25 the water, gas, and light bills."
Somewhere in the walls, relays clicked, memory tapes glided under electric eyes.
Eight-one, tick-tock, eight-one
30 *o'clock, off to school, off to work, run, run, eight-one!* But no doors slammed, no carpets took the soft tread of rubber heels. It was raining outside. The weather box on the
35 front door sang quietly: "Rain, rain, go away; rubbers, raincoats for to-day . . ." And the rain tapped on the empty house, echoing.
Outside, the garage chimed
40 and lifted its door to reveal the wait-ing car. After a long wait the door swung down again.
At eight-thirty the eggs were shriveled and the toast was like

45   stone. An aluminum wedge scraped
them into the sink, where hot water
whirled them down a metal throat
which digested and flushed them
away to the distant sea. The dirty
50   dishes were dropped into a hot
washer and emerged twinkling dry.

    —Ray Bradbury, excerpted from
"There Will Come Soft Rains," 1950

12. The house in the excerpt is best
described as

  (1) messy
  (2) deserted
  (3) dirty
  (4) haunted
  (5) aging

13. How are the details in the excerpt
organized?

  (1) order of importance
     (least significant details
     presented first)
  (2) flashback (past events
     interspersed with events
     currently happening)
  (3) general to specific (a
     general statement followed
     by specific details)
  (4) time order (events presented
     in the order in which they
     might actually happen)
  (5) main idea and example (a
     major point followed by
     specific instances)

14. The tone, or mood, of the excerpt
can best be described as

  (1) humorous
  (2) cheerful
  (3) sarcastic
  (4) bitter
  (5) lonely

15. Given the details in the excerpt,
you can tell that the family

  (1) liked doing housework
  (2) enjoyed cooking breakfast
     together
  (3) thought it was important to
     be well organized
  (4) hated to be told what to do
  (5) was unemployed and out
     of money

16. Which of the following TV
programs would be the most
likely to include an episode based
on the excerpt?

  (1) "Science Fiction Stories,"
     which features dramas
     showing the interaction of
     people and technology of
     the future
  (2) "The Model Home," which
     takes prospective home buyers
     on tours of houses that have
     the latest in home gadgets
  (3) "Tomorrow Is Here," which
     presents documentaries on
     scientific innovations that are
     sweeping the United States
  (4) "Comedy Showcase," which
     specializes in funny skits on
     subjects that are currently in
     the news
  (5) "Tell Me How," which takes
     new inventions and explains to
     children how they work and
     who developed them

Questions 17–21 refer to the following excerpt from a short story.

LIKE FATHER, LIKE SON?

The last time I saw my father was in Grand Central Station. I was going from my grandmother's in the Adirondacks to a cottage on the

5 Cape that my mother had rented, and I wrote my father that I would be in New York between trains for an hour and a half, and asked if we could have lunch together. His sec-

10 retary wrote to say that he would meet me at the information booth at noon, and at twelve-o'clock sharp I saw him coming through the crowd. He was a stranger to me—my

15 mother divorced him three years ago and I hadn't been with him since—but as soon as I saw him I felt that he was my father, my flesh and blood, my future and my doom.

20 I knew that when I was grown I would be something like him; I would have to plan my campaigns within his limitations. He was a big, good-looking man, and I was terri-

25 bly happy to see him again. He struck me on the back and shook my hand. "Hi, Charlie," he said. "Hi, boy. I'd like to take you up to my club, but it's in the Sixties, and if you

30 have to catch an early train I guess we'd better get something to eat around here." He put his arm around me, and I smelled my father the way my mother sniffs a rose. It was a

35 rich compound of whiskey, after-shave lotion, shoe polish, woolens, and the rankness of a mature male. I hoped that someone would see us together. I wished that we could be

40 photographed. I wanted some rec-ord of our having been together.

—John Cheever,
excerpted from "Reunion," 1952

17. The father responded to his son's invitation by

   (1) calling him on the telephone
   (2) having his secretary write a note
   (3) asking the boy's mother to call
   (4) sending a messenger
   (5) ignoring the boy's request

18. How did the son feel about seeing his father?

   (1) angry and hostile
   (2) nervous and hopeful
   (3) happy and proud
   (4) suspicious and wary
   (5) bored and uninterested

19. What does the son mean when he says, "I knew that when I was grown I would be something like him [the father]; I would have to plan my campaigns within his limitations" (lines 20–23)?

   (1) In the future, his father will try to tell him what to do.
   (2) Like his father, he will have limited funds.
   (3) As a man, he will have some of the same faults as his father.
   (4) As an adult, he will support the same political party as his father.
   (5) When he is grown, he will plan his life around his father's activities.

20. The fact that the father and son meet in a train station shows that the

   (1) father is living in the streets
   (2) two do not have a close relationship
   (3) son has an unusually busy schedule
   (4) rest of the family dislikes the two
   (5) mother fears the father will hurt the son

21. Which of the following books would the father be most likely to read?

    (1) *The Frantic Father: How to Juggle Work and Family*
    (2) *Making a Killing: Your Guide to Increasing Business Profits*
    (3) *A Man's Right: You Can Win Custody of Your Child*
    (4) *Husband and Wife: Improving Communication with Your Spouse*
    (5) *Back to Work: How to Survive Unemployment and Find a Good Job*

Questions 22–27 refer to the following excerpt from a short story.

IS HE HIS MOTHER'S FAVORITE?

    Life was very hard for the Whipples. It was hard to feed all the hungry mouths, it was hard to keep the children in flannels during the
5 winter, short as it was: "God knows what would become of us if we lived north," they would say: keeping them decently clean was hard. "It looks like our luck won't never let up
10 on us," said Mr. Whipple, but Mrs. Whipple was all for taking what was sent and calling it good, anyhow when the neighbors were in earshot. "Don't ever let a soul hear us com-
15 plain," she kept saying to her husband. She couldn't stand to be pitied. "No, not if it comes to it that we have to live in a wagon and pick cotton around the country," she said,
20 "nobody's going to get a chance to look down on us."
    Mrs. Whipple loved her second son, the simple-minded one, better than she loved the other two chil-
25 dren put together. She was forever saying so, and when she talked with certain of her neighbors, she would even throw in her husband and her mother for good measure.
30   "You needn't keep on saying it around," said Mr. Whipple, "you'll make people think nobody else has any feelings about Him but you."

    "It's natural for a mother," Mrs.
35 Whipple would remind him. "You know yourself it's more natural for a mother to be that way. People don't expect so much of fathers, some way."
40   This didn't keep the neighbors from talking plainly among themselves. "A Lord's pure mercy if He should die," they said. "It's the sins of the fathers," they agreed among
45 themselves. "There's bad blood and bad doings somewhere, you can bet on that." This behind the Whipples' backs. To their faces everybody said, "He's not so bad off. He'll be all
50 right yet. Look how He grows!"
    Mrs. Whipple hated to talk about it, she tried to keep her mind off it, but every time anybody set foot in the house, the subject always
55 came up, and she had to talk about Him first, before she could get on to anything else. It seemed to ease her mind. "I wouldn't have anything happen to Him for all the world, but
60 it just looks like I can't keep Him out of mischief. He's so strong and active, He's always into everything; He was like that since He could walk. It's actually funny sometimes, the
65 way He can do anything; it's laughable to see Him up to His tricks."

    —Katherine Anne Porter, excerpted from "He," 1935

22. The second son suffers from

    (1) a dangerous blood disease
    (2) stunted growth
    (3) the effects of malnutrition
    (4) a severe learning disability
    (5) a crippling muscular disorder

23. Which of the following phrases best describes the Whipple family?

    (1) poor and struggling
    (2) isolated and feared
    (3) popular and admired
    (4) arrogant and conceited
    (5) open and honest

24. You learn about the Whipple family mainly through

    (1) descriptions made by the person telling the story
    (2) Mrs. Whipple's unspoken thoughts
    (3) dialogue between the Whipples and their neighbors
    (4) Mr. Whipple's comments to the reader
    (5) the interaction between the parents and their children

25. Mrs. Whipple fears that

    (1) she will have to become a migrant farm worker to earn a living
    (2) the second son's problems are God's punishment for being sinful
    (3) her husband and children think she doesn't love them
    (4) her family is angry with her for complaining too much
    (5) the neighbors might look down on her and the rest of the family

26. Imagine that you are planning to make a film version of the excerpt. Which of the following places would make the best setting for the story?

    (1) an urban neighborhood of high-rise apartments
    (2) a wealthy resort community in the mountains
    (3) a white-collar suburb of a large eastern city
    (4) an oceanside retirement village on the west coast
    (5) a small town in a southern state

27. That the Whipples refer to their second son as "He" instead of by name shows that they

    (1) think of the child as someone important
    (2) did not give much thought to their children's names
    (3) do not want the child to know when they are talking about him
    (4) view the child as different from their other children
    (5) want to draw people's attention to the child

Questions 28–30 refer to the following poem.

DID THESE FORMER CLASSMATES ENJOY THEIR REUNION?

25th High School Reunion

We come to hear the endings
of all the stories
in our anthology
of false starts:
5 how the girl who seemed
as hard as nails
was hammered into shape;
how the athletes ran
out of races;
10 how under the skin
our skulls rise
to the surface
like rocks in the bed
of a drying stream.
15 Look! We have all
turned into
ourselves.

—Linda Pastan, 1978

28. According to the speaker in the poem, the former classmates attend their twenty-fifth high school reunion to

(1) see what kind of physical shape everyone is in
(2) find out how people's lives have turned out
(3) reminisce about their school experiences
(4) cheer on the school's former athletic stars
(5) compare how much they all have aged

29. What is the meaning of the following comparison "under the skin / our skulls rise / to the surface / like rocks in the bed / of a drying stream" (lines 10–14)?

(1) The former students' facial features are as sharp and pointed as the rocks a person might find in a stream.
(2) Rocks that are located beneath the surface of a stream become visible when the water dries up.
(3) Just as rocks become prominent when a stream begins to dry up, so the skulls of the ex-classmates have become more prominent with age.
(4) The once-young students are now as old and shriveled as a stream that is losing its water supply.
(5) The manner in which the sun has dried out the skin of the former classmates is similar to the manner in which the sun dries out rocks in a stream.

30. The language used in the poem might best be described as

(1) flowery and poetic
(2) complex and hard to understand
(3) formal and scholarly
(4) unusual and original
(5) simple and conversational

Questions 31–34 refer to the following excerpt from a play.

DO THIS MOTHER AND SON SHARE IN THE AMERICAN DREAM?

DOLORES: I'll never be okay until I go home again.

JAVIER: [*Crossing to chair*]: Oh Mom . . .

5　DOLORES: What's wrong with you? The first sky you saw was a Puerto Rican sky. Your first drink of water was Puerto Rican water. But you don't re-
10　member. You were just a baby! But I remember. Son, I want to see chickens run across my yard, all year round. I want to hear my language spoken by
15　everyone I meet, even little children. Spanish is so beautiful when children speak it. I left everything I cared about when I left Puerto Rico.

20　JAVIER: Hasn't this ever been home?

DOLORES: Never. This place has never been any good to any of us—

25　JAVIER: It's been good to me. I think I can go far here. [*He crosses to Dolores and takes her hand.*]

DOLORES: I don't doubt that for a moment. But Ramon is not
30　you.

JAVIER: Is that why you can't accept this as your home?

DOLORES [*Crosses to her altar*]: This "home" took away my lit-
35　tle girl . . .

JAVIER: Mom, you've got to let her go. You've got to bury her. You can't blame this house for—

DOLORES: Yes I can!

40　JAVIER: It would have happened down there. She would have died down there—

DOLORES: For six days she lived here! This cold house killed her!

45

JAVIER: She was born sickly, Mom; anything could've—

DOLORES: She was strong. I could feel how strong she was. I

50 could feel it in her hands. I could see it in her busy, red face. I heard it when she cried. [*Trying not to cry*] I came to her. I warmed her. I held her

55 against me, keeping her from the cold air in this dying house. For six days Ramon worked on the furnace, trying to make it start, but it wouldn't start. One

60 day, as I was making the coffee, while Ramon was at work, she died. I . . . stood by that window for a whole day, facing Puerto Rico. And poor Ramon.

65 He almost went crazy. [*She starts to cry openly.*]

JAVIER: Oh Mom, don't do that.

—Jose Rivera, excerpted from *The House of Ramon Iglesia*, 1983

31. In the excerpt, Dolores is experiencing an inner conflict, or psychological struggle, over the

(1) negative attitude her son has developed toward his new home
(2) difficulty of speaking Spanish in an English-speaking community
(3) difference between life in Puerto Rico and life in the United States
(4) inability of her husband, Ramon, to find a job with a future
(5) family's move to a chicken farm in a Hispanic community

32. Dolores blames her daughter's death on

(1) Ramon
(2) a birth defect
(3) Javier
(4) the cold air
(5) dirty water

33. Read the stage directions for the character of Javier in line 3 and lines 26–27. The character's actions and his conversation with Dolores reveal him to be

(1) nervous
(2) explosive
(3) rigid
(4) shy
(5) caring

34. How does Javier feel about his future?

(1) confident
(2) worried
(3) depressed
(4) angry
(5) confused

Questions 35–40 refer to the following excerpt from a review of a play.

WHAT IS THE PLAY ABOUT?

Fifty years ago, a struggle erupted in Munich that sadly seems timely today also: Five brave university students published and distrib-
5 uted throughout Germany and Austria anonymous anti-Nazi leaflets entitled "The White Rose." Their propaganda was a rare public act of defiance against the vicious Third
10 Reich.

Arrested by the Gestapo on February 22, 1943, the freedom fighters of the White Rose were quickly put on trial for high treason and
15 denied the defense of a jury, press coverage or the opportunity to appeal. The punishment was grimly predictable.

Honoring these young idealists
20 and chronicling the moral struggle
of the security officer who must decide their fate, "The White Rose," . . .
written by Lillian Garrett-Groag, . . .
is inspired in part by the experience
25 of the playwright's father, an Aus-
trian who fled Vienna in 1938 to
avoid the Nazis' takeover.

Even more relevantly, the play
reminds us how history can repeat
30 itself, as in the recent resurgence of
neo-Nazi intolerance at home and
abroad.

Director Russell Vanden-
broucke believes that this history
35 play speaks to the present. "The
playwright uses the story not so
much to talk about the kids, who
were educated and cultured idealists, but about the man in whose
40 hands their fate lies. Unlike many
today, they put their ideas to action
and they had the audacity to believe
the things their teachers taught
them about free thinking and
45 justice.

"What's hard is for the audience
to see themselves, not in these cou-
rageous students, but in the police-
man, a man who is also forced to
50 take a stand. In reality, the Gestapo
officer gave Sophie Scholl, a member of the White Rose, a chance to
escape; she refused."

—Lawrence Bommer,
" 'White Rose' Celebrates Anti-Nazi
Heroes," *Chicago Tribune*,
March 5, 1993

35. According to the excerpt, the
playwright was inspired to write
The White Rose as a result of her

(1) arrest by the Gestapo in
Nazi Germany
(2) experiences as a World War II
journalist in Munich
(3) father's escape from the Nazis
in Vienna
(4) friendship with anti-Nazi
artists in Berlin
(5) participation in the trial of
freedom fighters in Austria

36. The white rose of the play's title
refers to

(1) the main character of the play
(2) a group of students and the
leaflets they published
(3) the European village where
the play takes place
(4) a German officer and his
special force of soldiers
(5) the flower the townspeople
presented to their slain leader

37. The primary purpose of the first
three paragraphs of the excerpt
is to

(1) let readers know whether the
play is worth seeing
(2) give background information
about events dramatized in
the play
(3) publicize the play and
generate interest in seeing it
(4) summarize the content of the
first act of the play
(5) describe the strengths and
weaknesses of the play's plot

38. According to the excerpt, on
which of the following aspects of
the play does the director focus?

(1) the idealism of the upper class
in Germany
(2) Sophie Scholl's refusal
to escape
(3) neo-Nazism in the United
States and Europe
(4) the difficult moral decision
made by the Gestapo officer
(5) the punishment that the
government inflicted on
its enemies

39. The central situation of the play is similar to which of the following more recent world events? The

(1) Chinese government's execution of young people who protested in Tiananmen Square for government reform

(2) disbanding of the Union of Soviet Socialist Republics (U.S.S.R.) after the collapse of the communist government

(3) United Nations relief mission into Somalia to maintain order and distribute food and medical supplies

(4) conflict between people of different ethnic groups in the formerly communist state of Yugoslavia

(5) trial and acquittal in Israel of "Ivan the Terrible," a retired autoworker accused of murdering prisoners in a Nazi death camp

40. The reviewer's writing style is characterized by the

(1) reliance on slang and other informal language

(2) lack of description and other vivid words

(3) development of a bitter, negative tone

(4) use of long, flowing sentences

(5) large number of witty puns

Questions 41–45 refer to the following excerpt from a book review.

WHAT IS THE BOOK *IN MY PLACE* ABOUT?

[Charlayne] Hunter-Gault, now a well-known television correspondent, was one of the two black students whose entrance to the University of Georgia in 1961 desegregated that institution—with much national attention and local uproar. Her graceful and unpretentious memoir, however, is concerned less with that civil-rights triumph than with what it was like to grow up as the daughter of a distinguished dynasty of preachers in a generally self-sufficient minority community. The Hunters were not poor—her father was an Army chaplain—and unpleasant collisions with neighboring whites were either unknown or have been omitted. The brick-throwing that greeted the author at the university is described without rancor, as her commitment to the cause of civil rights is described without heat. One learns about segregated schools (poor equipment, dedicated teachers), visits to farming relatives with lavish tables, prom dresses, and Ms. Hunter-Gault's early addiction to journalism by way of the *Brenda Starr* comic strip. Most of these amiable recollections—including the compulsory home-economics class in which she learned "how to make white sauce"—parallel white experience. Perhaps the implication of similarity was precisely Ms. Hunter-Gault's intention. It is only in the book's final chapter, containing her address to the graduating class of 1988 at the University of Georgia, that she speaks bluntly of the need for "acknowledging the guiding principles of fundamental human decency and then living by them" in "a waiting and needful world."

—Review of *In My Place*, *The Atlantic*, December 1992

41. According to the review, Hunter-Gault grew up

(1) on a prosperous farm
(2) near a university campus
(3) by the ocean
(4) in a poor neighborhood
(5) in a minority community

42. Hunter-Gault was a victim of racism when she

(1) went to her father's church
(2) visited relatives who farmed
(3) enrolled at the University of Georgia
(4) walked into her home economics class
(5) spoke at a graduation ceremony

43. Hunter-Gault might describe her childhood as

(1) happy
(2) violent
(3) insecure
(4) tragic
(5) lonely

44. Most of the review focuses on

(1) persuading readers that Hunter-Gault's book is badly written
(2) making suggestions on how the book might be improved
(3) pointing out and correcting factual errors in the book
(4) giving an overview of the contents of the book
(5) providing background information on Hunter-Gault's TV career

45. According to the review, Hunter-Gault's book consists mainly of

(1) her impressions of what it was like to grow up in her family and community
(2) an explanation of how the civil rights movement developed in the United States
(3) her recollections of racist acts committed by whites in her neighborhood
(4) an account of the profound difference between black and white life experiences
(5) her descriptions of life as the first African-American TV anchor

Answers begin on page 911.

PRACTICE TEST 4: LITERATURE AND THE ARTS ANSWER KEY

1. (1) In lines 14–18, the author says, "Any listener could have asked me: if things were so grand in San Francisco, what had brought me back to a dusty mote of Arkansas?"

2. (3) The author states in lines 7–9, "a pretension to worldliness was expected of me, and I was too happy to disappoint."

3. (2) The author refers to the town as "a dusty mote" and makes reference to "Southern rural blacks," and all the people in the town seem to know each other.

4. (4) In the last sentence of the excerpt, the author states that she was "flattered to receive such acceptance."

5. (5) Just before quoting the conversation, the author says, "the farmers acknowledged my maturity" and "found subtler ways to make their wants known." The conversation illustrates the subtler, more polite ways. In addition, the author says directly after the conversation, "I had seen the formality of black adult equals all my youth but had never considered that a time would come when I, too, could participate." This statement sums up the purpose of the conversation—to show proper etiquette among adults in her community.

6. (3) The excerpt states that in the value system of rural southern African-Americans, "age has more worth than wealth, and religious piety more value than beauty" (lines 49–51).

7. (5) Lines 4–5 state that Casey expects to become a first baseman for the Red Sox.

8. (3) According to line 30, "baseball cards clog her [Casey's] room."

9. (1) Throughout the excerpt, the author gives examples of women's and girls' participation in baseball. She mentions female sportswriters, fans, and a bat girl.

10. (4) In lines 30–37, the author says, "At spring training batting practice . . . I look down at the crowd of kids. Half of them are girls. This is new." The final sentence gives a specific example of another new development—the traditionally male job of bat boy now being filled by a female.

11. (1) Throughout the excerpt, the author is supportive of her daughter's and other females' interest in baseball.

12. (2) Lines 5–6 state that the house is empty.

13. (4) Details are arranged chronologically. At the beginning of the excerpt, it is 7:00 in the morning. The next major actions occur at 7:09, 8:01, and 8:30.

14. (5) Note the repetition of the words *empty* and *emptiness* and descriptions such as the following: "the rain tapped on the empty house, echoing" (lines 37–38).

15. (3) Given the number of electronic-voice messages that remind the family of important dates (a birthday, an anniversary, payments due), one can infer that the family valued being well organized.

16. (1) The excerpt is primarily about the interaction of people and technology of the future—more specifically, the absurdity of technology divorced from humanity.

17. (2) In lines 9–11, the son says, "His secretary wrote to say that he would meet me."

18. (3) The son expresses happiness when he says, "He was a big, good-looking man, and I was terribly happy to see him again" (lines 23–25). The son expresses pride when he says, "I hoped that someone would see us together. I wished that we could be photographed. I wanted some record of our having been together" (lines 37–41).

19. (3) In lines 17–19, the son says, "as soon as I saw him I felt that he was . . . my future and my doom." The use of the word *doom* indicates that the son expects to display some of the same weaknesses or failings as his father.

20. (2) Had the father and son shared a close relationship, it is likely that they would have met in a more intimate setting. The psychological distance between the two characters is underscored by the fact that they meet in a train station—an impersonal place where strangers sit side-by-side without communicating.

21. (2) The father's life appears to revolve around his job.

22. (4) Line 23 states that the son is "simple-minded," an old-fashioned way of saying that the child has a severe learning disability.

23. (1) According to the first two sentences of the excerpt, "Life was very hard for the Whipples. It was hard to feed all the hungry mouths, it was hard to keep the children in flannels during the winter, short as it was. . . ."

24. (1) Throughout the excerpt, the narrator, or person telling the story, describes what the Whipples are like. Note, for example, the first two sentences of the excerpt, all of the second paragraph, and the first two sentences of the last paragraph.

25. (5) Lines 10–17 state that "Mrs. Whipple was all for taking what was sent and calling it good, anyhow when the neighbors were in earshot. . . . She couldn't stand to be pitied."

26. (5) According to the excerpt, the story takes place in a location where the winters are short (line 5) and it is possible to pick cotton for a living (lines 18–19). These details point to a small southern town.

27. (4) By referring to the child only by pronoun, the parents set him apart from their other children.

28. (2) In the first two lines of the poem, the speaker says, "We come to hear the endings / of all the stories."

29. (3) This complex comparison rests on two analogies. The first similarity is between a stream that is drying up and an aging person whose life is "drying up." The second similarity is between rocks jutting out from a stream that is drying out and the increasing prominence of the facial bones of a person who is aging. Note that all the comparisons in the poem develop the idea of people changing and "turning into themselves" over the course of time.

30. (5) Typical of the poem's language is the vocabulary of the last three lines—"Look! We have all / turned into / ourselves." Note that the vocabulary in these lines is commonplace, easy to understand, and could be heard in an informal conversation between friends.

31. (3) Dolores's inner conflict is expressed in the first line of the excerpt—"I'll never be okay until I go home again."

32. (4) In lines 44–45, Dolores says, "This cold house killed her!"

33. (5) Javier shows a caring attitude toward his mother when he crosses the room to be closer to her, takes her hand in his, and tries to calm her by saying, "Oh Mom, don't do that."

34. (1) Javier displays confidence in his future when he says, "I think I can go far here" (lines 25–26).

35. (3) Lines 24–27 explain that the playwright was inspired to write the play because her father had fled Vienna to escape the Nazi takeover.

36. (2) The first sentence of the excerpt refers to the anti-Nazi leaflets as "The White Rose." Later, in lines 51–52, the reviewer quotes the director of the play as saying that Sophie Scholl was "a member of the White Rose." His statement indicates that the group of student freedom fighters took its name from the leaflets it published.

37. (2) Because the play is based on actual incidents involving people who are not well known, the reviewer needs to provide background information at the beginning of the review.

38. (4) In lines 35–40, the reviewer states, "The playwright uses the story not so much to talk about the kids, who were educated and cultured idealists, but about the [Gestapo officer] in whose hands their fate lies."

39. (1) In each incident—that which involved the White Rose and that which took place in Tiananmen Square—university students were executed for protesting against a government that they viewed as immoral.

40. (4) The sentence structure of the review tends to be sophisticated. Most of the sentences are complex, and even simple sentences contain many qualifying phrases.

41. (5) Line 14 states that Hunter-Gault grew up in a "self-sufficient minority community."

42. (3) The first sentence of the excerpt refers to Hunter-Gault's enrollment in the University of Georgia and the part she played in desegregating the school. Lines 19–21 mention that campus racists threw bricks at Hunter-Gault.

43. (1) The anecdotes that Hunter-Gault chose to include—recollections of attending dinners at relatives' farms, shopping for prom dresses, and reading newspaper comic strips—exemplify a happy and normal childhood. Note that the reviewer characterizes Hunter-Gault's recollections as "amiable" (line 31).

44. (4) The excerpt is primarily informational, focusing on the content of the book rather than on criticism. Note that the reviewer never makes mention of the quality of the writing or of the strengths and weaknesses of the book.

45. (1) The second sentence of the excerpt says, "[Hunter-Gault's] memoir . . . is concerned less with that civil-rights triumph [the desegregation of the University of Georgia] than with what it was like to grow up as the daughter of a distinguished dynasty of preachers in a generally self-sufficient minority community."

Use the answer key on pages 911–913 to check your answers to the Practice Test. Then find the item number of each question you missed and circle it on the chart below to determine the reading skill and content areas in which you need more practice. Pay particular attention to areas where you missed half or more of the questions. The reading skills are covered on pages 187–243. The page numbers for the content areas are listed below on the chart. Knowledge of reading skill and content area–based questions is absolutely essential for success on the GED Literature and the Arts Test. For those questions that you missed, review the pages indicated.

PRACTICE TEST 4: LITERATURE AND THE ARTS EVALUATION CHART

Skill Area/ Content Area	Comprehension (pages 189–195)	Application (pages 195–199)	Analysis (pages 200–210)
Prose Fiction (pages 453–482)	12, 15, 17, 18, 19, 20, 22, 23, 25, 27	16, 21, 26	13, 14, 24
Poetry (pages 483–502)	28		29, 30
Drama (pages 503–518)	31, 32, 34		33
Nonfiction Prose (pages 519–536)	1, 2, 3, 4, 7, 8, 9	6, 11	5, 10
Commentaries (pages 537–546)	35, 36, 38, 41, 42, 43, 44, 45	39	37, 40

PRACTICE TEST 5: MATHEMATICS

The Mathematics Practice Test will give you the opportunity to evaluate your readiness for the actual GED Mathematics Test.

The test contains 56 questions and should take approximately 90 minutes to complete. At the end of 90 minutes, stop and mark your place. Then finish the test. This will give you an idea of whether or not you can finish the real GED Test in the time allotted. Try to answer as many questions as you can. A blank will count as a wrong answer, so make a reasonable guess for answers to questions you are not sure of.

When you are finished with the test, check your answers and turn to the Evaluation Chart on page 926 and the GED Readiness Worksheet on page 927. Use the chart and worksheet to evaluate whether or not you are ready to take the actual GED Test and, if not, in what areas you need more work.

You may find the formulas on page 815 useful for some of the problems.

PRACTICE TEST 5: MATHEMATICS ANSWER GRID

1 ① ② ③ ④ ⑤	15 ① ② ③ ④ ⑤	29 ① ② ③ ④ ⑤	43 ① ② ③ ④ ⑤
2 ① ② ③ ④ ⑤	16 ① ② ③ ④ ⑤	30 ① ② ③ ④ ⑤	44 ① ② ③ ④ ⑤
3 ① ② ③ ④ ⑤	17 ① ② ③ ④ ⑤	31 ① ② ③ ④ ⑤	45 ① ② ③ ④ ⑤
4 ① ② ③ ④ ⑤	18 ① ② ③ ④ ⑤	32 ① ② ③ ④ ⑤	46 ① ② ③ ④ ⑤
5 ① ② ③ ④ ⑤	19 ① ② ③ ④ ⑤	33 ① ② ③ ④ ⑤	47 ① ② ③ ④ ⑤
6 ① ② ③ ④ ⑤	20 ① ② ③ ④ ⑤	34 ① ② ③ ④ ⑤	48 ① ② ③ ④ ⑤
7 ① ② ③ ④ ⑤	21 ① ② ③ ④ ⑤	35 ① ② ③ ④ ⑤	49 ① ② ③ ④ ⑤
8 ① ② ③ ④ ⑤	22 ① ② ③ ④ ⑤	36 ① ② ③ ④ ⑤	50 ① ② ③ ④ ⑤
9 ① ② ③ ④ ⑤	23 ① ② ③ ④ ⑤	37 ① ② ③ ④ ⑤	51 ① ② ③ ④ ⑤
10 ① ② ③ ④ ⑤	24 ① ② ③ ④ ⑤	38 ① ② ③ ④ ⑤	52 ① ② ③ ④ ⑤
11 ① ② ③ ④ ⑤	25 ① ② ③ ④ ⑤	39 ① ② ③ ④ ⑤	53 ① ② ③ ④ ⑤
12 ① ② ③ ④ ⑤	26 ① ② ③ ④ ⑤	40 ① ② ③ ④ ⑤	54 ① ② ③ ④ ⑤
13 ① ② ③ ④ ⑤	27 ① ② ③ ④ ⑤	41 ① ② ③ ④ ⑤	55 ① ② ③ ④ ⑤
14 ① ② ③ ④ ⑤	28 ① ② ③ ④ ⑤	42 ① ② ③ ④ ⑤	56 ① ② ③ ④ ⑤

Solve each problem.

1. Compact discs are on sale at Super Sounds for $6.89 each. Which of the following is closest to the price of five discs?

   (1) $25
   (2) $35
   (3) $40
   (4) $45
   (5) $49

2. Gonzalo is a brick mason. Let x stand for the hourly wage he pays his apprentice. Gonzalo makes $5 more than three times the wage of his apprentice. Which of the following expresses Gonzalo's hourly wage?

   (1) $3x + 5$
   (2) $3(x + 5)$
   (3) $3x + 3$
   (4) $x + 5$
   (5) $3x$

3. Assuming no waste, how many boards each $1\frac{1}{2}$ feet long can be cut from a board that is 12 feet long?

   (1) 6
   (2) 8
   (3) 9
   (4) 15
   (5) 18

4. The figure below shows the plan of the living room and the dining room of a house. What is the area in square feet of the floors of both rooms?

   (1) 68
   (2) 140
   (3) 280
   (4) 420
   (5) not enough information is given

5. What is the perimeter of the figure pictured below?

   (1) 20
   (2) 22
   (3) 32
   (4) 40
   (5) 44

6. Each of the four members of the Rodriguez family bought a ticket for a music festival. A total of 360 tickets were sold. If one ticket holder will win the grand prize, what is the probability that the winner will be someone in the Rodriguez family?

(1) $\frac{1}{200}$

(2) $\frac{1}{100}$

(3) $\frac{1}{90}$

(4) $\frac{1}{36}$

(5) $\frac{1}{4}$

7. When Abdul was 20 years old, he weighed 150 pounds. When he was 40, he weighed 180 pounds. By what percent did his weight increase in those years?

(1) 10
(2) 20
(3) 30
(4) $33\frac{1}{3}$
(5) 40

8. If $3m + 6 = 30$, what is the value of m?

(1) 4
(2) 6
(3) 8
(4) 10
(5) 12

9. In a recent year, 327,000 Americans were employed as fire fighters. What is this number rounded to the nearest 10,000?

(1) 320,000
(2) 325,000
(3) 327,000
(4) 328,000
(5) 330,000

Use the following information to answer questions 10 and 11.

A man's shirt is listed in a catalog for $30. Below is a list of prices for the same shirt at several stores.

Clyde's Clothes	$24
Sam's Supply	$32
Florence's Fashion	$33
Dave's Duds	$27
Alma's Apparel	$35

10. For which store is the price of the shirt *10% less* than the catalog price?

(1) Clyde's Clothes
(2) Sam's Supply
(3) Florence's Fashion
(4) Dave's Duds
(5) Alma's Apparel

11. For a Labor Day sale, Florence's Fashion has all clothes marked $\frac{1}{3}$ off the regular price. What will be the price of the shirt during the sale?

(1) $11
(2) $22
(3) $27
(4) $30
(5) $32

12. Below is a plan of a rectangular vegetable garden. Which of the following represents the number of feet of fencing required to enclose the garden?

40 ft

(1) 40×15
(2) $40 + 15$
(3) $2(40) + 15$
(4) $(40 + 15)^2$
(5) $2(40) + 2(15)$

13. What is the value of $20^2 + 2^3$?

    (1) 46
    (2) 48
    (3) 392
    (4) 408
    (5) 484

14. What is the ratio of the width to the height of the door illustrated below?

27 in

81 in

    (1) 2:3
    (2) 1:2
    (3) 1:3
    (4) 2:7
    (5) 1:8

15. For the rectangle pictured below, which side is parallel to AB?

    (1) AC
    (2) AD
    (3) BC
    (4) BD
    (5) CD

The graph below shows the percent of the U.S. population living in each of the four major areas in the continental United States. Use the graph to answer questions 16 and 17.

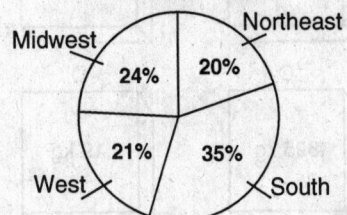

**DISTRIBUTION OF
U.S. POPULATION**

Midwest   Northeast
24%   20%
21%   35%
West   South

16. What fraction of the population lives in the South?

    (1) $\frac{1}{5}$
    (2) $\frac{1}{4}$
    (3) $\frac{1}{3}$
    (4) $\frac{7}{20}$
    (5) $\frac{13}{20}$

17. The population of the United States is about 250,000,000. Approximately how many people live in the Northeast?

    (1) 15 million
    (2) 20 million
    (3) 25 million
    (4) 35 million
    (5) 50 million

18. Arrange the packages pictured below in order from *lightest to heaviest*.

(1) A, D, C, B
(2) D, B, C, A
(3) B, D, C, A
(4) A, B, D, C
(5) B, A, C, D

Use the figure below to answer questions 19 and 20.

19. What is the distance between *P* and *R*?

(1) 1
(2) 2
(3) 3
(4) 4
(5) 5

20. What is the distance between *P* and *Q*?

(1) 3
(2) $\sqrt{3^2 + 3^2}$
(3) 5
(4) 3^2
(5) 5^2

21. If $4n - 9 = 31$, then

(1) $n = 4$
(2) $n = 5$
(3) $n = 8$
(4) $n = 10$
(5) $n = 12$

22. The figure below shows the plan of a pool. Which of the following is closest in feet to the distance around the pool?

(1) 1.57
(2) 15.7
(3) 157
(4) 314
(5) 1963

Use the following information to answer questions 23–25.

The Martins bought a house that cost $80,000. They made a down payment of $12,000. They will have to pay $420 a month in mortgage payments and $700 a year in real estate taxes.

23. The down payment was what percent of the total cost of the house?

(1) 9
(2) 10
(3) 12
(4) 15
(5) 20

24. Which expression represents the Martins' yearly mortgage payments and real estate taxes?

(1) $\frac{\$420}{12}$
(2) $\frac{\$700}{12}$
(3) 12($420)
(4) 12($700)
(5) 12($420) + $700

25. The difference between the total cost of the house and the down payment is the amount of the mortgage. How much is their mortgage?

(1) $63,000
(2) $68,000
(3) $73,000
(4) $85,000
(5) $92,000

---

26. A team can assemble 15 machine parts in two hours. How many parts can it assemble in a 40-hour workweek?

(1) 180
(2) 200
(3) 240
(4) 300
(5) 360

27. What is the diagonal distance *JL* for the rectangle pictured below?

(1) 30
(2) 40
(3) 50
(4) 60
(5) 70

28. Find the distance in meters around a monument whose base is a square measuring 4.5 meters on each side.

(1) 4(4.5)
(2) $\frac{2.5}{2}$
(3) 2(4.5)
(4) $(4.5)^2$
(5) 4.5 + 4.5

29. The Greek letter π (pi) is defined as the ratio of the circumference (*C*) divided by the diameter (*d*) of a circle. Which of the following represents π?

(1) $\frac{C}{d}$
(2) $\frac{(C + d)}{2}$
(3) $\frac{d}{C}$
(4) $\frac{Cd}{2}$
(5) $\frac{(C - d)}{2}$

30. Which of the following represents the volume in cubic inches of the rectangular box pictured below?

(1) 12 × 8
(2) 12 + 8
(3) 12 × 8 × 6
(4) 2(12 + 8)
(5) 6(8 + 12)

31. If $12a - 5 = 4a + 11$, then $a =$

(1) 2
(2) 3
(3) 5
(4) 8
(5) 12

32. The choices below list the price of an 8-ounce package of fish sticks at five different stores. Which is least expensive?

(1) 2 for $3
(2) $1.29 each
(3) 10 for $9
(4) $4.49 for 4
(5) $3.99 for 3

33. The expression $3a - 12$ is the same as which of the following?

    (1) $3(a - 4)$
    (2) $3(a - 12)$
    (3) $12(a - 3)$
    (4) $3(4a)$
    (5) $3a(12)$

34. Find the number of degrees in $\angle C$ of the triangle pictured below.

    (1) 25
    (2) 35
    (3) 60
    (4) 70
    (5) 90

Use the number line below to answer question 35.

35. How many units apart are points A and B?

    (1) 2
    (2) 5
    (3) 7
    (4) 12
    (5) 35

36. If $y = 2x - 5$, what is the value of y when $x = 3$?

    (1) -1
    (2) 0
    (3) 1
    (4) 3
    (5) 7

37. Which of the following equals $(1.5)^2$?

    (1) .75
    (2) 2.25
    (3) 3
    (4) 4.5
    (5) 15

38. Which of the following represents the area of the figure below?

    (1) $2 \times 13 \times 7$

    (2) 13×7

    (3) $2(13) + 2(7)$

    (4) $\frac{1}{2}(13 + 7)$

    (5) $\frac{1}{2} \times 13 \times 7$

39. Giorgos drove for three hours at an average speed of 55 mph and then for another two hours at 40 mph. Which of the following represents the total distance that he drove?

    (1) 5×45

    (2) 5×95

    (3) $55 \times 3 + 2$

    (4) $55 \times 3 + 40 \times 2$

    (5) $\frac{(55 + 40)}{5}$

40. For the figure below, $QR = 120$. What is the length of PQ?

   (1) 15
   (2) 24
   (3) 64
   (4) 75
   (5) 100

41. If $x - 6 > 24$, then

   (1) $x > 4$
   (2) $x > 6$
   (3) $x > 24$
   (4) $x > 28$
   (5) $x > 30$

42. At the rate of $9 an hour, how much does Shirley make in $1\frac{1}{2}$ hours?

   (1) $4.50
   (2) $11.50
   (3) $13.50
   (4) $18
   (5) not enough information is given

43. Find the slope of the line that passes through the two points indicated on the graph below.

   (1) 2
   (2) 3
   (3) 4
   (4) 6
   (5) 7

44. The scale on a map is 1 inch = 60 miles. Two towns are 80 miles apart. Find the distance in inches between the towns on the map.

   (1) $1\frac{1}{3}$
   (2) $1\frac{3}{4}$
   (3) 2
   (4) $2\frac{1}{3}$
   (5) $2\frac{2}{3}$

45. Sam bought 2 brushes for $8 each and 3 gallons of paint for $15 each. Which of the following represents the total dollar cost of the purchases?

   (1) $2(8) + 3(15)$
   (2) $2(15) + 3(8)$
   (3) $5(23)$
   (4) $(2 + 3) \times (8 + 15)$
   (5) $\frac{(2 + 8 + 15)}{3}$

46. The diameter of the cylinder pictured below is 10. What is the volume of the cylinder?

   (1) 10
   (2) 100
   (3) 314
   (4) 3140
   (5) not enough information is given

47. If 7 more than 6 times a number is 19, what is the number?

   (1) 1
   (2) 2
   (3) 3
   (4) 6
   (5) 9

Use the illustration below to answer question 48.

Scale: 1 in = 12 mi

48. What is the distance in miles from Brocton to Lakeview by way of Summit?

(1) 18
(2) 24
(3) 30
(4) 36
(5) 42

---

49. Which of the following expresses "3 less than a number squared?"

(1) $2x - 3$
(2) $x^2 - 3$
(3) $x^3 - 2$
(4) $3x - 2$
(5) $2(x - 3)$

50. Maxine is 20 years older than her daughter Pilar. Let y stand for Maxine's age. Which equation expresses the sum of Maxine's and her daughter's ages if the sum of their ages equals 58?

(1) $y + 20 = 58$
(2) $y - 20 = 58$
(3) $2y - 20 = 58$
(4) $20y = 58$
(5) $\frac{y}{20} = 58$

51. Simplify the expression $7s - 4s$.

(1) $28s$
(2) $11s$
(3) $11s^2$
(4) $3s$
(5) s

Use the graph below to answer questions 52 and 53.

PER-CAPITA CONSUMPTION
OF COFFEE AND SOFT DRINKS
(IN GALLONS)

Key:
Coffee   Soft drinks

52. Approximately how many gallons of coffee were consumed per capita in 1975?

(1) 22
(2) 27
(3) 31
(4) 35
(5) 42

53. By approximately how many gallons did the yearly consumption of soft drinks increase from 1975 to 1990?

(1) 5
(2) 10
(3) 15
(4) 20
(5) 25

54. In a recent year, the U.S. government received $98,000,000,000 in corporate income tax. Which of the following expresses that number in scientific notation?

   (1) 98×10^6
   (2) 9.8×10^6
   (3) 9.8×10^8
   (4) 9.8×10^{10}
   (5) 9.8×10^{12}

55. At a cost of $.90 per linear foot, what is the price of a board that is 78 inches long?

   (1) $4.95
   (2) $5.40
   (3) $5.85
   (4) $7.02
   (5) $7.20

56. Which of the following expresses the relationship among the sides of the figure below?

   (1) $x = 6 + 6$
   (2) $x = 2(6)$
   (3) $x = 2(6) + 2(6)$
   (4) $x = \dfrac{(6+6)}{2}$
   (5) $x^2 = 6^2 + 6^2$

Answers begin on page 924.

PRACTICE TEST 5: MATHEMATICS ANSWER KEY

1. **(2) $35**
$c = nr$
$c = 5 \times \$6.89$
$c = \$34.45$
The closest is $35.
$r = \$6.89 \cong \$7$
$c \cong 5 \times \$7$
$c \cong \$35$

2. **(1) $3x + 5$**

3. **(2) 8**
$12 \div 1\frac{1}{2} =$
$\frac{12}{1} \div \frac{3}{2}$
$\frac{12}{1} \times \frac{2}{3} = \frac{24}{3} = 8$

4. **(5) not enough information is given**
You do not know the width of the dining room.

5. **(3) 32**
$P = a + b + c$
$P = 10 + 10 + 12$
$P = 32$

6. **(3) $\frac{1}{90}$**
$\frac{\text{family members}}{\text{total tickets}} \quad \frac{4}{360} = \frac{1}{90}$

7. **(2) 20%**
180
$- 150$
30
$\frac{30}{150} = \frac{x}{100}$
$150x = 3000$
$x = 20\%$

8. **(3) 8**
$3m + 6 = 30$
$- 6 \quad - 6$
$\frac{3m}{3} = \frac{24}{3}$
$m = 8$

9. **(5) 330,000**
3$\underline{2}$7,000 to the nearest 10,000 is 330,000.

10. **(4) Dave's Duds**
$\frac{x}{\$30} = \frac{10}{100}$
$\$30$
$- \$3$
$\$27$
$100x = \$300$
$x = \$3$

11. **(2) $22**
$\frac{1}{3} \times \frac{33}{1}$
$\$33$
$-\$11$
$\$22$

12. **(5) 2(40) + 2(15)**
$P = 2l + 2w$
$P = 2(40) + 2(15)$

13. **(4) 408**
$20^2 + 2^3 =$
$20 \times 20 + 2 \times 2 \times 2 =$
$400 + 8 = 408$

14. **(3) 1:3**
width:height = 27:81 = 1:3

15. **(5) CD**

16. **(4) $\frac{7}{20}$**
$35\% = \frac{35}{100} = \frac{7}{20}$

17. **(5) 50 million**
$20\% = \frac{1}{5}$
$\frac{1}{5} \times 250,000,000 = 50,000,000$

18. **(3) B, D, C, A**
A = 0.9 = 0.900
B = 0.09 = 0.090
C = 0.895
D = 0.19 = 0.190

19. **(3) 3**
R is 3 units to the right of P.

20. **(2) $\sqrt{3^2 + 3^2}$**
$d = \sqrt{(x_2 - x_1)^2 + (y_2 - y_1)^2}$
$d = \sqrt{(5 - 2)^2 + (5 - 2)^2}$
$d = \sqrt{3^2 + 3^2}$

21. **(4) $n = 10$**
$4n - 9 = \quad 31$
$+ 9 \qquad + 9$
$\frac{4n}{4} = \quad \frac{40}{4}$
$n = \quad 10$

22. **(3) 157**
$C = \pi d$
$C = 3.14 \times 50$
$C = 157$

23. **(4) 15**
$\frac{\$12,000}{\$80,000} = \frac{3}{20}$
$\frac{3}{20} = \frac{x}{100}$
$20x = 300$
$x = 15\%$

24. **(5) 12($420) + $700**

25. **(2) $68,000**
total cost $\qquad \$80,000$
down payment $\quad -\$12,000$
mortgage $\qquad \$68,000$

26. **(4) 300**
$\frac{\text{parts}}{\text{hours}} \quad \frac{15}{2} = \frac{x}{40}$
$2x = 600$
$x = 300$

27. **(3) 50**
$c^2 = a^2 + b^2$
$c^2 = 40^2 + 30^2$
$c^2 = 1600 + 900$
$c = \sqrt{2500}$
$c = 50$

28. **(1) 4(4.5)**
$P = 4s$
$P = 4(4.5)$

29. **(1) $\frac{C}{d}$**

30. **(3) $12 \times 8 \times 6$**
$V = lwh$
$V = 12 \times 8 \times 6$

31. (1) 2

$$12a - 5 = 4a + 11$$
$$\underline{-4a \qquad\qquad -4a}$$
$$8a - 5 = 11$$
$$\underline{+5 \qquad +5}$$
$$\frac{8a}{8} = \frac{16}{8}$$
$$a = 2$$

32. (3) 10 for $9

Choice (1) is $3 ÷ 2 = $1.50 each.
Choice (2) is $1.29 each.
Choice (3) is $9 ÷ 10 = $.90 each.
Choice (4) is $4.49 ÷ 4 = $1.12 each.
Choice (5) is $3.99 ÷ 3 = $1.33 each.

33. (1) $3(a - 4)$

Divide each term by 3:
$3a - 12 = 3(a - 4)$

34. (2) 35

$$105° \qquad\quad 180°$$
$$\underline{+\ 40°} \qquad \underline{-\ 145°}$$
$$145° \qquad\quad 35°$$

35. (4) 12

Point A is 5 units to the left of 0.
Point B is 7 units to the right of 0.
The points are 5 + 7 = 12 units apart.

36. (3) 1

$$y = 2(3) - 5$$
$$y = 6 - 5$$
$$y = 1$$

37. (2) 2.25

$(1.5)^2 = 1.5 \times 1.5 = 2.25$

38. (5) $\frac{1}{2} \times 13 \times 7$

$$A = \tfrac{1}{2}bh$$
$$A = \tfrac{1}{2} \times 13 \times 7$$

39. (4) $55 \times 3 + 40 \times 2$

40. (4) 75

$$\frac{MR}{MN} = \frac{QR}{PQ}$$
$$\frac{8}{5} = \frac{120}{x}$$
$$8x = 600$$
$$x = 75$$

41. (5) $x > 30$

$$x - 6 > 24$$
$$\underline{+6 \qquad +6}$$
$$x > 30$$

42. (3) $13.50

$$1\tfrac{1}{2} \times \$9 =$$
$$\tfrac{3}{2} \times \frac{\$9}{1} = \frac{\$27}{2}$$

43. (1) 2

$$\frac{\text{change in } y}{\text{change in } x} \qquad \frac{6}{3}$$

44. (1) $1\frac{1}{3}$

$$\frac{1}{60} = \frac{x}{80}$$
$$60x = 80$$
$$x = \frac{80}{60} = 1\tfrac{1}{3}$$

45. (1) $2(8) + 3(15)$

46. (5) not enough information is given

You do not know the height of the cylinder.

47. (2) 2

$$6x + 7 = 19$$
$$\underline{-7 \qquad -7}$$
$$\frac{6x}{6} = \frac{12}{6}$$
$$x = 2$$

48. (5) 42

$$2 \qquad\qquad 3\tfrac{1}{2} \times 12 =$$
$$\underline{+\ 1\tfrac{1}{2}} \qquad \frac{7}{2} \times \frac{12}{1} = 42$$
$$3\tfrac{1}{2}$$

49. (2) $x^2 - 3$

50. (3) $2y - 20 = 58$

Maxine = y
Pilar = $y - 20$
sum: $y + y - 20 = 58$
$\qquad\quad 2y - 20 = 58$

51. (4) $3s$

$7s - 4s = 3s$

52. (3) 31

53. (4) 20

$$1990 \qquad 42 \text{ gal}$$
$$1975 \quad \underline{-\ 22}$$
$$20 \text{ gal}$$

54. (4) 9.8×10^{10}

55. (3) $5.85

$$6\tfrac{1}{2} \times \$.90 =$$
$$\frac{13}{2} \times \frac{\$.90}{1} = \$5.85$$

56. (5) $x^2 = 6^2 + 6^2$

$$c^2 = a^2 + b^2$$
$$x^2 = 6^2 + 6^2$$

Use the answer key on pages 924–925 to check your answers to the Practice Test. Then find the item number of each question you missed and circle it on the chart below to determine the mathematics content areas in which you need more practice. Pay particular attention to areas where you missed half or more of the questions. The page numbers for the content areas are listed below on the chart. The numbers in boldface are questions based on graphics. For those questions that you missed, review the pages indicated.

PRACTICE TEST 5: MATHEMATICS EVALUATION CHART

Skill Area/ Content Area	Item Number	Review Pages
Whole Numbers & Problem Solving	1, 9, 25, 26, 32, 39, 44, 45, 48	559–572
Decimals	37, 42, 55	573–586
Fractions	3, 11, **16**	587–604
Ratio & Proportion	**14**	605–610
Percent	7, 10, **17**, 23	611–620
Measurement	**35**	621–636
Graphs, Statistics, & Probability	6, **52**, **53**	637–648
Numeration	**18**, 47	649–656
Geometry	**4**, **5**, **12**, 13, **15**, **22**, **27**, 28, 29, 30, **34**, **38**, **40**, **46**, **56**	657–674
Algebra	2, 8, 19, 20, 21, 24, 31, 33, 36, 41, 43, 49, 50, 51, 54	675–710

GED READINESS WORKSHEET

Congratulations! You have finished the five Practice Tests, checked your answers, and filled out the Evaluation Charts at the end of each test. At this point, it's important to know if you are ready to take the actual GED Tests. Use the chart and the directions below to help you make that decision.

You will use the number of correct answers to estimate what is called your standard score. Every GED examinee's test results are reported as a *standard score*, so it is important to see how your numbers relate to the standard scores.

TEST	Number Correct	STANDARD SCORES									Standard Score	Required Score
		25	**30**	**35**	**40**	**45**	**50**	**55**	**60**	**65**		
Writing Skills	See page 848 for evaluation, and then refer to the Important Note on page 754 for final scoring.											
Social Studies		12	15	20	27	35	44	50	55	58		___ / ___
Science		13	15	20	28	35	43	49	54	57		___ / ___
Literature and the Arts		8	10	15	20	26	32	36	38	40		___ / ___
Mathematics		11	13	18	24	32	39	43	48	50		___ / ___
										Average		

1. **Fill in the number of answers that you got correct** in the column labeled **Number Correct**. Do this for all of the tests except Writing Skills. (Because evaluation of the writing sample makes this test more complicated, consult pages 754 and 848 to determine your readiness for the Writing Skills Test.)

2. **Figure your approximate standard score for each test.** Look across each row and find the number that is closest to your number of correct answers. The number in bold type at the top of that column will be your **Standard Score**.

   For example, Henry got 19 questions right on the Social Studies Test. This is closest to the given number of 20 correct answers. Now look at the top of the column that 20 falls in. This represents a standard score of 35. Henry would fill in 35 as his standard score in Social Studies. On Science, Henry got 37 right. This is closest to the given number of 35, which corresponds to the standard score of 45, so Henry would fill in 45 as his standard score for Science. As this example shows, you may estimate up or down, depending on which given number of correct answers you are closest to.

   Following this example, estimate your standard scores for Tests 2–5.

3. **Compare your standard scores to those required by your state, province, or territory.** There are two scores that you must look at: the *minimum score per test* and the *minimum average score*. To find out the scores required in your area, consult the listing on page 929. Write the minimum and minimum average numbers for your area in the column titled **Required Score**.

Are You Ready?

Here are some guidelines to help you decide whether or not you are ready to take any or all of the GED Tests.

If any of your standard scores are at or below the first minimum score that is given on page 929, you need more review before you take the GED Tests. (In most cases, the minimum score is a 35 or 40.) Any score below the minimum will keep you from passing that test and from getting the average score needed for all of the five tests.

If this is the case, use the Evaluation Charts following each Practice Test to determine which areas of the book you need to study more.

If all of your scores exceed the first minimum score that is given and are around the second score (in most cases this is 45), you are probably ready to take the GED Tests. Some scores can be a little higher and some can be a little lower because the second score given is really an average.

Be sure to consult your evaluation of the Writing Skills Practice Test before making any final decisions.

Remember, if you try the GED Tests and do not pass the first time, you will have the opportunity to study some more and retake all or some of the tests. (See page xvii for advice on this.)

Published by Kaplan Publishing, a division of Kaplan, Inc.
750 Third Avenue
New York, NY 10017

ISBN: 978-1-5062-2330-8
10 9 8 7 6 5 4 3 2

Kaplan Publishing print books are available at special quantity discounts to use for sales promotions, employee premiums, or educational purposes. For more information or to purchase books, please call the Simon & Schuster special sales department at 866-506-1949.

PART TWO: GAME TYPES UNLOCKED

Your Kaplan Resources— Getting Started

HOW TO USE THIS BOOK

Three Keys: Practice, Personalization, and Expertise

Some LSAT prep materials are written to demonstrate the author's mastery of the test, but *Logic Games Unlocked* is designed to build your mastery and raise your score. Empirical evidence makes it clear that the majority of test takers consider the Logic Games section to be the most difficult section on the test. However, it is equally clear that, on average, Kaplan students make their biggest improvements in this section. The three keys to their success are practice, personalization, and expertise, and those keys distinguish Logic Games Unlocked from any other title.

Practice. No matter who you are—no matter your starting point or ultimate goal—practice is the foundation for LSAT mastery. In *Logic Games Unlocked*, you'll find **over 30 real logic games** from officially released LSAT PrepTests (more than in any other Logic Games–specific title available). Each is accompanied by Kaplan's exclusive **"worked example" explanations** that break down each game's setup and all of its questions, step by step. In addition, this book contains **hundreds of exercises** that target all of the skills and strategies you'll learn. In the book's online resources, there are video lessons (The **LSAT Channel Spotlight** features) that highlight special topics and exclusive strategies from some of Kaplan's most highly rated LSAT instructors. Also online, you'll find the **LSAT Logic Games Training Camp** which contains sets of skill-building exercises to help you get sharp and stay sharp with everything you'll learn. In short, everything you need for Logic Games mastery is right here.

Personalization. LSAT logic games are consistent, but LSAT test takers vary. Your strengths, weaknesses, learning style, study time, and motivations are not exactly like anyone else's. *Logic Games Unlocked* was created with that in mind. Every lesson in this book ends with an **assessment** that will help you **evaluate your own, personal performance**, and each assessment is accompanied by **recommendations tailored to your results.** When you knock a particular skill or game type out of the park, the recommendations give you next steps and suggestions for advanced practice. When you run into an area that requires more work, the recommendations guide you to further practice with the fundamentals.

Expertise. In these pages, you'll encounter the knowledge and experience of more than a dozen Kaplan LSAT experts—not only **teachers**, but also **instructional designers** and even **psychometricians,** who analyze the test's design, scoring, and validity. Collectively, this team of top scorers has trained tens of thousands of LSAT test takers, helping them to achieve their goal scores and gain acceptance to the nation's top law schools. They know the LSAT. They know LSAT test takers. Most importantly, **they are now your team**.

The skills tested on the LSAT—including those tested in the Logic Games section—are strongly correlated to your performance in law school. Indeed, they are skills you will use throughout your legal career. This book gives you everything you need to master the Logic Games section, and thus, to get a head start on the reasoning skills you'll use as an attorney. **Welcome to the start of your legal education**.

Take a few minutes to learn how *Logic Games Unlocked* is designed, how you can get the most out of each chapter, and how you can design a study schedule that fits your life as you learn to unlock LSAT logic games.

This Book's Organization

For you to master LSAT logic games, you'll need to learn the skills involved, practice them, and assess your performance on each of them. This book is designed to allow you to take all three of those steps with each of the skills that form the foundation for success on logic games. To make the process as efficient and effective as possible, the book is divided into four sections.

Getting Started

This is where you are right now. Here, you'll learn how to use the book (and its associated online features) to maximize your performance. You'll see how the lessons in this book have been designed by Kaplan's Learning Science and Instructional Design teams to maximize efficacy and retention for every learner. This includes information about how to assess your own performance and personalized recommendations for further practice on each skill. Also included here are three model study schedules, tailored to different lengths of preparation.

Next, you'll find information about how to log into your online Study Plan, what's available there, and how and when to use it. *Logic Games Unlocked* is more than just a book. The LSAT Channel Spotlight features also give you the opportunity to learn from some of our finest instructors, and the LSAT Course Preview includes valuable study and practice resources.

The final portion of the Getting Started material introduces you to the LSAT, and then specifically to the Logic Games section. You'll learn about the test's structure and format, the core skills that it tests, how it's scored, and how law schools use those scores to evaluate applicants. After this, there is a short introduction to the Logic Games section, which includes an LSAT Channel Spotlight lesson on the secrets that Kaplan's expert instructors tell their students who are just beginning their Logic Games preparation. You'll learn more about The LSAT Channel Spotlight lessons in the section of this introduction focused on your online resources.

Part I: Logic Games Method and Strategy

The foundation of success on logic games is the five-step Kaplan Logic Games Method. By mastering the Logic Games Method, you'll learn to handle logic games effectively within the short amount of time provided on the LSAT (four logic games in 35 minutes).

KAPLAN LOGIC GAMES METHOD

- Step 1: Overview—Ask four key questions to assess the game's entities and action(s).
- Step 2: Sketch—Create a simple framework in which to record the game's rules and deductions.
- Step 3: Rules—Analyze and draw the game's explicit rules.
- Step 4: Deductions—Combine the game's rules and restrictions to reveal what must, can, and cannot be true within the game.
- Step 5: Questions—Approach each question strategically to maximize the number of correct answers in the shortest amount of time.

This section has four chapters. Chapter 1 introduces the Logic Games Method and demonstrates how LSAT experts use it to handle full logic games. Chapter 2 goes deeper into Steps 1 and 2, and gives you the opportunity to practice and assess your performance on these Steps. Chapter 3 breaks down Steps 3 and 4, again with ample practice and self-evaluation. Chapter 4 introduces the question types found in the Logic Games section, provides strategies for answering each type, and then allows you to practice and assess with full, officially released LSAT logic games.

There are two more LSAT Channel Spotlight lessons in this part of the book. One, at the end of Chapter 3, focuses on Limited Options, a powerful type of deduction LSAT experts use to simplify and speed up their performance on certain games. The other, at the end of Chapter 4, examines how LSAT experts use previous work to unlock certain LSAT questions quickly and accurately.

Part II: Game Types

In the second part of the book, you'll learn to apply the Logic Games Method to specific game types. This part of the book has seven chapters:

- Chapter 5: Basic Strict Sequencing Games
- Chapter 6: Complex Strict Sequencing Games
- Chapter 7: Loose Sequencing Games
- Chapter 8: Formal Logic and Selection Games
- Chapter 9: Matching and Distribution Games
- Chapter 10: Hybrid Games
- Chapter 11: Rare Games

In each of Chapters 5–10, you'll learn how to identify the game type and how the testmaker introduces variations within the tasks. Then, you'll have the opportunity to practice applying each step of the Logic Games Method to the game type in question. When you're ready, you'll assess your mastery of the game type with full officially released LSAT games. Each chapter ends with recommendations for additional practice on games at three skill levels: Foundations, Mid-Level, and Advanced. Chapter 6 ends with an LSAT Channel Spotlight feature on Circular Sequencing, a rare but challenging variation on this common game type. Chapter 10 ends with an LSAT Channel Spotlight feature on the Dinosaur game, a Hybrid game that some consider the hardest game ever to appear on an officially released LSAT test.

Chapter 8—the chapter covering Selection games—also includes a section with lessons covering everything you need to know to master Formal Logic as it is tested in the LSAT Logic Games section. Formal Logic is tested more comprehensively in the LSAT's Logical Reasoning section, so this section may improve your performance on the LSAT beyond the Logic Games section, as well. The Formal Logic section features an LSAT Channel Spotlight feature on two conditional statements that hold the key to unlocking many Selection games. Even if you're a Formal Logic whiz, this Spotlight will be worth your time.

Chapter 11—on the two rarest game types: Process and Mapping—is shorter than the other chapters in this part of the book. Although you are unlikely to encounter one of these games, understanding their defining features and having practice with officially released examples of each type will give you confidence that there is nothing you could see on Test Day that you aren't familiar with. The LSAT Channel Spotlight in this chapter covers a Process game from December 2016, the first game of these rare types to show up on a released LSAT in more than a decade.

Appendices

At the end of the book, you'll find helpful information collected into a handful of short appendices:

- Appendix I: Logic Games—Timing and Section Management—A short essay filled with tips and strategies LSAT experts use to finish the section faster and to maximize their scores.
- Appendix II: The Countdown to Test Day—Advice about how best to study and practice during the week (and on the day) before your official exam.
- Appendix III: Logic Games Index—A list of every logic game on every officially released LSAC PrepTest, including section, question numbers, and game type.
- Appendix IV: Logic Games Strategies—A quick reference digest covering the Logic Games Method, game types, model sketches, and rules.
- Appendix V: Formal Logic Statements and Translations—A quick reference digest covering conditional statements, contrapositives, and cause-effect relationships.

You'll want to read Appendices I and II after you've done the bulk of your work in this book. Appendix I is especially helpful if you plan to take full-length LSAT tests or complete Logic Games sections as practice in your run-up to Test Day.

The remaining Appendices are there for your reference. Familiarizing yourself with Appendix IV, in particular, may be the best way for you to put your finger on a particular definition or sketch pattern when you need it.

This Book's Instructional Design

"Instructional Design" is a fancy way of talking about how this book helps you learn, practice, and retain skills. In each chapter of this book, you will find one or more lessons, each focused on a specific Learning Objective, or on two or three related objectives. To get the most out of this book, it is helpful for you to become familiar with each piece of a lesson.

Learning Objective

Each Learning Objective is a measurable performance goal that contributes to your mastery of the LSAT Logic Games section. Here's one from Chapter 3:

LEARNING OBJECTIVES

In this section of Chapter 3, you'll learn to

- Analyze and draw logic games rules effectively.

Pay attention to the Learning Objective that forms the basis for the lesson you're in. Logic games are complex, and it is easy to become distracted by an interesting feature of a sample game or question on which you are working. This can lead you off on tangents that take your focus away from the goal of the lesson. Each lesson culminates with a quiz or a series of exercises that allow you to evaluate your performance on the lesson's learning objective. Keep your focus on the "need to know," and don't get caught up in the "nice to know."

Prepare

Accompanying the Learning Objective is the Prepare portion of the lesson. Here, you'll learn the terms, definitions, and concepts you need to know for the lesson. These are often illustrated with relevant examples. Study the Prepare section carefully so that you will be ready to put the strategies and tactics outlined there into practice.

Practice

This portion of the lesson gives you the opportunity to apply what you've learned in context. Practice exercises will range from the analysis and drawing of individual rules all the way up to practice on full games. In the practice sections, work at your own pace, and make your best effort to apply the lesson's skills to the examples at hand. When you have completed a Practice exercise, compare your work to the analysis of Kaplan LSAT experts, always found at the end of the Practice section. Don't merely check to see that you got the correct answer. Read the experts' analyses thoroughly to see their thought processes and to make sure your analysis was as effective and efficient as possible.

Throughout this book—especially in the Practice and Perform portions of lessons—you'll see the analyses of Kaplan LSAT experts depicted in a couple of ways. The first format is called a "worked example," and it provides you with a chance to think along with a Logic Games superstar as he or she approaches all or part of a logic game. Expert analysis is always laid out with the test material in the left-hand column and the expert's thinking immediately to the right or beneath. Where the LSAT is demonstrating more than one step of the Logic Games Method, you'll see the steps in bold to help you train yourself to take the most effective route through the game setup or question.

Here are a few things to be aware of whenever you study expert analyses:

This column contains test material; always read it first, so you know what the expert is analyzing.

In this column, you'll see the LSAT expert's analysis of each part of the test question—here's your coach "thinking out loud" for your benefit.

Analyze the question in the same order as the expert to train yourself in using proven methods on the LSAT.

When studying, the expert will always analyze all of the answer choices—correct and incorrect.

From time to time, you'll have practice exercises in which you'll have the chance to analyze a question. Use the spaces in the right-hand column to record your own analysis. In the answers and explanations, we'll always provide expert analysis so that you can compare your thinking to that of an LSAT expert.

Question 3:

LSAT Question	Analysis

A showroom contains exactly six new cars—T, V, W, X, Y, and Z—each equipped with at least one of the following three options: power windows, leather interior, and sunroof. No car has any other options. The following conditions must apply:

- V has power windows and a sunroof.
- W has power windows and a leather interior.
- W and Y have no options in common.
- X has more options than W.
- V and Z have exactly one option in common.
- T has fewer options than Z.

3. If all the cars that have leather interiors also have power windows, which one of the following must be false?

(A) T has power windows.

(B) T has a sunroof.

(C) V has power windows.

(D) Z has power windows.

(E) Z has a sunroof.

PrepTest35 Sec3 Q8

The format of our expert analyses is the result of work by leading academics in learning science. Merely answering LSAT questions and checking to see whether you got the right answer is fine, but studies indicate that studying expert thinking alongside actual test material produces better results and is a more effective (and faster) way to master LSAT skills. As you complete the questions, don't just check to see if you got them right or wrong. Use each question as an opportunity to better understand the patterns of the test as well as your own strengths and weaknesses.

When you complete full games (as in the Full Game Practice and Perform sections for Chapters 4-11), the worked examples containing the expert analyses will be found in your online resources. These are in PDF files that you can review on your computer, or download and print out, as you prefer.

In other cases—particularly when you are practicing rules and deductions—the exercises are laid out to provide more space for you to record your answers.

Practice 2

Directions: Take a couple of minutes to review the game setup, summarize your Overview analysis, and recreate the initial Sketch. Then, one at a time, analyze the rules, answer the questions about each one, and draw the rule either inside or underneath the sketch framework.

A novelty-item sales representative is tasked with arranging on a shelf six new products—an art kit, a bandanna, a charm bracelet, a disco ball, a pair of earrings, and a fleece pullover—bearing the logo of a popular band. Strict company guidelines dictate that in arranging the items from left to right, one at a time, the sales representative must conform to the following restrictions:

The art kit must be in one of the middle two spaces.
The charm bracelet must be in a space next to one of the end spaces.
The fleece pullover must be two spaces to the left of the disco ball.
The art kit must never be placed immediately to the left of the fleece pullover.
The earrings must be somewhere to the left of the bandanna.

1. [Step 1] Summarize your Overview analysis:

2. [Step 2] Create an initial Sketch:

3. [Step 3] Analyze and draw the Rules:
   - For each rule, answer the following questions and draw the rule in the appropriate box.
     - What does the rule restrict, and what does it leave open?
     - What are the rule's negative implications, if any?
     - Can the rule be depicted inside the sketch framework?

Rule 1:	Rule 4:
Rule 2:	Rule 5:
Rule 3:	

For these exercises, you'll find the expert analysis in italics.

Practice 2

A novelty-item sales representative is tasked with arranging on a shelf six new products—an art kit, a bandanna, a charm bracelet, a disco ball, a pair of earrings, and a fleece pullover—bearing the logo of a popular band. Strict company guidelines dictate that in arranging the items from left to right, one at a time, the sales representative must conform to the following restrictions:

> The art kit must be in one of the middle two spaces.
> The charm bracelet must be in a space next to one of the end spaces.
> The fleece pullover must be two spaces to the left of the disco ball.
> The art kit must never be placed immediately to the left of the fleece pullover.
> The earrings must be somewhere to the left of the bandanna.

1. [Step 1] Summarize your Overview analysis: *A Strict Sequencing game in which a sales rep is placing six items in order from left to right, one per position, along a shelf.*

- Can the rule be depicted inside the sketch framework? *Yes.*
- Draw the rule:

  A B C D E F

- Rule 2:
  - What does the rule restrict, and what does it leave open? *This rule restricts C to one of two positions (slot 2 or slot 5).*
  - What are the rule's negative implications, if any? *Simply that C will not be in slots 1, 3, 4, or 6.*
  - Can the rule be depicted inside the sketch framework? *Yes.*
  - Draw the rule:

    A B C D E F

Perform

In the Perform portion of each lesson, you will put your new skills to the test. Perform exercises look and feel just like those you do in the Practice portion of each lesson, but they come with timing guidelines. Your goal here is not perfection, but valid self-assessment. Do your best under the timing guidelines, and then, when you're done, compare your work to that of a Kaplan LSAT expert. Thorough review is a great learning opportunity, not just to find out what you got right and wrong, but to see how top scorers applied the Logic Games Method and its associated strategies and tactics to maximum effect.

For Chapters 4-11, the answers and explanations for complete game Perform quizzes are found in your online resources. Review them on your computer, or download and print them, as you prefer, but make sure to review them thoroughly.

Assess

Most Perform exercises are followed by specific criteria that you can use to evaluate your performance. For Perform exercises with full LSAT logic games, the assessment criteria will be the number of logic games questions you answered correctly. For Perform exercises that lack a numerical value (such as number correct), the assessment will outline how you should compare your performance to that of an LSAT expert to get a clear perspective on your skill level. Assessments are accompanied by recommended next steps for each level of mastery.

For the assessments accompanying the game-type chapters in Part II, the recommended additional practice refers to games from officially released LSAT tests. Here's the recommended additional practice from Chapter 5:

Recommended Additional Practice: Basic Strict Sequencing

All of the following games will provide good practice on basic Strict Sequencing games. They are grouped by difficulty as determined from empirical student practice results. All PrepTests included are available individually, or in bundles of ten as part of the LSAC's *10 Actual, Official LSAT PrepTests* series.

Foundations
PrepTest 70, Section 3, Game 1: Benefit Concert*

PrepTest 67, Section 3, Game 2: Literary Theory Lectures*

PrepTest 63, Section 2, Game 2: Skydiving Team*

PrepTest 62, Section 3, Game 4: Testifying Witnesses*

PrepTest 57, Section 1, Game 1: Student Activities**

Mid-Level
PrepTest 66, Section 3, Game 2: Shopping Center Businesses*

PrepTest 64, Section 2, Game 1: Employee Parking*

PrepTest 62, Section 3, Game 1: Motel Service Appointments*

PrepTest 56, Section 1, Game 1: Saxophone Auditions**

PrepTest 54, Section 3, Game 3: Cake Layers**

Advanced
PrepTest 71, Section 2, Game 4: Paintings in a Museum*

PrepTest 69, Section 2, Game 1: Manuscript Ages*

PrepTest 63, Section 2, Game 3: Vehicle Service*

PrepTest 59, Section 1, Game 2: Museum Photographs**

PrepTest 59, Section 1, Game 4: Organization's Annual Meetings**

*Game included in *10 Actual, Official LSAT PrepTests Volume V: PrepTests 62-71*; complete answers and explanations written by Kaplan LSAT experts available via the eBook: *LSAT PrepTests 62-71 Unlocked: Exclusive Data, Analysis & Explanations for 10 Actual, Official LSAT PrepTests Volume V.*

**Game included in *10 New Actual, Official LSAT PrepTests with Comparative Reading (PrepTests 52-61)*; complete answers and explanations written by Kaplan LSAT experts available via the eBook: *LSAT PrepTests 52-61 Unlocked: Exclusive Data, Analysis & Explanations for 10 New Actual, Official LSAT PrepTests with Comparative Reading.* [Explanations title coming soon.]

LSAC (the organization that writes and administers the LSAT) sells all released LSATs individually. The games for recommended additional practice, however, can also be found in the two 10-test volumes sold by LSAC mentioned after the recommendations. None of the LSAC PrepTests or 10-test volumes contains explanations. Kaplan offers complete explanations and analyses of those tests in the eBooks listed below the recommendations. Note that the eBook explanations for PrepTests 52-61 are expected to be available in 2018.

Reflect

At the very end of each lesson, you'll see a series of short thought exercises that will keep what you've learned fresh in your mind. Some students find it helpful to write out their answers to make their reflection more concrete. In any case, review the Reflect questions and keep them in mind until you come back to the book for your next lesson.

Model Study Schedules

Logic Games Unlocked is written so that you can, time permitting, start at page 1 and work straight through to the end. Indeed, to the LSAT experts who worked on this book, that would be ideal: take it all in, and absorb everything you can. To do that, you'll need to start your logic games preparation about a month and half (or more) before your official Test Day. Because not every student can start that early (or may not have as much time during the week), the following condensed schedules focus on the material that will likely be the most important to your LSAT score—the fundamental concepts and the most common game types on recent tests.

The following models should be used as a starting point as you design your own study schedule. They are based on the rough assumption that you can dedicate around 10–12 hours per week to logic games preparation. If you have more time, you may be able to finish these plans faster, of course. Be sure to consider other factors—school, work, other LSAT prep, and so on—as you plan your personal roadmap to Logic Games mastery. Note that the weeks count down to Test Day.

Comprehensive (6 weeks or more)

By getting an early start on your Logic Games prep, you will likely have the opportunity to complete the work in this book and additional practice from other sources.

Week 6
Logic Games Unlocked

Getting Started
LSAT Channel Spotlight: Secrets of Logic Games Preparation
Chapter 1: The Logic Games Method
Chapter 2: Logic Game Types and Sketches
Chapter 3: Logic Games Rules and Deductions (up through "How to Interpret and Sketch Rules")
Chapter 8: Formal Logic and Selection Games Unlocked (complete "Formal Logic in LSAT Logic Games")

Online Study Plan

Video: *Getting Started*
LSAT Channel Spotlight Video: *Secrets of Logic Games Preparation*
[If recommended] Quiz: "Game Types and Sketches Fundamentals"
[If recommended] Quiz: "Identifying and Sketching Rules Fundamentals"
[Optional] LSAT Channel lesson: Fundamentals of Formal Logic (found in the LSAT Course Preview)

Additional Practice

None

Week 5
Logic Games Unlocked

Chapter 3: Rules and Deductions (starting with "How to Combine Rules to Make Deductions")
LSAT Channel Spotlight: Limited Options
Chapter 4: Logic Games Questions
LSAT Channel Spotlight: Using Previous Work
Chapter 5: Basic Strict Sequencing Games Unlocked

Online Study Plan

LSAT Channel Spotlight Video: *Limited Options*
LSAT Channel Spotlight Video: *Using Previous Work*
[If recommended] Quiz: "Deductions Fundamentals"
[If recommended] Quiz: "Question Types Fundamentals"

Additional Practice

See "Recommended Additional Practice" for Chapter 5.

Week 4
Logic Games Unlocked

Chapter 6: Complex Strict Sequencing Games Unlocked
[Optional] LSAT Channel Spotlight: Circular Sequencing
Chapter 7: Loose Sequencing Games Unlocked

Online Study Plan

[Optional] LSAT Channel Spotlight video: *Circular Sequencing*

Additional Practice

See "Recommended Additional Practice" for Chapter 6.
See "Recommended Additional Practice" for Chapter 7.

Week 3
Logic Games Unlocked

Chapter 8: Formal Logic and Selection Games Unlocked (If you have already done "Formal Logic in LSAT Logic Games," complete all of the sections on Selection Games)
LSAT Channel Spotlight: Minimum Increasers and Maximum Decreasers
Chapter 9: Matching and Distribution Games Unlocked (up through "Matching Games—Full Games with Questions")

Online Study Plan

LSAT Channel Spotlight video: *Minimum Increasers and Maximum Decreasers*

Additional Practice

See "Recommended Additional Practice" for Chapter 8.
See "Recommended Additional Practice" for Chapter 9 (Matching Games).

Week 2
Logic Games Unlocked

Chapter 9: Matching and Distribution Games Unlocked (complete the sections on Distribution Games)
Chapter 10: Hybrid Games Unlocked
LSAT Channel Spotlight: The Dinosaur Game

<u>Online Study Plan</u>

LSAT Channel Spotlight video: *The Dinosaur Game*

<u>Additional Practice</u>

See "Recommended Additional Practice" for Chapter 9 (Distribution Games).
See "Recommended Additional Practice" for Chapter 10.

Week 1
<u>Logic Games Unlocked</u>

Review Chapters 1-4
Appendix I: Logic Games—Timing and Section Management
Appendix II: The Countdown to Test Day
[Optional] Chapter 11: Rare Games Unlocked—Process and Matching
[Optional] LSAT Channel Spotlight: 2016—The Return of Process

<u>Online Study Plan</u>

[Optional] LSAT Channel Spotlight Video: *2016—The Return of Process*
Timed Practice: Take and review the Logic Games section from PrepTest June 2007 (found in LSAT Course Preview)

<u>Additional Practice</u>

Timed Practice: Take and review at least one more Logic Games section from another officially released PrepTest.

Test Day
Take the LSAT and crush the Logic Games section.

Efficient (4 to 5 weeks)

With about a month until your Test Day, you may be able to complete the entire book, but your time is limited. This schedule will help you be judicious about where to focus your efforts. Work through the chapters and sections in this model schedule first. Then, if you find that you have more time than expected, complete the remaining chapters of the book.

Week 4
<u>Logic Games Unlocked</u>

Getting Started
LSAT Channel Spotlight: Secrets of Logic Games Preparation
Chapter 1: The Logic Games Method
Chapter 2: Logic Game Types and Sketches
Chapter 3: Logic Games Rules and Deductions
LSAT Channel Spotlight: Limited Options

Online Study Plan

Video: *Getting Started*
LSAT Channel Spotlight Video: *Secrets of Logic Games Preparation*
LSAT Channel Spotlight Video: *Limited Options*
[If recommended] Quiz: "Game Types and Sketches Fundamentals"
[If recommended] Quiz: "Identifying and Sketching Rules Fundamentals"
[If recommended] Quiz: "Deductions Fundamentals"

Additional Practice

None

Week 3
Logic Games Unlocked

Chapter 4: Logic Games Questions
LSAT Channel Spotlight: Using Previous Work
Chapter 5: Basic Strict Sequencing Games Unlocked
Chapter 7: Loose Sequencing Games Unlocked

Online Study Plan

LSAT Channel Spotlight Video: *Using Previous Work*
[If recommended] Quiz: "Question Types Fundamentals"

Additional Practice

See "Recommended Additional Practice" for Chapter 5.
See "Recommended Additional Practice" for Chapter 7.

Week 2
Logic Games Unlocked

Chapter 6: Complex Strict Sequencing Games Unlocked
Chapter 9: Matching and Distribution Games Unlocked (read the chapter introduction and "Real-Life Distribution," and then complete the sections on Distribution games)

Online Study Plan

None

Additional Practice

See "Recommended Additional Practice" for Chapter 6.
See "Recommended Additional Practice" for Chapter 9 (Distribution Games).

Week 1

Logic Games Unlocked

[Optional] LSAT Channel Spotlight: Minimum Increasers and Maximum Decreasers (Chapter 8)
Chapter 10: Hybrid Games Unlocked
[Optional] LSAT Channel Spotlight: The Dinosaur Game
Appendix I: Logic Games—Timing and Section Management
Appendix II: The Countdown to Test Day

Online Study Plan

[Optional] LSAT Channel Spotlight video: *Minimum Increasers and Maximum Decreasers*
Timed Practice: Take and review the Logic Games section from PrepTest June 2007 (found in LSAT Course Preview)

Additional Practice

See "Recommended Additional Practice" for Chapter 10.

Test Day
Take the LSAT and crush the Logic Games section.

Last-Minute (2 to 3 weeks)

With just two weeks until Test Day, you will need to make some hard choices. The material outlined in this schedule provides the fundamentals of the Logic Games Method and its associated strategies, and focuses your practice on the game types you are most likely to encounter on Test Day.

Week 2

Logic Games Unlocked

Getting Started
LSAT Channel Spotlight: Secrets of Logic Games Preparation
Chapter 1: The Logic Games Method
Chapter 2: Logic Game Types and Sketches*
Chapter 3: Logic Games Rules and Deductions*
[Optional] LSAT Channel Spotlight: Limited Options
Chapter 4: Logic Games Questions*
*You may need to cut out some or all Practice exercises to complete these chapters.

Online Study Plan

Video: *Getting Started*
LSAT Channel Spotlight Video: *Secrets of Logic Games Preparation*
[Optional] LSAT Channel Spotlight Video: *Limited Options*
[If recommended] Quiz: "Game Types and Sketches Fundamentals"
[If recommended] Quiz: "Identifying and Sketching Rules Fundamentals"
[If recommended] Quiz: "Deductions Fundamentals"

Additional Practice

If time permits more work during this week, you should move on to Chapter 5: Basic Strict Sequencing Games Unlocked. Strict Sequencing is, by far, the most common game type on the LSAT.

Week 1

Logic Games Unlocked

Chapter 5: Basic Strict Sequencing Games Unlocked
Chapter 7: Loose Sequencing Games Unlocked
Chapter 9: Matching and Distribution Games Unlocked (read the chapter introduction and "Real-Life Distribution," and then complete the sections on Distribution games)
Appendix I: Logic Games—Timing and Section Management
Appendix II: The Countdown to Test Day

Online Study Plan

None

Additional Practice

See "Recommended Additional Practice" for Chapter 5.
See "Recommended Additional Practice" for Chapter 7.
See "Recommended Additional Practice" for Chapter 9 (Distribution Games).

The model Last-Minute schedule cuts out a lot of material, but focuses on what you are most likely to see on Test Day, and on the areas in which you can make the greatest impact on your score in a short amount of time.

Note: You can use the LSAT Logic Games Training Camp exercises at any time. They are fast-paced drills designed to hone your skills, and they are done online. Use them to supplement your more intensive study sessions when you're away from your desk, or when you want a quick workout or warmup.

HOW TO USE YOUR ONLINE RESOURCES

Logic Games Unlocked comes with a wealth of online resources. They provide additional instruction, practice, and feedback that will aid your logic games preparation and improve your LSAT score. In this section, you'll learn how to access these resources, what they include, and how to use them.

Log In to Your Online Study Plan

The online Study Plan gives you access to even more Logic Games content and instruction, including The LSAT Channel Spotlight videos.

Register for your Online Center using these simple steps:

1. Go to **kaptest.com/booksonline** and find the appropriate book listed. Click the "Register" button next to it.
2. Enter the password as directed and click on "Next."
3. The Online Center will appear in your shopping cart free of charge. Click "Proceed to checkout" and complete your registration.
4. Once registered, click on the "personalized Student Homepage" link to access your online materials.

Please have your book with you because you will need information from the book to access your account.

Access to the Online Center is limited to the original owner of this book and is nontransferable. Kaplan is not responsible for providing access to the Online Center for customers who purchase or borrow used copies of this book. Access to the Online Center expires one year after you register.

Take a minute to log in now. Get familiar with the contents and organization of the online Study Plan. That way, you'll be ready to use the resources as they come up in your work with this book.

What's In the Online Study Plan

Here's what you have in your online resources:

- Video: Getting Started—Hear from Kaplan's lead instructional designer about how to make the most of your prep with *Logic Games Unlocked*.
- Full-game Perform Quiz explanations—In Chapters 4-11, your self-evaluation will be done on complete officially released LSAT games. There is an answer key in the book that you can use to quickly score your results, but the complete worked examples with in-depth expert analysis are found in your online resources. They are PDF files, so you can review them on your computer, or download and print them, as you prefer.
- LSAT Channel Spotlight videos—Each LSAT Channel Spotlight feature in *Logic Games Unlocked* is accompanied by a video lesson from one or more of Kaplan's top LSAT instructors. The videos present full answers and explanations for logic games found in LSAT Channel Spotlight features in the book. After the title of each video in this list, you'll see the location of the corresponding Spotlight feature in the book:
  - *Secrets of Logic Games Preparation* (Getting Started)
  - *Limited Options* (Chapter 3)
  - *Using Previous Work* (Chapter 4)
  - *Circular Sequencing* (Chapter 6)
  - *Minimum Increasers and Maximum Decreasers* (Chapter 8)
  - *The Dinosaur Game* (Chapter 10)
  - *2016—The Return of Process* (Chapter 11)

- The LSAT Logic Games Training Camp. This is a place for you to hone the skills you're learning in this book. It is made up of sets of fast-paced online drills to give you "reps" on deductions and strategies central to Logic Games mastery. There are Training Camp drills for each of Chapters 2-10, and they are broken up into Foundations, Mid-Level, and Advanced sets to fit your individual strengths and opportunities. Training Camp drills can be done at any time, as a warmup, a refresher, or just to keep you sharp.
- "Fundamentals" quizzes—For Chapters 2–4, each Assessment may recommend that you practice and review an additional quiz on the foundations of each lesson topic.
- LSAT Course Preview—This section contains a variety of resources to familiarize you with everything contained in Kaplan's comprehensive LSAT prep courses. Two of the items are especially relevant to your study and practice with *Logic Games Unlocked*:
  - PrepTest June 2007—This is a full, released LSAT test in PDF format. You can download and print it, and then take the full test for practice, or take just the Logic Games section for timing and section management practice after reading Appendix I on Timing and Section Management. From the same tab in which you access the test PDF, you can launch a webgrid that will score your test and provide access to complete answers and explanations.
  - A full LSAT Channel episode video—"Black Tie Optional: Formal Logic Basics"—that provides an excellent supplement to Chapter 8: Formal Logic and Selection Games Unlocked.

When to Use Your Online Resources

Your online resources are always available. You should watch the "Getting Started" video as soon as possible, along with this section of the book. At the end of this section, you'll find The LSAT Channel Spotlight feature "Secrets of Logic Games Prep," so watch its corresponding video as well. You'll meet The LSAT Channel faculty that deliver the other Spotlight lessons and get valuable tips that these top scorers give their students at the beginning of class.

Other LSAT Channel Spotlight videos correspond to the Spotlight features in the book, so watch them after reading those special sections. As previously mentioned, whenever a Spotlight feature contains a practice logic game, the teacher will give complete answers and explanations in the video, along with unique instruction containing special tips and strategies for attacking the Logic Games section on Test Day.

You will want to review the Full-Game Perform explanations thoroughly after every Perform quiz in Chapters 4 through 11. Studying the expert analyses will not only allow you to understand the right and wrong answers, it will provide a model of efficiency and strategy for you to emulate on test day.

The Logic Games Training Camp drills, on the other hand, can be used at any time. They provide quick, skills-based practice that sharpens and refines your approach to the Logic Games section. Since they are entirely online, you can even do them when you are on the go, or outside of your routine, scheduled study time.

The "Fundamentals" quizzes accompany the Perform exercises and Assessments in Chapters 2–4. If your Assessment recommends any of these quizzes, you should definitely take and review them accordingly. The quizzes provide excellent additional practice for the topics covered in these chapters, so you should feel free to try them out any time you want additional practice.

PrepTest June 2007 (contained in the LSAT Course Preview) is a complete, officially released LSAT test, and like any released PrepTest, it offers authentic LSAT practice. It is not included in any of the 10-test volumes sold as part of the *LSAC's 10 Actual, Official LSAT PrepTests* series. If you have purchased other LSAC-released PrepTests, then the June 2007 exam offers one more opportunity for full-length LSAT practice. If you don't have other official PrepTests as part of your prep library, save PrepTest 2007 until the end of your study with *Logic Games Unlocked* and use it to practice the section management principles outlined in Appendix I: Logic Games—Timing and Section Management. Note: For more information about using *Logic Games Unlocked* in conjunction with LSAC PrepTests, see the comments at the end of the next section.

LOOKING FOR MORE?

Kaplan LSAT Prep Books and Courses

At Kaplan, we're thrilled you've chosen us to help you on your journey to law school. Beyond this book, there's a wealth of additional resources that we invite you to check out. All of them will aid you with your LSAT preparation and your law school application.

- Logic Games Unlocked Complete Prep—Throughout this book, you'll find recommendations for further practice. If you are looking for every official LSAT logic game in one place, look no further. Our new Logic Games Unlocked Complete Prep study program contains every real logic game ever released (over 320 of them), along with complete explanations. Logic Games Unlocked Complete Prep also features dozens of instructional videos and episodes from *The LSAT Channel* to give you comprehensive instruction and practice for the Logic Games section.

- Free events—Take a real, previously released LSAT under proctored conditions, enroll in an LSAT Preview Class, experience what it's like being Inside the Classroom, Inside The LSAT Channel, and more. We host many free live online events each month. Check out our full schedule of upcoming free events at **kaplanlsat.com**.

- Comprehensive LSAT Courses—Of course, we'd be remiss if we did not mention the world's most popular LSAT preparation courses. Visit our website to learn about our comprehensive prep options. Choose from In Person, Live Online, Self-Paced, and Private Tutoring options depending on your needs and learning style. View course options and upcoming class schedules at **kaplanlsat.com**.

- ((⋅))—*The LSAT Channel*—Kaplan's new course feature, The LSAT Channel, features over 100 unique episodes of live, online instruction on every facet of the LSAT by our best teachers. Learn more at **kaplanlsat.com**. You have access to recordings of select LSAT Channel episodes in the Online Center that accompanies this book.

- ⓕ 🐦 YouTube—Facebook, Twitter, YouTube—Kaplan is wherever you are. Like us. Follow us. Subscribe to us. Get regular tips throughout the course of your study.

You have a lot to do. Ready to get started? Let's do this!

Using LSAC PrepTests with *Logic Games Unlocked*

The LSAT is somewhat unique among standardized tests because LSAC (the Law School Admissions Council), the organization that makes and administers the LSAT, releases three official tests to the public every year. Most standardized testing organizations release few, if any, of their official tests.

The LSAC calls their released LSATs "PrepTests," and, at the time that this book went to print, there were over 80 official PrepTests available for students to purchase and use. That's a terrific "library" of practice materials for students prepping for the LSAT—so terrific, in fact, that Kaplan provides access to every released PrepTest to students in our comprehensive LSAT prep courses.

If you are not in one of our comprehensive courses, you may have purchased LSAC PrepTests to take on your own. Logic Games Unlocked is designed for use with LSAC PrepTests, especially with the 20 PrepTests contained in two of LSAC's top-selling books:

10 Actual, Official LSAT PrepTests Volume V: PrepTests 62–71
10 New Actual, Official LSAT PrepTests with Comparative Reading (PrepTests 52–61)

All of the Recommended Additional Practice sections for Chapters 5–10 refer to logic games found in these two volumes. LSAC PrepTests are also available individually.

While LSAC PrepTests contain genuine, released LSAT tests that provide great practice, they do not have explanations or analysis. Complete answers and explanations written by Kaplan LSAT experts are available in two eBook companions to those LSAC volumes:

LSAT PrepTests 62–71 Unlocked: Exclusive Data, Analysis & Explanations for 10 Actual, Official LSAT PrepTests Volume V, and
LSAT PrepTests 52–61 Unlocked: Exclusive Data, Analysis & Explanations for 10 New Actual, Official LSAT PrepTests with Comparative Reading. [This title coming soon.]

If you are using the official PrepTests, we strongly recommend getting the accompanying eBook explanation, so that you can review your work. The explanations match the Logic Games Method and strategies found in *Logic Games Unlocked*, and will reinforce everything you are learning here.

LSAT REASONING AND STRATEGY

Why the LSAT?

You're reading this book because you want to be a law student. Well, your legal education starts now.

Every year, Kaplan surveys the admissions officers from law schools all around the country, and every year, the majority of them tell us that the LSAT is the most important factor in your law school application—more important than GPA, the personal statement, letters of recommendation, and other application requirements. Admissions officers routinely cite poor LSAT scores as the biggest "application killer," and they tell us it is the part of the application that they check first. You may already know how important the LSAT is, but what you may not know is why. The LSAT tests skills relevant to law school and to the practice of law. Moreover, the LSAT is the one factor common to all applications. It levels the playing field for candidates regardless of background. The LSAT doesn't care what you majored in or where you went to school.

The LSAT is probably unlike any other test you've taken in your academic career. Most tests you've encountered in high school and college have been content-based—that is, they required you to recall a certain body of facts, formulas, theorems, or other acquired knowledge. But the LSAT is a skills-based test. It doesn't ask you to repeat memorized facts or to apply learned formulas to specific problems. You will be rewarded for familiarity with patterns that make the LSAT predictable, and ultimately all you'll be asked to do on the LSAT is think—thoroughly, quickly, and strategically. There's no required content to study! Sound too good to be true? Well, before you get the idea that you can skate into the most important test of your life without preparing, consider the skills that you'll need to build. Admissions officers care about your score because the LSAT tests the skills you'll use on a daily basis in law school. It's the best predictor law schools have of the likelihood of your success at their institution.

That begins to explain why law schools value the LSAT so highly. But, even so, why would this test include logic games as a way of evaluating potential law students?

Why Logic Games?

One question that LSAT instructors hear over and over from students is "What in the world do logic games have to do with law school?" It's a good question. The answer is "Quite a bit, actually." But, seeing why that's the case requires us to step back and take a broader look at both law school and the LSAT.

In law school, you'll hear professors tell you that it is their job—the school's job—to teach you "how to think like a lawyer." That's a clever way of saying that, in law school, you learn and practice and refine the *skills* that attorneys use every day. These include logical reasoning skills such as the ability to assess the validity of arguments, to strengthen and weaken those arguments with relevant information, and to determine what can be deduced from a set of facts. Likewise, law school—and the practice of law—requires adept reading comprehension to sort quickly and accurately through dense, lengthy statutes, cases, contracts, and reports. So far, so good, but what does any of that have to do with logic games?

On the surface, logic games are little puzzles about obviously fictional people, places, and things. Sometimes, the scenarios you're given (Mixtapes? Movie studios? Toy dinosaurs???) seem almost whimsical. Even the colloquial name—logic *games*—implies that they're supposed to be fun, and, separated from the pressure and anxiety of the exam, you have to admit that they are fun (at least kind of). All of that masks the fact that logic games test a crucial set of law school skills.

When you look at an officially released LSAT test, notice that the testmaker (LSAC) refers to the Logic Games section as Analytical Reasoning. Already, that sounds more important than playing a "game," but a closer look at the kinds of analysis you do in Analytical Reasoning really tells the story. Logic games always reward the correct application of a set of rules to a situation or pattern, and usually to hypothetical variations on the pattern. Subject matter aside, the notorious Dinosaur Game (discussed in detail following Chapter 10 of this book) is a perfect example. In that game, you are told that, to create a window display, a toy store has to select from several kinds of toy dinosaurs, each in a number of colors. There are six rules about the kinds and colors that the store must choose. Then, the test asks you six questions about what must, can, or cannot be true about the window display. Here are three of them:

13. If the tyrannosaur is not included in the display, then the display must contain each of the following EXCEPT:

14. Which one of the following is a pair of toys that could be included in the display together?

16. If both the iguanadon and the ultrasaur are included in the display, then the display must contain which one of the following?

PrepTest57 Sec1 Qs 13, 14, and 16

In law school, you will be asked to read hundreds of legal cases, statutes, and administrative guidelines. When you come to class, your professors will question you to make sure you accurately distilled the rules of law contained in those cases and documents. (That's the reading comprehension part.) Then, they will grill and test you on the application of those rules to various real and fictional scenarios. In the process of doing that, the professors will present you with "hypotheticals." That is, they will add or change facts in the case and ask you which of the rules are still applicable or how the outcome under the rules might be different. The analytical reasoning skills you'll need for this are quite similar to those you will use to solve logic games. In this section, the LSAT strips away the lengthy passages and gives you the rules directly, so that they can focus on your ability to analyze and apply rules to given patterns. Law schools use your LSAT score to determine how prepared you are for the rigors of legal education, and your ability to quickly and accurately apply complex rule sets to various situations is central to their assessment.

So why would the testmaker use something as trivial (and downright bizarre) as a window display of toy dinosaurs to test this all-important law-school skill? One reason is you, the "collective you" of all law-school applicants. You come from a variety of academic and professional backgrounds, from English to Engineering to Criminal Justice. Law schools want that diversity of backgrounds and expertise in every incoming class. Thus, they want the law-school admissions test to be neutral in terms of subject matter. It is not in their interest to favor chemists or philosophers or anyone else by having the test focus on areas of expertise or knowledge. Another reason is probably just for fun. You've got three years of the emoluments clause and the parol evidence rule ahead of you. Enjoy playing with the plastic dinosaurs while you can.

So, that helps explain why the LSAT includes the Logic Games section, which is the focus of this book. Before making Logic Games your full-time job, however, take a few minutes to consider the context of the full LSAT test.

Four Core Skills—What The LSAT Tests

Now you may be thinking, "What does the Logic Games section have to do with torts? How can Logical Reasoning predict my success in Civil Procedure?" In this book, you are going to be taught a series of Learning Objectives, which are bundled around four key skills—key because they're what the LSAT rewards, key because they're what law school demands. We'll call them the Core Skills:

Reading Strategically

Reading for structure and anticipating what the author will say is what Strategic Reading is all about. Both your law professors and the LSAT want you to cut through the jargon and explain what the case or passage says. Reading strategically helps you zero in on exactly what opinions are present and how that knowledge will be rewarded in the question set.

Analyzing Arguments

The essence of Logical Reasoning and the essence of lawyering is Analyzing Arguments. To analyze an argument in the LSAT sense, you must distinguish the argument's conclusion from its evidence. Then, determine what the person making the argument is taking for granted. The assumptions the author makes are what allow you to strengthen or challenge arguments on the LSAT. Likewise, in a courtroom, attorneys will need to understand, analyze, evaluate, manipulate, and draw conclusions from the arguments of their opponent, their own clients, and the judge.

Understanding Formal Logic

Conditional, or "If-Then" statements, are incredibly important in rules of law. "If-Thens" tell you what must, can, or can't be true in a given situation or when a particular rule is or isn't applicable. The very first chapter will train you to seek out the Formal Logic embedded in LSAT questions and logic games and to manage the implications flawlessly. For a lot of students, this is the most intimidating of the Core Skills, but facing up to it is incredibly valuable. It brings a rigor to your reasoning that will allow you to answer questions—on the LSAT and in law school—with precision.

Making Deductions

Making Deductions is rewarded in every section of the test, but it is key in Logic Games. In that section, you're given a set of conditions and rules and then asked to apply them to various hypothetical cases: "If J goes on Wednesday, what must be true . . ." "If the van has more miles than the sedan, and the sedan has more miles than the motorcycle, what could be false . . ." That's just what law school exams demand. In law school, the rules and restrictions come from the dozens (potentially hundreds) of cases and statutes you will read during a semester. Just as you'll learn to do with Logic Games rules, judges synthesize rules in order to determine the outcome of a case.

The Structure of the LSAT

The LSAT consists of five multiple-choice sections: two Logical Reasoning sections, one Logic Games section, one Reading Comprehension section, and one unscored "experimental" section that will look exactly like one of the other multiple-choice sections. These five multiple-choice sections can appear in any order on Test Day. A 15-minute break will come between the third and fourth sections of the test. The unscored, 35-minute Writing Sample essay section is always administered after the multiple-choice sections are concluded.

Section	→	Number of Questions	→	Minutes	
Logical Reasoning		24–26		35	May occur in any order
Logical Reasoning		24–26		35	
Reading Comprehension		26–28		35	
Logic Games		22–24		35	
"Experimental"		22–28		35	
Writing Sample		One essay		35	

Familiarize yourself with the structure of each section.

Logical Reasoning

Each of the two Logical Reasoning sections consists of 24–26 questions based on short passages, which we'll call *stimuli*, that are typically two to five sentences each. Each stimulus may be a short argument or a series of statements of fact. Each stimulus will also have one corresponding question that tests your ability to do such things as spot the structure of arguments, identify assumptions and flaws, strengthen or weaken arguments, or find inferences. Together, the two Logical Reasoning sections comprise the most important part of the test, counting for approximately half of your overall score.

Reading Comprehension

This section consists of three passages, typically made up of two to five paragraphs—about 55–65 lines of text (i.e., about 500 words apiece)—and one set of paired passages, together about the same length as each of the three longer passages. Each passage is accompanied by anywhere from five to eight questions. A Reading Comprehension section can have 26–28, questions, but every released test since 2007 has had 27 questions. Reading Comprehension on the LSAT is an exercise in reading for structure and for multiple points of view. You'll learn to trace the outline of the passage as you read and to distinguish the author's viewpoint from the viewpoints of others mentioned in the passage, as well as to stay a step ahead of where the author is going by reading predictively.

Logic Games (Analytical Reasoning)

Analytical Reasoning, known popularly and in this book as Logic Games, consists of four game scenarios along with accompanying rules. Each game is accompanied by 5–7 questions. A Logic Games section can have 22–24 questions, but every LSAT released since 2007 has had 23 questions. With only 23 questions, it is the least valuable of the scored sections. Logic Games may nevertheless be the section you fear the most—many students do. Others, however, immediately take to the puzzle aspect of the section. Logic Games tests your ability to apply, combine, and manipulate rules and to deduce what can and cannot happen as a result. While the games may look daunting at first, they can be mastered with a systematic technique and proper use of scratchwork.

Experimental

The experimental section is an additional, unscored section of Logical Reasoning, Reading Comprehension, or Logic Games. You will not know what type of section you will get, and it can show up anywhere, including after the break. You'll have to bring your A-game for the entire test, as there is no reliable way to determine which section is experimental while you're taking the test. In case you're wondering, the LSAC includes an experimental section on the LSAT as a way to test questions for future administrations of the exam.

The Writing Sample

After you complete the five multiple-choice sections of the test, you'll write a short essay in which you choose between courses of action and explain your choice. While unscored, your Writing Sample is submitted to all law schools to which you apply, and law schools use it as part of the evaluation process.

LSAT Scored Sections

Logic Games
One section with four games and 22–24 questions
Logic Games questions reward you for sequencing, matching, distributing, or selecting entities on the basis of rules that combine to limit the acceptable arrangements.

Logical Reasoning
Two sections with 24–26 questions each
Logical Reasoning questions reward you for analyzing arguments to strengthen or weaken them or to identify their assumptions and flaws. Other LR questions require you to draw valid inferences from a set of facts.

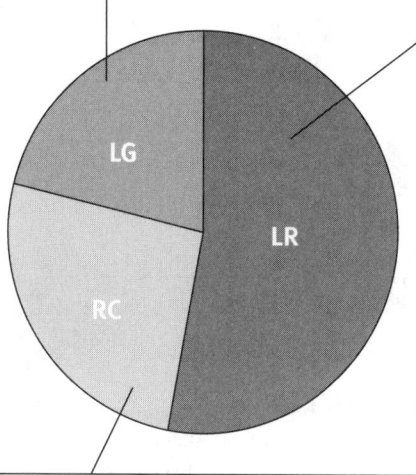

Reading Comprehension
One section with four passages and 26–28 questions
Reading Comp questions reward you for identifying the author's purpose and main idea, drawing valid inferences from the passage, and determining how and why the author uses certain details.

How the LSAT Is Scored

Here's how the LSAT is scored. Your performance is assessed on three scales: raw score (# correct), scaled score, and percentile.

Percentile (Scaled score)	10th (139)	20th (143)	30th (146)	40th (149)	50th (151)	60th (154)	70th (156)	80th (160)	90th (164)	95th (167)	99th (172)
# Correct	38	44	49	54	58	63	67	74	80	85	92

Source – PrepTest 74 (December 2014)

LSAT Score Breakdown

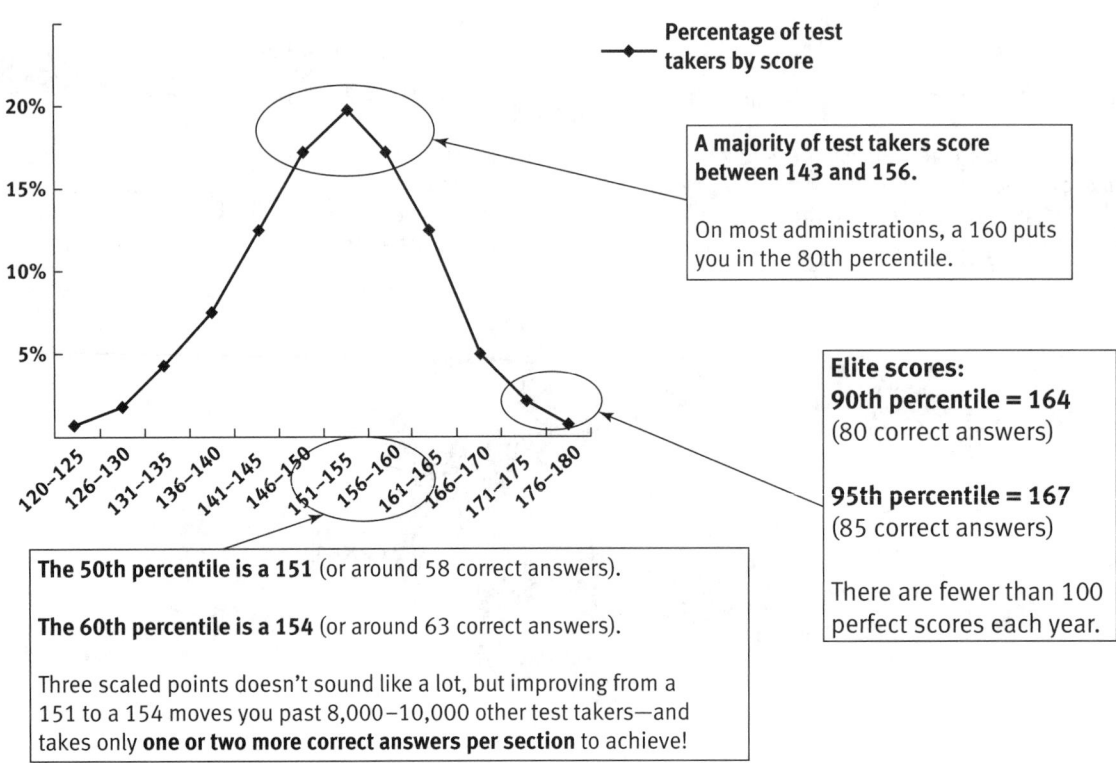

Percentage of test takers by score

A majority of test takers score between 143 and 156.

On most administrations, a 160 puts you in the 80th percentile.

Elite scores:
90th percentile = 164 (80 correct answers)

95th percentile = 167 (85 correct answers)

There are fewer than 100 perfect scores each year.

The 50th percentile is a 151 (or around 58 correct answers).

The 60th percentile is a 154 (or around 63 correct answers).

Three scaled points doesn't sound like a lot, but improving from a 151 to a 154 moves you past 8,000–10,000 other test takers—and takes only **one or two more correct answers per section** to achieve!

Raw score is simply the number of questions answered correctly.

Scaled score, the familiar 120–180 number, is a conversion of the raw score. Here, a raw score of 67—that is, 67 correct answers—converts to a scaled score of 156. A raw score of 58—meaning 58 correct answers—converts to a scaled score of 151. On a different test, a raw score of 58 might convert to a 150 or a 152. To account for differences in overall difficulty, each test has a slightly different raw score-to-scaled score conversion table.

Percentile score indicates how a test taker performed relative to other test takers over a three-year period. The conversion from scaled score to percentile score remains relatively stable, with only minor variations over the years. Test after test, a 151 scaled score is approximately a 50th percentile score.

The way in which the LSAT is scored has three important implications for your performance:

- First, the number of *right* answers determines your score. There is no guessing penalty. Never leave a question blank on the LSAT.
- Second, every question is worth the same, regardless of how hard it is. Learn to spot difficult questions and leave them for the end of each section. Find the easy questions and rack up points. If you're going to run out of time or need to guess, you want to do so on the tough stuff.
- Third, every additional correct answer can leapfrog you ahead of hundreds—or even thousands—of other test takers, your competition. How's that for inspiration?

What's a Good LSAT Score?

What you consider a good LSAT score depends on your own expectations and goals, but here are a few interesting statistics.

If you got about half of all of the scored questions right (a raw score of roughly 50), you'd earn a scaled score of roughly 146 or 147, putting you in about the 30th percentile—not a great performance. However, as you just saw, a little improvement goes a long way. Getting only one additional question right every 10 minutes (throughout the scored sections) would give you a raw score of 64, pushing you up to 154, which is about the 60th percentile—a huge improvement.

So, you don't have to be perfect to do well. On a typical LSAT, you can still get 25 wrong and end up in the 160s— or about 20 wrong and get a 164, a 90th percentile score. Even a perfect score of 180 often allows for a question or two to be missed.

Here is a chart detailing some top law schools and the scores of their admitted students.

Rank*	School	25th–75th %ile LSAT* (Scaled)	25th–75th %ile UGPA*	25th–75th %ile LSAT** (Raw)
1	Yale University	170–175	3.79–3.97	90–96
6	New York University	166–171	3.65–3.89	84–92
10	Duke University	167–170	3.59–3.84	86–91
12	University of California–Berkeley	163–169	3.65–3.89	79–89
14	University of Texas–Austin	162–168	3.41–3.84	77–88
19	University of Southern California	162–166	3.56–3.85	77–85
26	Boston College	161–163	3.32–3.65	76–80
30	University of Wisconsin–Madison	156–163	3.30–3.72	66–80
41	University of Florida	156–161	3.33–3.77	66–76
51	Tulane University	155–160	3.22–3.62	64–75
65	Northeastern University	154–163	3.30–3.69	62–80
72	University of Cincinnati	153–158	3.24–3.76	61–71
86	University of Oregon	154–159	3.20–3.64	62–73

* *U.S. News & World Report*, 2018 Law School Rankings
** LSAT PrepTest 80, December 2016 Exam

Registration for and Administration of The LSAT

As of the time that this book goes to print, the LSAT is administered by the Law School Admission Council (LSAC) (**www.lsac.org**) four times each year.

LSAT FACTS

In 2017, the LSAT is administered on:

- A Saturday morning in February
- A Monday afternoon in June
- A Saturday morning in late September or early October
- A Saturday morning in December

There are some exceptions. For example, Saturday Sabbath observers have the option to take the test on a specified weekday following a typical Saturday administration. Dates and times may also be different for tests administered outside the United States, Canada, and the Caribbean. Note: Beginning in the 2018-2019 testing cycle, the LSAC plans to move to six tests per year, with one in each of July, September, November, January, March, and June. Specific dates for that cycle had not been announced at the time that this book went to print. Check www.lsac.org for updates.

How do I register for the LSAT? Register for the LSAT online at **www.lsac.org**. Check the LSAC website for details on the procedures, deadlines, and fee schedules.

When should I register? Register as soon as you have chosen your test date. Test sites may fill up quickly. Registration is typically due about five weeks before Test Day, with an additional week of registration allowed subject to a "Late Registration" fee.

Can I change my test date or location? You can change your test dates or locations (subject to an additional "change" fee) via the LSAC website. Timely changes of test date are not reported to schools; "no shows" are reported, however.

What is the CAS? Upon signing up for the LSAT, you also need to register with the Credential Assembly Service (CAS) as part of the application process required by every ABA-approved law school. CAS receives your undergraduate transcripts and distributes a summary of your undergraduate performance, along with your letters of recommendation, evaluations, and LSAT score report to each of the law schools to which you apply. **www.lsac.org** lists the fees and sign-up details for CAS.

When are law schools' application deadlines? All law schools provide their application deadlines on their websites. Some schools require that the LSAT be taken by December for admission the following fall; others will accept a February LSAT score. Because most schools use a "rolling admissions" process, taking the test in June or September/October is preferable; also, taking the test earlier gives the test taker a chance to repeat the LSAT prior to most application deadlines.

Can I repeat the LSAT? As of June 2017, there is no limit to the number of times a test taker may take the LSAT. Any test taker who wishes to take the test a second time will need to reregister for the test. Law schools will receive scores for every LSAT an applicant has taken.

How do law schools view multiple LSAT scores? This varies from school to school. Few schools now average multiple scores, as was the policy in the past, but most consider *all scores from a five-year period* when evaluating applications. Applicants cannot choose which scores to report with their application. Find more information on repeating the test at **www.lsac.org/jd/lsat/about-the-lsat**.

Accommodations

If you have a disability, you may be able to receive testing accommodations for the LSAT. Accommodations are granted for physical, learning, and cognitive impairments severe enough to qualify as a disability relevant to test taking. A wide variety of accommodations are available. You must be registered for a test date before you can request accommodations, however, so register early. Your application for accommodations will require you to submit a full evaluation by a qualified professional who specializes in your particular disability as well as score reports from previous standardized admissions tests (SAT, GRE, etc.), any records of accommodations you received for those tests, and any records of accommodations you received from your undergraduate institution(s). All of these things can take time to prepare and must be submitted several weeks before your test date, so start your process as early as possible. If for any reason you move test dates, you will be required to resubmit your application, so be sure to hold on to copies of your records just in case.

Be aware that qualifying for accommodations on the LSAT is generally harder than it is for undergraduate accommodations, though recent policy changes by the LSAC now treat prior accommodations on other standardized admissions tests as sufficient evidence to grant you similar accommodations for the LSAT. Keep in mind that LSAC grants accommodations only when documentation clearly demonstrates disability in an area directly related to test taking. If you are denied accommodations and feel the denial was in error, you can submit an appeal with additional documentation provided that there is enough time for the LSAC to process the appeal before Test Day.

If you are granted accommodations from LSAC, your score will not be flagged as accommodated on your official score report. Law schools are now unable to distinguish an accommodated score from a score received under standard testing conditions. Given that the greatest difficulty many test takers face on Test Day is the timing demands of the LSAT, you should seek out accommodations as soon as possible if you feel you are qualified for them.

If you believe you have a disability that requires testing accommodations, start by reviewing the accommodations page on the LSAC website to get the most updated information on deadlines and required forms. Remember that this process is subject to change by LSAC at any time, so it is crucial that you get the most recent information directly from LSAC. Full information about accommodated testing is available at **www.lsac.org/jd/lsat/accommodated-testing**.

LSAT Study Skills

Imagine you want to lose a few pounds, so you get yourself a gym membership. Will the gym membership be sufficient for you to shed the weight? Of course not. You actually have to use the gym. And, once you get started, you'll need to use proper technique to maximize your results. If you're not sure how to get started, if you're overwhelmed by all the machines you find, or if you try to take shortcuts and don't put in the appropriate time and effort, you may not see the results you were hoping for.

You see where this is going. Kaplan is your gym. We're your mental workout. You've already committed to using our materials. But just as showing up at the gym is not enough for you to lose weight, picking up this book is not enough to raise your score either. You need to work out. You've been provided with a suite of assets, both print and online. But it's up to you to use them. And here's the best part: The work of dozens of Kaplan teachers, researchers, and testing experts has gone into creating not only the expert analysis in this book but also the Smart Reports® analytics, online material, and study plans that accompany it.

The LSAT is entirely a skills-based test. It is coachable. It is practicable. And there are lots of ways to practice. Some methods are great; others, not so much. Expect us to show you the best ways to practice. Expect us to show you the patterns of the test and how to tackle every question type. Expect us to show you how to manage every section.

To reach your full potential on the LSAT, you're going to need to work hard. We will show you precisely what you need to do, but ultimately it's up to you to do it.

LSAT Strategy and the Three Levels of Practice

On Test Day, you'll be asked to deal with stringent testing policies and procedures, answer approximately 125 multiple-choice questions (of which typically 101 will count toward your score), and write a short essay. It's grueling and intense. And, depending on how efficient your test proctors are, the entire process may end up lasting five or more hours.

For those sections that count toward your score, taking control means increasing your speed only to the extent you can do so without sacrificing accuracy. Your goal is not to attempt as many questions as possible; your goal is to get as many questions correct as possible.

For many people, the single biggest challenge of the LSAT is time. If you had unlimited time to take this test, you'd likely perform quite well. But you don't. You have a strict 35 minutes to complete each section, and many students are not able to tackle every question in the time allotted. For you, this means three things:

- It's important that you learn not only how to answer the questions effectively but also how to answer them efficiently.
- It's important to approach each section strategically, knowing which questions to attack first and which questions to save for last.
- It's important that you prepare for the rigors of 3½ hours of testing. You'll want to maintain your focus in the final section as well as you did in the first.

Achieving these goals won't happen overnight. Obviously you need to put in the work to get better. Specifically, though, you need to work on your foundational knowledge first, then improve on moving through the test more quickly and efficiently. To achieve your goals, you'll want to incorporate three levels of practice: Mastery, Timing, and Endurance.

Mastery is about learning the patterns of the exam and how to identify them in new questions. You'll gain command of new efficient, effective techniques that you will repeatedly practice on specific drills as well as on individual question types. You'll study the answers and explanations to learn how the testmaker builds questions and answer choices. You'll identify why right answers are right and why wrong answers are wrong. What traps do you consistently fall into? How do you avoid them? That's precisely what Mastery practice is for.

Once you've learned the skills individually, it's time to try full-length section practice, or *Timing*. At 3½ hours, the LSAT can seem like a marathon, but it's really a series of sprints—five 35-minute tests, plus a writing sample. Section management—how to recognize and apply the patterns you've learned efficiently to maximize the number of questions you get correct—is what Timing practice teaches you to do.

And finally, there's *Endurance*. Can you maintain your ability to identify and apply these patterns efficiently throughout the whole exam? Some students discover that they are great at focusing for two hours, then struggle through the last two sections of the test. Taking practice tests will help you build your stamina. But a word of warning: The single biggest trap students fall into as they prepare for the LSAT is taking test after test after test. Think about it like learning a musical instrument. If you're trying to learn the piano, do you schedule a piano recital every other day? No, of course not. It's the piano *practice* that allows you to improve. While practice tests are important, they should be spaced out and taken only when you're sure you've made some improvement through your Mastery and Timing practice.

By approaching your preparation this way—starting with Mastery and then layering in Timing first and then Endurance—you'll be fully and properly prepared by Test Day.

Keeping Time on the LSAT

One of the most common concerns heard about the LSAT is "If I only had more time, I would be able to get through all the Games/Reading Comp passages/Logical Reasoning questions." Though it may seem unfortunate that you only have 35 minutes for each section, keep in mind that this timing constraint is deliberate. You are not alone in thinking that it's difficult to get through the sections in the given time. But the timing constraint isn't necessarily a hindrance to success; precisely *because* concerns about timing are so universal, you can get a big leg up on your competition by understanding how to maximize your performance in those 35 minutes.

Initially, your goal when working on Mastery questions is to understand and use Kaplan Methods while becoming more familiar with question types and gaining greater competency. Once a degree of mastery has been attained, it is time to turn your attention to completing a section within the 35-minute time period.

On Test Day, you cannot count on being able to see a clock in the testing room. The proctors may put the start and stop time of each section on the board and will occasionally note the time; a verbal five-minute warning will be given toward the end of the section. However, it is ultimately your responsibility to keep track of the time. While it is rare, proctors have been known to forget to give five-minute warnings, and in some facilities, clocks don't keep accurate time. As you begin your LSAT prep, invest in the purchase of a watch—one with a large face and easy-to-read numbers. Remember, LSAC does not allow the use of digital watches, stopwatches, or timers; you are allowed to use only a good, old-fashioned watch with hands, known as an analog watch.

Get used to using your watch. During timing practice, use your watch to read and Roadmap a passage or to set up a game in four minutes. Keep track of how long it is taking to work through Logical Reasoning questions.

Here is a quick tip for efficiency on Test Day: As you begin every section, set your watch back to 12:00. At a glance, you will be able to tell how much time you have used and how much time is left until 12:35, when the section will end. This way, you won't need to waste precious time calculating the minutes left.

LSAT Attitude

In the following chapters, we will arm you with the tools you need—both content and strategy—to do well on the LSAT. But you must wield this LSAT arsenal with the right spirit. This involves taking a certain stance toward the entire test.

Those who approach the LSAT as an obstacle and rail against the necessity of taking it don't fare as well as those who see the LSAT as an opportunity. Think about it: This is your chance to show law schools your proficiency in the Core Skills. A great LSAT score will distinguish your application from those of your competition.

- Look at the LSAT as a challenge but try not to obsess over it; you certainly don't want to psych yourself out of the game.
- Remember that the LSAT is important, but this one test will not single-handedly determine the outcome of your life.
- Try to have fun with the test. Learning how to unlock the test's patterns and to approach its content in the way the testmaker rewards can be very satisfying, and the skills you'll acquire will benefit you in law school and your career.

Confidence

Confidence in your ability leads to quick, sure answers and a sense of well-being that translates into more points. Confidence feeds on itself; unfortunately, so does self-doubt. If you lack confidence, you end up reading sentences and answer choices two, three, or four times, until you confuse yourself and get off track. This leads to timing difficulties that perpetuate a downward spiral of anxiety, rushing, and poor performance.

If you subscribe to the proper LSAT mindset, however, you'll gear all of your practice toward taking control of the test. When you've achieved that goal—armed with the principles, techniques, strategies, and methods Kaplan has to offer—you'll be ready to face the LSAT with confidence.

Stamina

The LSAT is a grueling experience, and some test takers simply run out of gas before it's over. To avoid this, take full-length practice tests in the weeks before the test. That way, five sections plus a writing sample will seem like a breeze (well, maybe not a breeze, but at least not a hurricane). On the other hand, don't just rush from one practice test right into another. Learn what you can from your review of each test, then work on your weaknesses and build your strengths before tackling another full-length test. You should plan on spending just as much time to review your practice tests as you did to take them.

Managing Stress

Take Control. Research shows that if you don't have a sense of control over what's happening in your life, you can easily end up feeling helpless and hopeless. Try to identify the sources of the stress you feel. Which of these can you do something about?

Set Realistic Goals. Facing your problem areas gives you some distinct advantages. What do you want to accomplish in the time remaining? Make a list of realistic goals. You can't help but feel more confident when you know you're actively improving your chances of earning a higher test score.

Acknowledge Your Strengths. Make a list of your strengths that will help you do well on the test. Many students are experts at listing which aspects of the test they struggle with. But students who also have knowledge of their ever-expanding list of strengths will have more confidence and a better perspective on what to target to improve.

Get Exercise and Eat Well. Whether it is jogging, biking, yoga, or a pickup basketball game, physical exercise stimulates your mind and body and improves your ability to think and concentrate. Likewise, good nutrition helps you focus and think clearly. A surprising number of students fall out of good habits in these areas, ironically because they're spending so much time preparing for the test.

Keep Breathing. Conscious attention to breathing is an excellent way to manage stress. Most of the people who get into trouble during tests take shallow breaths. They breathe using only their upper chests and shoulder muscles and may even hold their breath for long periods of time. Breathe deeply in a slow, relaxed manner.

Stretch. If you find yourself getting spaced out or burned out as you're studying for or taking the test, stop for a brief moment and stretch. Stretching will help to refresh you and refocus your thoughts.

Imagine Yourself Succeeding. If you are continually filled with self-doubt about the test, it will be difficult to overcome those feelings and perform well on the test. Although preparing for the test can take many weeks or months of extensive practice, you must be able to visualize that you will gain confidence and take control of the test. Confidence gained through preparation will lead to better performance. Do not wait for it to occur the other way around.

The LSAT Mindset

You may have heard something about a popular concept known as "Growth Mindset." It has a great deal of applicability to any challenge that seems daunting—and the LSAT in general, and Logic Games in particular, can certainly seem daunting.

The idea, coined by noted researcher Dr. Carol Dweck and promoted by many others, is that how you feel about the likelihood of your success has a lot to do with whether you'll be successful. Specifically, if you believe that success (in whatever endeavor) is based on factors over which you have no control—like I.Q., schooling, social class, or luck—you're said to have a *fixed mindset*. People with a fixed mindset about an activity tend to get discouraged quicker and give up sooner, when early negative results confirm the notion that "I can't do this."

On the other hand, those with a *growth mindset* firmly believe that it's effort, training, and learning that always make the big difference. In study after study, those with a growth mindset tend to keep working hard, even in the face of setbacks. They "hang in there" past the pain points and eventually see breakthroughs. Talent, they believe (and Dr. Dweck confirms), can be acquired, *if* your attitudes allow talent to grow.

Can you think of instances in your life when you said "I can't do this" and were proven right? And other times when you firmly believed in your success, and success came to pass? Dr. Dweck is the first to point out that all of us hold a mix of fixed and growth attitudes, a fact that would be foolish to deny. What we have to do—and this gets us back to Logic Games—is stay very, very watchful of our fixed-mindset thoughts and deeds, so that we can move closer to a growth mindset in what we think and do.

Here are some tactics that can help foster a growth mindset in your logic games work:

- Never say "I can't do games." It's okay to say "I can't do games *yet*."
- Always seek out feedback on your work. If the game went well, how could it have gone better? If you crashed and burned, where did you go wrong, and is there another approach you could've taken? (Kaplan's answer explanations are a fantastic, 24/7 source of feedback and insights, and they're full of positive messaging too.)
- The basic sequencing or matching game lays the groundwork for the tougher games, so don't pooh-pooh your success on lower-difficulty material. "Work hard on the fundamentals," Dr. Dweck advises, echoing famous basketball coach John Wooden. Incidentally, Dr. Dweck warns against the idea of "the mistake-free game" promoted by coach Bobby Knight. Your goal, she says, shouldn't be mistake-free performance, but "full preparation and full effort."
- Never credit "your smarts" (whatever *that* means!) with creating the right sketch, interpreting a rule correctly, or getting a question right. And of course "I'm not smart enough" isn't the reason you had a setback. Your *effort* earns you success, and more (or different) *effort* will overcome today's setbacks and lead to learning and improvement over time. Give yourself A's for Effort always.

Shifting to a growth mindset isn't easy, and Carol Dweck herself reminds us, "the path to a growth mindset is a journey, not a proclamation." Instead of announcing, to others or to yourself, that you're going to "Go Growth," just start practicing—and reacting to practice—with these ideas in mind. You may be amazed at how your point of view, and your performance, start to change.

In The LSAT Channel Spotlight feature that follows, you'll learn some of the secrets for successful prep that Kaplan's top faculty members impart to their students. In the video that accompanies the Spotlight you'll see and hear from these outstanding coaches and mentors.

Secrets of Logic Games Preparation

by The LSAT Channel Faculty

 Watch the video lesson for this Spotlight in your online Study Plan.

Students who come to *The LSAT Channel* get to hear from some of Kaplan's most experienced and highly rated LSAT faculty. When it comes to logic games, the message they hear most clearly is: Kaplan knows logic games—inside out, forward, and backward—and we've got the method and strategies that will (with practice) help you get them, too. Each of these coaches and mentors has his or her own special insights, as well. In the video that accompanies this Spotlight, you'll meet The LSAT Channel faculty, and hear what each of them tells students at the beginning of their logic games prep. Here are a few of the themes they hit upon:

You Do Logic Games All the Time

If you've ever ranked the *Star Wars* movies from best to worst, chosen teams for a pick-up basketball game, or separated clothes into laundry and dry cleaning, you've done a logic game. While it may be true that you've never before had to answer questions quite like these *on a test*, you engage in logic games tasks every day. Logic games present you with small, real-world puzzles that may, at first, seem abstract or technical, but are really quite practical. And, you *can* do them.

There Is Always Enough Information to Answer Every Question

There are two criteria for a good game—not just for logic games, but even games we play with friends or against

the computer—they need to be challenging, and they need to be fair. If we're honest, challenging games are more fun. We quickly lose interest in puzzles that are too easy to solve, or in games we always win. Logic games are challenging, but always fair. Before a game appears on an official LSAT, it has been tested on thousands of test takers to make sure it has all of the information needed to answer every question. You'll find the confidence that you can extract that information every time.

Patience Can Make You Faster

The Logic Games section gives you 35 minutes for four games. That means you have approximately 8½ minutes for each game and its accompanying questions. The time pressure *is* real, but the best response to that pressure is counterintuitive. To increase your efficiency on logic games, you need patience. LSAT experts know that creating a thorough, accurate setup and sketch depicting all of the game's rules and deductions will allow them to get through the questions much more quickly. For some games, the setup may be so complete that you can answer the questions in a matter of a few seconds apiece.

Logic Games "Feel" Harder than They Really Are

Fact-based, data-driven analysis is at the heart of Kaplan's approach to LSAT preparation. When it comes to logic games, the data reveals a big lesson: Test takers' perception of logic games is out of line with their performance. For many years now, Kaplan has surveyed LSAT test takers after every exam, and, no surprise, they consistently rate Logic Games as the hardest section on the test.

**Percent of Test Takers Who Said
Each Section Was the Hardest, 2012–16**

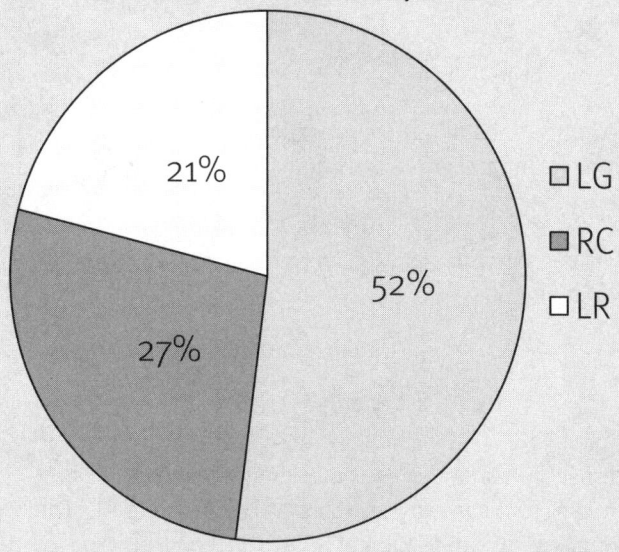

At Kaplan, we also record the actual results that students receive when they take official LSAC tests for practice. The students' performance tells a different story. On most LSATs, the Logic Games section is not noticeably harder than the other sections, and on some tests, it's actually the easiest section overall.

Percent Incorrect by Section, 2012–16

Experienced LSAT instructors know that students often make their biggest improvements in the Logic Games section. The bottom line: Don't let logic games'

reputation intimidate you. Don't listen to the chatter. You, like thousands of successful students before you, can learn to master this section of the LSAT.

Small Improvements Produce Big Results

You saw this demonstrated earlier, in the section about LSAT scoring. There are only 101 questions on the typical LSAT test, and given that the LSAT is scored on a curve, adding just five more correct answers to your score can move you past 10 percent of test takers. Depending on your starting score, 10 additional correct answers could move your score past a quarter of all law school applicants. That means the improvements you make in just the Logic Games section can have an enormous impact on your law school application.

The LSAT Channel

Kaplan launched *The LSAT Channel* in 2015 to bring nightly live instruction from our most highly rated LSAT teachers to every student enrolled in a comprehensive LSAT prep course. Since then, students all over the country (and the world) have had access to over 100 unique hours of instruction for every testing cycle. The *LSAT Channel* faculty is constantly creating new lessons on special topics to provide their strategic insights to ambitious test takers.

Now, The *LSAT Channel* instructors have developed several Spotlight lessons exclusively for *Logic Games Unlocked*. Whenever you see one of these Spotlight features in the book, you'll not only get the expertise provided on the page, but also have a chance to practice the strategies explained there, and to learn directly from the instructors through the videos in your online Study Plan.

Take a few minutes to meet the faculty, here and in the accompanying video. They'll motivate you and set you on the path to logic games success. Ready to get started?

JEFF BOUDREAU

"I love teaching logic games because once you understand them, they're actually fun, and if studying for the LSAT can be enjoyable, getting the score you want is a whole lot easier."

DESCRIBES TEACHING STYLE AS: Excited, fun-loving, caring

BOBBY GAUTAM

"Doing games is relaxing and addicting. Teaching them is arguably even more fun because once students see the moves and patterns, the games virtually teach themselves, and engagement is high."

DESCRIBES TEACHING STYLE AS: Clear, compassionate, lively, humorous, passionate

HANNAH GIST

"Logic Games are based on patterns: the same things show up over and over. This means you can memorize the common tricks to stay one step ahead of the LSAT. The payoff from practicing and teaching Logic Games is huge!"

DESCRIBES TEACHING STYLE AS: Patient, energetic, encouraging, accessible, proficient

GENE SUHIR

"I love teaching logic games because I love seeing students have a 'lightbulb' moment when they realize that one or two key deductions unlock the whole game for them! And then students can really bust through those questions and collect the rewards over and over again when they spot those patterns!"

DESCRIBES TEACHING STYLE AS: Energetic, passionate, entertaining, coherent

BOB VERINI

"I love doing puzzles where I know, at the end, there will be a clear, unambiguious solution. Even more, I love showing people who think they can't solve puzzles, how to become good at it!"

DESCRIBES TEACHING STYLE AS: Dynamic, scaffolded, realistic, tactical, idealistic

PART ONE

Logic Games Method and Strategy

CHAPTER 1

The Logic Games Method

In the Logic Games section of the LSAT, your goal—as it is throughout the test—is to answer the questions correctly. That statement may seem absurdly obvious, but it is also easy to overlook. As you work through this book, you'll encounter a variety of game types, numerous patterns and sketches that reflect them, rules for formal logic, and detailed strategies for handling everything you'll encounter in this section of the test. Don't lose sight of the real goal: getting the questions right.

With that in mind, take a look at a typical LSAT Logic Games question.

4. If exactly three of the trucks are green, then which one of the following trucks must be green?

    (A) S
    (B) T
    (C) U
    (D) W
    (E) Z

PrepTest37 Sec3 Q9

Here's another absurdly obvious statement: You cannot answer this question, at least not without more information. All Logic Games questions ask you about what must, can, or cannot be true given a particular situation and the rules and restrictions surrounding it. Here, you lack the context—what's all this about trucks and colors?—to make sense of the situation.

Pulling this question out from the rest of the game highlights a key point of this chapter: The background information, the rules, and sketches you'll make to take control of them are all there to provide the context that allows you to answer the questions. Indeed, when you've learned to effectively interpret and set up logic games, you'll discover that answering at least some of the questions is a snap, and you'll gain the confidence of knowing that you always have the information you need to find the correct answer to every question.

Now, take a look at that question within the context of the full game. Notice that the question is the fourth one in the game's question set. To the LSAT expert, the questions are simply applications of the situation, rules, and restrictions described in the opening scenario. The rest of this chapter will show you the method that experts use to turn that information into a sketch or diagram that they apply to answer all of the questions confidently and efficiently.

Analysis: This paragraph sets out the task. It defines the players or entities for which you must account, tells you what to do with them—in this case, to put the entities in order and to assign them certain attributes (colors)—and provides rules and limitations on how the entities can be arranged. This "setup" always contains all of the information you need to answer every question.

Questions 1–6

In a single day, exactly seven trucks—S, T, U, W, X, Y, and Z—are the only arrivals at a warehouse. No truck arrives at the same time as any other truck, and no truck arrives more than once that day. Each truck is either green or red (but not both). The following conditions apply:

> No two consecutive arrivals are red.
> Y arrives at some time before both T and W.
> Exactly two of the trucks that arrive before Y are red.
> S is the sixth arrival.
> Z arrives at some time before U.

1. Which one of the following could be the order, from first to last, in which the trucks arrive?

    (A) X, Z, U, Y, W, S, T
    (B) X, Y, Z, U, W, S, T
    (C) Z, W, U, T, Y, S, X
    (D) Z, U, T, Y, W, S, X
    (E) U, Z, Y, T, S, W, X

2. For which one of the following pairs of trucks is it the case that they CANNOT both be red?

    (A) S and X
    (B) T and S
    (C) U and W
    (D) W and T
    (E) X and Z

3. If X is the third arrival, then which one of the following trucks must be green?

    (A) S
    (B) T
    (C) U
    (D) W
    (E) Z

4. If exactly three of the trucks are green, then which one of the following trucks must be green?

    (A) S
    (B) T
    (C) U
    (D) W
    (E) Z

5. For exactly how many of the seven trucks can one determine exactly how many trucks arrived before it?

    (A) one
    (B) two
    (C) three
    (D) four
    (E) five

6. Which one of the following pairs of trucks CANNOT arrive consecutively at the warehouse?

    (A) U and Y
    (B) X and Y
    (C) Y and T
    (D) Y and W
    (E) Y and Z

PrepTest37 Sec3 Qs 6–11

Analysis: All of the questions reward an understanding of what is and is not possible given the game's action and restrictions. In one way or another, they all ask you to distinguish what must be true from what could be false or what must be false from what could be true. The first question seeks an acceptable sequence of the entities. The second and sixth questions ask you to identify impossibilities in the context of this game. The third and fourth questions both present hypothetical variations within the game, and ask for what must be true within those variations. The fifth question, a rare one, asks for the number of entities whose placement can be precisely determined once and for all.

The analyses on this page reflect what the LSAT expert sees at a glance. Over the remainder of this chapter, you'll learn the 5-step method that the expert uses to translate the game's information into correct answers.

LEARNING OBJECTIVES

In this chapter, you'll learn to

- List the steps of the Kaplan Logic Games Method and articulate the purpose of each step.

Prepare

The method you'll learn in this chapter provides an effective approach to all logic games you will encounter on the LSAT. Learning and practicing the method will make you efficient with your time as you manage all of the game's information, and confident as you apply that information to correctly answer the questions.

THE KAPLAN LOGIC GAMES METHOD

Step 1: Overview
Step 2: Sketch
Step 3: Rules
Step 4: Deductions
Step 5: Questions

In Chapters 2 through 4, we'll go into more detail about these steps and the skills associated with each of them. For now, your task is simply to learn them, and to learn what each step accomplishes as an LSAT expert uses them to tackle a logic game.

First, we'll walk you through an expert's step-by-step application of the Logic Games Method to the game you just saw. Then, you'll practice on another game. After that, you'll assess your mastery of the steps in the method.

Step 1: Overview

Before you can accomplish anything in a logic game, you need to understand your assignment, your *task*, if you will. The LSAT describes game scenarios as small, well defined, real-world jobs. In the next few chapters, for example, you will be asked to arrange some dresses in a closet with numbered hangers, divide a group of boaters into two boats, and match models of cars to the standard features they offer. In any case, you should always take a few seconds to make sure you understand the task. Doing so allows you to make a useful, accurate sketch in which to record the specific details and to account for all of the game's moving parts.

To make the overview process as efficient as possible, LSAT experts ask four questions—the SEAL questions—while conducting the Overview step.

STEP 1: OVERVIEW—THE SEAL QUESTIONS

Situation—What is the real-world scenario being described? What is the deliverable information—an ordered list, a calendar, a chart showing what's matched up?

Entities—Who or what are the "moving parts," the people or things I'm trying to sequence, select, distribute, or match up?

Action—What is the specific action—sequencing, selection, distribution, matching (or a combination of those)—that I'm performing on the entities?

Limitations—Does the game state parameters (e.g., "select four of seven" or "sequence the entities one per day") that restrict how I will set up or sketch the game?

Here's how an LSAT expert might answer the SEAL questions in the Truck Arrivals game.

LSAT Question	Analysis
In a single day, exactly seven trucks—S, T, U, W, X, Y, and Z—are the only arrivals at a warehouse. No truck arrives at the same time as any other truck, and no truck arrives more than once that day. Each truck is either green or red (but not both). The following conditions apply: *PrepTest37 Sec3 Qs 6–11*	**Step 1: Overview** What is the game's **situation**? Trucks are arriving in a particular order, and each truck is either red or green. What **entities** are involved in this game? The trucks—S, T, U, W, X, Y, and Z. → What is/are this game's **action**(s)? Sequencing (the order in which the trucks arrive) and Matching (the color of each truck). Are there any **limitations** on this game's entities or action? The trucks arrive one at a time, and each is only one color.

With practice, you'll be able to complete an Overview in a few seconds. Indeed, the expert's internal monologue probably sounds more like this.

LSAT Question	Analysis
In a single day, exactly seven trucks—S, T, U, W, X, Y, and Z—are the only arrivals at a warehouse. No truck arrives at the same time as any other truck, and no truck arrives more than once that day. Each truck is either green or red (but not both). The following conditions apply: *PrepTest37 Sec3 Qs 6–11*	This is a Sequencing/Matching Hybrid. Seven trucks arrive one at a time, and each is either green or red.

The LSAT expert then translates that simple description into a powerful tool: the game's sketch.

Step 2: Sketch

The actual picture of the game that you draw on the page—your Sketch—is the result of the clear mental picture you develop in the Overview. Logic games are nearly impossible if you try to keep all of the information in your head. A strong sketch is simple, easy to read, and often based on something familiar: If a game's action involves scheduling, for example, your sketch may mimic a calendar, or if the game involves putting people or items into different groups, the sketch might be a table.

STEP 2: SKETCH

Create a sketch that depicts the game's action(s) and limitations.

Aim for a sketch that is easy to read, quick to replicate, and able to account for what is certain and uncertain based on the game's rules.

S, T, U, W, X, Y, Z

_ _ _ _ _ _ _

G/R →

For the Truck Arrivals game, the LSAT expert would prepare something like this.

LSAT Question	Analysis
In a single day, exactly seven trucks—S, T, U, W, X, Y, and Z—are the only arrivals at a warehouse. No truck arrives at the same time as any other truck, and no truck arrives more than once that day. Each truck is either green or red (but not both). The following conditions apply:	**Step 1:** This is a Sequencing/Matching Hybrid. Seven trucks arrive one at a time, and each is either green or red.

$\longrightarrow$

Step 2: Sketch

S T U W X Y Z

___ ___ ___ ___ ___ ___ ___
1   2   3   4   5   6   7

PrepTest37 Sec3 Qs 6–11

g/r ___ ___ ___ ___ ___ ___ ___

You'll learn to think of this as a standard sketch pattern for Sequencing-Matching Hybrid games. Here, the top line allows you to keep track of information about the order in which the trucks arrive while the bottom line is where you can record each truck's color. You'll soon see that certain game actions produce similar sketches time after time, resulting in some time-saving patterns. Don't become complacent about sketching, however. A useful sketch must reflect the game's task, and sometimes you'll need to render unique twists on standard sketch patterns.

Step 3: Rules

Once you have the basic framework of your sketch, you're ready to record the game's rules. The rules are always listed under the game's opening paragraph, and they're indented in the test booklet so that they're easy to distinguish from the background scenario.

STEP 3: RULES

- Whenever possible, add information directly into your Sketch framework.
- If you cannot build the rule directly into the Sketch framework, make a shorthand graphical representation of it below or beside the framework.
- Write out the rules in a way that matches the style and conventions of the Sketch framework.
- Consider both the positive and negative implications of the rule.
- Write similar rules consistently, the same way from game to game.

Here's the LSAT expert's depiction of the rules in the Truck Arrivals game. Take a moment to review them and match up each new diagram to its corresponding rule.

LSAT Question	Analysis

LSAT Question

In a single day, exactly seven trucks—S, T, U, W, X, Y, and Z—are the only arrivals at a warehouse. No truck arrives at the same time as any other truck, and no truck arrives more than once that day. Each truck is either green or red (but not both). The following conditions apply:

    No two consecutive arrivals are red.

    Y arrives at some time before both T and W.

    Exactly two of the trucks that arrive before Y are red.

    S is the sixth arrival.

    Z arrives at some time before U.

PrepTest37 Sec3 Qs 6–11

Analysis

Step 3: Rules

S̸ T U W X Y Z

   — — — — — S̲ —
  1   2   3   4   5   6   7

g/r — — — — — — —

⟶

never | r r |

             T
Y ∴
             W

r . . . r . . . Y

Z . . . U

You'll learn much more about depicting rules in Chapter 3. For now, a few of the things that the LSAT expert has done are worth noting. 1) Rule 4 is built directly into the sketch; Truck S will never move. 2) The note "Never" followed by the box around the two Rs indicates Rule 1: Red trucks never arrive consecutively. 3) Rules 2 and 3 both involve Truck Y, so the expert has depicted them in relationship to one another.

LOGIC GAMES STRATEGY

Never make assumptions in logic games. Any restrictions must be explicitly stated, or deduced from the stated rules.

In the Truck Arrivals game, you are told that red trucks never arrive consecutively. That does not mean that green trucks cannot arrive consecutively. Some test takers want to assume that each arrival is a different color than the one before it, but you would need more information to reach that conclusion.

Having the rules depicted as a part of the overall sketch is a big step toward answering a game's questions efficiently and effectively, but it is the next step that can make the biggest difference.

Step 4: Deductions

This is the step that most untrained test takers overlook. Even those who instinctively understand the value of making a sketch and depicting the rules often fail to take the time to determine what must be true or must be false beyond what the game's rules explicitly state.

An LSAT expert, however, knows that in most games, it is possible to combine rules (or to combine rules with the game's overall limitations) in ways that reveal greater certainty within the game. As you practice, you'll start to make valuable deductions even as you are working through the rules. For now, though, be systematic and rigorous in this step to train yourself to get all of a game's potential deductions.

The vast majority of deductions come from one of five patterns, easily remembered with the mnemonic BLEND. Use this as a checklist, not a series of steps. You don't need to look for Blocks of Entities first, necessarily, but you don't want to miss any blocks that may produce additional information.

STEP 4: DEDUCTIONS

Blocks of Entities—two or more players that are always grouped together

Limited Options—rules or restrictions that limit the overall setup to one or the other of two acceptable arrangements

Established Entities—a player locked into a specific space or group

Number Restrictions—rules or limitations that provide guidance about the number of entities assigned to a group or space

Duplications—entities that appear in two or more rules and allow the rules to be combined

---

To make deductions as efficiently as possible, an LSAT expert begins by taking note of the entities that are most restricted or constrained by the rules. Note that Truck S is an Established Entity stuck in space 6. Which other entity is most constrained by the rules in the Truck Arrivals game? Examining the sketch, an LSAT expert immediately identifies Truck Y as an important entity in this game. Truck Y is a perfect example of a Duplication (the fifth item in the BLEND checklist).

LSAT Question	Analysis

In a single day, exactly seven trucks—S, T, U, W, X, Y, and Z—are the only arrivals at a warehouse. No truck arrives at the same time as any other truck, and no truck arrives more than once that day. Each truck is either green or red (but not both). The following conditions apply:
 	
    No two consecutive arrivals are red.
    Y arrives at some time before both T and W.
    Exactly two of the trucks that arrive before Y are red.
    S is the sixth arrival.
    Z arrives at some time before U.
 	
<p align="center">*PrepTest37 Sec3 Qs 6–11*</p>
	Steps 1–3:

Step 4: Deductions

Truck Y appears in both Rule 2 and Rule 3, and as a result, it is constrained by two red trucks that must come before it and Trucks T and W that must come after it. Because of Rule 1, the two red trucks that come before Truck Y must be separated by at least one green truck: r-g-r . . . Y. Thus, the earliest slot in which Truck Y can appear is slot 4. Likewise, because Truck Y must be followed by Trucks T and W, and because Rule 4 places Truck S in slot 6, the latest Truck Y can appear is also slot 4.

Because of Rule 1, the truck arriving in slot 4 (you now know that this is Truck Y) must be green.

Step 4: (cont.)

The only undecided arrivals are in slots 1, 2, and 3. Those must be Trucks Z and U, in that order (Rule 5) and Truck X (the unrestricted, or *floater*, entity in this game). In other words, slots 1–3 could be X-Z-U, Z-X-U, or Z-U-X.

We'll refer to the final sketch, with all of the deductions in place, as the Master Sketch. With the Master Sketch as a point of reference, the LSAT expert can now expect to make relatively short work of the questions.

Step 5: Questions

The first four steps of the Logic Games Method—conducting the Overview, making a useful Sketch, depicting the Rules, and making the available Deductions—are necessary, but not sufficient to success in the Logic Games section. LSAT experts know that the ultimate goal is to answer the question not just correctly, but also quickly. Remember that you have about 8 ½ minutes per game on Test Day. To get through all of the questions in that amount of time, you'll have to leverage the Master Sketch to save time. Don't be surprised if you spend three or four minutes setting up the game and making the deductions. You'll find that you can answer the questions much more quickly and confidently with all of that work clearly laid out on the page.

> ## STEP 5: QUESTIONS
>
> Be able to characterize both correct and incorrect answers.
>
> Know the different question types and how to approach each one.
>
> Don't hesitate to draw a new sketch in New-"If" questions.
>
> Use deductions and previous work to eliminate answers quickly.

Here's how an LSAT expert would manage each of the questions in the Truck Arrivals game.

Partial Acceptability Question

The majority of logic games open with an Acceptability question. The correct answer is the one that breaks none of the rules. All four of the wrong answers violate at least one of the game's rules or limitations. The expert's strategy is simple, and remarkably efficient: Apply the rules, one by one, to the answer choices, and eliminate answer choices that violate the rule.

LSAT Question	Analysis
In a single day, exactly seven trucks—S, T, U, W, X, Y, and Z—are the only arrivals at a warehouse. No truck arrives at the same time as any other truck, and no truck arrives more than once that day. Each truck is either green or red (but not both). The following conditions apply: 　No two consecutive arrivals are red. 　Y arrives at some time before both T and W. 　Exactly two of the trucks that arrive before Y are red. 　S is the sixth arrival. 　Z arrives at some time before U.	**Steps 1–4:** $\not{S}$ T U W X $\not{Y}$ Z （diagram showing positions 1–7 with 4=Y, 5=T/W, 6=S, 7=W/T; color row: g/r r g r g _ _ _; never [r r]; Z…U）

---

1. Which one of the following could be the order, from first to last, in which the trucks arrive?

Step 5: Questions

The answer choices show only the trucks, not their colors, so Rule 1 is of no help in this question. Rule 2 knocks out two answer choices: (C) and (D), in which either W or T appears earlier than Y. Strike those two choices. Rule 3 knocks out choice (B), where Y is placed too early to have two red trucks precede it in the sequence. Rule 4 eliminates choice (E), where S is fifth, not sixth in order.

(A)	X, Z, U, Y, W, S, T	Correct. This choice abides by all of the rules.
(B)	X, Y, Z, U, W, S, T	Violates Rule 3 by placing Truck Y too early in the sequence. Eliminate.
(C)	Z, W, U, T, Y, S, X	Violates Rule 2 by placing Trucks W and T earlier in the sequence than Truck Y. Eliminate.
(D)	Z, U, T, Y, W, S, X	Violates Rule 2 by placing Truck T earlier in the sequence than Truck Y. Eliminate.
(E)	U, Z, Y, T, S, W, X	Violates Rule 4 by placing S fifth instead of sixth in the sequence. Eliminate.

PrepTest37 Sec3 Q6

By approaching Acceptability questions this way—using the rules to eliminate answer choices that violate them—LSAT experts usually answer them in a matter of seconds. Trying to tackle these questions the other way around—testing each answer choice against the rules—is inefficient. You may wind up going back and forth between the rules several times before finding out which rule it violates, or finding out that it happens to be the answer that does not violate any of the rules.

Must Be False Question

Sometimes, the testmaker will ask you straight out, "Which one of the following must be false?" A question like this—which asks for an impossible situation within the game's context—is just a variation on that. To tackle these questions, the LSAT expert simply consults the Master Sketch containing all of the rules and deductions.

LSAT Question	Analysis

In a single day, exactly seven trucks—S, T, U, W, X, Y, and Z—are the only arrivals at a warehouse. No truck arrives at the same time as any other truck, and no truck arrives more than once that day. Each truck is either green or red (but not both). The following conditions apply:
    No two consecutive arrivals are red.
    Y arrives at some time before both T and W.
    Exactly two of the trucks that arrive before Y are red.
    S is the sixth arrival.
    Z arrives at some time before U.
	Steps 1–4:
	 $\cancel{S}$ T U W X $\cancel{Y}$ Z
	
	 X
	 ⏜
	 __ __ __ 4 T/W S W/T
	 1 2 3 4 5 6 7
	 g/r r g r g __ __ __
	
	 never [r r] Z...U ZUX / ZXY / XZU

2. For which one of the following pairs of trucks is it the case that they CANNOT both be red?	**Step 5: Questions** Consult the Master Sketch to evaluate the answer choices. The trucks in the correct answer cannot both be red. The trucks in the wrong answers *could* both be red.
(A) S and X	S could be red if the trucks in slots 5 and 7 are green, and X could be in slot 1 or 3. Both could be red. Eliminate.
(B) T and S	Correct. T and S will be in consecutive slots (whether T is fifth or seventh). Rule 1 prevents consecutive trucks from both being red. T and S *cannot* both be red.
(C) U and W	W could be red in either the fifth or seventh slot, as long as slot 6 is green, and U could be in slot 3. Both could be red. Eliminate.
(D) W and T	Slots 5 and 7 could both be red, as long as slot 6 is green. Both could be red. Eliminate.
(E) X and Z *PrepTest37 Sec3 Q7*	Z could be in slot 1 and X could be in slot 3. Both could be red. Eliminate.

Notice how the expert characterized both the correct *and* the incorrect answer choices before evaluating the answer choices. It may be easier for you to spot answers in which both trucks can be red. Knowing that this characterizes a wrong answer makes working through the choices much faster.

LOGIC GAMES STRATEGY

Once you are certain of the correct answer, you do not need to evaluate the remaining choices.

If an LSAT expert evaluated the answer choices for Question 2 in order, starting with (A), she could move on to the next question after testing (B). She would not have to check (C), (D), or (E) provided that she is certain of the criteria for the correct answer.

Every question has one demonstrably correct answer and four demonstrably incorrect answers. Early on in your practice, it's probably worth the time to check every answer choice to develop your evaluative skills. As you gain familiarity and confidence, you will be able to take advantage of time-saving tips like this one.

New-"If"/Must Be True Question

This next question is a New-"If" question. The LSAT expert knows to redraw the Master Sketch, adding the question's new stipulation ("X is the third arrival"), and making any additional deductions triggered by the new information. The correct answer here will name a truck that must be green under this question's new stipulation.

LSAT Question	Analysis
In a single day, exactly seven trucks—S, T, U, W, X, Y, and Z—are the only arrivals at a warehouse. No truck arrives at the same time as any other truck, and no truck arrives more than once that day. Each truck is either green or red (but not both). The following conditions apply:	**Steps 1–4:**

No two consecutive arrivals are red.
Y arrives at some time before both T and W.
Exactly two of the trucks that arrive before Y are red.
S is the sixth arrival.
Z arrives at some time before U.

$\longrightarrow$

S̸ T U W X Y̸ Z

X
⎧‾‾‾‾‾⎫
__ __ __   Y T/W S W/T
 1   2   3   4   5   6   7

g/r r g r g __ __ __

never [r r]   Z...U

3. If X is the third arrival, then which one of the following trucks must be green?

Step 5: Questions

Placing Truck X in slot 3 means than Truck Z must take slot 1 and Truck U must take slot 2.

S̸ T U̸ W X̸ Y̸ Z̸

$\longrightarrow$

Z   U   X   Y T/W S W/T
1   2   3   4   5   6   7

g/r r g r g __ __ __

Thus, truck U must be green.

(A)	S	$\longrightarrow$ Truck S could be either green or red. Eliminate.
(B)	T	$\longrightarrow$ Truck T could be either green or red. Eliminate.
(C)	U	$\longrightarrow$ Correct. Under this question's conditions, Truck U must be green.
(D)	W	$\longrightarrow$ Truck W could be either green or red. Eliminate.
(E)	Z	$\longrightarrow$ Under this question's conditions, Truck Z must be red. Eliminate.

PrepTest37 Sec3 Q8

LOGIC GAMES STRATEGY

Leave the Master Sketch alone. For New-"If" questions, copy the Master Sketch next to or below the question, and add the question's new information there.

It may be tempting to save time by adding a New-"If" question's new condition into the Master Sketch and making any additional deductions there, but you will likely need the Master Sketch again to answer further Must Be True/Must Be False type questions, or you may have additional New-"If" questions with different conditions (indeed, the next question in this game is just that). Either way, trying to erase the work you've done for one question in order to restore the Master Sketch leads to confusion and mistakes.

New-"If"/Must Be True Question

This question is very similar to question 3, but the conditions have changed. Once again, the LSAT expert quickly copies the Master Sketch and adds this question's new information to the copy, making her additional deductions there.

LSAT Question	Analysis

In a single day, exactly seven trucks—S, T, U, W, X, Y, and Z—are the only arrivals at a warehouse. No truck arrives at the same time as any other truck, and no truck arrives more than once that day. Each truck is either green or red (but not both). The following conditions apply:
    No two consecutive arrivals are red.
    Y arrives at some time before both T and W.
    Exactly two of the trucks that arrive before Y are red.
    S is the sixth arrival.
    Z arrives at some time before U.
	Steps 1–4:
	S̶ T U W X Y̶ Z
	
	X
	⌒
	___ ___ ___ Y T/W S W/T
	1 2 3 4 5 6 7
	
	g/r r g r g ___ ___ ___
	
	never [r r] Z...U

4.	If exactly three of the trucks are green, then which one of the following trucks must be green?	**Step 5: Questions** The trucks in slots 2 and 4 are always green. If there is to be just one more green truck, it will have to take slot 6 to prevent having any red trucks arrive consecutively (Rule 1). S̶ T U W X Y̶ Z X ⌒ ___ ___ ___ Y T/W S W/T 1 2 3 4 5 6 7 g/r r g r g r g r Z...U Thus, Truck S must be green.
	(A) S	Correct. Under this question's conditions, Truck S must be green.
	(B) T	Under this question's conditions, Truck T must be red, whether it is fifth or seventh. Eliminate.
	(C) U	Truck U could be either green or red. Eliminate.
	(D) W	Under this question's conditions, Truck W must be red, whether it is fifth or seventh. Eliminate.
	(E) Z	Truck Z could be either green or red. Eliminate.

PrepTest37 Sec3 Q9

"How Many" Question

This question type is pretty rare. It asks for the number of entities—the number of trucks in this case—that are placed with certainty once and for all. There is no New-"If" condition, so an LSAT expert recognizes that this question can be answered directly from the Master Sketch.

LSAT Question	Analysis

In a single day, exactly seven trucks—S, T, U, W, X, Y, and Z—are the only arrivals at a warehouse. No truck arrives at the same time as any other truck, and no truck arrives more than once that day. Each truck is either green or red (but not both). The following conditions apply:
 	
    No two consecutive arrivals are red.
    Y arrives at some time before both T and W.
    Exactly two of the trucks that arrive before Y are red.
    S is the sixth arrival.
    Z arrives at some time before U.
	Steps 1–4:
	
	S̶ T U W X Ȳ Z
	
	X
	
	‾‾‾‾‾‾‾ Y T/W S W/T
	_ _ _ 4 5 6 7
	1 2 3
	
	g/r r g r g _ _ _
	
	never [r r] Z...U

5.	For exactly how many of the seven trucks can one determine exactly how many trucks arrived before it?	**Step 5: Questions** Rule 4 established the placement of Truck S. Combining Rule 2 with Rules 1 and 4 established that Truck Y must take slot 4. Those are the only two trucks whose placement is determined once and for all.
(A)	one	
(B)	two	Correct. The placements of Trucks S and Y are completely determined.
(C)	three	
(D)	four	
(E)	five	

PrepTest37 Sec3 Q10

"How Many" questions, like this one, fall under the category of Numerical Questions. Related questions may ask for the minimum or maximum number of entities that may be selected or placed in a certain grouping, or the earliest or latest that an entity can appear within a sequence. You'll learn about all of the question types in Chapter 5. For the time being, recognizing that this question does not contain a New-"If" condition and can, therefore, be answered directly from the deductions in the Master Sketch, is all that you need to know.

Must Be False Question

This one is quite similar to the second question in this game's set.

LSAT Question	Analysis
In a single day, exactly seven trucks—S, T, U, W, X, Y, and Z—are the only arrivals at a warehouse. No truck arrives at the same time as any other truck, and no truck arrives more than once that day. Each truck is either green or red (but not both). The following conditions apply: No two consecutive arrivals are red. Y arrives at some time before both T and W. Exactly two of the trucks that arrive before Y are red. S is the sixth arrival. Z arrives at some time before U.	**Steps 1–4:** S̶ T U W X Y̶ Z X ⏞ _ _ _ Y T/W S W/T 1 2 3 4 5 6 7 g/r r g r g _ _ _ never [r r] Z...U
6. Which one of the following pairs of trucks CANNOT arrive consecutively at the warehouse?	**Step 5: Questions** Test each answer choice against the Master Sketch. Eliminate any choice in which the pair of trucks *could* arrive consecutively. The correct answer cites a pair of trucks that *cannot* arrive consecutively.
(A) U and Y	Truck Y is always in slot 4. Truck U could be in slot 3. Eliminate.
(B) X and Y	Truck Y is always in slot 4. Truck X could be in slot 3. Eliminate.
(C) Y and T	Truck Y is always in slot 4. Truck T could be in slot 5. Eliminate.
(D) Y and W	Truck Y is always in slot 4. Truck W could be in slot 5. Eliminate.
(E) Y and Z *PrepTest37 Sec3 Q11*	Correct. Truck Y is always in slot 4. Truck Z can be only in slots 1 or 2. These trucks can never be consecutive.

That's a look at the Logic Games Method in action. Once the LSAT expert analyzed the setup and made all of the deductions, answering the questions was fairly straightforward. Now, not all games have as many deductions as this one did, but it is always important that you know everything about the game—about what must, can, and cannot be true of the entities—that you can.

In the next portion of this chapter, you can practice the steps of the Logic Games Method on a new setup. Don't worry if you make mistakes at this point; you have lots of practice ahead of you. Concentrate on the steps of the Method, and on the purpose of each step.

Practice

Directions: Perform steps 1–4 of the Logic Games Method on the following game setup and rules, and answer the accompanying questions. When you're finished, compare your work to the expert analysis on the following pages.

A little league baseball team manager has to schedule his rotation of six starting pitchers—Atwood, Blevins, Chen, Dante, Engle, and Fuentes—for the first six games of the season. Each pitcher will start exactly once. The manager has decided to strictly adhere to the advice of his pitching coach as follows:

Chen, the team's strongest pitcher, will start the first game.
Atwood will start the game immediately after the game Dante starts due to the two pitchers' contrasting styles.
Fuentes will start a later game than the game Atwood starts.
Engle will not start the game immediately after the game Chen starts.

Step 1

1. What is Step 1 of the Logic Games Method, and what is its purpose?

    The overview. To understand the task

2. What are the four questions you ask in Step 1?

    What is the situation?   What limitations?
    Who or what are the entities?
    What is the action? → sequencing, selection, distribution, matching, or combo/hybrid?

3. What is your Step 1 analysis of this particular game?

    Six pitchers' starting rotation in six games each appearing once

Step 2

4. What is Step 2 of the Logic Games Method, and what is its purpose?

    Sketch - create a visual representation based on overview analysis.

5. What is your Step 2 analysis of this particular game?

    _ _ _ _ _ _
    1 2 3 4 5 6
    A B C D E F

Step 3

6. What is Step 3 of the Logic Games Method, and what is its purpose?

Rules. You are creating a clearer mental picture by adding the given rules of game to the sketch.

7. What is your Step 3 analysis of this particular game?

- Rule 1: *C*
- Rule 2: *always DA...F*
- Rule 3:
- Rule 4: *Never CE*

A B C D E F

C — DAEF
DAFE
EDAF

CBD ____

1 2 3 4 5 6

Step 4

8. What is Step 4 of the Logic Games Method, and what is its purpose?

Deductions. To rule out certain possibilities; determine True/False

9. What are five patterns you always look for during Step 4?

BLEND. Blocks of entities (2 or more together), Limited options, Established Entities, Number restrictions (number of entities assigned to a group or space),

10. What is your Step 4 analysis of this particular game?

- Which entities appear in two rules? What can you learn from combining those rules?

You can learn E won't be in slot 2. You can learn that F will always be after DA

- In which slots would Dante NOT be allowed?

3, 6

- In which slots would Atwood NOT be allowed?

2, 6

- In which slots would Fuentes NOT be allowed?

2, 3

- Which entities COULD be in slot 2?

B, D,

- Is there a *floater*, in other words, an entity that is unrestricted by any rule or limitation? If so, which one(s)?

no

C B ____
C B D A E/F F/E
C B E D A F
C D A ___

B E F
B F E
E B F
E F B
F B E
F E B

Step 5

11. What is Step 5 of the Logic Games Method, and what is its purpose?

    Questions, to answer the question quickly and correctly. 8 ½ mins/question

12. What strategy should you use for the following question?

    "Which one of the following could be the order, from first to last, of the little league team's starting rotation?"

    Compare each to master sketch

    - Which rule does the sequence C, E, B, D, A, F violate?

      Rule Never CE

13. What strategy should you use for the following question?

    "Which one of the following is a pitcher who could pitch in the team's second game?"

    Only B or D can appear in slot 2. Eliminate all others.

    - Which pitchers could be the correct answer to that question?

      B, D

14. What strategy should you use for the following question?

    "If Atwood pitches third in the team's rotation, then which one of the following could be true?"

    Create a new sketch with A in game 3, and D in game 2

    - What would the characteristic of the four wrong answers be to that question?

      Anything where C D A ... isn't the answer
                       1 2 3

    - Would the statement "Fuentes pitches fourth" be a correct or incorrect answer to that question?

      Correct

    - Would the statement "Blevins pitches second" be a correct or incorrect answer to that question?

      incorrect

15. [Bonus, high difficulty question] Placing Engle in which slot would completely determine the team's pitching rotation?

    Third Slot

    C B/D E __ __ __
    1   2   3   4   5   6

    C B E D A F

Explanations

The LSAT expert's answers are given in italics. Compare your answers to the expert's, and if you missed anything, revisit the game's setup to see where you went off track.

A little league baseball team manager has to schedule his rotation of six starting pitchers—Atwood, Blevins, Chen, Dante, Engle, and Fuentes—for the first six games of the season. Each pitcher will start exactly once. The manager has decided to strictly adhere to the advice of his pitching coach as follows:

> Chen, the team's strongest pitcher, will start the first game.
> Atwood will start the game immediately after the game Dante starts due to the two pitchers' contrasting styles.
> Fuentes will start a later game than the game Atwood starts.
> Engle will not start the game immediately after the game Chen starts.

Step 1

1. What is Step 1 of the Logic Games Method, and what is its purpose? *Step 1 is Overview—in other words, reviewing the game's opening paragraph to understand the game's task and its moving parts.*

2. What are the four questions you ask in Step 1? *The SEAL questions: What is the SITUATION? Who or what are the ENTITIES? What is the game's ACTION? What LIMITATIONS are given in the game's opening paragraph?*

3. What is your Step 1 analysis of this particular game? *The SITUATION is creating a baseball team's six-person starting rotation, so the task is just to write out the list in an acceptable order. The ENTITIES are the pitchers—A, B, C, D, E, and F. The game's ACTION is basic Strict Sequencing*, with the intuitive LIMITATION of one pitcher per spot in the rotation.*

    *You will learn the names of all the standard game types in Chapter 2.

Step 2

4. What is Step 2 of the Logic Games Method, and what is its purpose? *Step 2 is Sketch, and its purpose is to write out a simple, easily repeatable framework in which to record the details of the game's rules and restrictions.*

5. What is your Step 2 analysis of this particular game? *Here, the sketch will just consist of a shorthand list of the pitchers and six numbered slots. The slots could be arranged horizontally or vertically, whichever seems most natural.*

$$A \quad B \quad C \quad D \quad E \quad F$$

$$\overline{1} \quad \overline{2} \quad \overline{3} \quad \overline{4} \quad \overline{5} \quad \overline{6}$$

Step 3

6. What is Step 3 of the Logic Games Method, and what is its purpose? *Step 3 is Rules, and its purpose is to analyze each of the rules (considering both their positive and negative restrictions) and to record them in a way that aligns with the sketch framework.*

7. What is your Step 3 analysis of this particular game?

   - Rule 1:

   $$\frac{C}{1} \quad \overline{2} \quad \overline{3} \quad \overline{4} \quad \overline{5} \quad \overline{6}$$

   - Rule 2:

   $$\boxed{D \quad A}$$

   - Rule 3:

   $$A \ldots F$$

   - Rule 4:

   Never

Here's the sketch at the end of Step 3.

A B ~~C~~ D E F

$$\frac{C}{1} \quad \frac{}{2} \quad \frac{}{3} \quad \frac{}{4} \quad \frac{}{5} \quad \frac{}{6}$$

[D̲ A̲]

A . . . F

Never [C̲ E̲]

Step 4

8. What is Step 4 of the Logic Games Method, and what is its purpose? *Step 4 is Deductions, and its purpose is to combine rules to determine what must be true or must be false in the game.*

9. What are five patterns you always look for during Step 4? *BLEND: Blocks of Entities, Limited Options, Established Entities, Number Restrictions, and Duplications*

10. What is your Step 4 analysis of this particular game?

    • Which entities appear in two rules? What can you learn from combining those rules? *Atwood appears in Rules 2 and 3. Chen appears in Rules 1 and 4. Rules 2 and 3 can be combined to deduce that the string DA . . . F will always appear in that order. Rules 1 and 4 combine to deduce that Engle will never be the second pitcher in the rotation.*

    A B ~~C~~ D E F

    $$\frac{C}{1} \quad \frac{}{2} \quad \frac{}{3} \quad \frac{}{4} \quad \frac{}{5} \quad \frac{}{6}$$
    ~E

    [D̲ A̲] . . . F

• In which slots would Dante NOT be allowed? *Because Dante has to pitch before Atwood and Fuentes, Dante can never pitch fifth or sixth.*

• In which slots would Atwood NOT be allowed? *Because Atwood must pitch after Dante and before Fuentes, and because Chen is always the first pitcher, Atwood cannot pitch second or sixth.*

• In which slots would Fuentes NOT be allowed? *Because Fuentes must pitch after Dante and after Atwood, and because Chen always pitches first, Fuentes cannot pitch second or third.*

A B ~~C~~ D E F

$$\frac{C}{1} \quad \frac{}{2} \quad \frac{}{3} \quad \frac{}{4} \quad \frac{}{5} \quad \frac{}{6}$$
~E ~F   ~D ~D
~A   ~A
~F

[D̲ A̲] . . . F

• Which entities COULD be in slot 2? *Because Chen is already assigned to slot 1, and because Engle (Rule 4) and Atwood and Fuentes (Rules 2 and 3) are all prevented from pitching second, the only pitchers who could pitch second are Blevins and Dante.*

• Is there a *floater*, in other words, an entity that is unrestricted by any rule or limitation? If so, which one(s)? *There are no rules or restrictions on Blevins. Aside from slot 1 (which is always Chen's spot), Blevins can pitch in any position.*

This is the game's Master Sketch.

A B ~~C~~ D E F

$$\frac{C}{1} \quad \frac{B/D}{2} \quad \frac{}{3} \quad \frac{}{4} \quad \frac{}{5} \quad \frac{}{6}$$
~E ~F   ~D ~D
~A   ~A
~F

[D̲ A̲] . . . F

Step 5

11. What is Step 5 of the Logic Games Method, and what is its purpose? *Step 5 is Questions, and its purpose is to answer the questions as quickly and confidently as possible by using the appropriate strategy for each question type.*

12. What strategy should you use for the following question?

    "Which one of the following could be the order, from first to last, of the little league team's starting rotation?" *This is an Acceptability question. The fastest, surest way to answer it is to apply each rule to the answer choices and eliminate any answers that violate the rule.*

    - Which rule does the sequence C, E, B, D, A, F violate? *That violates Rule 4, which prevents Engle from pitching immediately after Chen.*

13. What strategy should you use for the following question?

    "Which one of the following is a pitcher who could pitch in the team's second game?" *This is a Could Be True question; just test the answer choices against the Master Sketch to see which one is possible. The four wrong answers will all name pitchers who CANNOT pitch second.*

    - Which pitcher(s) could be in the correct answer to that question? *The correct answer must be either Blevins or Dante, the only two pitchers who can take the second spot in the rotation.*

14. What strategy should you use for the following question?

    "If Atwood pitches third in the team's rotation, then which one of the following could be true?" *This is a New-"If" question. The best way to approach it is to make a copy of the Master Sketch next to the question, enter in the*

question's new conditional information, and make any additional deductions available as a result. For the record, if Atwood pitches third, then Dante pitches second. Blevins, Engle, and Fuentes would take slots 4, 5, and 6, but they could be in any order.

- What would the characteristic of the four wrong answers be in that question? *The four wrong answers Must Be False.*
- Would the statement "Fuentes pitches fourth" be a correct or incorrect answer in that question? *That statement could be true, so this would be a correct answer.*
- Would the statement "Blevins pitches second" be a correct or incorrect answer in that question? *That statement must be false— Dante pitches second in this question—so this would be an incorrect answer.*

15. [Bonus, high difficulty question] Placing Engle in which slot would completely determine the team's pitching rotation? *Giving Engle the third spot in the rotation would determine every pitchers' position. With Engle third, Blevins must pitch second. The remaining pitchers— Atwood, Dante, and Fuentes—must pitch in order determined by Rules 2 and 3, that is, they must go DA ... F. With only slots 4, 5, and 6 open to them, the rotation is entirely determined.*

$$\underset{1}{\underline{C}} \quad \underset{2}{\underline{B}} \quad \underset{3}{\underline{E}} \quad \underset{4}{\underline{D}} \quad \underset{5}{\underline{A}} \quad \underset{6}{\underline{F}}$$

Test out Engle in slots 4, 5, and 6 if you like. None of those placements will completely determine the rotation.

On the following pages, you'll find the Perform quiz (your self-assessment) for Chapter 1. After you complete it, compare your answers to those in the Answer Key. Because Chapter 1 provides the foundation for everything you'll be doing, you want to make sure you know the Logic Games Method by heart before moving on to the chapters that break down the steps of the Method and apply them to all of the various game types.

Perform

Fill in the following blanks, listing the steps and strategies associated with the Logic Games Method.

Kaplan Logic Games Method

Step 1: _Overview_

→ 4 questions to ask before Step 2
- What is the situation?
- Who or what are the entities?
- What limitations?
- What is the action? Sequencing, selection, distribution, matching, hybrid

Step 2: _Sketch_

Step 3: _Rules_

Step 4: _Deductions_

→ 6 things to look for before Step 5
- Blocks
- Limited entities
- Establish entities
- Number restrictions (# of entities assigned to group or space
- Duplications (entities
- Note any unused entities known as _Floaters_

Step 5: _____

Logic Games Questions

What is the strategy for Acceptability questions?

Apply the rules to the answer choices, 1 by 1.

What is the strategy for Must Be/Could Be questions?

Consult the master sketch

What is the strategy for New-"If" questions?

Draw new master sketch with rule added

Explanations

Kaplan Logic Games Method

Step 1: *Overview*

→ 4 questions to ask before Step 2
- Situation
- Entities
- Action
- Limitations

Step 2: *Sketch*

Step 3: *Rules*

Step 4: *Deductions*

→ 6 things to look for before Step 5
- **Blocks of Entities**
- **Limited Options**
- **Established Entities**
- **Numbers**
- **Duplication**
- Note any unused entities known as **Floaters**

Step 5: *Questions*

Logic Games Questions

What is the strategy for Acceptability questions?

Go rule by rule to eliminate each answer choice that violates a rule.

What is the strategy for Must Be/Could Be questions?

Consult the Master Sketch to see if the question can be answered immediately. If not, use sketches from New-"If"s, as well as the Acceptability question correct answer, to eliminate answers. The sketch from a New-"If" could also help pick a Could Be True answer. If multiple answer choices still remain use trial and error.

What is the strategy for New-"If" questions?

Draw a new sketch that incorporates the new information.

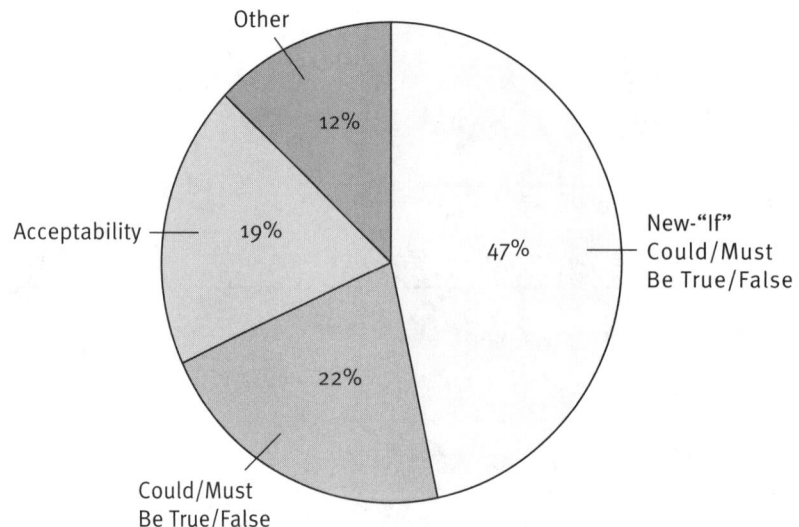

Types of Questions By Percentage, 2012–2016

- Other — 12%
- Acceptability — 19%
- Could/Must Be True/False — 22%
- New-"If" Could/Must Be True/False — 47%

*PrepTests 66–80; released 2012–2016

Assess

The self-assessment criteria for this chapter's Perform quiz is necessarily more strict than those in later chapters. To get the most out of all the study and practice available in this book, you *must* know the steps of the Logic Games Method by heart.

If you were able to list out the steps accurately: congratulations. You're ready for the valuable strategies and tactics you'll learn for each step.

If there were any steps you misidentified or forgot: Study the Logic Games Method once more before moving on to the following chapters, in which you'll drill down into each step in detail.

If you missed any of the question strategies, you'll have the opportunity to practice those thoroughly in Chapter 4. For now, the most important thing to remember is that you will use the sketch and deductions you make to answer the questions, so your work with Steps 1–4 is essential to success in the Logic Games section of the LSAT. The work you'll do in the next two chapters will introduce you to the basic logic game types seen on the test, and will give you the tools and strategies to analyze and sketch the setups, rules, and deductions you will encounter most often.

Reflect

Now that you've seen the Logic Games Method, take a few minutes to reflect on the following questions:

- What is the purpose of Step 1, and why does an expert always take that step?

- What is the purpose of Step 2, and why does an expert always take that step?

- What is the purpose of Step 3, and why does an expert always take that step?

- What is the purpose of Step 4, and why does an expert always take that step?

- What is the purpose of Step 5, and why does an expert always take that step?

- Did any part of the Logic Games Method surprise you?

- Are there specific steps in the Logic Games Method that excite you?

- Were any of the steps confusing? How will you get additional practice with those steps?

- How will you approach Logic Games differently the next time you practice them?

- What techniques did you see applied to the game in this chapter that you can immediately put to use the next time you practice Logic Games?

As you practice Logic Games further, review the explanations thoroughly. The explanations will cover each step in the Logic Games Method and help make clear how every game can be done most efficiently and effectively.

CHAPTER 2

Logic Game Types and Sketches

In this chapter, you get to drill down into Steps 1 and 2 of the Logic Games Method. You'll learn the most common game types and begin collecting a library of the most common sketch patterns.

Game types are based on the action or task you're expected to complete. For example, the Truck Arrivals game in Chapter 1 was a Sequencing/Matching Hybrid game because you were asked to determine the order in which the trucks arrived at the warehouse, and you had to match a color (green or red) to each truck. Even though that game had two actions, the sketch allowed you to depict the task clearly, and the rules and deductions left very little ambiguity about the final arrangement.

There are four basic actions in logic games: Sequencing, Selection, Distribution, and Matching. As you learn to identify the game types, it is helpful to associate them with real-world situations. The truth is that you handle these kinds of tasks all the time. When you rank the *Star Wars* movies from best to worst, or when you decide the order in which your friends will take turns bowling, you're doing a Sequencing game. When you choose who to invite or not invite to dinner, you're engaged in Selection. Any time you choose teams for a pick-up basketball game, you're completing a Distribution task. Keep it simple, and look for the real-world model to the task described in the game.

Associating logic game tasks with real-world situations will help you make clear, useful sketches, too. If you're deciding on a class schedule, you probably use a calendar so that you can make sure no day is too busy or that nothing overlaps. So, in a game that asks you to account for appointments on a person's work calendar, it would be natural for you to jot five spaces horizontally, and label them *M-Tu-W-Th-F*. The examples you will encounter in this chapter will provide a great starting point for how to sketch the games you'll see on Test Day, but always read the game setup carefully to have your sketch reflect the situation, entities, action, and limitations described.

HOW TO IDENTIFY AND SKETCH THE GAME TYPES

Prepare

In this chapter, you'll practice Steps 1 and 2 of the Logic Games Method together. That's because the sketch (Step 2) is the direct result of your Overview analysis (Step 1). Said another way, the best test of your work in Step 1 is the accuracy of your work in Step 2.

LEARNING OBJECTIVES

In this chapter, you'll learn to

- Identify the actions and limitations that characterize common LSAT logic game types
- Create clear, useful sketches for each logic game type

At the end of this chapter, you will test your ability to recognize six types of logic games based on their actions, and to create accurate sketches for each type.

Refresh (Activate Prior Knowledge)

To get the ball rolling, review the Step 1 and Step 2 analysis that the LSAT expert applied to the game you saw in Chapter 1.

> In a single day, exactly seven trucks—S, T, U, W, X, Y, and Z—are the only arrivals at a warehouse. No truck arrives at the same time as any other truck, and no truck arrives more than once that day. Each truck is either green or red (but not both). The following conditions apply:

PrepTest37 Sec3 Qs 6–11

Step 1: First, the expert conducted an overview of the game's opening paragraph by asking the SEAL questions.

- What is the game's **situation**? Trucks are arriving in a particular order, and each truck is either red or green.
- What **entities** are involved in this game? The trucks—S, T, U, W, X, Y, and Z
- What is/are this game's **action**(s)? Sequencing (the order in which the trucks arrive) and Matching (the color of each truck)
- Are there any **limitations** on this game's entities or action? The trucks arrive one at a time, and each is only one color.

Step 2: Based on the Step 1 analysis, the expert created a sketch that depicts the game's action(s) and limitations. The sketch should be easy to read, quick to replicate, and able to account for what is certain and uncertain based on the game's rules. This was the result:

S T U W X Y Z

‾ ‾ ‾ ‾ ‾ ‾ ‾
1 2 3 4 5 6 7

g/r __ __ __ __ __ __ __

Now, compare that analysis to another expert's work on a game you haven't seen before. See how well you can anticipate the expert's analysis here. Take a minute to consider the setup:

> On one afternoon, Patterson meets individually with each of exactly five clients—Reilly, Sanchez, Tang, Upton, and Yansky—and also goes to the gym by herself for a workout. Patterson's workout and her five meetings each start at either 1:00, 2:00, 3:00, 4:00, 5:00, or 6:00. The following conditions must apply:

PrepTest45 Sec3 Qs 1–6

Step 1: First, the expert conducts an overview of the game's opening paragraph by asking the SEAL questions.

- What is the game's **situation**? A woman scheduling five meetings and a workout for the afternoon.
- What **entities** are involved in this game? five clients—R, S, T, U, and Y—and the workout—W
- What is/are this game's **action**(s)? Sequencing
- Are there any **limitations** on this game's entities or action? She meets each client once, one at a time, and the meetings and the workout happen on the hour, from 1:00 through 6:00.

Step 2: Here, the Step 1 analysis shows a game with one action—Sequencing. The sketch should reflect the calendar-like description of the setup.

R S T U W Y

‾ ‾ ‾ ‾ ‾ ‾
1   2   3   4   5   6

As it turned out, this game is a Strict Sequencing game, the most common game type on the LSAT.

In this chapter, you'll learn to analyze various game types you could encounter on Test Day. The game types are defined by their action or actions. The pie chart that follows the definitions shows you how often each game type has appeared on released LSAT exams administered over the past five years.

GAME TYPE ACTIONS

- **Strict Sequencing:** Ordering or ranking entities with respect to defined positions
- **Loose Sequencing:** Ordering or ranking entities with respect to each other
- **Selection:** Choosing a smaller group of entities from a larger group
- **Matching:** Matching two kinds of entities to each other, or matching attributes to a list of entities
- **Distribution:** Separating entities into two or more smaller groups
- **Hybrid:** Performing a task that involves two or more of the actions described above; e.g., Sequencing/Matching, Distribution/Sequencing, or Selection/Distribution

Type of Games By Percentage, 2012–2016

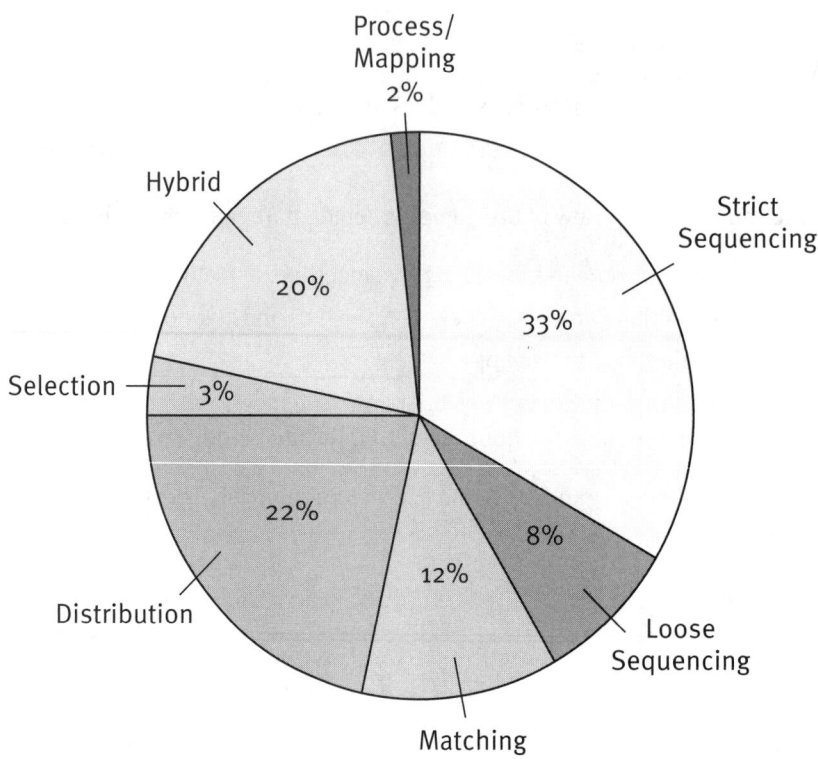

PrepTests 66–80; released 2012–2016

Logic Game Types Illustrated

Take a closer look at the game actions we defined in the previous Logic Games Strategy box. For each, you'll see a model game setup and a suggested sketch.

> ### LOGIC GAMES STRATEGY
>
> As you practice logic games, develop and maintain a library of common sketch frameworks for each game type. There are a limited number of game actions that correspond to sketch templates that will be useful again and again.

Strict Sequencing Games

Sequencing games are, by far, the most common games on recent LSATs. The testmaker uses several variations on Sequencing, as you'll see here, and in even more detail in Chapters 5, 6, and 7.

LOGIC GAMES STRATEGY

Sequencing games ask you to put things in order:

- Chronologically (either using units of time—years, weeks, days, or hours—or simply using the notions of "earlier" and "later")
- Spatially (either horizontally or vertically, and with specific positions—for example, runners in lanes 1 through 6—or by using notions such as "higher and lower" or "east and west")
- By rank or result (such as first place through seventh place, or "best to worst")
- By size or amount (such as "most to least expensive")

Most Sequencing games (more than 80 percent, in fact) are Strict Sequencing games, meaning that the positions are numbered (1, 2, 3...) or named (Monday, Tuesday, Wednesday...) and that the rules refer to specific positions or to a precise number of positions between entities (e.g., "B sits in the sixth chair," "C and D are in adjacent lanes," or "E speaks later than F and exactly one speech is given in between them"). Strict Sequencing games may include rules that provide a relative relationship between entities ("P speaks later than Q speaks"), but will always provide one or more rules related to the *strict* positions. Basic Strict Sequencing games are covered in detail in Chapter 5.

Here's a model Strict Sequencing setup and its initial sketch:

Six figurines—A, B, C, D, E, and F—are arranged in a line from left to right on a shelf, with each figurine in a different spot. The following conditions apply:

→

Step 1:
Situation: Arranging figurines in a single line along a shelf

Entities: Six figurines—A, B, C, D, E, and F

Action: Sequencing

Limitations: One figurine per position

Step 2:

A B C D E F

―   ―   ―   ―   ―   ―
1   2   3   4   5   6

Because Strict Sequencing games are so common, you will see a number of variations on this game type. For example, the testmaker could ask you to sequence five entities two times in different orders. Another variation might involve a difference between the number of entities and positions. If the game tasks you with sequencing seven appointments over five days, you would know that at least one or two of the days have multiple appointments. On the other hand, if the game asked you to sequence five events over the course of seven years, you would know that at least two of the years saw none of the events occur. These "complex" Strict Sequencing games are covered in detail in Chapter 6.

LOGIC GAMES STRATEGY

Never *assume* anything in a logic game. Rather, pay close attention to the limitations in the game's setup.

If a Strict Sequencing game lists seven people to schedule for appointments over seven days, your instinct will be that one person is scheduled per day. But, for that limitation to apply, the setup or rules must state "one appointment per day."

Here's a "double sequencing" twist on Strict Sequencing and its suggested sketch.

In a blind taste test, two professional food critics—Peters and Quimby—will each sample five breakfast cereals—Berry Bombs, Cocoa Clusters, Fruity Freaks, Marshmallow Mouthfuls, and NutriNuggets—one at a time. To ensure fairness, each critic will test the cereals in a different order, in accordance with the following restrictions:	**Step 1:** Situation: Two critics testing the same five cereals, but in a different order Entities: The cereals—B, C, F, M, and N Action: Double Sequencing, five items are sequenced two times → Limitations: "one at a time" and a "different order" for each critic **Step 2:** B C F M N P: _ _ _ _ _ Q: _ _ _ _ _ 1 2 3 4 5

The sketch for that "complex" Strict Sequencing game isn't all that different from one for a standard Strict Sequencing setup. It simply provides two lines of slots, one for each food critic, in accordance with the action and limitations described in the paragraph.

Loose Sequencing Games

While not nearly as common as Strict Sequencing, Loose Sequencing games have accounted for about 10 percent of all games on released LSATs over the past five years.

The opening setup of a Loose Sequencing game may not appear any different than that of a Strict Sequencing game. It is the *rules* that distinguish Loose Sequencing. In Loose Sequencing, none of the rules refer to specific positions, and none of the rules separate entities by a specific number of positions. In Loose Sequencing, all of the rules relate entities relative to one another (e.g., "B is ranked higher than C" or "H is opened later than L").

The reason that it is important to distinguish Loose Sequencing from Strict Sequencing is because Loose Sequencing is best managed with a different kind of sketch. Because Loose Sequencing rules relate the entities to one another, you can create a kind of "branching tree" that will show the relationships among the entities as they are restricted by the rules. Loose Sequencing games are covered in detail in Chapter 7.

Here's a model Loose Sequencing game and its accompanying *branching tree* sketch:

Seven magazines—G, H, J, K, L, M, and N—are ranked from most honest to least honest by an organization concerned with journalistic integrity. Each magazine receives a different rank, and no other magazines are ranked. The following conditions apply:

Both H and L are ranked higher than M.
J is ranked lower than G.
N is ranked lower than M.
K is ranked lower than N.
M is ranked higher than J.

Step 1:

Situation: A "most to least" ranking of magazines

Entities: The magazines—G, H, J, K, L, M, and N

Action: Sequencing, specifically Loose Sequencing, because all of the rules give relative relationships among the entities

$\longrightarrow$ Limitations: No ties

Step 2:

```
H        L
 \      /
  \    /      G
   \  /      /
    M        
   / \       /
  /   \     /
 N     J
 |
 K
```

By the way, it is common in Loose Sequencing for the rules to account for every entity, such that they all appear in the sketch's "tree" as they do in this example.

NOTE: For the Practice and Perform quizzes in this chapter, we won't include the rules. Thus, for some of the Sequencing setups you see, it may be unclear whether you would ultimately use a Strict or Loose Sequencing sketch. That's fine. Make a note of the ambiguity and jot down what the Strict Sequencing sketch would look like.

Selection Games

In recent years, Selection games have been quite rare, accounting for less than five percent of the games on released LSATs. Unlike Sequencing games, Selection games do not appear on every test.

LOGIC GAMES STRATEGY

Selection games ask you to choose some items and reject others from a list of items. Selection games may:

- Stipulate the number to be chosen (e.g., "the manager will interview exactly four of the seven applicants"),
- Limit the number to be chosen ("Mark will invite at most five of the seven marketers to the company retreat"), or
- Leave the number to be chosen ambiguous (e.g., "From among seven dishes on the catering menu . . . Carol will decide which to serve at the reception").

On Selection games that do not provide a specific number of entities to choose from the initial list, most LSAT experts forego making a sketch. Instead, they simply write out the initial list of entities, circle those that are chosen, and cross out those that are rejected. This is the most efficient approach for New-"If" questions (e.g., "If A is selected, then which one of the following must be true") because re-writing the list of entities takes almost no time at all. Here's an example:

A child is selecting stickers to put on her notebook. She can choose from six stickers, one each representing an apple, a banana, a cat, a dog, an egg, and a fan. The following conditions apply:	**Step 1:** Situation: A girl choosing stickers for her notebook Entities: The stickers—A, B, C, D, E, and F → Action: Selection Limitations: None (no minimum or maximum given) **Step 2** Ⓐ B C D̸ E F

In Selection games that provide no limitations, expect to see questions that ask you about the minimum or maximum number of entities that can be selected (e.g., "Which one of the following is the maximum number of stickers the child could put on her notebook?"). When the game's setup limits or establishes the number of items you will select, they cannot ask that kind of question, of course.

For Selection games in which the number of entities to be selected is precisely established, many LSAT experts choose to use an "In/Out" sketch. These sketches are slightly more complicated, but they clearly represent the number of items that need to be selected or rejected to complete an acceptable solution to the game. Here's an example of this variation on Selection games:

From a list of eight songs—O, P, Q, R, S, T, U, and V—Mary will choose five songs to sing at an event. The following conditions apply:	**Step 1:** Situation: A woman choosing five of eight songs to perform at an event Entities: The songs—O, P, Q, R, S, T, U, and V Action: Selection → Limitations: Choose exactly five **Step 2** O P Q R S T U V in out _ _ _ _ _ | _ _ _ 1 2 3 4 5 | 6 7 8

Over the years, roughly half of Selection games have specified a number of entities for you to choose. More recently, there has been a roughly equal three-way split among Selection games that stipulate an exact number, those that limit the number (e.g., "pick at least four"), and those that leave the number open.

Selection games will be covered in detail in Chapter 8.

Distribution and Matching Games

Distribution and Matching games are similar, so much so that even LSAT experts will sometimes argue about the category to which a particular game should belong. Giving a game the "right" name is less important than accurately analyzing its setup and drawing a useful sketch. The most important distinction between Distribution and Matching games is the number of times entities may be used.

LOGIC GAMES STRATEGY

To distinguish between Distribution and Matching games consider the entities.

In Distribution, entities are divided into two or more groups or teams, and each entity is placed into *exactly one* of the groups. In Matching, entities may be assigned *one or more* attributes, tasks, or items.

In a standard Distribution game, you are given a list of entities and asked to divide them into two or more subgroups. Each entity is an individual person or item, and can be placed into only one group at a time. Think of dividing up 10 people into two five-person basketball teams. Each player goes to one team or the other, not both.

Here's a standard Distribution set up and sketch:

Becky is adding six new baseball cards—one each for players named Morgan, Nettles, Oliver, Palmer, Quisenberry, and Rodriguez—to her card collection. She will place each of the cards into one of two binders, labeled Binder 1 and Binder 2. The following conditions apply:

Step 1:

Situation: A girl adding cards to one of two binders

Entities: Six cards—M, N, O, P, Q, and R

Action: Distribution

Limitations: Each card goes into one binder, but there are no restrictions on how many cards she may add to each binder.

$\longrightarrow$ **Step 2:**

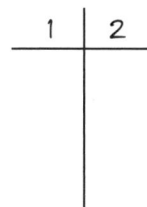

In the typical Matching game, you are provided with a list of people, places, or things, and then with another list of attributes, features, or items that you will assign to the first group. The big difference from Distribution is that, in a Matching game, the attributes, features, or items may be assigned to *one or more* of the "anchor" entities in the first list. Think of five basketball players. One or more may be wearing a wristband. One or more may have a knee brace. One or more may be wearing a particular brand of shoes.

Here's an example of a Matching game setup and sketch:

A restaurateur is opening five new locations—one each in the towns Gascon, Henderson, Junction City, Klondike, and Loredo. Each new location will feature one or more of his chef's famous desserts—apple tart, cheesecake, plum pudding, and strudel. The following conditions apply:

Step 1:

Situation: A restaurateur deciding which desserts to offer at five restaurant locations

Entities: The restaurants—G, H, J, K, and L—and the desserts—a, c, p, and s*

Action: Matching

Limitations: At least one dessert per location, but no limitation on how many restaurants may feature each dessert

Step 2:

or

	G	H	J	K	L
a					
c					
p					
s					

*Note that the LSAT expert uses capital letters to represent the restaurants, and lower case letters to represent the desserts. Being able to distinguish between the two lists of entities in Matching games is always helpful.

**Note that you are given two options for the sketch that should accompany this Matching game. There is no evidence to suggest that one is better than the other, and for LSAT experts, the choice between a list and a grid is simply a matter of taste. Practice setting up Matching games both ways so that you can see which sketch template works best for you.

Distribution and Matching games are covered in detail in Chapter 9.

Hybrid Games

Hybrid games are those that combine two (or, very rarely, three) of the standard logic game actions (Sequencing, Selection, Distribution, and Matching). Hybrid games are not always harder than single-action games, but they always reward careful attention in the Overview phase. Once you identify that there are two actions within the game, consider how the actions affect one another so that you can represent them effectively in your sketch. Usually, one action is primary and the other secondary. If a Hybrid combines Selection and Sequencing, for example, you will need to know who is selected before you can determine their order.

LOGIC GAMES STRATEGY

The most common Hybrid games on recent tests have been:

- Sequencing/Matching (put a number of entities in order, and assign an attribute—such as a color or job—to each entity or position)
- Distribution/Sequencing (divide a larger group into smaller groups—usually just two—and then put the members of each subgroup in order)
- Selection/Sequencing (choose a smaller group from a larger one, and then put the members of the smaller group in order)
- Selection/Distribution (choose a smaller group from a larger one, and then subdivide the selected entities into subgroups)

Although Hybrid games always contain at least two actions, they usually feature simple versions of those actions. For example, in a Sequencing/Matching Hybrid game, you may have to put six runners into six lanes, one per lane, and then assign each runner a jersey color, say blue, green, or red. You are unlikely to see any twists, such as double sequencing or uneven numbers, in the Sequencing action of a Hybrid game. Likewise, if Matching is one of the actions, you will likely need to match just one attribute to each entity.

Take a look at some model setups and sketches for the Hybrid games discussed in the Logic Games Strategy box.

Sequencing/Matching Hybrid Games

In Sequencing/Matching Hybrids, you are asked to arrange several entities in order, and then match an attribute (it is almost always just one attribute) to each entity or position in the sequence. Here's an example:

Each of seven records—S, T, U, V, W, X, and Y—is placed on a shelf in one of seven spots, with spot 1 on the far left of the shelf and spot 7 on the far right. No spot contains more than one record, and each record contains music from a single genre: country, hip-hop, or jazz. The following conditions apply:

→

Step 1:
Situation: Lining up records on a shelf and identifying the genre of each record

Entities: Seven records—S, T, U, V, W, X, and Y—and three genres—c, h, and j

Action: Sequencing/Matching Hybrid

Limitations: Records sequenced one per position, and each record has exactly one genre

Step 2:

— — — — — — —   S T U V W X Y Z

‾ ‾ ‾ ‾ ‾ ‾ ‾ c h j
1 2 3 4 5 6 7

Distribution/Sequencing Hybrid Games

Distribution/Sequencing Hybrids task you with divvying up a set of entities into teams or groups (almost always two), and then sequencing the entities within each team. Here's a typical Distribution/Sequencing Hybrid game setup:

Eastern State University's Dance team has been asked to join the school's marching band for a parade. The dance team has eight dancers—Benton, Carlson, Davis, Esai, Farrell, Gabrielson, Hutchins, and Joro. The eight dancers will be split into two dance lines—Line A and Line B—and the dancers in each line will be assigned positions—1 through 4— in which to march. The dancers' arrangement will obey the following restrictions:

Step 1:

Situation: A dance team lining up for a parade

Entities: Eight dancers—B, C, D, E, F, G, H, and J

Action: Distribution/Sequencing Hybrid

Limitations: Each team has four dancers, sequenced one per position

Step 2:

B C D E F G H J

	A	B
1	—	—
2	—	—
3	—	—
4	—	—

Selection/Sequencing Hybrid Games

In Selection/Sequencing Hybrid games, your job is to select a handful of members out of the initial entity list, and then to put the selected entities in order. Selection/Sequencing Hybrid games often look something like this:

From among seven witnesses to an industrial accident—Cirillo, Emegwale, Garrison, Hunt, Legrande, Petarski, and Taylor—a plaintiff's attorney will select four to be deposed at his office. Each of the four witnesses selected will be deposed on a single day from Monday through Thursday of the upcoming week. The attorney will consider the following restrictions:

Step 1:

Situation: An attorney scheduling depositions

Entities: Seven witnesses—C, E, G, H, L, P, and T

Action: Selection/Sequencing Hybrid

Limitations: Choose exactly four of seven, one deposition per day, M–Th

Step 2:

C E G H L P T

—	—	—	—	—	—	—
M	Tu	W	Th		out	

Selection/Distribution Hybrid Games

In Selection/Distribution Hybrids, the task is to select a handful of members out of the initial entity list, and then to divide them into two (or, rarely, three) groups. Here's a model Selection/Distribution Hybrid game setup:

Next week, the seven members of Woodbury's town council—Allen, Bennett, Chen, Dillard, Emery, Flippo, and Guilini—will meet to determine the composition of two subcommittees, one on parks and one on schools. Each subcommittee will have three members, and no council member may serve on more than one subcommittee. The following restrictions apply:

Step 1:

Situation: A town council creating two subcommittees

Entities: Seven council members—A, B, C, D, E, F, and G

Action: Selection/Distribution Hybrid

Limitations: Choose six out of seven, and divide those chosen into two three-person subcommittees

Step 2:

→ A B C D E F G

P	S	out
—	—	—
—	—	
—	—	

The testmaker could combine any of the standard game actions to create a Hybrid game, but the four Hybrids just illustrated are, by far, the most common. The other combinations are rare enough that they don't warrant too much of your study and practice time. For good measure, you will see a rare Selection/Matching Hybrid game in the Special Feature called "The Dinosaur Game" after Chapter 10.

Hybrid Games are covered in detail in Chapter 10.

Rare Game Types: Process and Mapping Games

There are two extremely rare game types that the test has featured in the past: Process games and Mapping games. Indeed, they are so rare that you should focus on learning all of the standard actions and common Hybrids before diving into them.

Process games were fairly common in LSATs administered in the early 1990s, but then disappeared from the test for more than two decades. PrepTest 80 (December 2016) surprisingly featured a Process game, the first to appear on a released test in more than 20 years. At this point, there is no way to know if this game signals a return to Process by the testmaker, or if it was just a one off. You can study that game in the Special Feature titled "2016: The Return of Process" in the middle of Chapter 11.

The LSAT has featured only five mapping games among the more than 80 officially released tests. Four of those appeared in 1992 and 1995. There was one more on PrepTest40 (June 2003). Since that time, the testmaker appears to have abandoned Mapping as a game type, and there has been nothing to indicate that a new Mapping game is imminent.

Chapter 11 covers what you need to know about these rare game types.

Practice

Now, practice your skills at identifying game types and creating sketches. This section contains two Practice Sets, each with eight model logic game setups. Practice Set 1 contains relatively simple setups, while in Practice Set 2, some of the setups are a little more complex. After each set, you can see analysis and sketches of LSAT experts, and get advice about how to compare your work to theirs.

Practice Set 1

Directions: Take no more than 16 minutes to perform Steps 1 and 2 of the Logic Games Method on the following eight model setups. For each, conduct the Overview by answering the SEAL questions, and then create a simple, accurate initial Sketch.

Logic Game setup		My Analysis
1. The judge at a dog show is determining the final rankings of seven dogs—an affenpinscher, a bulldog, a collie, a dachshund, a mastiff, a pointer, and a Westie. The dogs are ranked from first through seventh with no ties. The following conditions apply to the judge's decisions:	⟶	**Step 1:** Situation: Entities: Action: Limitations: **Step 2:**
2. A natural history museum curator is deciding which of the following animal models—a Camelops, a Dire Wolf, a Glyptodon, an Irish Elk, a Mastodon, a Sabre-tooth Cat, and a Wooly Mammoth—to feature in a diorama on extinct Ice Age mammals. The curator's decisions must accord with the following considerations:	⟶	**Step 1:** Situation: Entities: Action: Limitations: **Step 2:**

K

Logic Game setup	My Analysis

3. A police precinct captain must assign six officers—Johnson, Lemond, Mtumbe, Norton, Oliver, and Pate—to various duties patrolling a parade. Four of the officers will be assigned to specific positions numbered 1 through 4 along the parade route. The other two officers will "float," walking up and down the parade route to monitor the crowd. The officers' assignments must conform to the following constraints:

$\longrightarrow$

Step 1:
Situation:

Entities:

Action:

Limitations:

Step 2:

4. A student is getting ready to move home from her dormitory at the end of the Spring semester. From among nine items of clothing—four sweaters, one each of the colors blue, green, red, and yellow, and five blouses, one each in the colors blue, green, red, white, and yellow—she will choose four items to take home, four items to donate to charity, and one item to wear. The following conditions apply:

$\longrightarrow$

Step 1:
Situation:

Entities:

Action:

Limitations:

Step 2:

5. Five friends—Emily, Gabriela, Lawrence, Maren, and Thomasina—are creating costumes for their town's upcoming Renaissance Faire. As part of their costumes, each friend will carry between one and three of the following decorative weapons: an axe, a crossbow, a dagger, a pike, and a shield. The friends select the decorative weapons for their costumes according to the following conditions:

$\longrightarrow$

Step 1:
Situation:

Entities:

Action:

Limitations:

Step 2:

Logic Game setup	My Analysis

6. A software company is developing four new apps codenamed Projects A, B, C, and D. Four of the company's employees—Grayson, Hiller, Lutowski, and Mihn—will each work on between one and three projects, and on no other projects. The assignment of employees to projects is subject to the following restrictions:

→

Step 1:

Situation:

Entities:

Action:

Limitations:

Step 2:

7. A quality control manager will sample six soda pop flavors—cola, ginger ale, lemon-lime, orange, raspberry, and tamarind—to ensure that each one meets the company's standards for flavor and quality. She will sample each flavor one time according to the following conditions:

→

Step 1:

Situation:

Entities:

Action:

Limitations:

Step 2:

8. This year, the theme of North Grove Elementary School's fall pageant is ecology. For a song about coral reefs, six students—Jiro, Kandace, Maurice, Rutger, Sudeepa, and Teri—will stand in six positions from stage left to stage right, one student for each position. Each of the students will be dressed in one of three costumes— anemone, clownfish, or dugong. The assignments of position and costume accord with the following conditions:

→

Step 1:

Situation:

Entities:

Action:

Limitations:

Step 2:

Explanations

Compare your work to that of the LSAT experts. Pay close attention to each game's action and sketch. If you missed any of the games' actions, go back to the description and illustration of that game type to clear up any confusion. Don't worry if the language you use to answer the SEAL questions is different than that of the experts as long as your analysis is accurate. When comparing sketches, look for cases in which the expert's analysis was clearer, simpler, or easier to recreate than yours was.

Logic Game setup	My Analysis
1. The judge at a dog show is determining the final rankings of seven dogs—an affenpinscher, a bulldog, a collie, a dachshund, a mastiff, a pointer, and a Westie. The dogs are ranked from first through seventh with no ties. The following conditions apply to the judge's decisions:	**Step 1:** Situation: A judge determining the final standings at a dog show Entities: Seven dogs—A, B, C, D, M, P, and W Action: Sequencing. If the rules refer to specific positions, this will be Strict Sequencing. If the rules give only relative positions among the dogs, this will be Loose Sequencing. Limitations: No ties, one dog per position **Step 2:** This is the Strict Sequencing sketch: A B C D M P W $\overline{}\ \overline{}\ \overline{}\ \overline{}\ \overline{}\ \overline{}\ \overline{}$ 1　2　3　4　5　6　7 If the game turns out to be Loose Sequencing, the sketch will be a "tree" showing the dogs' relative positions to one another.
2. A natural history museum curator is deciding which of the following animal models—a Camelops, a Dire Wolf, a Glyptodon, an Irish Elk, a Mastodon, a Sabre-tooth Cat, and a Wooly Mammoth—to feature in a diorama on extinct Ice Age mammals. The curator's decisions must accord with the following considerations:	**Step 1:** Situation: A museum curator choosing models for a diorama Entities: Seven models—C, D, G, I, M, S, and W Action: Selection Limitations: None **Step 2:** C D G I M S W

Logic Game setup	My Analysis
3. A police precinct captain must assign six officers—Johnson, Lemond, Mtumbe, Norton, Oliver, and Pate—to various duties patrolling a parade. Four of the officers will be assigned to specific positions numbered 1 through 4 along the parade route. The other two officers will "float," walking up and down the parade route to monitor the crowd. The officers' assignments must conform to the following constraints:	**Step 1:** Situation: A police captain choosing officers for specific and general assignments at a parade Entities: Six officers—J, L, M, N, O, and P Action: Selection/Sequencing Hybrid Limitations: Four of the six selected for specific assignments, one per position **Step 2:** J L M N O P $\underline{\ \ }$ $\underline{\ \ }$ $\underline{\ \ }$ $\underline{\ \ }$	$\underline{\ \ }$ $\underline{\ \ }$ 1 2 3 4 float

4. A student is getting ready to move home from her dormitory at the end of the Spring semester. From among nine items of clothing—four sweaters, one each of the colors blue, green, red, and yellow, and five blouses, one each in the colors blue, green, red, white, and yellow—she will choose four items to take home, four items to donate to charity, and one item to wear. The following conditions apply:

Step 1:
Situation: A student separating clothes to pack, donate, and wear

Entities: Nine clothing items—B_S, G_S, R_S, Y_S, B_B, G_B, R_B, W_B, and Y_B

Action: Distribution

Limitations: Take home four, donate four, wear one

Step 2:
B_s G_s R_s Y_s
B_b G_b R_b W_b Y_b

T	D	W
$\underline{\ \ }$	$\underline{\ \ }$	$\underline{\ \ }$
$\underline{\ \ }$	$\underline{\ \ }$	
$\underline{\ \ }$	$\underline{\ \ }$	
$\underline{\ \ }$	$\underline{\ \ }$	

Logic Game setup	My Analysis

5. Five friends—Emily, Gabriela, Lawrence, Maren, and Thomasina—are creating costumes for their town's upcoming Renaissance Faire. As part of their costumes, each friend will carry between one and three of the following decorative weapons: an axe, a crossbow, a dagger, a pike, and a shield. The friends select the decorative weapons for their costumes according to the following conditions:

→

Step 1:

Situation: Friends selecting items for costumes

Entities: Five friends—E, G, L, M, and T—and five weapons—a, c, d, p, and s

Action: Matching

Limitations: Each friend chooses between one and three weapons.

Step 2:

a c d p s

E	G	L	M	T
—	—	—	—	—

6. A software company is developing four new apps codenamed Projects A, B, C, and D. Four of the company's employees—Grayson, Hiller, Lutowski, and Mihn—will each work on between one and three projects, and on no other projects. The assignment of employees to projects is subject to the following restrictions:

→

Step 1:

Situation: Software company assigning employees to projects

Entities: Four projects—a, b, c, and d—and four employees—G, H, L, and M

Action: Matching

Limitations: Each employee is assigned to between one and three of the projects.

Step 2:

a b c d

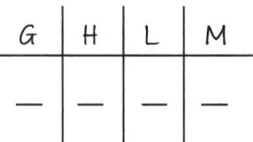

G	H	L	M
—	—	—	—

Logic Game setup	My Analysis
7. A quality control manager will sample six soda pop flavors—cola, ginger ale, lemon-lime, orange, raspberry, and tamarind—to ensure that each one meets the company's standards for flavor and quality. She will sample each flavor one time according to the following conditions:	**Step 1:** Situation: A manager sampling six different flavors of soda Entities: Six flavors—C, G, L, O, R, and T Action: Sequencing. If the rules refer to specific positions, this will be Strict Sequencing. If the rules give only relative positions among the soda flavors, this will be Loose Sequencing. Limitations: Each flavor sampled one time **Step 2:** This is the Strict Sequencing sketch: C G L O R T — — — — — — 1 2 3 4 5 6 If the game turns out to be Loose Sequencing, the sketch will be a "tree" showing the sodas' relative positions to one another.
8. This year, the theme of North Grove Elementary School's fall pageant is ecology. For a song about coral reefs, six students—Jiro, Kandace, Maurice, Rutger, Sudeepa, and Teri—will stand in six positions from stage left to stage right, one student for each position. Each of the students will be dressed in one of three costumes—anemone, clownfish, or dugong. The assignments of position and costume accord with the following conditions:	**Step 1:** Situation: Students taking positions on stage for an ecology pageant Entities: Six students—J, K, M, R, S, and T—and three costumes—a, c, and d Action: Sequencing/Matching Hybrid Limitations: One student per position, and one costume per student **Step 2:** — — — — — — J K M R S T — — — — — — a c d 1 2 3 4 5 6

When you're ready, practice Steps 1 and 2 of the Logic Games Method on Practice Set 2, in which you'll see somewhat more complex setups.

Practice Set 2

Directions: Take no more than 16 minutes to perform Steps 1 and 2 of the Logic Games Method on the following eight model setups. For each, conduct the Overview by answering the SEAL questions, and then create a simple, accurate initial Sketch.

Logic Game setup	My Analysis
9. At a switching yard, seven freight cars—T, U, V, W, X, Y, and Z—are assigned to seven positions— numbered 1 (closest to the front of the train) through 7 (closest to the back of the train). Each freight car carries one type of product—dry goods, foodstuffs, or machinery. The order of the cars and the cargo each carries are subject to the following restrictions: →	**Step 1:** Situation: Entities: Action: Limitations: **Step 2:**
10. Officials are determining the order in which six gymnasts—Quinn, Roland, and Sung from Bradley School; Tucker and Umali from Carlton Academy; and Winters from Dearborn Prep—will compete in the floor exercises portion of a gymnastics competition. Gymnasts from the same school may not compete consecutively. The officials must adhere to the following criteria: →	**Step 1:** Situation: Entities: Action: Limitations: **Step 2:**

Logic Game setup	My Analysis

11. The environmental agency of Country X is assembling a scientific research team to assess conditions in a remote mountainous region of the country. The team will consist of four of the following eight candidates: botanists Able and Barker; cartographers Dennis, Elwood, and Fuqua; and zoologists Montrose, Norwood, and Olague. Selection of the research team will be determined by the following restrictions:

→

Step 1:

Situation:

Entities:

Action:

Limitations:

Step 2:

12. During the upcoming week, Professor Howser must schedule exactly two appointments with each of four graduate students—Aaliyah, Clark, Jennifer, and Marcus—and hold open office hours exactly two times. Professor Howser has two appointment times, one in the morning and one in the afternoon, each day, Monday through Friday. The professor's schedule for the upcoming week will conform to the following constraints:

→

Step 1:

Situation:

Entities:

Action:

Limitations:

Step 2:

13. A homeowner is arranging six houseplants—an aloe, a cactus, a dracaena, an ivy, a lily, and a spider plant—by placing each on the left, center, or right of one of two shelves—an upper shelf and a lower shelf. The placement of the plants corresponds to the following considerations:

→

Step 1:

Situation:

Entities:

Action:

Limitations:

Step 2:

Logic Game setup	My Analysis

14. El Dorado Middle School's Chess Club has eight students—8th Graders Cole, Morimoto, Peters, and Stein, and 7th Graders Dillard, Francis, Nowak, and Orban. The club will enter two four-person teams—called Team 1 and Team 2—into an upcoming tournament. Each club member is assigned to exactly one team. One player on each team is designated as that team's captain. The teams must adhere to the following restrictions:

→

Step 1:
Situation:

Entities:

Action:

Limitations:

Step 2:

15. Three dancers—Kathryn, Martha, and Twyla—will each wear costumes consisting of a dress, a shawl, and a hat. Each piece of clothing is a single color—floral white, pale green, or sky blue. The following restrictions apply to the dancers' choice of colors:

→

Step 1:
Situation:

Entities:

Action:

Limitations:

Step 2:

16. Eight players—A, B, C, D, E, F, G, and H—and one dealer are seated around a poker table. Each player is assigned to one of eight seats, numbered 1 through 8 clockwise from the dealer's left. The assignment of players to seats will conform to the following conditions:

→

Step 1:
Situation:

Entities:

Action:

Limitations:

Step 2:

Explanations

Compare your work to that of the LSAT experts. Pay close attention to each game's action and sketch. If you missed any of the games' actions, go back to the description and illustration of that game type to clear up any confusion. Don't worry if the language you use to answer the SEAL questions is different than that of the experts as long as your analysis is accurate. When comparing sketches, look for cases in which the expert's analysis was clearer, simpler, or easier to recreate than yours was.

Logic Game setup	Analysis
9. At a switching yard, seven freight cars—T, U, V, W, X, Y, and Z—are assigned to seven positions—numbered 1 (closest to the front of the train) through 7 (closest to the back of the train). Each freight car carries one type of product—dry goods, foodstuffs, or machinery. The order of the cars and the cargo each carries are subject to the following restrictions:	**Step 1:** Situation: Putting freight cars in order for a train, and determining the cargo of each car Entities: Seven train cars—T, U, V, W, X, Y, and Z—and three types of cargo—d, f, and m Action: Sequencing/Matching Hybrid Limitations: One car per position, and one type of cargo per car **Step 2:** $$\underbrace{-\ \ -\ \ -\ \ -\ \ -\ \ -}_{1\ \ 2\ \ 3\ \ 4\ \ 5\ \ 6}\ \ \underset{\overline{d\ f\ m}}{\ }\ \ \begin{array}{l}T\,U\,V\,W\,X\,Y\,Z\\ \\ d\ f\ m\end{array}$$
10. Officials are determining the order in which six gymnasts—Quinn, Roland, and Sung from Bradley School; Tucker and Umali from Carlton Academy; and Winters from Dearborn Prep—will compete in the floor exercises portion of a gymnastics competition. Gymnasts from the same school may not compete consecutively. The officials must adhere to the following criteria:	**Step 1:** Situation: Determining the order in which six gymnasts will perform floor exercises Entities: Three students from Bradley—Q, R, and S—two from Carlton—T and U—and one from Dearborn—W Action: Strict Sequencing (The limitation on students from the same school would be unlikely in a Loose Sequencing game.) Limitations: One student per position; never consecutive positions for students from the same school **Step 2:** <table><tr><td>B</td><td>C</td><td>D</td></tr><tr><td>QRS</td><td>TU</td><td>W</td></tr></table> $$\overline{1}\ \ \overline{2}\ \ \overline{3}\ \ \overline{4}\ \ \overline{5}\ \ \overline{6}$$

Logic Game setup	**Analysis**

11. The environmental agency of Country X is assembling a scientific research team to assess conditions in a remote mountainous region of the country. The team will consist of four of the following eight candidates: botanists Able and Barker; cartographers Dennis, Elwood, and Fuqua; and zoologists Montrose, Norwood, and Olague. Selection of the research team will be determined by the following restrictions:

→

Step 1:

Situation: Choosing scientists for a research team

Entities: Two botanists—A and B—three cartographers—D, E, and F—and three zoologists—M, N, and O

Action: Selection

Limitations: Choose four of the eight scientists

Step 2:

B	C	Z
A B	D E F	M N O

— — — —│— — — —

in   out

12. During the upcoming week, Professor Howser must schedule exactly two appointments with each of four graduate students—Aaliyah, Clark, Jennifer, and Marcus—and hold open office hours exactly two times. Professor Howser has two appointment times, one in the morning and one in the afternoon, each day, Monday through Friday. The professor's schedule for the upcoming week will conform to the following constraints:

→

Step 1:

Situation: A professor schedules office hours and meetings with graduate students

Entities: Four students—A, C, J, and M—and two office hours spots

Action: Strict Sequencing (Double)

Limitations: Two appointments with each student

Step 2:

A_1 C_1 J_1 M_1 O_1
A_2 C_2 J_2 M_2 O_2

	M	Tu	W	Th	F
AM					
PM					

Logic Game setup	Analysis

13. A homeowner is arranging six houseplants—an aloe, a cactus, a dracaena, an ivy, a lily, and a spider plant—by placing each on the left, center, or right of one of two shelves—an upper shelf and a lower shelf. The placement of the plants corresponds to the following considerations:

Step 1:

Situation: A homeowner arranging houseplants on shelves

Entities: Six houseplants—A, C, D, I, L, and S

Action: Distribution/Sequencing Hybrid

Limitations: Three plants per shelf, one plant per position

→ **Step 2:**

A C D I L S

	left	center	right
upper			
lower			

14. El Dorado Middle School's Chess Club has eight students—8th Graders Cole, Morimoto, Peters, and Stein, and 7th Graders Dillard, Francis, Nowak, and Orban. The club will enter two four-person teams—called Team 1 and Team 2—into an upcoming tournament. Each club member is assigned to exactly one team. One player on each team is designated as that team's captain. The teams must adhere to the following restrictions:

Step 1:

Situation: Dividing students into teams, and designating team captains

Entities: Four seventh graders—D, F, N, and O—and four eighth graders—C, M, P, and S

Action: Distribution

Limitations: Four students per team, one captain per team

Step 2:

→

7	8
D F N O	C M P S

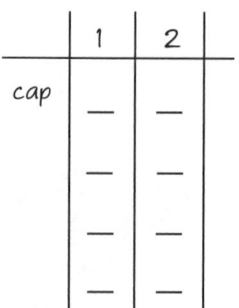

Logic Game setup	Analysis
15. Three dancers—Kathryn, Martha, and Twyla—will each wear costumes consisting of a dress, a shawl, and a hat. Each piece of clothing is a single color—floral white, pale green, or sky blue. The following restrictions apply to the dancers' choice of colors:	**Step 1:** Situation: Assigning costume pieces with different colors to three dancers Entities: Three dancers—K, M, and T—and three costume pieces—D, S, and H—each in one of three colors—fw, pg, and sb Action: Matching Limitations: One color per costume piece for each dancer

$\longrightarrow$ **Step 2:**

fw pg sb

	K	M	T
dress			
shawl			
hat			

| 16. Eight players—A, B, C, D, E, F, G, and H—and one dealer are seated around a poker table. Each player is assigned to one of eight seats, numbered 1 through 8 clockwise from the dealer's left. The assignment of players to seats will conform to the following conditions: | **Step 1:**

Situation: Arranging card players around a table

Entities: Eight players—A, B, C, D, E, F, G, and H

Action: Sequencing (Circular)

Limitations: One player per seat |

Step 2:

A B C D E F G H

$\longrightarrow$

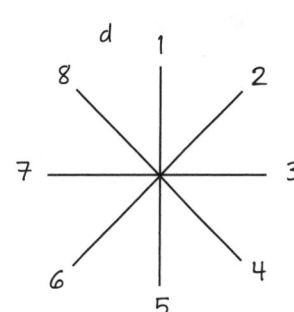

After comparing your work on the Practice Sets with that of the experts, do any review and study you feel is warranted to correct any mistakes you may have made. When you're ready, turn to the self-assessment in the Perform quiz.

Perform

Use the following quiz to assess your mastery of Steps 1 and 2 of the Logic Games Method.

Directions: Take no more than 22 minutes to perform Steps 1 and 2 of the Logic Games Method on the following eleven model setups. For each, conduct the Overview by answering the SEAL questions, and then create a simple, accurate initial Sketch.

Logic Game setup	My Analysis
1. A florist is delivering seven bouquets—A, B, C, D, E, F, and G—to seven different clients. Each client will receive exactly one of the bouquets. The order of the deliveries, from earliest to latest, conforms to the following rules: ⟶	**Step 1:** Situation: Entities: Action: Limitations: **Step 2:**
2. The manager of a department store is deciding which five pieces of furniture to display in a store window. There are seven pieces for the manager to choose from—a bookcase, a chair, a desk, a lamp, a mirror, a nightstand, and a table. The manager will make her selection based on the following rules: ⟶	**Step 1:** Situation: Entities: Action: Limitations: **Step 2:**

Logic Game setup	My Analysis

3. A coin collector is preparing to sell some of his coins. He has five coins—A, B, C, D, and E—that he will place in a display box. Each coin will occupy one of five spots, numbered one through five and arranged from left to right. Each of the coins will be assigned a different value, the cheapest coin being priced at $10 and the most expensive coin at $30. The other coins are priced at $5 increments between those values. The following conditions apply:

→

Step 1:
Situation:

Entities:

Action:

Limitations:

Step 2:

4. A grocer is determining the location in which to place a number of new food items. Each one of the following products—avocado juice, banana yogurt, cashew bars, kale bread, pistachio butter, quinoa flour, and yellow rice—will be placed in exactly one of the following aisles: 1, 2, or 3. The grocer makes her decisions based on the following rules:

→

Step 1:
Situation:

Entities:

Action:

Limitations:

Step 2:

5. A pharmaceutical company is planning on releasing a series of six new medications tentatively named N, P, Q, R, S, and T. Each medication will be released at a different time, and each medication will be marketed to exactly one of the following demographics: people who suffer from insomnia, people who suffer from migraines, or people who suffer from ulcers. The following conditions apply:

→

Step 1:
Situation:

Entities:

Action:

Limitations:

Step 2:

Logic Game setup	My Analysis

6. In order to learn more about the new students in her class, a teacher attempts to determine which extracurricular activities these students are involved in. Each of her new students—J, K, L, M, and N—participate in at least one and at most three of the following activities: archery team, basketball, chess club, foreign language club, and glee club. The students' activities correspond to the following conditions: $\longrightarrow$

Step 1:
Situation:

Entities:

Action:

Limitations:

Step 2:

7. An arborist is determining the order in which to plant a series of trees. He will plant one tree of each of the following varieties—elm, gingko, maple, oak, sycamore, tulip, and willow—along the top of a ridge. Each tree will be separated from the next tree by ten feet, and each tree will be numbered 1 through 7, moving from east to west, according to the following stipulations: $\longrightarrow$

Step 1:
Situation:

Entities:

Action:

Limitations:

Step 2:

8. Pamela is throwing a surprise party for her friend Sam. In considering which of the following friends—F, G, H, J, K, L, and M—to invite to the party, Pamela adheres to the following conditions: $\longrightarrow$

Step 1:
Situation:

Entities:

Action:

Limitations:

Step 2:

	Logic Game setup		**My Analysis**

9. A dental student is learning how to identify different teeth. Teeth always fit this pattern, moving from the front of the mouth to the back: central incisor, lateral incisor, canine, first premolar, second premolar, and first molar. She has six teeth labeled A, B, C, D, E, and F. Each tooth is a different type, and each fits one of the labels described above. As she attempts to match each tooth to its proper place in the mouth, she must adhere to the following conditions:

⟶

Step 1:

Situation:

Entities:

Action:

Limitations:

Step 2:

10. At an architectural firm, each of seven employees—A, B, C, D, E, F, and G—will be assigned to either Project X or Project Y, but not both. Each team has at least two team members. After the completion of each team's project, the team members will be evaluated and ranked according to their performance among members of the group. No team member shares the rank of any other team member. The following conditions apply:

⟶

Step 1:

Situation:

Entities:

Action:

Limitations:

Step 2:

11. During an observational experiment, a scientist notices a chimpanzee select exactly four of six possible objects—a book, a rubber duck, a marble, a ping pong paddle, a shoe, and a toy train—and then place each of the selected items on a different shelf. The shelves are numbered from 1 (the lowest) to 4 (the highest). The scientist makes the following observations:

⟶

Step 1:

Situation:

Entities:

Action:

Limitations:

Step 2:

Explanations

Compare your analysis and sketches to those of LSAT experts. Keep track of any case in which you misidentified the Action in the model setup, and any case in which you drew a sketch framework that does not match the game type.

Logic Game setup	My Analysis
1. A florist is delivering seven bouquets—A, B, C, D, E, F, and G—to seven different clients. Each client will receive exactly one of the bouquets. The order of the deliveries, from earliest to latest, conforms to the following rules:	**Step 1:** Situation: A florist is deciding the order of the deliveries she will make. Entities: The seven bouquets—A, B, C, D, E, F, and G Action: Sequencing. If the rules mention specific positions or separate entities by a specific number of spaces, this will be Strict Sequencing. If the rules mention only the relative positions of the entities, this will be Loose Sequencing. → Limitations: Because each of the deliveries will be to one client, no client gets multiple bouquets or zero bouquets. **Step 2:** If the game is Strict Sequencing, this is the opening sketch A B C D E F G (earliest) _ _ _ _ _ _ _ (latest) 　　　　　1　2　3　4　5　6　7 If the game is Loose Sequencing, the sketch will be a "tree" as established by the rules.
2. The manager of a department store is deciding which five pieces of furniture to display in a store window. There are seven pieces for the manager to choose from—a bookcase, a chair, a desk, a lamp, a mirror, a nightstand, and a table. The manager will make her selection based on the following rules:	**Step 1:** Situation: A store manager is deciding which pieces of furniture she wants to put on display. Entities: Seven pieces of furniture—B, C, D, L, M, N, and T Action: Selection. Pick five of the seven pieces of furniture. → Limitations: Exactly five of the seven pieces will be selected. **Step 2:** Because there is a pre-determined number of pieces of furniture to choose, use an in-out sketch: B C D L M N T in　　　　　　　out _ _ _ _ _ | _ _

Logic Game setup	My Analysis

3. A coin collector is preparing to sell some of his coins. He has five coins—A, B, C, D, and E—that he will place in a display box. Each coin will occupy one of five spots, numbered one through five and arranged from left to right. Each of the coins will be assigned a different value, the cheapest coin being priced at $10 and the most expensive coin at $30. The other coins are priced at $5 increments between those values. The following conditions apply:

Step 1:
Situation: A coin collector is arranging coins in a display box, and each coin has a different monetary value.

Entities: The five coins—A, B, C, D, and E—and the five values—$10, $15, $20, $25, and $30

Action: Sequencing/Matching Hybrid. Put the coins in order, and determine the value of each coin.

→ Limitations: Each coin will be used, and each spot will have a coin.

Step 2:
Some rules might match a dollar value to a coin, but ultimately each coin will occupy a single spot, and so will each dollar value. Set up a sketch that has two layers, one for the coins and one for the values.

```
—  —  —  —  — A B C D E
—  —  —  —  — 10, 15, 20, 25, 30
1  2  3  4  5
```

4. A grocer is determining the location in which to place a number of new food items. Each one of the following products—avocado juice, banana yogurt, cashew bars, kale bread, pistachio butter, quinoa flour, and yellow rice—will be placed in exactly one of the following aisles: 1, 2, or 3. The grocer makes her decisions based on the following rules:

Step 1:
Situation: A grocer is trying to figure out where to place new food items.

Entities: The food items—A, B, C, K, P, Q, and Y

Action: Distribution. Sort the seven food items into the three aisles.

Limitations: Each food item will be placed into exactly one of the three aisles.

→ **Step 2:**
Because each item is going to be placed into exactly one aisle, this is a Distribution game. Set up a table:
A B C K P Q Y

1	2	3

K 63

Logic Game setup	My Analysis

5. A pharmaceutical company is planning on releasing a series of six new medications tentatively named N, P, Q, R, S, and T. Each medication will be released at a different time, and each medication will be marketed to exactly one of the following demographics: people who suffer from insomnia, people who suffer from migraines, or people who suffer from ulcers. The following conditions apply:

→

Step 1:

Situation: A drug company is scheduling a roll out of new medications.

Entities: The six new drugs—N, P, Q, R, S, and T—and the people to whom the drugs will be marketed—i, m, and u

Action: Sequencing/Matching Hybrid. In addition to determining the order of the release of the drugs, also determine each drug's type.

Limitations: Every drug gets its own release date, and every drug is marketed to only one group. There are no limitations yet on how many drugs are of each type.

Step 2:

```
—  —  —  —  —  —   N P Q R S T
—  —  —  —  —  —   i m u
1  2  3  4  5  6
```

6. In order to learn more about the new students in her class, a teacher attempts to determine which extracurricular activities these students are involved in. Each of her new students—J, K, L, M, and N—participate in at least one and at most three of the following activities: archery team, basketball, chess club, foreign language club, and glee club. The students' activities correspond to the following conditions:

→

Step 1:

Situation: A teacher is figuring out which activities her students are involved in.

Entities: The five students—J, K, L, M, and N—and the five distinct activities—a, b, c, f, and g

Action: Matching. Determine which activities each student participates in.

Limitations: Each student will participate in a minimum of one and a maximum of three of the listed activities. There is no limit on how many students can participate in each activity—for example, it's possible that none of the students participate in glee club, but it's also possible that they all do.

Step 2:

Set up a table with the students affixed at the top of the sketch.

```
        a   b   c   f   g

   |  J  |  K  |  L  |  M  |  N  |
   |  —  |  —  |  —  |  —  |  —  |
```

Logic Game setup	My Analysis
7. An arborist is determining the order in which to plant a series of trees. He will plant one tree of each of the following varieties—elm, gingko, maple, oak, sycamore, tulip, and willow—along the top of a ridge. Each tree will be separated from the next tree by ten feet, and each tree will be numbered 1 through 7, moving from east to west, according to the following stipulations:	**Step 1:** Situation: An arborist is arranging trees in a line. Entities: The seven tree varieties—E, G, M, O, S, T, and W Action: Sequencing. If the rules mention specific positions or separate entities by a specific number of spaces, this will be Strict Sequencing. If the rules mention only the relative positions of the entities, this will be Loose Sequencing. → Limitations: Each tree gets its own spot, and the arrangement is horizontal—east to west. **Step 2:** If the game is Strict Sequencing, this is the opening sketch (keep in mind you will need to correctly label the sketch east and west): E G M O S T W west _ _ _ _ _ _ _ east 7 6 5 4 3 2 1
8. Pamela is throwing a surprise party for her friend Sam. In considering which of the following friends—F, G, H, J, K, L, and M—to invite to the party, Pamela adheres to the following conditions:	**Step 1:** Situation: A person is making a list of friends to invite to a party. Entities: Seven friends—F, G, H, J, K, L, and M Action: Selection. Pamela is deciding which friends to invite to the party. → Limitations: None so far. Pamela could decide to invite none or all of the friends. **Step 2:** In an open-ended Selection game like this, your sketch is simply the roster of entities. You can then circle or cross out entities as they are selected or rejected in specific questions. F G H J K L M

Logic Game setup	My Analysis
9. A dental student is learning how to identify different teeth. Teeth always fit this pattern, moving from the front of the mouth to the back: central incisor, lateral incisor, canine, first premolar, second premolar, and first molar. She has six teeth labeled A, B, C, D, E, and F. Each tooth is a different type, and each fits one of the labels described above. As she attempts to match each tooth to its proper place in the mouth, she must adhere to the following conditions:	**Step 1:** Situation: A dental student matching teeth to a fixed pattern. Entities: The teeth—A, B, C, D, E, and F—and the different positions—CI, LI, CAN, P1, P2, M1. Action: Sequencing. The student must arrange the teeth according to a fixed layout. Limitations: Six spots for the teeth, and six different teeth. Each tooth will fit into one of the six spots. **Step 2:** Set up a Strict Sequencing sketch, and clearly label the pattern of teeth. A B C D E F front _ _ _ _ _ _ back CI LI CAN P1 P2 M1
10. At an architectural firm, each of seven employees—A, B, C, D, E, F, and G—will be assigned to either Project X or Project Y, but not both. Each team has at least two team members. After the completion of each team's project, the team members will be evaluated and ranked according to their performance among members of the group. No team member shares the rank of any other team member. The following conditions apply:	**Step 1:** Situation: Determining the projects to which different employees will be assigned, and the rank each employee achieves. Entities: The employees—A, B, C, D, E, F, and G Action: Sequencing/Distribution Hybrid. Limitations: Each employee will be placed in exactly one group, and each employee receives a separate rank. **Step 2:** In a Distribution/Sequencing game, anchor your sketch around the Distribution action. A B C D E F G

	X	Y
1	—	—
2	—	—
3		
4		
5		

Logic Game setup	My Analysis

11. During an observational experiment, a scientist notices a chimpanzee select exactly four of six possible objects—a book, a rubber duck, a marble, a ping pong paddle, a shoe, and a toy train—and then place each item on a different shelf. The shelves are numbered from 1 (the lowest) to 4 (the highest). The scientist makes the following observations:

Step 1:

Situation: In a research facility, a scientist watches a chimpanzee perform certain actions.

Entities: The six objects—B, D, M, P, S, and T

Action: Selection/Sequencing Hybrid. Determine the four items that are selected, and put them in order from lowest to highest.

Limitations: Exactly four of the six items are selected.

Step 2:

A vertical sketch matches the physical arrangement of the shelves. In addition to the four shelves, find a way to account for the two objects that are not selected.

B D M P S T

4 _ | _
3 _ | _
2 _ | out
1 _ |

Assess

If your analysis was accurate and your sketch was appropriate in:

9–11 of the model sketches: Congratulations! You're well on your way to mastering Steps 1 and 2 of the Logic Games Method. Move on to Chapter 3 to study and practice Steps 3 (Rules) and 4 (Deductions).

6–8 of the model sketches: Good work! You have a solid foundation for Steps 1 and 2 of the Logic Games Method, but still have room to improve your skills in identifying and sketching game types. Make a note of the game types you misidentified, and study the description and illustration of those game types once more before moving on to Chapter 3. Keep the list to help you remember the game types to which you will want to give extra attention in Chapters 5–10.

1–5 of the model sketches: Keep at it. On Test Day, you'll need to make quick, accurate assessments of each game type you encounter, and you'll want to have a "library" of standard sketches committed to memory. First, study the Prepare portion of this chapter again to make sure you understand any of the game types you misidentified in the Perform quiz. Then, take and review the quiz titled "Game Types and Sketches Fundamentals" found in your online center. As you move forward, pay attention to the Step 1 and Step 2 analysis of each game you encounter, even in cases where the book is focusing on later steps of the Logic Games Method.

To stay sharp, practice the drills in the Logic Games Training Camp for this chapter in your Online Study Plan. Training Camp drills are divided into Fundamentals, Mid-Level, and Advanced sets.

Reflect

Think back over the work you did in this chapter.

Did you consistently conduct an Overview by answering the SEAL questions for each game setup?
How does mentally picturing a game's Situation help you understand the game's task and turn it into a useful sketch framework?
What do the entities tell you about a game's action? What may be different when the setup includes two or more *types* of entities? What may be different when the entities are subdivided in the setup?
What are four basic logic game actions? What are the most common Hybrid combinations of those actions?
What kinds of limitations does the testmaker impose upon a game in the game's setup? Were there any cases in which you took limitations for granted even though the limitations were not explicit?

In the coming days, take note of real-life jobs and tasks that mimic the standard game actions:

Sequencing: making schedules, or ranking or prioritizing items
Selection: choosing what to serve or who to invite to something
Distribution: creating teams, or separating things into different boxes or drawers
Matching: assigning items or tasks to different people, or matching attributes to different items

Try to envision how the testmaker would turn such tasks into logic games. What kinds of limitations would the test impose? What kinds of rules and restrictions might apply?

Logic Games Rules and Deductions

THE ROLE OF RULES AND DEDUCTIONS IN LOGIC GAMES

Most LSAT experts would agree that the skills you'll learn in this chapter are the most important tools you can add to your logic games repertoire. Here, you'll learn to analyze and draw a game's rules and then—and this is what sets real Logic Games masters apart from the crowd—to combine the game's rules and limitations to determine everything that can be deduced about what must, can, and cannot be true about the arrangement of entities. Gaining mastery of the skills in this chapter is your ticket to handling the questions quickly and accurately on a consistent basis.

To this point, you've seen how LSAT experts conduct the Overview and Sketch steps of the Logic Games Method. They analyze the Situation, Entities, Action, and overall Limitations to form a clear mental picture of their task. Then, they translate that mental picture into a diagram that will hold all of the relevant restrictions. In Chapter 2, you focused on clearly analyzing a game's big picture. Now, you'll see the rules of the games as well, and you'll use the next two steps of the Logic Games Method to produce a comprehensive Master Sketch for each game. Here, you'll have plenty of opportunities to practice analyzing and sketching rules and then combining them to make all available deductions.

When LSAT experts draw out a game's rules, they depict them clearly, in a way that matches and fits into the framework of their sketch and accounts for what the rule does and does not mean. In the first part of this chapter, you'll see how LSAT experts are able to do that within each of the common game types using the typical sketches introduced in Chapter 2.

In the second part of this chapter, you'll learn how experts then combine the rules to determine what must, can, and cannot be true of the entities in the game. LSAT experts use a checklist of five common patterns to ensure that they spot all of the game's deductions and are able to tackle the game's questions with confidence, knowing that they have maximized the available information. At the end of the chapter, you'll see a Special Feature on one of those patterns—Limited Options—that can, in some games, double the power of your Master Sketch.

HOW TO INTERPRET AND SKETCH RULES

LEARNING OBJECTIVES

In this section of Chapter 3, you'll learn to:

- Analyze and depict Logic Games rules effectively

  Before jotting down a rule, LSAT experts make sure that they understand the rule thoroughly. They are careful not to read more into a rule than what it says while, at the same time, accounting for all of the restrictions that the rule imposes within the game.

Prepare

LSAT experts know that rules are their best friends. With no rules, a Strict Sequencing game that asks you to arrange seven entities into seven slots, one per slot, has 5,040 acceptable arrangements. Add just one rule—"P is placed sixth"—and you reduce the number of acceptable arrangements to just 720. Depending on the additional rules, it's not uncommon for such a game on the LSAT to have fewer than 20 possible solutions. In short, it is the rules that make games manageable.

In this section of the chapter, you'll see the strategies and tactics that LSAT experts use to analyze and depict Logic Games rules in the most helpful way. First, you'll learn the most common rule patterns. Then, you'll look at sets of rules within the context of game setups. You'll have the opportunity to practice analyzing and drawing the rules associated with game setups. Finally, you'll assess your skill level with four more model and official game setups.

LOGIC GAMES STRATEGY

When analyzing and drawing a rule, always ask:

- Who/what does the rule restrict?
- Who/what does the rule leave undetermined?
- Is the rule stated in affirmative or negative terms?
- If stated affirmatively, can I learn something concrete from its negative implications (or vice versa)?
- Can I place the rule directly into the sketch framework?
- If not, how can I best draw the rule to account for what it does and does not restrict?

Common Rule Patterns

Rules, of course, are specific to the logic game setups they accompany. They restrict the entities within the given framework. But, just as there are a handful of game actions that occur again and again, so are there standard types of rules. Take a look at the affirmative and negative implications of the most common rules that appear in logic games.

Established Entities Rules

Established entities are committed to a particular position or placement throughout the game. *Affirmative* rules creating established entities are clear and concrete, and should be written directly into the sketch framework. For example, in a Sequencing game, you might see:

Lana is the fourth presenter.

$$\frac{\quad}{1} \quad \frac{\quad}{2} \quad \frac{\quad}{3} \quad \frac{L}{4} \quad \frac{\quad}{5} \quad \frac{\quad}{6}$$

Similarly, you might see the following in a Distribution game:

Quincy is assigned to Team 2.

Teams

1	2	3
—	Q	—
—	—	—

The *negative* implications of these rules are equally straightforward: The established entity does *not* go anywhere else. Because an established entity's placement is so clear, there is no reason to record the negative implications in the sketch.

There are two similar types of rules worth mentioning here.

Rules that limit an entity's placement

The most common rules of this type *affirmatively* restrict an entity to one of two positions. Like pure established entity rules, these rules can usually be depicted within the sketch framework. The Sequencing game example would state something such as:

Tom presents either first or sixth.

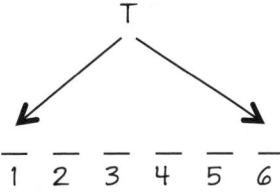

In a Distribution game, such a rule would look something like this:

Percy is assigned to either Team 2 or Team 3.

Teams

Here, again, the negative implications are clear: The entity restricted by the rule *cannot* appear in any other position.

Note: If the entity that is restricted to one of two positions directly impacts additional entities and determines or restricts their placements, you may choose to draw out two sketches so that you can depict the resulting deductions. These so-called Limited Options sketches are discussed along with other deductions in the second half of this chapter, and in the Special Feature at the end of this chapter.

Rules forbidding a particular placement

The terminology may be a little confusing here because these are rules that *affirmatively* forbid an entity from taking a particular slot or placement. While these rules are far less restrictive than those establishing an entity's placement, they are just as easy to add to the sketch. A typical Sequencing game example would be:

Frank does not give the second presentation.

$$\frac{\quad}{1} \ \frac{\quad}{2} \ \frac{\quad}{3} \ \frac{\quad}{4} \ \frac{\quad}{5} \ \frac{\quad}{6}$$
~F

The *negative* implication of that rule is that Frank *can* present in any other position. If you tried to indicate all of the places Frank could go, your sketch would get far too cluttered and confusing.

If you see a rule forbidding placement in a Matching game, you might depict it within a grid. Imagine a game with four employees—A, B, C, and D—assigned one or more of four tasks—w, x, y, or z.

Employee A does not perform Task *y*.

	A	B	C	D
w				
x				
y	✕			
z				

Ordering Rules

These rules are the bread and butter of Sequencing games or of Hybrid games that include a Sequencing task. They *affirmatively* restrict two or more entities relative to one another. The simplest examples say something such as:

George presents before Dawn presents.

$$\underset{1}{\_} \quad \underset{2}{\_} \quad \underset{3}{\_} \quad \underset{4}{\_} \quad \underset{5}{\_} \quad \underset{6}{\_}$$

G . . . D

That rule cannot effectively be drawn into the sketch framework because it leaves open too many possible placements for the two entities. It is best to depict it beneath or beside the sketch using ellipses to indicate that the distance between the two entities is not determined. You can, however, add its *negative* implications to the sketch. Since George must present before Dawn presents, Dawn cannot present first, and George cannot present last.

$$\underset{1}{\_} \quad \underset{2}{\_} \quad \underset{3}{\_} \quad \underset{4}{\_} \quad \underset{5}{\_} \quad \underset{6}{\_}$$
~D   ~G

G . . . D

If an ordering rule includes three entities, it is even more restrictive. Consider the following, and note how the expert drew out both the affirmative and negative aspects of the rule:

Michael presents at an earlier time than Oscar, but at a later time than Stephanie.

$$\underset{1}{\_} \quad \underset{2}{\_} \quad \underset{3}{\_} \quad \underset{4}{\_} \quad \underset{5}{\_} \quad \underset{6}{\_}$$
~O ~O   ~S ~S
~M   ~M

S . . . M . . . O

Another common example might be worded like this:

David and Hiromi both present after Candace presents.

$$\underset{1}{\_} \quad \underset{2}{\_} \quad \underset{3}{\_} \quad \underset{4}{\_} \quad \underset{5}{\_} \quad \underset{6}{\_}$$
~D   ~C ~C
~H

```
        ·D
C·.
        ·. H
```

Note that while David and Hiromi both follow Candace in that rule, you learn nothing about David and Hiromi relative to one another. Be sure not to read more into a rule than what it explicitly states.

By the way, some LSAT experts always add the negative implications to the sketch, while others are comfortable with just jotting down the affirmative rule underneath. Go with what works best for you, but be certain that you understand a rule's negative implications even if you don't write them out.

Distance Rules

This category of rules is associated specifically with Strict Sequencing games and Hybrid games with a Strict Sequencing component. They *affirmatively* tell you how close to one another two entities are placed (but they may not tell you anything about the entities' relative order). Here are some examples from a game that determines the lanes in which sprinters will run:

A and B run in consecutively numbered lanes.

$$\overline{1} \quad \overline{2} \quad \overline{3} \quad \overline{4} \quad \overline{5} \quad \overline{6}$$

$$\underline{A} \quad \underline{B} \quad \text{or} \quad \underline{B} \quad \underline{A}$$

The lanes in which J and K run are separated by exactly one lane.

$$\overline{1} \quad \overline{2} \quad \overline{3} \quad \overline{4} \quad \overline{5} \quad \overline{6}$$

$$\underline{K/J} \quad \_ \quad \underline{J/K}$$

The lanes in which X and Y run are separated by at least one lane.

$$\overline{1} \quad \overline{2} \quad \overline{3} \quad \overline{4} \quad \overline{5} \quad \overline{6}$$

$$\underline{X/Y} \quad \_ \quad ... \quad \underline{Y/X}$$

Notice that none of those rules tell you anything about the order in which the runners are sequenced, only about how far from one another they are. LSAT experts are careful not to add restrictions that are not explicitly stated in the rules. Because the rules say nothing about the order of the entities, there is little to learn from the *negative* implications of these rules beyond the obvious statement that the entities cannot be closer or farther apart than what the rule states.

If, however, a rule indicates both distance *and* order, you can add the negative implications to the sketch. For example:

E runs in a lane numbered exactly two higher than the lane in which L runs.

$$\overline{1} \quad \overline{2} \quad \overline{3} \quad \overline{4} \quad \overline{5} \quad \overline{6}$$
$$\text{~E} \quad \text{~E} \qquad\qquad \text{~L} \quad \text{~L}$$

$$\underline{L} \quad \_ \quad \underline{E}$$

Blocks of Entities Rules

Blocks of Entities are created whenever a rule *affirmatively* states that two entities must "travel together." In Strict Sequencing games, this occurs whenever two entities must be placed consecutively or when two entities are separated by an exact number of spaces. Some LSAT experts will draw a box around Blocks of Entities rules to remind themselves that the block will take up a certain number of slots.

$$\boxed{\underline{A} \,/\, \underline{B}}$$

$$\boxed{\underline{K/J} \ \_\_ \ \underline{J/K}}$$

Rules creating blocks of entities are also quite common in Distribution games. The wording is usually straightforward.

Oliver plays on the same team as Priscilla.

Teams

Notice how the LSAT expert depicted that rule in a way that matches the sketch framework.

Blocks of entities become very important in the deductions step of the Logic Games Method. There, you can see how other rules intervene to limit the acceptable placement of the block. On their own, they don't carry many *negative* implications beyond requiring that the two entities in the block stay together.

It is worth noting that you will occasionally see rules that force entities to stay apart. You can think of them as "anti-blocks."

T and U do not run in consecutively numbered lanes.

never $\boxed{\underline{T} \,/\, \underline{U}}$

Barbara and Colin do not play on the same team.

never $\boxed{\dfrac{B}{C}}$

On a tactical note, if the rule about Barbara and Colin appeared in a Distribution game with exactly two teams—let's call them Team Red and Team Blue—you could record this rule inside the sketch framework.

Teams

Red	Blue
B/C	C/B
—	—
—	—

Conditional (Formal Logic) Rules

You can recognize conditional rules from their "if-then" format, although they may be worded in a number of ways. The rule "If X is selected, then Y is selected" is exactly the same as "X is selected only if Y is selected" or even "X is not selected unless Y is selected." That's because the rule's "If" clause is sufficient to trigger its "then" clause, and its "then" clause is necessary for its "If" clause.

Most LSAT experts choose to jot down these rules in a standard shorthand.

If Carla is selected, then David is also selected.

If $C \longrightarrow D$

Clearly, that rule applies whenever Carla is selected (her selection is sufficient to ensure his). The rule is also triggered when David is *not* selected (his selection is necessary for hers). LSAT experts will routinely jot down the contrapositive of any conditional Formal Logic rule by reversing and negating the entities in the rule. For the rule about Carla and David, that would look like this:

If $\sim D \longrightarrow \sim C$

(Think of the tildes (~) as meaning "not.")

While you will occasionally run across a conditional rule in other types of games, these rules are at the core of Selection games. So close is this association that you'll find a large portion of Chapter 8—the chapter on Selection games—devoted to everything you need to know to use Formal Logic in LSAT logic games. You can study that section at any time, but conditional rules are rare enough in game types other than Selection that you are probably safe waiting until you study that chapter before taking the deep dive into Formal Logic. (As an aside, Formal Logic is much more common in the Logical Reasoning section of the LSAT than it is in the Logic Games section, so learning how to interpret conditional statements may improve your overall LSAT score even beyond the work you are doing in this book.)

Number Rules

These rules are most consistently associated with Matching and Distribution games. They sometimes *affirmatively* specify the number of entities that can be assigned to a group, as in this Distribution game:

Exactly three of the students are assigned to Team Red.

Red	Blue
—	
—	
=	

Or, they might restrict the number of entities or attributes assigned to two groups or individuals relatively, as in this Matching game (the axes of the grid represent employees A, B, C, and D, and tasks w, x, y, and z):

Employee B is assigned more of the tasks than Employee D is assigned.

$$B > D$$

	A	B	C	D
w				
x				
y				
z				

Number rules become very important in Step 4 of the Logic Games Method because they may trigger several deductions. Take the rule about the two employees. If other rules or restrictions make it clear that Employee D performs two of the tasks, you now know that Employee B must perform three or four of the tasks. On the other hand, if it turned out that Employee B performs two of the tasks, you would now know that Employee D can perform only one task, at most.

Rules In Context

Knowing the types of rules you will encounter is helpful, but it is only within a game's full context or setup that you can fully appreciate the rules' impact on the entities. Start your work here by reviewing a game you've already seen.

Refresh (Activate Prior Knowledge)

Here are the setup and rules from the Truck Arrivals game that you saw in Chapter 1.

> In a single day, exactly seven trucks—S, T, U, W, X, Y, and Z—are the only arrivals at a warehouse. No truck arrives at the same time as any other truck, and no truck arrives more than once that day. Each truck is either green or red (but not both). The following conditions apply:
>
> No two consecutive arrivals are red.
> Y arrives at some time before both T and W.
> Exactly two of the trucks that arrive before Y are red.
> S is the sixth arrival.
> Z arrives at some time before U.

PrepTest37 Sec3 Qs 6–11

Steps 1 and 2: You will recall that this is a Sequencing/Matching Hybrid game. Your tasks are to account for the order in which the trucks arrive and to assign each truck a color.

$$S \quad T \quad U \quad W \quad X \quad Y \quad Z$$

$$\underline{\quad} \quad \underline{\quad} \quad \underline{\quad} \quad \underline{\quad} \quad \underline{\quad} \quad \underline{\quad} \quad \underline{\quad}$$
$$1 \quad 2 \quad 3 \quad 4 \quad 5 \quad 6 \quad 7$$

g/r $\underline{\quad} \quad \underline{\quad} \quad \underline{\quad} \quad \underline{\quad} \quad \underline{\quad} \quad \underline{\quad} \quad \underline{\quad}$

Step 3: Now, review how the LSAT expert analyzed and drew each rule with the common rule patterns in mind.

> No two consecutive arrivals are red.

This is a negative rule about the distance between two entities (referred to previously as an "anti-block"). Since it doesn't provide enough information to draw anything into the sketch, depict it underneath the framework.

$$\underline{\quad} \quad \underline{\quad} \quad \underline{\quad} \quad \underline{\quad} \quad \underline{\quad} \quad \underline{\quad} \quad \underline{\quad}$$
$$1 \quad 2 \quad 3 \quad 4 \quad 5 \quad 6 \quad 7$$

g/r $\underline{\quad} \quad \underline{\quad} \quad \underline{\quad} \quad \underline{\quad} \quad \underline{\quad} \quad \underline{\quad} \quad \underline{\quad}$

never $\boxed{r \quad r}$

     Y arrives at some time before both T and W.

This is an ordering rule involving three entities. It tells you that Y precedes T and W, but does not give any information about the relative order of T and W. Note that you now know that Y cannot arrive sixth or seventh, and that neither T nor W can arrive first. The rule cannot be drawn into the framework, so write it underneath in a way that orients it to the sketch layout.

$$\begin{array}{ccccccc} \overline{} & \overline{} & \overline{} & \overline{} & \overline{} & \overline{} & \overline{} \\ 1 & 2 & 3 & 4 & 5 & 6 & 7 \end{array}$$

g/r _ _ _ _ _ _ _

never $\boxed{r \quad r}$

$$y \begin{array}{l} \cdot T \\ \cdot W \end{array}$$

     Exactly two of the trucks that arrive before Y are red.

This is another relative ordering rule that tells you that two of the trucks arriving before Y are red. You now know that Y cannot arrive first or second (and, if you remember Rule 1, which prevents consecutive red arrivals, you know that Y cannot arrive third, either). You cannot write this rule directly into the sketch, but because Y has already been mentioned in Rule 2, you can combine your sketch for Rule 1 with your sketch for Rule 2. If that doesn't occur to you, it's okay, because you will combine them during Step 4 as you make deductions.

$$\begin{array}{ccccccc} \overline{} & \overline{} & \overline{} & \overline{} & \overline{} & \overline{} & \overline{} \\ 1 & 2 & 3 & 4 & 5 & 6 & 7 \end{array}$$

g/r _ _ _ _ _ _ _

never $\boxed{r \quad r}$

$$r \ldots r \ldots y \begin{array}{l} \cdot T \\ \cdot W \end{array}$$

     S is the sixth arrival.

This rule establishes the position of S once and for all. Build this one directly into the sketch framework.

$$\begin{array}{ccccccc} \overline{} & \overline{} & \overline{} & \overline{} & \overline{} & \overline{S} & \overline{} \\ 1 & 2 & 3 & 4 & 5 & 6 & 7 \end{array}$$

g/r _ _ _ _ _ _ _

never $\boxed{r \quad r}$

$$r \ldots r \ldots y \begin{array}{l} \cdot T \\ \cdot W \end{array}$$

> Z arrives at some time before U.

This is one more relative ordering rule: Z arrives before U arrives. You now know that Z cannot arrive seventh, and that U cannot arrive first. Jot down the rule in shorthand underneath the sketch.

$$\overline{}\quad\overline{}\quad\overline{}\quad\overline{}\quad\overline{}\quad\overset{S}{\overline{}}\quad\overline{}$$
$$\;\;1\quad\;2\quad\;3\quad\;4\quad\;5\quad\;6\quad\;7$$

g/r $\overline{}\quad\overline{}\quad\overline{}\quad\overline{}\quad\overline{}\quad\overline{}\quad\overline{}$

never $\boxed{r \quad r}$

r ... r ... y .·⋰ T
        ·⋱ W

Z ... U

Because you've seen that game before, you may already be looking ahead to the deductions you can make by combining the rules. That's great. On Test Day, you will roll right from the Rules step into the Deductions. In fact, you'll have the chance to revisit the deductions in the Truck Arrivals game in the next section of this chapter, which covers Step 4.

First, though, take a look at an expert's analysis of the rules step in another game—Patterson's Meetings. You saw this game's setup, but not its rules, in Chapter 2. Take a minute or two to review the setup, and then try to anticipate how the expert will analyze and draw each rule.

> On one afternoon, Patterson meets individually with each of exactly five clients—Reilly, Sanchez, Tang, Upton, and Yansky—and also goes to the gym by herself for a workout. Patterson's workout and her five meetings each start at either 1:00, 2:00, 3:00, 4:00, 5:00, or 6:00. The following conditions must apply:
>
> > Patterson meets with Sanchez at some time before her workout.
> > Patterson meets with Tang at some time after her workout.
> > Patterson meets with Yansky either immediately before or immediately after her workout.
> > Patterson meets with Upton at some time before she meets with Reilly.

PrepTest45 Sec3 Qs 1–6

Steps 1 and 2: You will recall that this is a Strict Sequencing game. The task is to account for the order in which Patterson conducts her five meetings and her workout.

R S T U W Y

$$\overline{}\quad\overline{}\quad\overline{}\quad\overline{}\quad\overline{}\quad\overline{}$$
$$\;\;1\quad\;2\quad\;3\quad\;4\quad\;5\quad\;6$$

K

Step 3: Now, take a look how the LSAT expert analyzed and drew each rule with the common rule patterns in mind. Take note of cases in which you accurately anticipated the way in which the expert would draw out the rules, and anywhere your anticipated analysis differs from the expert's.

> Patterson meets with Sanchez at some time before her workout.

This is an ordering rule. You know that the Sanchez meeting precedes the workout, but you don't know by how many hours it precedes the workout. Since the rule doesn't provide enough information to draw anything into the sketch, depict it underneath the framework.

$$\overline{} \quad \overline{} \quad \overline{} \quad \overline{} \quad \overline{} \quad \overline{}$$
$$1 \quad 2 \quad 3 \quad 4 \quad 5 \quad 6$$

$$S\ldots W$$

> Patterson meets with Tang at some time after her workout.

This is another ordering rule. It tells you that the workout precedes the meeting with Tang, but not by how much. The rule cannot be drawn into the framework, so it, too, will go underneath the framework. If you noticed that the workout was also mentioned in Rule 1, you can combine the rules in your drawing. If you didn't notice that immediately, you will combine Rules 1 and 2 during the Deductions step.

$$\overline{} \quad \overline{} \quad \overline{} \quad \overline{} \quad \overline{} \quad \overline{}$$
$$1 \quad 2 \quad 3 \quad 4 \quad 5 \quad 6$$

$$S\ldots W\ldots T$$

> Patterson meets with Yansky either immediately before or immediately after her workout.

This is a distance rule—the Yansky meeting and the workout are consecutive—but it does not tell you about the order of the two meetings. Like Rules 1 and 2, this rule mentions the workout. Again, if you noticed that, you can combine this rule with the first two, or you can depict it separately and make that combination in the Deductions step.

$$\overline{} \quad \overline{} \quad \overline{} \quad \overline{} \quad \overline{} \quad \overline{}$$
$$1 \quad 2 \quad 3 \quad 4 \quad 5 \quad 6$$

$$S\ldots \boxed{W/Y} \ldots T$$

> Patterson meets with Upton at some time before she meets with Reilly.

Here, you have one more ordering rule. The Upton meeting precedes the Reilly meeting, but there is no information about the distance between the two meetings. Depict the rule underneath the framework.

$$\overline{} \quad \overline{} \quad \overline{} \quad \overline{} \quad \overline{} \quad \overline{}$$
$$1 \quad 2 \quad 3 \quad 4 \quad 5 \quad 6$$

$$S\ldots \boxed{W/Y} \ldots T$$
$$U\ldots R$$

You'll return to Patterson's Meetings in the second part of this chapter to make all of the deductions that follow from these rules.

Before turning to practice and assessment in the Rules step, take a look at an expert's analysis of one more logic game's setup and rules. This one is more complex than Patterson's Meetings, and you haven't seen it before at all. Once again, take a minute or two to review the game's setup and rules, and try to anticipate the expert's work.

Exactly six people–Lulu, Nam, Ofelia, Pachai, Santiago, and Tyrone–are the only contestants in a chess tournament. The tournament consists of four games, played one after the other. Exactly two people play in each game, and each person plays in at least one game. The following conditions must apply:

Tyrone does not play in the first or third game.
Lulu plays in the last game.
Nam plays in only one game and it is not against Pachai.
Santiago plays in exactly two games, one just before and one just after the only game that Ofelia plays in.

PrepTest45 Sec3 Qs 7–12

Steps 1 and 2: The Situation is a chess tournament with six players and four games, and the task is to schedule the players in each game. The Entities are the players—L, N, O, P, S, and T. The Action here is Strict Sequencing, but the Limitations introduce added complexity. Each game has exactly two players, so with four games to play, there are eight slots to fill. Because there are only six players, however, at least one player must appear in more than one game. Here is the initial sketch:

L N O P S T

1   2   3   4

—   —   —   —

—   —   —   —

Step 3: Now, take a look how the LSAT expert analyzed and drew each rule with the common rule patterns in mind. Take note of cases in which you accurately anticipated the way in which the expert would draw out the rules, and anywhere your anticipated analysis differs from the expert's.

Tyrone does not play in the first or third game.

This rule prevents Tyrone from playing in two of the games, Games 1 and 3. It does not tell you whether he plays in one or both of the remaining games.

L N O P S T

1   2   3   4

—   —   —   —

—   —   —   —
~T   ~T

K

Lulu plays in the last game.

This rule creates a "quasi-Established Entity." While Lulu will definitely play in Game 4, remember that, in this game, an entity may be scheduled more than once. Draw L in Game 4 within the sketch framework, but don't forget that, without further restrictions, Lulu may play again.

```
        L N O P S T

        1   2   3   4

        _   _   _   L

        _   _   _   _
       ~T      ~T
```

Nam plays in only one game and it is not against Pachai.

This rule contains a number restriction—Nam plays only one game—and creates an "anti-block"—Nam and Pachai are never in the same game. Note the number restriction above N in the roster of entities, and note the rule that prevents the N-P pairing next to or underneath the sketch framework.

```
          1
        L N O P S T

        1   2   3   4      never    N
                                     ─
        _   _   _   L                P

        _   _   _   _
       ~T      ~T
```

Santiago plays in exactly two games, one just before and one just after the only game that Ofelia plays in.

Here is a rule that contains two number restrictions—Santiago plays in two games, and Ofelia plays in one—and creates a block of three consecutive spaces: S-O-S. Note the number restrictions above the roster of entities, and represent the block next to or underneath the framework.

```
          1 1   2
        L N O P S T                never    N
                                            ─
        1   2   3   4                       P

        _   _   _   L              ┌─────────┐
                                   │ S  O  S │
        _   _   _   _              └─────────┘
       ~T      ~T
```

With that sketch, you will be ready to make all of the deductions in the Chess Tournament game (and, by the way, there are a lot to make in that one). Before moving on to Step 4, however, take time to practice analyzing and drawing the rules in context. You'll have three new model setups, and then a new official LSAC game setup. Because you haven't seen these game setups before, you'll need to start with Steps 1 and 2 to identify the games' actions and produce their initial sketches. Then, do your best to analyze and sketch the games' rules as the LSAT experts did in the preceding games in this chapter.

Practice

Directions: Read and analyze the game setup and record your analysis as indicated. In this practice section, work at your own pace, and answer every question thoroughly. Explanations for all four practice game setups follow the practice section.

Practice 1

A geologist is organizing a display of seven gemstones—amethyst, beryl, diamond, emerald, fluorite, garnet, and jade. The gemstones will be arranged in a single row in a glass display case, labeled 1 through 7 consecutively from left to right, with one stone occupying each position. The arrangement of the gemstones must conform to the following conditions:

> The diamond must occupy a higher-numbered position than the amethyst, but a lower-numbered position than the garnet.
>
> The emerald and the fluorite must occupy consecutively numbered positions.
>
> The beryl must occupy a higher-numbered position than the emerald.
>
> The diamond must occupy position number 3.

1. [Step 1] Summarize your Overview analysis:

2. [Step 2] Create an initial Sketch:

3. [Step 3] Analyze and draw the Rules:
   - For each rule, answer the following questions and then draw the rule in the appropriate box.
     - What does the rule restrict, and what does it leave open?
     - What are the rule's negative implications, if any?
     - Can the rule be depicted inside the sketch framework?

Rule 1:	Rule 2:
Rule 3:	Rule 4:

Practice 2

A chocolatier is putting together boxes of truffles for fundraisers at three local schools—X, Y, and Z. Each school will get a box with at least one of the five available flavors—hazelnut, maple walnut, peanut butter, raspberry, and white chocolate. Each flavor will be included in at least one of the boxes, subject to the following conditions:

> The box for school X will include hazelnut truffles.
> Maple walnut truffles will be used in more boxes than white chocolate truffles.
> Peanut butter truffles will be used in exactly one box, and no other flavor will be included in that box.

1.   [Step 1] Summarize your Overview analysis:

2.   [Step 2] Create an initial Sketch:

3.   [Step 3] Analyze and draw the Rules:
     - For each rule, answer the following questions and then draw the rule in the appropriate box.
       - What does the rule restrict, and what does it leave open?
       - What are the rule's negative implications, if any?
       - Can the rule be depicted inside the sketch framework?

Rule 1:	Rule 2:
Rule 3:	

Practice 3

An accountant is scheduling meetings with six clients—Able, Baker, Charlie, Delphine, Erica, and Frankie—over a four-day period, from Monday through Thursday. On each day, two appointments are available, one in the morning and one in the afternoon. In addition, two staff meetings will be scheduled over the same period. Each client and staff meeting must be assigned a different appointment time. The schedule is governed by the following conditions:

> The staff meetings are not scheduled in the afternoon.
> Charlie's and Frankie's meetings are scheduled for the same day.
> Delphine's meeting is scheduled for some time prior to Frankie's meeting.
> Baker's meeting is scheduled in the morning.
> The accountant will meet with Erica and Baker on different days.

1. [Step 1] Summarize your Overview analysis:

2. [Step 2] Create an initial Sketch:

3. [Step 3] Analyze and draw the Rules:
    - For each rule, answer the following questions and then draw the rule in the appropriate box.
      - What does the rule restrict, and what does it leave open?
      - What are the rule's negative implications, if any?
      - Can the rule be depicted inside the sketch framework?

Rule 1:	Rule 2:
Rule 3:	Rule 4:
Rule 5:	

K

Practice 4

A showroom contains exactly six new cars—T, V, W, X, Y, and Z—each equipped with at least one of the following three options: power windows, leather interior, and sunroof. No car has any other options. The following conditions must apply:

V has power windows and a sunroof.
W has power windows and a leather interior.
W and Y have no options in common.
X has more options than W.
V and Z have exactly one option in common.
T has fewer options than Z.

PrepTest35 Sec3 Qs 6–12

1. [Step 1] Summarize your Overview analysis:

2. [Step 2] Create an initial Sketch:

3. [Step 3] Analyze and draw the Rules:
   - For each rule, answer the following questions and then draw the rule in the appropriate box.
     - What does the rule restrict, and what does it leave open?
     - What are the rule's negative implications, if any?
     - Can the rule be depicted inside the sketch framework?

Rule 1:	Rule 2:
Rule 3:	Rule 4:
Rule 5:	Rule 6:

Explanations

Compare your work to that of an LSAT expert. Pay close attention to how the expert analyzed each rule and then depicted it within or beneath the game's initial sketch.

Practice 1

A geologist is organizing a display of seven gemstones—amethyst, beryl, diamond, emerald, fluorite, garnet, and jade. The gemstones will be arranged in a single row in a glass display case, labeled 1 through 7 consecutively from left to right, with one stone occupying each position. The arrangement of the gemstones must conform to the following conditions:

> The diamond must occupy a higher-numbered position than the amethyst, but a lower-numbered position than the garnet.
> The emerald and the fluorite must occupy consecutively numbered positions.
> The beryl must occupy a higher-numbered position than the emerald.
> The diamond must occupy position number 3.

1. [Step 1] Summarize your Overview analysis: *A geologist is arranging seven stones in positions numbered 1 through 7, one stone per position. This is a Strict Sequencing game as indicated by rules 2 and 4.*

2. [Step 2] Create an initial Sketch: *This calls for a standard Strict Sequencing sketch framework.*

A B D E F G J

    1 2 3 4 5 6 7

3. [Step 3] Analyze and draw the Rules:
   - Rule 1:
     - What does the rule restrict, and what does it leave open? *This rule gives the relative relationship among three of the stones: A-D-G. The rule does not say how close or how far the three entities are from one another.*

   - What are the rule's negative implications, if any? *Amethyst cannot occupy positions 6 or 7. Diamond cannot occupy positions 1 or 7. Garnet cannot occupy positions 1 or 2.*
   - Can the rule be depicted inside the sketch framework? *No.*
   - Draw the rule:

A B D E F G J

    1 2 3 4 5 6 7

A . . . D . . . G

- Rule 2:
  - What does the rule restrict, and what does it leave open? *This rule creates a block of entities by dictating that the emerald and the fluorite are placed consecutively. The rule does not dictate the order in which the two are placed.*
  - What are the rule's negative implications, if any? *None, apart from the fact that the entities may not be split up.*
  - Can the rule be depicted inside the sketch framework? *No.*
  - Draw the rule:

A B D E F G J

    __ __ __ __ __ __ __
    1   2   3   4   5   6   7

A . . . D . . . G

    ┌─────┐
    │ E / F │
    └─────┘

- Rule 3:
  - What does the rule restrict, and what does it leave open? *This rule gives the relative order of the emerald and the beryl, but does not say how close or far away the two entities must be.*
  - What are the rule's negative implications, if any? *The emerald cannot occupy position 7, and the beryl cannot occupy position 1.*
  - Can the rule be depicted inside the sketch framework? *No. Because you already know that emerald and fluorite are a block, you may make the deduction that beryl comes after the block and simply append this rule to Rule 2. If you don't do that now, you will when making the deductions in Step 4.*
  - Draw the rule:

    A B D E F G J

    <u> </u> <u> </u> <u> </u> <u> </u> <u> </u> <u> </u> <u> </u>
     1   2   3   4   5   6   7

    A . . . D . . . G
    ┌─────────┐
    │ E / F │ . . . B
    └─────────┘

- Rule 4:
  - What does the rule restrict, and what does it leave open? *This rule establishes the diamond's position once and for all. It leaves nothing open.*
  - What are the rule's negative implications, if any? *No other entity can occupy position 3.*
  - Can the rule be depicted inside the sketch framework? *Yes.*
  - Draw the rule:

    A B D E F G J

            D
    <u> </u> <u> </u> <u> </u> <u> </u> <u> </u> <u> </u> <u> </u>
     1   2   3   4   5   6   7

    A . . . D . . . G
    ┌─────────┐
    │ E / F │ . . . B
    └─────────┘

Practice 2

A chocolatier is putting together boxes of truffles for fundraisers at three local schools—X, Y, and Z. Each school will get a box with at least one of the five available flavors—hazelnut, maple walnut, peanut butter, raspberry, and white chocolate. Each flavor will be included in at least one of the boxes, subject to the following conditions:

> The box for school X will include hazelnut truffles.
> Maple walnut truffles will be used in more boxes than white chocolate truffles.
> Peanut butter truffles will be used in exactly one box, and no other flavor will be included in that box.

1. [Step 1] Summarize your Overview analysis: *The situation finds a chocolate shop putting together three different boxes, each with truffles of five different flavors. Flavors can appear in more than one of the boxes, so this is a Matching game. The key limitation is that each flavor must appear at least once among the three boxes.*

2. [Step 2] Create an initial Sketch: *This is a standard Matching game, so the initial sketch may be a list*

   hn mw pb rb wc

	X	Y	Z

or a grid.

	X	Y	Z
hn			
mw			
pb			
rb			
wc			

3. [Step 3] Analyze and draw the Rules:
   - Rule 1:
     - What does the rule restrict, and what does it leave open? *This rule establishes one placement for hazelnut, in the box for School X. Note that hazelnut may appear in more than one box, and that School X may have other flavors in its box.*
     - What are the rule's negative implications, if any? *Nothing yet.* (Note: If this were a Distribution game, in which each flavor could appear only one time, you would know hazelnut's only placement. Since this is a Matching game, however, the flavor may show up in another box as well.)
     - Can the rule be depicted inside the sketch framework? *Yes.*
     - Draw the rule: *Here's Rule 1 in the list-style sketch.*

       hn mw pb rb wc

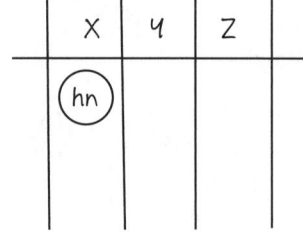

And here it is in the grid-style sketch.

	X	Y	Z
hn	✓		
mw			
pb			
rb			
wc			

   - Rule 2:
     - What does the rule restrict, and what does it leave open? *This rule provides relative number restriction: Maple walnut will be used more times than white chocolate. We don't yet know if maple walnut is used two or three times, or if white chocolate is used one or two times.*
     - What are the rule's negative implications, if any? *Maple walnut cannot be used only once, and white chocolate cannot be used more than twice.*
     - Can the rule be depicted inside the sketch framework? *No.*
     - Draw the rule: *Underneath either the list-style or the grid-style sketch, add this:*

       mw > wc

   - Rule 3:
     - What does the rule restrict, and what does it leave open? *This rule provides two restrictions on the peanut butter flavor: Peanut butter can appear in only one box, and it must be the only flavor in that box.*
     - What are the rule's negative implications, if any? *No other flavor can appear in a box with peanut butter.*

- Can the rule be depicted inside the sketch framework? *You could anticipate the deduction that because hazelnut is already in School X's box, peanut butter cannot be in that box, and indicate that peanut butter must be in either School Y's or School Z's box. (Note: You will explore the full implications of this deduction when you come back to this game in Step 4.)*

- Draw the rule: *This is the final sketch (including Rule 3) in the list-style sketch.*

1

hn mw pb rb wc

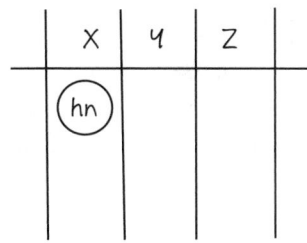

mw > wc

pb = alone

And here it is in the grid-style sketch.

	X	ч	Z
hn	✓		
mw			
1 = pb			
rb			
wc			

mw > wc

pb = alone

Practice 3

An accountant is scheduling meetings with six clients—Able, Baker, Charlie, Delphine, Erica, and Frankie—over a four-day period, from Monday through Thursday. On each day, two appointments are available, one in the morning and one in the afternoon. In addition, two staff meetings will be scheduled over the same period. Each client and staff meeting must be assigned a different appointment time. The schedule is governed by the following conditions:

> The staff meetings are not scheduled in the afternoon.
> Charlie's and Frankie's meetings are scheduled for the same day.
> Delphine's meeting is scheduled for some time prior to Frankie's meeting.
> Baker's meeting is scheduled in the morning.
> The accountant will meet with Erica and Baker on different days.

1. [Step 1] Summarize your Overview analysis: *In this situation, the task is to create a four-day—Monday through Thursday—schedule for an accountant's office. Each day has two appointment slots—AM and PM. Over the four days in question, the accountant schedules six client meetings and two staff meetings (the eight entities). This is a complex Strict Sequencing game. The explicit limitation in the setup is intuitive: Each of the eight meetings is scheduled for a different one of the eight appointment slots.*

2. [Step 2] Create an initial Sketch: *The sketch must account for the two appointment slots each day.*

A B C D E F S$_1$ S$_2$

M Tu W Th

AM __ __ __ __

PM __ __ __ __

3. [Step 3] Analyze and draw the Rules:
   - Rule 1:
     - What does the rule restrict, and what does it leave open? *This rule prevents either of the two staff meetings from being scheduled in the afternoon. It does not, however, tell us the days on which the staff meetings are scheduled.*
     - What are the rule's negative implications, if any? *Because the rule is negative, its "negative implication" is affirmative: The staff meetings are scheduled for the morning.*
     - Can the rule be depicted inside the sketch framework? *Because specific days are not stipulated, the rule cannot go inside the framework. It can, however, sit right next to the AM and PM lines of the sketch.*
     - Draw the rule:

       M Tu W Th

       AM __ __ __ __ S_1 S_2
       PM __ __ __ __ $\not{S_1}$ $\not{S_2}$

   - Rule 2:
     - What does the rule restrict, and what does it leave open? *This rule creates a block of entities: C and F are scheduled on the same day. The rule does not tell you which of the two entities takes the morning or the afternoon.*
     - What are the rule's negative implications, if any? *None, apart from the fact that no other entities are on the same day as either C or F.*
     - Can the rule be depicted inside the sketch framework? *No.*
     - Draw the rule: *Note the rule underneath the sketch framework.*

       $\boxed{\dfrac{C}{F}}$ or $\boxed{\dfrac{F}{C}}$ C, F = same day

   - Rule 3:
     - What does the rule restrict, and what does it leave open? *This rule gives the relative order of D and F, but does not tell us how close or far apart their appointments are.* (Note: Be careful not to assume, without further information, that D and F must be on different days. D's appointment could be in the morning and F's appointment in the afternoon of the same day and still abide by this rule's parameters.)
     - What are the rule's negative implications, if any? *D's appointment cannot be Thursday afternoon, and F's appointment cannot be Monday morning.*
     - Can the rule be depicted inside the sketch framework? *No.*
     - Draw the rule: *Note the rule underneath the sketch framework.*

       D . . . F

   - Rule 4:
     - What does the rule restrict, and what does it leave open? *This rule limits B's appointment to one of the morning slots, but does not say anything about the day on which B is scheduled.*
     - What are the rule's negative implications, if any? *B's appointment cannot be in the afternoon.*
     - Can the rule be depicted inside the sketch framework? *Because specific days are not stipulated, the rule cannot go inside the framework. It can, however, sit right next to the AM and PM lines of the sketch.*
     - Draw the rule:

       M Tu W Th

       AM __ __ __ __ S_1 S_2 B
       PM __ __ __ __ $\not{S_1}$ $\not{S_2}$ $\not{B}$

- Rule 5:
  - What does the rule restrict, and what does it leave open? *This rule creates an "anti-block" by stipulating that B and E will never be on the same day. It says nothing about the two entities' relative order. B might have an appointment before or after E's appointment.*
  - What are the rule's negative implications, if any? *This is a negative rule, so its "negative implication" is affirmative: B and E have appointments on different days.*
  - Can the rule be depicted inside the sketch framework? *No*
  - Draw the rule: *Note the rule underneath the sketch framework.*

never $\boxed{\begin{array}{c} E \\ \hline B \end{array}}$ or $\boxed{\begin{array}{c} B \\ \hline E \end{array}}$ E, B = different days

Here is the game's sketch including all of the rules.

A B C D E F S₁ S₂

M Tu W Th

AM __ __ __ __ S₁ S₂ B
PM __ __ __ __ S̶₁ S̶₂ B̶

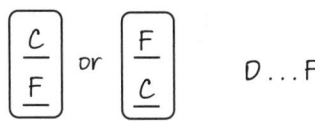

never $\boxed{\begin{array}{c} E \\ \hline B \end{array}}$ or $\boxed{\begin{array}{c} B \\ \hline E \end{array}}$

Practice 4

A showroom contains exactly six new cars—T, V, W, X, Y, and Z—each equipped with at least one of the following three options: power windows, leather interior, and sunroof. No car has any other options. The following conditions must apply:

> V has power windows and a sunroof.
> W has power windows and a leather interior.
> W and Y have no options in common.
> X has more options than W.
> V and Z have exactly one option in common.
> T has fewer options than Z.

PrepTest35 Sec3 Qs 6–12

1. [Step 1] Summarize your Overview analysis: *The situation here involves determining which of three features (the entities) correspond to each of six cars in a showroom. The features may appear on more than one car, so this is a Matching game. The key limitations are that each car has at least one of the features, and there are no other features.*

2. [Step 2] Create an initial Sketch: *As a Matching game, this can be sketched using a list*

pw li sr

T	V	W	X	Y	Z

or as a grid.

	T	V	W	X	Y	Z
pw						
li						
sr						

3. [Step 3] Analyze and draw the Rules:

- Rule 1:
  - What does the rule restrict, and what does it leave open? *This rule affirmatively assigns two features—power windows and a sunroof—to Car V. It does not say that these are Car V's only features.*
  - What are the rule's negative implications, if any? *None, for now.*
  - Can the rule be depicted inside the sketch framework? *Yes.*
  - Draw the rule: *Record the feature assignments in Car V's list*

  pw li sr

T	V	W	X	Y	Z
	pw				
	sr				

  or inside the grid.

	T	V	W	X	Y	Z
pw		✓				
li						
sr		✓				

- Rule 2:
  - What does the rule restrict, and what does it leave open? *This is the same kind of rule as Rule 1, but it assigns two features—power window and leather interior—to car W. Again, without additional rules, you don't know that these are Car W's only features.*
  - What are the rule's negative implications, if any? *None, for now.*
  - Can the rule be depicted inside the sketch framework? *Yes.*

- Draw the rule: *Record the assignments in Car W's list*

  pw li sr

T	V	W	X	Y	Z
	pw	pw			
	sr	li			

  or inside of the grid.

	T	V	W	X	Y	Z
pw		✓	✓			
li			✓			
sr		✓				

- Rule 3:
  - What does the rule restrict, and what does it leave open? *This is a negative assertion: Cars W and Y have no features in common.*
  - What are the rule's negative implications, if any? *You could phrase this affirmatively: The features for Car W are totally different than those for Car Y.*
  - Can the rule be depicted inside the sketch framework? *If you anticipate the deductions that (as a result of Rule 2) Car Y will have a sunroof and no other features, and that Car W will not have a sunroof, you could record those inside the sketch. If not, you will get to those when you return to the game for Step 4 of the Logic Games Method.*
  - Draw the rule: *For now, record the restriction underneath the sketch.*

  W ≠ Y Nothing in common

- Rule 4:
  - What does the rule restrict, and what does it leave open? *This rule provides a relative number restriction: Car X has more features than Car W.*
  - What are the rule's negative implications, if any? *You should be able to phrase the inverse of this rule: Car W has fewer features than Car X.*
  - Can the rule be depicted inside the sketch framework? *If you anticipate the deductions that (as a result of Rule 2) Car X will have all three features, and that Car W will not have a sunroof, you could record those inside the sketch. If not, you will get to those when you return to the game for Step 4 of the Logic Games Method.*
  - Draw the rule: *For now, record the restriction underneath the sketch.*

$$X > W$$

- Rule 5:
  - What does the rule restrict, and what does it leave open? *This rule provides an affirmative assertion: Cars V and Z have exactly one feature in common. It does, however, not say anything about what that feature is.*
  - What are the rule's negative implications, if any? *You may anticipate the deduction that (as a result of Rule 1) Car Z will not have both power windows and a sunroof. If it did, that would violate Rule 5 because Cars V and Z would have two features (not exactly one) in common.*
  - Can the rule be depicted inside the sketch framework? *No.*
  - Draw the rule: *For now, record the rule underneath the sketch.*

$$V = Z \text{ exactly 1 in common}$$

- Rule 6:
  - What does the rule restrict, and what does it leave open? *This rule provides another relative number restriction: Car T has fewer features than Car Z.*

- What are the rule's negative implications, if any? *The inverse phrasing for this rule is that Car Z has more features than Car T.*
- Can the rule be depicted inside the sketch framework? *You can record the fact that Car Z will have either two or three features while Car T will have either one or two. The deductions will refine the number restrictions even further.*
- Draw the rule: *For now, record the rule underneath the sketch.*

$$T < Z$$

In a list-style sketch, here is a depiction of all of the rules.

pw li sr

T	V	W	X	4	Z
	pw	pw			
	sr	li			

$X > W$ $W \neq 4$ Nothing in common

$T < Z$ $V = Z$ exactly 1 in common

In a grid-style sketch, the sketch with all of the rules would look like this.

	T	V	W	X	4	Z
pw		✓	✓			
li			✓			
sr		✓				

$X > W$ $W \neq 4$ Nothing in common

$T < Z$ $V = Z$ exactly 1 in common

Now that you have practiced analyzing and depicting the rules on several games, assess your skill level with the following Perform exercise. In format, the Perform section will be identical to the Practice exercise you just completed. You will have four logic game setups accompanied by their rules, and you will analyze them in the same way.

Perform

Directions: Take no more than four minutes to read and analyze the game setup and record your analysis as indicated. Explanations for each practice game setup follow the practice section.

Perform 1

A filmmaker is planning to create a short film with exactly five scenes. The scenes will all be shot in one day and will be filmed in order, with each scene completed before filming begins on the next. Each scene will feature at least one of four actors—Jenkins, Kwan, Lozano, and Millstone—and no others. Each actor will appear in exactly two of the scenes. The schedule must conform to the following conditions:

> No actor's second scene will be filmed at the same time as another actor's second scene.
> Exactly one actor will appear in the third scene of the film.
> Millstone's first scene will be filmed before Lozano's first scene.
> Any scene in which Lozano is filmed will feature at least one other actor.

1. [Step 1] Summarize your Overview analysis:

2. [Step 2] Create an initial Sketch:

3. [Step 3] Analyze and draw the Rules:
   - For each rule, answer the following questions and then draw the rule in the appropriate box.
     - What does the rule restrict, and what does it leave open?
     - What are the rule's negative implications, if any?
     - Can the rule be depicted inside the sketch framework?

Rule 1:	Rule 2:
Rule 3:	Rule 4:

Perform 2

Eight students—Bonham, Cullen, Dao, Farina, Gerber, Holt, Karlsson, and Logan—are assigned to do research on three court cases—R, S, and T. Each student will research exactly one case in accordance with the following:

Bonham is assigned to research case R.
Farina and Logan are not assigned to research the same case.
Karlsson is assigned to research a case with exactly two other students.
Gerber and Holt are assigned to research a case together, with no other student assigned to research that case.

1. [Step 1] Summarize your Overview analysis:

2. [Step 2] Create an initial Sketch:

3. [Step 3] Analyze and draw the Rules:
    - For each rule, answer the following questions and then draw the rule in the appropriate box.
        - What does the rule restrict, and what does it leave open?
        - What are the rule's negative implications, if any?
        - Can the rule be depicted inside the sketch framework?

Rule 1:	Rule 2:
Rule 3:	Rule 4:

Perform 3

Every Sunday, a zookeeper gives presentations on each of five snakes—an eastern indigo snake, a king snake, a milk snake, a python, and a rat snake. The presentations are held at 1:00, 2:00, 3:00, 4:00, and 5:00. Exactly one snake is exhibited at each presentation. Visitors are invited to hold some, but not all, of the snakes. Visitors are allowed to observe, but not to hold, the others. The schedule of presentations must conform to the following conditions:

> Visitors are invited to hold the king snake and at least one other snake.
> Visitors are allowed to observe, but not to hold, the last snake presented.
> The milk snake is presented before the king snake.
> The python is presented before any snake that visitors are invited to hold.

1. [Step 1] Summarize your Overview analysis:

2. [Step 2] Create an initial Sketch:

3. [Step 3] Analyze and draw the Rules:
    - For each rule, answer the following questions and then draw the rule in the appropriate box.
        - What does the rule restrict, and what does it leave open?
        - What are the rule's negative implications, if any?
        - Can the rule be depicted inside the sketch framework?

Rule 1:	Rule 2:
Rule 3:	Rule 4:

Perform 4

A closet contains exactly six hangers—1, 2, 3, 4, 5, and 6—hanging, in that order, from left to right. It also contains exactly six dresses—one gauze, one linen, one polyester, one rayon, one silk, and one wool—a different dress on each of the hangers, in an order satisfying the following conditions:

> The gauze dress is on a lower-numbered hanger than the polyester dress.
> The rayon dress is on hanger 1 or hanger 6.
> Either the wool dress or the silk dress is on hanger 3.
> The linen dress hangs immediately to the right of the silk dress.

PrepTest41 Sec2 Qs 1–7

1. [Step 1] Summarize your Overview analysis:

2. [Step 2] Create an initial Sketch:

3. [Step 3] Analyze and draw the Rules:
   - For each rule, answer the following questions and then draw the rule in the appropriate box.
     - What does the rule restrict, and what does it leave open?
     - What are the rule's negative implications, if any?
     - Can the rule be depicted inside the sketch framework?

Rule 1:	Rule 2:
Rule 3:	Rule 4:

Explanations

Compare your work to that of an LSAT expert. Pay close attention to how the expert depicted the rules within or beneath the game's initial sketch.

Perform 1

A filmmaker is planning to create a short film with exactly five scenes. The scenes will all be shot in one day and will be filmed in order, with each scene completed before filming begins on the next. Each scene will feature at least one of four actors—Jenkins, Kwan, Lozano, and Millstone—and no others. Each actor will appear in exactly two of the scenes. The schedule must conform to the following conditions:

> No actor's second scene will be filmed at the same time as another actor's second scene.
> Exactly one actor will appear in the third scene of the film.
> Millstone's first scene will be filmed before Lozano's first scene.
> Any scene in which Lozano is filmed will feature at least one other actor.

1. [Step 1] Summarize your Overview analysis: *A filmmaker is filming five scenes. Because they are filmed "in order," this is a Sequencing game. The actors will be assigned in order. Each scene features at least one actor, and each actor will be assigned twice, for a total of eight assignments. With more assignments than scenes, some scenes must feature multiple actors.*

2. [Step 2] Create an initial Sketch: *Set up a horizontal sequence of five scenes, with one slot in each scene. The entities should be listed by initial, with two of each initial. Because order is important, use a subscript 1 and 2 to differentiate each actor's first and second scene.*

$$J_1 \; J_2 \; K_1 \; K_2 \; L_1 \; L_2 \; M_1 \; M_2$$

3. [Step 3] Analyze and draw the Rules:
    -   Rule 1:
        -   What does the rule restrict, and what does it leave open? *This is a negative assertion. No two actors will film their second scenes together.*
        -   What are the rule's negative implications, if any? *Essentially, this means every actor's second scene will be a different scene.*
        -   Can the rule be depicted inside the sketch framework? *As presented, no. Some clever test takers may realize that an actor's second scene cannot be scene 1, so the four actors' second scenes will appear in scenes 2 through 5. In that case, a 2 can be established in each slot under those scenes.*
        -   Draw the rule:

    -   Rule 2:
        -   What does the rule restrict, and what does it leave open? *This is a number rule, establishing a single actor in scene 3. However, it could be any of the actors.*
        -   What are the rule's negative implications, if any? *There cannot be two or more actors in scene 3.*
        -   Can the rule be depicted inside the sketch framework? *Yes. Use a double-line to indicate that no more slots will be added to that column.*
        -   Draw the rule:

- Rule 3:
  - What does the rule restrict, and what does it leave open? *This rule indicates* order (Millstone's first scene must be before Lozano's first scene) but not "distance" (you don't know how many spaces earlier Millstone's first scene must be).
  - What are the rule's negative implications, if any? *Millstone's first scene cannot be scene 4 or 5, and Lozano's first scene cannot be scene 1.*
  - Can the rule be depicted inside the sketch framework? *No.*
  - Draw the rule:

    $$M_1 \ldots L_1$$

- Rule 4:
  - What does the rule restrict, and what does it leave open? *This rule invokes numbers to create an open-ended block. Any scene with Lozano will have at least a second actor, but could have more. It does not indicate which scenes they are, nor who will be in the scene with Lozano.*
  - What are the rule's negative implications, if any? *Lozano cannot be in a scene alone.*
  - Can the rule be depicted inside the sketch framework? *No.*
  - Draw the rule:

    Never L alone

Perform 2

Eight students—Bonham, Cullen, Dao, Farina, Gerber, Holt, Karlsson, and Logan—are assigned to do research on three court cases—R, S, and T. Each student will research exactly one case in accordance with the following:

> Bonham is assigned to research case R.
> Farina and Logan are not assigned to research the same case.
> Karlsson is assigned to research a case with exactly two other students.
> Gerber and Holt are assigned to research a case together, with no other student assigned to research that case.

1. [Step 1] Summarize your Overview analysis: *Eight students are being assigned to research three court cases. Each student is assigned to exactly one case, making this a Distribution game. There's no limit to the number of students on any given case.*

2. [Step 2] Create an initial Sketch:

   B C D F G H K L

   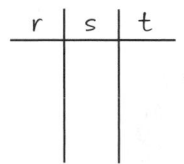

3. [Step 3] Analyze and draw the Rules:
   - Rule 1:
     - What does the rule restrict, and what does it leave open? *This rule establishes Bonham to case R. Other students can be assigned to case R, but Bonham is done.*
     - What are the rule's negative implications, if any? *Bonham is not assigned to case S or T.*
     - Can the rule be depicted inside the sketch framework? *Yes.*
     - Draw the rule:

       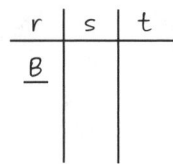

   - Rule 2:
     - What does the rule restrict, and what does it leave open? *This rule creates an anti-block. Farina and Logan cannot be together, but they could each still be assigned to any case.*
     - What are the rule's negative implications, if any? *The positive spin is that Farina and Logan will appear on different cases.*

- Can the rule be depicted inside the sketch framework? *No.*
- Draw the rule:

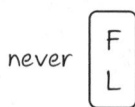

- Rule 3:
  - What does the rule restrict, and what does it leave open? *This rule sets a numeric restriction, creating an open-ended block. One case will have exactly three students, one of whom will be Karlsson. It could be any of the three cases, and there's no restriction on the other two students.*
  - What are the rule's negative implications, if any? *Karlsson cannot be alone, with just one other student, or with three or more other students.*
  - Can the rule be depicted inside the sketch framework? *No.*
  - Draw the rule:

- Rule 4:
  - What does the rule restrict, and what does it leave open? *This rule creates a block of Gerber and Holt, and nobody else. It does not indicate which case this will be.*
  - What are the rule's negative implications, if any? *Neither Gerber nor Holt can be assigned with anybody else.*
  - Can the rule be depicted inside the sketch framework? *No.*
  - Draw the rule:

Perform 3

Every Sunday, a zookeeper gives presentations on each of five snakes—an eastern indigo snake, a king snake, a milk snake, a python, and a rat snake. The presentations are held at 1:00, 2:00, 3:00, 4:00, and 5:00. Exactly one snake is exhibited at each presentation. Visitors are invited to hold some, but not all, of the snakes. Visitors are allowed to observe, but not to hold, the others. The schedule of presentations must conform to the following conditions:

> Visitors are invited to hold the king snake and at least one other snake.
> Visitors are allowed to observe, but not to hold, the last snake presented.
> The milk snake is presented before the king snake.
> The python is presented before any snake that visitors are invited to hold.

1. [Step 1] Summarize your Overview analysis: *Five snakes are being presented at a zoo. Determine the order in which they are presented, and determine which ones can be held and which ones can solely be observed. This is a classic Sequencing/Matching hybrid. Each snake appears once, with one slot for each, so the sequencing is standard one-to-one. At least one snake can be held, but at least one snake will be observed only. The exact numbers are not defined.*

2. [Step 2] Create an initial Sketch:

```
   1   2   3   4   5
   _   _   _   _   _    E K M P R
   _   _   _   _   _    h o
```

3. **[Step 3] Analyze and draw the Rules:**

   - Rule 1:
     - What does the rule restrict, and what does it leave open? *This rule presents two pieces of information: a number requirement (at least two snakes can be held) and an established match (the king snake can be held). The second snake is still unknown, and there could still be other snakes that are held. Also, there's no indication when these presentations occur in the sequence.*
     - What are the rule's negative implications, if any? *None.*
     - Can the rule be depicted inside the sketch framework? *No.*
     - Draw the rule:

       2+ h   [K / h]

   - Rule 2:
     - What does the rule restrict, and what does it leave open? *The last snake (5:00) is not held, just observed. It's still not mentioned which snake it is.*
     - What are the rule's negative implications, if any? *None.*
     - Can the rule be depicted inside the sketch framework? *Yes.*
     - Draw the rule:

       1   2   3   4   5
       __ __ __ __ __   E K M P R
       __ __ __ __ ᴅ   h ᴅ

   - Rule 3:
     - What does the rule restrict, and what does it leave open? *This rule presents ordering: the milk snake before the king snake. It's not mentioned how far apart they are.*
     - What are the rule's negative implications, if any? *Because the milk snake comes earlier, it cannot be last. And because the king snake comes later, it cannot be first.*

   - Can the rule be depicted inside the sketch framework? *No.*
   - Draw the rule:

     M . . . K

   - Rule 4:
     - What does the rule restrict, and what does it leave open? *This rule presents more ordering: The python is presented before any snake that is held. It's not mentioned how much before, so the python can appear any number of spaces before the first held snake.*
     - What are the rule's negative implications, if any? *Because the python comes earlier, it cannot be last. And because snakes that are held come later, the first snake cannot be held. This also implies that the python itself cannot be held, so it must be observed only.*
     - Can the rule be depicted inside the sketch framework? *No.*
     - Draw the rule:

       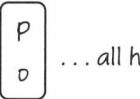 . . . all h

Perform 4

A closet contains exactly six hangers—1, 2, 3, 4, 5, and 6—hanging, in that order, from left to right. It also contains exactly six dresses—one gauze, one linen, one polyester, one rayon, one silk, and one wool—a different dress on each of the hangers, in an order satisfying the following conditions:

> The gauze dress is on a lower-numbered hanger than the polyester dress.
> The rayon dress is on hanger 1 or hanger 6.
> Either the wool dress or the silk dress is on hanger 3.
> The linen dress hangs immediately to the right of the silk dress.

PrepTest41 Sec2 Qs 1–7

1. **[Step 1] Summarize your Overview analysis:** *There are dresses hanging on numbered hangers in a closet. As the hangers are "in order," this is a Sequencing game. Each dress is on a different hanger. With six dresses and six hangers, this is standard one-to-one sequencing.*

2. [Step 2] Create an initial Sketch:

G L P R S W

1   2   3   4   5   6

—   —   —   —   —   —

3. [Step 3] Analyze and draw the Rules:

- Rule 1:
  - What does the rule restrict, and what does it leave open? *This rule indicates ordering. Gauze will appear before polyester. There can be any number of spaces in between, or they could be next to one another.*
  - What are the rule's negative implications, if any? *Because gauze comes earlier, it cannot be on hanger 6. And because polyester comes later, it cannot be on hanger 1.*
  - Can the rule be depicted inside the sketch framework? *No.*
  - Draw the rule:

    G . . . P

- Rule 2:
  - What does the rule restrict, and what does it leave open? *This rule limits the rayon dress to two hangers: 1 or 6. Any other dress can occupy the other slot.*
  - What are the rule's negative implications, if any? *The rayon dress cannot be on any hanger from 2 through 5.*
  - Can the rule be depicted inside the sketch framework? *Yes, or it can be simply notated to the side.*
  - Draw the rule:

    1   2   3   4   5   6

    —   —   —   —   —   —

    R

- Rule 3:
  - What does the rule restrict, and what does it leave open? *This establishes one of two entities on hanger 3: the silk dress or the wool dress. The other dress can still hang anywhere else.*
  - What are the rule's negative implications, if any? *No other dress can hang on hanger 3.*
  - Can the rule be depicted inside the sketch framework? *Yes.*
  - Draw the rule:

    1   2   3   4   5   6

    —   —   S/W   —   —   —

- Rule 4:
  - What does the rule restrict, and what does it leave open? *This rule creates a block of silk immediately before linen. There's no restriction on where this block can appear in the sequencing.*
  - What are the rule's negative implications, if any? *Because the silk dress comes earlier, it cannot be on hanger 6. And because the linen dress comes later, it cannot be on hanger 1.*
  - Can the rule be depicted inside the sketch framework? *No.*
  - Draw the rule:

    S L

Assess

Assess your performance according to the following criteria:

Game Types and Initial Sketches

At this point, you should be able to identify the action(s) of the standard game types. If you got all four of them correct here, well done. If there were any games you misidentified, return to Chapter 2 to review the definitions and illustrations of Logic Games actions and types.

Your initial sketches do not need to be exact replicas of those the LSAT experts drew. Superficial or stylistic differences are irrelevant. Assess your sketch frameworks by noting three considerations:

1) Did your framework fit the game's action (i.e., was it appropriate for the game type)? If "Yes," you are in great shape. If, for any of the setups, you chose a format that did not match the game type appropriately, return to Chapter 2 and review the model sketches there.

2) Was it accurate (with the correct number and orientation of positions)? If "Yes," well done. If there were any errors in your sketch frameworks, consider whether they were "sloppy" errors (e.g., the game had six positions, but you put seven), or whether you fundamentally misunderstood a description or limitation within the game's setup. Disciplining yourself to read with precision and accuracy is a key overarching skill for LSAT success.

3) Was it as simple as possible given the game's setup? This assessment is somewhat more subjective. On Test Day, accuracy is far more important than "elegance." LSAT experts, however, know that they will likely need to copy the Master Sketch one or more times when answering the questions (you may remember this from the New-"If" questions in Chapter 1), and thus, they strive to make their sketch frameworks as simple as possible. If there were cases in which your sketches were unnecessarily complicated, learn how to simplify them from the expert examples.

Rules

Assuming your analyses of the game types and your initial sketches were accurate, evaluate your performance on the rules as follows.

If you correctly analyzed and drew **more than 75%** of the rules in this Perform exercise correctly: Great job. Review any rules that you misunderstood or drew incorrectly to determine if there are any patterns. For example, did you miss rules associated with a particular game type or rules that describe certain types of restrictions, such as relative position or blocks of entities?

If you correctly analyzed and drew **51% to 75%** of the rules: Review the descriptions and illustrations of the rule types in the Prepare section of this chapter. Additionally, note the game types in which you mischaracterized any rules. In Chapters 5, 8, 9, and 10, you will have the opportunity to again study and practice the rule patterns associated with the standard game types. Make a note to yourself to study those sections carefully.

If you correctly analyzed and drew **50% or less** of the rules: You have some work to do. From this point forward, the book will assume that you can analyze and sketch rules with a fair degree of confidence and accuracy. First, review the Prepare section of this chapter. Then, try the quiz titled "Analyzing and Sketching Rules Fundamentals" found in your online center. Once you have completed that, you should feel far more confident with Step 3 of the Logic Games Method.

To stay sharp, practice the drills in the Logic Games Training Camp for this chapter in your Online Study Plan. Training Camp drills are divided into Fundamentals, Mid-Level, and Advanced sets.

Reflect

Think back over the work you did in this section of Chapter 3.

- Are you beginning to recognize the standard game types as they are described in the games' setups?
- Can you associate certain types of rules with particular game types (e.g., relative order rules occur in Sequencing games)?
- Do you recognize rules that can be depicted within a game's sketch framework, and distinguish them from those that must be written underneath or beside the sketch?
- Are you becoming more confident that you can draw out a rule in a way that matches the sketch?
- When you look at the way you've drawn out a rule, does it clearly reflect the way in which that rule did *and did not* restrict the entities?

In the coming days and weeks, take note of real-life considerations that mimic Logic Games rules. They pop up in all sorts of unexpected places. Some examples might be:

- You go out with a group of friends and you make sure that two of them sit next to each other: Tom and Becky will sit in adjacent positions.
- You have two coworkers who don't get along, so no one wants them assigned to the same project: Ellie and Mitchell will not both be assigned to work on the Taylor account.
- Even something as simple as the food you order could be described in logic games terms: If I order a muffin, then I will definitely get coffee.

Logic games mimic real world tasks, although they often seem to impose arbitrary and abstract rules upon them. In real life, you usually know the reason behind the rule, which makes your decisions more concrete. Noting when day-to-day tasks impose restrictions similar to those found on the test can help to demystify the logic games experience and makes you feel more immersed in the kinds of reasoning and analysis you'll do on Test Day.

HOW TO COMBINE RULES TO MAKE DEDUCTIONS

LEARNING OBJECTIVES

In this section of Chapter 3, you'll learn to

- Combine rules and restrictions to make valid deductions in logic games.

Prepare

Now that you've learned to analyze and draw the rules, you're ready for Step 4 of the Logic Games Method—Deductions. In this section, you'll learn to catalog the restrictions and rules limiting the possible arrangements within a game and to combine them to establish what must, can, and cannot be true in all cases. More than any of the other steps, this is the one that separates the LSAT expert from other test takers. Making all of the available deductions within a game will put you in control of the questions to a degree others cannot match.

Although making deductions stands as a distinct step within the Logic Games Method, you've actually had a bit of a head start on the thinking and analysis you'll do here. Considering the negative implications of rules can help you add information to a game's sketch. For example, a rule such as "Jonathan is scheduled for an earlier day of the week than Edith is scheduled" allows you to conclude that Edith will not take the first day of the schedule and Jonathan will not take the last day. Deductions of this sort make explicit the implications of a rule. A similar example stems from a rule such as "Hwang and Munoz will not be drafted by the same team." In a Distribution game with exactly two teams, you could deduce that each team drafts at least one player, either Hwang or Munoz.

The work you'll do in this section takes making deductions a step further. Here, instead of making the implications of a single rule explicit, you'll learn to combine two or more rules and bring the implications of that combination to light. To see a simple example, imagine that a Sequencing game with six positions has the following rules:

> Barney may not occupy the first position.
>
> Judith will be assigned a higher-numbered position than Barney's position.

From Rule 1 alone, you can exclude Barney from Position 1. From the second rule alone, you know Judith may not take Position 1 and Barney may not take Position 6.

$$\overline{1} \quad \overline{2} \quad \overline{3} \quad \overline{4} \quad \overline{5} \quad \overline{6}$$

~B · · · · · · · · · · · · · ~B

~J

B . . . J

By combining these two rules, you can deduce that the earliest position Judith may occupy is Position 3, and thus, exclude her from Position 2 as well.

$$\overline{1} \quad \overline{2} \quad \overline{3} \quad \overline{4} \quad \overline{5} \quad \overline{6}$$

```
 1   2   3   4   5   6
~B  ~J              ~B
~J

B . . . J
```

Deductions such as this may not seem earth-shattering, but knowing with certainty (and noting in your Master Sketch) that an entity cannot occupy a particular position will help you answer one or more of the questions. The testmaker may reward you directly with a correct answer that mirrors the deduction or indirectly by including wrong answers suggesting that an arrangement you've determined is impossible is actually acceptable.

When they first approach Step 4, the Deductions step, some students feel that something mysterious or almost magical is happening as so much of the game takes shape. The LSAT expert, however, knows that nothing could be further from the truth. The step of making deductions is thoroughly practical and methodical. You work from what is most certain and concrete in the game and check for anything else that information allows you to determine. Moreover, the LSAT expert knows that deductions stem from combinations of five types of rules, easily memorized with the BLEND checklist you first saw in Chapter 1.

To master Step 4 of the Logic Games Method, you'll need to hone your ability to do three things.

LOGIC GAMES STRATEGY

To make the deductions in a logic game efficiently and effectively, follow these steps:

1. Identify the most restricted entities and positions within the game.
2. Use the BLEND checklist to make all available deductions.
3. Identify *floaters* (unrestricted entities) after making all available deductions.

Before practicing this step on logic games setups, take a closer look at the process of making deductions.

Making Deductions Effectively and Efficiently

Spot the Most Restricted Entities and Positions

As you read earlier in this chapter, rules and restrictions are your greatest allies in solving logic games. Without the rules, there are hundreds (or, in some games, thousands) of possible arrangements. After you add in the rules, however, there will be only a handful of acceptable solutions, and the game will be much more manageable. In the Deductions step of the Logic Games Method, you are making those limitations explicit, and adding them to the sketch, your visual description of the game.

Established entities—those whose position is set once and for all—are obviously the most restricted entities within a game. They can't move. Always check to see if other entities are related by rule to the established entity, as their position will be affected as well. Take, for example, a distribution game with two rowing teams that includes the following rules:

> Brenda rows in boat 2.
>
> Sabrina and Brenda do not row in the same boat.

Given that Brenda's position is established, Rule 2 allows you to confidently place Sabrina in Boat 1.

Boat 1	Boat 2
S	B
—	—
—	—
—	—

In some games, there are no established entities, or the established entities are not directly related to other entities. In that case, seek out the entities or positions that have the greatest amount of restriction placed upon them by the rules. Truck Y in the Truck Arrivals game provides a great example.

Refresh (Activate Prior Knowledge)

In a single day, exactly seven trucks—S, T, U, W, X, Y, and Z—are the only arrivals at a warehouse. No truck arrives at the same time as any other truck, and no truck arrives more than once that day. Each truck is either green or red (but not both). The following conditions apply:

> No two consecutive arrivals are red.
> Y arrives at some time before both T and W.
> Exactly two of the trucks that arrive before Y are red.
> S is the sixth arrival.
> Z arrives at some time before U.

PrepTest37 Sec3 Qs 6–11

S̸ T U W X Y Z

					S	
—	—	—	—	—	—	—
1	2	3	4	5	6	7

g/r — — — — — — —

never [r r]

$Y \cdots \begin{matrix} T \\ W \end{matrix}$

r . . . r . . . y

Z . . . U

Here, Rule 4 establishes the position of Truck S (it arrives sixth), but no other rules relate another entity to Truck S or to the sixth slot. Thus, to make effective deductions, you'll want to move on to the next most restricted entity. Truck Y should pop out because it is mentioned in two rules (Rules 2 and 3). Truck Y is restricted by two trucks (Trucks T and W) that must *follow* it, and by two positions (both occupied by red trucks) that must *precede* it. That alone would tell you that Truck Y is restricted to the third, fourth or fifth positions.

$$r \ldots r \ldots y \therefore \begin{matrix} \cdot\cdot\,T \\ \cdot\cdot\,W \end{matrix}$$

Now, however, the established entity—Truck S in the sixth slot—comes into play. Since both Truck T and Truck W must follow Truck Y, the fifth slot is denied to Truck Y, as well, limiting Truck Y to only the third or fourth positions. But, there is yet another restriction that limits Truck Y. Rule 1 stipulates that red trucks may not arrive consecutively. If the first three trucks that arrive are red, green, and red respectively, Truck Y must arrive fourth.

$$\cancel{S} \; T \; U \; W \; X \; \cancel{Y} \; Z$$

$$\overset{\displaystyle X}{\overbrace{\underline{\quad}\;\underline{\quad}\;\underline{\quad}}} \; \underset{4}{\underline{y}} \; \underset{5}{\underline{T/W}} \; \underset{6}{\underline{S}} \; \underset{7}{\underline{W/T}}$$

$$g/r \;\; \underset{}{\underline{r}} \; \underset{}{\underline{g}} \; \underset{}{\underline{r}} \; \underset{}{\underline{g}} \; \underline{\quad} \; \underline{\quad} \; \underline{\quad}$$

$$never \; \boxed{r \;\; r} \quad Z \ldots U$$

Making those deductions solves a huge chunk of the game. Two of the trucks' arrival positions are established. Two more trucks are limited to a pair of positions. The colors of the first three arrivals are established as well. Concentrating on the most restricted entities made it possible to spot those deductions effectively and efficiently.

The Truck Arrivals game also illustrates the value of the BLEND checklist. Rules 2 and 3, in particular, exemplify the D in BLEND, Duplications. When two rules share a common entity, they can be combined to reveal additional restrictions within the game. The next portion of this chapter zeroes in on BLEND to show you how to find all of a game's deductions.

Use the BLEND Checklist to Make All Available Deductions

Not every game has deductions as strong as those in the Truck Arrivals game, but nearly every game has some additional information for you to uncover. The best way to ensure that you're spotting all of this extra help is by using the BLEND checklist, which catalogs the five patterns most likely to result in valid deductions in logic games.

STEP 4: DEDUCTIONS

BLEND

- **B**locks of Entities—two or more players that are always grouped together
- **L**imited Options—rules or restrictions that limit the overall setup to one or the other of two acceptable arrangements
- **E**stablished Entities—a player locked into a specific space or group
- **N**umber Restrictions—rules or limitations that provide guidance about the number of entities assigned to a group or space
- **D**uplications—entities that appear in two or more rules and allow the rules to be combined

Remember that BLEND is not a series of steps, and not all games contain all five types of rules and restrictions. As you note down a game's limitations and rules, learn to ask which of the five BLEND elements they represent. That way, you'll head into Step 4 anticipating the deductions you're most likely to make.

Blocks of Entities

Blocks of entities—two entities that must be placed together—are very common in Sequencing games. In these games, the strongest blocks are created by rules requiring entities to occupy consecutive positions in a particular order. For example:

Gregory must occupy the position immediately after Dawn's position.

To place that block within the game's framework, you'll have to find two consecutive open positions that are acceptable for both D and G. Blocks of entities may interact with established entities or with other blocks to produce deductions. Adding a little context for this rule helps to illustrate this. Picture a six-position Strict Sequencing game with the following rules.

Gregory must occupy the position immediately after Dawn's position.
Tom occupies the third position.
Farrah's position is earlier than Tom's.

Because the position of T is fixed, and because F must occupy one of the two slots that precede T's position, the D-G block can occupy only the fourth and fifth or the fifth and sixth positions.

Other Sequencing rules can produce blocks that are slightly less restrictive. Take a rule requiring the entities to occupy consecutive spaces in either order. You'll still need two consecutive open spaces for this block, but the entities within the block can swap positions.

> Charles and Hillary occupy consecutive positions.

$$\boxed{\underline{C}\ \ \underline{H}}\ \ or\ \ \boxed{\underline{H}\ \ \underline{C}}$$

A rule that gives the relative order of two entities, but does not limit how close or how far apart they must be, creates a "loose block." These are far less restrictive, but still worth considering as you make deductions.

> Rupa occupies a position later than Quincy's.

$$Q \ldots R$$

Blocks can also lead to powerful deductions in a Distribution game. Consider the following model game setup.

> The intelligence minister of a small nation will place seven spies—code named M, N, Q, R, S, T, and U—as follows: one will be assigned to the embassy in Ankara; three are assigned to the embassy in Budapest; and three are assigned to the embassy in Cairo. Each spy receives exactly one placement in accordance with the following restrictions:
>
> Q and S are assigned to the same embassy.

In Distribution games, blocks of entities most often lead to deductions when they interact with number restrictions. In this case, the number restrictions outlined in the game's setup allow the Q-S block only two acceptable assignments. Depending on what the game's additional rules contain, you may be able to limit the Q-S block to a specific group, or you may find out that it is valuable to create sketches for both of the possible placements of the block. When you create two parallel sketches, you are making the deduction called Limited Options.

Limited Options

Limited Options can be one of the most powerful deductions that you can make. Discovering that a game breaks down into just two (or, very rarely, three) distinct patterns can make handling the questions a snap. But, it takes practice to recognize when this deduction is available. There is a Special Feature on Limited Options at the end of this chapter that breaks down the types of rules that can lead to Limited Options. It is accompanied by a video in which an LSAT Channel expert illustrates Limited Options on a logic game you haven't tried before.

To spot the opportunity to use Limited Options in a game, look for a rule or a combination of rules that creates two distinct patterns, each of which then triggers additional deductions. To illustrate this definition, add a couple more rules to the model game setup about the spies in three cities.

The intelligence minister of a small nation will place seven spies—code named M, N, Q, R, S, T, and U—as follows: one will be assigned to the embassy in Ankara; three are assigned to the embassy in Budapest; and three are assigned to the embassy in Cairo. Each spy receives exactly one placement in accordance with the following restrictions:

> Q and S are assigned to the same embassy.
> Neither M nor U is assigned to the embassy in Ankara.
> S and U are not assigned to the same embassy.
> T is assigned to the embassy in Cairo.

M N Q R S T U

Here, Rule 1 combined with the number restrictions outlined in the game's setup led to the deduction that the Q-S block can be placed only in Budapest or Cairo. Because the placement of S triggers a further restriction in Rule 3, it is worth creating dual Limited Options sketches to explore what happens in each of two acceptable patterns. Then, add Rule 3 to each of the two options.

M N Q̸ R S̸ T U

Now, add Rules 2 and 4 to each option's sketch.

M N Q̸ R S̸ T̸ U

Opt. 1

A	B	C
—	Q	T
	S	—
	·	—

~Q ~U
~S
~M
~U

Opt. 2

A	B	C
—	—	Q
	—	S
	—	T

~Q   ~U
~S
~M
~U

The two options make it possible to learn more about Spy U. In Option I, Spy U must be assigned to Cairo. In Option II, Spy U will go to Budapest. Note, too, that in either option, only Spy N or Spy R is available for placement in Ankara.

M N Q̸ R S̸ T̸ Ų̸

Opt. 1

A	B	C
N/R	Q	T
	S	U
	—	—

~Q   ~U
~S
~M
~U

Opt. 2

A	B	C
N/R	U	Q
	—	S
	—	T

~Q   ~U
~S
~M
~U

Finally, because there is no room left for placements in Cairo in Option II, you can now place Spy M firmly in Budapest. Thus, in Option II, the third spy placed in Budapest will be either Spy N or Spy R, whichever does not go to Ankara.

M N Ø R Ø T̸ M̸

Opt. 1

A	B	C
N/R	Q	T
	S	U
	—	—

~Q
~S
~M
~U

Opt. 2

A	B	C
N/R	U	Q
	M	S
	N/R	T

~Q
~S
~M
~U

In logic games that break down into Limited Options, it is quite common for one of the two options to result in a more complete Master Sketch. Here, Option II is nearly "solved," with only the placements for Spies N and R undetermined. In Option I, on the other hand, three spies—M, N, and R—can still swap positions.

Refresh (Activate Prior Knowledge)

Another game you've worked with already—the one about the Chess Tournament—breaks down into Limited Options. Take a moment to review the setup and rules of that game, and try to anticipate how an LSAT expert will proceed through the Deductions step.

Exactly six people—Lulu, Nam, Ofelia, Pachai, Santiago, and Tyrone—are the only contestants in a chess tournament. The tournament consists of four games, played one after the other. Exactly two people play in each game, and each person plays in at least one game. The following conditions must apply:

Tyrone does not play in the first or third game.
Lulu plays in the last game.
Nam plays in only one game and it is not against Pachai.
Santiago plays in exactly two games, one just before and one just after the only game that Ofelia plays in.

PrepTest45 Sec3 Qs 7–12

$$\overset{\overset{\text{1 \quad 1 \quad 2}}{}}{\text{L \quad N \quad O \quad P \quad S \quad T}}$$

```
       1   2   3   4

       _   _   _   L
       ___ ___ ___ ___
       ~T      ~T
```

never $\boxed{\dfrac{N}{P}}$

$\boxed{\text{S \quad O \quad S}}$

What is the most restrictive rule in this game? Rule 2 establishes one placement for Lulu, but remember, in this game's setup, Lulu might play twice. Rule 4, however, creates a block of three entities (S-O-S) that will have to fit into a schedule of just four games. For the LSAT expert, that leads to Limited Options: The S-O-S block will fit only in games 1–3 or games 2–4.

$$\overset{\overset{\text{1 \quad 1 \quad 2}}{}}{\text{L \quad N \quad \cancel{O} \quad P \quad \cancel{S} \quad T}}$$

<u>Opt. 1</u>

```
   1   2   3   4

   S   O   S   L
   ___ ___ ___ ___
   ~T      ~T
```

<u>Opt. 2</u>

```
   1   2   3   4

   _   _   _   L
   ___ ___ ___ ___
   ~T  S   O   S
       ~T
```

never $\boxed{\dfrac{N}{P}}$

Each of those options accounts for all of the possible placements for Santiago and Ofelia. Thus, in both options, there are four open slots. In Option I, you know that Tyrone will play in game 2, game 4, or both, but you can't go much further than that. In Option II, however, Tyrone's only available game is game 2. What else can you determine in Option II?

```
        1   1   2
    L   N   P   P   T
```

Opt. 1

```
1   2   3   4

S   O   S   L
―   ―   ―   ―
~T      ~T
```

Opt. 2

```
1   2   3   4

_   T   _   L
―   ―   ―   ―
    S   O   S
―   ―   ―   ―
~T      ~T
```

never
```
N
―
P
```

Consider the role of Rule 3 in Option II. Nam and Pachai cannot play against each other. Thus, one of them will play in game 1 and one of them in game 3. Regardless of which one plays in game 1, the opponent in that game must be Lulu, the only player eligible to take Option II's final slot.

```
        1   1   2
    L   N   P   P   T
```

Opt. 1

```
1   2   3   4

S   O   S   L
―   ―   ―   ―
~T      ~T
```

Opt. 2

```
1    2    3    4

P/N  T   N/P  L
―    ―   ―    ―
L    S   O    S
―    ―   ―    ―
~T       ~T
```

never
```
N
―
P
```

Typically, just one of the games in an LSAT Logic Games section will break down into Limited Options (sometimes, none of them do, and rarely, two), so don't try to force every game into dual sketches. Learn to spot the patterns that divide a game into two patterns leading to additional deductions. When you do, the Limited Options deduction can help you answer the game's questions more quickly and confidently.

Established Entities

Established entities are those that are, by rule, placed in one permanent position. While that alone is helpful, deductions follow from established entities when they affect the placement of other entities. Always check to see if the established entity is mentioned in any other rule, and whether its placement prevents a block of entities from taking certain positions (in Sequencing games) or being placed on certain teams (in Distribution games).

Number Restrictions

Number restrictions are most prominent (and most helpful) in Distribution and Matching games. That's because the size of the groups into which you're divvying up the entities (Distribution) or the number of attributes, items, or tasks you're trying to assign (Matching) determines much of the game's outcome.

In Distribution games, you may find number restrictions in a game's setup. In the model game about the spies, for example, the numbers in each group were explicit: "one [spy] will be assigned to the embassy in Ankara; three are assigned to the embassy in Budapest; and three are assigned to the embassy in Cairo." In those cases, look for the impact that the number restrictions have on the placement of blocks of entities. It is routine for the testmaker to set up Distribution games in a way that limits blocks of entities to only one or two groups.

If a Distribution game's setup paragraph does not state or limit the number of entities that will be assigned to each group, look for a rule that does. Consider this model setup:

> A group of seven friends—Adam, Benji, Carole, Deng, Esther, Felicia, and Graham—is attending a soccer game. Each friend will wear a shirt in exactly one of the home team's colors—red and yellow. The friends' decisions about which color to wear must accord with the following considerations:

> More of the friends will wear red shirts than wear yellow shirts.

A B C D E F G

4-7	0-3
R	Y

From that comparative number restriction, you can conclude that the maximum number of yellow-shirted friends is three. Any more than that, and yellow shirts would outnumber red. There is still a lot of leeway, however. In fact, from that rule alone, you don't know that anyone wears a yellow shirt.

In a typical Distribution game, you will get a little more assistance from the rules, even if the rules do not explicitly mention the number of entities per team. For example:

> A group of seven friends—Adam, Benji, Carole, Deng, Esther, Felicia, and Graham—is attending a soccer game. Each friend will wear a shirt in exactly one of the home team's colors—red and yellow. The friends' decisions about which color to wear must accord with the following considerations:

> More of the friends will wear red shirts than wear yellow shirts.
> Graham wears a yellow shirt.
> Deng and Esther wear shirts of different colors.

A B C D E F G

4-7	0-3
R	Y
D/E	G
	E/D
—	
—	

Adding the established entity—Graham—to the yellow-shirt column, and depicting the "anti-block" pair—Deng and Esther—within the sketch framework, has a dramatic impact on the game's numbers. With at least two of the friends wearing yellow shirts, you now have only two options: two yellow shirts and five red shirts or three yellow shirts and four red shirts. Depending on the game's subsequent rules, you might choose to depict this with the following Limited Options sketches. In fact, in the case in which there are only two yellow shirts, you can virtually complete the sketch.

A B C D E F G

	Opt. 1			Opt. 2	
	4-7	0-3		4-7	0-3
	R	Y		R	Y
	D/E	G		D/E	G
	—	E/D		A	E/D
	—	—		B	
	—			C	
				F	

In Matching games, the initial setup might limit the number of attributes you can match to each of the recipients (the people, places, or things to which you are matching), but it will almost never determine the exact number for each recipient. Additional number restrictions are often found in the rules. Here's an example:

In preparation for a lecture, each of four archaeologists—Rand, Singer, Tulsi, and Wang—will study at least one and at most three of the following artifacts recovered from a prehistoric dwelling—an arrow point, a bowl, a diadem, and an effigy. In determining who will study each item, the archaeologists conform to the following considerations:

Rand will study more of the items than Singer.
Wang studies the diadem.
Rand does not study any item that Wang studies.

R > S   1-3 ea. arch

	2-3	1-2		
	R	S	T	W
a				
b				
d	✕			✓
e				

In this example, the opening setup limits the archaeologists to between one and three of the items, i.e., everyone studies something, but no one studies everything. The first rule further limits the numbers for Rand and Singer. If Singer studies just one item, then Rand may study either two or three. If Singer studies two of the items, then Rand will definitely study three. Rules 2 and 3 combine to prevent Rand from studying the diadem, so if Singer studies two of the items, Rand will study the arrow point, the bowl, and the effigy.

Number restrictions are relatively rare in Sequencing games. For the most part, Sequencing games have an equal number of entities and positions, and they tell you straight out that there are no ties among the entities. In those games, the numbers are already as simple as they can be (six entities, six slots, one-per-slot), and there is no way to further restrict the game's framework. In a complex Strict Sequencing game in which you have to schedule, say, seven appointments over five days, you might get a rule that sets or limits the number of entities per day (e.g., "Exactly one appointment will be scheduled for Wednesday," or "Tuesday is a day on which two of the appointments are scheduled"), but for the most part, Sequencing games lack this item from the BLEND checklist.

In Selection games, your task is to choose some of the entities and reject others. Roughly half of all Selection games purposely do not tell you the number of entities to select because that is what they ask about.

> What is the maximum number of employees who could be chosen to attend the company retreat?
> If Joanna is chosen to attend the company retreat, how many other employees must be chosen to attend the retreat?

In games of that type, the game setup stipulates merely that "some" or "at least one" of the entities is selected. You will use the game's conditional rules (e.g., "If Joanna is chosen to attend the retreat, then Matt is also chosen, but Kim is not") to determine the minimum or maximum number selected, or the numbers selected in various circumstances.

The other "half" of Selection games, however, tell you in the setup precisely how many entities to select. Number restrictions can come into play with Selection games of this type if the entities are subdivided into different categories. Here's an example:

> From among eight city employees—two city council members: Addams and Bernard; three police officers: Klaus, Lemark, and McCaffrey; and three teachers: Ritchie, Sanchez, and Xavier—the mayor will name exactly five to represent the city as a delegation to the city's sister municipality in another country. The mayor's selections conform to the following restrictions:
>
> Exactly two police officers will be named to the delegation.
> Ritchie and Sanchez cannot both be named to the delegation.

5 of 8

1 – 2	2	1 – 2
council	police	teach
A B	K L M	R S X

never R and S

Here, the first rule states an explicit number restriction: Exactly two police officers are selected. Because Ritchie and Sanchez are both teachers, the second rule implicitly limits the number of teachers who may be selected to a maximum of two. As a result, you know that at least one city council member will join the delegation (notice that nothing in the game's setup required that).

If you run across a game of this type, it is always valuable to determine how the numbers selected from among the subgroups of entities break down. In this game, the mayor could choose either one city council member, two police officers, and two teachers, or the mayor could choose two city council members, two police officers, and one teacher. Because the numbers break down into exactly two acceptable patterns, a Limited Options sketch may be helpful.

5 of 8

```
1-2      2    1-2
council police teach
A B    K L M  R S X
```

never R and S

<u>Opt I</u>   _ | _ _ | _ _

<u>Opt II</u> _ _ | _ _ | _

With dual Limited Options sketches in place, two things are clear, even from the partial set of rules presented here: In Opt I, Xavier will be selected, along with one of the other teachers (who cannot both be selected), and in Opt II, both Council members must be selected.

5 of 8

```
1-2      2    1-2
council police teach
A B    K L M  R S X
```

never R and S

<u>Opt I</u>   _ | _ _ | R/S X

<u>Opt II</u> A B | _ _ | _

Duplications

Duplications may be the last item in the BLEND checklist, but they are probably the most common type of deductions. Duplications occur anytime an entity is mentioned in two rules. This "duplicator" entity allows the rules to be combined, and doing so almost always reveals additional restrictions within the game.

In Sequencing games, a rule creating a "loose" block of entities very often shares an entity with another rule that creates a block (or "loose" block) of entities. For example:

> R's position is later than M's position.
> T's position is earlier than M's position.

$$T \ldots M \ldots R$$

In Strict Sequencing games, these "strings" of relative ordering relationships may sometimes include as many as four or five of the entities, but three is the most common.

In a typical Loose Sequencing game, all of the rules combine to create a "tree" of relative relationships. Here's an example:

A film festival advisory committee must determine the order in which to present awards in each of six categories—comedy, documentary, foreign, historical, independent, and nature—on the festival's closing night. Exactly one award will be presented for each film category, and no awards are presented at the same time. The committee will adhere to the following guidelines to determine the order of the presentations:

The award for foreign film is always presented at some time before the award for comedy.
The award for comedy is always presented at some time after the award for documentaries.
The award for foreign film is always presented at some time after the awards for historical and nature films.
The award for independent films is always presented before the award for historical films.

You will revisit this model game setup in Chapter 7, which focuses specifically on Loose Sequencing. For now, take notice of the following: 1) every rule stipulates the relative order between two or among three entities, 2) every rule shares a "duplicator" entity with at least one other rule, and 3) by the end of the rules, all six entities have been accounted for in the Master Sketch. Those criteria make this an example of the archetypal Loose Sequencing game.

Duplications also play a huge role in Selection games. Because virtually all of the rules in Selection games are conditional, the result of one rule may trigger another rule. Here's a typical example:

If A is selected, then C is selected.
If C is selected, then E is not selected.

If A $\longrightarrow$ C $\longrightarrow$ ~E

By combining those two rules, you can deduce that anytime A is selected, E will be rejected. It's not hard to spot a connection like that one—in which the result of one rule is the explicit trigger of another—but there can be more to creating these "strings" of conditions. Inherent in every conditional (Formal Logic) rule is a parallel rule known as the contrapositive. If you are familiar with that much of Formal Logic, you could also deduce from the rules above that anytime E is selected, both C and A will be rejected. If you aren't familiar with Formal Logic, make sure to study the section of Chapter 8 that covers this topic in detail. Learning this small slice of Formal Logic tested in LSAT Logic Games will also help you master the Logical Reasoning section of the test.

In Distribution and Matching, Duplications can occur in a variety of settings. Any two rules that share a common entity can be combined. The Matching game setup describing the archaeologists provided a couple of examples.

In preparation for a lecture, each of four archaeologists—Rand, Singer, Tulsi, and Wang—will study at least one and at most three of the following artifacts recovered from a prehistoric dwelling—an arrow point, a bowl, a diadem, and an effigy. In determining who will study each item, the archaeologists conform to the following considerations:

Rand will study more of the items than Singer.
Wang studies the diadem.
Rand does not study any item that Wang studies.

R > S   1-3 ea. arch

2-3   1-2

	R	S	T	W
a				
b				
d	✕			✓
e				

Here, Rules 2 and 3 share Wang, and by combining them, you can conclude that Rand does not study the diadem. Moreover, because Rules 1 and 3 both mention Rand, you are able to conclude that Rand will study at least two, and maybe all three of the arrow point, the bowl, and the effigy.

You have ample opportunity to practice making deductions in all of the common game types featured on the LSAT. In each of Chapters 5–10, you'll find a section that outlines the types of deductions most often found in the game type covered in detail in the chapter along with model setups and rules on which to hone your skills. At the end of each of those chapters, there are full games in which you will, of course, need to use all five steps of the Logic Games Method (Deductions included) to answer the questions.

Refresh (Activate Prior Knowledge)

Before moving on, take time to review an LSAT expert's Step 4 analyses for one more game you've worked with before, the one on Patterson's meetings. Take a couple of minutes to refresh your memory of the game's setup and rules; then, try to anticipate the deductions that the expert will make.

On one afternoon, Patterson meets individually with each of exactly five clients—Reilly, Sanchez, Tang, Upton, and Yansky—and also goes to the gym by herself for a workout. Patterson's workout and her five meetings each start at either 1:00, 2:00, 3:00, 4:00, 5:00, or 6:00. The following conditions must apply:

Patterson meets with Sanchez at some time before her workout.
Patterson meets with Tang at some time after her workout.
Patterson meets with Yansky either immediately before or immediately after her workout.
Patterson meets with Upton at some time before she meets with Reilly.

PrepTest45 Sec3 Qs 1–6

R S T U Y W

— — — — — —
1 2 3 4 5 6

S...W

W...T

[W Y]   or   [Y W]

U...R

First, the LSAT expert looks for the most restricted entity in the game. It is the workout, which is mentioned in Rules 1, 2, and 3, making it a kind of "super duplicator," if you will. Combining all three rules produces the following string:

$$S \ldots \boxed{\underline{W / Y}} \ldots T$$

The expert then uses that string to make explicit the negative implications of those three combined rules. Because Sanchez is, at a minimum, followed by the workout, Yansky, and Tang, the meeting with Sanchez may not be at 4:00, 5:00, or 6:00. Conversely, because Tang is, at a minimum, preceded by Sanchez, the workout, and Yansky, the meeting with Tang cannot be at 1:00, 2:00, or 3:00. Because the workout and Yansky are bookended by Sanchez and Tang, neither the workout nor the meeting with Yansky can be at 1:00 or at 6:00.

R S T U Y W

—	—	—	—	—	—
1	2	3	4	5	6
~T	~T	~T	~S	~S	~S
~W					~W
~Y					~Y

$$S \ldots \boxed{\underline{W / Y}} \ldots T$$

Finally, the expert can record the negative implications of Rule 4: the meeting with Reilly cannot be at 1:00, and the meeting with Upton cannot be at 6:00. Given all of the restrictions on the first and final slots in the game, the expert can deduce that Patterson meets with either Sanchez or Upton at 1:00, and with either Reilly or Tang at 6:00.

R S T U Y W

S/U	—	—	—	—	T/R
1	2	3	4	5	6
~T	~T	~T	~S	~S	~S
~W					~W
~Y					~Y
~R					~U

$$S \ldots \boxed{\underline{W / Y}} \ldots T$$

$$U \ldots R$$

Even though this game had no established entities, by focusing on the most restricted entity and using the Duplications found among the rules, the expert was able to make several deductions that will prove valuable in answering the game's questions.

Note the Floaters

After you've used the BLEND checklist, always take a moment to account for all of the entities in the game: Which are now established in a single position? Which ones are limited to only some of the possible positions? And which ones are "floaters," still unconstrained by any rule or restriction? In your initial roster of the entities, mark the floaters in some way. Many LSAT veterans will use a little star, asterisk, or question mark above a floater. Likewise, they may choose to cross out the established entities in the roster, knowing that they will not need to account for those entities going forward. By the end of Step 4 in the Truck Arrivals game, the positions of Trucks S and Y are established, but Truck X remains a floater.

$$\cancel{S}\ T\ U\ W\ X\ \cancel{Y}\ Z$$

How to Know When You've Made All of the Game's Deductions

An irony of learning to make deductions is that it's sometimes hard to stop. That is to say that, on some games, you may find yourself looking for additional deductions that just aren't there. All LSAT instructors have heard students say, "I got behind on time because I kept thinking that there must be more to figure out, and then I didn't have enough time to answer the questions."

So, how do you know when to move on to the questions? There are two ways to answer this question, and they amount to the same thing. The first way to think about this is: When you have exhausted the BLEND checklist and have made all of the deductions available from it, you're ready for the questions. The other way to express this idea is to say: When deduction gives way to speculation, you've made all of the available deductions. Deductions are the certain results of rules and restrictions. Speculations are guesses about what *might* happen if something were true.

There will always be some ambiguity left in the game. If there weren't, there would be no "game," no puzzle left to solve. As you practice with the setups that follow, stay aware of your own thought process. Are you combining rules to determine ineluctable results, or are you merely trying out arrangements to see if they work? When you find yourself doing the latter, get back to the BLEND checklist. As you continue to practice, your confidence that you can make the available deductions will grow, as will your ability to discern when you have all of the useful information recorded and it is time to move on to the questions.

Practice

Directions: In each game setup, first reacquaint yourself with the setup and rules. Then, combine the rules and restrictions to make all available deductions, recording your analyses as indicated. Finally, test your deductions by answering the questions that accompany each game. You can find expert analysis and explanations at the end of the Practice section.

Practice 1

A geologist is organizing a display of seven gemstones—amethyst, beryl, diamond, emerald, fluorite, garnet, and jade. The gemstones will be arranged in a single row in a glass display case, labeled 1 through 7 consecutively from left to right, with one stone occupying each position. The arrangement of the gemstones must conform to the following conditions:

> The diamond must occupy a higher-numbered position than the amethyst, but a lower-numbered position than the garnet.
> The emerald and the fluorite must occupy consecutively numbered positions.
> The beryl must occupy a higher-numbered position than the emerald.
> The diamond must occupy position number 3.

Here is the sketch for this game after Step 3: Rules.

$$A \; B \; D \; E \; F \; G \; J$$

$$\underline{} \; \underline{} \; \overset{D}{\underline{}} \; \underline{} \; \underline{} \; \underline{} \; \underline{}$$
$$1 \quad 2 \quad 3 \quad 4 \quad 5 \quad 6 \quad 7$$

$$A \ldots D \ldots G$$

$$\boxed{E \; F} \;\; \text{or} \;\; \boxed{F \; E}$$

$$E \ldots B$$

1. Which entities or positions are the most restricted in this game? Why?

2. Which elements from the BLEND checklist can you identify in this game? Are there
   - Blocks of entities? If so, what are they?
   - Limited Options? If so, which rule(s) trigger them?
   - Established Entities? If so, which ones?
   - Number Restrictions? If so, describe them.
   - Duplications? If so, which rules share an entity?

3. Combine the rules and restrictions to create a Master Sketch depicting all of the deductions available in this game:

4. Evaluate your sketch by answering the following questions:
   - Which positions are available for the amethyst?
   - Provide a complete and accurate list of the entities that could be assigned to position 4.
   - Which entities *must* appear in positions numbered lower than the garnet's position?
   - In which position(s) could jade appear?

Practice 2

A chocolatier is putting together boxes of truffles for fundraisers at three local schools—X, Y, and Z. Each school will get a box with at least one of the five available flavors—hazelnut, maple walnut, peanut butter, raspberry, and white chocolate. Each flavor will be included in at least one of the boxes, subject to the following conditions:

The box for school X will include hazelnut truffles.
Maple walnut truffles will be used in more boxes than white chocolate truffles.
Peanut butter truffles will be used in exactly one box, and no other flavor will be included in that box.

Here is the sketch for this game after Step 3: Rules.

	X	Y	Z
hn	✓		
mw			
① pb			
rb			
wc			

mw > wc   pb = alone

1. Which entities or positions are the most restricted in this game? Why?

2. Which elements from the BLEND checklist can you identify in this game? Are there
   - Blocks of entities? If so, what are they?
   - Limited Options? If so, which rule(s) trigger them?
   - Established Entities? If so, which ones?
   - Number Restrictions? If so, describe them.
   - Duplications? If so, which rules share an entity?

3. Combine the rules and restrictions to create a Master Sketch depicting all of the deductions available in this game:

4. Evaluate your sketch by answering the following questions:
   - Would the following be an acceptable arrangement of flavors? School X: hazelnut, raspberry, white chocolate; School Y: peanut butter; School Z: hazelnut, maple walnut.
   - What is the maximum number of boxes that could contain white chocolate truffles?
   - Which school's box must contain maple walnut truffles?
   - If School Y's box contains hazelnut truffles, which flavor(s) cannot be used in School Y's box?

Practice 3

An accountant is scheduling meetings with six clients—Able, Baker, Charlie, Delphine, Erica, and Frankie—over a four-day period, from Monday through Thursday. On each day, two appointments are available, one in the morning and one in the afternoon. In addition, two staff meetings will be scheduled over the same period. Each client and staff meeting must be assigned a different appointment time. The schedule is governed by the following conditions:

> The staff meetings are not scheduled in the afternoon.
> Charlie's and Frankie's meetings are scheduled for the same day.
> Delphine's meeting is scheduled for some time prior to Frankie's meeting.
> Baker's meeting is scheduled in the morning.
> The accountant will meet with Erica and Baker on different days.

Here is the sketch for this game after Step 3: Rules.

$$A \ B \ C \ D \ E \ F \ S_1 \ S_2$$

$$M \ \ Tu \ \ W \ \ Th$$

$$AM \ \_ \ \_ \ \_ \ \_ \ \ S_1 \ S_2 \ B$$
$$PM \ \_ \ \_ \ \_ \ \_ \ \ \cancel{S_1} \ \cancel{S_2} \ \cancel{B}$$

1. Which entities or positions are the most restricted in this game? Why?
2. Which elements from the BLEND checklist can you identify in this game? Are there
   - Blocks of entities? If so, what are they?
   - Limited Options? If so, which rule(s) trigger them?
   - Established Entities? If so, which ones?
   - Number Restrictions? If so, describe them.
   - Duplications? If so, which rules share an entity?
3. Combine the rules and restrictions to create a Master Sketch depicting all of the deductions available in this game:

4. Evaluate your sketch by answering the following questions:
   - Write out a complete and accurate list of meetings that cannot be scheduled for Monday.
   - Write out a complete and accurate list of meetings that must be scheduled for a morning (regardless of day).
   - Write out a complete and accurate list of meetings that must be scheduled for an afternoon (regardless of day).
   - If Baker's meeting is scheduled for Tuesday morning, who are the clients whose meetings could be scheduled on Tuesday afternoon?

Practice 4

A showroom contains exactly six new cars—T, V, W, X, Y, and Z—each equipped with at least one of the following three options: power windows, leather interior, and sunroof. No car has any other options. The following conditions must apply:

V has power windows and a sunroof.
W has power windows and a leather interior.
W and Y have no options in common.
X has more options than W.
V and Z have exactly one option in common.
T has fewer options than Z.

PrepTest35 Sec3 Qs 6–12

Here is the sketch for this game after Step 3: Rules.

$$T < Z \quad W < X$$

	T	V	W	X	Y	Z
pw		✓	✓			
li			✓			
sr		✓				

W ≠ Y – <u>nothing</u> in common

V = Z exactly 1 in common

1. Which entities or positions are the most restricted in this game? Why?

2. Which elements from the BLEND checklist can you identify in this game? Are there

   - Blocks of entities? If so, what are they?
   - Limited Options? If so, which rule(s) trigger them?
   - Established Entities? If so, which ones?
   - Number Restrictions? If so, describe them.
   - Duplications? If so, which rules share an entity?

3. Combine the rules and restrictions to create a Master Sketch depicting all of the deductions available in this game:

4. Evaluate your sketch by answering the following questions:

   - Is any car permitted to have all three options? If so, which one(s)?
   - How many of the cars will have exactly one of the options? Which ones are they?
   - Which cars may not have a leather interior?
   - What is the maximum number of cars that could have a sunroof?

Explanations

Compare your work to that of an LSAT expert. Pay close attention to how the LSAT experts combined the rules and restrictions to make deductions, and how they depicted those deductions within the sketch frameworks.

Practice 1

A geologist is organizing a display of seven gemstones—amethyst, beryl, diamond, emerald, fluorite, garnet, and jade. The gemstones will be arranged in a single row in a glass display case, labeled 1 through 7 consecutively from left to right, with one stone occupying each position. The arrangement of the gemstones must conform to the following conditions:

> The diamond must occupy a higher-numbered position than the amethyst, but a lower-numbered position than the garnet.
>
> The emerald and the fluorite must occupy consecutively numbered positions.
>
> The beryl must occupy a higher-numbered position than the emerald.
>
> The diamond must occupy position number 3.

Here is the sketch for this game after Step 3: Rules.

A B D E F G J

```
 __  __  D  __  __  __  __
  1   2   3   4   5   6   7
```

A . . . D . . . G

[E F] or [F E]

E . . . B

1. Which entities or positions are the most restricted in this game? Why? *The diamond is established in position 3 (Rule 4), locking the amethyst into either of positions 1 or 2 (Rule 1).*

2. Which elements from the BLEND checklist can you identify in this game? Are there

   - Blocks of entities? If so, what are they? *Rule 1 creates a "loose" block of A . . . D . . . G. Rule 2 stipulates that E and F must be consecutive, in either order. Rule 3 creates a "loose" block of E . . . B.*

   - Limited Options? If so, which rule(s) trigger them? *N/A*

   - Established Entities? If so, which ones? *The diamond, in position 3 (Rule 4).*

   - Number Restrictions? If so, describe them. *N/A*

   - Duplications? If so, which rules share an entity? *Rules 1 and 4 share D. Rules 2 and 3 share E.*

3. Combine the rules and restrictions to create a Master Sketch depicting all of the deductions available in this game: *Because D is established in position 3 (Rule 4), and also part of a three-entity string (A . . . D . . . G, Rule 1), A is restricted to either position 1 or position 2, while G must take one of positions 4–7.*

```
                         G
                      _____
 A/   /A   D  __  __  __  __
  1    2   3   4   5   6   7
```

Combine Rules 2 and 3 to create a string of E/F . . . B.

```
                         G
                      _____
 A/   /A   D  __  __  __  __
  1    2   3   4   5   6   7
```

[E / F] . . . B

Because E and F are a block of entities that requires two consecutive positions, neither E nor F may go in positions 1 or 2. Thus, J, the only remaining unrestricted entity, must take whichever of positions 1 or 2 not taken by A.

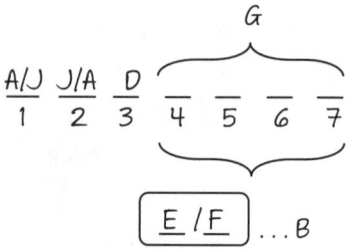

There are no floaters.

4. Evaluate your sketch by answering the following questions:

   • Which positions are available for the amethyst? *Positions 1 or 2.*

   • Provide a complete and accurate list of the entities that could be assigned to position 4? *Emerald, fluorite, garnet.*

   • Which entities *must* appear in positions numbered lower than the garnet's position? *Amethyst, jade, diamond. Note: Emerald, fluorite, and beryl could appear in positions numbered lower than the garnet's positions, but they do not have to.*

   • In which position(s) could jade appear? *Positions 1 or 2.*

Practice 2

A chocolatier is putting together boxes of truffles for fundraisers at three local schools—X, Y, and Z. Each school will get a box with at least one of the five available flavors—hazelnut, maple walnut, peanut butter, raspberry, and white chocolate. Each flavor will be included in at least one of the boxes, subject to the following conditions:

> The box for school X will include hazelnut truffles.
> Maple walnut truffles will be used in more boxes than white chocolate truffles.
> Peanut butter truffles will be used in exactly one box, and no other flavor will be included in that box.

Here is the sketch for this game after Step 3: Rules.

	X	Y	Z
hn	✓		
mw			
① pb			
rb			
wc			

mw > wc   pb = alone

1. Which entities or positions are the most restricted in this game? Why? *The most restricted flavor is peanut butter, which cannot be mixed with any other flavors. Hazelnut flavor is established in School X's box, but it may appear in another box as well.*

2. Which elements from the BLEND checklist can you identify in this game? Are there

   • Blocks of entities? If so, what are they? *N/A*

   • Limited Options? If so, which rule(s) trigger them? *The three rules combine to produce a Limited Options scenario involving peanut butter and maple walnut, but it takes a couple of steps to reach this deduction. See the explanation for question 3.*

   • Established Entities? If so, which ones? *Hazelnut is "quasi-established": It must be used in School X's box, but because this is a Matching game, it may be used in another box, too.*

   • Number Restrictions? If so, describe them. *1) Peanut butter flavor can appear in exactly one box. 2) Maple walnut flavor is used in more boxes than white chocolate.*

   • Duplications? If so, which rules share an entity? *N/A*

3. Combine the rules and restrictions to create a Master Sketch depicting all of the deductions available in this game: *Hazelnut will be used in School X's box (Rule 1), and peanut butter cannot be mixed with any other flavor, so peanut butter cannot be used in School X's box.*

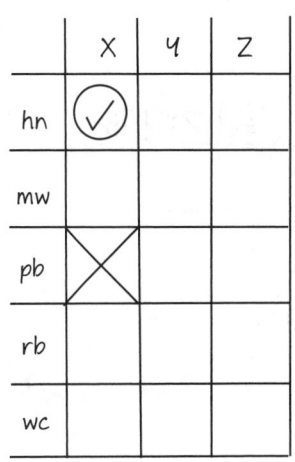

Since peanut butter must be used in exactly one box, it will go <u>alone</u> into either School Y's or School Z's box, and cannot be used in any other box. This creates a Limited Options scenario calling for dual sketches.

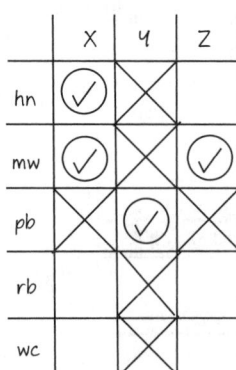

Maple walnut must be used in more boxes than white chocolate (Rule 2). The Limited Options make clear that, in either scenario, maple walnut will be used in two boxes and white chocolate in one box. Maple walnut will always be used in School X's box, and again in either School Y's or School Z's, whichever does not contain peanut butter. Fill in the placements for maple walnut, and mark white chocolate with a "1" as a reminder that it may not be used twice.

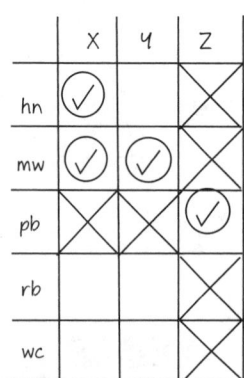

Raspberry flavor is a floater. It may appear in one or two boxes, but not in all three because of the rule requiring peanut butter to be alone (Rule 1).

4. Evaluate your sketch by answering the following questions:

- Would the following be an acceptable arrangement of flavors? School X: hazelnut, raspberry, white chocolate; School Y: peanut butter; School Z: hazelnut, maple walnut. *No, Rule 2 requires that maple walnut be used in more boxes than white chocolate is used.*

- What is the maximum number of boxes that could contain white chocolate truffles? *One.*

- Which school's box must contain maple walnut truffles? *School X.*

- If School Y's box contains hazelnut truffles, which flavor(s) cannot be used in School Y's box? *Peanut butter.*

Practice 3

An accountant is scheduling meetings with six clients—Able, Baker, Charlie, Delphine, Erica, and Frankie—over a four-day period, from Monday through Thursday. On each day, two appointments are available, one in the morning and one in the afternoon. In addition, two staff meetings will be scheduled over the same period. Each client and staff meeting must be assigned a different appointment time. The schedule is governed by the following conditions:

The staff meetings are not scheduled in the afternoon.
Charlie's and Frankie's meetings are scheduled for the same day.
Delphine's meeting is scheduled for some time prior to Frankie's meeting.
Baker's meeting is scheduled in the morning.
The accountant will meet with Erica and Baker on different days.

Here is the sketch for this game after Step 3: Rules.

A B C D E F S$_1$ S$_2$

M Tu W Th

AM _ _ _ _ S$_1$ S$_2$ B
PM _ _ _ _ ~~S$_1$~~ ~~S$_2$~~ ~~B~~

$\boxed{\dfrac{C}{F}}$ or $\boxed{\dfrac{F}{C}}$ D . . . F

never $\boxed{\dfrac{E}{B}}$ or $\boxed{\dfrac{B}{E}}$

1. Which entities or positions are the most restricted in this game? Why? *Frankie, who must follow Delphine and share a day with Charlie.*

2. Which elements from the BLEND checklist can you identify in this game? Are there

   • Blocks of entities? If so, what are they? *Charlie and Frankie must have their meetings on the same day (Rule 2). Delphine and Frankie are a "loose" block: D . . . F (Rule 3).*

   • Limited Options? If so, which rule(s) trigger them? *N/A*

   • Established Entities? If so, which ones? *N/A*

   • Number Restrictions? If so, describe them. *N/A*

   • Duplications? If so, which rules share an entity? *Rules 2 and 3 share Frankie and can be combined.*

3. Combine the rules and restrictions to create a Master Sketch depicting all of the deductions available in this game: *This game has no established entities and only one duplication. Combine Rules 2 and 3 (if you didn't do so when writing out the rules).*

D . . . $\boxed{\dfrac{C}{F}}$ or $\boxed{\dfrac{F}{C}}$

Note the negative implications of the D . . . C/F deduction: C/F cannot take Monday, and D will not have a meeting on Thursday.

A B C D E F S$_1$ S$_2$

M Tu W Th

AM _ _ _ _ S$_1$ S$_2$ B
PM _ _ _ _ ~~S$_1$~~ ~~S$_2$~~ ~~B~~
   ~C   ~D
   ~F

D . . . $\boxed{\dfrac{C}{F}}$ or $\boxed{\dfrac{F}{C}}$

never $\boxed{\dfrac{E}{B}}$ or $\boxed{\dfrac{B}{E}}$

Now, note that either C or F will take one morning slot and one afternoon slot. Because B's meeting and the two staff meetings are also in the morning, the meetings with A, D, and E will all be in the afternoon.

A B C D E F S$_1$ S$_2$

M Tu W Th

AM _ _ _ _ S$_1$ S$_2$ B C/F
PM _ _ _ _ ~~S$_1$~~ ~~S$_2$~~ ~~B~~ F/C A, D, E
   ~C   ~D
   ~F

D . . . $\boxed{\dfrac{C}{F}}$ or $\boxed{\dfrac{F}{C}}$

never $\boxed{\dfrac{E}{B}}$ or $\boxed{\dfrac{B}{E}}$

That's as far as the deductions go. You know the four meetings that will be scheduled in the morning slots, and the four for the afternoon slots, but you don't know the specific day on which any meeting will be scheduled.

4. Evaluate your sketch by answering the following questions:

   • Write out a complete and accurate list of meetings that cannot be scheduled for Monday. *Charlie, Frankie.*

   • Write out a complete and accurate list of meetings that must be scheduled for a morning (regardless of day). *Baker and both staff meetings.*

   • Write out a complete and accurate list of meetings that must be scheduled for an afternoon (regardless of day). *Able, Delphine, Erica.*

   • If Baker's meeting is scheduled for Tuesday morning, who are the clients whose meetings could be scheduled on Tuesday afternoon? *Able and Delphine; Charlie and Frankie must be on the same day (Rule 2), and Erica's meeting cannot be on the same day as Baker's (Rule 4).*

Practice 4

A showroom contains exactly six new cars—T, V, W, X, Y, and Z—each equipped with at least one of the following three options: power windows, leather interior, and sunroof. No car has any other option. The following conditions must apply:

> V has power windows and a sunroof.
> W has power windows and a leather interior.
> W and Y have no options in common.
> X has more options than W.
> V and Z have exactly one option in common.
> T has fewer options than Z.

PrepTest35 Sec3 Qs 6–12

Here is the sketch for this game after Step 3: Rules.

T < Z   W < X

	T	V	W	X	Y	Z
pw		✓	✓			
li			✓			
sr		✓				

W ≠ Y – <u>nothing</u> in common

V = Z exactly 1 in common

1. Which entities or positions are the most restricted in this game? Why? *Car W is at the center of three rules (Rules 2, 3, and 4) which assign it two features and limit it in relationship to two other cars (X and Y).*

2. Which elements from the BLEND checklist can you identify in this game? Are there

   • Blocks of entities? If so, what are they? *N/A*

   • Limited Options? If so, which rule(s) trigger them? *N/A*

   • Established Entities? If so, which ones? *Rule 1 gives Car V two features, and Rule 2 gives Car W two features. Because this is a Matching game, however, the features may be given to other cars as well.*

   • Number Restrictions? If so, describe them. *1) Rule 4 stipulates that Car X has more features than Car W. 2) Rule 6 requires that Car Z have more features than Car T.*

   • Duplications? If so, which rules share an entity? *There are three: 1) Car W is shared by Rules 2, 3, and 4; 2) Car V is shared by Rules 1 and 5; and 3) Car Z is shared by Rules 5 and 6.*

3. Combine the rules and restrictions to create a Master Sketch depicting all of the deductions available in this game: *Begin with Car W, which already has power windows and a leather interior (Rule 2). Combine that with Rule 3. If W and Y have nothing in common, then Car Y must have a sunroof, and cannot have either of the other features. By the same token, Car W may not have a sunroof.*

	T	V	W	X	Y	Z
pw		✓	✓		✗	
li			✓		✗	
sr		✓	✗		✓	✓

Then, combine Rule 2 with Rule 4. For Car X to have more features than Car W, Car X must have all three features.

	T	V	W	X	Y	Z
pw		✓	✓	✓	✗	
li			✓	✓		
sr		✓	✗	✓	✓	

At this point, Cars W, X, and Y are completely determined. Consider the rules that restrict Cars T, V, and Z. You know Car V already has power windows and a sunroof (Rule 1). Rule 5 requires that V and Z have exactly one feature in common, so Car Z will have either power windows or a sunroof, but not both.

	T	V	W	X	Y	Z
pw		✓	✓	✓	✗	
li			✓	✓		
sr		✓	✗	✓	✓	

pw or sr
<u>not both</u>

Rule 6 now allows for additional deductions about Cars T, V, and Z. For Car Z to have more features than Car T, Car Z must have either two or three features. It cannot have three, or it would break Rule 5, so it must have two features. One of Car Z's features must be a leather interior (remember, its other feature will be the one feature it has in common with Car V, either power windows or a sunroof, but not both). Since Car Z will have a leather interior, Car V will not (again, so that the two cars do not violate Rule 5). Finally, because Car Z has two features, Car T must have just one. Car T's one feature could be any of the three features available in the game.

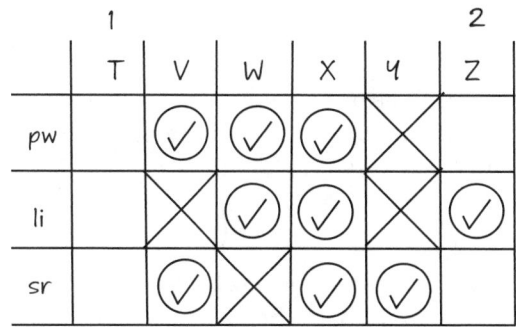

pw or sr
<u>not both</u>

That game had an extraordinary number of deductions. In four of the six cars that anchor the game, the feature sets are completely determined. That's unusually high, but by following through on the BLEND checklist and making all of those deductions, you're in a position to answer the questions much more quickly and confidently than you would be without the deductions in place.

4. Evaluate your sketch by answering the following questions:

   - Are any of the cars permitted to have all three options? If so, which one(s)? *Car X is the only car that may have all three options. In fact, it is required to have all three.*

   - Which cars, if any, will have exactly one of the options? *Cars T and Y will have exactly one of the options.*

   - Which cars may not have a leather interior? *Cars V and Y may not have leather interiors.*

   - What is the maximum number of cars that could have a sunroof? *Five cars —T, V, X, Y, and Z—could have sunroofs.*

Perform

Directions: Take one minute to refresh your memory of each game's setup and rules. Then, take no more than five minutes to catalog the rules and combine them to make all available deductions. Test your deductions by answering the questions at the end of each exercise.

Perform 1

A filmmaker is planning to create a short film with exactly five scenes. The scenes will all be shot in one day and will be filmed in order, with each scene completed before filming begins on the next. Each scene will feature at least one of four actors—Jenkins, Kwan, Lozano, and Millstone—and no others. Each actor will appear in exactly two of the scenes. The schedule must conform to the following conditions:

> No actor's second scene will be filmed at the same time as another actor's second scene.
> Exactly one actor will appear in the third scene of the film.
> Millstone's first scene will be filmed before Lozano's first scene.
> Any scene in which Lozano is filmed will feature at least one other actor.

Here is the sketch for this game after Step 3: Rules.

$$J_1 \ J_2 \ K_1 \ K_2 \ L_1 \ L_2 \ M_1 \ M_2$$

1	2	3	4	5
—	—	—	—	—

$$never \begin{array}{|c|} \hline 2 \\ 2 \\ \hline \end{array} \quad M_1 \ldots L_1$$

never L alone

1. Which entities or positions are the most restricted in this game? Why?

2. Which elements from the BLEND checklist can you identify in this game? Are there
   - Blocks of entities? If so, what are they?
   - Limited Options? If so, which rule(s) trigger them?
   - Established Entities? If so, which ones?
   - Number Restrictions? If so, describe them.
   - Duplications? If so, which rules share an entity?

3. Combine the rules and restrictions to create a Master Sketch depicting all of the deductions available in this game:

4. Evaluate your sketch by answering the following questions:
   - Which scenes could be Millstone's second scene?
   - Which scenes could be Kwan's first scene?
   - What is the maximum number of actors that can appear in any scene?
   - If Jenkins appeared in scene 3, who could appear in scene 5?

Perform 2

Eight students—Bonham, Cullen, Dao, Farina, Gerber, Holt, Karlsson, and Logan—are assigned to do research on three court cases—R, S and T. Each student will research exactly one case in accordance with the following:

> Bonham is assigned to research case R.
> Farina and Logan are not assigned to research the same case.
> Karlsson is assigned to research a case with exactly two other students.
> Gerber and Holt are assigned to research a case together, with no other student assigned to research that case.

Here is the sketch for this game after Step 3: Rules.

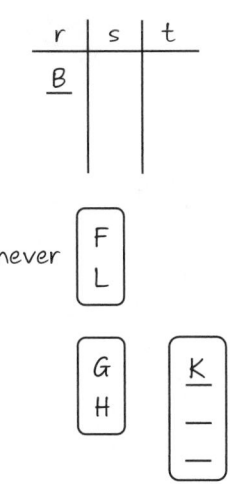

1. Which entities or positions are the most restricted in this game? Why?
2. Which elements from the BLEND checklist can you identify in this game? Are there
   - Blocks of entities? If so, what are they?
   - Limited Options? If so, which rule(s) trigger them?
   - Established Entities? If so, which ones?
   - Number Restrictions? If so, describe them.
   - Duplications? If so, which rules share an entity?
3. Combine the rules and restrictions to create a Master Sketch depicting all of the deductions available in this game:

4. Evaluate your sketch by answering the following questions:
   - Who are all of the students that CANNOT be assigned to case R?
   - Which students could be assigned to any of the three cases?
   - What is the minimum number of students for any case?
   - If Cullen and Dao are together, who could be the third person assigned to that case?

Perform 3

Every Sunday, a zookeeper gives presentations on each of five snakes—an eastern indigo snake, a king snake, a milk snake, a python, and a rat snake. The presentations are held at 1:00, 2:00, 3:00, 4:00, and 5:00. Exactly one snake is exhibited at each presentation. Visitors are invited to hold some, but not all, of the snakes. Visitors are allowed to observe, but not to hold, the others. The schedule of presentations must conform to the following conditions:

Visitors are invited to hold the king snake and at least one other snake.
Visitors are allowed to observe, but not to hold, the last snake presented.
The milk snake is presented before the king snake.
The python is presented before any snake that visitors are invited to hold.

Here is the sketch for this game after Step 3: Rules.

1. Which entities or positions are the most restricted in this game? Why?
2. Which elements from the BLEND checklist can you identify in this game? Are there
   - Blocks of entities? If so, what are they?
   - Limited Options? If so, which rule(s) trigger them?
   - Established Entities? If so, which ones?
   - Number Restrictions? If so, describe them.
   - Duplications? If so, which rules share an entity?
3. Combine the rules and restrictions to create a Master Sketch depicting all of the deductions available in this game:

4. Evaluate your sketch by answering the following questions:
   - What is the earliest time a snake could be held?
   - What is the maximum number of snakes that could be held?
   - Which snakes could be presented at 4:00?
   - What snake would be presented at 5:00 if the eastern indigo snake could be held?

Perform 4

A closet contains exactly six hangers—1, 2, 3, 4, 5, and 6—hanging, in that order, from left to right. It also contains exactly six dresses—one gauze, one linen, one polyester, one rayon, one silk, and one wool—a different dress on each of the hangers, in an order satisfying the following conditions:

> The gauze dress is on a lower-numbered hanger than the polyester dress.
> The rayon dress is on hanger 1 or hanger 6.
> Either the wool dress or the silk dress is on hanger 3.
> The linen dress hangs immediately to the right of the silk dress.

PrepTest41 Sec2 Qs 1–7

Here is the sketch for this game after Step 3: Rules.

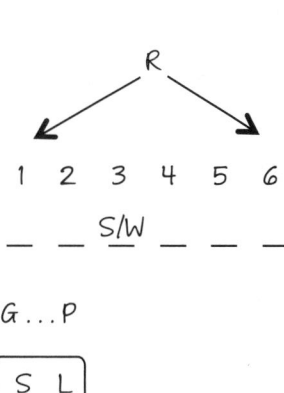

1. Which entities or positions are the most restricted in this game? Why?

2. Which elements from the BLEND checklist can you identify in this game? Are there

   - Blocks of entities? If so, what are they?

   - Limited Options? If so, which rule(s) trigger them?

   - Established Entities? If so, which ones?

   - Number Restrictions? If so, describe them.

   - Duplications? If so, which rules share an entity?

3. Combine the rules and restrictions to create a Master Sketch depicting all of the deductions available in this game:

4. Evaluate your sketch by answering the following questions:

   - Which dress (or dresses) could be on any of the six hangers?

   - Which dresses could be on hanger 6?

   - Which dresses could be immediately to the left of the rayon dress?

   - How many dresses can you determine if the silk dress is on hanger 1?

Explanations

Compare your work to that of an LSAT expert. Pay close attention to how the LSAT experts combined the rules and restrictions to make deductions, and how they depicted those deductions within the sketch frameworks.

Perform 1

A filmmaker is planning to create a short film with exactly five scenes. The scenes will all be shot in one day and will be filmed in order, with each scene completed before filming begins on the next. Each scene will feature at least one of four actors—Jenkins, Kwan, Lozano, and Millstone—and no others. Each actor will appear in exactly two of the scenes. The schedule must conform to the following conditions:

> No actor's second scene will be filmed at the same time as another actor's second scene.
> Exactly one actor will appear in the third scene of the film.
> Millstone's first scene will be filmed before Lozano's first scene.
> Any scene in which Lozano is filmed will feature at least one other actor.

Here is the sketch for this game after Step 3: Rules.

$$J_1 \ J_2 \ K_1 \ K_2 \ L_1 \ L_2 \ M_1 \ M_2$$

1	2	3	4	5
—	—	—	—	—

never $\begin{array}{|c|} \hline 2 \\ 2 \\ \hline \end{array}$ $M_1 \ldots L_1$

never L alone

1. Which entities or positions are the most restricted in this game? Why? *The most restricted actor is Lozano, who has to wait until Millstone appears first, and also cannot appear alone.*

2. Which elements from the BLEND checklist can you identify in this game? Are there

   • Blocks of entities? If so, what are they? *Nothing concrete, but Lozano will always be part of a block with somebody, and that will be important.*

   • Limited Options? If so, which rule(s) trigger them? *N/A*

   • Established Entities? If so, which ones? *N/A*

   • Number Restrictions? If so, describe them. *By Rule 1, the four actors will all have different scenes for their second scene. That means four separate scenes will feature an actor's second scene. Rule 2 limits scene 3 to one actor, and Rule 4 requires any scene with Lozano to feature at least two actors.*

   • Duplications? If so, which rules share an entity? *Lozano is mentioned in Rules 3 and 4.*

3. Combine the rules and restrictions to create a Master Sketch depicting all of the deductions available in this game:

   Numbers are most important here, so start there. Logically, all actors' first scenes precede their second scenes, so scene 1 cannot be any actor's second scene, and scene 5 cannot be any actor's first scene. By Rule 1, four different scenes feature an actor's second scene. They must be scenes 2 through 5, one actor in each.

1	2	3	4	5
—	2	2	2	2

Chapter 3: Logic Games Rules and Deductions

Scene 3 is now finished, with a single actor's second scene. Scene 5 cannot feature an actor's first scene, and can only have one actor's second scene. So, scene 5 is now closed off.

1	2	3	4	5
—	$_2$	$\underline{\underline{_2}}$	$_2$	$\underline{\underline{_2}}$

Lozano cannot be alone, so Lozano cannot be in scene 3 or scene 5. Also, Lozano cannot be in scene 1 because Millstone's first appearance has to be before Lozano's. So, Lozano must appear in scenes 2 and 4. Scene 2 will be Lozano's first scene, and must be shared with somebody else's second scene, at least. Scene 4 will be Lozano's second scene, and must be shared with someone else's first scene.

1	2	3	4	5
—	L_1	$\underline{\underline{_2}}$	$_1$	$\underline{\underline{_2}}$
	$_2$		L_2	

Millstone's first scene must precede Lozano's, so Millstone's first scene must be scene 1.

1	2	3	4	5
$\underline{M_1}$	L_1	$\underline{\underline{_2}}$	$_1$	$\underline{\underline{_2}}$
	$_2$		L_2	

Scene 4 has to include someone's first scene. Lozano's and Millstone's are established elsewhere, so it must be either Jenkins's or Kwan's. That actor's second scene will be the one in scene 5. Thus, scene 4 cannot be the first scene for both Jenkins and Kwan, so it will just be one of them. That closes off scene 4.

1	2	3	4	5
$\underline{M_1}$	L_1	$\underline{\underline{_2}}$	$\underline{\underline{J/K_1}}$	J/K_2
	$_2$		L_2	

There are now seven slots in the sketch, and there need to be eight (two for each actor). With scenes 3, 4, and 5 closed off, the final slot can be added to either scene 1 or scene 2.

4. Evaluate your sketch by answering the following questions:

- Which scenes could be Millstone's second scene? *Scene 2 or 3. Scene 4 is Lozano's second scene, and scene 5 has to be the second scene for the actor's whose first scene is scene 4.*

- Which scenes could be Kwan's first scene? *Scene 1, 2 or 4; Scene 3 can only have someone's second scene.*

- What is the maximum number of actors that can appear in any scene? *Three; the one slot that is left to add could be added to scene 2, allowing scene 2 to have Lozano's first scene, Millstone's second scene, and one other actor's first scene (either Jenkins or Kwan).*

- If Jenkins appeared in scene 3, who could appear in scene 5? *It would have to be Kwan, who would be the only person left whose first scene could be scene 4.*

Perform 2

Eight students - Bonham, Cullen, Dao, Farina, Gerber, Holt, Karlsson, and Logan—are assigned to do research on three court cases—R, S and T. Each student will research exactly one case in accordance with the following:

> Bonham is assigned to research case R.
> Farina and Logan are not assigned to research the same case.
> Karlsson is assigned to research a case with exactly two other students.
> Gerber and Holt are assigned to research a case together, with no other student assigned to research that case.

Here is the sketch for this game after Step 3: Rules.

B C D F G H K L

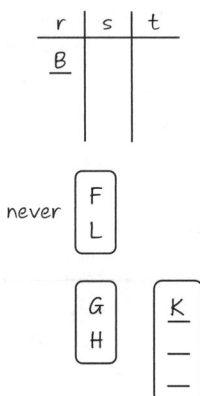

1. Which entities or positions are the most restricted in this game? Why? *Gerber and Holt must be in a group all by themselves, and case R is already occupied partially by someone else.*

2. Which elements from the BLEND checklist can you identify in this game? Are there

   - Blocks of entities? If so, what are they? *Gerber and Holt have to be together.*

   - Limited Options? If so, which rule(s) trigger them? *N/A*

   - Established Entities? If so, which ones? *Bonham is already established on case R.*

   - Number Restrictions? If so, describe them. *Rules 3 and 4 set numbers for two cases: one will have three students (including Karlsson) and another will have two (Gerber and Holt).*

   - Duplications? If so, which rules share an entity? *N/A*

3. Combine the rules and restrictions to create a Master Sketch depicting all of the deductions available in this game:

   The block of Gerber and Holt cannot be placed on case R because Bonham is already there. Thus, Gerber and Holt can only be assigned to case S or T.

By Rule 3, one case will have exactly three students (including Karlsson). By Rule 4, a second case will have exactly two students (Gerber and Holt). With eight students in total, the third case will have the remaining three students.

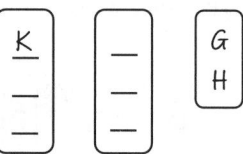

The case with two students is filled. That leaves the two cases with three students. One has Karlsson. Farina and Logan cannot be together, so one will be with Karlsson, and the other will be on the other case.

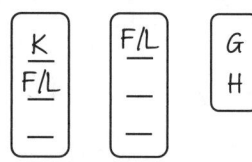

Case R cannot be the case with two students, so it will have three students. It could be the one with Karlsson or the one without Karlsson. Either way, though, it will also include Farina or Logan.

4. Evaluate your sketch by answering the following questions:

- Who are all of the students that CANNOT be assigned to case R? *Gerber and Holt, who must be by themselves and thus cannot be with Bonham.*

- Which students could be assigned to any of the three cases? *Cullen, Dao, Farina, Karlsson, and Logan.*

- What is the minimum number of students for any case? *Two—the case with Gerber and Holt; the other cases have three students each.*

- If Cullen and Dao are together, who could be the third person assigned to that case? *Farina or Logan; if it were anyone else, a second case would have Gerber and Holt, and Farina and Logan would be assigned together to the remaining case, violating Rule 2.*

Perform 3

Every Sunday, a zookeeper gives presentations on each of five snakes—an eastern indigo snake, a king snake, a milk snake, a python, and a rat snake. The presentations are held at 1:00, 2:00, 3:00, 4:00, and 5:00. Exactly one snake is exhibited at each presentation. Visitors are invited to hold some, but not all, of the snakes. Visitors are allowed to observe, but not to hold, the others. The schedule of presentations must conform to the following conditions:

Visitors are invited to hold the king snake and at least one other snake.
Visitors are allowed to observe, but not to hold, the last snake presented.
The milk snake is presented before the king snake.
The python is presented before any snake that visitors are invited to hold.

Here is the sketch for this game after Step 3: Rules.

1. Which entities or positions are the most restricted in this game? Why? *The king snake is most restricted because it must be held and it must come after the milk snake, as well as the python. The python is also heavily restricted because it has to be presented before every snake that's held. The 5:00 position is also very restricted because it must have a snake that is only observed, and there are multiple snakes that must appear earlier.*

2. Which elements from the BLEND checklist can you identify in this game? Are there

- Blocks of entities? If so, what are they? *Matching the king snake as held limits its placement as if it were a block.*

- Limited Options? If so, which rule(s) trigger them? *N/A*

- Established Entities? If so, which ones? *Rule 2 establishes the 5:00 snake as observed only.*

- Number Restrictions? If so, describe them. *Rule 1 sets a minimum of 2 snakes held, the king snake and at least one other.*

- Duplications? If so, which rules share an entity? *Rules 1 and 3 both mention the king snake.*

3. Combine the rules and restrictions to create a Master Sketch depicting all of the deductions available in this game:

    The king snake is most significant. It must be held, so it cannot be presented at 5:00. And because it's held, it has to be presented later than the python, so it cannot be at 1:00. It also has to be presented later than the milk snake, so it cannot be at 2:00. That means it will be presented at 3:00 or 4:00.

    The latest the king snake can appear is 4:00, and the python and the milk snake must both be earlier. So neither one can be presented at 4:00 or 5:00. That leaves just the eastern indigo or the rat snake for the 5:00 presentation.

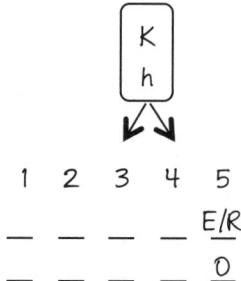

    The python has to appear before all snakes that are held. That means the python itself cannot be held, so the python will just be observed. That also means the snake at 1:00 cannot be held, so it must be just observed.

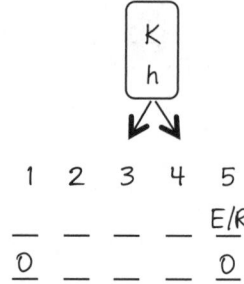

    At least two snakes are held, and the python must appear before them both. Also the 5:00 snake is just observed. The python must appear before that snake, too, so the python could only be presented at 1:00 or 2:00.

4. Evaluate your sketch by answering the following questions:

    -   What is the earliest time a snake could be held? *It would be 2:00, allowing the python to be displayed at 1:00.*

    -   What is the maximum number of snakes that could be held? *Three; the 5:00 is not held, and the 1:00 cannot be held because of the python. But, if the python was at 1:00, the three snakes at 2:00, 3:00, and 4:00 could all be held.*

    -   Which snakes could be presented at 4:00? *The eastern indigo, the king snake, or the rat snake.*

    -   What snake would be presented at 5:00 if the eastern indigo snake could be held? *The rat snake. The 5:00 snake is observed only. The other snakes are either held or have to be presented earlier.*

Perform 4

A closet contains exactly six hangers—1, 2, 3, 4, 5, and 6—hanging, in that order, from left to right. It also contains exactly six dresses—one gauze, one linen, one polyester, one rayon, one silk, and one wool—a different dress on each of the hangers, in an order satisfying the following conditions:

> The gauze dress is on a lower-numbered hanger than the polyester dress.
> The rayon dress is on hanger 1 or hanger 6.
> Either the wool dress or the silk dress is on hanger 3.
> The linen dress hangs immediately to the right of the silk dress.

PrepTest41 Sec2 Qs 1–7

Here is the sketch for this game after Step 3: Rules.

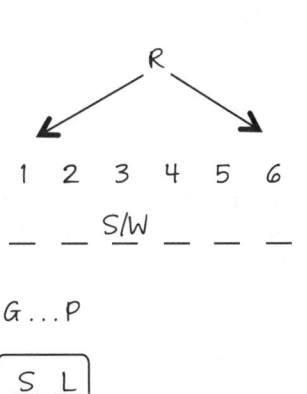

1. Which entities or positions are the most restricted in this game? Why? *Rayon, which is limited to two positions. And hanger 3 is similarly limited to just two dresses.*

2. Which elements from the BLEND checklist can you identify in this game? Are there

   - Blocks of entities? If so, what are they? *Yes, the silk and the linen dresses are consecutive, in that order.*

   - Limited Options? If so, which rule(s) trigger them? *No; Rules 2 and 3 each provide only two options, but neither one provides enough substantial deductions to warrant two sketches.*

   - Established Entities? If so, which ones? *Rule 3 establishes the silk or wool on hanger 3.*

   - Number Restrictions? If so, describe them. *N/A*

   - Duplications? If so, which rules share an entity? *The silk dress is mentioned in both rules 3 and 4.*

3. Combine the rules and restrictions to create a Master Sketch depicting all of the deductions available in this game:

   There's very little to find here. The fact that the gauze dress has to be lower than the polyester dress means that the gauze dress cannot be on hanger 6 and the polyester dress cannot be on hanger 1.

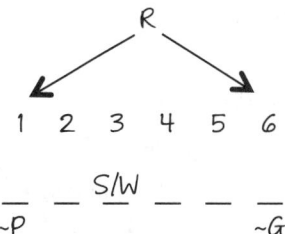

Similarly, because the silk dress has to be lower than the linen dress, the silk dress cannot be on hanger 6 and the linen dress cannot be on hanger 1. Further, the one place this block cannot go is hangers 2 and 3, because the linen dress cannot be on hanger 3. So, the silk dress cannot be on hanger 2.

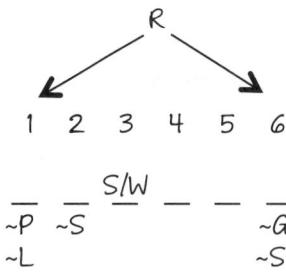

4. Evaluate your sketch by answering the following questions:

   - Which dress (or dresses) could be on any of the six hangers? *The wool dress; the other dresses all need to come before or after other dresses, or are limited to certain positions.*

   - Which dresses could be on hanger 6? *Linen, polyester, rayon, or wool.*

   - Which dresses could be immediately to the left of the rayon dress? *This would require the rayon dress to be on hanger 6. In that case, hanger 5 cannot be the gauze dress (Rule 2) or the silk dress (Rule 3). So, it could only be the polyester, the linen, or the wool dress.*

   - How many dresses can you determine if the silk dress is on hanger 1? *All six; this would put the linen on hanger 2, the wool on hanger 3, and the rayon on hanger 6. The gauze and polyester would then be on hangers 4 and 5, in that order.*

Assess

Assess your performance according to the following criteria. If you were able to make

All or most of the deductions in 3 to 4 of the logic games: Congratulations! That is outstanding work at this point in the book. Move on to Chapter 4 and dive into Step 5 of the Logic Games Method covering the strategies LSAT experts use to answer logic games questions quickly and accurately.

All of the deductions in at least 2 of the games, or at least some of the deductions in 3 to 4 of the games: Review your work to determine the game types and deductions types on which you will need more work. Review the deduction types as they are described in the Prepare portion of this subchapter, and make a note to study the Deductions step in the appropriate game type chapter (Chapters 5–8).

All of the deductions in only 1 of the games, or only some of the deductions in 2 to 3 of the games: First, review this subchapter thoroughly. Second, take the "Deductions Fundamentals" quiz found in your online center. Third, make sure to review the expert analysis for Step 4 of the Logic Games Method on all games you study or practice in the remainder of this book.

To stay sharp, practice the drills in the Logic Games Training Camp for this chapter in your Online Study Plan. Training Camp drills are divided into Fundamentals, Mid-Level, and Advanced sets.

Reflect

Think back over the work you did in this portion of Chapter 3.

- Are you now able to identify the most restricted entities and/or positions within a game's framework?
- Can you identify each of the five common deductions in the BLEND checklist?
- Are you able to more quickly and accurately note into your Master Sketch the additional information revealed by deductions?
- Do you now look for and spot unrestricted floaters among the entities?
- Are you better able to assess when you have made all of a game's deductions and know that you are ready to move on to the questions?

In the coming days and weeks leading up to Test Day, take note of real-world situations in which you make deductions.

- Are you able to state day-to-day rules affirmatively and negatively, (e.g., "disabled parking only" means that cars without a disability tag are forbidden)?
- Are you able to identify the constraints or rules that lead to valid deductions?
- Can you distinguish authentic deductions (the necessary result of two or more "rules") from mere preferences or assumptions?

The LSAT Channel Spotlight

Limited Options

By Gene Suhir

 Watch the video lesson for this Spotlight in your online Study Plan.

Limited Options, the situation in which an entire logic game breaks down into two (or, rarely, three) acceptable patterns, is often the most helpful deduction you can make. Unfortunately, Limited Options can also be one of the hardest deductions for test takers to spot. Here are a few rules of thumb that will help you exploit this powerful deduction tool.

Think of Limited Options as the testmaker's way of saying "either ... or." Indeed, at times, the rule giving rise to Limited Options is just that literal, e.g., "George must be interviewed fourth or sixth." With Limited Options, you draw two sketches of the game, one for each of the acceptable patterns. Once you've created the dual sketches and have filled in the additional deductions that arise within each one, you're usually left with only a handful of acceptable arrangements. You'll be close to seeing all of the ways that the game can be completed.

Limited Options stem from one of three conditions. It's worth remembering what they are.

A "Key Player"

This describes a situation in which a particular entity can take exactly two positions or placements, either of which gives rise to additional restrictions among the remaining entities. Take a look:

Six students—Becca, Charles, David, Edwina, George, and Hiromi—will be interviewed one at a time by a reporter for the school newspaper. The interviews will be conducted consecutively, first through sixth, according to the following restrictions.

> George must be interviewed fourth or sixth.
> Hiromi's interview will be conducted immediately before or immediately after George's interview.

Opt I

$$\overset{\displaystyle H}{\underset{1 \quad 2 \quad 3 \quad \overset{G}{4} \quad 5 \quad 6}{\text{—} \quad \text{—} \quad \text{—} \quad \text{—} \quad \text{—} \quad \text{—}}}$$

Opt II

$$\underset{1 \quad 2 \quad 3 \quad 4 \quad \overset{H}{5} \quad \overset{G}{6}}{\text{—} \quad \text{—} \quad \text{—} \quad \text{—} \quad \text{—} \quad \text{—}}$$

Since George is restricted to exactly two interview slots, and since his placement explicitly affects Hiromi's placement, George is a "Key Player," and dual Limited Options sketches are called for. Additional rules in this game should be built into both sketches whenever possible.

Number Restrictions

Number restrictions can occur in any type of game, but they are especially helpful in Distribution and Matching games. When the groups you are creating must fall into one of two number patterns, it is almost always worth it to create dual Limited Options sketches. Here's an example.

Five citizens—P, Q, X, Y, and Z—will vote in Country Y's upcoming parliamentary elections. Each citizen will vote for exactly one of three parties—the Conservative Party, the Economic Party, or the Reform Party. Each party receives a vote from at least one of the citizens. Votes are subject to the following criteria:

 Either two or three of the five citizens votes for the Economic Party.
 Q and Z both vote for the same party.

P Q X Y Z

Opt I

Con	Econ	Ref
— (—)	— —	— (—)

Opt II

Con	Econ	Ref
—	Q Z —	—

In this game, Option II, in which three citizens vote for the Economic Party, gives you an additional deduction: Q and Z, who must vote the same way, will definitely vote Economic because there is insufficient room for two votes in either of the other parties. Without additional rules, you can't make that same deduction in Option I because either Conservative or Reform could receive two votes (as represented by the slots in parentheses) in this option. Other rules in this game may allow you to make additional deductions in one or both options.

Blocks of Entities

In the previous example, the voting block of Q and Z could be placed concretely in one of the numbers-based options. In other games, however, it may be a block of entities that creates the Limited Option situation. Consider this Strict Sequencing example.

Six freshmen at a military academy—A, B, C, D, E, and G—will be assigned to six bunks, numbered 1 through 6, in the freshman dormitory. Each freshman is assigned to exactly one bunk.

 A is assigned to a bunk numbered two higher than the bunk to which G is assigned.
 D is assigned to bunk 4.

A̶ B C D̶ E G̶

Opt I	G	_	A	D	_	_
	1	2	3	4	5	6

Opt II	_	_	G	D	A	_
	1	2	3	4	5	6

Because D is an Established Entity, assigned once and for all to bunk 4, the block created by the G_A rule can be placed in exactly two places. Once you've created the dual sketches, you should incorporate this game's other rules into both sketches.

Limited Options can, in some cases, take you from dozens of possible arrangements down to just a handful, maybe as few as five or six. Indeed, it's not uncommon for one of the two options to be filled in entirely by the time you're done making all of the game's deductions.

In this Spotlight video, an LSAT Channel coach will take you through the game on the following pages. You'll see the awesome power of Limited Options in action.

Questions 1–6

On a Tuesday, an accountant has exactly seven bills—
numbered 1 through 7—to pay by Thursday of the same week.
The accountant will pay each bill only once according to the
following rules:

> Either three or four of the seven bills must be paid on
> Wednesday, the rest on Thursday.
> Bill 1 cannot be paid on the same day as bill 5.
> Bill 2 must be paid on Thursday.
> Bill 4 must be paid on the same day as bill 7.
> If bill 6 is paid on Wednesday, bill 7 must be paid on
> Thursday.

1. If exactly four bills are paid on Wednesday, then those
   four bills could be

   (A) 1, 3, 4, and 6
   (B) 1, 3, 5, and 6
   (C) 2, 4, 5, and 7
   (D) 3, 4, 5, and 7
   (E) 3, 4, 6, and 7

2. Which one of the following is a complete and accurate list of the bills any one of which could be among the bills paid on Wednesday?

(A) 3, 5, and 6
(B) 1, 3, 4, 6, and 7
(C) 1, 3, 4, 5, 6, and 7
(D) 2, 3, 4, 5, 6, and 7
(E) 1, 2, 3, 4, 5, 6, and 7

3. If bill 2 and bill 6 are paid on different days from each other, which one of the following must be true?

(A) Exactly three bills are paid on Wednesday.
(B) Exactly three bills are paid on Thursday.
(C) Bill 1 is paid on the same day as bill 4.
(D) Bill 2 is paid on the same day as bill 3.
(E) Bill 5 is paid on the same day as bill 7.

4. If bill 6 is paid on Wednesday, which one of the following bills must also be paid on Wednesday?

(A) 1
(B) 3
(C) 4
(D) 5
(E) 7

5. If bill 4 is paid on Thursday, which one of the following is a pair of bills that could also be paid on Thursday?

(A) 1 and 5
(B) 1 and 7
(C) 3 and 5
(D) 3 and 6
(E) 6 and 7

6. Which one of the following statements must be true?

(A) If bill 2 is paid on Thursday, bill 3 is paid on Wednesday.
(B) If bill 4 is paid on Thursday, bill 1 is paid on Wednesday.
(C) If bill 4 is paid on Thursday, bill 3 is paid on Wednesday.
(D) If bill 6 is paid on Thursday, bill 3 is also paid on Thursday.
(E) If bill 6 is paid on Thursday, bill 4 is also paid on Thursday.

PrepTest29 Sec3 Qs 1–6

Complete answers and explanations are provided in The LSAT Channel Spotlight video "Limited Options" in your online Study Plan.

CHAPTER 4

Logic Games Questions

This is where all of your work on Logic Games pays off. All that you've learned so far—how to conduct an Overview, build a Sketch, populate it with the Rules, and combine the rules to make Deductions—has prepared you for the skills you'll learn and practice here. If you've taken the preceding chapters seriously—if you've really conquered Steps 1 through 4 of the Logic Games Method—you may be surprised by how quickly and confidently you are able to answer Logic Games questions. Indeed, that's the reason that LSAT experts spend 3–4 minutes before tackling a game's questions doing the setup and critical-thinking steps that you've been practicing up to this point.

Nonetheless, there are still a few skills to learn to handle the Logic Games question sets efficiently and to avoid needless and costly mistakes. One of the biggest components of mastery in this chapter involves identifying, quickly and accurately, what each question is calling for. Many test takers lose points in the Logic Games section because, after having done strong analyses, they simply answer the wrong question. They might, for example, choose an answer that clearly must be true even though the question stem calls for the choice that could be false. Or, they pick out a scenario that could be true when the question credits only the choice that must be true. In the section of this chapter dedicated to Must Be/Could Be questions, you will learn to assess levels of certainty and truth values, a skill that will pay off when you practice New-"If" questions as well. Make sure to study these concepts carefully.

Other mistakes that poorly trained test takers make with Logic Games questions lead to wasted time and effort even when they don't lead to wrong answers. Students who try to test every choice by drawing innumerable diagrams lose time that an LSAT expert, confident in the deductions he has made in the Master Sketch, is able to preserve. Others, who are in too much of a hurry to draw even one new sketch (to account for a new condition in a New-"If" question stem, let's say), become so confused trying to hold dozens of arrangements in their heads that they can't quickly or confidently eliminate wrong answers.

In this chapter, you'll learn how best to handle every Logic Games question. We'll break the questions into a handful of question types and show you effective strategies for each one.

HOW TO ANSWER LOGIC GAMES QUESTIONS STRATEGICALLY

LEARNING OBJECTIVES

In this chapter, you'll learn to

- Identify the Logic Games question types,
- Characterize the correct and incorrect answer choices in each question type, and
- Apply the appropriate strategy to each question type.

Prepare

To answer a Logic Games question correctly, you will need to recognize the question type and be able to characterize the one correct and four incorrect answer choices. To then answer the question quickly and confidently, you'll need to apply the appropriate strategy. In the first part of this chapter, you'll learn all of the question types that appear in the Logic Games section of the LSAT, and the strategies and tactics associated with each one. The Prepare portion of the chapter is thus fairly lengthy. Whenever there is a question type that you saw in Chapter 1, you'll revisit it here to help activate your prior knowledge and make the strategies come to life.

To practice and assess your skill level in Logic Games questions you will, naturally, need full games. You can't answer the questions (at least not effectively) without the work you've done in the Overview, Sketch, Rules, and Deductions steps of the Logic Games Method. Therefore, in the Practice and Perform portions of this chapter, you will have the opportunity to answer all of the questions from the officially released games you've been setting up and analyzing in the previous chapters. You'll have additional opportunities to practice answering Logic Games questions in all of the game-type chapters that follow (Chapters 5–11).

LOGIC GAMES STRATEGY

Question Types appearing in the Logic Games section include:

- Acceptability Questions
- Must Be/Could Be Questions
- New-"If" Questions
- Other Question Types:
  - Complete and Accurate List Questions
  - Completely Determine Questions
  - Numerical Questions
    - Minimum/Maximum
    - Earliest/Latest
    - "How Many"
  - Rule Alteration Questions
    - Rule Change
    - Rule Substitution
  - Supply the "If" Questions

The first three items in that list—Acceptability, Must Be/Could Be, and New-"If" questions—are, by far, the most frequent question types in the Logic Games section, and you'll spend the bulk of your practice time on them. The remaining question types are fairly infrequent, and on some tests, some of them may not appear at all. While it is important that you are able to recognize them and to understand what they are asking for, you do not need to dedicate as much study and practice to them. If one of these question types comes up in a game you're studying, and you don't remember how LSAT experts approach it efficiently, come back to this chapter to refresh your memory.

Types of Questions By Percentage, 2012–16

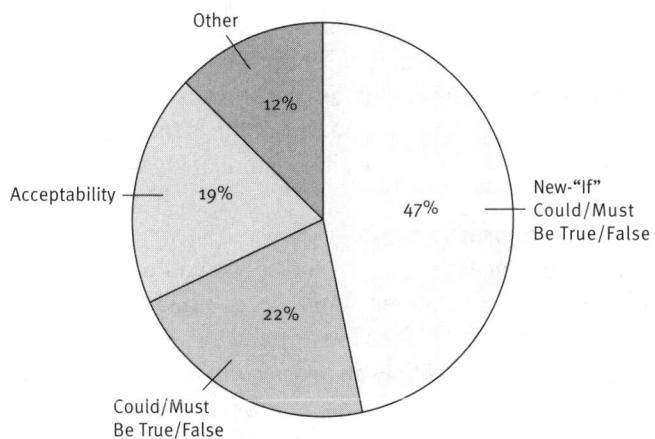

PrepTests 66–80; released 2012–2016

Logic Games Question Types

Now, take a look at the various question types in more detail.

Acceptability Questions

Most LSAT logic games feature one Acceptability question, and usually, it is the first question in the set. On rare occasions, you'll find a game with no Acceptability question, and very rarely, a game with two. You'll learn to look forward to Acceptability questions because they can be answered correctly in a matter of seconds once you learn to use the suggested strategy.

Identifying Acceptability Questions

Acceptability questions ask for an arrangement or selection of the entities in the game that does not violate any of the game's rules or restrictions. You can recognize Acceptability questions from question stems like these:

> Which one of the following is an acceptable schedule of all of the dentist's appointments for the day?

> Which one of the following could be an accurate account of the doctors who work at each of the town's three clinics?

> Which one of the following could be a complete and accurate list of employees chosen to attend the company retreat?

Note: From time to time, you will see Partial Acceptability questions that ask for an acceptable arrangement of part of the game's full setup. The question stems for Partial Acceptability might look like this:

> Which one of the following is an acceptable schedule of the dentist's first three appointments for the day?

> Which one of the following could be an accurate account of the doctors who work in Clinics A and B?

Don't let Partial Acceptability question stems throw you. The characteristics of the right and wrong answers, and the strategy you will use to answer these questions, are exactly the same as those in regular Acceptability questions. Just make sure you are concentrating on the parts of the game's setup designated by the question stem.

Characterizing the Answer Choices in Acceptability Questions

It is almost tautological to say that the correct answer to an Acceptability question is "acceptable." A more helpful characterization of the correct answer choice here is that it is the one answer choice that does *not* violate any of the game's rules or restrictions. The reason that definition is more helpful is that it allows you to easily comprehend the four wrong answers; they are the answers that *do* violate one or more of the game's rules or restrictions.

Answering Acceptability Questions Strategically

By characterizing the one correct and four incorrect answer choices as you've just seen, you avail yourself of one of the Logic Games section's biggest time saving strategies: Answer Acceptability questions by testing the rules one by one against the answer choices. Start with Rule 1. Cross out any and all answer choices that break this rule. Indeed, strike through the entire answer choice; once you know an answer violates one rule, there is no need to check it against any of the others. Move on to Rule 2, and repeat the process on only those answer choices that did not violate Rule 1. Continue this process with the remaining rules until only one choice remains. That's the correct answer, the one that violates none of the rules. Circle it, and move on to the next question.

Untrained test takers will often instinctively try to answer Acceptability questions "backward," by checking each answer choice to see if it violates any of the rules. This is terribly time consuming because, when you check answer choice (A), you don't know if it violates Rule 1, Rule 2, Rule 3, or Rule 4, or if it is the correct answer and does not violate any of the rules. The same applies to choices (B), (C), (D), and (E). You could wind up checking each answer choice against multiple rules before settling on the correct answer.

Refresh (Activate Prior Knowledge)

Take another look at the Acceptability question from the Truck Arrivals game that you first saw in Chapter 1. This time, it will be broken down so that you can see the LSAT expert's analysis rule-by-rule, as described in the strategy. Take a moment to refresh your memory of the game, and then try applying the strategy to the question. After you've given it a shot, follow along as the expert tests the rules against the answer choices.

LSAT Question	Analysis
In a single day, exactly seven trucks—S, T, U, W, X, Y, and Z—are the only arrivals at a warehouse. No truck arrives at the same time as any other truck, and no truck arrives more than once that day. Each truck is either green or red (but not both). The following conditions apply: No two consecutive arrivals are red. Y arrives at some time before both T and W. Exactly two of the trucks that arrive before Y are red. S is the sixth arrival. Z arrives at some time before U.	**Steps 1-4:** $\cancel{S}$ T U W X $\cancel{Y}$ Z X $\overbrace{\rule{2cm}{0pt}}$ __ __ __ Y T/W S W/T 1 2 3 4 5 6 7 g/r r g r g __ __ __ never [r r] Z...U

1.	Which one of the following could be the order, from first to last, in which the trucks arrive?	**Step 5: Questions** → An Acceptability question: Test the rules, one by one, against the answer choices.
	(A) X, Z, U, Y, W, S, T	→
	(B) X, Y, Z, U, W, S, T	→
	(C) Z, W, U, T, Y, S, X	→
	(D) Z, U, T, Y, W, S, X	→
	(E) U, Z, Y, T, S, W, X	→

PrepTest37 Sec3 Q6

Test Rule 1:

LSAT Question	Analysis

In a single day, exactly seven trucks—S, T, U, W, X, Y, and Z—are the only arrivals at a warehouse. No truck arrives at the same time as any other truck, and no truck arrives more than once that day. Each truck is either green or red (but not both). The following conditions apply:

    No two consecutive arrivals are red.

    Y arrives at some time before both T and W.

    Exactly two of the trucks that arrive before Y are red.

    S is the sixth arrival.

    Z arrives at some time before U.

Steps 1-4:

S̸ T U W X Y̸ Z

X
⎧‾‾‾‾‾‾‾‾⎫
__ __ __ Y T/W S W/T
 1   2   3   4   5   6   7

g/r   r   g   r   g   __ __ __

never [r r]   Z...U

---

1. Which one of the following could be the order, from first to last, in which the trucks arrive?

Step 5: Questions

An Acceptability question: Test the rules, one by one, against the answer choices. The answer choices show only the trucks, not their colors, so Rule 1 is of no help here.

  (A)   X, Z, U, Y, W, S, T

  (B)   X, Y, Z, U, W, S, T

  (C)   Z, W, U, T, Y, S, X

  (D)   Z, U, T, Y, W, S, X

  (E)   U, Z, Y, T, S, W, X

PrepTest37 Sec3 Q6

Technically, this is a Partial Acceptability question, since this question asks only about the order of the trucks' arrivals (Sequencing) while the full game also calls for you to assign each truck a color (Matching). Remember that the same strategy still applies. It happens from time to time, as it did here, that a rule doesn't eliminate any of the answer choices in an Acceptability or Partial Acceptability question. An LSAT expert just moves on to test Rule 2:

LSAT Question	Analysis
In a single day, exactly seven trucks—S, T, U, W, X, Y, and Z—are the only arrivals at a warehouse. No truck arrives at the same time as any other truck, and no truck arrives more than once that day. Each truck is either green or red (but not both). The following conditions apply: No two consecutive arrivals are red. Y arrives at some time before both T and W. Exactly two of the trucks that arrive before Y are red. S is the sixth arrival. Z arrives at some time before U.	**Steps 1-4:**

1.	Which one of the following could be the order, from first to last, in which the trucks arrive?	**Step 5: Questions** The answer choices show only the trucks, not their colors, so Rule 1 is of no help in this question. Rule 2 knocks out two answer choices: (C) and (D), in which either W or T appears earlier than Y. Strike through those two choices.
	(A) X, Z, U, Y, W, S, T	
	(B) X, Y, Z, U, W, S, T	
	(C) ~~Z, W, U, T, Y, S, X~~	Violates Rule 2 by placing Trucks W and T earlier in the sequence than Truck Y. Eliminate.
	(D) ~~Z, U, T, Y, W, S, X~~	Violates Rule 2 by placing Truck T earlier in the sequence than Truck Y. Eliminate.
	(E) U, Z, Y, T, S, W, X	

PrepTest37 Sec3 Q6

Now, that's progress. Keep going, and test Rule 3:

LSAT Question	Analysis

In a single day, exactly seven trucks—S, T, U, W, X, Y, and Z—are the only arrivals at a warehouse. No truck arrives at the same time as any other truck, and no truck arrives more than once that day. Each truck is either green or red (but not both). The following conditions apply:

    No two consecutive arrivals are red.
    Y arrives at some time before both T and W.
    Exactly two of the trucks that arrive before Y are red.
    S is the sixth arrival.
    Z arrives at some time before U.

Steps 1-4:

$\not{S}$ T U W X $\not{Y}$ Z

never [r r]   Z...U

1.   Which one of the following could be the order, from first to last, in which the trucks arrive?

Step 5: Questions

The answer choices show only the trucks, not their colors, so Rule 1 is of no help in this question. Rule 2 knocks out two answer choices: (C) and (D), in which either W or T appears earlier than Y. Strike through those two choices. Rule 3 knocks out choice (B), where Y is placed too early to have two red trucks precede it in the sequence.

(A)   X, Z, U, Y, W, S, T

(B)   ~~X, Y, Z, U, W, S, T~~

Violates Rule 3 by placing Y in a position that cannot be preceded by two red trucks. Eliminate.

(C)   ~~Z, W, U, T, Y, S, X~~

Violates Rule 2 by placing Trucks W and T earlier in the sequence than Truck Y. Eliminate.

(D)   ~~Z, U, T, Y, W, S, X~~

Violates Rule 2 by placing Truck T earlier in the sequence than Truck Y. Eliminate.

(E)   U, Z, Y, T, S, W, X

PrepTest37 Sec3 Q6

K

Now, you need eliminate only more answer choice, and you'll have the correct answer spotted. Test Rule 4:

LSAT Question	Analysis
In a single day, exactly seven trucks—S, T, U, W, X, Y, and Z—are the only arrivals at a warehouse. No truck arrives at the same time as any other truck, and no truck arrives more than once that day. Each truck is either green or red (but not both). The following conditions apply: 　No two consecutive arrivals are red. 　Y arrives at some time before both T and W. 　Exactly two of the trucks that arrive before Y are red. 　S is the sixth arrival. 　Z arrives at some time before U. $\longrightarrow$	**Steps 1-4:**

1.	Which one of the following could be the order, from first to last, in which the trucks arrive?	$\longrightarrow$	**Step 5: Questions** The answer choices show only the trucks, not their colors, so Rule 1 is of no help in this question. Rule 2 knocks out two answer choices: (C) and (D), in which either W or T appears earlier than Y. Strike through those two choices. Rule 3 knocks out choice (B), in which Y is placed too early to have two red trucks precede it in the sequence. Rule 4 knocks out choice (E), in which S is fifth, not sixth.
(A)	X, Z, U, Y, W, S, T	$\longrightarrow$	Correct. This answer choice does not violate any of the rules.
(B)	~~X, Y, Z, U, W, S, T~~	$\longrightarrow$	Violates Rule 3 by placing Truck Y in a position that cannot be preceded by two red trucks. Eliminate.
(C)	~~Z, W, U, T, Y, S, X~~	$\longrightarrow$	Violates Rule 2 by placing Trucks W and T earlier in the sequence than Truck Y. Eliminate.
(D)	~~Z, U, T, Y, W, S, X~~	$\longrightarrow$	Violates Rule 2 by placing Truck T earlier in the sequence than Truck Y. Eliminate.
(E)	~~U, Z, Y, T, S, W, X~~ *PrepTest37 Sec3 Q6*	$\longrightarrow$	Violates Rule 4 by placing Truck S fifth, not sixth. Eliminate.

By crossing out the wrong answer choices as soon as it is clear that they violate even one of the rules, the LSAT expert makes short work of any Acceptability question. Practice this strategy whenever you encounter an Acceptability question associated with any of the games throughout the remainder of this book. You will soon get to the point where you can confidently answer these questions in a matter of 30 seconds or less.

A Note on Complete and Accurate List Questions

One of the model question stems in the description of Acceptability questions had the following wording:

> Which one of the following could be a complete and accurate list of employees chosen to attend the company retreat?

That particular wording amounts to asking for an acceptable selection, and the correct answer will represent one possible "solution" to the game.

It's worth noting, however, that the testmaker will occasionally use the phrase "complete and accurate list" for questions that focus on a narrower part of the game. In a Sequencing game, for example, one of these questions might ask for "a complete and accurate list of the days on which Johnson's appointment may be scheduled." In a Distribution game, on the other hand, you might run across a question such as "Which one of the following is a complete and accurate list of all players who could play on Team B?"

For Complete and Accurate List questions such as these, the correct answer must contain any and all of the acceptable slots or entities called for by the question stem. In other words, each wrong answer will either be incomplete—it will not contain all of the days on which Johnson's appointment can be scheduled, or it will be missing players who are eligible for Team B—or the wrong answer will be inaccurate—it will include days on which Johnson's appointment cannot be scheduled or players ineligible for Team B. That makes sense when you think about the question. If the right answer is "complete and accurate," all four wrong answers must be incomplete or inaccurate (or both).

You will recognize Complete and Accurate List questions from question stems like the following, but don't spend too much time trying to hunt down examples of this rare question type.

> Which one of the following is a complete and accurate list of the cars any one of which could be among the cars washed on Tuesday?

> Which one of the following is a complete and accurate list of the days on which Isobel could shop for groceries?

When you do come across Complete and Accurate List questions, don't panic or change your strategic approach to logic games. These questions are too rare to be a type that makes or breaks your score. Just distinguish them from Acceptability questions and remember that the wrong answers are always inaccurate or incomplete (or both). Once you've characterized the answer choices, you just consult the Master Sketch to eliminate the violators and find the right answer.

Must Be/Could Be Questions

The majority of games in any administration of the LSAT have at least one, and often two or more, Must Be/Could Be questions. These questions simply test what must, can, or cannot be true of the arrangement or selection of the entities in the game. Must Be/Could Be question stems do not add any additional conditions or stipulations to the game's original rules and restrictions, and thus, they can always be answered with reference to the Master Sketch containing all of the game's available deductions.

Identifying Must Be/Could Be Questions

Some Must Be/Could Be question stems are straightforward and easy to recognize:

Which one of the following must be true?

Which one of the following could be true?

Which one of the following must be false?

Which one of the following could be false?

Other Must Be/Could Be question stems ask for the same types of analysis by introducing a negative term:

Each of the following could be false EXCEPT: (Note that the correct answer here *must be true*)

Which one of the following CANNOT be true? (Note that the correct answer here *must be false*)

Each of the following must be true EXCEPT: (Note that the correct answer here *could be false*)

Finally, some Must Be/Could Be questions include information that is specific to the setup or entities in the game:

Which one of the following lists a pair of doctors who must work at the same clinic?

Which one of the following is a patient that the dentist CANNOT see at 2:00 PM?

Must Be/Could Be questions are easy to identify. The challenge in these questions is to make sure that you are absolutely clear about the characteristics of the correct and incorrect answers.

Characterizing the Answer Choices in Must Be/Could Be Questions

In real life, you rarely think in "negatives" as you make decisions. It would seem strange, for example, to look at a menu and ask, "Which one of these sandwiches can I *not* choose for lunch?" Even on most tests you've taken in school, the *correct* answer has always equated to the *true* answer. On the LSAT, however, many questions ask for what must be false or what could be false, so you must characterize what you are looking for before evaluating the answer choices.

LOGIC GAMES STRATEGY

On the LSAT, never confuse *true* and *false* statements with *right* and *wrong* answers. Always characterize what you're looking for before evaluating the answer choices.

Some LSAT experts even find it helpful to note what they're looking for in the test booklet. For example, next to a Must Be False question, they might jot down "1 MBF/4 CBT" to signify that the correct answer must be false while the four incorrect answer choices could be true.

Even when the characteristics of the correct answer are clear in your mind, it may be easier to identify incorrect answers as you are evaluating the choices. You've seen a variation of this in Acceptability questions, where applying the rules makes it faster to eliminate the four *unacceptable* choices than it would be to ask repeatedly "Is this answer choice acceptable? How about this one?" and so on.

In Logic Games, the answer choices are never equivocal; there is one choice that meets the criteria of the question stem, and four choices that do not. LSAT experts always identify the characteristics of both the correct and incorrect answers before evaluating the answer choices. The following chart shows how the right and wrong answer characteristics line up.

When the correct answer . . .	Then, the wrong answers . . .
Must Be True	Could Be False*
Could Be True	Must Be False
Must Be False	Could Be True**
Could Be False	Must Be True

*Any answer choice that must be false would qualify as a wrong answer in this case. After all, any statement that must be false certainly could be false.

**Any answer choice that must be true would qualify as a wrong answer in this case. After all, any statement that must be true certainly could be true.

Having that chart memorized will help you avoid costly mistakes on Test Day. If you evaluate an answer choice and conclude that the statement it contains *must be true*, the chart indicates whether that choice is correct or incorrect. To see this in action, consider the following scenario:

In Country X, exactly one person serves as president at any given time. Thompkins was Country X's first president. Evaluate the truth value of the following statements:

- Jerome was the first president of Country X. [Must be false]
- Jerome was the second president of Country X. [Could be true or false]
- Jerome was not the first president of Country X. [Must be true]

Now, imagine that a question asked, "Which one of the statements must be true?" In that case, the correct answer would be the third statement, and the first two statements would be incorrect. On the other hand, if the question asked, "Which one of the statements must be false?" then the first statement would be the correct answer while the second and third would be incorrect.

Try your hand at characterizing the one right and four wrong answer choices in a handful of question stems. When you're finished, compare your analysis to that of an LSAT expert.

Exercise

Directions: For each of the following question stems, characterize the one correct and the four incorrect answer choices. An LSAT expert's analysis is shown on the pages following the exercise.

Question Stem	My Analysis
1. Which of the following must be true? $\longrightarrow$	The correct answer: The four wrong answer choices:
2. Which of the following could be false? $\longrightarrow$	The correct answer: The four wrong answer choices:
3. Which of the following applicants CANNOT be selected for the managerial position? $\longrightarrow$	The correct answer: The four wrong answer choices:
4. If the painting is the fourth item sold, which of the following could be the fifth item sold? $\longrightarrow$	The correct answer: The four wrong answer choices:
5. Each of the following could be true EXCEPT: $\longrightarrow$	The correct answer: The four wrong answer choices:
6. Which of the following is an acceptable order in which the cars are repaired? $\longrightarrow$	The correct answer: The four wrong answer choices:

Question Stem		My Analysis
7. Alexander could be placed on a team with any of the following EXCEPT:	→	The correct answer: The four wrong answer choices:
8. Which of the following is a pair of items that CANNOT both be included in the display?	→	The correct answer: The four wrong answer choices:
9. Each of the following must be false EXCEPT:	→	The correct answer: The four wrong answer choices:
10. If Brianna is assigned to the history project, then which of the following students must be assigned to the science project?	→	The correct answer: The four wrong answer choices:
11. Which of the following speeches could be presented third?	→	The correct answer: The four wrong answer choices:
12. Which of the following musicians must perform on Monday if Evan performs on Friday?	→	The correct answer: The four wrong answer choices:
13. If Samantha travels to France, then Taylor must travel to	→	The correct answer: The four wrong answer choices:

Question Stem		My Analysis
14. Which of the following could be a complete and accurate assignment of interns to the company's departments?	→	The correct answer: The four wrong answer choices:
15. The color of the fourth garment purchased CANNOT be	→	The correct answer: The four wrong answer choices:
16. The violinist must be seated immediately next to	→	The correct answer: The four wrong answer choices:
17. If astronomy is offered, it could be offered on any day of the week EXCEPT:	→	The correct answer: The four wrong answer choices:
18. Which of the following pieces of furniture could be placed with the divan in the Woodcrest Room?	→	The correct answer: The four wrong answer choices:
19. Which of the following dogs could be scheduled for the first appointment?	→	The correct answer: The four wrong answer choices:
20. Bacon must be included in which of the following meals?	→	The correct answer: The four wrong answer choices:

Expert Analysis

Here's how an LSAT expert would characterize the correct and incorrect answer choices for each of those question stems.

1.	Which of the following must be true?	The correct answer must be true.
	→	The four wrong answer choices could be false (or must be false).

2.	Which of the following could be false?	The correct answer could be false.
	→	The four wrong answer choices must be true.

3.	Which of the following applicants CANNOT be selected for the managerial position?	The correct answer must be false. Here, that means someone who must not be selected for the managerial position.
	→	Wrong answer choices will list applicants who could or must be selected for the managerial position.

4.	If the painting is the fourth item sold, which of the following could be the fifth item sold?	The correct answer could be true, which in this case means could be sold fifth.
	→	Wrong answer choices must be false, which means they must not be sold fifth.

5.	Each of the following could be true EXCEPT:	The correct answer must be false.
	→	Wrong answer choices could be true (or must be true).

6.	Which of the following is an acceptable order in which the cars are repaired?	An "acceptable order" is one that could be true.
	→	Wrong answer choices will be unacceptable, which means they must be false.

7. Alexander could be placed on a team with any of the following EXCEPT:

→

The correct answer must be false, which here means a person with whom Alexander must not be teamed.

Wrong answer choices will list people who could (or must) be on a team with Alexander.

8. Which of the following is a pair of items that CANNOT both be included in the display?

→

The correct answer must be false, which here means the two items must not be included together. They may be included individually, but not *together*.

Wrong answer choices will list pairs of items that could be included together.

9. Each of the following must be false EXCEPT:

→

The correct answer could (or must) be true.

Wrong answer choices must be false.

10. If Brianna is assigned to the history project, then which of the following students must be assigned to the science project?

→

The correct answer must be true, which here means someone who must be assigned to the science project.

Wrong answer choices could be false, i.e., students who may not (or cannot) be assigned to the science project.

11. Which of the following speeches could be presented third?

→

The correct answer could be true. In this case, a speech that could be third.

Wrong answer choices must be false, i.e., speeches that must not be third.

12. Which of the following musicians must perform on Monday if Evan performs on Friday?

→ The correct answer must be true, which here means a musician who must perform on Monday.

Wrong answer choices could be false, which means musicians who might not (or cannot) perform on Monday.

13. If Samantha travels to France, then Taylor must travel to

→ The correct answer must be true, which here means a place to which Taylor must travel.

Wrong answer choices could be false, which means places to which Taylor may not (or does not) travel.

14. Which of the following could be a complete and accurate assignment of interns to the company's departments?

→ The correct answer could be true, which here means an acceptable assignment of interns.

Wrong answer choices must be false, which means they describe assignments that are impossible.

15. The color of the fourth garment purchased CANNOT be

→ The correct answer must be false, which here means a color that fourth garment must not be.

Wrong answer choices could be true, which means they list colors the fourth garment could be.

16. The violinist must be seated immediately next to

→ The correct answer must be true, which here means someone who must sit next to the violinist.

Wrong answer choices could be false, which means people who might not (or do not) sit next to the violinist.

17. If astronomy is offered, it could be offered on any day of the week EXCEPT:

→ The correct answer must be false, which here means a day on which astronomy must not be offered.

Wrong answer choices could be true, which means days on which astronomy could be offered.

18. Which of the following pieces of furniture could be placed with the divan in the Woodcrest Room?

The correct answer could be true, which here means a piece of furniture that could be placed in the Woodcrest Room along with the divan.

$\longrightarrow$

Wrong answer choices must be false, which means pieces of furniture that cannot be placed in the Woodcrest Room along with the divan.

19. Which of the following dogs could be scheduled for the first appointment?

The correct answer could be true, which here means a dog that could be scheduled first.

$\longrightarrow$

Wrong answer choices must be false, which means dogs that must not be scheduled first.

20. Bacon must be included in which of the following meals?

The correct answer must be true, which here means a meal which must include bacon.

$\longrightarrow$

Wrong answer choices could be false, which means meals that might not (or definitely do not) include bacon—a sad thought, for sure.

Once you are comfortable characterizing the answer choices in Must Be/Could Be questions, the hardest part is over. Most of these questions can be answered simply by consulting the Master Sketch.

Answering Must Be/Could Be Questions Strategically

Must Be/Could Be questions reveal how important Steps 1 through 4 of the Logic Games Method are. By taking the time to sketch out a framework for the game's action, draw the rules into or underneath it, and make the available deductions, you uncover all that can be known about what must, could, and cannot be true within the game. Now, you can evaluate any answer choice in a Must Be/Could Be question by comparing it to the Master Sketch: "Can this statement be true? Does it have to be false?" and so on.

In some cases, your sketch will be so precise that you can even anticipate what the testmaker might ask. Imagine a Sequencing game in which you can deduce that a dentist's second appointment is with Matt. It's common, in such cases, for the test to ask a Must Be True question for which the correct answer is "The dentist sees Matt second." Likewise, in a Distribution game, you may be able to deduce that Catherine is never on Team 2. That deduction would lend itself perfectly to a Must Be False question.

Even when questions don't relate quite so obviously to the deductions, the Master Sketch contains the information you need to evaluate the answer choices. You can see this in the two Must Be/Could Be questions associated with the Truck Arrivals game from Chapter 1.

Refresh (Activate Prior Knowledge)

The first Must Be/Could Be question in the Truck Arrivals game was a Must Be False variant. That question asked for a pair of trucks that could *not* both be red. Review the LSAT expert's analysis of the question.

LSAT Question	Analysis
In a single day, exactly seven trucks—S, T, U, W, X, Y, and Z—are the only arrivals at a warehouse. No truck arrives at the same time as any other truck, and no truck arrives more than once that day. Each truck is either green or red (but not both). The following conditions apply: No two consecutive arrivals are red. Y arrives at some time before both T and W. Exactly two of the trucks that arrive before Y are red. S is the sixth arrival. Z arrives at some time before U.	**Steps 1-4:** $\cancel{S}$ T U W X $\cancel{Y}$ Z X ⎴ __ __ __ Y T/W S W/T 1 2 3 4 5 6 7 g/r r g r g __ __ __ never ⬚ r r ⬚ Z...U
2. For which one of the following pairs of trucks is it the case that they CANNOT both be red?	**Step 5: Questions** A Must Be False question: Consult the Master Sketch to evaluate the answer choices. The Trucks in the correct answer cannot both be red. The Trucks in the wrong answers *could* both be red.
(A) S and X	S could be red if the trucks in slots 5 and 7 are green, and X could be in slot 1 or 3. Both could be red. Eliminate.
(B) T and S	Correct. T and S will be in consecutive slots (whether T is fifth or seventh). Rule 1 prevents consecutive trucks from both being red. T and S *cannot* both be red.
(C) U and W	W could be red in either the fifth or seventh slot, as long as slot 6 is green, and U could be in slot 3. Both could be red. Eliminate.
(D) W and T	Slots 5 and 7 could both be red, as long as slot 6 is green. Both could be red. Eliminate.
(E) X and Z	Z could be in slot 1 and X could be in slot 3. Both could be red. Eliminate.

PrepTest37 Sec3 Q7

Notice how the LSAT expert characterized the one right and four wrong answers before evaluating the choices. Because the LSAT expert has recorded Rule 1 (which prevents consecutive trucks from both being red) and has added Trucks S and T to the Master Sketch, it is clear that choice (B) must be false, and is, therefore, correct.

The final question from that game was another Must Be False variant. Review the expert's analysis.

LSAT Question	Analysis
In a single day, exactly seven trucks—S, T, U, W, X, Y, and Z—are the only arrivals at a warehouse. No truck arrives at the same time as any other truck, and no truck arrives more than once that day. Each truck is either green or red (but not both). The following conditions apply: No two consecutive arrivals are red. Y arrives at some time before both T and W. Exactly two of the trucks that arrive before Y are red. S is the sixth arrival. Z arrives at some time before U.	**Steps 1-4:**

Steps 1-4:

~~S~~ T U W X ~~Y~~ Z

$$X$$

never $\boxed{r \quad r}$ Z...U

6.	Which one of the following pairs of trucks CANNOT arrive consecutively at the warehouse?	→	**Step 5: Questions** A Must Be False question: Test each answer choice against the Master Sketch. Eliminate any choice in which the pair of trucks *could* arrive consecutively. The correct answer cites a pair of trucks that *cannot* arrive consecutively.
	(A) U and Y	→	Truck Y is always in slot 4. Truck U could be in slot 3. Eliminate.
	(B) X and Y	→	Truck Y is always in slot 4. Truck X could be in slot 3. Eliminate.
	(C) Y and T	→	Truck Y is always in slot 4. Truck T could be in slot 5. Eliminate.
	(D) Y and W	→	Truck Y is always in slot 4. Truck W could be in slot 5. Eliminate.
	(E) Y and Z *PrepTest37 Sec3 Q11*	→	Correct. Truck Y is always in slot 4. Truck Z can be only in slots 1 or 2. These trucks can never be consecutive.

Once again, adding the deductions to the Master Sketch proves decisive. Once the LSAT expert has characterized the correct answer (a pair of trucks that *cannot* arrive consecutively), choice (E) is clearly the winner. By also characterizing the four wrong answer choices (a pair of trucks that can arrive consecutively), the expert can quickly eliminate (A), (B), (C), and (D).

Evaluating the Answer Choices by Making Sketches

Every once in a while, you may encounter a Must Be/Could Be question in which you need to sketch out the implications of an answer choice to know for certain whether it must, can, or cannot be true. In such cases, first eliminate any answers that are clearly incorrect based on the Master Sketch. As you do so, you may locate the correct answer, in which case, you're done, and there is no reason to continue checking the remaining choices. If, however, you still need to test two or more answer choices, quickly copy the Master Sketch framework, and fill in the information from one of the remaining answer choices so that you can evaluate that choice against the criteria of the correct and incorrect answers. Continue this process until you have spotted the right answer, or you have eliminated all four wrong answers.

Don't fall into the pattern of always sketching out every answer choice. That is unnecessarily time consuming. Look first to test the answer choices against the Master Sketch. In most cases, that will be sufficient.

Evaluating Conditional Answer Choices

One rare case that calls for new sketches happens when a Must Be/Could Be question has answer choices that are conditional. For example, you might see something like this:

> Which one of the following must be true?
> (A)   If the dentist sees Joanna third, then he must see Kim fifth.
> (B)   If the dentist sees Kim at some time after he sees Matt, then he must see Carlton fourth.
> (C)   . . . .

While it may be possible for you to picture the condition described in the first clause of each answer choice in your mind and to see its implications, it is safer to quickly copy the Master Sketch and to add the condition in writing. Once you've made any additional deductions triggered by the condition, you can evaluate your new sketch against the rules to determine if the statement in the second clause of the answer choice must, can, or cannot be true.

If all five of the answer choices are conditional (an extremely rare case, indeed), these questions can be quite time consuming. You may find it more strategic to skip the question and come back to it only if you have time remaining for the game. If not, you are probably better off guessing on a question like this and saving your time for the next game and all of its questions.

Evaluating Answer Choices by Using Previous Work

If you are stuck on a particular Must Be/Could Be question, you may be able to use the work you've done on another question to help you evaluate one or more of the answer choices. For example, once you have completed an Acceptability question, its correct answer serves as one acceptable "solution" for the game. Thus, any arrangement seen in that answer choice *could be true*. Thus, if an answer choice in a subsequent Must Be False question describes an arrangement seen in the correct answer of the Acceptability question, that answer choice will be *incorrect* in the Must Be False question.

The Special Feature that follows this chapter goes into the strategy of Using Previous Work in detail and illustrates it with a game you haven't seen before in this book. If you have time in your study schedule, read that Special Feature section and watch the accompanying video. The LSAT Channel expert will show you the ins and outs of using this strategy.

New-"If" Questions

New-"If" questions are the most common question type in every Logic Games section. Most (though not all) games have two or more New-"If" questions. Such a question is distinguished by the first clause of its question stem, which always adds a condition to the game's original setup and rules. While this makes the question stem longer (and seemingly more complicated) than most Must Be/Could Be question stems, the additional restriction serves to limit the number of acceptable arrangements in the game, and thus, often makes New-"If" questions even easier to answer.

Identifying New-"If" Questions

These questions are easy to spot; their question stems almost always begin with the word "If." Every once in a while, you might see "Suppose" or another synonym for "If" at the beginning of the stem, but once you spot the fact that the stem is adding a new condition, you'll know you have a question of this type. Here are some model New-"If" question stems:

> If the dentist sees Kim third, then which one of the following must be false?

> If two doctors are assigned to work at Clinic 3, then each of the following could be false EXCEPT

> Suppose that Karl is chosen to attend the company retreat; in that case, which one of the following is a pair of employees who CANNOT both attend the retreat?

In each case, it is the stem's first clause—the newly added condition—that distinguishes these as New-"If" questions.

Characterizing the Answer Choices in New-"If" Questions

It may have struck you that the second clause in each of those stems sounds like a Must Be/Could Be question. That's typical, and it means that once you are comfortable characterizing the one right and four wrong answers in Must Be/Could Be questions, you can do so just as efficiently and effectively in New-"If" questions, too. Here's how an LSAT expert would characterize the answer choices for the question stems you just saw.

> If the dentist sees Kim third, then which one of the following must be false?

Given this question's new condition (Kim has the third appointment), the correct answer must be false, and the four wrong answers could (or must) be true.

> If two doctors are assigned to work at Clinic 3, then each of the following could be false EXCEPT

Given this question's new condition (two doctors serve at Clinic 3), the correct answer must be true, and the four wrong answers could be false.

> Suppose that Karl is chosen to attend the company retreat; in that case, which one of the following is a pair of employees who CANNOT both attend the retreat?

Given this question's new condition (Karl is selected), the correct answer is a pair of employees who cannot both be selected, and the four wrong answers are pairs of employees who *can* both be selected.

Answering New-"If" Questions Strategically

The strategic aspect of dealing with New-"If" questions relates to how you account for the question's new condition. In most cases, you will do so by creating a new sketch for each specific New-"If" question. The best approach is to copy your Master Sketch framework next to the New-"If" question, add in the new rule or restriction given in the question stem, and make any additional deductions available. Once it's complete, you can use the resulting sketch to evaluate the New-"If" question's answer choices.

Don't balk at the prospect of making these new sketches; doing so actually *saves* time. Every time you add a rule or restriction to a logic game, it reduces the number of acceptable outcomes in the game. The sketches that result from New-"If" question stems usually have very little ambiguity, so you can be quick and confident when evaluating the answer choices. Trying to hold all of the game's information in your head along with the question's new condition will lead to hesitation and mistakes.

Refresh (Activate Prior Knowledge)

The Truck Arrivals game had two New-"If" questions, and both of them illustrate the new sketch strategy. Take a few minutes to review the expert's work on the first of these questions.

LSAT Question	Analysis

In a single day, exactly seven trucks—S, T, U, W, X, Y, and Z—are the only arrivals at a warehouse. No truck arrives at the same time as any other truck, and no truck arrives more than once that day. Each truck is either green or red (but not both). The following conditions apply:

    No two consecutive arrivals are red.
    Y arrives at some time before both T and W.
    Exactly two of the trucks that arrive before Y are red.
    S is the sixth arrival.
    Z arrives at some time before U.

→

Steps 1-4:

S̸ T U W X Ẏ Z

       X

			Y	T/W	S	W/T
__	__	__	__	__	__	__
1	2	3	4	5	6	7

g/r   r   g   r   g   _   _   _

never | r   r | Z...U

---

3. If X is the third arrival, then which one of the following trucks must be green?

→

Step 5: Questions

Placing Truck X in slot 3 means than Truck Z must take slot 1 and Truck U must take slot 2.

S̸ T Ủ W X̸ Ẏ Z̸

→

Z	U	X	Y	T/W	S	W/T
1	2	3	4	5	6	7

g/r   r   g   r   g   _   _   _

Thus, truck U must be green.

(A)	S	→ Truck S could be either green or red. Eliminate.
(B)	T	→ Truck T could be either green or red. Eliminate.
(C)	U	→ Correct. Under this question's conditions, Truck U must be green.
(D)	W	→ Truck W could be either green or red. Eliminate.
(E)	Z	→ Under this question's conditions, Truck Z must be red. Eliminate.

PrepTest37 Sec3 Q8

In that question, the new condition (placing Truck X third) resulted in five of the seven trucks' positions being firmly established. Evaluating the choices took the expert only a few seconds with the new sketch in place.

The second New-"If" question in that game required a bit more in the way of deductions, but the results were equally clear. Take a few minutes to look it over again now.

LSAT Question	Analysis
In a single day, exactly seven trucks—S, T, U, W, X, Y, and Z—are the only arrivals at a warehouse. No truck arrives at the same time as any other truck, and no truck arrives more than once that day. Each truck is either green or red (but not both). The following conditions apply: 　No two consecutive arrivals are red. 　Y arrives at some time before both T and W. 　Exactly two of the trucks that arrive before Y are red. 　S is the sixth arrival. 　Z arrives at some time before U.	**Steps 1-4:** S̷ T U W X Y̷ Z 　　　　X 　⎛‾‾‾‾⎞ 　__ __ __ Y T/W S W/T 　1　2　3　4　5　6　7 g/r　r　g　r　g　__ __ __ never [r　r]　Z…U

4. If exactly three of the trucks are green, then which one of the following trucks must be green?

Step 5: Questions

The trucks in slots 2 and 4 are always green. If there is to be just one more green truck, it will have to take slot 6 to prevent having any red trucks arrive consecutively (Rule 1).

S̷ T U W X Y̷ Z

　　　　X
　⎛‾‾‾‾⎞
　__ __ __ Y T/W S W/T
　1　2　3　4　5　6　7
g/r　r　g　r　g　r　g　r
　　　Z…U

Thus, Truck S must be green.

(A)	S	Correct. Under this question's conditions, Truck S must be green.
(B)	T	Under this question's conditions, Truck T must be red, whether it is fifth or seventh. Eliminate.
(C)	U	Truck U could be either green or red. Eliminate.
(D)	W	Under this question's conditions, Truck W must be red, whether it is fifth or seventh. Eliminate.
(E)	Z	Truck Z could be either green or red. Eliminate.

PrepTest37 Sec3 Q9

This time, the new condition fell on the line accounting for the trucks' colors rather than the one designating their arrival order. However, once the new sketch was in place, the expert could see the color that corresponds to each position, and again, evaluating the answer choices was a snap. Those questions are representative of most New-"If" questions you will encounter, and you will have ample opportunity to practice more New-"If"s on almost every game throughout this book.

One more word of caution: Some untrained test takers are tempted to add a New-"If" question's new condition into the Master Sketch and to work out the condition's implications there. The problem with this approach is that the New-"If" question's condition applies *only* to that specific question. Once you finish working on the New-"If" question, you would need to erase its specific conditions and try to restore the Master Sketch to its original state. That leads to confusion and mistakes, and doesn't really save any time in the long run.

Answering New-"If" Questions Using Limited Options

One case in which you may be able to avoid creating new sketches for New-"If" questions is when the game's deductions break down into Limited Options. Because Limited Options deductions lead to dual Master Sketches covering each of the game's two fundamental patterns, many of the game's New-"If" questions will lead you directly to one of the two options. Then, depending on the level of certainty you've been able to deduce, you may be able to use the appropriate option's sketch to evaluate the answer choices.

The Special Feature at the end of Chapter 3 covers Limited Options deductions in detail. If you have time, and you haven't already watched the video accompanying that Special Feature, do so now. Not every game breaks down into Limited Options, but it's not unusual to see it once (or, if you're lucky, twice) per test.

Other Question Types

Completely Determine Questions

From time to time, the LSAT will pose a question asking you for a statement that would completely determine the sequence, selection, matching, or distribution of all entities in the game. Completely Determine questions are not common—among the 60 logic games (345 questions) released from 2012 through 2016, there were only eight of these questions.

Should you run into one of these questions, you can recognize it from a question stem like one of these:

The order of the dentist's appointments for the day is completely determined if which one of the following is true?

The assignment of doctors to the three clinics is completely determined if which one of the following pairs of doctors is assigned to Clinic 2?

Characterizing the answer choices is straightforward in Completely Determine questions. The correct answer is the only one that, if true, provides a complete solution to the game (all entities sequenced, distributed, matched, or selected). The wrong answer choices all leave one or more of the entities' placements undetermined.

Unfortunately, there is usually no way to avoid testing the answer choices one by one, usually by making new sketches. Nonetheless, you can be strategic by testing certain entities first. Because they are the hardest entities to pin down in any game, an unrestricted *floater* entity is often your prime suspect. Test any answer choice that establishes the placement of a floater first. If it completely determines the game's arrangement, you're done.

If none of the answer choices places a floater, or if the answer choice(s) placing a floater doesn't completely determine the arrangement, move on to answer choices placing entities that restrict numerous other entities. For example, imagine you have the following rules in a Strict Sequencing game:

> P will speak sometime after S, but sometime before L.
> P and M will deliver consecutive speeches.

$$S \ldots \boxed{M / P} \ldots L$$

Here, the placement of M or P is much more likely to completely the determine the sequence than are the placements of S or L. Establishing the position of S or L might force the string of entities to move into earlier or later positions, but will not determine the order of M and P. A strategic test taker would evaluate answer choices establishing the position of M or P before evaluating answer choices that address S or L.

You actually used the same reasoning skills associated with Completely Determine questions in the Practice exercise in Chapter 1. Take a look back at question 15 in that exercise, the one that asked "Placing Engle in which slot would completely determine the team's pitching rotation?" The explanation for that question illustrates an analysis identical to what you would use for a Completely Determine question.

Numerical Questions
In earlier chapters, you saw several ways in which the the number restrictions on a game's setup could help you set up a game, make deductions, and answer questions. Numerical questions focus directly on the number limits within a game.

Minimum/Maximum Questions
The test might, for example, ask you to determine the minimum or maximum number of entities that may be selected (in a Selection game) or placed within a certain group (in a Distribution game, for instance). The question stem will be worded more or less like this one:

> What is the maximum number of employees who may be selected for the company retreat?

A question like this one would, of course, be part of the question set for a Selection game. You will use your expertise in Formal Logic to determine the maximum number of students you could choose. Any rule of the type "If A →~B" reduces the maximum number of entities that may be selected. Rules in that pattern translate to "Never AB."

Because you must exclude one of the two entities, the maximum available for selection has been reduced by one. On the flip side, rules fitting the pattern "If ~C → D" establish that at least one of C and D must be selected and so increase the minimum by one. (See Chapter 6 on Formal Logic and Selection games; there, you'll also find a Special Feature on the types of rules that decrease the maximum or increase the minimum number of entities that may be selected.)

The answer choices are always listed in numerical order, either lowest to highest or the other way around. The correct answer cites the precise minimum or maximum number. The wrong answers are either too high or too low.

In terms of strategy, you will always be able to use the rules to establish the minimum or maximum number of entities selected or placed within a particular group. Figure out that number and select the correct answer choice.

It is also possible that you will see a variant of the Minimum/Maximum question that has a New-"If" condition. Here's an example:

> If Milos is chosen to attend the company retreat, what is the maximum number of employees who could be chosen to attend the retreat?

Treat the first part of a question like that one just as you would a conventional New-"If" question. Copy the Master Sketch next to the question, add the new condition, and make any newly available deductions. Use the resulting sketch to determine what the correct answer will be.

On tests released from 2012 to 2016, there were three Minimum/Maximum questions, one of which had a New-"If" condition preceding the question.

Earliest/Latest Questions
In Sequencing games (and Hybrid games with a Sequencing action), you may see a similar question type: the Earliest/Latest question. The question stems are straightforward:

> The earliest that Kim's appointment could be scheduled is

The correct answer gives the precise position that represents the earliest or latest that the entity in question may appear. The incorrect answers are either too early or too late. Like those in Minimum/Maximum questions, the answer choices will be arranged in order, in this case from earliest to latest.

Treat these questions just as you would a Minimum/Maximum question. Simply consult the Master Sketch to determine the correct answer. Keep in mind that you could see a New-"If" variation of this question type, too.

Earliest/Latest questions are easy to understand, and if you've made all of the deductions during Step 4 of the Logic Games Method, they can turn into a quick point on Test Day. It's too bad you're not more likely to see one. On released tests from 2012 to 2016, there were only two Earliest/Latest questions, one of which had a New-"If" clause at the beginning.

"How Many" Questions
These questions ask you about numbers that can be firmly established in the game. There's little chance you'll misinterpret one of these stems. They tend to be extremely straightforward:

> How many of the interviews are there that could be the one given on Tuesday morning?

> How many of the dentist's patients are there any one of whom could be scheduled for an appointment at 1:00 PM?

> Exactly how many of the state senators are there any one of whom could be assigned to the Highways committee?

The correct answer gives the correct number, and the four wrong answers are either too high or too low. After consulting the Master Sketch, you should be able to predict the correct answer precisely before evaluating the choices.

Refresh (Activate Prior Knowledge)

The question set for the Truck Arrivals game featured one "How Many" question. Take a few minutes to review the LSAT expert's analysis. Note how she was able to determine the correct answer before checking the answer choices.

LSAT Question	Analysis
In a single day, exactly seven trucks—S, T, U, W, X, Y, and Z—are the only arrivals at a warehouse. No truck arrives at the same time as any other truck, and no truck arrives more than once that day. Each truck is either green or red (but not both). The following conditions apply: No two consecutive arrivals are red. Y arrives at some time before both T and W. Exactly two of the trucks that arrive before Y are red. S is the sixth arrival. Z arrives at some time before U.	**Steps 1-4:**

Steps 1-4:

$\cancel{S}$ T U W X $\cancel{Y}$ Z

			Y	T/W	S	W/T
1	2	3	4	5	6	7

g/r r g r g _ _ _

never [r r]   Z . . . U

5. For exactly how many of the seven trucks can one determine exactly how many trucks arrived before it?	**Step 5: Questions** Rule 4 established the placement of Truck S. Combining Rule 2 with Rules 1 and 4 established that Truck Y must take slot 4. Those are the only two trucks whose placement is determined once and for all.
(A) one	
(B) two	Correct. The placements of Trucks S and Y are completely determined.
(C) three	
(D) four	
(E) five	

PrepTest37 Sec3 Q10

Among the tests released between 2012 and 2016 (with a total of 345 Logic Games questions), there were only six "How Many" questions, four of which were of the New-"If" variety. Here's an example:

If Dr. Shelby is assigned to Clinic 2, exactly how many of the doctors are assigned to Clinic 1?

Should you encounter one of these questions in practice or on Test Day, treat the first clause of the question stem as you would any other New-"If" question. Copy the Master Sketch, add in the new condition, and make all newly available deductions. Consult the resulting sketch to determine the correct answer.

Rule Alteration Questions

Some tests feature no questions from this subcategory, and historically, those that do almost always have exactly one. That's good news because these questions tend to be difficult for most test takers, and they are time-consuming even for those who get them right.

Rule Substitution Questions

These questions didn't make their debut on the LSAT until PrepTest 57 (administered in June 2009). Since that time, there has been exactly one on each released administration of the exam except for PrepTests 60, 67, 68, and 79 (on which there were none), and PrepTest 71 (on which there were two). In a Rule Substitution question, the stem asks you to find a rule that would have the same effect on the game that one of the game's original rules has. For example:

> Which one of the following, if substituted for the condition that Barbara's appointment is later than Matt's appointment, would have the same effect on the game?

The correct answer will state a rule that has exactly the same effect on the game as the rule cited in the question stem. That is, the rule in the correct answer will restrict all of the entities restricted by the original rule, and in exactly the same ways. To illustrate this, imagine that the game associated with the model question stem had the following rules:

> Barbara's appointment is later than Matt's appointment.
> Matt and Rebekkah have consecutive appointments.
>
> [M / R] . . . B

In that case, an answer choice that stated "Rebekkah's appointment is earlier than Barbara's appointment" would have precisely the same effect on the game as the rule cited in the question stem, and would be correct. The rules stated in the four wrong answers will leave something restricted by the original rule unrestricted, or will over-restrict the entities in a way that the original rule did not.

To answer these questions, consult the original rule within the context of the Master Sketch. Ask which entities it explicitly restricts, and which entities it restricts as a result of additional deductions. Then test the answer choices by substituting them for the rule in question. If an answer choice does not create the same restrictions for all entities concerned (or if it over-restricts them), eliminate it. Once you find the rule that produces the exact effects produced by the original rule, you're done.

Analyzing the effect of the rules stated in the answer choices can be complicated, and sometimes, you'll need to redraw the sketch to work out the new rule's exact effects. That's a good way to proceed, but it can become time consuming. If the work required to answer a Rule Substitution question threatens to cut into the time you'll need to tackle additional games, your best strategy may be to guess and move on. Never take so much time answering one question that you run out of time for five to ten additional questions on later games.

Rule Change Questions

In times past, Rule Change questions were more common than they have been in recent years. In fact, between 2012 and 2016, there were no Rule Change questions among all 60 released logic games. (It seems possible that Rule Substitution questions have replaced them permanently.) There's a strong chance that you won't encounter a question of this type on Test Day. On the off chance that you do—every once in a while, the testmaker brings back questions or games that have not been used in a long time—here's what you should know. Rule Change question stems tell you to ignore one of the rules cited in the game's setup and to use another rule (described in the stem) instead. Then, based on these altered circumstances, the stem will usually pose a Must Be/Could Be-type question. Here is an example that you will work with shortly in the Practice section of this chapter:

> Assume that the original condition that the linen dress hangs immediately to the right of the silk dress is replaced by the condition that the wool dress hangs immediately to the right of the silk dress. If all the other initial conditions remain in effect, which one of the following must be false?

PrepTest 41 Sec2 Q7

Notice that the question stem's final clause tells you how to characterize the answer choices. In this case, treat the answer choices just as you would in a Must Be False question.

Since the opening sentence of the question stem changes the game's rules, you can think of Rule Change questions as a cousin of the New-"If" question. The main difference is that New-"If" questions add an additional restriction while preserving the original rules, whereas Rule Change questions alter or suspend one of the original rules. Should you happen across a Rule Change question, your instinct should be to create a new sketch and consult it as you evaluate the answer choices. Just make sure you actively undo the part of the Master Sketch suspended in the Rule Change question stem along with any deductions you drew using that rule.

Supply the "If" Questions

There's one more very rare question type: the Supply the "If" question. Between 2012 and 2016, there were only three of these questions among the 60 logic games released by the LSAC. It is pretty unlikely that you'll see one. If you do, you can recognize it from question stems like these:

> Joanna's appointment must be at 4:00 PM if which one of the following is true?

> Team H will compete later than Team J if which one of the following is true?

Perhaps the best way to think about these unusual questions is that they are New-"If" questions in reverse. The question stem gives you the necessary result and asks you for the sufficient condition. Thus, the correct answer will supply a condition that ensures the result cited in the question stem. The four wrong answers will supply conditions in which the result cited in the question stem could be false.

LSAT experts know that the best approach is to use the Master Sketch to see the possibilities for the entity or slot in question, and then use that analysis to determine the kind of additional restriction that would guarantee the desired result.

As you've learned, the questions covered in this "Other Question Types" section are not common. You're best served by trying these questions if and when they appear among your practice games and tests but not by spending time trying to find more examples of them in older tests. It is your facility with Acceptability, Must Be/Could Be, and New-"If" questions that will make or break your LSAT logic games performance. In contrast, you'll likely see only a single example of one or two of these rare question types on your official LSAT. If you do, analyze the question stem patiently, consult your Master Sketch, and remember that the testmaker always includes all of the information you need to answer every question the test asks.

Practice

Now it's time to practice what you've learned about Logic Games questions. There are three Practice sets. The first is an exercise with 12 question stems. For each stem, you will need to identify the question type, characterize the correct and incorrect answers, and note how to answer the question strategically. The second and third practice sets are the full question sets for two officially released logic games that you have worked with in previous chapters, in which you can practice answering the questions in context.

Expert analysis for all of the practice follows the third Practice set.

Practice 1

Directions: Read the question stems and provide the following analyses: 1) identify the question type, 2) characterize the one correct and four incorrect answer choices, and 3) outline the strategy to answer the question efficiently and effectively. For this Practice set, take your time and answer each question thoroughly.

Question		Analysis
1. If the acrobat is wearing a yellow jacket, which of the following must be true?	$\longrightarrow$	
2. Which of the following could be an acceptable schedule of the doctor's appointments from first through seventh?	$\longrightarrow$	
3. If the brown vase is in position 2, then what is the maximum number of vases that could be in position 5?	$\longrightarrow$	
4. Each of the following could be true EXCEPT	$\longrightarrow$	
5. Which of the following is a complete and accurate list of the participants, any one of whom could attend the conference on Day 1?	$\longrightarrow$	
6. If Emerson gives the fifth audition, which of the following could be true?	$\longrightarrow$	
7. Which of the following dishes must be selected?	$\longrightarrow$	

8. If K is in position 4, which of the following CANNOT be in position 6? $\longrightarrow$

9. Which of the following, if true, would completely determine the order of the houses from left to right? $\longrightarrow$

10. Which of the following could be a complete and accurate ranking of the songs from most to least popular? $\longrightarrow$

11. Which of the following, if substituted for the condition that Johnson must perform after Landry, would have the same effect in determining the order of the performances? $\longrightarrow$

12. If pasta is one of the dishes selected, which of the following dishes could be excluded? $\longrightarrow$

Practice 2

Directions: You have seen this game's setup, rules and deductions in the preceding chapters of this book. First, review the Master Sketch and reconstruct the work you did in Steps 1-4 of the Logic Games Method. Then, answer the game's questions. For practice, take time to analyze each question thoroughly and enter your analysis for each step and answer choice blank. Complete worked example expert analysis can be found in your online resources.

Question 1:

LSAT Question	Analysis
A closet contains exactly six hangers—1, 2, 3, 4, 5, and 6—hanging, in that order, from left to right. It also contains exactly six dresses—one gauze, one linen, one polyester, one rayon, one silk, and one wool—a different dress on each of the hangers, in an order satisfying the following conditions: The gauze dress is on a lower-numbered hanger than the polyester dress. The rayon dress is on hanger 1 or hanger 6. Either the wool dress or the silk dress is on hanger 3. The linen dress hangs immediately to the right of the silk dress.	**Steps 1-4:** G L P R S W R W/S 1 2 3 4 5 6 ~P ~G ~L ~S G . . . P [S L]

1. Which one of the following could be an accurate matching of the hangers to the fabrics of the dresses that hang on them? $\longrightarrow$

   (A) 1: wool; 2: gauze; 3: silk; 4: linen; 5: polyester; 6: rayon $\longrightarrow$

   (B) 1: rayon; 2: wool; 3: gauze; 4: silk; 5: linen; 6: polyester $\longrightarrow$

   (C) 1: polyester; 2: gauze; 3: wool; 4: silk; 5: linen; 6: rayon $\longrightarrow$

   (D) 1: linen; 2: silk; 3: wool; 4: gauze; 5: polyester; 6: rayon $\longrightarrow$

   (E) 1: gauze; 2: rayon; 3: silk; 4: linen; 5: wool; 6: polyester $\longrightarrow$

   PrepTest41 Sec2 Q1

Question 2:

LSAT Question	Analysis
A closet contains exactly six hangers—1, 2, 3, 4, 5, and 6—hanging, in that order, from left to right. It also contains exactly six dresses—one gauze, one linen, one polyester, one rayon, one silk, and one wool—a different dress on each of the hangers, in an order satisfying the following conditions: The gauze dress is on a lower-numbered hanger than the polyester dress. The rayon dress is on hanger 1 or hanger 6. Either the wool dress or the silk dress is on hanger 3. The linen dress hangs immediately to the right of the silk dress.	**Steps 1-4:** 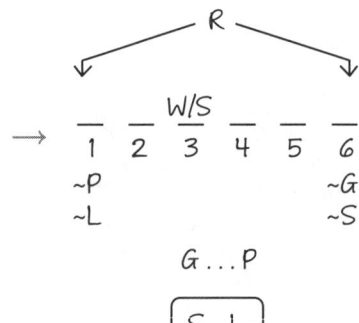

2. If both the silk dress and the gauze dress are on odd-numbered hangers, then which one of the following could be true?

   (A) The polyester dress is on hanger 1.

   (B) The wool dress is on hanger 2.

   (C) The polyester dress is on hanger 4.

   (D) The linen dress is on hanger 5.

   (E) The wool dress is on hanger 6.
       PrepTest41 Sec2 Q2

Question 3:

LSAT Question	**Analysis**

A closet contains exactly six hangers—1, 2, 3, 4, 5, and 6—hanging, in that order, from left to right. It also contains exactly six dresses—one gauze, one linen, one polyester, one rayon, one silk, and one wool—a different dress on each of the hangers, in an order satisfying the following conditions:

The gauze dress is on a lower-numbered hanger than the polyester dress.

The rayon dress is on hanger 1 or hanger 6.

Either the wool dress or the silk dress is on hanger 3.

The linen dress hangs immediately to the right of the silk dress.

→

Steps 1-4:

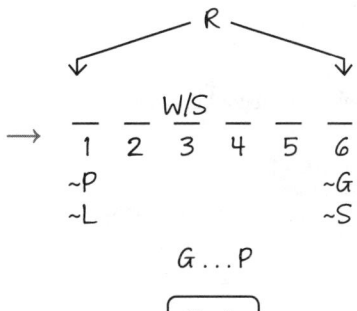

3. If the silk dress is on an even-numbered hanger, which one of the following could be on the hanger immediately to its left?   →

(A)   the gauze dress   →

(B)   the linen dress   →

(C)   the polyester dress   →

(D)   the rayon dress   →

(E)   the wool dress   →

PrepTest41 Sec2 Q3

Question 4:

LSAT Question	Analysis

A closet contains exactly six hangers—1, 2, 3, 4, 5, and 6—hanging, in that order, from left to right. It also contains exactly six dresses—one gauze, one linen, one polyester, one rayon, one silk, and one wool—a different dress on each of the hangers, in an order satisfying the following conditions:

> The gauze dress is on a lower-numbered hanger than the polyester dress.
> The rayon dress is on hanger 1 or hanger 6.
> Either the wool dress or the silk dress is on hanger 3.
> The linen dress hangs immediately to the right of the silk dress.

$\longrightarrow$

Steps 1-4:

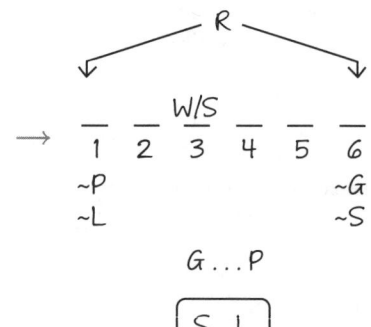

4. If the polyester dress is on hanger 2, then which one of the following must be true? $\longrightarrow$

(A)   The silk dress is on hanger 1. $\longrightarrow$

(B)   The wool dress is on hanger 3. $\longrightarrow$

(C)   The linen dress is on hanger 4. $\longrightarrow$

(D)   The linen dress is on hanger 5. $\longrightarrow$

(E)   The rayon dress is on hanger 6. $\longrightarrow$

PrepTest41 Sec2 Q4

Question 5:

LSAT Question	Analysis

A closet contains exactly six hangers—1, 2, 3, 4, 5, and 6—hanging, in that order, from left to right. It also contains exactly six dresses—one gauze, one linen, one polyester, one rayon, one silk, and one wool—a different dress on each of the hangers, in an order satisfying the following conditions:

The gauze dress is on a lower-numbered hanger than the polyester dress.

The rayon dress is on hanger 1 or hanger 6.

Either the wool dress or the silk dress is on hanger 3.

The linen dress hangs immediately to the right of the silk dress.

Steps 1-4:

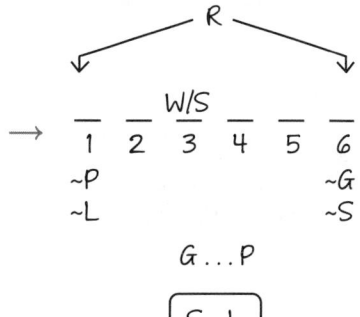

$\longrightarrow$

5.   Which one of the following CANNOT be true? $\longrightarrow$

(A)   The linen dress hangs immediately next to the gauze dress. $\longrightarrow$

(B)   The polyester dress hangs immediately to the right of the rayon dress. $\longrightarrow$

(C)   The rayon dress hangs immediately to the left of the wool dress. $\longrightarrow$

(D)   The silk dress is on a lower-numbered hanger than the gauze dress. $\longrightarrow$

(E)   The wool dress is on a higher-numbered hanger than the rayon dress. $\longrightarrow$

PrepTest41 Sec2 Q5

Question 6:

LSAT Question	Analysis
A closet contains exactly six hangers—1, 2, 3, 4, 5, and 6—hanging, in that order, from left to right. It also contains exactly six dresses—one gauze, one linen, one polyester, one rayon, one silk, and one wool—a different dress on each of the hangers, in an order satisfying the following conditions: The gauze dress is on a lower-numbered hanger than the polyester dress. The rayon dress is on hanger 1 or hanger 6. Either the wool dress or the silk dress is on hanger 3. The linen dress hangs immediately to the right of the silk dress.	**Steps 1-4:** 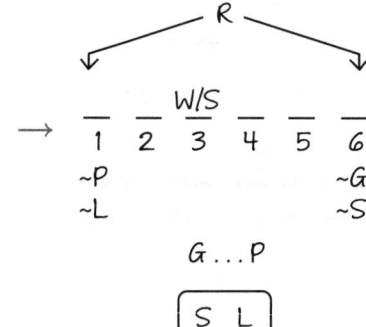

6. Which one of the following CANNOT hang immediately next to the rayon dress? $\longrightarrow$

(A)   the gauze dress $\longrightarrow$

(B)   the linen dress $\longrightarrow$

(C)   the polyester dress $\longrightarrow$

(D)   the silk dress $\longrightarrow$

(E)   the wool dress $\longrightarrow$

PrepTest41 Sec2 Q6

K

Question 7:

LSAT Question	Analysis

A closet contains exactly six hangers—1, 2, 3, 4, 5, and 6—hanging, in that order, from left to right. It also contains exactly six dresses—one gauze, one linen, one polyester, one rayon, one silk, and one wool—a different dress on each of the hangers, in an order satisfying the following conditions:

    The gauze dress is on a lower-numbered hanger than the polyester dress.

    The rayon dress is on hanger 1 or hanger 6.

    Either the wool dress or the silk dress is on hanger 3.

    The linen dress hangs immediately to the right of the silk dress.

$\longrightarrow$

Steps 1-4:

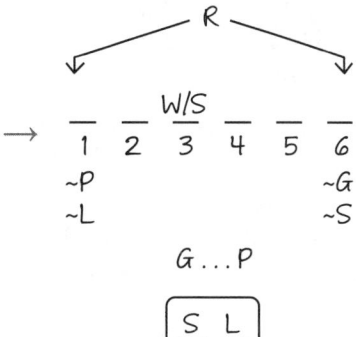

7.   Assume that the original condition that the linen dress hangs immediately to the right of the silk dress is replaced by the condition that the wool dress hangs immediately to the right of the silk dress. If all the other initial conditions remain in effect, which one of the following must be false? $\longrightarrow$

(A)   The linen dress is on hanger 1. $\longrightarrow$

(B)   The gauze dress is on hanger 2. $\longrightarrow$

(C)   The wool dress is on hanger 4. $\longrightarrow$

(D)   The silk dress is on hanger 5. $\longrightarrow$

(E)   The polyester dress is on hanger 6. $\longrightarrow$

PrepTest41 Sec2 Q7

Practice 3

Directions: You have seen this game's setup, rules and deductions in the preceding chapters of this book. First, review the Master Sketch and reconstruct the work you did in Steps 1–4 of the Logic Games Method. Then, answer the game's questions. For practice, take time to analyze each question thoroughly and enter your analysis for each step and answer choice blank. Complete worked example expert analysis can be found in your online resources.

Question 1:

LSAT Question	Analysis

Exactly six people—Lulu, Nam, Ofelia, Pachai, Santiago, and Tyrone—are the only contestants in a chess tournament. The tournament consists of four games, played one after the other. Exactly two people play in each game, and each person plays in at least one game. The following conditions must apply:

Tyrone does not play in the first or third game.

Lulu plays in the last game.

Nam plays in only one game and it is not against Pachai.

Santiago plays in exactly two games, one just before and one just after the only game that Ofelia plays in.

Steps 1-4:

1 1 2
L N Ø P Ş T

Opt. 1

1	2	3	4
S	O	S	L
~T		~T	

Opt. 2

1	2	3	4
P/N	T	N/P	L
L	S	O	S
~T		~T	

never $\dfrac{N}{P}$

1. Which one of the following could be an accurate list of the contestants who play in each of the four games?

(A) first game: Pachai, Santiago; second game: Ofelia, Tyrone; third game: Pachai, Santiago; fourth game: Lulu, Nam

(B) first game: Lulu, Nam; second game: Pachai, Santiago; third game: Ofelia, Tyrone; fourth game: Lulu, Santiago

(C) first game: Pachai, Santiago; second game: Lulu, Tyrone; third game: Nam, Ofelia; fourth game: Lulu, Nam

(D) first game: Nam, Santiago; second game: Nam, Ofelia; third game: Pachai, Santiago; fourth game: Lulu, Tyrone

(E) first game: Lulu, Nam; second game: Santiago, Tyrone; third game: Lulu, Ofelia; fourth game: Pachai, Santiago

PrepTest45 Sec3 Q7

Question 2:

LSAT Question	Analysis

Exactly six people—Lulu, Nam, Ofelia, Pachai, Santiago, and Tyrone—are the only contestants in a chess tournament. The tournament consists of four games, played one after the other. Exactly two people play in each game, and each person plays in at least one game. The following conditions must apply:

Tyrone does not play in the first or third game.

Lulu plays in the last game.

Nam plays in only one game and it is not against Pachai.

Santiago plays in exactly two games, one just before and one just after the only game that Ofelia plays in.

Steps 1-4:

```
    1  1   2
 L  N  Ø  P  Ø  T
```

Opt. 1

```
 1  2  3  4
 S  O  S  L
 ~T    ~T
```

Opt. 2

```
 1    2  3    4
P/N   T  N/P  L
 L    S  O    S
~T       ~T
```

never N/P

2. Which one of the following contestants could play in two consecutive games?

(A) Lulu

(B) Nam

(C) Ofelia

(D) Santiago

(E) Tyrone

PrepTest45 Sec3 Q8

Question 3:

LSAT Question	Analysis

Exactly six people—Lulu, Nam, Ofelia, Pachai, Santiago, and Tyrone—are the only contestants in a chess tournament. The tournament consists of four games, played one after the other. Exactly two people play in each game, and each person plays in at least one game. The following conditions must apply:

    Tyrone does not play in the first or third game.

    Lulu plays in the last game.

    Nam plays in only one game and it is not against Pachai.

    Santiago plays in exactly two games, one just before and one just after the only game that Ofelia plays in.

Steps 1-4:

$$\overset{1\quad 1\quad 2}{L\ N\ \cancel{O}\ P\ \cancel{S}\ T}$$

Opt. 1

1	2	3	4
S	O	S	L
~T		~T	

Opt. 2

1	2	3	4
P/N	T	N/P	L
L	S	O	S
~T		~T	

$$never\ \boxed{\begin{array}{c}N\\ \hline P\end{array}}$$

3.   If Tyrone plays in the fourth game, then which one of the following could be true?

    (A)   Nam plays in the second game.

    (B)   Ofelia plays in the third game.

    (C)   Santiago plays in the second game.

    (D)   Nam plays a game against Lulu.

    (E)   Pachai plays a game against Lulu.

PrepTest45 Sec3 Q9

Question 4:

LSAT Question	Analysis

Exactly six people—Lulu, Nam, Ofelia, Pachai, Santiago, and Tyrone—are the only contestants in a chess tournament. The tournament consists of four games, played one after the other. Exactly two people play in each game, and each person plays in at least one game. The following conditions must apply:

    Tyrone does not play in the first or third game.
    Lulu plays in the last game.
    Nam plays in only one game and it is not against
      Pachai.
    Santiago plays in exactly two games, one just before
      and one just after the only game that Ofelia plays in.

Steps 1-4:

$$\overset{1\ \ 1\ \ 2}{L\ N\ \cancel{O}\ P\ \cancel{S}\ T}$$

Opt. 1

1	2	3	4
S	O	S	L
~T		~T	

Opt. 2

1	2	3	4
P/N	T	N/P	L
L	S	O	S
~T		~T	

never $\boxed{\dfrac{N}{P}}$

---

4.   Which one of the following could be true?   →

(A)   Pachai plays against Lulu in the first game.   →

(B)   Pachai plays against Nam in the second game.   →

(C)   Santiago plays against Ofelia in the second game.   →

(D)   Pachai plays against Lulu in the third game.   →

(E)   Nam plays against Santiago in the fourth game.   →

PrepTest45 Sec3 Q10

Question 5:

LSAT Question	Analysis

Exactly six people—Lulu, Nam, Ofelia, Pachai, Santiago, and Tyrone—are the only contestants in a chess tournament. The tournament consists of four games, played one after the other. Exactly two people play in each game, and each person plays in at least one game. The following conditions must apply:

Tyrone does not play in the first or third game.
Lulu plays in the last game.
Nam plays in only one game and it is not against Pachai.
Santiago plays in exactly two games, one just before and one just after the only game that Ofelia plays in.

→

Steps 1-4:

$$\overset{1}{L} \; \overset{1}{N} \; \cancel{O} \; \overset{2}{P} \; \cancel{S} \; T$$

Opt. 1			
1	2	3	4
S	O	S	L
~T		~T	

Opt. 2			
1	2	3	4
P/N	T	N/P	L
L	S	O	S
~T		~T	

never $\dfrac{N}{P}$

5. Which one of the following is a complete and accurate list of the contestants who CANNOT play against Tyrone in any game?   →

(A) Lulu, Pachai   →

(B) Nam, Ofelia   →

(C) Nam, Pachai   →

(D) Nam, Santiago   →

(E) Ofelia, Pachai   →

PrepTest45 Sec3 Q11

Question 6:

LSAT Question	Analysis

Exactly six people—Lulu, Nam, Ofelia, Pachai, Santiago, and Tyrone—are the only contestants in a chess tournament. The tournament consists of four games, played one after the other. Exactly two people play in each game, and each person plays in at least one game. The following conditions must apply:

    Tyrone does not play in the first or third game.

    Lulu plays in the last game.

    Nam plays in only one game and it is not against Pachai.

    Santiago plays in exactly two games, one just before and one just after the only game that Ofelia plays in.

Steps 1-4:

$$\overset{1\ \ 1\ \ 2}{L\ N\ \cancel{O}\ P\ \cancel{S}\ T}$$

<u>Opt. 1</u>

1	2	3	4
<u>S</u>	<u>O</u>	<u>S</u>	<u>L</u>
~T	—	~T	—

<u>Opt. 2</u>

1	2	3	4
P/N	T	N/P	L
L	S	O	S
~T		~T	

never $\boxed{\dfrac{N}{P}}$

---

6.   If Ofelia plays in the third game, which one of the following must be true?

    (A)   Lulu plays in the third game.

    (B)   Nam plays in the third game.

    (C)   Pachai plays in the first game.

    (D)   Pachai plays in the third game.

    (E)   Tyrone plays in the second game.

PrepTest45 Sec3 Q12

Explanations

Compare your work to that of an LSAT expert. Pay close attention to how the expert identified each question type, characterized the one correct and four incorrect answer choices, and chose the best strategy for answering the question efficiently and effectively.

Practice 1

Question	Analysis
1. If the acrobat is wearing a yellow jacket, which of the following must be true?	Q-type: New-"If"/Must Be True. Correct answer: must be true; four incorrect choices: could be or must be false. Strategy: Create a new sketch, add the rule from the stem, and make any deductions. The correct answer will be something that is drawn into the new sketch or that must happen within the new sketch.
2. Which of the following could be an acceptable schedule of the doctor's appointments from first through seventh?	Q-type: Acceptability. Correct answer: could be true; four incorrect choices: must be false. Strategy: Apply the rules one by one; four incorrect choices violate one or more rules (or, in rare cases, a deduction). The one remaining choice will be correct.
3. If the brown vase is in position 2, what is the maximum number of vases that could be in position 5?	Q-type: New-"If"/Maximum. Correct answer: the total number of entities that can be in position 5. Strategy: Create a new sketch, add the rule from the stem, and make any deductions. Determine which entities *cannot* be in position 5 given the new If, in order to determine how many (i.e., the remaining entities) *could* be.
4. Each of the following could be true EXCEPT	Q-type: Must Be False. Correct answer: must be false; four incorrect choices: could be true. Strategy: Find a choice that is impossible in the Master Sketch (the correct answer), or use previous work to eliminate choices that could be true (four incorrect choices).
5. Which of the following is a complete and accurate list of the participants, any one of whom could attend the conference on Day 1?	Q-type: Complete and Accurate List. The correct answer will list all of the entities who could attend the conference on Day 1, and only those entities. The incorrect choices will include entities who could not attend the conference on Day 1, or exclude entities who could. Strategy: Save for later in the game, after the New-"If" questions. Use previous work to eliminate choices.
6. If Emerson gives the fifth audition, which of the following could be true?	Q-type: New-"If"/Could Be True. Correct answer: could be true, given the new If; four wrong choices: must be false. Strategy: Create a new sketch, add the rule from the stem, and make any deductions. Compare the choices to the sketch, eliminating the four that are impossible given the question's new condition.

Question	Analysis
7. Which of the following dishes must be selected?	Q-type: Must Be True. In this case, "true" means "included." The correct answer is an entity that must be included according to the game's rules and restrictions; four incorrect choices are entities that could be excluded. Strategy: Look for a deduction made in the Master Sketch, or use previous work to eliminate the choices that could be "false," or excluded.
8. If K is in position 4, which of the following CANNOT be in position 6?	Q-type: New-"If"/Must Be False. Correct answer: an entity that cannot be in position 6; four incorrect choices: entities that could be in position 6. Strategy: Create a new sketch, add the rule from the stem, and make any deductions. Eliminate the choices that list entities acceptable for position 6.
9. Which of the following, if true, would completely determine the order of the houses from left to right?	Q-type: Completely Determine. Correct answer will allow for only one possible placement for each entity, while four incorrect choices will allow for multiple possibilities. Strategy: Test answer choices, starting with choices that definitively place any floaters.
10. Which of the following could be a complete and accurate ranking of the songs from most to least popular?	Q-type: Acceptability (if ranking is the only action) or Partial Acceptability (if it is a Hybrid that requires you to rank the songs and then match some attribute to each one). Correct answer is a possible ranking; four wrong choices violate one or more rules. Strategy: Apply the rules one by one; eliminate the answer choices that violate each rule.
11. Which of the following, if substituted for the condition that Johnson must perform after Landry, would have the same effect in determining the order of the performances?	Q-type: Rule Substitution. The correct answer will have exactly the same effect on the game as the original rule, while wrong answer choices will either restrict an entity or placement not restricted by the original rule, or fail to restrict an entity in the same way that the original rule does. Strategy: Do this one last in the set, or even consider skipping it if short on time.
12. If pasta is one of the dishes selected, which of the following dishes could be excluded?	Q-type: New-"If"/Could Be False. The correct answer is an entity that does not have to be selected; the four incorrect choices are entities that must be selected, given the new If. Strategy: Create a new sketch, add the rule from the stem, and make any deductions. Compare the choices to the sketch, eliminating those that must be selected.

Practice 2

Answer Key

1.   (A)
2.   (B)
3.   (E)
4.   (E)
5.   (B)
6.   (D)
7.   (D)

Practice 3

Answer Key

1.   (A)
2.   (A)
3.   (A)
4.   (A)
5.   (C)
6.   (E)

Worked example explanations of these questions with complete expert analysis can be found in your Online Study Plan under Chapter 4. View or download the PDF titled "Chapter 4 Practice Full Games Explanations."

Perform

Now, assess your skill level in the strategies and tactics associated with answering logic games questions.

Perform 1

Directions: Take no more than 12 minutes to read the question stems and provide the following analyses: 1) identify the question type, 2) characterize the one correct and four incorrect answer choices, and 3) outline the strategy to answer the question efficiently and effectively.

Question	Analysis
1. If Holmes does not travel to Norway, which of the following could be true? $\longrightarrow$	
2. Which of the following is NOT an acceptable matching of animals to habitats? $\longrightarrow$	
3. Each of the following must be false EXCEPT $\longrightarrow$	
4. If the fourth cake baked is chocolate, which of the following CANNOT be the first cake baked? $\longrightarrow$	
5. What are the minimum and maximum numbers of people who can serve on the Board at the same time? $\longrightarrow$	
6. Which of the following could be a complete and accurate list of the projects assigned to Group A? $\longrightarrow$	

Question	Analysis
7. If the fourth phone call is from Lisa, which of the following must be true?	→
8. If no cars of the same color can be placed consecutively, then in exactly how many distinct orders can the cars be arranged?	→
9. The matching of tutors to students would be completely determined if which of the following were true?	→
10. If roses are not selected, what is the maximum number of flowers that can be in the bouquet?	→
11. Suppose that the condition that Ames and Barnes serve on the same committee is replaced with a condition stating that Ames and Barnes may not serve on the same committee. If all other conditions remain the same, which of the following must be true?	→
12. Suppose that J can never be the fourth audition and K can never be the first audition. Which of the following must be false?	→

Perform 2

Directions: You have seen this game's setup, rules and deductions in the preceding chapters of this book. Take two minutes to review the Master Sketch and reconstruct the work you did in Steps 1–4 of the Logic Games Method. Then, take no more than seven minutes to answer the game's questions. Complete worked example expert analysis can be found in your online resources.

Question 1:

LSAT Question	Analysis

On one afternoon, Patterson meets individually with each of exactly five clients—Reilly, Sanchez, Tang, Upton, and Yansky—and also goes to the gym by herself for a workout. Patterson's workout and her five meetings each start at either 1:00, 2:00, 3:00, 4:00, 5:00, or 6:00. The following conditions must apply:
 	
    Patterson meets with Sanchez at some time before her workout.
    Patterson meets with Tang at some time after her workout.
    Patterson meets with Yansky either immediately before or immediately after her workout.
    Patterson meets with Upton at some time before she meets with Reilly.
	Steps 1-4:
	R S T U Y W
	
	S/U _ _ _ _ T/R
	1 2 3 4 5 6
	~T ~T ~T ~S ~S ~S
	~W ~W
	~Y ~Y
	~R ~U
	
	S ... [W / Y] ... T
	
	U ... R

1. Which one of the following could be an acceptable schedule of Patterson's workout and meetings, in order from 1:00 to 6:00?

    (A)   Yansky, workout, Upton, Reilly, Sanchez, Tang

    (B)   Upton, Tang, Sanchez, Yansky, workout, Reilly

    (C)   Upton, Reilly, Sanchez, workout, Tang, Yansky

    (D)   Sanchez, Yansky, workout, Reilly, Tang, Upton

    (E)   Sanchez, Upton, workout, Yansky, Tang, Reilly

PrepTest45 Sec3 Q1

Question 2:

LSAT Question	Analysis

LSAT Question

On one afternoon, Patterson meets individually with each of exactly five clients—Reilly, Sanchez, Tang, Upton, and Yansky—and also goes to the gym by herself for a workout. Patterson's workout and her five meetings each start at either 1:00, 2:00, 3:00, 4:00, 5:00, or 6:00. The following conditions must apply:

Patterson meets with Sanchez at some time before her workout.

Patterson meets with Tang at some time after her workout.

Patterson meets with Yansky either immediately before or immediately after her workout.

Patterson meets with Upton at some time before she meets with Reilly.

Analysis

Steps 1-4:

R S T U Y W

S/U	_	_	_	_	T/R
1	2	3	4	5	6
~T	~T	~T	~S	~S	~S
~W					~W
~Y					~Y
~R					~U

S ... [W / Y] ... T

U ... R

---

2. How many of the clients are there, any one of whom could meet with Patterson at 1:00? $\longrightarrow$

(A) one $\longrightarrow$

(B) two $\longrightarrow$

(C) three $\longrightarrow$

(D) four $\longrightarrow$

(E) five

PrepTest45 Sec3 Q2 $\longrightarrow$

K

Question 3:

LSAT Question	Analysis

On one afternoon, Patterson meets individually with each of exactly five clients—Reilly, Sanchez, Tang, Upton, and Yansky—and also goes to the gym by herself for a workout. Patterson's workout and her five meetings each start at either 1:00, 2:00, 3:00, 4:00, 5:00, or 6:00. The following conditions must apply:

Patterson meets with Sanchez at some time before her workout.

Patterson meets with Tang at some time after her workout.

Patterson meets with Yansky either immediately before or immediately after her workout.

Patterson meets with Upton at some time before she meets with Reilly.

Steps 1-4:

R S T U Y W

S/U	_	_	_	_	T/R
1	2	3	4	5	6
~T	~T	~T	~S	~S	~S
~W					~W
~Y					~Y
~R					~U

S... [W / Y] ...T

U...R

3. Patterson CANNOT meet with Upton at which one of the following times?

(A) 1:00

(B) 2:00

(C) 3:00

(D) 4:00

(E) 5:00

Question 4:

LSAT Question	Analysis

On one afternoon, Patterson meets individually with each of exactly five clients—Reilly, Sanchez, Tang, Upton, and Yansky—and also goes to the gym by herself for a workout. Patterson's workout and her five meetings each start at either 1:00, 2:00, 3:00, 4:00, 5:00, or 6:00. The following conditions must apply:

    Patterson meets with Sanchez at some time before her workout.

    Patterson meets with Tang at some time after her workout.

    Patterson meets with Yansky either immediately before or immediately after her workout.

    Patterson meets with Upton at some time before she meets with Reilly.

Steps 1-4:

R S T U Y W

S/U	_	_	_	_	T/R
1	2	3	4	5	6
~T	~T	~T	~S	~S	~S
~W					~W
~Y					~Y
~R					~U

S ... [W / Y] ... T

U ... R

---

4.   If Patterson meets with Sanchez the hour before she meets with Yansky, then each of the following could be true EXCEPT:

    (A)   Patterson meets with Reilly at 2:00.

    (B)   Patterson meets with Yansky at 3:00.

    (C)   Patterson meets with Tang at 4:00.

    (D)   Patterson meets with Yansky at 5:00.

    (E)   Patterson meets with Tang at 6:00.

PrepTest45 Sec3 Q4

Question 5:

LSAT Question	Analysis

On one afternoon, Patterson meets individually with each of exactly five clients—Reilly, Sanchez, Tang, Upton, and Yansky—and also goes to the gym by herself for a workout. Patterson's workout and her five meetings each start at either 1:00, 2:00, 3:00, 4:00, 5:00, or 6:00. The following conditions must apply:

    Patterson meets with Sanchez at some time before her workout.

    Patterson meets with Tang at some time after her workout.

    Patterson meets with Yansky either immediately before or immediately after her workout.

    Patterson meets with Upton at some time before she meets with Reilly.

Steps 1-4:

$$R \quad S \quad T \quad U \quad Y \quad W$$

S/U	_	_	_	_	T/R
1	2	3	4	5	6
~T	~T	~T	~S	~S	~S
~W					~W
~Y					~Y
~R					~U

$$S \dots \boxed{W / Y} \dots T$$

$$U \dots R$$

---

5.   If Patterson meets with Tang at 4:00, then which one of the following must be true?

(A)   Patterson meets with Reilly at 5:00.

(B)   Patterson meets with Upton at 5:00.

(C)   Patterson meets with Yansky at 2:00.

(D)   Patterson meets with Yansky at 3:00.

(E)   Patterson's workout is at 2:00.

PrepTest45 Sec3 Q5

Question 6:

LSAT Question	Analysis

On one afternoon, Patterson meets individually with each of exactly five clients—Reilly, Sanchez, Tang, Upton, and Yansky—and also goes to the gym by herself for a workout. Patterson's workout and her five meetings each start at either 1:00, 2:00, 3:00, 4:00, 5:00, or 6:00. The following conditions must apply:

> Patterson meets with Sanchez at some time before her workout.
> Patterson meets with Tang at some time after her workout.
> Patterson meets with Yansky either immediately before or immediately after her workout.
> Patterson meets with Upton at some time before she meets with Reilly.

Steps 1-4:

R S T U Y W

S/U	_	_	_	_	T/R
1	2	3	4	5	6
~T	~T	~T	~S	~S	~S
~W					~W
~Y					~Y
~R					~U

S... [W / Y] ...T

U...R

6. Which one of the following could be the order of Patterson's meetings, from earliest to latest?

   (A)   Upton, Yansky, Sanchez, Reilly, Tang

   (B)   Upton, Reilly, Sanchez, Tang, Yansky

   (C)   Sanchez, Yansky, Reilly, Tang, Upton

   (D)   Sanchez, Upton, Tang, Yansky, Reilly

   (E)   Sanchez, Upton, Reilly, Yansky, Tang

PrepTest45 Sec3 Q6

Perform 3

Directions: You have seen this game's setup, rules and deductions in the preceding chapters of this book. Take two minutes to review the Master Sketch and reconstruct the work you did in Steps 1-4 of the Logic Games Method. Then, take no more than seven minutes to answer the game's questions. Complete worked example expert analysis can be found in your online resources.

Question 1:

LSAT Question	Analysis

A showroom contains exactly six new cars—T, V, W, X, Y, and Z—each equipped with at least one of the following three options: power windows, leather interior, and sunroof. No car has any other options. The following conditions must apply:

    V has power windows and a sunroof.
    W has power windows and a leather interior.
    W and Y have no options in common.
    X has more options than W.
    V and Z have exactly one option in common.
    T has fewer options than Z.

Steps 1-4:

① ②

T	V	W	X	Y	Z
	(pw)	(pw)	(pw)	(sr)	(li)
	(sr)	(li)	(li)	~li	
	~li	~sr	(sr)	~pw	

pw or sr
<u>not both</u>

1.   For exactly how many of the six cars is it possible to determine exactly which options each one has?

    (A)   two

    (B)   three

    (C)   four

    (D)   five

    (E)   six

PrepTest35 Sec3 Q6

Question 2:

LSAT Question	Analysis

A showroom contains exactly six new cars—T, V, W, X, Y, and Z—each equipped with at least one of the following three options: power windows, leather interior, and sunroof. No car has any other options. The following conditions must apply:

    V has power windows and a sunroof.
    W has power windows and a leather interior.
    W and Y have no options in common.
    X has more options than W.
    V and Z have exactly one option in common.
    T has fewer options than Z.

$\longrightarrow$

Steps 1-4:

①

T	V	W	X	Y	② Z
	pw	pw	pw	sr	li
	sr	li	li	~li	
	~li	~sr	sr	~pw	

pw or sr
not both

2.   Which one of the following must be false? $\longrightarrow$

(A)   Exactly five of the six cars have leather interiors. $\longrightarrow$

(B)   Exactly five of the six cars have sunroofs. $\longrightarrow$

(C)   Exactly four of the six cars have leather interiors. $\longrightarrow$

(D)   Exactly four of the six cars have power windows. $\longrightarrow$

(E)   Exactly four of the six cars have sunroofs. $\longrightarrow$

PrepTest35 Sec3 Q7

Question 3:

LSAT Question	Analysis

A showroom contains exactly six new cars—T, V, W, X, Y, and Z—each equipped with at least one of the following three options: power windows, leather interior, and sunroof. No car has any other options. The following conditions must apply:

    V has power windows and a sunroof.
    W has power windows and a leather interior.
    W and Y have no options in common.
    X has more options than W.
    V and Z have exactly one option in common.
    T has fewer options than Z.

⟶

Steps 1-4:

①   ②

T	V	W	X	Y	Z
	(pw)	(pw)	(pw)	(sr)	(li)
	(sr)	(li)	(li)	~li	
~li	~li	~sr	(sr)	~pw	

pw or sr
<u>not both</u>

3.   If all the cars that have leather interiors also have power windows, which one of the following must be false?   ⟶

(A)   T has power windows.   ⟶

(B)   T has a sunroof.   ⟶

(C)   V has power windows.   ⟶

(D)   Z has power windows.   ⟶

(E)   Z has a sunroof.   ⟶

PrepTest35 Sec3 Q8

Question 4:

LSAT Question	**Analysis**

A showroom contains exactly six new cars—T, V, W, X, Y, and Z—each equipped with at least one of the following three options: power windows, leather interior, and sunroof. No car has any other options. The following conditions must apply:

    V has power windows and a sunroof.
    W has power windows and a leather interior.
    W and Y have no options in common.
    X has more options than W.
    V and Z have exactly one option in common.
    T has fewer options than Z.

$\longrightarrow$

Steps 1-4:

①

T	V	W	X	Y	Z
	(pw)	(pw)	(pw)	sr	li
	(sr)	(li)	(li)	~li	
	~li	~sr	(sr)	~pw	

②

pw or sr
<u>not both</u>

---

4.   If Z has no options in common with T but has at least one option in common with every other car, then which one of the following must be false?

$\longrightarrow$

    (A)   T has power windows.

$\longrightarrow$

    (B)   Z has a sunroof.

$\longrightarrow$

    (C)   Exactly four of the six cars have power windows.

$\longrightarrow$

    (D)   Exactly four of the six cars have leather interiors.

$\longrightarrow$

    (E)   Exactly four of the six cars have sunroofs.

PrepTest35 Sec3 Q9

$\longrightarrow$

Question 5:

LSAT Question	Analysis

A showroom contains exactly six new cars—T, V, W, X, Y, and Z—each equipped with at least one of the following three options: power windows, leather interior, and sunroof. No car has any other options. The following conditions must apply:

    V has power windows and a sunroof.
    W has power windows and a leather interior.
    W and Y have no options in common.
    X has more options than W.
    V and Z have exactly one option in common.
    T has fewer options than Z.

$\longrightarrow$

Steps 1-4:

①②

T	V	W	X	Y	Z
	pw	pw	pw	sr	li
	sr	li	li	~li	
	~li	~sr	sr	~pw	

pw or sr
not both

5.   Suppose that no two cars have exactly the same options as one another. In that case, each of the following could be true EXCEPT:

$\longrightarrow$

(A)   Exactly three of the six cars have power windows. $\longrightarrow$

(B)   Exactly four of the six cars have power windows. $\longrightarrow$

(C)   Exactly three of the six cars have sunroofs. $\longrightarrow$

(D)   Exactly four of the six cars have sunroofs. $\longrightarrow$

(E)   Exactly four of the six cars have leather interiors. $\longrightarrow$

PrepTest35 Sec3 Q10

Question 6:

LSAT Question	Analysis

A showroom contains exactly six new cars—T, V, W, X, Y, and Z—each equipped with at least one of the following three options: power windows, leather interior, and sunroof. No car has any other options. The following conditions must apply:

V has power windows and a sunroof.
W has power windows and a leather interior.
W and Y have no options in common.
X has more options than W.
V and Z have exactly one option in common.
T has fewer options than Z.

Steps 1-4:

①   ②

T	V	W	X	Y	Z
	pw	pw	pw	sr	li
	sr	li	li	~li	
	~li	~sr	sr	~pw	

pw or sr
not both

6. If exactly four of the six cars have leather interiors, and exactly four of the six cars have power windows, then each of the following must be true EXCEPT:

(A) T and V have no options in common.

(B) T and Y have no options in common.

(C) T and Z have exactly one option in common.

(D) W and Z have exactly one option in common.

(E) Y and Z have no options in common.

PrepTest35 Sec3 Q11

Question 7:

LSAT Question	**Analysis**

A showroom contains exactly six new cars—T, V, W, X, Y, and Z—each equipped with at least one of the following three options: power windows, leather interior, and sunroof. No car has any other options. The following conditions must apply:

    V has power windows and a sunroof.
    W has power windows and a leather interior.
    W and Y have no options in common.
    X has more options than W.
    V and Z have exactly one option in common.
    T has fewer options than Z.

$\longrightarrow$

Steps 1-4:

① ②

T	V	W	X	Y	Z
	(pw)	(pw)	(pw)	(sr)	(li)
	(sr)	(li)	(li)	~li	
	~li	~sr	(sr)	~pw	

pw or sr
__not both__

7. Suppose that the condition requiring that X has more options than W is replaced by a new condition requiring that X and W have exactly two options in common. If all of the other original conditions remain in effect, which one of the following must be false?

$\longrightarrow$

(A) T and X have no options in common. $\longrightarrow$

(B) V and X have exactly one option in common. $\longrightarrow$

(C) V and X have exactly two options in common. $\longrightarrow$

(D) X and Z have no options in common. $\longrightarrow$

(E) X and Z have exactly two options in common. $\longrightarrow$

PrepTest35 Sec3 Q12

Explanations

Perform 1

Question	Analysis
1. If Holmes does not travel to Norway, which of the following could be true?	→ Q-type: New-"If"/Could Be True. Correct answer: could be true (given the new If); four incorrect choices: must be false. Strategy: Create a new sketch, add the rule from the stem, and make any deductions. Compare the choices to the sketch, eliminating the four that are impossible.
2. Which of the following is NOT an acceptable matching of animals to habitats?	→ Q-type: Acceptability EXCEPT. The correct answer violates one or more rules (i.e., must be false). The four incorrect choices could be true. Strategy: Test the rules one by one against the answer choices. If you don't find a rule violator, then check for a choice that violates a deduction.
3. Each of the following must be false EXCEPT	→ Q-type: Could Be True. Correct answer: could be or must be true; four incorrect choices: must be false. Strategy: Eliminate choices that are impossible under the Master sketch and rules.
4. If the fourth cake baked is chocolate, which of the following CANNOT be the first cake baked?	→ Q-type: New-"If"/Must Be False. The correct answer will list an entity that must be false (i.e., cannot be first), given the new If, while four incorrect choices will list entities that could be true (i.e., first). Strategy: Create a new sketch, add the rule from the stem, and make any deductions. Eliminate the choices that could or must be true (i.e., first).
5. What are the minimum and maximum numbers of people who can serve on the Board at the same time?	→ Q-type: Min/Max. The correct answer will list the minimum and maximum, in that order. Incorrect choices will include the wrong minimum, the wrong maximum, or both. Strategy: Use rules and deductions to find either the minimum or the maximum first, and narrow the options accordingly.

Question		Analysis
6. Which of the following could be a complete and accurate list of the projects assigned to Group A?	→	Q-type: Complete and Accurate List. The correct answer includes one possible complete assignment of projects to Group A. Incorrect choices will typically list incompatible entities or force incompatible pairings among entities NOT assigned to Group A. Strategy: First, apply the rules one by one; eliminate any answer choices that violate one or more rules. If more than one choice remains, consider what impact the choice will have on the remaining group(s) and eliminate any choices that would force a violation of the rules.
7. If the fourth phone call is from Lisa, which of the following must be true?	→	Q-type: New-"If"/Must Be True. Correct answer: must be true, given the new "If"; four wrong choices could be false. Strategy: Create a new sketch, add the rule from the stem, and make any deductions. The correct answer will be something drawn into the new sketch or that must happen within the new sketch. Eliminate any choices that must be false or are merely possible.
8. If no cars of the same color can be placed consecutively, then in exactly how many distinct orders can the cars be arranged?	→	Q-type: New-"If"/Could Be True. The correct answer identifies the number of orders that could be true, given the new If. Strategy: Create a new sketch, add the rule from the stem, and make any deductions. Determine how many arrangements do not violate the new rule and/or the other rules of the game.
9. The matching of tutors to students would be completely determined if which of the following were true?	→	Q-type: Completely Determine. The correct answer provides a new rule that allows you to match all tutors and students; four incorrect choices will leave entities unmatched or uncertain. Strategy: Test answer choices, starting with choices that definitively place any floaters.

Question	Analysis
10. If roses are not selected, what is the maximum number of flowers that can be in the bouquet?	⟶ Q-type: New-"If"/Maximum. The correct answer will identify the maximum possible number of flowers, given the new "If." Incorrect choices will be too high or too low. Strategy: Create a new sketch, add the rule from the stem, and make any deductions. The correct answer will reflect every entity that can be selected without violating the new and existing rules.
11. Suppose that the condition that Ames and Barnes serve on the same committee is replaced with a condition stating that Ames and Barnes may not serve on the same committee. If all other conditions remain the same, which of the following must be true?	⟶ Q-type: Rule Change/Must Be True. Correct answer: must be true, given the rule change; incorrect answers: could be false. Strategy: Rework Master Sketch to reflect the change in the rule. Make any deductions based on the rule change. Find something that must be true given the changed rule. Eliminate choices that could be false. Because of the time involved, save for last in the question set.
12. Suppose that J can never be the fourth audition and K can never be the first audition. Which of the following must be false?	⟶ Q-type: New-"If"/Must Be False. Correct answer: must be false, given the two new conditions; four incorrect choices: could be true. Strategy: Create a new sketch, add the two rules from the stem, and make any deductions. Eliminate the choices that could or must be true.

Perform 2

Answer Key

1. (E)
2. (B)
3. (C)
4. (D)
5. (B)
6. (E)

Perform 3

Answer Key

1. (C)
2. (A)
3. (E)
4. (D)
5. (C)
6. (D)
7. (D)

Worked example explanations of these questions with complete expert analysis can be found in your Online Study Plan under Chapter 4. View or download the PDF titled "Chapter 4 Perform Full Games Explanations."

Assess

Evaluate your performance according to the following criteria:

Logic Games Question Types (Perform 1)

If you correctly identified and analyzed:

10–12 of the question stems: Excellent work! You have a solid understanding of the various question types and of how to approach them. Take time to identify those you missed and review the discussion of them in the Prepare portion of this part of Chapter 4.

7–9 of the question stems: Review your work critically. Check the types of question stems you misidentified or mischaracterized and study their definitions and illustrations in the Prepare portion of this chapter. As you review your performance on the two full games (Perform 2 and Perform 3), check to see whether you answered questions of those types correctly. If not, review the expert analyses carefully, and make a note to review questions of those types whenever you encounter them until you are confident that you can identify and answer them without hesitation.

0–6 of the question stems: Reinforce your fundamental knowdedge of logic games question types and strategies. First, review the Prepare portion of this chapter. Second, review the question stems you misidentified or mischaracterized to ensure that they make sense to you. Third, complete the Fundamentals of Question Types and Strategies quiz in your online center. On Test Day, you need to know what each question is asking, and how to characterize the one correct and four incorrect answers so that you can choose the best strategy for approaching the question quickly and confidently.

To stay sharp, practice the drills in the Logic Games Training Camp for this chapter in your Online Study Plan. Training Camp drills are divided into Fundamentals, Mid-Level, and Advanced sets.

Full-Games and Question Sets (Perform 2 and Perform 3)

If you correctly answered:

11–13 of the questions in the two games: Outstanding! You're well on your way to a strong logic games performance on Test Day. Consider whether there were questions that took you too long to answer (even if you got the right answer). On those questions, review the expert analysis to see if there was a more efficient strategy or approach you might have used.

7–10 of the questions in the two games: You're off to a good start. Consider ways in which to build on this performance. First, review the expert analysis of the games thoroughly. If you missed the majority of questions in one of the two games, review the game setup, rules, and deductions as they were analyzed in earlier chapters. Make a note study this game type thoroughly in Part II. If, on the other hand, you recognize that a particular question type (as opposed to game type) is giving you trouble, review the description and illustration of that question type in the Prepare portion of this chapter, and make a note to review your performance on questions of this type going forward. Mostly, practice, practice, practice. Part II of this book has hundreds of questions and exercises to help you develop and refine your skills, and recommendations for dozens of additional games appropriate to your skill level.

0–6 of the questions in the two games: It's time to dig in and create a plan to establish the foundation of strong logic games performance on which you can build your expertise. Here are the recommended steps. 1) Review the Perform games, questions thoroughly, those you got right as well as those you got wrong. This will help you identify the parts of the games you understood and distinguish those that gave you trouble. 2) In your online resources, complete the quiz titled "Question Type Fundamentals." 3) Diagnose the source of your misunderstanding. Did you comprehend the game's setup, rules, and deductions, but struggle with the questions? If so, review the question types and practice characterizing right and wrong answer choices. Or, did you miss something in the Master Sketch? If that's the case, review Chapters 2 and 3 as they relate to the game you're reviewing, and then try the questions again. 4) When you move into Part II of this book, begin with Chapter 5 (on basic Strict Sequencing games). Then, move on to Chapters 7 and 9 (on Loose Sequencing and Matching and Distribution games, respectively) to keep your focus on the most common game types you will encounter on Test Day. There is enormous opportunity for you to improve your logic games performance, and steady practice is the surest path to expertise.

Reflect

Think back over the work you've been doing in Chapter 4.

- Are you able to distinguish among the common Logic Games question types?
- Do you consistently answer Acceptability questions strategically, by applying the rules one by one to the answer choices?
- When answering a Must Be/Could Be question, can you quickly and accurately characterize the one correct and four incorrect answer choices?
- How do you approach New-"If" questions? Can you calmly create a new sketch, add in the question's new condition, and make the available deductions?
- How does a Limited Options sketch help you save time analyzing and answering some questions?

In the coming days and weeks, take note of real-life cases in which people ask you questions similar to those found in LSAT logic games. You'll find that people are constantly posing Must Be/Could Be and New-"If" type questions:

- If Jamie doesn't have to work on Saturday, what do you guys want to do?
- Who could we have work on the Martinez account next week?
- If they are out of prawns, what will you order?

Pay special attention to whether you are answering these questions by speculating or stating your opinion. The primary distinction between day-to-day questions and those on the LSAT is that LSAT logic games questions will always provide information sufficient to provide a single, correct answer. Reflecting on the information you use to answer real-life questions—by distinguishing speculation and opinion from reasoning and deduction, as it were—can help make you aware of instances on the LSAT in which you are speculating rather than making deductions.

The LSAT Channel Spotlight

Using Previous Work

By Bobby Gautam

 Watch the video lesson for this Spotlight in your online Study Plan.

Occasionally, an opportunity will arise for you to make short work of a question or two by using work you've done on previous questions. In the Special Feature video that accompanies this page, one of The LSAT Channel instructors will show you the strategy in action on a complex Strict Sequencing game. The following example illustrates the strategy so that you'll know how it works and be able to spot chances to use it.

Take a couple minutes to set up this simple model Strict Sequencing game.

A vice-principal is arranging six trophies—one each for baseball, chess, debate, golf, lacrosse, and softball—on six pedestals, numbered 1 through 6, in her school's trophy case. The arrangement of the trophies is subject to the following constraints:

> The baseball trophy cannot be placed on Pedestal 1.
> The softball trophy is placed on a pedestal numbered higher than the pedestal on which the debate trophy is placed.
> The golf trophy is placed on Pedestal 3.
> The trophies for chess and debate are placed on consecutively numbered pedestals.

Your Master Sketch should look something like this:

$$ B \quad C \quad D \quad \cancel{G} \quad L \quad S $$

$$ \underline{} \quad \underline{} \quad \overset{G}{\underline{}} \quad \underline{} \quad \underline{} \quad \underline{} $$
$$ 1 \quad\; 2 \quad\; 3 \quad\; 4 \quad\; 5 \quad\; 6 $$
$$ \sim B $$

$$ \boxed{C \,/\, D} \ldots S $$

It would be quite common for the first question in this game's question set to be an Acceptability question. To cut to the chase, assume its correct answer is (C), as shown.

1. Which one of the following could be an acceptable arrangement of the trophies on the pedestals?

   (A)

   (B)

   (C) chess, debate, golf, softball, baseball, lacrosse

   (D)

   (E)

You have already learned to solve Acceptability questions quickly by applying the rules to the answer choices. Use the rules to knock out the wrong answers and you have a point on this game. But, more importantly for our present purposes, you now have at least one acceptable arrangement of the trophies. Remember that when you come across a question like this one.

4.   Which one of the following must be false?

    (A)   The chess trophy is placed on Pedestal 1.

    (B)   The debate trophy is placed on Pedestal 1.

    (C)   The softball trophy is placed on a pedestal numbered lower than the pedestal on which the lacrosse trophy is placed.

    (D)   The debate trophy is placed on a pedestal numbered lower than the pedestal on which the baseball trophy is placed.

    (E)   . . .

For many test takers, the first instinct on a question like this one is to test the answer choices one by one until they find the one that must be false. An LSAT expert, on the other hand, will characterize the question's wrong answers: They could be true. The expert also knows that he has at least one place—the correct answer to the Acceptability question—to check a pattern that could be true. He can see quickly that answer choices (A), (C),

and (D) are all present in the Acceptability question's correct answer. Thus, they are all wrong answers for this Must Be False question. That leaves only choices (B) and (E). Indeed, once he notices that chess and debate can always swap positions, he can even eliminate choice (B) as one that could be true in Question 4, leaving (E) as the correct answer. It doesn't even matter what choice (E) says. He has eliminated the four demonstrably wrong answers, so it must be false, and therefore, correct.

To use previous work effectively, you will need to 1) know where you have found acceptable solutions, 2) be able to characterize the correct and incorrect answer choices in later questions, and 3) be able to accurately compare answer choices to previously identified patterns. Because the LSAT expert was able to do those three things, her analysis of Question 4 in the example was far more efficient than writing out sketches to test each answer choice.

Follow along with the game on the following pages, as The LSAT Channel expert takes you even deeper into this helpful strategy.

Questions 19–24

A swim team with exactly five members—Jacobson, Kruger, Lu, Miller, Ortiz—swims a ten-lap relay race. Each team member swims exactly two of the laps: one swims laps 1 and 6, one swims laps 2 and 7, one swims laps 3 and 8, one swims laps 4 and 9, and one swims laps 5 and 10. The following conditions apply:

> Neither of Kruger's laps is immediately before either of Lu's.
>
> Jacobson does not swim lap 9.
>
> Ortiz's first lap is after (but not necessarily immediately after) Miller's.
>
> At least one of Jacobson's laps is immediately after one of Ortiz's laps.

19. Which one of the following could be an accurate list of the swimmers of the first five laps, in order from lap 1 through lap 5?

(A) Jacobson, Kruger, Miller, Lu, Ortiz
(B) Kruger, Miller, Ortiz, Jacobson, Lu
(C) Lu, Miller, Jacobson, Kruger, Ortiz
(D) Ortiz, Kruger, Miller, Lu, Jacobson
(E) Miller, Ortiz, Jacobson, Kruger, Lu

20. If Jacobson swims lap 8, then for exactly how many of the ten laps can one determine which team member swims the lap?

(A) ten
(B) eight
(C) six
(D) four
(E) two

21. If Ortiz swims lap 4, then which one of the following could be true?

(A) Jacobson swims lap 1.
(B) Jacobson swims lap 3.
(C) Kruger swims lap 5.
(D) Lu swims lap 3.
(E) Miller swims lap 5.

22. Which one of the following could be true?

(A) Jacobson swims lap 4.
(B) Kruger swims lap 5.
(C) Lu swims lap 5.
(D) Miller swims lap 10.
(E) Ortiz swims lap 6.

23. Jacobson CANNOT swim which one of the following laps?

(A) lap 1
(B) lap 2
(C) lap 3
(D) lap 6
(E) lap 10

24. Which one of the following could be an accurate list of the swimmers of the last five laps, in order from lap 6 through lap 10?

(A) Jacobson, Miller, Kruger, Ortiz, Lu
(B) Kruger, Lu, Miller, Ortiz, Jacobson
(C) Lu, Kruger, Miller, Ortiz, Jacobson
(D) Miller, Kruger, Ortiz, Jacobson, Lu
(E) Ortiz, Jacobson, Kruger, Miller, Lu

PrepTest37 Sec3 Qs 19–24

Complete answers and explanations are provided in The LSAT Channel Spotlight video "Limited Options" in your online Study Plan.

PART TWO

Game Types Unlocked

In this part of the book, each chapter focuses on one or more specific game types.

- Chapter 5: Basic Strict Sequencing Games
- Chapter 6: Complex Strict Sequencing Games
- Chapter 7: Loose Sequencing Games
- Chapter 8: Formal Logic and Selection Games
- Chapter 9: Matching and Distribution Games
- Chapter 10: Hybrid Games
- Chapter 11: Rare Games (Process and Mapping)

Sequencing games are so common on the LSAT that they are broken up into three chapters to give you the practice you'll need to master all of the Sequencing varieties. In the chapter on Selection games, you'll also find a section that thoroughly covers the aspects of Formal Logic ("If → then" statements) tested in LSAT Logic Games. Matching and Distribution games are similar to one another, and so, are covered together in Chapter 9.

In Chapters 5–10, the Learning Objective is to apply all five steps of the Logic Games Method to the various game types. You will begin with an overall Prepare that introduces the definitions and information you need about the patterns in each game type. Then, you'll have the opportunity to practice on each of Steps 1–4 of the Method. Finally, you will assess your skills with a comprehensive Perform section containing several full, official LSAT games of the type covered in the chapter. Thus, each of these chapters has five sections.

- In Real Life: Prepare for the chapter with a brief section illustrating real-life tasks that mirror the actions found in LSAT logic games.
- Tasks and Sketches: Practice on Steps 1 and 2 of the Logic Games Method, analyzing the game Overview and creating initial sketches.
- Rules: Practice on Step 3 of the Logic Games Method, analyzing and drawing the rules.
- Deductions: Practice on Step 4 of the Logic Games Method, combining rules and restrictions to reveal valid deductions within the game.
- Full Games with Questions: Assess your skill in the game type with several officially released Logic Games, followed by complete explanations and expert analysis.

(Note: In Chapter 7, due to the unusual characteristics of Loose Sequencing games, the sections on Steps 1–4 of the Logic Games Method are combined, but you will still practice all of the steps.)

These chapters will give you the ability to drill down into the specifics and details of specific game types while reinforcing your skills in each step of the Logic Games Method. You can use any of these chapters independently. To focus on the game types most commonly featured on the test, work through Chapters 5, 7, and 9. If you have limited time before Test Day, make sure to prioritize those important game types.

Chapter 11 is shorter than any of Chapters 5–10. The rare games featured there have appeared very infrequently in recent years, but they are included for students who want the most complete Logic Games preparation possible.

Throughout this part of the book, you'll find a number of LSAT Channel Special Feature pages as well, each accompanied by a video lesson from an LSAT Channel expert.

- At the end of Chapter 6, there is a special feature on Circular Sequencing, a rare but challenging Sequencing variation.
- Along with the Formal Logic section in Chapter 8, there is a special feature on Minimum Increasers and Maximum Decreasers, two of the most important "If → then" statements used in Selection games.
- At the end of Chapter 10, there is a special feature on the Dinosaur Game, a Selection-Matching Hybrid game considered by many to be the most difficult LSAT logic game of all time.
- Along with the discussion of Process games in Chapter 11, there is a special feature on a Process game from PrepTest 80 (administered in December 2016), the first Process game to appear on an official, released LSAT in more than 20 years.

CHAPTER 5

Basic Strict Sequencing Games Unlocked

LEARNING OBJECTIVES

In this chapter, you'll learn to

- Apply the Logic Games Method to basic Strict Sequencing games.

Prepare

By far, the most common game type is Strict Sequencing. Over the past five years, over one-third of the games on all officially released tests have been Strict Sequencing games.

Types of Games By Percentage, 2012–2016

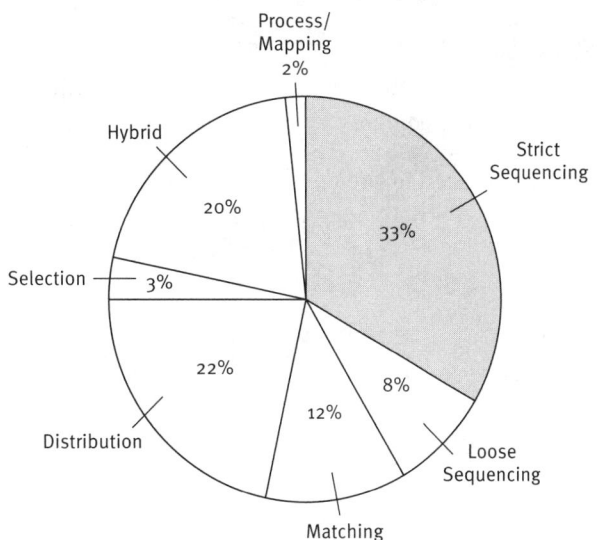

PrepTests 66–80; released 2012–2016

Given their prominence, Strict Sequencing games are central to your score in the Logic Games section of the LSAT.

Strict Sequencing games run the gamut from some of the easiest games on the test to some of the hardest. Strict Sequencing actions on the easier end of the spectrum tend to be simple and concrete, e.g., you are asked to place six entities in order in six numbered positions, one entity per position.

A B C D E F

$$\underline{} \quad \underline{} \quad \underline{} \quad \underline{} \quad \underline{} \quad \underline{}$$
1 2 3 4 5 6

Alternatively, your task could be scheduling one appointment for each of seven entities over the course of seven days, one appointment per day.

G H J K L N O

$$\underline{} \quad \underline{} \quad \underline{} \quad \underline{} \quad \underline{} \quad \underline{} \quad \underline{}$$
Su M Tu W Th F Sa

Along with this kind of simple action, the easiest Strict Sequencing games also tend to have quite restrictive rules that allow for solid deductions. We'll cover these basic Strict Sequencing games in this chapter.

Harder Strict Sequencing games often include variations that make the action more complex, e.g., over the course of five days, you will need to schedule two separate appointments for each of four entities, with a maximum of two appointments per day.

$$T_1 \ U_1 \ X_1 \ Y_1$$
$$T_2 \ U_2 \ X_2 \ Y_2$$

M Tu W Th F

$$\underline{} \quad \underline{} \quad \underline{} \quad \underline{} \quad \underline{}$$

$$\underline{} \quad \underline{} \quad \underline{} \quad \underline{} \quad \underline{}$$

Not only is this setup more complex, but it also contains some ambiguity about which days will have two appointments and which will have one or none. Complex Strict Sequencing games are covered in Chapter 6.

On recent tests, you've been virtually guaranteed to see one (or more) Strict Sequencing games, so work through Chapter 5 regardless of your skill level. Even if Strict Sequencing is your strong suit, practice with this important game type is essential.

BASIC STRICT SEQUENCING IN REAL LIFE

If you think about it, you'll realize that there's probably not a day in your adult life in which you don't sequence something. Every time you alphabetize, schedule, rank, or decide the order of steps in a process, you're sequencing.

The most common scenario—the default, if you will—is that things in the sequence happen one at a time or that items are ranked without ties, one per space. If asked to rank your 10 favorite songs, you probably wouldn't ask, "Are three songs supposed to be tied at number 2?" or "Should I avoid repeating the same song twice in my list?" You might have difficulty ranking your favorites, but you'd assume that the list is intended to have 10 songs and 10 slots with one song per slot.

Many real-world Sequencing tasks have obvious, or even visual, criteria that would make the task too easy to use on the LSAT. It wouldn't be much of a challenge, for example, to arrange six spice jars on a shelf *alphabetically*: "allspice is before basil"; "basil is before cumin"; and so on. But the test could give you a sequencing game that mimics the steps in a recipe: "add basil before adding allspice"; "add cumin fourth"; and so on.

$$A \quad B \quad C \quad D \quad R \quad S$$

$$\underline{\quad} \quad \underline{\quad} \quad \underline{\quad} \quad \underline{\quad} \quad \underline{\quad} \quad \underline{\quad}$$
$$1 \quad 2 \quad 3 \quad 4 \quad 5 \quad 6$$

Never assume anything on LSAT logic games. While it's true that a large majority of Sequencing games contain one-at-a-time, one-per-space restrictions, the testmaker must be, and will be, explicit about all restrictions that are to apply. Make sure you always pay attention to the overall limitations that affect a game's action and account for them in your sketch.

Even in basic Strict Sequencing, your assumptions can lead you astray. If the test asked you to create a sequence of six departments' offices in a certain company, your default would almost certainly be to start with a sketch like this:

$$A \quad C \quad H \quad M \quad Q \quad T$$

$$\underline{\quad} \quad \underline{\quad} \quad \underline{\quad} \quad \underline{\quad} \quad \underline{\quad} \quad \underline{\quad}$$
$$1 \quad 2 \quad 3 \quad 4 \quad 5 \quad 6$$

Our default orientations are generally left to right or top to bottom. Now, imagine that the six departments occupy one floor each in an six-story building. If the test includes a rule like "Human Resources occupies a higher floor than Marketing," your sketch needs to be numbered from the bottom up. You would have no problem with this task if it were part of your real-world job because you would already be thinking about your company's offices. But, on the test, you need to read the setup carefully before creating your initial sketch.

$$A \quad C \quad H \quad M \quad Q \quad T$$

6 —

5 —
            H
4 —
            ⋮
3 —
            M

2 —

1 —

The same confusion can be avoided by paying attention to the differences between games that mirror two more real-world tasks: ranking versus ordering. Consider two examples: If a game setup tells you that seven salespeople will be ranked on their performance over the past quarter, a rule such as "Barber ranks lower than Carty" should be depicted like this:

```
                                          1 __
           A B C D E F G                  2 __
                                   or     3 __        C
                                                      :
        __ __ __ __ __ __ __              4 __        B
         1  2  3  4  5  6  7              5 __
              C ... B                     6 __
                                          7 __
```

Being ranked lower means taking a position closer to number seven.

On the other hand, if the game asks you to assign seven salespeople to seven offices, numbered 1 through 7, the rule "Baker is assigned a lower-numbered office than the office to which Carty is assigned" should be written like this:

```
           A B C D E F G

        __ __ __ __ __ __ __
         1  2  3  4  5  6  7
              B ... C
```

Here, having a lower-numbered office means taking an office closer to number 1.

The testmaker can even reward you for paying attention to the criterion on which items are ranked. Imagine a game show host telling you, "Put these five products in order by price"; you'd make sure to know whether you are supposed to arrange the products from cheapest to most expensive, or vice versa. In the real world, when the gym teacher says, "Line up by height," she might gesture in a way that makes it clear whether you are supposed to go from tallest to shortest or the other way around. The testmaker must, and will, always be explicit about the order you're supposed to use. Over the years, there have been many examples of relatively simple Strict Sequencing games that challenged or confused test takers who failed to catch these distinctions.

As you conduct an Overview analysis in Step 1 of the Logic Games Method, use the real-world scenario described in the game's setup to your advantage. Ask the logical questions about your task and make sure you reflect all of the game's restrictions or definitions in your sketch framework. It's better to jot down "Cheapest" at the top of your sketch and "Most Expensive" at the bottom than to set up the whole game incorrectly and have to start over from scratch.

BASIC STRICT SEQUENCING GAMES TASKS AND SKETCHES

LEARNING OBJECTIVES

In this section of the chapter, you'll practice

- Applying Steps 1 and 2 of the Logic Games Method to basic Strict Sequencing games by
  - Asking the SEAL questions to analyze the game's Overview, and then
- Creating a simple, useful Sketch framework

Prepare

Although the scenario may vary, Sequencing games always task you with putting people, places, or items in order.

LOGIC GAMES STRATEGY

Sequencing games ask you to put things in order

- Chronologically—either using units of time such as years, weeks, days, or hours, or simply using the ideas of "earlier" and "later"
- Spatially—horizontally or vertically; imagine runners about to run a race taking their positions in numbered lanes, or a wedding cake with different layers, one on top of the other
- By rank—similar to a top 10 list, or the finishing order of a competition
- By size or amount—imagine a wish list with items arranged from most to least expensive

In basic Strict Sequencing, the entities are arranged one per position, and the number of entities is equal to the number of positions.

On one evening at a political convention, six politicians—Jones, Kasim, Laurence, Marcos, Nguyen, and Pearson—will give speeches. Each politician will speak once, and only one politician will speak at a time. The order of the speeches is determined in accordance with the following considerations:

J K L M N P

‾ ‾ ‾ ‾ ‾ ‾
1 2 3 4 5 6

Try Steps 1 and 2 on the model game setups that follow.

Practice

Directions: Conduct an Overview of each game's setup by asking the SEAL questions, and create an initial sketch framework for the game's action.

Practice 1

A novelty-item sales representative is tasked with arranging on a shelf six new products—an art kit, a bandanna, a charm bracelet, a disco ball, a pair of earrings, and a fleece pullover—bearing the logo of a popular band. Strict company guidelines dictate that in arranging the items from left to right, one at a time, the sales representative must conform to the following restrictions:

1. [Step 1] Conduct an Overview analysis:
    *   What is this game's Situation?
    *   Who or what are the game's Entities?
    *   What is the game's Action?
    *   What are the Limitations explicit in the game setup?

2. [Step 2] Create an initial Sketch:

Practice 2

A park ranger surveyed different parks in her district for various species of medium-sized predators—bobcat, coyote, lynx, marten, ocelot and wolverine—and ranked them from most to least common, with no ties. The results indicated:

1. [Step 1] Conduct an Overview analysis:
    *   What is this game's Situation?
    *   Who or what are the game's Entities?
    *   What is the game's Action?
    *   What are the Limitations explicit in the game setup?

2. [Step 2] Create an initial Sketch:

Practice 3

Note: To complete Steps 1 and 2 for this game, you will need to use one of the rules.

Throughout the course of a day, an executive will attend exactly seven different business presentations. Each of the presentations is on exactly one of four topics: Distribution, Logistics, Marketing, and Sales. She attends the meetings according to the following constraints:

> She attends exactly three presentations on Logistics, exactly two presentations on Marketing, and exactly one presentation each on Distribution and Sales.

1. [Step 1] Conduct an Overview analysis:
   - What is this game's Situation?
   - Who or what are the game's Entities?
   - What is the game's Action?
   - What are the Limitations explicit in the game setup?

2. [Step 2] Create an initial Sketch:

Explanations

Compare your work to that of an LSAT expert. Keep track of any case in which you incorrectly characterized the action described in the setup, and any case in which you drew a sketch framework that does not match the details of the game's situation.

Practice 1

A novelty-item sales representative is tasked with arranging on a shelf six new products—an art kit, a bandanna, a charm bracelet, a disco ball, a pair of earrings, and a fleece pullover—bearing the logo of a popular band. Strict company guidelines dictate that in arranging the items from left to right, one at a time, the sales representative must conform to the following restrictions:

1. [Step 1] Conduct an Overview analysis:

   • What is this game's Situation? *A sales representative is arranging six items in order along a shelf.*

   • Who or what are the game's Entities? *Six types of items—A, B, C, D, E, and F—each bearing a band's logo.*

   • What is the game's Action? *Sequencing (assuming that any of the rules mention specific positions or numbers of positions between entities, this is Strict Sequencing)*

   • What are the Limitations explicit in the game setup? *"One at a time," i.e., one item per position*

2. [Step 2] Create an initial Sketch:

   A B C D E F

   — — — — — —
   1 2 3 4 5 6

Practice 2

A park ranger surveyed different parks in her district for various species of medium-sized predators—bobcat, coyote, lynx, marten, ocelot and wolverine—and ranked them from most to least common, with no ties. The results indicated:

1. [Step 1] Conduct an Overview analysis:

   • What is this game's Situation? *A survey of the populations of six animal species in various parks.*

   • Who or what are the game's Entities? *The six animal species—B, C, L, M, O, and W*

   • What is the game's Action? *Sequencing (assuming that any of the rules mention specific positions or numbers of positions between entities, this is Strict Sequencing)*

   • What are the Limitations explicit in the game setup? *"with no ties," i.e., one species per position in the ranking*

2. [Step 2] Create an initial Sketch:

   B C L M O W

            or

   — — — — — —
   1 2 3 4 5 6

   1 —
   2 —
   3 —
   4 —
   5 —
   6 —

Practice 3

Note: To complete Steps 1 and 2 for this game, you will need to use one of the rules.

> Throughout the course of a day, an executive will attend exactly seven different business presentations. Each of the presentations is on exactly one of four topics: Distribution, Logistics, Marketing, and Sales. She attends the meetings according to the following constraints:
>
> > She attends exactly three presentations on Logistics, exactly two presentations on Marketing, and exactly one presentation each on Distribution and Sales.

1. [Step 1] Conduct an Overview analysis:
   - What is this game's Situation? *An executive's itinerary of seven presentations on one day of a business conference.*
   - Who or what are the game's Entities? *Four presentation topics—D, L, M, and S; because of the game's first rule, you know topics of all seven presentations that the executive will attend—D, L_1, L_2, L_3, M_1, M_2, and S.*

- What is the game's Action? *Sequencing (assuming that any of the rules mention specific positions or numbers of positions between entities, this is Strict Sequencing)*
- What are the Limitations explicit in the game setup? *Each presentation is on one of the topics.*

2. [Step 2] Create an initial Sketch:

$$D \quad L_1 \quad L_2 \quad L_3 \quad M_1 \quad M_2 \quad S$$

$$\overline{} \quad \overline{} \quad \overline{} \quad \overline{} \quad \overline{} \quad \overline{} \quad \overline{}$$
$$1 \quad 2 \quad 3 \quad 4 \quad 5 \quad 6 \quad 7$$

You'll see these model game setups again as you practice Step 3, analyzing and drawing the rules, and Step 4, making deductions in basic Strict Sequencing games.

BASIC STRICT SEQUENCING GAMES RULES

LEARNING OBJECTIVES

In this section of the chapter, you'll practice

- Applying Step 3 of the Logic Games Method to basic Strict Sequencing games by analyzing and sketching the rules

Prepare

Strict Sequencing games ask you to assign entities to specific positions. Knowing that should help you anticipate the kinds of rules you'll encounter in these games.

LOGIC GAMES STRATEGY

Strict Sequencing rules basically tell you one or more of the following:

- The order in which two or more entities are placed
- The number of spaces between two or more entities
- The slot(s) in which a given entity can or cannot be placed

In Strict Sequencing, a few types of rules may be drawn directly into the sketch framework.

> C is in position 3.
>
> D is either in position 1 or else in position 6.
>
> F is not in position 5.

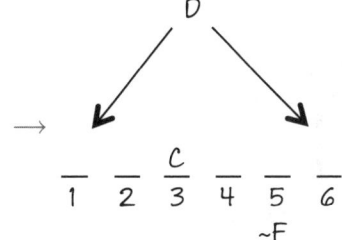

Most Strict Sequencing rules, however, stipulate the relative order or distance (or both) between two entities, and will be depicted underneath the sketch.

> H occupies a higher-numbered position than J.
>
> L and M occupy adjacent positions.
>
> P's position is at least two spaces earlier than Q's position.

$$\overline{1} \quad \overline{2} \quad \overline{3} \quad \overline{4} \quad \overline{5} \quad \overline{6}$$

$$J \ldots H$$

$$\rightarrow \quad \boxed{\underline{L}\ \ M} \quad or \quad \boxed{M\ \ L}$$

$$\underline{P} \ \_ \ \ldots \ \underline{Q}$$

Very rarely, you may see a conditional Formal Logic rule in a Strict Sequencing game; for example:

> If R is delivered sixth, then Q is delivered second.

$$\text{If R6} \quad \longrightarrow \quad \text{Q2}$$
$$\text{If ~Q2} \quad \longrightarrow \quad \text{~R6}$$

A rule like this only applies in two situations: when R *is* in the sixth slot (in which case Q must be in the second slot), or when Q is *not* in the second slot (in which case, R *cannot* be in the sixth slot). Formal Logic is most common in Selection games, and the process of analyzing and diagramming Formal Logic is discussed in detail in Chapter 8 along with the Selection games deep dive.

The following chart shows a handful of common Strict Sequencing rules and suggested drawings for each.

Rule	Analysis
C and D must be next to each other.	$\boxed{\underline{C/D}\ \underline{D/C}}$ or: $\boxed{\underline{C}\quad\underline{D}}$ or $\boxed{\underline{D}\quad\underline{C}}$
There are at least two people in line after A but before B.	$\underline{A}\ \_\ \_\ \ldots\ \underline{B}$
E appears on some day before F.	E . . . F
C's appointment is on the day before D's appointment.	$\boxed{C\ D}$
There is exactly one day between C's lecture and D's lecture.	$\boxed{\underline{C/D}\ \_\ \underline{D/C}}$ or: $\boxed{\underline{C}\ \_\ \underline{D}}$ or $\boxed{\underline{D}\ \_\ \underline{C}}$
Either V comes before W or V comes before X, but not both.	W . . . V . . . X or X . . . V . . . W
E performs some time before both F and G.	E . . . F E . . . G or E ╱ ╲ F G
If A is in position 2, B is in position 5.	If A2 $\longrightarrow$ B5 If ~B5 $\longrightarrow$ ~A2
C and D cannot be adjacent to each other.	never $\boxed{C\ D}$ never $\boxed{D\ C}$
A must appear before B, but after C.	C . . . A . . . B

Practice

Now, practice Strict Sequencing rules by completing four exercises. In the first, you'll see rules listed out as in the preceding table. Your job is to analyze and draw them accurately. The next three exercises add rules to the three Strict Sequencing game setups you sketched earlier. Analyze the rules, answer the questions about them, and draw them into or underneath the sketch frameworks.

Practice 1

Directions: Analyze and draw each of the following Strict Sequencing game rules.

Rule	My Analysis
1. There are exactly three appointments between D's appointment and C's appointment.	
2. There is, at most, one spot between H's spot and J's spot.	
3. If L is the second car, then M is the first car.	
4. J and K both have lower-numbered positions than H, or H has a lower-numbered position than both J and K.	
5. D is in position 4.	
6. C is immediately after D but before E.	
7. S is after both T and V.	
8. P finishes later than Q, but earlier than R.	
9. M's position is at least two positions later than J's position.	
10. N arrives exactly two hours before Z arrives.	
11. X is either in position 1 or position 6.	
12. B is not fifth.	

Practice 2

Directions: Take a couple of minutes to review the game setup, summarize your Overview analysis, and recreate the initial Sketch. Then, one at a time, analyze the rules, answer the questions about each one, and draw the rule either inside or underneath the sketch framework.

A novelty-item sales representative is tasked with arranging on a shelf six new products—an art kit, a bandanna, a charm bracelet, a disco ball, a pair of earrings, and a fleece pullover—bearing the logo of a popular band. Strict company guidelines dictate that in arranging the items from left to right, one at a time, the sales representative must conform to the following restrictions:

> The art kit must be in one of the middle two spaces.
> The charm bracelet must be in a space next to one of the end spaces.
> The fleece pullover must be two spaces to the left of the disco ball.
> The art kit must never be placed immediately to the left of the fleece pullover.
> The earrings must be somewhere to the left of the bandanna.

1. [Step 1] Summarize your Overview analysis:

2. [Step 2] Create an initial Sketch:

3. [Step 3] Analyze and draw the Rules:
   - For each rule, answer the following questions and draw the rule in the appropriate box.
     - What does the rule restrict, and what does it leave open?
     - What are the rule's negative implications, if any?
     - Can the rule be depicted inside the sketch framework?

Rule 1:	Rule 4:
Rule 2:	Rule 5:
Rule 3:	

Practice 3

Directions: Take a couple of minutes to review the game setup, summarize your Overview analysis, and recreate the initial Sketch. Then, one at a time, analyze the rules, answer the questions about each one, and draw the rule either inside or underneath the sketch framework.

A park ranger surveyed different parks in her district for various species of medium-sized predators—bobcat, coyote, lynx, marten, ocelot and wolverine—and ranked them from most to least common, with no ties. The results indicated:

In all parks, coyotes were the most or second most common species.
Bobcat and lynx were never both among the three most common species in the same park.
In every park, both bobcat and lynx were more common than both marten and wolverine.

1. [Step 1] Summarize your Overview analysis:

2. [Step 2] Create an initial Sketch:

3. [Step 3] Analyze and draw the Rules:
   - For each rule, answer the following questions and draw the rule in the appropriate box.
     - What does the rule restrict, and what does it leave open?
     - What are the rule's negative implications, if any?
     - Can the rule be depicted inside the sketch framework?

Rule 1:	Rule 3:
Rule 2:	

Practice 4

Directions: Take a couple of minutes to review the game setup, summarize your Overview analysis, and recreate the initial Sketch. Then, one at a time, analyze the rules, answer the questions about each one, and draw the rule either inside or underneath the sketch framework.

Throughout the course of a day, an executive will attend exactly seven different business presentations. Each of the presentations is on exactly one of four topics: Distribution, Logistics, Marketing, and Sales. She attends the meetings according to the following constraints:

She attends exactly three presentations on Logistics, exactly two presentations on Marketing, and exactly one presentation each on Distribution and Sales.
She never attends consecutive meetings on Logistics.
She attends the meeting on Sales immediately after she attends the meeting on Distribution.
Either the first or last presentation she attends, or both, will be a Marketing presentation.

1. [Step 1] Summarize your Overview analysis:

2. [Step 2] Create an initial Sketch:

3. [Step 3] Analyze and draw the Rules:
   - For each rule, answer the following questions and draw the rule in the appropriate box.
     - What does the rule restrict, and what does it leave open?
     - What are the rule's negative implications, if any?
     - Can the rule be depicted inside the sketch framework?

Rule 1:	Rule 3:
Rule 2:	Rule 4:

Explanations

Compare your work to that of an LSAT expert. Pay close attention to how the expert analyzed each rule and then depicted it within or beneath the game's initial sketch.

Practice 1

Rule		My Analysis
1.	There are exactly three appointments between D's appointment and C's appointment.	$\rightarrow$ D/C _ _ _ C/D
2.	There is, at most, one spot between H's spot and J's spot.	$\rightarrow$ [H / J] or H/J _ J/H
3.	If L is the second car, then M is the first car.	$\rightarrow$ If L2 $\rightarrow$ M1 If M~1 $\rightarrow$ L~2
4.	J and K both have lower-numbered positions than H or H has a lower-numbered position than both J and K.	$\rightarrow$ J .. ∴ H or H ∴ .. J K .· ·. K
5.	D is in position 4.	$\rightarrow$ $\frac{\quad}{1}$ $\frac{\quad}{2}$ $\frac{\quad}{3}$ $\frac{D}{4}$ $\frac{\quad}{5}$ $\frac{\quad}{6}$
6.	C is immediately after D but before E.	$\rightarrow$ [D C] ...E
7.	S is after both T and V.	$\rightarrow$ T ·. ∴ S V ·'
8.	P finishes later than Q, but earlier than R.	$\rightarrow$ Q...P...R
9.	M's position is at least two positions later than J's position.	$\rightarrow$ $\underline{J}$ _ ...$\underline{M}$
10.	N arrives exactly two hours before Z arrives.	$\rightarrow$ [N _ _ Z]
11.	X is in either position 1 or position 6.	X ↙ ↘ $\rightarrow$ $\frac{\quad}{1}$ $\frac{\quad}{2}$ $\frac{\quad}{3}$ $\frac{\quad}{4}$ $\frac{\quad}{5}$ $\frac{\quad}{6}$
12.	B is not fifth.	$\rightarrow$ $\frac{\quad}{1}$ $\frac{\quad}{2}$ $\frac{\quad}{3}$ $\frac{\quad}{4}$ $\frac{\quad}{5}$ $\frac{\quad}{6}$ ~B

Practice 2

A novelty-item sales representative is tasked with arranging on a shelf six new products—an art kit, a bandanna, a charm bracelet, a disco ball, a pair of earrings, and a fleece pullover—bearing the logo of a popular band. Strict company guidelines dictate that in arranging the items from left to right, one at a time, the sales representative must conform to the following restrictions:

> The art kit must be in one of the middle two spaces.
>
> The charm bracelet must be in a space next to one of the end spaces.
>
> The fleece pullover must be two spaces to the left of the disco ball.
>
> The art kit must never be placed immediately to the left of the fleece pullover.
>
> The earrings must be somewhere to the left of the bandanna.

1. [Step 1] Summarize your Overview analysis: *A Strict Sequencing game in which a sales rep is placing six items in order from left to right, one per position, along a shelf.*

2. [Step 2] Create an initial Sketch:

A B C D E F

$$\overline{}\ \overline{}\ \overline{}\ \overline{}\ \overline{}\ \overline{}$$
1   2   3   4   5   6

3. [Step 3] Analyze and draw the Rules:
    - Rule 1:
        - What does the rule restrict, and what does it leave open? *This rule restricts A to one of two positions (slot 3 or slot 4).*
        - What are the rule's negative implications, if any? *Simply that A won't be in slots 1, 2, 5, or 6.*

- Can the rule be depicted inside the sketch framework? *Yes.*
- Draw the rule:

A B C D E F

$$\overline{}\ \overline{}\ \overline{}\ \overline{}\ \overline{}\ \overline{}$$
1   2   3   4   5   6

- Rule 2:
    - What does the rule restrict, and what does it leave open? *This rule restricts C to one of two positions (slot 2 or slot 5).*
    - What are the rule's negative implications, if any? *Simply that C will not be in slots 1, 3, 4, or 6.*
    - Can the rule be depicted inside the sketch framework? *Yes.*
    - Draw the rule:

A B C D E F

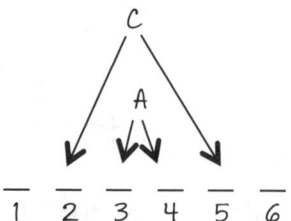

$$\overline{}\ \overline{}\ \overline{}\ \overline{}\ \overline{}\ \overline{}$$
1   2   3   4   5   6

- Rule 3:
    - What does the rule restrict, and what does it leave open? *This rule determines the order and distance between D and F: F will be exactly two slots to the left of D.*
    - What are the rule's negative implications, if any? *None beyond the fact that the relationship between D and F cannot be otherwise.*

- Can the rule be depicted inside the sketch framework? *No.*
- Draw the rule:

A B C D E F

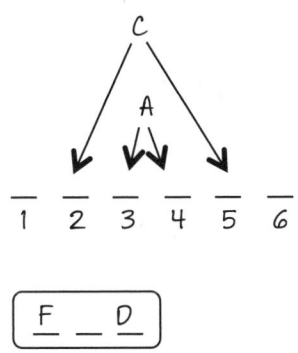

- Rule 4:
  - What does the rule restrict, and what does it leave open? *This is a negative rule that prevents A from being immediately to the left of F.*
  - What are the rule's negative implications, if any? *Either F is to the left of A, or A is two or more spaces to the left of F.*
  - Can the rule be depicted inside the sketch framework? *No.*
  - Draw the rule:

A B C D E F

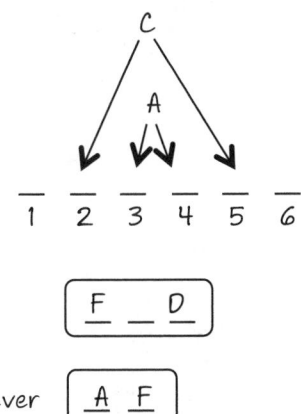

- Rule 5:
  - What does the rule restrict, and what does it leave open? *This creates a "loose" block: E . . . B. It says nothing about how close or far apart E and B are from one another.*

- What are the rule's negative implications, if any? *B is never to the left of E.*
- Can the rule be depicted inside the sketch framework? *No.*
- Draw the rule:

A B C D E F

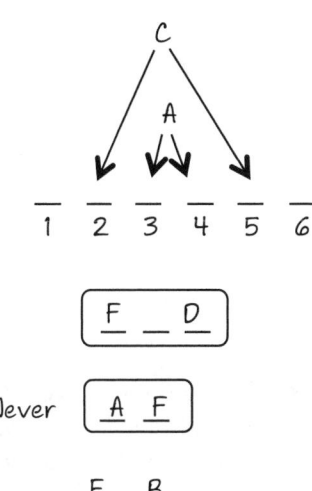

E . . . B

Practice 3

A park ranger surveyed different parks in her district for various species of medium-sized predators—bobcat, coyote, lynx, marten, ocelot and wolverine—and ranked them from most to least common, with no ties. The results indicated:

> In all parks, coyotes were the most or second most common species.
> Bobcat and lynx were never both among the three most common species in the same park.
> In every park, both bobcat and lynx were more common than both marten and wolverine.

1. [Step 1] Summarize your Overview analysis: *A Strict Sequencing game that accounts for the population sizes of six animal species in various parks.*

2. [Step 2] Create an initial Sketch: *Earlier, you saw this game depicted both horizontally and vertically. While either layout is fine, you'll see only the horizontal layout in the remainder of this chapter.*

3. [Step 3] Analyze and draw the Rules:
   - Rule 1:
     - What does the rule restrict, and what does it leave open? *This rule places C in either slot 1 or slot 2.*
     - What are the rule's negative implications, if any? *Simply that C is not in slots 3–6.*
     - Can the rule be depicted inside the sketch framework? *Yes.*
     - Draw the rule:

   - Rule 2:
     - What does the rule restrict, and what does it leave open? *This rule forbids both B and L from being among the top three slots. Note: The rule does not require either B or L to be among the top three; it simply says that if one of them is among the top three, the other will not be among the top three.*
     - What are the rule's negative implications, if any? *The top three spots will not consist of B, C, and L.*
     - Can the rule be depicted inside the sketch framework? *Yes, at least in a negative sense.*

- Draw the rule:

  B C L M O W

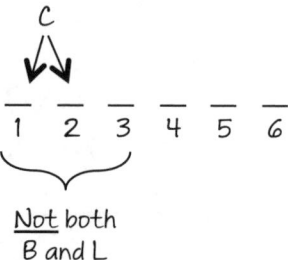

- Rule 3:
  - What does the rule restrict, and what does it leave open? *This is really two rules in one: B is ranked higher than M and W, and L is ranked higher than M and W. It does not give the relative order between B and L, or between M and W, nor does it restrict the distances among any of these entities.*
  - What are the rule's negative implications, if any? *Neither M nor W can be ranked higher than either B or L; neither M nor W can ever be ranked first or second, and neither B nor L can be ranked fifth or sixth.*
  - Can the rule be depicted inside the sketch framework? *No.*
  - Draw the rule:

    B C L M O W

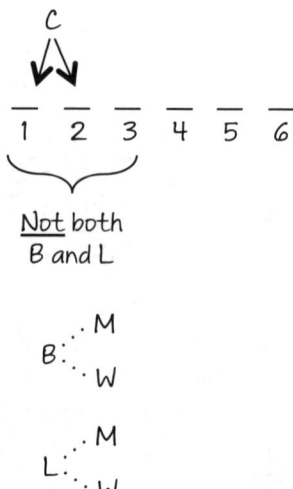

Practice 4

Throughout the course of a day, an executive will attend exactly seven different business presentations. Each of the presentations is on exactly one of four topics: Distribution, Logistics, Marketing, and Sales. She attends the meetings according to the following constraints:

> She attends exactly three presentations on Logistics, exactly two presentations on Marketing, and exactly one presentation each on Distribution and Sales.
> She never attends consecutive meetings on Logistics.
> She attends the meeting on Sales immediately after she attends the meeting on Distribution.
> Either the first or last presentation she attends, or both, will be a Marketing presentation.

1. [Step 1] Summarize your Overview analysis: *A Strict Sequencing game that accounts for an executive's itinerary of seven presentations over the course of one day. There are four types of presentations—D, L, M, and S—but we don't know the number of each type of presentation that the executive will see until Rule 1.*

2. [Step 2] Create an initial Sketch:

   $$D\ L\ M\ S$$

   $$\underline{\quad}\ \underline{\quad}\ \underline{\quad}\ \underline{\quad}\ \underline{\quad}\ \underline{\quad}\ \underline{\quad}$$
   $$\ \ 1\ \ \ \ 2\ \ \ \ 3\ \ \ \ 4\ \ \ \ 5\ \ \ \ 6\ \ \ \ 7$$

3. [Step 3] Analyze and draw the Rules:
   - Rule 1:
     - What does the rule restrict, and what does it leave open? *This rule defines the number of each type of presentation the executive will see—one D, three Ls, two Ms, and an S.*
     - What are the rule's negative implications, if any? *None. The number of each meeting type is now completely determined.*
     - Can the rule be depicted inside the sketch framework? *No, but this rule's details can be added to the roster of entities.*

   - Draw the rule:

     $$D\ L_1\ L_2\ L_3\ M_1\ M_2\ S$$

     $$\underline{\quad}\ \underline{\quad}\ \underline{\quad}\ \underline{\quad}\ \underline{\quad}\ \underline{\quad}\ \underline{\quad}$$
     $$\ \ 1\ \ \ \ 2\ \ \ \ 3\ \ \ \ 4\ \ \ \ 5\ \ \ \ 6\ \ \ \ 7$$

   - Rule 2:
     - What does the rule restrict, and what does it leave open? *This rule forbids consecutive presentations on Logistics.*
     - What are the rule's negative implications, if any? *At least one other type of presentation will always intervene between two Logistics presentations.*
     - Can the rule be depicted inside the sketch framework? *No.*
     - Draw the rule:

       $$D\ L_1\ L_2\ L_3\ M_1\ M_2\ S$$

       $$\underline{\quad}\ \underline{\quad}\ \underline{\quad}\ \underline{\quad}\ \underline{\quad}\ \underline{\quad}\ \underline{\quad}$$
       $$\ \ 1\ \ \ \ 2\ \ \ \ 3\ \ \ \ 4\ \ \ \ 5\ \ \ \ 6\ \ \ \ 7$$

       Never $\boxed{L\ \ L}$

   - Rule 3:
     - What does the rule restrict, and what does it leave open? *This rule creates a block of entities: D-S.*
     - What are the rule's negative implications, if any? *S cannot come before D, and the two can never be separated.*
     - Can the rule be depicted inside the sketch framework? *No.*
     - Draw the rule:

       $$D\ L_1\ L_2\ L_3\ M_1\ M_2\ S$$

       $$\underline{\quad}\ \underline{\quad}\ \underline{\quad}\ \underline{\quad}\ \underline{\quad}\ \underline{\quad}\ \underline{\quad}$$
       $$\ \ 1\ \ \ \ 2\ \ \ \ 3\ \ \ \ 4\ \ \ \ 5\ \ \ \ 6\ \ \ \ 7$$

       Never $\boxed{L\ \ L}$

       $\boxed{D\ \ S}$

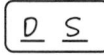   251

- Rule 4:
  - What does the rule restrict, and what does it leave open? *This rule dictates that Marketing will be the first presentation, the last presentation, or both.*
  - What are the rule's negative implications, if any? *None.*
  - Can the rule be depicted inside the sketch framework? *Partially—It is easy to show that an M needs to be in either slot 1 or slot 7, but the "or both" should be noted separately, as well.*

- Draw the rule:

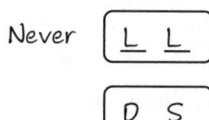

With the rules in place, you may already be anticipating the deductions that can be made in each of these practice game setups. You'll have a chance to add those in the next section of this chapter covering Step 4 of the Logic Games Method in basic Strict Sequencing games.

BASIC STRICT SEQUENCING GAMES DEDUCTIONS

LEARNING OBJECTIVES

In this section of the chapter, you'll practice

- Applying Step 4 of the Logic Games Method to Simple Strict Sequencing games by combining rules and restrictions to make all valid deductions in the game.

Prepare

Strict Sequencing games involve putting entities in order in numbered or named positions. It stands to reason, then, that the most concrete restrictions within these games come from rules that place an entity precisely (Established Entities) and those involving the relative positions of two or more entities (Blocks of Entities).

Keep in mind, though, that a rule such as "Brianna is placed exactly one position after Feng" is much more restrictive than one saying "Brianna's position is at some point after Feng's position." The first of those rules creates a block of entities that must occupy two consecutive positions, and depending on the other rules in the game, there may be only one or two places within the game's framework where you can find two consecutive open slots.

Whenever you're making deductions in a Strict Sequencing game, look for Duplications (rules that can be combined because they share a common entity). Knowing, for example, that L comes before J or that N comes before L is helpful, of course. But knowing that the three entities are all related (N . . . L . . . J), and thus all restrict one another, is far more restrictive within the game, and will lead to further deductions.

LOGIC GAMES STRATEGY

In Sequencing games, deductions are most likely to stem from:

- **Blocks of Entities**—Two or more entities that are linked together; when one is placed, the other's placement is determined or restricted.
- **Duplications**—Entities shared by two or more rules; duplications are always at the heart of Loose Sequencing games.
- **Established Entities**—Entities placed into a specific position; even if no rule directly provides for an Established Entity, you may be able to determine an entity's exact position by combining other rules.

In Sequencing games, deductions may involve:

- **Limited Options**—The situation arises when a Block of Entities or a key player (an entity affecting the positions of other entities) is restricted to either of two positions; when this occurs, draw dual Limited Options sketches.
- **Number Restrictions**—Limitations or rules affecting the number of entities that can be placed in a given position; this is rare in Sequencing games— typically, the stated limitation is one entity per position.

Practice

Directions: In each game setup, first reacquaint yourself with the setup and rules. Then, combine the rules and restrictions to make all available deductions, recording your analyses as indicated. Finally, test your deductions by answering the questions that accompany each game. You can find expert analysis and explanations at the end of the Practice section.

Practice 1

A novelty-item sales representative is tasked with arranging on a shelf six new products—an art kit, a bandanna, a charm bracelet, a disco ball, a pair of earrings, and a fleece pullover—bearing the logo of a popular band. Strict company guidelines dictate that in arranging the items from left to right, one at a time, the sales representative must conform to the following restrictions:

The art kit must be in one of the middle two spaces.
The charm bracelet must be in a space next to one of the end spaces.
The fleece pullover must be two spaces to the left of the disco ball.
The art kit must never be placed immediately to the left of the fleece pullover.
The earrings must be somewhere to the left of the bandanna.

Steps 1–3:

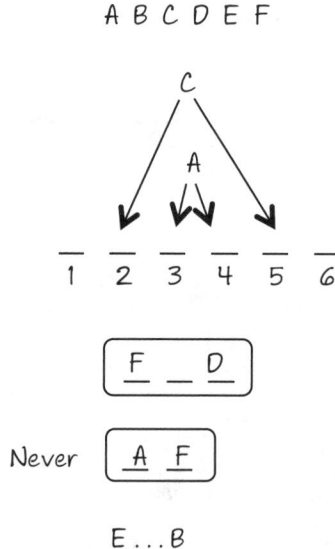

1. Which entities or positions are the most restricted in this game? Why?

2. Which elements from the BLEND checklist can you identify in this game? Are there
   - Blocks of entities? If so, what are they?
   - Limited Options? If so, which rule(s) trigger them?
   - Established Entities? If so, which ones?
   - Number Restrictions? If so, describe them.
   - Duplications? If so, which rules share an entity?

3. Combine the rules and restrictions to create a Master Sketch depicting all of the deductions available in this game:

4. Evaluate your sketch by answering the following questions:
   - Write out a complete and accurate list of the entities that could acceptably occupy position 1.
   - If the art kit is in position 3, which entity or entities could be in position 5?
   - If the art kit is in position 4, which entity or entities could be in position 2?
   - How many entities could acceptably occupy position 6?

Practice 2

A park ranger surveyed different parks in her district for various species of medium-sized predators—bobcat, coyote, lynx, marten, ocelot and wolverine—and ranked them from most to least common, with no ties. The results indicated:

> In all parks, coyotes were the most or second most common species.
> Bobcat and lynx were never both among the three most common species in the same park.
> In every park, both bobcat and lynx were more common than both marten and wolverine.

Steps 1–3:

BCLMOW

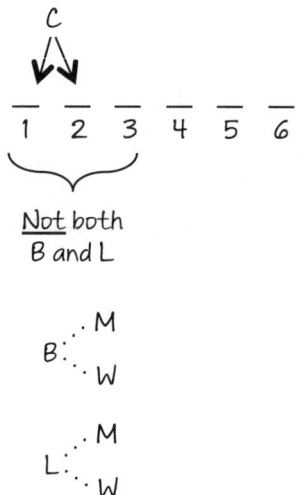

1. Which entities or positions are the most restricted in this game? Why?

2. Which elements from the BLEND checklist can you identify in this game? Are there
   - Blocks of entities? If so, what are they?
   - Limited Options? If so, which rule(s) trigger them?
   - Established Entities? If so, which ones?
   - Number Restrictions? If so, describe them.
   - Duplications? If so, which rules share an entity?

3. Combine the rules and restrictions to create a Master Sketch depicting all of the deductions available in this game:

4. Evaluate your sketch by answering the following questions:
   - Write out a complete and accurate list of species that could be the fourth most common at one of the parks.
   - Write out a complete and accurate list of the positions that martens could acceptably occupy.
   - Write out a complete and accurate list of the species that could be the most common at one of the parks.
   - If bobcats are the second most common species at one of the parks, what else *must be true* about species population at that park?

Practice 3

Throughout the course of a day, an executive will attend exactly seven different business presentations. Each of the presentations is on exactly one of four topics: Distribution, Logistics, Marketing, and Sales. She attends the meetings according to the following constraints:

> She attends exactly three presentations on Logistics, exactly two presentations on Marketing, and exactly one presentation each on Distribution and Sales.
>
> She never attends consecutive meetings on Logistics.
>
> She attends the meeting on Sales immediately after she attends the meeting on Distribution.
>
> Either the first or last presentation she attends, or both, will be a Marketing presentation.

Steps 1–3:

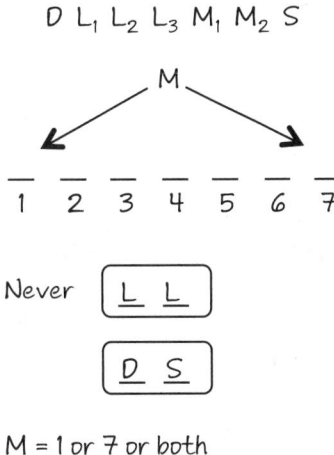

1. Which entities or positions are the most restricted in this game? Why?

2. Which elements from the BLEND checklist can you identify in this game? Are there

   - Blocks of entities? If so, what are they?

   - Limited Options? If so, which rule(s) trigger them?

   - Established Entities? If so, which ones?

   - Number Restrictions? If so, describe them.

   - Duplications? If so, which rules share an entity?

3. Combine the rules and restrictions to create a Master Sketch depicting all of the deductions available in this game:

4. Evaluate your sketch by answering the following questions:

   - If the executive sees the Sales presentation fourth, for how many of the positions can the topic of the presentation be precisely determined?

   - If the executive sees a Logistics presentation second, in which positions could she see the Distribution presentation?

   - If the executive sees a Marketing presentation first, which of the topics could be the topic she sees in the seventh presentation?

   - Write out a complete and accurate list of all the topics that could not be the topic covered by the first presentation.

Explanations

Compare your work to that of an LSAT expert. Pay close attention to how the expert combined the rules and restrictions to make additional deductions, and to how the expert depicted the deductions within the sketch framework.

Practice 1

A novelty-item sales representative is tasked with arranging on a shelf six new products—an art kit, a bandanna, a charm bracelet, a disco ball, a pair of earrings, and a fleece pullover—bearing the logo of a popular band. Strict company guidelines dictate that in arranging the items from left to right, one at a time, the sales representative must conform to the following restrictions:

> The art kit must be in one of the middle two spaces.
>
> The charm bracelet must be in a space next to one of the end spaces.
>
> The fleece pullover must be two spaces to the left of the disco ball.
>
> The art kit must never be placed immediately to the left of the fleece pullover.
>
> The earrings must be somewhere to the left of the bandanna.

Steps 1–3:

A B C D E F

C
↓ ↓ ↓
A
↘↙
1 2 3 4 5 6

F _ D

Never A F

E . . . B

1. Which entities or positions are the most restricted in this game? Why? *Both A and C are restricted to just two positions each (Rules 1 and 2), but A is even more restricted because it cannot be to the immediate left of F (Rule 4).*

2. Which elements from the BLEND checklist can you identify in this game? Are there

   - Blocks of entities? If so, what are they? *Rule 3 creates a block of two entities over three positions: F_D. Rule 5 creates a "loose" block: E . . . B.*

   - Limited Options? If so, which rule(s) trigger them? *Both Rules 1 and 2 create potential Limited Options scenarios by limiting A and C to just two positions each. Test Rule 1 first, however, because Rule 4 also restricts A in relationship to F, which is, in turn restricted by D (Rule 3).*

   - Established Entities? If so, which ones? *N/A*

   - Number Restrictions? If so, describe them. *N/A, entities are placed one per position.*

   - Duplications? If so, which rules share an entity? *Rules 1 and 4 share A, and Rules 3 and 4 share F.*

3. Combine the rules and restrictions to create a Master Sketch depicting all of the deductions available in this game: *Begin by recording the negative implications of the blocks of entities. Because of Rule 3, D will never take positions 1 and 2, and F will never take positions 5 or 6. Likewise, because of Rule 5, B will never take position 1 and E will never take position 6. Add those deductions to the sketch.*

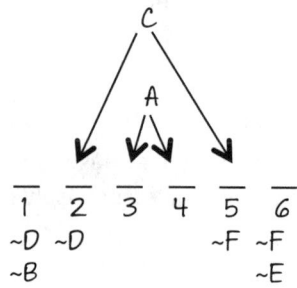

The only entities available for position 1 are thus E and F, and the only entities available for position 6 are thus B and D.

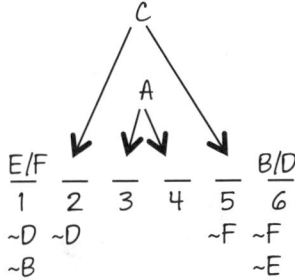

Now, because Rule 1 limits A to positions 3 or 4, and because the placement of A triggers another restriction in Rule 4, make a Limited Options framework to test out each of A's potential positions.

Opt. I
$$\frac{E/F}{1} \quad \frac{}{2} \quad \frac{A}{3} \quad \frac{}{4} \quad \frac{}{5} \quad \frac{B/D}{6}$$

Opt. II
$$\frac{E/F}{1} \quad \frac{}{2} \quad \frac{}{3} \quad \frac{A}{4} \quad \frac{}{5} \quad \frac{B/D}{6}$$

First, explore Option I. Because of Rule 4, F cannot occupy position 4 with A in position 3. Where could the F_D block be placed in this option? It can go only in positions 2 and 4. That means E will take position 1, and B will take position 6. In this option, C must take position 5, the only position that remains open.

Opt. I
$$\frac{E}{1} \quad \frac{F}{2} \quad \frac{A}{3} \quad \frac{D}{4} \quad \frac{C}{5} \quad \frac{B}{6}$$

Now, work out the deductions in Option II. With A in position 4, the F_D block could fit in positions 1 and 3, or in positions 3 and 5. In either case, B will take position 6.

Opt. II
$$\frac{E/F}{1} \quad \frac{}{2} \quad \frac{}{3} \quad \frac{A}{4} \quad \frac{}{5} \quad \frac{B}{6}$$
$$\phantom{\frac{E/F}{1}} \quad F \quad \quad D$$
$$\phantom{\frac{E/F}{1}} \quad \quad F \quad \quad D$$

With the two options worked out to that degree, you should be able to answer any question that the test might throw at you about this game.

Note: If you wanted to, you could continue to push the deductions in Option II even further. For example, when the F_D block takes positions 1 and 3, then C and E take will take positions 2 and 5 in either order. And when the F_D block takes positions 3 and 5, then E must take position 1 and C must take position 2. The decision to take the deductions that far on Test Day would be a matter of time, and of how much additional help you think it would be in answering the questions.

Opt. II
$$\frac{F}{1} \quad \frac{C/E}{2} \quad \frac{D}{3} \quad \frac{A}{4} \quad \frac{E/C}{5} \quad \frac{B}{6}$$

$$\frac{E}{1} \quad \frac{C}{2} \quad \frac{F}{3} \quad \frac{A}{4} \quad \frac{D}{5} \quad \frac{B}{6}$$

4. Evaluate your sketch by answering the following questions:

- Which entities could acceptably occupy position 1? *The earrings or the fleece pullover.*

- If the art kit is in position 3, which entity or entities could be in position 5? *Only the charm bracelet.*

- If the art kit is in position 4, which entity or entities could be in position 2? *The earrings or the charm bracelet.*

- How many entities could acceptably occupy position 6? *Just one, the bandanna.*

Practice 2

A park ranger surveyed different parks in her district for various species of medium-sized predators—bobcat, coyote, lynx, marten, ocelot and wolverine—and ranked them from most to least common, with no ties. The results indicated:

> In all parks, coyotes were the most or second most common species.
> Bobcat and lynx were never both among the three most common species in the same park.
> In every park, both bobcat and lynx were more common than both marten and wolverine.

Steps 1–3:

B C L M O W

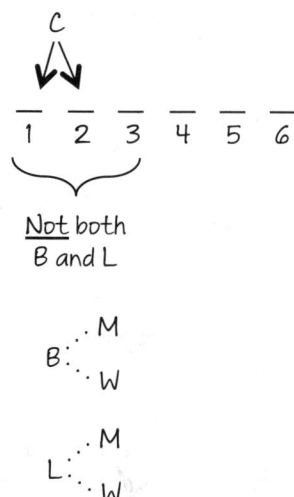

1. Which entities or positions are the most restricted in this game? Why? *While C is restricted to just two acceptable positions (Rule 1), B and L are both restricted by two rules (Rules 2 and 3). Both B and L must have larger populations than M and W, but only one of B or L is permitted to be among the top three largest populations.*

2. Which elements from the BLEND checklist can you identify in this game? Are there

   - Blocks of entities? If so, what are they? *Rule 3 creates two loose blocks: B is larger than M and W, and L is larger than M and W.*

   - Limited Options? If so, which rule(s) trigger them? *N/A*

   - Established Entities? If so, which ones? *C is restricted to two positions, but no entity's position is completely established.*

   - Number Restrictions? If so, describe them. *N/A; the arrangement is already one per position ("no ties").*

   - Duplications? If so, which rules share an entity? *Rules 2 and 3 share B and L.*

3. Combine the rules and restrictions to create a Master Sketch depicting all of the deductions available in this game: *The duplication of two entities in Rules 2 and 3 make B and L the focus of the deductions here. Because both B and L must rank higher than M and W, the lowest B or L could be is fourth. Because only one of B or L is allowed to among the top three species, you know that either B or L is always fourth.*

$$\overset{C}{\underset{\underset{1 \quad 2 \quad 3 \quad 4 \quad 5 \quad 6}{\rule{0pt}{0pt}}}{\text{\_\_ \_\_ \_\_ B/L M/W W/M}}}$$

That sketch also shows that M and W will be fifth and sixth, in either order, because both of them must be ranked lower than either B or L.

With one of B or L in fourth place, you can deduce that the other will be among the top three species. You already know (from Rule 1) that C is either first or second. That means that O, the only remaining entity, will also be among the top three.

$$\overset{C}{\text{\_\_ \_\_ \_\_ B/L M/W W/M}}$$
1 2 3 4 5 6

C, O, L/B

It is not worth the time it would take to work out all the possible arrangements of the first through third spots. Those positions would come into play in New-"If" questions, and the question stem would give you the information necessary to work out what you would need to know.

4. Evaluate your sketch by answering the following questions:

   • Write out a complete and accurate list of species that could be the fourth most common at one of the parks. *Bobcat and lynx.*

   • Write out a complete and accurate list of the positions that martens could acceptably occupy. *Fifth or sixth.*

   • Write out a complete and accurate list of the species that could be the most common at one of the parks. *Bobcat, coyote, lynx, and ocelot.*

   • If bobcats are the second most common species at one of the parks, what else *must be true* about species population at that park? *In that case, 1) coyotes are the most common species, 2) ocelots are the third most common species, and 3) lynx are the fourth most common species at that park.*

Practice 3

Throughout the course of a day, an executive will attend exactly seven different business presentations. Each of the presentations is on exactly one of four topics: Distribution, Logistics, Marketing, and Sales. She attends the meetings according to the following constraints:

> She attends exactly three presentations on Logistics, exactly two presentations on Marketing, and exactly one presentation each on Distribution and Sales.
> She never attends consecutive meetings on Logistics.
> She attends the meeting on Sales immediately after she attends the meeting on Distribution.
> Either the first or last presentation she attends, or both, will be a Marketing presentation.

Steps 1–3:

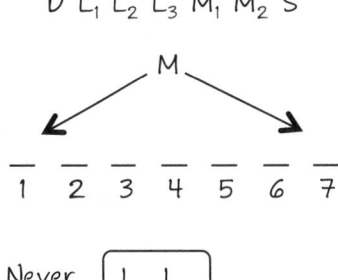

$D \; L_1 \; L_2 \; L_3 \; M_1 \; M_2 \; S$

M = 1 or 7 or both

1. Which entities or positions are the most restricted in this game? Why? *With the unusual set of entities in this game, the place to begin will be with the three presentations on Logistics (noted as L_1, L_2, and L_3 in the sketch), none of which can be consecutive.*

2. Which elements from the BLEND checklist can you identify in this game? Are there

   • Blocks of entities? If so, what are they? *Rule 3 creates a strict block: D-S.*

   • Limited Options? If so, which rule(s) trigger them? *N/A*

   • Established Entities? If so, which ones? *N/A*

   • Number Restrictions? If so, describe them. *N/A; although the assignment of entities to positions is one-to-one, Rule 1 creates a quasi-number restriction by stipulating that there are three Logistics presentations and two Marketing presentations.*

   • Duplications? If so, which rules share an entity? *All four entities appear in Rule 1 and in one other rule (Logistics in Rule 2, Distribution and Sales in Rule 3, and Marketing in Rule 4).*

3. Combine the rules and restrictions to create a Master Sketch depicting all of the deductions available in this game: *Start with the combination of Rules 1 and 2. If there are to be three Ls, and if none of them can be consecutive, they can be depicted like this:*

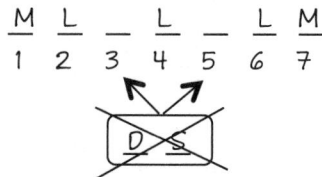

Note that the string of Ls takes up at least five of the game's seven positions. Next, consider the two Ms. At least one of them must be first or seventh, and Rule 3 allows for them to be both first and seventh. However, if Ms were both first and seventh, you would find yourself in this situation:

$$
\begin{array}{ccccccc}
\underline{M} & \underline{L} & \underline{} & \underline{L} & \underline{} & \underline{L} & \underline{M} \\
1 & 2 & 3 & 4 & 5 & 6 & 7
\end{array}
$$

$$\cancel{\boxed{D \ S}}$$

In that case, there is no place for the D-S block. You now know that if one M is first, the other cannot be seventh, and vice versa. To find room for the D-S block, it will need to go in between two Ls, and one of the Ms will also have to go in between two Ls.

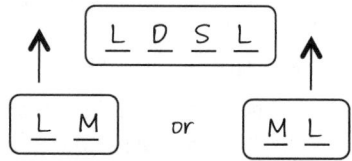

The remaining M can go on either side of one of these six-entity blocks. That helps you to see that whenever M is first, an L will be

seventh, and whenever an M is seventh, an L will be first.

$$
\begin{array}{ccccccc}
\underset{1}{\overset{M/L}{\underline{}}} & \underset{2}{\underline{}} & \underset{3}{\underline{}} & \underset{4}{\underline{}} & \underset{5}{\underline{}} & \underset{6}{\underline{}} & \underset{7}{\overset{L/M}{\underline{}}}
\end{array}
$$

↑ [L D S L] ↑

[L M] or [M L]

4. Evaluate your sketch by answering the following questions:

- If the executive sees the Sales presentation fourth, for how many of the positions can the topic of the presentation be precisely determined? *All seven positions can be determined. With S in the fourth position, the only acceptable arrangement is: M, L, D, S, L, M, L*

- If the executive sees a Logistics presentation second, in which positions could she see the Distribution presentation? *If an L is second, there are two acceptable arrangements, either M, L, D, S, L, M, L or M, L, M, L, D, S, L; thus, with an L in the second position, the D could be third or sixth.*

- If the executive sees a Marketing presentation first, which of the topics could be the topic she sees in the seventh presentation? *If an M is first, an L must be seventh.*

- Write out a complete and accurate list of all the topics that could not be the topic covered by the first presentation. *The first presentation must be an M or an L. Thus, D and S are the topics that <u>cannot</u> be first.*

The number of deductions available in Strict Sequencing games varies widely. In some, the deductions are so concrete that you will be left with only a handful of acceptable arrangements by the time you've finished Step 4. In others, the testmaker leaves much more ambiguity among the entities and within the framework. In games with fewer deductions, expect to see more New-"If" questions, as each of those questions' stems introduces a new rule or restriction into the mix. If you find yourself feeling stuck in Step 4, glance at the questions. If almost all of them are New-"If"s, you may have found all of the deductions available. Move on, creating new sketches for each of the New-"If" scenarios, and make the deductions for each question there.

In the next (and final) section of this chapter, put all of your skills together to handle some full basic Strict Sequencing games and their questions.

BASIC STRICT SEQUENCING GAMES—FULL GAMES WITH QUESTIONS

LEARNING OBJECTIVES

In this section, you'll assess your ability to

- Apply the Logic Games Method to basic Strict Sequencing games.

Perform

Here is your opportunity to put all of the pieces together and assess your skills on basic Strict Sequencing games. On the following pages, you'll find three full-length games along with their question sets. All of these games are from officially released LSAT tests, and all are representative of basic Strict Sequencing games you could see on Test Day. You can take the games one at a time or all together, but for your self-evaluation to be as accurate as possible, adhere to the timing guidelines set forth in the directions.

An answer key follows the games. Complete worked example analyses can be found in your online resources.

After you complete and review all three games, assess your performance using the evaluation guidelines. There you'll find recommendations for additional Easy, Medium, and Hard basic Strict Sequencing games from officially released LSAT exams that you can practice to continue honing your skills and raising your score.

Directions: Take no more than 9 minutes per game to complete the following three games and all of their questions.

Perform 1

<u>Questions 1–5</u>

A producer is positioning exactly seven music pieces—F, G, H, J, K, L, and M—one after another on a music recording, not necessarily in that order. Each piece will fill exactly one of the seven sequential tracks on the recording, according to the following conditions:

  F must be second.
  J cannot be seventh.
  G can come neither immediately before nor immediately after H.
  H must be in some track before that of L.
  L must be in some track before that of M.

1. Which one of the following could be the order, from first to seventh, of the pieces on the recording?

(A) F, K, G, J, H, L, M
(B) G, F, H, K, L, J, M
(C) G, F, H, K, L, M, J
(D) K, F, G, H, J, L, M
(E) K, F, L, J, H, M, G

2. If M fills some track before that of J and also before that of K on the recording, which one of the following must be true?

    (A) G is first.
    (B) K is seventh.
    (C) L is third.
    (D) H comes either immediately before or immediately after F.
    (E) L comes either immediately before or immediately after G.

3. Which one of the following is a complete and accurate list of the pieces any of which could be first on the recording?

    (A) G, J, K
    (B) G, H, J, K
    (C) G, H, J, L
    (D) G, J, K, L
    (E) H, J, K, L, M

4. The earliest track that M can fill is the

    (A) first
    (B) third
    (C) fourth
    (D) fifth
    (E) sixth

5. If G is to come immediately before H but all the other conditions remain in effect, any of the following could be true EXCEPT:

    (A) J comes immediately before F.
    (B) K comes immediately before G.
    (C) J comes immediately after L.
    (D) J comes immediately after K.
    (E) K comes immediately after M.

PrepTest23 Sec1 Qs 1-5

Perform 2

<u>Questions 6–10</u>

Five people—Harry, Iris, Kate, Nancy, and Victor—are to be scheduled as contestants on a television show, one contestant per day, for five consecutive days from Monday through Friday. The following restrictions governing the scheduling of contestants must be observed:

Nancy is not scheduled for Monday.

If Harry is scheduled for Monday, Nancy is scheduled for Friday.

If Nancy is scheduled for Tuesday, Iris is scheduled for Monday.

Kate is scheduled for the next day after the day for which Victor is scheduled.

6. Victor can be scheduled for any day EXCEPT

(A) Monday
(B) Tuesday
(C) Wednesday
(D) Thursday
(E) Friday

7. If Iris is scheduled for the next day after Harry, which one of the following lists all those days any one of which could be the day for which Harry is scheduled?

  (A) Monday, Tuesday
  (B) Monday, Wednesday
  (C) Monday, Thursday
  (D) Monday, Tuesday, Wednesday
  (E) Monday, Wednesday, Thursday

8. If Kate is scheduled for Wednesday, which one of the following could be true?

  (A) Iris is scheduled for Friday.
  (B) Nancy is scheduled for Tuesday.
  (C) Nancy is scheduled for an earlier day than the day for which Harry is scheduled.
  (D) Nancy is scheduled for an earlier day than the day for which Iris is scheduled.
  (E) Nancy is scheduled for an earlier day than the day for which Kate is scheduled.

9. If Kate is scheduled for Friday, which one of the following must be true?

  (A) Harry is scheduled for Tuesday.
  (B) Harry is scheduled for Wednesday.
  (C) Iris is scheduled for Monday.
  (D) Iris is scheduled for Wednesday.
  (E) Nancy is scheduled for Wednesday.

10. If Iris is scheduled for Wednesday, which one of the following must be true?

  (A) Harry is scheduled for an earlier day than the day for which Nancy is scheduled.
  (B) Harry is scheduled for an earlier day than the day for which Kate is scheduled.
  (C) Kate is scheduled for an earlier day than the day for which Harry is scheduled.
  (D) Nancy is scheduled for an earlier day than the day for which Kate is scheduled.
  (E) Nancy is scheduled for an earlier day than the day for which Iris is scheduled.

PrepTest13 Sec1 Qs 7-11

Perform 3

<u>Questions 11–17</u>

During a period of six consecutive days—day 1 through day 6—each of exactly six factories—F, G, H, J, Q, and R—will be inspected. During this period, each of the factories will be inspected exactly once, one factory per day. The schedule for the inspections must conform to the following conditions:

    F is inspected on either day 1 or day 6.

    J is inspected on an earlier day than Q is inspected.

    Q is inspected on the day immediately before R is inspected.

    If G is inspected on day 3, Q is inspected on day 5.

11. Which one of the following could be a list of the factories in the order of their scheduled inspections, from day 1 through day 6?

    (A)   F, Q, R, H, J, G
    (B)   G, H, J, Q, R, F
    (C)   G, J, Q, H, R, F
    (D)   G, J, Q, R, F, H
    (E)   J, H, G, Q, R, F

12. Which one of the following must be false?

    (A) The inspection of G is scheduled for day 4.
    (B) The inspection of H is scheduled for day 6.
    (C) The inspection of J is scheduled for day 4.
    (D) The inspection of Q is scheduled for day 3.
    (E) The inspection of R is scheduled for day 2.

13. The inspection of which one of the following CANNOT be scheduled for day 5?

    (A) G
    (B) H
    (C) J
    (D) Q
    (E) R

14. The inspection scheduled for day 3 and day 5, respectively, could be those of

    (A) G and H
    (B) G and R
    (C) H and G
    (D) R and J
    (E) R and H

15. If the inspection of R is scheduled for the day immediately before the inspection of F, which one of the following must be true about the schedule?

    (A) The inspection of either G or H is scheduled for day 1.
    (B) The inspection of either G or J is scheduled for day 1.
    (C) The inspection of either G or J is scheduled for day 2.
    (D) The inspection of either H or J is scheduled for day 3.
    (E) The inspection of either H or J is scheduled for day 4.

16. If the inspection of G and of H are scheduled, not necessarily in that order, for days as far apart as possible, which one of the following is a complete and accurate list of the factories any one of which could be scheduled for inspection for day 1?

    (A) F, J
    (B) G, H
    (C) G, H, J
    (D) F, G, H
    (E) F, G, H, J

17. If the inspection of G is scheduled for the day immediately before the inspection of Q, which one of the following could be true?

    (A) The inspection of G is scheduled for day 5.
    (B) The inspection of H is scheduled for day 6.
    (C) The inspection of J is scheduled for day 2.
    (D) The inspection of Q is scheduled for day 4.
    (E) The inspection of R is scheduled for day 3.

PrepTest19 Sec1 Qs 1-7

Answer Key

Perform 1

1. (B)
2. (D)
3. (B)
4. (C)
5. (D)

Perform 2

6. (E)
7. (E)
8. (C)
9. (C)
10. (C)

Perform 3

11. (B)
12. (E)
13. (C)
14. (E)
15. (D)
16. (D)
17. (C)

Worked example explanations of these questions with complete expert analysis can be found in your Online Study Plan under Chapter 5. View or download the PDF titled "Chapter 5 Perform Full Games Explanations."

Assess

Use the following criteria to evaluate your results on the Perform games.

If, under timed conditions, you correctly answered

14–17 of the questions: Outstanding! You have demonstrated a strong skill level in basic Strict Sequencing games. For further practice in basic Strict Sequencing, use any of the Recommended Additional Practice sets, including the Advanced set. Then, move on to Chapter 6 on complex Strict Sequencing.

10–13 of the questions: Good work! You have a solid foundation in basic Strict Sequencing games. For further practice in basic Strict Sequencing, begin with the Foundations or Mid-Level Recommended Additional Practice set. Then, move on to Chapter 6 on complex Strict Sequencing. If you have time before Test Day, try the Advanced Recommended Additional Practice set, as well.

0–9 of the questions: Keep working. Strict Sequencing games are central to your logic games performance, and continued practice will help you improve your score. Begin by reviewing this chapter. Then, try the games in the Foundations Recommended Additional Practice set. As you continue to progress, move on to the Mid-Level Recommended Additional Practice set, and then to Chapter 6 on complex Strict Sequencing games.

To stay sharp, practice the drills in the Logic Games Training Camp for this chapter in your Online Study Plan. Training Camp drills are divided into Fundamentals, Mid-Level, and Advanced sets.

Recommended Additional Practice: Basic Strict Sequencing

All of the following games will provide good practice on basic Strict Sequencing games. They are grouped by difficulty as determined from empirical student practice results. All PrepTests included are available individually, or in bundles of 10 as part of the LSAC's *10 Actual, Official LSAT PrepTests* series.

Foundations
PrepTest 70, Section 3, Game 1: Benefit Concert*

PrepTest 67, Section 3, Game 2: Literary Theory Lectures*

PrepTest 63, Section 2, Game 2: Skydiving Team*

PrepTest 62, Section 3, Game 4: Testifying Witnesses*

PrepTest 57, Section 1, Game 1: Student Activities**

Mid-Level
PrepTest 66, Section 3, Game 2: Shopping Center Businesses*

PrepTest 64, Section 2, Game 1: Employee Parking*

PrepTest 62, Section 3, Game 1: Motel Service Appointments*

PrepTest 56, Section 1, Game 1: Saxophone Auditions**

PrepTest 54, Section 3, Game 3: Cake Layers**

Advanced

PrepTest 71, Section 2, Game 4: Paintings in a Museum*

PrepTest 69, Section 2, Game 1: Manuscript Ages*

PrepTest 63, Section 2, Game 3: Vehicle Service*

PrepTest 59, Section 1, Game 2: Museum Photographs**

PrepTest 59, Section 1, Game 4: Organization's Annual Meetings**

*Game included in *10 Actual, Official LSAT PrepTests Volume V: PrepTests 62–71*; complete answers and explanations written by Kaplan LSAT experts available via the eBook: *LSAT PrepTests 62–71 Unlocked: Exclusive Data, Analysis & Explanations for 10 Actual, Official LSAT PrepTests Volume V.*

**Game included in *10 New Actual, Official LSAT PrepTests with Comparative Reading (PrepTests 52–61)*; complete answers and explanations written by Kaplan LSAT experts available via the eBook: *LSAT PrepTests 52–61 Unlocked: Exclusive Data, Analysis & Explanations for 10 New Actual, Official LSAT PrepTests with Comparative Reading.* [Explanations title coming soon.]

Reflect

Think back over the study and practice you did in this chapter.

- Are you able to identify basic Strict Sequencing games from their setups?
- Do you have a default sketch framework for Strict Sequencing actions?
- What kinds of rules do you anticipate seeing in Strict Sequencing games?
- Are you comfortable analyzing Strict Sequencing rules and determining whether to record them within or underneath the sketch framework?
- Are you making the available deductions efficiently and effectively in Strict Sequencing games?

In the coming days and weeks before Test Day, take note of real-world tasks that reflect basic Strict Sequencing tasks. Consider how they mirror the setups and questions in LSAT Strict Sequencing, and how they differ. Try to reframe real-life sequencing tasks using the terms, rules, and restrictions used by the testmaker.

CHAPTER 6

Complex Strict Sequencing Games Unlocked

LEARNING OBJECTIVES

In this chapter, you'll learn to

- Apply the Logic Games Method to complex Strict Sequencing games.

Prepare

On LSATs administered over the past five years, around 60 percent of all Strict Sequencing games qualify as "complex." Now, just because a Strict Sequencing game is complex doesn't mean that it's hard. While the complex Strict Sequencing variants are, on average, somewhat more challenging than their basic counterparts, they nevertheless run the gamut from games on the easier end of the spectrum to games that are among the hardest found on the LSAT. Don't be intimidated by a complex setup. Once these games are familiar—and nothing builds familiarity like practice does—you'll be able to apply the Logic Games Method just as you do on other game types. And, remember, the LSAT always provides all of the information you need to answer the questions.

The defining characteristic of basic Strict Sequencing games is a one-to-one matchup of entities to positions. Complex Strict Sequencing games alter the setup in a variety of ways. Some may ask you to sequence the entities two (or even three) times. Imagine a game in which five hurdlers at a track meet will take different starting positions in each of three heats.

```
        A  B  C  D  E
Heat
 1     __ __ __ __ __
        1  2  3  4  5

 2     __ __ __ __ __
        1  2  3  4  5

 3     __ __ __ __ __
        1  2  3  4  5
```

Another common variant has different numbers of entities and positions. You could be asked, for example, to schedule seven entities over the course of five days, with one *or two* each day.

J K L M N P Q

M   Tu   W   Th   F
—   —   —   —   —

—   —   —   —   —

Alternatively, the setup might call for you to figure out when each of six events occurred over the course of eight years.

C   D   F   G   H   J

—   —   —   —   —   —   —   —
05 06 07 08 09 10 11 12

Perhaps the most common complex Strict Sequencing variant is one in which the framework is doubled. This could involve two different people performing the same tasks in different orders.

F   H   K   L   M   O

Jones —   —   —   —   —   —
       1   2   3   4   5   6
Smith —   —   —   —   —   —
       1   2   3   4   5   6

It could also be a schedule of appointments with morning and afternoon meeting times.

Q   R   S   T   V   X

          M   Tu   W   Th

AM   —   —   —   —

PM   —   —   —   —

There is one complex Strict Sequencing setup so rare that it warrants a separate discussion. In the Special Feature that follows this chapter, you'll learn about Circular Sequencing, in which the entities are arranged around a table, or in some other type of round scenario. While it's unlikely that you'll see a Circular Sequencing game, those that were released in the past were challenging, and students who want the most comprehensive Logic Games preparation will enjoy the video in which a Kaplan LSAT Channel instructor takes you through one of the toughest complex Sequencing games ever to appear on the LSAT.

The Overview step of the Logic Games Method takes on added importance in complex games. You'll want to quickly understand the situation and have a clear picture of the task before you create your initial sketch.

COMPLEX STRICT SEQUENCING IN REAL LIFE

When you think about Sequencing tasks in real life, you likely default to those corresponding to basic Strict Sequencing—a group of people or items arranged in a row, one at a time. You won't have to brainstorm too long, however, to come up with real-life scenarios that mirror the LSAT's complex Strict Sequencing tasks.

In one or more of your college classes, you probably had to meet with a professor more than one time during the semester. For example, a professor may have required one meeting to discuss and approve your research topic, a second meeting to approve your list of sources, and then a third to review your first draft. Stick that scenario into a logic game that describes a seminar course with six students, and you have a ready-made complex Strict Sequencing game.

```
        A  C  J  L  S  V

meetings
     1   __ __ __ __ __ __
         1  2  3  4  5  6
     2   __ __ __ __ __ __

     3   __ __ __ __ __ __
```

A class schedule presents another easily understandable variation. It might be that a law student has some classes only on Tuesdays and Thursdays, and others only on Mondays, Wednesdays, and Fridays. For good measure, throw one of those long, once-per-week classes into the mix. You have no problem interpreting this student's schedule at a glance.

	M	Tu	W	Th	F
9:30AM	Torts	___	Torts	___	Torts
10:30AM	___	CivPro	___	CivPro	___
1PM	___	Property	___	Property	___
2:30-5:30PM	Crim Law	___	___	___	___

In real-life sequencing tasks, you sometimes have to account for subgroups among the people or things you're putting in order. In a photograph or a game, for example, you may want to arrange people "boy-girl-boy-girl." If you have six pictures to hang on a wall, you would take into account the fact that three have blue backgrounds and three have red backgrounds. You might want to keep those with the same background color together, or you might want to intersperse them with pictures of the other color. Either way, you would not ignore the differences in the groups. The LSAT sometimes mirrors these real-life situations by subdividing the entities in a Sequencing game. You might run into a game in which you are deciding the speaking order of seven foreign policy experts: four who specialize in the Balkans—A, B, C, and D—and three who specialize in North Africa—M, P, S.

```
   Bal        N.Afr
  _____     _____
  A B C D     m p s


  __ __ __ __ __ __ __
  1  2  3  4  5  6  7
```

Because the entities are subdivided, that game would qualify as "complex" Strict Sequencing, even though the ratio of entities to slots is one-to-one. When you encounter a situation like this, expect the rules or restrictions to explicitly group or break up entities in one or both of the subgroups within the sequence.

Even if a game asks you to use some entities multiple times, to leave some slots open, or to account for subdivisions among the entities, it's nothing you haven't done before. In the next section of this chapter, you'll have the chance to practice Steps 1 and 2 of the Logic Games Method on a handful of complex Strict Sequencing games. Pay close attention as you conduct your overview, and see if you can translate the situation described there into a clear, helpful sketch.

COMPLEX STRICT SEQUENCING GAMES TASKS AND SKETCHES

LEARNING OBJECTIVES

In this section of the chapter, you'll practice

- Applying Steps 1 and 2 of the Logic Games Method to complex Strict Sequencing games by
  - Asking the SEAL questions to analyze the game's Overview, and then
  - Creating a simple, useful Sketch framework

Prepare

While the situations described in complex Strict Sequencing setups offer an additional layer to action, the underlying tasks are identical to those in basic Strict Sequencing.

LOGIC GAMES STRATEGY

Sequencing games ask you to put things in order in one of the following ways:

- Chronologically—either using units of time such as years, weeks, days, or hours, or simply using the ideas of "earlier" and "later"
- Spatially—horizontally or vertically; imagine runners about to run a race taking their positions in numbered lanes, or a wedding cake with different layers, one on top of the other
- By rank—similar to a top 10 list, or the finishing order of a competition
- By size or amount—imagine a wish list with items arranged from most to least expensive

In complex Strict Sequencing, pay special attention to the list of entities—are the entities used once, twice, or three times each?—and to the description of the framework for the game—can each position in the game accommodate one or more than one entity?

At a chili cook-off, two judges—Rodriguez and Stanton—will each sample chili prepared by six contestants—Berghoff, Charlton, Dominguez, Ellis, Ferguson, and Gascon—although not necessarily in the same order. Each judge samples one bowl of chili from each contestant. The order in which each judge samples the chili will conform to the following restrictions:

$$B \quad C \quad D \quad E \quad F \quad G$$

$$\begin{array}{cccccccc} \text{Rod} & \underline{} & \underline{} & \underline{} & \underline{} & \underline{} & \underline{} \\ & 1 & 2 & 3 & 4 & 5 & 6 \\ \text{Stan} & \underline{} & \underline{} & \underline{} & \underline{} & \underline{} & \underline{} \\ & 1 & 2 & 3 & 4 & 5 & 6 \end{array}$$

In that game, each of the entities will be used twice, once in each judge's row.

Try Steps 1 and 2 of the Logic Games Method on the following game setups. Be on the lookout for the variations that make them examples of *complex* Strict Sequencing.

Practice

Directions: Conduct an Overview of each game's setup by asking the SEAL questions, and create an initial sketch framework for the game's action.

Practice 1

A committee of teachers at Lakeside High School is planning the spring exam schedule for freshmen and sophomores for a given week, Monday through Friday. The committee must schedule four freshman exams—algebra, biology, English 1 and world history; four sophomore exams—chemistry, English 2, geometry and US history; and no other exams. Each exam will be administered once during the week, either at 8 AM or at 11 AM, and no exams may be administered simultaneously. The following conditions must be met:

1. [Step 1] Conduct an Overview analysis:
    *   What is this game's Situation?
    *   Who or what are the game's Entities?
    *   What is the game's Action?
    *   What are the Limitations explicit in the game setup?

2. [Step 2] Create an initial Sketch:

Practice 2

An apartment building has five floors. Each floor has either one or two apartments. There are exactly eight apartments in the building. The residents of the building are J, K, L, M, N, O, P, and Q, who each live in a different apartment.

PrepTest2 Sec3 Qs 6–12

1. [Step 1] Conduct an Overview analysis:
    *   What is this game's Situation?
    *   Who or what are the game's Entities?
    *   What is the game's Action?
    *   What are the Limitations explicit in the game setup?

2. [Step 2] Create an initial Sketch:

Practice 3

Exactly seven professors—Madison, Nilsson, Orozco, Paton, Robinson, Sarkis, and Togo—were hired in the years 1989 through 1995. Each professor has one or more specialties, and any two professors hired in the same year or in consecutive years do not have a specialty in common. The professors were hired according to the following conditions:

PrepTest35 Sec3 Qs 18–23

1. [Step 1] Conduct an Overview analysis:
   - What is this game's Situation?
   - Who or what are the game's Entities?
   - What is the game's Action?
   - What are the Limitations explicit in the game setup?

2. [Step 2] Create an initial Sketch:

Explanations

Compare your work to that of an LSAT expert. Keep track of any case in which you incorrectly characterized the action described in the setup, and any case in which you drew a sketch framework that does not match the details of the game's situation.

Practice 1

A committee of teachers at Lakeside High School is planning the spring exam schedule for freshmen and sophomores for a given week, Monday through Friday. The committee must schedule four freshman exams—algebra, biology, English 1 and world history; four sophomore exams—chemistry, English 2, geometry and US history; and no other exams. Each exam will be administered once during the week, either at 8 AM or at 11 AM, and no exams may be administered simultaneously. The following conditions must be met:

1. [Step 1] Conduct an Overview analysis:

   - What is this game's Situation? *The task here is to schedule eight different exams—four each for two different groups of students— over the course of one school week.*

   - Who or what are the game's Entities? *Eight exams—A, B, E_1, and G for the freshmen, and C, E_2, G, and U for the sophomores.*

   - What is the game's Action? *Complex Strict Sequencing—there may be one or two exams per day given at 8 AM or 11 AM.*

   - What are the Limitations explicit in the game setup? *No exams given simultaneously.*

2. [Step 2] Create an initial Sketch:

   fresh   soph
   a b e_1 w   C E_2 G U

   M Tu W Th F
   8 __ __ __ __ __
   11 __ __ __ __ __

Practice 2

An apartment building has five floors. Each floor has either one or two apartments. There are exactly eight apartments in the building. The residents of the building are J, K, L, M, N, O, P, and Q, who each live in a different apartment.

PrepTest2 Sec3 Qs 6–12

1. [Step 1] Conduct an Overview analysis:

   - What is this game's Situation? *The task is to figure out which of five floors of an apartment building eight different people live on.*

   - Who or what are the game's Entities? *Eight residents—J, K, L, M, N, O, P, and Q.*

   - What is the game's Action? *Complex Strict Sequencing—some floors will have more than one resident.*

   - What are the Limitations explicit in the game setup? *Each floor has either one or two apartments, and each resident lives alone.*

2. [Step 2] Create an initial Sketch:

   J K L M N O P Q

   5 __ (__)
   4 __ (__)
   3 __ (__)
   2 __ (__)
   1 __ (__)

Practice 3

Exactly seven professors—Madison, Nilsson, Orozco, Paton, Robinson, Sarkis, and Togo—were hired in the years 1989 through 1995. Each professor has one or more specialties, and any two professors hired in the same year or in consecutive years do not have a specialty in common. The professors were hired according to the following conditions:

PrepTest35 Sec3 Qs 18–23

1. [Step 1] Conduct an Overview analysis:

   - What is this game's Situation? *The task is to determine the hiring year of seven professors who were each hired between 1989 and 1995.*

   - Who or what are the game's Entities? *Seven professors—M, N, O, P, R, S, and T.*

- What is the game's Action? *Complex Strict Sequencing—more than one professor may have been hired in a given year (the setup offers qualifications for "any two professors hired in the same year"), and thus, some years may have no hirings.*

- What are the Limitations explicit in the game setup? *Some of the professors share specialties, a characteristic that will prevent them from being hired in the same year or consecutive years to professors with the same specialty.*

2. [Step 2] Create an initial Sketch:

   M N O P R S T

   89 90 91 92 93 94 95

You'll see these model game setups again as you practice Step 3, analyzing and drawing the rules, and Step 4, making deductions in basic Strict Sequencing games. When you come back to the Professors' Hire Dates game, pay special attention to the rules that describe professors who share specialties. When logic games introduce unique terms (like "specialties" in that game), they will always define the term and use it to create restrictions within the game.

COMPLEX STRICT SEQUENCING RULES

LEARNING OBJECTIVES

In this section of the chapter, you'll practice

- Applying Step 3 of the Logic Games Method to complex Strict Sequencing games by analyzing and sketching the rules

Prepare

The rules in complex Strict Sequencing games aren't much different than those found in basic Strict Sequencing. In both, the rules restrict entities in relationship to specific positions or relative to one another.

LOGIC GAMES STRATEGY

Strict Sequencing rules basically tell you one or more of the following:

- The order in which two or more entities are placed
- The number of spaces between two or more entities
- The slot(s) in which a given entity can or cannot be placed

There are a couple of instances in which a complex Strict Sequencing sketch framework can work a little differently than its standard counterpart. Consider what the following rules mean in a game in which you are asked to schedule appointments for either a morning or an afternoon from Monday to Friday.

Becky's appointment is some time before Craig's appointment.
Greg's appointment is on an earlier day of the week than Rachel's appointment.

```
     M  Tu  W  Th  F
AM  __  __  __ __  __
PM  __  __  __ __  __
```

B...C

G ... R , never G/R

In the first of those rules, Becky's appointment could be in the morning of the same day on which Craig has an appointment in the afternoon. In the second rule, that case would be unacceptable.

If a game asks you to schedule entities more than one time apiece, pay close attention to the wording of rules that stipulate one of the entity's positions. For example, in a game where six employees are scheduled for two shifts each, you could see rules like the following:

> The second day on which Carlos works is Wednesday.
> Firuz works on Thursday.

$$\overbrace{}^{C_1}$$

$\underline{M}$	$\underline{Tu}$	$\underline{W}$	$\underline{Th}$	$\underline{F}$
		$\underline{C_2}$	$\underline{F}$	

Did you catch the distinction? The first rule states that Carlos's second shift is on Wednesday, meaning that his first shift must be on Monday or Tuesday. In Firuz's case, however, you learn only that *one of* his shifts is on Thursday, but not whether it is his first or second shift.

In the following exercises, the rules have been added to the three setups you analyzed in the previous section of this chapter. Practice analyzing and drawing the rules in the context of each setup.

Practice

Directions: Take a couple minutes to review each game's setup, summarize your Overview analysis, and recreate the initial Sketch. Then, one at a time, analyze the rules, answer the questions about each one, and draw the rule either inside or underneath the sketch framework.

Practice 1

A committee of teachers at Lakeside High School is planning the spring exam schedule for freshmen and sophomores for a given week, Monday through Friday. The committee must schedule four freshman exams—algebra, biology, English 1 and world history; four sophomore exams—chemistry, English 2, geometry and US history; and no other exams. Each exam will be administered once during the week, either at 8 AM or at 11 AM, and no exams may be administered simultaneously. The following conditions must be met:

> No two freshman exams may be given on the same day.
> Exactly one freshman exam is administered at 8 AM.
> The geometry exam and the US history exam must be administered on the same day.
> No exam will be administered on Friday at 11 AM.
> The algebra exam and the biology exam must be administered at the same time of day on consecutive days.

1. [Step 1] Summarize your Overview analysis:

2. [Step 2] Create an initial Sketch:

3. [Step 3] Analyze and draw the Rules:
   - For each rule, answer the following questions and draw the rule in the appropriate box.
     - What does the rule restrict, and what does it leave open?
     - What are the rule's negative implications, if any?
     - Can the rule be depicted inside the sketch framework?

Rule 1:	Rule 2:
Rule 3:	Rule 4:
Rule 5:	

Practice 2

An apartment building has five floors. Each floor has either one or two apartments. There are exactly eight apartments in the building. The residents of the building are J, K, L, M, N, O, P, and Q, who each live in a different apartment.

J lives on a floor with two apartments.
K lives on the floor directly above P.
The second floor is made up of only one apartment.
M and N live on the same floor.
O does not live on the same floor as Q.
L lives in the only apartment on her floor.
Q does not live on the first or second floor.

PrepTest2 Sec3 Qs 6–12

1. [Step 1] Summarize your Overview analysis:

2. [Step 2] Create an initial Sketch:

3. [Step 3] Analyze and draw the Rules:
   - For each rule, answer the following questions and draw the rule in the appropriate box.
     - What does the rule restrict, and what does it leave open?
     - What are the rule's negative implications, if any?
     - Can the rule be depicted inside the sketch framework?

Rule 1:	Rule 2:
Rule 3:	Rule 4:
Rule 5:	Rule 6:
Rule 7:	

Practice 3

Exactly seven professors—Madison, Nilsson, Orozco, Paton, Robinson, Sarkis, and Togo—were hired in the years 1989 through 1995. Each professor has one or more specialties, and any two professors hired in the same year or in consecutive years do not have a specialty in common. The professors were hired according to the following conditions:

Madison was hired in 1993, Robinson in 1991.
There is at least one specialty that Madison, Orozco, and Togo have in common.
Nilsson shares a specialty with Robinson.
Paton and Sarkis were each hired at least one year before Madison and at least one year after Nilsson.
Orozco, who shares a specialty with Sarkis, was hired in 1990.

PrepTest35 Sec3 Qs 18–23

1. [Step 1] Summarize your Overview analysis:

2. [Step 2] Create an initial Sketch:

3. [Step 3] Analyze and draw the Rules:
   - For each rule, answer the following questions and draw the rule in the appropriate box.
     - What does the rule restrict, and what does it leave open?
     - What are the rule's negative implications, if any?
     - Can the rule be depicted inside the sketch framework?

Rule 1:	Rule 2:
Rule 3:	Rule 4:
Rule 5:	

Explanations

Compare your work to that of an LSAT expert. Pay close attention to how the expert analyzed each rule and then depicted it within or beneath the game's initial sketch.

Practice 1

A committee of teachers at Lakeside High School is planning the spring exam schedule for freshmen and sophomores for a given week, Monday through Friday. The committee must schedule four freshman exams—algebra, biology, English 1 and world history; four sophomore exams—chemistry, English 2, geometry and US history; and no other exams. Each exam will be administered once during the week, either at 8 AM or at 11 AM, and no exams may be administered simultaneously. The following conditions must be met:

> No two freshman exams may be given on the same day.
> Exactly one freshman exam is administered at 8 AM.
> The geometry exam and the US history exam must be administered on the same day.
> No exam will be administered on Friday at 11 AM.
> The algebra exam and the biology exam must be administered at the same time of day on consecutive days.

1. [Step 1] Summarize your Overview analysis: *The task is to schedule eight exams—four each for two different groups of students—over the course of one week, with either one or two exams per day (and no exams administered at the same time).*

2. [Step 2] Create an initial Sketch:

   fresh   soph
   a b e_1 w   C E_2 G U

       M   Tu   W   Th   F

   8   __   __   __   __   __

   11   __   __   __   __   __

3. [Step 3] Analyze and draw the Rules:
   - Rule 1:
     - What does the rule restrict, and what does it leave open? *This rule forbids scheduling two freshman exams for the same day.*
     - What are the rule's negative implications, if any? *Because this rule is phrased negatively, its corollary is positive: All freshman exams will be on different days.*
     - Can the rule be depicted inside the sketch framework? *No.*
   - Draw the rule:

     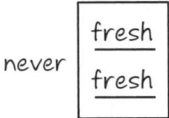

   - Rule 2:
     - What does the rule restrict, and what does it leave open? *This limits the number of freshman exams at 8 AM to just one. This means that three of the freshman exams will be at 11 AM. You can record that now or in Step 4 when making the deductions.*
     - What are the rule's negative implications, if any? *N/A*
     - Can the rule be depicted inside the sketch framework? *Next to the 8 AM line*
     - Draw the rule:

       ┌─┐
       │ 1 │ fresh   8   __   __   __   __   __
       └─┘

   - Rule 3:
     - What does the rule restrict, and what does it leave open? *This rule creates a vertical block of G and U, in either order.*
     - What are the rule's negative implications, if any? *G and U can never be on different days.*

- Can the rule be depicted inside the sketch framework? *No.*
- Draw the rule:

$$\boxed{\begin{array}{c} \underline{G/U} \\ \underline{U/G} \end{array}}$$

- Rule 4:
  - What does the rule restrict, and what does it leave open? *This prevents any exams from being scheduled at 11 AM on Friday.*
  - What are the rule's negative implications, if any? *N/A*
  - Can the rule be depicted inside the sketch framework? *Yes.*
  - Draw the rule:

  11 __ __ __ __ ✕

- Rule 5:
  - What does the rule restrict, and what does it leave open? *This rule creates a horizontal block for a and b. They will be at the same time on consecutive days.*
  - What are the rule's negative implications, if any? *Tests a and b cannot be on the same day nor at different times than one another.*
  - Can the rule be depicted inside the sketch framework? *No.*
  - Draw the rule:

$$\boxed{a/b \;\; b/a}$$

Here is the sketch with all of the rules depicted.

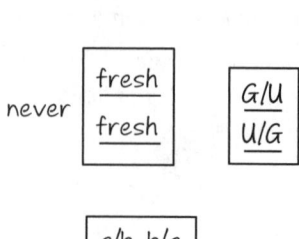

```
        fresh              soph
       a b e₁ w          C E₂ G U


          M  Tu  W  Th  F
┌─┐
│1│ fresh 8  __  __  __  __  __
└─┘
        11  __  __  __  __  ✕


              ┌───────┐     ┌─────┐
         never│ fresh │     │ G/U │
              │ fresh │     │ U/G │
              └───────┘     └─────┘

              ┌───────────┐
              │ a/b  b/a  │
              └───────────┘
```

Practice 2

An apartment building has five floors. Each floor has either one or two apartments. There are exactly eight apartments in the building. The residents of the building are J, K, L, M, N, O, P, and Q, who each live in a different apartment.

> J lives on a floor with two apartments.
> K lives on the floor directly above P.
> The second floor is made up of only one apartment.
> M and N live on the same floor.
> O does not live on the same floor as Q.
> L lives in the only apartment on her floor.
> Q does not live on the first or second floor.

PrepTest2 Sec3 Qs 6–12

1. [Step 1] Summarize your Overview analysis: *The task is to determine which of five floors in an apartment building eight residents live on. Each floor has one or two apartments, and each resident lives alone in one of the apartments.*

2. [Step 2] Create an initial Sketch:

   J K L M N O P Q

   5 __ (__)
   4 __ (__)
   3 __ (__)
   2 __ (__)
   1 __ (__)

3. [Step 3] Analyze and draw the Rules:
   - Rule 1:
     - What does the rule restrict, and what does it leave open? *This rule stipulates that resident J has a neighbor on the same floor. Without more information, you have no idea which floor this may or may not be.*
     - What are the rule's negative implications, if any? *Resident J cannot live on a floor that has only one apartment.*
     - Can the rule be depicted inside the sketch framework? *No.*
     - Draw the rule:

$$\boxed{\underline{J} \;\; \underline{}}$$

- Rule 2:
  - What does the rule restrict, and what does it leave open? *This creates a vertical block of entities: K is one floor above P. Without more information, however, it does not determine which floor either lives on.*
  - What are the rule's negative implications, if any? *K cannot be on floor 1 and P cannot be on floor 5.*
  - Can the rule be depicted inside the sketch framework? *No.*
  - Draw the rule:

- Rule 3:
  - What does the rule restrict, and what does it leave open? *This rule restricts floor 2 to only one apartment.*
  - What are the rule's negative implications, if any? *Anyone who lives on a floor with two apartments cannot live on floor 2. Note: If you notice that this affects resident J (Rule 1), you can eliminate J from floor 2 now. If not, you will catch that interaction in Step 4, when making the deductions.*
  - Can the rule be depicted inside the sketch framework? *Yes.*
  - Draw the rule:

$$5 \ \_\_ \ (\_)$$
$$4 \ \_\_ \ (\_)$$
$$3 \ \_\_ \ (\_)$$
$$2 \ \_\_ \ \bowtie$$
$$1 \ \_\_ \ (\_)$$

- Rule 4:
  - What does the rule restrict, and what does it leave open? *This rule creates a horizontal block: residents M and N are same-floor neighbors.*
  - What are the rule's negative implications, if any? *Residents M and N cannot live on any floor that has only one apartment. Note: Here, again, if you notice that this*

rule interacts with Rule 3, you can eliminate residents M and N from floor 2. If not, you'll catch this deduction in Step 4.

  - Can the rule be depicted inside the sketch framework? *No.*
  - Draw the rule:

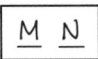

- Rule 5:
  - What does the rule restrict, and what does it leave open? *This rule creates a horizontal "anti-block": residents O and Q do not live on the same floor.*
  - What are the rule's negative implications, if any? *None. Residents O and Q could live on any floor, and they may or may not have same-floor neighbors (just not each other).*
  - Can the rule be depicted inside the sketch framework? *No.*
  - Draw the rule:

- Rule 6:
  - What does the rule restrict, and what does it leave open? *This rule means that resident L lives on a floor with only one apartment. Floor 2 is a possibility, but not a certainty, for resident L's apartment.*
  - What are the rule's negative implications, if any? *Resident L cannot live on a floor with two apartments.*
  - Can the rule be depicted inside the sketch framework? *No.*
  - Draw the rule:

$$\boxed{\underline{L}}$$

- Rule 7:
  - What does the rule restrict, and what does it leave open? *This negative rule prevents Q from taking an apartment on floors 1 or 2. The other floors remain open to him.*
  - What are the rule's negative implications, if any? *The rule is phrased negatively. Its affirmative implication is that Q lives on one of floors 3, 4, or 5.*
  - Can the rule be depicted inside the sketch framework? *Yes.*
  - Draw the rule:

$$
\begin{array}{ccc}
5 & \_ & (\_) \\
4 & \_ & (\_) \\
3 & \_ & (\_) \\
\sim Q \; 2 & \_ & \bowtie \\
\sim Q \; 1 & \_ & (\_)
\end{array}
$$

Here is the sketch at the end of Step 3, with all of the rules depicted.

J K L M N O P Q

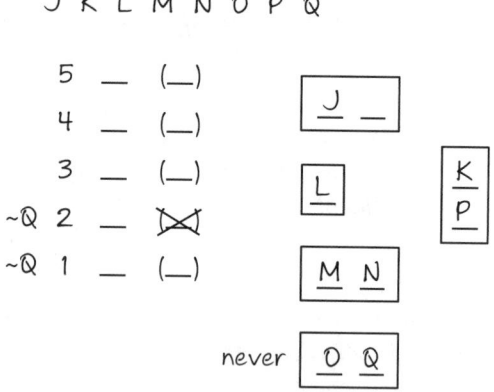

never ☐ O Q

Practice 3

Exactly seven professors—Madison, Nilsson, Orozco, Paton, Robinson, Sarkis, and Togo—were hired in the years 1989 through 1995. Each professor has one or more specialties, and any two professors hired in the same year or in consecutive years do not have a specialty in common. The professors were hired according to the following conditions:

Madison was hired in 1993, Robinson in 1991.
There is at least one specialty that Madison, Orozco, and Togo have in common.
Nilsson shares a specialty with Robinson.

Paton and Sarkis were each hired at least one year before Madison and at least one year after Nilsson.
Orozco, who shares a specialty with Sarkis, was hired in 1990.

PrepTest35 Sec3 Qs 18–23

[Steps 1 and 2] Here is this game's Overview and initial Sketch: *The task is to figure out the year (from 1989 to 1995) in which each of seven professors were hired. More than one professor may be hired during a given year, meaning that some years may have seen no professors hired. The professors have specialties, and cannot be hired during the same year or in years consecutive to other professors with the same specialty.*

M N O P R S T

89 90 91 92 93 94 95

1. [Step 3] Analyze and draw the Rules:
   - Rule 1:
     - What does the rule restrict, and what does it leave open? *This rule creates two established entities: M was hired in 1993, and R was hired in 1991. Remember, other professors may have been hired during those years, too.*
     - What are the rule's negative implications, if any? *N/A*
     - Can the rule be depicted inside the sketch framework? *Yes.*
     - Draw the rule:

M N O P R S T

$$
\begin{array}{ccccccc}
89 & 90 & 91 & 92 & 93 & 94 & 95 \\
& & R & & M & &
\end{array}
$$

   - Rule 2:
     - What does the rule restrict, and what does it leave open? *This rule tells you that three professors—M, O, and T—share a specialty. Remember that this means they were not hired during the same year, nor in adjacent years.*

- What are the rule's negative implications, if any? *Remember that this sharing a specialty means none of these professors were hired during the same year, nor in adjacent years.*
- Can the rule be depicted inside the sketch framework? *No.*
- Draw the rule:

  M N O P R S T

  89   90   91   92   93   94   95
            R   M

  share spec
  ————————————
  M = O = T

- Rule 3:
  - What does the rule restrict, and what does it leave open? *This is another rule about shared specialties, this time between N and R.*
  - What are the rule's negative implications, if any? *Remember that this sharing a specialty means that these professors were not hired during the same year, nor in adjacent years.*
  - Can the rule be depicted inside the sketch framework? *No.*
  - Draw the rule:

    M N O P R S T

    89   90   91   92   93   94   95
              R   M

    share spec
    ————————————
    M = O = T
    N = R

- Rule 4:
  - What does the rule restrict, and what does it leave open? *This rule provides the relative order of hiring among four of the professors: N was hired before P and S, and M was hired after P and S. The rule does not state the relationship between P and S.*
  - What are the rule's negative implications, if any? *N/A*

- Can the rule be depicted inside the sketch framework? *No.*
- Draw the rule:

  M N O P R S T

  89   90   91   92   93   94   95
            R   M

  share spec
  ————————————
  M = O = T
  N = R

  N < P , S   > M
      (P over S)

- Rule 5:
  - What does the rule restrict, and what does it leave open? *This rule establishes professor O's position—1990—and adds that O shares a specialty with professor S.*
  - What are the rule's negative implications, if any? *Remember that this sharing a specialty means that these professors were not hired during the same year, nor in adjacent years.*
  - Can the rule be depicted inside the sketch framework? *Partially. Write in O under the 1990 slot, and record the specialty rule with the rest of the shared specialty list.*
  - Draw the rule:

    M N O P R S T

    89   90   91   92   93   94   95
         O   R   M

    share spec
    ————————————
    M = O = T
    N = R
    O = S

    N < P , S   > M
      (P over S)

The Professors' Hire Dates game initially appeared to be quite complicated. After all, more than one professor may be hired in a given year, some years may be empty, and the setup introduced the unique term *specialty*. The rules, however, have already established the positions of three of the seven entities, reducing the game's complexity dramatically. By the time you add all of the deductions that stem from the "shared specialty" rules, this one won't seem so bad at all.

With the rules in place, you may already be anticipating the deductions that can be made in each of those practice game setups. You'll have a chance to add those in the next section of this chapter covering Step 4 of the Logic Games Method in basic Strict Sequencing games.

COMPLEX STRICT SEQUENCING GAMES DEDUCTIONS

LEARNING OBJECTIVES

In this section of the chapter, you'll practice

- Applying Step 4 of the Logic Games Method to complex Strict Sequencing games by combining rules and restrictions to make all valid deductions in the game.

Prepare

The added complexity in the games in this chapter means that you have to be especially careful and precise with setup and sketch framework to be sure that you are correctly interpreting and representing the situation described. That extra scrutiny will often pay off in Step 4, where extra complexity may produce several key deductions.

LOGIC GAMES STRATEGY

In Sequencing games, deductions are most likely to stem from:

- **Blocks of Entities**—Two or more entities that are linked together; when one is placed, the other's placement is determined or restricted
- **Duplications**—Entities shared by two or more rules; duplications are always at the heart of Loose Sequencing games.
- **Established Entities**—Entities placed into a specific position; even if no rule directly provides for an Established Entity, you may be able to determine an entity's exact position by combining other rules.

In Sequencing games, deductions may involve:

- **Limited Options**—The situation arises when a Block of Entities or a key player (an entity affecting the positions of other entities) is restricted to either of two positions; when this occurs, draw dual Limited Options sketches.
- **Number Restrictions**—Limitations or rules affecting the number of entities that can be placed in a given position; this is rare in Sequencing games— typically, the stated limitation is one entity per position.

The kinds of deductions you're looking for in these games are not much different than those in basic Strict Sequencing, but with all the moving parts in these games, you'll want to make sure you are able to get them all.

Practice Step 4 on the setups you've been working with throughout this chapter.

Practice

Directions: In each game setup, first reacquaint yourself with the setup and rules. Then, combine the rules and restrictions to make all available deductions, recording your analyses as indicated. Finally, test your deductions by answering the questions that accompany each game. You can find expert analysis and explanations at the end of the Practice section.

Practice 1

A committee of teachers at Lakeside High School is planning the spring exam schedule for freshmen and sophomores for a given week, Monday through Friday. The committee must schedule four freshman exams—algebra, biology, English 1 and world history; four sophomore exams—chemistry, English 2, geometry and US history; and no other exams. Each exam will be administered once during the week, either at 8 AM or at 11 AM, and no exams may be administered simultaneously. The following conditions must be met:

> No two freshman exams may be given on the same day.
> Exactly one freshman exam is administered at 8 AM.
> The geometry exam and the US history exam must be administered on the same day.
> No exam will be administered on Friday at 11 AM.
> The algebra exam and the biology exam must be administered at the same time of day *on consecutive days*.

Steps 1–3:

1. Which entities or positions are the most restricted in this game? Why?

2. Which elements from the BLEND checklist can you identify in this game? Are there

   - Blocks of entities? If so, what are they?
   - Limited Options? If so, which rule(s) trigger them?
   - Established Entities? If so, which ones?
   - Number Restrictions? If so, describe them.
   - Duplications? If so, which rules share an entity?

3. Combine the rules and restrictions to create a Master Sketch depicting all of the deductions available in this game:

4. Evaluate your sketch by answering the following questions:

   - How many of the exams will be administered at 11 AM?
   - Which exams could be the one administered at 8 AM on Friday?
   - How many sophomore exams must be administered at 8 AM?
   - Which freshman exams must be administered at 11 AM?

Practice 2

An apartment building has five floors. Each floor has either one or two apartments. There are exactly eight apartments in the building. The residents of the building are J, K, L, M, N, O, P, and Q, who each live in a different apartment.

> J lives on a floor with two apartments.
> K lives on the floor directly above P.
> The second floor is made up of only one apartment.
> M and N live on the same floor.
> O does not live on the same floor as Q.
> L lives in the only apartment on her floor.
> Q does not live on the first or second floor.

PrepTest2 Sec3 Qs 6–12

Steps 1–3:

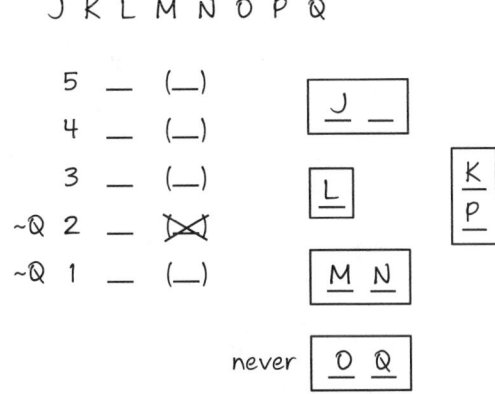

1. Which entities or positions are the most restricted in this game? Why?

2. Which elements from the BLEND checklist can you identify in this game? Are there
   - Blocks of entities? If so, what are they?
   - Limited Options? If so, which rule(s) trigger them?
   - Established Entities? If so, which ones?
   - Number Restrictions? If so, describe them.
   - Duplications? If so, which rules share an entity?

3. Combine the rules and restrictions to create a Master Sketch depicting all of the deductions available in this game:

4. Evaluate your sketch by answering the following questions:
   - Write a complete and accurate list of the residents who could live on the second floor.
   - If resident L lives on the third floor, and resident M lives on the fifth floor, what can you deduce about resident K?
   - Write a complete and accurate list of the residents who may <u>not</u> live on the first floor.
   - If resident P lives on the second floor, who are the residents who <u>cannot</u> live on the third floor?

Practice 3

Exactly seven professors—Madison, Nilsson, Orozco, Paton, Robinson, Sarkis, and Togo—were hired in the years 1989 through 1995. Each professor has one or more specialties, and any two professors hired in the same year or in consecutive years do not have a specialty in common. The professors were hired according to the following conditions:

Madison was hired in 1993, Robinson in 1991.

There is at least one specialty that Madison, Orozco, and Togo have in common.

Nilsson shares a specialty with Robinson.

Paton and Sarkis were each hired at least one year before Madison and at least one year after Nilsson.

Orozco, who shares a specialty with Sarkis, was hired in 1990.

PrepTest35 Sec3 Qs 18–23

Steps 1–3:

$$M \quad N \quad O \quad P \quad R \quad S \quad T$$

$$\underline{89} \quad \underline{90} \quad \underline{91} \quad \underline{92} \quad \underline{93} \quad \underline{94} \quad \underline{95}$$
$$\quad\;\; O \quad\;\; R \quad\quad\;\; M$$

$$\frac{\text{share spec}}{\begin{array}{c} M = O = T \\ N = R \\ O = S \end{array}}$$

$$N \begin{array}{c} \nearrow P \searrow \\ \searrow S \nearrow \end{array} M$$

1. Which entities or positions are the most restricted in this game? Why?

2. Which elements from the BLEND checklist can you identify in this game? Are there
    *   Blocks of entities? If so, what are they?
    *   Limited Options? If so, which rule(s) trigger them?
    *   Established Entities? If so, which ones?
    *   Number Restrictions? If so, describe them.
    *   Duplications? If so, which rules share an entity?

3. Combine the rules and restrictions to create a Master Sketch depicting all of the deductions available in this game:

4. Evaluate your sketch by answering the following questions:
    *   For how many of the seven professors can the exact year in which they were hired be determined? Who are they?
    *   In which of the seven years is it possible that none of the professors were hired?
    *   In which of the seven years is it possible that more than one of the professors were hired?
    *   If Paton and Orozco share a specialty, in how many of the seven years could Paton have been hired? Which one(s)?

Explanations

Compare your work to that of an LSAT expert. Pay close attention to how the expert combined the rules and restrictions to make additional deductions, and to how the expert depicted the deductions within the sketch framework.

Practice 1

A committee of teachers at Lakeside High School is planning the spring exam schedule for freshmen and sophomores for a given week, Monday through Friday. The committee must schedule four freshman exams—algebra, biology, English 1 and world history; four sophomore exams—chemistry, English 2, geometry and US history; and no other exams. Each exam will be administered once during the week, either at 8 AM or at 11 AM, and no exams may be administered simultaneously. The following conditions must be met:

No two freshman exams may be given on the same day.

Exactly one freshman exam is administered at 8 AM.

The geometry exam and the US history exam must be administered on the same day.

No exam will be administered on Friday at 11 AM.

The algebra exam and the biology exam must be administered at the same time of day *on consecutive days*.

1. Which entities or positions are the most restricted in this game? Why? *The entire category of freshman tests is highly restricted. One must be at 8 AM, three at 11:00 AM. Moreover, Tests a and b have to be at the same time (which you can now deduce will be at 11:00 AM).*

2. Which elements from the BLEND checklist can you identify in this game? Are there

    *   Blocks of entities? If so, what are they? *Tests G and U are a vertical block; they must be on the same day. Tests a and b are a horizontal block; they must be at the same time on consecutive days.*

    *   Limited Options? If so, which rule(s) trigger them? *N/A*

    *   Established Entities? If so, which ones? *None; Friday at 11 AM has been established as a time at which no test may be scheduled.*

    *   Number Restrictions? If so, describe them. *Because exactly one freshman exam is at 8 AM, three freshman exams are at 11 AM (Rule 1).*

    *   Duplications? If so, which rules share an entity? *Rules 1, 2, and 5 are all about freshman exams.*

3. Combine the rules and restrictions to create a Master Sketch depicting all of the deductions available in this game: *Consider where the freshman block AB (Rule 5) may be placed: since only one freshman exam may be given at 8 AM, the algebra and biology exams must be given at 11 AM.*

Another 11 AM slot must be taken up by one of G and U:

This leaves one remaining 11 AM slot for a third freshman exam:

Now, consider when the 8 AM freshman exam could be given. Three 11 AM slots are taken by freshman exams, and the other one is occupied by a sophomore exam (G/U) that must be preceded in the 8 AM slot by another sophomore exam (U/G). Therefore, the only day that the 8 AM freshman exam could be given is on Friday:

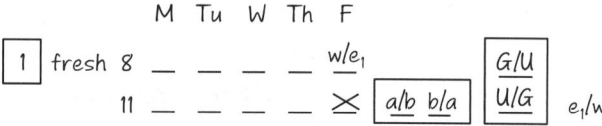

The remaining two sophomore exams—chemistry and English 2—must be offered at 8 AM, and one 8 AM slot will remain open:

```
       M  Tu  W  Th  F
 1  fresh 8  _  _  _  _  w/e₁  C  E₂  G/U  ✕
        11  _  _  _  _  ✕  a/b b/a  U/G  e₁/w
```

4. Evaluate your sketch by answering the following questions:

   • How many of the exams will be administered at 11 AM? *Four; three of the freshman exams (including Tests a and b), and one sophomore exam (either Test G or U) will be administered at 11 AM.*

   • Which exams could be the one administered at 8 AM on Friday? *Either Test e₁ or Test w must be administered at 8 AM on Friday.*

   • How many sophomore exams must be administered at 8 AM? *Three; one of G or U must be administered at 11 AM. The other of G or U, plus C and E₂, must be administered at 8 AM.*

   • Which freshman exams must be administered at 11 AM? *Because of Rules 1, 2, and 5, Tests a and b must be administered at 11 AM. One more freshman exam must also be administered at 11 AM, but there is no way to say which one that is.*

Practice 2

An apartment building has five floors. Each floor has either one or two apartments. There are exactly eight apartments in the building. The residents of the building are J, K, L, M, N, O, P, and Q, who each live in a different apartment.

> J lives on a floor with two apartments.
> K lives on the floor directly above P.
> The second floor is made up of only one apartment.
> M and N live on the same floor.
> O does not live on the same floor as Q.
> L lives in the only apartment on her floor.
> Q does not live on the first or second floor.

PrepTest2 Sec3 Qs 6–12

Steps 1–3:

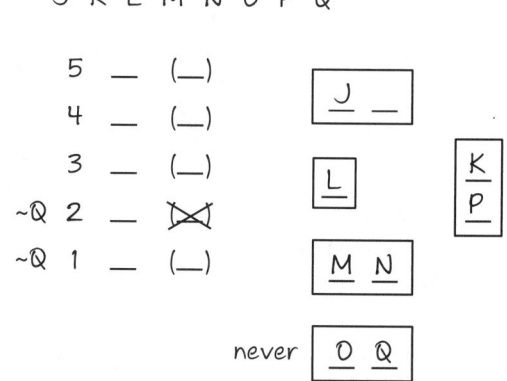

1. Which entities or positions are the most restricted in this game? Why? *The most restricted position is floor 2, which can have only one apartment. All of the entities have some restriction, but none stands out yet as central to the deduction-making process.*

2. Which elements from the BLEND checklist can you identify in this game? Are there

   • Blocks of entities? If so, what are they? *Rule 2 created a vertical block—K above P. Rule 4 created a horizontal block—M and N on the same floor. Rule 1 creates a quasi-block because J has a same-floor neighbor, but the rule doesn't specify who that neighbor is.*

   • Limited Options? If so, which rule(s) trigger them? *N/A*

- Established Entities? If so, which ones? *N/A*
- Number Restrictions? If so, describe them. *Rule 3 requires that floor 2 have only one apartment.*
- Duplications? If so, which rules share an entity? *1) Rule 3, which restricts floor 2 to one apartment, interacts with Rules 1 and 4, which dictate that residents J, M, and N live on floors with two apartments. 2) While resident Q appears in Rules 5 and 7, there isn't much to deduce from this Duplication because both of those rules are negative.*

3. Combine the rules and restrictions to create a Master Sketch depicting all of the deductions available in this game: *Start with floor 2. It can have only one apartment (Rule 3). Record the negative implications of Rules 1 and 4 here. J, M, and N cannot live on floor 2.*

```
        J  K  L  M  N  O  P  Q

        5  __  (__)              ┌──────┐
                                 │  J   │
        4  __  (__)              │ __ __│
                                 └──────┘
        3  __  (__)     ┌──┐            ┌──┐
                        │ L│            │ K│
~J ~M ~N ~Q  2  __   ✕  │__│            │ P│
                        └──┘            │__│
        ~Q  1  __  (__)                 └──┘
                               ┌──────┐
                               │ M  N │
                               │ __ __│
                               └──────┘

                   never  ┌──────┐
                          │ O  Q │
                          │ __ __│
                          └──────┘
```

Don't forget to record the negative implications of the vertical block created by Rule 2: Resident P cannot live on floor 5, and resident K cannot live on floor 1.

```
          J  K  L  M  N  O  P  Q

  ~P     5  __  (__)             ┌──────┐
                                 │  J   │
         4  __  (__)             │ __ __│
                                 └──────┘
         3  __  (__)    ┌──┐           ┌──┐
                        │ L│           │ K│
~J ~M ~N ~Q  2  __   ✕  │__│           │ P│
                        └──┘           │__│
  ~K ~Q  1  __  (__)                   └──┘
                              ┌──────┐
                              │ M  N │
                              │ __ __│
                              └──────┘

                  never  ┌──────┐
                         │ O  Q │
                         │ __ __│
                         └──────┘
```

Beyond this point, deduction gives way to speculation. There are dozens of "What if … ?" questions that you could ask at this point, but none of them lead to any additional certainties. You can be confident that the sketch above has all of the information you will need to answer the questions.

4. Evaluate your sketch by answering the following questions:
   - Write a complete and accurate list of the residents who could live on the second floor. *Residents K, L, O, and P could live on floor 2.*
   - If resident L lives on the third floor, and resident M lives on the fifth floor, what can you deduce about resident K? *Because L must live on a floor with one apartment (Rule 6), and because M must live on the same floor as N (Rule 4), the only place that the vertical K-P block (Rule 2) would fit is floors 1 and 2. Thus, under this question's conditions, K must live on floor 2.*
   - Write a complete and accurate list of the residents who may not live on the first floor. *Residents Q (Rule 7) and K (Rule 2) cannot live on floor 1.*
   - If resident P lives on the second floor, who are the residents who cannot live on the third floor? *If resident P lives on floor 2, then resident K will live on floor 3 (Rule 2). With K living on floor 3, residents L (Rule 6), M, and N (Rule 4) cannot live on floor 3.*

Practice 3

Exactly seven professors—Madison, Nilsson, Orozco, Paton, Robinson, Sarkis, and Togo—were hired in the years 1989 through 1995. Each professor has one or more specialties, and any two professors hired in the same year or in consecutive years do not have a specialty in common. The professors were hired according to the following conditions:

> Madison was hired in 1993, Robinson in 1991.
> There is at least one specialty that Madison, Orozco, and Togo have in common.
> Nilsson shares a specialty with Robinson.
> Paton and Sarkis were each hired at least one year before Madison and at least one year after Nilsson.
> Orozco, who shares a specialty with Sarkis, was hired in 1990.

PrepTest35 Sec3 Qs 18–23

Steps 1–3:

M N O P R S T

89	90	91	92	93	94	95
	O	R		M		

share spec
_____
M = O = T
N = R
O = S

N < P > M / < S >

1. Which entities or positions are the most restricted in this game? Why? *Professor T, who shares a specialty with two established entities (Professors O and M).*

2. Which elements from the BLEND checklist can you identify in this game? Are there

   - Blocks of entities? If so, what are they? *Rule 4 created a long, loose string: N before P and S, and P and S before M. Each shared specialty rule (Rules 2, 3, and 5) create "anti-blocks" that prevent professors who share specialties from being hired in the same or adjacent years.*

   - Limited Options? If so, which rule(s) trigger them? *N/A*

   - Established Entities? If so, which ones? *Professors M (Rule 1), O (Rule 5), and R (Rule 1) are all locked in.*

   - Number Restrictions? If so, describe them. *N/A; remember that more than one professor may be hired in the same year, and that there may be years in which no professors were hired.*

   - Duplications? If so, which rules share an entity? *Yes, five of them: 1) Rules 1, 2, and 4 all share M; 2) Rules 1 and 3 share R; 3) Rules 2 and 5 share O; 4) Rules 3 and 4 share N; and 5) Rules 4 and 5 share S.*

3. Combine the rules and restrictions to create a Master Sketch depicting all of the deductions available in this game: *Start with Professor T. Because T shares a specialty with O (Rule 2), T could not have been hired in '89, '90, or '91. Because T shares a specialty with M (also Rule 2), T could not have been hired in '92, '93, or '94. Thus, T must have been hired in 1995. Add T under '95 and cross out all of the established entities in the roster of entities above the sketch framework.*

Ṁ N Ø P Ṙ S Ṫ

89	90	91	92	93	94	95
	O	R		M		T

share spec
_____
M = O = T
N = R
O = S

N < P > M / < S >

Next, turn to Professor S, who shares a specialty with O (Rule 5) and must be after N and before M (Rule 4). Because S shares a specialty with O, S could not have been hired in '89, '90, or '91. That leaves only '92 as a year before M's hire date in which S could have been hired. Write S under '92, and cross out S in the roster of entities.

M̶ N Ø P R̶ S̶ T̶

89	90	91	92	93	94	95
	O	R	S	M		T

share spec
_____

M = O = T
N = R
O = S

N < P / S > M

Remarkably, six of the seven professors' hire dates are now determined once and for all. Only Professor P remains. Rule 4 places P's hire date between those of N and M, in other words, between '90 and '92. Professor P has no other restrictions, so simply indicate the acceptable range of dates for P, and you're done.

M̶ N̶ Ø P R̶ S̶ T̶

89	90	91	92	93	94	95
N	O	R	S	M		T

P (under 90–92)

share spec
_____

M = O = T
N = R
O = S

N < P / S > M

Determining that Professor S was hired in '92 means that Professor N could only have been hired in '89, '90 or '91 (Rule 4). However, remember that N shares a specialty with R (Rule 3), ruling out '90 or '91 as N's hire date. That means that N was hired in '89. Write in N under '89 and cross out N in the roster of entities.

M̶ N̶ Ø P R̶ S̶ T̶

89	90	91	92	93	94	95
N	O	R	S	M		T

share spec
_____

M = O = T
N = R
O = S

N < P / S > M

4. Evaluate your sketch by answering the following questions:

   • For how many of the seven professors can the exact year in which they were hired be determined? Who are they? *Six: N in '89, O in '90, R in '91, S in '92, M in '93, and T in '95.*

   • In which of the seven years is it possible that none of the professors were hired? *1994.*

   • In which of the seven years is it possible that more than one of the professors were hired? *1990, 1991, and 1992.*

   • If Paton and Orozco share a specialty, in how many of the seven years could Paton have been hired? Which one(s)? *Only one: 1992.*

Because the game setups in Practice 2 and Practice 3 come from officially released LSAT tests, you will have the opportunity to practice answering their questions in the next section of this chapter. After that, in the Perform section, you'll see two brand new games that you can use to assess your overall skill level on complex Strict Sequencing games.

COMPLEX STRICT SEQUENCING GAMES—FULL GAMES WITH QUESTIONS

In this section of the chapter, you will practice full-length complex Strict Sequencing games accompanied by their question sets. Look for all of the question types you encountered in Chapter 4, and apply the appropriate strategies to answer each as efficiently and accurately as possible. Given the complex nature of these games' setups and deductions, look for opportunities to turn the Master Sketch into quick points on Must Be/Could Be questions.

The two games in the Practice exercise are Apartment Floors and Professors' Hire Dates, games on which you've already worked through Steps 1–4. If you skipped the sections on those steps, go back and work through the practice exercises there.

Then, in the Perform section, you'll see two new games. On those, you can assess your skill level at applying all five steps of the Logic Games Method to complex Strict Sequencing.

Practice

Directions: You have seen this game's setup, rules and deductions in the preceding sections of this chapter. For each question, first review the Master Sketch and reconstruct the work you did in Steps 1–4 of the Logic Games Method. Then, answer the question. For practice, take time to analyze each question thoroughly and enter your analysis for each step and answer choice blank. Complete, worked example expert analyses can be found in your Online Study Plan in the PDF labeled "Chapter 6 Full Game Practice Explanations."

Question 1:

LSAT Question	Analysis

An apartment building has five floors. Each floor has either one or two apartments. There are exactly eight apartments in the building. The residents of the building are J, K, L, M, N, O, P, and Q, who each live in a different apartment.

    J lives on a floor with two apartments.
    K lives on the floor directly above P.
    The second floor is made up of only one apartment.
    M and N live on the same floor.
    O does not live on the same floor as Q.
    L lives in the only apartment on her floor.
    Q does not live on the first or second floor.

Steps 1-4:

J K L M N O P Q

~P 5 __ (__)

4 __ (__)

3 __ (__)

~J ~M ~N ~Q 2 __ ⊠

~K ~Q 1 __ (__)

J _ · L · K/P

M N

never O Q

---

1.   Which one of the following must be true?   →   **Step 5: Questions**

  (A) Q lives on the third floor.   →

  (B) Q lives on the fifth floor.   →

  (C) L does not live on the fourth floor.   →

  (D) N does not live on the second floor.   →

  (E) J lives on the first floor.   →
               PrepTest2 Sec3 Q6

Question 2:

LSAT Question	Analysis
An apartment building has five floors. Each floor has either one or two apartments. There are exactly eight apartments in the building. The residents of the building are J, K, L, M, N, O, P, and Q, who each live in a different apartment.	**Steps 1-4:**

An apartment building has five floors. Each floor has either one or two apartments. There are exactly eight apartments in the building. The residents of the building are J, K, L, M, N, O, P, and Q, who each live in a different apartment.

    J lives on a floor with two apartments.
    K lives on the floor directly above P.
    The second floor is made up of only one apartment.
    M and N live on the same floor.
    O does not live on the same floor as Q.
    L lives in the only apartment on her floor.
    Q does not live on the first or second floor.

$\longrightarrow$

Steps 1-4:

J K L M N O P Q

~P 5 __ (__)

4 __ (__)

3 __ (__)

~J ~M ~N ~Q 2 __ ⋈

~K ~Q 1 __ (__)

J _

L

K
P

M N

never O Q

---

2.   Which one of the following CANNOT be true? $\longrightarrow$ **Step 5: Questions**

(A)   K lives on the second floor. $\longrightarrow$

(B)   M lives on the first floor. $\longrightarrow$

(C)   N lives on the fourth floor. $\longrightarrow$

(D)   O lives on the third floor. $\longrightarrow$

(E)   P lives on the fifth floor.

                   PrepTest2 Sec3 Q7 $\longrightarrow$

Question 3:

LSAT Question	Analysis

An apartment building has five floors. Each floor has either one or two apartments. There are exactly eight apartments in the building. The residents of the building are J, K, L, M, N, O, P, and Q, who each live in a different apartment.
 	
    J lives on a floor with two apartments.
    K lives on the floor directly above P.
    The second floor is made up of only one apartment.
    M and N live on the same floor.
    O does not live on the same floor as Q.
    L lives in the only apartment on her floor.
    Q does not live on the first or second floor.
	Steps 1-4:

$\longrightarrow$

Steps 1-4:

J K L M N O P Q

~P 5 __ (__)

4 __ (__)

3 __ (__)

~J ~M ~N ~Q 2 __ ⧖

~K ~Q 1 __ (__)

J boxed / __

L boxed

K / P boxed

M N boxed

never O Q boxed

---

3.   If J lives on the fourth floor and K lives on the fifth floor, which one of the following can be true? $\longrightarrow$ **Step 5: Questions**

    (A)   O lives on the first floor. $\longrightarrow$

    (B)   Q lives on the fourth floor. $\longrightarrow$

    (C)   N lives on the fifth floor. $\longrightarrow$

    (D)   L lives on the fourth floor. $\longrightarrow$

    (E)   P lives on the third floor. $\longrightarrow$

PrepTest2 Sec3 Q8

Question 4:

LSAT Question	Analysis

Steps 1-4:

An apartment building has five floors. Each floor has either one or two apartments. There are exactly eight apartments in the building. The residents of the building are J, K, L, M, N, O, P, and Q, who each live in a different apartment.

    J lives on a floor with two apartments.
    K lives on the floor directly above P.
    The second floor is made up of only one apartment.
    M and N live on the same floor.
    O does not live on the same floor as Q.
    L lives in the only apartment on her floor.
    Q does not live on the first or second floor.

J K L M N O P Q

~P 5 __ (__)

4 __ (__)

→ 3 __ (__)

~J ~M ~N ~Q 2 __ ⋈

~K ~Q 1 __ (__)

J __

L

M N

K
P

never O Q

---

4. If O lives on the second floor, which one of the following CANNOT be true?

→ **Step 5: Questions**

(A)   K lives on the fourth floor.   →

(B)   K lives on the fifth floor.   →

(C)   L lives on the first floor.   →

(D)   L lives on the third floor.   →

(E)   L lives on the fourth floor.   →

PrepTest2 Sec3 Q9

Question 5:

LSAT Question	Analysis
An apartment building has five floors. Each floor has either one or two apartments. There are exactly eight apartments in the building. The residents of the building are J, K, L, M, N, O, P, and Q, who each live in a different apartment.	**Steps 1-4:**

An apartment building has five floors. Each floor has either one or two apartments. There are exactly eight apartments in the building. The residents of the building are J, K, L, M, N, O, P, and Q, who each live in a different apartment.
  J lives on a floor with two apartments.
  K lives on the floor directly above P.
  The second floor is made up of only one apartment.
  M and N live on the same floor.
  O does not live on the same floor as Q.
  L lives in the only apartment on her floor.
  Q does not live on the first or second floor.

$\longrightarrow$

Steps 1-4:

J K L M N O P Q

~P 5 __ (__)

4 __ (__)

3 __ (__)

~J ~M ~N ~Q 2 __ ⊠

~K ~Q 1 __ (__)

J / __

L

K / P

M N

never O Q

---

5. If M lives on the fourth floor, which one of the following must be false? $\longrightarrow$ **Step 5: Questions**

(A) O lives on the fifth floor. $\longrightarrow$

(B) J lives on the first floor. $\longrightarrow$

(C) L lives on the second floor. $\longrightarrow$

(D) Q lives on the third floor. $\longrightarrow$

(E) P lives on the first floor. $\longrightarrow$

PrepTest2 Sec3 Q10

Question 6:

LSAT Question	Analysis

An apartment building has five floors. Each floor has either one or two apartments. There are exactly eight apartments in the building. The residents of the building are J, K, L, M, N, O, P, and Q, who each live in a different apartment.

    J lives on a floor with two apartments.
    K lives on the floor directly above P.
    The second floor is made up of only one apartment.
    M and N live on the same floor.
    O does not live on the same floor as Q.
    L lives in the only apartment on her floor.
    Q does not live on the first or second floor.

Steps 1-4:

J K L M N O P Q

~P 5 __ (__)

4 __ (__)

3 __ (__)

~J ~M ~N ~Q 2 __ ⋈

~K ~Q 1 __ (__)

J	_

L

K
P

M	N

never
O	Q

6.   Which one of the following must be true?   → **Step 5: Questions**

(A)   If J lives on the fourth floor, then Q does not live on the fifth floor.

(B)   If O lives on the second floor, then L does not live on the fourth floor.

(C)   If N lives on the fourth floor, then K does not live on the second floor.

(D)   If K lives on the third floor, then O does not live on the fifth floor.

(E)   If P lives on the fourth floor, then M does not live on the third floor.

PrepTest2 Sec3 Q11

Question 7:

LSAT Question	Analysis

An apartment building has five floors. Each floor has either one or two apartments. There are exactly eight apartments in the building. The residents of the building are J, K, L, M, N, O, P, and Q, who each live in a different apartment.

    J lives on a floor with two apartments.
    K lives on the floor directly above P.
    The second floor is made up of only one apartment.
    M and N live on the same floor.
    O does not live on the same floor as Q.
    L lives in the only apartment on her floor.
    Q does not live on the first or second floor.

Steps 1-4:

J K L M N O P Q

~P 5 __ (__)

4 __ (__)

3 __ (__)

~J ~M ~N ~Q 2 __ ☒

~K ~Q 1 __ (__)

J _ / L / K P / M N / never O Q

7. If O lives on the fourth floor and P lives on the second floor, which one of the following must be true?

Step 5: Questions

(A) L lives on the first floor.

(B) M lives on the third floor.

(C) Q lives on the third floor.

(D) N lives on the fifth floor.

(E) Q lives on the fifth floor.

PrepTest2 Sec3 Q12

Practice 2

Directions: You have seen this game's setup, rules and deductions in the preceding sections of this chapter. For each question, first review the Master Sketch and reconstruct the work you did in Steps 1–4 of the Logic Games Method. Then, answer the question. For practice, take time to analyze each question thoroughly and enter your analysis for each step and answer choice blank. Complete expert analysis can be found in your Online Study Plan in the PDF labeled "Chapter 6 Full Game Practice Explanations."

Question 8:

LSAT Question	Analysis
Exactly seven professors—Madison, Nilsson, Orozco, Paton, Robinson, Sarkis, and Togo—were hired in the years 1989 through 1995. Each professor has one or more specialties, and any two professors hired in the same year or in consecutive years do not have a specialty in common. The professors were hired according to the following conditions: Madison was hired in 1993, Robinson in 1991. There is at least one specialty that Madison, Orozco, and Togo have in common. Nilsson shares a specialty with Robinson. Paton and Sarkis were each hired at least one year before Madison and at least one year after Nilsson. Orozco, who shares a specialty with Sarkis, was hired in 1990.	**Steps 1–4:** M̶ N̶ O̶ P R̶ S̶ T̶ 89 90 91 92 93 94 95 N O R S M T └─P─┘ share spec M = O = T N = R O = S N ⟨ P / S ⟩ M
8. Which one of the following is a complete and accurate list of the professors who could have been hired in the years 1989 through 1991?	**Step 5: Questions**
(A) Nilsson, Orozco, Robinson	
(B) Orozco, Robinson, Sarkis	
(C) Nilsson, Orozco, Paton, Robinson	
(D) Nilsson, Orozco, Paton, Sarkis	
(E) Orozco, Paton, Robinson, Sarkis *PrepTest35 Sec3 Q18*	

Question 9:

LSAT Question	Analysis
Exactly seven professors—Madison, Nilsson, Orozco, Paton, Robinson, Sarkis, and Togo—were hired in the years 1989 through 1995. Each professor has one or more specialties, and any two professors hired in the same year or in consecutive years do not have a specialty in common. The professors were hired according to the following conditions: Madison was hired in 1993, Robinson in 1991. There is at least one specialty that Madison, Orozco, and Togo have in common. Nilsson shares a specialty with Robinson. Paton and Sarkis were each hired at least one year before Madison and at least one year after Nilsson. Orozco, who shares a specialty with Sarkis, was hired in 1990.	**Steps 1-4:** M̶ N̶ Ø P R̶ S̶ T̶ $\underline{89}$ $\underline{90}$ $\underline{91}$ $\underline{92}$ $\underline{93}$ $\underline{94}$ $\underline{95}$ 　N　O　R　S　M　　　T 　　　　⎵⎵⎵ 　　　　P share spec M = O = T N = R O = S N ⟨ P / S ⟩ M

9.	If exactly one professor was hired in 1991, then which one of the following could be true?	**Step 5: Questions**
(A)	Madison and Paton share a specialty.	
(B)	Robinson and Sarkis share a specialty.	
(C)	Paton was hired exactly one year after Orozco.	
(D)	Exactly one professor was hired in 1994.	
(E)	Exactly two professors were hired in 1993.	

PrepTest35 Sec3 Q19

Question 10:

LSAT Question	Analysis

Exactly seven professors—Madison, Nilsson, Orozco, Paton, Robinson, Sarkis, and Togo—were hired in the years 1989 through 1995. Each professor has one or more specialties, and any two professors hired in the same year or in consecutive years do not have a specialty in common. The professors were hired according to the following conditions:

    Madison was hired in 1993, Robinson in 1991.

    There is at least one specialty that Madison, Orozco, and Togo have in common.

    Nilsson shares a specialty with Robinson.

    Paton and Sarkis were each hired at least one year before Madison and at least one year after Nilsson.

    Orozco, who shares a specialty with Sarkis, was hired in 1990.

$\longrightarrow$

Steps 1-4:

M̶ N̶ O̶ P R̶ S̶ T̶

89	90	91	92	93	94	95
N	O	R	S	M		T

(brace under O R S) P

share spec
M = O = T
N = R
O = S

N — P — M (diamond) with S below (N to P, P to M, N to S, S to M)

---

10. Which one of the following must be false? $\longrightarrow$ **Step 5: Questions**

(A)   Nilsson was hired in 1989. $\longrightarrow$

(B)   Paton was hired in 1990. $\longrightarrow$

(C)   Paton was hired in 1991. $\longrightarrow$

(D)   Sarkis was hired in 1992. $\longrightarrow$

(E)   Togo was hired in 1994. $\longrightarrow$

PrepTest35 Sec3 Q20

Question 11:

LSAT Question	Analysis

Exactly seven professors—Madison, Nilsson, Orozco, Paton, Robinson, Sarkis, and Togo—were hired in the years 1989 through 1995. Each professor has one or more specialties, and any two professors hired in the same year or in consecutive years do not have a specialty in common. The professors were hired according to the following conditions:

    Madison was hired in 1993, Robinson in 1991.

    There is at least one specialty that Madison, Orozco, and Togo have in common.

    Nilsson shares a specialty with Robinson.

    Paton and Sarkis were each hired at least one year before Madison and at least one year after Nilsson.

    Orozco, who shares a specialty with Sarkis, was hired in 1990.

→

Steps 1-4:

M̶ N̶ Ø P R̶ S̶ T̶

89	90	91	92	93	94	95
N	O	R	S	M		T

(brace under 91–92: P)

$$\frac{\text{share spec}}{\begin{array}{c}M = O = T\\N = R\\O = S\end{array}}$$

N ⟨ P / S ⟩ M

11. Which one of the following must be true? → **Step 5: Questions**

    (A) Orozco was hired before Paton. →

    (B) Paton was hired before Sarkis. →

    (C) Sarkis was hired before Robinson. →

    (D) Robinson was hired before Sarkis. →

    (E) Madison was hired before Sarkis.

PrepTest35 Sec3 Q21 →

Question 12:

LSAT Question	Analysis
Exactly seven professors—Madison, Nilsson, Orozco, Paton, Robinson, Sarkis, and Togo—were hired in the years 1989 through 1995. Each professor has one or more specialties, and any two professors hired in the same year or in consecutive years do not have a specialty in common. The professors were hired according to the following conditions:	**Steps 1–4:**

Madison was hired in 1993, Robinson in 1991.
There is at least one specialty that Madison, Orozco, and Togo have in common.
Nilsson shares a specialty with Robinson.
Paton and Sarkis were each hired at least one year before Madison and at least one year after Nilsson.
Orozco, who shares a specialty with Sarkis, was hired in 1990.

M̶ N̶ Ø P R̶ S̶ T̶

89	90	91	92	93	94	95
N	O	R	S	M		T

(P under 90–92)

share spec

M = O = T
N = R
O = S

N — P — M (with S below between P and M)

12. If exactly two professors were hired in 1992, then which one of the following could be true? → **Step 5: Questions**

(A) Orozco, Paton, and Togo share a specialty. →

(B) Madison, Paton, and Togo share a specialty. →

(C) Exactly two professors were hired in 1991. →

(D) Exactly two professors were hired in 1993. →

(E) Paton was hired in 1991. →

PrepTest35 Sec3 Q22 →

Question 13:

LSAT Question	Analysis

Exactly seven professors—Madison, Nilsson, Orozco, Paton, Robinson, Sarkis, and Togo—were hired in the years 1989 through 1995. Each professor has one or more specialties, and any two professors hired in the same year or in consecutive years do not have a specialty in common. The professors were hired according to the following conditions:

    Madison was hired in 1993, Robinson in 1991.

    There is at least one specialty that Madison, Orozco, and Togo have in common.

    Nilsson shares a specialty with Robinson.

    Paton and Sarkis were each hired at least one year before Madison and at least one year after Nilsson.

    Orozco, who shares a specialty with Sarkis, was hired in 1990.

$\longrightarrow$

Steps 1-4:

M̶ N̶ Ø P R̶ S̶ T̶

89	90	91	92	93	94	95
N	O	R	S	M		T

(brace under 91–92) P

share spec
M = O = T
N = R
O = S

N $<$ P $>$ M (over S) — N $<$ P / S $>$ M

13.   If Paton and Madison have a specialty in common, then which one of the following must be true? $\longrightarrow$ **Step 5: Questions**

(A)   Nilsson does not share a specialty with Paton. $\longrightarrow$

(B)   Exactly one professor was hired in 1990. $\longrightarrow$

(C)   Exactly one professor was hired in 1991. $\longrightarrow$

(D)   Exactly two professors were hired in each of two years. $\longrightarrow$

(E)   Paton was hired at least one year before Sarkis. $\longrightarrow$

PrepTest35 Sec3 Q23

Answer Key

Practice 1

1. (D)
2. (E)
3. (A)
4. (E)
5. (C)
6. (B)
7. (C)

Practice 2

8. (C)
9. (A)
10. (E)
11. (D)
12. (A)
13. (E)

Worked example explanations of these questions with complete expert analysis can be found in your Online Study Plan under Chapter 6. View or download the PDF titled "Chapter 6 Practice Full Games Explanations."

Perform

Here is your opportunity to put all of the pieces together and assess your skills on complex Strict Sequencing games. On the following pages, you'll find two full-length games along with their question sets. All of these games are from officially released LSAT tests, and all are representative of complex Strict Sequencing games you could see on Test Day. You can take the games one at a time or all together, but for your self-evaluation to be as accurate as possible, adhere to the timing guidelines set forth in the directions.

An answer key follows the games. Complete worked example expert analyses can be found in your online resources.

After you complete and review both games, assess your performance using the evaluation guidelines. There, you'll find recommendations for additional Easy, Medium, and Hard complex Strict Sequencing games from officially released LSAT exams that you can practice to continue honing your skills and raising your score.

Directions: Take no more than 9 minutes per game to complete the following two games and all of their questions.

Perform 1

Questions 1–7

A committee ranks five towns—Palmdale, Quietville, Riverdale, Seaside, Tidetown—from first (best) to fifth (worst) on each of three criteria: climate, location, friendliness.

> For each of the three criteria, none of the five towns receives the same ranking as any other town does.
> In climate, Tidetown is ranked third and Seaside fourth.
> In location, Quietville is ranked second, Riverdale third, and Palmdale fourth.
> In friendliness, Tidetown's ranking is better than Palmdale's, Quietville is ranked fourth and Seaside fifth.
> Riverdale receives a better ranking in climate than in friendliness.
> Quietville's three rankings are all different from each other.

1. Which of the following is a complete and accurate list of the rankings any one of which could be the ranking on climate given to Riverdale?

(A) first
(B) first, second
(C) first, fifth
(D) second, fifth
(E) first, second, fifth

2.   Which of the following is a town that CANNOT be ranked fifth on any one of the three criteria?

(A)   Palmdale
(B)   Quietville
(C)   Riverdale
(D)   Seaside
(E)   Tidetown

3.   Which of the following could be true?

(A)   Palmdale is ranked first in both climate and friendliness.
(B)   Quietville is ranked second in both climate and location.
(C)   Riverdale is ranked first in climate and third in both location and friendliness.
(D)   Seaside is ranked fifth in friendliness and fourth in both climate and location.
(E)   Tidetown is ranked third in both climate and friendliness.

4.   If Quietville is ranked first in climate, then it must be true that

(A)   Palmdale is ranked second in climate
(B)   Palmdale is ranked third in friendliness
(C)   Riverdale is ranked second in friendliness
(D)   Riverdale is ranked third in friendliness
(E)   Tidetown is ranked fifth in location

5.   If Palmdale is ranked second in climate, then which one of the following can be true?

(A)   Palmdale is ranked second in friendliness.
(B)   Quietville is ranked first in climate.
(C)   Riverdale is ranked first in friendliness.
(D)   Riverdale is ranked fifth in climate.
(E)   Tidetown is ranked third in friendliness.

6.   If Tidetown is ranked first in location and Riverdale is ranked second in friendliness, then it is possible to deduce with certainty all three rankings for exactly how many of the towns?

(A)   One
(B)   Two
(C)   Three
(D)   Four
(E)   Five

7.   Which one of the following statements CANNOT be true?

(A)   Palmdale is ranked first in climate.
(B)   Quietville is ranked fifth in climate.
(C)   Riverdale is ranked third in friendliness.
(D)   Seaside is ranked first in location.
(E)   Tidetown is ranked second in friendliness.

PrepTest5 Sec2 Qs 18–24

Perform 2

<u>Questions 8–13</u>

A disc jockey will play a sequence consisting of exactly seven different songs: three ballads—F, G, and H—and four dance tunes—R, S, V, and X. The following conditions must be met:

  No dance tune can be played immediately after another dance tune.

  H must be played earlier in the sequence than V.

  V and S must be separated from each other by exactly one song.

  S must be played immediately before or immediately after F.

  F must be played immediately after R, unless G is played earlier than R.

8. Which one of the following could be the order of the songs in the sequence?

(A) G, H, S, X, V, F, R

(B) R, H, X, G, S, F, V

(C) S, F, X, G, R, H, V

(D) V, F, S, H, X, G, R

(E) X, G, R, H, S, F, V

9. Which one of the following must be true about the sequence?

    (A) The first song is X.
    (B) The fifth song is S.
    (C) No ballad is played immediately after a dance tune.
    (D) No ballad is played immediately after another ballad.
    (E) No dance tune is played immediately after a ballad.

10. Which one of the following could be the fourth song in the sequence?

    (A) G
    (B) R
    (C) S
    (D) V
    (E) X

11. Which one of the following could be the first song in the sequence?

    (A) R
    (B) S
    (C) V
    (D) F
    (E) G

12. If the third song in the sequence is S, which one of the following must be the sixth song?

    (A) G
    (B) H
    (C) R
    (D) V
    (E) X

13. If the seventh song in the sequence is R, which one of the following could be the fifth song?

    (A) F
    (B) G
    (C) H
    (D) V
    (E) X

PrepTest25 Sec3 Qs 19–24

Answer Key

Perform 1

1. (B)
2. (C)
3. (C)
4. (D)
5. (A)
6. (E)
7. (E)

Perform 2

8. (E)
9. (D)
10. (A)
11. (A)
12. (A)
13. (D)

Worked example explanations of these questions with complete expert analysis can be found in your Online Study Plan under Chapter 6. View or download the PDF titled "Chapter 6 Perform Full Games Explanations."

Assess

Use the following criteria to evaluate your results on the Perform games.

If, under timed conditions, you correctly answered

11–13 of the questions: Outstanding! You have demonstrated a strong skill level in complex Strict Sequencing games. For further practice in complex Strict Sequencing, use any of the Recommended Additional Practice sets, including the Advanced set. Then, move on to Chapter 7 on Loose Sequencing.

8–11 of the questions: Good work! You have a solid foundation in complex Strict Sequencing games. For further practice in complex Strict Sequencing, begin with the Foundations or Mid-Level Recommended Additional Practice set. Then, move on to Chapter 7 on Loose Sequencing. If you have time before Test Day, try the Advanced Recommended Additional Practice set, as well.

0–7 of the questions: Keep working. Strict Sequencing games are central to your logic games performance, and continued practice will help you improve your score. Begin by reviewing this chapter. Then, try the games in the Foundations Recommended Additional Practice set. As you continue to progress, move on to the Mid-Level Recommended Additional Practice set, and then to Chapter 7 on Loose Sequencing games.

To stay sharp, practice the drills in the Logic Games Training Camp for this chapter in your Online Study Plan. Training Camp drills are divided into Fundamentals, Mid-Level, and Advanced sets.

Recommended Additional Practice: Complex Strict Sequencing

All of the following games will provide good practice on complex Strict Sequencing games. They are grouped by difficulty as determined from empirical student practice results. All PrepTests included are available individually, or in bundles of 10 as part of the LSAC's *10 Actual, Official LSAT PrepTests* series.

Foundations
PrepTest 69, Section 2, Game 2: Storing Petri Dishes (Vertical/Multiple Entities per Slot)*

PrepTest 68, Section 4, Game 1: Realtor Showings (Slot Groupings)*

PrepTest 65, Section 2, Game 2: Crafts Presentations (Entity Subsets)*

PrepTest 64, Section 2, Game 4: Bookcase Shelves (Vertical/Multiple Entities per Slot)*

PrepTest 60, Section 2, Game 1: Arts and Crafts Workshops (Calendar)**

Mid-Level
PrepTest 69, Section 2, Game 3: Juice and Snack Deliveries (Double Sequencing)*

PrepTest 67, Section 3, Game 3: Toy Store Aisles (Multiple Entities per Slot)*

PrepTest 54, Section 3, Game 2: CD Star Ratings (Entities Repeat/Multiple Entities per Slot)**

Advanced

PrepTest 68, Section 4, Game 4: Article Editing (Entity Subsets)*

PrepTest 65, Section 2, Game 4: TV Scheduling (Entity Sizes Vary)*

PrepTest 63, Section 2, Game 4: Street Entertainer (Vertical/Entities Repeat)*

*Game included in *10 Actual, Official LSAT PrepTests Volume V: PrepTests 62-71*; complete answers and explanations written by Kaplan LSAT experts available via the eBook: *LSAT PrepTests 62-71 Unlocked: Exclusive Data, Analysis & Explanations for 10 Actual, Official LSAT PrepTests Volume V.*

**Game included in *10 New Actual, Official LSAT PrepTests with Comparative Reading (PrepTests 52-61)*; complete answers and explanations written by Kaplan LSAT experts available via the eBook: *LSAT PrepTests 52-61 Unlocked: Exclusive Data, Analysis & Explanations for 10 New Actual, Official LSAT PrepTests with Comparative Reading.* [Explanations title coming Fall 2018.]

Reflect

Think back over the study and practice you did in this chapter.

- Are you able to identify complex Strict Sequencing games from their setups?
- Do you have default sketch frameworks for various complex Strict Sequencing variations?
- What kinds of rules do you anticipate seeing in complex Strict Sequencing games? In what ways are they similar to or different from those in basic Strict Sequencing?
- Are you comfortable analyzing complex Strict Sequencing rules and determining whether to record them within or underneath the sketch framework?
- Are you making the available deductions efficiently and effectively in complex Strict Sequencing games?

In the coming days and weeks before Test Day, take note of real-world tasks that reflect complex Strict Sequencing tasks. Consider how they mirror the setups and questions in LSAT Strict Sequencing, and how they differ. Try to reframe real-life sequencing tasks using the terms, rules, and restrictions employed by the testmaker.

Circular Sequencing

By Jeff Boudreau

 Watch the video lesson for this Spotlight in your online Study Plan.

Of all the variations on Strict Sequencing that the LSAT has featured, the most unusual is Circular Sequencing. At the time of this book's writing, Circular Sequencing has appeared on released LSAT tests only twice, most recently on PrepTest 41 (October 2003), and before that, on PrepTest 1 (June 1991). Depending on how you look at it, you could use those dates to conclude that Circular Sequencing games are a thing of the past, or that we're overdue for another one.

Circular Sequencing is just what it sounds like. The game's setup calls for you to determine the order of a set of entities, but instead of arranging them in a line, you must place them at points around a circle. In both of the Circular Sequencing games that have been officially released, the situation described people sitting around a circular table. It's not too hard to imagine other scenarios the testmaker might use—people taking their spots for a circle dance, items arranged around the points of a sundial, or maybe decorative flowers around the rim of a wedding cake—but, so far, it has always been people sitting at a round table.

In PrepTest 1's Circular Sequencing game, six trade representatives were seated in numbered chairs (1 through 6), and all of the rules centered around entities that were required to or prevented from sitting in adjacent seats. The only real trick there was remembering that, because the table is round, Seats 1 and 6 are adjacent seats. Okay, no more spoilers about that game in case you want to try it after this Special Feature.

The Circular Sequencing game from PrepTest 41 was less concrete. Notably, the seats in this case were not numbered.

Eight people—Fiona, George, Harriet, Ingrid, Karl, Manuel, Olivia, and Peter—are sitting, evenly spaced, around a circular picnic table. Any two of them are said to be sitting directly across from one another if and only if there are exactly three other people sitting between them, counting in either direction around the table. The following conditions apply:

> Fiona sits directly across from George.
> Harriet sits immediately next to neither Fiona nor Karl.
> Ingrid sits immediately next to, and immediately clockwise from, Olivia.

PrepTest41 Sec2 Qs 18-24

You may have noticed that this complex game has only three rules, and that they restrict only six of the eight entities. It's not surprising, then, that student results demonstrate that this is a difficult logic game.

In the video that accompanies this page, an LSAT Channel expert will walk you through the Picnic Table game, which is printed in full on the following pages. Try it on your own first, if you like. The expert's lesson provides a great example of how the Logic Games Method allows you to effectively tackle even unusual and unexpected games.

Questions 18–24

Eight people—Fiona, George, Harriet, Ingrid, Karl, Manuel, Olivia, and Peter—are sitting, evenly spaced, around a circular picnic table. Any two of them are said to be sitting directly across from one another if and only if there are exactly three other people sitting between them, counting in either direction around the table. The following conditions apply:

Fiona sits directly across from George.
Harriet sits immediately next to neither Fiona nor Karl.
Ingrid sits immediately next to, and immediately clockwise from, Olivia.

18. Which one of the following could be the order in which four of the people are seated, with no one else seated between them, counting clockwise around the table?

(A) George, Peter, Karl, Fiona
(B) Harriet, Olivia, Ingrid, Karl
(C) Ingrid, Fiona, Peter, Manuel
(D) Olivia, Manuel, Karl, George
(E) Peter, Harriet, Karl, Fiona

19. If Harriet and Olivia each sits immediately next to George, then which one of the following could be the two people each of whom sits immediately next to Peter?

   (A) Fiona and Karl
   (B) Fiona and Olivia
   (C) Harriet and Ingrid
   (D) Harriet and Karl
   (E) Karl and Manuel

20. If George does not sit immediately next to Harriet, then which one of the following could be the two people each of whom sits immediately next to Manuel?

   (A) Fiona and Harriet
   (B) Fiona and Peter
   (C) George and Karl
   (D) George and Peter
   (E) Harriet and Peter

21. If Manuel sits immediately next to Olivia, then which one of the following people must sit immediately next to Fiona?

   (A) Harriet
   (B) Ingrid
   (C) Karl
   (D) Manuel
   (E) Peter

22. What is the minimum possible number of people sitting between Ingrid and Manuel, counting clockwise from Ingrid around the table?

   (A) zero
   (B) one
   (C) two
   (D) three
   (E) four

23. If Karl sits directly across from Ingrid, then each of the following people could sit immediately next to Olivia EXCEPT:

   (A) Fiona
   (B) George
   (C) Harriet
   (D) Manuel
   (E) Peter

24. If Karl sits directly across from Harriet, then what is the minimum possible number of people sitting between George and Karl, counting clockwise from George to Karl?

   (A) zero
   (B) one
   (C) two
   (D) three
   (E) four

PrepTest41 Sec2 Qs 18–24

Complete answers and explanations are provided in The LSAT Channel Spotlight video "Limited Options" in your online Study Plan.

Loose Sequencing Games Unlocked

Prepare

Loose Sequencing games are far less common than the Strict Sequencing games you've seen in the two preceding chapters. Even so, Loose Sequencing has accounted for a little less than 10 percent of all logic games on LSAT tests released in the past five years.

Types of Games By Percentage, 2012–2016

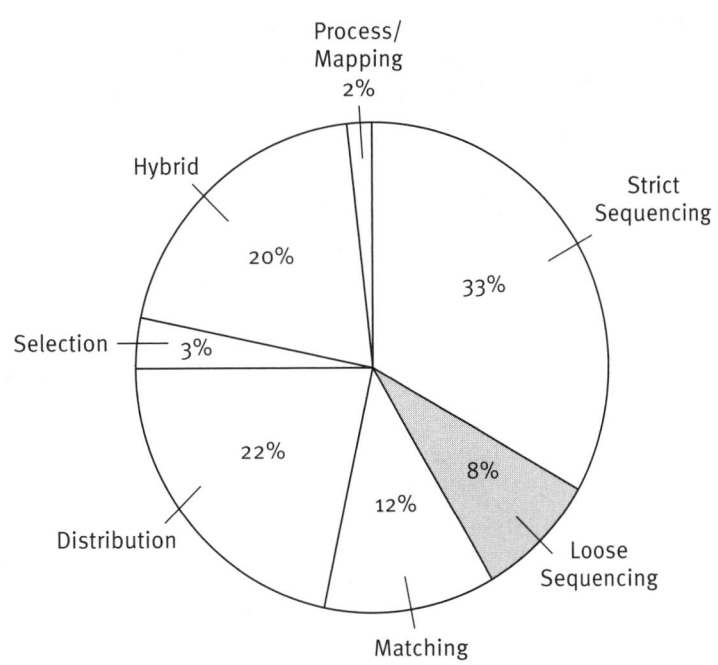

The opening paragraph of a Loose Sequencing game—its setup, if you will—is often no different than that of any other Sequencing game. The setup will define an ordering task such as ranking or scheduling, and it will always use language that tells you that the entities are to be arranged one per position with no ties.

> At a retirement party, exactly seven employees—Arias, Barnhard, Carmichael, Deng, Evans, Furillo, and Gillis—will give toasts honoring a retiring coworker. The employees will give their toasts one at a time in an order subject to the following considerations:

So far, that looks like any basic Strict Sequencing game.

The defining characteristic of Loose Sequencing games appears in the rules. All of the rules will stipulate the relative positions between or among the entities. For example:

> Gillis will give a toast before Carmichael and Furillo give toasts.
> Deng will give a toast after Carmichael.
> Arias gives a toast at some time before Carmichael, but at some time later than Barnhard.
> Evans will give a toast at some time before Gillis.

Notice, too, that every entity in the game is mentioned in at least one rule, and some are mentioned in two. This is typical of Loose Sequencing, and it leads to a special sketch framework that you'll learn for this game type.

Loose Sequencing games never present a rule that establishes an entity in a particular named or numbered position, that stipulates the exact number of positions by which two entities are separated, or that dictates that two entities are in adjacent positions. You might, on occasion, see a conditional rule (e.g., "If A ranks higher than C, then D ranks lower than F") or one that gives two alternative orders (e.g., "Either G ranks higher than B and lower than E, or G ranks lower than B and higher than A"). Rules like these are rare, and always indicate a more difficult Loose Sequencing game.

LOOSE SEQUENCING IN REAL LIFE

Because Loose Sequencing is defined by the relative nature of the rules, finding analogies in day-to-day life means thinking about the information you have when deciding how to put things in order. In real life, ranking things—deciding which ones you like better than others—often approximates Loose Sequencing.

Imagine you are relaxing with a social media page and you come across a poll titled "Rank the Greatest Classic Rock Bands." The poll lists seven bands—call them A, B, K, L, P, R, and W. As you look over the list, you probably don't think "I'll put W and L in consecutive positions, but I might like either one better than the other." Almost certainly, you don't think "I haven't considered the other bands here, but R is definitely third," or "K is ranked exactly two positions lower than W." Those "strict" rules seem inherently out of place in this kind of task.

Given the "loose" nature of ranking favorites, you study the list, and probably start with thoughts such as, "Well, I like L better than A, but not as well as R," and "I have to put R higher than W," and so on. For a simple task like this, you probably wouldn't need to sketch anything, but if you did, your "rules" would start to look like this:

R — L — A
  \
   W

At this point, you've ranked W relative to R, but not yet relative to L or A. Likewise, A is ranked relative to R and L, but not relative to W. In the real-life game, you will add more of these relative decisions—your "rules," if you like—until, in the end, you'll decide on a specific order, first through seventh.

On the LSAT, a Loose Sequencing game will stop short of giving you enough information to decide on just one final order. To see what a Master Sketch will look like on the test, add a couple more decisions to your classic rock list: "B and P both rank higher than R" and "K ranks below W." Here's what you know so far:

At this point, you know that one of B or P is your favorite among the seven bands, and the other is your second favorite. You've now determined that R is, for sure, your third favorite. Band A might be your least favorite of the seven, but it could still wind up as high as fifth because you haven't yet ranked it against W or K.

The sketch represents a typical LSAT Loose Sequencing game's Master Sketch, including all of the rules and deductions. By giving you that much information, the game's questions can ask you about any number of cases that must, could, or cannot be true. Given the "rules" recorded so far, for example, it must be true that you like P more than W, but it could be true or false that you like W more than L. The test may also ask New-"If" questions by giving conditions that further restrict something so far undetermined within the game: "If L is your fourth favorite of the seven bands, which one of the following must/could be true/false?"

When you notice sequencing tasks in your everyday routine, stop to consider whether the "rules" inherent in them are "strict" or "loose." Keep in mind that, on the LSAT, most Strict Sequencing games contain one or more loose, relative-relationship rules along with those that mention named or numbered positions and others that provide for strict relationships among the entities. LSAT Loose Sequencing games, however, provide only relative relationships. In the next section, you'll learn how LSAT experts handle sketches and deductions a little differently in Loose Sequencing than they do in other game types.

LOOSE SEQUENCING GAMES RULES

LEARNING OBJECTIVES

In this section of the chapter, you'll practice

- Applying Steps 1 and 2 of the Logic Games Method to Loose Sequencing games by
  - Asking the SEAL questions to analyze the game's Overview, and then
  - Building the rules into a simple, useful framework
- Applying Step 3 of the Logic Games Method to Loose Sequencing games by analyzing and sketching the rules
- Applying Step 4 of the Logic Games Method to Loose Sequencing games by combining rules and restrictions to make all valid deductions in the game

Prepare

Steps 1, 2, and 3 in Loose Sequencing Games

Because Loose Sequencing setups are often indistinguishable from their Strict counterparts, there isn't much to add about Step 1. As you ask the SEAL questions, you'll discover a game that asks you to put people or items in order or to schedule them, one per position with no ties. As a result, your instinct in Step 2 will be to draw out a standard Strict Sequencing sketch framework. That's fine. But, when you turn to the rules and find out you have a Loose Sequencing game—that is, when you discover that *all* of the rules provide *only* relative relationships among the entities—you'll know that you are going to build the rules into a branching "tree" of relationships, and won't depict any of them within a framework of numbered slots.

LOGIC GAMES STRATEGY

To distinguish Loose Sequencing games from Strict Sequencing games, modify **SEAL** to **SEAL'R**. In other words, if your answers to the SEAL questions in the Step 1 produce the following results:

- The **S**ituation poses an ordering or scheduling task,
- The roster of **E**ntities has no subdivisions,
- The **A**ction is Sequencing, and
- The **L**imitations specify a one per position/no ties arrangement

then quickly review the **R**ules.

- If all of the rules provide only relative relationships between or among the entities, this is a Loose Sequencing game.
- If any of the rules establishes an entity's position, provide an exact number of spaces between two (or more) entities, or stipulate that two entities are adjacent, this is a Strict Sequencing game.

As you practice, you'll begin to instinctively add that quick review of the rules to the Overview step. Most of the time, the rules will reveal a basic Strict Sequencing game (they are simply more common on the LSAT), but from time to time, you'll uncover a Loose Sequencing game.

To make the distinction concrete, consider the setup from the introduction to this chapter.

> At a retirement party, exactly seven employees—Arias, Barnhard, Carmichael, Deng, Evans, Furillo, and Gillis—will give toasts honoring a retiring coworker. The employees will give their toasts one at a time in an order subject to the following considerations:

While it is clear that the Action here is basic Sequencing, you don't yet know whether it is Strict or Loose. Now, consider two potential sets of rules to accompany that setup:

Rule Set I

> Deng gives the seventh toast.
> Exactly one employee gives a toast between Gillis and Carmichael.
> Barnhard's toast is some time before Arias's toast.
> Gillis's toast is before Evans's toast but after Furillo's.

ABCDEFG

1	2	3	4	5	6	7
—	—	—	—	—	—	D

G/C _ C/G

B...A

F...G...E

The first two rules distinguish Set I as belonging to a Strict Sequencing game. Rule 1 is depicted directly within the sketch framework, and Rule 2 is written out to reflect the spacing and orientation of the framework.

Rule Set II

> Gillis will give a toast before Carmichael and Furillo give toasts.
> Deng will give a toast after Carmichael.
> Arias gives a toast at some time before Carmichael, but at some time later than Barnhard.
> Evans will give a toast at some time before Gillis.

ABCDEFG

B — A
E — G
C — D
F

Rule Set II indicates a Loose Sequencing game. All of the rules outline relative relationships among the entities. In another distinguishing characteristic of Loose Sequencing games, notice that all of the game's entities are mentioned in at least one of the rules. The resulting sketch doesn't correspond to a framework, but it contains all of the information needed to answer the game's questions.

Steps 3 and 4 in Loose Sequencing

While examining the Loose Sequencing example provided by Rule Set II, it may have struck you that the LSAT expert combined all of the rules into a single "tree" of relationships. In essence, the expert combined Steps 3 and 4 while writing out the rules. To see how that happened, take the rules one at a time, and note how the expert adds each rule to the existing branches of the "tree":

At a retirement party, exactly seven employees—Arias, Barnhard, Carmichael, Deng, Evans, Furillo, and Gillis—will give toasts honoring a retiring coworker. The employees will give their toasts one at a time in an order subject to the following considerations:

Gillis will give a toast before Carmichael and Furillo give toasts.

A B C D E F G

Deng will give a toast after Carmichael.

A B C D E F G

Arias gives a toast at some time before Carmichael, but at some time later than Barnhard.

A B C D E F G

Evans will give a toast at some time before Gillis.

A B C D E F G

The value of a tree-like depiction of Loose Sequencing rules is that the resulting sketch allows you to determine the acceptable positions for every entity. To do this, count the number of entities that must come before, and the number of entities that must come after, the entity in question.

Take Gillis, for example, in the Retirement Toasts game: Gillis must follow Evans, and must precede Furillo, Carmichael, and Deng. Thus, Gillis could be no earlier than second, and no later than fourth. None of the rules relates Gillis directly to Barnhard or Arias. Gillis may give a toast earlier than both of them, later than both of them, or in between the two.

Now, consider Carmichael. What is the earliest and latest she could give her toast?

Carmichael must follow Evans, Gillis, Barnhard, and Arias, so the earliest toast she could give is fifth. Carmichael must precede Deng, so the latest toast she could give is sixth. The only employee not directly related to Carmichael by the rules is Furillo. Carmichael could give her toast before or after Furillo's toast.

For good measure, try one more. Determine the earliest and latest positions that are acceptable for Arias.

Arias must be preceded by Barnhard, so the earliest Arias could give a toast is second. Arias must be followed by Carmichael and Deng, so the latest Arias could give a toast is fifth. Note that Arias is not related to Evans, Gillis, or Furillo in any way by the rules.

Most Loose Sequencing games contain straightforward rules that state the relative order of two or three entities. From time to time, the LSAT will increase the complexity of Loose Sequencing games by adding conditional rules, or rules that allow for more than one order among certain entities.

LOGIC GAMES STRATEGY

In Loose Sequencing games, the rules basically tell you:

- The order in which two or more entities are positioned.

Occasionally, Loose Sequencing rules give you:

- A condition under which the order between entities can change; e.g., If C ranks higher than D, then F ranks higher than E.
- Two alternative orders among three entities; e.g., P ranks higher than either M or N, but not both. (This means that either of M-P-N or N-P-M is acceptable, but in no case can both M and N precede or follow P.)

Because Loose Sequencing games use so few types of rules, the deductions come from a limited number of sources.

LOGIC GAMES STRATEGY

In Loose Sequencing games, deductions are most likely to stem from:

- **"Loose" Blocks of Entities**—Two or more entities that must appear in a particular order, but are not restricted by the number of spaces between them, and
- **Duplications**—Entities shared by two or more rules; duplications are always at the heart of Loose Sequencing games.

In Loose Sequencing games, deductions may involve:

- **Limited Options**—The situation arises when a "loose" Block of Entities is restricted to either of two acceptable orders; when this occurs, draw dual Limited Options sketches.

In Loose Sequencing games, deductions never involve:

- **Established Entities**—Entities placed into a specific position.
- **Number Restrictions**—Limitations or rules affecting the number of entities that can be placed in a given position.

To see how the test might construct a complex Loose Sequencing game that results in Limited Options, revisit the "real-life" scenario of ranking classic rock bands.

Carla is ranking seven classic rock bands—A, B, K, L, P, R, and W—and no others from most to least favorite. She will rank each band once, with no ties. Her rankings correspond to the following considerations:

She ranks P higher than she ranks R.
She ranks B lower than she ranks L.
She ranks A higher than she ranks both P and W.
She ranks one of L or A, but not both, higher than she ranks K.

In this game, Rule 4 provides exactly two ways in which Karen might rank A, K, and L.

$$A — K — L \quad or \quad L — K — A$$

That provides a perfect starting point from which to build out dual Limited Options sketches. Because Rule 3 and Rule 4 share A, you can attach Rule 3 to both options.

Opt. I
$$A — K — L$$
with P and W branching from A

Opt. II
$$L — K — A$$
with P and W branching from A

Likewise, because Rule 2 and Rule 4 share L, you can attach Rule 2 to each option.

And, finally, because P is already placed in each option, there are clear places to attach Rule 1 to the "trees."

Rule 4 clearly makes this game more complex than a Loose Sequencing game without any rules that provide for alternative orders. Within each of the two options, however, you can still determine the highest or lowest that a given entity might appear.

Consider K, for example. In Option I, K is preceded by only A, so K could be ranked as high as second. In Option I, K is followed by only L and B, and could thus rank as low as fifth. In this option, K is not directly related to P, R, or W.

In Option II, K is preceded only by L, and again, could rank as high as second. However, in the second option, K is followed by A, P, R, and W, and so can only rank as low as third. In this option, K is directly related to every entity except B.

Remember that Loose Sequencing games with Limited Options are pretty rare. Should you see one, however, you will really appreciate being able to quickly and accurately assess the dual sketches. If a New-"If" question opened with "If Carla ranks K fifth ... ", then you would know you are in Option I (because K can't rank fifth in Option II), you would know that A ranks first (because it always does in Option I), and you would know that L ranks sixth and that B ranks seventh (because they must follow K in Option I). You could quickly draw a sketch for that question, and you would have high confidence that you could assess what must, could, and cannot be true as a result.

Now, it's time for a little practice with Loose Sequencing setups, rules, and deductions. You already know what you're going to see in the setup—a basic Sequencing action—and you know that, because these are Loose Sequencing games, you won't need a sketch framework. Therefore, the practice exercises focus on Steps 3 and 4, and especially on your ability to "read" the tree-like sketch (or sketches) that you will build.

Practice

Directions: In each practice exercise, work through Steps 1 through 4 of the Logic Games Method. After you complete your Master Sketch, assess its utility by determining the acceptable positions for each of the game's entities.

Practice 1

The order of presentation of six film award categories—comedy, documentary, foreign, historical, independent, and nature—at an annual film festival always adheres to the following guidelines established by the festival advisory committee:

No two award presentations will be made concurrently.
The award for foreign films is always presented at some time before the award for comedies.
The award for comedies is always presented at some time after the award for documentaries.
The award for foreign films is always presented at some time after the awards for historical and nature films.
The award for independent films is always presented before the award for historical films.

1. [Steps 1–4] Record your Master Sketch in the following space:

2. Evaluate your sketch by answering the following questions:
   - What are the earliest and latest positions in which the award for comedy may be presented?
   - What are the earliest and latest positions in which the award for documentary may be presented?
   - What are the earliest and latest positions in which the award for foreign film may be presented?
   - What are the earliest and latest positions in which the award for historical film may be presented?
   - What are the earliest and latest positions in which the award for independent film may be presented?
   - What are the earliest and latest positions in which the award for nature film may be presented?
   - If the nature film award is the third award presented, how many categories of awards are there that could be the second award category presented? Which categories are they?
   - If the foreign film award is the fourth award presented, which category of awards is presented fifth?
   - If the historical film award is the second award presented, how many categories of awards are there that could be the third award category presented? Which categories are they?

Practice 2

A music producer is sequencing seven instrumental music pieces—*Atmosphere, Botanica, Clouds, Dynamic, Ecologica, Fireflies,* and *Gyrate*—for a New Age relaxation CD. Each piece will appear exactly one time, and none of the pieces overlap. In order to achieve a harmonic progression in mood, the producer will adhere to the following guidelines:

> *Botanica* can neither appear earlier on the CD than *Fireflies* nor later on the CD than *Dynamic*.
> *Atmosphere* must appear earlier on the CD than *Fireflies* in any sequence in which *Gyrate* appears earlier than *Dynamic*.
> *Ecologica* must appear earlier on the CD than both *Clouds* and *Fireflies*.
> *Dynamic* must appear earlier on the CD than *Atmosphere*.

1. [Steps 1–4] Record your Master Sketch in the following space:

2. Evaluate your sketch by answering the following questions:
   - What are the earliest and latest positions in which *Atmosphere* may appear on the CD?
   - What are the earliest and latest positions in which *Botanica* may appear on the CD?
   - What are the earliest and latest positions in which *Clouds* may appear on the CD?
   - What are the earliest and latest positions in which *Dynamic* may appear on the CD?
   - What are the earliest and latest positions in which *Ecologica* may appear on the CD?
   - What are the earliest and latest positions in which *Fireflies* may appear on the CD?
   - What are the earliest and latest positions in which *Gyrate* may appear on the CD?
   - If *Botanica* is the fourth track on the CD, how many tracks are there that could be second track? Which ones are they?
   - If *Dynamic* is the fourth track on the CD, how many tracks are there that could be the fifth track? Which ones are they?

Explanations

Compare your work to that of an LSAT expert. Make sure that your sketch accurately reflects all of the restrictions given in the rules. Then, compare your answers to those of the expert on each of the assessment questions. If your answers differ, review the rules and your sketch to see why your analysis was mistaken.

Practice 1

The order of presentation of six film award categories—comedy, documentary, foreign, historical, independent, and nature—at the annual film festival always adheres to the following guidelines established by the festival advisory committee:

> No two award presentations will be made concurrently.
> The award for foreign films is always presented at some time before the award for comedies.
> The award for comedies is always presented at some time after the award for documentaries.
> The award for foreign films is always presented at some time after the awards for historical and nature films.
> The award for independent films is always presented before the award for historical films.

1. [Steps 1–4] Record your Master Sketch in the following space:

C D F H I N

2. Evaluate your sketch by answering the following questions:

- What are the earliest and latest positions in which the award for comedy may be presented? *The comedy award must be presented sixth; it is preceded by all five of the other entities.*

- What are the earliest and latest positions in which the award for documentary may be presented? *The earliest that the documentary award may be presented is first (no entities*

must precede it); the latest the documentary award may be presented is fifth (it is followed by comedy).

- What are the earliest and latest positions in which the award for foreign film may be presented? *The earliest that the foreign film award may be presented is fourth (it is preceded by independent, historical, and nature); the latest the foreign film award may be presented is fifth (it is followed by comedy).*

- What are the earliest and latest positions in which the award for historical film may be presented? *The earliest that the historical film award may be presented is second (it is preceded by independent); the latest the historical film award may be presented is fourth (it is followed by foreign film and comedy).*

- What are the earliest and latest positions in which the award for independent film may be presented? *The earliest that the independent film award may be presented is first (no entities must precede it); the latest the independent award may be presented is third (it is followed by historical film, foreign film, and comedy).*

- What are the earliest and latest positions in which the award for nature film may be presented? *The earliest that the nature film award may be presented is first (no entities must precede it); the latest the nature award may be presented is fourth (it is followed by foreign film and comedy).*

- If the nature film award is the third award presented, how many categories of awards are there that could be the second award category presented? Which categories are they? *When the nature film award is presented third, there are three categories that could be presented second:*

documentary, historical, and independent. Presenting the nature film award third allows for either of these sequence patterns:

```
(1-2)
 I
  \
   \     N — H — F — C
   /     3   4   5   6
  /
 D
(1-2)
```

```
            (4-5)
              F
            /   \
 I — H — N       C
 1   2   3  \   / 6
             \ /
              D
            (4-5)
```

- If the foreign film award is the fourth award presented, which category of awards is presented fifth? *When the foreign film award is fourth, then the fifth award must be for documentary.*

```
(1-2) (2-3)
 I — H
       \
        \   F — D — C
        /   4   5   6
       /
      N
    (1-3)
```

- If the historical film award is the second award presented, how many categories of awards are there that could be the third award category presented? Which categories are they? *When the historical film award is presented second, there are two categories that could be presented third: nature film or drama.*

```
 I — H  \ (4-5)
 1   2   \ F
          / \
         N   \   C
       (3-4)  \ / 6
               D
             (3-5)
```

Practice 2

A music producer is sequencing seven instrumental music pieces—*Atmosphere, Botanica, Clouds, Dynamic, Ecologica, Fireflies,* and *Gyrate*—for a New Age relaxation CD. Each piece will appear exactly one time, and none of the pieces overlap. In order to achieve a harmonic progression in mood, the producer will adhere to the following guidelines:

Botanica can neither appear earlier on the CD than *Fireflies* nor later on the CD than *Dynamic*.

Atmosphere must appear earlier on the CD than *Fireflies* in any sequence in which *Gyrate* appears earlier than *Dynamic*.

Ecologica must appear earlier on the CD than both *Clouds* and *Fireflies*.

Dynamic must appear earlier on the CD than *Atmosphere*.

1. [Steps 1–4] Record your Master Sketch in the following space: *Rule 1 translates into the following sketch:*

$$F — B — D$$

Rule 2 is conditional. For the moment, write it off to the side.

$$F — B — D$$

$$\text{If } G — D \rightarrow A — F$$

$$\text{If } F — A \rightarrow D — G$$

Rules 3 and 4 can be attached to Rule 1.

```
      / F — B — D — A
   E <
      \ C
```

$$\text{If } G — D \rightarrow A — F$$

$$\text{If } F — A \rightarrow D — G$$

Now, consider Rule 2 in light of what the sketch reveals about A and F. For G to be earlier than D, A must be earlier than F. But, A is locked into a position later than F. That means that G can never be in a position earlier than D. Add G to the sketch following D.

```
      / F — B — D — A
   E <                \
      \ C              G
```

At this point, the sketch is complete, and you can use it to determine acceptable positions for each entity.

2. Evaluate your sketch by answering the following questions:

- What are the earliest and latest positions in which *Atmosphere* may appear on the CD? Atmosphere *can take any position from fifth through seventh. It is preceded by E, F, B, and D, but is unrelated to C and G.*

- What are the earliest and latest positions in which *Botanica* may appear on the CD? Botanica *can be third or fourth. It is preceded by E and F, followed by D, A, and G, and is unrelated to C.*

- What are the earliest and latest positions in which *Clouds* may appear on the CD? Clouds *can take any position from second through seventh. It is preceded by E, but is unrelated to any other entity.*

- What are the earliest and latest positions in which *Dynamic* may appear on the CD? Dynamic *can be fourth or fifth. It is preceded by E, F, and B, followed by A and G, and is unrelated to C.*

- What are the earliest and latest positions in which *Ecologica* may appear on the CD? Ecologica *must be the first track on the CD. It is followed by every other piece of music.*

- What are the earliest and latest positions in which *Fireflies* may appear on the CD? Fireflies *could be second or third. It is preceded by E, followed by B, D, A, and G, and is unrelated to C.*

- What are the earliest and latest positions in which *Gyrate* may appear on the CD? Gyrate *can take any position from fifth through seventh. It is preceded by E, F, B, and D, but is unrelated to C and A.*

- If *Botanica* is the fourth track on the CD, how many tracks are there that could be second track? Which ones are they? *When* Botanica *is fourth, there are two options for the second track:* Fireflies *and* Clouds.

- If *Dynamic* is the fourth track on the CD, how many tracks are there that could be the fifth track? Which ones are they? *When* Dynamic *is fourth, there are three options for track five:* Atmosphere, Clouds, *and* Gyrate.

Now that you've learned the ins and outs of setting up Loose Sequencing games, test your skills on two officially released LSAT games in the Perform section.

LOOSE SEQUENCING GAMES—FULL GAMES WITH QUESTIONS

LEARNING OBJECTIVES

In this section of the chapter, you'll assess your ability to

- Apply the Logic Games Method to Loose Sequencing games.

Perform

Here is your opportunity to put all of the pieces together and assess your skills on Loose Sequencing games. On the following pages, you'll find two full-length games along with their question sets. Both of these games are from officially released LSAT tests, and are representative of Loose Sequencing games you could see on Test Day. You can take the games one at a time or together, but for your self-evaluation to be as accurate as possible, adhere to the timing guidelines set forth in the directions.

An answer key follows the games. Complete worked example expert analyses can be found in your online resources.

After you complete and review both games, assess your performance using the evaluation guidelines. There, you'll find recommendations for additional Easy, Medium, and Hard Loose Sequencing games from officially released LSAT exams that you can practice to continue honing your skills and raising your score.

Directions: Take no more than 9 minutes per game to complete the following two games and all of their questions.

Perform 1

<u>Questions 1–7</u>

A rowing team uses a boat with exactly six seats arranged in single file and numbered sequentially 1 through 6, from the front of the boat to the back. Six athletes—Lee, Miller, Ovitz, Singh, Valerio, and Zita—each row at exactly one of the seats. The following restrictions must apply:

>Miller rows closer to the front than Singh.
>Singh rows closer to the front than both Lee and Valerio.
>Valerio and Zita each row closer to the front than Ovitz.

1. Which one of the following could be an accurate matching of athletes to seats?

    (A) Miller: seat 1; Valerio: seat 5; Lee: seat 6
    (B) Singh: seat 3; Valerio: seat 4; Zita: seat 5
    (C) Miller: seat 1; Valerio: seat 3; Lee: seat 6
    (D) Lee: seat 3; Valerio: seat 4; Ovitz: seat 5
    (E) Zita: seat 2; Valerio: seat 3; Ovitz: seat 6

2. If Valerio rows at seat 5, then which one of the following must be true?

    (A) Miller rows at seat 1.
    (B) Singh rows at seat 2.
    (C) Zita rows at seat 3.
    (D) Lee rows at seat 4.
    (E) Ovitz rows at seat 6.

3. If Lee rows at seat 3, then each of the following could be true EXCEPT:

    (A) Zita rows immediately behind Valerio.
    (B) Ovitz rows immediately behind Valerio.
    (C) Ovitz rows immediately behind Zita.
    (D) Valerio rows immediately behind Lee.
    (E) Singh rows immediately behind Zita.

4. Which one of the following CANNOT be true?

    (A) Ovitz rows closer to the front than Singh.
    (B) Zita rows closer to the front than Miller.
    (C) Lee rows closer to the front than Valerio.
    (D) Singh rows closer to the front than Zita.
    (E) Valerio rows closer to the front than Lee.

5. Exactly how many different seats could be the seat occupied by Zita?

    (A) two
    (B) three
    (C) four
    (D) five
    (E) six

6. If Valerio rows closer to the front than Zita, then which one of the following must be true?

    (A) Miller rows immediately in front of Singh.
    (B) Lee rows immediately in front of Valerio.
    (C) Zita rows immediately in front of Ovitz.
    (D) Singh rows immediately in front of Lee.
    (E) Singh rows immediately in front of Valerio.

7. Suppose the restriction that Miller rows closer to the front than Singh is replaced by the restriction that Singh rows closer to the front than Miller. If the other two restrictions remain in effect, then each of the following could be an accurate matching of athletes to seats EXCEPT:

    (A) Singh: seat 1; Zita: seat 2; Miller: seat 6
    (B) Singh: seat 1; Valerio: seat 3; Ovitz: seat 5
    (C) Singh: seat 3; Lee: seat 4; Valerio: seat 5
    (D) Valerio: seat 3; Miller: seat 4; Lee: seat 5
    (E) Valerio: seat 4; Miller: seat 5; Ovitz: seat 6

    PrepTest43 Sec4 Qs 6–12

Perform 2

<u>Questions 8–12</u>

Each of seven television programs—H, J, L, P, Q, S, V—is assigned a different rank: from first through seventh (from most popular to least popular). The ranking is consistent with the following conditions:

J and L are each less popular than H.
J is more popular than Q.
S and V are each less popular than L.
P and S are each less popular than Q.
S is not seventh.

8. Which one of the following could be the order of the programs, from most popular to least popular?

(A) J, H, L, Q, V, S, P
(B) H, L, Q, J, S, P, V
(C) H, J, Q, L, S, V, P
(D) H, J, V, L, Q, S, P
(E) H, L, V, J, Q, P, S

9. If J is more popular than L, and S is more popular than P, then which one of the following must be true of the ranking?

    (A) J is second.
    (B) J is third.
    (C) L is third.
    (D) Q is third.
    (E) P is seventh.

10. Which one of the following programs CANNOT be ranked third?

    (A) L
    (B) J
    (C) Q
    (D) V
    (E) P

11. If V is more popular than Q and J is less popular than L, then which one of the following could be true of the ranking?

    (A) P is more popular than S.
    (B) S is more popular than V.
    (C) P is more popular than L.
    (D) J is more popular than V.
    (E) Q is more popular than V.

12. If Q is more popular than L, then each of the following must be true of the ranking EXCEPT:

    (A) H is first.
    (B) L is fourth.
    (C) V is not fourth.
    (D) J is not third.
    (E) Q is third.

PrepTest33 Sec4 Qs 1–5

Answer Key

Perform 1

1. (C)
2. (E)
3. (E)
4. (A)
5. (D)
6. (A)
7. (C)

Perform 2

8. (C)
9. (A)
10. (E)
11. (D)
12. (B)

Worked example explanations of these questions with complete expert analysis can be found in your Online Study Plan under Chapter 7. View or download the PDF titled "Chapter 7 Perform Full Games Explanations."

Assess

Use the following criteria to evaluate your results on the Perform games.

If, under timed conditions, you correctly answered

10–12 of the questions: Outstanding! You have demonstrated a strong skill level in Loose Sequencing games. For further practice in Loose Sequencing, use any of the Recommended Additional Practice sets, including the Advanced set. Then, move on to either Chapter 8 on Selection games, or if you have limited time before Test Day, skip to Chapter 9 on Matching and Distribution games.

7–9 of the questions: Good work! You have a solid foundation in Loose Sequencing games. For further practice in Loose Sequencing, begin with the Foundations or Mid-Level Recommended Additional Practice set. If you have ample time before Test Day, try the Advanced Recommended Additional Practice set, as well. Then, move on to either Chapter 8 on Selection games, or if you have limited time before Test Day, skip to Chapter 9 on Matching and Distribution games.

0–6 of the questions: Keep working. Loose Sequencing games are not as central to your logic games performance as Strict Sequencing games are, but they appear regularly, and continued practice will help you improve your score. Begin by reviewing this chapter. Then, try the games in the Foundations Recommended Additional Practice set. As you continue to progress, move on to the Mid-Level Recommended Additional Practice set, and then on to Chapter 8 on Selection games, or if you have limited time before Test Day, skip to Chapter 9 on Matching and Distribution games.

To stay sharp, practice the drills in the Logic Games Training Camp for this chapter in your Online Study Plan. Training Camp drills are divided into Fundamentals, Mid-Level, and Advanced sets.

Recommended Additional Practice: Loose Sequencing

All of the following games will provide good practice on Loose Sequencing. They are grouped by difficulty as determined from empirical student practice results. All PrepTests included are available individually, or in bundles of 10 as part of the LSAC's *10 Actual, Official LSAT PrepTests* series.

Foundations
PrepTest 71, Section 2, Game 1: Film Releases*
PrepTest 65, Section 2, Game 1: Piano Recital Solos*

Mid-Level
PrepTest 61, Section 3, Game 2: Ancient Artifacts**
PrepTest 60, Section 2, Game 2: Actors in Opening Credits**

Advanced
PrepTest 52, Section 2, Game 1: Water Valves**
PrepTest 52, Section 2, Game 4: Bread Truck Deliveries**

*Game included in *10 Actual, Official LSAT PrepTests Volume V: PrepTests 62–71*; complete answers and explanations written by Kaplan LSAT experts available via the eBook: *LSAT PrepTests 62–71 Unlocked: Exclusive Data, Analysis & Explanations for 10 Actual, Official LSAT PrepTests Volume V.*

**Game included in *10 New Actual, Official LSAT PrepTests with Comparative Reading (PrepTests 52–61)*; complete answers and explanations written by Kaplan LSAT experts available via the eBook: *LSAT PrepTests 52–61 Unlocked: Exclusive Data, Analysis & Explanations for 10 New Actual, Official LSAT PrepTests with Comparative Reading.* [Explanations title coming Fall 2018.]

Reflect

Think back over the study and practice you did in this chapter.

- Are you able to distinguish Loose Sequencing games from Strict Sequencing? What makes the difference?
- Do you understand why LSAT experts combine Steps 3 and 4 of the Logic Games Method in Loose Sequencing?
- What kinds of rules do you anticipate seeing in complex Loose Sequencing games? In what ways are they similar to or different from those in basic Strict Sequencing?
- Are you making the available deductions efficiently and effectively in Loose Sequencing games?

In the coming days and weeks before Test Day, take note of real-world tasks that reflect Loose Sequencing tasks, especially those that ask you to rank things. Consider how the day-to-day tasks mirror the setups and questions in LSAT Loose Sequencing, and how they differ. Try to reframe real-life sequencing tasks using the terms, rules, and restrictions employed by the testmaker.

CHAPTER 8

Formal Logic and Selection Games Unlocked

LEARNING OBJECTIVES

In this chapter, you'll learn to

- Apply the Logic Games Method to Selection games
- Identify, translate, and apply Formal Logic statements used in logic games rules

On recent LSATs, Selection games have been rare, accounting for just 3 percent of the games on tests released over the last five years. Of the 60 games that appeared in released LSATs during that period, only two were true Selection games.

Types of Games By Percentage, 2012–2016

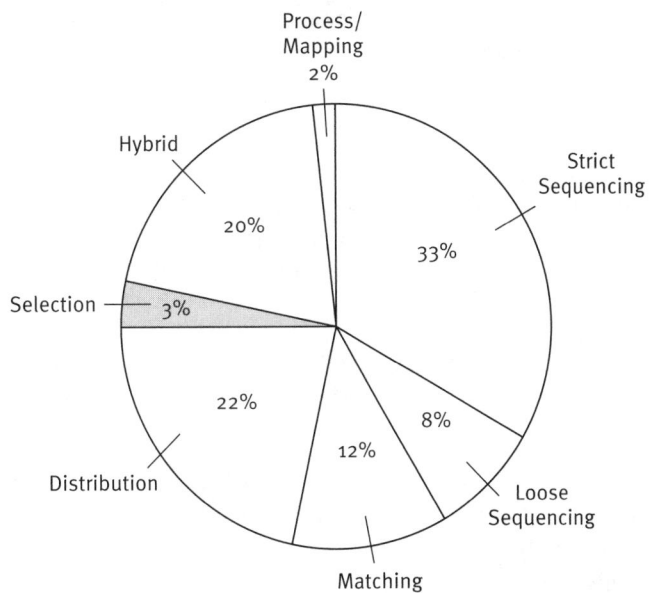

PrepTests 66–80; released 2012–2016

That number is unusually low compared to earlier periods in the LSAT's history, so it may be that the coming years will see the percentage shift back toward the mean. It's also worth noting that 5 of the 12 Hybrid games to appear on tests released in the past five years had a Selection element. So, the work you do in this chapter will not be for nothing. (If you have very little time between now and Test Day, however, you should probably complete Chapter 9 on the more common Matching and Distribution games first).

Another reason that this chapter is important to your LSAT performance is that this is where you'll learn to analyze, interpret, and sketch out Formal Logic. On the LSAT, Formal Logic is primarily tested through conditional (or "If-then") statements. The reason Formal Logic is covered in this chapter is that virtually all Selection game rules are conditional. Even when they aren't explicitly stated with an "if" clause and a "then" clause, they can be translated into that format for easy analysis. As an aside, the work you do on Formal Logic may turn out to be a bigger help to you in the LSAT's Logical Reasoning section than in Logic Games. On a typical LSAT, around 38 percent of the questions touch on Formal Logic in some way, and unless you run into a Selection game, the large majority of those questions are in Logical Reasoning.

The defining characteristic of Selection games is a setup that provides you with a list of entities, and then asks you to choose some of those entities to form a smaller group. You can easily recognize this action from verbs like *select*, *choose*, or *pick*.

The main variations in Selection games arise from how specific a game's setup is about the number of entities you will choose. In a little under half of games, the test gives no guidance at all. The setup simply says something along the lines of "From among seven photographs—A, B, C, D, E, F, and G—Karen will choose which to post on her home page." The rules will help to define how few or how many she selects, of course, but the setup itself will provide no limitations. For a game of this type, the best sketch is simply a list of the entities. Circle those she chooses, and cross out those she rejects for any given question.

$$A \quad B \quad \textcircled{C} \quad D \quad \textcircled{E} \quad \cancel{F} \quad G$$

Occasionally, the test will provide a maximum number of entities to choose. In a game of this type, the setup might say, "From among seven flavors of ice cream—chocolate, fudge ripple, mocha, praline pecan, rocky road, strawberry, and vanilla—Jack will choose at most five to serve at his child's birthday party." Since you don't know the exact number selected or rejected, you should still use a list of the entities as your initial sketch. It's easy to copy, and you can circle or cross out entities as necessary for each question.

$$C \quad \cancel{F} \quad \textcircled{M} \quad \textcircled{P} \quad R \quad \cancel{S} \quad V$$

A little more than half of the time, Selection games specify the exact number of entities to be selected. A typical setup of this type would contain phrasing like this: "From among seven data sets labeled M, N, O, P, Q, R, and S, a statistician will select exactly four to analyze for a demographic study." In this case, some LSAT experts prefer to use an "in-out" sketch to help them keep track of the numbers of entities selected and rejected.

M N O P Q R S

in   out

— — — —|— — —

You'll have the chance to work with setups and games in which the number to be selected is defined and others in which that number is left open-ended. In both types, your ability to accurately analyze and sketch rules written in Formal Logic will be the key to your success.

SELECTION GAMES IN REAL LIFE

You make selections all the time in your day-to-day life. You might be deciding which guests to invite to a wedding or a dinner. At work, you might need to choose which of six employees to send to a conference or meeting. Preparing to go to the conference, you might need to choose which of your suits or dresses to pack for the trip. Often, the toughest part of real-life selection lies in figuring out what not to include. That's true on the LSAT as well. Always remember that coming up with a complete and accurate list of which entities are not chosen is just as valuable as the list of which ones are. In real life, these tasks involve wildly different numbers of choices, professional considerations, and even personal feelings. Fortunately, the LSAT always limits you to choosing from among a limited set of options, typically from among five to nine entities.

Real-life selection tasks mirror the variations that the testmaker uses when designing these games. Here's a typical case: Imagine that you and a roommate are going to throw a party; maybe you have friends coming over to watch a big football game. One of you asks, "What snacks should we have?" In real life, that question is open-ended. You could have as many or as few snacks as you like. As you try to make your decision, it's likely that your first question will be, "How many kinds of snacks will we serve?" When the answer to that question is not inherent in the task, it's up to you to come up with a minimum or maximum number. Likewise, when LSAT Selection games do not provide you with a specific number of entities to choose, one or more of the questions accompanying the game will ask you to determine the minimum or maximum number of entities that may be chosen.

In the real-life version of the task, there are sometimes additional considerations. You could, for example, buy all of the snacks for the party, make all of them at home, or decide on some combination of the two. You and your roommate might say, "We're too busy to make anything; let's just buy the snacks." Or you might decide, "Let's make two snacks and buy two others." It will always be important to note whether the testmaker has designated subdivisions within the entities. In turning this scenario into a logic game, the testmaker could, for example, say simply, "The roommates will choose from among eight snacks: almonds, cupcakes, garlic bread, licorice, meatballs, pretzels, tortilla chips, and wings." Or they could put the snacks into two categories, like so: "The roommates will choose from among four homemade snacks—cupcakes, garlic bread, meatballs, and wings—and four store-bought snacks—almonds, licorice, pretzels, and tortilla chips." When the testmaker subdivides the entities, look for restrictions based on those categories, with rules like "At least two homemade snacks and at least two store-bought snacks must be served."

However the entity set is constructed, you can anticipate the types of rules that will be used. They're the same kinds of "rules" that guide your real-world decision. You might say, "If we serve pretzels, let's not have tortilla chips," or "If we have wings, then we have to have garlic bread." That leads to one of the friendliest features of Selection games: your sketch is basically no different than what you'd do in real life. "Okay, let's list out our potential snacks. We'll circle the ones we're going to serve and cross out the ones we're not."

$$A \quad C \quad \textcircled{G} \quad L \quad M \quad \textcircled{P} \quad \cancel{T} \quad \textcircled{W}$$

Selection tasks are probably more common in everyday life than Selection games are on the test. This is one area where you should have no trouble spotting analogies to what you'll see on the LSAT. Take advantage of your experience when the opportunity arises. Recontextualizing a seemingly difficult LSAT task by seeing it reflected in a simple, real-life scenario will help you build confidence, and improve your performance on Test Day.

SELECTION GAMES TASKS AND SKETCHES

LEARNING OBJECTIVES

In this section of the chapter, you'll practice

- Applying Steps 1 and 2 of the Logic Games Method to Selection games by
  - Asking the SEAL questions to analyze the game's Overview, and then
  - Creating a simple, useful Sketch framework

Prepare

Selection tasks are straightforward, and there is little chance that you will miss the action. Fortunately, the key question about Selection games' limitations is almost instinctive as well: "How many can I/must I choose?"

LOGIC GAMES STRATEGY

Selection games ask you to choose a smaller group of entities out of a larger one; the number you'll choose may be

- Open-ended—the game's setup will tell you that "some" or "at least one" of the entities is selected, but gives you no further guidance,
- A minimum of y and/or a maximum of x—the game's setup will set a floor or ceiling (or both) on the number of entities that may be selected, but will not state a specific number, or
- A specific number—the game's setup will explicitly state a limitation such as "five of the nine" or "four out of seven."

As discussed in the introduction to this chapter, your choice of sketch will depend largely on how clear-cut the number restrictions are in the game's setup. When the number selected is unclear, simply copy the list of entities, and circle those selected and cross out those rejected in each question.

$$A \quad B \quad \text{C⃝} \quad D \quad \text{E⃝} \quad \cancel{F} \quad G$$

When the game's setup provides a precise number of entities to select out of the initial list, you may choose to employ an "in-out" sketch.

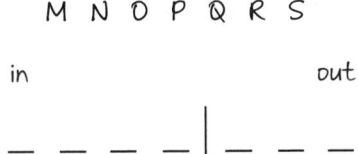

Practice applying Steps 1 and 2 of the Logic Games Method to some Selection games setups. Keep an eye out for the verb that signals the Selection task. Use the limitations on the number of entities to be selected to help you decide which sketch framework to use.

Practice

Directions: Conduct an Overview of each game's setup by asking the SEAL questions, and create an initial sketch framework for the game's action.

Practice 1

A graphic designer must choose colors for a new logo from among the seven—fuchsia, grapefruit, hibiscus, indigo, jade, kiwi, and lemon—suggested by the client. The color selection must conform to the following conditions:

1. [Step 1] Conduct an Overview analysis:
    - What is this game's Situation?

    - Who or what are the game's Entities?

    - What is the game's Action?

    - What are the Limitations explicit in the game setup?

2. [Step 2] Create an initial Sketch:

Practice 2

Melanie is planning a series of performances to promote her new relaxation CD. At each performance, she will play at least four of the pieces—*Atmosphere*, *Beats*, *Clouds*, *Dynamic*, *Ecologica*, *Firefly*, and *Glaciers*—that appear on the CD. Her selection for each performance is based on the following conditions:

1. [Step 1] Conduct an Overview analysis:
    - What is this game's Situation?

    - Who or what are the game's Entities?

    - What is the game's Action?

    - What are the Limitations explicit in the game setup?

2. [Step 2] Create an initial Sketch:

Practice 3

Writers for a science magazine submitted eight articles to their editor, each on a different topic—anatomy, biochemistry, climatology, ecology, genetics, hydrology, immunology, and neuroscience. The editor will select exactly four of the articles for publication in the next issue, based on the following guidelines:

1. [Step 1] Conduct an Overview analysis:

   - What is this game's Situation?

   - Who or what are the game's Entities?

   - What is the game's Action?

   - What are the Limitations explicit in the game setup?

2. [Step 2] Create an initial Sketch:

Explanations

Compare your work to that of an LSAT expert. Keep track of any case in which you incorrectly characterized the action described in the setup, and any case in which you drew a sketch framework that does not match the details of the game's situation.

Practice 1

A graphic designer must choose colors for a new logo from among the seven—fuchsia, grapefruit, hibiscus, indigo, jade, kiwi, and lemon—suggested by the client. The color selection must conform to the following conditions:

1. [Step 1] Conduct an Overview analysis:

    - What is this game's Situation? *A graphic designer choosing colors for a new logo.*

    - Who or what are the game's Entities? *Seven colors—F, G, H, I, J, K, and L.*

    - What is the game's Action? *Selection.*

    - What are the Limitations explicit in the game setup? *None; no minimum or maximum is provided.*

2. [Step 2] Create an initial Sketch:

       F   G   H   I   J   K   L

Practice 2

Melanie is planning a series of performances to promote her new relaxation CD. At each performance, she will play at least four of the pieces—*Atmosphere, Beats, Clouds, Dynamic, Ecologica, Firefly,* and *Glaciers*—that appear on the CD. Her selection for each performance is based on the following conditions:

1. [Step 1] Conduct an Overview analysis:

    - What is this game's Situation? *A musician scheduling a series of performances.*

    - Who or what are the game's Entities? *Seven songs—A, B, C, D, E, F, and G.*

    - What is the game's Action? *Selection; while the overview suggests multiple performances, the goal is to figure out which songs are selected for any given performance.*

    - What are the Limitations explicit in the game setup? *At least four songs will be used, but no maximum.*

2. [Step 2] Create an initial Sketch:

       A   B   C   D   E   F   G   4⁺ selected

Practice 3

Writers for a science magazine submitted eight articles to their editor, each on a different topic—anatomy, biochemistry, climatology, ecology, genetics, hydrology, immunology, and neuroscience. The editor will select exactly four of the articles for publication in the next issue, based on the following guidelines:

1. [Step 1] Conduct an Overview analysis:

    - What is this game's Situation? *An editor of a science magazine deciding which articles to publish.*

    - Who or what are the game's Entities? *Eight articles, by topic—A, B, C, E, G, H, I, and N.*

    - What is the game's Action? *Selection.*

    - What are the Limitations explicit in the game setup? *Exactly four will be selected, which means the other four will not.*

2. [Step 2] Create an initial Sketch:

       A   B   C   E   G   H   I   N

    in   out

    ___ ___ ___ ___ | ___ ___ ___ ___

The most important work you'll do on Selection games happens in Step 3. Interpreting and drawing out the Formal Logic contained in these games' rules is crucial to answering the questions efficiently and effectively. The next section of this chapter goes into detail and provides ample practice on everything you need to know about conditional statements in LSAT logic games.

If you are already a master of "If-then" statements and contrapositives, you may choose to skip the next section and move on to practicing with Selection rules in context. If not, you'll want to work through the next section carefully. Do all of the practice exercises and review them with the expert analysis that follows. Then, assess your own skill level with the Perform quizzes. Formal Logic can seem tricky at first, but with practice and review, you can master the fundamentals of conditional statements and contrapositives and use these reasoning principles with great confidence on the LSAT.

FORMAL LOGIC IN LSAT LOGIC GAMES

> ## LEARNING OBJECTIVES
>
> In this section, you'll learn to:
>
> - Identify what is and what is not a conditional statement (that is, understand what it means for a statement to be a conditional statement)

Before you can work with conditional statements to make valid deductions and inferences (and answer questions), you must be able to identify such statements.

This section of Chapter 8 contains nine Learning Objectives that, taken together, cover the breadth of knowledge you'll need to use Formal Logic in LSAT logic games. Each Learning Objective builds upon the ones before it, so you are encouraged to take them in the order presented.

Conditional Statements

In some Logic Games, and always in Selection games, the rules provided can be written as conditional statements. These statements always have two parts—a sufficient term and a necessary result or requirement—and can always be translated into an "If-then" format.

Conditional statements will appear in LSAT questions in all three sections of the test, but are most important in Logical Reasoning and Logic Games. The following chart shows the relative importance of Formal Logic on the LSAT.

LSAT Qs Testing Formal Logic, 2012–16

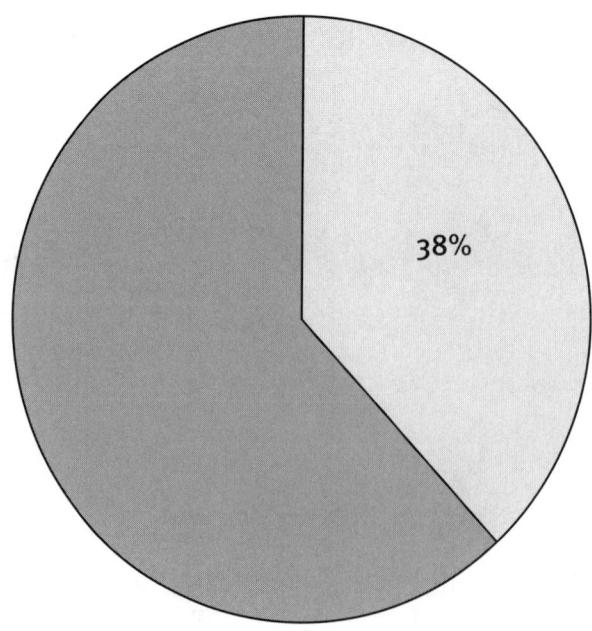

38%

PrepTests 66–90, released 2012–2016

LOGIC GAMES STRATEGY

Although Formal Logic appears in a minority of Logic Games, its importance is heightened by two considerations:

Most test takers have not refined the skill of understanding Formal Logic prior to preparing for the LSAT. Familiarity with Formal Logic will give you a competitive advantage.

Expertise in understanding and applying Formal Logic makes the correct answer to many LSAT questions unequivocal. There is little room for doubt or error if you have analyzed conditional statements correctly.

Identify Conditional Statements

Prepare

LOGIC GAMES STRATEGY

Every conditional statement has two parts:

- A *sufficient term*, also known as the "trigger" or "If" term.
- A *necessary term*, also known as the "result/requirement" or "then" term.

Consider this conditional statement:

> If the flashlight is working, then it must have batteries.

The flashlight working is a *sufficient* condition. That means knowing the flashlight works provides sufficient (i.e., enough) information to logically make a deduction: that it has batteries.

Batteries are a *necessary* condition. That means the batteries are required for the sufficient term to be present. In this case, the batteries are needed for the flashlight to work. If there were no batteries, the flashlight couldn't work.

But be careful. The sufficient condition is not required. In other words, the flashlight does not need to work in order for there to be batteries. Similarly, the necessary condition does not guarantee anything. It's possible for batteries to be installed without the flashlight working; after all, the light bulb could be broken.

Conditional relationships can be expressed in many ways other than "If . . . then" sentence structure. The key is to look for an absolute condition—either a condition that is always sufficient to produce a particular result, or one that is always necessary for something else to happen. Take a look at how an LSAT expert identifies conditional statements.

Premises		Analysis
Is each of the following a conditional statement?		
Every person who orders a cheeseburger also orders french fries.	$\longrightarrow$	Yes; the word *every* indicates that french fries will be ordered any time someone orders a cheeseburger. Ordering a cheeseburger is a *sufficient* condition.
John will participate in the race only if he runs first.	$\longrightarrow$	Yes; if John participates in the race, then he must run first. The phrase *only if* indicates that being first is a *necessary* condition for John to participate.
Apples, grapes, and strawberries are available for use in the fruit salad.	$\longrightarrow$	No; this just defines what is available, but nothing is sufficient to use these fruits and nothing is required.
Any Picasso painting in the exhibit must be placed directly to the left of a Renoir painting.	$\longrightarrow$	Yes; if a Picasso is included, then there must be a Renoir directly to its right. This is true for *any* Picasso painting. So including a Picasso is a *sufficient* condition, triggering its placement next to a Renoir.

Practice

In the following exercise, read each statement and decide whether it expresses a conditional relationship. If it does, which term is *sufficient* and which is *necessary*?

Premises	My Analysis
1. Square-shaped blocks are always placed in box 1. $\longrightarrow$	
2. Each member assigned to the advisory council is a college graduate. $\longrightarrow$	
3. The carpenter may receive several requests for estimates. $\longrightarrow$	
4. Robert will present in the Gold Room only if Jenson presents in the Black Room. $\longrightarrow$	

Explanations

Here's how an LSAT expert would analyze those statements.

Premises	Analysis
1. Square-shaped blocks are always placed in box 1.	Yes; the word *always* indicates that every square-shaped block is placed in box 1. This could be written: *If it's square-shaped, then it is placed in box 1.* Knowing that a block is square-shaped is *sufficient* to determine that it is placed in the box 1. And being placed in the box 1 is a *necessary* condition of all square-shaped blocks.
2. Each member assigned to the advisory council is a college graduate.	Yes; the word *each* indicates that being assigned to the advisory council is *sufficient* to know that that person is a college graduate. This could be written: *If a person is assigned to the advisory council, then he or she is a college graduate.* Being a college graduate is *necessarily* true of all of the members of the advisory council.
3. The carpenter may receive several requests for estimates.	No; conditional statements are statements of certainty. The use of language such as *may* and *several* often indicate that a statement is not conditional. Ask yourself: Is this statement saying that if one thing is true, then another thing must be true? No, this statement is just describing what might happen.
4. Robert will present in the Gold Room only if Jenson presents in the Black Room.	Yes; the phrase "only if" indicates that Jenson presenting in the Black Room is a *requirement* for Robert presenting in the Gold Room. This could be written: *If Robert presents in the Gold Room, then Jenson will present in the Black Room.* Robert presenting in the Gold Room is *sufficient* to know that Jenson is presenting in the Black Room.

Perform

In the following exercise, read each statement and decide whether it expresses a conditional relationship. If it does, which term is *sufficient* and which is *necessary*?

Premises		My Analysis
5. Certain medications can be prescribed to the patient.	$\longrightarrow$	
6. Kaylie will not participate in the Denver chess tournament unless she participates in at least two other tournaments.	$\longrightarrow$	
7. Robert will watch a movie at 8:00 PM if he does not go to the gym at 6:00 PM.	$\longrightarrow$	
8. The zebra will be transferred to the zoo only if the giraffe is also transferred.	$\longrightarrow$	

Explanations

Here's how an LSAT expert would analyze those statements.

Premises	Analysis
5. Certain medications can be prescribed to the patient.	No; conditional statements are statements of certainty. Just because medications "can" be prescribed doesn't mean they necessarily will. Ask yourself: Is this statement saying that if one thing is true, then another thing must be true? Here, the answer is no.
6. Kaylie will not participate in the Denver chess tournament unless she participates in at least two other tournaments.	Yes; the word *unless* indicates that Kaylie participating in at least two other tournaments is *necessary* for her to participate in the Denver chess tournament. This could be written: *If Kaylie competes in the Denver chess tournament, then she also participates in at least two other tournaments.* Knowing that Kaylie participates in the Denver tournament is *sufficient* to know that she will participate in at least two other tournaments.
7. Robert will watch a movie at 8:00 PM if he does not go to the gym at 6:00 PM.	Yes; the word *if* indicates a *sufficient* condition. This could be written: *If Robert does not go to the gym at 6:00 PM, then he will watch a movie at 8:00 PM.* Watching a movie at 8 PM is a *necessary* result of Robert not going to the gym at 6 PM.
8. The zebra will be transferred to the zoo only if the giraffe is also transferred.	Yes; the phrase "only if" indicates that the giraffe being transferred is *necessary* for the zebra to be transferred. This could be written: *If the zebra is transferred, then the giraffe is also transferred.* The zebra being transferred would be *sufficient* to know that the giraffe was also transferred.

Understand Conditional Statements with *And* and *Or*

Some conditional statements will also contain the words *and* or *or*. The two terms have quite different effects in conditional statements.

Prepare

LOGIC GAMES STRATEGY

In Formal Logic:

And means both terms are needed for a sufficient condition to trigger a result or for a necessary condition to be fulfilled.

Or means that at least one of the terms (the first or the second or both) is needed for a sufficient condition to trigger a result or for a necessary condition to be fulfilled.

Note how an LSAT expert analyzes conditional statements containing *and* or *or*.

Conditional Statement		Analysis
If Anthony and Brendan attend the concert, then so does Evan.	$\rightarrow$	One way to guarantee Evan attending the concert is to have Anthony and Brendan attend. Having Anthony or Brendan attend without the other does not guarantee that Evan will attend.
If the tour includes the planetarium, then it also includes the meteorite exhibit and the space shuttle exhibit.	$\rightarrow$	When the planetarium is included, it is guaranteed that both the meteorite and the space shuttle exhibits are included. It's not possible to include the planetarium and then include only one of the other exhibits.

| If Luisa or Steve performs in the orchestra, then Fiona performs in the choir. | $\longrightarrow$ | If either Luisa or Steve joins the orchestra, it is guaranteed that Fiona will join the choir. Even if *both* Luisa and Steve join the orchestra, it is still guaranteed Fiona will join the choir. And if Luisa and Steve *don't* join the orchestra, it's still possible for Fiona to join the choir. |
| If the factory does not manufacture chairs, then it must manufacture bookshelves or easels. | $\longrightarrow$ | If chairs are not made, then it's guaranteed that either bookshelves or easels are. It's also possible that both bookshelves *and* easels are made. And if chairs *are* made, then nothing is known about bookshelves and easels. It's possible that all three products are made in the factory. |

Practice

Check your understanding by analyzing the following conditional statements.

Conditional Statement	My Analysis

If Manny and Nouman are both assigned to Honduras, then Peggy will be assigned to Belize.

9. What do we know if we are told that Manny is assigned to Honduras?

$\longrightarrow$

10. What do we know if we are told that Peggy is assigned to Belize?

$\longrightarrow$

11. What do we know if we are told that Peggy is not assigned to Belize?

$\longrightarrow$

Any person who takes a picture by the tide pools will also take a picture by the lighthouse or by the harbor.

12. What do we know if we are told that Bonnie takes a picture by the lighthouse?

$\longrightarrow$

13. What do we know if we are told that Porter does not take a picture by the tide pools?

$\longrightarrow$

14. What do we know if we are told that Tamara takes a picture by neither the lighthouse nor the harbor

$\longrightarrow$

Explanations

Here's how an LSAT expert would analyze the questions about each conditional statement in the exercise.

Conditional Statement		Analysis
If Manny and Nouman are both assigned to Honduras, then Peggy will be assigned to Belize.		
9. What do we know if we are told that Manny is assigned to Honduras?	$\longrightarrow$	Nothing additional; we need to know that Manny and Nouman are *both* assigned to Honduras before we can confirm that Peggy must be assigned to Belize.
10. What do we know if we are told that Peggy is assigned to Belize?	$\longrightarrow$	Nothing additional; Peggy being assigned to Belize is a result of Manny and Nouman being assigned to Honduras. But Peggy being assigned to Belize does not, by itself, trigger anything.
11. What do we know if we are told that Peggy is not assigned to Belize?	$\longrightarrow$	If this is true, then there is no way that both Manny and Nouman are assigned to Honduras. So, we know that either Manny or Nouman (or both) is not assigned to Honduras.
Any person who takes a picture by the tide pools will also take a picture by the lighthouse or by the harbor.		
12. What do we know if we are told that Bonnie takes a picture by the lighthouse?	$\longrightarrow$	Nothing additional; taking a picture by the lighthouse is not sufficient to know anything else about Bonnie.
13. What do we know if we are told that Porter does not take a picture by the tide pools?	$\longrightarrow$	Nothing additional; it is still possible that Porter takes a picture by the lighthouse and the harbor.
14. What do we know if we are told that Tamara takes a picture by neither the lighthouse nor the harbor?	$\longrightarrow$	In this case, we would know that Tamara also does not take a picture by the tide pools; otherwise, she would have taken a picture by either the lighthouse or the harbor.

Perform

Check your understanding by analyzing the following conditional statements.

Conditional Statement	My Analysis
If a blue jelly bean is added to the jar, then a red jelly bean and a green jelly bean will also be added to the jar.	
15. What do we know if we are told that no red jelly beans are added to the jar?	$\longrightarrow$
16. What do we know if we are told that no blue jelly beans are added to the jar?	$\longrightarrow$
17. What do we know if we are told both red and green jelly beans are added to the jar?	$\longrightarrow$
Whenever a motorcycle or a bicycle is advertised in the magazine, there must be at least one advertisement for helmets.	
18. What do we know if we are told that the magazine contains an advertisement for helmets?	$\longrightarrow$
19. What do we know if we are told that the magazine features advertisements for both motorcycles and bicycles?	$\longrightarrow$
20. What do we know if we are told that there are no helmets advertised in the magazine?	$\longrightarrow$

Explanations

Here's how an LSAT expert would analyze the questions about each conditional statement in the exercise.

Conditional Statement		Analysis
If a blue jelly bean is added to the jar, then a red jelly bean and a green jelly bean will also be added to the jar.		
15. What do we know if we are told that no red jelly beans are added to the jar?	→	If no red jelly beans are added to the jar, then no blue jelly beans can be added to the jar. Otherwise, there would have to be red jelly beans (along with green ones).
16. What do we know if we are told that no blue jelly beans are added to the jar?	→	Nothing additional; even without blue jelly beans, it's still possible that red and green jelly beans are added.
17. What do we know if we are told both red and green jelly beans are added to the jar?	→	Nothing additional; blue jelly beans may or may not be added to the jar.
Whenever a motorcycle or a bicycle is advertised in the magazine, there must be at least one advertisement for helmets.		
18. What do we know if we are told that the magazine contains an advertisement for helmets?	→	Nothing additional; while it's possible that the magazine features advertisements for a motorcycle or a bicycle, it's also possible that there are only ads for helmets (or perhaps other products).
19. What do we know if we are told that the magazine features advertisements for both motorcycles and bicycles?	→	The magazine will also include at least one other advertisement for helmets.
20. What do we know if we are told that there are no helmets advertised in the magazine?	→	If there are no advertisements for helmets, then the magazine features ads for neither motorcycles nor bicycles. Otherwise, there would have been a helmet advertisement.

Translate Conditional Statements into If-Then Format

LEARNING OBJECTIVES

In this section, you'll learn to:

- Translate a sentence that expresses a conditional relationship into If-Then format.

Prepare

It's helpful to develop a simple system of notation for conditional statements. Whenever you see a conditional statement in Logic Games, translate it into something that looks like this:

If Trigger (sufficient) → *Result/Requirement (necessary)*

Write the sufficient term on the left, the necessary term on the right, and an arrow in the middle pointing from left to right (to indicate the direction in which the logic flows).

Here's how an LSAT expert takes several conditional statements and turns them into "If-then" statements.

Conditional Statement		Analysis
If Ricardo is in the tournament, then he's on the blue team.	→	*If Ricardo in → Blue team* "If" indicates the sufficient condition, with "blue team" being the necessary result.
Copper is used in every experiment that includes acetone.	→	*If acetone → copper* The word *every* indicates the sufficient condition. The presence of acetone is enough to guarantee the presence of copper.
The project will involve glue only if it involves cotton balls.	→	*If glue → cotton balls* The phrase "only if" indicates cotton balls are a necessary condition. They are required for glue to be used.
The platter is not selected unless the tureen or the gravy boat is selected.	→	*If platter → tureen OR gravy boat* The word *unless* indicates that a tureen or gravy boat is necessary in order for the platter to be selected.
Any two people who are assigned to the same group must be of the same rank.	→	*If same group → same rank* *Any* indicates sufficiency, and *must* indicates necessity. Being in the same group is enough to deduce that two people are of the same rank. That's required.

Translating The Prose of Common Conditional Statements

Conditional statements can be phrased in many different ways; you'll see that some of those are more common than others in Logic Games, but they all appear from time to time. You will need to learn to quickly distill the language into a notation like the following.

Formal Logic Statement		Analysis
If A, then B	$\longrightarrow$	If A $\rightarrow$ B
All C are D	$\longrightarrow$	If C $\rightarrow$ D
Every E is F	$\longrightarrow$	If E $\rightarrow$ F
If G, then not H	$\longrightarrow$	If G $\rightarrow$ ~H
No I are J	$\longrightarrow$	If I $\rightarrow$ ~J
Only K are L	$\longrightarrow$	If L $\rightarrow$ K
M only if N	$\longrightarrow$	If M $\rightarrow$ N
The only O are P	$\longrightarrow$	If O $\rightarrow$ P
No Q unless R	$\longrightarrow$	If Q $\rightarrow$ R
S unless T	$\longrightarrow$	If ~S $\rightarrow$ T
No U without V	$\longrightarrow$	If U $\rightarrow$ V
Without W, no X	$\longrightarrow$	If X $\rightarrow$ W
Y if, but only if, Z	$\longrightarrow$	If Y $\rightarrow$ Z If Z $\rightarrow$ Y
AA if, and only if, BB	$\longrightarrow$	If AA $\rightarrow$ BB If BB $\rightarrow$ AA
If CC, then neither DD nor EE	$\longrightarrow$	If CC $\rightarrow$ ~DD and ~EE
FF if GG	$\longrightarrow$	If GG $\rightarrow$ FF
HH is always II	$\longrightarrow$	If HH $\rightarrow$ II

It's okay if your shorthand is different from what is shown here, but it must be consistent and accurate to ensure your success on the test.

Practice

Using the previous statements as reference, translate each of the following statements, each of which expresses a sufficient and necessary relationship, into simple shorthand.

Formal Logic Statement	My Analysis
21. None of the first three songs on the album are country songs. $\longrightarrow$	
22. Only red bicycles can be placed in the fourth storage shed. $\longrightarrow$	
23. Monica will not go fishing unless Charlie goes dancing. $\longrightarrow$	
24. All of the photographs in Norton Hall are panoramas. $\longrightarrow$	
25. Anna is going to attend the basketball game only if Beth also attends. $\longrightarrow$	
26. Every bowl on the third shelf is ceramic. $\longrightarrow$	
27. Students may attend the conference unless they are currently on academic probation. $\longrightarrow$	
28. Danielle will play golf tomorrow at 7 AM if Esther goes swimming at 9 AM. $\longrightarrow$	
29. The only banks with secure vaults are on the north side of the street. $\longrightarrow$	
30. Peg will order the pork chop if, but only if, she orders the collard greens. $\longrightarrow$	

Explanations

This is how an LSAT expert might abbreviate each of the statements from the exercise.

Formal Logic Statement		Analysis
21. None of the first three songs on the album are country songs.	→	If one of first three songs on album → not country song
22. Only red bicycles can be placed in the fourth storage shed.	→	If in 4th shed → red bicycle
23. Monica will not go fishing unless Charlie goes dancing.	→	If Monica fishing → Charlie dancing
24. All of the photographs in Norton Hall are panoramas.	→	If Norton Hall → panorama
25. Anna is going to attend the basketball game only if Beth also attends.	→	If Anna attends → Beth attends
26. Every bowl on the third shelf is ceramic.	→	If bowl on third shelf → ceramic
27. Students may attend the conference unless they are currently on academic probation.	→	If a student can't attend the conference → that student is on academic probation
28. Danielle will play golf tomorrow at 7 AM if Esther goes swimming at 9 AM.	→	If Esther swimming 9 AM → Danielle golf 7 AM
29. The only banks with secure vaults are on the north side of the street.	→	If bank has secure vault → north side of street
30. Peg will order the pork chop if, but only if, she orders the collard greens.	→	If Peg orders pork chop → orders collard greens If Peg orders collard greens → orders pork chop

Perform

Using the previous statements as reference, translate each of the following statements, each of which expresses a sufficient and necessary relationship, into simple shorthand.

	Formal Logic Statement		My Analysis
31.	Whenever the orangutan pulls the blue lever, she is given a pear.	$\longrightarrow$	
32.	Euchre club is always on Friday.	$\longrightarrow$	
33.	The photographer cannot go to Peru without an editor also going to Peru.	$\longrightarrow$	
34.	The purple book is placed in the bedroom only when the red book is placed in the den.	$\longrightarrow$	
35.	All of the cookies in the small jar were made by Julia.	$\longrightarrow$	
36.	Pamela won't join the bowling team if Zoe is on the team.	$\longrightarrow$	
37.	Every time the band visits Columbus, they play "Groovy."	$\longrightarrow$	
38.	Unless the batteries are to the right of the candle, the dagger is to the left of the gizmo.	$\longrightarrow$	
39.	Only divers who have previously won a local diving competition will be invited to the state tournament.	$\longrightarrow$	
40.	If the park does not have a slide, then it will have a jungle gym.	$\longrightarrow$	

Explanations

This is how an LSAT expert might abbreviate each of the statements from the exercise.

Formal Logic Statement		Analysis
31. Whenever the orangutan pulls the blue lever, she is given a pear.	→	If pull blue lever → pear
32. Euchre club is always on Friday.	→	If Euchre club → Friday
33. The photographer cannot go to Peru without an editor also going to Peru.	→	If photographer Peru → editor Peru
34. The purple book is placed in the bedroom only when the red book is placed in the den.	→	If purple book in bedroom → red book in den
35. All of the cookies in the small jar were made by Julia.	→	If cookie in small jar → made by Julia
36. Pamela won't join the bowling team if Zoe is on the team.	→	If Zoe on bowling team → Pamela not on bowling team
37. Every time the band visits Columbus, they play "Groovy."	→	If band visits Columbus → play "Groovy"
38. Unless the batteries are to the right of the candle, the dagger is to the left of the gizmo.	→	If dagger not left of the gizmo → batteries right of the candle
39. Only divers who have previously won a local diving competition will be invited to the state tournament.	→	If invited to state tourn. → previously won local comp.
40. If the park does not have a slide, then it will have a jungle gym.	→	If no slide → jungle gym

Make Valid Deductions from Conditional Statements

LEARNING OBJECTIVES

In this section, you'll learn to:

- Make deductions on the basis of conditional statements

Prepare

LOGIC GAMES STRATEGY

Any time the necessary or "result" clause of one statement matches the sufficient or "If" clause of another, the two statements can be combined. For example:

$$\text{If } B \rightarrow \sim D$$
$$\text{If } \sim D \rightarrow \sim F$$
$$\text{If } B \rightarrow \sim D \rightarrow \sim F$$

Deduction:

$$\text{If } B \rightarrow \sim F$$

Connecting Conditional Statements

Now that you understand conditional relationships and how to spot them, you're ready to think about how to combine them to make new deductions.

Formal Logic Statements		Analysis
If A then B If B then C	$\longrightarrow$	If $A \rightarrow B \rightarrow C$
If D then E If F then E	$\longrightarrow$	If D OR $F \rightarrow E$
If G then H If G then I	$\longrightarrow$	If $G \rightarrow H$ and I

Practice

Translate the given conditional statements and use them to create a chain of logic. Then, answer questions about what we must know, given the chain.

Formal Logic Statements		My Analysis
(1) If the zebra is chosen, then so is the antelope	$\longrightarrow$	
(2) If the tortoise is chosen, then so is the zebra	$\longrightarrow$	
(3) If the antelope is chosen, then so is the gorilla	$\longrightarrow$	

Chain of logic:

What do we know if ...

41. the zebra is chosen?

$\longrightarrow$

42. the gorilla is chosen?

$\longrightarrow$

43. the tortoise is chosen?

$\longrightarrow$

Explanations

Here's how an LSAT expert would translate and combine the conditional statements in the previous exercise.

Formal Logic Statements		Analysis
(1)	If the zebra is chosen, then so is the antelope	$\longrightarrow$ If Z → A
(2)	If the tortoise is chosen, then so is the zebra	$\longrightarrow$ If T → Z
(3)	If the antelope is chosen, then so is the gorilla	$\longrightarrow$ If A → G
Chain of logic:		$\longrightarrow$ If T → Z → A → G

What do we know if . . .

41.	the zebra is chosen?	$\longrightarrow$ If the zebra is chosen, then the antelope and the gorilla are chosen. Z → A → G
42.	the gorilla is chosen?	$\longrightarrow$ Choosing the gorilla does not lead to any further deduction.
43.	the tortoise is chosen?	$\longrightarrow$ If the tortoise is chosen, then all of the animals in the list will be chosen. T → Z → A → G

Perform

Translate the given conditional statements and use them to create a chain of logic. Then, answer questions about what we must know, given the chain.

Formal Logic Statements	My Analysis
(1) If Craig brings his map, then he also brings his compass →	
(2) If Craig brings his compass, then he also brings his notebook and his binoculars →	
(3) If Craig does not bring his binoculars, then he does not bring his journal. →	
(4) If Craig brings his binoculars, then he also brings his guidebook. →	

Chain of logic:

What do we know if . . .

44. Craig brings his notebook?

    →

45. Craig brings his compass?

    →

46. Craig brings his binoculars?

    →

Explanations

Here's how an LSAT expert would translate and combine the conditional statements in the previous exercise.

Formal Logic Statements		Analysis
(1)	If Craig brings his map, then he also brings his compass	$\longrightarrow$ If M → C
(2)	If Craig brings his compass, then he also brings his notebook and his binoculars	$\longrightarrow$ If C → N and B
(3)	If Craig does not bring his binoculars, then he does not bring his journal.	$\longrightarrow$ If ~B → ~J
(4)	If Craig brings his binoculars, then he also brings his guidebook.	$\longrightarrow$ If B → G
Chain of logic:		$\longrightarrow$ If M → C → N and B If B → G

What do we know if ...

44. Craig brings his notebook?	$\longrightarrow$	Nothing else can be determined. Having the notebook is not sufficient to know anything else.
45. Craig brings his compass?	$\longrightarrow$	If Craig brings the compass, then he also brings the notebook and binoculars. And bringing the binoculars means he brings the guidebook. If C → N and B If B → G
46. Craig brings his binoculars?	$\longrightarrow$	If Craig brings the binoculars, then he also brings the guidebook. If B → G

Contrapositives

LEARNING OBJECTIVES

In this section, you'll learn to:

- Translate a conditional statement into its contrapositive
- Make valid deductions from the contrapositive of a conditional statement
- Make valid deductions from conditional statements containing *And* and *Or*
- Make valid deductions from conditional statements containing an "Exclusive Or" provision

Despite the many ways to express conditional statements, the logic underlying conditional statements is remarkably consistent. One more feature of these statements that is crucial for making deductions is the contrapositive.

Translating "If-then" Statements into Contrapositives: The contrapositive of a conditional statement is just another way of phrasing the sufficient/necessary relationship described in that statement. Take the following statement as an example:

All team leaders must be an adult.

If team leader → adult

Now, what happens if a team member is not an adult? Well, that person can't be team leader. That's the contrapositive of the statement. It looks like this:

If NOT adult → NOT team leader

That's the basis for the contrapositive: What happens if the *necessary* condition is negated, if it cannot happen? In that case, the sufficient condition cannot happen either. Every contrapositive is formed in exactly that way.

Conditional statements with two terms in the necessary condition: When the necessary term of a conditional statement has two terms, check to see whether both are necessary (B *and* C) or whether just one or the other is necessary (B *or* C). If both are necessary, then the absence of either will make the sufficient term impossible. In short, the "and" in the necessary term becomes "or" in the sufficient term of the contrapositive. If just one of the terms is necessary, then it is the absence of both that will render the sufficient term impossible. In other words, the "or" in the necessary clause becomes "and" in the sufficient clause of the contrapositive. For example:

Roberts will not be assigned to the project unless Tang and Wilhelm are assigned.

Abbreviate that statement in Formal Logic shorthand:

If Roberts → Tang AND Wilhelm

Now, what happens if either one of the two necessary conditions is not met?

If NO Tang   →   NO Roberts

If NO Wilhelm   →   NO Roberts

Thus, to form the contrapositive of the first statement, the *and* in the necessary condition must become *or* in the sufficient condition of the contrapositive:

If NO Tang OR NO Wilhelm   →   NO Roberts

Translating "If"-then Statements Into Contrapositives

LEARNING OBJECTIVES

In this section, you'll learn to:

- Translate a conditional statement into its contrapositive

Prepare

LOGIC GAMES STRATEGY

To form the contrapositive:

- Reverse the sufficient and necessary terms.
- Negate each term.
- Change *and* to *or* and change *or* to *and* (whenever applicable).

Here is a chart of the most common Formal Logic statements and their contrapositives.

Formal Logic Statements		Analysis
All A are B	$\longrightarrow$	If A → B If ~B → ~A
No C are D	$\longrightarrow$	If C → ~D If D → ~C
E unless F	$\longrightarrow$	If ~E → F If ~F → E
If G, then neither H nor I	$\longrightarrow$	If G → ~H and ~I If H or I → ~G
If J or K, then no L	$\longrightarrow$	If J or K → ~L If L → ~J and ~K

Practice

Translate each of the following statements into simple shorthand, and form the correct contrapositive of each.

Formal Logic Statement	My Analysis
47. None of the attendees at the programming seminar are enrolled in a four-week course.	$\longrightarrow$
48. The chef won't add onions to any salad that doesn't also contain tomatoes.	$\longrightarrow$
49. Businesses with offices on the third floor must also have offices on the fifth floor.	$\longrightarrow$
50. If the red car is not chosen for display, then the green car will be chosen.	$\longrightarrow$

51. Jake will finish fourth if and only if Nancy finishes sixth.

$\longrightarrow$

52. The Spanish club will not go to Mexico unless the French club goes to Cameroon and the Portuguese club goes to Brazil.

$\longrightarrow$

53. Only those with a severe condition will be allowed to participate in Trial B.

$\longrightarrow$

54. All of the members of the kayaking team have orange helmets.

$\longrightarrow$

55. There must be at least three members on any committee to which Jolene is assigned.

$\longrightarrow$

Explanations

Here's how an LSAT expert might abbreviate the statements and form the contrapositives.

	Formal Logic Statement		Analysis
47.	None of the attendees at the programming seminar are enrolled in a four-week course.	→	If at programming seminar → ~ 4-week course
			If 4-week course → ~ at programming seminar
48.	The chef won't add onions to any salad that doesn't also contain tomatoes.	→	If ~ tomatoes in salad → ~ onions
			If onions in salad → tomatoes
49.	Businesses with offices on the third floor must also have offices on the fifth floor.	→	If bus. has 3rd floor office → 5th floor office
			If ~ 5th floor office → ~ 3rd floor office
50.	If the red car is not chosen for display, then the green car will be chosen.	→	If ~ red car → green car
			If ~ green car → red car
51.	Jake will finish fourth if and only if Nancy finishes sixth.		If Jake 4th → Nancy 6th
			If ~ Nancy 6th → ~ Jake 4th
		→	
			If Nancy 6th → Jake 4th
			If ~ Jake 4th → ~ Nancy 6th
52.	The Spanish club will not go to Mexico unless the French club goes to Cameroon and the Portuguese club goes to Brazil.		If Spanish club to Mexico → French club to Cameroon AND Portuguese club to Brazil
		→	If ~French club to Cameroon OR ~ Portuguese club to Brazil → ~ Spanish club to Mexico
53.	Only those with a severe condition will be allowed to participate in Trial B.	→	If in Trial B → severe condition
			If ~ severe condition → ~ Trial B
54.	All of the members of the kayaking team have orange helmets.	→	If on kayaking team → orange helmet
			If ~ orange helmet → ~ on kayaking team
55.	There must be at least three members on any committee to which Jolene is assigned.		If Jolene on committee → 3+ members on that committee
		→	If ~ 3+ members on committee → ~ Jolene on that committee

Perform

Translate each of the following statements into simple shorthand, and form the correct contrapositive of each.

Formal Logic Statement	My Analysis
56. Janine is a member of every club that Marie is a member of. $\longrightarrow$	
57. Every tree planted in Big Park is either a magnolia or a gingko. $\longrightarrow$	
58. Allison will select a mauve dress if she selects either the black shoes or the white necklace. $\longrightarrow$	
59. The purple rug is selected only if the yellow rug is selected. $\longrightarrow$	
60. Unless medication A is prescribed, medication B will be prescribed. $\longrightarrow$	
61. If the first track is hip-hop, the second track will be country or jazz. $\longrightarrow$	
62. Whenever Bob and Jerami are both on Team A, Taina is on Team D. $\longrightarrow$	
63. All of the passengers in row 3 are wearing blue shirts. $\longrightarrow$	
64. The only kind of snack in the first bag is pretzels. $\longrightarrow$	

Explanations

Here's how an LSAT expert might abbreviate the statements and form the contrapositives.

Formal Logic Statement		Analysis
56. Janine is a member of every club that Marie is a member of.	→	If Marie in club → Janine in club If ~ Janine in club → ~ Marie in club
57. Every tree planted in Big Park is either a magnolia or a gingko.	→	If planted in Big Park → magnolia OR gingko If ~ magnolia AND ~ gingko → ~ planted in Big Park
58. Allison will select a mauve dress if she selects either the black shoes or the white necklace.	→	If black shoes OR white necklace → mauve dress If ~ mauve dress → ~ black shoes AND ~ white necklace
59. The purple rug is selected only if the yellow rug is selected.	→	If purple rug → yellow rug If ~ yellow rug → ~ purple rug
60. Unless medication A is prescribed, medication B will be prescribed.	→	If ~ medication B → medication A If ~ medication A → medication B
61. If the first track is hip-hop, the second track will be country or jazz.	→	If hip-hop 1st → country 2nd OR jazz 2nd If ~ country 2nd AND ~ jazz 2nd → ~ hip-hop 1st
62. Whenever Bob and Jerami are both on Team A, Taina is on Team D.	→	If Bob on Team A AND Jerami on Team A → Taina on Team D If ~ Taina on Team D → ~ Bob on Team A OR ~ Jerami on Team A
63. All of the passengers in row 3 are wearing blue shirts.	→	If in row 3 → blue shirt If ~ blue shirt → ~ in row 3
64. The only kind of snack in the first bag is pretzels.	→	If snack in first bag → pretzels If ~ pretzels → ~ snack in first bag

Make Valid Deductions from the Contrapositives of Conditional Statements

LEARNING OBJECTIVES

In this section, you'll learn to:

- Make valid deductions from the contrapositive of a conditional statement

In the previous section, you learned how to make contrapositives. You can use the contrapositive of any Formal Logic statement to help in making deductions about what must be true.

Prepare

When the contrapositive is formed, it provides a second sufficient condition (i.e., trigger). If that new sufficient condition is triggered, then the arrow can be followed to deduce the necessary result of that logic. Deductions can only be made when a sufficient condition is triggered. When a necessary condition (or result) is met, it cannot be logically deduced that the sufficient condition was met.

Conditional Statement		Analysis
If the clown has blue balloons, then she also has red balloons.	$\longrightarrow$	If blue → red If ~ red → ~ blue
What do we know if ...		
the clown has blue balloons?	$\longrightarrow$	If the clown has blue balloons, that is sufficient to deduce that the clown also has red balloons.
the clown does not have blue balloons?	$\longrightarrow$	Nothing; blue balloons are sufficient, but they are not necessary. It is possible for the clown to have red balloons without blue balloons.
the clown has red balloons?	$\longrightarrow$	Nothing; red balloons are merely a necessary result of having blue balloons. However, having red balloons is not sufficient, and thus does not trigger any result.
the clown does not have red balloons?	$\longrightarrow$	The red balloons are necessary. An absence of red balloons, triggers the contrapositive, resulting in the deduction that the clown cannot have blue balloons.

Practice

Review the deduction exercise you tried earlier, and then complete the practice on the next page.

Formal Logic Statements		Analysis
(1) If the zebra is chosen, then so is the antelope.	$\longrightarrow$	If Z $\rightarrow$ A
(2) If the tortoise is chosen, then so is the zebra.	$\longrightarrow$	If T $\rightarrow$ Z
(3) If the antelope is chosen, then so is the gorilla.	$\longrightarrow$	If A $\rightarrow$ G
Chain of logic:	$\longrightarrow$	If T $\rightarrow$ Z $\rightarrow$ A $\rightarrow$ G

What do we know if ...

the zebra is chosen?	$\longrightarrow$	If the zebra is chosen, then the antelope and the gorilla are chosen. If Z $\rightarrow$ A $\rightarrow$ G
the gorilla is chosen?	$\longrightarrow$	Choosing the gorilla does not lead to any further deduction.
the tortoise is chosen?	$\longrightarrow$	If the tortoise is chosen, then all of the animals in the list will be chosen. If T $\rightarrow$ Z $\rightarrow$ A $\rightarrow$ G

For each of the following statements, form the contrapositive of the statement and add it to the My Analysis column. Then answer the questions that follow.

Formal Logic Statements		My Analysis
(1)	If the zebra is chosen, then so is the antelope.	→ If Z → A
(2)	If the tortoise is chosen, then so is the zebra.	→ If T → Z
(3)	If the antelope is chosen, then so is the gorilla.	→ If A → G
Chain of logic:		→ If T → Z → A → G

What do we know if ...

65. the zebra is not chosen?

   →

66. the gorilla is not chosen?

   →

67. the tortoise is not chosen?

   →

68. the antelope is not chosen?

   →

Explanations

Here's how an LSAT expert would analyze the previous statements and answer the associated questions.

Formal Logic Statements	Analysis
(1) If the zebra is chosen, then so is the antelope.	If Z → A If ~A → ~Z
(2) If the tortoise is chosen, then so is the zebra.	If T → Z If ~Z → ~T
(3) If the antelope is chosen, then so is the gorilla.	If A → G If ~G → ~A
Chain of logic:	If T → Z → A → G If ~G → ~A → ~Z → ~T

What do we know if ...

65. the zebra is not chosen?	If the zebra is not chosen, then the tortoise cannot be chosen. If ~Z → ~T
66. the gorilla is not chosen?	Not choosing the gorilla means that none of the other animals can be selected either. If ~G → ~A → ~Z → ~T
67. the tortoise is not chosen?	If the tortoise is not chosen, no further deduction can be made.
68. the antelope is not chosen?	If the antelope is not chosen, then the zebra is not chosen, which means the tortoise is also not chosen. If ~A → ~Z → ~T

In the practice sets on the following pages, you will need to make the initial translations and abbreviations for the conditional statements, and then form the contrapositives before moving on to answer the questions.

Perform

For each of the following statements, turn it into shorthand, form the contrapositive, and then make notes about how each can be combined with other conditional statements in the same set to make deductions.

Formal Logic Statements		My Analysis
(1) If the vitamins are selected, the spinach will not be selected.	$\longrightarrow$	
(2) If the tea is selected, the vitamins will be selected.	$\longrightarrow$	
(3) If the milk is selected, the spinach will be selected.	$\longrightarrow$	
Chain of logic:	$\longrightarrow$	

What do we know if ...

69. the spinach is selected?	$\longrightarrow$	
70. the milk is not selected?	$\longrightarrow$	
71. the vitamins are not selected?	$\longrightarrow$	
72. the tea is not selected?	$\longrightarrow$	

Explanations

Here's how an LSAT expert would analyze the previous statements and answer the associated questions.

Formal Logic Statements		Analysis
(1)	If the vitamins are selected, the spinach will not be selected. $\longrightarrow$	If V $\rightarrow$ ~S If S $\rightarrow$ ~V
(2)	If the tea is selected, the vitamins will be selected. $\longrightarrow$	If T $\rightarrow$ V If ~V $\rightarrow$ ~T
(3)	If the milk is selected, the spinach will be selected. $\longrightarrow$	If M $\rightarrow$ S If ~S $\rightarrow$ ~M
Chain of logic:	$\longrightarrow$	If T $\rightarrow$ V $\rightarrow$ ~S $\rightarrow$ ~M If M $\rightarrow$ S $\rightarrow$ ~V $\rightarrow$ ~T

What do we know if ...

69. the spinach is selected?	$\longrightarrow$	If the spinach is selected, then the vitamins are not selected and the tea is not selected. If S $\rightarrow$ ~V $\rightarrow$ ~T
70. the milk is not selected?	$\longrightarrow$	Nothing additional can be deduced.
71. the vitamins are not selected?	$\longrightarrow$	If the vitamins are not selected, then the tea is not selected. If ~V $\rightarrow$ ~T
72. the tea is not selected?	$\longrightarrow$	Nothing additional can be deduced.

Make Valid Deductions from Conditional Statements Containing *And* and *Or*

Prepare

Earlier in this chapter, you learned that when a conditional statement includes an *and* or an *or* in one of its conditions, you must swap *and* for *or* (and vice versa) when forming the contrapositive. Here's another example to refresh your memory.

Whenever lentil soup is offered on Tuesday, then minestrone or gumbo is offered on Wednesday.

In a Formal Logic abbreviation, that statement would become:

If lentil on Tue. → minestrone on Wed. OR gumbo on Wed.

To form the contrapositive, reverse and negate the terms and swap the *or* for *and*.

NO minestrone on Wed. AND NO gumbo on Wed. → NO lentil on Tue.

So, consider what you know in each of the following cases:

If we know that ...		then we also know that ...
lentil soup is offered on Tuesday	→	at least one of minestrone or gumbo is offered on Wednesday, perhaps both.
lentil soup is not offered on Tuesday	→	we cannot deduce anything. Lentil soup is sufficient, not necessary. It's possible to have minestrone or gumbo on Wednesday even without lentil soup on Tuesday.
minestrone is offered on Wednesday, but not gumbo	→	we cannot deduce anything. Minestrone on Wednesday is merely a necessary condition. It is not sufficient by itself to guarantee lentil soup on Tuesday.
gumbo is offered on Wednesday, but not minestrone	→	we cannot deduce anything. Gumbo on Wednesday is merely a necessary condition. It is not sufficient by itself to guarantee lentil soup on Tuesday.
both gumbo and minestrone are offered on Wednesday	→	we cannot deduce anything. Gumbo and/or minestrone on Wednesday is merely a necessary condition. It is not sufficient by itself to guarantee lentil soup on Tuesday.
neither gumbo nor minestrone is offered on Wednesday	→	lentil soup cannot be offered on Tuesday.

The following chart shows the correct contrapositives for a variety of complex conditional statements.

Formal Logic Statement		Contrapositive
If A → B or C	→	If ~B and ~C → ~A
If D → E and F	→	If ~E or ~F → ~D
If G or H → J	→	If ~J → ~G and ~H
If K and L → M	→	If ~M → ~K or ~L
If N and O → P and R	→	If ~P or ~R → ~N or ~O
If S or T → U and V	→	If ~U or ~V → ~S and ~T
If W and X → Y or Z	→	If ~Y and ~Z → ~W or ~X
If AA or BB → CC or DD	→	If ~CC and ~DD → ~AA and ~BB

Here is an example of an LSAT expert's analysis of the implications of a complex conditional statement that contains two terms in its necessary clause.

Conditional Statement		Analysis
Whenever Ezra performs, Gloria and Horatio also perform.	→	If E → G and H If ~G or ~H → ~E

Is each of the following an acceptable group of people who perform?

Ezra, Gloria, and Horatio together	→	Yes
Ezra and Gloria, but not Horatio	→	No
Ezra and Horatio, but not Gloria	→	No
Gloria and Horatio, but not Ezra	→	Yes
Ezra alone	→	No
Gloria alone	→	Yes
Horatio alone	→	Yes

Practice

In this exercise, translate the conditional statement to Formal Logic abbreviations and form the correct contrapositive of the statement. Then, answer the questions beneath the statement using your work.

Conditional Statement		My Analysis
Yolanda will not join the sales team unless Xavier joins the accounting team and Wanda joins the development team.	$\longrightarrow$	
73. If Xavier joins the accounting team and Wanda joins the development team, will Yolanda join the sales team?	$\longrightarrow$	
74. If Xavier and Wanda both join the development team (and no other teams), will Yolanda join the sales team?	$\longrightarrow$	
75. If Yolanda does not join the sales team, do you know anything about where Xavier or Wanda can or cannot be assigned?	$\longrightarrow$	

Explanations

Here's how an LSAT expert would analyze the previous statements and answer the questions.

Conditional Statement		Analysis
Yolanda will not join the sales team unless Xavier joins the accounting team and Wanda joins the development team.	$\longrightarrow$	If Ys → Xa AND Wd If ~Xa OR ~Wd → ~Ys
73. If Xavier joins the accounting team and Wanda joins the development team, will Yolanda join the sales team?	$\longrightarrow$	This could happen, but it doesn't have to happen. Knowing the teams that Xavier and Wanda join is necessary but not sufficient for knowing the team that Yolanda joins.
74. If Xavier and Wanda both join the development team (and no other teams), will Yolanda join the sales team?	$\longrightarrow$	No, she won't. If Xavier does not join the accounting team, then Yolanda cannot join the sales team.
75. If Yolanda does not join the sales team, do you know anything about where Xavier or Wanda can or cannot be assigned?	$\longrightarrow$	No, nothing is known. If Yolanda were assigned to sales, we would know where Xavier and Wanda are assigned. But since Yolanda is not assigned there, we don't know anything about Xavier and Wanda.

Perform

In this exercise, translate the conditional statements to Formal Logic abbreviations and form the correct contrapositive of the statement. Then, answer the questions beneath the statement using your work.

Conditional Statement	My Analysis
Every gumdrop in the third bowl is red and apple-flavored. $\longrightarrow$	
76. If a gumdrop is blue, can it be apple flavored? $\longrightarrow$	
77. If a gumdrop is not apple-flavored, can it be in the third bowl? $\longrightarrow$	
78. If a gumdrop is red and apple-flavored, must it be in the third bowl? $\longrightarrow$	

Explanations

Here's how an LSAT expert would analyze the previous statements and answer the questions.

Conditional Statement		Analysis
Every gumdrop in the third bowl is red and apple-flavored.	$\longrightarrow$	If gumdrop in bowl 3 → red AND apple If ~ apple OR ~ red → ~ gumdrop in bowl 3
76. If a gumdrop is blue, can it be apple flavored?	$\longrightarrow$	This is possible. We don't know anything about gumdrops that are in other bowls.
77. If a gumdrop is not apple-flavored, can it be in the third bowl?	$\longrightarrow$	No, this isn't possible. Every gumdrop in the third bowl is apple-flavored.
78. If a gumdrop is red and apple-flavored, must it be in the third bowl?	$\longrightarrow$	No. It could be in the third bowl, but it could also be in other bowls.

Make Valid Deductions from Conditional Statements Containing an "Exclusive Or" Provision

LEARNING OBJECTIVES

In this section, you'll learn to:

- Make valid deductions from conditional statements containing an "Exclusive Or" provision

Prepare

So far, you've learned the fact that *or*, by itself, does not denote mutual exclusivity in conditional Formal Logic statements. However, if the LSAT adds a phrase such as "but not both," then, and only then, does it become a case of mutual exclusivity. Such statements are rare on the LSAT, but they warrant enough practice that you won't be thrown by them on Test Day.

Here's how an LSAT expert would translate such statements:

Formal Logic Statements	Analysis
If A, then B or C, but not both.	If A → B or C If ~B and ~C → ~A → If A → ~(B and C) If B and C → ~A The sufficient condition results in the selection of exactly one entity (not both).
If D or E, but not both, then F.	If exactly one of D or E → F If ~F → (D and E) or (~D and ~E) [both or neither] → The selection of exactly one triggers the result. Without the necessary result, then either both conditions occurred or both did not occur.

Practice

Record each of the following statements in If-Then format, and form both parts of their contrapositive.

Formal Logic Statements	My Analysis
79. Each member who attends the purchasing conference will also attend the sales conference or the marketing conference, but not both. →	
80. Students who take exactly one of either math or economics will also take biology. →	

Explanations

Here's how an LSAT expert might analyze the statements on the previous page.

Formal Logic Statements	Analysis	
79. Each member who attends the purchasing conference will also attend the sales conference or the marketing conference, but not both. →	If purchasing	→ sales OR marketing (but not both)
	If ~ sales AND ~ marketing	→ ~ purchasing
	If sales AND marketing	→ ~ purchasing
80. Students who take exactly one of either math or economics will also take biology. →	If math or econ. (but not both) → bio	
	If ~ bio	→ either [both math AND econ] OR [~ math AND ~ econ]

Perform

In this exercise, take each of the Formal Logic statements, turn it into "If-then" format, and make both parts of the contrapositive.

Formal Logic Statements	My Analysis
81. If Orson joins the dance team, he will also join the chess club or the glee club, but not both. $\longrightarrow$	
82. Whenever a box contains a peanut or a cashew (but not both), that box will be painted black. $\longrightarrow$	

Explanations

Here's how an LSAT expert might analyze the statements on the previous page.

Formal Logic Statements	My Analysis	
81. If Orson joins the dance team, he will also join the chess club or the glee club, but not both.	If dance	→ chess or glee (but not both)
	If ~ chess AND ~ glee	→ ~ dance
	If chess AND glee	→ ~ dance
82. Whenever a box contains a peanut or a cashew (but not both), that box will be painted black.	If peanut OR cashew (but not both)	→ black box
	If ~ black box	→ either [no peanuts AND no cashews] OR [peanuts AND cashews]

Numerical Deductions from Conditional Statements

LEARNING OBJECTIVES

In this section, you'll learn to:

- Determine the valid deduction from If X → ~Y and from If ~X → Y

Prepare

Numerical deductions are often rewarded on the LSAT, especially in Logic Games. This section highlights two such deductions that frequently arise from conditional Formal Logic statements.

Determining the Valid Deduction From If X → ~Y

The trigger involves something that *does* happen, and the result is something else that *cannot* happen. This reduces the number of terms by at least one.

In this case, the deduction is this: You cannot have both. (And you might have neither.)

If the contracting company services plumbing, it does not service roofing.

If plumbing   →   ~ roofing
If roofing   →   ~ plumbing

The company will not service both. It can service just plumbing, just roofing, or neither.

Determining the Valid Deduction From If ~X → Y

The trigger involves something that *doesn't* happen, and the result is something that *must* happen. This increases the number of terms chosen by at least one.

In this case, the deduction is this: You must have at least one. (And you might have both.)

If the story does not include metaphors, then it must include symbolism.

If ~ metaphor   →   symbolism
If ~ symbolism   →   metaphor

The story will definitely include at least one of those two literary devices. It will include symbolism, metaphor, or possibly both.

LOGIC GAMES STRATEGY

The triggers of a Formal Logic statement and its contrapositive can never occur simultaneously. You can have the sufficient and necessary terms of the original statement, the sufficient and necessary terms of the contrapositive, or both necessary terms—but never both sufficient terms at once.

Formal Logic Statements	Analysis
No X are Y	If X → ~Y
	→ You cannot have both X and Y. You may have X without Y, Y without X, or neither X nor Y.
If no U, then V	If ~U → V
	→ You must have at least one of U or V. You can either have just U, just V, or both U and V.
All those with J don't have K	If J → ~K
	→ You cannot have both J and K. You may have J without K, have K without J, or have neither J nor K.
R unless S	If ~R → S
	→ You must have at least one of R and S. You can either have just R, just S, or both R and S.

Practice

For each of the following statements, write out the statement in shorthand, and indicate whether a numerical deduction can be made based on the statement.

Formal Logic Statements	My Analysis
83. If the arrow is not selected, the hammer will be selected.	
$\longrightarrow$	
84. Any time the bake sale has brownies, it does not have cupcakes.	
$\longrightarrow$	
85. The oak tree will be planted in the orchard only if the maple tree is also planted in the orchard.	
$\longrightarrow$	

Explanations

Here's how an LSAT expert might translate and analyze the statements in the exercise.

Formal Logic Statements	Analysis
83. If the arrow is not selected, the hammer will be selected.	If ~ arrow → hammer If ~ hammer → arrow This statement increases the minimum of selected items by one. At the very least, either the hammer or the arrow will always be selected. It's possible that both are selected.
84. Any time the bake sale has brownies, it does not have cupcakes.	If brownies → ~ cupcakes If cupcakes → ~ brownies This statement decreases the maximum number of items at the bake sale. It will never have both brownies and cupcakes. It's possible the sale has neither.
85. The oak tree will be planted in the orchard only if the maple tree is also planted in the orchard.	If oak → maple If ~ maple → ~ oak No numerical deduction can be made here. It's possible to plant both trees in the park, it's possible to plant neither of the trees in the park, and it's also possible to plant a maple tree and not an oak tree.

K

Perform

For each of the following statements, write out the statement in shorthand, and indicate whether a numerical deduction can be made based on the statement.

Formal Logic Statements	My Analysis
86. Whenever the photographer is not selected, the writer is not selected. $\longrightarrow$	
87. Kyle is on every committee that Hector is not on. $\longrightarrow$	
88. If the poppy is included in the painting, then the rose will not be included. $\longrightarrow$	

Explanations

Here's how an LSAT expert might translate and analyze the statements in the exercise.

Formal Logic Statements	My Analysis
86. Whenever the photographer is not selected, the writer is not selected.	If ~ photographer → ~ writer If writer → photographer No numerical deduction can be made here. It's possible that both are selected, it's possible that neither are selected, and it's possible that the photographer is selected but not the writer.
87. Kyle is on every committee that Hector is not on.	If ~ Hector → Kyle If ~ Kyle → Hector This statement assures that every committee will have at least one member—either Hector or Kyle. As soon as one of them is NOT on a committee, the other person is assigned to that committee. It's also possible that they are on a committee together.
88. If the poppy is included in the painting, then the rose will not be included.	If poppy → ~ rose If rose → ~ poppy The painting cannot include both the poppy and the rose, so the maximum number of flowers in the painting is reduced by one. It's possible that the painting contains neither the rose nor the poppy.

Although this last learning objective about numerical deductions in Formal Logic comes all the way at the end of the section, the types of rules discussed here are very valuable when they appear in Selection games. In The LSAT Channel Special Feature that follows this section, a Kaplan expert will explain why these rules are so important, and illustrate them in action in a classic open-ended Selection game. If you want to push your mastery of LSAT Formal Logic over the top, don't miss this Special Feature.

Assess

Mastering Formal Logic takes repetition. No matter how you did on the exercises in this section, hone your edge and stay sharp by doing the Formal Logic drills in the Logic Games Training Camp in your online Study Plan.

Reflect

Look back over your practice:

Did you take the time to understand each conditional statement before noting it down in shorthand?

If you couldn't immediately see how to write it down in one sentence, did you translate it into "If-then" form and make the contrapositive? (If so, that's great!)

When forming contrapositives, did you remember to always negate and reverse the terms? Did you always remember that the result (the necessary condition) can occur without the trigger (the sufficient condition), but not vice versa?

Minimum Increasers and Maximum Decreasers

By Hannah Gist

 Watch the video lesson for this Spotlight in your online Study Plan.

While a conditional Formal Logic rule could appear in almost any game type, Formal Logic is at the heart of Selection games. Nearly all of the rules in Selection games will provide triggers and results based on the selection or rejection of an entity; e.g., "If A is selected, then B is also selected" or "C is not selected unless D is also selected." The lengthy section of Chapter 8 that precedes this Special Feature is dedicated to helping you build mastery and confidence with just these types of statements.

Even with that work under your belt, there are two Formal Logic rules that deserve extra attention:

> If G is selected, then H is not selected.

and

> If L is not selected, M is selected.

These rules appear frequently in Selection games, and they are frequently misunderstood, leading to confusion and wrong answers. That's unfortunate, of course, but there is a bright side. When these rules are handled correctly, they not only help you solve the questions, they also give you direct insight into the minimum and maximum number of entities that may be selected. Here's the how and why of it.

Take the first rule: If G is selected, then H is not selected. This pattern—if positive, then negative—is a "maximum decreaser." It simply means that G and H cannot both be selected. Putting the rule into Formal Logic shorthand demonstrates this:

> If $G \rightarrow$ ~H

Reverse and negate to get the contrapositive:

> If $H \rightarrow$ ~G

Any time G or H is selected, the other is rejected. The maximum number of entities that may be selected is reduced by one. Some LSAT experts just cut to the chase and jot down the rule like this:

> ~GH

That insight is almost certain to help you get points in a Selection game featuring this rule. But, the rule has a pitfall, a simple mistake that many students make that costs them points: They think the rule means that either G or H must be selected. It does not. Selecting G or selecting H are the triggers. The rule says nothing about rejecting them. Memorize the results of "maximum decreasers" like this: If $G \rightarrow$ ~H means that we could 1) select G and reject H, 2) select H and reject G, or 3) reject both G and H. We cannot, however, select both G and H.

The other rule, illustrated with the previous example "If L is not selected, then M is selected," has the inverse pattern—negative to positive. This is a "minimum increaser." Again, write it out in Formal Logic shorthand:

If ~L → M

and form the contrapositive:

If ~M → L

You could shorten this one to:

At least one of M or L

or

M, L, or ML

Now, the minimum number of entities that must be selected is increased by one. Any time L is rejected, M is selected. And any time M is rejected, L is selected. Since the "minimum increaser" is the inverse of the "maximum decreaser," test takers are at risk of making the inverse mistake. That is, they mistakenly assume that at least one of the two entities must be rejected. Nope. The triggers this time are the rejection, not selection, of one of the entities. It's possible that both are selected, simply because selecting one of the entities does not trigger anything (nothing prevents the selection of both entities).

Memorize the results of "minimum increasers" like this: If ~L → M means that we could 1) reject L and select M, 2) reject M and select L, or 3) select both L and M. We cannot, however, reject both L and M.

In the video that accompanies this Special Feature, an LSAT Channel expert will demonstrate a game that features both a maximum decreaser and a minimum increaser. The game is printed on the next two pages. Try it out on your own, if you like, but pay special attention to the rules that operate just like the ones discussed here. They are key to unlocking the game you're about to do.

Questions 6–12

Bird-watchers explore a forest to see which of the following six kinds of birds—grosbeak, harrier, jay, martin, shrike, wren—it contains. The findings are consistent with the following conditions:

   If harriers are in the forest, then grosbeaks are not.
   If jays, martins, or both are in the forest, then so are harriers.
   If wrens are in the forest, then so are grosbeaks.
   If jays are not in the forest, then shrikes are.

6.   Which one of the following could be a complete and accurate list of the birds NOT in the forest?

   (A)   jays, shrikes
   (B)   harriers, grosbeaks
   (C)   grosbeaks, jays, martins
   (D)   grosbeaks, martins, shrikes, wrens
   (E)   martins, shrikes

7. If both martins and harriers are in the forest, then which one of the following must be true?

    (A) Shrikes are the only other birds in the forest.
    (B) Jays are the only other birds in the forest.
    (C) The forest contains neither jays nor shrikes.
    (D) There are at least two other kinds of birds in the forest.
    (E) There are at most two other kinds of birds in the forest.

8. If jays are not in the forest, then which one of the following must be false?

    (A) Martins are in the forest.
    (B) Harriers are in the forest.
    (C) Neither martins nor harriers are in the forest.
    (D) Neither martins nor shrikes are in the forest.
    (E) Harriers and shrikes are the only birds in the forest.

9. Which one of the following is the maximum number of the six kinds of birds the forest could contain?

    (A) two
    (B) three
    (C) four
    (D) five
    (E) six

10. Which one of the following pairs of birds CANNOT be among those birds contained in the forest?

    (A) jays, wrens
    (B) jays, shrikes
    (C) shrikes, wrens
    (D) jays, martins
    (E) shrikes, martins

11. If grosbeaks are in the forest, then which one of the following must be true?

    (A) Shrikes are in the forest.
    (B) Wrens are in the forest.
    (C) The forest contains both wrens and shrikes.
    (D) At most two kinds of birds are in the forest.
    (E) At least three kinds of birds are in the forest.

12. Suppose the condition is added that if shrikes are in the forest, then harriers are not. If all other conditions remain in effect, then which one of the following could be true?

    (A) The forest contains both jays and shrikes.
    (B) The forest contains both wrens and shrikes.
    (C) The forest contains both martins and shrikes.
    (D) Jays are not in the forest, whereas martins are.
    (E) Only two of the six kinds of birds are not in the forest.

PrepTest33 Sec4 Qs 6–12

 Complete answers and explanations are provided in The LSAT Channel Spotlight video "Limited Options" in your online Study Plan.

SELECTION GAMES RULES

LEARNING OBJECTIVES

In this section of the chapter, you'll practice

- Applying Step 3 of the Logic Games Method to Selection games by analyzing and sketching the rules

Prepare

Now that you've worked through the section of this chapter on Formal Logic, there's not much more to say about Selection games rules. Aside from the occasional "established entity" rule (e.g., "Y is selected"), virtually everything you'll see will be expressed in conditional ("If"-then) terms.

LOGIC GAMES STRATEGY

Selection rules tell you one or more of the following:

- One entity's selection is dependent on another entity being selected.
- At least one of two entities must be selected.
- At least one of two entities must be rejected.
- Two entities must be selected or rejected as a pair (one cannot be selected and the other rejected).

Before moving on to the practice exercises, take a few moments to review some of the most common Selection rules. In the expert analysis you'll see them written in Formal Logic shorthand, and accompanied by their contrapositives.

Rules		Analysis
R is never selected without W.	$\longrightarrow$	If R → W If ~W → ~R
If A is chosen, then Z will not be chosen.	$\longrightarrow$	If A → ~Z If Z → ~A or Never AZ
T will be selected for the display if G is not selected.	$\longrightarrow$	If ~G → T If ~T → G or Must have G or T (or both)
H will be chosen only if T is chosen.	$\longrightarrow$	If H → T If ~T → ~H
If B is chosen, then either C or D (but not both) will also be chosen.	$\longrightarrow$	If B → C or D If B → ~[both C and D] If ~C and ~D → ~B If C and D → ~B
At least one of either K or L will be selected.	$\longrightarrow$	If ~K → L If ~L → K or Must have K or L (or both)
Whenever J is not chosen, P is not chosen.	$\longrightarrow$	~J → ~P P → J
Only when O and X are selected is E selected.	$\longrightarrow$	E → O and X ~O or ~X → ~E
F and Y cannot both be selected.	$\longrightarrow$	If F → ~Y If Y → ~F or Never FY
M is a member of every group of which N is a member.	$\longrightarrow$	If N → M If ~M → ~N

In a Selection game in which the entities are subdivided, you may see number restrictions expressed in the rules. For example, in a game that tasks you with selecting a team of researchers from among four biologists and four chemists, a rule such as "Exactly two biologists will be selected for the research team" is likely. Such rules are almost always straightforward and easy to add to your sketch by simply noting the number above that subgroup of entities.

There are four practice exercises. In the first, you'll analyze and draw out 12 rules. In the next three, you'll see the model game setups you worked with in the section of this chapter covering Steps 1 and 2, but now accompanied by their rules. Analyze the rules, answer the questions posed about them, and draw them as you would on Test Day.

Practice

Practice 1

Directions: Analyze and draw each of the following Selection game rules, and record their contrapositives.

	Rules		Analysis
1.	If Dan is picked for the dance team, then Elaine will also be picked for the dance team.	$\longrightarrow$	
2.	The blue toy will be selected only if the red toy is not selected.	$\longrightarrow$	
3.	If A is chosen, then neither B nor C is chosen.	$\longrightarrow$	
4.	Juan will become a member only if Levi becomes a member.	$\longrightarrow$	
5.	If X is not selected for inclusion, then Z will be selected.	$\longrightarrow$	
6.	Nanda will not be selected unless Opal is selected.	$\longrightarrow$	
7.	Uriah cannot be chosen for the group without either Van or Walker being chosen.	$\longrightarrow$	
8.	If D is picked, then T is not picked.	$\longrightarrow$	
9.	Glen must be selected for the medical trial unless Jack is not selected for the medical trial.	$\longrightarrow$	
10.	Only if Z is chosen will K be chosen.	$\longrightarrow$	
11.	Patty will be selected if Ben is not selected.	$\longrightarrow$	
12.	If R and S are selected, then Q is selected.	$\longrightarrow$	

Practice 2

Directions: Take a couple of minutes to review the game setup, summarize your Overview analysis, and recreate the initial Sketch. Then, one at a time, analyze the rules, answer the questions about each one, and draw the rule either inside or underneath the sketch framework.

A graphic designer must choose colors for a new logo from among the seven—fuchsia, grapefruit, hibiscus, indigo, jade, kiwi, and lemon—suggested by the client. The color selection must conform to the following conditions:

If grapefruit is used, then lemon cannot be used.
If jade is used, then indigo must also be used.
If indigo is used, then lemon must also be used.
If fuchsia is not used, then grapefruit must be used.
Hibiscus and kiwi cannot both be used.

1. [Step 1] Summarize your Overview analysis:

2. [Step 2] Create an initial Sketch:

3. [Step 3] Analyze and draw the Rules:
   - For each rule, answer the following questions and draw the rule in the appropriate box.
     - What does the rule restrict, and what does it leave open?
     - What are the rule's negative implications, if any?
     - Can the rule be depicted inside the sketch framework?

Rule 1:	Rule 2:
Rule 3:	Rule 4:
Rule 5:	

Practice 3

Directions: Take a couple of minutes to review the game setup, summarize your Overview analysis, and recreate the initial Sketch. Then, one at a time, analyze the rules, answer the questions about each one, and draw the rule either inside or underneath the sketch framework.

Melanie is planning a series of performances to promote her new relaxation CD. At each performance, she will play at least four of the pieces—*Atmosphere*, *Beats*, *Clouds*, *Dynamic*, *Ecologica*, *Firefly*, and *Glaciers*—that appear on the CD. Her selection for each performance is based on the following conditions:

Beats must be played at any performance that includes *Glaciers*.
Firefly will not be played at any performance that includes *Glaciers*.
Ecologica will not be played at any performance that includes both *Beats* and *Glaciers*.
If *Dynamic* is played, then *Atmosphere* is as well.
Clouds will be played at every performance.

1. [Step 1] Summarize your Overview analysis:

2. [Step 2] Create an initial Sketch:

3. [Step 3] Analyze and draw the Rules:
   - For each rule, answer the following questions and draw the rule in the appropriate box.
     - What does the rule restrict, and what does it leave open?
     - What are the rule's negative implications, if any?
     - Can the rule be depicted inside the sketch framework?

Rule 1:	Rule 2:
Rule 3:	Rule 4:
Rule 5:	

Practice 4

Directions: Take a couple of minutes to review the game setup, summarize your Overview analysis, and recreate the initial Sketch. Then, one at a time, analyze the rules, answer the questions about each one, and draw the rule either inside or underneath the sketch framework.

Writers for a science magazine submitted eight articles to their editor, each on a different topic—anatomy, biochemistry, climatology, ecology, genetics, hydrology, immunology, and neuroscience. The editor will select exactly four of the articles for publication in the next issue, based on the following guidelines:

The issue will include an article on either climatology or neuroscience, but not both.
If the article on biochemistry is not included, then the article on ecology will be included.
The article on genetics will not be included unless the article on immunology is included.
If the article on hydrology is included, then the article on anatomy is not included.
The article on ecology will be included if, but only if, the article on anatomy is included.

1. [Step 1] Summarize your Overview analysis:

2. [Step 2] Create an initial Sketch:

3. [Step 3] Analyze and draw the Rules:
   - For each rule, answer the following questions and draw the rule in the appropriate box.
     - What does the rule restrict, and what does it leave open?
     - What are the rule's negative implications, if any?
     - Can the rule be depicted inside the sketch framework?

Rule 1:	Rule 2:
Rule 3:	Rule 4:
Rule 5:	

Explanations

Compare your work to that of an LSAT expert. Pay close attention to how the expert analyzed each rule and then depicted it within or beneath the game's initial sketch.

Practice 1

Rules	Analysis
1. If Dan is picked for the dance team, then Elaine will also be picked for the dance team.	If D → E If ~E → ~D
2. The blue toy will be selected only if the red toy is not selected.	If B → ~R If R → ~B or Never BR
3. If A is chosen, then neither B nor C is chosen.	If A → ~B and ~C If B or C → ~A or Never AB Never AC
4. Juan will become a member only if Levi becomes a member.	If J → L If ~L → ~J
5. If X is not selected for inclusion, then Z will be selected.	If ~X → Z If ~Z → X or Must have X or Z (or both)
6. Nanda will not be selected unless Opal is selected.	If N → O If ~O → ~N
7. Uriah cannot be chosen for the group without either Van or Walker being chosen.	If U → V or W If ~V and ~W → ~U
8. If D is picked, then T is not picked.	If D → ~T If T → ~D or Never DT
9. Glen must be selected for the medical trial unless Jack is not selected for the medical trial.	If J → G If ~G → ~J
10. Only if Z is chosen will K be chosen.	If K → Z If ~Z → ~K
11. Patty will be selected if Ben is not selected.	If ~B → P If ~P → B or Must have B or P (or both)
12. If R and S are selected, then Q is selected.	If R and S → Q If ~Q → ~R or ~S

Practice 2

A graphic designer must choose colors for a new logo from among the seven—fuchsia, grapefruit, hibiscus, indigo, jade, kiwi, and lemon—suggested by the client. The color selection must conform to the following conditions:

> If grapefruit is used, then lemon cannot be used.
> If jade is used, then indigo must also be used.
> If indigo is used, then lemon must also be used.
> If fuchsia is not used, then grapefruit must be used.
> Hibiscus and kiwi cannot both be used.

1. [Step 1] Summarize your Overview analysis: *A Selection game in which an unspecific number of colors will be chosen by a graphic designer for a new logo.*

2. [Step 2] Create an initial Sketch:

   F G H I J K L

3. [Step 3] Analyze and draw the Rules:
   - Rule 1:
     - What does the rule restrict, and what does it leave open? *If grapefruit is selected, then lemon is not.*
     - What are the rule's negative implications, if any? *By contrapositive, if lemon is selected, then grapefruit is not. This means the designer cannot select both.*
     - Can the rule be depicted inside the sketch framework? *No.*
     - Draw the rule:
       If G → ~L
       If L → ~G   Never $\boxed{G\ L}$
   - Rule 2:
     - What does the rule restrict, and what does it leave open? *If jade is selected, then indigo is selected.*
     - What are the rule's negative implications, if any? *If indigo is not selected, then jade is not selected.*
     - Can the rule be depicted inside the sketch framework? *No.*
     - Draw the rule:
       If J → I
       If ~I → ~J
   - Rule 3:
     - What does the rule restrict, and what does it leave open? *If indigo is selected, then lemon is selected.*
     - What are the rule's negative implications, if any? *If lemon is not selected, then indigo is not selected.*
     - Can the rule be depicted inside the sketch framework? *No.*
     - Draw the rule:
       If I → L
       If ~L → ~I
   - Rule 4:
     - What does the rule restrict, and what does it leave open? *If fuchsia is not selected, then grapefruit is.*
     - What are the rule's negative implications, if any? *If grapefruit is not selected, then fuchsia is. This means at least one (if not both) of these colors will be selected.*
     - Can the rule be depicted inside the sketch framework? *No.*
     - Draw the rule:
       If ~F → G
       If ~G → F   F or G (or both)
   - Rule 5:
     - What does the rule restrict, and what does it leave open? *Hibiscus and kiwi cannot both be selected, but it's also possible they're both left out.*
     - What are the rule's negative implications, if any? *N/A*
     - Can the rule be depicted inside the sketch framework? *No.*
     - Draw the rule:

       Never $\boxed{H\ K}$

Practice 3

Melanie is planning a series of performances to promote her new relaxation CD. At each performance, she will play at least four of the pieces—*Atmosphere, Beats, Clouds, Dynamic, Ecologica, Firefly,* and *Glaciers*—that appear on the CD. Her selection for each performance is based on the following conditions:

> *Beats* must be played at any performance that includes *Glaciers.*
> *Firefly* will not be played at any performance that includes *Glaciers.*
> *Ecologica* will not be played at any performance that includes both *Beats* and *Glaciers.*
> If *Dynamic* is played, then *Atmosphere* is as well.
> *Clouds* will be played at every performance.

1. [Step 1] Summarize your Overview analysis: *A Selection game in which a musician selects at least four pieces of music for each of her performances.*

2. [Step 2] Create an initial Sketch:

   A B C D E F G   4⁺ selected

3. [Step 3] Analyze and draw the Rules:
   - Rule 1:
     - What does the rule restrict, and what does it leave open? *If Glaciers is performed, then so is Beats.*
     - What are the rule's negative implications, if any? *If Beats is not performed, then Glaciers is not.*
     - Can the rule be depicted inside the sketch framework? *No.*
     - Draw the rule:
       If G → B
       If ~B → ~G

   - Rule 2:
     - What does the rule restrict, and what does it leave open? *If Glaciers is performed, then Firefly is not performed.*
     - What are the rule's negative implications, if any? *If Firefly is performed, then Glaciers is not.*
     - Can the rule be depicted inside the sketch framework? *No.*
     - Draw the rule:
       If G → ~F
       If F → ~G   Never [F G]

   - Rule 3:
     - What does the rule restrict, and what does it leave open? *If both Beats and Glaciers are performed, then Ecologica is not.*
     - What are the rule's negative implications, if any? *If Ecologica is performed, then either Beats or Glaciers is not performed. It's also possible none of these pieces are played. The one certainty is that all three pieces cannot be performed.*
     - Can the rule be depicted inside the sketch framework? *No.*
     - Draw the rule:
       If B and G → ~E
       If E   → ~B or ~G   Never [B G E]

   - Rule 4:
     - What does the rule restrict, and what does it leave open? *If Dynamic is performed, then so is Atmosphere.*
     - What are the rule's negative implications, if any? *If Atmosphere is not performed, then neither is Dynamic.*
     - Can the rule be depicted inside the sketch framework? *No.*
     - Draw the rule:
       If D → A
       If ~A → ~D

- Rule 5:
  - What does the rule restrict, and what does it leave open? *Clouds is always performed.*
  - What are the rule's negative implications, if any? *N/A*
  - Can the rule be depicted inside the sketch framework? *Yes.*
  - Draw the rule:

    A B Ⓒ D E F G

Practice 4

Writers for a science magazine submitted eight articles to their editor, each on a different topic—anatomy, biochemistry, climatology, ecology, genetics, hydrology, immunology, and neuroscience. The editor will select exactly four of the articles for publication in the next issue, based on the following guidelines:

> The issue will include an article on either climatology or neuroscience, but not both.
> If the article on biochemistry is not included, then the article on ecology will be included.
> The article on genetics will not be included unless the article on immunology is included.
> If the article on hydrology is included, then the article on anatomy is not included.
> The article on ecology will be included if, but only if, the article on anatomy is included.

1. [Step 1] Summarize your Overview analysis: *A Selection game in which exactly four articles will be selected for inclusion in a magazine. The other four articles will be left out.*

2. [Step 2] Create an initial Sketch:

    A B C E G H I N

    in   out

    __ __ __ __ | __ __ __ __

3. [Step 3] Analyze and draw the Rules:
   - Rule 1:
     - What does the rule restrict, and what does it leave open? *Of climatology and neuroscience, exactly one will be selected.*
     - What are the rule's negative implications, if any? *One of them will be out.*
     - Can the rule be depicted inside the sketch framework? *Yes.*
     - Draw the rule:

       in   out

       C/N __ __ __ | N/C __ __ __

   - Rule 2:
     - What does the rule restrict, and what does it leave open? *If the biochemistry article is not selected, then the ecology article is.*
     - What are the rule's negative implications, if any? *If the ecology article is not selected, then the biochemistry article is. That means at least one of them (or both) must be selected.*
     - Can the rule be depicted inside the sketch framework? *Yes, along with the Formal Logic.*
     - Draw the rule:

       in   out

       C/N B/E __ __ | N/C __ __ __

       If ~B → E
       If ~E → B

   - Rule 3:
     - What does the rule restrict, and what does it leave open? *If the genetics article is selected, then so is the immunology article.*
     - What are the rule's negative implications, if any? *If the immunology article is not selected, then the genetics article is not.*
     - Can the rule be depicted inside the sketch framework? *No.*
     - Draw the rule:

       If G → I
       If ~I → ~G

- Rule 4:
  - What does the rule restrict, and what does it leave open? *If the hydrology article is selected, then the anatomy article is not.*
  - What are the rule's negative implications, if any? *If the anatomy article is selected, then the hydrology article is not. Essentially, they cannot both be selected. There could be just one, or perhaps neither one.*
  - Can the rule be depicted inside the sketch framework? *Yes, along with the Formal Logic.*
  - Draw the rule:

  in   out

  C/N B/E __ __ | N/C A/H __ __

  If H → ~A
  If A → ~H   Never [A H]

- Rule 5:
  - What does the rule restrict, and what does it leave open? *If the ecology article is selected, then so is the anatomy article ... and vice versa: if the anatomy article is selected, then the ecology must be, too.*
  - What are the rule's negative implications, if any? *By contrapositive of both parts of the logic, if either one is not selected, then the other one is out, too. In short, either both are selected, or they're both out.*
  - Can the rule be depicted inside the sketch framework? *No.*
  - Draw the rule:

  [A E] or neither

As you worked with all of those rules, you may already have noticed rules that can be combined into strings because the result of one matches the trigger of another. In some Selection games, these strings will grow to four or five entities long, and the same thing with their contrapositives in the other direction. You'll practice decoding those strings, and determining which rules do or don't combine, in the next section of this chapter on Step 4 of the Logic Games Method.

SELECTION GAMES DEDUCTIONS

LEARNING OBJECTIVES

In this section of the chapter, you'll practice

- Applying Step 4 of the Logic Games Method to Selection games by combining rules and restrictions to make all valid deductions in the game.

Prepare

The most common pattern of deductions in Selection games occurs when the result of one conditional rule matches the trigger of another conditional rule. This allows the rules to be combined into a "string" or "chain" of deductions. This is easily illustrated with two rules:

If $A \rightarrow B$

If $B \rightarrow C$

Because the result of the first rule matches the trigger of the second, these two rules combine into a string:

If $A \rightarrow B \rightarrow C$

Yielding the deduction:

If $A \rightarrow C$

Don't forget that in every such case, the rules' contrapositives can also be combined:

If $\sim B \rightarrow \sim A$

If $\sim C \rightarrow \sim B$

Because the result of the second rule's contrapositive matches the trigger of the first rule's contrapositive, the two rules combine into a string:

If $\sim C \rightarrow \sim B \rightarrow \sim A$

Yielding the deduction:

If $\sim C \rightarrow \sim A$

LOGIC GAMES STRATEGY

In Selection games, deductions are likely to stem from:

- **Duplications**—Entities shared by two or more rules; Selection games often feature "strings" or "chains" of deductions from Formal Logic statements that can be linked by shared entities.
- **Numbers Restrictions**—Restrictions or limitations on the number of entities to be selected or determinations of the minimum or maximum numbers that can be selected given the game's rules.

In Selection games, deductions may involve:

- **Limited Options**—The situation that arises when a rule specifies that exactly two selection patterns are possible (e.g., either G is selected and F is not selected, or F is selected and G is not selected, in every case)
- **Blocks of Entities**—Two or more entities that must be selected or rejected as a pair
- **Established Entities**—Entities that must be selected or rejected; this is very rare in Selection games where all or most rules are conditional; occasionally, the Numbers Restrictions will allow you to determine that a specific entity can never be selected.

There is a debate among LSAT experts about whether to actually write out all of the strings that can be found among a Selection game's rules. While writing out all of the deductions may help you spot all of the chains, it can be time consuming, and if the chains are long, stringing together three or four rules, your Master Sketch can become too cluttered. As long as you have written the rules neatly, and have lined up the "If"s and the "then"s of your Formal Logic, you should be able to spot any case in which one rule (or contrapositive) triggers another rule (or contrapositive).

Any time that LSAT experts disagree, it means that there is no one "correct" or "proper" way to do something on the test. (After all, the experts all got very high scores on the LSAT by doing it their own ways, right?) During practice, experiment a little with Selection rules and deductions. Try one game by writing out the chains of logic you discover. Then, try another by leaving your rules as-is and spotting the chains as they arise during the questions. You'll discover what works best for you when you are actually working in context.

You can try that out here, as you revisit the model games you've been working on throughout this chapter.

Practice

Directions: In each game setup, first reacquaint yourself with the setup and rules. Then, combine the rules and restrictions to make all available deductions, recording your analyses as indicated. Finally, test your deductions by answering the questions that accompany each game. You can find expert analysis and explanations at the end of the Practice section.

Practice 1

A graphic designer must choose colors for a new logo from among the seven—fuchsia, grapefruit, hibiscus, indigo, jade, kiwi, and lemon—suggested by the client. The color selection must conform to the following conditions:

If grapefruit is used, then lemon cannot be used.
If jade is used, then indigo must also be used.
If indigo is used, then lemon must also be used.
If fuchsia is not used, then grapefruit must be used.
Hibiscus and kiwi cannot both be used.

1. Which entities or positions are the most restricted in this game? Why?

2. Which elements from the BLEND checklist can you identify in this game? Are there
   - Blocks of entities? If so, what are they?
   - Limited Options? If so, which rule(s) trigger them?
   - Established Entities? If so, which ones?
   - Number Restrictions? If so, describe them.
   - Duplications? If so, which rules share an entity?

3. Combine the rules and restrictions to create a Master Sketch depicting all of the deductions available in this game:

4. Evaluate your sketch by answering the following questions:
   - What is the maximum number of colors that could be selected?
   - If just one color was used, what could it be?
   - Which colors directly guarantee the selection of another color?
   - If lemon is used, what other color(s) must ultimately be used?

Practice 2

Melanie is planning a series of performances to promote her new relaxation CD. At each performance, she will play at least four of the pieces—*Atmosphere*, *Beats*, *Clouds*, *Dynamic*, *Ecologica*, *Firefly*, and *Glaciers*—that appear on the CD. Her selection for each performance is based on the following conditions:

> *Beats* must be played at any performance that includes *Glaciers*.
> *Firefly* will not be played at any performance that includes *Glaciers*.
> *Ecologica* will not be played at any performance that includes both *Beats* and *Glaciers*.
> If *Dynamic* is played, then *Atmosphere* is as well.
> *Clouds* will be played at every performance.

1. Which entities or positions are the most restricted in this game? Why?

2. Which elements from the BLEND checklist can you identify in this game? Are there
   - Blocks of entities? If so, what are they?
   - Limited Options? If so, which rule(s) trigger them?
   - Established Entities? If so, which ones?
   - Number Restrictions? If so, describe them.
   - Duplications? If so, which rules share an entity?

3. Combine the rules and restrictions to create a Master Sketch depicting all of the deductions available in this game:

4. Evaluate your sketch by answering the following questions:
   - What is the maximum number of pieces at any performance?
   - What is the maximum number of pieces that are *not* performed at any performance?
   - What pieces must be performed?
   - What piece(s) cannot be performed if *Firefly* is performed?

Practice 3

Writers for a science magazine submitted eight articles to their editor, each on a different topic—anatomy, biochemistry, climatology, ecology, genetics, hydrology, immunology, and neuroscience. The editor will select exactly four of the articles for publication in the next issue, based on the following guidelines:

> The issue will include an article on either climatology or neuroscience, but not both.
> If the article on biochemistry is not included, then the article on ecology will be included.
> The article on genetics will not be included unless the article on immunology is included.
> If the article on hydrology is included, then the article on anatomy is not included.
> The article on ecology will be included if, but only if, the article on anatomy is included.

1. Which entities or positions are the most restricted in this game? Why?

2. Which elements from the BLEND checklist can you identify in this game? Are there
    - Blocks of entities? If so, what are they?
    - Limited Options? If so, which rule(s) trigger them?
    - Established Entities? If so, which ones?
    - Number Restrictions? If so, describe them.
    - Duplications? If so, which rules share an entity?

3. Combine the rules and restrictions to create a Master Sketch depicting all of the deductions available in this game:

4. Evaluate your sketch by answering the following questions:
    - How many of the submitted articles will not be included?
    - Which article(s) must be selected?
    - If the ecology article is selected, which other article(s) must also be selected?
    - Which articles cannot be selected if the climatology article is selected?

Explanations

Compare your work to that of an LSAT expert. Pay close attention to how the expert combined the rules and restrictions to make additional deductions, and to how the expert depicted the deductions within the sketch framework.

Practice 1

A graphic designer must choose colors for a new logo from among the seven—fuchsia, grapefruit, hibiscus, indigo, jade, kiwi, and lemon— suggested by the client. The color selection must conform to the following conditions:

> If grapefruit is used, then lemon cannot be used.
> If jade is used, then indigo must also be used.
> If indigo is used, then lemon must also be used.
> If fuchsia is not used, then grapefruit must be used.
> Hibiscus and kiwi cannot both be used.

1. Which entities or positions are the most restricted in this game? Why? *Lots of entities are mentioned multiple times, so no single entity stands out as the most significant.*

2. Which elements from the BLEND checklist can you identify in this game? Are there

   • Blocks of entities? If so, what are they? *N/A*

   • Limited Options? If so, which rule(s) trigger them? *N/A*

   • Established Entities? If so, which ones? *N/A*

   • Number Restrictions? If so, describe them. *Rule 1 prevents two colors from being together, dropping the maximum to six total colors. Rule 5 prevents two other colors from being together, dropping the maximum to five total colors.*

   • Duplications? If so, which rules share an entity? *Rules 1 and 3 mention lemon. Rules 1 and 4 mention grapefruit. Rules 2 and 3 mention indigo.*

3. Combine the rules and restrictions to create a Master Sketch depicting all of the deductions available in this game: *It's possible to combine various pieces of logic. For example, if lemon is used, then grapefruit is not, which then means fuchsia is. However, when every rule (or almost every rule) is based on Formal Logic, it's often not worth drawing every possible string. Simply have the triggers lined up. If a trigger produces a result, see if that new result triggers another piece of logic.*

   F G H I J K L

   If G → ~L   Never ⟨G L⟩
   If L → ~G

   If J → I
   If ~I → ~J

   If I → L
   If ~L → ~I

   If ~F → G   F or G (or both)
   If ~G → F

   Never ⟨H K⟩

4. Evaluate your sketch by answering the following questions:

   • What is the maximum number of colors that could be selected? *Five. Of the seven, the selection can't have both grapefruit and lemon, and can't have both hibiscus and kiwi.*

   • If just one color was used, what could it be? *Fuchsia or grapefruit.*

   • Which colors directly guarantee the selection of another color? *Jade (which guarantees indigo) and indigo (which guarantees lemon).*

   • If lemon is used, what other color(s) must ultimately be used? *Fuchsia; with lemon, there can be no grapefruit, which means fuchsia must be used.*

Practice 2

Melanie is planning a series of performances to promote her new relaxation CD. At each performance, she will play at least four of the pieces—*Atmosphere*, *Beats*, *Clouds*, *Dynamic*, *Ecologica*, *Firefly*, and *Glaciers*—that appear on the CD. Her selection for each performance is based on the following conditions:

> *Beats* must be played at any performance that includes *Glaciers*.
> *Firefly* will not be played at any performance that includes *Glaciers*.
> *Ecologica* will not be played at any performance that includes both *Beats* and *Glaciers*.
> If *Dynamic* is played, then *Atmosphere* is as well.
> *Clouds* will be played at every performance.

1. Which entities or positions are the most restricted in this game? Why? *Glaciers is mentioned in each of the first three rules, so it will have the most impact.*

2. Which elements from the BLEND checklist can you identify in this game? Are there

   - Blocks of entities? If so, what are they? *N/A*
   - Limited Options? If so, which rule(s) trigger them? *N/A*
   - Established Entities? If so, which ones? *Rule 5 established Clouds as selected.*
   - Number Restrictions? If so, describe them. *Rule 2 prevents two pieces from being together, reducing the maximum to 6 pieces. Rule 3 also prevents every piece from being used, but the repeated use of Glaciers does not allow for further reductions after Rule 2.*
   - Duplications? If so, which rules share an entity? *Rules 1, 2, and 3 mention Glaciers. Rules 1 and 3 mention Beats.*

3. Combine the rules and restrictions to create a Master Sketch depicting all of the deductions available in this game: *Although Clouds is selected, that leads to no further deductions. The rest of the rules are based on Formal Logic, so no concrete deductions can be made. Any remaining song can be selected or not, depending on what else is selected.*

A   B   Ⓒ   D   E   F   G   4-6 selected

If G	→ B	
If ~B	→ ~G	
If G	→ ~F	Never $\boxed{G\ F}$
If F	→ ~G	
If B and G	→ ~E	Never $\boxed{B\ G\ E}$
If E	→ ~B or ~G	
If D	→ A	
IF ~A	→ ~D	

4. Evaluate your sketch by answering the following questions:

   - What is the maximum number of pieces at any performance? *Six; Glaciers would prevent other pieces from being performed. However, if Glaciers is out, everything else could be in without violating any rules.*
   - What is the maximum number of pieces that are *not* performed at any performance? *Three; at least four are in, so only three can be out.*
   - What pieces must be performed? *Only Clouds; everything else can be in or out, depending on what else is performed.*
   - What piece(s) cannot be performed if *Firefly* is performed? *Glaciers.*

Practice 3

Writers for a science magazine submitted eight articles to their editor, each on a different topic—anatomy, biochemistry, climatology, ecology, genetics, hydrology, immunology, and neuroscience. The editor will select exactly four of the articles for publication in the next issue, based on the following guidelines:

> The issue will include an article on either climatology or neuroscience, but not both.
> If the article on biochemistry is not included, then the article on ecology will be included.
> The article on genetics will not be included unless the article on immunology is included.
> If the article on hydrology is included, then the article on anatomy is not included.
> The article on ecology will be included if, but only if, the article on anatomy is included.

1. Which entities or positions are the most restricted in this game? Why? *Anatomy and ecology, as the last rule severely restricts their selection and each one affects the selection of other entities.*

2. Which elements from the BLEND checklist can you identify in this game? Are there

    • Blocks of entities? If so, what are they? *Rule 5 effectively makes anatomy and ecology a block, as they will be both in or both out.*

    • Limited Options? If so, which rule(s) trigger them? *Rule 5 provides two outcomes: either anatomy and ecology are both in, or they're both out.*

    • Established Entities? If so, which ones? *Rule 1 establishes one of the articles as either climatology or neuroscience.*

    • Number Restrictions? If so, describe them. *The Overview sets the numbers of exactly four in and four out.*

    • Duplications? If so, which rules share an entity? *Rules 2 and 5 mention ecology, while rules 4 and 5 mention anatomy.*

3. Combine the rules and restrictions to create a Master Sketch depicting all of the deductions available in this game:

The last rule creates two options. In the first option, both the anatomy and ecology articles are selected. That means the hydrology article is out.

```
     in                      out
 A   E  __  __  |  H   __  __  __
```

In that case, a third article included will be on either climatology or neuroscience. The other will be a second article out.

```
     in                      out
 A   E  C/N  __ |  H   N/C  __  __
```

One more article needs to be included. All that remains are biochemistry, genetics, and immunology. However, genetics can't be included without immunology, so genetics must be out. The last article will be either biochemistry or immunology.

```
     in                      out
 A   E  C/N  B/I|  H   N/C  G   I/B
```

In the second option, the anatomy and ecology articles are both out.

```
     in                      out
 __  __  __  __ |  A   E   __  __
```

That means the biochemistry article must be included. A second article included will be on either climatology or neuroscience. The other will be a third article out.

```
     in                      out
 B   C/N  __  __|  A   E   N/C  __
```

That leaves genetics, hydrology, and immunology. Only one more can be left out. However, immunology can't be left out without also leaving out genetics. So, immunology must be included, along with either genetics or hydrology. The remaining article will be the final one out.

in out

B C/N I G/H | A E N/C H/G

4. Evaluate your sketch by answering the following questions:

- How many of the submitted articles will not be included? *Four.*

- Which article(s) must be selected? *None; each of the eight articles could be selected depending on what else is selected.*

- If the ecology article is selected, which other article(s) must also be selected? *Anatomy.*

- Which articles cannot be selected if the climatology article is selected? *Neuroscience.*

You've done a lot of work building up your expertise in Selection games, especially so if you started this chapter as a Formal Logic novice. In the last section of Chapter 8, evaluate your mastery of these new skills with two officially released Selection games.

SELECTION GAMES—FULL GAMES WITH QUESTIONS

> ## LEARNING OBJECTIVES
>
> In this section, you'll assess your ability to
>
> - Apply the Logic Games Method to Selection games.

Perform

Here is your opportunity to put all of the pieces together and assess your skills on Selection games. On the following pages, you'll find two full-length games along with their question sets. Both of these games are from officially released LSAT tests, and are representative of Selection games you could see on Test Day. You can take the games one at a time or together, but for your self-evaluation to be as accurate as possible, adhere to the timing guidelines set forth in the directions.

An answer key follows the games. Complete worked example expert analyses can be found in your online resources.

After you complete and review both games, assess your performance using the evaluation guidelines. There, you'll find recommendations for additional Easy, Medium, and Hard Selection games from officially released LSAT exams that you can practice to continue honing your skills and raising your score.

Directions: Take no more than 9 minutes per game to complete the following two games and all of their questions.

Perform 1

Questions 1–6

Fu, Gunsel, Jackson, Kowalski, Lee, Mayer, and Ordoveza are the only applicants being considered for some positions at a nonprofit organization. Only applicants who are interviewed will be hired. The hiring process must meet the following constraints:

    If Gunsel is interviewed, Jackson is interviewed.
    If Jackson is interviewed, Lee is interviewed.
    Fu is interviewed.
    Fu is not hired, unless Kowalski is interviewed.
    Kowalski is not hired, unless Mayer is interviewed.
    If Mayer is hired, and Lee is interviewed, Ordoveza is hired.

1. Which one of the following could be a complete and accurate list of the applicants that are interviewed?

    (A)   Fu, Gunsel
    (B)   Fu, Jackson
    (C)   Fu, Lee
    (D)   Fu, Gunsel, Lee
    (E)   Fu, Gunsel, Jackson

2. Which one of the following could be true?

   (A) Lee and Mayer are the only applicants interviewed.
   (B) Fu, Jackson, and Kowalski are the only applicants interviewed.
   (C) Gunsel and one other applicant are the only applicants interviewed.
   (D) Gunsel and two other applicants are the only applicants interviewed.
   (E) Gunsel and three other applicants are the only applicants interviewed.

3. If Mayer is not interviewed, which one of the following must be true?

   (A) Kowalski is not interviewed.
   (B) Kowalski is interviewed but not hired.
   (C) Fu is not hired.
   (D) Fu is hired but Kowalski is not hired.
   (E) Fu is interviewed but Kowalski is not hired.

4. If Gunsel and five other applicants are the only applicants interviewed, and if exactly three applicants are hired, then which one of the following could be an accurate list of the applicants hired?

   (A) Fu, Lee, Mayer
   (B) Fu, Kowalski, Mayer
   (C) Kowalski, Lee, Ordoveza
   (D) Gunsel, Jackson, Mayer
   (E) Gunsel, Jackson, Lee

5. If every applicant that is interviewed is hired, and if Lee is hired, then each of the following applicants must be interviewed EXCEPT:

   (A) Fu
   (B) Jackson
   (C) Kowalski
   (D) Mayer
   (E) Ordoveza

6. If Ordoveza is not interviewed, and if exactly four applicants are hired, then which one of the following must be false?

   (A) Lee is hired.
   (B) Mayer is hired.
   (C) Jackson is interviewed.
   (D) Kowalski is interviewed.
   (E) Gunsel is interviewed.

PrepTest23 Sec1 Qs 6–11

Perform 2

<u>Questions 7–12</u>

From a group of seven people—J, K, L, M, N, P, and Q—
exactly four will be selected to attend a diplomat's retirement
dinner. Selection must conform to the following conditions:

    Either J or K must be selected, but J and K cannot both
      be selected.

    Either N or P must be selected, but N and P cannot both
      be selected.

    N cannot be selected unless L is selected.

    Q cannot be selected unless K is selected.

7. Which one of the following could be the four people
selected to attend the retirement dinner?

(A) J, K, M, P
(B) J, L, N, Q
(C) J, M, N, Q
(D) K, M, P, Q
(E) L, M, N, P

8. Among the people selected to attend the retirement dinner there must be

    (A) K or Q or both
    (B) L or M or both
    (C) N or M or both
    (D) N or Q or both
    (E) P or Q or both

9. Which one of the following is a pair of people who CANNOT both be selected to attend the retirement dinner?

    (A) J and N
    (B) J and Q
    (C) K and L
    (D) K and N
    (E) N and Q

10. If M is not selected to attend the retirement dinner, the four people selected to attend must include which one of the following pairs of people?

    (A) J and Q
    (B) K and L
    (C) K and P
    (D) L and P
    (E) N and Q

11. If P is not selected to attend the retirement dinner, then exactly how many different groups of four are there each of which would be an acceptable selection?

    (A) one
    (B) two
    (C) three
    (D) four
    (E) five

12. There is only one acceptable group of four that can be selected to attend the retirement dinner if which one of the following pairs of people is selected?

    (A) J and L
    (B) K and M
    (C) L and N
    (D) L and Q
    (E) M and Q

PrepTest9 Sec3 Qs 8–13

Answer Key

Perform 1
1. (C)
2. (E)
3. (E)
4. (E)
5. (B)
6. (B)

Perform 2
7. (D)
8. (B)
9. (B)
10. (B)
11. (C)
12. (E)

Worked example explanations of these questions with complete expert analysis can be found in your Online Study Plan under Chapter 8. View or download the PDF titled "Chapter 8 Perform Full Games Explanations."

Assess

Use the following criteria to evaluate your results on the Perform games.

If, under timed conditions, you correctly answered

10–12 of the questions: Outstanding! You have demonstrated a strong skill level in Selection games. For further practice in Selection, use any of the Recommended Additional Practice sets, including the Advanced set. Then, move on to Chapter 9 on Matching and Distribution games.

7–9 of the questions: Good work! You have a solid foundation in Selection games. For further practice in basic Selection, begin with the Foundations or Mid-Level Recommended Additional Practice set. Then, move on to Chapter 9 on Matching and Distribution games. If you have time before Test Day, try the Advanced Recommended Additional Selection Practice set, as well.

0–6 of the questions: Keep working. Selection games do not show up frequently, but the practice with Formal Logic will pay off in other game types and on Logical Reasoning as well. Continued practice will help you improve your score. Begin by reviewing this chapter. Then, try the games in the Foundations Recommended Additional Practice set. As you continue to progress, move on to the Mid-Level Recommended Additional Practice set. Then, move on to Chapter 9 on Matching and Distribution games.

To stay sharp, practice the drills in the Logic Games Training Camp for this chapter in your Online Study Plan. Training Camp drills are divided into Fundamentals, Mid-Level, and Advanced sets.

Recommended Additional Practice: Selection

All of the following games will provide good practice on Selection. They are grouped by difficulty as determined from empirical student practice results. All PrepTests included are available individually, or in bundles of ten as part of the LSAC's *10 Actual, Official LSAT PrepTests* series.

> **Foundations**
> PrepTest 58, Section 3, Game 2: Day Care Volunteers**
> PrepTest 54, Section 3, Game 1: Dancers on Stage**
>
> **Mid-Level**
> PrepTest 70, Section 3, Game 2: Corporate Research Team*
> PrepTest 65, Section 2, Game 3: Luncheon Foods*
>
> **Advanced**
> PrepTest 59, Section 1, Game 3: Alicia's Courses**
> PrepTest 58, Section 3, Game 4: Summer School Courses**

*Game included in *10 Actual, Official LSAT PrepTests Volume V: PrepTests 62-71*; complete answers and explanations written by Kaplan LSAT experts available via the eBook: *LSAT PrepTests 62-71 Unlocked: Exclusive Data, Analysis & Explanations for 10 Actual, Official LSAT PrepTests Volume V.*

**Game included in *10 New Actual, Official LSAT PrepTests with Comparative Reading (PrepTests 52-61)*; complete answers and explanations written by Kaplan LSAT experts available via the eBook: *LSAT PrepTests 52-61 Unlocked: Exclusive Data, Analysis & Explanations for 10 New Actual, Official LSAT PrepTests with Comparative Reading.* [Explanations title coming Fall 2018.]

Reflect

Think back over the study and practice you did in this chapter.

- Are you able to identify Selection games from their setups?
- Do you have a default sketch framework for Selection actions?
- What kinds of rules do you anticipate seeing in Selection games?
- Are you comfortable analyzing Selection rules, translating them to Formal Logic and writing their contrapositives?
- Are you making the available deductions efficiently and effectively when a rule is triggered in a Selection game?

In the coming days and weeks before Test Day, take note of real-world tasks that reflect Selection tasks. Consider how they mirror the setups and questions in LSAT Selection, and how they differ. Try to reframe real-life sequencing tasks using the terms, rules, and restrictions used by the testmaker.

CHAPTER 9

Matching and Distribution Games Unlocked

LEARNING OBJECTIVES

In this chapter, you'll learn to

- Apply the Logic Games Method to Matching games
- Apply the Logic Games Method to Distribution games

Taken together, Matching and Distribution games have been about as common as Strict Sequencing games on LSAT tests released over the past five years. This is due largely to the recent popularity of Distribution games, which have accounted for over 20 percent of games on the 15 LSATs released from 2012 through 2016. That's a dramatic increase from 2007 to 2011, during which time Distribution accounted for just under seven percent of all games. Matching games haven't seen a similar increase in recent years, but they account for just under 12 percent of all games on tests released from 2012 through 2016.

Types of Games By Percentage, 2012–2016

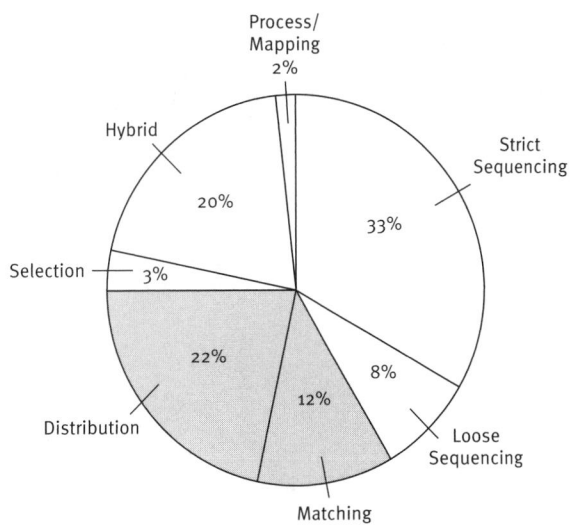

There is a reason to cover Matching and Distribution games in the same chapter. They are similar, so much so that LSAT experts will sometimes argue about which of the two categories a particular game falls into. Both involve grouping entities under two or more headings, and at times, their initial sketches can look quite similar. There is, however, an important distinction between the two game types, and covering them side by side will help you spot it and appreciate its importance.

The primary distinction between the two game types concerns the number of times each of the entities may be used in the game. In a standard Distribution game, you are tasked with dividing up a set of entities into two or more groups or teams. In most Distribution games, once an entity is placed into a group, the entity cannot be placed anywhere else. If Johnny plays for the Red Team, it stands to reason that he can't play for the Blue Team at the same time.

Blue	Red
—	J
—	—
—	—

In Matching, on the other hand, you have two sets of entities, and your job is to assign items or attributes in one set to each of the individuals in the other set. Matching tasks allow you assign the same item or attribute more than once. In a game in which you are matching colors to pieces of clothing, for example, nothing seems inherently strange about saying that two skiers both wear blue parkas.

	S	T	V
hat			
parka	b		b
gloves			

b = blue
g = gold
r = red

As you work through the practice exercises and full games in this chapter, keep that fundamental difference between the two game types in mind. Mastery of these games will provide a huge boost to your success in the Logic Games section of the LSAT.

MATCHING AND DISTRIBUTION GAMES IN REAL LIFE

Real-life Matching

Like all logic game tasks, Matching games correspond to real-life situations that you deal with regularly. Making decisions about what each of several guests will have for dinner provides a perfect illustration. Imagine you have five friends or family members coming over for a meal; call them A, B, C, D, and E. You've prepared plenty of food for everyone. You have two kinds of soup: split pea and minestrone. You have three different entrées: ham, pasta, and roast beef. You've even made a dessert. In real life, absent any artificial rules, your guests could say, "Oh, I want to try both soups," or "I'll have a little ham and a little of the pasta." Some of your guests will have dessert, and some might be too full. Your main concern—and this is what corresponds with the Matching task in a logic game—is that there's plenty for everyone. You can give B ham and still have some left to serve to D and E if they'd like to have it, too. Nothing (except running out) prevents you from serving everyone the roast beef, or anything else.

Now, you can see how the LSAT imposes restrictions on this kind of game. The testmaker can limit the number of entrées each guest has. (The simplest games would simply say, "Each guest will have exactly one kind of soup and exactly one entrée.") They could set restrictions among the guests, e.g., "C will not have any kind of food that A has," or, "B and D will have the same kind of soup." Likewise, they can impose restrictions based on the foods, e.g., "Any guest who has the split pea soup will have ham for an entrée," or, "No guest will have both the minestrone soup and the pasta." Number restrictions are just as important in Matching games as they are in Selection games—or, as you will soon see, Distribution games—but because the items to be matched can be reused, the numbers will play out along two dimensions of the game. In our dinner example, you'll need to pay attention to how many kinds of food you serve to individual guests and how many servings of each kind of food you serve. It's always valuable in Matching to have a clear orientation (an *x*-axis and *y*-axis, if you will) for each part of your task.

$$
\begin{array}{cccccc}
 & A & B & C & D & E \\
m/sp & \_ & \_ & \_ & \_ & \_ \\
h/p/rb & \_ & \_ & \_ & \_ & \_ \\
des\ y/n & \_ & \_ & \_ & \_ & \_ \\
\end{array}
$$

Record the number restrictions along the appropriate rows and columns. That diagram isn't tough to understand, although this fictional menu is more complicated than any Matching game that has actually appeared on the LSAT over the last 10 years.

Real-life Distribution

You engage in Distribution tasks whenever you choose teams for a game, decide which piece of clothing goes in which drawer, assign people to certain locations, or even when you deal out cards from a deck. The key thing to notice is that, in Distribution tasks, once you assign someone or something to a team or a place, you cannot simultaneously assign it somewhere else; the grey suit can't hang in the hall closet and the bedroom closet at the same time; Joe can't be at the New York office and the Boston office concurrently. Think of the entities in Distribution games as individual physical beings or objects. You might move the green chair from the living room to the den, but it can't be in both places at once.

Because real-world models for Distribution so often spring from activities like games and sports, your default assumption will often be that the teams or groups must be made up of equal numbers of players or entities. In most real-world games, each player gets the same number of cards or playing pieces to start. As you've already read (and will again), check your assumptions at the door when you approach logic games. The testmaker must be explicit about number restrictions in Distribution games. If they aren't, don't impose your own limitations.

While there are examples of Distribution tasks that follow an "equal groups" model, there are plenty that don't. A real-world model for Distribution games with unequal teams is a work assignment in which your boss tells you to assign eight employees to three different projects—logistics, marketing, and real estate, let's say—one project per person.

B C E J N O P R

log	mktg	r/e

Your first question might be, "How many people do you want on each task?" But your boss responds, "You tell me. I want those projects finished ASAP. If the marketing initiative needs more bodies than the real estate plan, so be it." Like a Distribution setup on the test, your boss might impose some limits without giving you exact numbers: for example, "Just don't put more than four people on the real estate plan."

B C E J N O P R

		(max 4)
log	mktg	r/e

You might wish that your boss would be more definite, but you wouldn't let this response stop you from making the proposed assignments. Don't let the lack of numbers stop you from attacking a Distribution game, either.

What's definite in almost any real-world Distribution task is that there are certain people or items you'll want to keep together and certain ones you'll want to keep apart. In choosing basketball teams, you might say, "Tom and Dave are team captains," in order to keep the two tallest guys from being on the same team. Arranging your furniture, you might think, "The chair could go in the living room or the den, but either way, the ottoman has to go with it."

Even your boss might tell you, "I don't care which project you put Peggy on, but don't assign Chuck to the same one," or, "Just make sure Evelyn and Nancy are working together; they're a good team."

B C E J N O P R

		(max 4)
log	mktg	r/e

Never
C
P

E
N

Thinking about how common such restrictions are in real life should take a lot of the sting out of the Formal Logic rules that sometimes appear in Distribution games. It's unlikely that you'd wring your hands or get confused if your boss said, "Look, if you assign Evelyn to the marketing campaign, then put Rosa on the real estate planning team."

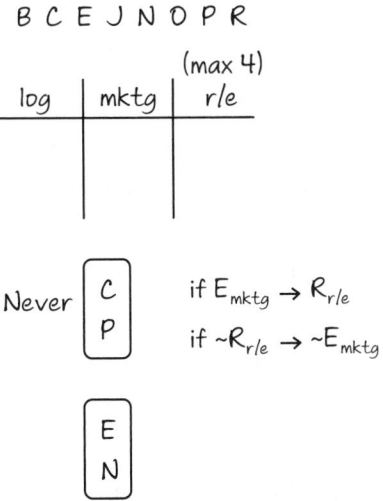

Don't let the testmaker undermine your confidence by using formal conditions, either.

Keep these everyday tasks in mind as you practice Steps 1–4 on Matching and Distribution setups. Logic Games setups almost always present tasks that you would feel confident handling in real life.

MATCHING GAMES TASKS AND SKETCHES

LEARNING OBJECTIVES

In this section of the chapter, you'll practice

- Applying Steps 1 and 2 of the Logic Games Method to Matching games by
  - Asking the SEAL questions to analyze the game's Overview, and then
  - Creating a simple, useful Sketch framework

Prepare

The key to recognizing a Matching game is to find what appears to be two sets of entities. One set is unchanging—the "anchor" set of the game, if you will—and is made up of the people, places, or things receiving items or attributes from the second set. The second set is flexible; some of the people or places in the first set will get all of the items or attributes in the second set, while others may get only some of the items or attributes. Most importantly, in Matching games, the items or attributes in the second set can be matched to more than one of the "anchor" entities.

LOGIC GAMES STRATEGY

Matching games ask you to match

- Attributes, items, or tasks to a certain set of people, places, or things, or
- Attributes (such as color) to a set of items belonging to a certain set of people.

To make the definition of Matching tasks more concrete, consider the following game setup, and consider how an LSAT expert decided to depict its initial sketch.

In downtown Farlow, there are three doughnut shops, one each on H Street, J Street, and L Street. Each of the shops sells between two and four of the following kinds of doughnuts—crullers, glazed, old fashioned, and sprinkles. The following conditions apply:

c g o s

H	J	L
—	—	—
—	—	—
(—)	(—)	(—)
(—)	(—)	(—)

The game's task is to determine the types of doughnuts sold at each of three shops. The shops serve as the "anchor" set of entities. They are unchanging. The doughnuts are the items that will be matched to each shop. The shops can have different numbers of doughnuts. Some may sell one or more types sold in another shop. This is a classic Matching game task.

For the record, that game (and virtually all Matching games) could also be depicted with a grid sketch. LSAT experts vary on which type of sketch they prefer. Whenever high scorers use slightly different tactics with equal success, it's a good idea for you to practice a bit with both approaches to see which works best for you.

2 – 4 *each*

	H	J	L
c			
g			
D			
S			

As an aside, students often ask how they can know which set of entities should go on the *x*-axis of their sketch and which should go on the *y*-axis. The answer is that it really doesn't matter as long it's consistent throughout the game. Most people instinctively place the "anchor" set horizontally along the *x*-axis. But, as a practical matter, if you find that the orientation of your sketch is confusing you, stop. Redraw the sketch in the way you've discovered makes more sense, and then get back to the game. Struggling through a game for several minutes with a sketch your brain doesn't fully comprehend will cost you time and, potentially, points on the test. Taking a few seconds to "fix" the sketch is well worth the small effort it takes.

Practice identifying and sketching Matching tasks with the model game setups that follow. Complete expert analysis can be found on the pages following the exercise.

Practice

Directions: Conduct an Overview of each game's setup by asking the SEAL questions, and create an initial sketch framework for the game's action.

Practice 1

A chef will prepare each of three entrées—K, L, and M—each of which will contain at least three of the following ingredients—buttermilk, garlic, onion, paprika, and salt. Each ingredient is used at least once. Preparation of the entrées must also conform to the following conditions:

1. [Step 1] Conduct an Overview analysis:
   - What is this game's Situation?

   - Who or what are the game's Entities?

   - What is the game's Action?

   - What are the Limitations explicit in the game setup?

2. [Step 2] Create an initial Sketch:

Practice 2

A financial advisor is meeting with four clients—Jordan, Klaus, Lisa, and Marie. Each client is investing in at least one of five mutual funds—energy, financials, gold, healthcare, and international—and no others. Investing choices must conform to the following conditions:

1. [Step 1] Conduct an Overview analysis:
   - What is this game's Situation?

   - Who or what are the game's Entities?

   - What is the game's Action?

   - What are the Limitations explicit in the game setup?

2. [Step 2] Create an initial Sketch:

Practice 3

A video game designer is creating a game for young children that involves players progressing through four separate levels, from level 1 to level 4. On each level, players are offered at least one reward—an apple, a bagel, or a cookie—and will encounter at least one obstacle—a mud pit, an oil slick, or quicksand. The designer is limited by the following constraints:

1. [Step 1] Conduct an Overview analysis:

    - What is this game's Situation?

    - Who or what are the game's Entities?

    - What is the game's Action?

    - What are the Limitations explicit in the game setup?

2. [Step 2] Create an initial Sketch:

Explanations

Compare your work to that of an LSAT expert. Keep track of any case in which you incorrectly characterized the action described in the setup, and any case in which you drew a sketch framework that does not match the details of the game's situation.

Practice 1

A chef will prepare each of three entrées—K, L, and M—each of which will contain at least three of the following ingredients—buttermilk, garlic, onion, paprika, and salt. Each ingredient is used at least once. Preparation of the entrées must also conform to the following conditions:

1. [Step 1] Conduct an Overview analysis:

    • What is this game's Situation? *A chef preparing three entrées.*

    • Who or what are the game's Entities? *Three entrées—K, L, and M—and five ingredients—b, g, o, p, and s.*

    • What is the game's Action? *Matching; determine which ingredients will be used in each entrée.*

    • What are the Limitations explicit in the game setup? *Each entrée will receive at least three ingredients. Each ingredient needs to be used at least once.*

2. [Step 2] Create an initial Sketch:

b g o p s

K	L	M
—	—	—
—	—	—
—	—	—

Practice 2

A financial advisor is meeting with four clients—Jordan, Klaus, Lisa, and Marie. Each client is investing in at least one of five mutual funds—energy, financials, gold, healthcare, and international—and no others. Investing choices must conform to the following conditions:

1. [Step 1] Conduct an Overview analysis:

    • What is this game's Situation? *Clients making investments into mutual funds.*

    • Who or what are the game's Entities? *Four clients—J, K, L, and M—and five mutual funds—e, f, g, h, i.*

    • What is the game's Action? *Matching; determine the mutual funds in which each person invests.*

    • What are the Limitations explicit in the game setup? *Each person invested in at least one fund, but there's no limit to how many people can invest in each fund. It's possible some funds go unused.*

2. [Step 2] Create an initial Sketch:

e f g h i

J	K	L	M
—	—	—	—

Practice 3

A video game designer is creating a game for young children that involves players progressing through four separate levels, from level 1 to level 4. On each level, players are offered at least one reward—an apple, a bagel, or a cookie—and will encounter at least one obstacle—a mud pit, an oil slick, or quicksand. The designer is limited by the following constraints:

1. [Step 1] Conduct an Overview analysis:

   - What is this game's Situation? *A video game designer creating levels for a kid's game.*

   - Who or what are the game's Entities? *Four levels—1, 2, 3, and 4—and six items— rewards A, B, and C; obstacles m, o, and q.*

- What is the game's Action? *Matching; for each level, determine which rewards and/or obstacles will appear.*

- What are the Limitations explicit in the game setup? *Each floor will include at least one reward and at least one obstacle. No limits are set, so it's possible that some rewards or obstacles will not appear in the game.*

2. [Step 2] Create an initial Sketch:

	1	2	3	4	
rew:	_	_	_	_	A B C
obst:	_	_	_	_	m o q

With your sketches in place, it's time to add in the rules. Practice applying Step 2 of the Logic Games Method to Matching games in the next section.

MATCHING GAMES RULES

Prepare

Numbers are at the heart of Matching games, and it's likely that one or more rules will present some restriction on how many attributes can be matched to particular "anchor" entities, and that other rules will establish or limit the number of "anchor" entities to which a particular attribute can be matched. Those number restrictions—along with simpler rules that stipulate that a particular anchor must or cannot have a given attribute, or that certain attributes must or cannot be matched to the same "anchor"—usually lead to important deductions during Step 4 in Matching games.

LOGIC GAMES STRATEGY

Matching rules tell you one or more of the following:

- Attributes that must or cannot be matched to the same entity.
- The number of attributes that must, can, or cannot be assigned to an entity, or the relative numbers among entities (e.g., Frances is assigned to review more books than Greg is).
- Conditions triggering the assignment of an attribute to a particular entity (e.g., if Horace's painting has blue in it, then Inez's painting has red in it).

How you choose to depict the rules in Matching games depends a lot on how you chose to draw the initial sketch. To see this in action, here is the doughnut–shop setup along with four typical Matching rules.

In downtown Farlow, there are three doughnut shops, one each on H Street, J Street, and L Street. Each of the shops sells between two and four of the following kinds of doughnuts—crullers, glazed, old fashioned, and sprinkles. The following conditions apply:

Exactly two shops sell old fashioned doughnuts.
Any shop that sells crullers does not sell glazed doughnuts.
The shop on L Street sells more kinds of doughnuts than the shop on J Street.
The shop on H Street sells glazed doughnuts.

Take a look at those rules depicted in the sketch you saw in the preceding section.

The LSAT expert noted Rule 1 above the "o" (for old fashioned) in the roster of entities to be matched. She jotted down Rule 2 in shorthand underneath the sketch. She noted Rule 3 just to the side of the columns representing the "anchor" entities, and it is built into the sketch in two ways: first, J's fourth slot is crossed off (if L sells more types of doughnuts than J, then J does not sell all four), and the possible numbers of doughnut types for J and L are recorded above their respective columns. Finally, Rule 4 was drawn directly into H's column. The expert even anticipated one of the deductions in this game. Because H sells glazed doughnuts, Rule 2 prevents it from selling crullers. Most rules in Matching games can be depicted in and around the initial sketch in ways that logically relate them to the entities they restrict.

Here's how those rules would appear in a grid sketch. Notice that the expert follows the same principles—depicting the rules in and around the entities they restrict—even though the sketch framework is slightly different.

Review the following expert analyses of a handful of other common Matching game rules. Here, again, pay attention to how the rules are depicted in ways that fit the game's sketch.

Rule	Analysis
A game in which three theaters—1, 2 and 3—each show at least one of five movies—a comedy, a drama, a fantasy, a horror film, and a mystery. C D F H M 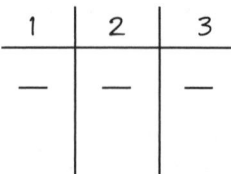	
Exactly two theaters will show the fantasy.	$\longrightarrow$ F = 2x
Exactly two films will be shown in theater 1.	$\longrightarrow$ 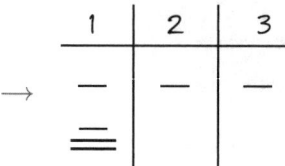
If theater 2 shows the horror film, then theater 3 shows the comedy.	$\longrightarrow$ If H in 2 → C in 3 If ~C in 3 → ~H in 2
A game in which four athletes—J, K, L, and M—each participate in at least one of three sports—rugby, soccer, or tennis. r s t J | K | L | M — — — —	
M participates in rugby.	$\longrightarrow$ J | K | L | M — — — r
J participates in exactly the same sports as K.	$\longrightarrow$ J = K
If L participates in soccer, then M participates in tennis.	$\longrightarrow$ If L = s → M = t If M ≠ t → L ≠ s

Now, practice analyzing and drawing Matching game rules. There are four exercises. The first provides 12 Matching game rules associated with four simple descriptions of the setups with which they are associated. Then, you'll see three exercises that add full sets of rules to each of the three setups you worked with in the previous section of this chapter.

Practice

Practice 1

Directions: Analyze and draw each of the following Matching game rules. Use the brief game description to guide your depiction of the game's framework.

Rule	My Analysis
A game in which three riders—L, M, and N—each ride at least one of six horses—a black horse, a champagne horse, a gray horse, a roan horse, a sorrel horse, and a white horse.	
1. L rides the gray horse. $\longrightarrow$	
2. The champagne horse and the white horse are never ridden by the same person. $\longrightarrow$	
3. M rides exactly two of the horses. $\longrightarrow$	
A game in which each of six albums—R, S, T, V, W, and X—contains at least one of three musical genres—classical, jazz, and opera.	
4. If R contains jazz, then S contains classical. $\longrightarrow$	
5. T and X have no musical genres in common. $\longrightarrow$	
6. Exactly three of the albums contain jazz. $\longrightarrow$	
A game in which four dresses each use at least one of six colors—green, orange, red, white, violet, and yellow.	
7. Any dress that contains red also contains white. $\longrightarrow$	
8. A dress contains yellow if, and only if, it contains green. $\longrightarrow$	
9. No dress can contain both orange and violet. $\longrightarrow$	
A game in which five houses—1, 2, 3, 4, and 5—each contain at least one of four features—balcony, fireplace, patio, and skylight.	
10. House 2 contains neither a patio nor a skylight. $\longrightarrow$	
11. No house contains both a balcony and a patio. $\longrightarrow$	
12. Houses 1 and 4 have no features in common. $\longrightarrow$	

Practice 2

Directions: Take a couple of minutes to review the game setup, summarize your Overview analysis, and recreate the initial Sketch. Then, one at a time, analyze the rules, answer the questions about each one, and draw the rule either inside or underneath the sketch framework.

A chef will prepare each of three entrées—K, L, and M—each of which will contain at least three of the following ingredients—buttermilk, garlic, onion, paprika, and salt. Each ingredient is used at least once. Preparation of the entrées must also conform to the following conditions:

No entrée contains all five ingredients.
Entrée L does not contain onion.
Garlic is used in exactly two of the entrées.
Entrée L contains more of these ingredients than entrée K.

1. [Step 1] Summarize your Overview analysis:

2. [Step 2] Create an initial Sketch:

3. [Step 3] Analyze and draw the Rules:
   - For each rule, answer the following questions and draw the rule in the appropriate box.
     - What does the rule restrict, and what does it leave open?
     - What are the rule's negative implications, if any?
     - Can the rule be depicted inside the sketch framework?

Rule 1:	Rule 2:
Rule 3:	Rule 4:

Practice 3

Directions: Take a couple of minutes to review the game setup, summarize your Overview analysis, and recreate the initial Sketch. Then, one at a time, analyze the rules, answer the questions about each one, and draw the rule either inside or underneath the sketch framework.

A financial advisor is meeting with four clients—Jordan, Klaus, Lisa, and Marie. Each client is investing in at least one of five mutual funds—energy, financials, gold, healthcare, and international—and no others. Investing choices must conform to the following conditions:

Lisa invests in gold.
Klaus invests in neither energy nor healthcare.
At least three of the clients invest in financials.
Klaus invests in every fund that Marie invests in.

1. [Step 1] Summarize your Overview analysis:

2. [Step 2] Create an initial Sketch:

3. [Step 3] Analyze and draw the Rules:
   - For each rule, answer the following questions and draw the rule in the appropriate box.
     - What does the rule restrict, and what does it leave open?
     - What are the rule's negative implications, if any?
     - Can the rule be depicted inside the sketch framework?

Rule 1:	Rule 2:
Rule 3:	Rule 4:

Practice 4

Directions: Take a couple of minutes to review the game setup, summarize your Overview analysis, and recreate the initial Sketch. Then, one at a time, analyze the rules, answer the questions about each one, and draw the rule either inside or underneath the sketch framework.

A video game designer is creating a game for young children that involves players progressing through four separate levels, from level 1 to level 4. On each level, players are offered at least one reward—an apple, a bagel, or a cookie—and will encounter at least one obstacle—a mud pit, an oil slick, or quicksand. The designer is limited by the following constraints:

No reward or obstacle can appear more than once on any level.
No reward can appear on three consecutive levels.
Level 2 has an apple, and level 3 has both a mud pit and quicksand.
Level 4 has a greater combined total of rewards and obstacles than does level 2.
Level 2 has a greater number of obstacles than each of level 3 and level 4.

1. [Step 1] Summarize your Overview analysis:

2. [Step 2] Create an initial Sketch:

3. [Step 3] Analyze and draw the Rules:
   - For each rule, answer the following questions and draw the rule in the appropriate box.
     - What does the rule restrict, and what does it leave open?
     - What are the rule's negative implications, if any?
     - Can the rule be depicted inside the sketch framework?

Rule 1:	Rule 2:
Rule 3:	Rule 4:
Rule 5:	

K

Explanations

Compare your work to that of an LSAT expert. Pay close attention to how the expert analyzed each rule and then depicted it within or beneath the game's initial sketch.

Practice 1

Rule	Analysis

A game in which three riders—L, M, and N, each ride at least one of six horses—a black horse, a champagne horse, a gray horse, a roan horse, a sorrel horse, and a white horse.

b c g r s w

L	M	N
—	—	—

1. L rides the gray horse.

$\longrightarrow$

L	M	N
g	—	—

2. The champagne horse and the white horse are never ridden by the same person.

$\longrightarrow$ never $\boxed{\begin{matrix} c \\ w \end{matrix}}$

3. M rides exactly two of the horses.

$\longrightarrow$

L	M	N
—	—	—
	=	

A game in which each of six albums—R, S, T, V, W, and X—contains at least one of three musical genres—classical, jazz, and opera.

c j o

R	S	T	V	W	X
—	—	—	—	—	—

4. If R contains jazz, then S contains classical.

$\longrightarrow$ If R = j → S = c

If S ≠ c → R ≠ j

5. T and X have no musical genres in common.

$\longrightarrow$ T ≠ X

6. Exactly three of the albums contain jazz.

$\longrightarrow$
c j o
  j   OR: exactly 3 j
  j
  =

A game in which four dresses each use at least one of six colors—green, orange, red, white, violet, and yellow.

G O R W V Y

1	2	3	4
—	—	—	—

---

7. Any dress that contains red also contains white.

⟶   If R → W

     If ~W → ~R

---

8. A dress contains yellow if, and only if, it contains green.

⟶   If Y → G   If G → Y

     If ~G → ~Y   If ~Y → ~G

---

9. No dress can contain both orange and violet.

⟶   never $\boxed{\begin{array}{c}O\\V\end{array}}$

A game in which each of five houses—1, 2, 3, 4, and 5—contains at least one of four features—balcony, fireplace, patio, and skylight.

B F P S

1	2	3	4	5
—	—	—	—	—

---

10. House 2 contains neither a patio nor a skylight.

⟶

1	2	3	4	5
—	B/F	—	—	—
	~P			
	~S			
	(BF?)			

---

11. No house contains both a balcony and a patio.

⟶   never $\boxed{\begin{array}{c}B\\P\end{array}}$

---

12. Houses 1 and 4 have no features in common.

⟶   1 ≠ 4

Practice 2

A chef will prepare each of three entrées—K, L, and M—each of which will contain at least three of the following ingredients—buttermilk, garlic, onion, paprika, and salt. Each ingredient is used at least once. Preparation of the entrées must also conform to the following conditions:

> No entrée contains all five ingredients.
> Entrée L does not contain onion.
> Garlic is used in exactly two of the entrées.
> Entrée L contains more of these ingredients than entrée K.

1. [Step 1] Summarize your Overview analysis: *A Matching game in which a chef will use at least three of five ingredients in each of three entrées. Ingredients can be used in multiple entrées, and each ingredient will be used at least once.*

2. [Step 2] Create an initial Sketch:

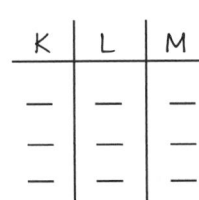

3. [Step 3] Analyze and draw the Rules:
   - Rule 1:
     - What does the rule restrict, and what does it leave open? *The rule prevents any entrée from having all five ingredients.*
     - What are the rule's negative implications, if any? *Because an entrée has at least three but can't have all five, an entrée is limited to either three or four ingredients.*
     - Can the rule be depicted inside the sketch framework? *No.*
     - Draw the rule:
       never all 5 ing.

- Rule 2:
  - What does the rule restrict, and what does it leave open? *Entrée L won't get onion, but it could still get anything else.*
  - What are the rule's negative implications, if any? *Either entrée K or M gets onion, if not both.*
  - Can the rule be depicted inside the sketch framework? *Yes.*
  - Draw the rule:

K	L	M
—	—	—
—	—	—
—	—	—
	~o	

- Rule 3:
  - What does the rule restrict, and what does it leave open? *Exactly two entrées get garlic, but it could be any pair.*
  - What are the rule's negative implications, if any? *One entrée will not get garlic.*
  - Can the rule be depicted inside the sketch framework? *No.*
  - Draw the rule:

  b g o p s
     g
     =

  Or: exactly 2g

- Rule 4:
  - What does the rule restrict, and what does it leave open? *Entrée L gets more ingredients than K.*
  - What are the rule's negative implications, if any? *Entrée L cannot have the minimum of three.*
  - Can the rule be depicted inside the sketch framework? *Yes; add a fourth slot to L, and draw a double line under K's three slots to indicate that it cannot have more ingredients.*

- Draw the rule:

$$
\begin{array}{c|c}
L & K \\
\hline
- & - \\
- & - \\
- & - \\
- & = \\
\end{array}
$$

Practice 3

A financial advisor is meeting with four clients—Jordan, Klaus, Lisa, and Marie. Each client has decided to invest in at least one of five mutual funds—energy, financials, gold, healthcare, and international—and no others. Investing choices must conform to the following conditions:

> Lisa invests in gold.
> Klaus invests in neither energy nor healthcare.
> At least three of the clients invest in financials.
> Klaus invests in every fund that Marie
>   invests in.

1. [Step 1] Summarize your Overview analysis: *A Matching game in which four people invest in one or more of five different mutual funds.*

2. [Step 2] Create an initial Sketch:

$$
e \ f \ g \ h \ i
$$

$$
\begin{array}{c|c|c|c}
J & K & L & M \\
\hline
- & - & - & - \\
\end{array}
$$

3. [Step 3] Analyze and draw the Rules:
   - Rule 1:
     - What does the rule restrict, and what does it leave open? *Lisa invests in gold, but could invest in other funds. Also, other people can invest in gold, too.*
     - What are the rule's negative implications, if any? *N/A*
     - Can the rule be depicted inside the sketch framework? *Yes.*

- Draw the rule:

$$
\begin{array}{c|c|c|c}
J & K & L & M \\
\hline
- & - & \underset{g}{} & - \\
\end{array}
$$

- Rule 2:
  - What does the rule restrict, and what does it leave open? *Energy and healthcare are ruled out for Klaus.*
  - What are the rule's negative implications, if any? *Klaus still has to invest in at least one of financials, gold, or international.*
  - Can the rule be depicted inside the sketch framework? *Yes.*
  - Draw the rule:

$$
\begin{array}{c|c|c|c}
J & K & L & M \\
\hline
- & - & \underset{g}{} & - \\
 & \sim e & & \\
 & \sim h & & \\
\end{array}
$$

- Rule 3:
  - What does the rule restrict, and what does it leave open? *At least three of the clients invest in financials, but it could be any of the three or all four.*
  - What are the rule's negative implications, if any? *At most, only one of the investors will not invest in financials.*
  - Can the rule be depicted inside the sketch framework? *No; remember that the rule says "at least three," not exactly three.*
  - Draw the rule:

$$
\text{at least } 3 \text{ f}
$$

- Rule 4:
  - What does the rule restrict, and what does it leave open? *If Maria invests in something, then so does Klaus. Klaus could invest in more, but has to have at least as many investments as Maria.*
  - What are the rule's negative implications, if any? *By contrapositive, if Klaus doesn't invest in a particular fund, then Maria can't invest in that fund.*

- Can the rule be depicted inside the sketch framework? *No.*
- Draw the rule:

    If M → K

    If ~K → ~M

Practice 4

A video game designer is creating a game for young children that involves players progressing through four separate levels, from level 1 to level 4. On each level, players are offered at least one reward—an apple, a bagel, or a cookie—and will encounter at least one obstacle—a mud pit, an oil slick, or quicksand. The designer is limited by the following constraints:

> No reward or obstacle can appear more than once on any level.
> No reward can appear on three consecutive levels.
> Level 2 has an apple, and level 3 has both a mud pit and quicksand.
> Level 4 has a greater combined total of rewards and obstacles than does level 2.
> Level 2 has a greater number of obstacles than each of level 3 and level 4.

1. [Step 1] Summarize your Overview analysis: *A Matching game in which at least one of three rewards and at least one of three obstacles are assigned to each of four levels in a kids' video game. Rewards and obstacles can be repeated on different levels.*

2. [Step 2] Create an initial Sketch:

	1	2	3	4	
rew:	_	_	_	_	A B C
obst:	_	_	_	_	m o q

3. [Step 3] Analyze and draw the Rules:
   - Rule 1:
     - What does the rule restrict, and what does it leave open? *Entities can be used only once on each level.*

- What are the rule's negative implications, if any? *Entities cannot appear multiple times on any given level.*
- Can the rule be depicted inside the sketch framework? *No.*
- Draw the rule:

    no dupl. in level

- Rule 2:
   - What does the rule restrict, and what does it leave open? *No reward can appear on three consecutive levels. This does not put the same restriction on obstacles.*
   - What are the rule's negative implications, if any? *No reward will appear on all four levels. And if a reward is used three times in the game, it would be on levels 1, 2, and 4 or levels 1, 3, and 4.*
   - Can the rule be depicted inside the sketch framework? *No.*
   - Draw the rule:

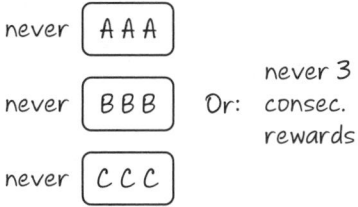

- Rule 3:
   - What does the rule restrict, and what does it leave open? *A reward is established in level 2 and two obstacles are established in level 3. Level 2 still needs an obstacle and level 3 still needs a reward.*
   - What are the rule's negative implications, if any? *N/A*
   - Can the rule be depicted inside the sketch framework? *Yes.*
   - Draw the rule:

	1	2	3	4	
rew:	_	A	_	_	A B C
obst:	_	_	m q	_	m o q

- Rule 4:
  - What does the rule restrict, and what does it leave open? *The total number of items in level 4 is greater than the total number of items in level 2. The exact numbers are unknown.*
  - What are the rule's negative implications, if any? *Level 2 cannot get everything. It has a maximum of five items.*
  - Can the rule be depicted inside the sketch framework? *No.*
  - Draw the rule:

    total: 4 > 2

- Rule 5:
  - What does the rule restrict, and what does it leave open? *Level 2 has more obstacles than level 3 and level 4, So, level 2 will have at least two obstacles, but it could be any two—or all three.*
  - What are the rule's negative implications, if any? *Neither level 3 nor level 4 will get all three obstacles.*
  - Can the rule be depicted inside the sketch framework? *No.*
  - Draw the rule:

    obst: 2 > 3

    obst: 2 > 4

Matching games typically have multiple deductions, often centered around the number restrictions and duplications among the various entities. You may have spotted some of them already as you were analyzing and drawing out the rules. If there were any you missed, you'll have the chance to discover them as you rigorously apply Step 4 of the Logic Games Method to these games in the next section of this chapter.

MATCHING GAMES DEDUCTIONS

LEARNING OBJECTIVES

In this section of the chapter, you'll practice

- Applying Step 4 of the Logic Games Method to Matching games by combining rules and restrictions to make all valid deductions in the game.

Prepare

In the section on Matching games rules, you saw the importance of drawing the rules in ways that reflect the visual orientation of the game's setup. Whether you prefer to use list-style or grid-style sketch frameworks for Matching games, continue that emphasis on accurate visual depiction of the game as you add the deductions.

LOGIC GAMES STRATEGY

In Matching games, deductions are likely to stem from:

- **Duplications**—Entities shared by two or more rules; one rule might match a certain attribute to entity X, and another might tell you that entity Y has more attributes to it than X does.
- **Number Restrictions**—Limitations on the number of attributes that can be assigned to a given entity of limitations on the number of entities to which an attribute can be matched.
- **Established Entities**—Matches between entities and attributes that must be maintained throughout the game (e.g., Luis uses blueberries in his pie); Established Entities are quite common in Matching games.

In Matching games, deductions may involve:

- **Blocks of Entities**—Two or more entities that must be assigned a given attribute, or two or more attributes that must be assigned to the same entity or entities; Blocks are somewhat rare in Matching games.
- **Limited Options**—The situation that arises when a rule or a combination of rules makes all acceptable arrangements fall into one of two patterns; Limited Options is a rare deduction to find in Matching games.

In any Matching game, pay attention to numbers restrictions that affect multiple entities. For example, in the model setup about the three doughnut shops, Rule 3 required L to sell more kinds of doughnuts than J. From that, the LSAT expert was able to deduce that J could not sell all four kinds of doughnuts mentioned in the game, and built that deduction into the sketch at the same time as she recorded the rule.

In downtown Farlow, there are three doughnut shops, one each on H Street, J Street, and L Street. Each of the shops sells between two and four of the following kinds of doughnuts—crullers, glazed, old fashioned, and sprinkles. The following conditions apply:

Exactly two shops sell old fashioned doughnuts.
Any shop that sells crullers does not sell glazed doughnuts.
The shop on L Street sells more kinds of doughnuts than the shop on J Street.
The shop on H Street sells glazed doughnuts.

The expert also made a deduction from the duplication of *g* in Rules 2 and 4, that H cannot sell crullers because it sells glazed doughnuts.

You'll spot similar deductions as you practice applying Step 4 of the Logic Games Method to the now familiar model game setups you've been working with. Just as the LSAT expert did with the doughnut shop game, you may already have spotted some of these deductions as you were analyzing and drawing the rules.

Practice

Directions: In each game setup, first reacquaint yourself with the setup and rules. Then, combine the rules and restrictions to make all available deductions, recording your analyses as indicated. Finally, test your deductions by answering the questions that accompany each game. You can find expert analysis and explanations at the end of the Practice section.

Practice 1

A chef will prepare each of three entrées—K, L, and M—each of which will contain at least three of the following ingredients—buttermilk, garlic, onion, paprika, and salt. Each ingredient is used at least once. Preparation of the entrées must also conform to the following conditions:

No entrée contains all five ingredients.
Entrée L does not contain onion.
Garlic is used in exactly two of the entrées.
Entrée L contains more of these ingredients than entrée K.

```
        b  g  o  p  s
           g
           ‗

           <
      K |  L |  M
      ―    ―    ―        never all 5 ing.
      ―    ―    ―        L > K
      ―    ―    ―        exactly 2g
           ~o |
```

1. Which entities or positions are the most restricted in this game? Why?

2. Which elements from the BLEND checklist can you identify in this game? Are there
    *   Blocks of entities? If so, what are they?
    *   Limited Options? If so, which rule(s) trigger them?
    *   Established Entities? If so, which ones?
    *   Number Restrictions? If so, describe them.
    *   Duplications? If so, which rules share an entity?

3. Combine the rules and restrictions to create a Master Sketch depicting all of the deductions available in this game:

4. Evaluate your sketch by answering the following questions:
    *   How many entrées can include onion?
    *   Which ingredients can be used in all three entrées?
    *   Which ingredients can entrées K and M have in common?
    *   What is the maximum total number of ingredients that can be used in all three entrées?

Practice 2

A financial advisor is meeting with four clients—Jordan, Klaus, Lisa, and Marie. Each client is investing in at least one of five mutual funds—energy, financials, gold, healthcare, and international—and no others. Investing choices must conform to the following conditions:

Lisa invests in gold.
Klaus invests in neither energy nor healthcare.
At least three of the clients invest in financials.
Klaus invests in every fund that Marie invests in.

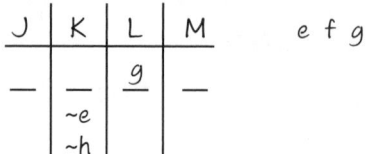

at least 3 f

If M → K

If ~K → ~M

1. Which entities or positions are the most restricted in this game? Why?

2. Which elements from the BLEND checklist can you identify in this game? Are there
   - Blocks of entities? If so, what are they?
   - Limited Options? If so, which rule(s) trigger them?
   - Established Entities? If so, which ones?
   - Number Restrictions? If so, describe them.
   - Duplications? If so, which rules share an entity?

3. Combine the rules and restrictions to create a Master Sketch depicting all of the deductions available in this game:

4. Evaluate your sketch by answering the following questions:
   - What is the maximum number of investments that Marie can make?
   - Which clients can invest in energy?
   - Which funds can be invested in by all four clients?
   - Who can invest in financials if Lisa invests in only one fund?

Practice 3

A video game designer is creating a game for young children that involves players progressing through four separate levels, from level 1 to level 4. On each level, players are offered at least one reward—an apple, a bagel, or a cookie—and will encounter at least one obstacle—a mud pit, an oil slick, or quicksand. The designer is limited by the following constraints:

> No reward or obstacle can appear more than once on any level.
> No reward can appear on three consecutive levels.
> Level 2 has an apple, and level 3 has both a mud pit and quicksand.
> Level 4 has a greater combined total of rewards and obstacles than does level 2.
> Level 2 has a greater number of obstacles than each of level 3 and level 4.

	1	2	3	4	
rew:	_	A	_	_	A B C
obst:	_	_	m q	_	m o q

never [A A A]   no dupl. in level

never [B B B]   total: 4 > 2

never [C C C]   obst: 2 > 3

                                        obst: 2 > 4

1. Which entities or positions are the most restricted in this game? Why?

2. Which elements from the BLEND checklist can you identify in this game? Are there
   - Blocks of entities? If so, what are they?
   - Limited Options? If so, which rule(s) trigger them?
   - Established Entities? If so, which ones?
   - Number Restrictions? If so, describe them.
   - Duplications? If so, which rules share an entity?

3. Combine the rules and restrictions to create a Master Sketch depicting all of the deductions available in this game:

4. Evaluate your sketch by answering the following questions:
   - Which rewards can appear on level 3?
   - Which rewards or obstacles can appear on all four levels?
   - Which levels can include both a cookie and an oil slick?
   - What is the maximum total rewards and obstacles for any level?

Explanations

Compare your work to that of an LSAT expert. Pay close attention to how the expert combined the rules and restrictions to make additional deductions, and to how the expert depicted the deductions within the sketch framework.

Practice 1

A chef will prepare each of three entrées—K, L, and M—each of which will contain at least three of the following ingredients—buttermilk, garlic, onion, paprika, and salt. Each ingredient is used at least once. Preparation of the entrées must also conform to the following conditions:

> No entrée contains all five ingredients.
> Entrée L does not contain onion.
> Garlic is used in exactly two of the entrées.
> Entrée L contains more of these ingredients than entrée K.

Which entities or positions are the most restricted in this game? Why? *Entrée L, because it needs more ingredients than entrée K yet cannot use onion.*

5. Which elements from the BLEND checklist can you identify in this game? Are there

   - Blocks of entities? If so, what are they? *N/A*

   - Limited Options? If so, which rule(s) trigger them? *N/A*

   - Established Entities? If so, which ones? *N/A*

   - Number Restrictions? If so, describe them. *Rule 1 reduces the maximum number of ingredients in a entrée. Rule 3 limits garlic to just two entrées. Rule 4 gives entrée L more ingredients than entrée K.*

   - Duplications? If so, which rules share an entity? *Rules 2 and 4 both mention entrée L.*

6. Combine the rules and restrictions to create a Master Sketch depicting all of the deductions available in this game:

   K has to have at least three ingredients. L has to have more, so it has to have at least four, but it can't have all five. So L has exactly four, limiting K to just three.

L cannot have onion, so its four ingredients must be buttermilk, garlic, paprika, and salt.

L has garlic, which means only one more entrée—K or M—will have garlic.

7. Evaluate your sketch by answering the following questions:

   - How many entrées can include onion? *Two; it's not in entrée L, but it could be in both K and M.*

   - Which ingredients can be used in all three entrées? *Buttermilk, paprika, and salt; garlic is in only two entrées, and L doesn't use onion.*

   - Which ingredients can entrées K and M have in common? *Any three of buttermilk, onion, paprika, and salt.*

   - What is the maximum total number of ingredients that can be used in all three entrées? *Eleven; K and L are set at three and four, respectively. M cannot have all five, but can have four.*

Practice 2

A financial advisor is meeting with four clients—Jordan, Klaus, Lisa, and Marie. Each client is investing in at least one of five mutual funds—energy, financials, gold, healthcare, and international—and no others. Investing choices must conform to the following conditions:

> Lisa invests in gold.
> Klaus invests in neither energy nor healthcare.
> At least three of the clients invest in financials.
> Klaus invests in every fund that Marie invests in.

1. Which entities or positions are the most restricted in this game? Why? *Klaus, who cannot have energy or healthcare, but needs to share investments with Marie.*

2. Which elements from the BLEND checklist can you identify in this game? Are there

   - Blocks of entities? If so, what are they? *N/A*

   - Limited Options? If so, which rule(s) trigger them? *N/A*

   - Established Entities? If so, which ones? *Rule 1 establishes gold for Lisa.*

   - Number Restrictions? If so, describe them. *Rule 3 sets a minimum of three clients getting the financials fund.*

   - Duplications? If so, which rules share an entity? *Rules 2 and 4 mention Klaus.*

3. Combine the rules and restrictions to create a Master Sketch depicting all of the deductions available in this game: *By the contrapositive of Rule 4, if Klaus doesn't invest in a fund, then Marie can't invest in that fund. That means Marie can't invest in energy or healthcare.*

J	K	L	M
—	—	_g_	—
	~e		~e
	~h		~h

The contrapositive also effects financials. If Klaus didn't invest in financials, then Marie couldn't. That would leave just two clients who

could invest in financials, which would not be enough to satisfy Rule 3. So, Klaus must invest in financials.

J	K	L	M
—	_f_	_g_	—
	~e		~e
	~h		~h

4. Evaluate your sketch by answering the following questions:

   - What is the maximum number of investments that Marie can make? *Three—financials, gold, and international.*

   - Which clients can invest in energy? *Jordan and Lisa.*

   - Which funds can be invested in by all four clients? *Financials, gold, and international.*

   - Who must invest in financials if Lisa invests in only one fund? *Jordan, Klaus, and Marie; three people must invest in financials, and Lisa must invest in gold.*

Practice 3

A video game designer is creating a game for young children that involves players progressing through four separate levels, from level 1 to level 4. On each level, players are offered at least one reward—an apple, a bagel, or a cookie—and will encounter at least one obstacle—a mud pit, an oil slick, or quicksand. The designer is limited by the following constraints:

> No reward or obstacle can appear more than once on any level.
> No reward can appear on three consecutive levels.
> Level 2 has an apple, and level 3 has both a mud pit and quicksand.
> Level 4 has a greater combined total of rewards and obstacles than does level 2.
> Level 2 has a greater number of obstacles than each of level 3 and level 4.

1. Which entities or positions are the most restricted in this game? Why? *Level 2, which is limited by what's on levels 3 and 4.*

2. Which elements from the BLEND checklist can you identify in this game? Are there

   - Blocks of entities? If so, what are they? *N/A*
   - Limited Options? If so, which rule(s) trigger them? *N/A*
   - Established Entities? If so, which ones? *Rule 3 establishes three items on two of the levels.*
   - Number Restrictions? If so, describe them. *Rules 4 and 5 require some levels to have more of certain items than others.*
   - Duplications? If so, which rules share an entity? *Rules 3, 4, and 5 all mention level 2; Rules 3 and 5 mention level 3; and Rules 4 and 5 mention level 4.*

3. Combine the rules and restrictions to create a Master Sketch depicting all of the deductions available in this game: *Level 3 has two obstacles to begin with. That means level 2 must get all three obstacles.*

	1	2	3	4
rew:	_	A	_	_
obst:	_	m o q	m q	_

That gives level 2 at least four items total (one reward and three obstacles). So level 4 has to have at least five items total. However, level 4 cannot have all three obstacles, so it must have

exactly five items: all three rewards and just two obstacles.

	1	2	3	4
rew:	_	A	_	A B C
obst:	_	m o q	m q	_ _ ‖

Level 2 is thus done with four items total. Level 3 cannot have any more obstacles, but can have more rewards. Level 1 is unlimited. Levels 2 and 4 both contain the apple as a reward, so level 3 cannot contain an apple.

	1	2	3	4
rew:	_	A‖	_	A B C
obst:	_	m o q‖	m q‖	_ _ ‖
			~A	

4. Evaluate your sketch by answering the following questions:

   - Which rewards can appear on level 3? *Bagel or cookie, or both*
   - Which rewards or obstacles can appear on all four levels? *Mud pit or quicksand, or both.*
   - Which levels can include both a cookie and an oil slick? *Levels 1 or 4, or both; level 2 doesn't offer a cookie, and level 3 has no oil slick.*
   - What is the maximum total rewards and obstacles for any level? *Six; level 1 is unlimited and thus can offer everything.*

Now, put your Matching games skills to the test. In the next section, you can evaluate your performance and get recommendations for further practice.

MATCHING GAMES—FULL GAMES WITH QUESTIONS

LEARNING OBJECTIVES

In this section, you'll assess your ability to

- Apply the Logic Games Method to Matching games.

Perform

Here is your opportunity to put all of the pieces together and assess your skills on Matching games. On the following pages, you'll find two full-length games along with their question sets. Both of these games are from officially released LSAT tests, and all are representative of Matching games you could see on Test Day. You can take the games one at a time or both together, but for your self-evaluation to be as accurate as possible, adhere to the timing guidelines set forth in the directions.

An answer key follows the games. Complete worked example expert analyses can be found in your online resources.

After you complete and review both games, assess your performance using the evaluation guidelines. There, you'll find recommendations for additional Easy, Medium, and Hard Matching games from officially released LSAT exams that you can practice to continue honing your skills and raising your score.

Directions: Take no more than 9 minutes per game to complete the following two games and all of their questions.

Perform 1

<u>Questions 1–7</u>

Three couples—John and Kate, Lewis and Marie, and Nat and Olive have dinner in a restaurant together. Kate, Marie, and Olive are women; the other three are men. Each person orders one and only one of the following kinds of entrees: pork chops, roast beef, swordfish, tilefish, veal cutlet. The six people order in a manner consistent with the following conditions:

    The two people in each couple do not order the same kind of entree as each other.
    None of the men orders the same kind of entree as any of the other men.
    Marie orders swordfish.
    Neither John nor Nat orders a fish entree.
    Olive orders roast beef.

1. Which one of the following is a complete and accurate list of the entrees any one of which Lewis could order?

    (A)   pork chops, roast beef
    (B)   pork chops, veal cutlet
    (C)   pork chops, swordfish, veal cutlet
    (D)   pork chops, roast beef, tilefish, veal cutlet
    (E)   pork chops, roast beef, swordfish, tilefish, veal cutlet

2. Which one of the following statements could be true?

   (A) John orders the same kind of entree as Marie does.
   (B) Kate orders the same kind of entree as Nat does.
   (C) Lewis orders the same kind of entree as Nat does.
   (D) Marie orders the same kind of entree as Olive does.
   (E) Nat orders the same kind of entree as Olive does.

3. Which one of the following statements must be true?

   (A) One of the men orders pork chops or veal cutlet.
   (B) One of the men orders swordfish or veal cutlet.
   (C) Two of the women order tilefish.
   (D) None of the men orders a fish entree.
   (E) Exactly one of the women orders a fish entree.

4. If John orders veal cutlet, then which one of the following statements must be true?

   (A) Kate orders roast beef.
   (B) Kate orders swordfish.
   (C) Lewis orders tilefish.
   (D) Lewis orders veal cutlet.
   (E) Nat orders pork chops.

5. If none of the six people orders pork chops, then which one of the following statements must be true?

   (A) John orders veal cutlet.
   (B) Kate orders tilefish.
   (C) Lewis orders tilefish.
   (D) One of the men orders swordfish.
   (E) One of the women orders tilefish.

6. If Lewis orders pork chops, then which one of the following is a complete and accurate list of the entrees any one of which John could order?

   (A) roast beef
   (B) veal cutlet
   (C) roast beef, veal cutlet
   (D) roast beef, swordfish
   (E) pork chops, roast beef, swordfish

7. Suppose that the people in each couple both order the same kind of entree as each other rather than order different kinds of entrees. If all other conditions remain the same, and no two women order the same kind of entree, then which one of the following statements could be true?

   (A) John orders roast beef.
   (B) John orders swordfish.
   (C) Kate orders roast beef.
   (D) Two of the people order pork chops.
   (E) Two of the people order tilefish.

PrepTest3 Sec1 Qs 1–7

Perform 2

<u>Questions 8–12</u>

A store sells shirts only in small, medium, and large sizes, and only in red, yellow, and blue colors. Casey buys exactly three shirts from the store.

> A shirt type consists of both a size and a color.
> Casey does not buy two shirts of the same type.
> Casey does not buy both a small shirt and a large shirt.
> No small red shirts are available.
> No large blue shirts are available.

8. Which one of the following must be false?

   (A) Two of the shirts that Casey buys are small and two are red.

   (B) Two of the shirts that Casey buys are medium and two are red.

   (C) Two of the shirts that Casey buys are large and two are red.

   (D) Two of the shirts that Casey buys are small, one is yellow, and one is blue.

   (E) Two of the shirts that Casey buys are medium, one is yellow, and one is blue.

9. If Casey buys a small blue shirt, which one of the following must be false?

   (A) Casey buys two blue shirts.
   (B) Casey buys two red shirts.
   (C) Casey buys two yellow shirts.
   (D) Casey buys two small shirts.
   (E) Casey buys two medium shirts.

10. If Casey does not buy a medium yellow shirt, which one of the following must be true?

   (A) Casey buys either a medium red shirt or a small blue shirt.
   (B) Casey buys either a medium red shirt or a medium blue shirt.
   (C) Casey buys either a large red shirt or a small blue shirt.
   (D) Casey buys either a large red shirt or a medium red shirt.
   (E) Casey buys either a large yellow shirt or a small yellow shirt.

11. If Casey buys exactly one medium shirt and does not buy two shirts of the same color, then she cannot buy which one of the following?

   (A) a medium red shirt
   (B) a medium yellow shirt
   (C) a medium blue shirt
   (D) a large red shirt
   (E) a large yellow shirt

12. If neither large red shirts nor small blue shirts are available, which one of the following must Casey buy?

   (A) a red shirt
   (B) a medium yellow shirt
   (C) either a large shirt or a small shirt
   (D) either a medium red shirt or a medium blue shirt
   (E) either a large yellow shirt or a medium blue shirt

PrepTest5 Sec2 Qs 7–11

Answer Key

Perform 1

1. (D)
2. (B)
3. (A)
4. (E)
5. (C)
6. (A)
7. (D)

Perform 2

8. (A)
9. (B)
10. (B)
11. (B)
12. (D)

Worked example explanations of these questions with complete expert analysis can be found in your Online Study Plan under Chapter 9. View or download the PDF titled "Chapter 9 Matching Perform Full Games Explanations."

Assess

Use the following criteria to evaluate your results on the Perform games.

If, under timed conditions, you correctly answered

10–12 of the questions: Outstanding! You have demonstrated a strong skill level in Matching games. For further practice in Matching, use any of the Recommended Additional Practice sets, including the Advanced set. Then, move on to the Distribution section of this chapter and to Chapter 10 on Hybrid games.

7–9 of the questions: Good work! You have a solid foundation in Matching games. For further practice in Matching, begin with the Foundations or Mid-Level Recommended Additional Practice set. Then, move on to the Distribution section of this chapter and to Chapter 10 on Hybrid games. If you have time before Test Day, try the Advanced Recommended Additional Matching Practice set, as well.

0–6 of the questions: Keep working. Matching, along with its close cousin Distribution, shows up on more than a third of games as a pure action or as part of a hybrid. Continued practice will help you improve your score. Begin by reviewing this chapter. Then, try the games in the Foundations Recommended Additional Practice set. As you continue to progress, move on to the Mid-Level Recommended Additional Practice set. Then, move on to the Distribution section of this chapter and to Chapter 10 on Hybrid games.

To stay sharp, practice the drills in the Logic Games Training Camp for this chapter in your Online Study Plan. Training Camp drills are divided into Fundamentals, Mid-Level, and Advanced sets.

Recommended Additional Practice: Matching

All of the following games will provide good practice on Matching. They are grouped by difficulty as determined from empirical student practice results. All PrepTests included are available individually, or in bundles of ten as part of the LSAC's *10 Actual, Official LSAT PrepTests* series.

Foundations
PrepTest 67, Section 3, Game 1: Student Speeches*
PrepTest 56, Section 1, Game 3: Parks and Trees**

Mid-Level
PrepTest 64, Section 2, Game 3: Bicycle Testers*
PrepTest 62, Section 3, Game 2: Stained Glass Windows*
PrepTest 56, Section 1, Game 2: Furniture Moving**

Advanced
PrepTest 68, Section 4, Game 3: Maintenance Service Targets*
PrepTest 67, Section 3, Game 4: Development Zones*

*Game included in *10 Actual, Official LSAT PrepTests Volume V: PrepTests 62–71*; complete answers and explanations written by Kaplan LSAT experts available via the eBook: *LSAT PrepTests 62–71 Unlocked: Exclusive Data, Analysis & Explanations for 10 Actual, Official LSAT PrepTests Volume V.*

**Game included in *10 New Actual, Official LSAT PrepTests with Comparative Reading (PrepTests 52–61)*; complete answers and explanations written by Kaplan LSAT experts available via the eBook: *LSAT PrepTests 52–61 Unlocked: Exclusive Data, Analysis & Explanations for 10 New Actual, Official LSAT PrepTests with Comparative Reading.* [Explanations title coming Fall 2018.]

Reflect

Think back over the study and practice you did in this chapter.

- Are you able to identify Matching games from their setups?
- Do you have a default sketch framework for Matching actions?
- What kinds of rules do you anticipate seeing in Matching games?
- Are you comfortable analyzing Matching rules and determining whether to record them within or underneath the sketch framework?
- Are you making the available deductions efficiently and effectively in Matching games?

In the coming days and weeks before Test Day, take note of real-world tasks that reflect Matching tasks. Consider how they mirror the setups and questions in LSAT Matching, and how they differ. Try to reframe real-life sequencing tasks using the terms, rules, and restrictions used by the testmaker.

DISTRIBUTION GAMES TASKS AND SKETCHES

LEARNING OBJECTIVES

In this section of the chapter, you'll practice

- Applying Steps 1 and 2 of the Logic Games Method to Distribution games by
  - Asking the SEAL questions to analyze the game's Overview, and then
- Creating a simple, useful Sketch framework

Prepare

As soon as you discern that the situation in a game involves splitting the entities into groups, you know that you have a Distribution game. You will almost instinctively ask the two questions that will guide how you set up the game: "How many groups/teams are there?" and "How many items/people go into each group?" The setup will almost always answer the first question, and will usually provide names for the groups or teams involved. In some games, the setup will answer the second question as well—e.g., "three teams, each with three players"—but, in other games, you will need to use the rules or limitations to determine the number of entities acceptable within each group. In many real-life situations, we assume that we want groups or teams with equal numbers. That is not the case in Distribution games *unless* the setup or rules explicitly establish that condition.

LOGIC GAMES STRATEGY

Distribution games ask you to

- Divide an initial set of entities into two, three, or four groups

In Distribution games, there are two things to keep in mind about the entities. First, unlike the attributes or items you are matching to other entities in Matching games, each of the entities in most Distribution games can be assigned to just one group or team. Think of them as physical individuals that cannot exist in two places at once.

Second, always note when the game's setup subdivides the entities. Most Distribution setups will provide an undifferentiated list of entities, in which all of them are to be treated equally. When the setup designates subgroups, however, it will always supply rules that treat entities in the two subgroups differently. For example, if a Distribution game tasks you with dividing a group of eight hikers into two smaller groups with four hikers each *and* tells you that three of the hikers are experienced and five are inexperienced, then there will almost certainly be a rule requiring at least one experienced hiker on each team.

Keep these considerations in mind as you apply Steps 1 and 2 to three model Distribution setups in the following practice section.

Directions: Conduct an Overview of each game's setup by asking the SEAL questions, and create an initial sketch framework for the game's action.

Practice 1

A homeowner has purchased exactly seven fruit trees—a kiwi tree, a lemon tree, a mango tree, a nectarine tree, an orange tree, a plum tree, and a quince tree—to plant in his front and back yards. The planting of trees must adhere to the following guidelines:

1. [Step 1] Conduct an Overview analysis:

    • What is this game's Situation?

    • Who or what are the game's Entities?

    • What is the game's Action?

    • What are the Limitations explicit in the game setup?

2. [Step 2] Create an initial Sketch:

Practice 2

Seven graduate students—Arroyo, Baxter, Chen, Domingo, Erickson, Farrel, and Goya—are being assigned as teaching assistants for three professors—Sheffield, Tran, and Umberto. Each student will be assigned to exactly one professor, and each professor will receive at least one student. Arroyo, Baxter, Domingo, and Erickson are studying mathematics, while Chen, Farrel, and Goya are studying physics. The following restrictions apply:

1. [Step 1] Conduct an Overview analysis:

    • What is this game's Situation?

    • Who or what are the game's Entities?

    • What is the game's Action?

    • What are the Limitations explicit in the game setup?

2. [Step 2] Create an initial Sketch:

Practice 3

A theater director is scheduling auditions for seven actors—Anh, Behn, Chang, Dien, Enge, Fein, and Gus. The actors will audition either alone or in groups. The director will schedule at most four auditions, with each actor attending exactly one audition. The final schedule will be based on the following determinations:

1. [Step 1] Conduct an Overview analysis:
   - What is this game's Situation?
   - Who or what are the game's Entities?
   - What is the game's Action?
   - What are the Limitations explicit in the game setup?

2. [Step 2] Create an initial Sketch:

Explanations

Compare your work to that of an LSAT expert. Keep track of any case in which you incorrectly characterized the action described in the setup, and any case in which you drew a sketch framework that does not match the details of the game's situation.

Practice 1

A homeowner has purchased exactly seven fruit trees—a kiwi tree, a lemon tree, a mango tree, a nectarine tree, an orange tree, a plum tree, and a quince tree—to plant in his front and back yards. The planting of trees must adhere to the following guidelines:

1. [Step 1] Conduct an Overview analysis:
   - What is this game's Situation? *A homeowner planting trees in his front and back yards.*
   - Who or what are the game's Entities? *Seven trees—K, L, M, N, O, P, and Q.*
   - What is the game's Action? *Distribution. Determine in which yard each tree is planted.*
   - What are the Limitations explicit in the game setup? *There are "exactly seven trees," so no tree will be repeated. Thus, each tree will be assigned to just one yard—front or back.*

2. [Step 2] Create an initial Sketch:

Practice 2

Seven graduate students—Arroyo, Baxter, Chen, Domingo, Erickson, Farrel, and Goya—are being assigned as teaching assistants for three professors—Sheffield, Tran, and Umberto. Each student will be assigned to exactly one professor, and each professor will receive at least one student. Arroyo, Baxter, Domingo, and Erickson are studying mathematics, while Chen, Farrel, and Goya are studying physics. The following restrictions apply:

1. [Step 1] Conduct an Overview analysis:
   - What is this game's Situation? *Students being assigned as teaching assistants to a group of professors.*
   - Who or what are the game's Entities? *Seven students—math students A, B, D, and E; physics students c, f, and g.*
   - What is the game's Action? *Distribution; assign the students to the professors.*
   - What are the Limitations explicit in the game setup? *Each student is assigned to exactly one professor, and each professor gets at least one student.*

2. [Step 2] Create an initial Sketch:

$$\frac{\text{Math} \quad \text{Phys}}{A\,B\,D\,E \quad c\,f\,g}$$

Shef	Tran	Umb
—	—	—

Practice 3

A theater director is scheduling auditions for seven actors—Anh, Behn, Chang, Dien, Enge, Fein, and Gus. The actors will audition either alone or in groups. The director will schedule at most four auditions, with each actor attending exactly one audition. The final schedule will be based on the following determinations:

1. [Step 1] Conduct an Overview analysis:
   - What is this game's Situation? *A director scheduling auditions for a play.*
   - Who or what are the game's Entities? *Seven actors—A, B, C, D, E, F, and G.*
   - What is the game's Action? *Distribution; putting actors in groups for auditions.*

- What are the Limitations explicit in the game setup? *There are "at most four auditions," which means there could be fewer. For any audition, there's no limit. There could be one actor or it could be multiple actors—perhaps all seven. However, each actor will only be assigned to one audition.*

2. [Step 2] Create an initial Sketch:

In the next section of this chapter, we'll add the rules to these setups. There, you'll practice applying Step 3 of the Logic Games Method to Distribution games by analyzing and drawing the rules.

DISTRIBUTION GAMES RULES

Prepare

LOGIC GAMES STRATEGY

Distribution rules tell you one or more of the following:

- Entities that must or cannot be assigned to the same group.
- The number of entities that must, can, or cannot be assigned to a group, or the relative sizes among groups (e.g., the lighting crew must have more members than the props crew).
- Conditions triggering the assignment of an entity to a particular group (e.g., if the vase is exhibited in Percy Hall, then the sculpture is exhibited in Rowe Hall).

In both Distribution and Matching games, the setup and sketch have a big influence over how you will depict the rules. In Distribution, this is especially true of games with different numbers of groups. Consider the following rule:

Dan does not play on the Blue Team.

You will draw that rule differently in a game with two teams than you would in a game with three teams.

Red	Blue		Red	Blue	Green
_D_	—		—	—	—
—	—		—	—	—
				~D	

With only two teams, the rule forbidding Dan from playing on the Blue Team means that he will play on the Red Team. With three teams in the mix, however, the best you can do is to record the negative restriction on Dan beneath the Blue Team's column.

Take a look at an expert's analysis and drawing of common Distribution rules in a couple more game contexts.

Rules	Analysis
A game in which seven volunteers—A, B, C, D, E, F, and G—are each assigned to exactly one group—1, 2, or 3. A B C D E F G 	
If A is assigned to group 1, then B is assigned to group 2	$\longrightarrow$ If A = 1 $\rightarrow$ B = 2 If B $\neq$ 2 $\rightarrow$ A $\neq$ 1
E and F cannot be assigned to the same group.	$\longrightarrow$ never $\boxed{\begin{array}{c} E \\ F \end{array}}$
C and D are assigned to the same group.	$\longrightarrow$ $\boxed{\begin{array}{c} C \\ D \end{array}}$

A game in which six workers—J, K, L, M, N, and O—are each assigned to work on exactly one of two projects—1 or 2.

J K L M N O

1	2

Rules	Analysis
If J is assigned to project 1, then K is assigned to project 1.	$\longrightarrow$ If J = 1 $\rightarrow$ K = 1 If K = 2 $\rightarrow$ J = 2
K and L are assigned to different projects.	$\longrightarrow$ 1 | 2 K/L | L/K
Either exactly two or exactly three workers are assigned to project 1.	$\longrightarrow$ 1 | 2 1 | 2

Now, practice that kind of rule analysis and depiction in four exercises. The first is similar to the table, where the rules are grouped under brief game descriptions. In the next three practice exercises, full sets of rules are provided for the game setups you analyzed in the preceding section of this chapter.

Practice

Directions: Analyze and draw each of following Distribution game rules. Use the brief game description to guide your depiction of the game's framework.

Practice 1

Rules	Analysis
A game distributing seven animals—B, D, F, G, H, J, and K—into three habitats—1, 2, and 3, each of which must have at least one animal.	
1. B and D must be assigned to the same habitat. $\longrightarrow$	
2. If J is in habitat 1, then G is in habitat 3. $\longrightarrow$	
3. Habitat 2 has exactly twice as many animals as does habitat 1. $\longrightarrow$	
A game distributing five pieces of furniture—a bookcase, a couch, a hutch, an ottoman, and a table—into three rooms—a dining room, a living room, and a study.	
4. The table and the couch are placed in the same room. $\longrightarrow$	
5. If the couch is placed in the living room, the bookcase must go in the dining room. $\longrightarrow$	
6. The hutch is placed in the study. $\longrightarrow$	
A game in which six accountants—D, E, F, G, H, and I—are each assigned to exactly one of two projects—billing or collection.	
7. If D is not assigned to billing, then E must be. $\longrightarrow$	
8. If G is assigned to billing, then H is assigned to collection. $\longrightarrow$	
9. E and F must be assigned to different projects. $\longrightarrow$	
A game in which six departments—bedding, kitchen, lighting, pets, swimwear, and toys—are each placed on exactly one of three floors in a building—1, 2, and 3.	
10. Exactly one department will be on Floor 2. $\longrightarrow$	
11. Swimwear and toys will be assigned to different floors. $\longrightarrow$	
12. Lighting is not assigned to Floor 3. $\longrightarrow$	

K

Practice 2

Directions: Take a couple minutes to review the game setup, summarize your Overview analysis, and recreate the initial Sketch. Then, one at a time, analyze the rules, answer the questions about each one, and draw the rule either inside or underneath the sketch framework.

A homeowner has purchased exactly seven fruit trees—a kiwi tree, a lemon tree, a mango tree, a nectarine tree, an orange tree, a plum tree, and a quince tree—to plant in his front and back yards. The planting of trees must adhere to the following guidelines:

The kiwi tree and the mango tree cannot be planted in the same yard.
The quince tree and the orange tree cannot be planted in the same yard.
The lemon tree and the orange tree must be planted in the same yard.
If the nectarine tree is planted in the front yard, then the plum tree must also be planted in the front yard.
The quince tree must be planted in the front yard.

1. [Step 1] Summarize your Overview analysis:

2. [Step 2] Create an initial Sketch:

3. [Step 3] Analyze and draw the Rules:
   - For each rule, answer the following questions and draw the rule in the appropriate box.
     - What does the rule restrict, and what does it leave open?
     - What are the rule's negative implications, if any?
     - Can the rule be depicted inside the sketch framework?

Rule 1:	Rule 2:
Rule 3:	Rule 4:
Rule 5:	

Practice 3

Directions: Take a couple minutes to review the game setup, summarize your Overview analysis, and recreate the initial Sketch. Then, one at a time, analyze the rules, answer the questions about each one, and draw the rule either inside or underneath the sketch framework.

Seven graduate students—Arroyo, Baxter, Chen, Domingo, Erickson, Farrel, and Goya—are being assigned as teaching assistants for three professors—Sheffield, Tran, and Umberto. Each student will be assigned to exactly one professor, and each professor will receive at least one student. Arroyo, Baxter, Domingo, and Erickson are studying mathematics, while Chen, Farrel, and Goya are studying physics. The following restrictions apply:

No student studying physics can be assigned to the same professor as another student studying physics.
Baxter and Domingo will be assigned to the same professor.
Tran will be assigned more teaching assistants than will Sheffield.
If Erickson is assigned to Tran, then Arroyo cannot be assigned to Tran.

1. [Step 1] Summarize your Overview analysis:

2. [Step 2] Create an initial Sketch:

3. [Step 3] Analyze and draw the Rules:
   - For each rule, answer the following questions and draw the rule in the appropriate box.
     - What does the rule restrict, and what does it leave open?
     - What are the rule's negative implications, if any?
     - Can the rule be depicted inside the sketch framework?

Rule 1:	Rule 2:
Rule 3:	Rule 4:

Practice 4

Directions: Take a couple of minutes to review the game setup, summarize your Overview analysis, and recreate the initial Sketch. Then, one at a time, analyze the rules, answer the questions about each one, and draw the rule either inside or underneath the sketch framework.

A theater director is scheduling auditions for seven actors—Anh, Behn, Chang, Dien, Enge, Fein, and Gus. The actors will audition either alone or in groups. The director will schedule at most four auditions, with each actor attending exactly one audition. The final schedule will be based on the following determinations:

> Fein will audition alone.
> Anh and Enge will not be scheduled for the same audition.
> Chang and Enge will be not be scheduled for the same audition.
> Anh and Chang will not audition together unless Behn and Chang audition together.
> Dien and Anh will not audition together unless Behn auditions alone.

1. [Step 1] Summarize your Overview analysis:

2. [Step 2] Create an initial Sketch:

3. [Step 3] Analyze and draw the Rules:
   - For each rule, answer the following questions and draw the rule in the appropriate box.
     - What does the rule restrict, and what does it leave open?
     - What are the rule's negative implications, if any?
     - Can the rule be depicted inside the sketch framework?

Rule 1:	Rule 2:
Rule 3:	Rule 4:
Rule 5:	

Explanations

Compare your work to that of an LSAT expert. Pay close attention to how the expert analyzed each rule and then depicted it within or beneath the game's initial sketch.

Practice 1

Rules	Analysis

A game distributing seven animals—B, D, F, G, H, J, and K—into three habitats—1, 2, and 3, each of which must have at least one animal.

B D F G H J K

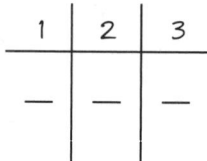

1. B and D must be assigned to the same habitat.

$\longrightarrow$ [B / D]

2. If J is in habitat 1, then G is in habitat 3.

$\longrightarrow$ If J = 1 → G = 3

If G ≠ 3 → J ≠ 1

3. Habitat 2 has exactly twice as many animals as does habitat 1.

$\longrightarrow$

1	2	3
—	—	—
	—	—
	—	
	—	

1	2	3
—	—	—
—	—	
	—	
	—	

A game distributing five pieces of furniture—a bookcase, a couch, a hutch, an ottoman, and a table—into three rooms—a dining room, a living room, and a study.

B C H O T

dr	lr	st

4. The table and the couch are placed in the same room.

$\longrightarrow$ [T / C]

5. If the couch is placed in the living room, the bookcase must go in the dining room.

$\longrightarrow$ If C = lr → B = dr

If B ≠ dr → C ≠ lr

6. The hutch is placed in the study.

$\longrightarrow$

dr	lr	st
		H

A game in which six accountants—D, E, F, G, H, and I—are each assigned to exactly one of two projects—billing or collection.

D E F G H I

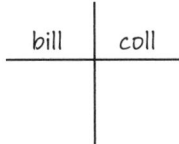

7. If D is not assigned to billing, then E must be.

    $\longrightarrow$ If D = coll → E = bill

    If E = coll → D = bill

8. If G is assigned to billing, then H is assigned to collection.

    $\longrightarrow$ If G = bill → H = coll

    If H = bill → G = coll

9. E and F must be assigned to different projects.

    $\longrightarrow$

bill	coll
E/F	F/E

A game in which six departments—bedding, kitchen, lighting, pets, swimwear, and toys—are each placed on exactly one of three floors in a building—1, 2, and 3.

B K L P S T

3:

2:

1:

10. Exactly one department will be on Floor 2.

     $\longrightarrow$
     3:
     2: __ ||
     1:

11. Swimwear and toys will be assigned to different floors.

     $\longrightarrow$ never [S T]

12. Lighting is not assigned to Floor 3.

     $\longrightarrow$
     3:    ~L
     2: __ ||
     1:

Practice 2

A homeowner has purchased exactly seven fruit trees—a kiwi tree, a lemon tree, a mango tree, a nectarine tree, an orange tree, a plum tree, and a quince tree—to plant in his front and back yards. The planting of trees must adhere to the following guidelines:

> The kiwi tree and the mango tree cannot be planted in the same yard.
> The quince tree and the orange tree cannot be planted in the same yard.
> The lemon tree and the orange tree must be planted in the same yard.
> If the nectarine tree is planted in the front yard, then the plum tree must also be planted in the front yard.
> The quince tree must be planted in the front yard.

1. [Step 1] Summarize your Overview analysis: *A Distribution game in which each of seven trees will be planted in exactly one of two yards. There is no limit, minimum or maximum, for each yard.*

2. [Step 2] Create an initial Sketch:

   K L M N O P Q

Front	Back

3. [Step 3] Analyze and draw the Rules:
   - Rule 1:
     - What does the rule restrict, and what does it leave open? *The kiwi and the mango trees cannot be together.*
     - What are the rule's negative implications, if any? *They must be in different yards. Since there are only two yards, one must be in the front, and one must be in the back.*
     - Can the rule be depicted inside the sketch framework? *Yes.*

   - Draw the rule:

Front	Back
K/M	M/K

   - Rule 2:
     - What does the rule restrict, and what does it leave open? *The quince and the orange trees cannot be in the same yard.*
     - What are the rule's negative implications, if any? *They must be in different yards. Since there are only two yards, one must be in the front, and one must be in the back.*
     - Can the rule be depicted inside the sketch framework? *Yes.*
     - Draw the rule:

Front	Back
K/M	M/K
O/Q	Q/O

   - Rule 3:
     - What does the rule restrict, and what does it leave open? *The lemon and orange trees are in the same yard, but it could be either yard.*
     - What are the rule's negative implications, if any? *These trees cannot be split up.*
     - Can the rule be depicted inside the sketch framework? *No.*
     - Draw the rule:

   - Rule 4:
     - What does the rule restrict, and what does it leave open? *If the nectarine is in the front yard, then the plum must be there, too. If the nectarine is in the back yard, the rule doesn't apply and the plum could be in either yard.*

- What are the rule's negative implications, if any? *By contrapositive, if the plum is not in the front yard (i.e., if it's in the back yard), then the nectarine can't be in the front yard (i.e., it must be in the back yard). Again, if the plum is in the back yard, the rule doesn't apply, and the nectarine could be in either yard.*

- Can the rule be depicted inside the sketch framework? *No.*

- Draw the rule:

  If N = front → P = front

  If P = back → N = back

- Rule 5:

  - What does the rule restrict, and what does it leave open? *The quince tree is established in the front yard.*

  - What are the rule's negative implications, if any? *It's not in the back yard.*

  - Can the rule be depicted inside the sketch framework? *Yes.*

  - Draw the rule:

Front	Back
Q̲	

Practice 3

Seven graduate students—Arroyo, Baxter, Chen, Domingo, Erickson, Farrel, and Goya—are being assigned as teaching assistants for three professors—Sheffield, Tran, and Umberto. Each student will be assigned to exactly one professor, and each professor will receive at least one student. Arroyo, Baxter, Domingo, and Erickson are studying mathematics, while Chen, Farrel, and Goya are studying physics. The following restrictions apply:

No student studying physics can be assigned to the same professor as another student studying physics.

Baxter and Domingo will be assigned to the same professor.

Tran will be assigned more teaching assistants than will Sheffield.

If Erickson is assigned to Tran, then Arroyo cannot be assigned to Tran.

1. [Step 1] Summarize your Overview analysis: *This is a Distribution game in which seven students will each be assigned to exactly one of three professors. Each professor will get at least one student. The students are split into two subgroups: math students and physics students.*

2. [Step 2] Create an initial Sketch:

Math	Phys
A B D E	c f g

Shef	Tran	Umb
—	—	—

3. [Step 3] Analyze and draw the Rules:

   - Rule 1:

     - What does the rule restrict, and what does it leave open? *None of the physics students (Chen, Farrel, and Goya) can be assigned to the same professor.*

     - What are the rule's negative implications, if any? *They each must be assigned to a different professor.*

     - Can the rule be depicted inside the sketch framework? *Yes. There are three physics students, and only three professors. Each professor must get one of the physics students. One each of c, f, and g will be with each professor.*

     - Draw the rule:

Shef	Tran	Umb
c/f/g	c/f/g	c/f/g

   - Rule 2:

     - What does the rule restrict, and what does it leave open? *Baxter and Domingo must be together, but they could be assigned to any teacher.*

     - What are the rule's negative implications, if any? *Baxter and Domingo cannot be separated.*

- Can the rule be depicted inside the sketch framework? *No.*
- Draw the rule:

- Rule 3:
  - What does the rule restrict, and what does it leave open? *Tran will get more students than Sheffield, but it's unknown how many more.*
  - What are the rule's negative implications, if any? *Tran cannot have just one student, so Tran will get at least two.*
  - Can the rule be depicted inside the sketch framework? *Generally, no; however, a second space can be added to Tran's column.*
  - Draw the rule:

- Rule 4:
  - What does the rule restrict, and what does it leave open? *If Erickson is assigned to Tran, then Arroyo is not.*
  - What are the rule's negative implications, if any? *By contrapositive, if Arroyo is assigned to Tran, Erickson is not. Essentially, they can't both be assigned to Tran—although they could be together with another professor.*
  - Can the rule be depicted inside the sketch framework? *No, but you can draw an anti-block under the Tran column.*
  - Draw the rule:

    If E = Tran → A ≠ Tran

    If A = Tran → E ≠ Tran

Practice 4

A theater director is scheduling auditions for seven actors—Anh, Behn, Chang, Dien, Enge, Fein, and Gus. The actors will audition either alone or in groups. The director will schedule at most four auditions, with each actor attending exactly one audition. The final schedule will be based on the following determinations:

> Fein will audition alone.
> Anh and Enge will not be scheduled for the same audition.
> Chang and Enge will be not be scheduled for the same audition.
> Anh and Chang will not audition together unless Behn and Chang audition together.
> Dien and Anh will not audition together unless Behn auditions alone.

1. [Step 1] Summarize your Overview analysis: *A Distribution game in which seven actors will each be assigned to exactly one of four auditions. There's a maximum of four auditions, so there could be fewer than four. There's no limit to the number of actors at each audition. The auditions don't have labels, so call them 1, 2, 3, and 4.*

2. [Step 2] Create an initial Sketch:

3. [Step 3] Analyze and draw the Rules:
   - Rule 1:
     - What does the rule restrict, and what does it leave open? *Fein will be alone.*
     - What are the rule's negative implications, if any? *Nobody could be with Fein, so there must be at least a second audition for the other actors.*
     - Can the rule be depicted inside the sketch framework? *No.*
     - Draw the rule:

- Rule 2:
  - What does the rule restrict, and what does it leave open? *Anh and Enge will not be together.*
  - What are the rule's negative implications, if any? *They must attend different auditions.*
  - Can the rule be depicted inside the sketch framework? *No.*
  - Draw the rule:

    never $\boxed{\begin{array}{c} A \\ E \end{array}}$

- Rule 3:
  - What does the rule restrict, and what does it leave open? *Chang and Enge will not be together.*
  - What are the rule's negative implications, if any? *They must attend different auditions.*
  - Can the rule be depicted inside the sketch framework? *No.*
  - Draw the rule:

    never $\boxed{\begin{array}{c} C \\ E \end{array}}$

- Rule 4:
  - What does the rule restrict, and what does it leave open? *If Anh and Cheng are to audition together, then Behn would also have to audition with Cheng, i.e., they would all be together.*

- What are the rule's negative implications, if any? *By contrapositive, if Behn and Cheng auditioned separately, then Anh and Cheng are separate, too.*
- Can the rule be depicted inside the sketch framework? *No.*
- Draw the rule:

  If $\boxed{\begin{array}{c} A \\ C \end{array}}$ → $\boxed{\begin{array}{c} A \\ B \\ C \end{array}}$

  If not $\boxed{\begin{array}{c} B \\ C \end{array}}$ → not $\boxed{\begin{array}{c} A \\ C \end{array}}$

- Rule 5:
  - What does the rule restrict, and what does it leave open? *If Ahn and Dien audition together, then Behn must audition alone.*
  - What are the rule's negative implications, if any? *By contrapositive, if Behn auditions with anybody else, then Ahn and Dien must audition separately.*
  - Can the rule be depicted inside the sketch framework? *No.*
  - Draw the rule:

    If $\boxed{\begin{array}{c} A \\ D \end{array}}$ → $\boxed{B}$ alone

    If not $\boxed{B}$ alone → not $\boxed{\begin{array}{c} A \\ D \end{array}}$

Rule analysis reveals another way in which Distribution and Matching games are similar. In both, deductions can often be made "on the fly" as you are analyzing and drawing out the rules. It is always fine to add a deduction to your sketch during Step 3 if you notice it as you are drawing out the rules. However, you should still take a moment to catalog the rules using the BLEND checklist to be sure you've made all of the available deductions. Practice that step in the next section of this chapter.

DISTRIBUTION GAMES DEDUCTIONS

LEARNING OBJECTIVES

In this section of the chapter, you'll practice

- Applying Step 4 of the Logic Games Method to Distribution games by combining rules and restrictions to make all valid deductions in the game.

Prepare

Distribution games are distinguished from Matching games because, instead of featuring attributes that can be assigned to multiple entities, Distribution games ask you to dole out individual entities among a number of groups. In Distribution games, once you've distributed an entity (assigned it to a group), the entity is "done," and you cannot assign it to a second group. This difference in task makes for a slight difference in where the LSAT expert expects to spot the game's deductions. In all Distribution games, Numbers Restrictions are paramount. If a game's Overview establishes the number of entities per group up front (e.g., three boats with three seats each), then the key deductions will involve entities that must stay together (Blocks of Entities) or must be assigned to different groups. When the game doesn't establish the number of entities per group up front, the LSAT expert focuses on rules that help establish or limit the possibilities. For example, if the game has two teams and you're told that X and Y must be assigned to different teams and that P and Q must be assigned to different teams, you now know that each team has at least two entities.

LOGIC GAMES STRATEGY

In Distribution games, deductions are likely to stem from:

- **Numbers Restrictions**—Limitations on the number of entities per group or determinations of the minimum and maximum number of entities per group; in Distribution games, rules preventing entities from being assigned to the same group may act as *de facto* Numbers Restrictions (e.g., Raul and Sylvia must be assigned to different groups; ergo, two groups have at least one person). Another Numbers Restriction involves games with only two groups: The binary structure of such games means that if an entity is not in one group, it must be in the other.
- **Blocks of Entities**—Two or more entities that must be placed in the same group.
- **Limited Options**—The situation that arises when there are only two possible patterns for the number of entities per group (e.g., either five students are assigned to project X and four students to project Y, or four students are assigned to project X and five students to project Y); In Distribution games, you can sometimes determine a Limited Options numbers scenario by applying other rules to the game's overall framework. Limited Options sketches may also be created if a Block of Entities is influential enough to warrant two or three sketches.
- **Duplications**—Entities shared by two or more rules; a common occurrence in Distribution games is one rule that says A and B will be in the same group and another rule that says A and C cannot be in the same group—from this, you can deduce that B and C cannot be in the same group.

In Distribution games, deductions may involve:

- **Established Entities**—Entities that are assigned to one group for the entire game; this is not very common in Distribution games.

Maintain your focus on numbers deductions and on rules that create blocks of entities (or forbid two entities from ever becoming a block) as you practice Step 4 by making the deductions in the model game setups you've been working with earlier in this chapter.

Practice

Directions: In each game setup, first reacquaint yourself with the setup and rules. Then, combine the rules and restrictions to make all available deductions, recording your analyses as indicated. Finally, test your deductions by answering the questions that accompany each game. You can find expert analysis and explanations at the end of the Practice section.

Practice 1

A homeowner has purchased exactly seven fruit trees—a kiwi tree, a lemon tree, a mango tree, a nectarine tree, an orange tree, a plum tree, and a quince tree—to plant in his front and back yards. The planting of trees must adhere to the following guidelines:

The kiwi tree and the mango tree cannot be planted in the same yard.
The quince tree and the orange tree cannot be planted in the same yard.
The lemon tree and the orange tree must be planted in the same yard.
If the nectarine tree is planted in the front yard, then the plum tree must also be planted in the front yard.
The quince tree must be planted in the front yard.

K L M N O P Q

Front	Back
K/M	M/K
O/Q	Q/O

L
O

In N = front → P = front
If P = back → N = back

1. Which entities or positions are the most restricted in this game? Why?

2. Which elements from the BLEND checklist can you identify in this game? Are there
   - Blocks of entities? If so, what are they?
   - Limited Options? If so, which rule(s) trigger them?
   - Established Entities? If so, which ones?
   - Number Restrictions? If so, describe them.
   - Duplications? If so, which rules share an entity?

3. Combine the rules and restrictions to create a Master Sketch depicting all of the deductions available in this game:

4. Evaluate your sketch by answering the following questions:
   - Which trees could be planted in either yard?
   - What is the minimum number of trees that must be planted in the front yard?
   - What is the maximum number of trees that could be planted in the same yard as the orange tree (not including the orange tree itself)?
   - If only two trees are planted in the front yard, what could they be?

Practice 2

Seven graduate students—Arroyo, Baxter, Chen, Domingo, Erickson, Farrel, and Goya—are being assigned as teaching assistants for three professors—Sheffield, Tran, and Umberto. Each student will be assigned to exactly one professor, and each professor will receive at least one student. Arroyo, Baxter, Domingo, and Erickson are studying mathematics, while Chen, Farrel, and Goya are studying physics. The following restrictions apply:

> No student studying physics can be assigned to the same professor as another student studying physics.
> Baxter and Domingo will be assigned to the same professor.
> Tran will be assigned more teaching assistants than will Sheffield.
> If Erickson is assigned to Tran, then Arroyo cannot be assigned to Tran.

$$\frac{Math}{A\ B\ D\ E} \quad \frac{Phys}{c\ f\ g}$$

(1-2)

Shef	Tran	Umb
c/f/g	c/f/g	c/f/g
	—	

$\boxed{\begin{matrix} B \\ D \end{matrix}}$

Tran > Shef

If E = Tran → A ≠ Tran

If A = Tran → E ≠ Tran

1. Which entities or positions are the most restricted in this game? Why?

2. Which elements from the BLEND checklist can you identify in this game? Are there
   - Blocks of entities? If so, what are they?
   - Limited Options? If so, which rule(s) trigger them?
   - Established Entities? If so, which ones?
   - Number Restrictions? If so, describe them.
   - Duplications? If so, which rules share an entity?

3. Combine the rules and restrictions to create a Master Sketch depicting all of the deductions available in this game:

4. Evaluate your sketch by answering the following questions:
   - Which math students can be assigned to any of the three professors?
   - Which professor could get both Arroyo and Erickson together?
   - What is the maximum number of students that could be assigned to Umberto?
   - If Umberto is assigned one student, who could it be?

Practice 3

A theater director is scheduling auditions for seven actors—Anh, Behn, Chang, Dien, Enge, Fein, and Gus. The actors will audition either alone or in groups. The director will schedule at most four auditions, with each actor attending exactly one audition. The final schedule will be based on the following determinations:

Fein will audition alone.
Anh and Enge will not be scheduled for the same audition.
Chang and Enge will be not be scheduled for the same audition.
Anh and Chang will not audition together unless Behn and Chang audition together.
Dien and Anh will not audition together unless Behn auditions alone.

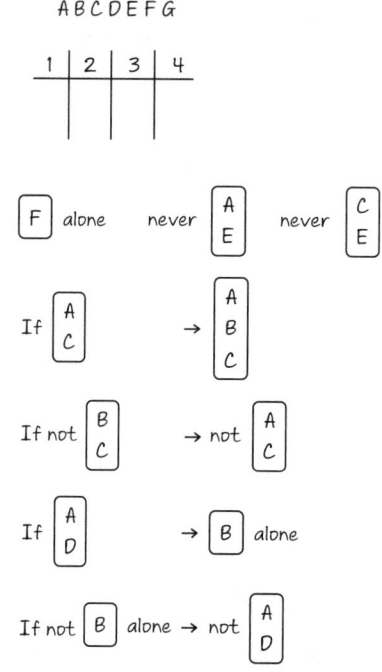

1. Which entities or positions are the most restricted in this game? Why?

2. Which elements from the BLEND checklist can you identify in this game? Are there
   - Blocks of entities? If so, what are they?
   - Limited Options? If so, which rule(s) trigger them?
   - Established Entities? If so, which ones?
   - Number Restrictions? If so, describe them.
   - Duplications? If so, which rules share an entity?

3. Combine the rules and restrictions to create a Master Sketch depicting all of the deductions available in this game:

4. Evaluate your sketch by answering the following questions:
   - What is the minimum number of auditions that must be held?
   - Who could Enge audition with?
   - Who could Chang audition with?
   - What is the maximum number of people in any audition?

K

Explanations

Compare your work to that of an LSAT expert. Pay close attention to how the expert combined the rules and restrictions to make additional deductions, and to how the expert depicted the deductions within the sketch framework.

Practice 1

A homeowner has purchased exactly seven fruit trees—a kiwi tree, a lemon tree, a mango tree, a nectarine tree, an orange tree, a plum tree, and a quince tree—to plant in his front and back yards. The planting of trees must adhere to the following guidelines:

> The kiwi tree and the mango tree cannot be planted in the same yard.
> The quince tree and the orange tree cannot be planted in the same yard.
> The lemon tree and the orange tree must be planted in the same yard.
> If the nectarine tree is planted in the front yard, then the plum tree must also be planted in the front yard.
> The quince tree must be planted in the front yard.

1. Which entities or positions are the most restricted in this game? Why? *The quince tree, which is established in the front yard, and the orange tree, which cannot be with the quince tree but must be with the lemon tree.*

2. Which elements from the BLEND checklist can you identify in this game? Are there
   - Blocks of entities? If so, what are they? *Rule 3 requires the lemon and orange trees to be together.*
   - Limited Options? If so, which rule(s) trigger them? *N/A*
   - Established Entities? If so, which ones? *Rule 5 establishes the quince tree in the front yard.*
   - Number Restrictions? If so, describe them. *Rules 1 and 2 each place one tree in each yard. Together, they establish at least two trees in each yard.*

- Duplications? If so, which rules share an entity? *Rules 2 and 5 both mention the quince tree. Rules 2 and 3 both mention the orange tree.*

3. Combine the rules and restrictions to create a Master Sketch depicting all of the deductions available in this game: *Start with the quince tree, which is established in the front yard. That means the orange tree (and thus also the lemon tree) must be in the back yard.*

Front	Back
Q̲	O̲
	L̲

The kiwi and mango trees are split, but either can be planted in either yard.

Front	Back
Q̲	O̲
K/M̲	L̲
	M/K̲

4. Evaluate your sketch by answering the following questions:
   - Which trees could be planted in either yard? *Kiwi, mango, nectarine, and plum.*
   - What is the minimum number of trees that must be planted in the front yard? *Two.*
   - What is the maximum number of trees that could be planted in the same yard as the orange tree (not including the orange tree itself)? *Four; lemon, nectarine, plum, and one more—either the kiwi or the mango.*
   - If only two trees are planted in the front yard, what could they be? *The quince and the kiwi, or the quince and the mango.*

Practice 2

Seven graduate students—Arroyo, Baxter, Chen, Domingo, Erickson, Farrel, and Goya—are being assigned as teaching assistants for three professors—Sheffield, Tran, and Umberto. Each student will be assigned to exactly one professor, and each professor will receive at least one student. Arroyo, Baxter, Domingo, and Erickson are studying mathematics, while Chen, Farrel, and Goya are studying physics. The following restrictions apply:

>   No student studying physics can be assigned to the same professor as another student studying physics.
>   Baxter and Domingo will be assigned to the same professor.
>   Tran will be assigned more teaching assistants than will Sheffield.
>   If Erickson is assigned to Tran, then Arroyo cannot be assigned to Tran.

1. Which entities or positions are the most restricted in this game? Why? *Sheffield, who must have fewer entities than Tran.*

2. Which elements from the BLEND checklist can you identify in this game? Are there

    •   Blocks of entities? If so, what are they? *Rule 2 puts Baxter and Domingo together.*

    •   Limited Options? If so, which rule(s) trigger them? *Not directly, but the Block from Rule 2 and the numbers of Rule 3 are restricted enough to present two options each.*

    •   Established Entities? If so, which ones? *Rule 1 establishes a physics student with each professor.*

    •   Number Restrictions? If so, describe them. *Rule 4 gives Tran at least two students, and limits Sheffield to fewer than Tran.*

    •   Duplications? If so, which rules share an entity? *Rules 3 and 4 both mention Tran, but not in a way that can be easily combined.*

3. Combine the rules and restrictions to create a Master Sketch depicting all of the deductions available in this game:

    Sheffield has to have fewer students than Tran. Sheffield can just have one student (a physics student) or two. If Sheffield got three students, Tran would need four, leaving nobody for Umberto. So Sheffield is limited to just one or two students.

    (1-2) <

Shef	Tran	Umb
c/f/g	c/f/g	c/f/g
___		___
	___	

    One of Sheffield's students must be a physics student. So, even if Sheffield got two students, it couldn't be both Baxter and Domingo.

    There are two opportunities for Limited Options. The first is based on the Block of Baxter and Domingo, which can only be assigned to Tran or Umberto. If they were assigned to Tran, that would set up five slots in the sketch, and nothing else.

Shef	Tran	Umb
c/f/g	c/f/g	c/f/g
	B	
	D	

    However, if Baxter and Domingo were assigned to Umberto, that would set up six slots. The second student for Tran would be Arroyo or Erickson.

Shef	Tran	Umb
c/f/g	c/f/g	c/f/g
___	A/E	B
		D

Tran cannot get both Arroyo and Erickson, so Tran will be finished with two students. That means Sheffield has just one. Whichever student Tran doesn't get (Arroyo or Erickson) will have to be assigned to Umberto.

Shef	Tran	Umb
c/f/g	c/f/g	c/f/g
═══	A/E	B
	═══	D
		A/E
		═══

The second opportunity for Limited Options is based on the number—whether Sheffield gets one or two students. If Sheffield gets just one student, that has no further effect on the numbers. Baxter and Domingo can be assigned to Tran or Umberto. Arroyo and Erickson cannot both be assigned to Tran, so at least one of them (if not both) must be assigned to Umberto.

Shef	Tran	Umb
c/f/g	c/f/g	c/f/g
═══	—	A/E
		═══

If Sheffield gets two students, then Tran gets at least three. Umberto could then only get one extra math student, so Baxter and Domingo must be assigned to Tran. Sheffield's second student will be Arroyo or Erickson. Whichever one is not assigned to Sheffield could go to Tran or Umberto.

Shef	Tran	Umb
c/f/g	c/f/g	c/f/g
A/E	B	
═══	D	

4. Evaluate your sketch by answering the following questions:
    *   Which math students can be assigned to any of the three professors? *Arroyo or Erickson.*

*   Which professor could get both Arroyo and Erickson together? *Umberto.*
*   What is the maximum number of students that could be assigned to Umberto? *Four.*
*   If Umberto is assigned one student, who could it be? *It must be a physics student: Chen, Farrel, or Goya.*

Practice 3

A theater director is scheduling auditions for seven actors—Anh, Behn, Chang, Dien, Enge, Fein, and Gus. The actors will audition either alone or in groups. The director will schedule at most four auditions, with each actor attending exactly one audition. The final schedule will be based on the following determinations:

> Fein will audition alone.
> Anh and Enge will not be scheduled for the same audition.
> Chang and Enge will be not be scheduled for the same audition.
> Anh and Chang will not audition together unless Behn and Chang audition together.
> Dien and Anh will not audition together unless Behn auditions alone.

1. Which entities or positions are the most restricted in this game? Why? *Anh, Chang, and Enge; Enge cannot be with the other two, and both Anh and Chang potentially affect other actors.*

2. Which elements from the BLEND checklist can you identify in this game? Are there
    *   Blocks of entities? If so, what are they? *N/A*
    *   Limited Options? If so, which rule(s) trigger them? *N/A*
    *   Established Entities? If so, which ones? *Rule 1 establishes F in an audition alone.*
    *   Number Restrictions? If so, describe them. *Rule 1 established that one audition will have exactly one actor, meaning there must be at least a second audition. Rules 2 and 3 also split up actors, requiring multiple auditions.*

- Duplications? If so, which rules share an entity? *Rules 2, 4, and 5 all mention Anh. Rules 2 and 3 mention Enge. Rules 3 and 4 mention Chang. Rules 4 and 5 mention Behn.*

3. Combine the rules and restrictions to create a Master Sketch depicting all of the deductions available in this game:

   The auditions are never referred to by name, and there's no order to the auditions. So, the audition labels are arbitrary, and actors can be placed into any audition at any time. So, start by placing Fein in audition 1 and closing it off.

1	2	3	4
F̲			

   After that, Anh and Enge must be separated, so put Ang in audition 2 and Enge in audition 3. Chang cannot go into audition 3 with Enge.

1	2	3	4
F̲	A	E	
		~C	

   That means there will be at least three auditions. Everything else is dependent on the Formal Logic. It can be noted that the result of

each Formal Logic rule triggers the contrapositive of the other. In other words, if Anh and Chang are together, then Behn is with them and thus not alone. So, Anh and Dien would be separate. Similarly, if Anh and Dien were separate, then Behn would be alone and thus couldn't be with Chang. That would mean Anh and Chang would have to be separate.*

4. Evaluate your sketch by answering the following questions:

   - What is the minimum number of auditions that must be held? *Three.*
   - Who could Enge audition with? *Behn, Dien, or Gus.*
   - Who could Chang audition with? *Anh, Behn, Dien, or Gus.*
   - What is the maximum number of people in any audition? *Four; nobody can be with Fein, and Enge can't audition with Chang. The remaining five (Anh, Behn, Chang, Dien, and Gus) cannot all be together. If Anh and Dien were together, Behn would have to be alone. However, If Dien was elsewhere, Anh, Behn, Chang and Gus could all be together.*

In both Matching and Distribution games, the deductions step can make or break your ability to answer the questions quickly and accurately. With all of the deductions in place, you can often handle the question set quite quickly and confidently. Make sure to give Step 4 due diligence, however, as you evaluate your skills in all five steps of the Logic Games Method on the full-length Distribution games in the next section of this chapter.

DISTRIBUTION GAMES—FULL GAMES WITH QUESTIONS

LEARNING OBJECTIVES

In this section, you'll assess your ability to

- Apply the Logic Games Method to Distribution games.

Perform

Here is your opportunity to put all of the pieces together and assess your skills on Distribution games. On the following pages, you'll find two full-length games along with their question sets. Both of these games are from officially released LSAT tests, and all are representative of Distribution games you could see on Test Day. You can take the games one at a time or both together, but for your self-evaluation to be as accurate as possible, adhere to the timing guidelines set forth in the directions.

An answer key follows the games. Complete worked example expert analyses can be found in your online resources.

After you complete and review both games, assess your performance using the evaluation guidelines. There, you'll find recommendations for additional Easy, Medium, and Hard Distribution games from officially released LSAT exams that you can practice to continue honing your skills and raising your score.

Directions: Take no more than 9 minutes per game to complete the following two games and all of their questions.

Perform 1

<u>Questions 1–5</u>

Planes 1, 2, 3, and 4—and no others—are available to fly in an air show.

> Pilots Anna, Bob, and Cindy are all aboard planes that are flying in the show and they are the only qualified pilots in the show.
>
> Copilots Dave, Ed, and Fran are all aboard planes that are flying in the show and they are the only qualified copilots in the show.
>
> No plane flies in the show without a qualified pilot aboard.
>
> No one but qualified pilots and qualified copilots flies in the show.
>
> Anna will only fly in either plane 1 or plane 4.
>
> Dave will only fly in either plane 2 or plane 3.

1. If Anna flies in plane 4 and Dave flies in plane 2, which one of the following must be true?

    (A) Cindy flies in either plane 1 or plane 3.
    (B) If Cindy flies in plane 3, Bob flies in plane 2.
    (C) Bob and one other person fly in plane 1.
    (D) If Bob is aboard plane 4, Cindy flies in plane 3.
    (E) If Cindy is in plane 2, Bob flies in plane 3.

2. If Bob and Anna fly on the same plane, which one of the following must be true?

    (A) Cindy flies with Dave and Ed.
    (B) Cindy flies with Ed.
    (C) Dave flies with Cindy.
    (D) Dave flies with Cindy, Ed, and Fran.
    (E) Fran flies with Ed.

3. If Cindy and Fran are the only people in one of the planes, which one of the following must be true?

    (A) Bob flies with Anna.
    (B) Dave flies with Ed.
    (C) Dave and Ed fly with Bob.
    (D) Dave flies with Bob.
    (E) Ed flies with Anna.

4. If plane 1 is used, its crew could consist of

    (A) Anna, Bob, Cindy, Fran
    (B) Anna, Bob, Ed, Fran
    (C) Bob, Cindy, Ed, Fran
    (D) Bob, Cindy, Dave, Ed
    (E) Bob, Dave, Ed, Fran

5. If as many of the pilots and copilots as possible fly in plane 4, that group will consist of

    (A) exactly two people
    (B) exactly three people
    (C) exactly four people
    (D) exactly five people
    (E) three pilots and two copilots

PrepTest3 Sec1 Qs 20–24

Perform 2

<u>Questions 6–11</u>

Eight camp counselors—Fran, George, Henry, Joan, Kathy, Lewis, Nathan, and Olga—must each be assigned to supervise exactly one of three activities—swimming, tennis, and volleyball. The assignment of counselors must conform to the following conditions:

Each activity is supervised by at least two, but not more than three, of the eight counselors.

Henry supervises swimming.

Neither Kathy nor Olga supervises tennis.

Neither Kathy nor Nathan supervises the same activity as Joan.

If George supervises swimming, both Nathan and Olga supervise volleyball.

6. Which one of the following is an acceptable assignment of the counselors to the activities?

(A) Swimming: Fran, George, Henry; Tennis: Joan, Lewis; Volleyball: Kathy, Nathan, Olga

(B) Swimming: George, Henry, Olga; Tennis: Fran, Joan, Lewis; Volleyball: Kathy, Nathan

(C) Swimming: Henry; Tennis: Fran, George, Joan, Lewis; Volleyball: Kathy, Nathan, Olga

(D) Swimming: Henry, Joan, Kathy; Tennis: George, Nathan; Volleyball: Fran, Lewis, Olga

(E) Swimming: Henry, Nathan; Tennis: Fran, Kathy, Lewis; Volleyball: George, Joan, Olga

7. Which one of the following is a pair of counselors who could be two of three counselors assigned to supervise swimming?

    (A) George and Nathan
    (B) George and Olga
    (C) Joan and Kathy
    (D) Joan and Nathan
    (E) Joan and Olga

8. Which one of the following is a pair of counselors who could together be assigned to supervise tennis?

    (A) Fran and Kathy
    (B) George and Nathan
    (C) Henry and Lewis
    (D) Joan and Nathan
    (E) Joan and Olga

9. If George and Kathy are two of three counselors assigned to supervise swimming, which one of the following could be true of the assignment?

    (A) Fran supervises swimming.
    (B) Henry supervises tennis.
    (C) Joan supervises volleyball.
    (D) Lewis supervises volleyball.
    (E) Nathan supervises tennis.

10. If Fran and Lewis are two of three counselors assigned to supervise swimming, which one of the following must be true of the assignment?

    (A) George supervises volleyball.
    (B) Henry supervises volleyball.
    (C) Joan supervises tennis.
    (D) Kathy supervises swimming.
    (E) Nathan supervises tennis.

11. If Joan is assigned to supervise the same activity as Olga, which one of the following CANNOT be true of the assignment?

    (A) Fran supervises swimming.
    (B) George supervises swimming.
    (C) Kathy supervises volleyball.
    (D) Lewis supervises volleyball.
    (E) Nathan supervises tennis.

PrepTest11 Sec1 Qs 1–6

Answer Key

Perform 1

1. (B)
2. (C)
3. (D)
4. (B)
5. (C)

Perform 2

6. (A)
7. (E)
8. (B)
9. (D)
10. (C)
11. (B)

Worked example explanations of these questions with complete expert analysis can be found in your Online Study Plan under Chapter 9. View or download the PDF titled "Chapter 9 Distribution Perform Full Games Explanations."

Assess

Use the following criteria to evaluate your results on the Perform games.

If, under timed conditions, you correctly answered

9–11 of the questions: Outstanding! You have demonstrated a strong skill level in Distribution games. For further practice in Distribution, use any of the Recommended Additional Practice sets, including the Advanced set. Then, move on to Chapter 10 on Hybrid games.

6–8 of the questions: Good work! You have a solid foundation in Distribution games. For further practice in Distribution, begin with the Foundations or Mid-Level Recommended Additional Practice set. Then, move on to Chapter 10 on Hybrid games. If you have time before Test Day, try the Advanced Recommended Additional Distribution Practice set, as well.

0–5 of the questions: Keep working. Distribution, along with its close cousin Matching, shows up on more than a third of games as a pure action or as part of a hybrid. Continued practice will help you improve your score. Begin by reviewing this chapter. Then, try the games in the Foundations Recommended Additional Practice set. As you continue to progress, move on to the Mid-Level Recommended Additional Practice set. Then, move on to Chapter 10 on Hybrid games.

To stay sharp, practice the drills in the Logic Games Training Camp for this chapter in your Online Study Plan. Training Camp drills are divided into Fundamentals, Mid-Level, and Advanced sets.

Recommended Additional Practice: Distribution

All of the following games will provide good practice on Distribution. They are grouped by difficulty as determined from empirical student practice results. All PrepTests included are available individually, or in bundles of ten as part of the LSAC's *10 Actual, Official LSAT PrepTests* series.

Foundations
PrepTest 68, Section 4, Game 2: Two Days of Witness Testimony*

PrepTest 63, Section 2, Game 1: Judicial Appointments*

Mid-Level
PrepTest 71, Section 2, Game 2: Application Evaluation*

PrepTest 66, Section 3, Game 3: Software Company Sales Zones*

PrepTest 61, Section 3, Game 1: Business Convention**

Advanced
PrepTest 69, Section 2, Game 4: Cases for Paralegals*

PrepTest 52, Section 2, Game 2: Field Trip Chaperones**

*Game included in *10 Actual, Official LSAT PrepTests Volume V: PrepTests 62–71*; complete answers and explanations written by Kaplan LSAT experts available via the eBook: *LSAT PrepTests 62–71 Unlocked: Exclusive Data, Analysis & Explanations for 10 Actual, Official LSAT PrepTests Volume V.*

**Game included in *10 New Actual, Official LSAT PrepTests with Comparative Reading (PrepTests 52–61)*; complete answers and explanations written by Kaplan LSAT experts available via the eBook: *LSAT PrepTests 52–61 Unlocked: Exclusive Data, Analysis & Explanations for 10 New Actual, Official LSAT PrepTests with Comparative Reading.* [Explanations title coming Fall 2018.]

Reflect

Think back over the study and practice you did in this chapter.

- Are you able to identify Distribution games from their setups?
- Do you have a default sketch framework for Distribution actions?
- What kinds of rules do you anticipate seeing in Distribution games?
- Are you comfortable analyzing Distribution rules and determining whether to record them within or underneath the sketch framework?
- Are you making the available deductions efficiently and effectively in Distribution games?

In the coming days and weeks before Test Day, take note of real-world tasks that reflect Distribution tasks. Consider how they mirror the setups and questions in LSAT Distribution, and how they differ. Try to reframe real-life distribution tasks using the terms, rules, and restrictions used by the testmaker.

Hybrid Games Unlocked

Hybrid games have made up 20 percent of the games on official LSATs released over the past five years.

Types of Games By Percentage, 2012–2016

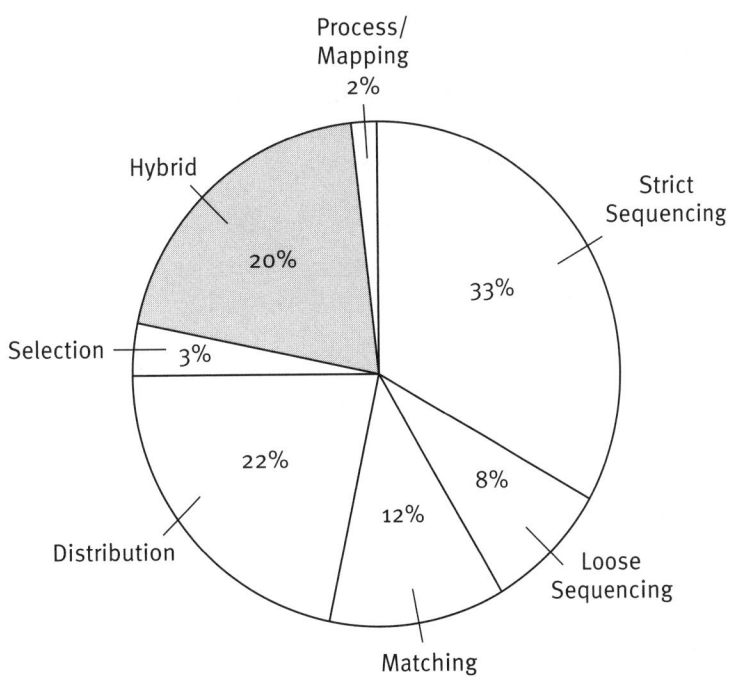

That looks like a lot, but don't think that you have to learn one-fifth of the Logic Games section in this chapter. In reality, you've learned most of what you'll be doing in this chapter already. That's because Hybrid games combine two (or, very rarely, three) of the standard game actions: Sequencing, Distribution, Matching, and Selection.

In theory, the test could combine any of the standard actions, but in practice, there are just four Hybrids that regularly appear on the LSAT. A look at the breakdown of Hybrid games on LSATs released from 2012 to 2016 show you what they are.

Hybrid Actions	# of games on LSATs released 2012–2016
Sequencing-Matching	4
Distribution-Sequencing	3
Selection-Sequencing	3
Selection-Distribution	2

In the next section of this chapter, you'll see default sketch frameworks suggested for each of those Hybrid actions.

Hybrid games have a reputation for being complicated, confusing, and downright hard. That's fair to an extent—Hybrids are, on average, slightly harder than other game types—but the difficulty of Hybrids is often exaggerated. The individual actions in Hybrid games are often quite simple. In a Sequencing-Matching Hybrid, for example, you might be asked to put six figurines in a row, one per position, and then assign each figurine one of two colors, black or tan. (By the way, did it strike you that the game just described is very similar to the Truck Arrivals game from Chapter 1? That, too, was a Sequencing-Matching Hybrid game.)

After the work you've already done, a six-entity basic Strict Sequencing game shouldn't sound too bad. Nor should a matching game with just two attributes. The only complexity introduced by this game's Hybrid nature is that you must account for each entity's position and color.

Throughout this chapter, you'll work with games that provide examples of the four common Hybrids. At the end of the chapter, there is an LSAT Channel Special Feature on one example of a rare Hybrid game—Selection-Matching—that has only appeared twice in LSAT history. The game covered in that Special Feature is famous (well, as famous as an LSAT logic game can be) as one of the hardest of all time. It's known as the Dinosaur game, and you will definitely want to check out The LSAT Channel experts giving their take on it.

HYBRID GAMES IN REAL LIFE

If you think about it, almost everything you do in real life is a Hybrid task. To make this statement concrete, think of the jobs involved in planning a wedding. You have to decide whom you'll invite. That's Selection. You have to plan who will (or won't) sit together at dinner, like a huge Distribution game. You even have to decide the pairs in the wedding party and the order in which they'll walk down the aisle; that's a Sequencing-Matching game. As you plan that task, you and your spouse-to-be will have some "rules" to determine who enters first, second, third, and so on, and other "rules" to determine who will walk with whom. This is exactly what the test would outline in a comparable logic game.

Ask anyone who has ever planned a wedding and they'll tell you it is a very complex task. While the wedding scenarios provide some helpful analogies, LSAT Hybrid games keep your job much simpler. The LSAT will never ask you to sequence seven bridesmaids and to assign each of them between one and three types of clothing, jewelry, and bouquets. They don't expect even the most expert test takers to able to complete a game like that in eight and half minutes. As you practice with the games in this chapter, take note of how the testmaker limits the scope of one or both of the tasks.

Here are four more real-life tasks that illustrate the standard sketch frameworks associated with the LSAT's most common Hybrid game types.

Sequencing-Matching

Arrange six plants labeled A, B, C, D, E, and F from left to right in a planter box with six spaces, one plant per space. Each plant flowers in exactly one of three colors—red, white, or yellow.

$$A \quad B \quad C \quad D \quad E \quad F$$

$$\overline{} \ \overline{} \ \overline{} \ \overline{} \ \overline{} \ \overline{}$$
$$ 1 \quad 2 \quad 3 \quad 4 \quad 5 \quad 6$$
$$r/w/y \ \_ \ \_ \ \_ \ \_ \ \_ \ \_$$

In real life, you'd have practical or aesthetic reasons for how you arrange the plants. Maybe the left side of the window box will get more sun. Or maybe you want flowers of the same color kept together or apart. In any case, the factors that go into your decisions translate easily into logic games rules: "Plants with the same color flowers cannot be in adjacent spaces" or "C is placed to the right of E."

Selection-Sequencing

From an envelope containing six family photos—one of mom, one of dad, one with mom and dad together, one of your sister as a baby, one of your sister as a teen, and one of your brother—choose four to display on the hallway wall. Then, choose the order in which to display them, one at a time, from left to right.

$$M, D, MD, S_1, S_2, B \quad (4 \text{ of } 6)$$

$$\overline{} \ \overline{} \ \overline{} \ \overline{}$$
$$1 \quad 2 \quad 3 \quad 4$$

You can already imagine how the rules might work. You will select only one picture of your sister. If you select both individual pictures of your mom and dad, you won't select the one of them together. You will hang the pictures of your siblings on either side of pictures of your parents. Simply substitute letters like A, B, C, and D for the pictures, and you have a ready-made Selection-Sequencing Hybrid game.

Selection-Distribution

From 10 articles of clothing—three blouses: one each in blue, red, and white; two dresses: one each in blue and white; two pairs of jeans: one each in blue and white; and three sweaters: one each in blue, red, and white—choose seven articles to keep. For each of the pieces kept, decide whether to hang it in the closet or put it in a drawer.

$$B_b \quad B_r \quad B_w \quad J_b \quad J_w$$
$$D_b \quad D_w \quad S_b \quad S_r \quad S_w \quad \text{Choose 7 of 10}$$

Closet	Drawer

This task might be hard in real life for emotional reasons ("oh, man, I love those jeans"), but it's pretty easy to picture, and certainly doesn't seem complicated. It's also pretty easy to see how your own rules—"I'll keep two of the three sweaters," "I'll keep two of the white things," or "Any dress I keep has to go in the closet"—would work in the context of an LSAT logic game.

This scenario actually has more entities and options than any recent Selection-Distribution game featured on the LSAT. It's good to remember how many factors there are in the everyday things we do, and use that to remind ourselves that LSAT logic games have quite limited and concrete tasks.

Distribution-Sequencing

From a group of eight sprinters—Q, R, S, T, W, X, Y, and Z—create two relay teams of four runners each. Assign each runner to run one leg—1st, 2nd, 3rd, or 4th—in the race.

$$Q \quad R \quad S \quad T \quad W \quad X \quad Y \quad Z$$

	Team 1	Team 2
1	—	—
2	—	—
3	—	—
4	—	—

This task would be routine for any track coach or PE teacher. In real life, you might have your reasons for making the two teams as equal as possible, or for making one much stronger than the other. Whatever your motive, the rules are easy to imagine: "Q and R will run on the same team," or "W is the fastest sprinter here, so she will run the anchor leg regardless of the team she's on."

With some grounding in the everyday nature of these tasks, and a good idea of the standard Hybrid sketches, you're ready to start analyzing these setups and games in the context that you'll see them on the LSAT.

HYBRID GAMES TASKS AND SKETCHES

LEARNING OBJECTIVES

In this section of the chapter, you'll learn to

- Apply Steps 1 and 2 of the Logic Games Method to Hybrid games by
  - Asking the SEAL questions to analyze the game's Overview, and then
  - Creating a simple, useful Sketch framework

Prepare

By reading the section on Hybrid Games in Real Life and taking careful note of the sample sketches, you've done the preparation needed to practice applying Steps 1 and 2 to Hybrid games.

LOGIC GAMES STRATEGY

Hybrid games ask you to combine two (or, rarely, three) of the standard game actions. The most common Hybrid games are

- Sequencing-Matching
- Distribution-Sequencing
- Selection-Sequencing
- Selection-Distribution

Not every Hybrid game fits one of the standard sketch frameworks exactly, of course. You've seen how LSAT experts adapt their default sketches to account for small "twists" or variations in all of the standard game types. The same thing applies here. Memorize the standard sketch formats—add them to your mental "library," if you will—and then be open to altering them as necessary to fit the situations described in various game setups.

Practice

Directions: Conduct an Overview of each game's setup by asking the SEAL questions, and create an initial sketch framework for the game's action.

Practice 1

Six witnesses—B, C, D, E, F, and G—are scheduled to testify in a court case. Three witnesses will be examined by the plaintiff's lead litigator, while the other three will be examined by the assistant attorney. Each witness will be examined once. The order in which they testify, and who examines them, are restricted by the following conditions:

Witness C will testify immediately after witness D.
Witness G will testify before witness F but after witness C.
Witness E will testify after witness D.
The lead litigator will examine the first and last witnesses.
The lead litigator will examine C.
The assistant attorney will not examine three consecutive witnesses.

1. [Step 1] Conduct an Overview analysis:
   - What is this game's Situation?
   - Who or what are the game's Entities?
   - What is the game's Action?
   - What are the Limitations explicit in the game setup?

2. [Step 2] Create an initial Sketch:

Practice 2

A company is conducting a quarterly review. Eight employees—Grant, Heather, Julia, Kendra, Lauren, Matthew, Nathan, and Oliver—will each attend a meeting with a supervisor on either Thursday or Friday of this week. One employee at a time will attend each meeting. The arrangement of the meetings is subject to the following restrictions:

If Heather attends her meeting on Thursday, then Lauren and Nathan will both attend their meetings on Friday.
Grant will attend his meeting on a different day than Matthew.
Julia will attend her meeting after Oliver and on the same day.
Friday will have no more than three meeting slots.
Julia's meeting is never the last meeting of the day.

1. [Step 1] Conduct an Overview analysis:

   - What is this game's Situation?

   - Who or what are the game's Entities?

   - What is the game's Action?

   - What are the Limitations explicit in the game setup?

2. [Step 2] Create an initial Sketch:

Practice 3

A senior partner is deciding how to organize the firm's associates for a new class action. Six of the eight associates—Ann, Brian, Courtney, David, Edwin, Frank, Gina, and Hannah—will be selected for either the Support team or the Trial team, each team needing at least two associates. The selection is governed by the following conditions:

> There are at most three associates selected for the Support team.
> If Edwin is on the Trial team, then Ann is on the Support team and David is not selected for either.
> If Ann is selected, then Hannah and Ann are placed on the same team.
> Brian and Courtney will never be placed on the same team.
> If Frank is placed on the Support team, then David is also placed on the Support team.

1. [Step 1] Conduct an Overview analysis:
   - What is this game's Situation?
   - Who or what are the game's Entities?
   - What is the game's Action?
   - What are the Limitations explicit in the game setup?

2. 2. [Step 2] Create an initial Sketch:

Explanations

Compare your work to that of an LSAT expert. Keep track of any case in which you incorrectly characterized the action described in the setup, and any case in which you drew a sketch framework that does not match the details of the game's situation.

Practice 1

Six witnesses—B, C, D, E, F, and G—are scheduled to testify in a court case. Three witnesses will be examined by the plaintiff's lead litigator, while the other three will be examined by the assistant attorney. Each witness will be examined once. The order in which they testify, and who examines them, are restricted by the following conditions:

> Witness C will testify immediately after witness D.
> Witness G will testify before witness F but after witness C.
> Witness E will testify after witness D.
> The lead litigator will examine the first and last witnesses.
> The lead litigator will examine witness C.
> The assistant attorney will not examine three consecutive witnesses.

1. [Step 1] Conduct an Overview analysis:

   • What is this game's Situation? *Witnesses testifying in a court case.*

   • Who or what are the game's Entities? *Six witnesses—B, C, D, E, F, and G—and two examiners—a (assistant attorney) and l (lead litigator).*

   • What is the game's Action? *Sequencing-Matching Hybrid. Determine the order in which the witnesses testify (Sequencing) and determine who examines each witness (Matching).*

   • What are the Limitations explicit in the game setup? *Each witness is examined once, making this standard one-to-one Sequencing. For the Matching action, each witness will be examined by one person; three by the lead litigator, and three by the assistant attorney.*

2. [Step 2] Create an initial Sketch:

```
 1   2   3   4   5   6
 _   _   _   _   _   _    B C D E F G
                          a a a l l l
```

Practice 2

A company is conducting a quarterly review. Eight employees—Grant, Heather, Julia, Kendra, Lauren, Matthew, Nathan, and Oliver—will each attend a meeting with a supervisor on either Thursday or Friday of this week. One employee at a time will attend each meeting. The arrangement of the meetings is subject to the following restrictions:

> If Heather attends her meeting on Thursday, then Lauren and Nathan will both attend their meetings on Friday.
> Grant will attend his meeting on a different day than Matthew.
> Julia will attend her meeting after Oliver and on the same day.
> Friday will have no more than three meeting slots.
> Julia's meeting is never the last meeting of the day.

1. [Step 1] Conduct an Overview analysis:

   • What is this game's Situation? *Employees getting their quarterly reviews.*

   • Who or what are the game's Entities? *Eight employees—G, H, J, K, L, M, N, and O.*

   • What is the game's Action? *Distribution-Sequencing Hybrid; determine the day on which each employee has a meeting (Distribution), followed by the order in which they have their meetings on each day (Sequencing).*

   • What are the Limitations explicit in the game setup? *Each employee will attend "a meeting," so that's one each, and they meet "one . . . at a time," so the sequencing is one-to-one.*

2. [Step 2] Create an initial Sketch:

G H J K L M N O

Practice 3

A senior partner is deciding how to organize the firm's associates for a new class action. Six of the eight associates—Ann, Brian, Courtney, David, Edwin, Frank, Gina, and Hannah—will be selected for either the Support or the Trial team, each team needing at least two associates. The selection is governed by the following conditions:

There are at most three associates selected for the Support team.
If Edwin is on the Trial team, then Ann is on the Support team and David is not selected for either.
If Ann is selected, then Hannah and Ann are placed on the same team.
Brian and Courtney will never be placed on the same team.
If Frank is placed on the Support team, then David is also placed on the Support team.

1. [Step 1] Conduct an Overview analysis:

- What is this game's Situation? *A law firm putting together teams of associates for a new class action.*

- Who or what are the game's Entities? *Eight associates—A, B, C, D, E, F, G, and H—and two teams—Support and Trial.*

- What is the game's Action? *Selection-Distribution Hybrid; determine which associates are going to be assigned to teams (Selection), then determine the team to which they will be assigned (Distribution).*

- What are the Limitations explicit in the game setup? *Exactly six of the eight are selected, so two will be out. The six that are selected will each be assigned to exactly one team.*

2. [Step 2] Create an initial Sketch:

A B C D E F G H

Supp	Trial	Out
—	—	—
—	—	=

Once you have your sketch in place for Hybrid games, take note of how each rule affects one or both of the Hybrid's two actions. Where and how you depict each rule will have much to do with the part(s) of the game it restricts. Keep that in mind as you turn to the next section and apply Step 3 to Hybrid games.

HYBRID GAMES RULES

LEARNING OBJECTIVES

In this section of the chapter, you'll practice

- Applying Step 3 of the Logic Games Method to Hybrid games by analyzing and sketching the rules

Prepare

The rules in Hybrid games will be of the same types as those in their single-action counterparts. The only difference is that within a Hybrid game, you will see a mix of different types of rules.

LOGIC GAMES STRATEGY

Hybrid rules tell you one of the following:

- How one action of the game is restricted
- How the actions are restricted simultaneously

When you are analyzing the rules in Hybrid games, pay attention to which of the actions each rule affects. In a Sequencing-Matching Hybrid, for example, some rules will exclusively apply to the Sequencing element, some to the Matching, and a couple may overlap. Here's the "real-life" game about flowers in the window box with several logic games-style rules appended to it.

An apartment dweller is arranging six plants—labeled A, B, C, D, E, and F—from left to right in a planter box with six spaces, with one plant occupying each space. Each plant flowers in exactly one of three colors—red, white, or yellow. His arrangement of the plants will correspond to the following considerations:

A and C are placed in adjacent boxes.
F is placed in a space to the left of D.
Plant E has yellow flowers.
Plant D does not have white flowers.
Plant C will occupy a space between two plants that have white flowers.

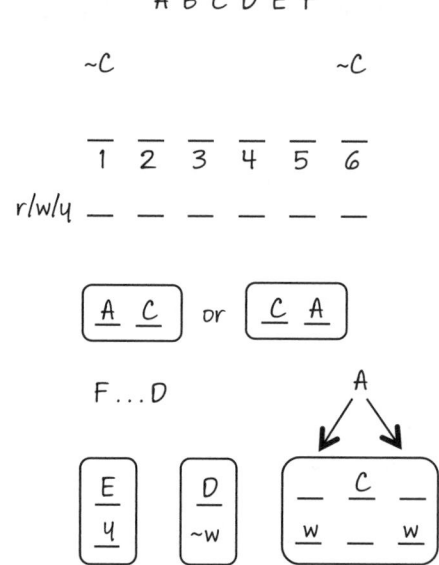

In this scenario, Rules 1 and 2 apply specifically to the Sequencing action. Rules 3 and 4 apply exclusively to the Matching action. Rule 5, however, touches both the Sequencing and Matching lines of the initial sketch. Because Rule 5 is a true "Hybrid rule," at least two deductions result from it: 1) It prevents C from being in either Space 1 or Space 6, and 2) it establishes A as having white flowers, because Rule 1 places A adjacent to C on the Sequencing line.

As you review the sample Hybrid rules in the following table, assess which part of the Hybrid games described each rule affects. Make a note of how the LSAT expert analyzes and draws "Hybrid rules" that affect both of the game's actions.

Rules	Analysis
A Sequencing-Matching Hybrid in which racers T, V, W, X, Y, and Z are arranged in six consecutive lanes at the starting line, and each one is wearing one brand of shoe—k, l, or m.	
V does not wear *k* unless X is in lane 6.	If $\dfrac{V}{k}$ → X = 6 If X ≠ 6 → ~$\dfrac{V}{k}$
Only one racer is wearing brand *m*, and that racer is in a higher-numbered lane than T and a lower-numbered lane than W	$\dfrac{T}{k/l}$ ... $\dfrac{\ }{m}$ ... $\dfrac{W}{k/l}$
Z wears brand *l* in lane 4, and no racer in a higher-numbered lane wears brand *l*.	1　2　3　4　5　6 — — — $\dfrac{Z}{l}$ $\dfrac{\ }{k/m}$ $\dfrac{\ }{k/m}$

A Selection-Sequencing Hybrid in which six out of eight collectibles—B, D, F, G, H, M, N, and P—are selected and arranged in 6 positions labeled 1 to 6 from left to right.

Rules	Analysis
F cannot appear to the left of G.	Never F . . . G
B is chosen only if D is not in position 6.	If B selected → D ≠ 6 If D = 6　　→ B not selected
If M appears to the right of P, then N is in position 3.	If P . . . M → N = 3 If N ≠ 3 → ~(P . . . M)

A Distribution-Selection game in which six of nine workers—F, G, H, J, K, L, M, N and P—are selected and assigned to either the front or back area.

Rules	Analysis
L does not work in the front area.	Front | Back ~L |
If H is assigned to the front area, then G is assigned to the back area.	If H = Front → G = Back If G = Front → H = Back

Now, get in some practice analyzing and drawing rules in Hybrid games. In the first exercise, consider the brief game descriptions to help you determine how best to draw the rules that follow. In exercises 2–4, you'll revisit the game setups you saw in the previous section of this chapter, now accompanied by full sets of rules.

Practice

Practice 1

Directions: Analyze and draw each of following Hybrid game rules. Use the brief game description to guide your depiction of the game's framework.

Rules		Analysis
A Sequencing-Matching Hybrid in which six cars—B, C, D, E, F, and G—are exhibited in order at a car show, and each car is from a different decade—1970s, 1980s, or 1990s.		
1. The third and sixth car must be from different decades.	$\longrightarrow$	
2. If C is presented before B, then the second car must be from an earlier decade than the sixth car.	$\longrightarrow$	
3. F is not from the 1970s unless D is immediately before E.	$\longrightarrow$	
A Distribution-Sequencing Hybrid in which six students—P, Q, R, S, T, and U—are each assigned to exactly one class— art or music—and are arranged in order of the presentations they give in class.		
4. Q is assigned to the music class.	$\longrightarrow$	
5. If T is assigned to the art class, then P and U must be assigned to the music class, with P presenting some time before U.	$\longrightarrow$	
6. R is assigned to the art class if S gives the last presentation in the music class.	$\longrightarrow$	
A Selection-Sequencing Hybrid that selects five out of eight artifacts—S, T, U, V, W, X, Y, and Z—and arranges them in order of presentation.		
7. V is selected only if X is presented at some time before it.	$\longrightarrow$	
8. T is not selected unless U and W are presented consecutively.	$\longrightarrow$	
9. S cannot be one of the first three artifacts presented.	$\longrightarrow$	
A Selection-Matching Hybrid in which exactly six of eight canvasses—A, B, C, D, E, F, G, and H—are selected and matched to exactly one of three colors—red, silver, or tan.		
10. B cannot be selected if it is red.	$\longrightarrow$	
11. If C and D are selected, then exactly two of the canvasses selected are silver.	$\longrightarrow$	
12. Exactly three of the canvasses selected are tan.	$\longrightarrow$	

Practice 2

Directions: Take a couple minutes to review the game setup, summarize your Overview analysis, and recreate the initial Sketch. Then, one at a time, analyze the rules, answer the questions about each one, and draw the rule either inside or underneath the sketch framework.

Six witnesses—B, C, D, E, F, and G—are scheduled to testify in a court case. Three witnesses will be examined by the plaintiff's lead litigator, while the other three will be examined by the assistant attorney. Each witness will be examined once. The order in which they testify, and who examines them, are restricted by the following conditions:

> Witness C will testify immediately after witness D.
> Witness G will testify before witness F but after witness C.
> Witness E will testify after witness D.
> The lead litigator will examine the first and last witnesses.
> The lead litigator will examine C.
> The assistant attorney will not examine three consecutive witnesses.

1. [Step 1] Summarize your Overview analysis:

2. [Step 2] Create an initial Sketch:

3. [Step 3] Analyze and draw the Rules:
   - For each rule, answer the following questions and draw the rule in the appropriate box.
     - What does the rule restrict, and what does it leave open?
     - What are the rule's negative implications, if any?
     - Can the rule be depicted inside the sketch framework?

Rule 1:	Rule 2:
Rule 3:	Rule 4:
Rule 5:	Rule 6:

Practice 3

Directions: Take a couple minutes to review the game setup, summarize your Overview analysis, and recreate the initial Sketch. Then, one at a time, analyze the rules, answer the questions about each one, and draw the rule either inside or underneath the sketch framework.

A company is conducting a quarterly review. Eight employees—Grant, Heather, Julia, Kendra, Lauren, Matthew, Nathan, and Oliver—will each attend a meeting with a supervisor on either Thursday or Friday of this week. One employee at a time will attend each meeting. The arrangement of the meetings is subject to the following restrictions:

If Heather attends her meeting on Thursday, then Lauren and Nathan will both attend their meetings on Friday.

Grant will attend his meeting on a different day than Matthew.

Julia will attend her meeting after Oliver and on the same day.

Friday will have no more than three meeting slots.

Julia's meeting is never the last meeting of the day.

1. [Step 1] Summarize your Overview analysis:

2. [Step 2] Create an initial Sketch:

3. [Step 3] Analyze and draw the Rules:
    - For each rule, answer the following questions and draw the rule in the appropriate box.
      - What does the rule restrict, and what does it leave open?
      - What are the rule's negative implications, if any?
      - Can the rule be depicted inside the sketch framework?

Rule 1:	Rule 2:
Rule 3:	Rule 4:
Rule 5:	

Practice 4

Directions: Take a couple minutes to review the game setup, summarize your Overview analysis, and recreate the initial Sketch. Then, one at a time, analyze the rules, answer the questions about each one, and draw the rule either inside or underneath the sketch framework.

A senior partner is deciding how to organize the firm's associates for a new class action. Six of the eight associates—Ann, Brian, Courtney, David, Edwin, Frank, Gina, and Hannah—will be selected for either the Support team or the Trial team, each team needing at least two associates. The selection is governed by the following conditions:

There are at most three associates selected for the Support team.
If Edwin is on the Trial team, then Ann is on the Support team and David is not selected for either.
If Ann is selected, then Hannah and Ann are placed on the same team.
Brian and Courtney will never be placed on the same team.
If Frank is placed on the Support team, then David is also placed on the Support team.

1. [Step 1] Summarize your Overview analysis:

2. [Step 2] Create an initial Sketch:

3. [Step 3] Analyze and draw the Rules:
   - For each rule, answer the following questions and draw the rule in the appropriate box.
     - What does the rule restrict, and what does it leave open?
     - What are the rule's negative implications, if any?
     - Can the rule be depicted inside the sketch framework?

Rule 1:	Rule 2:
Rule 3:	Rule 4:
Rule 5:	

Explanations

Compare your work to that of an LSAT expert. Pay close attention to how the expert analyzed each rule and then depicted it within or beneath the game's initial sketch.

Practice 1

Rules	Analysis

A Sequencing-Matching Hybrid in which six cars—B, C, D, E, F, and G—are exhibited in order at a car show, and each car is from a different decade—1970s, 1980s, or 1990s.

1.	The third and sixth car must be from different decades.	$\longrightarrow$ Dec: $3^{rd} \neq 6^{th}$
2.	If C is presented before B, then the second car must be from an earlier decade than the sixth car.	$\longrightarrow$ If C...B $\rightarrow$ $\begin{array}{c} 2^{nd} < 6^{th} \\ (Dec) \end{array}$ If $2^{nd} > 6^{th}$ (Dec) $\rightarrow$ B...C
3.	F is not from the 1970s unless D is immediately before E.	$\longrightarrow$ If $\dfrac{F}{70}$ $\rightarrow$ $\boxed{D\ E}$ If $\sim\boxed{D\ E}$ $\rightarrow$ $\sim\dfrac{F}{70}$

A Distribution-Sequencing Hybrid in which six students—P, Q, R, S, T, and U—are each assigned to exactly one class—art or music—and are arranged in order of the presentations they give in class.

4.	Q is assigned to the music class.	$\longrightarrow$
5.	If T is assigned to the art class, then P and U must be assigned to the music class, with P presenting some time before U.	$\longrightarrow$ 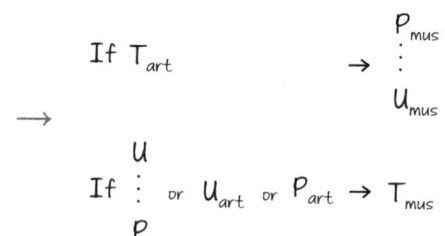
6.	R is assigned to the art class if S gives the last presentation in the music class.	$\longrightarrow$ If $S_{mus\ (last)} \rightarrow R_{art}$ If $R_{mus} \rightarrow S_{mus\ (not\ last)\ or\ art}$

A Selection-Sequencing Hybrid that selects five out of eight artifacts—S, T, U, V, W, X, Y, and Z—and arranges them in order of presentation.

7. V is selected only if X is presented at some time before it.

    $\longrightarrow$

    If V = Sel $\rightarrow$ X . . . V

    If X = 5 or X ≠ Sel $\rightarrow$ V ≠ Sel

8. T is not selected unless U and W are presented consecutively.

    $\longrightarrow$

    If T = Sel $\rightarrow$ [U W] or [W U]

    If ~[U W] and ~[W U] $\rightarrow$ T ≠ Sel

    If U ≠ Sel or W ≠ Sel $\rightarrow$ T ≠ Sel

9. S cannot be one of the first three artifacts presented.

    $\longrightarrow$

    S T U V W X Y Z

    $\underset{\sim S}{\underline{}}_{1}\ \underset{\sim S}{\underline{}}_{2}\ \underset{\sim S}{\underline{}}_{3}\ \underline{}_{4}\ \underline{}_{5}\ \bigg|\ \underset{out}{\underline{}\ \underline{}\ \underline{}}$

A Selection-Matching Hybrid in which exactly six of eight canvasses—A, B, C, D, E, F, G, and H—are selected and matched to exactly one of three colors—red, silver, or tan.

10. B cannot be selected if it is red.

    $\longrightarrow$ never $\boxed{\dfrac{B}{r}}$

11. If C and D are selected, then exactly two of the canvasses selected are silver.

    $\longrightarrow$

    If C and D $\rightarrow$ Exactly 2$_s$

    If ~ Exactly 2$_s$ $\rightarrow$ ~C or ~D

12. Exactly three of the canvasses selected are tan.

    $\longrightarrow$

    Exactly 3 t

    or

    r s t
      t
      $\underline{\underline{t}}$

Practice 2

Six witnesses—B, C, D, E, F, and G—are scheduled to testify in a court case. Three witnesses will be examined by the plaintiff's lead litigator, while the other three will be examined by the assistant attorney. Each witness will be examined once. The order in which they testify, and who examines them, are restricted by the following conditions:

> Witness C will testify immediately after witness D.
> Witness G will testify before witness F but after witness C.
> Witness E will testify after witness D.
> The lead litigator will examine the first and last witnesses.
> The lead litigator will examine C.
> The assistant attorney will not examine three consecutive witnesses.

1. [Step 1] Summarize your Overview analysis: *A Sequencing-Matching Hybrid that asks for the order in which six witnesses testify at a court case, as well as which one of the two lawyers will examine them. Three witnesses will be examined by the lead litigator, and three by the assistant attorney.*

2. [Step 2] Create an initial Sketch:

$$\begin{array}{cccccc} 1 & 2 & 3 & 4 & 5 & 6 \end{array}$$
$$\underline{\quad}\ \underline{\quad}\ \underline{\quad}\ \underline{\quad}\ \underline{\quad}\ \underline{\quad} \quad B\,C\,D\,E\,F\,G$$
$$a\,a\,a\,l\,l\,l$$

3. [Step 3] Analyze and draw the Rules:
   - Rule 1:
     - What does the rule restrict, and what does it leave open? *D and C will be in that order, consecutively.*
     - What are the rule's negative implications, if any? *C cannot be first and D cannot be last.*
     - Can the rule be depicted inside the sketch framework? *No.*
     - Draw the rule:

   - Rule 2:
     - What does the rule restrict, and what does it leave open? *In order, C, then G, then F will testify, but not necessarily consecutively.*
     - What are the rule's negative implications, if any? *With two people after, C cannot go fifth or sixth. G is in the middle, so cannot be first or sixth. F has to come after two people, so F cannot go first or second.*
     - Can the rule be depicted inside the sketch framework? *No.*
     - Draw the rule:

       $$C \ldots G \ldots F$$

   - Rule 3:
     - What does the rule restrict, and what does it leave open? *D will go before E, but with any amount of space in between.*
     - What are the rule's negative implications, if any? *D cannot go last and E cannot go first.*
     - Can the rule be depicted inside the sketch framework? *No.*
     - Draw the rule:

       $$D \ldots E$$

   - Rule 4:
     - What does the rule restrict, and what does it leave open? *This establishes the lead litigator in the first and sixth positions, but does not state who the witnesses will be.*
     - What are the rule's negative implications, if any? *N/A*
     - Can the rule be depicted inside the sketch framework? *Yes.*
     - Draw the rule:

       $$\begin{array}{cccccc} 1 & 2 & 3 & 4 & 5 & 6 \end{array}$$
       $$\underline{\quad}\ \underline{\quad}\ \underline{\quad}\ \underline{\quad}\ \underline{\quad}\ \underline{\quad}$$
       $$l \qquad\qquad\qquad\qquad l$$

   - Rule 5:
     - What does the rule restrict, and what does it leave open? *This matches C to the lead*

litigator, but does not establish when it will occur.

- What are the rule's negative implications, if any? *C will not be examined by the assistant attorney.*

- Can the rule be depicted inside the sketch framework? *No.*

- Draw the rule:

- Rule 6:

  - What does the rule restrict, and what does it leave open? *The assistant attorney will not appear in three consecutive positions.*

  - What are the rule's negative implications, if any? *The lead litigator will have to examine at least one witness in between the assistant attorney's witnesses.*

  - Can the rule be depicted inside the sketch framework? *No.*

  - Draw the rule:

never

Practice 3

A company is conducting a quarterly review. Eight employees—Grant, Heather, Julia, Kendra, Lauren, Matthew, Nathan, and Oliver—will each attend a meeting with a supervisor on either Thursday or Friday of this week. One employee at a time will attend each meeting. The arrangement of the meetings is subject to the following restrictions:

> If Heather attends her meeting on Thursday, then Lauren and Nathan will both attend their meetings on Friday.
> Grant will attend his meeting on a different day than Matthew.
> Julia will attend her meeting after Oliver and on the same day.
> Friday will have no more than three meeting slots.
> Julia's meeting is never the last meeting of the day.

1. [Step 1] Summarize your Overview analysis: *A Distribution-Sequencing Hybrid in which eight employees will be assigned to either a Thursday or Friday meeting, and the employees on each day will be arranged in order. Each employee meets on just one day, but there is no limit to the number of employees on either day.*

2. [Step 2] Create an initial Sketch:

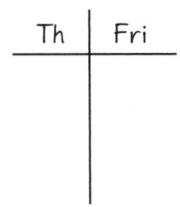

3. [Step 3] Analyze and draw the Rules:

   - Rule 1:

     - What does the rule restrict, and what does it leave open? *If Heather is on Thursday, then Lauren and Nathan are both on Friday.*

     - What are the rule's negative implications, if any? *By contrapositive, if either Lauren or Nathan is not on Friday (i.e., is on Thursday), then Heather is not on Thursday (i.e., is on Friday).*

     - Can the rule be depicted inside the sketch framework? *No.*

     - Draw the rule:

     If H = Th → L = Fr and N = Fr

     If L = Th or N = Th → H = Fr

   - Rule 2:

     - What does the rule restrict, and what does it leave open? *Grant and Matthew cannot be on the same day.*

     - What are the rule's negative implications, if any? *They must be on different days. With only two days, that means Grant is on one and Matthew is on the other.*

     - Can the rule be depicted inside the sketch framework? *Yes.*

- Draw the rule:

Th	Fri
G/M	M/G

- Rule 3:
  - What does the rule restrict, and what does it leave open? *Julia and Oliver are on the same day, with Oliver going before Julia. This still could happen on either day.*
  - What are the rule's negative implications, if any? *Julia will not be first on either day, and Oliver will not be last.*
  - Can the rule be depicted inside the sketch framework? *No.*
  - Draw the rule:

- Rule 4:
  - What does the rule restrict, and what does it leave open? *This sets a maximum of three spaces for Friday.*
  - What are the rule's negative implications, if any? *At least five employees have to be on Thursday, otherwise there would be too many left for Friday.*
  - Can the rule be depicted inside the sketch framework? *Not entirely; add the minimum slots to Thursday, and write in the minimum and maximum numbers above Thursday and Friday columns, respectively.*
  - Draw the rule:

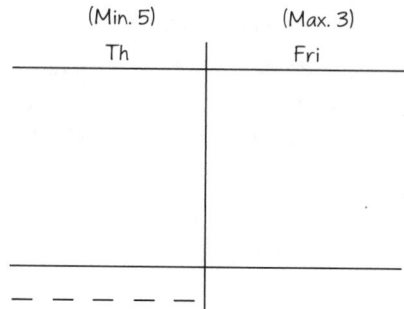

- Rule 5:
  - What does the rule restrict, and what does it leave open? *Julia cannot be last.*
  - What are the rule's negative implications, if any? *At least one person must come after Julia, regardless of the day.*
  - Can the rule be depicted inside the sketch framework? *No.*
  - Draw the rule:

Practice 4

A senior partner is deciding how to organize the firm's associates for a new class action. Six of the eight associates—Ann, Brian, Courtney, David, Edwin, Frank, Gina, and Hannah—will be selected for either the Trial team or Support team, each team needing at least two associates. The selection is governed by the following conditions:

> There are at most three associates selected for the Support team.
> If Edwin is on the Trial team, then Ann is on the Support team and David is not selected for either.
> If Ann is selected, then Hannah and Ann are placed on the same team.
> Brian and Courtney will never be placed on the same team.
> If Frank is placed on the Support team, then David is also placed on the Support team.

1. [Step 1] Summarize your Overview analysis: *A Selection-Distribution Hybrid in which six of eight associates are selected, and each one is placed on one of two teams: Trial or Support. Each team needs at least two associates, and exactly two associates will go unselected.*

2. [Step 2] Create an initial Sketch:

A B C D E F G H

Supp	Trial	Out
—	—	—
—	—	═

3. [Step 3] Analyze and draw the Rules:

- Rule 1:
  - What does the rule restrict, and what does it leave open? *The support team will have a maximum of three associates.*
  - What are the rule's negative implications, if any? *The support team has to have at least two associates, so it can only have two or three. If it had two, the Trial team would get four associates. If support had three, the Trial team would get three.*
  - Can the rule be depicted inside the sketch framework? *It can be drawn to the side, or incorporated into Limited Options.*
  - Draw the rule:

Supp	Trial	Out		Supp	Trial	Out
—	—	—		—	—	—
—	—	—	*or*	—	—	—
	—			—	—	
	—					

or

Supp: Max. 3

- Rule 2:
  - What does the rule restrict, and what does it leave open? *If Edwin is on the Trial team, then Ann is on the Support team and David is out.*
  - What are the rule's negative implications, if any? *By contrapositive, if Ann is not on the Support team or if David is not out, then Edwin cannot be on the Trial team.*
  - Can the rule be depicted inside the sketch framework? *No.*

- Draw the rule:

$$\text{If } E_{Tr} \rightarrow A_{Sup} \text{ and } D_{Out}$$

$$\text{If } {\sim}D_{Out} \text{ or } {\sim}A_{Sup} \rightarrow {\sim}E_{Tr}$$

- Rule 3:
  - What does the rule restrict, and what does it leave open? *If Ann is selected, then Hannah is also selected and on her team.*
  - What are the rule's negative implications, if any? *If Hannah is not selected, then neither is Ann—which would mean everyone else is.*
  - Can the rule be depicted inside the sketch framework? *No.*
  - Draw the rule:

$$\text{If } A_{Sup \text{ or } Tr} \rightarrow \boxed{\begin{array}{c} A \\ H \end{array}}$$

$$\text{If } H_{Out} \rightarrow A_{Out}$$

- Rule 4:
  - What does the rule restrict, and what does it leave open? *Brian and Courtney will never be assigned to the same team.*
  - What are the rule's negative implications, if any? *Don't assume they're just on separate teams. It's possible one is just not selected—or maybe they're both out!*
  - Can the rule be depicted inside the sketch framework? *No.*
  - Draw the rule:

$$\text{never } \boxed{\begin{array}{c} B \\ C \end{array}}$$

- Rule 5:
    - What does the rule restrict, and what does it leave open? *If Frank is on the Support team, then so is David.*
    - What are the rule's negative implications, if any? *If David is not on the Support team, then neither is Frank. That doesn't mean they're on the Trial team. One or both of them could be out.*

- Can the rule be depicted inside the sketch framework? *No.*
- Draw the rule:

$$\text{If } F_{Sup} \ \rightarrow \ D_{Sup}$$

$$\text{If } \sim D_{Sup} \ \rightarrow \ \sim F_{Sup}$$

As you've seen, the rules vary a great deal in Hybrid games that combine different actions. Once the rules are in place, however, deductions will turn out to spring from the same sources you've seen in all of the single-action games you've practiced. The BLEND checklist is still your go-to source for making all of the game's available deductions. Practice applying it to Hybrids in the next section of this chapter.

HYBRID GAMES DEDUCTIONS

LEARNING OBJECTIVES

In this section of the chapter, you'll practice

- Applying Step 4 of the Logic Games Method to Hybrid games by combining rules and restrictions to make all valid deductions in the game.

Prepare

The notion of Hybrid deductions is a bit of a misnomer. Because Hybrid games combine the actions of two (or occasionally three) of the standard logic games actions, the deductions you're likely to encounter correspond to the actions the testmaker has chosen to create the game. Thus, in Sequencing-Matching Hybrids (the most common Hybrid actions), Blocks of Entities are likely to form the basis for Sequencing deductions and Duplications and/or Numbers Restrictions will give you further certainty for the Matching component. On the other hand, if you have a Selection-Sequencing Hybrid game, expect to see Numbers Restrictions informing the Selection action and Blocks of Entities driving the Sequencing action. The one type of deduction unique to Hybrid games comes from rules and restrictions that cross over between the actions, providing deductions in one part of the game based on restrictions in the other.

LOGIC GAMES STRATEGY

In Hybrid games, deductions are likely to stem from:

- **BLEND**—Because Hybrid games may involve any of the standard logic games actions, all five of the BLEND elements are on the table.
- **"Cross Over" rules**—In Hybrid games, keep an eye out for rules that provide restrictions to multiple actions in the game.

Use all that you've learned about deductions thus far as you practice applying Step 4 of the Logic Games Method to Hybrid games.

Practice

Directions: In each game setup, first reacquaint yourself with the setup and rules. Then, combine the rules and restrictions to make all available deductions, recording your analyses as indicated. Finally, test your deductions by answering the questions that accompany each game. You can find expert analysis and explanations at the end of the Practice section.

Practice 1

Six witnesses—B, C, D, E, F, and G—are scheduled to testify in a court case. Three witnesses will be examined by the plaintiff's lead litigator, while the other three will be examined by the assistant attorney. Each witness will be examined once. The order in which they testify, and who examines them, are restricted by the following conditions:

> Witness C will testify immediately after witness D.
> Witness G will testify before witness F but after witness C.
> Witness E will testify after witness D.
> The lead litigator will examine the first and last witnesses.
> The lead litigator will examine C.
> The assistant attorney will not examine three consecutive witnesses.

1. Which entities or positions are the most restricted in this game? Why?

2. Which elements from the BLEND checklist can you identify in this game? Are there
   - Blocks of entities? If so, what are they?
   - Limited Options? If so, which rule(s) trigger them?
   - Established Entities? If so, which ones?
   - Number Restrictions? If so, describe them.
   - Duplications? If so, which rules share an entity?

3. Combine the rules and restrictions to create a Master Sketch depicting all of the deductions available in this game:

4. Evaluate your sketch by answering the following questions:
   - Which position could witness F be in?
   - What is the earliest position in which witness E could be scheduled?
   - Which witnesses must be examined by the assistant attorney?
   - Which witnesses must be examined by the lead litigator?

Practice 2

A company is conducting a quarterly review. Eight employees—Grant, Heather, Julia, Kendra, Lauren, Matthew, Nathan, and Oliver—will each attend a meeting with a supervisor on either Thursday or Friday of this week. One employee at a time will attend each meeting. The arrangement of the meetings is subject to the following restrictions:

> If Heather attends her meeting on Thursday, then Lauren and Nathan will both
> attend their meetings on Friday.
> Grant will attend his meeting on a different day than Matthew.
> Julia will attend her meeting after Oliver and on the same day.
> Friday will have no more than three meeting slots.
> Julia's meeting is never the last meeting of the day.

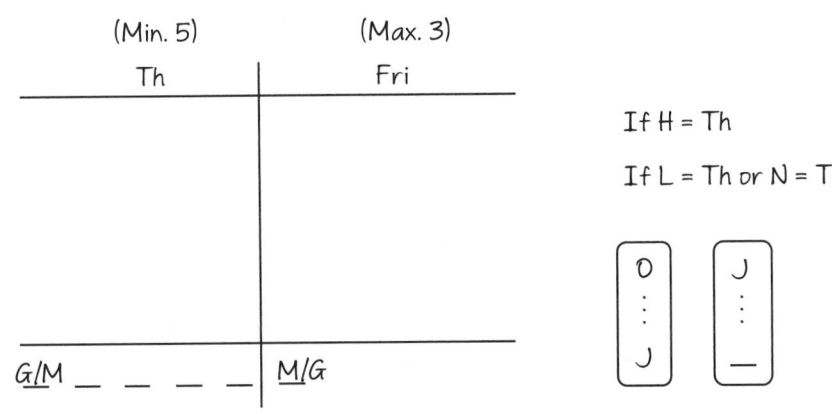

1. Which entities or positions are the most restricted in this game? Why?

2. Which elements from the BLEND checklist can you identify in this game? Are there
   - Blocks of entities? If so, what are they?
   - Limited Options? If so, which rule(s) trigger them?
   - Established Entities? If so, which ones?
   - Number Restrictions? If so, describe them.
   - Duplications? If so, which rules share an entity?

3. Combine the rules and restrictions to create a Master Sketch depicting all of the deductions available in this game:

4. Evaluate your sketch by answering the following questions:
   - What is the minimum number of people whose meetings are on Thursday?
   - On which day(s) could Julia's and Oliver's meetings be?
   - Who could have the last meeting on Thursday?
   - If Heather and Nathan had their meetings on the same day, what day(s) could it be?

Practice 3

A senior partner is deciding how to organize the firm's associates for a new class action. Six of the eight associates—Ann, Brian, Courtney, David, Edwin, Frank, Gina, and Hannah—will be selected for either the Support team or the Trial team, each team needing at least two associates. The selection is governed by the following conditions:

> There are at most three associates selected for the Support team.
> If Edwin is on the Trial team, then Ann is on the Support team and David is not selected for either.
> If Ann is selected, then Hannah and Ann are placed on the same team.
> Brian and Courtney will never be placed on the same team.
> If Frank is placed on the Support team, then David is also placed on the Support team.

ABCDEFGH

Supp	Trial	Out
—	—	—
—	—	=

Supp: Max 3

never $\begin{bmatrix} B \\ C \end{bmatrix}$

If E_{Tr} → A_{Sup} and

If $\sim D_{Out}$ or $\sim A_{Sup}$ → $\sim E_{Tr}$

If $A_{Sup\ or\ Tr}$ → $\begin{bmatrix} A \\ H \end{bmatrix}$

If H_{Out} → A_{Out}

If F_{Sup} → D_{Sup}

If $\sim D_{Sup}$ → $\sim F_{Sup}$

1. Which entities or positions are the most restricted in this game? Why?

2. Which elements from the BLEND checklist can you identify in this game? Are there
   - Blocks of entities? If so, what are they?
   - Limited Options? If so, which rule(s) trigger them?
   - Established Entities? If so, which ones?
   - Number Restrictions? If so, describe them.
   - Duplications? If so, which rules share an entity?

3. Combine the rules and restrictions to create a Master Sketch depicting all of the deductions available in this game:

4. Evaluate your sketch by answering the following questions:
   - What is the minimum number of associates on the Trial team?
   - What team(s), if any, could Hannah be on without Ann?
   - What team(s), if any, could David be on without Frank?
   - If Edwin is on the Trial team, who must be on the Support team?

Explanations

Compare your work to that of an LSAT expert. Pay close attention to how the expert combined the rules and restrictions to make additional deductions, and to how the expert depicted the deductions within the sketch framework.

Practice 1

Six witnesses—B, C, D, E, F, and G—are scheduled to testify in a court case. Three witnesses will be examined by the plaintiff's lead litigator, while the other three will be examined by the assistant attorney. Each witness will be examined once. The order in which they testify, and who examines them, are restricted by the following conditions:

> Witness C will testify immediately after witness D.
> Witness G will testify before witness F but after witness C.
> Witness E will testify after witness D.
> The lead litigator will examine the first and last witnesses.
> The lead litigator will examine C.
> The assistant attorney will not examine three consecutive witnesses.

1. Which entities or positions are the most restricted in this game? Why? *Witness C, who is already matched to the lead litigator and whose order is directly restricted by two other rules.*

2. Which elements from the BLEND checklist can you identify in this game? Are there

   - Blocks of entities? If so, what are they? *Rule 1 provides an absolute Block of D immediately before C.*

   - Limited Options? If so, which rule(s) trigger them? *N/A*

   - Established Entities? If so, which ones? *Rule 4 establishes the lead litigator to positions 1 and 6. Rule 5 establishes C with the lead litigator.*

   - Number Restrictions? If so, describe them. *Rule 6 prevents three consecutive positions with the assistant attorney.*

   - Duplications? If so, which rules share an entity? *Rules 1, 2, and 5 all mention witness C.*

Rules 1 and 3 mention witness D. Rules 4 and 5 mention the lead litigator.

3. Combine the rules and restrictions to create a Master Sketch depicting all of the deductions available in this game:

The Block of witnesses D and C must appear before witnesses G and F (in that order), as well as before witness E.

$$\boxed{D\ C}\ ...\ G\ ...\ F$$
$$\therefore\ E$$

That means D and C could only be in positions 1 and 2, or in positions 2 and 3. However, C is with the lead litigator. If C was in position 2, that would leave three consecutive positions (3, 4, and 5) for the assistant attorney. So, D and C must be positions 2 and 3.

1	2	3	4	5	6
_	D	C	_	_	_
l		l			l

That means witnesses 2, 4, and 5 will all be examined by the assistant attorney.

1	2	3	4	5	6
_	D	C	_	_	_
l	a	l	a	a	l

E, F, and G will be in the final three spots, with E in any of the three spots, and G and F, in that order, taking up the remaining spots. That leaves B for the first position.

E
$$\overbrace{4\quad 5\quad 6}$$

1	2	3	4	5	6
B	D	C	_	_	_
l	a	l	a	a	l

G ... F

4. Evaluate your sketch by answering the following questions:

- Which position could witness F be in? *5th or 6th.*

- What is the earliest position in which witness E could be scheduled? *4th.*

- Which witnesses must be examined by the assistant attorney? *D and G. (Note that G can be 4th or 5th, either way certainly being examined by the assistant attorney.)*

- Which witnesses must be examined by the lead litigator? *B and C.*

Practice 2

A company is conducting a quarterly review. Eight employees—Grant, Heather, Julia, Kendra, Lauren, Matthew, Nathan, and Oliver—will each attend a meeting with a supervisor on either Thursday or Friday of this week. One employee at a time will attend each meeting. The arrangement of the meetings is subject to the following restrictions:

> If Heather attends her meeting on Thursday, then Lauren and Nathan will both attend their meetings on Friday.
>
> Grant will attend his meeting on a different day than Matthew.
>
> Julia will attend her meeting after Oliver and on the same day.
>
> Friday will have no more than three meeting slots.
>
> Julia's meeting is never the last meeting of the day.

1. Which entities or positions are the most restricted in this game? Why? *Julia, who must be with Oliver and is the only employee with two restrictions on sequencing. Also, Friday is restricted to a maximum of three out of eight people.*

2. Which elements from the BLEND checklist can you identify in this game? Are there

- Blocks of entities? If so, what are they? *N/A*

- Limited Options? If so, which rule(s) trigger them? *The substantial results of the Formal Logic in Rule 1 offer a great opportunity.*

- Established Entities? If so, which ones? *Rule 2 essentially establishes that Grant or Matthew will occupy a spot on each day.*

- Number Restrictions? If so, describe them. *Rule 4 restricts the number of employees on Friday, which effectively sets a minimum number of employees on Thursday.*

- Duplications? If so, which rules share an entity? *Rules 3 and 5 mention Julia.*

3. Combine the rules and restrictions to create a Master Sketch depicting all of the deductions available in this game:

Julia is the only Duplicate. Oliver will be on the same day as her, and before her. There will also be at least one more person after her.

There's plenty of space on Thursday, but Friday's more of a problem. There's a maximum of three employees on Friday, and Grant or Matthew must be one. If Julia and Oliver were on Friday, that would reach the maximum, but that would put Heather on Thursday with Lauren and Nathan. Thats can't happen, so Julia and Oliver must be on Thursday.

If that wasn't immediately clear, it could be discovered by setting up Limited Options based on the first rule. The Formal Logic affects a lot of entities, so set up one sketch if Heather is on Thursday, and one if Heather is on Friday. If she's on Thursday, then Lauren and Nathan are on Friday along with Grant or Matthew. That's the maximum for Friday, so all the remaining employees (Julia, Kendra, and Oliver) are on Thursday.

Th	Fri
O	
:	
J	
:	
—	

H J K O G/M | L N M/G

If Heather is on Friday, the Formal Logic doesn't apply. However, there are now at least two employees on Friday. There's no longer room for both Julia and Oliver, so they must be on Thursday.

```
        Th              Fri
  _____|_____
        O         |
        :         |
        J         |
        :         |
        —         |
  _____|_____
  M/G  J  O  _  _ | G/M  H  _
```

4. Evaluate your sketch by answering the following questions:

   - What is the minimum number of people whose meetings are on Thursday? *Five.*

   - On which day(s) could Julia's and Oliver's meetings be? *They must be on Thursday.*

   - Who could have the last meeting on Thursday? *Grant, Heather, Kendra, Lauren, Matthew, or Nathan; basically, anybody but Oliver and Julia.*

   - If Heather and Nathan had their meetings on the same day, what day(s), if any, could it be? *Friday; if Heather was on Thursday, Nathan would be on Friday. However, Nathan could also be on Friday if Heather is there, too.*

Practice 3

A senior partner is deciding how to organize the firm's associates for a new class action. Six of the eight associates—Ann, Brian, Courtney, David, Edwin, Frank, Gina, and Hannah—will be selected for either the Support team or the Trial team, each team needing at least two associates. The selection is governed by the following conditions:

> There are at most three associates selected for the Support team.
> If Edwin is on the Trial team, then Ann is on the Support team and David is not selected for either.
> If Ann is selected, then Hannah and Ann are placed on the same team.

Brian and Courtney will never be placed on the same team.
If Frank is placed on the Support team, then David is also placed on the Support team.

1. Which entities or positions are the most restricted in this game? Why? *The Support team, which is referenced in three of the rules. As for the associates, Ann is the only one duplicated and hence the most limited.*

2. Which elements from the BLEND checklist can you identify in this game? Are there

   - Blocks of entities? If so, what are they? *N/A*

   - Limited Options? If so, which rule(s) trigger them? *Rule 1 sets up only two numerical outcomes.*

   - Established Entities? If so, which ones? *N/A*

   - Number Restrictions? If so, describe them. *Rule 1 has an effect on the numeric distribution.*

   - Duplications? If so, which rules share an entity? *Rules 1, 2, and 5 mention the Support team. Rules 2 and 3 mention Ann.*

3. Combine the rules and restrictions to create a Master Sketch depicting all of the deductions available in this game:

The Support team must have at least two associates, but no more than three. If it has only two, the Trial team will have four. If Support has three, the Trial team will have three. You can draw out both options.

Beyond that, the remaining rules are all abstract or conditional. The one rule with the biggest potential impact is the one with Ann and Hannah. If Hannah is out, then Ann must be out, which would mean everyone else is in. Drawing out Limited Options may provide some useful information.

If Hannah is out, then Ann is out, meaning Brian, Courtney, David, Edwin, Frank, and Gina are in. Brian and Courtney can't be together, so one will be on Support and one on Trial.

Supp	Trial	Out
B/C	C/B	A
—	—	H
		—

With Ann out, Edwin cannot be on Trial, so must be on Support. That leaves only one more possible space on Support. Frank cannot be on Support without David, so Frank would have to be on Trial. At least one more person is on Trial, and that will be either David or Gina. The other person could be on either team.

Supp	Trial	Out
B/C	C/B	A
E	F	H
		—

If Hannah is in, no concrete deductions can be made, so that would just leave the two numeric outcomes.

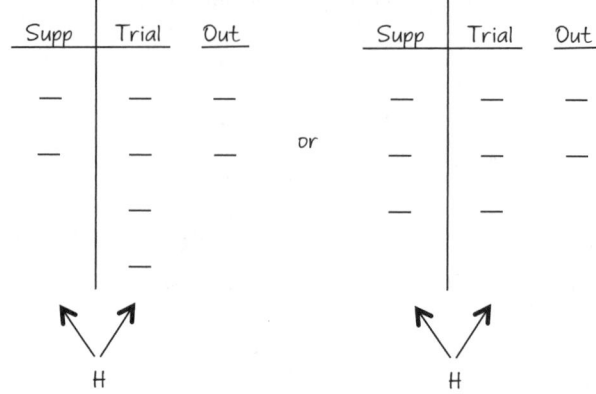

4. Evaluate your sketch by answering the following questions:

   • What is the minimum number of associates on the Trial team? *Three.*

   • What team(s), if any, could Hannah be on without Ann? *Either Support or Trial; Ann cannot be without Hannah, but Hannah can be without Ann if Ann is out.*

   • What team(s), if any, could David be on without Frank? *Either Support or Trial; David is only required to be with Frank if Frank is on the Support team. If Frank is on the Trial team or out, David can go anywhere.*

   • If Edwin is on the Trial team, who must be on the Support team? *Ann, which would also mean Hannah has to be there.*

As always, the true assessment of your skills comes with Step 5, the Questions. The full game section of this chapter is longer than you've seen previously. That's so that you can evaluate yourself on several different types of Hybrid games. Taking and reviewing those games will help you discover which of the Hybrid actions come more naturally to you, and which you still need to work on. The recommended practice is labeled by the type of Hybrid each game represents, so that you can more efficiently follow up with additional work.

HYBRID GAMES—FULL GAMES WITH QUESTIONS

LEARNING OBJECTIVES

In this section, you'll assess your ability to

- Apply the Logic Games Method to Hybrid games.

Perform

Here is your opportunity to put all of the pieces together and assess your skills on Hybrid games. On the following pages, you'll find five full-length games along with their question sets. All of these games are from officially released LSAT tests, and all are representative of Hybrid games you could see on Test Day. You can take the games one at a time or all together, but for your self-evaluation to be as accurate as possible, adhere to the timing guidelines set forth in the directions.

An answer key follows the games. Complete worked example expert analyses can be found in your online resources.

After you complete and review these games, assess your performance using the evaluation guidelines. There, you'll find recommendations for additional Easy, Medium, and Hard Hybrid games from officially released LSAT exams that you can practice to continue honing your skills and raising your score.

Directions: Take no more than 9 minutes per game to complete the following five games and all of their questions.

Perform 1

<u>Questions 1–6</u>

An official is assigning five runners—Larry, Ned, Olivia, Patricia, and Sonja—to parallel lanes numbered consecutively 1 through 5. The official will also assign each runner to represent a different charity—F, G, H, J, and K—not necessarily in order of the runners' names as given. The following ordering restrictions apply:

> The runner representing K is assigned to lane 4.
> Patricia is assigned to the only lane between the lanes of the runners representing F and G.
> There are exactly two lanes between Olivia's lane and the lane of the runner representing G.
> Sonja is assigned to a higher-numbered lane than the lane to which Ned is assigned.

1. Which one of the following is a possible assignment of runners to lanes by the charity they represent?

	1	2	3	4	5
(A)	F	G	H	K	J
(B)	G	H	J	K	F
(C)	G	K	F	J	H
(D)	H	J	G	K	F
(E)	J	H	F	K	G

2. The lane to which Patricia is assigned must be a lane that is

    (A) next to the lane to which Larry is assigned
    (B) next to the lane to which Ned is assigned
    (C) separated by exactly one lane from the lane to which Ned is assigned
    (D) separated by exactly one lane from the lane to which Olivia is assigned
    (E) separated by exactly one lane from the lane to which Sonja is assigned

3. If Olivia is assigned to lane 2, which one of the following assignments must be made?

	Charity	Lane
(A)	F	1
(B)	G	5
(C)	H	1
(D)	H	3
(E)	J	5

4. Which one of the following is a complete and accurate list of runners each of whom could be the runner representing F?

    (A) Larry, Ned
    (B) Patricia, Sonja
    (C) Larry, Ned, Olivia
    (D) Larry, Ned, Sonja
    (E) Ned, Patricia, Sonja

5. If Ned is the runner representing J, then it must be true that

    (A) the runner representing G is assigned to lane 1
    (B) the runner representing H is assigned to lane 2
    (C) Larry is the runner representing K
    (D) Olivia is the runner representing F
    (E) Patricia is the runner representing H

6. If Larry represents J, which one of the following could be the assignment of runners to lanes?

	1	2	3	4	5
(A)	Larry	Olivia	Ned	Patricia	Sonja
(B)	Larry	Ned	Olivia	Sonja	Patricia
(C)	Larry	Sonja	Patricia	Ned	Olivia
(D)	Ned	Olivia	Larry	Patricia	Sonja
(E)	Ned	Sonja	Olivia	Patricia	Larry

    PrepTest7 Sec2 Qs 19-24

Perform 2

Questions 7–12

An art teacher will schedule exactly six of eight lectures—fresco, history, lithography, naturalism, oils, pastels, sculpture, and watercolors—for three days—1, 2, and 3. There will be exactly two lectures each day—morning and afternoon. Scheduling is governed by the following conditions:

> Day 2 is the only day for which oils can be scheduled.
> Neither sculpture nor watercolors can be scheduled for the afternoon.
> Neither oils nor pastels can be scheduled for the same day as lithography.
> If pastels is scheduled for day 1 or day 2, then the lectures scheduled for the day immediately following pastels must be fresco and history, not necessarily in that order.

7. Which one of the following is an acceptable schedule of lectures for days 1, 2, and 3, respectively?

(A) Morning: lithography, history, sculpture
Afternoon: pastels, fresco, naturalism

(B) Morning: naturalism, oils, fresco
Afternoon: lithography, pastels, history

(C) Morning: oils, history, naturalism
Afternoon: pastels, fresco, lithography

(D) Morning: sculpture, lithography, naturalism
Afternoon: watercolors, fresco, pastels

(E) Morning: sculpture, pastels, fresco
Afternoon: lithography, history, naturalism

8. If lithography and fresco are scheduled for the afternoons of day 2 and day 3, respectively, which one of the following is a lecture that could be scheduled for the afternoon of day 1?

    (A)   history
    (B)   oils
    (C)   pastels
    (D)   sculpture
    (E)   watercolors

9. If lithography and history are scheduled for the mornings of day 2 and day 3, respectively, which one of the following lectures could be scheduled for the morning of day 1?

    (A)   fresco
    (B)   naturalism
    (C)   oils
    (D)   pastels
    (E)   sculpture

10. If oils and lithography are scheduled for the mornings of day 2 and day 3, respectively, which one of the following CANNOT be scheduled for any day?

    (A)   fresco
    (B)   history
    (C)   naturalism
    (D)   pastels
    (E)   sculpture

11. If neither fresco nor naturalism is scheduled for any day, which one of the following must be scheduled for day 1?

    (A)   history
    (B)   lithography
    (C)   oils
    (D)   pastels
    (E)   sculpture

12. If the lectures scheduled for the mornings are fresco, history, and lithography, not necessarily in that order, which one of the following could be true?

    (A)   Lithography is scheduled for day 3.
    (B)   Naturalism is scheduled for day 2.
    (C)   Fresco is scheduled for the same day as naturalism.
    (D)   History is scheduled for the same day as naturalism.
    (E)   History is scheduled for the same day as oils.

PrepTest13 Sec1 Qs 12-17

Perform 3

<u>Questions 13–19</u>

Exactly six tourists—Harry, Irene, Klaus, Laura, Michael, Norma—are to be assigned to four guides: Valois, Xerxes, Yossarian, Zalamea. Each tourist is assigned to exactly one guide, with at least one tourist assigned to each guide. Valois speaks only French. Xerxes speaks only Turkish and Spanish. Yossarian speaks only French and Turkish. Zalamea speaks only Spanish and Russian. Each tourist speaks exactly one of the languages spoken by his or her guide and speaks no other language.

The following rules govern the assignment of the tourists to the guides:

> At least Harry and Irene are assigned to Yossarian.
> At least Laura is assigned to Zalamea.
> If Klaus is assigned to Xerxes, then Michael speaks French.

13. Each of the following could be true EXCEPT:

    (A) Both Klaus and Harry speak Turkish.
    (B) Both Klaus and Michael speak French.
    (C) Both Klaus and Michael speak Russian.
    (D) Both Klaus and Norma speak French.
    (E) Both Klaus and Norma speak Spanish.

14. Which one of the following must be true?

   (A)   Zalamea is assigned fewer than three of the tourists.
   (B)   Xerxes is assigned fewer than two of the tourists.
   (C)   Yossarian is assigned exactly two of the tourists.
   (D)   Valois is assigned exactly one of the tourists.
   (E)   Zalamea is assigned exactly one of the tourists.

15. Each of the following could be true of the assignment of tourists to guides EXCEPT:

   (A)   It assigns Klaus to Valois and Michael to Xerxes.
   (B)   It assigns Klaus to Yossarian and Norma to Zalamea.
   (C)   It assigns Laura to Zalamea and Michael to Zalamea.
   (D)   It assigns Michael to Valois and Klaus to Zalamea.
   (E)   It assigns Michael to Xerxes and Klaus to Zalamea.

16. If Klaus and Laura speak the same language as each other, then which one of the following must be true?

   (A)   At least one of Michael and Norma speaks Spanish.
   (B)   At least two tourists speak Russian.
   (C)   Klaus and Laura speak Russian.
   (D)   At least two tourists speak French.
   (E)   At least one of Michael and Norma speaks French.

17. If Laura and Norma speak the same language as each other, then the maximum number of the tourists who could speak Turkish is

   (A)   two
   (B)   three
   (C)   four
   (D)   five
   (E)   six

18. If exactly two tourists are assigned to Xerxes, then which one of the following could be true?

   (A)   Norma speaks Russian and Laura speaks Russian.
   (B)   Norma speaks French and Michael speaks French.
   (C)   Norma speaks French and Klaus speaks Turkish.
   (D)   Michael speaks Spanish and Klaus speaks Spanish.
   (E)   Michael speaks French and Klaus speaks Spanish.

19. If Harry, Irene, Michael, and Norma all speak the same language as each other, then which one of the following could be true?

   (A)   Klaus speaks Russian.
   (B)   Exactly two of the tourists speak Russian.
   (C)   Exactly three of the tourists speak Spanish.
   (D)   Exactly two of the tourists speak Turkish.
   (E)   Klaus speaks French.

PrepTest25 Sec3 Qs 6-12

Perform 4

<u>Questions 20–26</u>

Exactly six of seven researchers—three anthropologists: Franklin, Jones, and Marquez; and four linguists: Neil, Osborne, Rice, and Samuels—will be included in two three-person teams—team 1 and team 2. No researcher will be included in more than one team. Each team must include at least one anthropologist and at least one linguist. The teams' composition must conform to the following conditions:

    Neither team includes both Franklin and Samuels.
    Neither team includes both Neil and Rice.
    If a team includes Marquez, it includes neither Rice nor Samuels.
    If team 1 includes Jones, team 2 includes Rice.

20. Which one of the following could be the list of the researchers on the two teams?

    (A)   team 1: Franklin, Marquez, Osborne
            team 2: Jones, Neil, Rice

    (B)   team 1: Franklin, Neil, Samuels
            team 2: Jones, Osborne, Rice

    (C)   team 1: Franklin, Osborne, Rice
            team 2: Jones, Neil, Samuels

    (D)   team 1: Jones, Marquez, Neil
            team 2: Osborne, Rice, Samuels

    (E)   team 1: Jones, Osborne, Rice
            team 2: Franklin, Marquez, Neil

21. If Jones is on team 1, which one of the following is a pair of researchers that must be on team 2 together?

    (A) Franklin and Rice
    (B) Marquez and Osborne
    (C) Neil and Osborne
    (D) Osborne and Samuels
    (E) Rice and Samuels

22. If Neil is on team 1, which one of the following is a pair of researchers that could be on team 1 together with Neil?

    (A) Franklin and Jones
    (B) Jones and Osborne
    (C) Jones and Rice
    (D) Jones and Samuels
    (E) Osborne and Samuels

23. If Franklin is on the same team as Marquez, which one of the following could be true?

    (A) Jones is on team 1.
    (B) Rice is on team 1.
    (C) Samuels is on team 2.
    (D) Both Neil and Osborne are on team 1.
    (E) Both Neil and Osborne are on team 2.

24. Each of the following is a pair of researchers that could be on team 2 together EXCEPT:

    (A) Franklin and Jones
    (B) Franklin and Marquez
    (C) Franklin and Rice
    (D) Jones and Marquez
    (E) Jones and Rice

25. Which one of the following could be true?

    (A) Franklin is on team 1 and Neil is on team 2.
    (B) Franklin is on team 2 and Jones is not on any team.
    (C) Franklin is on team 2 and Marquez is on team 2.
    (D) Franklin is not on any team and Jones is on team 1.
    (E) Jones is on team 1 and Neil is on team 2.

26. If Marquez is on team 2, which one of the following must also be on team 2?

    (A) Franklin
    (B) Jones
    (C) Osborne
    (D) Rice
    (E) Samuels

PrepTest23 Sec1 Qs 12-18

Perform 5

<u>Questions 27–31</u>

The members of two committees, a planting committee and a trails committee, are to be selected from among seven volunteers—F, G, H, J, K, L, and M. The following conditions govern the composition of the committees:

Each committee must have at least three members.

F cannot be on the same committee as K.

If K is on a committee, J must also be on that committee.

M must be on at least one of the committees.

The two committees must have at least one member in common.

27. Which one of the following represents an acceptable selection of volunteers for the committees?

(A) planting: F, G, H; trails: G, J, K, L

(B) planting: F, H, J; trails: G, H, L, M

(C) planting: F, H, M; trails: G, K, L, M

(D) planting: F, G, L, M; trails: F, H

(E) planting: F, H, J, K; trails: H, L, M

28. If the planting committee consists of F, H, L, and M, and if the trails committee consists of G, H, and J, then K could replace which one of the following committee members on a committee without violating any of the conditions governing the composition of the committees?

    (A) F
    (B) G
    (C) H
    (D) L
    (E) M

29. If the only members of the planting committee are G, H, and L and if the two committees are to have as many members in common as the conditions allow, then which one of the following must be true?

    (A) The trails committee and the planting committee have exactly one member in common.
    (B) The trails committee and the planting committee have exactly two members in common.
    (C) The trails committee and the planting committee have an equal number of members.
    (D) The trails committee has at least one more member than the planting committee.
    (E) The planting committee has exactly two more members than the trails committee.

30. If K is on both committees and L is also on both committees and if the planting committee has exactly three members, then which one of the following must be true?

    (A) F is on the planting committee.
    (B) F is on the trails committee.
    (C) G is on the planting committee.
    (D) M is on the planting committee.
    (E) M is on the trails committee.

31. The largest number of members that the planting committee and the trails committee could have in common is

    (A) three
    (B) four
    (C) five
    (D) six
    (E) seven

PrepTest25 Sec3 Qs 1-5

Answer Key

Perform 1
1. (E)
2. (D)
3. (B)
4. (D)
5. (B)
6. (A)

Perform 2
7. (B)
8. (A)
9. (E)
10. (D)
11. (B)
12. (E)

Perform 3
13. (C)
14. (A)
15. (B)
16. (E)
17. (B)
18. (E)
19. (E)

Perform 4
20. (C)
21. (A)
22. (D)
23. (C)
24. (B)
25. (A)
26. (B)

Perform 5
27. (B)
28. (B)
29. (D)
30. (E)
31. (D)

Worked example explanations of these questions with complete expert analysis can be found in your Online Study Plan under Chapter 10. View or download the PDF titled "Chapter 10 Perform Full Games Explanations."

Assess

Use the following criteria to evaluate your results on the Perform games.

If, under timed conditions, you correctly answered

25–31 of the questions: Outstanding! You have demonstrated a strong skill level in Hybrid games. For further practice in Hybrids, use any of the Recommended Additional Practice sets, including the Advanced set. Then, move on to Chapter 11 on Rare games, if you have time before Test Day.

17–24 of the questions: Good work! You have a solid foundation in Hybrid games. For further practice in Hybrids, begin with the Foundations or Mid-Level Recommended Additional Practice set. If you have time before Test Day, try the Advanced Recommended Additional Practice set, as well.

0–16 of the questions: Keep working. Hybrid games historically comprise more than a fifth of all games, so you're likely to see one on Test Day. Continued practice will help you improve your score. Begin by reviewing this chapter. Then, try the games in the Foundations Recommended Additional Practice set. As you continue to progress, move on to the Mid-Level Recommended Additional Practice set.

To stay sharp, practice the drills in the Logic Games Training Camp for this chapter in your Online Study Plan. Training Camp drills are divided into Fundamentals, Mid-Level, and Advanced sets.

Recommended Additional Practice: Hybrid

All of the following games will provide good practice on Hybrids. They are grouped by difficulty as determined from empirical student practice results. All PrepTests included are available individually, or in bundles of ten as part of the LSAC's *10 Actual, Official LSAT PrepTests* series.

Foundations

PrepTest 70, Section 3, Game 4: Bird Lectures* (Sequencing/Matching)

PrepTest 64, Section 2, Game 2: Ambassador Assignments* (Selection/Distribution)

PrepTest 58, Section 3, Game 3: Flyhigh & Getaway Airlines** (Sequencing/Matching)

Mid-Level

PrepTest 71, Section 2, Game 3: Literature Course* (Sequencing/Matching)

PrepTest 70, Section 3, Game 3: Repertory Theater Screenings* (Distribution/Sequencing)

PrepTest 61, Section 3, Game 3: Track Team** (Selection/Sequencing)

PrepTest 52, Section 2, Game 3: Sales Conference Seminars** (Distribution/Sequencing)

Advanced

PrepTest 66, Section 3, Game 4: Wayne & Zara's Piano Solos* (Sequencing/Matching)

PrepTest 60, Section 2, Game 4: Travel Magazine Interns** (Distribution/Matching)

PrepTest 56, Section 1, Game 4: Executives and Manufacturing Plants** (Distribution/Sequencing)

PrepTest 53, Section 2, Game 3: Burglary Suspects** (Sequencing/Matching)

*Game included in *10 Actual, Official LSAT PrepTests Volume V: PrepTests 62–71*; complete answers and explanations written by Kaplan LSAT experts available via the eBook: *LSAT PrepTests 62–71 Unlocked: Exclusive Data, Analysis & Explanations for 10 Actual, Official LSAT PrepTests Volume V.*

**Game included in *10 New Actual, Official LSAT PrepTests with Comparative Reading (PrepTests 52–61)*; complete answers and explanations written by Kaplan LSAT experts available via the eBook: *LSAT PrepTests 52–61 Unlocked: Exclusive Data, Analysis & Explanations for 10 New Actual, Official LSAT PrepTests with Comparative Reading.* [Explanations title coming Fall 2018.]

Reflect

Think back over the study and practice you did in this chapter.

- Are you able to identify Hybrid games and their individual actions from their setups?
- Do you have a default sketch framework for each of the common Hybrid action combinations?
- What kinds of rules do you anticipate seeing in Hybrid games?
- Are you comfortable identifying which action a rule describes and determining whether and how to record the rules within the sketch framework?
- Are you making the available deductions efficiently and effectively in Hybrid games?

In the coming days or weeks before Test Day, take note of real-world tasks that reflect Hybrid task combinations. Consider how they mirror the setups and questions in LSAT Hybrids, and how they differ. Try to reframe real-life hybrid tasks using the terms, rules, and restrictions used by the testmaker.

Turn the page to see an LSAT Channel Spotlight feature on the game many consider the hardest in LSAT history. ▶ ▶ ▶

The Dinosaur Game

By Bob Verini and Bobby Gautam

 Watch the video lesson for this Spotlight in your online Study Plan.

Being asked to arrange a display of five plastic dinosaur toys in different colors doesn't sound so bad, does it? Depending on the mood you're in, it might be downright fun. Well, LSAT test takers in June of 2009 didn't think so. The third logic game on their test—now known as PrepTest 57—had exactly that task, and boy, it stopped some folks in their tracks.

Each of seven toy dinosaurs—an iguanadon, a lambeosaur, a plateosaur, a stegosaur, a tyrannosaur, an ultrasaur, and a velociraptor—is completely colored either green, mauve, red, or yellow. A display is to consist entirely of exactly five of these toys. The display must meet the following specifications:
    Exactly two mauve toys are included.
    The stegosaur is red and is included.
    The iguanadon is included only if it is green.
    The plateosaur is included only if it is yellow.
    The velociraptor is included only if the ultrasaur is not.
    If both the lambeosaur and the ultrasaur are included, at
      least one of them is not mauve.

PrepTest57 Sec1 Qs 12–17

Given the whimsy of its subject matter, it seems ironic that this is the logic game that has gone down in LSAT folklore as maybe the hardest of all time, a game to fear and panic over. How did it become so notorious? What are the reasons that it strikes people as being so weird, and so difficult? Two factors stand out.

First, it is an unusual Hybrid—Selection and Matching—that had only appeared on a released LSAT once before* and never since. Not knowing a game's type is

paralyzing to some test takers. Familiarity with game types and setups is comforting, and quickly recognizing a game helps you feel that you have a head start on it. Still, you shouldn't feel too intimidated by a Selection game that asks you to choose five of seven toys, or by a Matching game that asks you to match a single color to each of five items. So, the game type itself cannot account for all of this game's bad reputation.

*There was a Selection-Matching Hybrid on PrepTest B, administered in February 1999.

The second factor that made the Dinosaur game intimidating is the wording of its rules. The first two are straightforward, but the next three are all Formal Logic, and they have the "only if" construction. Well-trained test takers know that "only if" translates to "then," indicating the necessary clause. But, for any test taker who misunderstands or mistranslates those rules, this game quickly goes off the rails. Whenever you draw a game's rules incorrectly, at least some of the questions will seem to make no sense at all. As if those three "only if" rules weren't enough for one game, the Dinosaur game's final rule offers another unusual construction, and thus, another opportunity to make a mistake. Patient test takers shouldn't be thrown off by the game's final rule, however, as it boils down to a simple prohibition: You can't put a mauve lambeosaur and a mauve ultrasaur together in the display. Come to think of it, maybe this game seemed so tough because nobody can ever remember exactly what color *mauve* is.

Bottom line, the Dinosaur game *is* legitimately challenging. Like all hard games, it demands respect. Likewise, it rewards careful, strategic reading and precision in translating the rules and making deductions. It is a terrific test of your expertise in using the Logic Games Method.

The Dinosaur game is a great example of one more thing that top scorers always develop: the ability to respond to unfamiliar games creatively. Anchored in the Logic Games Method, and confident in the fact that the LSAT always provides all of the information needed to answer every question, LSAT experts don't panic in the face of the unfamiliar (and, remember, even the most experienced LSAT guru could only have seen one of these games before). Indeed, LSAT experts respond to unfamiliar games with the same approach they do run of the mill games: They assess the game's Situation, Entities, Actions, and Limitations, and then create a sketch that will allow them

to account for the rules. That is the foundation for success on any LSAT logic game. On unfamiliar games, however, experts know that the sketch they need probably isn't sitting in their standard library of sketches. They adapt the familiar to account for the unique.

On a game as rare as the Dinosaur game, the sketches created by two different experts may not even match one another, but they will both fit the game. And both experts' sketches will be simple, accurate, and useful. In the video that accompanies this Special Feature, two LSAT Channel experts will show you how they handled the Dinosaur game, and how they got its questions right. Try the game yourself on the following pages (but don't expect to be perfect, even if you've been acing the Perform quizzes in this book). Then, let the experts walk you through it their way. Take note of the patterns they spotted, and of how they applied the Logic Games Method to turn the unfamiliar into something manageable. You may never tackle a Selection-Matching Hybrid game again, but the lessons you'll take away from this Special Feature will serve you well whenever you bump up against a game that gives other test takers nightmares.

<u>Questions 12–17</u>

Each of seven toy dinosaurs—an iguanadon, a lambeosaur, a plateosaur, a stegosaur, a tyrannosaur, an ultrasaur, and a velociraptor—is completely colored either green, mauve, red, or yellow. A display is to consist entirely of exactly five of these toys. The display must meet the following specifications:

> Exactly two mauve toys are included.
> The stegosaur is red and is included.
> The iguanadon is included only if it is green.
> The plateosaur is included only if it is yellow.
> The velociraptor is included only if the ultrasaur is not.
> If both the lambeosaur and the ultrasaur are included, at least one of them is not mauve.

12. Which one of the following could be the toys included in the display?

   (A) the lambeosaur, the plateosaur, the stegosaur, the ultrasaur, the velociraptor
   (B) the lambeosaur, the plateosaur, the stegosaur, the tyrannosaur, the ultrasaur
   (C) the iguanadon, the lambeosaur, the plateosaur, the stegosaur, the ultrasaur
   (D) the iguanadon, the lambeosaur, the plateosaur, the tyrannosaur, the velociraptor
   (E) the iguanadon, the lambeosaur, the stegosaur, the ultrasaur, the velociraptor

13. If the tyrannosaur is not included in the display, then the display must contain each of the following EXCEPT:

   (A) a green iguanadon
   (B) a mauve velociraptor
   (C) a mauve lambeosaur
   (D) a mauve ultrasaur
   (E) a yellow plateosaur

14. Which one of the following is a pair of toys that could be included in the display together?

   (A) a green lambeosaur and a mauve velociraptor
   (B) a green lambeosaur and a yellow tyrannosaur
   (C) a green lambeosaur and a yellow ultrasaur
   (D) a yellow tyrannosaur and a green ultrasaur
   (E) a yellow tyrannosaur and a red velociraptor

15. If the display includes a yellow tyrannosaur, then which one of the following must be true?

   (A) The iguanadon is included in the display.
   (B) The plateosaur is not included in the display.
   (C) The display includes two yellow toy dinosaurs.
   (D) The display contains a green lambeosaur.
   (E) The display contains a mauve velociraptor.

16. If both the iguanadon and the ultrasaur are included in the display, then the display must contain which one of the following?

   (A) a mauve tyrannosaur
   (B) a mauve ultrasaur
   (C) a yellow lambeosaur
   (D) a yellow plateosaur
   (E) a yellow ultrasaur

17. If the display includes two green toys, then which one of the following could be true?

   (A) There is exactly one yellow toy included in the display.
   (B) The tyrannosaur is included in the display and it is green.
   (C) Neither the lambeosaur nor the velociraptor is included in the display.
   (D) Neither the tyrannosaur nor the velociraptor is included in the display.
   (E) Neither the ultrasaur nor the velociraptor is included in the display.

PrepTest57 Sec1 Qs 12–17

Complete answers and explanations are provided in The LSAT Channel Spotlight video "Limited Options" in your online Study Plan.

CHAPTER 11

Rare Games Unlocked: Process and Mapping

The rare game types outlined in this chapter are truly rare. Since the LSAT established its current format in 1991, the LSAC has released more than 80 official exams containing more than 320 logic games. Of those, exactly seven have been Process games, and only five have been Mapping games. In the past five years, there has been only *one* of either of these game types on a released LSAT, which was a process game on PrepTest 80.

Types of Games By Percentage, 2012–2016

Process Games By the Numbers

Those meager numbers take on even more significance when you consider the dates of those tests. Of the seven released Process games, six are from tests administered in the 1990s. It is noteworthy that the one Process game that postdates the '90s appeared on the December 2016 LSAT (PrepTest 80). Seeing a Process game on a current administration of the exam surprised many, including LSAT experts. The reemergence of Process was so significant that you'll find an LSAT Channel Special Feature on that game following the discussion of Process games in this chapter. There, you'll have the opportunity to work through that game, and to see an LSAT Channel instructor's approach to it.

In the Special Feature, you'll also discover that Kaplan LSAT experts had taken note of several recent Sequencing games that may have signaled the testmaker's renewed interest in Process games. At present, the game on PrepTest 80 remains an anomaly, and there's no evidence that it foreshadows a new wave of Process games. Still, the return of Process after such a long period of dormancy is intriguing. Process games warrant a small amount of your study time if only for the peace of mind that you'll recognize a Process game should the LSAT decide to include another one on an upcoming administration.

Mapping Games By the Numbers

Of the five Mapping games ever to appear on officially released LSAT tests, the most recent is from PrepTest 40, administered in June 2003. Since that time, Mapping has been a dead letter on released exams, with nothing to suggest its return.

To be clear, the LSAC has never announced that it is abandoning Mapping games, so an unexpected return is not impossible. Nonetheless, if you have limited time between now and Test Day, and if you have more work to do on any of the important game types covered in earlier chapters of this book, your time will probably be better spent honing your mastery of Sequencing, Distribution, or Hybrid games than it would be seeking out further practice on this rarest of all games.

For true logic games mavens—those who want absolutely complete coverage of every game type—there are complete lists of all Process and Mapping games ever released at the end of each game type's respective section in this chapter.

PROCESS GAMES UNLOCKED

Prepare

In most LSAT logic games, your task is take a list of unassigned entities and place each of them into specific positions or groups. In Process games, the entities start out assigned to positions or groups (or, rarely, New-"If" question stems stipulate initial arrangements), and your task is to reassign them to new positions or groups. Here's a typical Process game setup:

> In a particular area of national forest, there are four fire lookouts—numbered 1 through 4—and a headquarters. In the current winter quarter, five rangers are assigned as follows: Adams is in Lookout 1, Benitez is in Lookout 2, Campbell is in Lookout 3, Davis is in Lookout 4, and Estavez is at headquarters. At the end of each quarter, and only then, the area supervisor will reassign the rangers according to exactly one of the following protocols:

In the Step 1 Overview, an LSAT expert would note three key features of this setup that identify this as a Process game: 1) the fact that an initial arrangement of the entities is provided, 2) the phrase "[a]t the end of each quarter," which indicates an iterative action, and 3) the word "reassign," which establishes the nature of the task.

In Step 2, the expert will sketch out what is given about the initial arrangement. In this case, the setup provides a complete picture of the rangers' initial assignments.

$$\begin{array}{ccccc} HQ & 1 & 2 & 3 & 4 \\ E & A & B & C & D \end{array}$$

In Step 3 of a Process game, an LSAT expert will begin by noting what the setup or rules say about how often change takes place. In this game, a reassignment is made "[a]t the end of each quarter." The setup tells you that the initial arrangement represents the winter quarter. That means that after one reassignment is made, you will have the arrangement for the spring quarter. After two reassignments have occurred, it will be summer. And so on. Always make a note of how often change occurs within the game.

After that, Step 3 for Process games is much the same as it is in any other game type. Analyze the rules and draw them out in a helpful shorthand or visual representation of the action.

In a particular area of national forest, there are four fire lookouts—numbered 1 through 4—and a headquarters. In the current winter quarter, five rangers are assigned as follows: Adams is at Lookout 1, Benitez is at Lookout 2, Campbell is at Lookout 3, Davis is at Lookout 4, and Estavez is at headquarters. At the end of each quarter, the area supervisor will reassign the rangers according to exactly one of the following protocols:

1. The ranger at headquarters will move to Lookout 1; the ranger at Lookout 1 will move to Lookout 4; and the ranger at Lookout 4 will move to headquarters.

2. The rangers in Lookouts 1 and 2 will change positions with one another.

3. The rangers in Lookouts 3 and 4 will change positions with one another.

winter

HQ	1	2	3	4
E	A	B	C	D

1 per quarter

1. HQ → 1
    1 → 4
    4 → HQ

2. 1 ↔ 2

3. 3 ↔ 4

Because of their iterative nature, Process games tend to have few solid deductions to make up front. If you see Duplications among the rules that lead to clear outcomes, you can note them. In this game, for example, you can quickly record the spring arrangements that result from the implementation of each protocol.

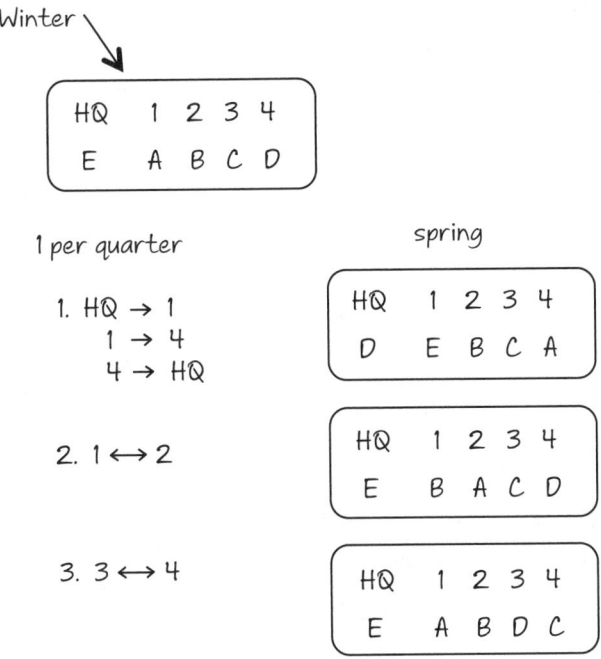

Avoid the inclination to speculate about all of the various ways that entities could be arranged after two or three reassignments. The questions that ask about the state of affairs after two or three iterations will always provide the information you need to determine what happened earlier in the process.

Step 5 in Process games is no different than it is in other game types. Process games are accompanied by all of the standard question types.

- Acceptability—e.g., "Which one of the following could be an acceptable assignment of the rangers during the spring quarter?"
- Must Be/Could Be—e.g., "Which one of the following must be false?" [*A potential correct answer for this question might be "Estavez is at Lookout 3 during the summer." No matter which reassignments the supervisor makes at the end of the winter and spring quarters, there is no way for Estavez to be at Lookout 3 before the fall.*]
- New-"If"—e.g., "If summer is the first quarter in which Adams is assigned to headquarters, which one of the following must have been true of the spring quarter?" [*For Adams to be assigned to headquarters in the summer, he must have been at Lookout 4 in the spring. Because he was assigned to Lookout 1 in the winter, the protocol implemented at the end of the winter must have been protocol 1. That means that in the spring, Davis was at headquarters, Estavez was at Lookout 1, Benitez was at Lookout 2, Campbell was at Lookout 3, and Adams was at Lookout 4. One of those assignments will be stated in the correct answer to this question.*]
- "How Many" or Minimum/Maximum questions—"What is the minimum number of quarters needed for a ranger assigned to Lookout 2 to be reassigned to headquarters?" [*The correct answer will be "three." The quickest way for a ranger to get from Lookout 2 to headquarters is via the implementation of protocol 2, then protocol 1, and then protocol 1 again.*]

Process games tend to expect you to be able to figure out possible arrangements for up to three iterations. In questions accompanying this game, you would almost certainly be asked about the arrangements found in the spring and summer quarters, and maybe even about the fall. It's very unlikely, however, that any question would take you beyond that point.

Practice

Directions: Practice applying the Logic Games Method to a full game and question set. An answer key follows the game. Complete worked example expert analysis can be found in your online resources.

Questions 1–5

Four apprentices—Louis, Madelyn, Nora, and Oliver—are initially assigned to projects Q, R, S, and T, respectively. During the year in which they are apprentices, two reassignments of apprentices to projects will be made, each time according to a different one of the following plans, which can be used in any order:

Plan 1. The apprentice assigned to project Q switches projects with the apprentice assigned to project S and the apprentice assigned to project R switches projects with the apprentice assigned to project T.

Plan 2. The apprentice assigned to project S switches projects with the apprentice assigned to project T.

Plan 3. Louis and Madelyn switch projects with each other.

1. Which one of the following must be true after the second reassignment of apprentices to projects during the year if that reassignment assigns Nora to project T ?

(A) Louis is assigned to project S.
(B) Madelyn is assigned to project R.
(C) Madelyn is assigned to project S.
(D) Oliver is assigned to project R.
(E) Oliver is assigned to project S.

2. Which one of the following could be true after only one reassignment during the year?

   (A)   Louis is assigned to project T.
   (B)   Nora is assigned to project R.
   (C)   Oliver is assigned to project Q.
   (D)   Louis and Nora each remain assigned to the same projects as before.
   (E)   Nora and Oliver each remain assigned to the same projects as before.

3. If at some time during the year, Louis is reassigned to project R, which one of the following could have been the assignment of apprentices to the projects immediately before the reassignment?

   (A)   Q: Louis;   R: Madelyn;   S: Oliver;   T: Nora
   (B)   Q: Louis;   R: Nora;   S: Oliver;   T: Madelyn
   (C)   Q: Nora;   R: Madelyn;   S: Louis;   T: Oliver
   (D)   Q: Nora;   R: Oliver;   S: Louis;   T: Madelyn
   (E)   Q: Oliver; R: Nora;   S: Louis;   T: Madelyn

4. Which one of the following is an acceptable assignment of apprentices to the projects after only one reassignment during the year?

   (A)   Q: Louis;   R: Madelyn; S: Nora;   T: Oliver
   (B)   Q: Madelyn;   R: Louis;   S: Nora;   T: Oliver
   (C)   Q: Madelyn;   R: Oliver;   S: Nora;   T: Louis
   (D)   Q: Nora;   R: Louis;   S: Oliver; T: Madelyn
   (E)   Q: Nora;   R: Madelyn; S: Oliver; T: Louis

5. If the first reassignment is made according to plan 1, which one of the following must be true?

   (A)   Louis is assigned to project T as a result of the second reassignment.
   (B)   Madelyn is assigned to project Q as a result of the second reassignment.
   (C)   Madelyn is assigned to project T as a result of the second reassignment.
   (D)   Oliver is assigned to project S as a result of the second reassignment.
   (E)   Oliver is assigned to project T as a result of the second reassignment.

PrepTest11 Sec1 Qs 20–24

Answer Key
Process Game Practice
1. (E)
2. (E)
3. (A)
4. (B)
5. (A)

Worked example explanations of these questions with complete expert analysis can be found in your Online Study Plan under Chapter 11. View or download the PDF titled "Chapter 11 Process Practice Full Game Explanations."

For further practice on Process games, start with the LSAT Channel Special Feature that follows this section. There, you can practice the one recent Process game (from PrepTest 80, December 2016), and then go to your online center to see an LSAT Channel expert explain the game and provide strategies and tactics for Process games.

For your convenience, here is a list of all of the Process games ever to appear in released LSAT tests. Unless you have ample time before Test Day, do not spend too much of your time on this rare game type.

Officially Released Process games
PrepTest 18, Section 1, Game 4 (Firm's Annual Review for Promotion)

PrepTest 10, Section 2, Game 3 (Words/Sentences Game)

PrepTest 11, Section 1, Game 4 (Apprentice Re-Assignment to Projects)*

PrepTest 12, Section 2, Game 4 (Four Colored Chemical Flasks)

PrepTest 16, Section 1, Game 4 (Tennis Matches Based on Rankings)

PrepTest 80, Section 3, Game 4 (Trading Buildings)**

*This is the game featured in this chapter. **This is the game featured in the Special Feature that follows this section of this chapter.

The Return of Process

By Bob Verini

 Watch the video lesson for this Spotlight in your online Study Plan.

In December 2016, a remarkable thing happened, but only a few thousand people knew about it. While the rest of the world was focused on holiday shopping, football, and the politics of a new presidential administration, these "lucky" people saw something that had not happened in more than 21 years.

Even in January of the new year, when a document was released that contained this amazing rarity, most of the world ignored it. But for the small group of us who follow the LSAT test, it was a stunner. LSAC PrepTest 80 contained a Process game!

A Process game is one in which the game setup provides an initial arrangement of entities, followed by a set of rules that specify conditions for the *rearrangement* of those entities.

Three real estate companies—RealProp, Southco, and Trustcorp—are considering trading buildings with one another. Each building they own is categorized as either class 1, class 2, or class 3, depending on its approximate value:

> RealProp owns the Garza Tower (class 1), the Yates House (class 3), and the Zimmer House (class 3).
> Southco owns the Flores Tower (class 1) and the Lynch Building (class 2).
> Trustcorp owns the King Building, the Meyer Building, and the Ortiz Building, all of which are class 2.

Each trade must be of exactly one of the following three kinds:

> Trading one building for one other building of the same class
> Trading one class 1 building for two class 2 buildings
> Trading one class 2 building for two class 3 buildings

PrepTest80 Sec3 Qs 19–23

Consider this December 2016 game. In a standard Matching game, you would be given the five towers F, G, T, Y, and Z, and then asked to match them up to the three real estate companies. But, the Process game is different. Its setup *states* the initial match-ups. But those initial match-ups are subject to change. So the rules explain the Process (get it?) by which those towers can be traded among the companies. And the questions, as you'll see when you attempt this game, go on to ask about the new match-ups that could result after one or more trades are made.

For a period of time in the 1990s, the LSAT featured Process games regularly. PrepTest 16 (the LSAT from September 1995) and PrepTest 18 (from December 1992) presented one Process game each. So did all four 1994 exams, published as PrepTests 10–13. Then there was no sign of Process for two decades. The LSAT simply stopped using Process as a game type. By the 2010s, most LSAT experts figured that it would never return.

The first hint that the testmaker might be open to bringing back Process games came in June 2014, when PrepTest 72 included a "quadruple Strict Sequencing" game (Summit Company Workpieces), which reminded LSAT watchers of the old Process games. Then, on PrepTest 77, in December 2015, a hybrid Sequencing/Matching game about office selection showed the influence of Process games. Almost a year later, in September 2016, PrepTest 79's fourth game (Computer Virus) was an unusual "branching Sequencing" game that was hotly debated among the Kaplan LSAT team.

Finally, in December 2016, it happened unequivocally: Process came back. The game was so unusual that we had to include it here. Try it out on the next two pages, and then watch the video that accompanies this Special Feature to see an LSAT Channel instructor take you through the game step-by-step.

Questions 19–23

Three real estate companies—RealProp, Southco, and Trustcorp—are considering trading buildings with one another. Each building they own is categorized as either class 1, class 2, or class 3, depending on its approximate value:

> RealProp owns the Garza Tower (class 1), the Yates House (class 3), and the Zimmer House (class 3).
>
> Southco owns the Flores Tower (class 1) and the Lynch Building (class 2).
>
> Trustcorp owns the King Building, the Meyer Building, and the Ortiz Building, all of which are class 2.

Each trade must be of exactly one of the following three kinds:

> Trading one building for one other building of the same class
>
> Trading one class 1 building for two class 2 buildings
>
> Trading one class 2 building for two class 3 buildings

19. Which one of the following could be the buildings owned by the three companies after only one trade is made?

(A) RealProp: the Flores Tower and the Garza Tower
Southco: the Lynch Building, the Yates House, and the Zimmer House
Trustcorp: the King Building, the Meyer Building, and the Ortiz Building

(B) RealProp: the Garza Tower, the King Building, and the Ortiz Building
Southco: the Flores Tower and the Lynch Building
Trustcorp: the Meyer Building, the Yates House, and the Zimmer House

(C) RealProp: the Garza Tower and the Lynch Building
Southco: the Flores Tower, the Yates House, and the Zimmer House
Trustcorp: the King Building, the Meyer Building, and the Ortiz Building

(D) RealProp: the Garza Tower, the Meyer Building, and the Yates House
Southco: the Flores Tower and the Lynch Building
Trustcorp: the King Building, the Ortiz Building, and the Zimmer House

(E) RealProp: the Garza Tower, the Yates House, and the Zimmer House
Southco: the Lynch Building and the Ortiz Building
Trustcorp: the Flores Tower, the King Building, and the Meyer Building

20. Which one of the following CANNOT be true, no matter how many trades are made?

(A) The buildings owned by RealProp are the Flores Tower and the Garza Tower.
(B) The buildings owned by Southco are the Flores Tower and the Meyer Building.
(C) The buildings owned by Southco are the Garza Tower and the Lynch Building.
(D) The buildings owned by Trustcorp are the Flores Tower and the Ortiz Building.
(E) The buildings owned by Trustcorp are the Garza Tower and the Meyer Building.

21. If RealProp owns only class 2 buildings after some number of trades, which one of the following must be true?

(A) Trustcorp owns a class 1 building.
(B) Trustcorp owns the Meyer Building.
(C) Southco owns a class 2 Building.
(D) Southco owns both of the class 3 buildings.
(E) Southco owns the Flores Tower.

22. If Trustcorp owns no class 2 buildings after some number of trades, which one of the following must be true?

(A) RealProp owns a class 1 building.
(B) Southco owns only class 2 buildings.
(C) Southco has made at least one trade with Trustcorp.
(D) Trustcorp owns the Garza Tower.
(E) Trustcorp owns the Zimmer House.

23. Which one of the following CANNOT be true, no matter how many trades are made?

(A) The buildings owned by RealProp are the Lynch Building, the Meyer Building, and the Ortiz Building.
(B) The buildings owned by Southco are the Garza Tower and the Meyer Building.
(C) The buildings owned by Southco are the King Building, the Meyer Building, and the Ortiz Building.
(D) The buildings owned by Trustcorp are the Flores Tower and the Yates House.
(E) The buildings owned by Trustcorp are the Garza Tower and the Lynch Building.

PrepTest80 Sec3 Qs 19–23

Complete answers and explanations are provided in The LSAT Channel Spotlight video "Limited Options" in your online Study Plan.

MAPPING GAMES UNLOCKED

Prepare

Mapping games, as the name implies, always describe a spatial layout of places, areas, or zones. In some Mapping games, each place is a distinct node connected to other distinct places by a network of paths, roads, or rails. An urban area's subway map provides a good real-world analogy to Mapping games of this type. The model setup you'll see here fits this description.

In other cases, the map may describe overlapping or distinct regions, each with a certain characteristic. A valid real-world example might be a map showing the dominant language groups within a larger region. In some areas, a single language is dominant, while in others, two or even three languages may coexist. As you'll see, the full-length Mapping game used as a practice exercise matches this description quite well.

Take a look at a model Mapping setup of the first type just described. Try to anticipate what an LSAT expert will do when applying Steps 1 and 2 of the Logic Games Method to it.

> On the grounds of a mansion, there is a large garden with exactly six features. Five of the features—a fountain, a gazebo, a pond, and a rose bed, and a topiary display—are arranged in that order in a semicircle from the mansion's left to its right. The hermitage lies outside the semicircle directly behind the pond. Gardeners are constructing paths that will connect features to the mansion or to one another according to the following criteria:

In Step 1, an LSAT expert would immediately notice the description of the physical layout of the garden. The order and positions of the features matter. In some Mapping games, the setup may provide a simple diagram to illustrate the positions of the places named in the setup. When, as here, no diagram is provided, it is incumbent on the test taker to carefully create a diagram that matches the description in the setup. Nothing is more important in Mapping games than having an accurate map.

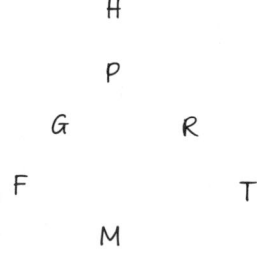

The expert would also note that while the drawing of the map will be based on the features in the garden, the action is based on creating connections—paths in this case—*between* features. From this, the expert can anticipate that the rules will cover how many paths may be built and restrict the features they may connect.

On the grounds of a mansion, there is a large garden with exactly six features. Five of the features—a fountain, a gazebo, a pond, and a rose bed, and a topiary display—are arranged in that order in a semi-circle from the mansion's left to its right. The hermitage lies outside the semi-circle directly behind the pond. Gardeners are constructing paths that will connect features to the mansion or to one another according to the following criteria:

Neither the mansion nor any of the features is connected by more than two paths.
Paths will connect the mansion to the fountain and to one other feature.
Paths will connect the pond to the gazebo and to the hermitage.
A path will connect the rose bed to the topiary display.
None of the paths may cross another path.
All of the paths are straight, and connect exactly two features or connect the mansion with exactly one feature.

As expected, all of the rules in this game define, limit, or establish paths. Rules 1, 5, and 6 limit how many paths may be built, and provide regulations for how they must be built. Rules 2, 3, and 4 establish four of the paths, which can be drawn directly into the sketch. In any game, it is always preferable to draw the rules inside of the sketch framework. That goes double in Mapping games, in which the visual and spatial elements are so strong.

In Mapping games, deductions will most likely spring from Duplications. When a place on the map is named in more than one rule, or a place is mentioned in one rule and a connection to that place is mentioned in another, there is likely a deduction to be made. In the game you've been exploring, the key Duplication arises in another way. Rule 1 limits the number of paths connecting any feature to two. Rule 3 creates two paths connecting connecting the pond to other features. Thus, the pond's connections are established once and for all in this game. Circle or box in P on your map to indicate this.

Turning to Step 5, you'll find that the types of questions associated with Mapping games depend a lot on the map itself. In games with points and connections, like the one you've been working on, there is a lot of counting. You could see questions that ask "What is minimum number of additional paths that must be built to walk from the mansion to the pond?" [*The answer would be "one," either by building a path from the mansion to the gazebo or from the fountain to the gazebo. Remember, a path cannot be build directly from the mansion to the pond because the pond has its limit of two paths already.*] New-"If" questions could explore the same territory; e.g., "If a path is built between the rose bed and the hermitage, what additional path must be built for a person to walk from the mansion to the hermitage taking only two paths?" [*The answer would be "a path from the mansion to the rose bed."*] There seems always to be a whiff of Sequencing in these Mapping games because so many of the questions center on the number of connections one must use or the number of points one must pass through to move from one point to another. The difference, of course, is that number of spaces moved is not always in a straight line in Mapping games.

In Mapping games with overlapping areas, the game is more likely to provide entities that must, can, or cannot be placed or stationed within certain areas. Although the basis of these game is still spatial, the action is closer to that in Matching games. As you'll see in the practice game, some entities may be placed in a single named area, while others, by being placed in an area of overlap, are placed in two named areas at the same time.

To get the feel of the second variety of Mapping games, try the practice exercise now. Feel free to compare your work to that of the LSAT expert—found on the pages following the game—in a step-by-step fashion. Complete Steps 1 and 2, and then compare your map to that of the expert. When you're comfortable that you understand the setup, move on to Steps 3 and 4, and then compare your work to the expert's once more before tackling the questions.

Practice

Directions: Practice applying the Logic Games Method to a full game and question set. An answer key follows the game. Complete worked example expert analysis can be found in your online resources.

Questions 1–7

The country of Zendu contains exactly four areas for radar detection: R, S, T, and U. Each detection area is circular and falls completely within Zendu. Part of R intersects T; part of S also intersects T; R does not intersect S. Area U is completely within R and also completely within T. At noon exactly four planes—J, K, L, M—are over Zendu, in a manner consistent with the following statements:

Each plane is in at least one of the four areas.
J is in area S.
K is not in any detection area that J is in.
L is not in any detection area that M is in.
M is in exactly one of the areas.

1. Which one of the following could be a complete listing of the planes located in the four areas at noon, with each plane listed in every area in which it is located?

(A)   R: J, L;   S: J, M;   T: L;   U: L
(B)   R: J, L;   S: K;   T: M;   U: none
(C)   R: K;   S: J;   T: L;   U: M
(D)   R: K, M;   S: J, L;   T: J;   U: none
(E)   R: M;   S: J, K;   T: J, L;   U: none

2. If at noon K is within exactly two of the four areas, then which one of the following CANNOT be true at that time?

   (A) J is within area T.
   (B) K is within area R.
   (C) K is within area T.
   (D) L is within area R.
   (E) L is within area T.

3. Which one of the following is a complete and accurate list of those planes any one of which could be within area T at noon?

   (A) M
   (B) J, L
   (C) J, L, M
   (D) K, L, M
   (E) J, K, L, M

4. Which one of the following statements CANNOT be true at noon about the planes?

   (A) K is within area T.
   (B) K is within area U.
   (C) L is within area R.
   (D) M is within area R.
   (E) M is within area U.

5. It CANNOT be true that at noon there is at least one plane that is within both area

   (A) R and area T
   (B) R and area U
   (C) S and area T
   (D) S and area U
   (E) T and area U

6. If at noon M is within area T, then which one of the following statements CANNOT be true at that time?

   (A) J is within area T.
   (B) L is within area R.
   (C) L is within area S.
   (D) K is within exactly two areas.
   (E) L is within exactly two areas.

7. If at noon plane L is within exactly three of the areas, which one of the following could be true at that time?

   (A) J is within exactly two of the areas.
   (B) J is within exactly three of the areas.
   (C) K is within area S.
   (D) M is within area R.
   (E) M is within area T.

PrepTest15 Sec4 Qs 7–13

Answer Key

Mapping Game Practice

1. (D)
2. (A)
3. (E)
4. (E)
5. (D)
6. (E)
7. (A)

Worked example explanations of these questions with complete expert analysis can be found in your Online Study Plan under Chapter 11. View or download the PDF titled "Chapter 11 Mapping Practice Full Game Explanations."

For further practice on Mapping games, consult the following list. Only five Mapping games have ever appeared on LSAC PrepTests, and even the most recent is more than a decade old (PrepTest 40 was administered in 2003). If you want to do one more, choose that one, but unless you have ample time before Test Day, do not spend too much of your time on this rare game type.

Officially Released Mapping games

PrepTest 4, Section 3, Game 4 (Ski Chalet Snow Shoveled Paths)

PrepTest 6, Section 4, Game 4 (Island Bridges)

PrepTest 18, Section 1, Game 3 (Five Subway Lines)

PrepTest 15, Section 4, Game 2 (Plane Zones)*

PrepTest 40, Section 2, Game 3 (Zephyr Airlines)

*This game is the game featured in this chapter.

PART THREE

Appendices

Logic Games—Timing and Section Management

The Logic Games section is the smallest of the scored sections with only 23 questions, on average. Nonetheless, for most test takers, time is tight in the Logic Games section. You must complete four games (and all of their associated questions) in 35 minutes. That means that you have roughly 8.5 minutes to tackle each game. After spending roughly three minutes to set up a game, you'll have just over a minute to tackle each question. Of course, these numbers rarely break down so evenly. Some games will take longer than others, and some questions take longer than others. Knowing your own strengths and weaknesses, knowing game actions, and knowing question types will put you in a position to strategically move through the games in a way that will ensure you get the most points possible.

In this chapter, we'll talk about how to maximize the time available to you in the Logic Games section. There is no one-size-fits-all strategy here. For some of you, your best bet will be to tackle three of the four games, giving yourself more time to fully understand rules and make valid deductions during the game setup. For others, you'll want to aim to get to all four games but be quick to strategically skip questions that you anticipate will be very difficult or time-consuming. In practice, you'll find the best strategy for you.

For every test taker, there are a few simple rules to keep in mind to help you maximize your performance in this section:

Slow down and think. Success in Logic Games ultimately comes from understanding the action (or actions, in Hybrid Games) in the initial game setup, interpreting rules correctly, and making deductions. Rushing through these steps to get to the questions quickly will lead to a poor understanding of the game, sloppy mistakes, and frustration.

Do the games in the order you want to do them. There is nothing that says that you have to do the games in the order in which they are presented to you. Quickly analyze a game's action(s), rules, and even the question stems themselves to determine if you'd like to do the game now, or save it for later.

Skip questions that you know will be overly difficult or time-consuming. Even easy games can have difficult questions. Some types, like Rule Substitution questions, nearly always have a 4-star difficulty rating. Instead of investing two or three minutes working through such a question, skip it and use that time to set up the next game.

Answer questions that you know are straightforward and simple. Even if you do skip a game, ask yourself if you can at least answer that game's Acceptability question. Remember, all you need to do to correctly answer an Acceptability question is to work through the rules and eliminate choices that violate those rules.

Use past work to answer more difficult questions. One of the benefits of creating sketches for "If" questions is that each of those sketches will provide a possible permutation of the game. Use those sketches to help you quickly select the right answer in a Could be True question, or eliminate wrong answers in Must be False questions.

When in doubt, sketch it out. Imagine you've exhausted your question specific strategies and you've referred to previous work to help you answer a question, and you're still stuck. Now what? Confident test takers know that there is no value in staring at questions, hoping the right answer magically appears to them. Instead, they aggressively dive into answer choices and sketch out what is and is not possible.

If you practice those strategies, you'll become a better, more efficient test taker. Let's take a look at each strategy in a bit more depth.

Slow Down to Speed Up

It might sound counterintuitive at first: "Slow down to speed up." But that's exactly the right approach to success in Logic Games. Here's why: Most students who struggle with timing in Logic Games do so because they rush through the game setup, then get bogged down in the questions. This is the wrong approach. Without a clear understanding of the game's mechanics, and without at least one or two concrete deductions, every question essentially becomes a completely new puzzle to solve. That is frustrating, and time consuming. You simply don't have time to sketch out possible scenarios for every single answer choice in every question. Instead, there is a better way: Be deliberate and precise in the first four steps of the method.

In Step 1, understanding the the game's action and limitations will help you set up an effective sketch in Step 2. In Step 3, reading and translating each rule is key, of course, but do you also sit with each rule and consider what the rule says *can't* happen? Do you consider *both* the positive and negative implications of every rule? Do you consider how each rule builds on and interacts with other rules in the game? In Step 4, read through the rules again and see if there are deductions you missed. Is this a game where you could set up two master sketches? Were there any duplicate entities that you overlooked? How did the rules modify any number limitations that might be present in the game? Excellent test takers know that it's better to sit and ponder (and, if necessary, sketch!) the answers to these mental questions than to simply rush to the game's questions. Give yourself time. The more you can figure out how the game "works," the better off you're going to be.

In practice, make note cards with the SEAL questions and the BLEND deductions written out on them. Place those note cards over the Acceptability question and force yourself to go through each list before moving on to the questions. After a while, this approach will become second nature to you, and you can start tackling new games without the note cards.

Game Triage

To maximize your performance in the Logic Games section, you also want to consider how strategic you are in your approach to the section as a whole. Everyone understands that the goal in the Logic Games section of the LSAT, like the goal in every other section of the test, is to correctly answer as many questions as possible. Unfortunately, many people interpret this task to mean that they should rush through each game in an effort to get to every question presented. But what many test takers soon discover in practice is that this strategy is actually counterproductive to the goal of getting as many questions correct as possible. By focusing so much on speed, they make crucial errors during the game setup. If this sounds like something that you've fallen victim to in your practice, consider slowing down and tackling fewer games, but spending more time interpreting rules, making deductions, and creating new sketches in the games that you do tackle.

As for the order in which you do the games, there is no rule that says you must do them in the order in which they are presented. Instead, take control of the section, and make it a point to do the games in the order in which *you* choose to do them. While it's possible that the first game is the easiest and the fourth game is the most difficult, it doesn't always work out that way. Take a look at the following chart, which breaks down the difficulty level of the questions in the Logic Games section of PrepTest 62.

Game 1 - Strict Sequencing

Question	Difficulty Level
1	★
2	★★
3	★★★
4	★★
5	★
6	★★★★

Game 2 - Matching

Question	Difficulty Level
7	★
8	★★★
9	★★★
10	★★★
11	★★★★
12	★★
13	★★★★

Game 3 - Hybrid: Sequencing-Matching

Question	Difficulty Level
14	★
15	★★★★
16	★★★★
17	★★★
18	★★★★

Game 4 - Strict Sequencing

Question	Difficulty Level
19	★
20	★
21	★
22	★★★
23	★★

Notice that any test taker who simply worked through the section from Game 1 to Game 4 would have had to work through the very difficult Game 3 before getting to the much easier Game 4. A strategic test taker, on the other hand, would have tackled games in the order in which she wanted to do them. Such a test taker would have wisely moved past Game 3, grabbed the easy points available in Game 4, and then returned to Game 3 in the time remaining.

This idea of evaluating the games and then deciding the order in which you choose to tackle them is what we call "game triage." There is no right way to triage games—the important thing is that you at least give yourself the opportunity to choose for yourself which games you are going to do, and the order in which you are going to do them.

Our data suggest that the most difficult game is rarely one of the first two games. Instead, there is a roughly equal chance that it will be Game 3 or Game 4. So, use this knowledge to your advantage. Some test takers make it a point to do Games 1 and 2 first, then stop and consider whether they'd prefer to do Game 3 or Game 4 next. Some test takers decide to triage the entire section by spending the first minute or two looking at all four games and then deciding a route that works for them. And then there are some test takers who simply work through the games in order, but are comfortable moving on from any game that is difficult to set up or in which very few deductions can be made.

When you think about game triage, consider factors that would cause you to tackle a game, or cause you to skip a game. Games that have straightforward actions, simple sketch setups, and rules that allow for many deductions are often going to be easier than games that have multiple actions, a difficult to imagine sketch setup, and few overlapping rules. For example, imagine Game 2 is a Selection/Sequencing/Matching Hybrid that involves selecting four or five entities out of eight possible entities, putting them in order and then matching each to a specific color. Game 3, on the other hand, is a Strict Sequencing game that simply involves putting six entities in order. Which game would you prefer to do first, and why? These are the types of questions strategic test takers ask themselves.

Tackling the Questions

Once you've taken the time to understand the game's limitations, rules, and deductions, it's time to get points by answering the questions. But not all questions are created equally. Acceptability questions, for example, are nearly always straightforward and require nothing more than an understanding of the game's rules. Other question types, like Rule Substitution, can be extremely difficult, or time-consuming, or both.

No matter your game triage strategy, try to make an effort to answer the Acceptability question in each of the four games. These questions can be answered even without a clear understanding of the game's setup and deductions. Simply look at the rules, eliminate choices that violate rules, and pick the choice that is left over.

As for tackling the rest of the questions in a game, your strategy will likely depend on the number of deductions you've been able to make during Steps 3 and 4. If you were able to make a key deduction—something like a certain entity being forced into exactly one spot in a Sequencing game, or discovering that two entities cannot be placed together in the same group in a Distribution game—then look to any Must Be True/False or Could Be True/False questions that directly test your understanding of that deduction.

If, on the other hand, you struggled to make any concrete deductions in a game, there is no need to panic. Instead, head to the "If" questions after tackling the Acceptability question. For each "If" question, sketch the new scenario or the new rule, and push yourself to make as many deductions as possible. Each "If" question is an opportunity to see how one permutation of the game could be constructed. For example, perhaps an "If" question demonstrates that by placing a certainty entity in spot 3, another entity is forced to occupy spot 2. This deduction isn't just helpful in answering that question, it's helpful in your overall understanding of the game.

After tackling the "If" questions, you can then return to any questions you might have skipped. Use all of the sketches you now have in your test booklet to help you either quickly select the right answer, or quickly eliminate wrong answers, in any Must Be True/False or Could Be True/False questions.

Other question types that are less common—Full and Complete List, Rule Substitution—can be left for the end of the game. For rare or uncommon question types, be sure to read slowly to understand fully the task at hand. If the question is overly confusing or if it appears that the route to the right answer is going to take too long, consider skipping that question and using the time saved to set up the next game in the section.

Using Past Work

Even if you work through a game's setup and its questions strategically, you still might find yourself struggling with one or two questions where the approach to the right answer does not seem obvious. In these questions, see if you can use your past work to answer the question correctly or, at the very least, eliminate clearly wrong answers. For example, imagine a game where seven different people are arranged in a line from left to right, in spots 1 through 7. There is a question that asks:

1. Paul CANNOT be assigned to which of the following spots?
   (A) first
   (B) second
   (C) thid
   (D) fourth
   (E) fifth

You look at your master sketch and notice that because Paul is always to the left of Mary, Paul can never be in the seventh spot. So, you look through the answer choices and...well, "seventh" isn't an answer choice. Now what? Well, first consider what would constitute a wrong answer. In this question, wrong answer choices will represent a spot to which Paul COULD be assigned. Look through the other questions in the set. The first question, the Acceptability question, shows an acceptable arrangement in which Paul is ranked second. So, because it is possible for Paul to be ranked second, choice B cannot be correct and can be eliminated. Now look to some of the sketches you created for "If" questions. Perhaps in one "If" question, you've discovered that it's possible for Paul to be in the first spot, and in another "If" question, it is possible to place Paul in the third spot. Eliminate choices A and C. Now you are simply left with two choices: D and E. Test one of them out, following the rules and limitations of the game. Imagine you try choice D, placing Paul in the fourth spot. If you discover that the placement of Paul in that spot *cannot* work, you've found the right answer. If on the other hand you discover that placing Paul in spot 4 is fine, and that the other rules and limitations of the game allow for other entities to be placed elsewhere on the sketch with no violations, then you know that D is incorrect and you can confidently select choice E.

One of the keys to getting more efficient in Logic Games is trying to do only enough work to get right answers, and no more than that. Relying on previous work is an excellent example of this principle.

When In Doubt, Sketch It Out

For every game, and for every question, you have a strategy, a plan of attack. You are going to do the games in the order in which you want to do them, and you have a system for getting through the questions strategically and efficiently. Even still, there may be times when a question has you stumped. You're not sure what you should do next, or how your past work will help you. When you hit such a roadblock, do one of two things: move on, or start sketching. Sitting and staring at a question and its answer choices won't help you. The right answer isn't going to magically come to you. You either don't know it (move on!) or you have to figure it out (start sketching!).

While excellent test takers might have slightly different approaches to game types, sketch setups, and question order, they do all tend to have a similar personality trait: an aggressive, confident attitude of "I'm going to figure this question out." Build this attitude within yourself. When you're stuck on a question, remember: The rules of the game are there on the page in front of you. The deductions you made during the game setup are sound. The "If" sketches you've created show possible avenues down which the game can go. You've got this. You can figure it out. If you need to make a sketch or two to figure out a new deduction, or to see if an entity can go in that spot, or to find out if two people can join the same group—do it. Make the sketch. Be confident, and be decisive.

Summing Up

A sound section management strategy in Logic Games will help you maximize your performance in this section. As you practice, remember to:

Slow down and think.

Understand the action(s) in the initial game setup, interpret rules correctly, and make solid, concrete deductions before moving to the questions.

Do the games in the order you want to do them. Analyze a game's action(s), rules, and questions stems to determine if you'd like to do the game now, or save it for later.

Skip difficult questions and tackle easy questions. Make it a point to tackle all of the Acceptability questions in the section, even if you don't have time to do a game fully. Strategically skip Rule Substitution questions that are notoriously difficult.

Use past work. The right answer to an Acceptability question and "If" sketches provide possible acceptable game scenarios. Use that information to quickly find right answers or quickly eliminate wrong answers.

When in doubt, sketch it out. Be confident. In questions where you cannot strategically use past work, aggressively dive into answer choices and sketch out what is and is not possible.

Put These Skills to the Test

The best way to practice the strategies and tactics described in this appendix is to take a timed Logic Games section. You can use the Logic Games section from PrepTest June 2007, available in your online Study Plan under the "LSAT Course Preview" tab, or any other released LSAT test. You may have one of the following LSAC 10 Actual, Official LSAT PrepTests series containing the Recommended Additional Practice assignments for Chapters 5–10:

10 Actual, Official LSAT PrepTests Volume V: PrepTests 62–71
10 New Actual, Official LSAT PrepTests with Comparative Reading (PrepTests 52–61)

If so, you can also practice timed sections from any of the tests in those books. Those tests provide outstanding practice opportunities because complete answers and explanations written by Kaplan LSAT experts are available in two eBook companions to those LSAC volumes:

LSAT PrepTests 62–71 Unlocked: Exclusive Data, Analysis & Explanations for 10 Actual, Official LSAT PrepTests Volume V, and
LSAT PrepTests 52–61 Unlocked: Exclusive Data, Analysis & Explanations for 10 New Actual, Official LSAT PrepTests with Comparative Reading. [Explanations title coming Fall 2018.]

The Countdown to Test Day

Is it starting to feel like your whole life is a buildup to the LSAT? You've known about it for years, worried about it for months, and now spent weeks in solid preparation for it. As the test gets closer, you may find that your anxiety is on the rise. You shouldn't worry. After the preparation you've done, you're in good shape. To calm any pre-test jitters you may have, though, here are a few strategies for the days before the test.

The Week Before the Test

Your goal during the week before the LSAT is to set yourself up for success on Test Day. Up until this point, you have been working to build your LSAT potential, but Test Day is about achievement. That process begins with taking care of your basic needs: food, sleep, and exercise. It's easy to get caught up in the stress of balancing your life with your studying, but if taking an extra hour to study every night leaves you sleep deprived and exhausted on Test Day, it's hurting you more than helping. Figure out what time you need to go to sleep the night before the exam and make sure you're in bed at that time every night the week before the exam. This is particularly important if you're a night owl who tends to get a second wind later in the evening. If at all possible, start doing some LSAT work—even if it's only a few problems—each morning at the same time as the test. Finally, if you are someone who regularly goes to the gym or engages in other physical activity, this is *not* the week to stop. Physical activity helps lower stress and increases production of dopamine and norepinephrine, two neurotransmitters that play a crucial role in memory, attention, and mood.

You should also take at least one trip to your test center sometime before the actual exam to figure out the logistics: how long it takes to get there, where to park, how to get to your room, and where the bathrooms and drinking fountains are. The last thing you want to end up doing the morning of the test is running into unexpected construction on your route or not being able to find your room when you arrive. If the test center is a classroom or public building, try to take a practice test or timed section in the room to get a feel for it. Pay close attention to things like noise levels and temperature while you're there. The more you can mentally prepare for these conditions, the less they will distract you on Test Day.

Early in the week, make sure to print out your admissions ticket from the LSAC website and check it against your government-issued ID. Be sure that the names match and that the ID isn't expired. (As of the time this book went to press, LSAC accepts photo IDs that expired *within 90 days* of the test date, but check the LSAC website for the latest information.) If the names don't match, contact LSAC *immediately* so you can remedy the situation. If that isn't fixed by Test Day, you will be denied admission to the exam. You will also need to upload a passport-style photo to your **LSAC.org** account. The photo must be a "recent and recognizable photo of only you." LSAC is strict about the photo requirements, so Kaplan recommends that you have your photos taken professionally at a place that specializes in passport photos, such as the post office, a chain drug store, or a photocopy shop.

For a complete list of the LSAC photo requirements, visit LSAC's website, **www.lsac.org**.

The kind of practice that you do the week before the exam is important. Resist the temptation to focus on your weaknesses and instead focus primarily on shoring up your strengths. It's all fine and good to grab two more points in games, for example, but if you start losing points in the other sections from neglect, you may very well end up worse off than you started. The reality is that you are more likely to grab a few points in your strengths at the last minute than you are in the areas you struggle with the most. Of course, be sure to work on all three areas during this time: no one section should be fully ignored. Also keep in mind that the actual LSAT is a test of timing and endurance. A majority of your work should be under timed conditions, and you should try to fit in a complete test or two if you have the time in your schedule. Having said that, do not fall into the trap of doing nothing but tests right before the LSAT. As always, there is a balancing act between test taking and review: Taking a test every day can make it difficult to find time to review them, which means you aren't learning from them. You also need to watch your stress levels carefully: Taking too many exams can lead to a stress spiral that is hard to climb out of.

Finally, the week before the exam is the time to decide whether or not you are ready to take your test. As of the time of writing, LSAC's policy allows you to withdraw your registration all the way up until 11:59 PM Eastern Standard Time the night before the exam without it showing up on your record. There is no right or wrong answer to the question of whether or not you are ready to take your exam, but if you are having any doubts, ask yourself two questions:

- What is the lowest score I would be okay with an admissions officer seeing?
- Am I scoring at least that high now?

You can choose your goals in life, but you can't always choose your timelines. If the answer to the second question was a resounding no, then it may be in your best interest to change your test date. Though there is a modest benefit to applying early, submitting a score that is well below a school's median early is more likely to result in a faster rejection than a surprise admission. Don't expect any miracles on Test Day. It's possible that your score will suddenly jump up to an all-time high on the day of the exam, but it isn't likely. More importantly, it's risky. This is especially important if you already have one score or cancellation within the last five years: Admissions officers can be understanding about one blemish on your record, but if you have two, it starts to look like a pattern.

LSAT STRATEGY

In the last week before the test:

- Print out your admission ticket.
- Get your body on schedule for the time of your test (either 8:30 AM or 12:30 PM).
- Visit the testing center.
- Don't take any practice tests within 48 hours of the test.
- Decide whether you want to take the test or withdraw.

The Day Before the Test

The day before the test is as important as the six days before it. The first instinct of most test takers is to cram as much as possible in hopes of grabbing a few last-second points. But the LSAT isn't an AP exam or your history final: You cannot "cram" for the LSAT. You should think of Test Day as Game Day. An athlete doesn't try to run 10 miles the day before a big race: He rests up to make sure that he can hit his potential when it counts. Though this advice is hard to follow, trust Kaplan's decades of experience with tens of thousands of students. You should make the day before the test a wonderful, relaxing day. There's a good chance that during the last few weeks or months, the stress of balancing prep with the rest of your life has meant you've had less time to yourself or with your family and loved ones. Spend a day with your significant other or kids. Go to the spa or spend the day in a movie marathon. Whatever you do, make sure that today is as restful and relaxing as possible. Put your LSAT materials away and leave them there because, while you aren't going to cram your way to a good score, you may cram your way into a bad one. Think of how you normally feel when you get a score on something that is less than you hoped for. Now imagine how it would feel the day before the exam and what that kind of anxiety could do to you on Test Day. The benefits to studying the day before are almost nonexistent, but the risks are sky-high.

Don't forget to cap off the day with a full meal for dinner and a good night of sleep. It's not going to be easy to fall asleep the night before the test, so make sure you are in bed on time. Resist the urge to stare at a television or computer screen: they tend to make it even harder to sleep. For what it's worth, however, the most important night of sleep isn't the night before the test; it's two nights before the test. For various reasons, the effects of sleep deprivation tend to skip a day, so getting a great night of sleep two nights before the exam will help make sure that you are well rested the day of the test.

LSAT STRATEGY

On the day before the test:

- Relax! Read a book, watch a movie, go shopping, etc.
- Get all of your materials together: your admission ticket, watch, snack, plastic bag, etc.
- Eat a full meal for dinner and get plenty of sleep.

You also want to make sure that everything you need for tomorrow is packed up and ready. Don't put yourself in the position of fumbling around the next morning trying to find everything you need. Everything you bring into the test center **must** be in a clear, one-gallon zip-top bag.

LSAT FACTS

The following items are required for admission on Test Day:

- Admissions ticket (which includes your uploaded passport photo)
- Government-issued ID
- Regular No. 2 pencils (no mechanical pencils)

In addition to those required items, there are a few other things you should bring with you as well:

> ## LSAT STRATEGY
>
> Kaplan recommends you bring the following items with you on Test Day:
>
> - A snack for the break (things like granola bars are best; avoid sugary snacks that might make you crash)
> - Bottled water or juice box (metal cans are not permitted)
> - Erasers
> - Pain reliever
> - Tissues (even if they end up being for someone else in the room with the sniffles)
> - A nondigital timing device (i.e., an analog watch)
> - A positive, upbeat attitude

On occasion, the LSAC will change its admissions requirements. Because of this, it's important that you consult its website (**www.lsac.org**) to get updated information on what is and is not acceptable to bring on Test Day.

The Morning of the Test

On the morning of the exam, you should obviously get up early to give yourself some time to wake up and to leave for the test center early. A relaxed morning is a much better start than a frantic, stressful one. After you wake up, make sure you have a great breakfast that is both high in protein and high in carbohydrates—you'll need the energy later. Also, make sure you pack an appropriate snack. While it's important to have a protein-rich breakfast, you want to *avoid* a protein-rich snack. You will have a chance to eat your snack during the 15-minute break after the third section, and you'll want the energy it provides as quickly as possible. Because carbohydrates digest much faster than protein, foods like fruit and granola are much more practical than peanut butter and jelly sandwiches. Try to avoid any processed sugars (as they could lead to a crash) or caffeine (a notorious diuretic). Finally, you are allowed a drink, but it must be contained in either a juice box or in a plastic bottle of no more than 20 ounces. Avoid energy drinks (as they are mostly sugar and caffeine) and instead opt for water or 100 percent juice.

When choosing what to wear, go for layers. It's hard to tell what the temperature will be in the room, and heating and cooling systems tend to kick in erratically. You want to be sure you can adjust your clothing as needed to stay as comfortable as possible. It's important to note, however, that you may not wear hats or hoods during the exam unless LSAC has given you a religious exemption.

Before you head to the test center, be sure to read LSAC's website one more time to see a complete and official list of what is and is not allowed into the room beforehand.

LSAT FACTS

The following items are prohibited:

- Cell phones (leave it at home or in the car)
- Electronic devices of any kind, including tablets, MP3 players, or digital watches
- Earplugs
- Backpacks or purses
- Mechanical pencils
- Papers or books
- Hats or hoods
- Fitness tracking devices
- Electronic cigarettes

This is not a complete list, so be sure to check the LSAC website to get the most updated information. But do know that once you check in, you may not have any of these items on your person. If you bring any of them into the testing center, you risk having your score immediately cancelled and a misconduct letter placed in your file. So, as hard as it may be for you to part with it, leave the cell phone in the car—it's not worth the risk.

LSAT STRATEGY

On the morning of the test:

- Get up early and plan accordingly for traffic and parking.
- Eat an appropriate breakfast.
- Dress in layers (but do not wear a hooded sweatshirt).
- Don't forget your one-gallon plastic bag with permissible items for the testing center.

At the LSAC Facility and During the Test

Aim to arrive at your testing facility at least 30 minutes before the test is scheduled to begin. Traffic, parking, and other unforeseen circumstances may delay you, so don't risk arriving late to the facility. The LSAC is strict about when the test begins—if you are even a minute late, the proctors have the right to deny you entry. Arriving early also allows you to familiarize yourself with your surroundings and to scope out where the bathrooms and drinking fountains are (though, as mentioned before, this is something you were hopefully able to do in the week leading up to the test).

There are also a number of things you'll want to do once you arrive at the testing facility. After all, if the only point of arriving 30 minutes early is to sit around and twiddle your thumbs, any anxiety you might feel would get worse, not better. That's why it's so important to have a game plan for what to do at the testing facility on Test Day. First of all, make sure you get a drink of water and go to the bathroom. Though that advice might seem like common sense, you'd be surprised by how many students get so nervous that they actually skip this important step. But going to the bathroom before the test is really important. After all, having to leave the testing room during Section 3 to go to the bathroom will cost you time and, in the process, undo the months of effort and practice you put into this test.

The other thing you'll want to do at the testing facility in the minutes before the test begins is get your brain in "LSAT mode." Bring with you a quick warm-up exercise to do while you wait to check in. Find a game, passage, or set of Logical Reasoning questions that you've done before and that you know well. Reviewing LSAT material and walking through the various steps you took to get to the right answer will get your brain prepared for the test to come. Many students find that if they don't do this, they start the test "cold." Don't wait until the second section to get your brain "warmed up." A word of caution: Be sure that your warm-up exercise is something you've already done. There's enough stress on Test Day without adding the anxiety of getting stumped by one of your warm-up questions right before the exam.

Because paper materials are not allowed in the testing room, do your warm-up exercise in a hallway or other room at the testing facility in the minutes leading up to the test start. While other students rush into the testing room 30 minutes before the test starts, take your time and review your material outside the testing room. Then, when there are 5–7 minutes to go, get in line and officially check in. Once you enter the testing room, you'll have little to do besides sit with your thoughts and wait for the proctors to begin the test. Remember, of course, to discard any practice materials prior to check-in.

Checking in on Test Day will involve showing your identification and having the proctors examine the materials you're bringing into the facility. Don't get flustered when they check your identification and belongings as you enter the testing room—this is standard operating procedure. The test administrators do this because (1) they want to make sure that everyone is who they say they are and (2) the materials used by each test taker should never distract others. That's one of the reasons why items like mechanical pencils (which can click) and cell phones (which can ring) are prohibited. To avoid any uncertainty or stress over what to bring, again, check the LSAC website for a list of acceptable and prohibited items. Additionally, make sure to follow the most up-to-date requirements for identification, lest all of your preparation be squandered when you are not allowed into the facility.

Once you enter the testing room and find your seat, you'll have to wait for the proctors to let everyone else in the room, pass out the test booklets, and recite a long list of rules. For some students, this time before the test can be nerve-racking. What thoughts will go through your head when this moment comes? Some students, no doubt, will think, "Gee, I hope I do well," or "I better not bomb this, or my life is over!" This time before the test begins is an opportunity for you to take control of your thoughts for the next four hours. Visualize yourself doing well. Walk through a logic game in your head. Identify the assumption from an old Strengthen question you've done. Tell yourself you will be successful. "I am going to do really well on this test. I'm well prepared and have seen thousands of LSAT problems. I know exactly how to tackle every question they throw at me. If they give me an Inference question, I'm going to read the stimulus and make deductions…" While the heads of the test takers around you fill with nervous thoughts, game-plan for the test and build your mental confidence.

After the test booklets have been handed out and once you've filled out the required information, the test will begin. Your proctor may or may not write the starting and ending time of each section in the front of the room, but the proctor should *always* announce a "five minutes remaining" warning. Even though this is one of the proctors' duties, don't rely solely on them for timing cues. Your watch is there to accurately measure time, so the only thing you need to hear from the proctor is "you may begin."

During the break, be sure to eat your snack, drink your beverage, and go to the bathroom. Stretch and move around a bit. Use the time during the break to recharge for the second half of the test. One thing you'll probably notice during the break is that people will talk—they'll talk about a section that was particularly hard, or particularly easy, or they may even talk about a section that you haven't even taken yet! That's because LSAT sections are organized differently in different test booklets. Your booklet may go LR, LG, LR in the first three sections, while the person next to you may have a booklet that goes RC, LR, LG. Additionally, you are never sure which section will end up being the experimental section until after the test is over. That's why the LSAC and the proctors will expressly prohibit discussion of the test during the break. Moral of the story? Don't worry about what people are talking about during the break; in fact, actively avoid anyone who seems to be discussing the test because it can lead to a misconduct letter or expulsion from the test. Focus only on yourself and your own progress. Forget about what happened during the first part of the test and turn your attention to the next three sections.

After the fifth section of the test, take a moment to relax and breathe. Congratulations. You have finished the scored sections of the LSAT. The only section that now remains is the Writing Sample. Though this section is not unimportant, it's nowhere near as important as the previous sections. Between the fifth and sixth sections, feel free to decompress before gathering yourself and moving forward to the Writing Sample.

LSAT STRATEGY

At the testing facility on Test Day:

- Arrive 30 minutes early.
- Find and use the drinking fountains and bathroom.
- Get into "LSAT mode" by reviewing previous work.
- Enter the testing room a few minutes before the test is set to begin.
- Use the time before the test begins to mentally prepare yourself for the test.
- Don't look backward—always keep moving through the test and stay focused on the section you're currently in, not sections you've already done or will do in the future.

After the Test

If it turns out that Test Day doesn't go *exactly* as planned, that's all right—it rarely, if ever, does, and the LSAT does not require perfection. All of your fellow test takers will likely experience some level of self-doubt as well; that's fairly typical.

If it turns out you feel like you did well on Test Day, then skip this section and head to the Post-LSAT Festivities section later in this chapter. If, however, you end up having a particularly unusual Test Day, you may think about canceling your score. Canceling your score means that neither you nor the law schools will have access to whatever your score would have been. But here's the rub: Law schools will still know that you took the test at that administration. For many law schools, a cancellation can raise a red flag. If you do cancel, you may want to consider attaching an addendum to your application explaining why you canceled.

You have two opportunities to cancel your score. The first opportunity is immediately after you finish the test on Test Day. In fact, there is a part of the scoring grid where you can indicate your wish to cancel. The second, less impetuous way, is to cancel your score via the LSAT Status page of your **LSAC.org** account. Cancellations must be made within six calendar days after the exam. If you're considering canceling, check the LSAC's website to verify the most recent means and deadlines for canceling your score.

Should You Cancel Your Score?

If you're wondering whether canceling is the right decision, the information on the next page should be helpful. If you feel confident in your Test Day abilities and are not considering canceling your score, feel free to skip this section entirely.

First, let's examine the **benefits** of not canceling your LSAT score.

No matter how you "feel" about how things went, you *don't know for sure*. You may have actually done much better than you think. According to LSAC, many test takers who cancel their score and then retest would've been better off sticking with the first score. (While the examinee never finds out the cancelled score, the LSAC still computes it internally and can compare the cancelled and subsequent results.)

Additionally, if you cancel your score, you will never have access to the answers you selected during Test Day. If you keep your score, you will receive an official score report and a PDF copy of the test you took (except for February administrations, for which the exam is not released). This information can be extremely helpful if you do choose to take the test again, as you will be able to review and evaluate the decisions you made during an official LSAT, when everything was on the line. Allowing your score to stay in place gives you access not only to the right answers but also to the answers *you* picked. Even weeks later, you'll be amazed as you go question by question through the sections of the exam and say, "Hmmm, now why did I find wrong answer (A) so alluring?" or "Shoot, I should've stuck with my first answer there!" By canceling your score, you forfeit access to this information.

Another reason why it may not be in your best interest to cancel a score is that in recent years, more and more law schools are *not* averaging scores. In fact, law schools have been given careful guidelines from LSAC *against* averaging. That doesn't mean that every school follows this policy, though, and remember this recommendation: The most preferable scenario is to take the test once and ace it. However, if your decision is between canceling and taking it again and *not* canceling and taking it again, it's likely that the latter option will be preferable. (Again, schools can see when you cancel.) Even a so-so score followed by a much better score won't hurt you as it might have in the past, when averaging was the common practice. As a rule, law schools want to assess you fairly, and most agree that the fairest thing is to take the better of two scores, irrespective of the order in which tests were taken. So, even if you decide you want to retest at the next administration, there will be less pressure next time if you don't cancel *this time*. By having a score already on record, you won't have the anxiety of thinking that you absolutely must use the retest score.

So, based on the benefits of not canceling, the following situations **would NOT warrant a score cancellation:**

- There were some minor distractions in the testing facility. Yes, it's hard to define exactly what counts as "minor" versus "major." Pencil tapping, coughing, and the humming of an air conditioner may all have been distractions, but that's also part of the test environment, and you'd likely experience the same things next time. It's highly unlikely you'll ever have a perfectly distraction-free atmosphere!

- You didn't get to finish or forgot to bubble in the last few questions of a section (or two), even though you usually finish those sections when you practice. Although these time-management issues are not ideal, they do not warrant a cancellation. Yes, a few questions here or there can affect your overall score, but the unanswered questions you saved for last may be of a higher level of difficulty, so even if you had completed those questions, there is no guarantee they would have markedly affected your score. Also, there is always the possibility that a section you struggled with was the Experimental section.

Now, let's talk about **when you should cancel your LSAT score:**

- If you have already taken the real test two or three (or more) times, you probably have a much better "feel" for whether or not a particular exam has truly gone well. Also, with two or three scores already on the record, one more cancellation isn't going to significantly damage your profile.

- If you had been consistently scoring in a certain range but became physically ill with flu or nausea on Test Day, or had some other serious difficulty during the test that prevented you from staying focused to the point that you were unable to complete large sections of the exam, then you should consider cancellation. This may have been due to test anxiety, lack of sleep the night before, personal stress not related to the LSAT, severe illness, and so on. To be clear, the situations described would have affected *every* section; they wouldn't cause just a moment of panic during a single section.

- If you realized that you made significant gridding mistakes for an entire section, thereby putting many questions in jeopardy of being incorrect, you should consider cancellation (e.g., #8 was gridded in spot #7, #9 in spot #8, etc.).

- Large-scale time issues, such as a proctor who mistakenly shorted time in a section (without having it immediately brought to his or her attention), can significantly change test performance. Minor issues related to the location of clocks, times written on the board, or the exact precision of a five-minute warning are all things that can be prevented by using one's own watch and only relying on the proctor for the words, "You may begin." So, a significant loss of time covering multiple sections could warrant a cancellation, but small, single-section timing issues will usually not.

- Remember that you can (and should) explain valid reasons for a score cancellation in an addendum to your law school application.

Post-LSAT Festivities

So, you've just taken the LSAT. After months of preparation and hard work, it's finally over. What to do now? First, give yourself a great big pat on the back. You've just completed (and hopefully rocked) the most important factor in law school admissions. Go celebrate and enjoy the moment—but of course, don't celebrate *too* hard. Law schools are in the business of recruiting future lawyers, which means they're typically not interested in applicants with criminal records. Don't be the person who destroys the LSAT in the morning, then acts inappropriately in the evening.

Instead, take a moment to reach out to anyone who has helped you prepare for the test—teachers, tutors, study buddies, friends, and family members who have invested in your decision to go to law school and become a lawyer. Let them know how you did and share your success with them.

After you've celebrated, and after you've taken a couple of days off from thinking about the LSAT and law school, it's time to once again start thinking about putting together the other pieces of your application. Be sure to get a good head start on your letters of recommendation, personal statement, and transcripts.

Congratulations on your journey!

Logic Games Index

The following is a list of every logic game to appear on an officially released LSAC PrepTest. You can use this list to find additional practice games of a certain type. There is a brief description of the situation described in the game's setup to help you avoid confusion, or to find a game if you remember what it was about, but not the PrepTest on which it appeared.

Note: The index lists games chronologically by the month and year in which they were administered. PrepTest numbers correspond to the order in which the tests were released to the public. In years past, the LSAC did not always release tests chronologically.

PrepTest	Section #	Game #	Q #s	Game Type	Game Name
1	2	Game 1	Qs 1–7	Sequencing—Strict (Circular)	Trade Negotiation Treaty Seating
1	2	Game 2	Qs 8–13	Matching	Computer and Printer Years
1	2	Game 3	Qs 14–18	Sequencing—Loose	Law Firm Partner Hiring
1	2	Game 4	Qs 19–24	Matching (Spatial)	Colored Railway Tickets for January/ February
2	3	Game 1	Qs 1–5	Sequencing—Loose	Mammoth Corp Hiring
2	3	Game 2	Qs 6–12	Sequencing—Strict	Five Floor Apartment Building
2	3	Game 3	Qs 13–17	Distribution	Hannah and Her Cities
2	3	Game 4	Qs 18–24	Hybrid—Matching/ Sequencing	Six Dogs at Dog Show; Breeds & Genders
3	1	Game 1	Qs 1–7	Matching	Three Couples at Dinner
3	1	Game 2	Qs 8–13	Sequencing—Strict	Seven Families in Houses
3	1	Game 3	Qs 14–19	Matching (Spatial)	Automobile Exhibition
3	1	Game 4	Qs 20–24	Distribution	Airshow Pilots & Copilots
4	3	Game 1	Qs 1–6	Sequencing—Loose	Law Firm Salaries
4	3	Game 2	Qs 7–11	Matching	Illness Symptoms

PrepTest	Section #	Game #	Q #s	Game Type	Game Name
4	3	Game 3	Qs 12–17	Sequencing—Strict	Street Cleaning Crew
4	3	Game 4	Qs 18–24	Mapping	Ski Chalet Snow Shoveled Paths
5	2	Game 1	Qs 1–6	Sequencing—Strict	Six Course Grades A-E
5	2	Game 2	Qs 7–11	Matching	Casey's Shirts
5	2	Game 3	Qs 12–17	Selection	Aquarium Fish & Plants
5	2	Game 4	Qs 18–24	Sequencing—Strict (Triple)	Town Rankings
6	4	Game 1	Qs 1–6	Distribution	Gerbils, Hamsters, Lizards, and Snakes
6	4	Game 2	Qs 7–12	Sequencing—Loose	Soft Drink Names
6	4	Game 3	Qs 13–19	Sequencing—Strict (Square)	Park Benches
6	4	Game 4	Qs 20–24	Mapping	Island Bridges
18	1	Game 1	Qs 1–6	Distribution	Students Visiting Three Canadian Cities
18	1	Game 2	Qs 7–13	Sequencing—Strict	Fall and Spring Course Folders
18	1	Game 3	Qs 14–19	Mapping	Five Subway Lines
18	1	Game 4	Qs 20–24	Process	Firm's Annual Review for Promotion
7	2	Game 1	Qs 1–7	Sequencing—Strict	Six Songs and One News Tape
7	2	Game 2	Qs 8–12	Matching (Spatial)	Dr. Yamata's Schedule
7	2	Game 3	Qs 13–18	Distribution	Judges Voting on Datalog Corp's Petition
7	2	Game 4	Qs 19–24	Hybrid—Matching/ Sequencing	Runners & Charities
8	2	Game 1	Qs 1–5	Sequencing—Strict	Gymnastics Coaching Sessions
8	2	Game 2	Qs 6–12	Selection	Square Parking Lot Lights
8	2	Game 3	Qs 13–17	Sequencing—Strict	Seven Boys/Girls in Seven Chairs
8	2	Game 4	Qs 18–24	Matching	Antibiotics and Organisms
9	3	Game 1	Qs 1–7	Matching	Corsages
9	3	Game 2	Qs 8–13	Selection	Diplomat Dinner Attendees
9	3	Game 3	Qs 14–18	Matching	Dance Recital Partnering
9	3	Game 4	Qs 19–24	Matching (Spatial)	Cities with Hospitals, Jails, and Universities
10	2	Game 1	Qs 1–5	Sequencing—Loose	Three Classes of Three Students Each

PrepTest	Section #	Game #	Q #s	Game Type	Game Name
10	2	Game 2	Qs 6–12	Distribution	Six Film Reviewers for Four Movies
10	2	Game 3	Qs 13–18	Process	Words/Sentences Game
10	2	Game 4	Qs 19–24	Hybrid - Selection/Sequencing	Giuliani, Rodrigo, and Vivaldi Concertos
11	1	Game 1	Qs 1–6	Distribution	Camp Counselors Supervising Activities
11	1	Game 2	Qs 7–11	Hybrid—Selection/Sequencing	Firefighter Schedules
11	1	Game 3	Qs 12–19	Selection	Housing Committee
11	1	Game 4	Qs 20–24	Process	Apprentice Re-Assignment to Projects
12	2	Game 1	Qs 1–6	Sequencing—Strict	Individual Piano Classes
12	2	Game 2	Qs 7–11	Distribution	Nine People in Three Canoes
12	2	Game 3	Qs 12–17	Matching	Street Vendor's Four Kinds of Food
12	2	Game 4	Qs 18–24	Process	Four Colored Chemical Flasks
13	1	Game 1	Qs 1–6	Distribution	Two Four-Person Consumer Groups
13	1	Game 2	Qs 7–11	Sequencing—Strict	TV Show Contestants
13	1	Game 3	Qs 12–17	Hybrid—Selection/Sequencing	Art Class Scheduling (Lecture)
13	1	Game 4	Qs 18–24	Matching (Spatial)	Clans in Annual Harvest Ceremonies
14	1	Game 1	Qs 1–6	Distribution	President, Manager, Technician
14	1	Game 2	Qs 7–12	Sequencing—Strict	Washing Dishes
14	1	Game 3	Qs 13–18	Distribution	Exhibited and Caged Birds
14	1	Game 4	Qs 19–24	Matching	Nikki's and Otto's Seasonal Sports
15	4	Game 1	Qs 1–6	Sequencing—Strict	Student Speeches
15	4	Game 2	Qs 7–13	Mapping	Plane Zones
15	4	Game 3	Qs 14–19	Sequencing—Strict	Four-Person Car Pool over Six Days
15	4	Game 4	Qs 20–24	Hybrid—Distribution/Selection	Experienced/Inexperienced Plumber Teams
16	1	Game 1	Qs 1–6	Distribution	Eight Students in Three Classes
16	1	Game 2	Qs 7–12	Sequencing - Strict	Lions and Tigers in Stalls
16	1	Game 3	Qs 13–18	Matching (Spatial)	Ranch, Split-Level, and Tudor Houses
16	1	Game 4	Qs 19–24	Process	Tennis Matches Based on Rankings
17	1	Game 1	Qs 1–5	Sequencing—Strict	Doctor's Seven Patients

PrepTest	Section #	Game #	Q #s	Game Type	Game Name
17	1	Game 2	Qs 6–12	Distribution	Policy, Quality, and Sales Committees
17	1	Game 3	Qs 13–17	Matching	Vladimir and Wendy's Meals
17	1	Game 4	Qs 18–24	Hybrid—Distribution/ Sequencing	Relay Race Teams
A	3	Game 1	Qs 1–5	Sequencing—Strict	Building Decks
A	3	Game 2	Qs 6–10	Hybrid—Distribution/ Matching	Sales Presentation
A	3	Game 3	Qs 11–17	Sequencing—Strict	Academic Office Assignments
A	3	Game 4	Qs 18–24	Selection	Wool/Silk and Rectangular/Oval Rugs
19	1	Game 1	Qs 1–7	Sequencing—Strict	Factory Inspections
19	1	Game 2	Qs 8–12	Sequencing—Strict	Theater Company Workshops
19	1	Game 3	Qs 13–19	Distribution	Adults and Children in Two Boats
19	1	Game 4	Qs 20–24	Distribution	Oceans, Recycling, and Wetlands Panels
20	3	Game 1	Qs 1–5	Sequencing—Strict	Nine Airplane Seats
20	3	Game 2	Qs 6–12	Selection	Library Budget Reductions
20	3	Game 3	Qs 13–18	Sequencing—Strict	String of Colored Beads
20	3	Game 4	Qs 19–24	Hybrid—Matching/ Sequencing	Evening Concert for Three Vocalists
21	1	Game 1	Qs 1–6	Distribution	Single, Double, and Triple Dormitory Rooms
21	1	Game 2	Qs 7–11	Matching	Colored Light Bulbs into Sockets
21	1	Game 3	Qs 12–17	Sequencing—Strict	Hostile and Non-Hostile Witness Interviews
21	1	Game 4	Qs 18–24	Sequencing—Strict	Product Advertisements Over Four Weeks
"Feb 1997"	4	Game 1	Qs 1–6	Sequencing—Strict	Upholsterer Jobs
"Feb 1997"	4	Game 2	Qs 7–13	Distribution	Rock-Climbing Teams and Organizer
"Feb 1997"	4	Game 3	Qs 14–18	Matching (Spatial)	Five Train Loops
"Feb 1997"	4	Game 4	Qs 19–24	Hybrid—Distribution/ Sequencing	Lectures in Library or Studio
22	3	Game 1	Qs 1–7	Distribution	Benefit Dinner

PrepTest	Section #	Game #	Q #s	Game Type	Game Name
22	3	Game 2	Qs 8–14	Hybrid—Matching/ Sequencing	Medical Training Sessions
22	3	Game 3	Qs 15–19	Matching (Spatial)	Paintings: Oil/Watercolor and 19th/20th
22	3	Game 4	Qs 20–24	Hybrid—Distribution/ Selection/Sequencing	Juggling Teams
23	1	Game 1	Qs 1–5	Sequencing—Strict	Music Recording
23	1	Game 2	Qs 6–11	Selection	Interviewing and Hiring
23	1	Game 3	Qs 12–18	Hybrid—Distribution/ Selection	Anthropologist and Linguist Teams
23	1	Game 4	Qs 19–24	Sequencing—Strict (Triple)	Mayoral Speeches
24	4	Game 1	Qs 1–5	Distribution	Recipe Contest for an Appetizer and a Main Dish
24	4	Game 2	Qs 6–10	Sequencing—Strict	Singing Competition
24	4	Game 3	Qs 11–17	Sequencing—Strict (Double)	Advanced/Introductory Textbook Evaluation
24	4	Game 4	Qs 18–23	Selection	Nine Treatments
25	3	Game 1	Qs 1–5	Hybrid—Distribution/ Selection	Planting and Trails Committee
25	3	Game 2	Qs 6–12	Hybrid—Distribution/ Matching	Guides, Tourists, and Languages
25	3	Game 3	Qs 13–18	Hybrid—Distribution/ Sequencing	Golf and Tennis Rankings
25	3	Game 4	Qs 19–24	Sequencing—Strict	Ballads and Dance Songs
26	1	Game 1	Qs 1–7	Sequencing—Strict (Two Sequences)	Laboratory Benches
26	1	Game 2	Qs 8–12	Sequencing—Strict	Messenger Delivering Packages
26	1	Game 3	Qs 13–18	Distribution	Movie, Restaurant, Soccer Game
26	1	Game 4	Qs 19–24	Selection	Lawmaker and Scientist Panel
27	2	Game 1	Qs 1–6	Sequencing—Strict	Investors Viewing a Building
27	2	Game 2	Qs 7–12	Hybrid—Distribution/ Matching/Sequencing	Snakes' and Reptiles' Zoo Habitats
27	2	Game 3	Qs 13–19	Distribution	Fellini, Hitchcock, and Kurosawa Films
27	2	Game 4	Qs 20–24	Sequencing—Strict	Orange, Purple, and Green Cars
B	2	Game 1	Qs 1–6	Sequencing—Loose	Boat Arrivals
B	2	Game 2	Qs 7–12	Selection	Trees in the Park

PrepTest	Section #	Game #	Q #s	Game Type	Game Name
B	2	Game 3	Qs 13–18	Sequencing—Strict (Circular)	Four Couples Around the Table
B	2	Game 4	Qs 19–24	Hybrid—Matching/ Selection	Zeno's Unfinished Furniture
28	2	Game 1	Qs 1–5	Sequencing—Strict	Race Horses
28	2	Game 2	Qs 6–12	Matching	Researchers and Languages
28	2	Game 3	Qs 13–18	Sequencing—Strict	Health Officer Inspecting Hotels & Restaurants
28	2	Game 4	Qs 19–23	Matching	Morrisville's Town Council Voting
29	3	Game 1	Qs 1–6	Distribution	Accountant Paying Bills over Two Days
29	3	Game 2	Qs 7–13	Matching	Mannequin Outfits
29	3	Game 3	Qs 14–19	Sequencing—Strict	Language Awards
29	3	Game 4	Qs 20–24	Sequencing—Strict	Piano Classes
30	1	Game 1	Qs 1–5	Matching	Bread Types & Sliced/Unsliced
30	1	Game 2	Qs 6–10	Hybrid—Selection/ Sequencing	Answering Machine Messages
30	1	Game 3	Qs 11–16	Hybrid—Matching/ Sequencing	Car Wash
30	1	Game 4	Qs 17–23	Sequencing—Strict	Toy Trucks
C	1	Game 1	Qs 1–5	Distribution	Boat Race and Rescue Exercise
C	1	Game 2	Qs 6–12	Sequencing—Loose	Restaurant Rankings
C	1	Game 3	Qs 13–19	Matching	Three Parks, Five Attractions
C	1	Game 4	Qs 20–24	Hybrid—Matching/ Sequencing	Dynamic Motors' Automobile Factories
31	1	Game 1	Qs 1–6	Sequencing—Strict	Lockers—Boys/Girls
31	1	Game 2	Qs 7–13	Selection	Music Store Sale—Genre & Used/ New
31	1	Game 3	Qs 14–18	Sequencing—Strict	Company Division Tours
31	1	Game 4	Qs 19–23	Hybrid—Distribution/ Selection	Installation Crew
32	3	Game 1	Qs 1–6	Hybrid—Selection/ Sequencing	Oral Reports Mon–Wed AM/PM
32	3	Game 2	Qs 7–11	Selection	Russian/French and Novels/Plays
32	3	Game 3	Qs 12–18	Sequencing—Strict	Concert Compositions

PrepTest	Section #	Game #	Q #s	Game Type	Game Name
32	3	Game 4	Qs 19–24	Sequencing—Strict (Two Sequences)	Pet Shop Puppies & Kittens
33	4	Game 1	Qs 1–5	Sequencing—Loose	Television Program Rankings
33	4	Game 2	Qs 6–12	Selection	Bird-watchers
33	4	Game 3	Qs 13–18	Selection	Jeweler—Ruby, Sapphire, and Topaz
33	4	Game 4	Qs 19–23	Matching (Spatial)	Oak Street Colored Lights
34	4	Game 1	Qs 1–7	Sequencing—Strict	Supermarket Stock Clerks
34	4	Game 2	Qs 8–12	Matching	Philosophy Lectures
34	4	Game 3	Qs 13–18	Sequencing—Strict	Train Arrivals
34	4	Game 4	Qs 19–24	Distribution	Doctors at Two Clinics
35	3	Game 1	Qs 1–5	Selection	Astronauts—Geologists/Radiobiologists
35	3	Game 2	Qs 6–12	Matching	Cars & Options
35	3	Game 3	Qs 13–17	Hybrid—Distribution/Sequencing	Opera Seats & Rows for Kim Family
35	3	Game 4	Qs 18–23	Sequencing—Strict	Professor Hiring 1989-1995
36	4	Game 1	Qs 1–6	Selection	Fruit Stand
36	4	Game 2	Qs 7–13	Hybrid—Matching/Sequencing	Radio Talk Show Calls
36	4	Game 3	Qs 14–18	Hybrid—Distribution/Sequencing	Bus Seats and Rows
36	4	Game 4	Qs 19–23	Sequencing—Strict (Two Sequences)	Flights With One Pilot and One Co-pilot
37	3	Game 1	Qs 1–5	Matching	Dormitory Wings
37	3	Game 2	Qs 6–11	Hybrid—Matching/Sequencing	Truck Arrivals, Green/Red
37	3	Game 3	Qs 12–18	Distribution	Bookshelves
37	3	Game 4	Qs 19–24	Sequencing—Strict	Swim Team Relay Race
38	2	Game 1	Qs 1–7	Sequencing—Loose	Clowns Getting Out of Car
38	2	Game 2	Qs 8–13	Hybrid—Matching/Sequencing	Farm Exhibition
38	2	Game 3	Qs 14–19	Distribution	Management, Production, and Sales Positions
38	2	Game 4	Qs 20–24	Sequencing—Strict	Musical Pieces with Two Instruments Each
39	1	Game 1	Qs 1–5	Sequencing—Strict	Red, Green, and Yellow Files

PrepTest	Section #	Game #	Q #s	Game Type	Game Name
39	1	Game 2	Qs 6–11	Matching	Capital Enterprises Three-Day Conference
39	1	Game 3	Qs 12–18	Hybrid—Matching/ Sequencing	Pohl Children—Right-/Left-Handed and Birth Years
39	1	Game 4	Qs 19–23	Selection	Barbara's Aquarium Fish
40	2	Game 1	Qs 1–5	Sequencing—Strict	Charlie's Soup
40	2	Game 2	Qs 6–10	Hybrid—Selection/ Sequencing	Cold Medication Testing
40	2	Game 3	Qs 11–17	Mapping	Zephyr Airlines
40	2	Game 4	Qs 18–23	Selection	Animal Behavioral Study
41	2	Game 1	Qs 1–7	Sequencing—Strict	Dresses in Closet
41	2	Game 2	Qs 8–12	Hybrid—Matching/ Sequencing	Children's Song Festival
41	2	Game 3	Qs 13–17	Distribution	Finance & Incentives Committees
41	2	Game 4	Qs 18–24	Sequencing—Strict (Circular)	Circular Picnic Table
42	1	Game 1	Qs 1–5	Selection	Scientist Panelists
42	1	Game 2	Qs 6–12	Sequencing—Strict	Loading Dock
42	1	Game 3	Qs 13–18	Sequencing—Strict	Bakery Cookies
42	1	Game 4	Qs 19–23	Matching	Play Reviews
43	4	Game 1	Qs 1–5	Sequencing—Strict	Civic Parade
43	4	Game 2	Qs 6–12	Sequencing—Loose	Rowing Team
43	4	Game 3	Qs 13–17	Hybrid—Distribution/ Sequencing	Museum & Art Collector
43	4	Game 4	Qs 18–22	Matching	Lunch Trucks
44	3	Game 1	Qs 1–6	Sequencing—Strict	Dignitary Meetings
44	3	Game 2	Qs 7–12	Distribution	Shelter Dog Placement
44	3	Game 3	Qs 13–17	Matching	Archaeological Sites
44	3	Game 4	Qs 18–22	Hybrid—Matching/ Sequencing	Parking Lots
45	3	Game 1	Qs 1–6	Sequencing—Strict	Meetings with Clients & Gym
45	3	Game 2	Qs 7–12	Sequencing—Strict	Chess Tournament
45	3	Game 3	Qs 13–17	Selection	Photographs
45	3	Game 4	Qs 18–22	Matching	Export Alliance
46	4	Game 1	Qs 1–6	Sequencing—Strict	Animal Guideposts
46	4	Game 2	Qs 7–11	Matching (Spatial)	Cassette Tapes

PrepTest	Section #	Game #	Q #s	Game Type	Game Name
46	4	Game 3	Qs 12–16	Hybrid—Matching/Sequencing	Town & Precipitation
46	4	Game 4	Qs 17–22	Matching	Secret Committees
47	4	Game 1	Qs 1–5	Sequencing—Strict	Product Ads
47	4	Game 2	Qs 6–11	Selection	Lighting Switches
47	4	Game 3	Qs 12–17	Matching	Record Stores
47	4	Game 4	Qs 18–22	Sequencing—Strict	Deli Staffing
48	2	Game 1	Qs 1–6	Selection	Electrical Appliances
48	2	Game 2	Qs 7–12	Sequencing—Loose	Harvesting Fields
48	2	Game 3	Qs 13–17	Matching	Technician Repairs
48	2	Game 4	Qs 18–22	Hybrid—Distribution/Sequencing	Folk & Rock Concert
49	1	Game 1	Qs 1–7	Hybrid—Selection/Sequencing	International Film Festival
49	1	Game 2	Qs 8–12	Distribution	Housemates & Mail
49	1	Game 3	Qs 13–17	Selection	Summer Courses
49	1	Game 4	Qs 18–22	Sequencing—Strict	Computer Chips
50	3	Game 1	Qs 1–5	Sequencing—Strict	Airline Stops
50	3	Game 2	Qs 6–11	Selection	Educational Committee
50	3	Game 3	Qs 12–17	Sequencing—Strict (Double)	Car & Graduation Dates
50	3	Game 4	Qs 18–22	Sequencing—Strict	Alphabet Soup
51	4	Game 1	Qs 1–5	Matching	Clown Costume
51	4	Game 2	Qs 6–10	Sequencing—Loose	Hotel Suites
51	4	Game 3	Qs 11–15	Hybrid—Matching/Sequencing	Guitarist's Demo CD
51	4	Game 4	Qs 16–22	Sequencing—Loose	Courier Deliveries
"June 2007"	1	Game 1	Qs 1–5	Sequencing—Strict	Product Codes
"June 2007"	1	Game 2	Qs 6–10	Hybrid—Matching/Sequencing	Film Club Festival
"June 2007"	1	Game 3	Qs 11–17	Sequencing—Strict	Cruise Line Voyages
"June 2007"	1	Game 4	Qs 18–23	Matching	Recycling Centers

PrepTest	Section #	Game #	Q #s	Game Type	Game Name
52	2	Game 1	Qs 1–7	Sequencing—Loose	Water Valves
52	2	Game 2	Qs 8–12	Distribution	Field Trip Chaperones
52	2	Game 3	Qs 13–17	Hybrid—Distribution/ Sequencing	Sales Conference Seminars
52	2	Game 4	Qs 18–23	Sequencing—Loose	Bread Truck Deliveries
53	2	Game 1	Qs 1–5	Distribution	Talent Agency Performers
53	2	Game 2	Qs 6–11	Sequencing—Loose	Architects' Designs
53	2	Game 3	Qs 12–17	Hybrid—Matching/ Sequencing	Burglary Suspects
53	2	Game 4	Qs 18–23	Hybrid—Distribution/ Sequencing	Debate Team Tourney
54	3	Game 1	Qs 1–5	Selection	Dancers on Stage
54	3	Game 2	Qs 6–12	Sequencing—Strict	CD Star Ratings
54	3	Game 3	Qs 13–17	Sequencing—Strict	Cake Layers
54	3	Game 4	Qs 18–23	Sequencing—Strict	Accepted Bid
55	4	Game 1	Qs 1–6	Hybrid—Distribution/ Matching	Trial Advocacy Teams
55	4	Game 2	Qs 7–12	Sequencing—Strict	E-Mail Messages
55	4	Game 3	Qs 13–18	Sequencing—Loose	Mercotek Productivity Rankings
55	4	Game 4	Qs 19–23	Sequencing—Strict (Two Sequences)	Shuttle Van Stops
56	1	Game 1	Qs 1–6	Sequencing—Strict	Saxophone Auditions
56	1	Game 2	Qs 7–11	Matching	Furniture Moving
56	1	Game 3	Qs 12–16	Matching	Parks and Trees
56	1	Game 4	Qs 17–23	Hybrid—Distribution/ Sequencing	Executives and Manufacturing Plants
57	1	Game 1	Qs 1–5	Sequencing—Strict	Student Activities
57	1	Game 2	Qs 6–11	Sequencing—Strict	Actor Auditions
57	1	Game 3	Qs 12–17	Hybrid—Matching/ Selection	Toy Dinosaurs
57	1	Game 4	Qs 18–23	Matching (Spatial)	Charitable Grants
58	3	Game 1	Qs 1–6	Sequencing—Strict	Construction of Monuments
58	3	Game 2	Qs 7–12	Selection	Day Care Volunteers
58	3	Game 3	Qs 13–17	Hybrid—Matching/ Sequencing	Flyhigh & Getaway Airlines
58	3	Game 4	Qs 18–23	Selection	Summer School Courses

PrepTest	Section #	Game #	Q #s	Game Type	Game Name
59	1	Game 1	Qs 1–5	Sequencing—Strict	Law Firm Departments
59	1	Game 2	Qs 6–10	Sequencing—Strict	Museum Photographs
59	1	Game 3	Qs 11–16	Selection	Alicia's Courses
59	1	Game 4	Qs 17–23	Sequencing—Strict	Organization Meetings
60	2	Game 1	Qs 1–6	Sequencing—Strict	Arts and Crafts Workshops
60	2	Game 2	Qs 7–12	Sequencing—Loose	Actors in Opening Credits
60	2	Game 3	Qs 13–17	Sequencing—Strict	Landscaper with Mulch and Stone
60	2	Game 4	Qs 18–23	Hybrid—Distribution/Matching	Travel Magazine Interns
61	3	Game 1	Qs 1–5	Distribution	Business Convention
61	3	Game 2	Qs 6–11	Sequencing—Loose	Ancient Artifacts
61	3	Game 3	Qs 12–17	Hybrid—Selection/Sequencing	Track Team
61	3	Game 4	Qs 18–23	Sequencing—Strict	Nurses
62	3	Game 1	Qs 1–6	Sequencing—Strict	Motel Service Appointments
62	3	Game 2	Qs 7–13	Matching	Stained Glass Windows
62	3	Game 3	Qs 14–18	Sequencing—Strict	Management Skills Conference
62	3	Game 4	Qs 19–23	Sequencing—Strict	Testifying Witnesses
63	2	Game 1	Qs 1–5	Distribution	Judicial Appointments to Appellate and Trial Courts
63	2	Game 2	Qs 6–10	Sequencing—Strict	Skydiving Team
63	2	Game 3	Qs 11–17	Sequencing—Strict	Vehicle Service
63	2	Game 4	Qs 18–23	Sequencing—Strict	Street Entertainer
64	2	Game 1	Qs 1–6	Sequencing—Strict	Employee Parking
64	2	Game 2	Qs 7–12	Hybrid—Distribution/Selection	Ambassador Assignments
64	2	Game 3	Qs 13–18	Matching	Bicycle Testers
64	2	Game 4	Qs 19–23	Sequencing—Strict	Bookcase Shelves
65	2	Game 1	Qs 1–5	Sequencing—Loose	Piano Recital Solos
65	2	Game 2	Qs 6–11	Sequencing—Strict	Crafts Presentations
65	2	Game 3	Qs 12–16	Selection	Luncheon Foods
65	2	Game 4	Qs 17–23	Sequencing—Strict	TV Scheduling
66	3	Game 1	Qs 1–5	Sequencing—Strict	Chemistry Class Lab Sessions
66	3	Game 2	Qs 6–11	Sequencing—Strict	Shopping Center Businesses

PrepTest	Section #	Game #	Q #s	Game Type	Game Name
66	3	Game 3	Qs 12–18	Distribution	Software Company Sales Zones
66	3	Game 4	Qs 19–23	Hybrid—Matching/Sequencing	Wayne & Zara's Piano Solos
67	3	Game 1	Qs 1–5	Matching	Student Speeches on Friendship and Liberty
67	3	Game 2	Qs 6–12	Sequencing—Strict	Literary Theory Lectures
67	3	Game 3	Qs 13–17	Sequencing—Strict	Toy Store Aisles
67	3	Game 4	Qs 18–23	Matching	Millville's Development Zones
68	4	Game 1	Qs 1–5	Sequencing—Strict	Realtor Showings
68	4	Game 2	Qs 6–10	Distribution	Three Days of Witness Testimony
68	4	Game 3	Qs 11–16	Matching	Maintenance Service Targets
68	4	Game 4	Qs 17–23	Sequencing—Strict	Article Editing
69	2	Game 1	Qs 1–5	Sequencing—Strict	Manuscript Ages
69	2	Game 2	Qs 6–11	Sequencing—Strict	Storing Petri Dishes
69	2	Game 3	Qs 12–17	Sequencing—Strict (Double)	Juice and Snack Deliveries
69	2	Game 4	Qs 18–23	Distribution	Cases for Paralegals
70	3	Game 1	Qs 1–7	Sequencing—Strict	Benefit Concert
70	3	Game 2	Qs 8–12	Selection	Corporate Research Team
70	3	Game 3	Qs 13–18	Hybrid—Distribution/Sequencing	Repertory Theater Screenings
70	3	Game 4	Qs 19–23	Hybrid—Matching/Sequencing	Bird Lectures
71	2	Game 1	Qs 1–5	Sequencing—Loose	Film Releases
71	2	Game 2	Qs 6–11	Distribution	Application Evaluation
71	2	Game 3	Qs 12–16	Hybrid—Matching/Sequencing	Literature Course
71	2	Game 4	Qs 17–23	Sequencing—Strict	Paintings in a Museum
72	4	Game 1	Qs 1–6	Hybrid—Distribution/Sequencing	Radio News Updates
72	4	Game 2	Qs 7–12	Sequencing—Strict	Realtor's Houses
72	4	Game 3	Qs 13–18	Distribution	Sunken Ship Artifacts
72	4	Game 4	Qs 19–23	Sequencing—Strict (Quadruple)	Summit Company Workpieces
73	3	Game 1	Qs 1–7	Sequencing—Loose	Instrumental CD

PrepTest	Section #	Game #	Q #s	Game Type	Game Name
73	3	Game 2	Qs 8–13	Hybrid—Distribution/ Sequencing	Symposium Speakers
73	3	Game 3	Qs 14–18	Distribution	Historic Building Owners
73	3	Game 4	Qs 19–23	Matching	Florist's Bouquets
74	2	Game 1	Qs 1–5	Sequencing—Loose	Band Solos
74	2	Game 2	Qs 6–10	Sequencing—Strict (Two Sequences)	Art Historians' Lectures
74	2	Game 3	Qs 11–16	Hybrid—Distribution/ Selection	Colored Rugs
74	2	Game 4	Qs 17–23	Hybrid—Distribution/ Selection	Graduation Photographers
75	4	Game 1	Qs 1–6	Distribution	Employee Bonuses
75	4	Game 2	Qs 7–11	Distribution	Landscaper's Trees
75	4	Game 3	Qs 12–18	Sequencing—Loose	Librarians' Desk Duty
75	4	Game 4	Qs 19–23	Matching (Spatial)	Business Newsletter
76	3	Game 1	Qs 1–6	Sequencing—Strict	Recruiting Criminal Accomplices
76	3	Game 2	Qs 7–13	Matching	Newspaper Photographs
76	3	Game 3	Qs 14–18	Sequencing—Strict	Campus Art Gallery
76	3	Game 4	Qs 19–23	Distribution	Publishing Cookbooks
77	3	Game 1	Qs 1–5	Sequencing—Strict	Community Festival Performances
77	3	Game 2	Qs 6–12	Hybrid—Selection/ Sequencing	Ceramic Bowl Display
77	3	Game 3	Qs 13–17	Hybrid—Matching/ Sequencing	Office Selection
77	3	Game 4	Qs 18–23	Matching	Community Committee Volunteers
78	2	Game 1	Qs 1–5	Selection	Special Project Workers
78	2	Game 2	Qs 6–11	Hybrid—Selection/ Sequencing	1920s History Archives Project
78	2	Game 3	Qs 12–17	Sequencing—Loose	Antique Dealer Auction
78	2	Game 4	Qs 18–23	Sequencing—Strict	Chorus Auditions
79	3	Game 1	Qs 1–5	Hybrid—Selection/ Sequencing	Bookmobile
79	3	Game 2	Qs 6–12	Distribution	National Park Rangers

PrepTest	Section #	Game #	Q #s	Game Type	Game Name
79	3	Game 3	Qs 13–17	Distribution	Economics TAs
79	3	Game 4	Qs 18–23	Sequencing—Strict	Computer Virus
80	3	Game 1	Qs 1–5	Distribution	Student Research Teams
80	3	Game 2	Qs 6–11	Sequencing—Strict	Mystery Novel Clues
80	3	Game 3	Qs 12–18	Distribution	Art Exhibition Paintings
80	3	Game 4	Qs 19–23	Process	Trading Buildings
81	4	Game 1	Qs 1–6	Hybrid—Matching/Sequencing	Rural and Urban Photo Essays
81	4	Game 2	Qs 7–11	Sequencing—Strict	Concert Musicians
81	4	Game 3	Qs 12–16	Sequencing—Strict	Amusement Center Obstacle Course
81	4	Game 4	Qs 17–23	Matching	Managers in Manila, Sydney, and Tokyo
82	2	Game 1	Qs 1–7	Hybrid—Distribution/Sequencing	Instructional Film Presentations
82	2	Game 2	Qs 8–12	Sequencing—Strict	Cafe Cosmopolitano Specials
82	2	Game 3	Qs 13–18	Hybrid—Matching/Sequencing	Investigators Interviewing Witnesses
82	2	Game 4	Qs 19–23	Matching	George, Rita, and Wendy's Student Presentations

Logic Games Strategies

Logic Games Method

STEP 1: OVERVIEW—THE SEAL QUESTIONS

Situation—What is the real-world scenario being described? What is the deliverable information—an ordered list, a calendar, a chart showing what's matched up?

Entities—Who or what are the "moving parts," the people or things I'm distributing, selecting, sequencing, or matching?

Action—What is the specific action—distribution, selection, sequencing, matching, or a combination of those—that I'm performing on the entities?

Limitations—Does the game state parameters (e.g., select four of seven, sequence the entities one per day) that restrict how I'll set up and sketch the game?

STEP 2: SKETCH

- Create a sketch that depicts the game's action(s) and limitations.
- Aim for a sketch that is easy to read, quick to replicate, and able to account for what is certain and uncertain based on the game's rules.

STEP 3: RULES

- Whenever possible, add information directly to your Master Sketch.
- If you cannot build a rule directly into the Master Sketch, make a shorthand graphical representation of it.
- Write the rules in a way that matches the style and conventions of the Master Sketch.
- Consider both the positive and negative implications of a rule.
- Write similar rules consistently, the same way from game to game.
- When analyzing and drawing rules, always ask the following:
  - What does the rule restrict?
  - What does the rule leave undetermined?
  - Is the rule stated in affirmative or negative terms?
  - If stated affirmatively, can I learn something concrete from its negative implications (or vice versa)?
  - Can I place the rule directly into the sketch framework?
  - If not, how can I best draw the rule to account for what it does and does not restrict?

STEP 4: DEDUCTIONS

Blocks of Entities—two or more players who are always grouped together

Limited Options—rules or restrictions that limit the overall setup to one of two acceptable arrangements

Established Entities—a player locked into a specific space or group

Number Restrictions—rules or limitations that provide guidance about the number of entities assigned to a group or space

Duplications—entities that appear in two or more rules and allow the rules to be combined

STEP 5: QUESTIONS

- Be able to characterize both correct and incorrect answer choices.
- Know the different question types and how to approach each one.
- Don't hesitate to draw a new sketch in "If" questions.
- Use deductions and past work to eliminate wrong answers quickly.

Logic Game Question Types

- **Acceptability:** Use the rules to eliminate violators.
- **Partial Acceptability:** Use the rules to eliminate violators, but some rules may not apply. It may be helpful to deduce the other entities that would be in a full acceptable arrangement.
- **Must Be/Could Be:** Characterize the one right and four wrong choices. Use deductions and previous work to eliminate wrong answers. Be strategic about testing answers.
- **New-"If"s:** Take the "new rule" through Steps 3 and 4 in a new sketch, or if the Master Sketch has Limited Options, check to see which option(s) apply.
- **Complete and Accurate List:** The sketches made for other questions in the game may help to narrow the possibilities. Test the remaining possibilities.
- **Completely Determine:** Pick the one answer that establishes every entity. Nailing down a duplicated entity or a Floater can be helpful.
- **Rule Substitution:** Identify what impact the removed rule had. Find another that has the same impact.
- **Rule Change/Suspension:** Repeat Steps 3 and 4 with the new information. Some deductions may have changed.
- **Maximum and Minimum:** Most often in Selection games. Use the Master Sketch, previous work, and number deductions from the Formal Logic rules to find the minimum/maximum known so far, then keep testing one more/less if necessary.
- **Earliest and Latest:** Most often in Sequencing games. Use the Master Sketch, previous work, and deductions to find the earliest/latest known so far, then keep testing one earlier/later if necessary.
- **Supply the If:** Use the Master Sketch to see the possibilities for the entity or slot in question and then use that analysis to determine the kind of additional restriction that would guarantee the desired result.
- **How Many:** Use deductions to count the relevant entities/slots.

Sample Logic Games Sketches

Strict Sequencing

A B C D E F

— — — — — —
1   2   3   4   5   6

Loose Sequencing

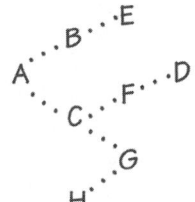

or

Distribution Games
All entities are used exactly one time.

```
        LMNOPRS
       1 | 2 | 3
      ___|___|___
      ___|___|___
         |   |___
```

Selection Games

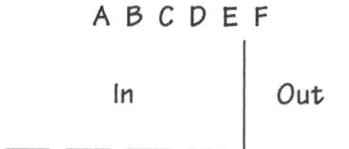

For Selection games defining a specific number of entities, some test takers prefer:

```
      A B C D E F

         In      |    Out

      __ __ __ __|__ __
```

Matching Games
Entities might be used multiple times.

```
              x y z
      A | B | C | D | E | F
        |   |   |   |   |
```

or

Sequencing/Matching Hybrid Games

```
      __ __ __ __ __ __  A B C D E F

      __ __ __ __ __ __  g/h
       1  2  3  4  5  6
```

Typical Rules

Sequencing Rules

A is in a lower numbered position than B.

A . . . B

A gets out at some time before B.

A . . . B

A gets out at some time after B.

B . . . A

A gets out at some time before B but after C.

C . . . A . . . B

A gets out immediately after B.

BA

A gets out immediately before B.

AB

Exactly one person gets out after A but before B.

A _ B

A is exactly two positions before B.

A _ B

At least one person gets out after A but before B.

A _ . . . B

Exactly one person gets out between A and B.

A/B _ B/A

A is immediately next to B.

AB or BA

M got out after either V or G but not both.

$$V \ldots M \ldots G \text{ or } G \ldots M \ldots V$$

or

$$V/G \ldots M \ldots G/V$$

(Exactly one of V or G is before M; the other comes afterward.)

P is ranked after T or before S, but not both.

(Both S and T come before P or both S and T come after P; P can't be in the middle.)

A can come neither immediately before nor immediately after B.

~~AB BA~~

If A is fourth, B is seventh.

$$A_4 \rightarrow B_7$$

$$B_{\sim 7} \rightarrow A_{\sim 4}$$

If A is not seventh, A is fifth.

$$A_{\sim 7} \rightarrow A_5$$

$$A_{\sim 5} \rightarrow A_7$$

(Or…A is either fifth or seventh. Consider Limited Options if there are further deductions to be made.)

If A is before B, then C is before B. (in a sequence with no ties)

$$A \ldots B \rightarrow C \ldots B$$

$$B \ldots C \rightarrow B \ldots A$$

Selection Rules

If she selects K, she must select M.

$$K \to M$$

$$\sim M \to \sim K$$

A is not selected unless B is selected.

$$A \to B$$

$$\sim B \to \sim A$$

If George buys A, then he does not buy B.

$$A \to \sim B$$

$$B \to \sim A$$

(This rule says we can never have both A and B—so it is often faster/more intuitive to just write "Never AB.")

If George does not buy A, then he buys B.

$$\sim A \to B$$

$$\sim B \to A$$

(This rule says we must have A, or B, or both.)

If she selects G, she can select neither H nor Y.

$$G \to \sim H \text{ and } \sim Y$$

$$H \text{ or } Y \to \sim G$$

(You can split an "and" result into two pieces—e.g., $G \to \sim H$; $G \to \sim Y$)
(You can split an "or" trigger into two pieces—e.g., $H \to \sim G$; $Y \to \sim G$)

Either A or B must be selected, but A and B cannot both be selected.

$$A/B$$

(Replace A and B with A/B in the entity list—you'll select exactly one.)

Matching/Distribution Rules

A cannot be in the same group as B.

NEVER AB

(Note that if there are only two groups, this means one of A and B is in the first group and the other is in the second group. This is important to help account for the numbers in each group.)

A is in a group with exactly 2 members.

A__

A and B are in the same group.

AB

Abstract rules and considerations

J and K have at least one symptom in common. (What symptom could that be?)

L has a greater number of symptoms than K. (How many could L have? How many could K have?)

Exactly twice as many people are in group 1 as in group 2. (How many people can be in group 1? This will often lead to Limited Options.)

Exactly one entity is in every group. (Which entity could that be? Must it be? Could it not be?)

How does the Testmaker make a game harder?

- Removing the "one entity per position" limitation in Sequencing or other "natural" limitations

- Altering the definition of a week—Monday to Friday? Monday to Sunday?—or other common unit

- Incorporating multiple hybrid actions

- Including tough rules—abstract, if/then, undefined group size (Distribution)

- Creating Sequencing games with some repeating elements (four entities, seven positions)

- Using scenarios in which not all entities must be used

- Incorporating challenging/time-consuming question types (Rule Substitution, Completely Determine, Partial Acceptability, Rule Change, Supply the If, etc.)

- Writing lengthy answer choices

- Including answer choices that contain conditional statements

Variations on Games

Sequencing

Double/Triple sequencing

Sequencing over a multiple-week period, but each week has the same schedule (watch for the overlap between the end of one week and the start of the next)

Adding a characteristic to each entity—might sequence children, some of whom are boys and some of whom are girls, and have rules about boys and girls

Circular sequencing—positions might be numbered or unnumbered; could also be along the perimeter of a square

Matching

Matching entities to schedules—looks like a Sequencing game at first glance, but not every entity must be used and some will be repeated

Distribution

Distribute a group of entities that consists of smaller subgroups (e.g., distribute nine people from five children and four adults)

The exact number of entities assigned to each group is unknown

Selection

Double selection—entities selected in the first group restrict who can be selected in the second group

Select from a group of entities that consists of smaller subgroups (e.g., select four committee members from five juniors and four seniors)

Hybrid

Sequence a group of entities, then match a second characteristic to each entity

Distribute a group of entities, then within each group create a sequence (Distribution then Sequencing)

Distribute a large group into two smaller groups, which don't account for all the entities (Selection then Distribution)

Formal Logic Statements and Translations

Keywords

Sufficient:	Necessity:	Mutually Exclusive:
If	Then	No
All	Requires	Incapable
Any	Guarantees	Impossible
Every	Must	Cannot
Each	Necessary	None
When	Bound to lead to	Neither...nor
Whenever	Are destined to	Never
Wherever	Only (if)	
The only	Results in	
	Produces	
	Sure to	
	Always	
	Unless	
	Depends on	
	Without	

Translating Conditional Statements into "If"-Then Format

Formal Logic Statement	Analysis
If A, then B	If A $\longrightarrow$ B
All C are D	If C $\longrightarrow$ D
Every E is F	If E $\longrightarrow$ F
If G, then not H	If G $\longrightarrow$ ~H
No I are J	If I $\longrightarrow$ ~J
Only K are L	If L $\longrightarrow$ K
M only if N	If M $\longrightarrow$ N
The only O are P	If O $\longrightarrow$ P
No Q unless R	If Q $\longrightarrow$ R
S unless T	If ~S $\longrightarrow$ T
No U without V	If U $\longrightarrow$ V
Without W, no X	If X $\longrightarrow$ W
Y if, but only if, Z	If Y $\longrightarrow$ Z If Z $\longrightarrow$ Y
AA if, and only if, BB	If AA $\longrightarrow$ BB If BB $\longrightarrow$ AA
If CC, then neither DD nor EE	If CC $\longrightarrow$ ~DD and ~EE
FF if GG	If GG $\longrightarrow$ FF
HH is always II	If HH $\longrightarrow$ II

Contrapositives

FORMING THE CONTRAPOSITIVE

- Reverse the sufficient and necessary terms.
- Negate each term.
- Change *and* to *or* and change *or* to *and* (whenever applicable).

Formal Logic Statement			Contrapositive		
If A	$\longrightarrow$	B or C	If ~B and ~C	$\longrightarrow$	~A
If D	$\longrightarrow$	E and F	If ~E or ~F	$\longrightarrow$	~D
If G or H	$\longrightarrow$	J	If ~J	$\longrightarrow$	~G and ~H
If K and L	$\longrightarrow$	M	If ~M	$\longrightarrow$	~K or ~L
If N and O	$\longrightarrow$	P and R	If ~P or ~R	$\longrightarrow$	~N or ~O
If S or T	$\longrightarrow$	U and V	If ~U or ~V	$\longrightarrow$	~S and ~T
If W and X	$\longrightarrow$	Y or Z	If ~Y and ~Z	$\longrightarrow$	~W or ~X
If AA or BB	$\longrightarrow$	CC or DD	If ~CC and ~DD	$\longrightarrow$	~AA and ~BB